Information Theory, Inference, and Learning Algorithms

David J.C. MacKay

PUBLISHED BY THE PRESS SYNDICATE OF THE UNIVERSITY OF CAMBRIDGE
The Pitt Building, Trumpington Sreet, Cambridge, United Kingdom

CAMBRIDGE UNIVERSITY PRESS
The Edinburgh Building, Cambridge CB2 2RU, UK
40 West 20th Sreet, New York, NY 10011-4211, USA
477 Williamstown Road, Port Melbourne, VIC 3207, Australia
Ruiz de Alarcón 13, 28014 Madrid, Spain
Dock House, The Waterfront, Cape Town 8001, South Africa

http://www.cambridge.org

First published 2003
Reprinted with corrections 2004

Printed in the United Kingdom at the University Press, Cambridge

Typeset in Computer Modern

A record for the book is available from the British Library

ISBN 0 521 64298 1

Contents

Preface

This book is aimed at senior undergraduates and graduate students in Engineering, Science, Mathematics, and Computing. It expects familiarity with calculus, probability theory, and linear algebra as taught in a first- or second-year undergraduate course on mathematics for scientists and engineers.

Conventional courses on information theory cover not only the beautiful *theoretical* ideas of Shannon, but also *practical* solutions to communication problems. This book goes further, bringing in Bayesian data modelling, Monte Carlo methods, variational methods, clustering algorithms, and neural networks.

Why unify information theory and machine learning? Because they are two sides of the same coin. In the 1960s, a single field, cybernetics, was populated by information theorists, computer scientists, and neuroscientists, all studying common problems. Information theory and machine learning still belong together. Brains are the ultimate compression and communication systems. And the state-of-the-art algorithms for both data compression and error-correcting codes use the same tools as machine learning.

How to use this book

The essential dependencies between chapters are indicated in the figure on the next page. An arrow from one chapter to another indicates that the second chapter requires some of the first.

Within Parts I, II, IV, and V of this book, chapters on advanced or optional topics are towards the end. All chapters of Part III are optional on a first reading, except perhaps for Chapter 16 (Message Passing).

The same system sometimes applies within a chapter: the final sections often deal with advanced topics that can be skipped on a first reading. For example in two key chapters – Chapter 4 (The Source Coding Theorem) and Chapter 10 (The Noisy-Channel Coding Theorem) – the first-time reader should detour at section 4.5 and section 10.4 respectively.

Pages vii–x show a few ways to use this book. First, I give the roadmap for a course that I teach in Cambridge: 'Information theory, pattern recognition, and neural networks'. The book is also intended as a textbook for traditional courses in information theory. The second roadmap shows the chapters for an introductory information theory course and the third for a course aimed at an understanding of state-of-the-art error-correcting codes. The fourth roadmap shows how to use the text in a conventional course on machine learning.

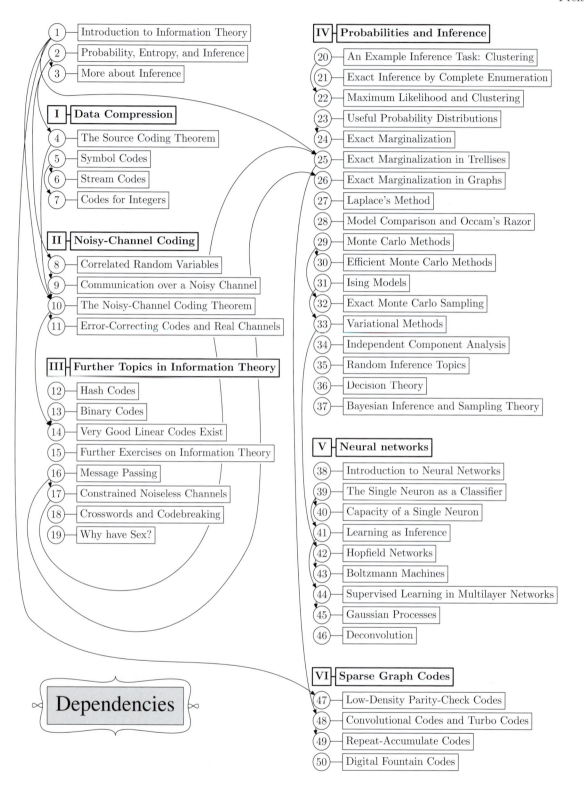

1 — Introduction to Information Theory
2 — Probability, Entropy, and Inference
3 — More about Inference

I — **Data Compression**

4 — The Source Coding Theorem
5 — Symbol Codes
6 — Stream Codes
7 — Codes for Integers

II — **Noisy-Channel Coding**

8 — Correlated Random Variables
9 — Communication over a Noisy Channel
10 — The Noisy-Channel Coding Theorem
11 — Error-Correcting Codes and Real Channels

III — **Further Topics in Information Theory**

12 — Hash Codes
13 — Binary Codes
14 — Very Good Linear Codes Exist
15 — Further Exercises on Information Theory
16 — Message Passing
17 — Constrained Noiseless Channels
18 — Crosswords and Codebreaking
19 — Why have Sex?

IV — **Probabilities and Inference**

20 — An Example Inference Task: Clustering
21 — Exact Inference by Complete Enumeration
22 — Maximum Likelihood and Clustering
23 — Useful Probability Distributions
24 — Exact Marginalization
25 — Exact Marginalization in Trellises
26 — Exact Marginalization in Graphs
27 — Laplace's Method
28 — Model Comparison and Occam's Razor
29 — Monte Carlo Methods
30 — Efficient Monte Carlo Methods
31 — Ising Models
32 — Exact Monte Carlo Sampling
33 — Variational Methods
34 — Independent Component Analysis
35 — Random Inference Topics
36 — Decision Theory
37 — Bayesian Inference and Sampling Theory

V — **Neural networks**

38 — Introduction to Neural Networks
39 — The Single Neuron as a Classifier
40 — Capacity of a Single Neuron
41 — Learning as Inference
42 — Hopfield Networks
43 — Boltzmann Machines
44 — Supervised Learning in Multilayer Networks
45 — Gaussian Processes
46 — Deconvolution

VI — **Sparse Graph Codes**

47 — Low-Density Parity-Check Codes
48 — Convolutional Codes and Turbo Codes
49 — Repeat-Accumulate Codes
50 — Digital Fountain Codes

Dependencies

My Cambridge Course on,
Information Theory,
Pattern Recognition,
and Neural Networks

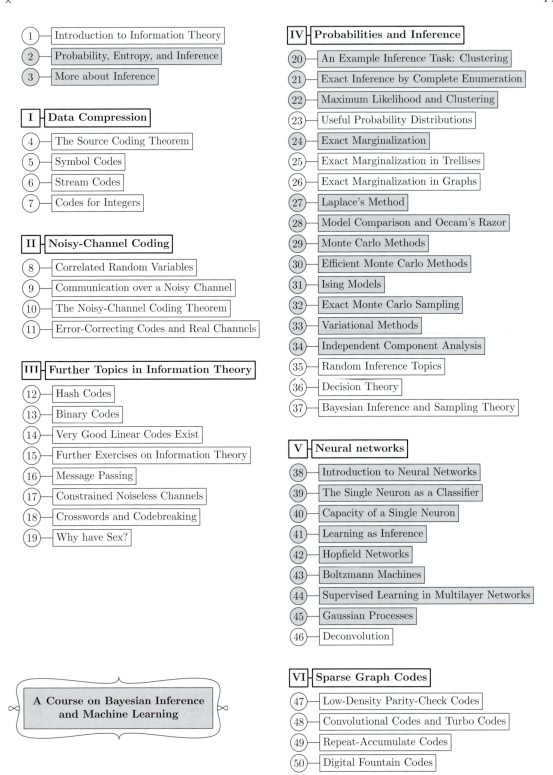

About the exercises

You can understand a subject only by creating it for yourself. The exercises play an essential role in this book. For guidance, each has a rating (similar to that used by Knuth (1968)) from 1 to 5 to indicate its difficulty.

In addition, exercises that are especially recommended are marked by a marginal encouraging rat. Some exercises that require the use of a computer are marked with a *C*.

Answers to many exercises are provided. Use them wisely. Where a solution is provided, this is indicated by including its page number alongside the difficulty rating.

Solutions to many of the other exercises will be supplied to instructors using this book in their teaching; please email `solutions@cambridge.org`.

Summary of codes for exercises

	Especially recommended	[1]	Simple (one minute)
		[2]	Medium (quarter hour)
▷	Recommended	[3]	Moderately hard
C	Parts require a computer	[4]	Hard
[p. 42]	Solution provided on page 42	[5]	Research project

Internet resources

The website

> http://www.inference.phy.cam.ac.uk/mackay/itila

contains several resources:

1. *Software.* Teaching software that I use in lectures, interactive software, and research software, written in `perl`, `octave`, `tcl`, `C`, and `gnuplot`. Also some animations.

2. *Corrections to the book.* Thank you in advance for emailing these!

3. *This book.* The book is provided in `postscript`, `pdf`, and `djvu` formats for on-screen viewing. The same copyright restrictions apply as to a normal book.

About this edition

In this second printing, a small number of typographical errors were corrected, and the design of the book was altered slightly. Page-numbering generally remains unchanged, except in chapters 1, 6, and 28, where a few paragraphs, figures, and equations have moved around. All equation, section, and exercise numbers are unchanged.

Acknowledgments

I am most grateful to the organizations who have supported me while this book gestated: the Royal Society and Darwin College who gave me a fantastic research fellowship in the early years; the University of Cambridge; the

Keck Centre at the University of California in San Francisco, where I spent a productive sabbatical; and the Gatsby Charitable Foundation, whose support gave me the freedom to break out of the Escher staircase that book-writing had become.

My work has depended on the generosity of free software authors. I wrote the book in LaTeX 2_ε. Three cheers for Donald Knuth and Leslie Lamport! Our computers run the GNU/Linux operating system. I use `emacs`, `perl`, and `gnuplot` every day. Thank you Richard Stallman, thank you Linus Torvalds, thank you everyone.

Many readers, too numerous to name here, have given feedback on the book, and to them all I extend my sincere acknowledgments. I especially wish to thank all the students and colleagues at Cambridge University who have attended my lectures on information theory and machine learning over the last nine years.

The members of the Inference research group have given immense support, and I thank them all for their generosity and patience over the last ten years: Mark Gibbs, Michelle Povinelli, Simon Wilson, Coryn Bailer-Jones, Matthew Davey, Katriona Macphee, James Miskin, David Ward, Edward Ratzer, Seb Wills, John Barry, John Winn, Phil Cowans, Hanna Wallach, Matthew Garrett, and especially Sanjoy Mahajan. Thank you too to Graeme Mitchison, Mike Cates, and Davin Yap.

Finally I would like to express my debt to my personal heroes, the mentors from whom I have learned so much: Yaser Abu-Mostafa, Andrew Blake, John Bridle, Peter Cheeseman, Steve Gull, Geoff Hinton, John Hopfield, Steve Luttrell, Robert MacKay, Bob McEliece, Radford Neal, Roger Sewell, and John Skilling.

Dedication

This book is dedicated to the campaign against the arms trade.

`www.caat.org.uk`

Peace cannot be kept by force.
It can only be achieved through understanding.
– Albert Einstein

About Chapter 1

In the first chapter, you will need to be familiar with the binomial distribution. And to solve the exercises in the text – which I urge you to do – you will need to know *Stirling's approximation* for the factorial function, $x! \simeq x^x\, e^{-x}$, and be able to apply it to $\binom{N}{r} = \frac{N!}{(N-r)!\,r!}$. These topics are reviewed below.

Unfamiliar notation?
See Appendix A, p.598.

The binomial distribution

Example 1.1. A bent coin has probability f of coming up heads. The coin is tossed N times. What is the probability distribution of the number of heads, r? What are the mean and variance of r?

Solution. The number of heads has a binomial distribution.

$$P(r \mid f, N) = \binom{N}{r} f^r (1-f)^{N-r}. \tag{1.1}$$

The mean, $\mathcal{E}[r]$, and variance, $\mathrm{var}[r]$, of this distribution are defined by

$$\mathcal{E}[r] \equiv \sum_{r=0}^{N} P(r \mid f, N)\, r \tag{1.2}$$

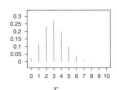

Figure 1.1. The binomial distribution $P(r \mid f = 0.3,\ N = 10)$.

$$\mathrm{var}[r] \equiv \mathcal{E}\left[(r - \mathcal{E}[r])^2\right] \tag{1.3}$$

$$= \mathcal{E}[r^2] - (\mathcal{E}[r])^2 = \sum_{r=0}^{N} P(r \mid f, N) r^2 - (\mathcal{E}[r])^2. \tag{1.4}$$

Rather than evaluating the sums over r in (1.2) and (1.4) directly, it is easiest to obtain the mean and variance by noting that r is the sum of N *independent* random variables, namely, the number of heads in the first toss (which is either zero or one), the number of heads in the second toss, and so forth. In general,

$$\begin{aligned}
\mathcal{E}[x + y] &= \mathcal{E}[x] + \mathcal{E}[y] & \text{for any random variables } x \text{ and } y; \\
\mathrm{var}[x + y] &= \mathrm{var}[x] + \mathrm{var}[y] & \text{if } x \text{ and } y \text{ are independent.}
\end{aligned} \tag{1.5}$$

So the mean of r is the sum of the means of those random variables, and the variance of r is the sum of their variances. The mean number of heads in a single toss is $f \times 1 + (1 - f) \times 0 = f$, and the variance of the number of heads in a single toss is

$$\left[f \times 1^2 + (1 - f) \times 0^2\right] - f^2 = f - f^2 = f(1 - f), \tag{1.6}$$

so the mean and variance of r are:

$$\mathcal{E}[r] = Nf \qquad \text{and} \qquad \mathrm{var}[r] = Nf(1 - f). \qquad \square \tag{1.7}$$

Approximating $x!$ and $\binom{N}{r}$

Let's derive Stirling's approximation by an unconventional route. We start from the Poisson distribution with mean λ,

$$P(r \mid \lambda) = e^{-\lambda} \frac{\lambda^r}{r!} \qquad r \in \{0, 1, 2, \ldots\}. \tag{1.8}$$

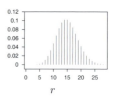

Figure 1.2. The Poisson distribution $P(r \mid \lambda = 15)$.

For large λ, this distribution is well approximated – at least in the vicinity of $r \simeq \lambda$ – by a Gaussian distribution with mean λ and variance λ:

$$e^{-\lambda} \frac{\lambda^r}{r!} \simeq \frac{1}{\sqrt{2\pi\lambda}} e^{-\frac{(r-\lambda)^2}{2\lambda}}. \tag{1.9}$$

Let's plug $r = \lambda$ into this formula.

$$e^{-\lambda} \frac{\lambda^\lambda}{\lambda!} \simeq \frac{1}{\sqrt{2\pi\lambda}} \tag{1.10}$$

$$\Rightarrow \lambda! \simeq \lambda^\lambda e^{-\lambda} \sqrt{2\pi\lambda}. \tag{1.11}$$

This is Stirling's approximation for the factorial function.

$$x! \simeq x^x e^{-x} \sqrt{2\pi x} \quad \Leftrightarrow \quad \ln x! \simeq x \ln x - x + \tfrac{1}{2} \ln 2\pi x. \tag{1.12}$$

We have derived not only the leading order behaviour, $x! \simeq x^x e^{-x}$, but also, at no cost, the next-order correction term $\sqrt{2\pi x}$. We now apply Stirling's approximation to $\ln \binom{N}{r}$:

$$\ln \binom{N}{r} \equiv \ln \frac{N!}{(N-r)!\, r!} \simeq (N-r) \ln \frac{N}{N-r} + r \ln \frac{N}{r}. \tag{1.13}$$

Since all the terms in this equation are logarithms, this result can be rewritten in any base. We will denote natural logarithms ($\log_e$) by 'ln', and logarithms to base 2 ($\log_2$) by 'log'.

Recall that $\log_2 x = \dfrac{\log_e x}{\log_e 2}$.

Note that $\dfrac{\partial \log_2 x}{\partial x} = \dfrac{1}{\log_e 2} \dfrac{1}{x}$.

If we introduce the *binary entropy function*,

$$H_2(x) \equiv x \log \frac{1}{x} + (1-x) \log \frac{1}{(1-x)}, \tag{1.14}$$

then we can rewrite the approximation (1.13) as

$$\log \binom{N}{r} \simeq N H_2(r/N), \tag{1.15}$$

or, equivalently,

$$\binom{N}{r} \simeq 2^{N H_2(r/N)}. \tag{1.16}$$

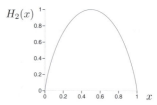

Figure 1.3. The binary entropy function.

If we need a more accurate approximation, we can include terms of the next order from Stirling's approximation (1.12):

$$\log \binom{N}{r} \simeq N H_2(r/N) - \tfrac{1}{2} \log \left[2\pi N \frac{N-r}{N} \frac{r}{N} \right]. \tag{1.17}$$

1

Introduction to Information Theory

> The fundamental problem of is that of reproducing at one point either exactly or approximately a message selected at another point.
> *(Claude Shannon, 1948)*

In the first half of this book we study how to measure information content; we learn how to compress data; and we learn how to communicate perfectly over imperfect communication channels.

We start by getting a feeling for this last problem.

▶ 1.1 How can we achieve perfect communication over an imperfect, noisy communication channel?

Some examples of noisy communication channels are:

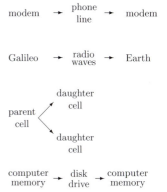

- an analogue telephone line, over which two modems communicate digital information;

- the radio communication link from Galileo, the Jupiter-orbiting spacecraft, to earth;

- reproducing cells, in which the daughter cells's DNA contains information from the parent cells;

- a disk drive.

The last example shows that communication doesn't have to involve information going from one *place* to another. When we write a file on a disk drive, we'll read it off in the same location – but at a later *time*.

These channels are noisy. A telephone line suffers from cross-talk with other lines; the hardware in the line distorts and adds noise to the transmitted signal. The deep space network that listens to Galileo's puny transmitter receives background radiation from terrestrial and cosmic sources. DNA is subject to mutations and damage. A disk drive, which writes a binary digit (a one or zero, also known as a *bit*) by aligning a patch of magnetic material in one of two orientations, may later fail to read out the stored binary digit: the patch of material might spontaneously flip magnetization, or a glitch of background noise might cause the reading circuit to report the wrong value for the binary digit, or the writing head might not induce the magnetization in the first place because of interference from neighbouring bits.

In all these cases, if we transmit data, e.g., a string of bits, over the channel, there is some probability that the received message will not be identical to the transmitted message. We would prefer to have a communication channel for which this probability was zero – or so close to zero that for practical purposes it is indistinguishable from zero.

Let's consider a noisy disk drive that transmits each bit correctly with probability $(1-f)$ and incorrectly with probability f. This model communication channel is known as the *binary symmetric channel* (figure 1.4).

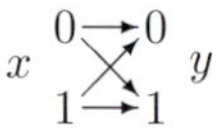

$$x \underset{1 \longrightarrow 1}{\overset{0 \longrightarrow 0}{\times}} y \qquad \begin{aligned} P(y=0\,|\,x=0) &= 1-f; & P(y=0\,|\,x=1) &= f; \\ P(y=1\,|\,x=0) &= f; & P(y=1\,|\,x=1) &= 1-f. \end{aligned}$$

Figure 1.4. The binary symmetric channel. The transmitted symbol is x and the received symbol y. The noise level, the probability that a bit is flipped, is f.

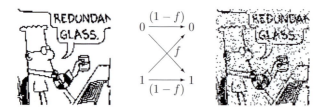

Figure 1.5. A binary data sequence of length 10 000 transmitted over a binary symmetric channel with noise level $f = 0.1$. [Dilbert image Copyright©1997 United Feature Syndicate, Inc., used with permission.]

As an example, let's imagine that $f = 0.1$, that is, ten per cent of the bits are flipped (figure 1.5). A useful disk drive would flip no bits at all in its entire lifetime. If we expect to read and write a gigabyte per day for ten years, we require a bit error probability of the order of 10^{-15}, or smaller. There are two approaches to this goal.

The physical solution

The physical solution is to improve the physical characteristics of the communication channel to reduce its error probability. We could improve our disk drive by

1. using more reliable components in its circuitry;

2. evacuating the air from the disk enclosure so as to eliminate the turbulence that perturbs the reading head from the track;

3. using a larger magnetic patch to represent each bit; or

4. using higher-power signals or cooling the circuitry in order to reduce thermal noise.

These physical modifications typically increase the cost of the communication channel.

The 'system' solution

Information theory and coding theory offer an alternative (and much more exciting) approach: we accept the given noisy channel as it is and add communication *systems* to it so that we can detect and correct the errors introduced by the channel. As shown in figure 1.6, we add an *encoder* before the channel and a *decoder* after it. The encoder encodes the source message **s** into a *transmitted* message **t**, adding *redundancy* to the original message in some way. The channel adds noise to the transmitted message, yielding a received message **r**. The decoder uses the known redundancy introduced by the encoding system to infer both the original signal **s** and the added noise.

Source

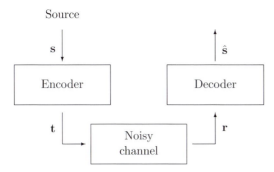

Figure 1.6. The 'system' solution for achieving reliable communication over a noisy channel. The encoding system introduces systematic redundancy into the transmitted vector **t**. The decoding system uses this known redundancy to deduce from the received vector **r** *both* the original source vector *and* the noise introduced by the channel.

Whereas physical solutions give incremental channel improvements only at an ever-increasing cost, system solutions can turn noisy channels into reliable communication channels with the only cost being a *computational* requirement at the encoder and decoder.

Information theory is concerned with the theoretical limitations and potentials of such systems. 'What is the best error-correcting performance we could achieve?'

Coding theory is concerned with the creation of practical encoding and decoding systems.

▶ ## 1.2 Error-correcting codes for the binary symmetric channel

We now consider examples of encoding and decoding systems. What is the simplest way to add useful redundancy to a transmission? [To make the rules of the game clear: we want to be able to detect *and* correct errors; and retransmission is not an option. We get only one chance to encode, transmit, and decode.]

Repetition codes

A straightforward idea is to repeat every bit of the message a prearranged number of times – for example, three times, as shown in table 1.7. We call this *repetition code* 'R$_3$'.

Imagine that we transmit the source message

$$\mathbf{s} = 0\ 0\ 1\ 0\ 1\ 1\ 0$$

over a binary symmetric channel with noise level $f = 0.1$ using this repetition code. We can describe the channel as 'adding' a sparse noise vector **n** to the transmitted vector – adding in modulo 2 arithmetic, i.e., the binary algebra in which 1+1=0. A possible noise vector **n** and received vector $\mathbf{r} = \mathbf{t} + \mathbf{n}$ are shown in figure 1.8.

Source sequence	Transmitted sequence
s	**t**
0	000
1	111

Table 1.7. The repetition code R$_3$.

```
s    0     0     1     0     1     1     0
     ⌒⌒⌒   ⌒⌒⌒   ⌒⌒⌒   ⌒⌒⌒   ⌒⌒⌒   ⌒⌒⌒   ⌒⌒⌒
t    000   000   111   000   111   111   000
n    000   001   000   000   101   000   000
     ───────────────────────────────────────
r    000   001   111   000   010   111   000
```

Figure 1.8. An example transmission using R$_3$.

How should we decode this received vector? The optimal algorithm looks at the received bits three at a time and takes a majority vote (algorithm 1.9).

Received sequence $\mathbf{r}$	Likelihood ratio $\frac{P(\mathbf{r}\mid s=1)}{P(\mathbf{r}\mid s=0)}$	Decoded sequence $\hat{s}$
000	γ^{-3}	0
001	γ^{-1}	0
010	γ^{-1}	0
100	γ^{-1}	0
101	γ^{1}	1
110	γ^{1}	1
011	γ^{1}	1
111	γ^{3}	1

Algorithm 1.9. Majority-vote decoding algorithm for R_3. Also shown are the likelihood ratios (1.23), assuming the channel is a binary symmetric channel; $\gamma \equiv (1-f)/f$.

At the risk of explaining the obvious, let's prove this result. The optimal decoding decision (optimal in the sense of having the smallest probability of being wrong) is to find which value of $\mathbf{s}$ is most probable, given $\mathbf{r}$. Consider the decoding of a single bit s, which was encoded as $\mathbf{t}(s)$ and gave rise to three received bits $\mathbf{r} = r_1 r_2 r_3$. By Bayes' theorem, the *posterior probability* of s is

$$P(s\mid r_1 r_2 r_3) = \frac{P(r_1 r_2 r_3 \mid s)P(s)}{P(r_1 r_2 r_3)}. \tag{1.18}$$

We can spell out the posterior probability of the two alternatives thus:

$$P(s=1\mid r_1 r_2 r_3) = \frac{P(r_1 r_2 r_3 \mid s=1)P(s=1)}{P(r_1 r_2 r_3)}; \tag{1.19}$$

$$P(s=0\mid r_1 r_2 r_3) = \frac{P(r_1 r_2 r_3 \mid s=0)P(s=0)}{P(r_1 r_2 r_3)}. \tag{1.20}$$

This posterior probability is determined by two factors: the *prior probability* $P(s)$, and the data-dependent term $P(r_1 r_2 r_3 \mid s)$, which is called the *likelihood* of s. The normalizing constant $P(r_1 r_2 r_3)$ needn't be computed when finding the optimal decoding decision, which is to guess $\hat{s}=0$ if $P(s=0\mid\mathbf{r}) > P(s=1\mid\mathbf{r})$, and $\hat{s}=1$ otherwise.

To find $P(s=0\mid\mathbf{r})$ and $P(s=1\mid\mathbf{r})$, we must make an assumption about the prior probabilities of the two hypotheses $s=0$ and $s=1$, and we must make an assumption about the probability of $\mathbf{r}$ given s. We assume that the prior probabilities are equal: $P(s=0) = P(s=1) = 0.5$; then maximizing the posterior probability $P(s\mid\mathbf{r})$ is equivalent to maximizing the likelihood $P(\mathbf{r}\mid s)$. And we assume that the channel is a binary symmetric channel with noise level $f < 0.5$, so that the likelihood is

$$P(\mathbf{r}\mid s) = P(\mathbf{r}\mid \mathbf{t}(s)) = \prod_{n=1}^{N} P(r_n \mid t_n(s)), \tag{1.21}$$

where $N = 3$ is the number of transmitted bits in the block we are considering, and

$$P(r_n \mid t_n) = \begin{cases} (1-f) & \text{if} \quad r_n = t_n \\ f & \text{if} \quad r_n \neq t_n. \end{cases} \tag{1.22}$$

Thus the likelihood ratio for the two hypotheses is

$$\frac{P(\mathbf{r}\mid s=1)}{P(\mathbf{r}\mid s=0)} = \prod_{n=1}^{N} \frac{P(r_n \mid t_n(1))}{P(r_n \mid t_n(0))}; \tag{1.23}$$

each factor $\frac{P(r_n\mid t_n(1))}{P(r_n\mid t_n(0))}$ equals $\frac{(1-f)}{f}$ if $r_n = 1$ and $\frac{f}{(1-f)}$ if $r_n = 0$. The ratio $\gamma \equiv \frac{(1-f)}{f}$ is greater than 1, since $f < 0.5$, so the winning hypothesis is the one with the most 'votes', each vote counting for a factor of γ in the likelihood ratio.

Thus the majority-vote decoder shown in algorithm 1.9 is the optimal decoder if we assume that the channel is a binary symmetric channel and that the two possible source messages 0 and 1 have equal prior probability.

We now apply the majority vote decoder to the received vector of figure 1.8. The first three received bits are all 0, so we decode this triplet as a 0. In the second triplet of figure 1.8, there are two 0s and one 1, so we decode this triplet as a 0 – which in this case corrects the error. Not all errors are corrected, however. If we are unlucky and two errors fall in a single block, as in the fifth triplet of figure 1.8, then the decoding rule gets the wrong answer, as shown in figure 1.10.

Figure 1.10. Decoding the received vector from figure 1.8.

$$
\begin{array}{c c c c c c c c}
\mathbf{s} & 0 & 0 & 1 & 0 & 1 & 1 & 0 \\
\mathbf{t} & \overbrace{000} & \overbrace{000} & \overbrace{111} & \overbrace{000} & \overbrace{111} & \overbrace{111} & \overbrace{000} \\
\mathbf{n} & 000 & 001 & 000 & 000 & 101 & 000 & 000 \\
\mathbf{r} & \underbrace{000} & \underbrace{001} & \underbrace{111} & \underbrace{000} & \underbrace{010} & \underbrace{111} & \underbrace{000} \\
\hat{\mathbf{s}} & 0 & 0 & 1 & 0 & 0 & 1 & 0 \\
\end{array}
$$

corrected errors   ⋆

undetected errors   ⋆

Exercise 1.2.[2, p.16] Show that the error probability is reduced by the use of R_3 by computing the error probability of this code for a binary symmetric channel with noise level f.

The exercise's rating, e.g.'[2]', indicates its difficulty: '1' exercises are the easiest. Exercises that are accompanied by a marginal rat are especially recommended. If a solution or partial solution is provided, the page is indicated after the difficulty rating; for example, this exercise's solution is on page 16.

The error probability is dominated by the probability that two bits in a block of three are flipped, which scales as f^2. In the case of the binary symmetric channel with $f = 0.1$, the R_3 code has a probability of error, after decoding, of $p_b \simeq 0.03$ per bit. Figure 1.11 shows the result of transmitting a binary image over a binary symmetric channel using the repetition code.

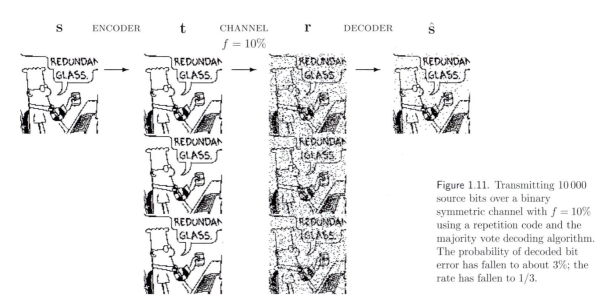

s	ENCODER	**t**	CHANNEL	**r**	DECODER	$\hat{\mathbf{s}}$

$f = 10\%$

Figure 1.11. Transmitting 10 000 source bits over a binary symmetric channel with $f = 10\%$ using a repetition code and the majority vote decoding algorithm. The probability of decoded bit error has fallen to about 3%; the rate has fallen to 1/3.

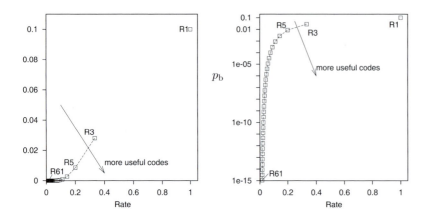

Figure 1.12. Error probability p_b versus rate for repetition codes over a binary symmetric channel with $f = 0.1$. The right-hand figure shows p_b on a logarithmic scale. We would like the rate to be large and p_b to be small.

The repetition code R_3 has therefore reduced the probability of error, as desired. Yet we have lost something: our *rate* of information transfer has fallen by a factor of three. So if we use a repetition code to communicate data over a telephone line, it will reduce the error frequency, but it will also reduce our communication rate. We will have to pay three times as much for each phone call. Similarly, we would need three of the original noisy gigabyte disk drives in order to create a one-gigabyte disk drive with $p_b = 0.03$.

Can we push the error probability lower, to the values required for a sellable disk drive – 10^{-15}? We could achieve lower error probabilities by using repetition codes with more repetitions.

 Exercise 1.3.[3, p.16] (a) Show that the probability of error of R_N, the repetition code with N repetitions, is

$$p_b = \sum_{n=(N+1)/2}^{N} \binom{N}{n} f^n (1-f)^{N-n}, \qquad (1.24)$$

for odd N.

(b) Assuming $f = 0.1$, which of the terms in this sum is the biggest? How much bigger is it than the second-biggest term?

(c) Use Stirling's approximation (p.2) to approximate the $\binom{N}{n}$ in the largest term, and find, approximately, the probability of error of the repetition code with N repetitions.

(d) Assuming $f = 0.1$, find how many repetitions are required to get the probability of error down to 10^{-15}. [Answer: about 60.]

So to build a *single* gigabyte disk drive with the required reliability from noisy gigabyte drives with $f = 0.1$, we would need *sixty* of the noisy disk drives. The tradeoff between error probability and rate for repetition codes is shown in figure 1.12.

Block codes – the $(7, 4)$ Hamming code

We would like to communicate with tiny probability of error *and* at a substantial rate. Can we improve on repetition codes? What if we add redundancy to *blocks* of data instead of encoding one bit at a time? We now study a simple *block code*.

A *block code* is a rule for converting a sequence of source bits **s**, of length K, say, into a transmitted sequence **t** of length N bits. To add redundancy, we make N greater than K. In a *linear* block code, the extra $N - K$ bits are linear functions of the original K bits; these extra bits are called *parity-check bits*. An example of a linear block code is the $(7, 4)$ *Hamming code*, which transmits $N = 7$ bits for every $K = 4$ source bits.

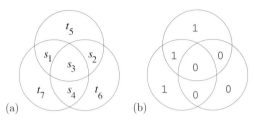

Figure 1.13. Pictorial representation of encoding for the $(7, 4)$ Hamming code.

The encoding operation for the code is shown pictorially in figure 1.13. We arrange the seven transmitted bits in three intersecting circles. The first four transmitted bits, $t_1 t_2 t_3 t_4$, are set equal to the four source bits, $s_1 s_2 s_3 s_4$. The parity-check bits $t_5 t_6 t_7$ are set so that the *parity* within each circle is even: the first parity-check bit is the parity of the first three source bits (that is, it is 0 if the sum of those bits is even, and 1 if the sum is odd); the second is the parity of the last three; and the third parity bit is the parity of source bits one, three and four.

As an example, figure 1.13b shows the transmitted codeword for the case **s** = 1000. Table 1.14 shows the codewords generated by each of the $2^4 =$ sixteen settings of the four source bits. These codewords have the special property that any pair differ from each other in at least three bits.

s	t	s	t	s	t	s	t
0000	0000000	0100	0100110	1000	1000101	1100	1100011
0001	0001011	0101	0101101	1001	1001110	1101	1101000
0010	0010111	0110	0110001	1010	1010010	1110	1110100
0011	0011100	0111	0111010	1011	1011001	1111	1111111

Table 1.14. The sixteen codewords $\{\mathbf{t}\}$ of the $(7, 4)$ Hamming code. Any pair of codewords differ from each other in at least three bits.

Because the Hamming code is a linear code, it can be written compactly in terms of matrices as follows. The transmitted codeword **t** is obtained from the source sequence **s** by a linear operation,

$$\mathbf{t} = \mathbf{G}^{\mathsf{T}} \mathbf{s}, \qquad (1.25)$$

where **G** is the *generator matrix* of the code,

$$\mathbf{G}^{\mathsf{T}} = \begin{bmatrix} 1 & 0 & 0 & 0 \\ 0 & 1 & 0 & 0 \\ 0 & 0 & 1 & 0 \\ 0 & 0 & 0 & 1 \\ 1 & 1 & 1 & 0 \\ 0 & 1 & 1 & 1 \\ 1 & 0 & 1 & 1 \end{bmatrix}, \qquad (1.26)$$

and the encoding operation (1.25) uses modulo-2 arithmetic ($1 + 1 = 0$, $0 + 1 = 1$, etc.).

In the encoding operation (1.25) I have assumed that **s** and **t** are column vectors. If instead they are row vectors, then this equation is replaced by

$$\mathbf{t} = \mathbf{s} \mathbf{G}, \qquad (1.27)$$

where

$$\mathbf{G} = \begin{bmatrix} 1 & 0 & 0 & 0 & 1 & 0 & 1 \\ 0 & 1 & 0 & 0 & 1 & 1 & 0 \\ 0 & 0 & 1 & 0 & 1 & 1 & 1 \\ 0 & 0 & 0 & 1 & 0 & 1 & 1 \end{bmatrix}. \tag{1.28}$$

I find it easier to relate to the right-multiplication (1.25) than the left-multiplication (1.27). Many coding theory texts use the left-multiplying conventions (1.27–1.28), however.

The rows of the generator matrix (1.28) can be viewed as defining four basis vectors lying in a seven-dimensional binary space. The sixteen codewords are obtained by making all possible linear combinations of these vectors.

Decoding the $(7, 4)$ Hamming code

When we invent a more complex encoder $\mathbf{s} \to \mathbf{t}$, the task of decoding the received vector $\mathbf{r}$ becomes less straightforward. Remember that *any* of the bits may have been flipped, including the parity bits.

If we assume that the channel is a binary symmetric channel and that all source vectors are equiprobable, then the optimal decoder identifies the source vector $\mathbf{s}$ whose encoding $\mathbf{t}(\mathbf{s})$ differs from the received vector $\mathbf{r}$ in the fewest bits. [Refer to the likelihood function (1.23) to see why this is so.] We could solve the decoding problem by measuring how far $\mathbf{r}$ is from each of the sixteen codewords in table 1.14, then picking the closest. Is there a more efficient way of finding the most probable source vector?

Syndrome decoding for the Hamming code

For the $(7, 4)$ Hamming code there is a pictorial solution to the decoding problem, based on the encoding picture, figure 1.13.

As a first example, let's assume the transmission was $\mathbf{t} = 1000101$ and the noise flips the second bit, so the received vector is $\mathbf{r} = 1000101 \oplus 0100000 = 1100101$. We write the received vector into the three circles as shown in figure 1.15a, and look at each of the three circles to see whether its parity is even. The circles whose parity is *not* even are shown by dashed lines in figure 1.15b. The decoding task is to find the smallest set of flipped bits that can account for these violations of the parity rules. [The pattern of violations of the parity checks is called the *syndrome*, and can be written as a binary vector – for example, in figure 1.15b, the syndrome is $\mathbf{z} = (1, 1, 0)$, because the first two circles are 'unhappy' (parity 1) and the third circle is 'happy' (parity 0).]

To solve the decoding task, we ask the question: can we find a unique bit that lies *inside* all the 'unhappy' circles and *outside* all the 'happy' circles? If so, the flipping of that bit would account for the observed syndrome. In the case shown in figure 1.15b, the bit r_2 lies inside the two unhappy circles and outside the happy circle; no other single bit has this property, so r_2 is the only single bit capable of explaining the syndrome.

Let's work through a couple more examples. Figure 1.15c shows what happens if one of the parity bits, t_5, is flipped by the noise. Just one of the checks is violated. Only r_5 lies inside this unhappy circle and outside the other two happy circles, so r_5 is identified as the only single bit capable of explaining the syndrome.

If the central bit r_3 is received flipped, figure 1.15d shows that all three checks are violated; only r_3 lies inside all three circles, so r_3 is identified as the suspect bit.

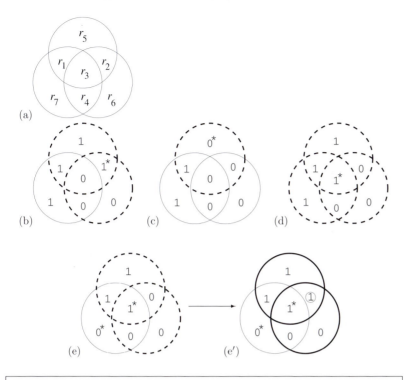

Figure 1.15. Pictorial representation of decoding of the Hamming $(7, 4)$ code. The received vector is written into the diagram as shown in (a). In (b,c,d,e), the received vector is shown, assuming that the transmitted vector was as in figure 1.13b and the bits labelled by $\star$ were flipped. The violated parity checks are highlighted by dashed circles. One of the seven bits is the most probable suspect to account for each 'syndrome', i.e., each pattern of violated and satisfied parity checks.

In examples (b), (c), and (d), the most probable suspect is the one bit that was flipped.

In example (e), two bits have been flipped, s_3 and t_7. The most probable suspect is r_2, marked by a circle in (e'), which shows the output of the decoding algorithm.

Syndrome $\mathbf{z}$	000	001	010	011	100	101	110	111
Unflip this bit	*none*	r_7	r_6	r_4	r_5	r_1	r_2	r_3

Algorithm 1.16. Actions taken by the optimal decoder for the $(7, 4)$ Hamming code, assuming a binary symmetric channel with small noise level f. The syndrome vector $\mathbf{z}$ lists whether each parity check is violated (1) or satisfied (0), going through the checks in the order of the bits r_5, r_6, and r_7.

If you try flipping any one of the seven bits, you'll find that a different syndrome is obtained in each case – seven non-zero syndromes, one for each bit. There is only one other syndrome, the all-zero syndrome. So if the channel is a binary symmetric channel with a small noise level f, the optimal decoder unflips at most one bit, depending on the syndrome, as shown in algorithm 1.16. Each syndrome could have been caused by other noise patterns too, but any other noise pattern that has the same syndrome must be less probable because it involves a larger number of noise events.

What happens if the noise actually flips more than one bit? Figure 1.15e shows the situation when two bits, r_3 and r_7, are received flipped. The syndrome, 110, makes us suspect the single bit r_2; so our optimal decoding algorithm flips this bit, giving a decoded pattern with three errors as shown in figure 1.15e'. If we use the optimal decoding algorithm, any two-bit error pattern will lead to a decoded seven-bit vector that contains three errors.

General view of decoding for linear codes: syndrome decoding

We can also describe the decoding problem for a linear code in terms of matrices. The first four received bits, $r_1r_2r_3r_4$, purport to be the four source bits; and the received bits $r_5r_6r_7$ purport to be the parities of the source bits, as defined by the generator matrix $\mathbf{G}$. We evaluate the three parity-check bits for the received bits, $r_1r_2r_3r_4$, and see whether they match the three received bits, $r_5r_6r_7$. The differences (modulo 2) between these two triplets are called the *syndrome* of the received vector. If the syndrome is zero – if all three parity checks are happy – then the received vector is a codeword, and the most probable decoding is

s   ENCODER   **t**   CHANNEL   **r**   DECODER   ŝ

$f = 10\%$

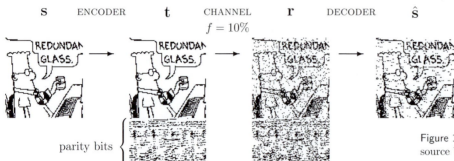

parity bits {

Figure 1.17. Transmitting 10 000 source bits over a binary symmetric channel with $f = 10\%$ using a $(7, 4)$ Hamming code. The probability of decoded bit error is about 7%.

given by reading out its first four bits. If the syndrome is non-zero, then the noise sequence for this block was non-zero, and the syndrome is our pointer to the most probable error pattern.

The computation of the syndrome vector is a linear operation. If we define the 3×4 matrix **P** such that the matrix of equation (1.26) is

$$\mathbf{G}^{\mathsf{T}} = \begin{bmatrix} \mathbf{I}_4 \\ \mathbf{P} \end{bmatrix}, \tag{1.29}$$

where $\mathbf{I}_4$ is the 4×4 identity matrix, then the syndrome vector is $\mathbf{z} = \mathbf{H}\mathbf{r}$, where the *parity-check matrix* **H** is given by $\mathbf{H} = \begin{bmatrix} -\mathbf{P} & \mathbf{I}_3 \end{bmatrix}$; in modulo 2 arithmetic, $-1 \equiv 1$, so

$$\mathbf{H} = \begin{bmatrix} \mathbf{P} & \mathbf{I}_3 \end{bmatrix} = \begin{bmatrix} 1 & 1 & 1 & 0 & 1 & 0 & 0 \\ 0 & 1 & 1 & 1 & 0 & 1 & 0 \\ 1 & 0 & 1 & 1 & 0 & 0 & 1 \end{bmatrix}. \tag{1.30}$$

All the codewords $\mathbf{t} = \mathbf{G}^{\mathsf{T}}\mathbf{s}$ of the code satisfy

$$\mathbf{H}\mathbf{t} = \begin{bmatrix} 0 \\ 0 \\ 0 \end{bmatrix}. \tag{1.31}$$

▷ Exercise 1.4.[1] Prove that this is so by evaluating the 3×4 matrix $\mathbf{H}\mathbf{G}^{\mathsf{T}}$.

Since the received vector **r** is given by $\mathbf{r} = \mathbf{G}^{\mathsf{T}}\mathbf{s} + \mathbf{n}$, the syndrome-decoding problem is to find the most probable noise vector **n** satisfying the equation

$$\mathbf{H}\mathbf{n} = \mathbf{z}. \tag{1.32}$$

A decoding algorithm that solves this problem is called a *maximum-likelihood decoder*. We will discuss decoding problems like this in later chapters.

Summary of the $(7, 4)$ Hamming code's properties

Every possible received vector of length 7 bits is either a codeword, or it's one flip away from a codeword.

Since there are three parity constraints, each of which might or might not be violated, there are $2 \times 2 \times 2 = 8$ distinct syndromes. They can be divided into seven non-zero syndromes – one for each of the one-bit error patterns – and the all-zero syndrome, corresponding to the zero-noise case.

The optimal decoder takes no action if the syndrome is zero, otherwise it uses this mapping of non-zero syndromes onto one-bit error patterns to unflip the suspect bit.

There is a *decoding error* if the four decoded bits $\hat{s}_1, \hat{s}_2, \hat{s}_3, \hat{s}_4$ do not all match the source bits s_1, s_2, s_3, s_4. The *probability of block error* p_{B} is the probability that one or more of the decoded bits in one block fail to match the corresponding source bits,

$$p_{\mathrm{B}} = P(\hat{\mathbf{s}} \neq \mathbf{s}). \tag{1.33}$$

The *probability of bit error* p_{b} is the average probability that a decoded bit fails to match the corresponding source bit,

$$p_{\mathrm{b}} = \frac{1}{K} \sum_{k=1}^{K} P(\hat{s}_k \neq s_k). \tag{1.34}$$

In the case of the Hamming code, a decoding error will occur whenever the noise has flipped more than one bit in a block of seven. The probability of block error is thus the probability that two or more bits are flipped in a block. This probability scales as $O(f^2)$, as did the probability of error for the repetition code R_3. But notice that the Hamming code communicates at a greater rate, $R = 4/7$.

Figure 1.17 shows a binary image transmitted over a binary symmetric channel using the $(7, 4)$ Hamming code. About 7% of the decoded bits are in error. Notice that the errors are correlated: often two or three successive decoded bits are flipped.

Exercise 1.5.[1] This exercise and the next three refer to the $(7, 4)$ Hamming code. Decode the received strings:

    (a) $\mathbf{r} = 1101011$

    (b) $\mathbf{r} = 0110110$

    (c) $\mathbf{r} = 0100111$

    (d) $\mathbf{r} = 1111111$.

Exercise 1.6.[2, p.17] (a) Calculate the probability of block error p_{B} of the $(7, 4)$ Hamming code as a function of the noise level f and show that to leading order it goes as $21f^2$.

    (b) [3] Show that to leading order the probability of bit error p_{b} goes as $9f^2$.

Exercise 1.7.[2, p.19] Find some noise vectors that give the all-zero syndrome (that is, noise vectors that leave all the parity checks unviolated). How many such noise vectors are there?

▷ Exercise 1.8.[2] I asserted above that a block decoding error will result whenever two or more bits are flipped in a single block. Show that this is indeed so. [In principle, there might be error patterns that, after decoding, led only to the corruption of the parity bits, with no source bits incorrectly decoded.]

Summary of codes' performances

Figure 1.18 shows the performance of repetition codes and the Hamming code. It also shows the performance of a family of linear block codes that are generalizations of Hamming codes, called BCH codes.

This figure shows that we can, using linear block codes, achieve better performance than repetition codes; but the asymptotic situation still looks grim.

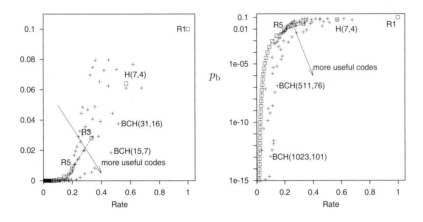

Figure 1.18. Error probability p_b versus rate R for repetition codes, the $(7, 4)$ Hamming code and BCH codes with block lengths up to 1023 over a binary symmetric channel with $f = 0.1$. The righthand figure shows p_b on a logarithmic scale.

Exercise 1.9.[4, p.19] Design an error-correcting code and a decoding algorithm for it, estimate its probability of error, and add it to figure 1.18. [Don't worry if you find it difficult to make a code better than the Hamming code, or if you find it difficult to find a good decoder for your code; that's the point of this exercise.]

Exercise 1.10.[3, p.20] A $(7, 4)$ Hamming code can correct any *one* error; might there be a $(14, 8)$ code that can correct any two errors?

Optional extra: Does the answer to this question depend on whether the code is linear or nonlinear?

Exercise 1.11.[4, p.21] Design an error-correcting code, other than a repetition code, that can correct any *two* errors in a block of size N.

▶ 1.3 What performance can the best codes achieve?

There seems to be a trade-off between the decoded bit-error probability p_b (which we would like to reduce) and the rate R (which we would like to keep large). How can this trade-off be characterized? What points in the (R, p_b) plane are achievable? This question was addressed by Claude Shannon in his pioneering paper of 1948, in which he both created the field of information theory and solved most of its fundamental problems.

At that time there was a widespread belief that the boundary between achievable and nonachievable points in the (R, p_b) plane was a curve passing through the origin $(R, p_b) = (0, 0)$; if this were so, then, in order to achieve a vanishingly small error probability p_b, one would have to reduce the rate correspondingly close to zero. 'No pain, no gain.'

However, Shannon proved the remarkable result that the boundary between achievable and nonachievable points meets the R axis at a *non-zero* value $R = C$, as shown in figure 1.19. For any channel, there exist codes that make it possible to communicate with *arbitrarily small* probability of error p_b at non-zero rates. The first half of this book (Parts I–III) will be devoted to understanding this remarkable result, which is called the *noisy-channel coding theorem*.

Example: $f = 0.1$

The maximum rate at which communication is possible with arbitrarily small p_b is called the *capacity* of the channel. The formula for the capacity of a

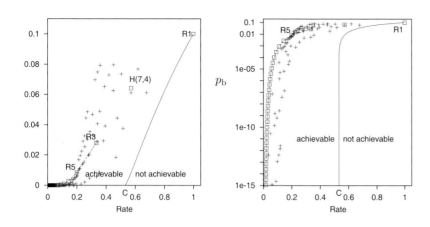

Figure 1.19. Shannon's noisy-channel coding theorem. The solid curve shows the Shannon limit on achievable values of (R, p_b) for the binary symmetric channel with $f = 0.1$. Rates up to $R = C$ are achievable with arbitrarily small p_b. The points show the performance of some textbook codes, as in figure 1.18.

The equation defining the Shannon limit (the solid curve) is $R = C/(1 - H_2(p_b))$, where C and H_2 are defined in equation (1.35).

binary symmetric channel with noise level f is

$$C(f) = 1 - H_2(f) = 1 - \left[f \log_2 \frac{1}{f} + (1 - f) \log_2 \frac{1}{1 - f} \right]; \qquad (1.35)$$

the channel we were discussing earlier with noise level $f = 0.1$ has capacity $C \simeq 0.53$. Let us consider what this means in terms of noisy disk drives. The repetition code R_3 could communicate over this channel with $p_b = 0.03$ at a rate $R = 1/3$. Thus we know how to build a single gigabyte disk drive with $p_b = 0.03$ from three noisy gigabyte disk drives. We also know how to make a single gigabyte disk drive with $p_b \simeq 10^{-15}$ from sixty noisy one-gigabyte drives (exercise 1.3, p.8). And now Shannon passes by, notices us juggling with disk drives and codes and says:

> 'What performance are you trying to achieve? 10^{-15}? You don't need *sixty* disk drives – you can get that performance with just *two* disk drives (since $1/2$ is less than 0.53). And if you want $p_b = 10^{-18}$ or 10^{-24} or anything, you can get there with two disk drives too!'

[Strictly, the above statements might not be quite right, since, as we shall see, Shannon proved his noisy-channel coding theorem by studying sequences of block codes with ever-increasing blocklengths, and the required blocklength might be bigger than a gigabyte (the size of our disk drive), in which case, Shannon might say 'well, you can't do it with those *tiny* disk drives, but if you had two noisy *terabyte* drives, you could make a single high quality terabyte drive from them'.]

▶ ## 1.4 Summary

The $(7, 4)$ Hamming Code

By including three parity-check bits in a block of 7 bits it is possible to detect and correct any single bit error in each block.

Shannon's noisy-channel coding theorem

Information can be communicated over a noisy channel at a non-zero rate with arbitrarily small error probability.

Information theory addresses both the *limitations* and the *possibilities* of communication. The noisy-channel coding theorem, which we will prove in Chapter 10, asserts both that reliable communication at any rate beyond the capacity is impossible, and that reliable communication at all rates up to capacity is possible.

The next few chapters lay the foundations for this result by discussing *how to measure information content* and the intimately related topic of *data compression*.

▶ 1.5 Further exercises

▷ **Exercise 1.12.**[2, p.21] Consider the repetition code R_9. One way of viewing this code is as a *concatenation* of R_3 with R_3. We first encode the source stream with R_3, then encode the resulting output with R_3. We could call this code 'R_3^2'. This idea motivates an alternative decoding algorithm, in which we decode the bits three at a time using the decoder for R_3; then decode the decoded bits from that first decoder using the decoder for R_3.

Evaluate the probability of error for this decoder and compare it with the probability of error for the optimal decoder for R_9.

Do the concatenated encoder and decoder for R_3^2 have advantages over those for R_9?

▶ 1.6 Solutions

Solution to exercise 1.2 (p.7). An error is made by R_3 if two or more bits are flipped in a block of three. So the error probability of R_3 is a sum of two terms: the probability that all three bits are flipped, f^3; and the probability that exactly two bits are flipped, $3f^2(1-f)$. [If these expressions are not obvious, see example 1.1 (p.1): the expressions are $P(r=3 \mid f, N=3)$ and $P(r=2 \mid f, N=3)$.]

$$p_b = p_B = 3f^2(1-f) + f^3 = 3f^2 - 2f^3. \tag{1.36}$$

This probability is dominated for small f by the term $3f^2$.

See exercise 2.38 (p.39) for further discussion of this problem.

Solution to exercise 1.3 (p.8). The probability of error for the repetition code R_N is dominated by the probability of $\lceil N/2 \rceil$ bits' being flipped, which goes (for odd N) as

$$\binom{N}{\lceil N/2 \rceil} f^{(N+1)/2}(1-f)^{(N-1)/2}. \tag{1.37}$$

Notation: $\lceil N/2 \rceil$ denotes the smallest integer greater than or equal to $N/2$.

The term $\binom{N}{K}$ can be approximated using the binary entropy function:

$$\frac{1}{N+1} 2^{NH_2(K/N)} \leq \binom{N}{K} \leq 2^{NH_2(K/N)} \Rightarrow \binom{N}{K} \simeq 2^{NH_2(K/N)}, \tag{1.38}$$

where this approximation introduces an error of order $\sqrt{N}$ – as shown in equation (1.17). So

$$p_b = p_B \simeq 2^N (f(1-f))^{N/2} = (4f(1-f))^{N/2}. \tag{1.39}$$

Setting this equal to the required value of 10^{-15} we find $N \simeq 2\frac{\log 10^{-15}}{\log 4f(1-f)} = 68$. This answer is a little out because the approximation we used overestimated $\binom{N}{K}$ and we did not distinguish between $\lceil N/2 \rceil$ and $N/2$.

A slightly more careful answer (short of explicit computation) goes as follows. Taking the approximation for $\binom{N}{K}$ to the next order, we find:

$$\binom{N}{N/2} \simeq 2^N \frac{1}{\sqrt{2\pi N/4}}. \tag{1.40}$$

This approximation can be proved from an accurate version of Stirling's approximation (1.12), or by considering the binomial distribution with $p = 1/2$ and noting

$$1 = \sum_K \binom{N}{K} 2^{-N} \simeq 2^{-N} \binom{N}{N/2} \sum_{r=-N/2}^{N/2} e^{-r^2/2\sigma^2} \simeq 2^{-N} \binom{N}{N/2} \sqrt{2\pi}\sigma, \tag{1.41}$$

where $\sigma = \sqrt{N/4}$, from which equation (1.40) follows. The distinction between $\lceil N/2 \rceil$ and $N/2$ is not important in this term since $\binom{N}{K}$ has a maximum at $K = N/2$.

Then the probability of error (for odd N) is to leading order

$$p_b \simeq \binom{N}{(N+1)/2} f^{(N+1)/2} (1-f)^{(N-1)/2} \tag{1.42}$$

$$\simeq 2^N \frac{1}{\sqrt{\pi N/2}} f[f(1-f)]^{(N-1)/2} \simeq \frac{1}{\sqrt{\pi N/8}} f[4f(1-f)]^{(N-1)/2} \tag{1.43}$$

The equation $p_b = 10^{-15}$ can be written

$$(N-1)/2 \simeq \frac{\log 10^{-15} + \log \frac{\sqrt{\pi N/8}}{f}}{\log 4f(1-f)} \tag{1.44}$$

which may be solved for N iteratively, the first iteration starting from $\hat{N}_1 = 68$:

$$(\hat{N}_2 - 1)/2 \simeq \frac{-15 + 1.7}{-0.44} = 29.9 \quad \Rightarrow \quad \hat{N}_2 \simeq 60.9 \tag{1.45}$$

This answer is found to be stable, so $N \simeq 61$ is the block length at which $p_b \simeq 10^{-15}$.

Solution to exercise 1.6 (p.13).

(a) The probability of block error of the Hamming code is a sum of six terms – the probabilities that 2, 3, 4, 5, 6, or 7 errors occur in one block.

$$p_B = \sum_{r=2}^{7} \binom{7}{r} f^r (1-f)^{7-r}. \tag{1.46}$$

To leading order, this goes as

$$p_B \simeq \binom{7}{2} f^2 = 21 f^2. \tag{1.47}$$

(b) The probability of bit error of the Hamming code is smaller than the probability of block error because a block error rarely corrupts all bits in the decoded block. The leading-order behaviour is found by considering the outcome in the most probable case where the noise vector has weight two. The decoder will erroneously flip a *third* bit, so that the modified received vector (of length 7) differs in three bits from the transmitted vector. That means, if we average over all seven bits, the probability that a randomly chosen bit is flipped is 3/7 times the block error probability, to leading order. Now, what we really care about is the probability that a source bit is flipped. Are parity bits or source bits more likely to be among these three flipped bits, or are all seven bits equally likely to be corrupted when the noise vector has weight two? The Hamming code is in fact completely symmetric in the protection it affords to the seven bits (assuming a binary symmetric channel). [This symmetry can be proved by showing that the role of a parity bit can be exchanged with a source bit and the resulting code is still a $(7,4)$ Hamming code; see below.] The probability that any one bit ends up corrupted is the same for all seven bits. So the probability of bit error (for the source bits) is simply three sevenths of the probability of block error.

$$p_{\mathrm{b}} \simeq \frac{3}{7} p_{\mathrm{B}} \simeq 9f^2. \tag{1.48}$$

Symmetry of the Hamming $(7,4)$ code

To prove that the $(7,4)$ code protects all bits equally, we start from the parity-check matrix

$$\mathbf{H} = \begin{bmatrix} 1 & 1 & 1 & 0 & 1 & 0 & 0 \\ 0 & 1 & 1 & 1 & 0 & 1 & 0 \\ 1 & 0 & 1 & 1 & 0 & 0 & 1 \end{bmatrix}. \tag{1.49}$$

The symmetry among the seven transmitted bits will be easiest to see if we reorder the seven bits using the permutation $(t_1 t_2 t_3 t_4 t_5 t_6 t_7) \rightarrow (t_5 t_2 t_3 t_4 t_1 t_6 t_7)$. Then we can rewrite $\mathbf{H}$ thus:

$$\mathbf{H} = \begin{bmatrix} 1 & 1 & 1 & 0 & 1 & 0 & 0 \\ 0 & 1 & 1 & 1 & 0 & 1 & 0 \\ 0 & 0 & 1 & 1 & 1 & 0 & 1 \end{bmatrix}. \tag{1.50}$$

Now, if we take any two parity constraints that $\mathbf{t}$ satisfies and add them together, we get another parity constraint. For example, row 1 asserts $t_5 + t_2 + t_3 + t_1 = \text{even}$, and row 2 asserts $t_2 + t_3 + t_4 + t_6 = \text{even}$, and the sum of these two constraints is

$$t_5 + 2t_2 + 2t_3 + t_1 + t_4 + t_6 = \text{even}; \tag{1.51}$$

we can drop the terms $2t_2$ and $2t_3$, since they are even whatever t_2 and t_3 are; thus we have derived the parity constraint $t_5 + t_1 + t_4 + t_6 = \text{even}$, which we can if we wish add into the parity-check matrix as a fourth row. [The set of vectors satisfying $\mathbf{Ht} = \mathbf{0}$ will not be changed.] We thus define

$$\mathbf{H'} = \begin{bmatrix} 1 & 1 & 1 & 0 & 1 & 0 & 0 \\ 0 & 1 & 1 & 1 & 0 & 1 & 0 \\ 0 & 0 & 1 & 1 & 1 & 0 & 1 \\ 1 & 0 & 0 & 1 & 1 & 1 & 0 \end{bmatrix}. \tag{1.52}$$

The fourth row is the sum (modulo two) of the top two rows. Notice that *the second, third, and fourth rows are all cyclic shifts of the top row.* If, having added the fourth redundant constraint, we drop the first constraint, we obtain a new parity-check matrix $\mathbf{H''}$,

$$\mathbf{H''} = \begin{bmatrix} 0 & 1 & 1 & 1 & 0 & 1 & 0 \\ 0 & 0 & 1 & 1 & 1 & 0 & 1 \\ 1 & 0 & 0 & 1 & 1 & 1 & 0 \end{bmatrix}, \tag{1.53}$$

which still satisfies $\mathbf{H''t} = 0$ for all codewords, and which looks just like the starting $\mathbf{H}$ in (1.50), except that all the columns have shifted along one to the right, and the rightmost column has reappeared at the left (a cyclic permutation of the columns).

This establishes the symmetry among the seven bits. Iterating the above procedure five more times, we can make a total of seven different $\mathbf{H}$ matrices for the same original code, each of which assigns each bit to a different role.

We may also construct the super-redundant seven-row parity-check matrix for the code,

$$\mathbf{H}''' = \begin{bmatrix} 1 & 1 & 1 & 0 & 1 & 0 & 0 \\ 0 & 1 & 1 & 1 & 0 & 1 & 0 \\ 0 & 0 & 1 & 1 & 1 & 0 & 1 \\ 1 & 0 & 0 & 1 & 1 & 1 & 0 \\ 0 & 1 & 0 & 0 & 1 & 1 & 1 \\ 1 & 0 & 1 & 0 & 0 & 1 & 1 \\ 1 & 1 & 0 & 1 & 0 & 0 & 1 \end{bmatrix}. \tag{1.54}$$

This matrix is 'redundant' in the sense that the space spanned by its rows is only three-dimensional, not seven.

This matrix is also a *cyclic* matrix. Every row is a cyclic permutation of the top row.

Cyclic codes: if there is an ordering of the bits $t_1 \ldots t_N$ such that a linear code has a *cyclic* parity-check matrix, then the code is called a *cyclic code*.

The codewords of such a code also have cyclic properties: any cyclic permutation of a codeword is a codeword.

For example, the Hamming $(7, 4)$ code, with its bits ordered as above, consists of all seven cyclic shifts of the codewords 1110100 and 1011000, and the codewords 0000000 and 1111111.

Cyclic codes are a cornerstone of the algebraic approach to error-correcting codes. We won't use them again in this book, however, as they have been superceded by sparse graph codes (Part VI).

Solution to exercise 1.7 (p.13). There are fifteen non-zero noise vectors which give the all-zero syndrome; these are precisely the fifteen non-zero codewords of the Hamming code. Notice that because the Hamming code is *linear*, the sum of any two codewords is a codeword.

Graphs corresponding to codes

Solution to exercise 1.9 (p.14). When answering this question, you will probably find that it is easier to invent new codes than to find optimal decoders for them. There are many ways to design codes, and what follows is just one possible train of thought. We make a linear block code that is similar to the $(7, 4)$ Hamming code, but bigger.

Many codes can be conveniently expressed in terms of graphs. In figure 1.13, we introduced a pictorial representation of the $(7, 4)$ Hamming code. If we replace that figure's big circles, each of which shows that the parity of four particular bits is even, by a 'parity-check node' that is connected to the four bits, then we obtain the representation of the $(7, 4)$ Hamming code by a *bipartite graph* as shown in figure 1.20. The 7 circles are the 7 transmitted bits. The 3 squares are the parity-check nodes (not to be confused with the 3 parity-check *bits*, which are the three most peripheral circles). The graph is a 'bipartite' graph because its nodes fall into two classes – bits and checks

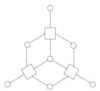

Figure 1.20. The graph of the $(7, 4)$ Hamming code. The 7 circles are the bit nodes and the 3 squares are the parity-check nodes.

– and there are edges only between nodes in different classes. The graph and the code's parity-check matrix (1.30) are simply related to each other: each parity-check node corresponds to a row of $\mathbf{H}$ and each bit node corresponds to a column of $\mathbf{H}$; for every 1 in $\mathbf{H}$, there is an edge between the corresponding pair of nodes.

Having noticed this connection between linear codes and graphs, one way to invent linear codes is simply to think of a bipartite graph. For example, a pretty bipartite graph can be obtained from a dodecahedron by calling the vertices of the dodecahedron the parity-check nodes, and putting a transmitted bit on each edge in the dodecahedron. This construction defines a parity-check matrix in which every column has weight 2 and every row has weight 3. [The weight of a binary vector is the number of 1s it contains.]

This code has $N = 30$ bits, and it appears to have $M_{\text{apparent}} = 20$ parity-check constraints. Actually, there are only $M = 19$ *independent* constraints; the 20th constraint is redundant (that is, if 19 constraints are satisfied, then the 20th is automatically satisfied); so the number of source bits is $K = N - M = 11$. The code is a $(30, 11)$ code.

It is hard to find a decoding algorithm for this code, but we can estimate its probability of error by finding its lowest weight codewords. If we flip all the bits surrounding one face of the original dodecahedron, then all the parity checks will be satisfied; so the code has 12 codewords of weight 5, one for each face. Since the lowest-weight codewords have weight 5, we say that the code has distance $d = 5$; the $(7, 4)$ Hamming code had distance 3 and could correct all single bit-flip errors. A code with distance 5 can correct all double bit-flip errors, but there are some triple bit-flip errors that it cannot correct. So the error probability of this code, assuming a binary symmetric channel, will be dominated, at least for low noise levels f, by a term of order f^3, perhaps something like

$$12 \binom{5}{3} f^3 (1 - f)^{27}. \tag{1.55}$$

Of course, there is no obligation to make codes whose graphs can be represented on a plane, as this one can; the best linear codes, which have simple graphical descriptions, have graphs that are more tangled, as illustrated by the tiny $(16, 4)$ code of figure 1.22.

Furthermore, there is no reason for sticking to linear codes; indeed some nonlinear codes – codes whose codewords cannot be defined by a linear equation like $\mathbf{Ht} = \mathbf{0}$ – have very good properties. But the encoding and decoding of a nonlinear code are even trickier tasks.

Solution to exercise 1.10 (p.14). First let's assume we are making a linear code and decoding it with syndrome decoding. If there are N transmitted bits, then the number of possible error patterns of weight up to two is

$$\binom{N}{2} + \binom{N}{1} + \binom{N}{0}. \tag{1.56}$$

For $N = 14$, that's $91 + 14 + 1 = 106$ patterns. Now, every distinguishable error pattern must give rise to a distinct syndrome; and the syndrome is a list of M bits, so the maximum possible number of syndromes is 2^M. For a $(14, 8)$ code, $M = 6$, so there are at most $2^6 = 64$ syndromes. The number of possible error patterns of weight up to two, 106, is bigger than the number of syndromes, 64, so we can immediately rule out the possibility that there is a $(14, 8)$ code that is 2-error-correcting.

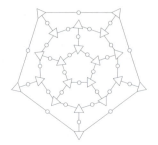

Figure 1.21. The graph defining the $(30, 11)$ dodecahedron code. The circles are the 30 transmitted bits and the triangles are the 20 parity checks. One parity check is redundant.

Figure 1.22. Graph of a rate-$\frac{1}{4}$ low-density parity-check code (Gallager code) with blocklength $N = 16$, and $M = 12$ parity-check constraints. Each white circle represents a transmitted bit. Each bit participates in $j = 3$ constraints, represented by $\boxplus$ squares. The edges between nodes were placed at random. (See Chapter 47 for more.)

The same counting argument works fine for nonlinear codes too. When the decoder receives $\mathbf{r} = \mathbf{t} + \mathbf{n}$, his aim is to deduce both $\mathbf{t}$ and $\mathbf{n}$ from $\mathbf{r}$. If it is the case that the sender can select any transmission $\mathbf{t}$ from a code of size $S_{\mathbf{t}}$, and the channel can select any noise vector from a set of size $S_{\mathbf{n}}$, and those two selections can be recovered from the received bit string $\mathbf{r}$, which is one of at most 2^N possible strings, then it must be the case that

$$S_{\mathbf{t}} S_{\mathbf{n}} \leq 2^N. \tag{1.57}$$

So, for a (N, K) two-error-correcting code, whether linear or nonlinear,

$$2^K \left[\binom{N}{2} + \binom{N}{1} + \binom{N}{0} \right] \leq 2^N. \tag{1.58}$$

Solution to exercise 1.11 (p.14). There are various strategies for making codes that can correct multiple errors, and I strongly recommend you think out one or two of them for yourself.

If your approach uses a linear code, e.g., one with a collection of M parity checks, it is helpful to bear in mind the counting argument given in the previous exercise, in order to anticipate how many parity checks, M, you might need.

Examples of codes that can correct any two errors are the $(30, 11)$ dodecahedron code in the previous solution, and the $(15, 6)$ pentagonful code to be introduced on p.221. Further simple ideas for making codes that can correct multiple errors from codes that can correct only one error are discussed in section 13.7.

Solution to exercise 1.12 (p.16). The probability of error of R_3^2 is, to leading order,

$$p_{\mathrm{b}}(\mathrm{R}_3^2) \simeq 3 \left[p_{\mathrm{b}}(\mathrm{R}_3) \right]^2 = 3(3f^2)^2 + \cdots = 27f^4 + \cdots, \tag{1.59}$$

whereas the probability of error of R_9 is dominated by the probability of five flips,

$$p_{\mathrm{b}}(\mathrm{R}_9) \simeq \binom{9}{5} f^5 (1 - f)^4 \simeq 126f^5 + \cdots. \tag{1.60}$$

The R_3^2 decoding procedure is therefore suboptimal, since there are noise vectors of weight four that cause it to make a decoding error.

It has the advantage, however, of requiring smaller computational resources: only memorization of three bits, and counting up to three, rather than counting up to nine.

This simple code illustrates an important concept. Concatenated codes are widely used in practice because concatenation allows large codes to be implemented using simple encoding and decoding hardware. Some of the best known practical codes are concatenated codes.

2

Probability, Entropy, and Inference

This chapter, and its sibling, Chapter 8, devote some time to notation. Just as the White Knight distinguished between the song, the name of the song, and what the name of the song was called (Carroll, 1998), we will sometimes need to be careful to distinguish between a random variable, the value of the random variable, and the proposition that asserts that the random variable has a particular value. In any particular chapter, however, I will use the most simple and friendly notation possible, at the risk of upsetting pure-minded readers. For example, if something is 'true with probability 1', I will usually simply say that it is 'true'.

▶ ## 2.1 Probabilities and ensembles

An ensemble X is a triple $(x, \mathcal{A}_X, \mathcal{P}_X)$, where the *outcome* x is the value of a random variable, which takes on one of a set of possible values, $\mathcal{A}_X = \{a_1, a_2, \ldots, a_i, \ldots, a_I\}$, having probabilities $\mathcal{P}_X = \{p_1, p_2, \ldots, p_I\}$, with $P(x = a_i) = p_i$, $p_i \geq 0$ and $\sum_{a_i \in \mathcal{A}_X} P(x = a_i) = 1$.

The name $\mathcal{A}$ is mnemonic for 'alphabet'. One example of an ensemble is a letter that is randomly selected from an English document. This ensemble is shown in figure 2.1. There are twenty-seven possible letters: a–z, and a space character '–'.

Abbreviations. Briefer notation will sometimes be used. For example, $P(x = a_i)$ may be written as $P(a_i)$ or $P(x)$.

Probability of a subset. If T is a subset of $\mathcal{A}_X$ then:

$$P(T) = P(x \in T) = \sum_{a_i \in T} P(x = a_i). \tag{2.1}$$

For example, if we define V to be vowels from figure 2.1, $V = \{a, e, i, o, u\}$, then

$$P(V) = 0.06 + 0.09 + 0.06 + 0.07 + 0.03 = 0.31. \tag{2.2}$$

A joint ensemble XY is an ensemble in which each outcome is an ordered pair x, y with $x \in \mathcal{A}_X = \{a_1, \ldots, a_I\}$ and $y \in \mathcal{A}_Y = \{b_1, \ldots, b_J\}$.

We call $P(x, y)$ the joint probability of x and y.

Commas are optional when writing ordered pairs, so $xy \Leftrightarrow x, y$.

N.B. In a joint ensemble XY the two variables are not necessarily independent.

i	a_i	p_i		
1	a	0.0575	a	
2	b	0.0128	b	
3	c	0.0263	c	
4	d	0.0285	d	
5	e	0.0913	e	
6	f	0.0173	f	
7	g	0.0133	g	
8	h	0.0313	h	
9	i	0.0599	i	
10	j	0.0006	j	
11	k	0.0084	k	
12	l	0.0335	l	
13	m	0.0235	m	
14	n	0.0596	n	
15	o	0.0689	o	
16	p	0.0192	p	
17	q	0.0008	q	
18	r	0.0508	r	
19	s	0.0567	s	
20	t	0.0706	t	
21	u	0.0334	u	
22	v	0.0069	v	
23	w	0.0119	w	
24	x	0.0073	x	
25	y	0.0164	y	
26	z	0.0007	z	
27	–	0.1928	–	

Figure 2.1. Probability distribution over the 27 outcomes for a randomly selected letter in an English language document (estimated from *The Frequently Asked Questions Manual for Linux*). The picture shows the probabilities by the areas of white squares.

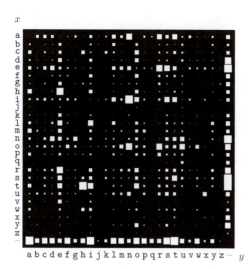

Figure 2.2. The probability distribution over the 27×27 possible bigrams xy in an English language document, *The Frequently Asked Questions Manual for Linux.*

Marginal probability. We can obtain the marginal probability $P(x)$ from the joint probability $P(x, y)$ by summation:

$$P(x=a_i) \equiv \sum_{y \in \mathcal{A}_Y} P(x=a_i, y). \tag{2.3}$$

Similarly, using briefer notation, the marginal probability of y is:

$$P(y) \equiv \sum_{x \in \mathcal{A}_X} P(x, y). \tag{2.4}$$

Conditional probability

$$P(x=a_i \mid y=b_j) \equiv \frac{P(x=a_i, y=b_j)}{P(y=b_j)} \text{ if } P(y=b_j) \neq 0. \tag{2.5}$$

[If $P(y=b_j) = 0$ then $P(x=a_i \mid y=b_j)$ is undefined.]

We pronounce $P(x=a_i \mid y=b_j)$ 'the probability that x equals a_i, given y equals b_j'.

Example 2.1. An example of a joint ensemble is the ordered pair XY consisting of two successive letters in an English document. The possible outcomes are ordered pairs such as aa, ab, ac, and zz; of these, we might expect ab and ac to be more probable than aa and zz. An estimate of the joint probability distribution for two neighbouring characters is shown graphically in figure 2.2.

This joint ensemble has the special property that its two marginal distributions, $P(x)$ and $P(y)$, are identical. They are both equal to the monogram distribution shown in figure 2.1.

From this joint ensemble $P(x, y)$ we can obtain conditional distributions, $P(y \mid x)$ and $P(x \mid y)$, by normalizing the rows and columns, respectively (figure 2.3). The probability $P(y \mid x=\mathsf{q})$ is the probability distribution of the second letter given that the first letter is a q. As you can see in figure 2.3a, the two most probable values for the second letter y given

x

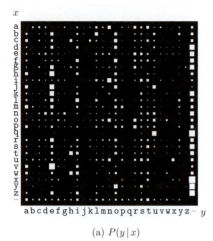

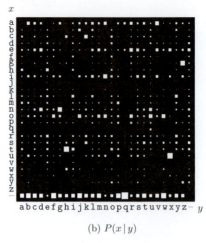

(a) $P(y\,|\,x)$ (b) $P(x\,|\,y)$

Figure 2.3. Conditional probability distributions. (a) $P(y\,|\,x)$: Each *row* shows the conditional distribution of the second letter, y, given the first letter, x, in a bigram xy. (b) $P(x\,|\,y)$: Each *column* shows the conditional distribution of the first letter, x, given the second letter, y.

that the first letter x is q are u and -. (The space is common after q because the source document makes heavy use of the word FAQ.)

The probability $P(x\,|\,y\!=\!\mathtt{u})$ is the probability distribution of the first letter x given that the second letter y is a u. As you can see in figure 2.3b the two most probable values for x given $y\!=\!\mathtt{u}$ are n and o.

Rather than writing down the joint probability directly, we often define an ensemble in terms of a collection of conditional probabilities. The following rules of probability theory will be useful. ($\mathcal{H}$ denotes assumptions on which the probabilities are based.)

Product rule – obtained from the definition of conditional probability:

$$P(x, y\,|\,\mathcal{H}) = P(x\,|\,y, \mathcal{H})P(y\,|\,\mathcal{H}) = P(y\,|\,x, \mathcal{H})P(x\,|\,\mathcal{H}). \qquad (2.6)$$

This rule is also known as the chain rule.

Sum rule – a rewriting of the marginal probability definition:

$$P(x\,|\,\mathcal{H}) = \sum_y P(x, y\,|\,\mathcal{H}) \qquad (2.7)$$

$$= \sum_y P(x\,|\,y, \mathcal{H})P(y\,|\,\mathcal{H}). \qquad (2.8)$$

Bayes' theorem – obtained from the product rule:

$$P(y\,|\,x, \mathcal{H}) = \frac{P(x\,|\,y, \mathcal{H})P(y\,|\,\mathcal{H})}{P(x\,|\,\mathcal{H})} \qquad (2.9)$$

$$= \frac{P(x\,|\,y, \mathcal{H})P(y\,|\,\mathcal{H})}{\sum_{y'} P(x\,|\,y', \mathcal{H})P(y'\,|\,\mathcal{H})}. \qquad (2.10)$$

Independence. Two random variables X and Y are *independent* (sometimes written $X \perp Y$) if and only if

$$P(x, y) = P(x)P(y). \qquad (2.11)$$

 Exercise 2.2.[1, p.40] Are the random variables X and Y in the joint ensemble of figure 2.2 independent?

I said that we often define an ensemble in terms of a collection of conditional probabilities. The following example illustrates this idea.

Example 2.3. Jo has a test for a nasty disease. We denote Jo's state of health by the variable a and the test result by b.

$$
\begin{aligned}
a = 1 & \quad \text{Jo has the disease} \\
a = 0 & \quad \text{Jo does not have the disease.}
\end{aligned}
\tag{2.12}
$$

The result of the test is either 'positive' ($b = 1$) or 'negative' ($b = 0$); the test is 95% reliable: in 95% of cases of people who really have the disease, a positive result is returned, and in 95% of cases of people who do not have the disease, a negative result is obtained. The final piece of background information is that 1% of people of Jo's age and background have the disease.

OK – Jo has the test, and the result was positive. What is the probability that Jo has the disease?

Solution. We write down all the provided probabilities. The test reliability specifies the conditional probability of b given a:

$$
\begin{aligned}
P(b{=}1 \mid a{=}1) = 0.95 & \quad P(b{=}1 \mid a{=}0) = 0.05 \\
P(b{=}0 \mid a{=}1) = 0.05 & \quad P(b{=}0 \mid a{=}0) = 0.95;
\end{aligned}
\tag{2.13}
$$

and the disease prevalence tells us about the marginal probability of a:

$$
P(a{=}1) = 0.01 \qquad P(a{=}0) = 0.99.
\tag{2.14}
$$

From the marginal $P(a)$ and the conditional probability $P(b \mid a)$ we can deduce the joint probability $P(a, b) = P(a)P(b \mid a)$ and any other probabilities we are interested in. For example, by the sum rule, the marginal probability of $b{=}1$ – the probability of getting a positive result – is

$$
P(b{=}1) = P(b{=}1 \mid a{=}1)P(a{=}1) + P(b{=}1 \mid a{=}0)P(a{=}0).
\tag{2.15}
$$

Jo has received a positive result $b{=}1$ and is interested in how plausible it is that she has the disease (i.e., that $a{=}1$). The man in the street might be duped by the statement 'the test is 95% reliable, so Jo's positive result implies that there is a 95% chance that Jo has the disease', but this is incorrect. The correct solution to an inference problem is found using Bayes' theorem.

$$
\begin{aligned}
P(a{=}1 \mid b{=}1) &= \frac{P(b{=}1 \mid a{=}1)P(a{=}1)}{P(b{=}1 \mid a{=}1)P(a{=}1) + P(b{=}1 \mid a{=}0)P(a{=}0)} \tag{2.16} \\
&= \frac{0.95 \times 0.01}{0.95 \times 0.01 + 0.05 \times 0.99} \tag{2.17} \\
&= 0.16 \tag{2.18}
\end{aligned}
$$

So in spite of the positive result, the probability that Jo has the disease is only 16%. □

▶ 2.2 The meaning of probability

Probabilities can be used in two ways.

Probabilities can describe *frequencies of outcomes in random experiments*, but giving noncircular definitions of the terms 'frequency' and 'random' is a challenge – what does it mean to say that the frequency of a tossed coin's

Notation. Let 'the degree of belief in proposition x' be denoted by $B(x)$. The negation of x (NOT-x) is written $\overline{x}$. The degree of belief in a conditional proposition, 'x, assuming proposition y to be true', is represented by $B(x\,|\,y)$.

Axiom 1. Degrees of belief can be ordered; if $B(x)$ is 'greater' than $B(y)$, and $B(y)$ is 'greater' than $B(z)$, then $B(x)$ is 'greater' than $B(z)$.

[Consequence: beliefs can be mapped onto real numbers.]

Axiom 2. The degree of belief in a proposition x and its negation $\overline{x}$ are related. There is a function f such that

$$B(x) = f[B(\overline{x})].$$

Axiom 3. The degree of belief in a conjunction of propositions x, y (x AND y) is related to the degree of belief in the conditional proposition $x\,|\,y$ and the degree of belief in the proposition y. There is a function g such that

$$B(x, y) = g\left[B(x\,|\,y), B(y)\right].$$

Box 2.4. The Cox axioms. If a set of beliefs satisfy these axioms then they can be mapped onto probabilities satisfying $P(\text{FALSE}) = 0$, $P(\text{TRUE}) = 1$, $0 \le P(x) \le 1$, and the rules of probability:

$$P(x) = 1 - P(\overline{x}),$$

and

$$P(x, y) = P(x\,|\,y)P(y).$$

coming up heads is $1/2$? If we say that this frequency is the average fraction of heads in long sequences, we have to define 'average'; and it is hard to define 'average' without using a word synonymous to probability! I will not attempt to cut this philosophical knot.

Probabilities can also be used, more generally, to describe *degrees of belief* in propositions that do not involve random variables – for example 'the probability that Mr. S. was the murderer of Mrs. S., given the evidence' (he either was or wasn't, and it's the jury's job to assess how probable it is that he was); 'the probability that Thomas Jefferson had a child by one of his slaves'; 'the probability that Shakespeare's plays were written by Francis Bacon'; or, to pick a modern-day example, 'the probability that a particular signature on a particular cheque is genuine'.

The man in the street is happy to use probabilities in both these ways, but some books on probability restrict probabilities to refer only to frequencies of outcomes in repeatable random experiments.

Nevertheless, degrees of belief *can* be mapped onto probabilities if they satisfy simple consistency rules known as the Cox axioms (Cox, 1946) (figure 2.4). Thus probabilities can be used to describe assumptions, and to describe inferences given those assumptions. The rules of probability ensure that if two people make the same assumptions and receive the same data then they will draw identical conclusions. This more general use of probability to quantify beliefs is known as the *Bayesian* viewpoint. It is also known as the *subjective* interpretation of probability, since the probabilities depend on assumptions. Advocates of a Bayesian approach to data modelling and pattern recognition do not view this subjectivity as a defect, since in their view,

you cannot do inference without making assumptions.

In this book it will from time to time be taken for granted that a Bayesian approach makes sense, but the reader is warned that this is not yet a globally held view – the field of statistics was dominated for most of the 20th century by non-Bayesian methods in which probabilities are allowed to describe only random variables. The big difference between the two approaches is that

Bayesians also use probabilities to describe *inferences*.

▶ 2.3 Forward probabilities and inverse probabilities

Probability calculations often fall into one of two categories: *forward probability* and *inverse probability*. Here is an example of a forward probability problem:

Exercise 2.4.[2, p.40] An urn contains K balls, of which B are black and $W = K - B$ are white. Fred draws a ball at random from the urn and replaces it, N times.

    (a) What is the probability distribution of the number of times a black ball is drawn, n_B?

    (b) What is the expectation of n_B? What is the variance of n_B? What is the standard deviation of n_B? Give numerical answers for the cases $N = 5$ and $N = 400$, when $B = 2$ and $K = 10$.

Forward probability problems involve a *generative model* that describes a process that is assumed to give rise to some data; the task is to compute the probability distribution or expectation of some quantity that depends on the data. Here is another example of a forward probability problem:

Exercise 2.5.[2, p.40] An urn contains K balls, of which B are black and $W = K - B$ are white. We define the fraction $f_B \equiv B/K$. Fred draws N times from the urn, exactly as in exercise 2.4, obtaining n_B blacks, and computes the quantity

$$z = \frac{(n_B - f_B N)^2}{N f_B (1 - f_B)}. \tag{2.19}$$

What is the expectation of z? In the case $N = 5$ and $f_B = 1/5$, what is the probability distribution of z? What is the probability that $z < 1$? [Hint: compare z with the quantities computed in the previous exercise.]

Like forward probability problems, *inverse probability problems* involve a generative model of a process, but instead of computing the probability distribution of some quantity *produced* by the process, we compute the conditional probability of one or more of the *unobserved variables* in the process, *given* the observed variables. This invariably requires the use of Bayes' theorem.

Example 2.6. There are eleven urns labelled by $u \in \{0, 1, 2, \ldots, 10\}$, each containing ten balls. Urn u contains u black balls and $10 - u$ white balls. Fred selects an urn u at random and draws N times with replacement from that urn, obtaining n_B blacks and $N - n_B$ whites. Fred's friend, Bill, looks on. If after $N = 10$ draws $n_B = 3$ blacks have been drawn, what is the probability that the urn Fred is using is urn u, from Bill's point of view? (Bill doesn't know the value of u.)

Solution. The joint probability distribution of the random variables u and n_B can be written

$$P(u, n_B \,|\, N) = P(n_B \,|\, u, N) P(u). \tag{2.20}$$

From the joint probability of u and n_B, we can obtain the conditional distribution of u given n_B:

$$P(u \,|\, n_B, N) = \frac{P(u, n_B \,|\, N)}{P(n_B \,|\, N)} \tag{2.21}$$

$$= \frac{P(n_B \,|\, u, N) P(u)}{P(n_B \,|\, N)}. \tag{2.22}$$

u

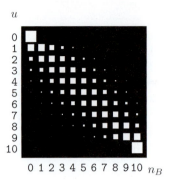

0 1 2 3 4 5 6 7 8 9 10 n_B

Figure 2.5. Joint probability of u and n_B for Bill and Fred's urn problem, after $N = 10$ draws.

The marginal probability of u is $P(u) = \frac{1}{11}$ for all u. You wrote down the probability of n_B given u and N, $P(n_B \mid u, N)$, when you solved exercise 2.4 (p.27). [You *are* doing the highly recommended exercises, aren't you?] If we define $f_u \equiv u/10$ then

$$P(n_B \mid u, N) = \binom{N}{n_B} f_u^{n_B} (1 - f_u)^{N-n_B}. \tag{2.23}$$

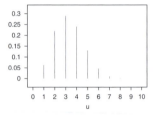

What about the denominator, $P(n_B \mid N)$? This is the marginal probability of n_B, which we can obtain using the sum rule:

$$P(n_B \mid N) = \sum_u P(u, n_B \mid N) = \sum_u P(u) P(n_B \mid u, N). \tag{2.24}$$

So the conditional probability of u given n_B is

$$P(u \mid n_B, N) = \frac{P(u) P(n_B \mid u, N)}{P(n_B \mid N)} \tag{2.25}$$

$$= \frac{1}{P(n_B \mid N)} \frac{1}{11} \binom{N}{n_B} f_u^{n_B} (1 - f_u)^{N-n_B}. \tag{2.26}$$

u	$P(u \mid n_B = 3, N)$
0	0
1	0.063
2	0.22
3	0.29
4	0.24
5	0.13
6	0.047
7	0.0099
8	0.00086
9	0.0000096
10	0

This conditional distribution can be found by normalizing column 3 of figure 2.5 and is shown in figure 2.6. The normalizing constant, the marginal probability of n_B, is $P(n_B = 3 \mid N = 10) = 0.083$. The posterior probability (2.26) is correct for all u, including the end-points $u = 0$ and $u = 10$, where $f_u = 0$ and $f_u = 1$ respectively. The posterior probability that $u = 0$ given $n_B = 3$ is equal to zero, because if Fred were drawing from urn 0 it would be impossible for any black balls to be drawn. The posterior probability that $u = 10$ is also zero, because there are no white balls in that urn. The other hypotheses $u = 1$, $u = 2$, ... $u = 9$ all have non-zero posterior probability. □

Figure 2.6. Conditional probability of u given $n_B = 3$ and $N = 10$.

Terminology of inverse probability

In inverse probability problems it is convenient to give names to the probabilities appearing in Bayes' theorem. In equation (2.25), we call the marginal probability $P(u)$ the *prior* probability of u, and $P(n_B \mid u, N)$ is called the *likelihood* of u. It is important to note that the terms likelihood and probability are not synonyms. The quantity $P(n_B \mid u, N)$ is a function of both n_B and u. For fixed u, $P(n_B \mid u, N)$ defines a *probability* over n_B. For fixed n_B, $P(n_B \mid u, N)$ defines the *likelihood* of u.

> Never say 'the likelihood of the data'. Always say 'the likelihood of the parameters'. The likelihood function is not a probability distribution.

(If you want to mention the data that a likelihood function is associated with, you may say 'the likelihood of the parameters given the data'.)

The conditional probability $P(u \mid n_B, N)$ is called the *posterior probability* of u given n_B. The normalizing constant $P(n_B \mid N)$ has no u-dependence so its value is not important if we simply wish to evaluate the relative probabilities of the alternative hypotheses u. However, in most data modelling problems of any complexity, this quantity becomes important, and it is given various names: $P(n_B \mid N)$ is known as the *evidence* or the *marginal likelihood*.

If $\boldsymbol{\theta}$ denotes the unknown parameters, D denotes the data, and $\mathcal{H}$ denotes the overall hypothesis space, the general equation:

$$P(\boldsymbol{\theta} \mid D, \mathcal{H}) = \frac{P(D \mid \boldsymbol{\theta}, \mathcal{H})P(\boldsymbol{\theta} \mid \mathcal{H})}{P(D \mid \mathcal{H})} \tag{2.27}$$

is written:

$$\text{posterior} = \frac{\text{likelihood} \times \text{prior}}{\text{evidence}}. \tag{2.28}$$

Inverse probability and prediction

Example 2.6 (continued). Assuming again that Bill has observed $n_B = 3$ blacks in $N = 10$ draws, let Fred draw another ball from the same urn. What is the probability that the next drawn ball is a black? [You should make use of the posterior probabilities in figure 2.6.]

Solution. By the sum rule,

$$P(\text{ball } N{+}1 \text{ is black} \mid n_B, N) = \sum_u P(\text{ball } N{+}1 \text{ is black} \mid u, n_B, N)P(u \mid n_B, N).$$
$$\tag{2.29}$$

Since the balls are drawn with replacement from the chosen urn, the probability $P(\text{ball } N{+}1 \text{ is black} \mid u, n_B, N)$ is just $f_u = u/10$, whatever n_B and N are. So

$$P(\text{ball } N{+}1 \text{ is black} \mid n_B, N) = \sum_u f_u P(u \mid n_B, N). \tag{2.30}$$

Using the values of $P(u \mid n_B, N)$ given in figure 2.6 we obtain

$$P(\text{ball } N{+}1 \text{ is black} \mid n_B{=}3, N{=}10) = 0.333. \quad \square \tag{2.31}$$

Comment. Notice the difference between this prediction obtained using probability theory, and the widespread practice in statistics of making predictions by first selecting the most plausible hypothesis (which here would be that the urn is urn $u = 3$) and then making the predictions assuming that hypothesis to be true (which would give a probability of 0.3 that the next ball is black). The correct prediction is the one that takes into account the uncertainty by *marginalizing* over the possible values of the hypothesis u. Marginalization here leads to slightly more moderate, less extreme predictions.

Inference as inverse probability

Now consider the following exercise, which has the character of a simple scientific investigation.

Example 2.7. Bill tosses a bent coin N times, obtaining a sequence of heads and tails. We assume that the coin has a probability f_H of coming up heads; we do not know f_H. If n_H heads have occurred in N tosses, what is the probability distribution of f_H? (For example, N might be 10, and n_H might be 3; or, after a lot more tossing, we might have $N = 300$ and $n_H = 29$.) What is the probability that the $N+1$th outcome will be a head, given n_H heads in N tosses?

Unlike example 2.6 (p.27), this problem has a subjective element. Given a restricted definition of probability that says 'probabilities are the frequencies of random variables', this example is different from the eleven-urns example. Whereas the urn u was a random variable, the bias f_H of the coin would not normally be called a random variable. It is just a fixed but unknown parameter that we are interested in. Yet don't the two examples 2.6 and 2.7 seem to have an essential similarity? [Especially when $N = 10$ and $n_H = 3$!]

To solve example 2.7, we have to make an assumption about what the bias of the coin f_H might be. This prior probability distribution over f_H, $P(f_H)$, corresponds to the prior over u in the eleven-urns problem. In that example, the helpful problem definition specified $P(u)$. In real life, we have to make assumptions in order to assign priors; these assumptions will be subjective, and our answers will depend on them. Exactly the same can be said for the other probabilities in our generative model too. We are assuming, for example, that the balls are drawn from an urn independently; but could there not be correlations in the sequence because Fred's ball-drawing action is not perfectly random? Indeed there could be, so the likelihood function that we use depends on assumptions too. In real data modelling problems, priors are subjective *and so are likelihoods*.

> Here $P(f)$ denotes a probability density, rather than a probability distribution.

> We are now using $P()$ to denote probability *densities* over continuous variables as well as probabilities over discrete variables and probabilities of logical propositions. The probability that a continuous variable v lies between values a and b (where $b > a$) is defined to be $\int_a^b dv\, P(v)$. $P(v)dv$ is dimensionless. The density $P(v)$ is a dimensional quantity, having dimensions inverse to the dimensions of v – in contrast to discrete probabilities, which are dimensionless. Don't be surprised to see probability densities greater than 1. This is normal, and nothing is wrong, as long as $\int_a^b dv\, P(v) < 1$ for any interval (a, b).

> Conditional and joint probability densities are defined in just the same way as conditional and joint probabilities.

▷ Exercise 2.8.[2] Assuming a uniform prior on f_H, $P(f_H) = 1$, solve the problem posed in example 2.7 (p.30). Sketch the posterior distribution of f_H and compute the probability that the $N+1$th outcome will be a head, for

(a) $N = 3$ and $n_H = 0$;

(b) $N = 3$ and $n_H = 2$;

(c) $N = 10$ and $n_H = 3$;

(d) $N = 300$ and $n_H = 29$.

You will find the beta integral useful:

$$\int_0^1 dp_a\, p_a^{F_a}(1 - p_a)^{F_b} = \frac{\Gamma(F_a + 1)\Gamma(F_b + 1)}{\Gamma(F_a + F_b + 2)} = \frac{F_a!F_b!}{(F_a + F_b + 1)!}. \quad (2.32)$$

You may also find it instructive to look back at example 2.6 (p.27) and equation (2.31).

People sometimes confuse assigning a prior distribution to an unknown parameter such as f_H with making an initial guess of the *value* of the parameter. But the prior over f_H, $P(f_H)$, is not a simple statement like 'initially, I would guess $f_H = 1/2$'. The prior is a probability density over f_H which specifies the prior degree of belief that f_H lies in any interval $(f, f + \delta f)$. It may well be the case that our prior for f_H is symmetric about $1/2$, so that the *mean of* f_H under the prior is $1/2$. In this case, the predictive distribution *for the first toss* x_1 would indeed be

$$P(x_1 = \text{head}) = \int \mathrm{d}f_H \, P(f_H) P(x_1 = \text{head} \mid f_H) = \int \mathrm{d}f_H \, P(f_H) f_H = 1/2.$$
(2.33)

But the prediction for subsequent tosses will depend on the whole prior distribution, not just its mean.

Data compression and inverse probability

Consider the following task.

Example 2.9. Write a computer program capable of compressing binary files like this one:

0000000000000000000010010001000000100000010000000000000000000000000000000000000101000000000000000110000
1000000000010000100000000010000000000000000000000001000000000000000000010000000011000001000000011000100
0000000001001000000000001000100000000000000000011000000000000000000000000000000001000000000000000100000000

The string shown contains $n_1 = 29$ 1s and $n_0 = 271$ 0s.

Intuitively, compression works by taking advantage of the predictability of a file. In this case, the source of the file appears more likely to emit 0s than 1s. A data compression program that compresses this file must, implicitly or explicitly, be addressing the question 'What is the probability that the next character in this file is a 1?'

Do you think this problem is similar in character to example 2.7 (p.30)? I do. One of the themes of this book is that data compression and data modelling are one and the same, and that they should both be addressed, like the urn of example 2.6, using inverse probability. Example 2.9 is solved in Chapter 6.

The likelihood principle

Please solve the following two exercises.

Example 2.10. Urn A contains three balls: one black, and two white; urn B contains three balls: two black, and one white. One of the urns is selected at random and one ball is drawn. The ball is black. What is the probability that the selected urn is urn A?

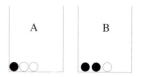

Figure 2.7. Urns for example 2.10.

Example 2.11. Urn A contains five balls: one black, two white, one green and one pink; urn B contains five hundred balls: two hundred black, one hundred white, 50 yellow, 40 cyan, 30 sienna, 25 green, 25 silver, 20 gold, and 10 purple. [One fifth of A's balls are black; two-fifths of B's are black.] One of the urns is selected at random and one ball is drawn. The ball is black. What is the probability that the urn is urn A?

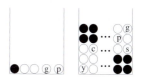

Figure 2.8. Urns for example 2.11.

What do you notice about your solutions? Does each answer depend on the detailed contents of each urn?

The details of the other possible outcomes and their probabilities are irrelevant. All that matters is the probability of the outcome that actually happened (here, that the ball drawn was black) given the different hypotheses. We need only to know the *likelihood*, i.e., how the probability of the data that happened varies with the hypothesis. This simple rule about inference is known as the *likelihood principle*.

> The likelihood principle: given a generative model for data d given parameters $\boldsymbol{\theta}$, $P(d \mid \boldsymbol{\theta})$, and having observed a particular outcome d_1, all inferences and predictions should depend only on the function $P(d_1 \mid \boldsymbol{\theta})$.

In spite of the simplicity of this principle, many classical statistical methods violate it.

▶ **2.4 Definition of entropy and related functions**

The Shannon information content of an outcome x is defined to be

$$h(x) = \log_2 \frac{1}{P(x)}. \tag{2.34}$$

It is measured in bits. [The word 'bit' is also used to denote a variable whose value is 0 or 1; I hope context will always make clear which of the two meanings is intended.]

In the next few chapters, we will establish that the Shannon information content $h(a_i)$ is indeed a natural measure of the information content of the event $x = a_i$. At that point, we will shorten the name of this quantity to 'the information content'.

The fourth column in table 2.9 shows the Shannon information content of the 27 possible outcomes when a random character is picked from an English document. The outcome $x = \mathsf{z}$ has a Shannon information content of 10.4 bits, and $x = \mathsf{e}$ has an information content of 3.5 bits.

The entropy of an ensemble X is defined to be the average Shannon information content of an outcome:

$$H(X) \equiv \sum_{x \in \mathcal{A}_X} P(x) \log \frac{1}{P(x)}, \tag{2.35}$$

with the convention for $P(x) = 0$ that $0 \times \log 1/0 \equiv 0$, since $\lim_{\theta \to 0^+} \theta \log 1/\theta = 0$.

Like the information content, entropy is measured in bits.

When it is convenient, we may also write $H(X)$ as $H(\mathbf{p})$, where $\mathbf{p}$ is the vector $(p_1, p_2, \ldots, p_I)$. Another name for the entropy of X is the uncertainty of X.

Example 2.12. The entropy of a randomly selected letter in an English document is about 4.11 bits, assuming its probability is as given in table 2.9. We obtain this number by averaging $\log 1/p_i$ (shown in the fourth column) under the probability distribution p_i (shown in the third column).

i	a_i	p_i	$h(p_i)$
1	a	.0575	4.1
2	b	.0128	6.3
3	c	.0263	5.2
4	d	.0285	5.1
5	e	.0913	3.5
6	f	.0173	5.9
7	g	.0133	6.2
8	h	.0313	5.0
9	i	.0599	4.1
10	j	.0006	10.7
11	k	.0084	6.9
12	l	.0335	4.9
13	m	.0235	5.4
14	n	.0596	4.1
15	o	.0689	3.9
16	p	.0192	5.7
17	q	.0008	10.3
18	r	.0508	4.3
19	s	.0567	4.1
20	t	.0706	3.8
21	u	.0334	4.9
22	v	.0069	7.2
23	w	.0119	6.4
24	x	.0073	7.1
25	y	.0164	5.9
26	z	.0007	10.4
27	-	.1928	2.4

$$\sum_i p_i \log_2 \frac{1}{p_i} \qquad 4.1$$

Table 2.9. Shannon information contents of the outcomes a–z.

We now note some properties of the entropy function.

- $H(X) \geq 0$ with equality iff $p_i = 1$ for one i. ['iff' means 'if and only if'.]

- Entropy is maximized if $\mathbf{p}$ is uniform:

$$H(X) \leq \log(|\mathcal{A}_X|) \quad \text{with equality iff } p_i = 1/|X| \text{ for all } i. \qquad (2.36)$$

  Notation: the vertical bars '$|\cdot|$' have two meanings. If $\mathcal{A}_X$ is a set, $|\mathcal{A}_X|$ denotes the number of elements in $\mathcal{A}_X$; if x is a number, then $|x|$ is the absolute value of x.

The *redundancy* measures the fractional difference between $H(X)$ and its maximum possible value, $\log(|\mathcal{A}_X|)$.

The redundancy of X is:

$$1 - \frac{H(X)}{\log|\mathcal{A}_X|}. \qquad (2.37)$$

We won't make use of 'redundancy' in this book, so I have not assigned a symbol to it.

The joint entropy of X, Y is:

$$H(X, Y) = \sum_{xy \in \mathcal{A}_X \mathcal{A}_Y} P(x, y) \log \frac{1}{P(x, y)}. \qquad (2.38)$$

Entropy is additive for independent random variables:

$$H(X, Y) = H(X) + H(Y) \quad \text{iff} \quad P(x, y) = P(x)P(y). \qquad (2.39)$$

Our definitions for information content so far apply only to discrete probability distributions over finite sets $\mathcal{A}_X$. The definitions can be extended to infinite sets, though the entropy may then be infinite. The case of a probability *density* over a continuous set is addressed in section 11.3. Further important definitions and exercises to do with entropy will come along in section 8.1.

▶ 2.5 Decomposability of the entropy

The entropy function satisfies a recursive property that can be very useful when computing entropies. For convenience, we'll stretch our notation so that we can write $H(X)$ as $H(\mathbf{p})$, where $\mathbf{p}$ is the probability vector associated with the ensemble X.

Let's illustrate the property by an example first. Imagine that a random variable $x \in \{0, 1, 2\}$ is created by first flipping a fair coin to determine whether $x = 0$; then, if x is not 0, flipping a fair coin a second time to determine whether x is 1 or 2. The probability distribution of x is

$$P(x{=}0) = \frac{1}{2}; \quad P(x{=}1) = \frac{1}{4}; \quad P(x{=}2) = \frac{1}{4}. \qquad (2.40)$$

What is the entropy of X? We can either compute it by brute force:

$$H(X) = \frac{1}{2}\log 2 + \frac{1}{4}\log 4 + \frac{1}{4}\log 4 = 1.5; \qquad (2.41)$$

or we can use the following decomposition, in which the value of x is revealed gradually. Imagine first learning whether $x{=}0$, and then, if x is not 0, learning which non-zero value is the case. The revelation of whether $x{=}0$ or not entails revealing a binary variable whose probability distribution is $\{1/2, 1/2\}$. This revelation has an entropy $H(1/2, 1/2) = \frac{1}{2} \log 2 + \frac{1}{2} \log 2 = 1$ bit. If x is not 0, we learn the value of the second coin flip. This too is a binary variable whose probability distribution is $\{1/2, 1/2\}$, and whose entropy is 1 bit. We only get to experience the second revelation half the time, however, so the entropy can be written:

$$H(X) = H(1/2, 1/2) + 1/2 \, H(1/2, 1/2). \tag{2.42}$$

Generalizing, the observation we are making about the entropy of any probability distribution $\mathbf{p} = \{p_1, p_2, \ldots, p_I\}$ is that

$$H(\mathbf{p}) = H(p_1, 1 - p_1) + (1 - p_1)H\left(\frac{p_2}{1 - p_1}, \frac{p_3}{1 - p_1}, \ldots, \frac{p_I}{1 - p_1}\right). \tag{2.43}$$

When it's written as a formula, this property looks regrettably ugly; nevertheless it is a simple property and one that you should make use of.

Generalizing further, the entropy has the property for any m that

$$
\begin{aligned}
H(\mathbf{p}) \;=\; & H\left[(p_1 + p_2 + \cdots + p_m), (p_{m+1} + p_{m+2} + \cdots + p_I)\right] \\
& + (p_1 + \cdots + p_m)H\left(\frac{p_1}{(p_1 + \cdots + p_m)}, \ldots, \frac{p_m}{(p_1 + \cdots + p_m)}\right) \\
& + (p_{m+1} + \cdots + p_I)H\left(\frac{p_{m+1}}{(p_{m+1} + \cdots + p_I)}, \ldots, \frac{p_I}{(p_{m+1} + \cdots + p_I)}\right).
\end{aligned}
\tag{2.44}
$$

Example 2.13. A source produces a character x from the alphabet $\mathcal{A} = \{0, 1, \ldots, 9, \mathsf{a}, \mathsf{b}, \ldots, \mathsf{z}\}$; with probability $1/3$, x is a numeral $(0, \ldots, 9)$; with probability $1/3$, x is a vowel $(\mathsf{a}, \mathsf{e}, \mathsf{i}, \mathsf{o}, \mathsf{u})$; and with probability $1/3$ it's one of the 21 consonants. All numerals are equiprobable, and the same goes for vowels and consonants. Estimate the entropy of X.

Solution. $\log 3 + \frac{1}{3}(\log 10 + \log 5 + \log 21) = \log 3 + \frac{1}{3} \log 1050 \simeq \log 30$ bits. $\square$

▶ 2.6 Gibbs' inequality

The relative entropy *or* **Kullback–Leibler divergence** between two probability distributions $P(x)$ and $Q(x)$ that are defined over the same alphabet $\mathcal{A}_X$ is

The 'ei' in **Lei**bler is pronounced the same as in **hei**st.

$$D_{\mathrm{KL}}(P||Q) = \sum_x P(x) \log \frac{P(x)}{Q(x)}. \tag{2.45}$$

The relative entropy satisfies *Gibbs' inequality*

$$D_{\mathrm{KL}}(P||Q) \geq 0 \tag{2.46}$$

with equality only if $P = Q$. Note that in general the relative entropy is not symmetric under interchange of the distributions P and Q: in general $D_{\mathrm{KL}}(P||Q) \neq D_{\mathrm{KL}}(Q||P)$, so D_{KL}, although it is sometimes called the 'KL distance', is not strictly a distance. The relative entropy is important in pattern recognition and neural networks, as well as in information theory.

Gibbs' inequality is probably the most important inequality in this book. It, and many other inequalities, can be proved using the concept of convexity.

▶ 2.7 Jensen's inequality for convex functions

The words 'convex ⌣' and 'concave ⌢' may be pronounced 'convex-smile' and 'concave-frown'. This terminology has useful redundancy: while one may forget which way up 'convex' and 'concave' are, it is harder to confuse a smile with a frown.

Convex ⌣ functions. A function $f(x)$ is *convex ⌣* over (a, b) if every chord of the function lies above the function, as shown in figure 2.10; that is, for all $x_1, x_2 \in (a, b)$ and $0 \le \lambda \le 1$,

$$f(\lambda x_1 + (1 - \lambda)x_2) \ \le \ \lambda f(x_1) + (1 - \lambda)f(x_2). \qquad (2.47)$$

A function f is *strictly convex ⌣* if, for all $x_1, x_2 \in (a, b)$, the equality holds only for $\lambda = 0$ and $\lambda = 1$.

Similar definitions apply to concave ⌢ and strictly concave ⌢ functions.

Some strictly convex ⌣ functions are

- x^2, e^x and e^{-x} for all x;

- $\log(1/x)$ and $x \log x$ for $x > 0$.

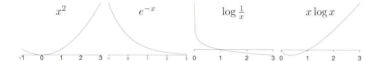

Figure 2.10. Definition of convexity.

Figure 2.11. Convex ⌣ functions.

Jensen's inequality. If f is a convex ⌣ function and x is a random variable then:

$$\mathcal{E}\left[f(x)\right] \ge f(\mathcal{E}[x]), \qquad (2.48)$$

where $\mathcal{E}$ denotes expectation. If f is strictly convex ⌣ and $\mathcal{E}\left[f(x)\right] = f(\mathcal{E}[x])$, then the random variable x is a constant.

Jensen's inequality can also be rewritten for a concave ⌢ function, with the direction of the inequality reversed.

A physical version of Jensen's inequality runs as follows.

If a collection of masses p_i are placed on a convex ⌣ curve $f(x)$ at locations $(x_i, f(x_i))$, then the centre of gravity of those masses, which is at $(\mathcal{E}[x], \mathcal{E}\left[f(x)\right])$, lies above the curve.

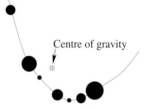

Centre of gravity

If this fails to convince you, then feel free to do the following exercise.

Exercise 2.14.[2, p.41] Prove Jensen's inequality.

Example 2.15. Three squares have average area $\bar{A} = 100\,\mathrm{m}^2$. The average of the lengths of their sides is $\bar{l} = 10\,\mathrm{m}$. What can be said about the size of the largest of the three squares? [Use Jensen's inequality.]

Solution. Let x be the length of the side of a square, and let the probability of x be $1/3, 1/3, 1/3$ over the three lengths l_1, l_2, l_3. Then the information that we have is that $\mathcal{E}[x] = 10$ and $\mathcal{E}\left[f(x)\right] = 100$, where $f(x) = x^2$ is the function mapping lengths to areas. This is a strictly convex ⌣ function. We notice that the equality $\mathcal{E}\left[f(x)\right] = f(\mathcal{E}[x])$ holds, therefore x is a constant, and the three lengths must all be equal. The area of the largest square is $100\,\mathrm{m}^2$. $\quad\square$

Convexity and concavity also relate to maximization

If $f(\mathbf{x})$ is concave $\frown$ and there exists a point at which

$$\frac{\partial f}{\partial x_k} = 0 \text{ for all } k, \tag{2.49}$$

then $f(\mathbf{x})$ has its maximum value at that point.

The converse does not hold: if a concave $\frown$ $f(\mathbf{x})$ is maximized at some $\mathbf{x}$ it is not necessarily true that the gradient $\nabla f(\mathbf{x})$ is equal to zero there. For example, $f(x) = -|x|$ is maximized at $x = 0$ where its derivative is undefined; and $f(p) = \log(p)$, for a probability $p \in (0,1)$, is maximized on the boundary of the range, at $p = 1$, where the gradient $df(p)/dp = 1$.

▶ 2.8 Exercises

Sums of random variables

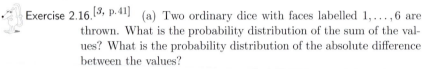

Exercise 2.16.[3, p.41] (a) Two ordinary dice with faces labelled $1, \ldots, 6$ are thrown. What is the probability distribution of the sum of the values? What is the probability distribution of the absolute difference between the values?

(b) One hundred ordinary dice are thrown. What, roughly, is the probability distribution of the sum of the values? Sketch the probability distribution and estimate its mean and standard deviation.

(c) How can two cubical dice be labelled using the numbers $\{0, 1, 2, 3, 4, 5, 6\}$ so that when the two dice are thrown the sum has a uniform probability distribution over the integers 1–12?

(d) Is there any way that one hundred dice could be labelled with integers such that the probability distribution of the sum is uniform?

Inference problems

Exercise 2.17.[2, p.41] If $q = 1 - p$ and $a = \ln p/q$, show that

$$p = \frac{1}{1 + \exp(-a)}. \tag{2.50}$$

Sketch this function and find its relationship to the hyperbolic tangent function $\tanh(u) = \frac{e^u - e^{-u}}{e^u + e^{-u}}$.

It will be useful to be fluent in base-2 logarithms also. If $b = \log_2 p/q$, what is b as a function of p?

▷ Exercise 2.18.[2, p.42] Let x and y be correlated random variables with x a binary variable taking values in $\mathcal{A}_X = \{0, 1\}$. Use Bayes' theorem to show that the log posterior probability ratio for x given y is

$$\log \frac{P(x=1 \mid y)}{P(x=0 \mid y)} = \log \frac{P(y \mid x=1)}{P(y \mid x=0)} + \log \frac{P(x=1)}{P(x=0)}. \tag{2.51}$$

▷ Exercise 2.19.[2, p.42] Let x, d_1 and d_2 be random variables such that d_1 and d_2 are conditionally independent given a binary variable x. Use Bayes' theorem to show that the posterior probability ratio for x given $\{d_i\}$ is

$$\frac{P(x=1 \mid \{d_i\})}{P(x=0 \mid \{d_i\})} = \frac{P(d_1 \mid x=1)}{P(d_1 \mid x=0)} \frac{P(d_2 \mid x=1)}{P(d_2 \mid x=0)} \frac{P(x=1)}{P(x=0)}. \tag{2.52}$$

Life in high-dimensional spaces

Probability distributions and volumes have some unexpected properties in high-dimensional spaces.

▷ Exercise 2.20.[2, p.42] Consider a sphere of radius r in an N-dimensional real space. Show that the fraction of the volume of the sphere that is in the surface shell lying at values of the radius between $r - \epsilon$ and r, where $0 < \epsilon < r$, is:

$$f = 1 - \left(1 - \frac{\epsilon}{r}\right)^N. \qquad (2.53)$$

Evaluate f for the cases $N=2$, $N=10$ and $N=1000$, with (a) $\epsilon/r=0.01$; (b) $\epsilon/r=0.5$.

Implication: points that are uniformly distributed in a sphere in N dimensions, where N is large, are very likely to be in a thin shell near the surface.

Expectations and entropies

You are probably familiar with the idea of computing the expectation of a function of x,

$$\mathcal{E}\left[f(x)\right] = \langle f(x) \rangle = \sum_x P(x) f(x). \qquad (2.54)$$

Maybe you are not so comfortable with computing this expectation in cases where the function $f(x)$ depends on the probability $P(x)$. The next few examples address this concern.

▷ Exercise 2.21.[1, p.43] Let $p_a=0.1$, $p_b=0.2$, and $p_c=0.7$. Let $f(a)=10$, $f(b)=5$, and $f(c)=10/7$. What is $\mathcal{E}\left[f(x)\right]$? What is $\mathcal{E}\left[1/P(x)\right]$?

▷ Exercise 2.22.[2, p.43] For an arbitrary ensemble, what is $\mathcal{E}\left[1/P(x)\right]$?

▷ Exercise 2.23.[1, p.43] Let $p_a=0.1$, $p_b=0.2$, and $p_c=0.7$. Let $g(a)=0$, $g(b)=1$, and $g(c)=0$. What is $\mathcal{E}\left[g(x)\right]$?

▷ Exercise 2.24.[1, p.43] Let $p_a=0.1$, $p_b=0.2$, and $p_c=0.7$. What is the probability that $P(x) \in [0.15, 0.5]$? What is

$$P\left(\left|\log \frac{P(x)}{0.2}\right| > 0.05\right)?$$

▷ Exercise 2.25.[3, p.43] Prove the assertion that $H(X) \leq \log(|X|)$ with equality iff $p_i = 1/|X|$ for all i. ($|X|$ denotes the number of elements in the set $\mathcal{A}_X$.) [Hint: use Jensen's inequality (2.48); if your first attempt to use Jensen does not succeed, remember that Jensen involves both a random variable and a function, and you have quite a lot of freedom in choosing these; think about whether your chosen function f should be convex or concave.]

▷ Exercise 2.26.[3, p.44] Prove that the relative entropy (equation (2.45)) satisfies $D_{\mathrm{KL}}(P||Q) \geq 0$ (Gibbs' inequality) with equality only if $P = Q$.

▷ Exercise 2.27.[2] Prove that the entropy is indeed decomposable as described in equations (2.43–2.44).

▷ Exercise 2.28.[2] A random variable $x \in \{0, 1, 2, 3\}$ is selected by flipping a bent coin with bias f to determine whether the outcome is in $\{0, 1\}$ or $\{2, 3\}$; then either flipping a second bent coin with bias g or a third bent coin with bias h respectively. Write down the probability distribution of x. Use the decomposability of the entropy (2.44) to find the entropy of X. [Notice how compact an expression is obtained if you make use of the binary entropy function $H_2(x)$, compared with writing out the four-term entropy explicitly.] Find the derivative of $H(X)$ with respect to f. [Hint: $\mathrm{d}H_2(x)/\mathrm{d}x = \log((1-x)/x)$.]

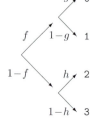

▷ Exercise 2.29.[2] An unbiased coin is flipped until one head is thrown. What is the entropy of the random variable $x \in \{1, 2, 3, \dots\}$, the number of flips? Repeat the calculation for the case of a biased coin with probability f of coming up heads. [Hint: solve the problem both directly and by using the decomposability of the entropy (2.43).]

▶ 2.9 Further exercises

Forward probability

▷ Exercise 2.30.[1] An urn contains w white balls and b black balls. Two balls are drawn, one after the other, without replacement. Prove that the probability that the first ball is white is equal to the probability that the second is white.

▷ Exercise 2.31.[2] A circular coin of diameter a is thrown onto a square grid whose squares are $b \times b$. $(a < b)$ What is the probability that the coin will lie entirely within one square? [Ans: $(1 - a/b)^2$]

▷ Exercise 2.32.[3] Buffon's needle. A needle of length a is thrown onto a plane covered with equally spaced parallel lines with separation b. What is the probability that the needle will cross a line? [Ans, if $a < b$: $2a/\pi b$] [Generalization – Buffon's noodle: on average, a random curve of length A is expected to intersect the lines $2A/\pi b$ times.]

Exercise 2.33.[2] Two points are selected at random on a straight line segment of length 1. What is the probability that a triangle can be constructed out of the three resulting segments?

Exercise 2.34.[2, p.45] An unbiased coin is flipped until one head is thrown. What is the expected number of tails and the expected number of heads?

Fred, who doesn't know that the coin is unbiased, estimates the bias using $\hat{f} \equiv h/(h + t)$, where h and t are the numbers of heads and tails tossed. Compute and sketch the probability distribution of $\hat{f}$.

NB, this is a forward probability problem, a sampling theory problem, not an inference problem. Don't use Bayes' theorem.

Exercise 2.35.[2, p.45] Fred rolls an unbiased six-sided die once per second, noting the occasions when the outcome is a six.

(a) What is the mean number of rolls from one six to the next six?

(b) Between two rolls, the clock strikes one. What is the mean number of rolls until the next six?

(c) Now think back before the clock struck. What is the mean number of rolls, going back in time, until the most recent six?

(d) What is the mean number of rolls from the six before the clock struck to the next six?

(e) Is your answer to (d) different from your answer to (a)? Explain.

Another version of this exercise refers to Fred waiting for a bus at a bus-stop in Poissonville where buses arrive independently at random (a Poisson process), with, on average, one bus every six minutes. What is the average wait for a bus, after Fred arrives at the stop? [6 minutes.] So what is the time between the two buses, the one that Fred just missed, and the one that he catches? [12 minutes.] Explain the apparent paradox. Note the contrast with the situation in Clockville, where the buses are spaced exactly 6 minutes apart. There, as you can confirm, the mean wait at a bus-stop is 3 minutes, and the time between the missed bus and the next one is 6 minutes.

Conditional probability

▷ **Exercise 2.36.**[2] You meet Fred. Fred tells you he has two brothers, Alf and Bob.

What is the probability that Fred is older than Bob?

Fred tells you that he is older than Alf. Now, what is the probability that Fred is older than Bob? (That is, what is the conditional probability that $F > B$ given that $F > A$?)

▷ **Exercise 2.37.**[2] The inhabitants of an island tell the truth one third of the time. They lie with probability 2/3.

On an occasion, after one of them made a statement, you ask another 'was that statement true?' and he says 'yes'.

What is the probability that the statement was indeed true?

▷ **Exercise 2.38.**[2, p.46] Compare two ways of computing the probability of error of the repetition code R_3, assuming a binary symmetric channel (you did this once for exercise 1.2 (p.7)) and confirm that they give the same answer.

Binomial distribution method. Add the probability of all three bits' being flipped to the probability of exactly two bits' being flipped.

Sum rule method. Using the sum rule, compute the marginal probability that **r** takes on each of the eight possible values, $P(\mathbf{r})$. $[P(\mathbf{r}) = \sum_s P(s)P(\mathbf{r}\,|\,s).]$ Then compute the posterior probability of s for each of the eight values of **r**. [In fact, by symmetry, only two example cases $\mathbf{r} = (000)$ and $\mathbf{r} = (001)$ need be considered.] Notice that some of the inferred bits are better determined than others. From the posterior probability $P(s\,|\,\mathbf{r})$ you can read out the case-by-case error probability, the probability that the more probable hypothesis is not correct, $P(\text{error}\,|\,\mathbf{r})$. Find the average error probability using the sum rule,

$$P(\text{error}) = \sum_{\mathbf{r}} P(\mathbf{r})P(\text{error}\,|\,\mathbf{r}). \qquad (2.55)$$

Equation (1.18) gives the posterior probability of the input s, given the received vector **r**.

▷ **Exercise 2.39.**[3C] The frequency p_n of the nth most frequent word in English is roughly approximated by

$$p_n \simeq \begin{cases} \frac{0.1}{n} & \text{for } n \in 1 \dots 12\,367 \\ 0 & n > 12\,367. \end{cases} \tag{2.56}$$

[This remarkable $1/n$ law is known as Zipf's law, and applies to the word frequencies of many languages (Zipf, 1949).] If we assume that English is generated by picking words at random according to this distribution, what is the entropy of English (per word)? [This calculation can be found in 'Prediction and entropy of printed English', C.E. Shannon, *Bell Syst. Tech. J.* **30**, pp.50–64 (1950), but, inexplicably, the great man made numerical errors in it.]

▶ 2.10 Solutions

Solution to exercise 2.2 (p.24).   No, they are not independent. If they were then all the conditional distributions $P(y \mid x)$ would be identical functions of y, regardless of x (c.f. figure 2.3).

Solution to exercise 2.4 (p.27).   We define the fraction $f_B \equiv B/K$.

(a) The number of black balls has a binomial distribution.

$$P(n_B \mid f_B, N) = \binom{N}{n_B} f_B^{n_B}(1 - f_B)^{N-n_B}. \tag{2.57}$$

(b) The mean and variance of this distribution are:

$$\mathcal{E}[n_B] = N f_B \tag{2.58}$$

$$\mathrm{var}[n_B] = N f_B(1 - f_B). \tag{2.59}$$

These results were derived in example 1.1 (p.1). The standard deviation of n_B is $\sqrt{\mathrm{var}[n_B]} = \sqrt{N f_B(1 - f_B)}$.

When $B/K = 1/5$ and $N = 5$, the expectation and variance of n_B are 1 and 4/5. The standard deviation is 0.89.

When $B/K = 1/5$ and $N = 400$, the expectation and variance of n_B are 80 and 64. The standard deviation is 8.

Solution to exercise 2.5 (p.27).   The numerator of the quantity

$$z = \frac{(n_B - f_B N)^2}{N f_B(1 - f_B)}$$

can be recognized as $(n_B - \mathcal{E}[n_B])^2$; the denominator is equal to the variance of n_B (2.59), which is by definition the expectation of the numerator. So the expectation of z is 1. [A random variable like z, which measures the deviation of data from the expected value, is sometimes called χ^2 (chi-squared).]

In the case $N = 5$ and $f_B = 1/5$, $N f_B$ is 1, and $\mathrm{var}[n_B]$ is 4/5. The numerator has five possible values, only one of which is smaller than 1: $(n_B - f_B N)^2 = 0$ has probability $P(n_B = 1) = 0.4096$; so the probability that $z < 1$ is 0.4096.

Solution to exercise 2.14 (p.35). We wish to prove, given the property

$$f(\lambda x_1 + (1 - \lambda)x_2) \leq \lambda f(x_1) + (1 - \lambda)f(x_2), \tag{2.60}$$

that, if $\sum p_i = 1$ and $p_i \geq 0$,

$$\sum_{i=1}^{I} p_i f(x_i) \geq f\left(\sum_{i=1}^{I} p_i x_i\right). \tag{2.61}$$

We proceed by recursion, working from the right-hand side. (This proof does not handle cases where some $p_i = 0$; such details are left to the pedantic reader.) At the first line we use the definition of convexity (2.60) with $\lambda = \frac{p_1}{\sum_{i=1}^{I} p_i} = p_1$; at the second line, $\lambda = \frac{p_2}{\sum_{i=2}^{I} p_i}$.

$$f\left(\sum_{i=1}^{I} p_i x_i\right) = f\left(p_1 x_1 + \sum_{i=2}^{I} p_i x_i\right)$$

$$\leq p_1 f(x_1) + \left[\sum_{i=2}^{I} p_i\right]\left[f\left(\sum_{i=2}^{I} p_i x_i \bigg/ \sum_{i=2}^{I} p_i\right)\right] \tag{2.62}$$

$$\leq p_1 f(x_1) + \left[\sum_{i=2}^{I} p_i\right]\left[\frac{p_2}{\sum_{i=2}^{I} p_i} f(x_2) + \frac{\sum_{i=3}^{I} p_i}{\sum_{i=2}^{I} p_i} f\left(\sum_{i=3}^{I} p_i x_i \bigg/ \sum_{i=3}^{I} p_i\right)\right],$$

and so forth. □

Solution to exercise 2.16 (p.36).

(a) For the outcomes $\{2, 3, 4, 5, 6, 7, 8, 9, 10, 11, 12\}$, the probabilities are $\mathcal{P} = \{\frac{1}{36}, \frac{2}{36}, \frac{3}{36}, \frac{4}{36}, \frac{5}{36}, \frac{6}{36}, \frac{5}{36}, \frac{4}{36}, \frac{3}{36}, \frac{2}{36}, \frac{1}{36}\}$.

(b) The value of one die has mean 3.5 and variance $35/12$. So the sum of one hundred has mean 350 and variance $3500/12 \simeq 292$, and by the central limit theorem the probability distribution is roughly Gaussian (but confined to the integers), with this mean and variance.

(c) In order to obtain a sum that has a uniform distribution we have to start from random variables some of which have a spiky distribution with the probability mass concentrated at the extremes. The unique solution is to have one ordinary die and one with faces 6, 6, 6, 0, 0, 0.

(d) Yes, a uniform distribution can be created in several ways, for example by labelling the rth die with the numbers $\{0, 1, 2, 3, 4, 5\} \times 6^r$.

Solution to exercise 2.17 (p.36).

$$a = \ln\frac{p}{q} \qquad \Rightarrow \qquad \frac{p}{q} = e^a \tag{2.63}$$

and $q = 1 - p$ gives

$$\frac{p}{1 - p} = e^a \tag{2.64}$$

$$\Rightarrow \qquad p = \frac{e^a}{e^a + 1} = \frac{1}{1 + \exp(-a)}. \tag{2.65}$$

The hyperbolic tangent is

$$\tanh(a) = \frac{e^a - e^{-a}}{e^a + e^{-a}} \tag{2.66}$$

so

$$f(a) \equiv \frac{1}{1 + \exp(-a)} = \frac{1}{2}\left(\frac{1 - e^{-a}}{1 + e^{-a}} + 1\right)$$

$$= \frac{1}{2}\left(\frac{e^{a/2} - e^{-a/2}}{e^{a/2} + e^{-a/2}} + 1\right) = \frac{1}{2}(\tanh(a/2) + 1). \qquad (2.67)$$

In the case $b = \log_2 p/q$, we can repeat steps (2.63–2.63), replacing e by 2, to obtain

$$p = \frac{1}{1 + 2^{-a}}. \qquad (2.68)$$

Solution to exercise 2.18 (p.36).

$$P(x\,|\,y) = \frac{P(y\,|\,x)P(x)}{P(y)} \qquad (2.69)$$

$$\Rightarrow \frac{P(x{=}1\,|\,y)}{P(x{=}0\,|\,y)} = \frac{P(y\,|\,x{=}1)}{P(y\,|\,x{=}0)}\frac{P(x{=}1)}{P(x{=}0)} \qquad (2.70)$$

$$\Rightarrow \log \frac{P(x{=}1\,|\,y)}{P(x{=}0\,|\,y)} = \log \frac{P(y\,|\,x{=}1)}{P(y\,|\,x{=}0)} + \log \frac{P(x{=}1)}{P(x{=}0)}. \qquad (2.71)$$

Solution to exercise 2.19 (p.36). The conditional independence of d_1 and d_2 given x means

$$P(x, d_1, d_2) = P(x)P(d_1\,|\,x)P(d_2\,|\,x). \qquad (2.72)$$

This gives a separation of the posterior probability ratio into a series of factors, one for each data point, times the prior probability ratio.

$$\frac{P(x{=}1\,|\,\{d_i\})}{P(x{=}0\,|\,\{d_i\})} = \frac{P(\{d_i\}\,|\,x{=}1)}{P(\{d_i\}\,|\,x{=}0)}\frac{P(x{=}1)}{P(x{=}0)} \qquad (2.73)$$

$$= \frac{P(d_1\,|\,x{=}1)}{P(d_1\,|\,x{=}0)}\frac{P(d_2\,|\,x{=}1)}{P(d_2\,|\,x{=}0)}\frac{P(x{=}1)}{P(x{=}0)}. \qquad (2.74)$$

Life in high-dimensional spaces

Solution to exercise 2.20 (p.37). The volume of a hypersphere of radius r in N dimensions is in fact

$$V(r, N) = \frac{\pi^{N/2}}{(N/2)!}r^N, \qquad (2.75)$$

but you don't need to know this. For this question all that we need is the r-dependence, $V(r, N) \propto r^N$. So the fractional volume in $(r - \epsilon, r)$ is

$$\frac{r^N - (r - \epsilon)^N}{r^N} = 1 - \left(1 - \frac{\epsilon}{r}\right)^N. \qquad (2.76)$$

The fractional volumes in the shells for the required cases are:

N	2	10	1000
$\epsilon/r = 0.01$	0.02	0.096	0.99996
$\epsilon/r = 0.5$	0.75	0.999	$1 - 2^{-1000}$

Notice that no matter how small ϵ is, for large enough N essentially all the probability mass is in the surface shell of thickness ϵ.

Solution to exercise 2.21 (p.37). $p_a = 0.1$, $p_b = 0.2$, $p_c = 0.7$. $f(a) = 10$,
$f(b) = 5$, and $f(c) = 10/7$.

$$\mathcal{E}\left[f(x)\right] = 0.1 \times 10 + 0.2 \times 5 + 0.7 \times 10/7 = 3. \tag{2.77}$$

For each x, $f(x) = 1/P(x)$, so

$$\mathcal{E}\left[1/P(x)\right] = \mathcal{E}\left[f(x)\right] = 3. \tag{2.78}$$

Solution to exercise 2.22 (p.37).   For general X,

$$\mathcal{E}\left[1/P(x)\right] = \sum_{x \in \mathcal{A}_X} P(x)1/P(x) = \sum_{x \in \mathcal{A}_X} 1 = |\mathcal{A}_X|. \tag{2.79}$$

Solution to exercise 2.23 (p.37). $p_a = 0.1$, $p_b = 0.2$, $p_c = 0.7$. $g(a) = 0$, $g(b) = 1$,
and $g(c) = 0$.

$$\mathcal{E}\left[g(x)\right] = p_b = 0.2. \tag{2.80}$$

Solution to exercise 2.24 (p.37).

$$P\left(P(x) \in [0.15, 0.5]\right) = p_b = 0.2. \tag{2.81}$$

$$P\left(\left|\log \frac{P(x)}{0.2}\right| > 0.05\right) = p_a + p_c = 0.8. \tag{2.82}$$

Solution to exercise 2.25 (p.37).   This type of question can be approached in
two ways: either by differentiating the function to be maximized, finding the
maximum, and proving it is a global maximum; this strategy is somewhat
risky since it is possible for the maximum of a function to be at the boundary
of the space, at a place where the derivative is not zero.   Alternatively, a
carefully chosen inequality can establish the answer. The second method is
much neater.

Proof by differentiation (not the recommended method).   Since it is slightly
easier to differentiate $\ln 1/p$ than $\log_2 1/p$, we temporarily define $H(X)$ to be
measured using natural logarithms, thus scaling it down by a factor of $\log_2 e$.

$$H(X) \;\; = \;\; \sum_i p_i \ln \frac{1}{p_i} \tag{2.83}$$

$$\frac{\partial H(X)}{\partial p_i} \;\; = \;\; \ln \frac{1}{p_i} - 1 \tag{2.84}$$

we maximize subject to the constraint $\sum_i p_i = 1$ which can be enforced with
a Lagrange multiplier:

$$G(\mathbf{p}) \;\; \equiv \;\; H(X) + \lambda \left(\sum_i p_i - 1\right) \tag{2.85}$$

$$\frac{\partial G(\mathbf{p})}{\partial p_i} \;\; = \;\; \ln \frac{1}{p_i} - 1 + \lambda. \tag{2.86}$$

At a maximum,

$$\ln \frac{1}{p_i} - 1 + \lambda \;\; = \;\; 0 \tag{2.87}$$

$$\Rightarrow \ln \frac{1}{p_i} \;\; = \;\; 1 - \lambda, \tag{2.88}$$

so all the p_i are equal. That this extremum is indeed a maximum is established
by finding the curvature:

$$\frac{\partial^2 G(\mathbf{p})}{\partial p_i \partial p_j} = -\frac{1}{p_i}\delta_{ij}, \tag{2.89}$$

which is negative definite. $\square$

Proof using Jensen's inequality (recommended method).   First a reminder of
the inequality.

If f is a convex $\smile$ function and x is a random variable then:

$$\mathcal{E}\left[f(x)\right] \geq f\left(\mathcal{E}[x]\right).$$

If f is strictly convex $\smile$ and $\mathcal{E}\left[f(x)\right] = f\left(\mathcal{E}[x]\right)$, then the random
variable x is a constant (with probability 1).

The secret of a proof using Jensen's inequality is to choose the right function and the right random variable. We could define

$$f(u) = \log \frac{1}{u} = -\log u \qquad (2.90)$$

(which is a convex function) and think of $H(X) = \sum p_i \log \frac{1}{p_i}$ as the mean of
$f(u)$ where $u = P(x)$, but this would not get us there – it would give us an
inequality in the wrong direction. If instead we define

$$u = 1/P(x) \qquad (2.91)$$

then we find:

$$H(X) = -\mathcal{E}\left[f(1/P(x))\right] \leq -f\left(\mathcal{E}[1/P(x)]\right); \qquad (2.92)$$

now we know from exercise 2.22 (p.37) that $\mathcal{E}[1/P(x)] = |\mathcal{A}_X|$, so

$$H(X) \leq -f\left(|\mathcal{A}_X|\right) = \log|\mathcal{A}_X|. \qquad (2.93)$$

Equality holds only if the random variable $u = 1/P(x)$ is a constant, which
means $P(x)$ is a constant for all x.   □

Solution to exercise 2.26 (p.37).

$$D_{\mathrm{KL}}(P||Q) = \sum_x P(x) \log \frac{P(x)}{Q(x)}. \qquad (2.94)$$

We prove Gibbs' inequality using Jensen's inequality. Let $f(u) = \log 1/u$ and
$u = \frac{Q(x)}{P(x)}$. Then

$$
\begin{aligned}
D_{\mathrm{KL}}(P||Q) &= \mathcal{E}[f(Q(x)/P(x))] & (2.95) \\
&\geq f\left(\sum_x P(x)\frac{Q(x)}{P(x)}\right) = \log\left(\frac{1}{\sum_x Q(x)}\right) = 0, & (2.96)
\end{aligned}
$$

with equality only if $u = \frac{Q(x)}{P(x)}$ is a constant, that is, if $Q(x) = P(x)$.   □

Second solution.   In the above proof the expectations were with respect to
the probability distribution $P(x)$. A second solution method uses Jensen's
inequality with $Q(x)$ instead. We define $f(u) = u \log u$ and let $u = \frac{P(x)}{Q(x)}$.
Then

$$
\begin{aligned}
D_{\mathrm{KL}}(P||Q) &= \sum_x Q(x)\frac{P(x)}{Q(x)} \log \frac{P(x)}{Q(x)} = \sum_x Q(x) f\left(\frac{P(x)}{Q(x)}\right) & (2.97) \\
&\geq f\left(\sum_x Q(x)\frac{P(x)}{Q(x)}\right) = f(1) = 0, & (2.98)
\end{aligned}
$$

with equality only if $u = \frac{P(x)}{Q(x)}$ is a constant, that is, if $Q(x) = P(x)$.   □

Solution to exercise 2.28 (p.38).

$$H(X) = H_2(f) + fH_2(g) + (1 - f)H_2(h).\qquad(2.99)$$

Solution to exercise 2.29 (p.38). The probability that there are $x - 1$ tails and then one head (so we get the first head on the xth toss) is

$$P(x) = (1 - f)^{x-1}f.\qquad(2.100)$$

If the first toss is a tail, the probability distribution for the future looks just like it did before we made the first toss. Thus we have a recursive expression for the entropy:

$$H(X) = H_2(f) + (1 - f)H(X).\qquad(2.101)$$

Rearranging,

$$H(X) = H_2(f)/f.\qquad(2.102)$$

Solution to exercise 2.34 (p.38). The probability of the number of tails t is

$$P(t) = \left(\frac{1}{2}\right)^t \frac{1}{2} \quad \text{for } t \geq 0.\qquad(2.103)$$

The expected number of heads is 1, by definition of the problem. The expected number of tails is

$$\mathcal{E}[t] = \sum_{t=0}^{\infty} t \left(\frac{1}{2}\right)^t \frac{1}{2},\qquad(2.104)$$

which may be shown to be 1 in a variety of ways. For example, since the situation after one tail is thrown is equivalent to the opening situation, we can write down the recurrence relation

$$\mathcal{E}[t] = \frac{1}{2}(1 + \mathcal{E}[t]) + \frac{1}{2}0 \;\Rightarrow\; \mathcal{E}[t] = 1.\qquad(2.105)$$

The probability distribution of the 'estimator' $\hat{f} = 1/(1 + t)$, given that $f = 1/2$, is plotted in figure 2.12. The probability of $\hat{f}$ is simply the probability of the corresponding value of t.

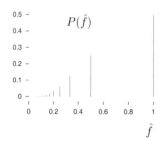

Figure 2.12. The probability distribution of the estimator $\hat{f} = 1/(1 + t)$, given that $f = 1/2$.

Solution to exercise 2.35 (p.38).

(a) The mean number of rolls from one six to the next six is six (assuming we start counting rolls after the first of the two sixes). The probability that the next six occurs on the rth roll is the probability of *not* getting a six for $r - 1$ rolls multiplied by the probability of then getting a six:

$$P(r_1 = r) = \left(\frac{5}{6}\right)^{r-1} \frac{1}{6}, \quad \text{for } r \in \{1, 2, 3, \dots\}.\qquad(2.106)$$

This probability distribution of the number of rolls, r, may be called an exponential distribution, since

$$P(r_1 = r) = e^{-\alpha r}/Z,\qquad(2.107)$$

where $\alpha = \ln(6/5)$, and Z is a normalizing constant.

(b) The mean number of rolls from the clock until the next six is six.

(c) The mean number of rolls, going back in time, until the most recent six is six.

(d) The mean number of rolls from the six before the clock struck to the six after the clock struck is the sum of the answers to (b) and (c), less one, that is, eleven.

(e) Rather than explaining the difference between (a) and (d), let me give another hint. Imagine that the buses in Poissonville arrive independently at random (a Poisson process), with, on average, one bus every six minutes. Imagine that passengers turn up at bus-stops at a uniform rate, and are scooped up by the bus without delay, so the interval between two buses remains constant. Buses that follow gaps bigger than six minutes become overcrowded. The passengers' representative complains that two-thirds of all passengers found themselves on overcrowded buses. The bus operator claims, 'no, no – only one third of our buses are overcrowded'. Can both these claims be true?

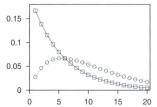

Figure 2.13. The probability distribution of the number of rolls r_1 from one 6 to the next (falling solid line),

$$P(r_1 = r) = \left(\frac{5}{6}\right)^{r-1} \frac{1}{6},$$

and the probability distribution (dashed line) of the number of rolls from the 6 before 1pm to the next 6, r_{tot},

$$P(r_{tot} = r) = r \left(\frac{5}{6}\right)^{r-1} \left(\frac{1}{6}\right)^2.$$

The probability $P(r_1 > 6)$ is about $1/3$; the probability $P(r_{tot} > 6)$ is about $2/3$. The mean of r_1 is 6, and the mean of r_{tot} is 11.

Solution to exercise 2.38 (p.39).

Binomial distribution method. From the solution to exercise 1.2, $p_B = 3f^2(1-f) + f^3$.

Sum rule method. The marginal probabilities of the eight values of **r** are illustrated by:

$$P(\mathbf{r} = 000) = \tfrac{1}{2}(1-f)^3 + \tfrac{1}{2}f^3, \tag{2.108}$$

$$P(\mathbf{r} = 001) = \tfrac{1}{2}f(1-f)^2 + \tfrac{1}{2}f^2(1-f) = \tfrac{1}{2}f(1-f). \tag{2.109}$$

The posterior probabilities are represented by

$$P(s = 1 \mid \mathbf{r} = 000) = \frac{f^3}{(1-f)^3 + f^3} \tag{2.110}$$

and

$$P(s = 1 \mid \mathbf{r} = 001) = \frac{(1-f)f^2}{f(1-f)^2 + f^2(1-f)} = f. \tag{2.111}$$

The probabilities of error in these representative cases are thus

$$P(\text{error} \mid \mathbf{r} = 000) = \frac{f^3}{(1-f)^3 + f^3} \tag{2.112}$$

and

$$P(\text{error} \mid \mathbf{r} = 001) = f. \tag{2.113}$$

Notice that while the average probability of error of R_3 is about $3f^2$, the probability (given **r**) that any *particular* bit is wrong is either about f^3 or f.

The average error probability, using the sum rule, is

$$
\begin{aligned}
P(\text{error}) &= \sum_{\mathbf{r}} P(\mathbf{r}) P(\text{error} \mid \mathbf{r}) \\
&= 2[\tfrac{1}{2}(1-f)^3 + \tfrac{1}{2}f^3] \frac{f^3}{(1-f)^3 + f^3} + 6[\tfrac{1}{2}f(1-f)]f.
\end{aligned}
$$

The first two terms are for the cases **r** = 000 and 111; the remaining 6 are for the other outcomes, which share the same probability of occurring and identical error probability, f.

So

$$P(\text{error}) = f^3 + 3f^2(1-f).$$

Solution to exercise 2.39 (p.40). The entropy is 9.7 bits per word.

About Chapter 3

If you are eager to get on to information theory, data compression, and noisy channels, you can skip to Chapter 4. Data compression and data modelling are intimately connected, however, so you'll probably want to come back to this chapter by the time you get to Chapter 6. Before reading Chapter 3, it might be good to look at the following exercises.

▷ Exercise 3.1.[2, p.59] A die is selected at random from two twenty-faced dice on which the symbols 1–10 are written with nonuniform frequency as follows.

Symbol	1	2	3	4	5	6	7	8	9	10
Number of faces of die A	6	4	3	2	1	1	1	1	1	0
Number of faces of die B	3	3	2	2	2	2	2	2	1	1

The randomly chosen die is rolled 7 times, with the following outcomes:

$$5, 3, 9, 3, 8, 4, 7.$$

What is the probability that the die is die A?

▷ Exercise 3.2.[2, p.59] Assume that there is a third twenty-faced die, die C, on which the symbols 1–20 are written once each. As above, one of the three dice is selected at random and rolled 7 times, giving the outcomes: 3, 5, 4, 8, 3, 9, 7.
What is the probability that the die is (a) die A, (b) die B, (c) die C?

Exercise 3.3.[3, p.48] Inferring a decay constant

Unstable particles are emitted from a source and decay at a distance x, a real number that has an exponential probability distribution with characteristic length λ. Decay events can only be observed if they occur in a window extending from $x = 1\,\mathrm{cm}$ to $x = 20\,\mathrm{cm}$. N decays are observed at locations $\{x_1, \ldots, x_N\}$. What is λ?

▷ Exercise 3.4.[3, p.55] Forensic evidence

Two people have left traces of their own blood at the scene of a crime. A suspect, Oliver, is tested and found to have type 'O' blood. The blood groups of the two traces are found to be of type 'O' (a common type in the local population, having frequency 60%) and of type 'AB' (a rare type, with frequency 1%). Do these data (type 'O' and 'AB' blood were found at scene) give evidence in favour of the proposition that Oliver was one of the two people present at the crime?

3

More about Inference

It is not a controversial statement that Bayes' theorem provides the correct language for describing the inference of a message communicated over a noisy channel, as we used it in Chapter 1 (p.6). But strangely, when it comes to other inference problems, the use of Bayes' theorem is not so widespread.

▶ 3.1 A first inference problem

When I was an undergraduate in Cambridge, I was privileged to receive supervisions from Steve Gull. Sitting at his desk in a dishevelled office in St. John's College, I asked him how one ought to answer an old Tripos question (exercise 3.3):

> Unstable particles are emitted from a source and decay at a distance x, a real number that has an exponential probability distribution with characteristic length λ. Decay events can only be observed if they occur in a window extending from $x = 1\,\mathrm{cm}$ to $x = 20\,\mathrm{cm}$. N decays are observed at locations $\{x_1, \ldots, x_N\}$. What is λ?

I had scratched my head over this for some time. My education had provided me with a couple of approaches to solving such inference problems: constructing 'estimators' of the unknown parameters; or 'fitting' the model to the data, or a processed version of the data.

Since the mean of an unconstrained exponential distribution is λ, it seemed reasonable to examine the sample mean $\bar{x} = \sum_n x_n/N$ and see if an estimator $\hat{\lambda}$ could be obtained from it. It was evident that the estimator $\hat{\lambda} = \bar{x} - 1$ would be appropriate for $\lambda \ll 20\,\mathrm{cm}$, but not for cases where the truncation of the distribution at the right-hand side is significant; with a little ingenuity and the introduction of ad hoc bins, promising estimators for $\lambda \gg 20$ cm could be constructed. But there was no obvious estimator that would work under all conditions.

Nor could I find a satisfactory approach based on fitting the density $P(x\,|\,\lambda)$ to a histogram derived from the data. I was stuck.

What is the general solution to this problem and others like it? Is it always necessary, when confronted by a new inference problem, to grope in the dark for appropriate 'estimators' and worry about finding the 'best' estimator (whatever that means)?

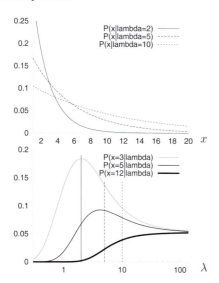

Figure 3.1. The probability density $P(x \mid \lambda)$ as a function of x.

Figure 3.2. The probability density $P(x \mid \lambda)$ as a function of λ, for three different values of x. When plotted this way round, the function is known as the *likelihood* of λ. The marks indicate the three values of λ, $\lambda = 2, 5, 10$, that were used in the preceding figure.

Steve wrote down the probability of one data point, given λ:

$$P(x \mid \lambda) = \begin{cases} \frac{1}{\lambda} e^{-x/\lambda}/Z(\lambda) & 1 < x < 20 \\ 0 & \text{otherwise} \end{cases} \tag{3.1}$$

where

$$Z(\lambda) = \int_1^{20} \mathrm{d}x \, \frac{1}{\lambda} e^{-x/\lambda} = \left(e^{-1/\lambda} - e^{-20/\lambda} \right). \tag{3.2}$$

This seemed obvious enough. Then he wrote *Bayes' theorem*:

$$P(\lambda \mid \{x_1, \ldots, x_N\}) = \frac{P(\{x\} \mid \lambda) P(\lambda)}{P(\{x\})} \tag{3.3}$$

$$\propto \frac{1}{(\lambda Z(\lambda))^N} \exp\left(-\sum_1^N x_n/\lambda \right) P(\lambda). \tag{3.4}$$

Suddenly, the straightforward distribution $P(\{x_1, \ldots, x_N\} \mid \lambda)$, defining the probability of the data given the hypothesis λ, was being turned on its head so as to define the probability of a hypothesis given the data. A simple figure showed the probability of a single data point $P(x \mid \lambda)$ as a familiar function of x, for different values of λ (figure 3.1). Each curve was an innocent exponential, normalized to have area 1. Plotting the same function as a function of λ for a fixed value of x, something remarkable happens: a peak emerges (figure 3.2). To help understand these two points of view of the one function, figure 3.3 shows a surface plot of $P(x \mid \lambda)$ as a function of x and λ.

For a dataset consisting of several points, e.g., the six points $\{x\}_{n=1}^N = \{1.5, 2, 3, 4, 5, 12\}$, the likelihood function $P(\{x\} \mid \lambda)$ is the product of the N functions of λ, $P(x_n \mid \lambda)$ (figure 3.4).

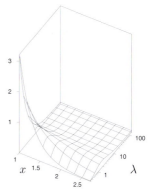

Figure 3.3. The probability density $P(x \mid \lambda)$ as a function of x and λ. Figures 3.1 and 3.2 are vertical sections through this surface.

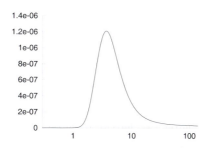

Figure 3.4. The likelihood function in the case of a six-point dataset, $P(\{x\} = \{1.5, 2, 3, 4, 5, 12\} \mid \lambda)$, as a function of λ.

Steve summarized Bayes' theorem as embodying the fact that

> what you know about λ after the data arrive is what you knew before $[P(\lambda)]$, and what the data told you $[P(\{x\} \mid \lambda)]$.

Probabilities are used here to quantify degrees of belief. To nip possible confusion in the bud, it must be emphasized that the hypothesis λ that correctly describes the situation is *not* a *stochastic* variable, and the fact that the Bayesian uses a probability distribution P does *not* mean that he thinks of the world as stochastically changing its nature between the states described by the different hypotheses. He uses the notation of probabilities to represent his *beliefs* about the mutually exclusive micro-hypotheses (here, values of λ), of which only one is actually true. That probabilities can denote degrees of belief, given assumptions, seemed reasonable to me.

The posterior probability distribution (3.4) represents the unique and complete solution to the problem. There is no need to invent 'estimators'; nor do we need to invent criteria for comparing alternative estimators with each other. Whereas orthodox statisticians offer twenty ways of solving a problem, and another twenty different criteria for deciding which of these solutions is the best, Bayesian statistics only offers one answer to a well-posed problem.

Assumptions in inference

Our inference is conditional on our assumptions [for example, the prior $P(\lambda)$]. Critics view such priors as a difficulty because they are 'subjective', but I don't see how it could be otherwise. How can one perform inference without making assumptions? I believe that it is of great value that Bayesian methods force one to make these tacit assumptions explicit.

First, once assumptions are made, the inferences are objective and unique, reproducible with complete agreement by anyone who has the same information and makes the same assumptions. For example, given the assumptions listed above, $\mathcal{H}$, and the data D, everyone will agree about the posterior probability of the decay length λ:

$$P(\lambda \mid D, \mathcal{H}) = \frac{P(D \mid \lambda, \mathcal{H}) P(\lambda \mid \mathcal{H})}{P(D \mid \mathcal{H})}. \tag{3.5}$$

Second, when the assumptions are explicit, they are easier to criticize, and easier to modify – indeed, we can quantify the sensitivity of our inferences to the details of the assumptions. For example, we can note from the likelihood curves in figure 3.2 that in the case of a single data point at $x = 5$, the likelihood function is less strongly peaked than in the case $x = 3$; the details of the prior $P(\lambda)$ become increasingly important as the sample mean $\bar{x}$ gets closer to the middle of the window, 10.5. In the case $x = 12$, the likelihood function doesn't have a peak at all – such data merely rule out small values of λ, and don't give any information about the relative probabilities of large values of λ. So in this case, the details of the prior at the small λ end of things are not important, but at the large λ end, the prior is important.

Third, when we are not sure which of various alternative assumptions is the most appropriate for a problem, we can treat this question as another inference task. Thus, given data D, we can compare alternative assumptions $\mathcal{H}$ using Bayes' theorem:

$$P(\mathcal{H} \mid D, I) = \frac{P(D \mid \mathcal{H}, I) P(\mathcal{H} \mid I)}{P(D \mid I)}, \tag{3.6}$$

If you have any difficulty understanding this chapter I recommend ensuring you are happy with exercises 3.1 and 3.2 (p.47) then noting their similarity to exercise 3.3.

where I denotes the highest assumptions, which we are not questioning.

Fourth, we can take into account our uncertainty regarding such assumptions when we make subsequent predictions. Rather than choosing one particular assumption $\mathcal{H}^*$, and working out our predictions about some quantity $\mathbf{t}$, $P(\mathbf{t} \mid D, \mathcal{H}^*, I)$, we obtain predictions that take into account our uncertainty about $\mathcal{H}$ by using the sum rule:

$$P(\mathbf{t} \mid D, I) = \sum_{\mathcal{H}} P(\mathbf{t} \mid D, \mathcal{H}, I) P(\mathcal{H} \mid D, I). \qquad (3.7)$$

This is another contrast with orthodox statistics, in which it is conventional to 'test' a default model, and then, if the test 'accepts the model' at some 'significance level', to use exclusively that model to make predictions.

Steve thus persuaded me that

> probability theory reaches parts that ad hoc methods cannot reach.

Let's look at a few more examples of simple inference problems.

▶ 3.2 The bent coin

A bent coin is tossed F times; we observe a sequence $\mathbf{s}$ of heads and tails (which we'll denote by the symbols a and b). We wish to know the bias of the coin, and predict the probability that the next toss will result in a head. We first encountered this task in example 2.7 (p.30), and we will encounter it again in Chapter 6, when we discuss adaptive data compression. It is also the original inference problem studied by Thomas Bayes in his essay published in 1763.

As in exercise 2.8 (p.30), we will assume a uniform prior distribution and obtain a posterior distribution by multiplying by the likelihood. A critic might object, 'where did this prior come from?' I will not claim that the uniform prior is in any way fundamental; indeed we'll give examples of nonuniform priors later. The prior is a subjective assumption. One of the themes of this book is:

> you can't do inference – or data compression – without making assumptions.

We give the name $\mathcal{H}_1$ to our assumptions. [We'll be introducing an alternative set of assumptions in a moment.] The probability, given p_{a}, that F tosses result in a sequence $\mathbf{s}$ that contains $\{F_{\mathsf{a}}, F_{\mathsf{b}}\}$ counts of the two outcomes is

$$P(\mathbf{s} \mid p_{\mathsf{a}}, F, \mathcal{H}_1) = p_{\mathsf{a}}^{F_{\mathsf{a}}} (1 - p_{\mathsf{a}})^{F_{\mathsf{b}}}. \qquad (3.8)$$

[For example, $P(\mathbf{s} = \mathsf{aaba} \mid p_{\mathsf{a}}, F = 4, \mathcal{H}_1) = p_{\mathsf{a}} p_{\mathsf{a}} (1 - p_{\mathsf{a}}) p_{\mathsf{a}}.$] Our first model assumes a uniform prior distribution for p_{a},

$$P(p_{\mathsf{a}} \mid \mathcal{H}_1) = 1, \quad p_{\mathsf{a}} \in [0, 1] \qquad (3.9)$$

and $p_{\mathsf{b}} \equiv 1 - p_{\mathsf{a}}$.

Inferring unknown parameters

Given a string of length F of which F_{a} are as and F_{b} are bs, we are interested in (a) inferring what p_{a} might be; (b) predicting whether the next character is an a or a b. [Predictions are always expressed as probabilities. So 'predicting whether the next character is an a' is the same as computing the probability that the next character is an a.]

Assuming $\mathcal{H}_1$ to be true, the posterior probability of p_a, given a string s of length F that has counts $\{F_a, F_b\}$, is, by Bayes' theorem,

$$P(p_a \,|\, s, F, \mathcal{H}_1) \;=\; \frac{P(s \,|\, p_a, F, \mathcal{H}_1)P(p_a \,|\, \mathcal{H}_1)}{P(s \,|\, F, \mathcal{H}_1)}. \tag{3.10}$$

The factor $P(s \,|\, p_a, F, \mathcal{H}_1)$, which, as a function of p_a, is known as the likelihood function, was given in equation (3.8); the prior $P(p_a \,|\, \mathcal{H}_1)$ was given in equation (3.9). Our inference of p_a is thus:

$$P(p_a \,|\, s, F, \mathcal{H}_1) \;=\; \frac{p_a^{F_a}(1 - p_a)^{F_b}}{P(s \,|\, F, \mathcal{H}_1)}. \tag{3.11}$$

The normalizing constant is given by the beta integral

$$P(s \,|\, F, \mathcal{H}_1) = \int_0^1 dp_a\, p_a^{F_a}(1 - p_a)^{F_b} = \frac{\Gamma(F_a + 1)\Gamma(F_b + 1)}{\Gamma(F_a + F_b + 2)} = \frac{F_a! F_b!}{(F_a + F_b + 1)!}. \tag{3.12}$$

Exercise 3.5.[2, p.59] Sketch the posterior probability $P(p_a \,|\, s = \text{aba}, F = 3)$. What is the most probable value of p_a (i.e., the value that maximizes the posterior probability density)? What is the mean value of p_a under this distribution?

Answer the same questions for the posterior probability $P(p_a \,|\, s = \text{bbb}, F = 3)$.

From inferences to predictions

Our prediction about the next toss, the probability that next toss is a a, is obtained by integrating over p_a. This has the effect of taking into account our uncertainty about p_a when making predictions. By the sum rule,

$$P(a \,|\, s, F) \;=\; \int dp_a\, P(a \,|\, p_a)P(p_a \,|\, s, F). \tag{3.13}$$

The probability of an a given p_a is simply p_a, so

$$P(a \,|\, s, F) = \int dp_a\, p_a \frac{p_a^{F_a}(1 - p_a)^{F_b}}{P(s \,|\, F)} \tag{3.14}$$

$$= \int dp_a\, \frac{p_a^{F_a+1}(1 - p_a)^{F_b}}{P(s \,|\, F)} \tag{3.15}$$

$$= \left[\frac{(F_a + 1)! F_b!}{(F_a + F_b + 2)!}\right] \bigg/ \left[\frac{F_a! F_b!}{(F_a + F_b + 1)!}\right] = \frac{F_a + 1}{F_a + F_b + 2}, \tag{3.16}$$

which is known as *Laplace's rule*.

▶ 3.3 The bent coin and model comparison

Imagine that a scientist introduces another theory for our data. He asserts that the source is not really a bent coin but is really a perfectly formed die with one face painted heads ('a') and the other five painted tails ('b'). Thus the parameter p_a, which in the original model, $\mathcal{H}_1$, could take any value between 0 and 1, is according to the new hypothesis, $\mathcal{H}_0$, not a free parameter at all; rather, it is equal to 1/6. [This hypothesis is termed $\mathcal{H}_0$ so that the suffix of each model indicates its number of free parameters.]

How can we compare these two models in the light of data? We wish to infer how probable $\mathcal{H}_1$ is relative to $\mathcal{H}_0$.

Model comparison as inference

In order to perform model comparison, we write down Bayes' theorem again, but this time with a different argument on the left-hand side. We wish to know how probable $\mathcal{H}_1$ is given the data. By Bayes' theorem,

$$P(\mathcal{H}_1 \mid \mathbf{s}, F) = \frac{P(\mathbf{s} \mid F, \mathcal{H}_1)P(\mathcal{H}_1)}{P(\mathbf{s} \mid F)}. \tag{3.17}$$

Similarly, the posterior probability of $\mathcal{H}_0$ is

$$P(\mathcal{H}_0 \mid \mathbf{s}, F) = \frac{P(\mathbf{s} \mid F, \mathcal{H}_0)P(\mathcal{H}_0)}{P(\mathbf{s} \mid F)}. \tag{3.18}$$

The normalizing constant in both cases is $P(\mathbf{s} \mid F)$, which is the total probability of getting the observed data. If $\mathcal{H}_1$ and $\mathcal{H}_0$ are the only models under consideration, this probability is given by the sum rule:

$$P(\mathbf{s} \mid F) = P(\mathbf{s} \mid F, \mathcal{H}_1)P(\mathcal{H}_1) + P(\mathbf{s} \mid F, \mathcal{H}_0)P(\mathcal{H}_0). \tag{3.19}$$

To evaluate the posterior probabilities of the hypotheses we need to assign values to the prior probabilities $P(\mathcal{H}_1)$ and $P(\mathcal{H}_0)$; in this case, we might set these to $1/2$ each. And we need to evaluate the data-dependent terms $P(\mathbf{s} \mid F, \mathcal{H}_1)$ and $P(\mathbf{s} \mid F, \mathcal{H}_0)$. We can give names to these quantities. The quantity $P(\mathbf{s} \mid F, \mathcal{H}_1)$ is a measure of how much the data favour $\mathcal{H}_1$, and we call it the *evidence* for model $\mathcal{H}_1$. We already encountered this quantity in equation (3.10) where it appeared as the normalizing constant of the first inference we made – the inference of p_a given the data.

> **How model comparison works:** The evidence for a model is usually the normalizing constant of an earlier Bayesian inference.

We evaluated the normalizing constant for model $\mathcal{H}_1$ in (3.12). The evidence for model $\mathcal{H}_0$ is very simple because this model has no parameters to infer. Defining p_0 to be $1/6$, we have

$$P(\mathbf{s} \mid F, \mathcal{H}_0) = p_0^{F_\mathrm{a}}(1 - p_0)^{F_\mathrm{b}}. \tag{3.20}$$

Thus the posterior probability ratio of model $\mathcal{H}_1$ to model $\mathcal{H}_0$ is

$$\frac{P(\mathcal{H}_1 \mid \mathbf{s}, F)}{P(\mathcal{H}_0 \mid \mathbf{s}, F)} = \frac{P(\mathbf{s} \mid F, \mathcal{H}_1)P(\mathcal{H}_1)}{P(\mathbf{s} \mid F, \mathcal{H}_0)P(\mathcal{H}_0)} \tag{3.21}$$

$$= \frac{\frac{F_\mathrm{a}!F_\mathrm{b}!}{(F_\mathrm{a}+F_\mathrm{b}+1)!}}{p_0^{F_\mathrm{a}}(1 - p_0)^{F_\mathrm{b}}}. \tag{3.22}$$

Some values of this posterior probability ratio are illustrated in table 3.5. The first five lines illustrate that some outcomes favour one model, and some favour the other. No outcome is completely incompatible with either model. With small amounts of data (six tosses, say) it is typically not the case that one of the two models is overwhelmingly more probable than the other. But with more data, the evidence against $\mathcal{H}_0$ given by any data set with the ratio $F_\mathrm{a} : F_\mathrm{b}$ differing from $1 : 5$ mounts up. You can't predict in advance how much data are needed to be pretty sure which theory is true. It depends what p_0 is.

The simpler model, $\mathcal{H}_0$, since it has no adjustable parameters, is able to lose out by the biggest margin. The odds may be hundreds to one against it. The more complex model can never lose out by a large margin; there's no data set that is actually *unlikely* given model $\mathcal{H}_1$.

F	Data (F_a, F_b)	$\dfrac{P(\mathcal{H}_1 \mid \mathbf{s}, F)}{P(\mathcal{H}_0 \mid \mathbf{s}, F)}$	
6	$(5,1)$	222.2	
6	$(3,3)$	2.67	
6	$(2,4)$	0.71	$= 1/1.4$
6	$(1,5)$	0.356	$= 1/2.8$
6	$(0,6)$	0.427	$= 1/2.3$
20	$(10,10)$	96.5	
20	$(3,17)$	0.2	$= 1/5$
20	$(0,20)$	1.83	

Table 3.5. Outcome of model comparison between models $\mathcal{H}_1$ and $\mathcal{H}_0$ for the 'bent coin'. Model $\mathcal{H}_0$ states that $p_a = 1/6$, $p_b = 5/6$.

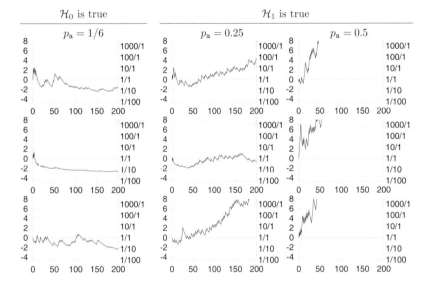

Figure 3.6. Typical behaviour of the evidence in favour of $\mathcal{H}_1$ as bent coin tosses accumulate under three different conditions. Horizontal axis is the number of tosses, F. The vertical axis on the left is $\ln \dfrac{P(\mathbf{s} \mid F, \mathcal{H}_1)}{P(\mathbf{s} \mid F, \mathcal{H}_0)}$; the right-hand vertical axis shows the values of $\dfrac{P(\mathbf{s} \mid F, \mathcal{H}_1)}{P(\mathbf{s} \mid F, \mathcal{H}_0)}$. (See also figure 3.8, p.60.)

▷ Exercise 3.6.[2] Show that after F tosses have taken place, the biggest value that the log evidence ratio

$$\log \frac{P(\mathbf{s} \mid F, \mathcal{H}_1)}{P(\mathbf{s} \mid F, \mathcal{H}_0)} \tag{3.23}$$

can have scales *linearly* with F if $\mathcal{H}_1$ is more probable, but the log evidence in favour of $\mathcal{H}_0$ can grow at most as $\log F$.

▷ Exercise 3.7.[3, p.60] Putting your sampling theory hat on, assuming F_a has not yet been measured, compute a plausible range that the log evidence ratio might lie in, as a function of F and the true value of p_a, and sketch it as a function of F for $p_a = p_0 = 1/6$, $p_a = 0.25$, and $p_a = 1/2$. [Hint: sketch the log evidence as a function of the random variable F_a and work out the mean and standard deviation of F_a.]

Typical behaviour of the evidence

Figure 3.6 shows the log evidence ratio as a function of the number of tosses, F, in a number of simulated experiments. In the left-hand experiments, $\mathcal{H}_0$ was true. In the right-hand ones, $\mathcal{H}_1$ was true, and the value of p_a is either 0.25 or 0.5.

We will discuss model comparison more in a later chapter.

▶ **3.4 An example of legal evidence**

The following example illustrates that there is more to Bayesian inference than the priors.

> Two people have left traces of their own blood at the scene of a crime. A suspect, Oliver, is tested and found to have type 'O' blood. The blood groups of the two traces are found to be of type 'O' (a common type in the local population, having frequency 60%) and of type 'AB' (a rare type, with frequency 1%). Do these data (type 'O' and 'AB' blood were found at scene) give evidence in favour of the proposition that Oliver was one of the two people present at the crime?

A careless lawyer might claim that the fact that the suspect's blood type was found at the scene is positive evidence for the theory that he was present. But this is not so.

Denote the proposition 'the suspect and one unknown person were present' by S. The alternative, $\bar{S}$, states 'two unknown people from the population were present'. The prior in this problem is the prior probability ratio between the propositions S and $\bar{S}$. This quantity is important to the final verdict and would be based on all other available information in the case. Our task here is just to evaluate the contribution made by the data D, that is, the likelihood ratio, $P(D\,|\,S,\mathcal{H})/P(D\,|\,\bar{S},\mathcal{H})$. In my view, a jury's task should generally be to multiply together carefully evaluated likelihood ratios from each independent piece of admissible evidence with an equally carefully reasoned prior probability. [This view is shared by many statisticians but learned British appeal judges recently disagreed and actually overturned the verdict of a trial because the jurors *had* been taught to use Bayes' theorem to handle complicated DNA evidence.]

The probability of the data given S is the probability that one unknown person drawn from the population has blood type AB:

$$P(D\,|\,S,\mathcal{H}) = p_{\text{AB}} \tag{3.24}$$

(since given S, we already know that one trace will be of type O). The probability of the data given $\bar{S}$ is the probability that two unknown people drawn from the population have types O and AB:

$$P(D\,|\,\bar{S},\mathcal{H}) = 2\,p_{\text{O}}\,p_{\text{AB}}. \tag{3.25}$$

In these equations $\mathcal{H}$ denotes the assumptions that two people were present and left blood there, and that the probability distribution of the blood groups of unknown people in an explanation is the same as the population frequencies.

Dividing, we obtain the likelihood ratio:

$$\frac{P(D\,|\,S,\mathcal{H})}{P(D\,|\,\bar{S},\mathcal{H})} = \frac{1}{2p_{\text{O}}} = \frac{1}{2 \times 0.6} = 0.83. \tag{3.26}$$

Thus the data in fact provide weak evidence *against* the supposition that Oliver was present.

This result may be found surprising, so let us examine it from various points of view. First consider the case of another suspect, Alberto, who has type AB. Intuitively, the data do provide evidence in favour of the theory S'

that this suspect was present, relative to the null hypothesis $\bar{S}$. And indeed the likelihood ratio in this case is:

$$\frac{P(D \mid S', \mathcal{H})}{P(D \mid \bar{S}, \mathcal{H})} = \frac{1}{2\, p_{\mathrm{AB}}} = 50. \tag{3.27}$$

Now let us change the situation slightly; imagine that 99% of people are of blood type O, and the rest are of type AB. Only these two blood types exist in the population. The data at the scene are the same as before. Consider again how these data influence our beliefs about Oliver, a suspect of type O, and Alberto, a suspect of type AB. Intuitively, we still believe that the presence of the rare AB blood provides positive evidence that Alberto was there. But does the fact that type O blood was detected at the scene favour the hypothesis that Oliver was present? If this were the case, that would mean that regardless of who the suspect is, the data make it more probable they were present; everyone in the population would be under greater suspicion, which would be absurd. The data may be *compatible* with any suspect of either blood type being present, but if they provide evidence *for* some theories, they must also provide evidence *against* other theories.

Here is another way of thinking about this: imagine that instead of two people's blood stains there are ten, and that in the entire local population of one hundred, there are ninety type O suspects and ten type AB suspects. Consider a particular type O suspect, Oliver: without any other information, and before the blood test results come in, there is a one in 10 chance that he was at the scene, since we know that 10 out of the 100 suspects were present. We now get the results of blood tests, and find that *nine* of the ten stains are of type AB, and *one* of the stains is of type O. Does this make it more likely that Oliver was there? No, there is now only a one in ninety chance that he was there, since we know that only one person present was of type O.

Maybe the intuition is aided finally by writing down the formulae for the general case where n_{O} blood stains of individuals of type O are found, and n_{AB} of type AB, a total of N individuals in all, and unknown people come from a large population with fractions $p_{\mathrm{O}}, p_{\mathrm{AB}}$. (There may be other blood types too.) The task is to evaluate the likelihood ratio for the two hypotheses: S, 'the type O suspect (Oliver) and $N-1$ unknown others left N stains'; and $\bar{S}$, 'N unknowns left N stains'. The probability of the data under hypothesis $\bar{S}$ is just the probability of getting $n_{\mathrm{O}}, n_{\mathrm{AB}}$ individuals of the two types when N individuals are drawn at random from the population:

$$P(n_{\mathrm{O}}, n_{\mathrm{AB}} \mid \bar{S}) = \frac{N!}{n_{\mathrm{O}}!\, n_{\mathrm{AB}}!} p_{\mathrm{O}}^{n_{\mathrm{O}}} p_{\mathrm{AB}}^{n_{\mathrm{AB}}}. \tag{3.28}$$

In the case of hypothesis S, we need the distribution of the $N-1$ other individuals:

$$P(n_{\mathrm{O}}, n_{\mathrm{AB}} \mid S) = \frac{(N-1)!}{(n_{\mathrm{O}}-1)!\, n_{\mathrm{AB}}!} p_{\mathrm{O}}^{n_{\mathrm{O}}-1} p_{\mathrm{AB}}^{n_{\mathrm{AB}}}. \tag{3.29}$$

The likelihood ratio is:

$$\frac{P(n_{\mathrm{O}}, n_{\mathrm{AB}} \mid S)}{P(n_{\mathrm{O}}, n_{\mathrm{AB}} \mid \bar{S})} = \frac{n_{\mathrm{O}}/N}{p_{\mathrm{O}}}. \tag{3.30}$$

This is an instructive result. The likelihood ratio, i.e. the contribution of these data to the question of whether Oliver was present, depends simply on a comparison of the frequency of his blood type in the observed data with the background frequency in the population. There is no dependence on the counts of the other types found at the scene, or their frequencies in the population.

If there are more type O stains than the average number expected under hypothesis $\bar{S}$, then the data give evidence in favour of the presence of Oliver. Conversely, if there are fewer type O stains than the expected number under $\bar{S}$, then the data reduce the probability of the hypothesis that he was there. In the special case $n_O/N = p_O$, the data contribute no evidence either way, regardless of the fact that the data are compatible with the hypothesis S.

▶ 3.5 Exercises

Exercise 3.8.[2, p.60] *The three doors, normal rules.*

On a game show, a contestant is told the rules as follows:

> There are three doors, labelled 1, 2, 3. A single prize has been hidden behind one of them. You get to select one door. Initially your chosen door will *not* be opened. Instead, the gameshow host will open one of the other two doors, and *he will do so in such a way as not to reveal the prize.* For example, if you first choose door 1, he will then open one of doors 2 and 3, and it is guaranteed that he will choose which one to open so that the prize will not be revealed.
>
> At this point, you will be given a fresh choice of door: you can either stick with your first choice, or you can switch to the other closed door. All the doors will then be opened and you will receive whatever is behind your final choice of door.

Imagine that the contestant chooses door 1 first; then the gameshow host opens door 3, revealing nothing behind the door, as promised. Should the contestant (a) stick with door 1, or (b) switch to door 2, or (c) does it make no difference?

Exercise 3.9.[2, p.61] *The three doors, earthquake scenario.*

Imagine that the game happens again and just as the gameshow host is about to open one of the doors a violent earthquake rattles the building and one of the three doors flies open. It happens to be door 3, and it happens not to have the prize behind it. The contestant had initially chosen door 1.

Repositioning his toupée, the host suggests, 'OK, since you chose door 1 initially, door 3 is a valid door for me to open, according to the rules of the game; I'll let door 3 stay open. Let's carry on as if nothing happened.'

Should the contestant stick with door 1, or switch to door 2, or does it make no difference? Assume that the prize was placed randomly, that the gameshow host does not know where it is, and that the door flew open because its latch was broken by the earthquake.

[A similar alternative scenario is a gameshow whose *confused host* forgets the rules, and where the prize is, and opens one of the unchosen doors at random. He opens door 3, and the prize is not revealed. Should the contestant choose what's behind door 1 or door 2? Does the optimal decision for the contestant depend on the contestant's beliefs about whether the gameshow host is confused or not?]

▷ Exercise 3.10.[2] *Another example in which the emphasis is not on priors.* You visit a family whose three children are all at the local school. You don't

know anything about the sexes of the children. While walking clum-
sily round the home, you stumble through one of the three unlabelled
bedroom doors that you know belong, one each, to the three children,
and find that the bedroom contains girlie stuff in sufficient quantities to
convince you that the child who lives in that bedroom is a girl. Later,
you sneak a look at a letter addressed to the parents, which reads 'From
the Headmaster: we are sending this letter to all parents who have male
children at the school to inform them about the following boyish matters. . .'.

These two sources of evidence establish that at least one of the three
children is a girl, and that at least one of the children is a boy. What
are the probabilities that there are (a) two girls and one boy; (b) two
boys and one girl?

▷ Exercise 3.11.[2, p.61] Mrs S is found stabbed in her family garden. Mr S
behaves strangely after her death and is considered as a suspect. On
investigation of police and social records it is found that Mr S had beaten
up his wife on at least nine previous occasions. The prosecution advances
this data as evidence in favour of the hypothesis that Mr S is guilty of the
murder. 'Ah no,' says Mr S's highly paid lawyer, '*statistically*, only one
in a thousand wife-beaters actually goes on to murder his wife.[1] So the
wife-beating is not strong evidence at all. In fact, given the wife-beating
evidence alone, it's extremely unlikely that he would be the murderer of
his wife – only a 1/1000 chance. You should therefore find him innocent.'

Is the lawyer right to imply that the history of wife-beating does not
point to Mr S's being the murderer? Or is the lawyer a slimy trickster?
If the latter, what is wrong with his argument?

[Having received an indignant letter from a lawyer about the preceding
paragraph, I'd like to add an extra inference exercise at this point: *Does
my suggestion that Mr. S.'s lawyer may have been a slimy trickster imply
that I believe* all *lawyers are slimy tricksters?* (Answer: No.)]

▷ Exercise 3.12.[2] A bag contains one counter, known to be either white or
black. A white counter is put in, the bag is shaken, and a counter
is drawn out, which proves to be white. What is now the chance of
drawing a white counter? [Notice that the state of the bag, after the
operations, is exactly identical to its state before.]

▷ Exercise 3.13.[2, p.62] You move into a new house; the phone is connected, and
you're pretty sure that the phone number is 740511, but not as sure as
you would like to be. As an experiment, you pick up the phone and
dial 740511; you obtain a 'busy' signal. Are you now more sure of your
phone number? If so, how much?

▷ Exercise 3.14.[1] In a game, two coins are tossed. If either of the coins comes
up heads, you have won a prize. To claim the prize, you must point to
one of your coins that is a head and say 'look, that coin's a head, I've
won'. You watch Fred play the game. He tosses the two coins, and he

---

[1]In the U.S.A., it is estimated that 2 million women are abused each year by their partners.
In 1994, 4739 women were victims of homicide; of those, 1326 women (28%) were slain by
husbands and boyfriends.
(Sources: http://www.umn.edu/mincava/papers/factoid.htm,
http://www.gunfree.inter.net/vpc/womenfs.htm)

points to a coin and says 'look, that coin's a head, I've won'. What is the probability that the *other* coin is a head?

▷ Exercise 3.15.[2, p.63] A statistical statement appeared in *The Guardian* on Friday January 4, 2002:

> When spun on edge 250 times, a Belgian one-euro coin came up heads 140 times and tails 110. 'It looks very suspicious to me', said Barry Blight, a statistics lecturer at the London School of Economics. 'If the coin were unbiased the chance of getting a result as extreme as that would be less than 7%'.

But *do* these data give evidence that the coin is biased rather than fair? [Hint: see equation (3.22).]

▶ 3.6 Solutions

Solution to exercise 3.1 (p.47). Let the data be D. Assuming equal prior probabilities,

$$\frac{P(A\,|\,D)}{P(B\,|\,D)} = \frac{1}{2}\frac{3}{2}\frac{1}{1}\frac{3}{2}\frac{1}{2}\frac{2}{2}\frac{1}{2} = 9/32 \tag{3.31}$$

and $P(A\,|\,D) = 9/41$.

Solution to exercise 3.2 (p.47). The probability of the data given each hypothesis is:

$$P(D\,|\,A) = \frac{3}{20}\frac{1}{20}\frac{2}{20}\frac{1}{20}\frac{3}{20}\frac{1}{20}\frac{1}{20} = \frac{18}{20^7}; \tag{3.32}$$

$$P(D\,|\,B) = \frac{2}{20}\frac{2}{20}\frac{2}{20}\frac{2}{20}\frac{2}{20}\frac{1}{20}\frac{2}{20} = \frac{64}{20^7}; \tag{3.33}$$

$$P(D\,|\,C) = \frac{1}{20}\frac{1}{20}\frac{1}{20}\frac{1}{20}\frac{1}{20}\frac{1}{20}\frac{1}{20} = \frac{1}{20^7}. \tag{3.34}$$

So

$$P(A\,|\,D) = \frac{18}{18 + 64 + 1} = \frac{18}{83}; \qquad P(B\,|\,D) = \frac{64}{83}; \qquad P(C\,|\,D) = \frac{1}{83}. \tag{3.35}$$

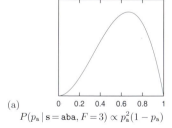

(a)

$P(p_a\,|\,\mathsf{s}=\mathsf{aba}, F=3) \propto p_a^2(1 - p_a)$

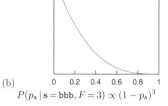

(b)

$P(p_a\,|\,\mathsf{s}=\mathsf{bbb}, F=3) \propto (1 - p_a)^3$

Figure 3.7. Posterior probability for the bias p_a of a bent coin given two different data sets.

Solution to exercise 3.5 (p.52).

(a) $P(p_a\,|\,\mathsf{s}=\mathsf{aba}, F=3) \propto p_a^2(1 - p_a)$. The most probable value of p_a (i.e., the value that maximizes the posterior probability density) is $2/3$. The mean value of p_a is $3/5$.

See figure 3.7a.

(b) $P(p_a \mid \mathbf{s} = \mathtt{bbb}, F = 3) \propto (1 - p_a)^3$. The most probable value of p_a (i.e., the value that maximizes the posterior probability density) is 0. The mean value of p_a is $1/5$.

See figure 3.7b.

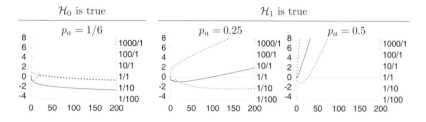

$\mathcal{H}_0$ is true $\mathcal{H}_1$ is true

Figure 3.8. Range of plausible values of the log evidence in favour of $\mathcal{H}_1$ as a function of F. The vertical axis on the left is $\log \frac{P(\mathbf{s} \mid F, \mathcal{H}_1)}{P(\mathbf{s} \mid F, \mathcal{H}_0)}$; the right-hand vertical axis shows the values of $\frac{P(\mathbf{s} \mid F, \mathcal{H}_1)}{P(\mathbf{s} \mid F, \mathcal{H}_0)}$. The solid line shows the log evidence if the random variable F_a takes on its mean value, $F_a = p_a F$. The dotted lines show (approximately) the log evidence if F_a is at its 2.5th or 97.5th percentile. (See also figure 3.6, p.54.)

Solution to exercise 3.7 (p.54). The curves in figure 3.8 were found by finding the mean and standard deviation of F_a, then setting F_a to the mean $\pm$ two standard deviations to get a 95% plausible range for F_a, and computing the three corresponding values of the log evidence ratio.

Solution to exercise 3.8 (p.57). Let $\mathcal{H}_i$ denote the hypothesis that the prize is behind door i. We make the following assumptions: the three hypotheses $\mathcal{H}_1$, $\mathcal{H}_2$ and $\mathcal{H}_3$ are equiprobable *a priori*, i.e.,

$$P(\mathcal{H}_1) = P(\mathcal{H}_2) = P(\mathcal{H}_3) = \frac{1}{3}. \tag{3.36}$$

The datum we receive, after choosing door 1, is one of $D = 3$ and $D = 2$ (meaning door 3 or 2 is opened, respectively). We assume that these two possible outcomes have the following probabilities. If the prize is behind door 1 then the host has a free choice; in this case we assume that the host selects at random between $D = 2$ and $D = 3$. Otherwise the choice of the host is forced and the probabilities are 0 and 1.

$$\left| \begin{array}{c|c|c} P(D{=}2 \mid \mathcal{H}_1) = {}^1\!/\!_2 & P(D{=}2 \mid \mathcal{H}_2) = 0 & P(D{=}2 \mid \mathcal{H}_3) = 1 \\ P(D{=}3 \mid \mathcal{H}_1) = {}^1\!/\!_2 & P(D{=}3 \mid \mathcal{H}_2) = 1 & P(D{=}3 \mid \mathcal{H}_3) = 0 \end{array} \right| \tag{3.37}$$

Now, using Bayes' theorem, we evaluate the posterior probabilities of the hypotheses:

$$P(\mathcal{H}_i \mid D{=}3) = \frac{P(D{=}3 \mid \mathcal{H}_i) P(\mathcal{H}_i)}{P(D{=}3)} \tag{3.38}$$

$$\left| P(\mathcal{H}_1 \mid D{=}3) = \frac{(1/2)(1/3)}{P(D{=}3)} \right| P(\mathcal{H}_2 \mid D{=}3) = \frac{(1)(1/3)}{P(D{=}3)} \left| P(\mathcal{H}_3 \mid D{=}3) = \frac{(0)(1/3)}{P(D{=}3)} \right| \tag{3.39}$$

The denominator $P(D{=}3)$ is $(1/2)$ because it is the normalizing constant for this posterior distribution. So

$$\left| P(\mathcal{H}_1 \mid D{=}3) = {}^1\!/\!_3 \, \right| P(\mathcal{H}_2 \mid D{=}3) = {}^2\!/\!_3 \, \left| P(\mathcal{H}_3 \mid D{=}3) = 0. \right| \tag{3.40}$$

So the contestant should switch to door 2 in order to have the biggest chance of getting the prize.

Many people find this outcome surprising. There are two ways to make it more intuitive. One is to play the game thirty times with a friend and keep track of the frequency with which switching gets the prize. Alternatively, you can perform a thought experiment in which the game is played with a million doors. The rules are now that the contestant chooses one door, then the game show host opens 999,998 doors in such a way as not to reveal the prize, leaving the *contestant's* selected door and *one other door* closed. The contestant may now stick or switch. Imagine the contestant confronted by a million doors, of which doors 1 and 234,598 have not been opened, door 1 having been the contestant's initial guess. Where do you think the prize is?

Solution to exercise 3.9 (p.57). If door 3 is opened by an earthquake, the inference comes out differently – even though visually the scene looks the same. The nature of the data, and the probability of the data, are both now different. The possible data outcomes are, firstly, that any number of the doors might have opened. We could label the eight possible outcomes $\mathbf{d} = (0,0,0), (0,0,1), (0,1,0), (1,0,0), (0,1,1), \ldots, (1,1,1)$. Secondly, it might be that the prize is visible after the earthquake has opened one or more doors. So the data D consists of the value of $\mathbf{d}$, and a statement of whether the prize was revealed. It is hard to say what the probabilities of these outcomes are, since they depend on our beliefs about the reliability of the door latches and the properties of earthquakes, but it is possible to extract the desired posterior probability without naming the values of $P(\mathbf{d}\,|\,\mathcal{H}_i)$ for each $\mathbf{d}$. All that matters are the relative values of the quantities $P(D\,|\,\mathcal{H}_1)$, $P(D\,|\,\mathcal{H}_2)$, $P(D\,|\,\mathcal{H}_3)$, for the value of D that actually occurred. [This is the *likelihood principle*, which we met in section 2.3.] The value of D that actually occurred is $\mathbf{d} = (0,0,1)$, and no prize visible. First, it is clear that $P(D\,|\,\mathcal{H}_3) = 0$, since the datum that no prize is visible is incompatible with $\mathcal{H}_3$. Now, assuming that the contestant selected door 1, how does the probability $P(D\,|\,\mathcal{H}_1)$ compare with $P(D\,|\,\mathcal{H}_2)$? Assuming that earthquakes are not sensitive to decisions of game show contestants, these two quantities have to be equal, by symmetry. We don't know how likely it is that door 3 falls off its hinges, but however likely it is, it's just as likely to do so whether the prize is behind door 1 or door 2. So, if $P(D\,|\,\mathcal{H}_1)$ and $P(D\,|\,\mathcal{H}_2)$ are equal, we obtain:

$$
\left|
\begin{array}{ll}
P(\mathcal{H}_1|D) = \frac{P(D|\mathcal{H}_1)(1/3)}{P(D)} \\[4pt]
\qquad\quad = 1/2
\end{array}
\right|
\begin{array}{ll}
P(\mathcal{H}_2|D) = \frac{P(D|\mathcal{H}_2)(1/3)}{P(D)} \\[4pt]
\qquad\quad = 1/2
\end{array}
\left|
\begin{array}{ll}
P(\mathcal{H}_3|D) = \frac{P(D|\mathcal{H}_3)(1/3)}{P(D)} \\[4pt]
\qquad\quad = 0.
\end{array}
\right.
\tag{3.41}
$$

The two possible hypotheses are now equally likely.

If we assume that the host knows where the prize is and might be acting deceptively, then the answer might be further modified, because we have to view the host's words as part of the data.

Confused? It's well worth making sure you understand these two gameshow problems. Don't worry, I slipped up on the second problem, the first time I met it.

There is a general rule which helps immensely in confusing probability problems:

> Always write down the probability of everything.
> *(Steve Gull)*

From this joint probability, any desired inference can be mechanically obtained (figure 3.9).

Solution to exercise 3.11 (p.58). The statistic quoted by the lawyer indicates the probability that a randomly selected wife-beater will also murder his wife. The probability that the husband was the murderer, *given that the wife has been murdered*, is a completely different quantity.

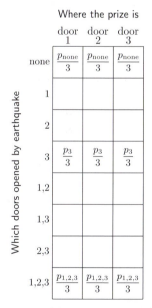

Figure 3.9. The probability of everything, for the second three-door problem, assuming an earthquake has just occurred. Here, p_3 is the probability that door 3 alone is opened by an earthquake.

To deduce the latter, we need to make further assumptions about the probability of the wife's being murdered by someone else. If she lives in a neighbourhood with frequent random murders, then this probability is large and the posterior probability that the husband did it (in the absence of other evidence) may not be very large. But in more peaceful regions, it may well be that the most likely person to have murdered you, if you are found murdered, is one of your closest relatives.

Let's work out some illustrative numbers with the help of the statistics on page 58. Let $m=1$ denote the proposition that a woman has been murdered; $h=1$, the proposition that the husband did it; and $b=1$, the proposition that he beat her in the year preceding the murder. The statement 'someone else did it' is denoted by $h=0$. We need to define $P(h \,|\, m=1)$, $P(b \,|\, h=1, m=1)$, and $P(b=1 \,|\, h=0, m=1)$ in order to compute the posterior probability $P(h=1 \,|\, b=1, m=1)$. From the statistics, we can read out $P(h=1 \,|\, m=1) = 0.28$. And if two million women out of 100 million are beaten, then $P(b=1 \,|\, h=0, m=1) = 0.02$. Finally, we need a value for $P(b \,|\, h=1, m=1)$: if a man murders his wife, how likely is it that this is the first time he laid a finger on her? I expect it's pretty unlikely; so maybe $P(b=1 \,|\, h=1, m=1)$ is 0.9 or larger.

By Bayes' theorem, then,

$$P(h=1 \,|\, b=1, m=1) = \frac{.9 \times .28}{.9 \times .28 + .02 \times .72} \simeq 95\%. \qquad (3.42)$$

One way to make obvious the sliminess of the lawyer on p.58 is to construct arguments, with the same logical structure as his, that are clearly wrong. For example, the lawyer could say 'Not only was Mrs. S murdered, she was murdered between 4.02pm and 4.03pm. *Statistically*, only one in a *million* wife-beaters actually goes on to murder his wife between 4.02pm and 4.03pm. So the wife-beating is not strong evidence at all. In fact, given the wife-beating evidence alone, it's extremely unlikely that he would murder his wife in this way – only a 1/1,000,000 chance.'

Solution to exercise 3.13 (p.58). There are two hypotheses. $\mathcal{H}_0$: your number is 740511; $\mathcal{H}_1$: it is another number. The data, D, are 'when I dialed 740511, I got a busy signal'. What is the probability of D, given each hypothesis? If your number is 740511, then we expect a busy signal with certainty:

$$P(D \,|\, \mathcal{H}_0) = 1.$$

On the other hand, if $\mathcal{H}_1$ is true, then the probability that the number dialled returns a busy signal is smaller than 1, since various other outcomes were also possible (a ringing tone, or a number-unobtainable signal, for example). The value of this probability $P(D \,|\, \mathcal{H}_1)$ will depend on the probability α that a random phone number similar to your own phone number would be a valid phone number, and on the probability β that you get a busy signal when you dial a valid phone number.

I estimate from the size of my phone book that Cambridge has about 75 000 valid phone numbers, all of length six digits. The probability that a random six-digit number is valid is therefore about $75\,000/10^6 = 0.075$. If we exclude numbers beginning with 0, 1, and 9 from the random choice, the probability α is about $75\,000/700\,000 \simeq 0.1$. If we assume that telephone numbers are clustered then a misremembered number might be more likely to be valid than a randomly chosen number; so the probability, α, that our guessed number would be valid, assuming $\mathcal{H}_1$ is true, might be bigger than

0.1. Anyway, α must be somewhere between 0.1 and 1. We can carry forward this uncertainty in the probability and see how much it matters at the end.

The probability β that you get a busy signal when you dial a valid phone number is equal to the fraction of phones you think are in use or off-the-hook when you make your tentative call. This fraction varies from town to town and with the time of day. In Cambridge, during the day, I would guess that about 1% of phones are in use. At 4am, maybe 0.1%, or fewer.

The probability $P(D \mid \mathcal{H}_1)$ is the product of α and β, that is, about $0.1 \times 0.01 = 10^{-3}$. According to our estimates, there's about a one-in-a-thousand chance of getting a busy signal when you dial a random number; or one-in-a-hundred, if valid numbers are strongly clustered; or one-in-10^4, if you dial in the wee hours.

How do the data affect your beliefs about your phone number? The posterior probability ratio is the likelihood ratio times the prior probability ratio:

$$\frac{P(\mathcal{H}_0 \mid D)}{P(\mathcal{H}_1 \mid D)} = \frac{P(D \mid \mathcal{H}_0)}{P(D \mid \mathcal{H}_1)} \frac{P(\mathcal{H}_0)}{P(\mathcal{H}_1)}. \tag{3.43}$$

The likelihood ratio is about 100-to-1 or 1000-to-1, so the posterior probability ratio is swung by a factor of 100 or 1000 in favour of $\mathcal{H}_0$. If the prior probability of $\mathcal{H}_0$ was 0.5 then the posterior probability is

$$P(\mathcal{H}_0 \mid D) = \frac{1}{1 + \frac{P(\mathcal{H}_1 \mid D)}{P(\mathcal{H}_0 \mid D)}} \simeq 0.99 \text{ or } 0.999. \tag{3.44}$$

Solution to exercise 3.15 (p.59). We compare the models $\mathcal{H}_0$ – the coin is fair – and $\mathcal{H}_1$ – the coin is biased, with the prior on its bias set to the uniform distribution $P(p|\mathcal{H}_1) = 1$. [The use of a uniform prior seems reasonable to me, since I know that some coins, such as American pennies, have severe biases when spun on edge; so the situations $p = 0.01$ or $p = 0.1$ or $p = 0.95$ would not surprise me.]

> When I mention $\mathcal{H}_0$ – the coin is fair – a pedant would say, 'how absurd to even consider that the coin is fair – any coin is surely biased to some extent'. And of course I would agree. So will pedants kindly understand $\mathcal{H}_0$ as meaning 'the coin is fair to within one part in a thousand, i.e., $p \in 0.5 \pm 0.001$'.

The likelihood ratio is:

$$\frac{P(D|\mathcal{H}_1)}{P(D|\mathcal{H}_0)} = \frac{\frac{140!110!}{251!}}{1/2^{250}} = 0.48. \tag{3.45}$$

Thus the data give scarcely any evidence either way; in fact they give weak evidence (two to one) in favour of $\mathcal{H}_0$!

'No, no', objects the believer in bias, 'your silly uniform prior doesn't represent *my* prior beliefs about the bias of biased coins – I was *expecting* only a small bias'. To be as generous as possible to the $\mathcal{H}_1$, let's see how well it could fare if the prior were presciently set. Let us allow a prior of the form

$$P(p|\mathcal{H}_1, \alpha) = \frac{1}{Z(\alpha)} p^{\alpha-1}(1-p)^{\alpha-1}, \quad \text{where } Z(\alpha) = \Gamma(\alpha)^2 / \Gamma(2\alpha) \tag{3.46}$$

(a Beta distribution, with the original uniform prior reproduced by setting $\alpha = 1$). By tweaking α, the likelihood ratio for $\mathcal{H}_1$ over $\mathcal{H}_0$,

$$\frac{P(D|\mathcal{H}_1, \alpha)}{P(D|\mathcal{H}_0)} = \frac{\Gamma(140+\alpha)\,\Gamma(110+\alpha)\,\Gamma(2\alpha)2^{250}}{\Gamma(250+2\alpha)\,\Gamma(\alpha)^2}, \tag{3.47}$$

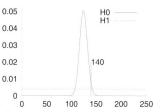

Figure 3.10. The probability distribution of the number of heads given the two hypotheses, that the coin is fair, and that it is biased, with the prior distribution of the bias being uniform. The outcome ($D = 140$ heads) gives weak evidence in favour of $\mathcal{H}_0$, the hypothesis that the coin is fair.

can be increased a little. It is shown for several values of α in figure 3.11. Even the most favourable choice of α ($\alpha \simeq 50$) can yield a likelihood ratio of only two to one in favour of $\mathcal{H}_1$.

In conclusion, the data are not 'very suspicious'. They can be construed as giving at most two-to-one evidence in favour of one or other of the two hypotheses.

> Are these wimpy likelihood ratios the fault of over-restrictive priors? Is there any way of producing a 'very suspicious' conclusion? The prior that is best-matched to the data, in terms of likelihood, is the prior that sets p to $f \equiv 140/250$ with probability one. Let's call this model $\mathcal{H}_*$. The likelihood ratio is $P(D|\mathcal{H}_*)/P(D|\mathcal{H}_0) = 2^{250} f^{140}(1-f)^{110} = 6.1$. So the strongest evidence that these data can possibly muster against the hypothesis that there is no bias is six-to-one.

While we are noticing the absurdly misleading answers that 'sampling theory' statistics produces, such as the p-value of 7% in the exercise we just solved, let's stick the boot in. If we make a tiny change to the data set, increasing the number of heads in 250 tosses from 140 to 141, we find that the p-value goes below the mystical value of 0.05 (the p-value is 0.0497). The sampling theory statistician would happily squeak 'the probability of getting a result as extreme as 141 heads is smaller than 0.05 – we thus reject the null hypothesis at a significance level of 5%'. The correct answer is shown for several values of α in figure 3.12. The values worth highlighting from this table are, first, the likelihood ratio when $\mathcal{H}_1$ uses the standard uniform prior, which is 1:0.61 in favour of the *null hypothesis* $\mathcal{H}_0$. Second, the most favourable choice of α, from the point of view of $\mathcal{H}_1$, can only yield a likelihood ratio of about 2.3:1 in favour of $\mathcal{H}_1$.

Be warned! A p-value of 0.05 is often interpreted as implying that the odds are stacked about twenty-to-one *against* the null hypothesis. But the truth in this case is that the evidence either slightly *favours* the null hypothesis, or disfavours it by at most 2.3 to one, depending on the choice of prior.

The p-values and 'significance levels' of classical statistics should be treated with *extreme caution*. Shun them! Here ends the sermon.

α	$\dfrac{P(D|\mathcal{H}_1, \alpha)}{P(D|\mathcal{H}_0)}$
.37	.25
1.0	.48
2.7	.82
7.4	1.3
20	1.8
55	1.9
148	1.7
403	1.3
1096	1.1

Figure 3.11. Likelihood ratio for various choices of the prior distribution's hyperparameter α.

α	$\dfrac{P(D'|\mathcal{H}_1, \alpha)}{P(D'|\mathcal{H}_0)}$
.37	.32
1.0	.61
2.7	1.0
7.4	1.6
20	2.2
55	2.3
148	1.9
403	1.4
1096	1.2

Figure 3.12. Likelihood ratio for various choices of the prior distribution's hyperparameter α, when the data are $D' = 141$ heads in 250 trials.

Part I

Data Compression

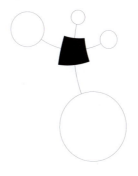

About Chapter 4

In this chapter we discuss how to measure the information content of the outcome of a random experiment.

This chapter has some tough bits. If you find the mathematical details hard, skim through them and keep going – you'll be able to enjoy Chapters 5 and 6 without this chapter's tools.

Before reading Chapter 4, you should have read Chapter 2 and worked on exercises 2.21–2.25 and 2.16 (pp.36–37), and exercise 4.1 below.

The following exercise is intended to help you think about how to measure information content.

Exercise 4.1.[2, p.69] – *Please work on this problem before reading Chapter 4.*

You are given 12 balls, all equal in weight except for one that is either heavier or lighter. You are also given a two-pan balance to use. In each use of the balance you may put any number of the 12 balls on the left pan, and the same number on the right pan, and push a button to initiate the weighing; there are three possible outcomes: either the weights are equal, or the balls on the left are heavier, or the balls on the left are lighter. Your task is to design a strategy to determine which is the odd ball *and* whether it is heavier or lighter than the others *in as few uses of the balance as possible.*

While thinking about this problem, you may find it helpful to consider the following questions:

(a) How can one measure *information*?

(b) When you have identified the odd ball and whether it is heavy or light, how much information have you gained?

(c) Once you have designed a strategy, draw a tree showing, for each of the possible outcomes of a weighing, what weighing you perform next. At each node in the tree, how much information have the outcomes so far given you, and how much information remains to be gained?

(d) How much information is gained when you learn (i) the state of a flipped coin; (ii) the states of two flipped coins; (iii) the outcome when a four-sided die is rolled?

(e) How much information is gained on the first step of the weighing problem if 6 balls are weighed against the other 6? How much is gained if 4 are weighed against 4 on the first step, leaving out 4 balls?

Notation

$x \in \mathcal{A}$	x is a *member* of the set $\mathcal{A}$
$S \subset \mathcal{A}$	S is a *subset* of the set $\mathcal{A}$
$S \subseteq \mathcal{A}$	S is a *subset of, or equal to,* the set $\mathcal{A}$
$\mathcal{V} = \mathcal{B} \cup \mathcal{A}$	$\mathcal{V}$ is the *union* of the sets $\mathcal{B}$ and $\mathcal{A}$
$\mathcal{V} = \mathcal{B} \cap \mathcal{A}$	$\mathcal{V}$ is the *intersection* of the sets $\mathcal{B}$ and $\mathcal{A}$
$|\mathcal{A}|$	number of elements in set $\mathcal{A}$

4

The Source Coding Theorem

▶ **4.1 How to measure the information content of a random variable?**

In the next few chapters, we'll be talking about probability distributions and random variables. Most of the time we can get by with sloppy notation, but occasionally, we will need precise notation. Here is the notation that we established in Chapter 2.

An ensemble X is a triple $(x, \mathcal{A}_X, \mathcal{P}_X)$, where the *outcome* x is the value of a random variable, which takes on one of a set of possible values, $\mathcal{A}_X = \{a_1, a_2, \ldots, a_i, \ldots, a_I\}$, having probabilities $\mathcal{P}_X = \{p_1, p_2, \ldots, p_I\}$, with $P(x = a_i) = p_i$, $p_i \geq 0$ and $\sum_{a_i \in \mathcal{A}_X} P(x = a_i) = 1$.

How can we measure the information content of an outcome $x = a_i$ from such an ensemble? In this chapter we examine the assertions

1. that the *Shannon information content*,

$$h(x = a_i) \equiv \log_2 \frac{1}{p_i}, \tag{4.1}$$

   is a sensible measure of the information content of the outcome $x = a_i$, and

2. that the *entropy* of the ensemble,

$$H(X) = \sum_i p_i \log_2 \frac{1}{p_i}, \tag{4.2}$$

   is a sensible measure of the ensemble's average information content.

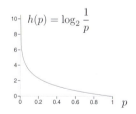

p	$h(p)$	$H_2(p)$
0.001	10.0	0.011
0.01	6.6	0.081
0.1	3.3	0.47
0.2	2.3	0.72
0.5	1.0	1.0

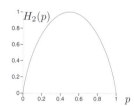

Figure 4.1. The Shannon information content $h(p) = \log_2 \frac{1}{p}$ and the binary entropy function $H_2(p) = H(p, 1-p) = p \log_2 \frac{1}{p} + (1 - p) \log_2 \frac{1}{(1-p)}$ as a function of p.

Figure 4.1 shows the Shannon information content of an outcome with probability p, as a function of p. The less probable an outcome is, the greater its Shannon information content. Figure 4.1 also shows the binary entropy function,

$$H_2(p) = H(p, 1-p) = p \log_2 \frac{1}{p} + (1 - p) \log_2 \frac{1}{(1 - p)}, \tag{4.3}$$

which is the entropy of the ensemble X whose alphabet and probability distribution are $\mathcal{A}_X = \{a, b\}$, $\mathcal{P}_X = \{p, (1 - p)\}$.

Information content of independent random variables

Why should $\log 1/p_i$ have anything to do with the information content? Why not some other function of p_i? We'll explore this question in detail shortly, but first, notice a nice property of this particular function $h(x) = \log 1/p(x)$.

Imagine learning the value of two *independent* random variables, x and y. The definition of independence is that the probability distribution is separable into a *product*:

$$P(x, y) = P(x)P(y). \tag{4.4}$$

Intuitively, we might want any measure of the 'amount of information gained' to have the property of *additivity* – that is, for independent random variables x and y, the information gained when we learn x and y should equal the sum of the information gained if x alone were learned and the information gained if y alone were learned.

The Shannon information content of the outcome x, y is

$$h(x, y) = \log \frac{1}{P(x, y)} = \log \frac{1}{P(x)P(y)} = \log \frac{1}{P(x)} + \log \frac{1}{P(y)} \tag{4.5}$$

so it does indeed satisfy

$$h(x, y) = h(x) + h(y), \text{ if } x \text{ and } y \text{ are independent.} \tag{4.6}$$

Exercise 4.2.[1] Show that, if x and y are independent, the entropy of the outcome x, y satisfies

$$H(X, Y) = H(X) + H(Y). \tag{4.7}$$

In words, entropy is additive for independent variables.

We now explore these ideas with some examples; then, in section 4.4 and in Chapters 5 and 6, we prove that the Shannon information content and the entropy are related to the number of bits needed to describe the outcome of an experiment.

The weighing problem: designing informative experiments

Have you solved the weighing problem (exercise 4.1, p.66) yet? Are you sure? Notice that in three uses of the balance – which reads either 'left heavier', 'right heavier', or 'balanced' – the number of conceivable outcomes is $3^3 = 27$, whereas the number of possible states of the world is 24: the odd ball could be any of twelve balls, and it could be heavy or light. So in principle, the problem might be solvable in three weighings – but not in two, since $3^2 < 24$.

If you know how you can determine the odd weight *and* whether it is heavy or light in *three* weighings, then you may read on. If you haven't found a strategy that always gets there in three weighings, I encourage you to think about exercise 4.1 some more.

Why is your strategy optimal? What is it about your series of weighings that allows useful information to be gained as quickly as possible? The answer is that at each step of an optimal procedure, the three outcomes ('left heavier', 'right heavier', and 'balance') are *as close as possible to equiprobable*. An optimal solution is shown in figure 4.2.

Suboptimal strategies, such as weighing balls 1–6 against 7–12 on the first step, do not achieve all outcomes with equal probability: these two sets of balls can never balance, so the only possible outcomes are 'left heavy' and 'right heavy'. Such a binary outcome only rules out half of the possible hypotheses,

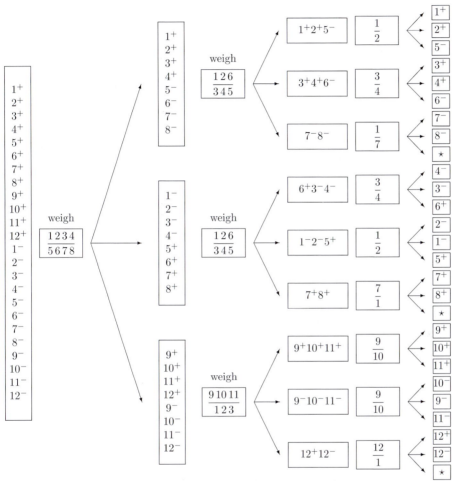

Figure 4.2. An optimal solution to the weighing problem. At each step there are two boxes: the left box shows which hypotheses are still possible; the right box shows the balls involved in the next weighing. The 24 hypotheses are written $1^+, \ldots, 12^-$, with, e.g., 1^+ denoting that 1 is the odd ball and it is heavy. Weighings are written by listing the names of the balls on the two pans, separated by a line; for example, in the first weighing, balls 1, 2, 3, and 4 are put on the left-hand side and 5, 6, 7, and 8 on the right. In each triplet of arrows the upper arrow leads to the situation when the left side is heavier, the middle arrow to the situation when the right side is heavier, and the lower arrow to the situation when the outcome is balanced. The three points labelled $\star$ correspond to impossible outcomes.

so a strategy that uses such outcomes must sometimes take longer to find the right answer.

The insight that the outcomes should be as near as possible to equiprobable makes it easier to search for an optimal strategy. The first weighing must divide the 24 possible hypotheses into three groups of eight. Then the second weighing must be chosen so that there is a 3:3:2 split of the hypotheses.

Thus we might conclude:

> the outcome of a random experiment is guaranteed to be most informative if the probability distribution over outcomes is uniform.

This conclusion agrees with the property of the entropy that you proved when you solved exercise 2.25 (p.37): the entropy of an ensemble X is biggest if all the outcomes have equal probability $p_i = 1/|\mathcal{A}_X|$.

Guessing games

In the game of twenty questions, one player thinks of an object, and the other player attempts to guess what the object is by asking questions that have yes/no answers, for example, 'is it alive?', or 'is it human?' The aim is to identify the object with as few questions as possible. What is the best strategy for playing this game? For simplicity, imagine that we are playing the rather dull version of twenty questions called 'sixty-three'.

Example 4.3. The game 'sixty-three'. What's the smallest number of yes/no questions needed to identify an integer x between 0 and 63?

Intuitively, the best questions successively divide the 64 possibilities into equal sized sets. Six questions suffice. One reasonable strategy asks the following questions:

> 1: is $x \geq 32$?
> 2: is $x \bmod 32 \geq 16$?
> 3: is $x \bmod 16 \geq 8$?
> 4: is $x \bmod 8 \geq 4$?
> 5: is $x \bmod 4 \geq 2$?
> 6: is $x \bmod 2 = 1$?

[The notation $x \bmod 32$, pronounced 'x modulo 32', denotes the remainder when x is divided by 32; for example, $35 \bmod 32 = 3$ and $32 \bmod 32 = 0$.]

The answers to these questions, if translated from $\{$yes, no$\}$ to $\{1, 0\}$, give the binary expansion of x, for example $35 \Rightarrow 100011$.   □

What are the Shannon information contents of the outcomes in this example? If we assume that all values of x are equally likely, then the answers to the questions are independent and each has Shannon information content $\log_2(1/0.5) = 1$ bit; the total Shannon information gained is always six bits. Furthermore, the number x that we learn from these questions is a six-bit binary number. Our questioning strategy defines a way of encoding the random variable x as a binary file.

So far, the Shannon information content makes sense: it measures the length of a binary file that encodes x. However, we have not yet studied ensembles where the outcomes have unequal probabilities. Does the Shannon information content make sense there too?

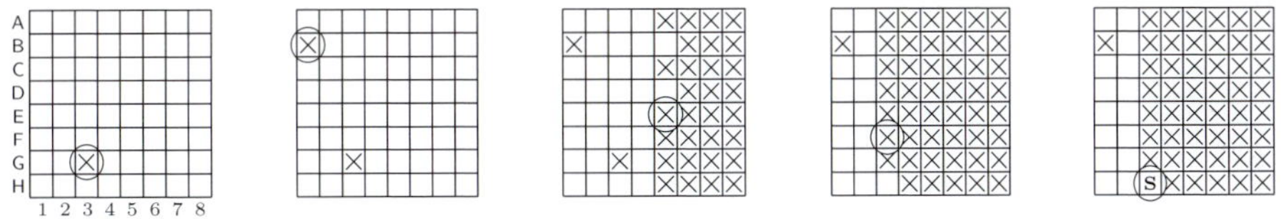

	1	2	32	48	49
move #	1	2	32	48	49
question	G3	B1	E5	F3	H3
outcome	$x = \mathbf{n}$	$x = \mathbf{n}$	$x = \mathbf{n}$	$x = \mathbf{n}$	$x = \mathbf{y}$
$P(x)$	$\dfrac{63}{64}$	$\dfrac{62}{63}$	$\dfrac{32}{33}$	$\dfrac{16}{17}$	$\dfrac{1}{16}$
$h(x)$	0.0227	0.0230	0.0443	0.0874	4.0
Total info.	0.0227	0.0458	1.0	2.0	6.0

Figure 4.3. A game of submarine. The submarine is hit on the 49th attempt.

The game of submarine: how many bits can one bit convey?

In the game of battleships, each player hides a fleet of ships in a sea represented by a square grid. On each turn, one player attempts to hit the other's ships by firing at one square in the opponent's sea. The response to a selected square such as 'G3' is either 'miss', 'hit', or 'hit and destroyed'.

In a boring version of battleships called **submarine**, each player hides just one submarine in one square of an eight-by-eight grid. Figure 4.3 shows a few pictures of this game in progress: the circle represents the square that is being fired at, and the ×s show squares in which the outcome was a miss, $x = \mathbf{n}$; the submarine is hit (outcome $x = \mathbf{y}$ shown by the symbol **s**) on the 49th attempt.

Each shot made by a player defines an ensemble. The two possible outcomes are $\{\mathbf{y}, \mathbf{n}\}$, corresponding to a hit and a miss, and their probabilities depend on the state of the board. At the beginning, $P(\mathbf{y}) = 1/64$ and $P(\mathbf{n}) = 63/64$. At the second shot, if the first shot missed, $P(\mathbf{y}) = 1/63$ and $P(\mathbf{n}) = 62/63$. At the third shot, if the first two shots missed, $P(\mathbf{y}) = 1/62$ and $P(\mathbf{n}) = 61/62$.

The Shannon information gained from an outcome x is $h(x) = \log(1/P(x))$. If we are lucky, and hit the submarine on the first shot, then

$$h(x) = h_{(1)}(\mathbf{y}) = \log_2 64 = 6 \text{ bits.} \tag{4.8}$$

Now, it might seem a little strange that one binary outcome can convey six bits. But we have learnt the hiding place, which could have been any of 64 squares; so we have, by one lucky binary question, indeed learnt six bits.

What if the first shot misses? The Shannon information that we gain from this outcome is

$$h(x) = h_{(1)}(\mathbf{n}) = \log_2 \frac{64}{63} = 0.0227 \text{ bits.} \tag{4.9}$$

Does this make sense? It is not so obvious. Let's keep going. If our second shot also misses, the Shannon information content of the second outcome is

$$h_{(2)}(\mathbf{n}) = \log_2 \frac{63}{62} = 0.0230 \text{ bits.} \tag{4.10}$$

If we miss thirty-two times (firing at a new square each time), the total Shannon information gained is

$$\log_2 \frac{64}{63} + \log_2 \frac{63}{62} + \cdots + \log_2 \frac{33}{32}$$
$$= 0.0227 + 0.0230 + \cdots + 0.0430 = 1.0 \text{ bits.} \tag{4.11}$$

Why this round number? Well, what have we learnt? We now know that the submarine is not in any of the 32 squares we fired at; learning that fact is just like playing a game of `sixty-three` (p.70), asking as our first question 'is x one of the thirty-two numbers corresponding to these squares I fired at?', and receiving the answer 'no'. This answer rules out half of the hypotheses, so it gives us one bit.

After 48 unsuccessful shots, the information gained is 2 bits: the unknown location has been narrowed down to one quarter of the original hypothesis space.

What if we hit the submarine on the 49th shot, when there were 16 squares left? The Shannon information content of this outcome is

$$h_{(49)}(\mathrm{y}) = \log_2 16 = 4.0 \,\text{bits}. \tag{4.12}$$

The total Shannon information content of all the outcomes is

$$\log_2 \frac{64}{63} + \log_2 \frac{63}{62} + \cdots + \log_2 \frac{17}{16} + \log_2 \frac{16}{1}$$
$$= \quad 0.0227 + 0.0230 + \cdots + 0.0874 + 4.0 \quad = \quad 6.0 \,\text{bits}. \tag{4.13}$$

So once we know where the submarine is, the total Shannon information content gained is 6 bits.

This result holds regardless of when we hit the submarine. If we hit it when there are n squares left to choose from — n was 16 in equation (4.13) — then the total information gained is:

$$\log_2 \frac{64}{63} + \log_2 \frac{63}{62} + \cdots + \log_2 \frac{n+1}{n} + \log_2 \frac{n}{1}$$
$$= \quad \log_2 \left[\frac{64}{63} \times \frac{63}{62} \times \cdots \times \frac{n+1}{n} \times \frac{n}{1} \right] \quad = \quad \log_2 \frac{64}{1} \quad = \quad 6 \,\text{bits}. \tag{4.14}$$

What have we learned from the examples so far? I think the `submarine` example makes quite a convincing case for the claim that the Shannon information content is a sensible measure of information content. And the game of `sixty-three` shows that the Shannon information content can be intimately connected to the size of a file that encodes the outcomes of a random experiment, thus suggesting a possible connection to data compression.

In case you're not convinced, let's look at one more example.

The Wenglish language

Wenglish is a language similar to English. Wenglish sentences consist of words drawn at random from the Wenglish dictionary, which contains $2^{15} = 32{,}768$ words, all of length 5 characters. Each word in the Wenglish dictionary was constructed at random by picking five letters from the probability distribution over a...z depicted in figure 2.1.

Some entries from the dictionary are shown in alphabetical order in figure 4.4. Notice that the number of words in the dictionary (32,768) is much smaller than the total number of possible words of length 5 letters, $26^5 \simeq 12{,}000{,}000$.

Because the probability of the letter `z` is about 1/1000, only 32 of the words in the dictionary begin with the letter `z`. In contrast, the probability of the letter `a` is about 0.0625, and 2048 of the words begin with the letter `a`. Of those 2048 words, two start `az`, and 128 start `aa`.

Let's imagine that we are reading a Wenglish document, and let's discuss the Shannon information content of the characters as we acquire them. If we

1	aaail
2	aaaiu
3	aaald
⋮	
129	abati
⋮	
2047	azpan
2048	aztdn
⋮	
16 384	odrcr
⋮	
⋮	
32 737	zatnt
⋮	
32 768	zxast

Figure 4.4. The Wenglish dictionary.

are given the text one word at a time, the Shannon information content of each five-character word is $\log 32{,}768 = 15$ bits, since Wenglish uses all its words with equal probability. The average information content per character is therefore 3 bits.

Now let's look at the information content if we read the document one character at a time. If, say, the first letter of a word is a, the Shannon information content is $\log 1/0.0625 \simeq 4$ bits. If the first letter is z, the Shannon information content is $\log 1/0.001 \simeq 10$ bits. The information content is thus highly variable at the first character. The total information content of the 5 characters in a word, however, is exactly 15 bits; so the letters that follow an initial z have lower average information content per character than the letters that follow an initial a. A rare initial letter such as z indeed conveys more information about what the word is than a common initial letter.

Similarly, in English, if rare characters occur at the start of the word (e.g. xyl...), then often we can identify the whole word immediately; whereas words that start with common characters (e.g. pro...) require more characters before we can identify them.

▶ 4.2 Data compression

The preceding examples justify the idea that the Shannon information content of an outcome is a natural measure of its information content. Improbable outcomes do convey more information than probable outcomes. We now discuss the information content of a source by considering how many bits are needed to describe the outcome of an experiment.

If we can show that we can compress data from a particular source into a file of L bits per source symbol and recover the data reliably, then we will say that the average information content of that source is at most L bits per symbol.

Example: compression of text files

A file is composed of a sequence of bytes. A byte is composed of 8 bits and can have a decimal value between 0 and 255. A typical text file is composed of the ASCII character set (decimal values 0 to 127). This character set uses only seven of the eight bits in a byte.

Here we use the word 'bit' with its meaning, 'a symbol with two values', not to be confused with the unit of information content.

▷ Exercise 4.4.[1, p.86] By how much could the size of a file be reduced given that it is an ASCII file? How would you achieve this reduction?

Intuitively, it seems reasonable to assert that an ASCII file contains 7/8 as much information as an arbitrary file of the same size, since we already know one out of every eight bits before we even look at the file. This is a simple example of redundancy. Most sources of data have further redundancy: English text files use the ASCII characters with non-equal frequency; certain pairs of letters are more probable than others; and entire words can be predicted given the context and a semantic understanding of the text.

Some simple data compression methods that define measures of information content

One way of measuring the information content of a random variable is simply to count the number of *possible* outcomes, $|\mathcal{A}_X|$. (The number of elements in a set $\mathcal{A}$ is denoted by $|\mathcal{A}|$.) If we gave a binary name to each outcome, the length of each name would be $\log_2 |\mathcal{A}_X|$ bits, if $|\mathcal{A}_X|$ happened to be a power of 2. We thus make the following definition.

The raw bit content of X is

$$H_0(X) = \log_2 |\mathcal{A}_X|. \tag{4.15}$$

$H_0(X)$ is a lower bound for the number of binary questions that are always guaranteed to identify an outcome from the ensemble X. It is an additive quantity: the raw bit content of an ordered pair x, y, having $|\mathcal{A}_X||\mathcal{A}_Y|$ possible outcomes, satisfies

$$H_0(X, Y) = H_0(X) + H_0(Y). \tag{4.16}$$

This measure of information content does not include any probabilistic element, and the encoding rule it corresponds to does not 'compress' the source data, it simply maps each outcome to a constant-length binary string.

Exercise 4.5.[2, p.86] Could there be a compressor that maps an outcome x to a binary code $c(x)$, and a decompressor that maps c back to x, such that *every possible outcome* is compressed into a binary code of length *shorter* than $H_0(X)$ bits?

Even though a simple counting argument shows that it is impossible to make a reversible compression program that reduces the size of *all* files, amateur compression enthusiasts frequently announce that they have invented a program that can do this – indeed that they can further compress compressed files by putting them through their compressor several times. Stranger yet, patents have been granted to these modern-day alchemists. See the `comp.compression` frequently asked questions for further reading.[1]

There are only two ways in which a 'compressor' can actually compress files:

1. A *lossy* compressor compresses some files, but maps some files to the *same* encoding. We'll assume that the user requires perfect recovery of the source file, so the occurrence of one of these confusable files leads to a failure (though in applications such as image compression, lossy compression is viewed as satisfactory). We'll denote by δ the probability that the source string is one of the confusable files, so a lossy compressor has a probability δ of failure. If δ can be made very small then a lossy compressor may be practically useful.

2. A *lossless* compressor maps all files to different encodings; if it shortens some files, it necessarily *makes others longer*. We try to design the compressor so that the probability that a file is lengthened is very small, and the probability that it is shortened is large.

In this chapter we discuss a simple lossy compressor. In subsequent chapters we discuss lossless compression methods.

4.3 Information content defined in terms of lossy compression

Whichever type of compressor we construct, we need somehow to take into account the *probabilities* of the different outcomes. Imagine comparing the information contents of two text files – one in which all 128 ASCII characters

---

[1] `http://sunsite.org.uk/public/usenet/news-faqs/comp.compression/`

are used with equal probability, and one in which the characters are used with their frequencies in English text. Can we define a measure of information content that distinguishes between these two files? Intuitively, the latter file contains less information per character because it is more predictable.

One simple way to use our knowledge that some symbols have a smaller probability is to imagine recoding the observations into a smaller alphabet – thus losing the ability to encode some of the more improbable symbols – and then measuring the raw bit content of the new alphabet. For example, we might take a risk when compressing English text, guessing that the most infrequent characters won't occur, and make a reduced ASCII code that omits the characters { !, @, #, %, ^, *, ~, <, >, /, \, _, {, }, [,], | }, thereby reducing the size of the alphabet by seventeen. The larger the risk we are willing to take, the smaller our final alphabet becomes.

We introduce a parameter δ that describes the risk we are taking when using this compression method: δ is the probability that there will be no name for an outcome x.

Example 4.6. Let

$$\mathcal{A}_X = \{\, \mathsf{a}, \mathsf{b}, \mathsf{c}, \mathsf{d}, \ \mathsf{e}, \ \mathsf{f}, \ \mathsf{g}, \ \mathsf{h} \,\},$$
$$\text{and} \quad \mathcal{P}_X = \{\, \tfrac{1}{4}, \tfrac{1}{4}, \tfrac{1}{4}, \tfrac{3}{16}, \tfrac{1}{64}, \tfrac{1}{64}, \tfrac{1}{64}, \tfrac{1}{64} \,\}. \tag{4.17}$$

The raw bit content of this ensemble is 3 bits, corresponding to 8 binary names. But notice that $P(x \in \{\mathsf{a}, \mathsf{b}, \mathsf{c}, \mathsf{d}\}) = 15/16$. So if we are willing to run a risk of $\delta = 1/16$ of not having a name for x, then we can get by with four names – half as many names as are needed if every $x \in \mathcal{A}_X$ has a name.

Table 4.5 shows binary names that could be given to the different outcomes in the cases $\delta = 0$ and $\delta = 1/16$. When $\delta = 0$ we need 3 bits to encode the outcome; when $\delta = 1/16$ we only need 2 bits.

$\delta = 0$		$\delta = 1/16$	
x	$c(x)$	x	$c(x)$
a	000	a	00
b	001	b	01
c	010	c	10
d	011	d	11
e	100	e	—
f	101	f	—
g	110	g	—
h	111	h	—

Table 4.5. Binary names for the outcomes, for two failure probabilities δ.

Let us now formalize this idea. To make a compression strategy with risk δ, we make the smallest possible subset S_δ such that the probability that x is not in S_δ is less than or equal to δ, i.e., $P(x \notin S_\delta) \leq \delta$. For each value of δ we can then define a new measure of information content – the log of the size of this smallest subset S_δ. [In ensembles in which several elements have the same probability, there may be several smallest subsets that contain different elements, but all that matters is their sizes (which are equal), so we will not dwell on this ambiguity.]

The smallest δ-sufficient subset S_δ is the smallest subset of $\mathcal{A}_X$ satisfying

$$P(x \in S_\delta) \geq 1 - \delta. \tag{4.18}$$

The subset S_δ can be constructed by ranking the elements of $\mathcal{A}_X$ in order of decreasing probability and adding successive elements starting from the most probable elements until the total probability is $\geq (1-\delta)$.

We can make a data compression code by assigning a binary name to each element of the smallest sufficient subset. This compression scheme motivates the following measure of information content:

The essential bit content of X is:

$$H_\delta(X) = \log_2 |S_\delta| \tag{4.19}$$

Note that $H_0(X)$ is the special case of $H_\delta(X)$ with $\delta = 0$ (if $P(x) > 0$ for all $x \in \mathcal{A}_X$). [Caution: do not confuse $H_0(X)$ and $H_\delta(X)$ with the function $H_2(p)$ displayed in figure 4.1.]

Figure 4.6 shows $H_\delta(X)$ for the ensemble of example 4.6 as a function of δ.

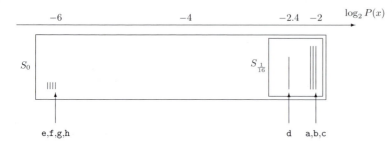

(a)

Figure 4.6. (a) The outcomes of X (from example 4.6 (p.75)), ranked by their probability. (b) The essential bit content $H_\delta(X)$. The labels on the graph show the smallest sufficient set as a function of δ. Note $H_0(X) = 3$ bits and $H_{1/16}(X) = 2$ bits.

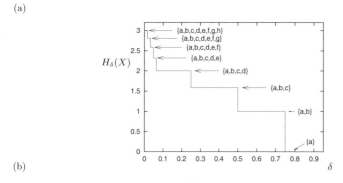

(b)

Extended ensembles

Is this compression method any more useful if we compress *blocks* of symbols from a source?

We now turn to examples where the outcome $\mathbf{x} = (x_1, x_2, \ldots, x_N)$ is a string of N independent identically distributed random variables from a single ensemble X. We will denote by X^N the ensemble $(X_1, X_2, \ldots, X_N)$. Remember that entropy is additive for independent variables (exercise 4.2 (p.68)), so $H(X^N) = NH(X)$.

Example 4.7. Consider a string of N flips of a bent coin, $\mathbf{x} = (x_1, x_2, \ldots, x_N)$, where $x_n \in \{0, 1\}$, with probabilities $p_0 = 0.9$, $p_1 = 0.1$. The most probable strings $\mathbf{x}$ are those with most 0s. If $r(\mathbf{x})$ is the number of 1s in $\mathbf{x}$ then

$$P(\mathbf{x}) = p_0^{N-r(\mathbf{x})} p_1^{r(\mathbf{x})}. \tag{4.20}$$

To evaluate $H_\delta(X^N)$ we must find the smallest sufficient subset S_δ. This subset will contain all $\mathbf{x}$ with $r(\mathbf{x}) = 0, 1, 2, \ldots$, up to some $r_{\max}(\delta) - 1$, and some of the $\mathbf{x}$ with $r(\mathbf{x}) = r_{\max}(\delta)$. Figures 4.7 and 4.8 show graphs of $H_\delta(X^N)$ against δ for the cases $N = 4$ and $N = 10$. The steps are the values of δ at which $|S_\delta|$ changes by 1, and the cusps where the slope of the staircase changes are the points where $r_{\max}$ changes by 1.

Exercise 4.8.[2, p.86] What are the mathematical shapes of the curves between the cusps?

For the examples shown in figures 4.6–4.8, $H_\delta(X^N)$ depends strongly on the value of δ, so it might not seem a fundamental or useful definition of information content. But we will consider what happens as N, the number of independent variables in X^N, increases. We will find the remarkable result that $H_\delta(X^N)$ becomes almost independent of δ – and for all δ it is very close to $NH(X)$, where $H(X)$ is the entropy of one of the random variables.

Figure 4.9 illustrates this asymptotic tendency for the binary ensemble of example 4.7. As N increases, $\frac{1}{N}H_\delta(X^N)$ becomes an increasingly flat function,

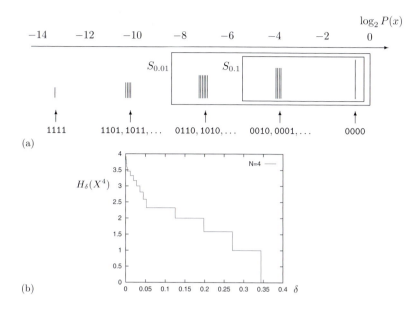

(a)

Figure 4.7. (a) The sixteen outcomes of the ensemble X^4 with $p_1 = 0.1$, ranked by probability. (b) The essential bit content $H_\delta(X^4)$. The upper schematic diagram indicates the strings's probabilities by the vertical lines's lengths (not to scale).

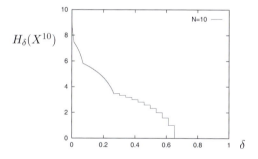

(b)

Figure 4.8. $H_\delta(X^N)$ for $N = 10$ binary variables with $p_1 = 0.1$.

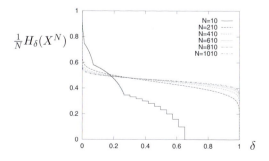

Figure 4.9. $\frac{1}{N} H_\delta(X^N)$ for $N = 10, 210, \ldots, 1010$ binary variables with $p_1 = 0.1$.

$\mathbf{x}$	$\log_2(P(\mathbf{x}))$
...1.........................1.....1...1.1.......1.........1..........1.........................1.....11...	-50.1
....................1.....1.....1.........1.....1.........1...1....	-37.3
........1...1..1...1....11..1.1.........11...................................1...1.1..1...1.................1.	-65.9
1.1...1.....................1...................11.1..1....................1.....1...1.1.11.......	-56.4
...11...........1...1.....1.1........1..........1.....1...1...1....1.............1...............	-53.2
..............1.....1.........1.1..........1.........1........1...1................................1.......	-43.7
.....1.......1.....1...1.........1.............1........1.....1...11...........................	-46.8
....1..1..1........111......................1.............1.........1.1...1...1............1	-56.4
........1.......1.....1.....1.........1...1.....................................1....	-37.3
.....1...........1............1.....1...1.1.1.1..1....................................1.	-43.7
1...................1.........1...1.................1...1...1.....1..11..1.1...1.......	-56.4
..........11.1........1...................1....1.......................1.....................	-37.3
.1.........1...1.1..............1......11........1.1...1.............1.............11..........	-56.4
......1...1..1....1..11.1.1.1...1............................1.........1..............1..1..........	-59.5
...........11.1.......1....1...1...........................1.......1............1.......1.........	-46.8
....	-15.2
1111111111111111111111111111111111111111111111111111111111111111111111111111111111111111111111111111	-332.1

Figure 4.10. The top 15 strings are samples from X^{100}, where $p_1 = 0.1$ and $p_0 = 0.9$. The bottom two are the most and least probable strings in this ensemble. The final column shows the log-probabilities of the random strings, which may be compared with the entropy $H(X^{100}) = 46.9$ bits.

except for tails close to $\delta = 0$ and 1. As long as we are allowed a tiny probability of error δ, compression down to NH bits is possible. Even if we are allowed a large probability of error, we still can compress only down to NH bits. This is the source coding theorem.

Theorem 4.1 Shannon's source coding theorem. *Let X be an ensemble with entropy $H(X) = H$ bits. Given $\epsilon > 0$ and $0 < \delta < 1$, there exists a positive integer N_0 such that for $N > N_0$,*

$$\left| \frac{1}{N} H_\delta(X^N) - H \right| < \epsilon. \tag{4.21}$$

▶ 4.4 Typicality

Why does increasing N help? Let's examine long strings from X^N. Table 4.10 shows fifteen samples from X^N for $N = 100$ and $p_1 = 0.1$. The probability of a string $\mathbf{x}$ that contains r 1s and $N-r$ 0s is

$$P(\mathbf{x}) = p_1^r (1 - p_1)^{N-r}. \tag{4.22}$$

The number of strings that contain r 1s is

$$n(r) = \binom{N}{r}. \tag{4.23}$$

So the number of 1s, r, has a binomial distribution:

$$P(r) = \binom{N}{r} p_1^r (1 - p_1)^{N-r}. \tag{4.24}$$

These functions are shown in figure 4.11. The mean of r is Np_1, and its standard deviation is $\sqrt{Np_1(1 - p_1)}$ (p.1). If N is 100 then

$$r \sim Np_1 \pm \sqrt{Np_1(1 - p_1)} \simeq 10 \pm 3. \tag{4.25}$$

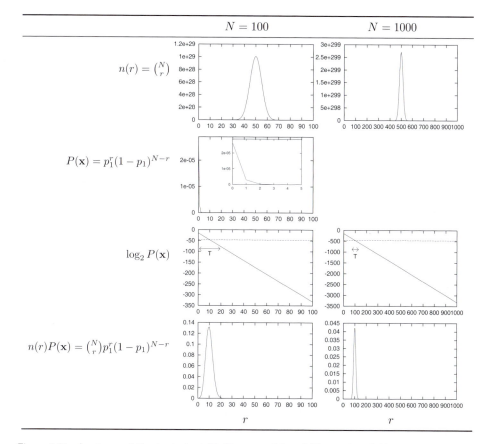

Figure 4.11. Anatomy of the typical set T. For $p_1 = 0.1$ and $N = 100$ and $N = 1000$, these graphs show $n(r)$, the number of strings containing r 1s; the probability $P(\mathbf{x})$ of a single string that contains r 1s; the same probability on a log scale; and the total probability $n(r)P(\mathbf{x})$ of all strings that contain r 1s. The number r is on the horizontal axis. The plot of $\log_2 P(\mathbf{x})$ also shows by a dotted line the mean value of $\log_2 P(\mathbf{x}) = -NH_2(p_1)$ which equals -46.9 when $N = 100$ and -469 when $N = 1000$. The typical set includes only the strings that have $\log_2 P(\mathbf{x})$ close to this value. The range marked T shows the set $T_{N\beta}$ (as defined in section 4.4) for $N = 100$ and $\beta = 0.29$ (left) and $N = 1000$, $\beta = 0.09$ (right).

If $N = 1000$ then

$$r \sim 100 \pm 10. \qquad (4.26)$$

Notice that as N gets bigger, the probability distribution of r becomes more concentrated, in the sense that while the range of possible values of r grows as N, the standard deviation of r only grows as $\sqrt{N}$. That r is most likely to fall in a small range of values implies that the outcome $\mathbf{x}$ is also most likely to fall in a corresponding small subset of outcomes that we will call the *typical set*.

Definition of the typical set

Let us define typicality for an arbitrary ensemble X with alphabet $\mathcal{A}_X$. Our definition of a typical string will involve the string's probability. A long string of N symbols will usually contain about $p_1 N$ occurrences of the first symbol, $p_2 N$ occurrences of the second, etc. Hence the probability of this string is roughly

$$P(\mathbf{x})_{\text{typ}} = P(x_1)P(x_2)P(x_3)\ldots P(x_N) \simeq p_1^{(p_1 N)} p_2^{(p_2 N)} \ldots p_I^{(p_I N)} \qquad (4.27)$$

so that the information content of a typical string is

$$\log_2 \frac{1}{P(\mathbf{x})} \simeq N \sum_i p_i \log_2 \frac{1}{p_i} \simeq NH. \qquad (4.28)$$

So the random variable $\log_2 {}^1/P(\mathbf{x})$, which is the information content of $\mathbf{x}$, is very likely to be close in value to NH. We build our definition of typicality on this observation.

We define the typical elements of $\mathcal{A}_X^N$ to be those elements that have probability close to 2^{-NH}. (Note that the typical set, unlike the smallest sufficient subset, does *not* include the most probable elements of $\mathcal{A}_X^N$, but we will show that these most probable elements contribute negligible probability.)

We introduce a parameter β that defines how close the probability has to be to 2^{-NH} for an element to be 'typical'. We call the set of typical elements the typical set, $T_{N\beta}$:

$$T_{N\beta} \equiv \left\{ \mathbf{x} \in \mathcal{A}_X^N : \left| \frac{1}{N} \log_2 \frac{1}{P(\mathbf{x})} - H \right| < \beta \right\}. \qquad (4.29)$$

We will show that whatever value of β we choose, the typical set contains almost all the probability as N increases.

This important result is sometimes called the 'asymptotic equipartition' principle.

'Asymptotic equipartition' principle. For an ensemble of N independent identically distributed (i.i.d.) random variables $X^N \equiv (X_1, X_2, \ldots, X_N)$, with N sufficiently large, the outcome $\mathbf{x} = (x_1, x_2, \ldots, x_N)$ is almost certain to belong to a subset of $\mathcal{A}_X^N$ having only $2^{NH(X)}$ members, each having probability 'close to' $2^{-NH(X)}$.

Notice that if $H(X) < H_0(X)$ then $2^{NH(X)}$ is a *tiny* fraction of the number of possible outcomes $|\mathcal{A}_X^N| = |\mathcal{A}_X|^N = 2^{NH_0(X)}$.

> The term equipartition is chosen to describe the idea that the members of the typical set have *roughly equal* probability. [This should not be taken too literally, hence my use of quotes around 'asymptotic equipartition'; see page 83.]

> A second meaning for equipartition, in thermal physics, is the idea that each degree of freedom of a classical system has equal average energy, $\frac{1}{2}kT$. This second meaning is not intended here.

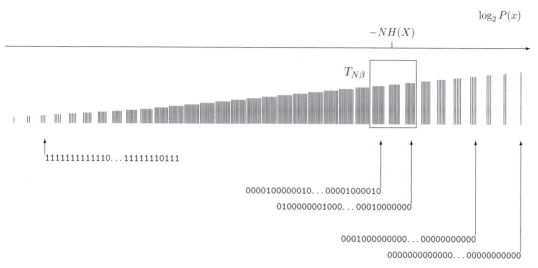

Figure 4.12. Schematic diagram showing all strings in the ensemble X^N ranked by their probability, and the typical set $T_{N\beta}$.

The 'asymptotic equipartition' principle is equivalent to:

Shannon's source coding theorem (verbal statement). N i.i.d. random variables each with entropy $H(X)$ can be compressed into more than $NH(X)$ bits with negligible risk of information loss, as $N \to \infty$; conversely if they are compressed into fewer than $NH(X)$ bits it is virtually certain that information will be lost.

These two theorems are equivalent because we can define a compression algorithm that gives a distinct name of length $NH(X)$ bits to each $\mathbf{x}$ in the typical set.

▶ 4.5 Proofs

This section may be skipped if found tough going.

The law of large numbers

Our proof of the source coding theorem uses the law of large numbers.

Mean and variance of a real random variable are $\mathcal{E}[u] = \bar{u} = \sum_u P(u)u$ and $\text{var}(u) = \sigma_u^2 = \mathcal{E}[(u - \bar{u})^2] = \sum_u P(u)(u - \bar{u})^2$.

> Technical note: strictly I am assuming here that u is a function $u(x)$ of a sample x from a finite discrete ensemble X. Then the summations $\sum_u P(u)f(u)$ should be written $\sum_x P(x)f(u(x))$. This means that $P(u)$ is a finite sum of delta functions. This restriction guarantees that the mean and variance of u do exist, which is not necessarily the case for general $P(u)$.

Chebyshev's inequality 1. Let t be a non-negative real random variable, and let α be a positive real number. Then

$$P(t \geq \alpha) \leq \frac{\bar{t}}{\alpha}. \qquad (4.30)$$

Proof: $P(t \geq \alpha) = \sum_{t \geq \alpha} P(t)$. We multiply each term by $t/\alpha \geq 1$ and obtain: $P(t \geq \alpha) \leq \sum_{t \geq \alpha} P(t)t/\alpha$. We add the (non-negative) missing terms and obtain: $P(t \geq \alpha) \leq \sum_t P(t)t/\alpha = \bar{t}/\alpha$. □

Chebyshev's inequality 2. Let x be a random variable, and let α be a positive real number. Then

$$P\left((x - \bar{x})^2 \geq \alpha\right) \leq \sigma_x^2/\alpha. \tag{4.31}$$

Proof: Take $t = (x - \bar{x})^2$ and apply the previous proposition. □

Weak law of large numbers. Take x to be the average of N independent random variables $h_1, \ldots, h_N$, having common mean $\bar{h}$ and common variance σ_h^2: $x = \frac{1}{N} \sum_{n=1}^{N} h_n$. Then

$$P((x - \bar{h})^2 \geq \alpha) \leq \sigma_h^2/\alpha N. \tag{4.32}$$

Proof: obtained by showing that $\bar{x} = \bar{h}$ and that $\sigma_x^2 = \sigma_h^2/N$. □

We are interested in x being very close to the mean (α very small). No matter how large σ_h^2 is, and no matter how small the required α is, and no matter how small the desired probability that $(x - \bar{h})^2 \geq \alpha$, we can always achieve it by taking N large enough.

Proof of theorem 4.1 (p. 78)

We apply the law of large numbers to the random variable $\frac{1}{N} \log_2 \frac{1}{P(\mathbf{x})}$ defined for $\mathbf{x}$ drawn from the ensemble X^N. This random variable can be written as the average of N information contents $h_n = \log_2(1/P(x_n))$, each of which is a random variable with mean $H = H(X)$ and variance $\sigma^2 \equiv \text{var}[\log_2(1/P(x_n))]$. (Each term h_n is the Shannon information content of the nth outcome.)

We again define the typical set with parameters N and β thus:

$$T_{N\beta} = \left\{ \mathbf{x} \in \mathcal{A}_X^N : \left[\frac{1}{N} \log_2 \frac{1}{P(\mathbf{x})} - H \right]^2 < \beta^2 \right\}. \tag{4.33}$$

For all $\mathbf{x} \in T_{N\beta}$, the probability of $\mathbf{x}$ satisfies

$$2^{-N(H+\beta)} < P(\mathbf{x}) < 2^{-N(H-\beta)}. \tag{4.34}$$

And by the law of large numbers,

$$P(\mathbf{x} \in T_{N\beta}) \geq 1 - \frac{\sigma^2}{\beta^2 N}. \tag{4.35}$$

We have thus proved the 'asymptotic equipartition' principle. As N increases, the probability that $\mathbf{x}$ falls in $T_{N\beta}$ approaches 1, for any β. How does this result relate to source coding?

We must relate $T_{N\beta}$ to $H_\delta(X^N)$. We will show that for any given δ there is a sufficiently big N such that $H_\delta(X^N) \simeq NH$.

Part 1: $\frac{1}{N} H_\delta(X^N) < H + \epsilon$.

The set $T_{N\beta}$ is not the best subset for compression. So the size of $T_{N\beta}$ gives an upper bound on H_δ. We show how *small* $H_\delta(X^N)$ must be by calculating how big $T_{N\beta}$ could possibly be. We are free to set β to any convenient value. The smallest possible probability that a member of $T_{N\beta}$ can have is $2^{-N(H+\beta)}$, and the total probability that $T_{N\beta}$ contains can't be any bigger than 1. So

$$|T_{N\beta}| 2^{-N(H+\beta)} < 1, \tag{4.36}$$

that is, the size of the typical set is bounded by

$$|T_{N\beta}| < 2^{N(H+\beta)}. \tag{4.37}$$

If we set $\beta = \epsilon$ and N_0 such that $\frac{\sigma^2}{\epsilon^2 N} \leq \delta$, then $P(T_{N\beta}) \geq 1 - \delta$, and the set $T_{N\beta}$ becomes a witness to the fact that $H_\delta(X^N) \leq \log_2 |T_{N\beta}| < N(H + \epsilon)$.

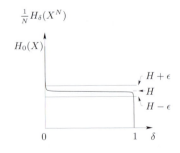

Figure 4.13. Schematic illustration of the two parts of the theorem. Given any δ and ϵ, we show that for large enough N, $\frac{1}{N} H_\delta(X^N)$ lies (1) below the line $H + \epsilon$ and (2) above the line $H - \epsilon$.

Part 2: $\frac{1}{N}H_\delta(X^N) > H - \epsilon$.

Imagine that someone claims this second part is not so – that, for any N, the smallest δ-sufficient subset S_δ is smaller than the above inequality would allow. We can make use of our typical set to show that they must be mistaken. Remember that we are free to set β to any value we choose. We will set $\beta = \epsilon/2$, so that our task is to prove that a subset S' having $|S'| \leq 2^{N(H-2\beta)}$ and achieving $P(\mathbf{x} \in S') \geq 1 - \delta$ cannot exist (for N greater than an N_0 that we will specify).

So, let us consider the probability of falling in this rival smaller subset S'. The probability of the subset S' is

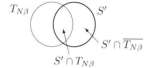

$$P(\mathbf{x} \in S') = P(\mathbf{x} \in S' \cap T_{N\beta}) + P(\mathbf{x} \in S' \cap \overline{T_{N\beta}}), \qquad (4.38)$$

where $\overline{T_{N\beta}}$ denotes the complement $\{\mathbf{x} \notin T_{N\beta}\}$. The maximum value of the first term is found if $S' \cap T_{N\beta}$ contains $2^{N(H-2\beta)}$ outcomes all with the maximum probability, $2^{-N(H-\beta)}$. The maximum value the second term can have is $P(\mathbf{x} \notin T_{N\beta})$. So:

$$P(\mathbf{x} \in S') \leq 2^{N(H-2\beta)}\, 2^{-N(H-\beta)} + \frac{\sigma^2}{\beta^2 N} = 2^{-N\beta} + \frac{\sigma^2}{\beta^2 N}. \qquad (4.39)$$

We can now set $\beta = \epsilon/2$ and N_0 such that $P(\mathbf{x} \in S') < 1 - \delta$, which shows that S' cannot satisfy the definition of a sufficient subset S_δ. Thus *any* subset S' with size $|S'| \leq 2^{N(H-\epsilon)}$ has probability less than $1 - \delta$, so by the definition of H_δ, $H_\delta(X^N) > N(H - \epsilon)$.

Thus for large enough N, the function $\frac{1}{N}H_\delta(X^N)$ is essentially a constant function of δ, for $0 < \delta < 1$, as illustrated in figures 4.9 and 4.13. □

▶ 4.6 Comments

The source coding theorem (p.78) has two parts, $\frac{1}{N}H_\delta(X^N) < H + \epsilon$, and $\frac{1}{N}H_\delta(X^N) > H - \epsilon$. Both results are interesting.

The first part tells us that even if the probability of error δ is extremely small, the number of bits per symbol $\frac{1}{N}H_\delta(X^N)$ needed to specify a long N-symbol string $\mathbf{x}$ with vanishingly small error probability does not have to exceed $H + \epsilon$ bits. We need to have only a tiny tolerance for error, and the number of bits required drops significantly from $H_0(X)$ to $(H + \epsilon)$.

What happens if we are yet more tolerant to compression errors? Part 2 tells us that even if δ is very close to 1, so that errors are made most of the time, the average number of bits per symbol needed to specify $\mathbf{x}$ must still be at least $H - \epsilon$ bits. These two extremes tell us that regardless of our specific allowance for error, the number of bits per symbol needed to specify $\mathbf{x}$ is H bits; no more and no less.

Caveat regarding 'asymptotic equipartition'

I put the words 'asymptotic equipartition' in quotes because it is important not to think that the elements of the typical set $T_{N\beta}$ really do have roughly the same probability as each other. They are similar in probability only in the sense that their values of $\log_2 \frac{1}{P(\mathbf{x})}$ are within $2N\beta$ of each other. Now, as β is decreased, how does N have to increase, if we are to keep our bound on the mass of the typical set, $P(\mathbf{x} \in T_{N\beta}) \geq 1 - \frac{\sigma^2}{\beta^2 N}$, constant? N must grow as $1/\beta^2$, so, if we write β in terms of N as $\alpha/\sqrt{N}$, for some constant α, then the most probable string in the typical set will be of order $2^{\alpha\sqrt{N}}$ times greater than the least probable string in the typical set. As β decreases, N increases, and this ratio $2^{\alpha\sqrt{N}}$ grows exponentially. Thus we have 'equipartition' only in a weak sense!

Why did we introduce the typical set?

The best choice of subset for block compression is (by definition) S_δ, not a typical set. So why did we bother introducing the typical set? The answer is, *we can count the typical set*. We know that all its elements have 'almost identical' probability (2^{-NH}), and we know the whole set has probability almost 1, so the typical set must have roughly 2^{NH} elements. Without the help of the typical set (which is very similar to S_δ) it would have been hard to count how many elements there are in S_δ.

▶ ## 4.7 Exercises

Weighing problems

▷ **Exercise 4.9.**[1] While some people, when they first encounter the weighing problem with 12 balls and the three-outcome balance (exercise 4.1 (p.66)), think that weighing six balls against six balls is a good first weighing, others say 'no, weighing six against six conveys *no* information at all'. Explain to the second group why they are both right and wrong. Compute the information gained about *which is the odd ball*, and the information gained about *which is the odd ball and whether it is heavy or light*.

▷ **Exercise 4.10.**[2] Solve the weighing problem for the case where there are 39 balls of which one is known to be odd.

▷ **Exercise 4.11.**[2] You are given 16 balls, all of which are equal in weight except for one that is either heavier or lighter. You are also given a bizarre two-pan balance that can report only two outcomes: 'the two sides balance' or 'the two sides do not balance'. Design a strategy to determine which is the odd ball in as few uses of the balance as possible.

▷ **Exercise 4.12.**[2] You have a two-pan balance; your job is to weigh out bags of flour with integer weights 1 to 40 pounds inclusive. How many weights do you need? [You are allowed to put weights on either pan. You're only allowed to put one flour bag on the balance at a time.]

Exercise 4.13.[4, p.86] (a) Is it possible to solve exercise 4.1 (p.66) (the weighing problem with 12 balls and the three-outcome balance) using a sequence of three *fixed* weighings, such that the balls chosen for the second weighing do not depend on the outcome of the first, and the third weighing does not depend on the first or second?

(b) Find a solution to the general N-ball weighing problem in which exactly one of N balls is odd. Show that in W weighings, an odd ball can be identified from among $N = (3^W - 3)/2$ balls.

Exercise 4.14.[3] You are given 12 balls and the three-outcome balance of exercise 4.1; this time, *two* of the balls are odd; each odd ball may be heavy or light, and we don't know which. We want to identify the odd balls and in which direction they are odd.

(a) *Estimate* how many weighings are required by the optimal strategy. And what if there are three odd balls?

(b) How do your answers change if it is known that all the regular balls weigh 100 g, that light balls weigh 99 g, and heavy ones weigh 110 g?

Source coding with a lossy compressor, with loss δ

▷ **Exercise 4.15.**[2, p.87] Let $\mathcal{P}_X = \{0.2, 0.8\}$. Sketch $\frac{1}{N} H_\delta(X^N)$ as a function of δ for $N = 1, 2$ and 1000.

▷ **Exercise 4.16.**[2] Let $\mathcal{P}_Y = \{0.5, 0.5\}$. Sketch $\frac{1}{N} H_\delta(Y^N)$ as a function of δ for $N = 1, 2, 3$ and 100.

▷ **Exercise 4.17.**[2, p.87] (For physics students.) Discuss the relationship between the proof of the 'asymptotic equipartition' principle and the equivalence (for large systems) of the Boltzmann entropy and the Gibbs entropy.

Distributions that don't obey the law of large numbers

The law of large numbers, which we used in this chapter, shows that the mean of a set of N i.i.d. random variables has a probability distribution that becomes narrower, with width $\propto 1/\sqrt{N}$, as N increases. However, we have proved this property only for discrete random variables, that is, for real numbers taking on a *finite* set of possible values. While many random variables with continuous probability distributions also satisfy the law of large numbers, there are important distributions that do not. Some continuous distributions do not have a mean or variance.

▷ **Exercise 4.18.**[3, p.88] Sketch the Cauchy distribution

$$P(x) = \frac{1}{Z}\frac{1}{x^2 + 1}, \quad x \in (-\infty, \infty). \tag{4.40}$$

What is its normalizing constant Z? Can you evaluate its mean or variance?

Consider the sum $z = x_1 + x_2$, where x_1 and x_2 are independent random variables from a Cauchy distribution. What is $P(z)$? What is the probability distribution of the mean of x_1 and x_2, $\bar{x} = (x_1 + x_2)/2$? What is the probability distribution of the mean of N samples from this Cauchy distribution?

Other asymptotic properties

Exercise 4.19.[3] Chernoff bound. We derived the weak law of large numbers from Chebyshev's inequality (4.30) by letting the random variable t in the inequality $P(t \geq \alpha) \leq \bar{t}/\alpha$ be a function, $t = (x - \bar{x})^2$, of the random variable x we were interested in.

Other useful inequalities can be obtained by using other functions. The Chernoff bound, which is useful for bounding the tails of a distribution, is obtained by letting $t = \exp(sx)$.

Show that

$$P(x \geq a) \leq e^{-sa} g(s), \quad \text{for any } s > 0 \tag{4.41}$$

and

$$P(x \leq a) \leq e^{-sa} g(s), \quad \text{for any } s < 0 \tag{4.42}$$

where $g(s)$ is the moment-generating function of x,

$$g(s) = \sum_x P(x)\, e^{sx}. \tag{4.43}$$

Curious functions related to $p \log 1/p$

Exercise 4.20.[4, p.89] This exercise has no purpose at all; it's included for the enjoyment of those who like mathematical curiosities.

Sketch the function

$$f(x) = x^{x^{x^{x^{\cdot^{\cdot^{\cdot}}}}}} \tag{4.44}$$

for $x \geq 0$. **Hint:** Work out the inverse function to f – that is, the function $g(y)$ such that if $x = g(y)$ then $y = f(x)$ – it's closely related to $p \log 1/p$.

▶ **4.8 Solutions**

Solution to exercise 4.2 (p.68).   Let $P(x, y) = P(x)P(y)$. Then

$$
\begin{aligned}
H(X,Y) &= \sum_{xy} P(x)P(y) \log \frac{1}{P(x)P(y)} & (4.45) \\
&= \sum_{xy} P(x)P(y) \log \frac{1}{P(x)} + \sum_{xy} P(x)P(y) \log \frac{1}{P(y)} & (4.46) \\
&= \sum_{x} P(x) \log \frac{1}{P(x)} + \sum_{y} P(y) \log \frac{1}{P(y)} & (4.47) \\
&= H(X) + H(Y). & (4.48)
\end{aligned}
$$

Solution to exercise 4.4 (p.73).   An ASCII file can be reduced in size by a factor of 7/8. This reduction could be achieved by a block code that maps 8-byte blocks into 7-byte blocks by copying the 56 information-carrying bits into 7 bytes, and ignoring the last bit of every character.

Solution to exercise 4.5 (p.74).   The pigeon-hole principle states: you can't put 16 pigeons into 15 holes without using one of the holes twice.

Similarly, you can't give $\mathcal{A}_X$ outcomes unique binary names of some length l shorter than $\log_2 |\mathcal{A}_X|$ bits, because there are only 2^l such binary names, and $l < \log_2 |\mathcal{A}_X|$ implies $2^l < |\mathcal{A}_X|$, so at least two different inputs to the compressor would compress to the same output file.

Solution to exercise 4.8 (p.76).   Between the cusps, all the changes in probability are equal, and the number of elements in T changes by one at each step. So H_δ varies logarithmically with $(-\delta)$.

Solution to exercise 4.13 (p.84). This solution was found by Dyson and Lyness in 1946 and presented in the following elegant form by John Conway in 1999. Be warned: the symbols A, B, and C are used to name the balls, to name the pans of the balance, to name the outcomes, and to name the possible states of the odd ball!

(a) Label the 12 balls by the sequences

   AAB   ABA   ABB   ABC   BBC   BCA   BCB   BCC   CAA   CAB   CAC   CCA

   and in the

```
1st                    AAB ABA ABB ABC           BBC BCA BCB BCC
2nd weighings put AAB CAA CAB CAC in pan A, ABA ABB ABC BBC in pan B.
3rd                    ABA BCA CAA CCA           AAB ABB BCB CAB
```

Now in a given weighing, a pan will either end up in the

- Canonical position (C) that it assumes when the pans are balanced, or

- Above that position (A), or

- Below it (B),

so the three weighings determine for each pan a sequence of three of these letters.

If both sequences are CCC, then there's no odd ball. Otherwise, for *just one* of the two pans, the sequence is among the 12 above, and names the odd ball, whose weight is Above or Below the proper one according as the pan is A or B.

(b) In W weighings the odd ball can be identified from among

$$N = (3^W - 3)/2 \tag{4.49}$$

balls in the same way, by labelling them with all the non-constant sequences of W letters from A, B, C whose first change is A-to-B or B-to-C or C-to-A, and at the wth weighing putting those whose wth letter is A in pan A and those whose wth letter is B in pan B.

Solution to exercise 4.15 (p.85). The curves $\frac{1}{N}H_\delta(X^N)$ as a function of δ for $N = 1, 2$ and 1000 are shown in figure 4.14. Note that $H_2(0.2) = 0.72$ bits.

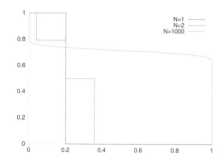

$N = 1$		
δ	$\frac{1}{N}H_\delta(\mathbf{X})$	$2^{H_\delta(\mathbf{X})}$
0–0.2	1	2
0.2–1	0	1

$N = 2$		
δ	$\frac{1}{N}H_\delta(\mathbf{X})$	$2^{H_\delta(\mathbf{X})}$
0–0.04	1	4
0.04–0.2	0.79	3
0.2–0.36	0.5	2
0.36–1	0	1

Figure 4.14. $\frac{1}{N}H_\delta(\mathbf{X})$ (vertical axis) against δ (horizontal), for $N = 1, 2, 100$ binary variables with $p_1 = 0.4$.

Solution to exercise 4.17 (p.85). The Gibbs entropy is $k_\mathrm{B} \sum_i p_i \ln \frac{1}{p_i}$, where i runs over all states of the system. This entropy is equivalent (apart from the factor of k_B) to the Shannon entropy of the ensemble.

Whereas the Gibbs entropy can be defined for any ensemble, the Boltzmann entropy is only defined for *microcanonical* ensembles, which have a probability distribution that is uniform over a set of accessible states. The Boltzmann entropy is defined to be $S_\mathrm{B} = k_\mathrm{B} \ln \Omega$ where Ω is the number of accessible states of the microcanonical ensemble. This is equivalent (apart from the factor of k_B) to the perfect information content H_0 of that constrained ensemble. The Gibbs entropy of a microcanonical ensemble is trivially equal to the Boltzmann entropy.

We now consider a thermal distribution (the *canonical* ensemble), where the probability of a state $\mathbf{x}$ is

$$P(\mathbf{x}) = \frac{1}{Z} \exp\left(-\frac{E(\mathbf{x})}{k_{\mathrm{B}}T}\right). \qquad (4.50)$$

With this canonical ensemble we can associate a corresponding microcanonical ensemble, an ensemble with total energy fixed to the mean energy of the canonical ensemble (fixed to within some precision ϵ). Now, fixing the total energy to a precision ϵ is equivalent to fixing the value of $\ln^{1/P(\mathbf{x})}$ to within $\epsilon k_{\mathrm{B}}T$. Our definition of the typical set $T_{N\beta}$ was precisely that it consisted of all elements that have a value of $\log P(\mathbf{x})$ very close to the mean value of $\log P(\mathbf{x})$ under the canonical ensemble, $-NH(X)$. Thus the microcanonical ensemble is equivalent to a uniform distribution over the typical set of the canonical ensemble.

Our proof of the 'asymptotic equipartition' principle thus proves – for the case of a system whose energy is separable into a sum of independent terms – that the Boltzmann entropy of the microcanonical ensemble is very close (for large N) to the Gibbs entropy of the canonical ensemble, if the energy of the microcanonical ensemble is constrained to equal the mean energy of the canonical ensemble.

Solution to exercise 4.18 (p.85). The normalizing constant of the Cauchy distribution

$$P(x) = \frac{1}{Z}\frac{1}{x^2 + 1}$$

is

$$Z = \int_{-\infty}^{\infty} \mathrm{d}x\,\frac{1}{x^2 + 1} = \left[\tan^{-1}x\right]_{-\infty}^{\infty} = \frac{\pi}{2} - \frac{-\pi}{2} = \pi. \qquad (4.51)$$

The mean and variance of this distribution are both undefined. (The distribution is symmetrical about zero, but this does not imply that its mean is zero. The mean is the value of a divergent integral.) The sum $z = x_1 + x_2$, where x_1 and x_2 both have Cauchy distributions, has probability density given by the convolution

$$P(z) = \frac{1}{\pi^2}\int_{-\infty}^{\infty}\mathrm{d}x_1\,\frac{1}{x_1^2 + 1}\frac{1}{(z - x_1)^2 + 1}, \qquad (4.52)$$

which after a considerable labour using standard methods gives

$$P(z) = \frac{1}{\pi^2}2\frac{\pi}{z^2 + 4} = \frac{2}{\pi}\frac{1}{z^2 + 2^2}, \qquad (4.53)$$

which we recognize as a Cauchy distribution with width parameter 2 (where the original distribution has width parameter 1). This implies that the mean of the two points, $\bar{x} = (x_1 + x_2)/2 = z/2$, has a Cauchy distribution with width parameter 1. Generalizing, the mean of N samples from a Cauchy distribution is Cauchy-distributed with the *same parameters* as the individual samples. The probability distribution of the mean does *not* become narrower as $1/\sqrt{N}$.

The central limit theorem does not apply to the Cauchy distribution, because it does not have a finite variance.

An alternative neat method for getting to equation (4.53) makes use of the Fourier transform of the Cauchy distribution, which is a biexponential $e^{-|\omega|}$. Convolution in real space corresponds to multiplication in Fourier space, so the Fourier transform of z is simply $e^{-|2\omega|}$. Reversing the transform, we obtain equation (4.53).

Solution to exercise 4.20 (p.86).   The function $f(x)$ has inverse function

$$g(y) = y^{1/y}. \tag{4.54}$$

Note

$$\log g(y) = 1/y \log y. \tag{4.55}$$

I obtained a tentative graph of $f(x)$ by plotting $g(y)$ with y along the vertical axis and $g(y)$ along the horizontal axis. The resulting graph suggests that $f(x)$ is single valued for $x \in (0, 1)$, and looks surprisingly well-behaved and ordinary; for $x \in (1, e^{1/e})$, $f(x)$ is two-valued. $f(\sqrt{2})$ is equal both to 2 and 4. For $x > e^{1/e}$ (which is about 1.44), $f(x)$ is infinite. However, it might be argued that this approach to sketching $f(x)$ is only partly valid, if we define f as the limit of the sequence of functions x, x^x, x^{x^x}, ...; this sequence does not have a limit for $0 \le x \le (1/e)^e \simeq 0.07$ on account of a pitchfork bifurcation at $x = (1/e)^e$; and for $x \in (1, e^{1/e})$, the sequence's limit is single-valued — the lower of the two values sketched in the figure.

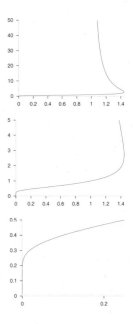

Figure 4.15. $f(x) = x^{x^{x^{x^{x^{\cdot^{\cdot^{\cdot}}}}}}}$ shown at three different scales.

About Chapter 5

In the last chapter, we saw a proof of the fundamental status of the entropy as a measure of average information content. We defined a data compression scheme using *fixed length block codes*, and proved that as N increases, it is possible to encode N i.i.d. variables $\mathbf{x} = (x_1, \ldots, x_N)$ into a block of $N(H(X) + \epsilon)$ bits with vanishing probability of error, whereas if we attempt to encode X^N into $N(H(X) - \epsilon)$ bits, the probability of error is virtually 1.

We thus verified the *possibility* of data compression, but the block coding defined in the proof did not give a practical algorithm. In this chapter and the next, we study practical data compression algorithms. Whereas the last chapter's compression scheme used large blocks of *fixed* size and was *lossy*, in the next chapter we discuss *variable-length* compression schemes that are practical for small block sizes and that are *not lossy*.

Imagine a rubber glove filled with water. If we compress two fingers of the glove, some other part of the glove has to expand, because the total volume of water is constant. (Water is essentially incompressible.) Similarly, when we shorten the codewords for some outcomes, there must be other codewords that get longer, if the scheme is not lossy. In this chapter we will discover the information-theoretic equivalent of water volume.

Before reading Chapter 5, you should have worked on exercise 2.26 (p.37).

We will use the following notation for intervals:
$$x \in [1, 2) \quad \text{means that } x \geq 1 \text{ and } x < 2;$$
$$x \in (1, 2] \quad \text{means that } x > 1 \text{ and } x \leq 2.$$

5

Symbol Codes

In this chapter, we discuss *variable-length symbol codes*, which encode one source symbol at a time, instead of encoding huge strings of N source symbols. These codes are *lossless:* unlike the last chapter's block codes, they are guaranteed to compress and decompress without any errors; but there is a chance that the codes may sometimes produce encoded strings longer than the original source string.

The idea is that we can achieve compression, on average, by assigning *shorter* encodings to the more probable outcomes and *longer* encodings to the less probable.

The key issues are:

What are the implications if a symbol code is *lossless*? If some codewords are shortened, by how much do other codewords have to be lengthened?

Making compression practical. How can we ensure that a symbol code is easy to decode?

Optimal symbol codes. How should we assign codelengths to achieve the best compression, and what is the best achievable compression?

We again verify the fundamental status of the Shannon information content and the entropy, proving:

Source coding theorem (symbol codes). There exists a variable-length encoding C of an ensemble X such that the average length of an encoded symbol, $L(C, X)$, satisfies $L(C, X) \in [H(X), H(X) + 1)$.

The average length is equal to the entropy $H(X)$ only if the codelength for each outcome is equal to its Shannon information content.

We will also define a constructive procedure, the Huffman coding algorithm, that produces optimal symbol codes.

Notation for alphabets. $\mathcal{A}^N$ denotes the set of ordered N-tuples of elements from the set $\mathcal{A}$, i.e., all strings of length N. The symbol $\mathcal{A}^+$ will denote the set of all strings of finite length composed of elements from the set $\mathcal{A}$.

Example 5.1. $\{0, 1\}^3 = \{000, 001, 010, 011, 100, 101, 110, 111\}$.

Example 5.2. $\{0, 1\}^+ = \{0, 1, 00, 01, 10, 11, 000, 001, \ldots\}$.

▶ 5.1 Symbol codes

A (binary) symbol code C for an ensemble X is a mapping from the range of x, $\mathcal{A}_X = \{a_1, \ldots, a_I\}$, to $\{0,1\}^+$. $c(x)$ will denote the *codeword* corresponding to x, and $l(x)$ will denote its length, with $l_i = l(a_i)$.

The *extended code* C^+ is a mapping from $\mathcal{A}_X^+$ to $\{0,1\}^+$ obtained by concatenation, without punctuation, of the corresponding codewords:

$$c^+(x_1 x_2 \ldots x_N) = c(x_1)c(x_2) \ldots c(x_N). \tag{5.1}$$

[The term 'mapping' here is a synonym for 'function'.]

Example 5.3. A symbol code for the ensemble X defined by

$$\begin{aligned} \mathcal{A}_X &= \{\ \text{a, b, c, d}\ \}, \\ \mathcal{P}_X &= \{\ 1/2, 1/4, 1/8, 1/8\ \}, \end{aligned} \tag{5.2}$$

is C_0, shown in the margin.

	a_i	$c(a_i)$	l_i
	a	1000	4
C_0:	b	0100	4
	c	0010	4
	d	0001	4

Using the extended code, we may encode acdbac as

$$c^+(\text{acdbac}) = 100000100001010010000010 \tag{5.3}$$

There are basic requirements for a useful symbol code. First, any encoded string must have a unique decoding. Second, the symbol code must be easy to decode. And third, the code should achieve as much compression as possible.

Any encoded string must have a unique decoding

A code $C(X)$ is uniquely decodeable if, under the extended code C^+, no two distinct strings have the same encoding, i.e.,

$$\forall \mathbf{x}, \mathbf{y} \in \mathcal{A}_X^+,\ \mathbf{x} \neq \mathbf{y} \implies c^+(\mathbf{x}) \neq c^+(\mathbf{y}). \tag{5.4}$$

The code C_0 defined above is an example of a uniquely decodeable code.

The symbol code must be easy to decode

A symbol code is easiest to decode if it is possible to identify the end of a codeword as soon as it arrives, which means that no codeword can be a *prefix* of another codeword. [A word c is a *prefix* of another word d if there exists a tail string t such that the concatenation ct is identical to d. For example, 1 is a prefix of 101, and so is 10.]

We will show later that we don't lose any performance if we constrain our symbol code to be a prefix code.

A symbol code is called a prefix code if no codeword is a prefix of any other codeword.

A prefix code is also known as an *instantaneous* or *self-punctuating* code, because an encoded string can be decoded from left to right without looking ahead to subsequent codewords. The end of a codeword is immediately recognizable. A prefix code is uniquely decodeable.

Prefix codes are also known as 'prefix-free codes' or 'prefix condition codes'.

Prefix codes correspond to trees.

Example 5.4. The code $C_1 = \{0, 101\}$ is a prefix code because 0 is not a prefix of 101, nor is 101 a prefix of 0.

Example 5.5. Let $C_2 = \{1, 101\}$. This code is not a prefix code because 1 is a prefix of 101.

Example 5.6. The code $C_3 = \{0, 10, 110, 111\}$ is a prefix code.

Example 5.7. The code $C_4 = \{00, 01, 10, 11\}$ is a prefix code.

Exercise 5.8.[1, p.104] Is C_2 uniquely decodeable?

Example 5.9. Consider exercise 4.1 (p.66) and figure 4.2 (p.69). Any weighing strategy that identifies the odd ball and whether it is heavy or light can be viewed as assigning a *ternary* code to each of the 24 possible states. This code is a prefix code.

The code should achieve as much compression as possible

The expected length $L(C, X)$ of a symbol code C for ensemble X is

$$L(C, X) = \sum_{x \in \mathcal{A}_X} P(x)\, l(x). \tag{5.5}$$

We may also write this quantity as

$$L(C, X) = \sum_{i=1}^{I} p_i l_i \tag{5.6}$$

where $I = |\mathcal{A}_X|$.

Example 5.10. Let

$$\begin{aligned} \mathcal{A}_X &= \{\, a,\ b,\ c,\ d\,\}, \\ \text{and} \quad \mathcal{P}_X &= \{\, 1/2, 1/4, 1/8, 1/8\,\}, \end{aligned} \tag{5.7}$$

and consider the code C_3. The entropy of X is 1.75 bits, and the expected length $L(C_3, X)$ of this code is also 1.75 bits. The sequence of symbols $\mathbf{x} = (\text{acdbac})$ is encoded as $c^+(\mathbf{x}) = 0110111100110$. C_3 is a prefix code and is therefore uniquely decodeable. Notice that the codeword lengths satisfy $l_i = \log_2(1/p_i)$, or equivalently, $p_i = 2^{-l_i}$.

Example 5.11. Consider the fixed length code for the same ensemble X, C_4. The expected length $L(C_4, X)$ is 2 bits.

Example 5.12. Consider C_5. The expected length $L(C_5, X)$ is 1.25 bits, which is less than $H(X)$. But the code is not uniquely decodeable. The sequence $\mathbf{x} = (\text{acdbac})$ encodes as 000111000, which can also be decoded as (cabdca).

Example 5.13. Consider the code C_6. The expected length $L(C_6, X)$ of this code is 1.75 bits. The sequence of symbols $\mathbf{x} = (\text{acdbac})$ is encoded as $c^+(\mathbf{x}) = 0011111010011$.

Is C_6 a prefix code? It is not, because $c(a) = 0$ is a prefix of $c(b)$ and $c(c)$.

C_1

C_3

C_4

Prefix codes can be represented on binary trees. *Complete* prefix codes correspond to binary trees with no unused branches. C_1 is an incomplete code.

C_3:

a_i	$c(a_i)$	p_i	$h(p_i)$	l_i
a	0	$1/2$	1.0	1
b	10	$1/4$	2.0	2
c	110	$1/8$	3.0	3
d	111	$1/8$	3.0	3

	C_4	C_5
a	00	0
b	01	1
c	10	00
d	11	11

C_6:

a_i	$c(a_i)$	p_i	$h(p_i)$	l_i
a	0	$1/2$	1.0	1
b	01	$1/4$	2.0	2
c	011	$1/8$	3.0	3
d	111	$1/8$	3.0	3

Is C_6 uniquely decodeable? This is not so obvious. If you think that it might *not* be uniquely decodeable, try to prove it so by finding a pair of strings $\mathbf{x}$ and $\mathbf{y}$ that have the same encoding. [The definition of unique decodeability is given in equation (5.4).]

C_6 certainly isn't *easy* to decode. When we receive '00', it is possible that $\mathbf{x}$ could start 'aa', 'ab' or 'ac'. Once we have received '001111', the second symbol is still ambiguous, as $\mathbf{x}$ could be 'abd...' or 'acd...'. But eventually a unique decoding crystallizes, once the next 0 appears in the encoded stream.

C_6 *is* in fact uniquely decodeable. Comparing with the prefix code C_3, we see that the codewords of C_6 are the reverse of C_3's. That C_3 is uniquely decodeable proves that C_6 is too, since any string from C_6 is identical to a string from C_3 read backwards.

▶ 5.2 What limit is imposed by unique decodeability?

We now ask, given a list of positive integers $\{l_i\}$, does there exist a uniquely decodeable code with those integers as its codeword lengths? At this stage, we ignore the probabilities of the different symbols; once we understand unique decodeability better, we'll reintroduce the probabilities and discuss how to make an *optimal* uniquely decodeable symbol code.

In the examples above, we have observed that if we take a code such as $\{00, 01, 10, 11\}$, and shorten one of its codewords, for example $00 \rightarrow 0$, then we can retain unique decodeability only if we lengthen other codewords. Thus there seems to be a constrained budget that we can spend on codewords, with shorter codewords being more expensive.

Let us explore the nature of this budget. If we build a code purely from codewords of length l equal to three, how many codewords can we have and retain unique decodeability? The answer is $2^l = 8$. Once we have chosen all eight of these codewords, is there any way we could add to the code another codeword of some *other* length and retain unique decodeability? It would seem not.

What if we make a code that includes a length-one codeword, '0', with the other codewords being of length three? How many length-three codewords can we have? If we restrict attention to prefix codes, then we can have only four codewords of length three, namely $\{100, 101, 110, 111\}$. What about other codes? Is there any other way of choosing codewords of length 3 that can give more codewords? Intuitively, we think this unlikely. A codeword of length 3 appears to have a cost that is 2^2 times smaller than a codeword of length 1.

Let's define a total budget of size 1, which we can spend on codewords. If we set the cost of a codeword whose length is l to 2^{-l}, then we have a pricing system that fits the examples discussed above. Codewords of length 3 cost $1/8$ each; codewords of length 1 cost $1/2$ each. We can spend our budget on any codewords. If we go over our budget then the code will certainly not be uniquely decodeable. If, on the other hand,

$$\sum_i 2^{-l_i} \leq 1, \tag{5.8}$$

then the code may be uniquely decodeable. This inequality is the Kraft inequality.

Kraft inequality. For any uniquely decodeable code C over the binary alphabet $\{0, 1\}$, the codeword lengths must satisfy:

$$\sum_{i=1}^{I} 2^{-l_i} \leq 1, \qquad (5.9)$$

where $I = |A_X|$.

Completeness. If a uniquely decodeable code satisfies the Kraft inequality with equality then it is called a *complete* code.

We want codes that are uniquely decodeable; prefix codes are uniquely decodeable, and are easy to decode. So life would be simpler for us if we could restrict attention to prefix codes. Fortunately, for any source there *is* an optimal symbol code that is also a prefix code.

Kraft inequality and prefix codes. Given a set of codeword lengths that satisfy the Kraft inequality, there exists a uniquely decodeable prefix code with these codeword lengths.

The Kraft inequality might be more accurately referred to as the Kraft–McMillan inequality: Kraft proved that if the inequality is satisfied, then a prefix code exists with the given lengths. McMillan (1956) proved the converse, that unique decodeability implies that the inequality holds.

Proof of the Kraft inequality. Define $S = \sum_i 2^{-l_i}$. Consider the quantity

$$S^N = \left[\sum_i 2^{-l_i} \right]^N = \sum_{i_1=1}^{I} \sum_{i_2=1}^{I} \cdots \sum_{i_N=1}^{I} 2^{-\left(l_{i_1} + l_{i_2} + \cdots l_{i_N}\right)} \qquad (5.10)$$

The quantity in the exponent, $(l_{i_1} + l_{i_2} + \cdots + l_{i_N})$, is the length of the encoding of the string $\mathbf{x} = a_{i_1} a_{i_2} \ldots a_{i_N}$. For every string $\mathbf{x}$ of length N, there is one term in the above sum. Introduce an array A_l that counts how many strings $\mathbf{x}$ have encoded length l. Then, defining $l_{\min} = \min_i l_i$ and $l_{\max} = \max_i l_i$:

$$S^N = \sum_{l=Nl_{\min}}^{Nl_{\max}} 2^{-l} A_l. \qquad (5.11)$$

Now assume C is uniquely decodeable, so that for all $\mathbf{x} \neq \mathbf{y}$, $c^+(\mathbf{x}) \neq c^+(\mathbf{y})$. Concentrate on the $\mathbf{x}$ that have encoded length l. There are a total of 2^l distinct bit strings of length l, so it must be the case that $A_l \leq 2^l$. So

$$S^N = \sum_{l=Nl_{\min}}^{Nl_{\max}} 2^{-l} A_l \leq \sum_{l=Nl_{\min}}^{Nl_{\max}} 1 \leq Nl_{\max}. \qquad (5.12)$$

Thus $S^N \leq l_{\max} N$ for all N. Now if S were greater than 1, then as N increases, S^N would be an exponentially growing function, and for large enough N, an exponential always exceeds a polynomial such as $l_{\max} N$. But our result ($S^N \leq l_{\max} N$) is true for *any* N. Therefore $S \leq 1$. $\square$

▷ Exercise 5.14.[3, p.104] Prove the result stated above, that for any set of codeword lengths $\{l_i\}$ satisfying the Kraft inequality, there is a prefix code having those lengths.

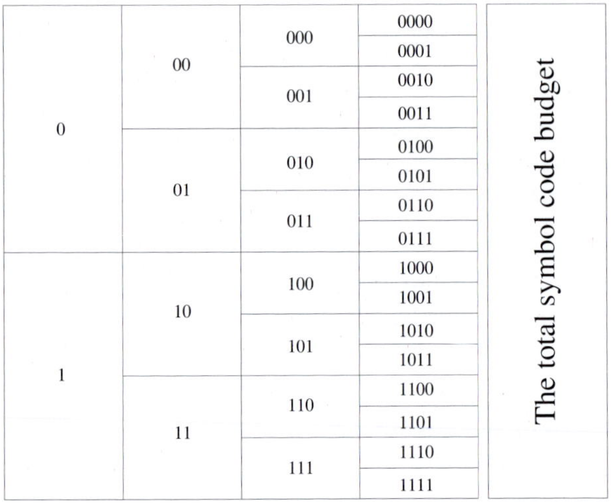

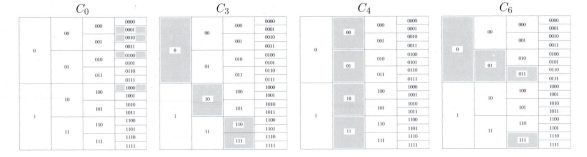

Figure 5.1. The symbol coding budget. The 'cost' 2^{-l} of each codeword (with length l) is indicated by the size of the box it is written in. The total budget available when making a uniquely decodeable code is 1.

You can think of this diagram as showing a *codeword supermarket*, with the codewords arranged in aisles by their length, and the cost of each codeword indicated by the size of its box on the shelf. If the cost of the codewords that you take exceeds the budget then your code will not be uniquely decodeable.

Figure 5.2. Selections of codewords made by codes C_0, C_3, C_4 and C_6 from section 5.1.

A pictorial view of the Kraft inequality may help you solve this exercise. Imagine that we are choosing the codewords to make a symbol code. We can draw the set of all candidate codewords in a supermarket that displays the 'cost' of the codeword by the area of a box (figure 5.1). The total budget available – the '1' on the right-hand side of the Kraft inequality – is shown at one side. Some of the codes discussed in section 5.1 are illustrated in figure 5.2. Notice that the codes that are prefix codes, C_0, C_3, and C_4, have the property that to the right of any selected codeword, there are no other selected codewords – because prefix codes correspond to trees. Notice that a *complete* prefix code corresponds to a *complete* tree having no unused branches.

We are now ready to put back the symbols's probabilities $\{p_i\}$. Given a set of symbol probabilities (the English language probabilities of figure 2.1, for example), how do we make the best symbol code – one with the smallest possible expected length $L(C, X)$? And what is that smallest possible expected length? It's not obvious how to assign the codeword lengths. If we give short codewords to the more probable symbols then the expected length might be reduced; on the other hand, shortening some codewords necessarily causes others to lengthen, by the Kraft inequality.

▶ **5.3 What's the most compression that we can hope for?**

We wish to minimize the expected length of a code,

$$L(C, X) \quad = \quad \sum_i p_i l_i. \tag{5.13}$$

As you might have guessed, the entropy appears as the lower bound on the expected length of a code.

Lower bound on expected length. The expected length $L(C, X)$ of a uniquely decodeable code is bounded below by $H(X)$.

Proof. We define the *implicit probabilities* $q_i \equiv 2^{-l_i}/z$, where $z = \sum_{i'} 2^{-l_{i'}}$, so that $l_i = \log 1/q_i - \log z$. We then use Gibbs' inequality, $\sum_i p_i \log 1/q_i \geq \sum_i p_i \log 1/p_i$, with equality if $q_i = p_i$, and the Kraft inequality $z \leq 1$:

$$L(C, X) \quad = \quad \sum_i p_i l_i = \sum_i p_i \log 1/q_i - \log z \tag{5.14}$$

$$\geq \quad \sum_i p_i \log 1/p_i - \log z \tag{5.15}$$

$$\geq \quad H(X). \tag{5.16}$$

The equality $L(C, X) = H(X)$ is achieved only if the Kraft equality $z = 1$ is satisfied, and if the codelengths satisfy $l_i = \log(1/p_i)$. □

This is an important result so let's say it again:

Optimal source codelengths. The expected length is minimized and is equal to $H(X)$ only if the codelengths are equal to the *Shannon information contents*:

$$l_i = \log_2(1/p_i). \tag{5.17}$$

Implicit probabilities defined by codelengths. Conversely, any choice of codelengths $\{l_i\}$ *implicitly* defines a probability distribution $\{q_i\}$,

$$q_i \equiv 2^{-l_i}/z, \tag{5.18}$$

for which those codelengths would be the optimal codelengths. If the code is complete then $z = 1$ and the implicit probabilities are given by $q_i = 2^{-l_i}$.

▶ 5.4 How much can we compress?

So, we can't compress below the entropy. How close can we expect to get to
the entropy?

Theorem 5.1 Source coding theorem for symbol codes. *For an ensemble X
there exists a prefix code C with expected length satisfying*

$$H(X) \leq L(C, X) < H(X) + 1. \tag{5.19}$$

Proof.   We set the codelengths to integers slightly larger than the optimum
lengths:

$$l_i = \lceil \log_2(1/p_i) \rceil \tag{5.20}$$

where $\lceil l^* \rceil$ denotes the smallest integer greater than or equal to l^*. [We
are not asserting that the *optimal* code necessarily uses these lengths,
we are simply choosing these lengths because we can use them to prove
the theorem.]

We check that there *is* a prefix code with these lengths by confirming
that the Kraft inequality is satisfied.

$$\sum_i 2^{-l_i} = \sum_i 2^{-\lceil \log_2(1/p_i) \rceil} \leq \sum_i 2^{-\log_2(1/p_i)} = \sum_i p_i = 1. \tag{5.21}$$

Then we confirm

$$L(C, X) = \sum_i p_i \lceil \log(1/p_i) \rceil < \sum_i p_i (\log(1/p_i) + 1) = H(X) + 1. \tag{5.22}$$

□

The cost of using the wrong codelengths

If we use a code whose lengths are not equal to the optimal codelengths, the
average message length will be larger than the entropy.

If the true probabilities are $\{p_i\}$ and we use a complete code with lengths
l_i, we can view those lengths as defining implicit probabilities $q_i = 2^{-l_i}$. Continuing from equation (5.14), the average length is

$$L(C, X) = H(X) + \sum_i p_i \log p_i/q_i, \tag{5.23}$$

i.e., it exceeds the entropy by the relative entropy $D_{\mathrm{KL}}(\mathbf{p}\|\mathbf{q})$ (as defined on
p.34).

x		$P(x)$
a	■	0.0575
b	·	0.0128
c	·	0.0263
d	·	0.0285
e	■	0.0913
f	·	0.0173
g	·	0.0133
h	·	0.0313
i	■	0.0599
j	·	0.0006
k	·	0.0084
l	·	0.0335
m	·	0.0235
n	■	0.0596
o	■	0.0689
p	·	0.0192
q	·	0.0008
r	■	0.0508
s	■	0.0567
t	■	0.0706
u	·	0.0334
v	·	0.0069
w	·	0.0119
x	·	0.0073
y	·	0.0164
z	·	0.0007
–	■	0.1928

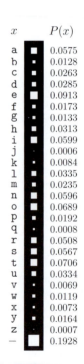

Figure 5.3. An ensemble in need of
a symbol code.

▶ 5.5 Optimal source coding with symbol codes: Huffman coding

Given a set of probabilities $\mathcal{P}$, how can we design an optimal prefix code?
For example, what is the best symbol code for the English language ensemble
shown in figure 5.3?   When we say 'optimal', let's assume our aim is to
minimize the expected length $L(C, X)$.

How not to do it

One might try to roughly split the set $\mathcal{A}_X$ in two, and continue bisecting the
subsets so as to define a binary tree from the root. This construction has the
right spirit, as in the weighing problem, but it is not necessarily optimal; it
achieves $L(C, X) \leq H(X) + 2$.

The Huffman coding algorithm

We now present a beautifully simple algorithm for finding an optimal prefix code. The trick is to construct the code *backwards* starting from the tails of the codewords; *we build the binary tree from its leaves.*

---

1. Take the two least probable symbols in the alphabet. These two symbols will be given the longest codewords, which will have equal length, and differ only in the last digit.

2. Combine these two symbols into a single symbol, and repeat.

Algorithm 5.4. Huffman coding algorithm.

Since each step reduces the size of the alphabet by one, this algorithm will have assigned strings to all the symbols after $|\mathcal{A}_X| - 1$ steps.

Example 5.15. Let $\quad \mathcal{A}_X = \{\, a, \quad b, \quad c, \quad d, \quad e \quad \}$
and $\quad \mathcal{P}_X = \{\, 0.25, 0.25, 0.2, 0.15, 0.15 \,\}$.

x	step 1	step 2	step 3	step 4
a	0.25 —	0.25 —	0.25 $\overset{0}{\nearrow}$	0.55 $\overset{0}{\nearrow}$ 1.0
b	0.25 —	0.25 $\overset{0}{\nearrow}$	0.45 $\diagup$	0.45 ⁄ 1
c	0.2 —	0.2 ⁄ 1		
d	0.15 $\overset{0}{\nearrow}$	0.3 —	0.3 ⁄ 1	
e	0.15 ⁄ 1			

a_i	p_i	$h(p_i)$	l_i	$c(a_i)$
a	0.25	2.0	2	00
b	0.25	2.0	2	10
c	0.2	2.3	2	11
d	0.15	2.7	3	010
e	0.15	2.7	3	011

Table 5.5. Code created by the Huffman algorithm.

The codewords are then obtained by concatenating the binary digits in reverse order: $C = \{00, 10, 11, 010, 011\}$. The codelengths selected by the Huffman algorithm (column 4 of table 5.5) are in some cases longer and in some cases shorter than the ideal codelengths, the Shannon information contents $\log_2 \frac{1}{p_i}$ (column 3). The expected length of the code is $L = 2.30$ bits, whereas the entropy is $H = 2.2855$ bits. □

If at any point there is more than one way of selecting the two least probable symbols then the choice may be made in any manner – the expected length of the code will not depend on the choice.

Exercise 5.16.[3, p. 105] Prove that there is no better symbol code for a source than the Huffman code.

Example 5.17. We can make a Huffman code for the probability distribution over the alphabet introduced in figure 2.1. The result is shown in figure 5.6. This code has an expected length of 4.15 bits; the entropy of the ensemble is 4.11 bits. Observe the disparities between the assigned codelengths and the ideal codelengths $\log_2 \frac{1}{p_i}$.

Constructing a binary tree top-down is suboptimal

In previous chapters we studied weighing problems in which we built ternary or binary trees. We noticed that balanced trees – ones in which, at every step, the two possible outcomes were as close as possible to equiprobable – appeared to describe the most efficient experiments. This gave an intuitive motivation for entropy as a measure of information content.

a_i	p_i	$\log_2 \frac{1}{p_i}$	l_i	$c(a_i)$
a	0.0575	4.1	4	0000
b	0.0128	6.3	6	001000
c	0.0263	5.2	5	00101
d	0.0285	5.1	5	10000
e	0.0913	3.5	4	1100
f	0.0173	5.9	6	111000
g	0.0133	6.2	6	001001
h	0.0313	5.0	5	10001
i	0.0599	4.1	4	1001
j	0.0006	10.7	10	1101000000
k	0.0084	6.9	7	1010000
l	0.0335	4.9	5	11101
m	0.0235	5.4	6	110101
n	0.0596	4.1	4	0001
o	0.0689	3.9	4	1011
p	0.0192	5.7	6	111001
q	0.0008	10.3	9	110100001
r	0.0508	4.3	5	11011
s	0.0567	4.1	4	0011
t	0.0706	3.8	4	1111
u	0.0334	4.9	5	10101
v	0.0069	7.2	8	11010001
w	0.0119	6.4	7	1101001
x	0.0073	7.1	7	1010001
y	0.0164	5.9	6	101001
z	0.0007	10.4	10	1101000001
–	0.1928	2.4	2	01

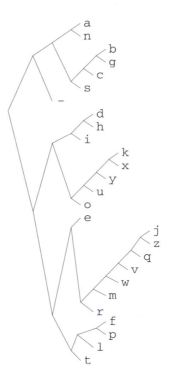

Figure 5.6. Huffman code for the English language ensemble (monogram statistics).

It is not the case, however, that optimal codes can *always* be constructed by a greedy top-down method in which the alphabet is successively divided into subsets that are as near as possible to equiprobable.

Example 5.18. Find the optimal binary symbol code for the ensemble:

$$\begin{array}{l} \mathcal{A}_X = \{ \text{ a, } \quad \text{b, } \quad \text{c, } \quad \text{d, } \quad \text{e, } \quad \text{f, } \quad \text{g } \} \\ \mathcal{P}_X = \{ 0.01, 0.24, 0.05, 0.20, 0.47, 0.01, 0.02 \} \end{array} . \qquad (5.24)$$

Notice that a greedy top-down method can split this set into two subsets $\{a, b, c, d\}$ and $\{e, f, g\}$ which both have probability 1/2, and that $\{a, b, c, d\}$ can be divided into subsets $\{a, b\}$ and $\{c, d\}$, which have probability 1/4; so a greedy top-down method gives the code shown in the third column of table 5.7, which has expected length 2.53. The Huffman coding algorithm yields the code shown in the fourth column, which has expected length 1.97. □

a_i	p_i	Greedy	Huffman
a	.01	000	000000
b	.24	001	01
c	.05	010	0001
d	.20	011	001
e	.47	10	1
f	.01	110	000001
g	.02	111	00001

Table 5.7. A greedily-constructed code compared with the Huffman code.

▶ 5.6 Disadvantages of the Huffman code

The Huffman algorithm produces an optimal symbol code for an ensemble, but this is not the end of the story. Both the word 'ensemble' and the phrase 'symbol code' need careful attention.

Changing ensemble

If we wish to communicate a sequence of outcomes from one unchanging ensemble, then a Huffman code may be convenient. But often the appropriate ensemble changes. If for example we are compressing text, then the symbol frequencies will vary with context: in English the letter u is much more probable after a q than after an e (figure 2.3). And furthermore, our knowledge of these context-dependent symbol frequencies will also change as we learn the statistical properties of the text source.

Huffman codes do not handle changing ensemble probabilities with any elegance. One brute-force approach would be to recompute the Huffman code every time the probability over symbols changes. Another attitude is to deny the option of adaptation, and instead run through the entire file in advance and compute a good probability distribution, which will then remain fixed throughout transmission. The code itself must also be communicated in this scenario. Such a technique is not only cumbersome and restrictive, it is also suboptimal, since the initial message specifying the code and the document itself are partially redundant. This technique therefore wastes bits.

The extra bit

An equally serious problem with Huffman codes is the innocuous-looking 'extra bit' relative to the ideal average length of $H(X)$ – a Huffman code achieves a length that satisfies $H(X) \leq L(C, X) < H(X)+1$, as proved in theorem 5.1. A Huffman code thus incurs an overhead of between 0 and 1 bits per symbol. If $H(X)$ were large, then this overhead would be an unimportant fractional increase. But for many applications, the entropy may be as low as one bit per symbol, or even smaller, so the overhead $L(C, X) - H(X)$ may dominate the encoded file length. Consider English text: in some contexts, long strings of characters may be highly predictable. For example, in the context 'strings_of_ch', one might predict the next nine symbols to be 'aracters_' with a probability of 0.99 each. A traditional Huffman code would be obliged to use at least one bit per character, making a total cost of nine bits where virtually no information is being conveyed (0.13 bits in total, to be precise). The entropy of English, given a good model, is about one bit per character (Shannon, 1948), so a Huffman code is likely to be highly inefficient.

A traditional patch-up of Huffman codes uses them to compress *blocks* of symbols, for example the 'extended sources' X^N we discussed in Chapter 4. The overhead per block is at most 1 bit so the overhead per symbol is at most $1/N$ bits. For sufficiently large blocks, the problem of the extra bit may be removed – but only at the expenses of (a) losing the elegant instantaneous decodeability of simple Huffman coding; and (b) having to compute the probabilities of all relevant strings and build the associated Huffman tree. One will end up explicitly computing the probabilities and codes for a huge number of strings, most of which will never actually occur. (See exercise 5.29 (p.103).)

Beyond symbol codes

Huffman codes, therefore, although widely trumpeted as 'optimal', have many defects for practical purposes. They *are* optimal *symbol* codes, but for practical purposes *we don't want a symbol code*.

The defects of Huffman codes are rectified by *arithmetic coding*, which dispenses with the restriction that each symbol must translate into an integer number of bits. Arithmetic coding is the main topic of the next chapter.

▶ **5.7 Summary**

Kraft inequality. If a code is *uniquely decodeable* its lengths must satisfy

$$\sum_i 2^{-l_i} \le 1. \tag{5.25}$$

For any lengths satisfying the Kraft inequality, there exists a prefix code with those lengths.

Optimal source codelengths for an ensemble are equal to the Shannon information contents

$$l_i = \log_2 \frac{1}{p_i}, \tag{5.26}$$

and conversely, any choice of codelengths defines *implicit probabilities*

$$q_i = \frac{2^{-l_i}}{z}. \tag{5.27}$$

The relative entropy $D_{\mathrm{KL}}(\mathbf{p}\|\mathbf{q})$ measures how many bits per symbol are wasted by using a code whose implicit probabilities are $\mathbf{q}$, when the ensemble's true probability distribution is $\mathbf{p}$.

Source coding theorem for symbol codes. For an ensemble X, there exists a prefix code whose expected length satisfies

$$H(X) \le L(C, X) < H(X) + 1. \tag{5.28}$$

The Huffman coding algorithm generates an optimal symbol code iteratively. At each iteration, the two least probable symbols are combined.

▶ **5.8 Exercises**

▷ Exercise 5.19.[2] Is the code $\{00, 11, 0101, 111, 1010, 100100, 0110\}$ uniquely decodeable?

▷ Exercise 5.20.[2] Is the ternary code $\{00, 012, 0110, 0112, 100, 201, 212, 22\}$ uniquely decodeable?

Exercise 5.21.[3, p.106] Make Huffman codes for X^2, X^3 and X^4 where $\mathcal{A}_X = \{0, 1\}$ and $\mathcal{P}_X = \{0.9, 0.1\}$. Compute their expected lengths and compare them with the entropies $H(X^2)$, $H(X^3)$ and $H(X^4)$.

Repeat this exercise for X^2 and X^4 where $\mathcal{P}_X = \{0.6, 0.4\}$.

Exercise 5.22.[2, p.106] Find a probability distribution $\{p_1, p_2, p_3, p_4\}$ such that there are *two* optimal codes that assign different lengths $\{l_i\}$ to the four symbols.

Exercise 5.23.[3] (Continuation of exercise 5.22.) Assume that the four probabilities $\{p_1, p_2, p_3, p_4\}$ are ordered such that $p_1 \ge p_2 \ge p_3 \ge p_4 \ge 0$. Let $\mathcal{Q}$ be the set of all probability vectors $\mathbf{p}$ such that there are *two* optimal codes with different lengths. Give a complete description of $\mathcal{Q}$. Find three probability vectors $\mathbf{q}^{(1)}$, $\mathbf{q}^{(2)}$, $\mathbf{q}^{(3)}$, which are the convex hull of $\mathcal{Q}$, i.e., such that any $\mathbf{p} \in \mathcal{Q}$ can be written as

$$\mathbf{p} = \mu_1 \mathbf{q}^{(1)} + \mu_2 \mathbf{q}^{(2)} + \mu_3 \mathbf{q}^{(3)}, \tag{5.29}$$

where $\{\mu_i\}$ are positive.

▷ Exercise 5.24.[1] Write a short essay discussing how to play the game of twenty questions optimally. [In twenty questions, one player thinks of an object, and the other player has to guess the object using as few binary questions as possible, preferably fewer than twenty.]

▷ Exercise 5.25.[2] Show that, if each probability p_i is equal to an integer power of 2 then there exists a source code whose expected length equals the entropy.

▷ Exercise 5.26.[2, p.106] Make ensembles for which the difference between the entropy and the expected length of the Huffman code is as big as possible.

▷ Exercise 5.27.[2, p.106] A binary source X has an alphabet of eleven characters

$$\{a, b, c, d, e, f, g, h, i, j, k\},$$

all of which have equal probability, $1/11$.

Find an optimal uniquely decodeable symbol code for this source. How much greater is the expected length of this optimal code than the entropy of X?

▷ Exercise 5.28.[2] Consider the optimal symbol code for an ensemble X with alphabet size I from which all symbols have identical probability $p = 1/I$. I is not a power of 2.

Show that the fraction f^+ of the I symbols that are assigned codelengths equal to

$$l^+ \equiv \lceil \log_2 I \rceil \tag{5.30}$$

satisfies

$$f^+ = 2 - \frac{2^{l^+}}{I} \tag{5.31}$$

and that the expected length of the optimal symbol code is

$$L = l^+ - 1 + f^+. \tag{5.32}$$

By differentiating the excess length $\Delta L \equiv L - H(X)$ with respect to I, show that the excess length is bounded by

$$\Delta L \leq 1 - \frac{\ln(\ln 2)}{\ln 2} - \frac{1}{\ln 2} = 0.086. \tag{5.33}$$

▷ Exercise 5.29.[2] Consider a sparse binary source with $\mathcal{P}_X = \{0.99, 0.01\}$. Discuss how Huffman codes could be used to compress this source *efficiently*. Estimate how many codewords your proposed solutions require.

▷ Exercise 5.30.[2] *Scientific American* carried the following puzzle in 1975.

The poisoned glass. 'Mathematicians are curious birds', the police commissioner said to his wife. 'You see, we had all those partly filled glasses lined up in rows on a table in the hotel kitchen. Only one contained poison, and we wanted to know which one before searching that glass for fingerprints. Our lab could test the liquid in each glass, but the tests take time and money, so we wanted to make as few of them as possible by simultaneously testing mixtures of small samples from groups of glasses. The university sent over a mathematics professor to help us. He counted the glasses, smiled and said:

' "Pick any glass you want, Commissioner. We'll test it first."

' "But won't that waste a test?" I asked.

' "No," he said, "it's part of the best procedure. We can test one glass first. It doesn't matter which one." '

'How many glasses were there to start with?' the commissioner's wife asked.

'I don't remember. Somewhere between 100 and 200.'

What was the exact number of glasses?

Solve this puzzle and then explain why the professor was in fact wrong and the commissioner was right. What is in fact the optimal procedure for identifying the one poisoned glass? What is the expected waste relative to this optimum if one followed the professor's strategy? Explain the relationship to symbol coding.

 Exercise 5.31.[2, p.106] Assume that a sequence of symbols from the ensemble X introduced at the beginning of this chapter is compressed using the code C_3. Imagine picking one bit at random from the binary encoded sequence $\mathbf{c} = c(x_1)c(x_2)c(x_3)\ldots$. What is the probability that this bit is a 1?

▷ Exercise 5.32.[2, p.107] How should the binary Huffman encoding scheme be modified to make optimal symbol codes in an encoding alphabet with q symbols? (Also known as 'radix q'.)

C_3:

a_i	$c(a_i)$	p_i	$h(p_i)$	l_i
a	0	$1/2$	1.0	1
b	10	$1/4$	2.0	2
c	110	$1/8$	3.0	3
d	111	$1/8$	3.0	3

Mixture codes

It is a tempting idea to construct a 'metacode' from several symbol codes that assign different-length codewords to the alternative symbols, then switch from one code to another, choosing whichever assigns the shortest codeword to the current symbol. Clearly we cannot do this for free. If one wishes to choose between two codes, then it is necessary to lengthen the message in a way that indicates which of the two codes is being used. If we indicate this choice by a single leading bit, it will be found that the resulting code is suboptimal because it is incomplete (that is, it fails the Kraft equality).

 Exercise 5.33.[3, p.108] Prove that this metacode is incomplete, and explain why this combined code is suboptimal.

▶ **5.9 Solutions**

Solution to exercise 5.8 (p.93).   Yes, $C_2 = \{1, 101\}$ is uniquely decodeable, even though it is not a prefix code, because no two different strings can map onto the same string; only the codeword $c(a_2) = 101$ contains the symbol 0.

Solution to exercise 5.14 (p.95).   We wish to prove that for any set of codeword lengths $\{l_i\}$ satisfying the Kraft inequality, there is a prefix code having those lengths. This is readily proved by thinking of the codewords illustrated in figure 5.8 as being in a 'codeword supermarket', with size indicating cost. We imagine purchasing codewords one at a time, starting from the shortest codewords (i.e., the biggest purchases), using the budget shown at the right of figure 5.8. We start at one side of the codeword supermarket, say the

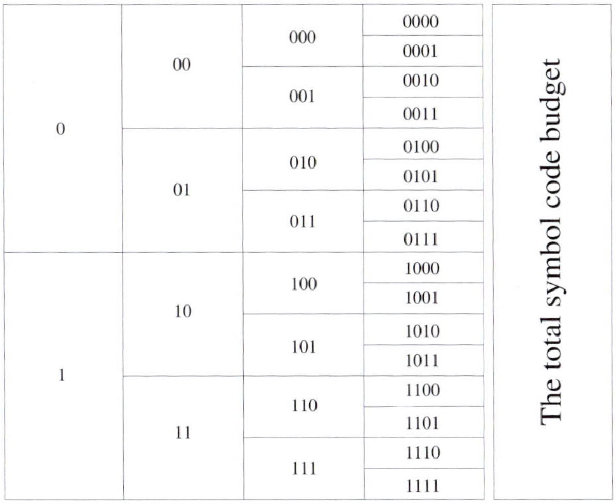

Figure 5.8. The codeword supermarket and the symbol coding budget. The 'cost' 2^{-l} of each codeword (with length l) is indicated by the size of the box it is written in. The total budget available when making a uniquely decodeable code is 1.

symbol	probability	Huffman codewords	Rival code's codewords	Modified rival code
a	p_a ☐	$c_{\mathrm{H}}(a)$	$c_{\mathrm{R}}(a)$	$c_{\mathrm{R}}(c)$
b	p_b ☐	$c_{\mathrm{H}}(b)$	$c_{\mathrm{R}}(b)$	$c_{\mathrm{R}}(b)$
c	p_c ☐	$c_{\mathrm{H}}(c)$	$c_{\mathrm{R}}(c)$	$c_{\mathrm{R}}(a)$

Figure 5.9. Proof that Huffman coding makes an optimal symbol code. We assume that the rival code, which is said to be optimal, assigns *unequal* length codewords to the two symbols with smallest probability, a and b. By interchanging codewords a and c of the rival code, where c is a symbol with rival codelength as long as b's, we can make a code better than the rival code. This shows that the rival code was not optimal.

top, and purchase the first codeword of the required length. We advance down the supermarket a distance 2^{-l}, and purchase the next codeword of the next required length, and so forth. Because the codeword lengths are getting longer, and the corresponding intervals are getting shorter, we can always buy an adjacent codeword to the latest purchase, so there is no wasting of the budget. Thus at the Ith codeword we have advanced a distance $\sum_{i=1}^{I} 2^{-l_i}$ down the supermarket; if $\sum 2^{-l_i} \leq 1$, we will have purchased all the codewords without running out of budget.

Solution to exercise 5.16 (p.99). The proof that Huffman coding is optimal depends on proving that the key step in the algorithm – the decision to give the two symbols with smallest probability equal encoded lengths – cannot lead to a larger expected length than any other code. We can prove this by contradiction.

Assume that the two symbols with smallest probability, called a and b, to which the Huffman algorithm would assign equal length codewords, do *not* have equal lengths in *any* optimal symbol code. The optimal symbol code is some other rival code in which these two codewords have unequal lengths l_a and l_b with $l_a < l_b$. Without loss of generality we can assume that this other code is a complete prefix code, because any codelengths of a uniquely decodeable code can be realized by a prefix code.

In this rival code, there must be some other symbol c whose probability p_c is greater than p_a and whose length in the rival code is greater than or equal to l_b, because the code for b must have an adjacent codeword of equal or greater length – a complete prefix code never has a solo codeword of the maximum length.

Consider exchanging the codewords of a and c (figure 5.9), so that a is encoded with the longer codeword that was c's, and c, which is more probable than a, gets the shorter codeword. Clearly this reduces the expected length of the code. The change in expected length is $(p_a - p_c)(l_c - l_a)$. Thus we have contradicted the assumption that the rival code is optimal. Therefore it is valid to give the two symbols with smallest probability equal encoded lengths. Huffman coding produces optimal symbol codes.   □

Solution to exercise 5.21 (p.102). A Huffman code for X^2 where $\mathcal{A}_X = \{0, 1\}$ and $\mathcal{P}_X = \{0.9, 0.1\}$ is $\{00, 01, 10, 11\} \rightarrow \{1, 01, 000, 001\}$. This code has $L(C, X^2) = 1.29$, whereas the entropy $H(X^2)$ is 0.938.

A Huffman code for X^3 is

$$\{000, 100, 010, 001, 101, 011, 110, 111\} \rightarrow$$
$$\{1, 011, 010, 001, 00000, 00001, 00010, 00011\}.$$

This has expected length $L(C, X^3) = 1.598$ whereas the entropy $H(X^3)$ is 1.4069.

A Huffman code for X^4 maps the sixteen source strings to the following codelengths:

$$\{0000, 1000, 0100, 0010, 0001, 1100, 0110, 0011, 0101, 1010, 1001, 1110, 1101,$$
$$1011, 0111, 1111\} \rightarrow \{1, 3, 3, 3, 4, 6, 7, 7, 7, 7, 7, 9, 9, 9, 10, 10\}.$$

This has expected length $L(C, X^4) = 1.9702$ whereas the entropy $H(X^4)$ is 1.876.

When $\mathcal{P}_X = \{0.6, 0.4\}$, the Huffman code for X^2 has lengths $\{2, 2, 2, 2\}$; the expected length is 2 bits, and the entropy is 1.94 bits. A Huffman code for X^4 is shown in table 5.10. The expected length is 3.92 bits, and the entropy is 3.88 bits.

a_i	p_i	l_i	$c(a_i)$
0000	0.1296	3	000
0001	0.0864	4	0100
0010	0.0864	4	0110
0100	0.0864	4	0111
1000	0.0864	3	100
1100	0.0576	4	1010
1010	0.0576	4	1100
1001	0.0576	4	1101
0110	0.0576	4	1110
0101	0.0576	4	1111
0011	0.0576	4	0010
1110	0.0384	5	00110
1101	0.0384	5	01010
1011	0.0384	5	01011
0111	0.0384	4	1011
1111	0.0256	5	00111

Table 5.10. Huffman code for X^4 when $p_0 = 0.6$. Column 3 shows the assigned codelengths and column 4 the codewords. Some strings whose probabilities are identical, e.g., the fourth and fifth, receive different codelengths.

Solution to exercise 5.22 (p.102). The set of probabilities $\{p_1, p_2, p_3, p_4\} = \{1/6, 1/6, 1/3, 1/3\}$ gives rise to two different optimal sets of codelengths, because at the second step of the Huffman coding algorithm we can choose any of the three possible pairings. We may either put them in a constant length code $\{00, 01, 10, 11\}$ or the code $\{000, 001, 01, 1\}$. Both codes have expected length 2.

Another solution is $\{p_1, p_2, p_3, p_4\} = \{1/5, 1/5, 1/5, 2/5\}$.
And a third is $\{p_1, p_2, p_3, p_4\} = \{1/3, 1/3, 1/3, 0\}$.

Solution to exercise 5.26 (p.103). Let $p_{\max}$ be the largest probability in $p_1, p_2, \ldots, p_I$. The difference between the expected length L and the entropy H can be no bigger than $\max(p_{\max}, 0.086)$ (Gallager, 1978).

See exercises 5.27–5.28 to understand where the curious 0.086 comes from.

Solution to exercise 5.27 (p.103). Length $-$ entropy $= 0.086$.

Solution to exercise 5.31 (p.104). There are two ways to answer this problem correctly, and one popular way to answer it incorrectly. Let's give the incorrect answer first:

Erroneous answer. "We can pick a random bit by first picking a random source symbol x_i with probability p_i, then picking a random bit from $c(x_i)$. If we define f_i to be the fraction of the bits of $c(x_i)$ that are 1s, we find

$$P(\text{bit is 1}) = \sum_i p_i f_i \qquad (5.34)$$

$$= 1/2 \times 0 + 1/4 \times 1/2 + 1/8 \times 2/3 + 1/8 \times 1 = 1/3." \qquad (5.35)$$

	a_i	$c(a_i)$	p_i	l_i
C_3:	a	0	$1/2$	1
	b	10	$1/4$	2
	c	110	$1/8$	3
	d	111	$1/8$	3

This answer is wrong because it falls for the bus-stop fallacy, which was introduced in exercise 2.35 (p.38): if buses arrive at random, and we are interested in 'the average time from one bus until the next', we must distinguish two possible averages: (a) the average time from a randomly chosen bus until the next; (b) the average time between the bus you just missed and the next bus. The second 'average' is twice as big as the first because, by waiting for a bus at a random time, you bias your selection of a bus in favour of buses that follow a large gap. You're unlikely to catch a bus that comes 10 seconds after a preceding bus! Similarly, the symbols c and d get encoded into longer-length binary strings than a, so when we pick a bit from the compressed string at random, we are more likely to land in a bit belonging to a c or a d than would be given by the probabilities p_i in the expectation (5.34). All the probabilities need to be scaled up by l_i, and renormalized.

Correct answer in the same style. Every time symbol x_i is encoded, l_i bits are added to the binary string, of which $f_i l_i$ are 1s. The expected number of 1s added per symbol is

$$\sum_i p_i f_i l_i; \tag{5.36}$$

and the expected total number of bits added per symbol is

$$\sum_i p_i l_i. \tag{5.37}$$

So the fraction of 1s in the transmitted string is

$$P(\text{bit is 1}) = \frac{\sum_i p_i f_i l_i}{\sum_i p_i l_i} \tag{5.38}$$

$$= \frac{1/2 \times 0 + 1/4 \times 1 + 1/8 \times 2 + 1/8 \times 3}{7/4} = \frac{7/8}{7/4} = 1/2.$$

For a general symbol code and a general ensemble, the expectation (5.38) is the correct answer. But in this case, we can use a more powerful argument.

Information-theoretic answer. The encoded string $\mathbf{c}$ is the output of an optimal compressor that compresses samples from X down to an expected length of $H(X)$ bits. We can't expect to compress this data any further. But if the probability $P(\text{bit is 1})$ were not equal to $1/2$ then it *would* be possible to compress the binary string further (using a block compression code, say). Therefore $P(\text{bit is 1})$ must be equal to $1/2$; indeed the probability of any sequence of l bits in the compressed stream taking on any particular value must be 2^{-l}. The output of a perfect compressor is always perfectly random bits.

To put it another way, if the probability $P(\text{bit is 1})$ were not equal to $1/2$, then the information content per bit of the compressed string would be at most $H_2(P(1))$, which would be less than 1; but this contradicts the fact that we can recover the original data from $\mathbf{c}$, so the information content per bit of the compressed string must be $H(X)/L(C, X) = 1$.

Solution to exercise 5.32 (p.104). The general Huffman coding algorithm for an encoding alphabet with q symbols has one difference from the binary case. The process of combining q symbols into 1 symbol reduces the number of symbols by $q-1$. So if we start with A symbols, we'll only end up with a complete q-ary tree if $A \bmod (q-1)$ is equal to 1. Otherwise, we know that whatever prefix code we make, it must be an incomplete tree with a number of missing leaves equal, modulo $(q-1)$, to $A \bmod (q-1) - 1$. For example, if a ternary tree is built for eight symbols, then there will unavoidably be one missing leaf in the tree.

The optimal q-ary code is made by putting these extra leaves in the longest branch of the tree. This can be achieved by adding the appropriate number of symbols to the original source symbol set, all of these extra symbols having probability zero. The total number of leaves is then equal to $r(q-1) + 1$, for some integer r. The symbols are then repeatedly combined by taking the q symbols with smallest probability and replacing them by a single symbol, as in the binary Huffman coding algorithm.

Solution to exercise 5.33 (p.104). We wish to show that a greedy metacode, which picks the code which gives the shortest encoding, is actually suboptimal, because it violates the Kraft inequality.

We'll assume that each symbol x is assigned lengths $l_k(x)$ by each of the candidate codes C_k. Let us assume there are K alternative codes and that we can encode which code is being used with a header of length $\log K$ bits. Then the metacode assigns lengths $l'(x)$ that are given by

$$l'(x) = \log_2 K + \min_k l_k(x). \qquad (5.39)$$

We compute the Kraft sum:

$$S = \sum_x 2^{-l'(x)} = \frac{1}{K} \sum_x 2^{-\min_k l_k(x)}. \qquad (5.40)$$

Let's divide the set $\mathcal{A}_X$ into non-overlapping subsets $\{\mathcal{A}_k\}_{k=1}^K$ such that subset $\mathcal{A}_k$ contains all the symbols x that the metacode sends via code k. Then

$$S = \frac{1}{K} \sum_k \sum_{x \in \mathcal{A}_k} 2^{-l_k(x)}. \qquad (5.41)$$

Now if one sub-code k satisfies the Kraft equality $\sum_{x \in \mathcal{A}_X} 2^{-l_k(x)} = 1$, then it must be the case that

$$\sum_{x \in \mathcal{A}_k} 2^{-l_k(x)} \leq 1, \qquad (5.42)$$

with equality only if all the symbols x are in $\mathcal{A}_k$, which would mean that we are only using one of the K codes. So

$$S \leq \frac{1}{K} \sum_{k=1}^K 1 = 1, \qquad (5.43)$$

with equality only if equation (5.42) is an equality for all codes k. But it's impossible for all the symbols to be in *all* the non-overlapping subsets $\{\mathcal{A}_k\}_{k=1}^K$, so we can't have equality (5.42) holding for *all* k. So $S < 1$.

Another way of seeing that a mixture code is suboptimal is to consider the binary tree that it defines. Think of the special case of two codes. The first bit we send identifies which code we are using. Now, in a complete code, any subsequent binary string is a valid string. But once we know that we are using, say, code A, we know that what follows can only be a codeword corresponding to a symbol x whose encoding is shorter under code A than code B. So some strings are invalid continuations, and the mixture code is incomplete and suboptimal.

For further discussion of this issue and its relationship to probabilistic modelling read about 'bits back coding' in section 28.3 and in Frey (1998).

About Chapter 6

Before reading Chapter 6, you should have read the previous chapter and worked on most of the exercises in it.

We'll also make use of some Bayesian modelling ideas that arrived in the vicinity of exercise 2.8 (p.30).

6

Stream Codes

In this chapter we discuss two data compression schemes.

Arithmetic coding is a beautiful method that goes hand in hand with the philosophy that compression of data from a source entails probabilistic modelling of that source. As of 1999, the best compression methods for text files use arithmetic coding, and several state-of-the-art image compression systems use it too.

Lempel–Ziv coding is a 'universal' method, designed under the philosophy that we would like a single compression algorithm that will do a reasonable job for *any* source. In fact, for many real life sources, this algorithm's universal properties hold only in the limit of unfeasibly large amounts of data, but, all the same, Lempel–Ziv compression is widely used and often effective.

▶ 6.1 The guessing game

As a motivation for these two compression methods, consider the redundancy in a typical English text file. Such files have redundancy at several levels: for example, they contain the ASCII characters with non-equal frequency; certain consecutive pairs of letters are more probable than others; and entire words can be predicted given the context and a semantic understanding of the text.

To illustrate the redundancy of English, and a curious way in which it could be compressed, we can imagine a guessing game in which an English speaker repeatedly attempts to predict the next character in a text file.

For simplicity, let us assume that the allowed alphabet consists of the 26 upper case letters A,B,C,..., Z and a space '-'. The game involves asking the subject to guess the next character repeatedly, the only feedback being whether the guess is correct or not, until the character is correctly guessed. After a correct guess, we note the number of guesses that were made when the character was identified, and ask the subject to guess the next character in the same way.

One sentence gave the following result when a human was asked to guess a sentence. The numbers of guesses are listed below each character.

```
T H E R E - I S - N O - R E V E R S E - O N - A - M O T O R C Y C L E -
1 1 1 5 1 1 2 1 1 2 1 1 15 1 17 1 1 1 2 1 3 2 1 2 2 7 1 1 1 1 4 1 1 1 1 1
```

Notice that in many cases, the next letter is guessed immediately, in one guess. In other cases, particularly at the start of syllables, more guesses are needed.

What do this game and these results offer us? First, they demonstrate the redundancy of English from the point of view of an English speaker. Second, this game might be used in a data compression scheme, as follows.

The string of numbers '1, 1, 1, 5, 1, ...', listed above, was obtained by presenting the text to the subject. The maximum number of guesses that the subject will make for a given letter is twenty-seven, so what the subject is doing for us is performing a time-varying mapping of the twenty-seven letters $\{A, B, C, \ldots, Z, -\}$ onto the twenty-seven numbers $\{1, 2, 3, \ldots, 27\}$, which we can view as symbols in a new alphabet. The total number of symbols has not been reduced, but since he uses some of these symbols much more frequently than others – for example, 1 and 2 – it should be easy to compress this new string of symbols.

How would the *uncompression* of the sequence of numbers '1, 1, 1, 5, 1, ...' work? At uncompression time, we do not have the original string 'THERE...', we have only the encoded sequence. Imagine that our subject has an absolutely identical twin who also plays the guessing game with us, as if we knew the source text. If we stop him whenever he has made a number of guesses equal to the given number, then he will have just guessed the correct letter, and we can then say 'yes, that's right', and move to the next character. Alternatively, if the identical twin is not available, we could design a compression system with the help of just one human as follows. We choose a window length L, that is, a number of characters of context to show the human. For every one of the 27^L possible strings of length L, we ask them, 'What would you predict is the next character?', and 'If that prediction were wrong, what would your next guesses be?'. After tabulating their answers to these 26×27^L questions, we could use two copies of these enormous tables at the encoder and the decoder in place of the two human twins. Such a language model is called an Lth order Markov model.

These systems are clearly unrealistic for practical compression, but they illustrate several principles that we will make use of now.

▶ 6.2 Arithmetic codes

When we discussed variable-length symbol codes, and the optimal Huffman algorithm for constructing them, we concluded by pointing out two practical and theoretical problems with Huffman codes (section 5.6).

These defects are rectified by *arithmetic codes*, which were invented by Elias, by Rissanen and by Pasco, and subsequently made practical by Witten *et al.* (1987). In an arithmetic code, the probabilistic modelling is clearly separated from the encoding operation. The system is rather similar to the guessing game. The human predictor is replaced by a *probabilistic model* of the source. As each symbol is produced by the source, the probabilistic model supplies a *predictive distribution* over all possible values of the next symbol, that is, a list of positive numbers $\{p_i\}$ that sum to one. If we choose to model the source as producing i.i.d. symbols with some known distribution, then the predictive distribution is the same every time; but arithmetic coding can with equal ease handle complex adaptive models that produce context-dependent predictive distributions. The predictive model is usually implemented in a computer program.

The encoder makes use of the model's predictions to create a binary string. The decoder makes use of an identical twin of the model (just as in the guessing game) to interpret the binary string.

Let the source alphabet be $\mathcal{A}_X = \{a_1, \ldots, a_I\}$, and let the Ith symbol a_I have the special meaning 'end of transmission'. The source spits out a sequence $x_1, x_2, \ldots, x_n, \ldots$. The source does *not* necessarily produce i.i.d. symbols. We will assume that a computer program is provided to the encoder that assigns a predictive probability distribution over a_i given the sequence that has occurred thus far, $P(x_n = a_i \mid x_1, \dots, x_{n-1})$. The receiver has an identical program that produces the same predictive probability distribution $P(x_n = a_i \mid x_1, \dots, x_{n-1})$.

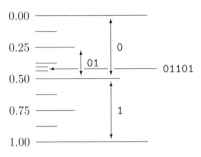

Figure 6.1. Binary strings define real intervals within the real line $[0,1)$. We first encountered a picture like this when we discussed the symbol-code supermarket in Chapter 5.

Concepts for understanding arithmetic coding

> Notation for intervals. The interval $[0.01, 0.10)$ is all numbers between 0.01 and 0.10, including $0.01\dot{0} \equiv 0.01000\dots$ but not $0.10\dot{0} \equiv 0.10000\dots$.

A binary transmission defines an interval within the real line from 0 to 1. For example, the string 01 is interpreted as a binary real number $0.01\dots$, which corresponds to the interval $[0.01, 0.10)$ in binary, i.e., the interval $[0.25, 0.50)$ in base ten.

The longer string 01101 corresponds to a smaller interval $[0.01101, 0.01110)$. Because 01101 has the first string, 01, as a prefix, the new interval is a sub-interval of the interval $[0.01, 0.10)$. A one-megabyte binary file (2^{23} bits) is thus viewed as specifying a number between 0 and 1 to a precision of about two million decimal places – two million decimal digits, because each byte translates into a little more than two decimal digits.

Now, we can also divide the real line $[0,1)$ into I intervals of lengths equal to the probabilities $P(x_1 = a_i)$, as shown in figure 6.2.

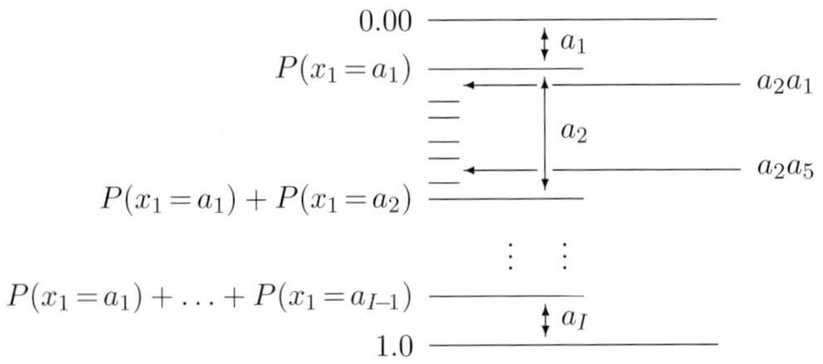

$$0.00 \quad \overline{} \quad a_1$$
$$P(x_1 = a_1) \quad \overline{} \quad a_2 a_1$$
$$a_2$$
$$a_2 a_5$$
$$P(x_1 = a_1) + P(x_1 = a_2) \quad \overline{}$$
$$P(x_1 = a_1) + \dots + P(x_1 = a_{I-1}) \quad \overline{} \quad a_I$$
$$1.0 \quad \overline{}$$

Figure 6.2. A probabilistic model defines real intervals within the real line $[0,1)$.

We may then take each interval a_i and subdivide it into intervals denoted $a_i a_1, a_i a_2, \dots, a_i a_I$, such that the length of $a_i a_j$ is proportional to $P(x_2 = a_j \mid x_1 = a_i)$. Indeed the length of the interval $a_i a_j$ will be precisely the joint probability

$$P(x_1 = a_i, x_2 = a_j) = P(x_1 = a_i)P(x_2 = a_j \mid x_1 = a_i). \qquad (6.1)$$

Iterating this procedure, the interval $[0, 1)$ can be divided into a sequence of intervals corresponding to all possible finite length strings $x_1 x_2 \dots x_N$, such that the length of an interval is equal to the probability of the string given our model.

```
u := 0.0
v := 1.0
p := v - u
for n = 1 to N {
        Compute the cumulative probabilities Qₙ and Rₙ (6.2, 6.3)
        v := u + pRₙ(xₙ | x₁, ..., xₙ₋₁)
        u := u + pQₙ(xₙ | x₁, ..., xₙ₋₁)
        p := v - u
}
```

Algorithm 6.3. Arithmetic coding. Iterative procedure to find the interval $[u, v)$ for the string $x_1 x_2 \ldots x_N$.

Formulae describing arithmetic coding

The process depicted in figure 6.2 can be written explicitly as follows. The intervals are defined in terms of the lower and upper cumulative probabilities

$$Q_n(a_i \,|\, x_1, \ldots, x_{n-1}) \;\equiv\; \sum_{i'=1}^{i-1} P(x_n = a_{i'} \,|\, x_1, \ldots, x_{n-1}), \qquad (6.2)$$

$$R_n(a_i \,|\, x_1, \ldots, x_{n-1}) \;\equiv\; \sum_{i'=1}^{i} P(x_n = a_{i'} \,|\, x_1, \ldots, x_{n-1}). \qquad (6.3)$$

As the nth symbol arrives, we subdivide the $n{-}1$th interval at the points defined by Q_n and R_n. For example, starting with the first symbol, the intervals 'a_1', 'a_2', and 'a_I' are

$$a_1 \leftrightarrow [Q_1(a_1), R_1(a_1)) = [0, P(x_1 = a_1)), \qquad (6.4)$$

$$a_2 \leftrightarrow [Q_1(a_2), R_1(a_2)) = [P(x = a_1), P(x = a_1) + P(x = a_2)), \qquad (6.5)$$

and

$$a_I \leftrightarrow [Q_1(a_I), R_1(a_I)) = [P(x_1 = a_1) + \ldots + P(x_1 = a_{I-1}), 1.0). \qquad (6.6)$$

Algorithm 6.3 describes the general procedure.

To encode a string $x_1 x_2 \ldots x_N$, we locate the interval corresponding to $x_1 x_2 \ldots x_N$, and send a binary string whose interval lies within that interval. This encoding can be performed on the fly, as we now illustrate.

Example: compressing the tosses of a bent coin

Imagine that we watch as a bent coin is tossed some number of times (c.f. example 2.7 (p.30) and section 3.2 (p.51)). The two outcomes when the coin is tossed are denoted a and b. A third possibility is that the experiment is halted, an event denoted by the 'end of file' symbol, '□'. Because the coin is bent, we expect that the probabilities of the outcomes a and b are not equal, though beforehand we don't know which is the more probable outcome.

Encoding

Let the source string be 'bbba□'. We pass along the string one symbol at a time and use our model to compute the probability distribution of the next symbol given the string thus far. Let these probabilities be:

Context (sequence thus far)	Probability of next symbol		
	$P(\mathsf{a})=0.425$	$P(\mathsf{b})=0.425$	$P(\square)=0.15$
b	$P(\mathsf{a}\,|\,\mathsf{b})=0.28$	$P(\mathsf{b}\,|\,\mathsf{b})=0.57$	$P(\square\,|\,\mathsf{b})=0.15$
bb	$P(\mathsf{a}\,|\,\mathsf{bb})=0.21$	$P(\mathsf{b}\,|\,\mathsf{bb})=0.64$	$P(\square\,|\,\mathsf{bb})=0.15$
bbb	$P(\mathsf{a}\,|\,\mathsf{bbb})=0.17$	$P(\mathsf{b}\,|\,\mathsf{bbb})=0.68$	$P(\square\,|\,\mathsf{bbb})=0.15$
bbba	$P(\mathsf{a}\,|\,\mathsf{bbba})=0.28$	$P(\mathsf{b}\,|\,\mathsf{bbba})=0.57$	$P(\square\,|\,\mathsf{bbba})=0.15$

Figure 6.4 shows the corresponding intervals. The interval b is the middle 0.425 of $[0,1)$. The interval bb is the middle 0.567 of b, and so forth.

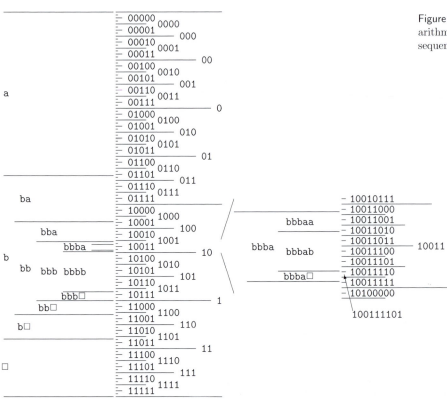

Figure 6.4. Illustration of the arithmetic coding process as the sequence bbba□ is transmitted.

When the first symbol 'b' is observed, the encoder knows that the encoded string will start '01', '10', or '11', but does not know which. The encoder writes nothing for the time being, and examines the next symbol, which is 'b'. The interval 'bb' lies wholly within interval '1', so the encoder can write the first bit: '1'. The third symbol 'b' narrows down the interval a little, but not quite enough for it to lie wholly within interval '10'. Only when the next 'a' is read from the source can we transmit some more bits. Interval 'bbba' lies wholly within the interval '1001', so the encoder adds '001' to the '1' it has written. Finally when the '□' arrives, we need a procedure for terminating the encoding. Magnifying the interval 'bbba□' (figure 6.4, right) we note that the marked interval '100111101' is wholly contained by bbba□, so the encoding can be completed by appending '11101'.

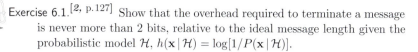

Exercise 6.1.[2, p.127] Show that the overhead required to terminate a message is never more than 2 bits, relative to the ideal message length given the probabilistic model $\mathcal{H}$, $h(\mathbf{x}\,|\,\mathcal{H}) = \log[1/P(\mathbf{x}\,|\,\mathcal{H})]$.

This is an important result. Arithmetic coding is very nearly optimal. The message length is always within two bits of the Shannon information content of the entire source string, so the expected message length is within two bits of the entropy of the entire message.

Decoding

The decoder receives the string '100111101' and passes along it one symbol at a time. First, the probabilities $P(a), P(b), P(\Box)$ are computed using the identical program that the encoder used and the intervals 'a', 'b' and '$\Box$' are deduced. Once the first two bits '10' have been examined, it is certain that the original string must have been started with a 'b', since the interval '10' lies wholly within interval 'b'. The decoder can then use the model to compute $P(a\,|\,b), P(b\,|\,b), P(\Box\,|\,b)$ and deduce the boundaries of the intervals 'ba', 'bb' and 'b$\Box$'. Continuing, we decode the second b once we reach '1001', the third b once we reach '100111', and so forth, with the unambiguous identification of 'bbba$\Box$' once the whole binary string has been read. With the convention that '$\Box$' denotes the end of the message, the decoder knows to stop decoding.

Transmission of multiple files

How might one use arithmetic coding to communicate several distinct files over the binary channel? Once the $\Box$ character has been transmitted, we imagine that the decoder is reset into its initial state. There is no transfer of the learnt statistics of the first file to the second file. If, however, we did believe that there is a relationship among the files that we are going to compress, we could define our alphabet differently, introducing a second end-of-file character that marks the end of the file but instructs the encoder and decoder to continue using the same probabilistic model.

The big picture

Notice that to communicate a string of N letters both the encoder and the decoder needed to compute only $N|\mathcal{A}|$ conditional probabilities – the probabilities of each possible letter in each context actually encountered – just as in the guessing game. This cost can be contrasted with the alternative of using a Huffman code with a large block size (in order to reduce the possible one-bit-per-symbol overhead discussed in section 5.6), where *all* block sequences that could occur must be considered and their probabilities evaluated.

Notice how flexible arithmetic coding is: it can be used with any source alphabet and any encoded alphabet. The size of the source alphabet and the encoded alphabet can change with time. Arithmetic coding can be used with any probability distribution, which can change utterly from context to context.

Furthermore, if we would like the symbols of the encoding alphabet (say, 0 and 1) to be used with *unequal* frequency, that can easily be arranged by subdividing the right-hand interval in proportion to the required frequencies.

How the probabilistic model might make its predictions

The technique of arithmetic coding does not force one to produce the predictive probability in any particular way, but the predictive distributions might

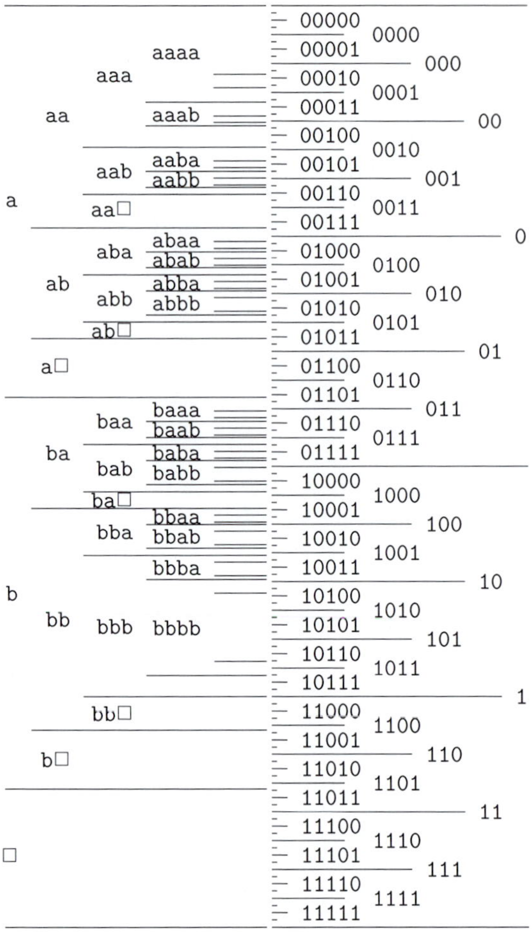

Figure 6.5. Illustration of the intervals defined by a simple Bayesian probabilistic model. The size of an intervals is proportional to the probability of the string. This model anticipates that the source is likely to be biased towards one of a and b, so sequences having lots of as or lots of bs have larger intervals than sequences of the same length that are 50:50 as and bs.

naturally be produced by a Bayesian model.

Figure 6.4 was generated using a simple model that always assigns a probability of 0.15 to □, and assigns the remaining 0.85 to a and b, divided in proportion to probabilities given by Laplace's rule,

$$P_{\mathrm{L}}(\mathsf{a}\,|\,x_1,\ldots,x_{n-1}) = \frac{F_\mathsf{a}+1}{F_\mathsf{a}+F_\mathsf{b}+2},\qquad(6.7)$$

where $F_\mathsf{a}(x_1,\ldots,x_{n-1})$ is the number of times that a has occurred so far, and F_b is the count of bs. These predictions corresponds to a simple Bayesian model that expects and adapts to a non-equal frequency of use of the source symbols a and b within a file.

Figure 6.5 displays the intervals corresponding to a number of strings of length up to five. Note that if the string so far has contained a large number of bs then the probability of b relative to a is increased, and conversely if many as occur then as are made more probable. Larger intervals, remember, require fewer bits to encode.

Details of the Bayesian model

Having emphasized that any model could be used – arithmetic coding is not wedded to any particular set of probabilities – let me explain the simple adaptive probabilistic model used in the preceding example; we first encountered this model in exercise 2.8 (p.30).

Assumptions

The model will be described using parameters $p_\square$, p_a and p_b, defined below, which should not be confused with the predictive probabilities *in a particular context*, for example, $P(a \mid s = baa)$. A bent coin labelled a and b is tossed some number of times l, which we don't know beforehand. The coin's probability of coming up a when tossed is p_a, and $p_b = 1 - p_a$; the parameters p_a, p_b are not known beforehand. The source string $s = baaba\square$ indicates that l was 5 and the sequence of outcomes was baaba.

1. It is assumed that the length of the string l has an exponential probability distribution

$$P(l) = (1 - p_\square)^l p_\square. \qquad (6.8)$$

   This distribution corresponds to assuming a constant probability $p_\square$ for the termination symbol '$\square$' at each character.

2. It is assumed that the non-terminal characters in the string are selected independently at random from an ensemble with probabilities $\mathcal{P} = \{p_a, p_b\}$; the probability p_a is fixed throughout the string to some unknown value that could be anywhere between 0 and 1. The probability of an a occurring as the next symbol, given p_a (if only we knew it), is $(1 - p_\square)p_a$. The probability, given p_a, that an unterminated string of length F is a given string s that contains $\{F_a, F_b\}$ counts of the two outcomes is the Bernoulli distribution

$$P(s \mid p_a, F) = p_a^{F_a}(1 - p_a)^{F_b}. \qquad (6.9)$$

3. We assume a uniform prior distribution for p_a,

$$P(p_a) = 1, \qquad p_a \in [0, 1] \qquad (6.10)$$

   and $p_b \equiv 1 - p_a$. It would be easy to assume other priors on p_a, with beta distributions being the most convenient to handle.

This model was studied in section 3.2. The key result we require is the predictive distribution for the next symbol, given the string so far, s. This probability of an a or b being the next character (assuming that it is not '$\square$') was derived in equation (3.16) and is precisely Laplace's rule (6.7).

▷ Exercise 6.2.[3] Compare the expected message length when an ASCII file is compressed by the following three methods.

Huffman-with-header. Read the whole file, find the empirical frequency of each symbol, construct a Huffman code for those frequencies, transmit the code by transmitting the lengths of the Huffman codewords, then transmit the file using the Huffman code. (The actual codewords don't need to be transmitted, since we can use a deterministic method for building the tree given the codelengths.)

Arithmetic code using the Laplace model.

$$P_L(a \mid x_1, \ldots, x_{n-1}) = \frac{F_a + 1}{\sum_{a'}(F_{a'} + 1)}. \qquad (6.11)$$

Arithmetic code using a Dirichlet model. This model's predictions are:

$$P_D(a \mid x_1, \ldots, x_{n-1}) = \frac{F_a + \alpha}{\sum_{a'}(F_{a'} + \alpha)}, \qquad (6.12)$$

where α is fixed to a number such as 0.01. This corresponds to a more responsive version of the Laplace model; the probability over characters is expected to be more nonuniform; $\alpha = 1$ reproduces the Laplace model.

Take care that the header of your Huffman message is self-delimiting. Special cases worth considering are (a) short files with just a few hundred characters; (b) large files in which some characters are never used.

▶ 6.3 Further applications of arithmetic coding

Efficient generation of random samples

Arithmetic coding not only offers a way to compress strings believed to come from a given model; it also offers a way to generate random strings from a model. Imagine sticking a pin into the unit interval at random, that line having been divided into subintervals in proportion to probabilities p_i; the probability that your pin will lie in interval i is p_i.

So to generate a sample from a model, all we need to do is feed ordinary random bits into an arithmetic *decoder* for that model. An infinite random bit sequence corresponds to the selection of a point at random from the line $[0, 1)$, so the decoder will then select a string at random from the assumed distribution. This arithmetic method is guaranteed to use very nearly the smallest number of random bits possible to make the selection – an important point in communities where random numbers are expensive! [This is not a joke. Large amounts of money are spent on generating random bits in software and hardware. Random numbers are valuable.]

A simple example of the use of this technique is in the generation of random bits with a nonuniform distribution $\{p_0, p_1\}$.

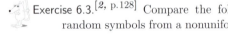 Exercise 6.3.[2, p. 128] Compare the following two techniques for generating random symbols from a nonuniform distribution $\{p_0, p_1\} = \{0.99, 0.01\}$:

(a) The standard method: use a standard random number generator to generate an integer between 1 and 2^{32}. Rescale the integer to $(0, 1)$. Test whether this uniformly distributed random variable is less than 0.99, and emit a 0 or 1 accordingly.

(b) Arithmetic coding using the correct model, fed with standard random bits.

Roughly how many random bits will each method use to generate a thousand samples from this sparse distribution?

Efficient data-entry devices

When we enter text into a computer, we make gestures of some sort – maybe we tap a keyboard, or scribble with a pointer, or click with a mouse; an *efficient* text entry system is one where the number of gestures required to enter a given text string is *small*.

Writing can be viewed as an inverse process to data compression. In data compression, the aim is to map a given text string into a *small* number of bits. In text entry, we want a small sequence of gestures to produce our intended text.

By inverting an arithmetic coder, we can obtain an information-efficient text entry device that is driven by continuous pointing gestures (Ward *et al.*,

Compression:
text $\rightarrow$ bits

Writing:
text $\leftarrow$ gestures

2000). In this system, called Dasher, the user zooms in on the unit interval to locate the interval corresponding to their intended string, in the same style as figure 6.4. A language model (exactly as used in text compression) controls the sizes of the intervals such that probable strings are quick and easy to identify. After an hour's practice, a novice user can write with one finger driving Dasher at about 25 words per minute – that's about half their normal ten-finger typing speed on a regular keyboard. It's even possible to write at 25 words per minute, *hands-free*, using gaze direction to drive Dasher (Ward and MacKay, 2002). Dasher is available as free software for various platforms.[1]

▶ ## 6.4 Lempel–Ziv coding

The Lempel–Ziv algorithms, which are widely used for data compression (e.g., the `compress` and `gzip` commands), are different in philosophy to arithmetic coding. There is no separation between modelling and coding, and no opportunity for explicit modelling.

Basic Lempel–Ziv algorithm

The method of compression is to replace a substring with a pointer to an earlier occurrence of the same substring. For example if the string is `1011010100010...`, we parse it into an ordered *dictionary* of substrings that have not appeared before as follows: λ, 1, 0, 11, 01, 010, 00, 10, ... We include the empty substring λ as the first substring in the dictionary and order the substrings in the dictionary by the order in which they emerged from the source. After every comma, we look along the next part of the input sequence until we have read a substring that has not been marked off before. A moment's reflection will confirm that this substring is longer by one bit than a substring that has occurred earlier in the dictionary. This means that we can encode each substring by giving a *pointer* to the earlier occurrence of that prefix and then sending the extra bit by which the new substring in the dictionary differs from the earlier substring. If, at the nth bit, we have enumerated $s(n)$ substrings, then we can give the value of the pointer in $\lceil \log_2 s(n) \rceil$ bits. The code for the above sequence is then as shown in the fourth line of the following table (with punctuation included for clarity), the upper lines indicating the source string and the value of $s(n)$:

source substrings	λ	1	0	11	01	010	00	10
$s(n)$	0	1	2	3	4	5	6	7
$s(n)_{\text{binary}}$	000	001	010	011	100	101	110	111
(pointer, bit)		(, 1)	(0, 0)	(01, 1)	(10, 1)	(100, 0)	(010, 0)	(001, 0)

Notice that the first pointer we send is empty, because, given that there is only one substring in the dictionary – the string λ – no bits are needed to convey the 'choice' of that substring as the prefix. The encoded string is `100011101100001000010`. The encoding, in this simple case, is actually a longer string than the source string, because there was no obvious redundancy in the source string.

▷ Exercise 6.4.[2] Prove that *any* uniquely decodeable code from $\{0, 1\}^+$ to $\{0, 1\}^+$ necessarily makes some strings longer if it makes some strings shorter.

---

[1] `www.inference.phy.cam.ac.uk/dasher/`

One reason why the algorithm described above lengthens a lot of strings is because it is inefficient – it transmits unnecessary bits; to put it another way, its code is not complete. Once a substring in the dictionary has been joined there by both of its children, then we can be sure that it will not be needed (except possibly as part of our protocol for terminating a message); so at that point we could drop it from our dictionary of substrings and shuffle them all along one, thereby reducing the length of subsequent pointer messages. Equivalently, we could write the second prefix into the dictionary at the point previously occupied by the parent. A second unnecessary overhead is the transmission of the new bit in these cases – the second time a prefix is used, we can be sure of the identity of the next bit.

Decoding

The decoder again involves an identical twin at the decoding end who constructs the dictionary of substrings as the data are decoded.

▷ Exercise 6.5.[2, p.128] Encode the string 000000000000100000000000 using the basic Lempel–Ziv algorithm described above.

▷ Exercise 6.6.[2, p.128] Decode the string

$$00101011101100100100011010101000011$$

that was encoded using the basic Lempel–Ziv algorithm.

Practicalities

In this description I have not discussed the method for terminating a string.

There are many variations on the Lempel–Ziv algorithm, all exploiting the same idea but using different procedures for dictionary management, etc. The resulting programs are fast, but their performance on compression of English text, although useful, does not match the standards set in the arithmetic coding literature.

Theoretical properties

In contrast to the block code, Huffman code, and arithmetic coding methods we discussed in the last three chapters, the Lempel–Ziv algorithm is defined without making any mention of a probabilistic model for the source. Yet, given any ergodic source (i.e., one that is memoryless on sufficiently long timescales), the Lempel–Ziv algorithm can be proven *asymptotically* to compress down to the entropy of the source. This is why it is called a 'universal' compression algorithm. For a proof of this property, see Cover and Thomas (1991).

It achieves its compression, however, only by *memorizing* substrings that have happened so that it has a short name for them the next time they occur. The asymptotic timescale on which this universal performance is achieved may, for many sources, be unfeasibly long, because the number of typical substrings that need memorizing may be enormous. The useful performance of the algorithm in practice is a reflection of the fact that many files contain multiple repetitions of particular short sequences of characters, a form of redundancy to which the algorithm is well suited.

Common ground

I have emphasized the difference in philosophy behind arithmetic coding and Lempel–Ziv coding. There is common ground between them, though: in principle, one can design adaptive probabilistic models, and thence arithmetic codes, that are 'universal', that is, models that will asymptotically compress *any source in some class* to within some factor (preferably 1) of its entropy. However, for practical purposes, I think such universal models can only be constructed if the class of sources is severely restricted. A general purpose compressor that can discover the probability distribution of *any* source would be a general purpose artificial intelligence! A general purpose artificial intelligence does not yet exist.

▶ 6.5 Demonstration

An interactive aid for exploring arithmetic coding, `dasher.tcl`, is available.[2]

A demonstration arithmetic-coding software package written by Radford Neal[3] consists of encoding and decoding modules to which the user adds a module defining the probabilistic model. It should be emphasized that there is no single general-purpose arithmetic-coding compressor; a new model has to be written for each type of source. Radford Neal's package includes a simple adaptive model similar to the Bayesian model demonstrated in section 6.2. The results using this Laplace model should be viewed as a basic benchmark since it is the simplest possible probabilistic model – it simply assumes the characters in the file come independently from a fixed ensemble. The counts $\{F_i\}$ of the symbols $\{a_i\}$ are rescaled and rounded as the file is read such that all the counts lie between 1 and 256.

A state-of-the-art compressor for documents containing text and images, `DjVu`, uses arithmetic coding.[4] It uses a carefully designed approximate arithmetic coder for binary alphabets called the Z-coder (Bottou *et al.*, 1998), which is much faster than the arithmetic coding software described above. One of the neat tricks the Z-coder uses is this: the adaptive model adapts only occasionally (to save on computer time), with the decision about when to adapt being pseudo-randomly controlled by whether the arithmetic encoder emitted a bit.

The JBIG image compression standard for binary images uses arithmetic coding with a context-dependent model, which adapts using a rule similar to Laplace's rule. PPM (Teahan, 1995) is a leading method for text compression, and it uses arithmetic coding.

There are many Lempel–Ziv-based programs. `gzip` is based on a version of Lempel–Ziv called 'LZ77'. `compress` is based on 'LZW'. In my experience the best is `gzip`, with `compress` being inferior on most files.

`bzip` is a *block-sorting file compressor*, which makes use of a neat hack called the *Burrows–Wheeler transform* (Burrows and Wheeler, 1994). This method is not based on an explicit probabilistic model, and it only works well for files larger than several thousand characters; but in practice it is a very effective compressor for files in which the context of a character is a good predictor for that character.[5]

---

[2]`http://www.inference.phy.cam.ac.uk/mackay/itprnn/softwareI.html`
[3]`ftp://ftp.cs.toronto.edu/pub/radford/www/ac.software.html`
[4]`http://www.djvuzone.org/`
[5]There is a lot of information about the Burrows–Wheeler transform on the net. `http://dogma.net/DataCompression/BWT.shtml`

Compression of a text file

Table 6.6 gives the computer time in seconds taken and the compression achieved when these programs are applied to the LaTeX file containing the text of this chapter, of size 20,942 bytes.

Method	Compression time / sec	Compressed size (%age of 20,942)	Uncompression time / sec
Laplace model	0.28	12 974 (61%)	0.32
gzip	0.10	8 177 (39%)	**0.01**
compress	0.05	10 816 (51%)	0.05
bzip		7 495 (36%)	
bzip2		7 640 (36%)	
ppmz		**6 800 (32%)**	

Table 6.6. Comparison of compression algorithms applied to a text file.

Compression of a sparse file

Interestingly, `gzip` does not always do so well. Table 6.7 gives the compression achieved when these programs are applied to a text file containing 10^6 characters, each of which is either 0 and 1 with probabilities 0.99 and 0.01. The Laplace model is quite well matched to this source, and the benchmark arithmetic coder gives good performance, followed closely by `compress`; `gzip`, interestingly, is worst. An ideal model for this source would compress the file into about $10^6 H_2(0.01)/8 \simeq 10\,100$ bytes. The Laplace model compressor falls short of this performance because it is implemented using only eight-bit precision. The `ppmz` compressor compresses the best of all, but takes much more computer time.

Method	Compression time / sec	Compressed size / bytes	Uncompression time / sec
Laplace model	0.45	14 143 (1.4%)	0.57
gzip	0.22	20 646 (2.1%)	0.04
gzip --best+	1.63	15 553 (1.6%)	0.05
compress	0.13	14 785 (1.5%)	0.03
bzip	0.30	10 903 (1.09%)	0.17
bzip2	0.19	11 260 (1.12%)	0.05
ppmz	533	**10 447 (1.04%)**	535

Table 6.7. Comparison of compression algorithms applied to a random file of 10^6 characters, 99% 0s and 1% 1s.

▶ **6.6 Summary**

In the last three chapters we have studied three classes of data compression codes.

Fixed-length block codes (Chapter 4). These are mappings from a fixed number of source symbols to a fixed length binary message. Only a tiny fraction of the source strings are given an encoding. These codes were fun for identifying the entropy as the measure of compressibility but they are of little practical use.

Symbol codes (Chapter 5). Symbol codes employ a variable length code for each symbol in the source alphabet, the codelengths being integer lengths determined by the probabilities of the symbols. Huffman's algorithm constructs an optimal symbol code for a given set of symbol probabilities.

Every source string has a uniquely decodeable encoding, and if the source symbols come from the assumed distribution then the symbol code will compress to an expected length L lying in the interval $[H, H+1)$. Statistical fluctuations in the source may make the actual length longer or shorter than this mean length.

If the source is not well matched to the assumed distribution then the mean length is increased by the relative entropy D_{KL} between the source distribution and the code's implicit distribution. For sources with small entropy, the symbol has to emit at least one bit per source symbol; compression below one bit per source symbol can only be achieved by the cumbersome procedure of putting the source data into blocks.

Stream codes. The distinctive property of stream codes, compared with symbol codes, is that they are not constrained to emit at least one bit for every symbol read from the source stream. So large numbers of source symbols may be coded into a smaller number of bits. This property could only be obtained using a symbol code if the source stream were somehow chopped into blocks.

- Arithmetic codes combine a probabilistic model with an encoding algorithm that identifies each string with a sub-interval of $[0, 1)$ of size equal to the probability of that string under the model. This code is almost optimal in the sense that the compressed length of a string **x** closely matches the Shannon information content of **x** given the probabilistic model. Arithmetic codes fit with the philosophy that good compression requires *data modelling*, in the form of an adaptive Bayesian model.

- Lempel–Ziv codes are adaptive in the sense that they memorize strings that have already occurred. They are built on the philosophy that we don't know anything at all about what the probability distribution of the source will be, and we want a compression algorithm that will perform reasonably well whatever that distribution is.

Both arithmetic codes and Lempel–Ziv codes will fail to decode correctly if any of the bits of the compressed file are altered. So if compressed files are to be stored or transmitted over noisy media, error-correcting codes will be essential. Reliable communication over unreliable channels is the topic of Part II.

▶ **6.7 Exercises on stream codes**

Exercise 6.7.[2] Describe an arithmetic coding algorithm to encode random bit strings of length N and weight K (i.e., K ones and $N - K$ zeroes) where N and K are given.

For the case $N = 5$, $K = 2$ show in detail the intervals corresponding to all source substrings of lengths 1–5.

▷ Exercise 6.8.[2, p.128] How many bits are needed to specify a selection of K objects from N objects? (N and K are assumed to be known and the selection of K objects is unordered.) How might such a selection be made at random without being wasteful of random bits?

▷ Exercise 6.9.[2] A binary source X emits independent identically distributed symbols with probability distribution $\{f_0, f_1\}$, where $f_1 = 0.01$. Find an optimal uniquely-decodeable symbol code for a string $\mathbf{x} = x_1 x_2 x_3$ of **three** successive samples from this source.

Estimate (to one decimal place) the factor by which the expected length of this optimal code is greater than the entropy of the three-bit string $\mathbf{x}$.

$[H_2(0.01) \simeq 0.08$, where $H_2(x) = x \log_2(1/x) + (1-x) \log_2(1/(1-x)).]$

An arithmetic code is used to compress a string of 1000 samples from the source X. Estimate the mean and standard deviation of the length of the compressed file.

▷ Exercise 6.10.[2] Describe an arithmetic coding algorithm to generate random bit strings of length N with density f (i.e., each bit has probability f of being a one) where N is given.

Exercise 6.11.[2] Use a modified Lempel–Ziv algorithm in which, as discussed on p.120, the dictionary of prefixes is pruned by writing new prefixes into the space occupied by prefixes that will not be needed again. Such prefixes can be identified when both their children have been added to the dictionary of prefixes. (You may neglect the issue of termination of encoding.) Use this algorithm to encode the string 0100001000100010101000001. Highlight the bits that follow a prefix on the second occasion that that prefix is used. (As discussed earlier, these bits could be omitted.)

Exercise 6.12.[2, p.128] Show that this modified Lempel–Ziv code is still not 'complete', that is, there are binary strings that are not encodings of any string.

▷ Exercise 6.13.[3, p.128] Give examples of simple sources that have low entropy but would not be compressed well by the Lempel–Ziv algorithm.

▶ 6.8 Further exercises on data compression

The following exercises may be skipped by the reader who is eager to learn about noisy channels.

Exercise 6.14.[3, p.130] Consider a Gaussian distribution in N dimensions,

$$P(\mathbf{x}) = \frac{1}{(2\pi\sigma^2)^{N/2}} \exp\left(-\frac{\sum_n x_n^2}{2\sigma^2}\right). \tag{6.13}$$

Define the radius of a point $\mathbf{x}$ to be $r = \left(\sum_n x_n^2\right)^{1/2}$. Estimate the mean and variance of the square of the radius, $r^2 = \left(\sum_n x_n^2\right)$.

You may find helpful the integral

$$\int dx \frac{1}{(2\pi\sigma^2)^{1/2}} x^4 \exp\left(-\frac{x^2}{2\sigma^2}\right) = 3\sigma^4, \tag{6.14}$$

though you should be able to estimate the required quantities without it.

Assuming that N is large, show that nearly all the probability of a Gaussian is contained in a thin shell of radius $\sqrt{N}\sigma$. Find the thickness of the shell.

Evaluate the probability density (6.13) at a point in that thin shell and at the origin $\mathbf{x} = 0$ and compare. Use the case $N = 1000$ as an example.

Notice that nearly all the probability mass is located in a different part of the space from the region of highest probability density.

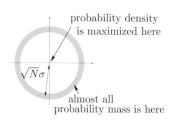

probability density is maximized here

$\sqrt{N}\sigma$

almost all probability mass is here

Figure 6.8. Schematic representation of the typical set of an N-dimensional Gaussian distribution.

Exercise 6.15.[2] Explain what is meant by an *optimal binary symbol code*.

Find an optimal binary symbol code for the ensemble:

$$\mathcal{A} = \{a, b, c, d, e, f, g, h, i, j\},$$

$$\mathcal{P} = \left\{ \frac{1}{100}, \frac{2}{100}, \frac{4}{100}, \frac{5}{100}, \frac{6}{100}, \frac{8}{100}, \frac{9}{100}, \frac{10}{100}, \frac{25}{100}, \frac{30}{100} \right\},$$

and compute the expected length of the code.

Exercise 6.16.[2] A string $\mathbf{y} = x_1 x_2$ consists of *two* independent samples from an ensemble

$$X : \mathcal{A}_X = \{a, b, c\}; \mathcal{P}_X = \left\{ \frac{1}{10}, \frac{3}{10}, \frac{6}{10} \right\}.$$

What is the entropy of $\mathbf{y}$? Construct an optimal binary symbol code for the string $\mathbf{y}$, and find its expected length.

Exercise 6.17.[2] Strings of N independent samples from an ensemble with $\mathcal{P} = \{0.1, 0.9\}$ are compressed using an arithmetic code that is matched to that ensemble. Estimate the mean and standard deviation of the compressed strings' lengths for the case $N = 1000$. [$H_2(0.1) \simeq 0.47$]

Exercise 6.18.[3] Source coding with variable-length symbols.

> In the chapters on source coding, we assumed that we were encoding into a binary alphabet $\{0, 1\}$ in which both symbols should be used with equal frequency. In this question we explore how the encoding alphabet should be used if the symbols take different times to transmit.

A poverty-stricken student communicates for free with a friend using a telephone by selecting an integer $n \in \{1, 2, 3 \ldots\}$, making the friend's phone ring n times, then hanging up in the middle of the nth ring. This process is repeated so that a string of symbols $n_1 n_2 n_3 \ldots$ is received. What is the optimal way to communicate? If large integers n are selected then the message takes longer to communicate. If only small integers n are used then the information content per symbol is small. We aim to maximize the rate of information transfer, per unit time.

Assume that the time taken to transmit a number of rings n and to redial is l_n seconds. Consider a probability distribution over n, $\{p_n\}$. Defining the average duration *per symbol* to be

$$L(\mathbf{p}) = \sum_n p_n l_n \tag{6.15}$$

and the entropy *per symbol* to be

$$H(\mathbf{p}) = \sum_n p_n \log_2 \frac{1}{p_n}, \qquad (6.16)$$

show that for the average information rate *per second* to be maximized, the symbols must be used with probabilities of the form

$$p_n = \frac{1}{Z} 2^{-\beta l_n} \qquad (6.17)$$

where $Z = \sum_n 2^{-\beta l_n}$ and β satisfies the implicit equation

$$\beta = \frac{H(\mathbf{p})}{L(\mathbf{p})}, \qquad (6.18)$$

that is, β is the rate of communication. Show that these two equations (6.17, 6.18) imply that β must be set such that

$$\log Z = 0. \qquad (6.19)$$

Assuming that the channel has the property

$$l_n = n \text{ seconds}, \qquad (6.20)$$

find the optimal distribution $\mathbf{p}$ and show that the maximal information rate is 1 bit per second.

How does this compare with the information rate per second achieved if $\mathbf{p}$ is set to $(1/2, 1/2, 0, 0, 0, 0, \ldots)$ — that is, only the symbols $n = 1$ and $n = 2$ are selected, and they have equal probability?

Discuss the relationship between the results (6.17, 6.19) derived above, and the Kraft inequality from source coding theory.

How might a random binary source be efficiently encoded into a sequence of symbols $n_1 n_2 n_3 \ldots$ for transmission over the channel defined in equation (6.20)?

▷ Exercise 6.19.[1] How many bits does it take to shuffle a pack of cards?

▷ Exercise 6.20.[2] In the card game Bridge, the four players receive 13 cards each from the deck of 52 and start each game by looking at their own hand and bidding. The legal bids are, in ascending order $1\clubsuit, 1\diamondsuit, 1\heartsuit, 1\spadesuit$, $1NT, 2\clubsuit, 2\diamondsuit, \ldots 7\heartsuit, 7\spadesuit, 7NT$, and successive bids must follow this order; a bid of, say, $2\heartsuit$ may only be followed by higher bids such as $2\spadesuit$ or $3\clubsuit$ or $7NT$. (Let us neglect the 'double' bid.)

The players have several aims when bidding. One of the aims is for two partners to communicate to each other as much as possible about what cards are in their hands.

Let us concentrate on this task.

(a) After the cards have been dealt, how many bits are needed for North to convey to South what her hand is?

(b) Assuming that E and W do not bid at all, what is the maximum total information that N and S can convey to each other while bidding? Assume that N starts the bidding, and that once either N or S stops bidding, the bidding stops.

▷ Exercise 6.21.[2] My old 'arabic' microwave oven had 11 buttons for entering cooking times, and my new 'roman' microwave has just five. The buttons of the roman microwave are labelled '10 minutes', '1 minute', '10 seconds', '1 second', and 'Start'; I'll abbreviate these five strings to the symbols M, C, X, I, □.   To enter one minute and twenty-three seconds (1:23), the arabic sequence is

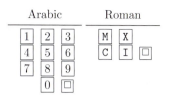

Arabic   Roman

Figure 6.9. Alternative keypads for microwave ovens.

$$123\square, \qquad (6.21)$$

and the roman sequence is

$$\texttt{CXXIII}\square. \qquad (6.22)$$

Each of these keypads defines a code mapping the 3599 cooking times from 0:01 to 59:59 into a string of symbols.

(a) Which times can be produced with two or three symbols? (For example, 0:20 can be produced by three symbols in either code: XX□ and 20□.)

(b) Are the two codes complete? Give a detailed answer.

(c) For each code, name a cooking time that it can produce in four symbols that the other code cannot.

(d) Discuss the implicit probability distributions over times to which each of these codes is best matched.

(e) Concoct a plausible probability distribution over times that a real user might use, and evaluate roughly the expected number of symbols, and maximum number of symbols, that each code requires. Discuss the ways in which each code is inefficient or efficient.

(f) Invent a more efficient cooking-time-encoding system for a microwave oven.

Exercise 6.22.[2, p.132] Is the standard binary representation for positive integers (e.g. $c_b(5) = 101$) a uniquely decodeable code?

Design a binary code for the positive integers, i.e., a mapping from $n \in \{1, 2, 3, \dots\}$ to $c(n) \in \{0, 1\}^+$, that is uniquely decodeable. Try to design codes that are prefix codes and that satisfy the Kraft equality $\sum_n 2^{-l_n} = 1$.

Motivations: any data file terminated by a special end of file character can be mapped onto an integer, so a prefix code for integers can be used as a self-delimiting encoding of files too. Large files correspond to large integers. Also, one of the building blocks of a 'universal' coding scheme – that is, a coding scheme that will work OK for a large variety of sources – is the ability to encode integers. Finally, in microwave ovens, cooking times are positive integers!

Discuss criteria by which one might compare alternative codes for integers (or, equivalently, alternative self-delimiting codes for files).

▶ **6.9 Solutions**

Solution to exercise 6.1 (p.115). The worst-case situation is when the interval to be represented lies just inside a binary interval. In this case, we may choose either of two binary intervals as shown in figure 6.10. These binary intervals

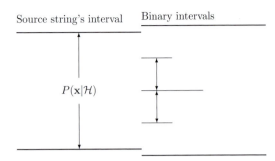

Source string's interval   Binary intervals

$P(\mathbf{x}|\mathcal{H})$

Figure 6.10. Termination of arithmetic coding in the worst case, where there is a two bit overhead. Either of the two binary intervals marked on the right-hand side may be chosen. These binary intervals are no smaller than $P(\mathbf{x}|\mathcal{H})/4$.

are no smaller than $P(\mathbf{x}|\mathcal{H})/4$, so the binary encoding has a length no greater than $\log_2 1/P(\mathbf{x}|\mathcal{H}) + \log_2 4$, which is two bits more than the ideal message length.

Solution to exercise 6.3 (p.118).   The standard method uses 32 random bits per generated symbol and so requires 32 000 bits to generate one thousand samples.

Arithmetic coding uses on average about $H_2(0.01) = 0.081$ bits per generated symbol, and so requires about 83 bits to generate one thousand samples (assuming an overhead of roughly two bits associated with termination).

Fluctuations in the number of 1s would produce variations around this mean with standard deviation 21.

Solution to exercise 6.5 (p.120).   The encoding is 010100110010110001100, which comes from the parsing

$$0, 00, 000, 0000, 001, 00000, 000000 \qquad (6.23)$$

which is encoded thus

$$(, 0), (1, 0), (10, 0), (11, 0), (010, 1), (100, 0), (110, 0). \qquad (6.24)$$

Solution to exercise 6.6 (p.120).   The decoding is
$$010000100010001010101000001.$$

Solution to exercise 6.8 (p.123).   This problem is equivalent to exercise 6.7 (p.123).

The selection of K objects from N objects requires $\lceil \log_2 \binom{N}{K} \rceil$ bits $\simeq N H_2(K/N)$ bits. This selection could be made using arithmetic coding. The selection corresponds to a binary string of length N in which the 1 bits represent which objects are selected. Initially the probability of a 1 is K/N and the probability of a 0 is $(N-K)/N$. Thereafter, given that the emitted string thus far, of length n, contains k 1s, the probability of a 1 is $(K-k)/(N-n)$ and the probability of a 0 is $1 - (K-k)/(N-n)$.

Solution to exercise 6.12 (p.124).   This modified Lempel–Ziv code is still not 'complete', because, for example, after five prefixes have been collected, the pointer could be any of the strings 000, 001, 010, 011, 100, but it cannot be 101, 110 or 111. Thus there are some binary strings that cannot be produced as encodings.

Solution to exercise 6.13 (p.124).   Sources with low entropy that are not well compressed by Lempel–Ziv include:

(a) Sources with some symbols that have long range correlations and intervening random junk. An ideal model should capture what's correlated and compress it. Lempel–Ziv can only compress the correlated features by memorizing all cases of the intervening junk. As a simple example, consider a telephone book in which every line contains an (old number, new number) pair:

$$285\text{-}3820\text{:}572\text{-}5892\square$$
$$258\text{-}8302\text{:}593\text{-}2010\square$$

The number of characters per line is 18, drawn from the 13-character alphabet $\{0, 1, \ldots, 9, -, :, \square\}$. The characters '$-$', '$:$' and '$\square$' occur in a predictable sequence, so the true information content per line, assuming all the phone numbers are seven digits long, and assuming that they are random sequences, is about 14 bans. (A ban is the information content of a random integer between 0 and 9.) A finite state language model could easily capture the regularities in these data. A Lempel–Ziv algorithm will take a long time before it compresses such a file down to 14 bans per line, however, because in order for it to 'learn' that the string $:ddd$ is always followed by $-$, for any three digits ddd, it will have to *see* all those strings. So near-optimal compression will only be achieved after thousands of lines of the file have been read.

Figure 6.11. A source with low entropy that is not well compressed by Lempel–Ziv. The bit sequence is read from left to right. Each line differs from the line above in $f = 5\%$ of its bits. The image width is 400 pixels.

(b) Sources with long range correlations, for example two-dimensional images that are represented by a sequence of pixels, row by row, so that vertically adjacent pixels are a distance w apart in the source stream, where w is the image width. Consider, for example, a fax transmission in which each line is very similar to the previous line (figure 6.11). The true entropy is only $H_2(f)$ per pixel, where f is the probability that a pixel differs from its parent. Lempel–Ziv algorithms will only compress down to the entropy once *all* strings of length $2^w = 2^{400}$ have occurred and their successors have been memorized. There are only about 2^{300} particles in the universe, so we can confidently say that Lempel–Ziv codes will *never* capture the redundancy of such an image.

Another highly redundant texture is shown in figure 6.12. The image was made by dropping horizontal and vertical pins randomly on the plane. It contains both long-range vertical correlations and long-range horizontal correlations. There is no practical way that Lempel–Ziv, fed with a pixel-by-pixel scan of this image, could capture both these correlations.

Biological computational systems can readily identify the redundancy in these images and in images that are much more complex; thus we might anticipate that the best data compression algorithms will result from the development of artificial intelligence methods.

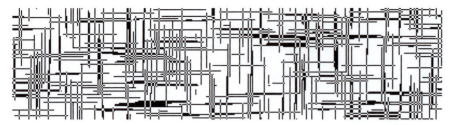

Figure 6.12. A texture consisting of horizontal and vertical pins dropped at random on the plane.

(c) Sources with intricate redundancy, such as files generated by computers. For example, a LaTeX file followed by its encoding into a PostScript file. The information content of this pair of files is roughly equal to the information content of the LaTeX file alone.

(d) A picture of the Mandelbrot set. The picture has an information content equal to the number of bits required to specify the range of the complex plane studied, the pixel sizes, and the colouring rule used.

(e) A picture of a ground state of a frustrated antiferromagnetic Ising model (figure 6.13), which we will discuss in Chapter 31. Like figure 6.12, this binary image has interesting correlations in two directions.

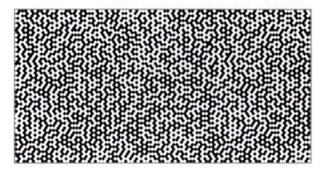

Figure 6.13. Frustrated triangular Ising model in one of its ground states.

(f) Cellular automata – figure 6.14 shows the state history of 100 steps of a cellular automaton with 400 cells. The update rule, in which each cell's new state depends on the state of five preceding cells, was selected at random. The information content is equal to the information in the boundary (400 bits), and the propagation rule, which here can be described in 32 bits. An optimal compressor will thus give a compressed file length which is essentially constant, independent of the vertical height of the image. Lempel–Ziv would only give this zero-cost compression once the cellular automaton has entered a periodic limit cycle, which could easily take about 2^{100} iterations.

In contrast, the JBIG compression method, which models the probability of a pixel given its local context and uses arithmetic coding, would do a good job on these images.

Solution to exercise 6.14 (p.124).   For a one-dimensional Gaussian, the variance of x, $\mathcal{E}[x^2]$, is σ^2. So the mean value of r^2 in N dimensions, since the components of $\mathbf{x}$ are independent random variables, is

$$\mathcal{E}[r^2] = N\sigma^2. \qquad (6.25)$$

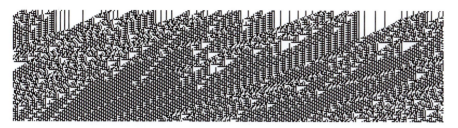

Figure 6.14. The 100-step time-history of a cellular automaton with 400 cells.

The variance of r^2, similarly, is N times the variance of x^2, where x is a one-dimensional Gaussian variable.

$$\text{var}(x^2) = \int dx \, \frac{1}{(2\pi\sigma^2)^{1/2}} x^4 \exp\left(-\frac{x^2}{2\sigma^2}\right) - \sigma^4. \qquad (6.26)$$

The integral is found to be $3\sigma^4$ (equation (6.14)), so $\text{var}(x^2) = 2\sigma^4$. Thus the variance of r^2 is $2N\sigma^4$.

For large N, the central limit theorem indicates that r^2 has a Gaussian distribution with mean $N\sigma^2$ and standard deviation $\sqrt{2N}\sigma^2$, so the probability density of r must similarly be concentrated about $r \simeq \sqrt{N}\sigma$.

The thickness of this shell is given by turning the standard deviation of r^2 into a standard deviation on r: for small $\delta r/r$, $\delta \log r = \delta r/r = (1/2)\delta \log r^2 = (1/2)\delta(r^2)/r^2$, so setting $\delta(r^2) = \sqrt{2N}\sigma^2$, r has standard deviation $\delta r = (1/2)r\delta(r^2)/r^2 = \sigma/\sqrt{2}$.

The probability density of the Gaussian at a point $\mathbf{x}_{\text{shell}}$ where $r = \sqrt{N}\sigma$ is

$$P(\mathbf{x}_{\text{shell}}) = \frac{1}{(2\pi\sigma^2)^{N/2}} \exp\left(-\frac{N\sigma^2}{2\sigma^2}\right) = \frac{1}{(2\pi\sigma^2)^{N/2}} \exp\left(-\frac{N}{2}\right). \qquad (6.27)$$

Whereas the probability density at the origin is

$$P(\mathbf{x}=0) = \frac{1}{(2\pi\sigma^2)^{N/2}}. \qquad (6.28)$$

Thus $P(\mathbf{x}_{\text{shell}})/P(\mathbf{x}=0) = \exp(-N/2)$. The probability density at the typical radius is $e^{-N/2}$ times smaller than the density at the origin. If $N = 1000$, then the probability density at the origin is e^{500} times greater.

7

Codes for Integers

This chapter is an aside, which may safely be skipped.

Solution to exercise 6.22 (p.127)

To discuss the coding of integers we need some definitions.

The standard binary representation of a positive integer n will be denoted by $c_{\mathrm{b}}(n)$, e.g., $c_{\mathrm{b}}(5) = 101$, $c_{\mathrm{b}}(45) = 101101$.

The standard binary length of a positive integer n, $l_{\mathrm{b}}(n)$, is the length of the string $c_{\mathrm{b}}(n)$. For example, $l_{\mathrm{b}}(5) = 3$, $l_{\mathrm{b}}(45) = 6$.

The standard binary representation $c_{\mathrm{b}}(n)$ is *not* a uniquely decodeable code for integers since there is no way of knowing when an integer has ended. For example, $c_{\mathrm{b}}(5)c_{\mathrm{b}}(5)$ is identical to $c_{\mathrm{b}}(45)$. It would be uniquely decodeable if we knew the standard binary length of each integer before it was received.

Noticing that all positive integers have a standard binary representation that starts with a 1, we might define another representation:

The headless binary representation of a positive integer n will be denoted by $c_{\mathrm{B}}(n)$, e.g., $c_{\mathrm{B}}(5) = 01$, $c_{\mathrm{B}}(45) = 01101$ and $c_{\mathrm{B}}(1) = \lambda$ (where λ denotes the null string).

This representation would be uniquely decodeable if we knew the length $l_{\mathrm{b}}(n)$ of the integer.

So, how can we make a uniquely decodeable code for integers? Two strategies can be distinguished.

1. **Self-delimiting codes.** We first communicate somehow the length of the integer, $l_{\mathrm{b}}(n)$, which is also a positive integer; then communicate the original integer n itself using $c_{\mathrm{B}}(n)$.

2. **Codes with 'end of file' characters.** We code the integer into blocks of length b bits, and reserve one of the 2^b symbols to have the special meaning 'end of file'. The coding of integers into blocks is arranged so that this reserved symbol is not needed for any other purpose.

The simplest uniquely decodeable code for integers is the unary code, which can be viewed as a code with an end of file character.

Unary code. An integer n is encoded by sending a string of $n-1$ 0s followed by a **1**.

n	$c_U(n)$
1	1
2	01
3	001
4	0001
5	00001
$\vdots$	
45	000000000000000000000000000000000000000000001

The unary code has length $l_U(n) = n$.

The unary code is the optimal code for integers if the probability distribution over n is $p_U(n) = 2^{-n}$.

Self-delimiting codes

We can use the unary code to encode the *length* of the binary encoding of n and make a self-delimiting code:

Code C_α. We send the unary code for $l_b(n)$, followed by the headless binary representation of n.

$$c_\alpha(n) = c_U[l_b(n)]c_B(n) \tag{7.1}$$

Table 7.1 shows the codes for some integers. The overlining indicates the division of each string into the parts $c_U[l_b(n)]$ and $c_B(n)$. We might equivalently view $c_\alpha(n)$ as consisting of a string of $(l_b(n) - 1)$ zeroes followed by the standard binary representation of n, $c_b(n)$.

The codeword $c_\alpha(n)$ has length $l_\alpha(n) = 2l_b(n) - 1$.

The implicit probability distribution over n for the code C_α is separable into the product of a probability distribution over the length l,

$$P(l) = 2^{-l}, \tag{7.2}$$

and a uniform distribution over integers having that length,

$$P(n|l) = \begin{cases} 2^{-l+1} & l_b(n) = l \\ 0 & \text{otherwise.} \end{cases} \tag{7.3}$$

Now, for the above code, the header that communicates the length always occupies the same number of bits as the standard binary representation of the integer (give or take one). If we are expecting to encounter large integers (large files) then this representation seems suboptimal, since it leads to all files occupying a size that is double their original uncoded size. Instead of using the unary code to encode the length $l_b(n)$, we could use C_α.

Code C_β. We send the length $l_b(n)$ using C_α, followed by the headless binary representation of n.

$$c_\beta(n) = c_\alpha[l_b(n)]c_B(n) \tag{7.4}$$

Iterating this procedure, we can define a sequence of codes.

Code C_γ.

$$c_\gamma(n) = c_\beta[l_b(n)]c_B(n) \tag{7.5}$$

Code C_δ.

$$c_\delta(n) = c_\gamma[l_b(n)]c_B(n) \tag{7.6}$$

n	$c_b(n)$	$l_b(n)$	$c_\alpha(n)$
1	1	1	$\overline{1}$
2	10	2	$\overline{0}10$
3	11	2	$\overline{0}11$
4	100	3	$\overline{00}100$
5	101	3	$\overline{00}101$
6	110	3	$\overline{00}110$
$\vdots$			
45	101101	6	$\overline{00000}101101$

Table 7.1. C_α.

n	$c_\beta(n)$	$c_\gamma(n)$
1	$\overline{1}$	$\overline{1}$
2	$\overline{0100}$	$\overline{01000}$
3	$\overline{0101}$	$\overline{01001}$
4	$\overline{01}100$	$\overline{010}100$
5	$\overline{01}101$	$\overline{010}101$
6	$\overline{01}110$	$\overline{010}110$
$\vdots$		
45	$\overline{0011}001101$	$\overline{01110}01101$

Table 7.2. C_β and C_γ.

Codes with end-of-file symbols

We can also make byte-based representations. (Let's use the term byte flexibly here, to denote any fixed-length string of bits, not just a string of length 8 bits.) If we encode the number in some base, for example decimal, then we can represent each digit in a byte. In order to represent a digit from 0 to 9 in a byte we need four bits. Because $2^4 = 16$, this leaves 6 extra four-bit symbols, $\{1010, 1011, 1100, 1101, 1110, 1111\}$, that correspond to no decimal digit. We can use these as end-of-file symbols to indicate the end of our positive integer.

Clearly it is redundant to have more than one end-of-file symbol, so a more efficient code would encode the integer into base 15, and use just the sixteenth symbol, 1111, as the punctuation character. Generalizing this idea, we can make similar byte-based codes for integers in bases 3 and 7, and in any base of the form $2^n - 1$.

These codes are almost complete. (Recall that a code's being 'complete' means that it satisfies the Kraft inequality with equality.) The codes's remaining inefficiency is that they provide the ability to encode the integer zero and the empty string, neither of which was required.

n	$c_3(n)$	$c_7(n)$
1	01 11	001 111
2	10 11	010 111
3	01 00 11	011 111
⋮		
45	01 10 00 00 11	110 011 111

Table 7.3. Two codes with end-of-file symbols, C_3 and C_7. Spaces have been included to show the byte boundaries.

▷ **Exercise 7.1.**[2, p.136] Consider the implicit probability distribution over integers corresponding to the code with an end-of-file character.

(a) If the code has eight-bit blocks (i.e., the integer is coded in base 255), what is the mean length in bits of the integer, under the implicit distribution?

(b) If one wishes to encode binary files of expected size about one hundred kilobytes using a code with an end-of-file character, what is the optimal block size?

Encoding a tiny file

To illustrate the codes we have discussed, we now use each code to encode a small file consisting of just 14 characters,

$$\boxed{\texttt{Claude Shannon}}.$$

• If we map the ASCII characters onto seven-bit symbols (e.g., in decimal, $\texttt{C} = 67$, $\texttt{l} = 108$, etc.), this 14 character file corresponds to the integer

$$n = 167\,987\,786\,364\,950\,891\,085\,602\,469\,870 \ \ (\text{decimal}).$$

• The unary code for n consists of this many (less one) zeroes, followed by a one. If all the oceans were turned into ink, and if we wrote a hundred bits with every cubic millimeter, there might be enough ink to write $c_U(n)$.

• The standard binary representation of n is this length 98 sequence of bits:

$$c_b(n) = \begin{array}{l} \texttt{10000111101100110000111101011100100110010101010000} \\ \texttt{101001110100011000011011101101110110111111101110.} \end{array}$$

▷ **Exercise 7.2.**[2] Write down or describe the following self-delimiting representations of the above number n: $c_\alpha(n)$, $c_\beta(n)$, $c_\gamma(n)$, $c_\delta(n)$, $c_3(n)$, $c_7(n)$, and $c_{15}(n)$. Which of these encodings is the shortest? [Answer: c_{15}.]

Comparing the codes

One could answer the question 'which of two codes is superior?' by a sentence of the form 'For $n > k$, code 1 is superior, for $n < k$, code 2 is superior' but I contend that such an answer misses the point: any complete code corresponds to a prior for which it is optimal; you should not say that any other code is superior to it. Other codes are optimal for other priors. These implicit priors should be thought about so as to achieve the best code for one's application.

Notice that one cannot, for free, switch from one code to another, choosing whichever is shorter. If one were to do this, then it would be necessary to lengthen the message in some way that indicates which of the two codes is being used. If this is done by a single leading bit, it will be found that the resulting code is suboptimal because it fails the Kraft equality, as was discussed in exercise 5.33 (p.104).

Another way to compare codes for integers is to consider a sequence of probability distributions, such as monotonic probability distributions over $n \geq 1$, and rank the codes as to how well they encode *any* of these distributions. A code is called a 'universal' code if for any distribution in a given class, it encodes into an average length that is within some factor of the ideal average length.

Let me say this again. We are meeting an alternative world view – rather than figuring out a good prior over integers, as advocated above, many theorists have studied the problem of creating codes that are reasonably good codes for *any* priors in a broad class. Here the class of priors conventionally considered is the set of priors that (a) assign a monotonically decreasing probability over integers and (b) have finite entropy.

Several of the codes we have discussed above are universal. Another code which elegantly transcends the sequence of self-delimiting codes is Elias's 'universal code for integers' (Elias, 1975), which effectively chooses from all the codes $C_\alpha, C_\beta, \ldots$. It works by sending a sequence of messages each of which encodes the length of the next message, and indicates by a single bit whether or not that message is the final integer (in its standard binary representation). Because a length is a positive integer and all positive integers begin with '1', all the leading 1s can be omitted.

```
Write '0'
Loop {
    If ⌊log n⌋ = 0 halt
    Prepend c_b(n) to the written string
    n:=⌊log n⌋
}
```

Algorithm 7.4. Elias's encoder for an integer n.

The encoder of C_ω is shown in algorithm 7.4. The encoding is generated from right to left. Table 7.5 shows the resulting codewords.

▷ Exercise 7.3.[2] Show that the Elias code is not actually the best code for a prior distribution that expects very large integers. (Do this by constructing another code and specifying how large n must be for your code to give a shorter length than Elias's.)

n	$c_\omega(n)$	n	$c_\omega(n)$	n	$c_\omega(n)$	n	$c_\omega(n)$
1	0	31	10100111110	9	1110010	256	1110001000000000
2	100	32	101011000000	10	1110100	365	1110001011011010
3	110	45	101011011010	11	1110110	511	1110001111111110
4	101000	63	101011111110	12	1111000	512	11100110000000000
5	101010	64	1011010000000	13	1111010	719	11100110110011110
6	101100	127	1011011111110	14	1111100	1023	11100111111111110
7	101110	128	10111100000000	15	1111110	1024	111010100000000000
8	1110000	255	10111111111110	16	10100100000	1025	111010100000000010

Table 7.5. Elias's 'universal' code for integers. Examples from 1 to 1025.

Solutions

Solution to exercise 7.1 (p.134).   The use of the end-of-file symbol in a code that represents the integer in some base q corresponds to a belief that there is a probability of $(1/(q+1))$ that the current character is the last character of the number. Thus the prior to which this code is matched puts an exponential prior distribution over the length of the integer.

(a) The expected number of characters is $q+1 = 256$, so the expected length of the integer is $256 \times 8 \simeq 2000$ bits.

(b) We wish to find q such that $q \log q \simeq 800\,000$ bits. A value of q between 2^{15} and 2^{16} satisfies this constraint, so 16-bit blocks are roughly the optimal size, assuming there is one end-of-file character.

Part II

Noisy-Channel Coding

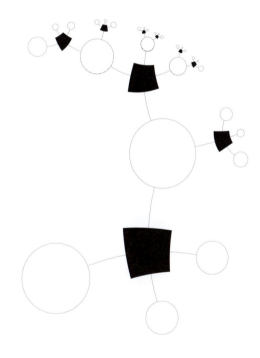

Correlated Random Variables

In the last three chapters on data compression we concentrated on random vectors $\mathbf{x}$ coming from an extremely simple probability distribution, namely the separable distribution in which each component x_n is independent of the others.

In this chapter, we consider *joint ensembles* in which the random variables are correlated. This material has two motivations. First, data from the real world have interesting correlations, so to do data compression well, we need to know how to work with models that include correlations. Second, a noisy channel with input x and output y defines a joint ensemble in which x and y are correlated – if they were independent, it would be impossible to communicate over the channel – so communication over noisy channels (the topic of chapters 9–11) is described in terms of the entropy of joint ensembles.

▶ 8.1 More about entropy

This section gives definitions and exercises to do with entropy, carrying on from section 2.4.

The joint entropy of X, Y is:

$$H(X,Y) = \sum_{xy \in \mathcal{A}_X \mathcal{A}_Y} P(x,y) \log \frac{1}{P(x,y)}. \tag{8.1}$$

Entropy is additive for independent random variables:

$$H(X,Y) = H(X) + H(Y) \text{ iff } P(x,y) = P(x)P(y). \tag{8.2}$$

The conditional entropy of X given $y = b_k$ is the entropy of the probability distribution $P(x \,|\, y = b_k)$.

$$H(X \,|\, y = b_k) \equiv \sum_{x \in \mathcal{A}_X} P(x \,|\, y = b_k) \log \frac{1}{P(x \,|\, y = b_k)}. \tag{8.3}$$

The conditional entropy of X given Y is the average, over y, of the conditional entropy of X given y.

$$
\begin{aligned}
H(X \,|\, Y) &\equiv \sum_{y \in \mathcal{A}_Y} P(y) \left[\sum_{x \in \mathcal{A}_X} P(x \,|\, y) \log \frac{1}{P(x \,|\, y)} \right] \\
&= \sum_{xy \in \mathcal{A}_X \mathcal{A}_Y} P(x,y) \log \frac{1}{P(x \,|\, y)}.
\end{aligned}
\tag{8.4}
$$

This measures the average uncertainty that remains about x when y is known.

The marginal entropy of X is another name for the entropy of X, $H(X)$, used to contrast it with the conditional entropies listed above.

Chain rule for information content. From the product rule for probabilities, equation (2.6), we obtain:

$$\log \frac{1}{P(x,y)} \;=\; \log \frac{1}{P(x)} + \log \frac{1}{P(y\,|\,x)} \qquad (8.5)$$

so

$$h(x,y) = h(x) + h(y\,|\,x). \qquad (8.6)$$

In words, this says that the information content of x and y is the information content of x plus the information content of y given x.

Chain rule for entropy. The joint entropy, conditional entropy and marginal entropy are related by:

$$H(X,Y) = H(X) + H(Y\,|\,X) = H(Y) + H(X\,|\,Y). \qquad (8.7)$$

In words, this says that the uncertainty of X and Y is the uncertainty of X plus the uncertainty of Y given X.

The mutual information between X **and** Y is

$$I(X;Y) \;\equiv\; H(X) - H(X\,|\,Y), \qquad (8.8)$$

and satisfies $I(X;Y) = I(Y;X)$, and $I(X;Y) \geq 0$. It measures the average reduction in uncertainty about x that results from learning the value of y; **or vice versa**, the average amount of information that x conveys about y.

The conditional mutual information between X **and** Y **given** $z = c_k$ is the mutual information between the random variables X and Y in the joint ensemble $P(x,y\,|\,z = c_k)$,

$$I(X;Y\,|\,z = c_k) = H(X\,|\,z = c_k) - H(X\,|\,Y, z = c_k). \qquad (8.9)$$

The conditional mutual information between X **and** Y **given** Z is the average over z of the above conditional mutual information.

$$I(X;Y\,|\,Z) = H(X\,|\,Z) - H(X\,|\,Y,Z). \qquad (8.10)$$

No other 'three-term entropies' will be defined. For example, expressions such as $I(X;Y;Z)$ and $I(X\,|\,Y;Z)$ are illegal. But you may put conjunctions of arbitrary numbers of variables in each of the three spots in the expression $I(X;Y\,|\,Z)$ – for example, $I(A,B;C,D\,|\,E,F)$ is fine: it measures how much information on average c and d convey about a and b, assuming e and f are known.

Figure 8.1 shows how the total entropy $H(X,Y)$ of a joint ensemble can be broken down. **This figure is important.** $*$

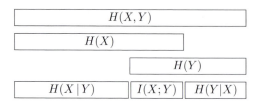

Figure 8.1. The relationship between joint information, marginal entropy, conditional entropy and mutual entropy.

▶ 8.2 Exercises

▷ **Exercise 8.1.**[1] Consider three independent random variables u, v, w with entropies H_u, H_v, H_w. Let $X \equiv (U, V)$ and $Y \equiv (V, W)$. What is $H(X, Y)$? What is $H(X \mid Y)$? What is $I(X; Y)$?

▷ **Exercise 8.2.**[3, p.142] Referring to the definitions of conditional entropy (8.3–8.4), confirm (with an example) that it is possible for $H(X \mid y = b_k)$ to exceed $H(X)$, but that the average, $H(X \mid Y)$ is less than $H(X)$. So data are helpful – they do not increase uncertainty, on average.

▷ **Exercise 8.3.**[2, p.143] Prove the chain rule for entropy, equation (8.7). $[H(X, Y) = H(X) + H(Y \mid X)]$.

Exercise 8.4.[2, p.143] Prove that the mutual information $I(X; Y) \equiv H(X) - H(X \mid Y)$ satisfies $I(X; Y) = I(Y; X)$ and $I(X; Y) \geq 0$.

[Hint: see exercise 2.26 (p.37) and note that

$$I(X; Y) = D_{\mathrm{KL}}(P(x, y) \| P(x) P(y)).] \qquad (8.11)$$

Exercise 8.5.[4] The 'entropy distance' between two random variables can be defined to be the difference between their joint entropy and their mutual information:

$$D_H(X, Y) \equiv H(X, Y) - I(X; Y). \qquad (8.12)$$

Prove that the entropy distance satisfies the axioms for a distance – $D_H(X, Y) \geq 0$, $D_H(X, X) = 0$, $D_H(X, Y) = D_H(Y, X)$, and $D_H(X, Z) \leq D_H(X, Y) + D_H(Y, Z)$. [Incidentally, we are unlikely to see $D_H(X, Y)$ again but it is a good function on which to practise inequality-proving.]

Exercise 8.6.[2] A joint ensemble XY has the following joint distribution.

$P(x, y)$			x		
		1	2	3	4
	1	1/8	1/16	1/32	1/32
y	2	1/16	1/8	1/32	1/32
	3	1/16	1/16	1/16	1/16
	4	1/4	0	0	0

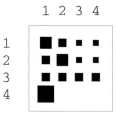

What is the joint entropy $H(X, Y)$? What are the marginal entropies $H(X)$ and $H(Y)$? For each value of y, what is the conditional entropy $H(X \mid y)$? What is the conditional entropy $H(X \mid Y)$? What is the conditional entropy of Y given X? What is the mutual information between X and Y?

Exercise 8.7.[2, p.143] Consider the ensemble XYZ in which $\mathcal{A}_X = \mathcal{A}_Y = \mathcal{A}_Z = \{0,1\}$, x and y are independent with $\mathcal{P}_X = \{p, 1-p\}$ and $\mathcal{P}_Y = \{q, 1-q\}$ and

$$z = (x+y) \bmod 2. \tag{8.13}$$

(a) If $q = 1/2$, what is $\mathcal{P}_Z$? What is $I(Z;X)$?

(b) For general p and q, what is $\mathcal{P}_Z$? What is $I(Z;X)$? Notice that this ensemble is related to the binary symmetric channel, with $x =$ input, $y =$ noise, and $z =$ output.

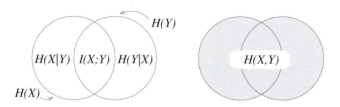

Figure 8.2. A misleading representation of entropies (contrast with figure 8.1).

Three term entropies

Exercise 8.8.[3, p.143] Many texts draw figure 8.1 in the form of a Venn diagram (figure 8.2). Discuss why this diagram is a misleading representation of entropies. Hint: consider the three-variable ensemble XYZ in which $x \in \{0,1\}$ and $y \in \{0,1\}$ are independent binary variables and $z \in \{0,1\}$ is defined to be $z = x + y \bmod 2$.

▶ 8.3 Further exercises

The data-processing theorem

The data processing theorem states that data processing can only destroy information.

Exercise 8.9.[3, p.144] Prove this theorem by considering an ensemble WDR in which w is the state of the world, d is data gathered, and r is the processed data, so that these three variables form a *Markov chain*

$$w \to d \to r, \tag{8.14}$$

that is, the probability $P(w,d,r)$ can be written as

$$P(w,d,r) = P(w)P(d\,|\,w)P(r\,|\,d). \tag{8.15}$$

Show that the average information that R conveys about W, $I(W;R)$, is less than or equal to the average information that D conveys about W, $I(W;D)$.

This theorem is as much a caution about our definition of 'information' as it is a caution about data processing!

Inference and information measures

Exercise 8.10.[2] The three cards.

    (a) One card is white on both faces; one is black on both faces; and one is white on one side and black on the other. The three cards are shuffled and their orientations randomized. One card is drawn and placed on the table. The upper face is black. What is the colour of its lower face? (Solve the inference problem.)

    (b) Does seeing the top face convey *information* about the colour of the bottom face? Discuss the *information contents* and *entropies* in this situation. Let the value of the upper face's colour be u and the value of the lower face's colour be l. Imagine that we draw a random card and learn both u and l. What is the entropy of u, $H(U)$? What is the entropy of l, $H(L)$? What is the mutual information between U and L, $I(U;L)$?

Entropies of Markov processes

▷ Exercise 8.11.[3] In the guessing game, we imagined predicting the next letter in a document starting from the beginning and working towards the end. Consider the task of predicting the *reversed* text, that is, predicting the letter that precedes those already known. Most people find this a harder task. Assuming that we model the language using an N-gram model (which says the probability of the next character depends only on the $N-1$ preceding characters), is there any difference between the average information contents of the reversed language and the forward language?

▶ 8.4 Solutions

Solution to exercise 8.2 (p.140). See exercise 8.6 (p.140) for an example where $H(X \mid y)$ exceeds $H(X)$ (set $y = 3$).

    We can prove the inequality $H(X \mid Y) \leq H(X)$ by turning the expression into a relative entropy (using Bayes' theorem) and invoking Gibbs' inequality (exercise 2.26 (p.37)):

$$
\begin{aligned}
H(X \mid Y) &\equiv \sum_{y \in \mathcal{A}_Y} P(y) \left[\sum_{x \in \mathcal{A}_X} P(x \mid y) \log \frac{1}{P(x \mid y)} \right] \\
&= \sum_{xy \in \mathcal{A}_X \mathcal{A}_Y} P(x, y) \log \frac{1}{P(x \mid y)} \quad\quad\quad (8.16) \\
&= \sum_{xy} P(x) P(y \mid x) \log \frac{P(y)}{P(y \mid x) P(x)} \quad\quad (8.17) \\
&= \sum_{x} P(x) \log \frac{1}{P(x)} + \sum_{x} P(x) \sum_{y} P(y \mid x) \log \frac{P(y)}{P(y \mid x)} (8.18)
\end{aligned}
$$

The last expression is a sum of relative entropies between the distributions $P(y \mid x)$ and $P(y)$. So

$$
H(X \mid Y) \leq H(X) + 0, \quad\quad\quad\quad (8.19)
$$

with equality only if $P(y \mid x) = P(y)$ for all x and y (that is, only if X and Y are independent).

Solution to exercise 8.3 (p.140). The chain rule for entropy follows from the decomposition of a joint probability:

$$H(X,Y) = \sum_{xy} P(x,y) \log \frac{1}{P(x,y)} \tag{8.20}$$

$$= \sum_{xy} P(x)P(y\,|\,x) \left[\log \frac{1}{P(x)} + \log \frac{1}{P(y\,|\,x)} \right] \tag{8.21}$$

$$= \sum_x P(x) \log \frac{1}{P(x)} + \sum_x P(x) \sum_y P(y\,|\,x) \log \frac{1}{P(y\,|\,x)} \tag{8.22}$$

$$= H(X) + H(Y\,|\,X). \tag{8.23}$$

Solution to exercise 8.4 (p.140). Symmetry of mutual information:

$$I(X;Y) = H(X) - H(X\,|\,Y) \tag{8.24}$$

$$= \sum_x P(x) \log \frac{1}{P(x)} - \sum_{xy} P(x,y) \log \frac{1}{P(x\,|\,y)} \tag{8.25}$$

$$= \sum_{xy} P(x,y) \log \frac{P(x\,|\,y)}{P(x)} \tag{8.26}$$

$$= \sum_{xy} P(x,y) \log \frac{P(x,y)}{P(x)P(y)}. \tag{8.27}$$

This expression is symmetric in x and y so

$$I(X;Y) = H(X) - H(X\,|\,Y) = H(Y) - H(Y\,|\,X). \tag{8.28}$$

We can prove that mutual information is positive two ways. One is to continue from

$$I(X;Y) = \sum_{x,y} P(x,y) \log \frac{P(x,y)}{P(x)P(y)} \tag{8.29}$$

which is a relative entropy and use Gibbs' inequality (proved on p.44), which asserts that this relative entropy is ≥ 0, with equality only if $P(x,y) = P(x)P(y)$, that is, if X and Y are independent.

The other is to use Jensen's inequality on

$$-\sum_{x,y} P(x,y) \log \frac{P(x)P(y)}{P(x,y)} \geq -\log \sum_{x,y} \frac{P(x,y)}{P(x,y)} P(x)P(y) = \log 1 = 0. \tag{8.30}$$

Solution to exercise 8.7 (p.141). $z = x + y \bmod 2$.

(a) If $q = 1/2$, $\mathcal{P}_Z = \{1/2, 1/2\}$ and $I(Z;X) = H(Z) - H(Z\,|\,X) = 1 - 1 = 0$.

(b) For general q and p, $\mathcal{P}_Z = \{pq + (1-p)(1-q), p(1-q) + q(1-p)\}$. The mutual information is $I(Z;X) = H(Z) - H(Z\,|\,X) = H_2(pq + (1-p)(1-q)) - H_2(q)$.

Three term entropies

Solution to exercise 8.8 (p.141). The depiction of entropies in terms of Venn diagrams is misleading for at least two reasons.

First, one is used to thinking of Venn diagrams as depicting sets; but what are the 'sets' $H(X)$ and $H(Y)$ depicted in figure 8.2, and what are the objects that are members of those sets? I think this diagram encourages the novice student to make inappropriate analogies. For example, some students imagine

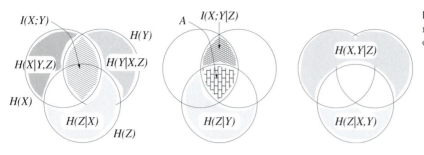

Figure 8.3. A misleading representation of entropies, continued.

that the random outcome (x, y) might correspond to a point in the diagram, and thus confuse entropies with probabilities.

Secondly, the depiction in terms of Venn diagrams encourages one to believe that all the areas correspond to positive quantities. In the special case of two random variables it is indeed true that $H(X \mid Y)$, $I(X; Y)$ and $H(Y \mid X)$ are positive quantities. But as soon as we progress to three-variable ensembles, we obtain a diagram with positive-looking areas that may actually correspond to negative quantities. Figure 8.3 correctly shows relationships such as

$$H(X) + H(Z \mid X) + H(Y \mid X, Z) = H(X, Y, Z). \qquad (8.31)$$

But it gives the misleading impression that the conditional mutual information $I(X; Y \mid Z)$ is *less than* the mutual information $I(X; Y)$. In fact the area labelled A can correspond to a *negative* quantity. Consider the joint ensemble (X, Y, Z) in which $x \in \{0, 1\}$ and $y \in \{0, 1\}$ are independent binary variables and $z \in \{0, 1\}$ is defined to be $z = x + y \bmod 2$. Then clearly $H(X) = H(Y) = 1$ bit. Also $H(Z) = 1$ bit. And $H(Y \mid X) = H(Y) = 1$ since the two variables are independent. So the mutual information between X and Y is zero. $I(X; Y) = 0$. However, if z is observed, X and Y become correlated — knowing x, given z, tells you what y is: $y = z - x \bmod 2$. So $I(X; Y \mid Z) = 1$ bit. Thus the area labelled A must correspond to -1 bits for the figure to give the correct answers.

The above example is not at all a capricious or exceptional illustration. The binary symmetric channel with input X, noise Y, and output Z is a situation in which $I(X; Y) = 0$ (input and noise are uncorrelated) but $I(X; Y \mid Z) > 0$ (once you see the output, the unknown input and the unknown noise are intimately related!).

The Venn diagram representation is therefore valid only if one is aware that positive areas may represent negative quantities. With this proviso kept in mind, the interpretation of entropies in terms of sets can be helpful (Yeung, 1991).

Solution to exercise 8.9 (p.141). For any joint ensemble XYZ, the following chain rule for mutual information holds.

$$I(X; Y, Z) = I(X; Y) + I(X; Z \mid Y). \qquad (8.32)$$

Now, in the case $w \rightarrow d \rightarrow r$, w and r are independent given d, so $I(W; R \mid D) = 0$. Using the chain rule twice, we have:

$$I(W; D, R) = I(W; D) \qquad (8.33)$$

and

$$I(W; D, R) = I(W; R) + I(W; D \mid R), \qquad (8.34)$$

so

$$I(W; R) - I(W; D) \leq 0. \qquad (8.35)$$

About Chapter 9

Before reading Chapter 9, you should have read Chapter 1 and worked on exercise 2.26 (p.37), and exercises 8.2–8.7 (pp.140–141).

9

Communication over a Noisy Channel

▶ 9.1 The big picture

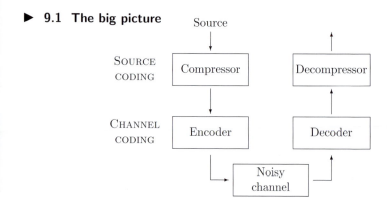

In Chapters 4–6, we discussed source coding with block codes, symbol codes and stream codes. We implicitly assumed that the channel from the compressor to the decompressor was noise-free. Real channels are noisy. We will now spend two chapters on the subject of noisy-channel coding – the fundamental possibilities and limitations of error-free communication through a noisy channel. The aim of channel coding is to make the noisy channel behave like a noiseless channel. We will assume that the data to be transmitted has been through a good compressor, so the bit stream has no obvious redundancy. The channel code, which makes the transmission, will put back redundancy of a special sort, designed to make the noisy received signal decodeable.

Suppose we transmit 1000 bits per second with $p_0 = p_1 = 1/2$ over a noisy channel that flips bits with probability $f = 0.1$. What is the rate of transmission of information? We might guess that the rate is 900 bits per second by subtracting the expected number of errors per second. But this is not correct, because the recipient does not know where the errors occurred. Consider the case where the noise is so great that the received symbols are independent of the transmitted symbols. This corresponds to a noise level of $f = 0.5$, since half of the received symbols are correct due to chance alone. But when $f = 0.5$, no information is transmitted at all.

Given what we have learnt about entropy, it seems reasonable that a measure of the information transmitted is given by the mutual information between the source and the received signal, that is, the entropy of the source minus the conditional entropy of the source given the received signal.

We will now review the definition of conditional entropy and mutual information. Then we will examine whether it is possible to use such a noisy channel to communicate *reliably*. We will show that for any channel Q there is a non-zero rate, the capacity $C(Q)$, up to which information can be sent with arbitrarily small probability of error.

▶ 9.2 Review of probability and information

As an example, we take the joint distribution XY from exercise 8.6 (p.140). The marginal distributions $P(x)$ and $P(y)$ are shown in the margins.

$P(x,y)$		x			$P(y)$
	1	2	3	4	
y 1	$1/8$	$1/16$	$1/32$	$1/32$	$1/4$
2	$1/16$	$1/8$	$1/32$	$1/32$	$1/4$
3	$1/16$	$1/16$	$1/16$	$1/16$	$1/4$
4	$1/4$	0	0	0	$1/4$
$P(x)$	$1/2$	$1/4$	$1/8$	$1/8$	

The joint entropy is $H(X,Y) = 27/8$ bits. The marginal entropies are $H(X) = 7/4$ bits and $H(Y) = 2$ bits.

We can compute the conditional distribution of x for each value of y, and the entropy of each of those conditional distributions:

$P(x\,|\,y)$		x			$H(X\,|\,y)/\text{bits}$
	1	2	3	4	
y 1	$1/2$	$1/4$	$1/8$	$1/8$	$7/4$
2	$1/4$	$1/2$	$1/8$	$1/8$	$7/4$
3	$1/4$	$1/4$	$1/4$	$1/4$	2
4	1	0	0	0	0
					$H(X\,|\,Y) = {}^{11}/_8$

Note that whereas $H(X\,|\,y\!=\!4) = 0$ is less than $H(X)$, $H(X\,|\,y\!=\!3)$ is greater than $H(X)$. So in some cases, learning y can *increase* our uncertainty about x. Note also that although $P(x\,|\,y\!=\!2)$ is a different distribution from $P(x)$, the conditional entropy $H(X\,|\,y\!=\!2)$ is equal to $H(X)$. So learning that y is 2 changes our knowledge about x but does not reduce the uncertainty of x, as measured by the entropy. On average though, learning y does convey information about x, since $H(X\,|\,Y) < H(X)$.

One may also evaluate $H(Y|X) = 13/8$ bits. The mutual information is $I(X;Y) = H(X) - H(X\,|\,Y) = 3/8$ bits.

▶ 9.3 Noisy channels

A discrete memoryless channel Q is characterized by an input alphabet $\mathcal{A}_X$, an output alphabet $\mathcal{A}_Y$, and a set of conditional probability distributions $P(y\,|\,x)$, one for each $x \in \mathcal{A}_X$.

These *transition probabilities* may be written in a matrix

$$Q_{j|i} = P(y\!=\!b_j\,|\,x\!=\!a_i). \qquad (9.1)$$

I usually orient this matrix with the output variable j indexing the rows and the input variable i indexing the columns, so that each column of $\mathbf{Q}$ is a probability vector. With this convention, we can obtain the probability of the output, $\mathbf{p}_Y$, from a probability distribution over the input, $\mathbf{p}_X$, by right-multiplication:

$$\mathbf{p}_Y = \mathbf{Q}\mathbf{p}_X. \qquad (9.2)$$

Some useful model channels are:

Binary symmetric channel. $\mathcal{A}_X = \{0, 1\}$. $\mathcal{A}_Y = \{0, 1\}$.

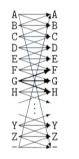

$$
\begin{aligned}
P(y=0\,|\,x=0) &= 1-f; & P(y=0\,|\,x=1) &= f; \\
P(y=1\,|\,x=0) &= f; & P(y=1\,|\,x=1) &= 1-f.
\end{aligned}
$$

Binary erasure channel. $\mathcal{A}_X = \{0, 1\}$. $\mathcal{A}_Y = \{0, ?, 1\}$.

$$
\begin{aligned}
P(y=0\,|\,x=0) &= 1-f; & P(y=0\,|\,x=1) &= 0; \\
P(y=?\,|\,x=0) &= f; & P(y=?\,|\,x=1) &= f; \\
P(y=1\,|\,x=0) &= 0; & P(y=1\,|\,x=1) &= 1-f.
\end{aligned}
$$

Noisy typewriter. $\mathcal{A}_X = \mathcal{A}_Y =$ the 27 letters {A, B, ..., Z, -}. The letters are arranged in a circle, and when the typist attempts to type B, what comes out is either A, B or C, with probability $1/3$ each; when the input is C, the output is B, C or D; and so forth, with the final letter '-' adjacent to the first letter A.

$$
\begin{aligned}
P(y=\mathrm{F}\,|\,x=\mathrm{G}) &= 1/3; \\
P(y=\mathrm{G}\,|\,x=\mathrm{G}) &= 1/3; \\
P(y=\mathrm{H}\,|\,x=\mathrm{G}) &= 1/3;
\end{aligned}
$$

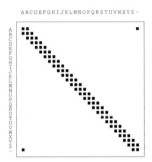

Z channel. $\mathcal{A}_X = \{0, 1\}$. $\mathcal{A}_Y = \{0, 1\}$.

$$
\begin{aligned}
P(y=0\,|\,x=0) &= 1; & P(y=0\,|\,x=1) &= f; \\
P(y=1\,|\,x=0) &= 0; & P(y=1\,|\,x=1) &= 1-f.
\end{aligned}
$$

▶ 9.4 Inferring the input given the output

If we assume that the input x to a channel comes from an ensemble X, then we obtain a joint ensemble XY in which the random variables x and y have the joint distribution:

$$P(x, y) = P(y\,|\,x)P(x). \tag{9.3}$$

Now if we receive a particular symbol y, what was the input symbol x? We typically won't know for certain. We can write down the posterior distribution of the input using Bayes' theorem:

$$P(x\,|\,y) = \frac{P(y\,|\,x)P(x)}{P(y)} = \frac{P(y\,|\,x)P(x)}{\sum_{x'} P(y\,|\,x')P(x')}. \tag{9.4}$$

Example 9.1. Consider a binary symmetric channel with probability of error $f = 0.15$. Let the input ensemble be $\mathcal{P}_X : \{p_0 = 0.9, p_1 = 0.1\}$. Assume we observe $y = 1$.

$$
\begin{aligned}
P(x=1\,|\,y=1) &= \frac{P(y=1\,|\,x=1)P(x=1)}{\sum_{x'} P(y\,|\,x')P(x')} \\
&= \frac{0.85 \times 0.1}{0.85 \times 0.1 + 0.15 \times 0.9} \\
&= \frac{0.085}{0.22} = 0.39.
\end{aligned}
\tag{9.5}
$$

Thus '$x=1$' is still less probable than '$x=0$', although it is not as improbable as it was before.

Exercise 9.2.[1, p.157] Now assume we observe $y=0$. Compute the probability of $x=1$ given $y=0$.

Example 9.3. Consider a Z channel with probability of error $f=0.15$. Let the input ensemble be $\mathcal{P}_X : \{p_0=0.9, p_1=0.1\}$. Assume we observe $y=1$.

$$
\begin{aligned}
P(x=1\,|\,y=1) &= \frac{0.85 \times 0.1}{0.85 \times 0.1 + 0 \times 0.9} \\
&= \frac{0.085}{0.085} = 1.0. \quad (9.6)
\end{aligned}
$$

So given the output $y=1$ we become certain of the input.

Exercise 9.4.[1, p.157] Alternatively, assume we observe $y=0$. Compute $P(x=1\,|\,y=0)$.

▶ **9.5 Information conveyed by a channel**

We now consider how much information can be communicated through a channel. In operational terms, we are interested in finding ways of using the channel such that all the bits that are communicated are recovered with negligible probability of error. In mathematical terms, assuming a particular input ensemble X, we can measure how much information the output conveys about the input by the mutual information:

$$
I(X;Y) \equiv H(X) - H(X\,|\,Y) = H(Y) - H(Y|X). \quad (9.7)
$$

Our aim is to establish the connection between these two ideas. Let us evaluate $I(X;Y)$ for some of the channels above.

Hint for computing mutual information

We will tend to think of $I(X;Y)$ as $H(X) - H(X\,|\,Y)$, i.e., how much the uncertainty of the input X is reduced when we look at the output Y. But for computational purposes it is often handy to evaluate $H(Y) - H(Y|X)$ instead.

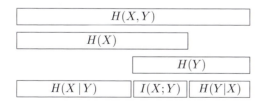

Figure 9.1. The relationship between joint information, marginal entropy, conditional entropy and mutual entropy. This figure is important, so I'm showing it twice.

Example 9.5. Consider the binary symmetric channel again, with $f=0.15$ and $\mathcal{P}_X : \{p_0=0.9, p_1=0.1\}$. We already evaluated the marginal probabilities $P(y)$ implicitly above: $P(y=0) = 0.78$; $P(y=1) = 0.22$. The mutual information is:

$$
I(X;Y) = H(Y) - H(Y|X).
$$

What is $H(Y|X)$? It is defined to be the weighted sum over x of $H(Y\,|\,x)$; but $H(Y\,|\,x)$ is the same for each value of x: $H(Y\,|\,x=0)$ is $H_2(0.15)$, and $H(Y\,|\,x=1)$ is $H_2(0.15)$. So

$$
\begin{aligned}
I(X;Y) &= H(Y) - H(Y|X) \\
&= H_2(0.22) - H_2(0.15) \\
&= 0.76 - 0.61 \; = \; 0.15 \text{ bits.} \qquad (9.8)
\end{aligned}
$$

This may be contrasted with the entropy of the source $H(X) = H_2(0.1) = 0.47$ bits.

Note: here we have used the binary entropy function $H_2(p) \equiv H(p, 1-p) = p\log_2\frac{1}{p} + (1-p)\log_2\frac{1}{(1-p)}$.

Example 9.6. And now the Z channel, with $\mathcal{P}_X$ as above. $P(y=1)=0.085$.

$$
\begin{aligned}
I(X;Y) &= H(Y) - H(Y|X) \\
&= H_2(0.085) - [0.9H_2(0) + 0.1H_2(0.15)] \\
&= 0.42 - (0.1 \times 0.61) = 0.36 \text{ bits.} \qquad (9.9)
\end{aligned}
$$

The entropy of the source, as above, is $H(X) = 0.47$ bits. Notice that the mutual information $I(X;Y)$ for the Z channel is bigger than the mutual information for the binary symmetric channel with the same f. The Z channel is a more reliable channel.

 Exercise 9.7.[1, p.157] Compute the mutual information between X and Y for the binary symmetric channel with $f=0.15$ when the input distribution is $\mathcal{P}_X = \{p_0=0.5, p_1=0.5\}$.

 Exercise 9.8.[2, p.157] Compute the mutual information between X and Y for the Z channel with $f = 0.15$ when the input distribution is $\mathcal{P}_X$: $\{p_0=0.5, p_1=0.5\}$.

Maximizing the mutual information

We have observed in the above examples that the mutual information between the input and the output depends on the chosen input ensemble.

Let us assume that we wish to maximize the mutual information conveyed by the channel by choosing the best possible input ensemble. We define the *capacity* of the channel to be its maximum mutual information.

The capacity of a channel Q is:

$$
C(Q) = \max_{\mathcal{P}_X} I(X;Y). \qquad (9.10)
$$

The distribution $\mathcal{P}_X$ that achieves the maximum is called the *optimal input distribution*, denoted by $\mathcal{P}_X^*$. [There may be multiple optimal input distributions achieving the same value of $I(X;Y)$.]

In Chapter 10 we will show that the capacity does indeed measure the maximum amount of error-free information that can be transmitted over the channel per unit time.

Example 9.9. Consider the binary symmetric channel with $f=0.15$. Above, we considered $\mathcal{P}_X = \{p_0=0.9, p_1=0.1\}$, and found $I(X;Y) = 0.15$ bits. How much better can we do? By symmetry, the optimal input distribu-

$I(X;Y)$

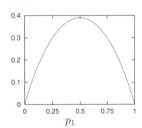

Figure 9.2. The mutual information $I(X;Y)$ for a binary symmetric channel with $f = 0.15$ as a function of the input distribution.

tion is $\{0.5, 0.5\}$ and the capacity is

$$C(Q_{\mathrm{BSC}}) = H_2(0.5) - H_2(0.15) = 1.0 - 0.61 = 0.39 \text{ bits}. \qquad (9.11)$$

We'll justify the symmetry argument later. If there's any doubt about the symmetry argument, we can always resort to explicit maximization of the mutual information $I(X;Y)$,

$$I(X;Y) = H_2((1-f)p_1 + (1-p_1)f) - H_2(f) \quad \text{(figure 9.2)}. \qquad (9.12)$$

Example 9.10. The noisy typewriter. The optimal input distribution is a uniform distribution over x, and gives $C = \log_2 9$ bits.

Example 9.11. Consider the Z channel with $f = 0.15$. Identifying the optimal input distribution is not so straightforward. We evaluate $I(X;Y)$ explicitly for $\mathcal{P}_X = \{p_0, p_1\}$. First, we need to compute $P(y)$. The probability of $y = 1$ is easiest to write down:

$$P(y=1) = p_1(1-f). \qquad (9.13)$$

Then the mutual information is:

$$
\begin{aligned}
I(X;Y) &= H(Y) - H(Y|X) \\
&= H_2(p_1(1-f)) - (p_0 H_2(0) + p_1 H_2(f)) \\
&= H_2(p_1(1-f)) - p_1 H_2(f). \qquad (9.14)
\end{aligned}
$$

This is a non-trivial function of p_1, shown in figure 9.3. It is maximized for $f = 0.15$ by $p_1^* = 0.445$. We find $C(Q_Z) = 0.685$. Notice that the optimal input distribution is not $\{0.5, 0.5\}$. We can communicate slightly more information by using input symbol 0 more frequently than 1.

$I(X;Y)$

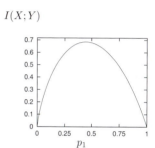

Figure 9.3. The mutual information $I(X;Y)$ for a Z channel with $f = 0.15$ as a function of the input distribution.

Exercise 9.12.[1, p.158] What is the capacity of the binary symmetric channel for general f?

Exercise 9.13.[2, p.158] Show that the capacity of the binary erasure channel with $f = 0.15$ is $C_{\mathrm{BEC}} = 0.85$. What is its capacity for general f? Comment.

▶ 9.6 The noisy-channel coding theorem

It seems plausible that the 'capacity' we have defined may be a measure of information conveyed by a channel; what is not obvious, and what we will prove in the next chapter, is that the capacity indeed measures the rate at which blocks of data can be communicated over the channel *with arbitrarily small probability of error*.

We make the following definitions.

An (N, K) block code for a channel Q is a list of $S = 2^K$ codewords

$$\{\mathbf{x}^{(1)}, \mathbf{x}^{(2)}, \dots, \mathbf{x}^{(2^K)}\}, \quad \mathbf{x}^{(s)} \in \mathcal{A}_X^N,$$

each of length N. Using this code we can encode a signal $s \in \{1, 2, 3, \dots, 2^K\}$ as $\mathbf{x}^{(s)}$. [The number of codewords S is an integer, but the number of bits specified by choosing a codeword, $K \equiv \log_2 S$, is not necessarily an integer.]

The *rate* of the code is $R = K/N$ bits per channel use.

[We will use this definition of the rate for any channel, not only channels with binary inputs; note however that it is sometimes conventional to define the rate of a code for a channel with q input symbols to be $K/(N \log q)$.]

A decoder for an (N, K) block code is a mapping from the set of length-N strings of channel outputs, $\mathcal{A}_Y^N$ to a codeword label $\hat{s} \in \{0, 1, 2, \ldots, 2^K\}$.

The extra symbol $\hat{s} = 0$ can be used to indicate a 'failure'.

The probability of block error of a code and decoder, for a given channel, and for a given probability distribution over the encoded signal $P(s_{\text{in}})$, is:

$$p_{\text{B}} = \sum_{s_{\text{in}}} P(s_{\text{in}}) P(s_{\text{out}} \neq s_{\text{in}} \mid s_{\text{in}}) \tag{9.15}$$

The maximal probability of block error is

$$p_{\text{BM}} = \max_{s_{\text{in}}} P(s_{\text{out}} \neq s_{\text{in}} \mid s_{\text{in}}) \tag{9.16}$$

The optimal decoder for a channel code is the one that minimizes the probability of block error. It decodes an output $\mathbf{y}$ as the input s that has maximum posterior probability $P(s \mid \mathbf{y})$.

$$P(s \mid \mathbf{y}) = \frac{P(\mathbf{y} \mid s) P(s)}{\sum_{s'} P(\mathbf{y} \mid s') P(s')} \tag{9.17}$$

$$\hat{s}_{\text{optimal}} = \arg\max P(s \mid \mathbf{y}). \tag{9.18}$$

A uniform prior distribution on s is usually assumed, in which case the optimal decoder is also the *maximum likelihood decoder*, i.e., the decoder that maps an output $\mathbf{y}$ to the input s that has maximum *likelihood* $P(\mathbf{y} \mid s)$.

The probability of bit error p_{b} is defined assuming that the codeword number s is represented by a binary vector $\mathbf{s}$ of length K bits; it is the average probability that a bit of $\mathbf{s}_{\text{out}}$ is not equal to the corresponding bit of $\mathbf{s}_{\text{in}}$ (averaging over all K bits).

Shannon's noisy-channel coding theorem (part one). Associated with each discrete memoryless channel, there is a non-negative number C (called the channel capacity) with the following property. For any $\epsilon > 0$ and $R < C$, for large enough N, there exists a block code of length N and rate $\geq R$ and a decoding algorithm, such that the maximal probability of block error is $< \epsilon$.

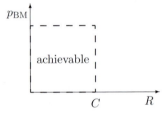

Figure 9.4. Portion of the R, p_{BM} plane asserted to be achievable by the first part of Shannon's noisy channel coding theorem.

Confirmation of the theorem for the noisy typewriter channel

In the case of the noisy typewriter, we can easily confirm the theorem, because we can create a completely error-free communication strategy using a block code of length $N = 1$: we use only the letters B, E, H, ..., Z, i.e., every third letter. These letters form a *non-confusable subset* of the input alphabet (see figure 9.5). Any output can be uniquely decoded. The number of inputs in the non-confusable subset is 9, so the error-free information rate of this system is $\log_2 9$ bits, which is equal to the capacity C, which we evaluated in example 9.10 (p. 151).

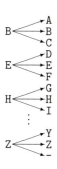

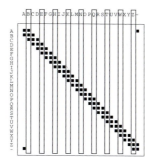

Figure 9.5. A non-confusable subset of inputs for the noisy typewriter.

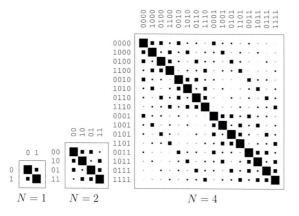

Figure 9.6. Extended channels obtained from a binary symmetric channel with transition probability 0.15.

$N = 1$ $N = 2$ $N = 4$

How does this translate into the terms of the theorem? The following table explains.

The theorem	How it applies to the noisy typewriter
Associated with each discrete memoryless channel, there is a non-negative number C.	The capacity C is $\log_2 9$.
For any $\epsilon > 0$ and $R < C$, for large enough N,	No matter what ϵ and R are, we set the block length N to 1.
there exists a block code of length N and rate $\geq R$	The block code is $\{B, E, \ldots, Z\}$. The value of K is given by $2^K = 9$, so $K = \log_2 9$, and this code has rate $\log_2 9$, which is greater than the requested value of R.
and a decoding algorithm,	The decoding algorithm maps the received letter to the nearest letter in the code;
such that the maximal probability of block error is $< \epsilon$.	the maximal probability of block error is zero, which is less than the given ϵ.

▶ 9.7 Intuitive preview of proof

Extended channels

To prove the theorem for a given channel, we consider the *extended channel* corresponding to N uses of the given channel. The extended channel has $|\mathcal{A}_X|^N$ possible inputs $\mathbf{x}$ and $|\mathcal{A}_Y|^N$ possible outputs. Extended channels obtained from a binary symmetric channel and from a Z channel are shown in figures 9.6 and 9.7, with $N = 2$ and $N = 4$.

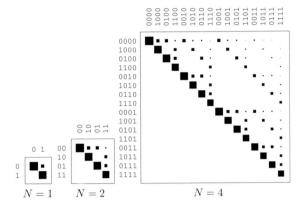

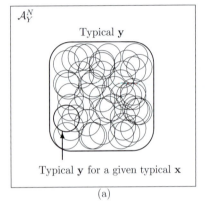

Figure 9.7. Extended channels obtained from a Z channel with transition probability 0.15. Each column corresponds to an input, and each row is a different output.

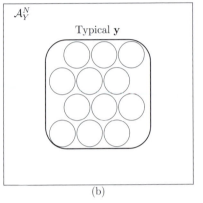

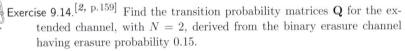

Figure 9.8. (a) Some typical outputs in $\mathcal{A}_Y^N$ corresponding to typical inputs $\mathbf{x}$. (b) A subset of the typical sets shown in (a) that do not overlap each other. This picture can be compared with the solution to the noisy typewriter in figure 9.5.

Exercise 9.14.[2, p.159] Find the transition probability matrices $\mathbf{Q}$ for the extended channel, with $N = 2$, derived from the binary erasure channel having erasure probability 0.15.

By selecting two columns of this transition probability matrix, we can define a rate-$1/2$ code for this channel with blocklength $N = 2$. What is the best choice of two columns? What is the decoding algorithm?

To prove the noisy-channel coding theorem, we make use of large block lengths N. The intuitive idea is that, if N is large, *an extended channel looks a lot like the noisy typewriter*. Any particular input $\mathbf{x}$ is very likely to produce an output in a small subspace of the output alphabet – the typical output set, given that input. So we can find a non-confusable subset of the inputs that produce essentially disjoint output sequences. For a given N, let us consider a way of generating such a non-confusable subset of the inputs, and count up how many distinct inputs it contains.

Imagine making an input sequence $\mathbf{x}$ for the extended channel by drawing it from an ensemble X^N, where X is an arbitrary ensemble over the input alphabet. Recall the source coding theorem of Chapter 4, and consider the number of probable output sequences $\mathbf{y}$. The total number of typical output sequences $\mathbf{y}$ is $2^{NH(Y)}$, all having similar probability. For any particular typical input sequence $\mathbf{x}$, there are about $2^{NH(Y|X)}$ probable sequences. Some of these subsets of $\mathcal{A}_Y^N$ are depicted by circles in figure 9.8a.

We now imagine restricting ourselves to a subset of the typical inputs $\mathbf{x}$ such that the corresponding typical output sets do not overlap, as shown in figure 9.8b. We can then bound the number of non-confusable inputs by dividing the size of the typical $\mathbf{y}$ set, $2^{NH(Y)}$, by the size of each typical-$\mathbf{y}$-

given-typical-**x** set, $2^{NH(Y|X)}$. So the number of non-confusable inputs, if they are selected from the set of typical inputs $\mathbf{x} \sim X^N$, is $\leq 2^{NH(Y)-NH(Y|X)} = 2^{NI(X;Y)}$.

The maximum value of this bound is achieved if X is the ensemble that maximizes $I(X;Y)$, in which case the number of non-confusable inputs is $\leq 2^{NC}$. Thus asymptotically up to C bits per cycle, and no more, can be communicated with vanishing error probability. □

This sketch has not rigorously proved that reliable communication really is possible – that's our task for the next chapter.

▶ ## 9.8 Further exercises

 Exercise 9.15.[3, p.159] Refer back to the computation of the capacity of the Z channel with $f = 0.15$.

(a) Why is p_1^* less than 0.5? One could argue that it is good to favour the 0 input, since it is transmitted without error – and also argue that it is good to favour the 1 input, since it often gives rise to the highly prized 1 output, which allows certain identification of the input! Try to make a convincing argument.

(b) In the case of general f, show that the optimal input distribution is

$$p_1^* = \frac{1/(1-f)}{1 + 2^{(H_2(f)/(1-f))}}. \qquad (9.19)$$

(c) What happens to p_1^* if the noise level f is very close to 1?

 Exercise 9.16.[2, p.159] Sketch graphs of the capacity of the Z channel, the binary symmetric channel and the binary erasure channel as a function of f.

▷ Exercise 9.17.[2] What is the capacity of the five-input, ten-output channel whose transition probability matrix is

$$
\begin{bmatrix}
0.25 & 0 & 0 & 0 & 0.25 \\
0.25 & 0 & 0 & 0 & 0.25 \\
0.25 & 0.25 & 0 & 0 & 0 \\
0.25 & 0.25 & 0 & 0 & 0 \\
0 & 0.25 & 0.25 & 0 & 0 \\
0 & 0.25 & 0.25 & 0 & 0 \\
0 & 0 & 0.25 & 0.25 & 0 \\
0 & 0 & 0.25 & 0.25 & 0 \\
0 & 0 & 0 & 0.25 & 0.25 \\
0 & 0 & 0 & 0.25 & 0.25
\end{bmatrix}
$$
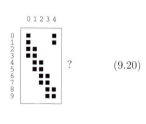
$$? \qquad (9.20)$$

 Exercise 9.18.[2, p.159] Consider a Gaussian channel with binary input $x \in \{-1, +1\}$ and *real* output alphabet $\mathcal{A}_Y$, with transition probability density

$$Q(y \,|\, x, \alpha, \sigma) = \frac{1}{\sqrt{2\pi\sigma^2}} e^{-\frac{(y-x\alpha)^2}{2\sigma^2}}, \qquad (9.21)$$

where α is the signal amplitude.

(a) Compute the posterior probability of x given y, assuming that the two inputs are equiprobable. Put your answer in the form

$$P(x=1 \,|\, y, \alpha, \sigma) = \frac{1}{1 + e^{-a(y)}}. \qquad (9.22)$$

Sketch the value of $P(x=1 \mid y, \alpha, \sigma)$ as a function of y.

(b) Assume that a single bit is to be transmitted. What is the optimal decoder, and what is its probability of error? Express your answer in terms of the signal to noise ratio α^2/σ^2 and the error function (the cumulative probability function of the Gaussian distribution),

$$\Phi(z) \equiv \int_{-\infty}^{z} \frac{1}{\sqrt{2\pi}} e^{-\frac{z^2}{2}} \, dz. \qquad (9.23)$$

[Note that this definition of the error function $\Phi(z)$ may not correspond to other people's.]

Pattern recognition as a noisy channel

We may think of many pattern recognition problems in terms of communication channels. Consider the case of recognizing handwritten digits (such as postcodes on envelopes). The author of the digit wishes to communicate a message from the set $\mathcal{A}_X = \{0, 1, 2, 3, \ldots, 9\}$; this selected message is the input to the channel. What comes out of the channel is a pattern of ink on paper. If the ink pattern is represented using 256 binary pixels, the channel Q has as its output a random variable $y \in \mathcal{A}_Y = \{0, 1\}^{256}$. An example of an element from this alphabet is shown in the margin.

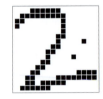

Exercise 9.19.[2] Estimate how many patterns in $\mathcal{A}_Y$ are recognizable as the character '2'. [The aim of this problem is to try to demonstrate the existence of *as many patterns as possible* that are recognizable as 2s.]

Discuss how one might model the channel $P(y \mid x=2)$. Estimate the entropy of the probability distribution $P(y \mid x=2)$.

One strategy for doing pattern recognition is to create a model for $P(y \mid x)$ for each value of the input $x = \{0, 1, 2, 3, \ldots, 9\}$, then use Bayes' theorem to infer x given y.

$$P(x \mid y) = \frac{P(y \mid x)P(x)}{\sum_{x'} P(y \mid x')P(x')}. \qquad (9.24)$$

This strategy is known as *full probabilistic modelling* or *generative modelling*. This is essentially how current speech recognition systems work. In addition to the channel model, $P(y \mid x)$, one uses a prior probability distribution $P(x)$, which in the case of both character recognition and speech recognition is a language model that specifies the probability of the next character/word given the context and the known grammar and statistics of the language.

Figure 9.9. Some more 2s.

Random coding

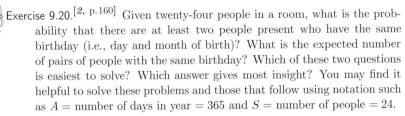Exercise 9.20.[2, p.160] Given twenty-four people in a room, what is the probability that there are at least two people present who have the same birthday (i.e., day and month of birth)? What is the expected number of pairs of people with the same birthday? Which of these two questions is easiest to solve? Which answer gives most insight? You may find it helpful to solve these problems and those that follow using notation such as A = number of days in year = 365 and S = number of people = 24.

▷ Exercise 9.21.[2] The birthday problem may be related to a coding scheme. Assume we wish to convey a message to an outsider identifying one of the twenty-four people. We could simply communicate a number s from $\mathcal{A}_S = \{1, 2, \ldots, 24\}$, having agreed a mapping of people onto numbers; alternatively, we could convey a number from $\mathcal{A}_X = \{1, 2, \ldots, 365\}$, identifying the day of the year that is the selected person's birthday (with apologies to leapyearians). [The receiver is assumed to know all the people's birthdays.] What, roughly, is the probability of error of this communication scheme, assuming it is used for a single transmission? What is the capacity of the communication channel, and what is the rate of communication attempted by this scheme?

▷ Exercise 9.22.[2] Now imagine that there are K rooms in a building, each containing q people. (You might think of $K = 2$ and $q = 24$ as an example.) The aim is to communicate a selection of one person from each room by transmitting an ordered list of K days (from $\mathcal{A}_X$). Compare the probability of error of the following two schemes.

(a) As before, where each room transmits the birthday of the selected person.

(b) To each K-tuple of people, one drawn from each room, an ordered K-tuple of randomly selected days from $\mathcal{A}_X$ is assigned (this K-tuple has nothing to do with their birthdays). This enormous list of $S = q^K$ strings is known to the receiver. When the building has selected a particular person from each room, the ordered string of days corresponding to that K-tuple of people is transmitted.

What is the probability of error when $q = 364$ and $K = 1$? What is the probability of error when $q = 364$ and K is large, e.g. $K = 6000$?

▶ 9.9 Solutions

Solution to exercise 9.2 (p.149).   If we assume we observe $y = 0$,

$$P(x=1 \mid y=0) = \frac{P(y=0 \mid x=1)P(x=1)}{\sum_{x'} P(y \mid x')P(x')} \tag{9.25}$$

$$= \frac{0.15 \times 0.1}{0.15 \times 0.1 + 0.85 \times 0.9} \tag{9.26}$$

$$= \frac{0.015}{0.78} = 0.019. \tag{9.27}$$

Solution to exercise 9.4 (p.149).   If we observe $y = 0$,

$$P(x=1 \mid y=0) = \frac{0.15 \times 0.1}{0.15 \times 0.1 + 1.0 \times 0.9} \tag{9.28}$$

$$= \frac{0.015}{0.915} = 0.016. \tag{9.29}$$

Solution to exercise 9.7 (p.150).   The probability that $y = 1$ is 0.5, so the mutual information is:

$$I(X;Y) = H(Y) - H(Y \mid X) \tag{9.30}$$

$$= H_2(0.5) - H_2(0.15) \tag{9.31}$$

$$= 1 - 0.61 = 0.39 \text{ bits.} \tag{9.32}$$

Solution to exercise 9.8 (p.150).   We again compute the mutual information using $I(X;Y) = H(Y) - H(Y \mid X)$. The probability that $y = 0$ is 0.575, and

$H(Y \mid X) = \sum_x P(x)H(Y \mid x) = P(x=1)H(Y \mid x=1) + P(x=0)H(Y \mid x=0)$

so the mutual information is:

$$
\begin{aligned}
I(X;Y) &= H(Y) - H(Y \mid X) &\text{(9.33)}\\
&= H_2(0.575) - [0.5 \times H_2(0.15) + 0.5 \times 0] &\text{(9.34)}\\
&= 0.98 - 0.30 = 0.679 \text{ bits.} &\text{(9.35)}
\end{aligned}
$$

Solution to exercise 9.12 (p.151). By symmetry, the optimal input distribution is $\{0.5, 0.5\}$. Then the capacity is

$$
\begin{aligned}
C = I(X;Y) &= H(Y) - H(Y \mid X) &\text{(9.36)}\\
&= H_2(0.5) - H_2(f) &\text{(9.37)}\\
&= 1 - H_2(f). &\text{(9.38)}
\end{aligned}
$$

Would you like to find the optimal input distribution without invoking symmetry? We can do this by computing the mutual information in the general case where the input ensemble is $\{p_0, p_1\}$:

$$
\begin{aligned}
I(X;Y) &= H(Y) - H(Y \mid X) &\text{(9.39)}\\
&= H_2(p_0 f + p_1(1 - f)) - H_2(f). &\text{(9.40)}
\end{aligned}
$$

The only p-dependence is in the first term $H_2(p_0 f + p_1(1 - f))$, which is maximized by setting the argument to 0.5. This value is given by setting $p_0 = 1/2$.

Solution to exercise 9.13 (p.151). Answer 1. By symmetry, the optimal input distribution is $\{0.5, 0.5\}$. The capacity is most easily evaluated by writing the mutual information as $I(X;Y) = H(X) - H(X \mid Y)$. The conditional entropy $H(X \mid Y)$ is $\sum_y P(y)H(X \mid y)$; when y is known, x is only uncertain if $y = ?$, which occurs with probability $f/2 + f/2$, so the conditional entropy $H(X \mid Y)$ is $fH_2(0.5)$.

$$
\begin{aligned}
C = I(X;Y) &= H(X) - H(X \mid Y) &\text{(9.41)}\\
&= H_2(0.5) - fH_2(0.5) &\text{(9.42)}\\
&= 1 - f. &\text{(9.43)}
\end{aligned}
$$

The binary erasure channel fails a fraction f of the time. Its capacity is precisely $1 - f$, which is the fraction of the time that the channel is reliable. This result seems very reasonable, but it is far from obvious how to encode information so as to communicate *reliably* over this channel.

Answer 2. Alternatively, without invoking the symmetry assumed above, we can start from the input ensemble $\{p_0, p_1\}$. The probability that $y = ?$ is $p_0 f + p_1 f = f$, and when we receive $y = ?$, the posterior probability of x is the same as the prior probability, so:

$$
\begin{aligned}
I(X;Y) &= H(X) - H(X \mid Y) &\text{(9.44)}\\
&= H_2(p_1) - fH_2(p_1) &\text{(9.45)}\\
&= (1 - f)H_2(p_1). &\text{(9.46)}
\end{aligned}
$$

This mutual information achieves its maximum value of $(1-f)$ when $p_1 = 1/2$.

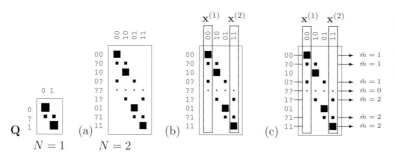

Figure 9.10. (a) The extended channel ($N = 2$) obtained from a binary erasure channel with erasure probability 0.15. (b) A block code consisting of the two codewords 00 and 11. (c) The optimal decoder for this code.

Solution to exercise 9.14 (p.153). The extended channel is shown in figure 9.10. The best code for this channel with $N = 2$ is obtained by choosing two columns that have minimal overlap, for example, columns 00 and 11. The decoding algorithm returns '00' if the extended channel output is among the top four and '11' if it's among the bottom four, and gives up if the output is '??'.

Solution to exercise 9.15 (p.155). In example 9.11 (p.151) we showed that the mutual information between input and output of the Z channel is

$$I(X;Y) = H(Y) - H(Y \mid X)$$
$$= H_2(p_1(1 - f)) - p_1 H_2(f). \tag{9.47}$$

We differentiate this expression with respect to p_1, taking care not to confuse $\log_2$ with $\log_e$:

$$\frac{\mathrm{d}}{\mathrm{d}p_1} I(X;Y) = (1 - f) \log_2 \frac{1 - p_1(1 - f)}{p_1(1 - f)} - H_2(f). \tag{9.48}$$

Setting this derivative to zero and rearranging using skills developed in exercise 2.17 (p.36), we obtain:

$$p_1^*(1 - f) = \frac{1}{1 + 2^{H_2(f)/(1-f)}}, \tag{9.49}$$

so the optimal input distribution is

$$p_1^* = \frac{1/(1 - f)}{1 + 2^{(H_2(f)/(1-f))}}. \tag{9.50}$$

As the noise level f tends to 1, this expression tends to $1/e$ (as you can prove using L'Hôpital's rule).

For all values of f, p_1^* is smaller than $1/2$. A rough intuition for why input 1 is used less than input 0 is that when input 1 is used, the noisy channel injects entropy into the received string; whereas when input 0 is used, the noise has zero entropy. Thus starting from $p_1 = 1/2$, a perturbation towards smaller p_1 will reduce the conditional entropy $H(Y \mid X)$ linearly while leaving $H(Y)$ unchanged, to first order. $H(Y)$ decreases only quadratically in $(p_1 - 1/2)$.

Solution to exercise 9.16 (p.155). The capacities of the three channels are shown in figure 9.11. For any $f < 0.5$, the BEC is the channel with highest capacity and the BSC the lowest.

Solution to exercise 9.18 (p.155). The logarithm of the posterior probability ratio, given y, is

$$a(y) = \log \frac{P(x = 1 \mid y, \alpha, \sigma)}{P(x = -1 \mid y, \alpha, \sigma)} = \log \frac{Q(y \mid x = 1, \alpha, \sigma)}{Q(y \mid x = -1, \alpha, \sigma)} = 2 \frac{\alpha y}{\sigma^2}. \tag{9.51}$$

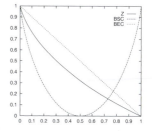

Figure 9.11. Capacities of the Z channel, binary symmetric channel, and binary erasure channel.

Using our skills picked up from exercise 2.17 (p.36), we rewrite this in the form

$$P(x=1\,|\,y,\alpha,\sigma) = \frac{1}{1+e^{-a(y)}}. \qquad (9.52)$$

The optimal decoder selects the most probable hypothesis; this can be done simply by looking at the sign of $a(y)$. If $a(y) > 0$ then decode as $\hat{x} = 1$.

The probability of error is

$$p_{\rm b} = \int_{-\infty}^{0} dy\, Q(y\,|\,x=1,\alpha,\sigma) = \int_{-\infty}^{-x\alpha} dy\, \frac{1}{\sqrt{2\pi\sigma^2}} e^{-\frac{y^2}{2\sigma^2}} = \Phi\left(-\frac{x\alpha}{\sigma}\right). \qquad (9.53)$$

Random coding

Solution to exercise 9.20 (p.156). The probability that $S = 24$ people whose birthdays are drawn at random from $A = 365$ days all have *distinct* birthdays is

$$\frac{A(A-1)(A-2)\ldots(A-S+1)}{A^q}. \qquad (9.54)$$

The probability that two (or more) people share a birthday is one minus this quantity, which, for $S = 24$ and $A = 365$, is about 0.5. This exact way of answering the question is not very informative since it is not clear for what value of S the probability changes from being close to 0 to being close to 1.

The number of pairs is $S(S-1)/2$, and the probability that a particular pair shares a birthday is $1/A$, so the *expected number* of collisions is

$$\frac{S(S-1)}{2}\frac{1}{A}. \qquad (9.55)$$

This answer is more instructive. The expected number of collisions is tiny if $S \ll \sqrt{A}$ and big if $S \gg \sqrt{A}$.

We can also approximate the probability that all birthdays are distinct, for small S, thus:

$$\frac{A(A-1)(A-2)\ldots(A-S+1)}{A^S} = (1)(1-{}^1\!/\!A)(1-{}^2\!/\!A)\ldots(1-{}^{(S-1)}\!/\!A)$$

$$\simeq \exp(0)\exp(-1/A)\exp(-2/A)\ldots\exp(-(S-1)/A) \qquad (9.56)$$

$$\simeq \exp\left(-\frac{1}{A}\sum_{i=1}^{S-1} i\right) = \exp\left(-\frac{S(S-1)/2}{A}\right). \qquad (9.57)$$

About Chapter 10

Before reading Chapter 10, you should have read Chapters 4 and 9. Exercise 9.14 (p.153) is especially recommended.

Cast of characters

Q	the noisy channel
C	the capacity of the channel
X^N	an ensemble used to create a random code
$\mathcal{C}$	a random code
N	the length of the codewords
$\mathbf{x}^{(s)}$	a codeword, the sth in the code
s	the number of a chosen codeword (mnemonic: the *source* selects s)
$S = 2^K$	the total number of codewords in the code
$K = \log_2 S$	the number of bits conveyed by the choice of one codeword from S, assuming it is chosen with uniform probability
$\mathbf{s}$	a binary representation of the number s
$R = K/N$	the rate of the code, in bits per channel use (sometimes called R' instead)
$\hat{s}$	the decoder's guess of s

10

The Noisy-Channel Coding Theorem

▶ **10.1 The theorem**

The theorem has three parts, two positive and one negative. The main positive result is the first.

1. For every discrete memoryless channel, the channel capacity

$$C = \max_{\mathcal{P}_X} I(X;Y) \qquad (10.1)$$

   has the following property. For any $\epsilon > 0$ and $R < C$, for large enough N, there exists a code of length N and rate $\geq R$ and a decoding algorithm, such that the maximal probability of block error is $< \epsilon$.

2. If a probability of bit error p_b is acceptable, rates up to $R(p_b)$ are achievable, where

$$R(p_b) = \frac{C}{1 - H_2(p_b)}. \qquad (10.2)$$

3. For any p_b, rates greater than $R(p_b)$ are not achievable.

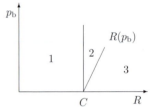

Figure 10.1. Portion of the R, p_b plane to be proved achievable $(1, 2)$ and not achievable (3).

▶ **10.2 Jointly typical sequences**

We formalize the intuitive preview of the last chapter.

We will define codewords $\mathbf{x}^{(s)}$ as coming from an ensemble X^N, and consider the random selection of one codeword and a corresponding channel output $\mathbf{y}$, thus defining a joint ensemble $(XY)^N$. We will use a *typical set decoder*, which decodes a received signal $\mathbf{y}$ as s if $\mathbf{x}^{(s)}$ and $\mathbf{y}$ are *jointly typical*, a term to be defined shortly.

The proof will then centre on determining the probabilities (a) that the true input codeword is *not* jointly typical with the output sequence; and (b) that a *false* input codeword is jointly typical with the output. We will show that, for large N, both probabilities go to zero as long as there are fewer than 2^{NC} codewords, and the ensemble X is the optimal input distribution.

Joint typicality. A pair of sequences $\mathbf{x}, \mathbf{y}$ of length N are defined to be jointly typical (to tolerance β) with respect to the distribution $P(x, y)$ if

$$\mathbf{x} \text{ is typical of } P(\mathbf{x}), \quad \text{i.e.,} \quad \left| \frac{1}{N} \log \frac{1}{P(\mathbf{x})} - H(X) \right| < \beta,$$

$$\mathbf{y} \text{ is typical of } P(\mathbf{y}), \quad \text{i.e.,} \quad \left| \frac{1}{N} \log \frac{1}{P(\mathbf{y})} - H(Y) \right| < \beta,$$

$$\text{and } \mathbf{x}, \mathbf{y} \text{ is typical of } P(\mathbf{x}, \mathbf{y}), \quad \text{i.e.,} \quad \left| \frac{1}{N} \log \frac{1}{P(\mathbf{x}, \mathbf{y})} - H(X, Y) \right| < \beta.$$

The jointly typical set $J_{N\beta}$ is the set of all jointly typical sequence pairs of length N.

Example. Here is a jointly typical pair of length $N = 100$ for the ensemble $P(x, y)$ in which $P(x)$ has $(p_0, p_1) = (0.9, 0.1)$ and $P(y \mid x)$ corresponds to a binary symmetric channel with noise level 0.2.

x 1111111111000000000000000000000000000000000000000000000000000000000000000000000000000000000000000000

y 0011111111100000000000000000000000000000000000000000000000000000000000000001111111111111111111111111

Notice that **x** has 10 1s, and so is typical of the probability $P(\mathbf{x})$ (at any tolerance β); and **y** has 26 1s, so it is typical of $P(\mathbf{y})$ (because $P(y = 1) = 0.26$); and **x** and **y** differ in 20 bits, which is the typical number of flips for this channel.

Joint typicality theorem. Let $\mathbf{x}, \mathbf{y}$ be drawn from the ensemble $(XY)^N$ defined by

$$P(\mathbf{x}, \mathbf{y}) = \prod_{n=1}^{N} P(x_n, y_n).$$

Then

1. the probability that $\mathbf{x}, \mathbf{y}$ are jointly typical (to tolerance β) tends to 1 as $N \to \infty$;

2. the number of jointly typical sequences $|J_{N\beta}|$ is close to $2^{NH(X,Y)}$. To be precise,

$$|J_{N\beta}| \le 2^{N(H(X,Y)+\beta)}; \tag{10.3}$$

3. if $\mathbf{x}' \sim X^N$ and $\mathbf{y}' \sim Y^N$, i.e., $\mathbf{x}'$ and $\mathbf{y}'$ are *independent* samples with the same marginal distribution as $P(\mathbf{x}, \mathbf{y})$, then the probability that $(\mathbf{x}', \mathbf{y}')$ lands in the jointly typical set is about $2^{-NI(X;Y)}$. To be precise,

$$P((\mathbf{x}', \mathbf{y}') \in J_{N\beta}) \le 2^{-N(I(X;Y)-3\beta)}. \tag{10.4}$$

Proof. The proof of parts 1 and 2 by the law of large numbers follows that of the source coding theorem in Chapter 4. For part 2, let the pair x, y play the role of x in the source coding theorem, replacing $P(x)$ there by the probability distribution $P(x, y)$.

For the third part,

$$
\begin{aligned}
P((\mathbf{x}', \mathbf{y}') \in J_{N\beta}) &= \sum_{(\mathbf{x}, \mathbf{y}) \in J_{N\beta}} P(\mathbf{x}) P(\mathbf{y}) & (10.5) \\
&\le |J_{N\beta}| \, 2^{-N(H(X)-\beta)} \, 2^{-N(H(Y)-\beta)} & (10.6) \\
&\le 2^{N(H(X,Y)+\beta)-N(H(X)+H(Y)-2\beta)} & (10.7) \\
&= 2^{-N(I(X;Y)-3\beta)}. \quad\square & (10.8)
\end{aligned}
$$

A cartoon of the jointly typical set is shown in figure 10.2. Two independent typical vectors are jointly typical with probability

$$P((\mathbf{x}', \mathbf{y}') \in J_{N\beta}) \simeq 2^{-N(I(X;Y))} \tag{10.9}$$

because the *total* number of independent typical pairs is the area of the dashed rectangle, $2^{NH(X)}2^{NH(Y)}$, and the number of jointly typical pairs is roughly $2^{NH(X,Y)}$, so the probability of hitting a typical pair is roughly

$$2^{NH(X,Y)} / 2^{NH(X)+NH(Y)} = 2^{-NI(X;Y)}. \tag{10.10}$$

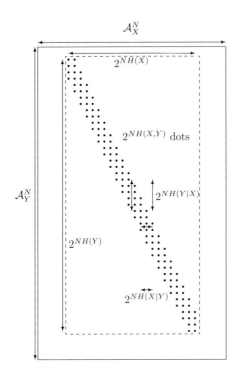

Figure 10.2. The jointly typical set. The horizontal direction represents $\mathcal{A}_X^N$, the set of all input strings of length N. The vertical direction represents $\mathcal{A}_Y^N$, the set of all output strings of length N. The outer box contains all conceivable input–output pairs. Each dot represents a jointly typical pair of sequences $(\mathbf{x}, \mathbf{y})$. The total number of jointly typical sequences is about $2^{NH(X,Y)}$.

▶ **10.3 Proof of the noisy-channel coding theorem**

Analogy

Imagine that we wish to prove that there is a baby in a class of one hundred babies who weighs less than 10 kg. Individual babies are difficult to catch and weigh. Shannon's method of solving the task is to scoop up all the babies and weigh them all at once on a big weighing machine. If we find that their *average* weight is smaller than 10 kg, there must exist *at least one* baby who weighs less than 10 kg – indeed there must be many! Shannon's method isn't guaranteed to reveal the existence of an underweight child, since it relies on there being a tiny number of elephants in the class. But if we use his method and get a total weight smaller than 1000 kg then our task is solved.

Figure 10.3. Shannon's method for proving one baby weighs less than 10 kg.

From skinny children to fantastic codes

We wish to show that there exists a code and a decoder having small probability of error. Evaluating the probability of error of any particular coding and decoding system is not easy. Shannon's innovation was this: instead of constructing a good coding and decoding system and evaluating its error probability, Shannon calculated the average probability of block error of *all* codes, and proved that this average is small. There must then exist individual codes that have small probability of block error.

Random coding and typical set decoding

Consider the following encoding–decoding system, whose rate is R'.

1. We fix $P(x)$ and generate the $S = 2^{NR'}$ codewords of a $(N, NR') =$

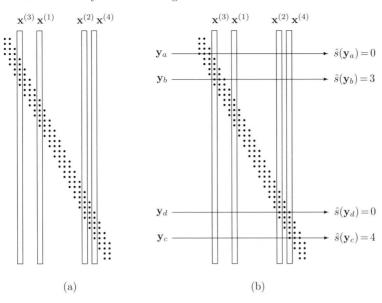

$\mathbf{x}^{(3)}\,\mathbf{x}^{(1)}$ $\mathbf{x}^{(2)}\,\mathbf{x}^{(4)}$

(a)

Figure 10.4. (a) A random code.
(b) Example decodings by the
typical set decoder. A sequence
that is not jointly typical with any
of the codewords, such as $\mathbf{y}_a$, is
decoded as $\hat{s} = 0$. A sequence that
is jointly typical with codeword
$\mathbf{x}^{(3)}$ alone, $\mathbf{y}_b$, is decoded as $\hat{s} = 3$.
Similarly, $\mathbf{y}_c$ is decoded as $\hat{s} = 4$.
A sequence that is jointly typical
with more than one codeword,
such as $\mathbf{y}_d$, is decoded as $\hat{s} = 0$.

(N, K) code $\mathcal{C}$ at random according to

$$P(\mathbf{x}) = \prod_{n=1}^{N} P(x_n). \qquad (10.11)$$

A random code is shown schematically in figure 10.4a.

2. The code is known to both sender and receiver.

3. A message s is chosen from $\{1, 2, \dots, 2^{NR'}\}$, and $\mathbf{x}^{(s)}$ is transmitted. The received signal is $\mathbf{y}$, with

$$P(\mathbf{y}\,|\,\mathbf{x}^{(s)}) = \prod_{n=1}^{N} P(y_n\,|\,x_n^{(s)}). \qquad (10.12)$$

4. The signal is decoded by *typical set decoding*.

   Typical set decoding. Decode $\mathbf{y}$ as $\hat{s}$ if $(\mathbf{x}^{(\hat{s})}, \mathbf{y})$ are jointly typical *and* there is no other s' such that $(\mathbf{x}^{(s')}, \mathbf{y})$ are jointly typical; otherwise declare a failure ($\hat{s} = 0$).

   This is not the optimal decoding algorithm, but it will be good enough, and easier to analyze. The typical set decoder is illustrated in figure 10.4b.

5. A decoding error occurs if $\hat{s} \neq s$.

   There are three probabilities of error that we can distinguish. First, there is the probability of block error for a particular code $\mathcal{C}$, that is,

$$p_{\mathrm{B}}(\mathcal{C}) \equiv P(\hat{s} \neq s\,|\,\mathcal{C}). \qquad (10.13)$$

This is a difficult quantity to evaluate for any given code.

Second, there is the average over all codes of this block error probability,

$$\langle p_{\mathrm{B}} \rangle \equiv \sum_{\mathcal{C}} P(\hat{s} \neq s\,|\,\mathcal{C})P(\mathcal{C}). \qquad (10.14)$$

Fortunately, this quantity is much easier to evaluate than the first quantity $P(\hat{s} \neq s \,|\, \mathcal{C})$.

Third, the maximal block error probability of a code $\mathcal{C}$,

$$p_{\mathrm{BM}}(\mathcal{C}) \equiv \max_s P(\hat{s} \neq s \,|\, s, \mathcal{C}), \qquad (10.15)$$

is the quantity we are most interested in: we wish to show that there exists a code $\mathcal{C}$ with the required rate whose maximal block error probability is small.

We will get to this result by first finding the average block error probability, $\langle p_{\mathrm{B}} \rangle$. Once we have shown that this can be made smaller than a desired small number, we immediately deduce that there must exist *at least one* code $\mathcal{C}$ whose block error probability is also less than this small number. Finally, we show that this code, whose block error probability is satisfactorily small but whose maximal block error probability is unknown (and could conceivably be enormous), can be modified to make a code of slightly smaller rate whose maximal block error probability is also guaranteed to be small. We modify the code by throwing away the worst 50% of its codewords.

We therefore now embark on finding the average probability of block error.

Probability of error of typical set decoder

There are two sources of error when we use typical set decoding. Either (a) the output $\mathbf{y}$ is not jointly typical with the transmitted codeword $\mathbf{x}^{(s)}$, or (b) there is some other codeword in $\mathcal{C}$ that is jointly typical with $\mathbf{y}$.

By the symmetry of the code construction, the average probability of error averaged over all codes does not depend on the selected value of s; we can assume without loss of generality that $s = 1$.

(a) The probability that the input $\mathbf{x}^{(1)}$ and the output $\mathbf{y}$ are not jointly typical vanishes, by the joint typicality theorem's first part (p. 163). We give a name, δ, to the upper bound on this probability, satisfying $\delta \to 0$ as $N \to \infty$; for any desired δ, we can find a blocklength $N(\delta)$ such that the $P((\mathbf{x}^{(1)}, \mathbf{y}) \notin J_{N\beta}) \leq \delta$.

(b) The probability that $\mathbf{x}^{(s')}$ and $\mathbf{y}$ are jointly typical, for a *given* $s' \neq 1$ is $\leq 2^{-N(I(X;Y) - 3\beta)}$, by part 3. And there are $(2^{NR'} - 1)$ rival values of s' to worry about.

Thus the average probability of error $\langle p_{\mathrm{B}} \rangle$ satisfies:

$$\langle p_{\mathrm{B}} \rangle \leq \delta + \sum_{s'=2}^{2^{NR'}} 2^{-N(I(X;Y) - 3\beta)} \qquad (10.16)$$

$$\leq \delta + 2^{-N(I(X;Y) - R' - 3\beta)}. \qquad (10.17)$$

The inequality (10.16) that bounds the total probability of error P_{ERR} by the sum of the probabilities $P_{s'}$ of all sorts of events s' each of which is sufficient to cause error,

$$P_{\mathrm{TOT}} \leq P_1 + P_2 + \cdots,$$

is called a 'union bound'. It is only an equality if the different events that cause error never occur at the same time as each other.

The average probability of error can be made $< 2\delta$ by increasing N if

$$R' < I(X;Y) - 3\beta. \qquad (10.18)$$

We are almost there. We make three modifications:

1. We choose $P(x)$ in the proof to be the optimal input distribution of the channel. Then the condition $R' < I(X;Y) - 3\beta$ becomes $R' < C - 3\beta$.

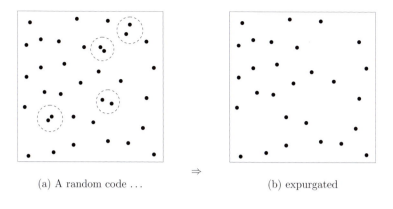

(a) A random code ... $\Rightarrow$ (b) expurgated

Figure 10.5. How expurgation works. (a) In a typical random code, a small fraction of the codewords are involved in collisions – pairs of codewords are sufficiently close to each other that the probability of error when either codeword is transmitted is not tiny. We obtain a new code from a random code by deleting all these confusable codewords. (b) The resulting code has slightly fewer codewords, so has a slightly lower rate, and its maximal probability of error is greatly reduced.

2. Since the average probability of error over all codes is $< 2\delta$, there must exist *a* code with mean probability of block error $p_B(\mathcal{C}) < 2\delta$.

3. To show that not only the average but also the maximal probability of error, p_{BM}, can be made small, we modify this code by throwing away the worst half of the codewords – the ones most likely to produce errors. Those that remain must all have *conditional* probability of error less than 4δ. We use these remaining codewords to define a new code. This new code has $2^{NR'-1}$ codewords, i.e., we have reduced the rate from R' to $R' - 1/N$ (a negligible reduction, if N is large), and achieved $p_{BM} < 4\delta$. This trick is called *expurgation* (figure 10.5). The resulting code may not be the best code of its rate and length, but it is still good enough to prove the noisy-channel coding theorem, which is what we are trying to do here.

In conclusion, we can 'construct' a code of rate $R' - 1/N$, where $R' < C - 3\beta$, with maximal probability of error $< 4\delta$. We obtain the theorem as stated by setting $R' = (R+C)/2$, $\delta = \epsilon/4$, $\beta < (C-R')/3$, and N sufficiently large for the remaining conditions to hold. The theorem's first part is thus proved. □

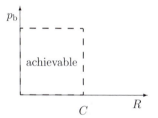

Figure 10.6. Portion of the R, p_b plane proved achievable in the first part of the theorem. [We've proved that the maximal probability of block error p_{BM} can be made arbitrarily small, so the same goes for the bit error probability p_b, which must be smaller than p_{BM}.]

▶ 10.4 Communication (with errors) above capacity

We have proved, for any discrete memoryless channel, the achievability of a portion of the R, p_b plane shown in figure 10.6. We have shown that we can turn any noisy channel into an essentially noiseless binary channel with rate up to C bits per cycle. We now extend the right-hand boundary of the region of achievability at non-zero error probabilities. [This is called *rate-distortion theory*.]

We do this with a new trick. Since we know we can make the noisy channel into a perfect channel with a smaller rate, it is sufficient to consider communication with errors over a *noiseless* channel. How fast can we communicate over a noiseless channel, if we are allowed to make errors?

Consider a noiseless binary channel, and assume that we force communication at a rate greater than its capacity of 1 bit. For example, if we require the sender to attempt to communicate at $R=2$ bits per cycle then he must effectively throw away half of the information. What is the best way to do this if the aim is to achieve the smallest possible probability of bit error? One simple strategy is to communicate a fraction $1/R$ of the source bits, and ignore the rest. The receiver guesses the missing fraction $1 - 1/R$ at random, and the average probability of bit error is

$$p_{\mathrm{b}} = \frac{1}{2}(1 - 1/R).$$ (10.19)

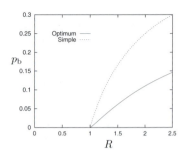

The curve corresponding to this strategy is shown by the dashed line in figure 10.7.

We can do better than this (in terms of minimizing p_{b}) by spreading out the risk of corruption evenly among all the bits. In fact, we can achieve $p_{\mathrm{b}} = H_2^{-1}(1 - 1/R)$, which is shown by the solid curve in figure 10.7. So, how can this optimum be achieved?

Figure 10.7. A simple bound on achievable points (R, p_{b}), and Shannon's bound.

We reuse a tool that we just developed, namely the (N, K) code for a noisy channel, and we turn it on its head, using the *decoder* to define a lossy compressor. Specifically, we take an excellent (N, K) code for the binary symmetric channel. Assume that such a code has a rate $R' = K/N$, and that it is capable of correcting errors introduced by a binary symmetric channel whose transition probability is q. Asymptotically, rate R' codes exist that have $R' \simeq 1 - H_2(q)$. Recall that, if we attach one of these capacity-achieving codes of length N to a binary symmetric channel then (a) the probability distribution over the outputs is close to uniform, since the entropy of the output is equal to the entropy of the source (NR') plus the entropy of the noise ($NH_2(q)$), and (b) the optimal decoder of the code, in this situation, typically maps a received vector of length N to a transmitted vector differing in qN bits from the received vector.

We take the signal that we wish to send, and chop it into blocks of length N (yes, N, not K). We pass each block through the *decoder*, and obtain a shorter signal of length K bits, which we communicate over the noiseless channel. To decode the transmission, we pass the K bit message to the *encoder* of the original code. The reconstituted message will now differ from the original message in some of its bits – typically qN of them. So the probability of bit error will be $p_{\mathrm{b}} = q$. The rate of this lossy compressor is $R = N/K = 1/R' = 1/(1 - H_2(p_{\mathrm{b}}))$.

Now, attaching this lossy compressor to our capacity-C error-free communicator, we have proved the achievability of communication up to the curve (p_{b}, R) defined by:

$$R = \frac{C}{1 - H_2(p_{\mathrm{b}})}. \qquad \qquad \Box$$ (10.20)

For further reading about rate-distortion theory, see Gallager (1968), p. 451, or McEliece (2002), p. 75.

▶ 10.5 The non-achievable region (part 3 of the theorem)

The source, encoder, noisy channel and decoder define a Markov chain: $s \to \mathbf{x} \to \mathbf{y} \to \hat{s}$

$$P(s, \mathbf{x}, \mathbf{y}, \hat{s}) = P(s)P(\mathbf{x} \mid s)P(\mathbf{y} \mid \mathbf{x})P(\hat{s} \mid \mathbf{y}).$$ (10.21)

The data processing inequality (exercise 8.9, p. 141) must apply to this chain: $I(s; \hat{s}) \leq I(\mathbf{x}; \mathbf{y})$. Furthermore, by the definition of channel capacity, $I(\mathbf{x}; \mathbf{y}) \leq NC$, so $I(s; \hat{s}) \leq NC$.

Assume that a system achieves a rate R and a bit error probability p_{b}; then the mutual information $I(s; \hat{s})$ is $\geq NR(1 - H_2(p_{\mathrm{b}}))$. But $I(s; \hat{s}) > NC$ is not achievable, so $R > \frac{C}{1-H_2(p_{\mathrm{b}})}$ is not achievable. $\Box$

Exercise 10.1.[3] Fill in the details in the preceding argument. If the bit errors between $\hat{s}$ and s are independent then we have $I(s; \hat{s}) = NR(1 - H_2(p_{\mathrm{b}}))$.

What if we have complex correlations among those bit errors? Why does the inequality $I(s; \hat{s}) \geq NR(1 - H_2(p_{\mathrm{b}}))$ hold?

► **10.6 Computing capacity**

We have proved that the capacity of a channel is the maximum rate at which reliable communication can be achieved. How can we compute the capacity of a given discrete memoryless channel? We need to find its optimal input distribution. In general we can find the optimal input distribution by a computer search, making use of the derivative of the mutual information with respect to the input probabilities.

▷ Exercise 10.2.[2] Find the derivative of $I(X;Y)$ with respect to the input probability p_i, $\partial I(X;Y)/\partial p_i$, for a channel with conditional probabilities $Q_{j|i}$.

Exercise 10.3.[2] Show that $I(X;Y)$ is a concave $\frown$ function of the input probability vector **p**.

Since $I(X;Y)$ is concave $\frown$ in the input distribution **p**, any probability distribution **p** at which $I(X;Y)$ is stationary must be a global maximum of $I(X;Y)$. So it is tempting to put the derivative of $I(X;Y)$ into a routine that finds a local maximum of $I(X;Y)$, that is, an input distribution $P(x)$ such that

$$\frac{\partial I(X;Y)}{\partial p_i} = \lambda \quad \text{for all } i, \tag{10.22}$$

where λ is a Lagrange multiplier associated with the constraint $\sum_i p_i = 1$. However, this approach may fail to find the right answer, because $I(X;Y)$ might be maximized by a distribution that has $p_i = 0$ for some inputs. A simple example is given by the ternary confusion channel.

Ternary confusion channel. $\mathcal{A}_X = \{0, ?, 1\}$. $\mathcal{A}_Y = \{0, 1\}$.

$$
\begin{array}{l}
0 \longrightarrow 0 \\
? \\
1 \longrightarrow 1
\end{array}
\qquad
\begin{array}{l}
P(y=0 \,|\, x=0) = 1; \quad P(y=0 \,|\, x=?) = 1/2; \quad P(y=0 \,|\, x=1) = 0; \\
P(y=1 \,|\, x=0) = 0; \quad P(y=1 \,|\, x=?) = 1/2; \quad P(y=1 \,|\, x=1) = 1.
\end{array}
$$

Whenever the input ? is used, the output is random; the other inputs are reliable inputs. The maximum information rate of 1 bit is achieved by making no use of the input ?.

▷ Exercise 10.4.[2, p.173] Sketch the mutual information for this channel as a function of the input distribution **p**. Pick a convenient two-dimensional representation of **p**.

The optimization routine must therefore take account of the possibility that, as we go up hill on $I(X;Y)$, we may run into the inequality constraints $p_i \geq 0$.

▷ Exercise 10.5.[2, p.174] Describe the condition, similar to equation (10.22), that is satisfied at a point where $I(X;Y)$ is maximized, and describe a computer program for finding the capacity of a channel.

Results that may help in finding the optimal input distribution

1. All outputs must be used.

2. $I(X,Y)$ is a convex $\smile$ function of the channel parameters.

3. There may be several optimal input distributions, but they all look the same at the output.

Reminder: The term 'convex $\smile$' means 'convex', and the term 'concave $\frown$' means 'concave'; the little smile and frown symbols are included simply to remind you what convex and concave mean.

▷ Exercise 10.6.[2] Prove that no output y is unused by an optimal input distribution, unless it is unreachable, that is, has $Q(y\,|\,x) = 0$ for all x.

Exercise 10.7.[2] Prove that $I(X,Y)$ is a convex $\smile$ function of $Q(y\,|\,x)$.

Exercise 10.8.[2] Prove that all optimal input distributions of a channel have the same output probability distribution $P(y) = \sum_x P(x)Q(y\,|\,x)$.

These results, along with the fact that $I(X;Y)$ is a concave $\frown$ function of the input probability vector $\mathbf{p}$, prove the validity of the symmetry argument that we have used when finding the capacity of symmetric channels. If a channel is invariant under a group of symmetry operations – for example, interchanging the input symbols and interchanging the output symbols – then, given any optimal input distribution that is not symmetric, i.e., is not invariant under these operations, we can create another input distribution by averaging together this optimal input distribution and all its permuted forms that we can make by applying the symmetry operations to the original optimal input distribution. The permuted distributions must have the same $I(X;Y)$ as the original, by symmetry, so the new input distribution created by averaging must have $I(X;Y)$ bigger than or equal to that of the original distribution, because of the concavity of I.

Symmetric channels

In order to use symmetry arguments, it will help to have a definition of a symmetric channel. I like Gallager's (1968) definition.

A discrete memoryless channel is a symmetric channel if the set of outputs can be partitioned into subsets in such a way that for each subset the matrix of transition probabilities has the property that each row (if more than 1) is a permutation of each other row and each column is a permutation of each other column.

Example 10.9. This channel

$$P(y=0\,|\,x=0) \;=\; 0.7; \quad P(y=0\,|\,x=1) \;=\; 0.1;$$
$$P(y=?\,|\,x=0) \;=\; 0.2; \quad P(y=?\,|\,x=1) \;=\; 0.2; \qquad (10.23)$$
$$P(y=1\,|\,x=0) \;=\; 0.1; \quad P(y=1\,|\,x=1) \;=\; 0.7.$$

is a symmetric channel because its outputs can be partitioned into $(0,1)$ and ?, so that the matrix can be rewritten:

$P(y=0\,|\,x=0)$	$= 0.7;$	$P(y=0\,|\,x=1)$	$= 0.1;$
$P(y=1\,|\,x=0)$	$= 0.1;$	$P(y=1\,|\,x=1)$	$= 0.7;$
$P(y=?\,|\,x=0)$	$= 0.2;$	$P(y=?\,|\,x=1)$	$= 0.2.$

(10.24)

Symmetry is a useful property because, as we will see in a later chapter, communication at capacity can be achieved over symmetric channels by *linear* codes.

Exercise 10.10.[2] Prove that for a symmetric channel with any number of inputs, the uniform distribution over the inputs is an optimal input distribution.

▷ Exercise 10.11.[2, p.174] Are there channels that are not symmetric whose optimal input distributions are uniform? Find one, or prove there are none.

▶ ## 10.7 Other coding theorems

The noisy-channel coding theorem that we proved in this chapter is quite general, applying to any discrete memoryless channel; but it is not very specific. The theorem only says that reliable communication with error probability ϵ and rate R can be achieved by using codes with *sufficiently large* blocklength N. The theorem does not say how large N needs to be to achieve given values of R and ϵ.

Presumably, the smaller ϵ is and the closer R is to C, the larger N has to be.

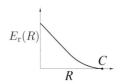

Figure 10.8. A typical random-coding exponent.

Noisy-channel coding theorem – version with explicit N-dependence

For a discrete memoryless channel, a blocklength N and a rate R, there exist block codes of length N whose average probability of error satisfies:

$$p_B \leq \exp\left[-NE_r(R)\right] \qquad (10.25)$$

where $E_r(R)$ is the *random-coding exponent* of the channel, a convex ⌣, decreasing, positive function of R for $0 \leq R < C$. The random-coding exponent is also known as the reliability function.

[By an expurgation argument it can also be shown that there exist block codes for which the *maximal* probability of error p_{BM} is also exponentially small in N.]

The definition of $E_r(R)$ is given in Gallager (1968), p. 139. $E_r(R)$ approaches zero as $R \to C$; the typical behaviour of this function is illustrated in figure 10.8. The computation of the random-coding exponent for interesting channels is a challenging task on which much effort has been expended. Even for simple channels like the binary symmetric channel, there is no simple expression for $E_r(R)$.

Lower bounds on the error probability as a function of blocklength

The theorem stated above asserts that there are codes with p_B smaller than $\exp\left[-NE_r(R)\right]$. But how small can the error probability be? Could it be much smaller?

For any code with blocklength N on a discrete memoryless channel, the probability of error assuming all source messages are used with equal probability satisfies

$$p_B \gtrsim \exp[-NE_{sp}(R)], \qquad (10.26)$$

where the function $E_{\text{sp}}(R)$, the *sphere-packing exponent* of the channel, is a convex $\smile$, decreasing, positive function of R for $0 \le R < C$.

For a precise statement of this result and further references, see Gallager (1968), p. 157.

▶ 10.8 Noisy-channel coding theorems and coding practice

Imagine a customer who wants to buy an error-correcting code and decoder for a noisy channel. The results described above allow us to offer the following service: if he tells us the properties of his channel, the desired rate R and the desired error probability p_{B}, we can, after working out the relevant functions C, $E_{\text{r}}(R)$, and $E_{\text{sp}}(R)$, advise him that there exists a solution to his problem using a particular blocklength N; indeed that almost any randomly chosen code with that blocklength should do the job. Unfortunately we have not found out how to implement these encoders and decoders in practice; the cost of implementing the encoder and decoder for a random code with large N would be exponentially large in N.

Furthermore, for practical purposes, the customer is unlikely to know exactly what channel he is dealing with. So Berlekamp (1980) suggests that the sensible way to approach error-correction is to design encoding-decoding systems and plot their performance on a *variety* of idealized channels as a function of the channel's noise level. These charts (one of which is illustrated on page 568) can then be shown to the customer, who can choose among the systems on offer without having to specify what he really thinks his channel is like. With this attitude to the practical problem, the importance of the functions $E_{\text{r}}(R)$ and $E_{\text{sp}}(R)$ is diminished.

▶ 10.9 Further exercises

Exercise 10.12.[2] A binary erasure channel with input x and output y has transition probability matrix:

$$\mathbf{Q} = \begin{bmatrix} 1-q & 0 \\ q & q \\ 0 & 1-q \end{bmatrix}$$

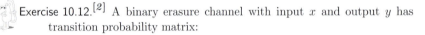

Find the *mutual information* $I(X;Y)$ between the input and output for general input distribution $\{p_0, p_1\}$, and show that the *capacity* of this channel is $C = 1 - q$ bits.

A Z channel has transition probability matrix:

$$\mathbf{Q} = \begin{bmatrix} 1 & q \\ 0 & 1-q \end{bmatrix}$$

Show that, using a $(2, 1)$ code, **two** uses of a Z channel can be made to emulate **one** use of an erasure channel, and state the erasure probability of that erasure channel. Hence show that the capacity of the Z channel, C_{Z}, satisfies $C_{\text{Z}} \ge \frac{1}{2}(1 - q)$ bits.

Explain why the result $C_{\text{Z}} \ge \frac{1}{2}(1 - q)$ is an inequality rather than an equality.

Exercise 10.13.[3, p.174] A transatlantic cable contains $N = 20$ indistinguishable electrical wires. You have the job of figuring out which wire is
which, that is, to create a consistent labelling of the wires at each end.
Your only tools are the ability to connect wires to each other in groups
of two or more, and to test for connectedness with a continuity tester.
What is the smallest number of transatlantic trips you need to make,
and how do you do it?

How would you solve the problem for larger N such as $N = 1000$?

As an illustration, if N were 3 then the task can be solved in two steps
by labelling one wire at one end a, connecting the other two together,
crossing the Atlantic, measuring which two wires are connected, labelling
them b and c and the unconnected one a, then connecting b to a and
returning across the Atlantic, whereupon on disconnecting b from c, the
identities of b and c can be deduced.

This problem can be solved by persistent search, but the reason it is
posed in this chapter is that it can also be solved by a greedy approach
based on maximizing the acquired *information*. Let the unknown permutation of wires be x. Having chosen a set of connections of wires $\mathcal{C}$ at
one end, you can then make measurements at the other end, and these
measurements y convey *information* about x. How much? And for what
set of connections is the information y conveys about x maximized?

▶ 10.10 Solutions

Solution to exercise 10.4 (p.169). If the input distribution is $\mathbf{p} = (p_0, p_?, p_1)$,
the mutual information is

$$I(X;Y) = H(Y) - H(Y|X) = H_2(p_0 + p_?/2) - p_?. \qquad (10.27)$$

We can build a good sketch of this function in two ways: by careful inspection
of the function, or by looking at special cases.

    For the plots, the two-dimensional representation of $\mathbf{p}$ I will use has p_0 and
p_1 as the independent variables, so that $\mathbf{p} = (p_0, p_?, p_1) = (p_0, (1-p_0-p_1), p_1)$.

By inspection. If we use the quantities $p_* \equiv p_0 + p_?/2$ and $p_?$ as our two
degrees of freedom, the mutual information becomes very simple: $I(X;Y) =
H_2(p_*) - p_?$. Converting back to $p_0 = p_* - p_?/2$ and $p_1 = 1 - p_* - p_?/2$,
we obtain the sketch shown at the left below. This function is like a tunnel
rising up the direction of increasing p_0 and p_1. To obtain the required plot of
$I(X;Y)$ we have to strip away the parts of this tunnel that live outside the
feasible simplex of probabilities; we do this by redrawing the surface, showing
only the parts where $p_0 > 0$ and $p_1 > 0$. A full plot of the function is shown
at the right.

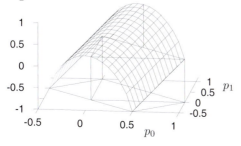
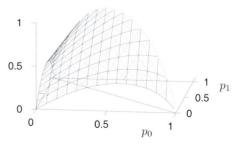

Special cases. In the special case $p_? = 0$, the channel is a noiseless binary channel, and $I(X;Y) = H_2(p_0)$.

In the special case $p_0 = p_1$, the term $H_2(p_0 + p_?/2)$ is equal to 1, so $I(X;Y) = 1 - p_?$.

In the special case $p_0 = 0$, the channel is a Z channel with error probability 0.5. We know how to sketch that, from the previous chapter (figure 9.3).

These special cases allow us to construct the skeleton shown in figure 10.9.

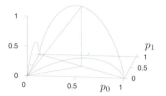

Figure 10.9. Skeleton of the mutual information for the ternary confusion channel.

Solution to exercise 10.5 (p.169). Necessary and sufficient conditions for $\mathbf{p}$ to maximize $I(X;Y)$ are

$$\left.\begin{array}{ll}\frac{\partial I(X;Y)}{\partial p_i} = \lambda & \text{and} \quad p_i > 0 \\[2mm] \frac{\partial I(X;Y)}{\partial p_i} \leq \lambda & \text{and} \quad p_i = 0\end{array}\right\} \quad \text{for all } i, \tag{10.28}$$

where λ is a constant related to the capacity by $C = \lambda + \log_2 e$.

This result can be used in a computer program that evaluates the derivatives and increments and decrements the probabilities p_i in proportion to the differences between those derivatives.

This result is also useful for lazy human capacity-finders who are good guessers. Having guessed the optimal input distribution, one can simply confirm that equation (10.28) holds.

Solution to exercise 10.11 (p.171). We certainly expect nonsymmetric channels with uniform optimal input distributions to exist, since when inventing a channel we have $I(J-1)$ degrees of freedom whereas the optimal input distribution is just $(I-1)$-dimensional; so in the $I(J-1)$-dimensional space of perturbations around a symmetric channel, we expect there to be a subspace of perturbations of dimension $I(J-1) - (I-1) = I(J-2) + 1$ that leave the optimal input distribution unchanged.

Here is an explicit example, a bit like a Z channel.

$$\mathbf{Q} = \begin{bmatrix} 0.9585 & 0.0415 & 0.35 & 0.0 \\ 0.0415 & 0.9585 & 0.0 & 0.35 \\ 0 & 0 & 0.65 & 0 \\ 0 & 0 & 0 & 0.65 \end{bmatrix} \tag{10.29}$$

Solution to exercise 10.13 (p.173). The labelling problem can be solved for any $N > 2$ with just two trips, one each way across the Atlantic.

The key step in the information-theoretic approach to this problem is to write down the information content of one *partition*, the combinatorial object that is the connecting together of subsets of wires. If N wires are grouped together into g_1 subsets of size 1, g_2 subsets of size 2, ..., then the number of such partitions is

$$\Omega = \frac{N!}{\prod_r (r!)^{g_r} g_r!}, \tag{10.30}$$

and the information content of one such partition is the log of this quantity. In a greedy strategy we choose the first partition to maximize this information content.

One game we can play is to maximize this information content with respect to the quantities g_r, treated as real numbers, subject to the constraint $\sum_r g_r r = N$. Introducing a Lagrange multiplier λ for the constraint, the derivative is

$$\frac{\partial}{\partial g_r}\left(\log \Omega + \lambda \sum_r g_r r\right) = -\log r! - \log g_r + \lambda r, \tag{10.31}$$

which, when set to zero, leads to the rather nice expression

$$g_r = \frac{e^{\lambda r}}{r!};\qquad(10.32)$$

the optimal g_r is proportional to a Poisson distribution! We can solve for the Lagrange multiplier by plugging g_r into the constraint $\sum_r g_r r = N$, which gives the implicit equation

$$N = \mu\,e^{\mu},\qquad(10.33)$$

where $\mu \equiv e^{\lambda}$ is a convenient reparameterization of the Lagrange multiplier. Figure 10.10a shows a graph of $\mu(N)$; figure 10.10b shows the deduced non-integer assignments g_r when $\mu = 2.2$, and nearby integers $g_r = \{1, 2, 2, 1, 1\}$ that motivate setting the first partition to (a)(bc)(de)(fgh)(ijk)(lmno)(pqrst).

This partition produces a random partition at the other end, which has an information content of $\log \Omega = 40.4$ bits, which is a lot more than half the total information content we need to acquire to infer the transatlantic permutation, $\log 20! \simeq 61$ bits. [In contrast, if all the wires are joined together in pairs, the information content generated is only about 29 bits.] How to choose the second partition is left to the reader. A Shannonesque approach is appropriate, picking a random partition at the other end, using the same $\{g_r\}$; you need to ensure the two partitions are as unlike each other as possible.

If $N \neq 2$, 5 or 9, then the labelling problem has solutions that are particularly simple to implement, called Knowlton–Graham partitions: partition $\{1, \ldots, N\}$ into disjoint sets in two ways A and B, subject to the condition that at most one element appears both in an A set of cardinality j and in a B set of cardinality k, for each j and k (Graham, 1966; Graham and Knowlton, 1968).

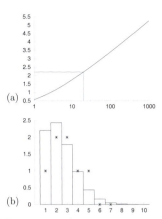

Figure 10.10. Approximate solution of the cable labelling problem using Lagrange multipliers. (a) The parameter μ as a function of N; the value $\mu(20) = 2.2$ is highlighted. (b) Non-integer values of the function $g_r = \mu^r/r!$ are shown by lines and integer values of g_r motivated by those non-integer values are shown by crosses.

About Chapter 11

Before reading Chapter 11, you should have read Chapters 9 and 10.

You will also need to be familiar with the *Gaussian distribution*.

One-dimensional Gaussian distribution. If a random variable y is Gaussian and has mean μ and variance σ^2, which we write:

$$y \sim \text{Normal}(\mu, \sigma^2), \text{ or } P(y) = \text{Normal}(y; \mu, \sigma^2), \qquad (11.1)$$

then the distribution of y is:

$$P(y|\mu, \sigma^2) = \frac{1}{\sqrt{2\pi\sigma^2}} \exp\left[-(y-\mu)^2/2\sigma^2\right]. \qquad (11.2)$$

[I use the symbol P for both probability densities and probabilities.]

The inverse-variance $\tau \equiv 1/\sigma^2$ is sometimes called the *precision* of the Gaussian distribution.

Multi-dimensional Gaussian distribution. If $\mathbf{y} = (y_1, y_2, \ldots, y_N)$ has a multivariate Gaussian distribution, then

$$P(\mathbf{y}|\mathbf{x}, \mathbf{A}) = \frac{1}{Z(\mathbf{A})} \exp\left(-\frac{1}{2}(\mathbf{y}-\mathbf{x})^{\mathsf{T}}\mathbf{A}(\mathbf{y}-\mathbf{x})\right), \qquad (11.3)$$

where $\mathbf{x}$ is the mean of the distribution, $\mathbf{A}$ is the inverse of the variance–covariance matrix, and the normalizing constant is $Z(\mathbf{A}) = (\det(\mathbf{A}/2\pi))^{-1/2}$.

This distribution has the property that the variance Σ_{ii} of y_i, and the covariance Σ_{ij} of y_i and y_j are given by

$$\Sigma_{ij} \equiv \mathcal{E}\left[(y_i - \bar{y}_i)(y_j - \bar{y}_j)\right] = A_{ij}^{-1}, \qquad (11.4)$$

where $\mathbf{A}^{-1}$ is the inverse of the matrix $\mathbf{A}$.

The marginal distribution $P(y_i)$ of one component y_i is Gaussian; the joint marginal distribution of any subset of the components is multivariate-Gaussian; and the conditional density of any subset, given the values of another subset, for example, $P(y_i|y_j)$, is also Gaussian.

11

Error-Correcting Codes & Real Channels

The noisy-channel coding theorem that we have proved shows that there exist reliable error-correcting codes for any noisy channel. In this chapter we address two questions.

First, many practical channels have real, rather than discrete, inputs and outputs. What can Shannon tell us about these continuous channels? And how should digital signals be mapped into analogue waveforms, and *vice versa*?

Second, how are practical error-correcting codes made, and what is achieved in practice, relative to the possibilities proved by Shannon?

▶ ## 11.1 The Gaussian channel

The most popular model of a real-input, real-output channel is the Gaussian channel.

The Gaussian channel has a real input x and a real output y. The conditional distribution of y given x is a Gaussian distribution:

$$P(y|x) = \frac{1}{\sqrt{2\pi\sigma^2}} \exp\left[-(y-x)^2/2\sigma^2\right]. \qquad (11.5)$$

This channel has a continuous input and output but is discrete in time. We will show below that certain continuous-time channels are equivalent to the discrete-time Gaussian channel.

This channel is sometimes called the additive white Gaussian noise (AWGN) channel.

As with discrete channels, we will discuss what rate of error-free information communication can be achieved over this channel.

Motivation in terms of a continuous-time channel

Consider a physical (electrical, say) channel with inputs and outputs that are continuous in time. We put in $x(t)$, and out comes $y(t) = x(t) + n(t)$.

Our transmission has a power cost. The average power of a transmission of length T may be constrained thus:

$$\int_0^T dt\, [x(t)]^2/T \le P. \qquad (11.6)$$

The received signal is assumed to differ from $x(t)$ by additive noise $n(t)$ (for example Johnson noise), which we will model as white Gaussian noise. The magnitude of this noise is quantified by the *noise spectral density* N_0.

How could such a channel be used to communicate information?   Consider transmitting a set of N real numbers $\{x_n\}_{n=1}^N$ in a signal of duration T made up of a weighted combination of orthonormal basis functions $\phi_n(t)$,

$$x(t) = \sum_{n=1}^{N} x_n \phi_n(t),\qquad(11.7)$$

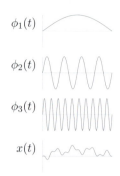

where $\int_0^T dt\, \phi_n(t)\phi_m(t) = \delta_{nm}$. The receiver can then compute the scalars:

$$
\begin{aligned}
y_n &\equiv \int_0^T dt\, \phi_n(t)y(t) &= x_n + \int_0^T dt\, \phi_n(t)n(t) \qquad(11.8)\\
&&\equiv x_n + n_n \qquad(11.9)
\end{aligned}
$$

for $n = 1\ldots N$. If there were no noise, then y_n would equal x_n. The white Gaussian noise $n(t)$ adds scalar noise n_n to the estimate y_n. This noise is Gaussian:

$$n_n \sim \text{Normal}(0, N_0/2),\qquad(11.10)$$

where N_0 is the spectral density introduced above. Thus a continuous channel used in this way is equivalent to the Gaussian channel defined above. The power constraint $\int_0^T dt\, [x(t)]^2 \le PT$ defines a constraint on the signal amplitudes x_n,

$$\sum_n x_n^2 \le PT \qquad\Rightarrow\qquad \overline{x_n^2} \le \frac{PT}{N}.\qquad(11.11)$$

Before returning to the Gaussian channel, we define the *bandwidth* (measured in Hertz) of the continuous channel to be:

$$W = \frac{N^{\max}}{2T},\qquad(11.12)$$

where $N^{\max}$ is the maximum number of orthonormal functions that can be produced in an interval of length T. This definition can be motivated by imagining creating a band-limited signal of duration T from orthonormal cosine and sine curves of maximum frequency W. The number of orthonormal functions is $N^{\max} = 2WT$. This definition relates to the Nyquist sampling theorem: if the highest frequency present in a signal is W, then the signal can be fully determined from its values at a series of discrete sample points separated by the Nyquist interval $\Delta t = 1/2W$ seconds.

So the use of a real continuous channel with bandwidth W, noise spectral density N_0 and power P is equivalent to $N/T = 2W$ uses per second of a Gaussian channel with noise level $\sigma^2 = N_0/2$ and subject to the signal power constraint $\overline{x_n^2} \le P/2W$.

Definition of E_{b}/N_0

Imagine that the Gaussian channel $y_n = x_n + n_n$ is used with an encoding system to transmit *binary* source bits at a rate of R bits per channel use. How can we compare two encoding systems that have different rates of communication R and that use different powers $\overline{x_n^2}$? Transmitting at a large rate R is good; using small power is good too.

It is conventional to measure the rate-compensated signal to noise ratio by the ratio of the power per source bit $E_{\mathrm{b}} = \overline{x_n^2}/R$ to the noise spectral density N_0:

$$E_{\mathrm{b}}/N_0 = \frac{\overline{x_n^2}}{2\sigma^2 R}.\qquad(11.13)$$

E_{b}/N_0 is one of the measures used to compare coding schemes for Gaussian channels.

Figure 11.1. Three basis functions, and a weighted combination of them, $x(t) = \sum_{n=1}^N x_n\phi_n(t)$, with $x_1 = 0.4$, $x_2 = -0.2$, and $x_3 = 0.1$.

E_{b}/N_0 is dimensionless, but it is usually reported in the units of decibels; the value given is $10\log_{10} E_{\mathrm{b}}/N_0$.

▶ 11.2 Inferring the input to a real channel

'The best detection of pulses'

In 1944 Shannon wrote a memorandum (Shannon, 1993) on the problem of best differentiating between two types of pulses of known shape, represented by vectors $\mathbf{x}_0$ and $\mathbf{x}_1$, given that one of them has been transmitted over a noisy channel. This is a pattern recognition problem. It is assumed that the noise is Gaussian with probability density

$$P(\mathbf{n}) = \left[\det\left(\frac{\mathbf{A}}{2\pi}\right)\right]^{1/2} \exp\left(-\frac{1}{2}\mathbf{n}^{\mathsf{T}}\mathbf{A}\mathbf{n}\right), \tag{11.14}$$

where $\mathbf{A}$ is the inverse of the variance–covariance matrix of the noise, a symmetric and positive-definite matrix. (If $\mathbf{A}$ is a multiple of the identity matrix, $\mathbf{I}/\sigma^2$, then the noise is 'white'. For more general $\mathbf{A}$, the noise is 'coloured'.) The probability of the received vector $\mathbf{y}$ given that the source signal was s (either zero or one) is then

$$P(\mathbf{y}|s) = \left[\det\left(\frac{\mathbf{A}}{2\pi}\right)\right]^{1/2} \exp\left(-\frac{1}{2}(\mathbf{y}-\mathbf{x}_s)^{\mathsf{T}}\mathbf{A}(\mathbf{y}-\mathbf{x}_s)\right). \tag{11.15}$$

The optimal detector is based on the posterior probability ratio:

$$\frac{P(s=1|\mathbf{y})}{P(s=0|\mathbf{y})} = \frac{P(\mathbf{y}|s=1)\,P(s=1)}{P(\mathbf{y}|s=0)\,P(s=0)} \tag{11.16}$$

$$= \exp\left(-\frac{1}{2}(\mathbf{y}-\mathbf{x}_1)^{\mathsf{T}}\mathbf{A}(\mathbf{y}-\mathbf{x}_1) + \frac{1}{2}(\mathbf{y}-\mathbf{x}_0)^{\mathsf{T}}\mathbf{A}(\mathbf{y}-\mathbf{x}_0) + \ln\frac{P(s=1)}{P(s=0)}\right)$$

$$= \exp\left(\mathbf{y}^{\mathsf{T}}\mathbf{A}(\mathbf{x}_1-\mathbf{x}_0) + \theta\right), \tag{11.17}$$

where θ is a constant independent of the received vector $\mathbf{y}$,

$$\theta = -\frac{1}{2}\mathbf{x}_1^{\mathsf{T}}\mathbf{A}\mathbf{x}_1 + \frac{1}{2}\mathbf{x}_0^{\mathsf{T}}\mathbf{A}\mathbf{x}_0 + \ln\frac{P(s=1)}{P(s=0)}. \tag{11.18}$$

If the detector is forced to make a decision (i.e., guess either $s=1$ or $s=0$) then the decision that minimizes the probability of error is to guess the most probable hypothesis. We can write the optimal decision in terms of a *discriminant function*:

$$a(\mathbf{y}) \equiv \mathbf{y}^{\mathsf{T}}\mathbf{A}(\mathbf{x}_1-\mathbf{x}_0) + \theta \tag{11.19}$$

with the decisions

$$\begin{aligned} a(\mathbf{y}) > 0 &\rightarrow \text{guess } s=1 \\ a(\mathbf{y}) < 0 &\rightarrow \text{guess } s=0 \\ a(\mathbf{y}) = 0 &\rightarrow \text{guess either.} \end{aligned} \tag{11.20}$$

Notice that $a(\mathbf{y})$ is a linear function of the received vector,

$$a(\mathbf{y}) = \mathbf{w}^{\mathsf{T}}\mathbf{y} + \theta, \tag{11.21}$$

where $\mathbf{w} \equiv \mathbf{A}(\mathbf{x}_1 - \mathbf{x}_0)$.

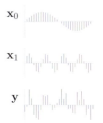

Figure 11.2. Two pulses $\mathbf{x}_0$ and $\mathbf{x}_1$, represented as 31-dimensional vectors, and a noisy version of one of them, $\mathbf{y}$.

Figure 11.3. The weight vector $\mathbf{w} \propto \mathbf{x}_1 - \mathbf{x}_0$ that is used to discriminate between $\mathbf{x}_0$ and $\mathbf{x}_1$.

▶ 11.3 Capacity of Gaussian channel

Until now we have only measured the joint, marginal, and conditional entropy of discrete variables. In order to define the information conveyed by continuous variables, there are two issues we must address – the infinite length of the real line, and the infinite precision of real numbers.

Infinite inputs

How much information can we convey in one use of a Gaussian channel? If
we are allowed to put *any* real number x into the Gaussian channel, we could
communicate an enormous string of N digits $d_1d_2d_3 \ldots d_N$ by setting $x =
d_1d_2d_3 \ldots d_N000 \ldots 000$. The amount of error-free information conveyed in
just a single transmission could be made arbitrarily large by increasing N,
and the communication could be made arbitrarily reliable by increasing the
number of zeroes at the end of x. There is usually some power cost associated
with large inputs, however, not to mention practical limits in the dynamic
range acceptable to a receiver. It is therefore conventional to introduce a
cost function $v(x)$ for every input x, and constrain codes to have an average
cost $\bar{v}$ less than or equal to some maximum value. A generalized channel
coding theorem, including a cost function for the inputs, can be proved – see
McEliece (1977). The result is a channel capacity $C(\bar{v})$ that is a function of
the permitted cost. For the Gaussian channel we will assume a cost

$$v(x) = x^2 \tag{11.22}$$

such that the 'average power' $\overline{x^2}$ of the input is constrained. We motivated this
cost function above in the case of real electrical channels in which the physical
power consumption is indeed quadratic in x. The constraint $\overline{x^2} = \bar{v}$ makes
it impossible to communicate infinite information in one use of the Gaussian
channel.

Infinite precision

It is tempting to define joint, marginal, and conditional entropies for real
variables simply by replacing summations by integrals, but this is not a well
defined operation. As we discretize an interval into smaller and smaller divi-
sions, the entropy of the discrete distribution diverges (as the logarithm of the
granularity) (figure 11.4). Also, it is not permissible to take the logarithm of
a dimensional quantity such as a probability density $P(x)$ (whose dimensions
are $[x]^{-1}$).

There is one information measure, however, that has a well-behaved limit,
namely the mutual information – and this is the one that really matters, since
it measures how much information one variable conveys about another. In the
discrete case,

$$I(X;Y) = \sum_{x,y} P(x,y) \log \frac{P(x,y)}{P(x)P(y)}. \tag{11.23}$$

Now because the argument of the log is a ratio of two probabilities over the
same space, it is OK to have $P(x,y)$, $P(x)$ and $P(y)$ be probability densities
and replace the sum by an integral:

$$I(X;Y) = \int \mathrm{d}x\,\mathrm{d}y\, P(x,y) \log \frac{P(x,y)}{P(x)P(y)} \tag{11.24}$$

$$= \int \mathrm{d}x\,\mathrm{d}y\, P(x)P(y|x) \log \frac{P(y|x)}{P(y)}. \tag{11.25}$$

We can now ask these questions for the Gaussian channel: (a) what probability
distribution $P(x)$ maximizes the mutual information (subject to the constraint
$\overline{x^2} = v$)? and (b) does the maximal mutual information still measure the
maximum error free communication rate of this real channel, as it did for the
discrete channel?

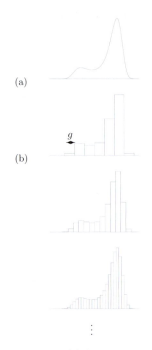

Figure 11.4. (a) A probability
density $P(x)$. Question: can we
define the 'entropy' of this
density? (b) We could evaluate
the entropies of a sequence of
probability distributions with
decreasing grain-size g, but these
entropies tend to

$$\int P(x) \log \frac{1}{P(x)g}\,\mathrm{d}x,$$ which is not

independent of g: the entropy
goes up by one bit for every
halving of g.

$$\int P(x) \log \frac{1}{P(x)}\,\mathrm{d}x$$ is an illegal

integral.

Exercise 11.1.[3, p.189] Prove that the probability distribution $P(x)$ that maximizes the mutual information (subject to the constraint $\overline{x^2} = v$) is a Gaussian distribution of mean zero and variance v.

▷ Exercise 11.2.[2, p.189] Show that the mutual information $I(X;Y)$, in the case of this optimized distribution, is

$$C = \frac{1}{2} \log \left(1 + \frac{v}{\sigma^2}\right). \tag{11.26}$$

This is an important result. We see that the capacity of the Gaussian channel is a function of the *signal to noise ratio* v/σ^2.

Inferences given a Gaussian input distribution

If $P(x) = \text{Normal}(x; 0, v)$ and $P(y|x) = \text{Normal}(y; x, \sigma^2)$ then the marginal distribution of y is $P(y) = \text{Normal}(y; 0, v + \sigma^2)$ and the posterior distribution of the input, given that the output is y, is:

$$P(x|y) \propto P(y|x)P(x) \tag{11.27}$$
$$\propto \exp(-(y-x)^2/2\sigma^2)\exp(-x^2/2v) \tag{11.28}$$
$$= \text{Normal}\left(x; \frac{v}{v+\sigma^2}\, y,\, \left(\frac{1}{v} + \frac{1}{\sigma^2}\right)^{-1}\right). \tag{11.29}$$

[The step from (11.28) to (11.29) is made by completing the square in the exponent.] This formula deserves careful study. The mean of the posterior distribution, $\frac{v}{v+\sigma^2}\, y$, can be viewed as a weighted combination of the value that best fits the output, $x = y$, and the value that best fits the prior, $x = 0$:

$$\frac{v}{v+\sigma^2}\, y = \frac{1/\sigma^2}{1/v + 1/\sigma^2}\, y + \frac{1/v}{1/v + 1/\sigma^2}\, 0. \tag{11.30}$$

The weights $1/\sigma^2$ and $1/v$ are the *precisions* of the two Gaussians that we multiplied together in equation (11.28): the prior and the likelihood.

The precision of the posterior distribution is the sum of these two precisions. This is a general property: whenever two independent sources contribute information, via Gaussian distributions, about an unknown variable, the precisions add. [This is the dual to the better known relationship 'when independent variables are added, their variances add'.]

Noisy-channel coding theorem for the Gaussian channel

We have evaluated a maximal mutual information. Does it correspond to a maximum possible rate of error-free information transmission? One way of proving that this is so is to define a sequence of discrete channels, all derived from the Gaussian channel, with increasing numbers of inputs and outputs, and prove that the maximum mutual information of these channels tends to the asserted C. The noisy-channel coding theorem for discrete channels applies to each of these derived channels, thus we obtain a coding theorem for the continuous channel. Alternatively, we can make an intuitive argument for the coding theorem specific for the Gaussian channel.

Geometrical view of the noisy-channel coding theorem: sphere packing

Consider a sequence $\mathbf{x} = (x_1, \ldots, x_N)$ of inputs, and the corresponding output $\mathbf{y}$, as defining two points in an N dimensional space. For large N, the noise power is very likely to be close (fractionally) to $N\sigma^2$. The output $\mathbf{y}$ is therefore very likely to be close to the surface of a sphere of radius $\sqrt{N\sigma^2}$ centred on $\mathbf{x}$. Similarly, if the original signal $\mathbf{x}$ is generated at random subject to an average power constraint $\overline{x^2} = v$, then $\mathbf{x}$ is likely to lie close to a sphere, centred on the origin, of radius $\sqrt{Nv}$; and because the total average power of $\mathbf{y}$ is $v + \sigma^2$, the received signal $\mathbf{y}$ is likely to lie on the surface of a sphere of radius $\sqrt{N(v + \sigma^2)}$, centred on the origin.

The volume of an N-dimensional sphere of radius r is

$$V(r, N) = \frac{\pi^{N/2}}{\Gamma(N/2+1)} r^N. \tag{11.31}$$

Now consider making a communication system based on non-confusable inputs $\mathbf{x}$, that is, inputs whose spheres do not overlap significantly. The maximum number S of non-confusable inputs is given by dividing the volume of the sphere of probable $\mathbf{y}$s by the volume of the sphere for $\mathbf{y}$ given $\mathbf{x}$:

$$S \leq \left(\frac{\sqrt{N(v + \sigma^2)}}{\sqrt{N\sigma^2}} \right)^N \tag{11.32}$$

Thus the capacity is bounded by:

$$C = \frac{1}{N} \log M \leq \frac{1}{2} \log \left(1 + \frac{v}{\sigma^2} \right). \tag{11.33}$$

A more detailed argument like the one used in the previous chapter can establish equality.

Back to the continuous channel

Recall that the use of a real continuous channel with bandwidth W, noise spectral density N_0 and power P is equivalent to $N/T = 2W$ uses per second of a Gaussian channel with $\sigma^2 = N_0/2$ and subject to the constraint $\overline{x_n^2} \leq P/2W$. Substituting the result for the capacity of the Gaussian channel, we find the capacity of the continuous channel to be:

$$C = W \log \left(1 + \frac{P}{N_0 W} \right) \text{ bits per second.} \tag{11.34}$$

This formula gives insight into the tradeoffs of practical communication. Imagine that we have a fixed power constraint. What is the best bandwidth to make use of that power? Introducing $W_0 = P/N_0$, i.e., the bandwidth for which the signal to noise ratio is 1, figure 11.5 shows $C/W_0 = W/W_0 \log(1 + W_0/W)$ as a function of W/W_0. The capacity increases to an asymptote of $W_0 \log e$. It is dramatically better (in terms of capacity for fixed power) to transmit at a low signal to noise ratio over a large bandwidth, than with high signal to noise in a narrow bandwidth; this is one motivation for wideband communication methods such as the 'direct sequence spread-spectrum' approach used in 3G mobile phones. Of course, you are not alone, and your electromagnetic neighbours may not be pleased if you use a large bandwidth, so for social reasons, engineers often have to make do with higher-power, narrow-bandwidth transmitters.

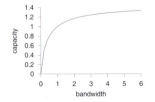

Figure 11.5. Capacity versus bandwidth for a real channel: $C/W_0 = W/W_0 \log(1 + W_0/W)$ as a function of W/W_0.

▶ 11.4 What are the capabilities of practical error-correcting codes?

Nearly all codes are good, but nearly all codes require exponential look-up tables for practical implementation of the encoder and decoder – exponential in the block length N. And the coding theorem required N to be large.

By a *practical* error-correcting code, we mean one that can be encoded and decoded in a reasonable amount of time, for example, a time that scales as a polynomial function of the block length N – preferably linearly.

The Shannon limit is not achieved in practice

The non-constructive proof of the noisy-channel coding theorem showed that good block codes exist for any noisy channel, and indeed that nearly all block codes are good. But writing down an explicit and practical encoder and decoder that are as good as promised by Shannon is still an unsolved problem.

Very good codes. Given a channel, a family of block codes that achieve arbitrarily small probability of error at any communication rate up to the capacity of the channel are called 'very good' codes for that channel.

Good codes are code families that achieve arbitrarily small probability of error at non-zero communication rates up to some maximum rate that may be *less than* the capacity of the given channel.

Bad codes are code families that cannot achieve arbitrarily small probability of error, or that can only achieve arbitrarily small probability of error by decreasing the information rate to zero. Repetition codes are an example of a bad code family. (Bad codes are not necessarily useless for practical purposes.)

Practical codes are code families that can be encoded and decoded in time and space polynomial in the block length.

Most established codes are linear codes

Let us review the definition of a block code, and then add the definition of a linear block code.

An (N, K) block code for a channel Q is a list of $S = 2^K$ codewords $\{\mathbf{x}^{(1)}, \mathbf{x}^{(2)}, \ldots, \mathbf{x}^{(2^K)}\}$, each of length N: $\mathbf{x}^{(s)} \in \mathcal{A}_X^N$. The signal to be encoded, s, which comes from an alphabet of size 2^K, is encoded as $\mathbf{x}^{(s)}$.

A linear (N, K) block code is a block code in which the codewords $\{\mathbf{x}^{(s)}\}$ make up a K-dimensional subspace of $\mathcal{A}_X^N$. The encoding operation can be represented by an $N \times K$ binary matrix $\mathbf{G}^\mathsf{T}$ such that if the signal to be encoded, in binary notation, is $\mathbf{s}$ (a vector of length K bits), then the encoded signal is $\mathbf{t} = \mathbf{G}^\mathsf{T}\mathbf{s}$ modulo 2.

The codewords $\{\mathbf{t}\}$ can be defined as the set of vectors satisfying $\mathbf{Ht} = \mathbf{0} \bmod 2$, where $\mathbf{H}$ is the *parity-check matrix* of the code.

For example the $(7, 4)$ Hamming code of section 1.2 takes $K = 4$ signal bits, $\mathbf{s}$, and transmits them followed by three parity-check bits. The $N = 7$ transmitted symbols are given by $\mathbf{G}^\mathsf{T}\mathbf{s} \bmod 2$.

Coding theory was born with the work of Hamming, who invented a family of practical error-correcting codes, each able to correct one error in a block of length N, of which the repetition code R_3 and the $(7, 4)$ code are

$$\mathbf{G}^\mathsf{T} = \begin{bmatrix} 1 & \cdot & \cdot & \cdot \\ \cdot & 1 & \cdot & \cdot \\ \cdot & \cdot & 1 & \cdot \\ \cdot & \cdot & \cdot & 1 \\ 1 & 1 & 1 & \cdot \\ \cdot & 1 & 1 & 1 \\ 1 & \cdot & 1 & 1 \end{bmatrix}$$

the simplest. Since then most established codes have been generalizations of Hamming's codes: Bose–Chaudhury–Hocquenhem codes, Reed–Müller codes, Reed–Solomon codes, and Goppa codes, to name a few.

Convolutional codes

Another family of linear codes are *convolutional codes*, which do not divide the source stream into blocks, but instead read and transmit bits continuously. The transmitted bits are a linear function of the past source bits. Usually the rule for generating the transmitted bits involves feeding the present source bit into a linear feedback shift register of length k, and transmitting one or more linear functions of the state of the shift register at each iteration. The resulting transmitted bit stream is the convolution of the source stream with a linear filter. The impulse response function of this filter may have finite or infinite duration, depending on the choice of feedback shift register.

We will discuss convolutional codes in Chapter 48.

Are linear codes 'good'?

One might ask, is the reason that the Shannon limit is not achieved in practice because linear codes are inherently not as good as random codes? The answer is no, the noisy-channel coding theorem can still be proved for linear codes, at least for some channels (see Chapter 14), though the proofs, like Shannon's proof for random codes, are non-constructive.

Linear codes are easy to implement at the encoding end. Is decoding a linear code also easy? Not necessarily. The general decoding problem (find the maximum likelihood $\mathbf{s}$ in the equation $\mathbf{G}^{\mathsf{T}}\mathbf{s} + \mathbf{n} = \mathbf{r}$) is in fact NP-complete (Berlekamp *et al.*, 1978). [NP-complete problems are computational problems that are all equally difficult and which are widely believed to require exponential computer time to solve in general.] So attention focuses on families of codes for which there is a fast decoding algorithm.

Concatenation

One trick for building codes with practical decoders is the idea of concatenation.

An encoder–channel–decoder system $\mathcal{C} \to Q \to \mathcal{D}$ can be viewed as defining a super-channel Q' with a smaller probability of error, and with complex correlations among its errors. We can create an encoder $\mathcal{C}'$ and decoder $\mathcal{D}'$ for this super-channel Q'. The code consisting of the outer code $\mathcal{C}'$ followed by the inner code $\mathcal{C}$ is known as a *concatenated code*.

$$\mathcal{C}' \to \underbrace{\mathcal{C} \to Q \to \mathcal{D}}_{Q'} \to \mathcal{D}'$$

Some concatenated codes make use of the idea of *interleaving*. We read the data in blocks, the size of each block being larger than the block lengths of the constituent codes $\mathcal{C}$ and $\mathcal{C}'$. After encoding the data of one block using code $\mathcal{C}'$, the bits are reordered within the block in such a way that nearby bits are separated from each other once the block is fed to the second code $\mathcal{C}$. A simple example of an interleaver is a *rectangular code* or *product code* in which the data are arranged in a $K_2 \times K_1$ block, and encoded horizontally using an (N_1, K_1) linear code, then vertically using a (N_2, K_2) linear code.

▷ Exercise 11.3.[3] Show that either of the two codes can be viewed as the inner code or the outer code.

As an example, figure 11.6 shows a product code in which we encode first with the repetition code R_3 (also known as the Hamming code $H(3,1)$)

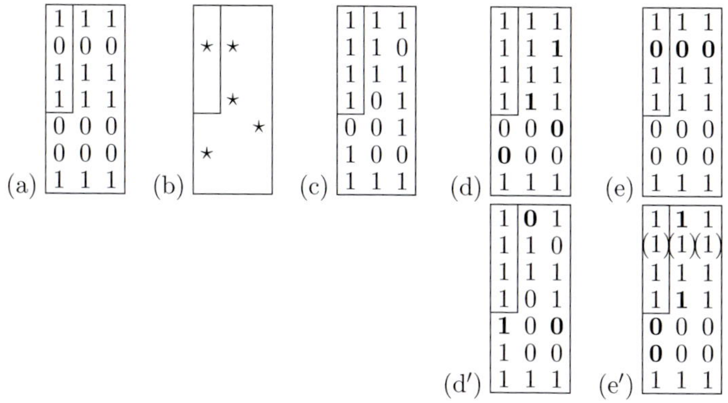

Figure 11.6. A product code. (a) A string 1011 encoded using a concatenated code consisting of two Hamming codes, $H(3,1)$ and $H(7,4)$. (b) a noise pattern that flips 5 bits. (c) The received vector. (d) After decoding using the horizontal $(3,1)$ decoder, and (e) after subsequently using the vertical $(7,4)$ decoder. The decoded vector matches the original.
(d', e') After decoding in the other order, three errors still remain.

horizontally then with $H(7,4)$ vertically. The block length of the concatenated code is 27. The number of source bits per codeword is four, shown by the small rectangle.

We can decode conveniently (though not optimally) by using the individual decoders for each of the subcodes in some sequence. It makes most sense to first decode the code which has the lowest rate and hence the greatest error-correcting ability.

Figure 11.6(c–e) shows what happens if we receive the codeword of figure 11.6a with some errors (five bits flipped, as shown) and apply the decoder for $H(3,1)$ first, and then the decoder for $H(7,4)$. The first decoder corrects three of the errors, but erroneously modifies the third bit in the second row where there are two bit errors. The $(7,4)$ decoder can then correct all three of these errors.

Figure 11.6(d'–e') shows what happens if we decode the two codes in the other order. In columns one and two there are two errors, so the $(7,4)$ decoder introduces two extra errors. It corrects the one error in column 3. The $(3,1)$ decoder then cleans up four of the errors, but erroneously infers the second bit.

Interleaving

The motivation for interleaving is that by spreading out bits that are nearby in one code, we make it possible to ignore the complex correlations among the errors that are produced by the inner code. Maybe the inner code will mess up an entire codeword; but that codeword is spread out one bit at a time over several codewords of the outer code. So we can treat the errors introduced by the inner code as if they are independent.

Other channel models

In addition to the binary symmetric channel and the Gaussian channel, coding theorists keep more complex channels in mind also.

Burst-error channels are important models in practice. Reed–Solomon codes use Galois fields (see Appendix C.1) with large numbers of elements (e.g. 2^{16}) as their input alphabets, and thereby automatically achieve a degree of burst-error tolerance in that even if 17 successive bits are corrupted, only 2 successive symbols in the Galois field representation are corrupted. Concatenation and interleaving can give further protection against burst errors. The concatenated Reed–Solomon codes used on digital compact discs are able to correct bursts of errors of length 4000 bits.

▷ Exercise 11.4.[2, p.189] The technique of interleaving, which allows bursts of errors to be treated as independent, is widely used, but is theoretically a poor way to protect data against burst errors, in terms of the amount of redundancy required. Explain why interleaving is a poor method, using the following burst-error channel as an example. Time is divided into chunks of length $N = 100$ clock cycles; during each chunk, there is a burst with probability $b = 0.2$; during a burst, the channel is a binary symmetric channel with $f = 0.5$. If there is no burst, the channel is an error-free binary channel. Compute the capacity of this channel and compare it with the maximum communication rate that could conceivably be achieved if one used interleaving and treated the errors as independent.

Fading channels are real channels like Gaussian channels except that the received power is assumed to vary with time. A moving mobile phone is an important example. The incoming radio signal is reflected off nearby objects so that there are interference patterns and the intensity of the signal received by the phone varies with its location. The received power can easily vary by 10 decibels (a factor of ten) as the phone's antenna moves through a distance similar to the wavelength of the radio signal (a few centimetres).

▶ 11.5 The state of the art

What are the best known codes for communicating over Gaussian channels? All the practical codes are linear codes, and are either based on convolutional codes or block codes.

Convolutional codes, and codes based on them

Textbook convolutional codes. The 'de facto standard' error-correcting code for satellite communications is a convolutional code with constraint length 7. Convolutional codes are discussed in Chapter 48.

Concatenated convolutional codes. The above convolutional code can be used as the inner code of a concatenated code whose outer code is a Reed–Solomon code with eight-bit symbols. This code was used in deep space communication systems such as the Voyager spacecraft. For further reading about Reed–Solomon codes, see Lin and Costello (1983).

The code for Galileo. A code using the same format but using a longer constraint length – 15 – for its convolutional code and a larger Reed–Solomon code was developed by the Jet Propulsion Laboratory (Swanson, 1988). The details of this code are unpublished outside JPL, and the decoding is only possible using a room full of special-purpose hardware. In 1992, this was the best known code of rate $1/4$.

Turbo codes. In 1993, Berrou, Glavieux and Thitimajshima reported work on *turbo codes*. The encoder of a turbo code is based on the encoders of two convolutional codes. The source bits are fed into each encoder, the order of the source bits being permuted in a random way, and the resulting parity bits from each constituent code are transmitted.

The decoding algorithm involves iteratively decoding each constituent code using its standard decoding algorithm, then using the output of the decoder as the input to the other decoder. This decoding algorithm

Figure 11.7. The encoder of a turbo code. Each box C_1, C_2, contains a convolutional code. The source bits are reordered using a permutation π before they are fed to C_2. The transmitted codeword is obtained by concatenating or interleaving the outputs of the two convolutional codes. The random permutation is chosen when the code is designed, and fixed thereafter.

is an instance of a *message-passing* algorithm called the *sum–product algorithm*.

Turbo codes are discussed in Chapter 48, and message passing in Chapters 16, 17, 25, and 26.

Block codes

Gallager's low-density parity-check codes. The best block codes known for Gaussian channels were invented by Gallager in 1962 but were promptly forgotten by most of the coding theory community. They were rediscovered in 1995 and shown to have outstanding theoretical and practical properties. Like turbo codes, they are decoded by message-passing algorithms.

We will discuss these beautifully simple codes in Chapter 47.

The performances of the above codes are compared for Gaussian channels in figure 47.17, p.568.

▶ **11.6 Summary**

Random codes are good, but they require exponential resources to encode and decode them.

Non-random codes tend for the most part not to be as good as random codes. For a non-random code, encoding may be easy, but even for simply-defined linear codes, the decoding problem remains very difficult.

The best practical codes (a) employ very large block sizes; (b) are based on semi-random code constructions; and (c) make use of probability-based decoding algorithms.

▶ **11.7 Nonlinear codes**

Most practically used codes are linear, but not all. Digital soundtracks are encoded onto cinema film as a binary pattern. The likely errors affecting the film involve dirt and scratches, which produce large numbers of 1s and 0s respectively. We want none of the codewords to look like all-1s or all-0s, so that it will be easy to detect errors caused by dirt and scratches. One of the codes used in digital cinema sound systems is a nonlinear $(8,6)$ code consisting of 64 of the $\binom{8}{4}$ binary patterns of weight 4.

▶ **11.8 Errors other than noise**

Another source of uncertainty for the receiver is uncertainty about the *timing* of the transmitted signal $x(t)$. In ordinary coding theory and information theory, the transmitter's time t and the receiver's time u are assumed to be perfectly synchronized. But if the receiver receives a signal $y(u)$, where the receiver's time, u, is an imperfectly known function $u(t)$ of the transmitter's time t, then the capacity of this channel for communication is reduced. The theory of such channels is incomplete, compared with the synchronized channels we have discussed thus far. Not even the *capacity* of channels with synchronization errors is known (Levenshtein, 1966; Ferreira *et al.*, 1997); codes for reliable communication over channels with synchronization errors remain an active research area (Davey and MacKay, 2001).

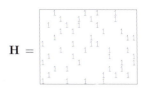

$$\mathbf{H} =$$

Figure 11.8. A low-density parity-check matrix and the corresponding graph of a rate-$^1\!/4$ low-density parity-check code with blocklength $N = 16$, and $M = 12$ constraints. Each white circle represents a transmitted bit. Each bit participates in $j = 3$ constraints, represented by ⊞ squares. Each constraint forces the sum of the $k = 4$ bits to which it is connected to be even. This code is a $(16, 4)$ code. Outstanding performance is obtained when the block length is increased to $N \simeq 10\,000$.

Further reading

For a review of the history of spread-spectrum methods, see Scholtz (1982).

▶ **11.9 Exercises**

The Gaussian channel

▷ Exercise 11.5.[2, p.190] Consider a Gaussian channel with a real input x, and signal to noise ratio v/σ^2.

(a) What is its capacity C?

(b) If the input is constrained to be binary, $x \in \{\pm\sqrt{v}\}$, what is the capacity C' of this constrained channel?

(c) If in addition the output of the channel is thresholded using the mapping

$$y \to y' = \begin{cases} 1 & y > 0 \\ 0 & y \le 0, \end{cases} \qquad (11.35)$$

what is the capacity C'' of the resulting channel?

(d) Plot the three capacities above as a function of v/σ^2 from 0.1 to 2. [You'll need to do a numerical integral to evaluate C'.]

▷ Exercise 11.6.[3] For large integers K and N, what fraction of all binary error-correcting codes of length N and rate $R = K/N$ are *linear* codes? [The answer will depend on whether you choose to define the code to be an *ordered* list of 2^K codewords, that is, a mapping from $s \in \{1, 2, \dots, 2^K\}$ to $\mathbf{x}^{(s)}$, or to define the code to be an unordered list, so that two codes consisting of the same codewords are identical. Use the latter definition: a code is a set of codewords; how the encoder operates is not part of the definition of the code.]

Erasure channels

▷ Exercise 11.7.[4] Design a code for the binary erasure channel, and a decoding algorithm, and evaluate their probability of error. [The design of good codes for erasure channels is an active research area (Spielman, 1996; Byers *et al.*, 1998); see also Chapter 50.]

▷ Exercise 11.8.[5] Design a code for the q-ary erasure channel, whose input x is drawn from $0, 1, 2, 3, \dots, (q-1)$, and whose output y is equal to x with probability $(1-f)$ and equal to ? otherwise. [This erasure channel is a good model for packets transmitted over the internet, which are either received reliably or are lost.]

Exercise 11.9.[2, p.190] How do redundant arrays of independent disks (RAID) work? These are information storage systems consisting of about ten disk drives, of which any two or three can be disabled and the others are able to still able to reconstruct any requested file. What codes are used, and how far are these systems from the Shannon limit for the problem they are solving? How would *you* design a better RAID system? Some information is provided in the solution section. See http://www.acnc.com/raid2.html; see also Chapter 50.

[Some people say RAID stands for 'redundant array of inexpensive disks', but I think that's silly – RAID would still be a good idea even if the disks were expensive!]

▶ 11.10 Solutions

Solution to exercise 11.1 (p.181). Introduce a Lagrange multiplier λ for the power constraint and another, μ, for the constraint of normalization of $P(x)$.

$$F = I(X;Y) - \lambda \int dx\, P(x) x^2 - \mu \int dx\, P(x) \tag{11.36}$$

$$= \int dx\, P(x) \left[\int dy\, P(y|x) \ln \frac{P(y|x)}{P(y)} - \lambda x^2 - \mu \right]. \tag{11.37}$$

Make the functional derivative with respect to $P(x^*)$.

$$\frac{\delta F}{\delta P(x^*)} = \int dy\, P(y|x^*) \ln \frac{P(y|x^*)}{P(y)} - \lambda x^{*2} - \mu$$

$$- \int dx\, P(x) \int dy\, P(y|x) \frac{1}{P(y)} \frac{\delta P(y)}{\delta P(x^*)}. \tag{11.38}$$

The final factor $\delta P(y)/\delta P(x^*)$ is found, using $P(y) = \int dx\, P(x)P(y|x)$, to be $P(y|x^*)$, and the whole of the last term collapses in a puff of smoke to 1, which can be absorbed into the μ term.

Substitute $P(y|x) = \exp(-(y-x)^2/2\sigma^2)/\sqrt{2\pi\sigma^2}$ and set the derivative to zero:

$$\int dy\, P(y|x) \ln \frac{P(y|x)}{P(y)} - \lambda x^2 - \mu' = 0 \tag{11.39}$$

$$\Rightarrow \int dy\, \frac{\exp(-(y-x)^2/2\sigma^2)}{\sqrt{2\pi\sigma^2}} \ln \left[P(y)\sigma \right] = -\lambda x^2 - \mu' - \frac{1}{2}. \tag{11.40}$$

This condition must be satisfied by $\ln[P(y)\sigma]$ for all x.

Writing a Taylor expansion of $\ln[P(y)\sigma] = a + by + cy^2 + \cdots$, only a quadratic function $\ln[P(y)\sigma] = a + cy^2$ would satisfy the constraint (11.40). (Any higher order terms y^p, $p > 2$, would produce terms in x^p that are not present on the right-hand side.) Therefore $P(y)$ is Gaussian. We can obtain this optimal output distribution by using a Gaussian input distribution $P(x)$.

Solution to exercise 11.2 (p.181). Given a Gaussian input distribution of variance v, the output distribution is Normal$(0, v + \sigma^2)$, since x and the noise are independent random variables, and variances add for independent random variables. The mutual information is:

$$I(X;Y) = \int dx\, dy\, P(x)P(y|x) \log P(y|x) - \int dy\, P(y) \log P(y) \tag{11.41}$$

$$= \frac{1}{2} \log \frac{1}{\sigma^2} - \frac{1}{2} \log \frac{1}{v + \sigma^2} \tag{11.42}$$

$$= \frac{1}{2} \log \left(1 + \frac{v}{\sigma^2} \right). \tag{11.43}$$

Solution to exercise 11.4 (p.186). The capacity of the channel is one minus the information content of the noise that it adds. That information content is, per chunk, the entropy of the selection of whether the chunk is bursty, $H_2(b)$, plus, with probability b, the entropy of the flipped bits, N, which adds up to $H_2(b) + Nb$ per chunk (roughly; accurate if N is large). So, per bit, the capacity is, for $N = 100$,

$$C = 1 - \left(\frac{1}{N} H_2(b) + b \right) = 1 - 0.207 = 0.793. \tag{11.44}$$

In contrast, interleaving, which treats bursts of errors as independent, causes the channel to be treated as a binary symmetric channel with $f = 0.2 \times 0.5 = 0.1$, whose capacity is about 0.53.

Interleaving throws away the useful information about the correlatedness of the errors. Theoretically, we should be able to communicate about $(0.79/0.53) \simeq 1.6$ times faster using a code and decoder that explicitly treat bursts as bursts.

Solution to exercise 11.5 (p.188).

(a) Putting together the results of exercises 11.1 and 11.2, we deduce that a Gaussian channel with real input x, and signal to noise ratio v/σ^2 has capacity

$$C = \frac{1}{2} \log \left(1 + \frac{v}{\sigma^2}\right). \tag{11.45}$$

(b) If the input is constrained to be binary, $x \in \{\pm\sqrt{v}\}$, the capacity is achieved by using these two inputs with equal probability. The capacity is reduced to a somewhat messy integral,

$$C'' = \int_{-\infty}^{\infty} dy\, N(y; 0) \log N(y; 0) - \int_{-\infty}^{\infty} dy\, P(y) \log P(y), \tag{11.46}$$

where $N(y; x) \equiv (1/\sqrt{2\pi}) \exp[(y - x)^2/2]$, $x \equiv \sqrt{v}/\sigma$, and $P(y) \equiv [N(y; x) + N(y; -x)]/2$. This capacity is smaller than the unconstrained capacity (11.45), but for small signal to noise ratio, the two capacities are close in value.

(c) If the output is thresholded, then the Gaussian channel is turned into a binary symmetric channel whose transition probability is given by the error function Φ defined on page 156. The capacity is

$$C'' = 1 - H_2(f), \text{ where } f = \Phi(\sqrt{v}/\sigma). \tag{11.47}$$

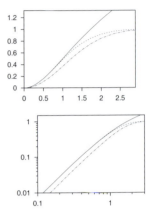

Figure 11.9. Capacities (from top to bottom in each graph) C, C', and C'', versus the signal to noise ratio ($\sqrt{v}/\sigma$). The lower graph is a log–log plot.

Solution to exercise 11.9 (p.188). There are several RAID systems. One of the easiest to understand consists of 7 disk drives which store data at rate $4/7$ using a $(7, 4)$ Hamming code: each successive four bits are encoded with the code and the seven codeword bits are written one to each disk. Two or perhaps three disk drives can go down and the others can recover the data. The effective channel model here is a binary erasure channel, because it is assumed that we can tell when a disk is dead.

It is not possible to recover the data for *some* choices of the three dead disk drives; can you see why?

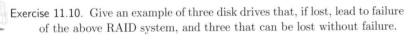 **Exercise 11.10.** Give an example of three disk drives that, if lost, lead to failure of the above RAID system, and three that can be lost without failure.

Solution to exercise 11.10 (p.190). The $(7, 4)$ Hamming code has codewords of weight 3. If any set of three disk drives corresponding to one of those codewords is lost, then the other four disks can only recover 3 bits of information about the four source bits; a fourth bit is lost. [c.f. exercise 13.13 (p.220) with $q = 2$: there are no binary MDS codes. This deficit is discussed further in section 13.11]

Any other set of three disk drives can be lost without problems because the corresponding four by four submatrix of the generator matrix is invertible. A better code would be the digital fountain – see Chapter 50.

Part III

Further Topics in Information Theory

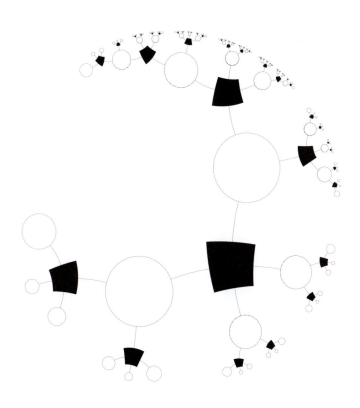

About Chapter 12

In Chapters 1–11, we concentrated on two aspects of information theory and coding theory: source coding – the compression of information so as to make efficient use of data transmission and storage channels; and channel coding – the redundant encoding of information so as to be able to detect and correct communication errors.

In both these areas we started by ignoring practical considerations, concentrating on the question of the theoretical limitations and possibilities of coding. We then discussed practical source-coding and channel-coding schemes, shifting the emphasis towards computational feasibility. But the prime criterion for comparing encoding schemes remained the efficiency of the code in terms of the channel resources it required: the best source codes were those that achieved the greatest compression; the best channel codes were those that communicated at the highest rate with a given probability of error.

In this chapter we now shift our viewpoint a little, thinking of *ease of information retrieval* as a primary goal. It turns out that the random codes which were theoretically useful in our study of channel coding are also useful for rapid information retrieval.

Efficient information retrieval is one of the problems that brains seem to solve effortlessly, and content-addressable memory is one of the topics we will study when we look at neural networks.

Hash Codes: Codes for Efficient Information Retrieval

▶ ## 12.1 The information retrieval problem

A simple example of an information retrieval problem is the task of implementing a phone directory service, which, in response to a person's *name*, returns (a) a confirmation that that person is listed in the directory; and (b) the person's phone number and other details. We could formalize this problem as follows, with S being the number of names that must be stored in the directory.

You are given a list of S binary strings of length N bits, $\{\mathbf{x}^{(1)}, \ldots, \mathbf{x}^{(S)}\}$, where S is considerably smaller than the total number of possible strings, 2^N. We will call the superscript 's' in $\mathbf{x}^{(s)}$ the *record number* of the string. The idea is that s runs over customers in the order in which they are added to the directory and $\mathbf{x}^{(s)}$ is the name of customer s. We assume for simplicity that all people have names of the same length. The name length might be, say, $N = 200$ bits, and we might want to store the details of ten million customers, so $S \simeq 10^7 \simeq 2^{23}$. We will ignore the possibility that two customers have identical names.

The task is to construct the inverse of the mapping from s to $\mathbf{x}^{(s)}$, i.e., to make a system that, given a string $\mathbf{x}$, returns the value of s such that $\mathbf{x} = \mathbf{x}^{(s)}$ if one exists, and otherwise reports that no such s exists. (Once we have the record number, we can go and look in memory location s in a separate memory full of phone numbers to find the required number.) The aim, when solving this task, is to use minimal computational resources in terms of the amount of memory used to store the inverse mapping from $\mathbf{x}$ to s and the amount of time to compute the inverse mapping. And, preferably, the inverse mapping should be implemented in such a way that further new strings can be added to the directory in a small amount of computer time too.

string length	$N \simeq 200$
number of strings	$S \simeq 2^{23}$
number of possible strings	$2^N \simeq 2^{200}$

Figure 12.1. Cast of characters.

Some standard solutions

The simplest and dumbest solutions to the information retrieval problem are a look-up table and a raw list.

The look-up table is a piece of memory of size $2^N \log_2 S$, $\log_2 S$ being the amount of memory required to store an integer between 1 and S. In each of the 2^N locations, we put a zero, except for the locations $\mathbf{x}$ that correspond to strings $\mathbf{x}^{(s)}$, into which we write the value of s.

The look-up table is a simple and quick solution, if only there is sufficient memory for the table, and if the cost of looking up entries in memory is independent of the memory size. But in our definition of the task, we assumed that N is about 200 bits or more, so the amount of memory required would be of size 2^{200}; this solution is completely out of the question. Bear in mind that the number of particles in the solar system is only about 2^{190}.

The raw list is a simple list of ordered pairs $(s, \mathbf{x}^{(s)})$ ordered by the value of s. The mapping from $\mathbf{x}$ to s is achieved by searching through the list of strings, starting from the top, and comparing the incoming string $\mathbf{x}$ with each record $\mathbf{x}^{(s)}$ until a match is found. This system is very easy to maintain, and uses a small amount of memory, about SN bits, but is rather slow to use, since on average five million pairwise comparisons will be made.

▷ Exercise 12.1.[2, p.202] Show that the average time taken to find the required string in a raw list, assuming that the original names were chosen at random, is about $S + N$ binary comparisons. (Note that you don't have to compare the whole string of length N, since a comparison can be terminated as soon as a mismatch occurs; show that you need on average two binary comparisons per incorrect string match.) Compare this with the worst-case search time – assuming that the devil chooses the set of strings and the search key.

The standard way in which phone directories are made improves on the look-up table and the raw list by using an *alphabetically ordered list*.

Alphabetical list. The strings $\{\mathbf{x}^{(s)}\}$ are sorted into alphabetical order. Searching for an entry now usually takes less time than was needed for the raw list because we can take advantage of the sortedness; for example, we can open the phonebook at its middle page, and compare the name we find there with the target string; if the target is 'greater' than the middle string then we know that the required string, if it exists, will be found in the second half of the alphabetical directory. Otherwise, we look in the first half. By iterating this splitting-in-the-middle procedure, we can identify the target string, or establish that the string is not listed, in $\lceil \log_2 S \rceil$ string comparisons. The expected number of binary comparisons per string comparison will tend to increase as the search progresses, but the total number of binary comparisons required will be no greater than $\lceil \log_2 S \rceil N$.

The amount of memory required is the same as that required for the raw list.

Adding new strings to the database requires that we insert them in the correct location in the list. To find that location takes about $\lceil \log_2 S \rceil$ binary comparisons.

Can we improve on the well-established alphabetized list? Let us consider our task from some new viewpoints.

The task is to construct a mapping $\mathbf{x} \to s$ from N bits to $\log_2 S$ bits. This is a pseudo-invertible mapping, since for any $\mathbf{x}$ that maps to a non-zero s, the customer database contains the pair $(s, \mathbf{x}^{(s)})$ that takes us back. Where have we come across the idea of mapping from N bits to M bits before?

We encountered this idea twice: first, in source coding, we studied block codes which were mappings from strings of N symbols to a selection of one label in a list. The task of information retrieval is similar to the task (which we never actually solved) of making an encoder for a typical-set compression code.

The second time that we mapped bit strings to bit strings of another dimensionality was when we studied channel codes. There, we considered codes that mapped from K bits to N bits, with N greater than K, and we made theoretical progress using *random* codes.

In hash codes, we put together these two notions. We will study random codes that map from N bits to M bits where M is *smaller* than N.

The idea is that we will map the original high-dimensional space down into a lower-dimensional space, one in which it is feasible to implement the dumb look-up table method which we rejected a moment ago.

string length	$N \simeq 200$
number of strings	$S \simeq 2^{23}$
size of hash function	$M \simeq 30$ bits
size of hash table	$T = 2^M$
	$\simeq 2^{30}$

Figure 12.2. Revised cast of characters.

▶ ## 12.2 Hash codes

First we will describe how a hash code works, then we will study the properties of idealized hash codes. A hash code implements a solution to the information retrieval problem, that is, a mapping from $\mathbf{x}$ to s, with the help of a pseudo-random function called a *hash function*, which maps the N-bit string $\mathbf{x}$ to an M-bit string $\mathbf{h}(\mathbf{x})$, where M is smaller than N. M is typically chosen such that the 'table size' $T \simeq 2^M$ is a little bigger than S – say, ten times bigger. For example, if we were expecting S to be about a million, we might map $\mathbf{x}$ into a 30-bit hash $\mathbf{h}$ (regardless of the size N of each item $\mathbf{x}$). The hash function is some fixed deterministic function which should ideally be indistinguishable from a fixed random code. For practical purposes, the hash function must be quick to compute.

Two simple examples of hash functions are:

Division method. The table size T is a prime number, preferably one that is not close to a power of 2. The hash value is the remainder when the integer $\mathbf{x}$ is divided by T.

Variable string addition method. This method assumes that $\mathbf{x}$ is a string of bytes and that the table size T is 256. The characters of $\mathbf{x}$ are added, modulo 256. This hash function has the defect that it maps strings that are anagrams of each other onto the same hash.

It may be improved by putting the running total through a fixed pseudorandom permutation after each character is added. In the *variable string exclusive-or method* with table size $\leq 65\,536$, the string is hashed twice in this way, with the initial running total being set to 0 and 1 respectively (algorithm 12.3). The result is a 16-bit hash.

Having picked a hash function $\mathbf{h}(\mathbf{x})$, we implement an information retriever as follows.

Encoding. A piece of memory called the *hash table* is created of size $2^M b$ memory units, where b is the amount of memory needed to represent an integer between 0 and S. This table is initially set to zero throughout. Each memory $\mathbf{x}^{(s)}$ is put through the hash function, and at the location in the hash table corresponding to the resulting vector $\mathbf{h}^{(s)} = \mathbf{h}(\mathbf{x}^{(s)})$, the integer s is written – unless that entry in the hash table is already occupied, in which case we have a *collision* between $\mathbf{x}^{(s)}$ and some earlier $\mathbf{x}^{(s')}$ which both happen to have the same hash code. Collisions can be handled in various ways – we will discuss some in a moment – but first let us complete the basic picture.

```
unsigned char Rand8[256];     // This array contains a random
                                 permutation from 0..255 to 0..255
int Hash(char *x) {           // x is a pointer to the first char;
    int h;                    //    *x is the first character
    unsigned char h1, h2;

    if (*x == 0) return 0;    // Special handling of empty string
    h1 = *x; h2 = *x + 1;     // Initialize two hashes
    x++;                      // Proceed to the next character
    while (*x) {
        h1 = Rand8[h1 ^ *x];  // Exclusive-or with the two hashes
        h2 = Rand8[h2 ^ *x];  //    and put through the randomizer
        x++;
    }                         // End of string is reached when *x=0
    h = ((int)(h1)<<8) |      // Shift h1 left 8 bits and add h2
        (int) h2 ;
    return h ;                // Hash is concatenation of h1 and h2
}
```

Algorithm 12.3. C code implementing the variable string exclusive-or method to create a hash h in the range $0 \ldots 65\,535$ from a string x. Author: Thomas Niemann.

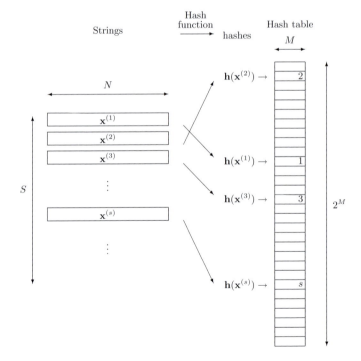

Figure 12.4. Use of hash functions for information retrieval. For each string $\mathbf{x}^{(s)}$, the hash $\mathbf{h} = \mathbf{h}(\mathbf{x}^{(s)})$ is computed, and the value of s is written into the $\mathbf{h}$th row of the hash table. Blank rows in the hash table contain the value zero. The table size is $T = 2^M$.

Decoding. To retrieve a piece of information corresponding to a target vector $\mathbf{x}$, we compute the hash $\mathbf{h}$ of $\mathbf{x}$ and look at the corresponding location in the hash table. If there is a zero, then we know immediately that the string $\mathbf{x}$ is not in the database. The cost of this answer is the cost of one hash function evaluation and one look-up in the table of size 2^M. If, on the other hand, there is a non-zero entry s in the table, there are two possibilities: either the vector $\mathbf{x}$ is indeed equal to $\mathbf{x}^{(s)}$; or the vector $\mathbf{x}^{(s)}$ is another vector that happens to have the same hash code as the target $\mathbf{x}$. (A third possibility is that this non-zero entry might have something to do with our yet-to-be-discussed collision-resolution system.)

To check whether $\mathbf{x}$ is indeed equal to $\mathbf{x}^{(s)}$, we take the tentative answer s, look up $\mathbf{x}^{(s)}$ in the original forward database, and compare it bit by bit with $\mathbf{x}$; if it matches then we report s as the desired answer. This successful retrieval has an overall cost of one hash-function evaluation, one look-up in the table of size 2^M, another look-up in a table of size S, and N binary comparisons – which may be much cheaper than the simple solutions presented in section 12.1.

▷ Exercise 12.2.[2, p.202] If we have checked the first few bits of $\mathbf{x}^{(s)}$ with $\mathbf{x}$ and found them to be equal, what is the probability that the correct entry has been retrieved, if the alternative hypothesis is that $\mathbf{x}$ is actually not in the database? Assume that the original source strings are random, and the hash function is a random hash function. How many binary evaluations are needed to be sure with odds of a billion to one that the correct entry has been retrieved?

The hashing method of information retrieval can be used for strings $\mathbf{x}$ of arbitrary length, if the hash function $\mathbf{h}(\mathbf{x})$ can be applied to strings of any length.

▶ 12.3 Collision resolution

We will study two ways of resolving collisions: appending in the table, and storing elsewhere.

Appending in table

When encoding, if a collision occurs, we continue down the hash table and write the value of s into the next available location in memory that currently contains a zero. If we reach the bottom of the table before encountering a zero, we continue from the top.

When decoding, if we compute the hash code for $\mathbf{x}$ and find that the s contained in the table doesn't point to an $\mathbf{x}^{(s)}$ that matches the cue $\mathbf{x}$, we continue down the hash table until we either find an s whose $\mathbf{x}^{(s)}$ does match the cue $\mathbf{x}$, in which case we are done, or else encounter a zero, in which case we know that the cue $\mathbf{x}$ is not in the database.

For this method, it is essential that the table be substantially bigger in size than S. If $2^M < S$ then the encoding rule will become stuck with nowhere to put the last strings.

Storing elsewhere

A more robust and flexible method is to use *pointers* to additional pieces of memory in which collided strings are stored. There are many ways of doing this. As an example, we could store in location **h** in the hash table a pointer (which must be distinguishable from a valid record number s) to a 'bucket' where all the strings that have hash code **h** are stored in a *sorted list*. The encoder sorts the strings in each bucket alphabetically as the hash table and buckets are created.

The decoder simply has to go and look in the relevant bucket and then check the short list of strings that are there by a brief alphabetical search.

This method of storing the strings in buckets allows the option of making the hash table quite small, which may have practical benefits. We may make it so small that almost all strings are involved in collisions, so all buckets contain a small number of strings. It only takes a small number of binary comparisons to identify which of the strings in the bucket matches the cue **x**.

▶ 12.4 Planning for collisions: a birthday problem

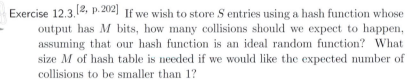

Exercise 12.3.[2, p.202] If we wish to store S entries using a hash function whose output has M bits, how many collisions should we expect to happen, assuming that our hash function is an ideal random function? What size M of hash table is needed if we would like the expected number of collisions to be smaller than 1?

What size M of hash table is needed if we would like the expected number of collisions to be a small fraction, say 1%, of S?

[Notice the similarity of this problem to exercise 9.20 (p.156).]

▶ 12.5 Other roles for hash codes

Checking arithmetic

If you wish to check an addition that was done by hand, you may find useful the method of *casting out nines*. In casting out nines, one finds the sum, modulo nine, of all the *digits* of the numbers to be summed and compares it with the sum, modulo nine, of the digits of the putative answer. [With a little practice, these sums can be computed much more rapidly than the full original addition.]

Example 12.4. In the calculation shown in the margin the sum, modulo nine, of the digits in 189+1254+238 is 7, and the sum, modulo nine, of 1+6+8+1 is 7. The calculation thus passes the casting-out-nines test.

$$
\begin{array}{r}
189 \\
+1254 \\
+\ 238 \\
\hline
1681
\end{array}
$$

Casting out nines gives a simple example of a hash function. For any addition expression of the form $a + b + c + \cdots$, where $a, b, c, \ldots$ are decimal numbers we define $h \in \{0, 1, 2, 3, 4, 5, 6, 7, 8\}$ by

$$h(a + b + c + \cdots) = \text{ sum modulo nine of all digits in } a, b, c ; \qquad (12.1)$$

then it is nice property of decimal arithmetic that if

$$a + b + c + \cdots = m + n + o + \cdots \qquad (12.2)$$

then the hashes $h(a + b + c + \cdots)$ and $h(m + n + o + \cdots)$ are equal.

▷ Exercise 12.5.[1, p.203] What evidence does a correct casting-out-nines match give in favour of the hypothesis that the addition has been done correctly?

Error detection among friends

Are two files the same? If the files are on the same computer, we could just compare them bit by bit. But if the two files are on separate machines, it would be nice to have a way of confirming that two files are identical without having to transfer one of the files from A to B. [And even if we did transfer one of the files, we would still like a way to confirm whether it has been received without modifications!]

This problem can be solved using hash codes. Let Alice and Bob be the holders of the two files; Alice sent the file to Bob, and they wish to confirm it has been received without error. If Alice computes the hash of her file and sends it to Bob, and Bob computes the hash of his file, using the same M-bit hash function, and the two hashes match, then Bob can deduce that the two files are almost surely the same.

Example 12.6. What is the probability of a false negative, i.e., the probability, given that the two files do differ, that the two hashes are nevertheless identical?

If we assume that the hash function is random and that the process that causes the files to differ knows nothing about the hash function, then the probability of a false negative is 2^{-M}. □

A 32-bit hash gives a probability of false negative of about 10^{-10}. It is common practice to use a linear hash function called a 32-bit cyclic redundancy check to detect errors in files. (A cyclic redundancy check is a set of 32 parity-check bits similar to the 3 parity-check bits of the $(7, 4)$ Hamming code.)

> To have a false-negative rate smaller than one in a billion, $M = 32$ bits is plenty, if the errors are produced by noise.

▷ Exercise 12.7.[2, p.203] Such a simple parity-check code only detects errors; it doesn't help correct them. Since error-*correcting* codes exist, why not use one of them to get some error-correcting capability too?

Tamper detection

What if the differences between the two files are not simply 'noise', but are introduced by an adversary, a clever *forger* called Fiona, who modifies the original file to make a forgery that purports to be Alice's file? How can Alice make a digital signature for the file so that Bob can confirm that no-one has tampered with the file? And how can we prevent Fiona from listening in on Alice's signature and attaching it to other files?

Let's assume that Alice computes a hash function for the file and sends it securely to Bob. If Alice computes a simple hash function for the file like the linear cyclic redundancy check, and Fiona knows that this is the method of verifying the file's integrity, Fiona can make her chosen modifications to the file and then easily identify (by linear algebra) a further 32-or-so single bits that, when flipped, restore the hash function of the file to its original value. *Linear hash functions give no security against forgers.*

We must therefore require that the hash function be *hard to invert* so that no-one can construct a tampering that leaves the hash function unaffected. We would still like the hash function to be easy to compute, however, so that Bob doesn't have to do hours of work to verify every file he received. Such a hash function – easy to compute, but hard to invert – is called a *one-way hash function.* Finding such functions is one of the active research areas of cryptography.

A hash-function that is widely used in the free software community to confirm that two files do not differ is MD5, which produces a 128 bit hash. The details of how it works are quite complicated, involving convoluted exclusive-or-ing and if-ing and and-ing.[1]

Even with a good one-way hash function, the digital signatures described above are still vulnerable to attack, if Fiona has access to the hash function. Fiona could take the tampered file and hunt for a further tiny modification to it such that its hash matches the original hash of Alice's file. This would take some time – on average, about 2^{32} attempts, if the hash function has 32 bits – but eventually Fiona would find a tampered file that matches the given hash. To be secure against forgery, digital signatures must either have enough bits for such a random search to take too long, or the hash function itself must be kept secret.

> Fiona has to hash 2^M files to cheat. 2^{32} file modifications is not very many, so a 32-bit hash function is not large enough for forgery prevention.

Another person who might have a motivation for forgery is Alice herself. For example, she might be making a bet on the outcome of a race, without wishing to broadcast her prediction publicly; a method for placing bets would be for her to send to Bob the bookie the hash of her bet. Later on, she could send Bob the details of her bet. Everyone can confirm that her bet is consistent with the previously publicized hash. [This method of secret publication was used by Isaac Newton and Robert Hooke when they wished to establish priority for scientific ideas without revealing them. Hooke's hash function was alphabetization as illustrated by the conversion of *UT TENSIO, SIC VIS* into the anagram CEIIINOSSSTTUV.] Such a protocol relies on the assumption that Alice cannot change her bet after the event without the hash coming out wrong. How big a hash function do we need to use to ensure that Alice cannot cheat? The answer is different from the size of the hash we needed in order to defeat Fiona above, because Alice is the author of *both* files. Alice could cheat by searching for two files that have identical hashes to each other. For example, if she'd like to cheat by placing two bets for the price of one, she could make a large number N_1 of versions of bet one (differing from each other in minor details only), and a large number N_2 of versions of bet two, and hash them all. If there's a collision between the hashes of two bets of different types, then she can submit the common hash and thus buy herself the option of placing either bet.

Example 12.8. If the hash has M bits, how big do N_1 and N_2 need to be for Alice to have a good chance of finding two different bets with the same hash?

This is a birthday problem like exercise 9.20 (p. 156). If there are N_1 Montagues and N_2 Capulets at a party, and each is assigned a 'birthday' of M bits, the expected number of collisions between a Montague and a Capulet is

$$N_1 N_2 2^{-M}, \tag{12.3}$$

---

[1]http://www.freesoft.org/CIE/RFC/1321/3.htm

so to minimize the number of files hashed, $N_1 + N_2$, Alice should make N_1 and N_2 equal, and will need to hash about $2^{M/2}$ files until she finds two that match. □

> Alice has to hash $2^{M/2}$ files to cheat. [This is the square root of the number of hashes Fiona had to make.]

If Alice has the use of $C = 10^6$ computers for $T = 10$ years, each computer taking $t = 1$ ns to evaluate a hash, the bet-communication system is secure against Alice's dishonesty only if $M \gg 2 \log_2 CT/t \simeq 160$ bits.

Further reading

I highly recommend the story of Doug McIlroy's `spell` program, as told in section 13.8 of *Programming Pearls* (Bentley, 2000). This astonishing piece of software makes use of a 64-kilobyte data structure to store the spellings of all the words of 75 000-word dictionary.

▶ 12.6 Further exercises

Exercise 12.9.[1] What is the shortest the address on a typical international letter could be, if it is to get to a unique human recipient? (Assume the permitted characters are [A-Z,0-9].) How long are typical email addresses?

Exercise 12.10.[2, p.203] How long does a piece of text need to be for you to be pretty sure that no human has written that string of characters before? How many notes are there in a new melody that has not been composed before?

▷ Exercise 12.11.[2, p.204] Pattern recognition by molecules.

Some proteins produced in a cell have a regulatory role. A regulatory protein controls the transcription of specific genes in the genome. This control often involves the protein's binding to a particular DNA sequence in the vicinity of the regulated gene. The presence of the bound protein either promotes or inhibits transcription of the gene.

(a) Use information-theoretic arguments to obtain a lower bound on the size of a typical protein that acts as a regulator specific to one gene in the whole human genome. Assume that the genome is a sequence of 3×10^9 nucleotides drawn from a four letter alphabet $\{A, C, G, T\}$; a protein is a sequence of amino acids drawn from a twenty letter alphabet. [Hint: establish how long the recognized DNA sequence has to be in order for that sequence to be unique to the vicinity of one gene, treating the rest of the genome as a random sequence. Then discuss how big the protein must be to recognize a sequence of that length uniquely.]

(b) Some of the sequences recognized by DNA-binding regulatory proteins consist of a subsequence that is repeated twice or more, for example the sequence

GCCCCCCACCCCTGCCCCC   (12.4)

is a binding site found upstream of the alpha-actin gene in humans. Does the fact that some binding sites consist of a repeated subsequence influence your answer to part (a)?

▶ 12.7 Solutions

Solution to exercise 12.1 (p.194). First imagine comparing the string $\mathbf{x}$ with another random string $\mathbf{x}^{(s)}$. The probability that the first bits of the two strings match is $1/2$. The probability that the second bits match is $1/2$. Assuming we stop comparing once we hit the first mismatch, the expected number of matches is 1, so the expected number of comparisons is 2 (exercise 2.34, p.38).

Assuming the correct string is located at random in the raw list, we will have to compare with an average of $S/2$ strings before we find it, which costs $2S/2$ binary comparisons; and comparing the correct strings takes N binary comparisons, giving a total expectation of $S + N$ binary comparisons, if the strings are chosen at random.

In the worst case (which may indeed happen in practice), the other strings are very similar to the search key, so that a lengthy sequence of comparisons is needed to find each mismatch. The worst case is when the correct string is last in the list, and all the other strings differ in the last bit only, giving a requirement of SN binary comparisons.

Solution to exercise 12.2 (p.197). The likelihood ratio for the two hypotheses, $\mathcal{H}_0$: $\mathbf{x}^{(s)} = \mathbf{x}$, and $\mathcal{H}_1$: $\mathbf{x}^{(s)} \neq \mathbf{x}$, contributed by the datum 'the first bits of $\mathbf{x}^{(s)}$ and $\mathbf{x}$ are equal' is

$$\frac{P(\text{Datum}|\mathcal{H}_0)}{P(\text{Datum}|\mathcal{H}_1)} = \frac{1}{1/2} = 2. \tag{12.5}$$

If the first r bits all match, the likelihood ratio is 2^r to one. On finding that 30 bits match, the odds are a billion to one in favour of $\mathcal{H}_0$, assuming we start from even odds. [For a complete answer, we should compute the evidence given by the prior information that the hash entry s has been found in the table at $\mathbf{h}(\mathbf{x})$. This fact gives further evidence in favour of $\mathcal{H}_0$.]

Solution to exercise 12.3 (p.198). Let the hash function have an output alphabet of size $T = 2^M$. If M were equal to $\log_2 S$ then we would have exactly enough bits for each entry to have its own unique hash. The probability that one particular pair of entries collide under a random hash function is $1/T$. The number of pairs is $S(S-1)/2$. So the expected number of collisions between pairs is exactly

$$S(S-1)/(2T). \tag{12.6}$$

If we would like this to be smaller than 1, then we need $T > S(S-1)/2$ so

$$M > 2\log_2 S. \tag{12.7}$$

We need *twice as many* bits as the number of bits, $\log_2 S$, that would be sufficient to give each entry a unique name.

If we are happy to have occasional collisions, involving a fraction f of the names S, then we need $T > S/f$ (since the probability that one particular name is collided-with is $f \simeq S/T$) so

$$M > \log_2 S + \log_2[1/f], \tag{12.8}$$

which means for $f \simeq 0.01$ that we need an extra 7 bits above $\log_2 S$.

The important point to note is the scaling of T with S in the two cases (12.7, 12.8). If we want the hash function to be collision-free, then we must have T greater than $\sim S^2$. If we are happy to have a small frequency of collisions, then T needs to be of order S only.

Solution to exercise 12.5 (p.198). The posterior probability ratio for the two hypotheses, $\mathcal{H}_+$ = 'calculation correct' and $\mathcal{H}_-$ = 'calculation incorrect' is the product of the prior probability ratio $P(\mathcal{H}_+)/P(\mathcal{H}_-)$ and the likelihood ratio, $P(\text{match}|\mathcal{H}_+)/P(\text{match}|\mathcal{H}_-)$. This second factor is the answer to the question. The numerator $P(\text{match}|\mathcal{H}_+)$ is equal to 1. The denominator's value depends on our model of errors. If we know that the human calculator is prone to errors involving multiplication of the answer by 10, or to transposition of adjacent digits, neither of which affects the hash value, then $P(\text{match}|\mathcal{H}_-)$ could be equal to 1 also, so that the correct match gives no evidence in favour of $\mathcal{H}_+$. But if we assume that errors are 'random from the point of view of the hash function' then the probability of a false positive is $P(\text{match}|\mathcal{H}_-) = 1/9$, and the correct match gives evidence 9:1 in favour of $\mathcal{H}_+$.

Solution to exercise 12.7 (p.199). If you add a tiny $M = 32$ extra bits of hash to a huge N-bit file you get pretty good error detection – the probability that an error is undetected is 2^{-M}, less than one in a billion. To do error *correction* requires far more check bits, the number depending on the expected types of corruption, and on the file size. For example, if just eight random bits in a megabyte file are corrupted, it would take about $\log_2 \binom{2^{23}}{8} \simeq 23 \times 8 \simeq 180$ bits to specify which are the corrupted bits, and the number of parity-check bits used by a successful error-correcting code would have to be at least this number, by the counting argument of exercise 1.10 (solution, p.20).

Solution to exercise 12.10 (p.201). We want to know the length L of a string such that it is very improbable that that string matches any part of the entire writings of humanity. Let's estimate that these writings total about one book for each person living, and that each book contains two million characters (200 pages with 10 000 characters per page) – that's 10^{16} characters, drawn from an alphabet of, say, 37 characters.

The probability that a randomly chosen string of length L matches at one point in the collected works of humanity is $1/37^L$. So the expected number of matches is $10^{16}/37^L$, which is vanishingly small if $L \geq 16/\log_{10} 37 \simeq 10$. Because of the redundancy and repetition of humanity's writings, it is possible that $L \simeq 10$ is an overestimate.

So, if you want to write something unique, sit down and compose a string of ten characters. But don't write `gidnebinzz`, because I already thought of that string.

As for a new melody, if we focus on the sequence of notes, ignoring duration and stress, and allow leaps of up to an octave at each note, then the number of choices per note is 23. The pitch of the first note is arbitrary. The number of melodies of length r notes in this rather ugly ensemble of Schönbergian tunes is 23^{r-1}; for example, there are 250 000 of length $r = 5$. Restricting the permitted intervals will reduce this figure; including duration and stress will increase it again. [If we restrict the permitted intervals to repetitions and tones or semitones, the reduction is particularly severe; is this why the melody of 'Ode to Joy' sounds so boring?] The number of recorded compositions is probably less than a million. If you learn 100 new melodies per week for every week of your life then you will have learned 250 000 melodies at age 50. Based on empirical experience of playing the game 'guess that tune', it seems to me that whereas many four-note sequences are shared in common between melodies, the number of collisions between five-note sequences is rather smaller – most famous five-note sequences are unique.

Solution to exercise 12.11 (p.201). (a) Let the DNA-binding protein recognize a sequence of length L nucleotides. That is, it binds preferentially to that DNA sequence, and not to any other pieces of DNA in the whole genome. (In reality, the recognized sequence may contain some wildcard characters, e.g., the * in TATAA*A, which denotes 'any of A, C, G and T'; so, to be precise, we are assuming that the recognized sequence contains L non-wildcard characters.)

Assuming the rest of the genome is 'random', i.e., that the sequence consists of random nucleotides A, C, G and T with equal probability – which is obviously untrue, but it shouldn't make too much difference to our calculation – the chance of there being no other occurrence of the target sequence in the whole genome, of length N nucleotides, is roughly

$$(1 - (1/4)^L)^N \simeq \exp(-N(1/4)^L), \tag{12.9}$$

which is close to one only if

$$N4^{-L} \ll 1, \tag{12.10}$$

that is,

$$L > \log N / \log 4. \tag{12.11}$$

Using $N = 3 \times 10^9$, we require the recognized sequence to be longer than $L_{\min} = 16$ nucleotides.

What size of protein does this imply?

- A weak lower bound can be obtained by assuming that the information content of the protein sequence itself is greater than the information content of the nucleotide sequence the protein prefers to bind to (which we have argued above must be at least 32 bits). This gives a minimum protein length of $32/\log_2(20) \simeq 7$ amino acids.

- Thinking realistically, the recognition of the DNA sequence by the protein presumably involves the protein coming into contact with all sixteen nucleotides in the target sequence. If the protein is a monomer, it must be big enough that it can simultaneously make contact with sixteen nucleotides of DNA. One helical turn of DNA containing ten nucleotides has a length of 3.4 nm, so a contiguous sequence of sixteen nucleotides has a length of 5.4 nm. The diameter of the protein must therefore be about 5.4 nm or greater. Egg-white lysozyme is a small globular protein with a length of 129 amino acids and a diameter of about 4 nm. Assuming that volume is proportional to sequence length and that volume scales as diameter cubed, a protein of diameter 5.4 nm must have a sequence of length $2.5 \times 129 \simeq 324$ amino acids.

(b) If, however, a target sequence consists of a twice-repeated sub-sequence, we can get by with a much smaller protein that recognizes only the sub-sequence, and that binds to the DNA strongly only if it can form a *dimer*, both halves of which are bound to the recognized sequence. Halving the diameter of the protein, we now only need a protein whose length is greater than $324/8 = 40$ amino acids. A protein of length smaller than this cannot by itself serve as a regulatory protein specific to one gene, because it's simply too small to be able to make a sufficiently specific match – its available surface does not have enough information content.

About Chapter 13

In Chapters 8–11, we established Shannon's noisy-channel coding theorem for a general channel with any input and output alphabets. A great deal of attention in coding theory focuses on the special case of channels with binary inputs. Constraining ourselves to these channels simplifies matters, and leads us into an exceptionally rich world, which we will only taste in this book.

One of the aims of this chapter is to point out a contrast between Shannon's aim of achieving reliable communication over a noisy channel and the apparent aim of many in the world of coding theory. Many coding theorists take as their fundamental problem the task of packing as many spheres as possible, with radius as large as possible, into an N-dimensional space, *with no spheres overlapping*. Prizes are awarded to people who find packings that squeeze in an extra few spheres. While this is a fascinating mathematical topic, we shall see that the aim of maximizing the distance between codewords in a code has only a tenuous relationship to Shannon's aim of reliable communication.

13

Binary Codes

We've established Shannon's noisy-channel coding theorem for a general channel with any input and output alphabets. A great deal of attention in coding theory focuses on the special case of channels with binary inputs, the first implicit choice being the binary symmetric channel.

The optimal decoder for a code, given a binary symmetric channel, finds the codeword that is closest to the received vector, closest in *Hamming distance*. The Hamming distance between two binary vectors is the number of coordinates in which the two vectors differ. Decoding errors will occur if the noise takes us from the transmitted codeword **t** to a received vector **r** that is closer to some other codeword. The *distances* between codewords are thus relevant to the probability of a decoding error.

▶ 13.1 Distance properties of a code

The *distance* of a code is the smallest separation between two of its codewords.

Example 13.1. The $(7, 4)$ Hamming code (p.8) has distance $d = 3$. All pairs of its codewords differ in at least 3 bits. The minimum number of errors it can correct is $t = 1$; in general a code with distance d is $\lfloor (d-1)/2 \rfloor$-error-correcting.

A more precise term for distance is the *minimum distance* of the code. The distance of a code is often denoted by d or $d_{\min}$.

We'll now constrain our attention to linear codes. In a linear code, all codewords have identical distance properties, so we can summarize all the distances between the code's codewords by counting the distances from the all-zero codeword.

The *weight enumerator function* of a code, $A(w)$, is defined to be the number of codewords in the code that have weight w. The weight enumerator function is also known as the *distance distribution* of the code.

Example 13.2. The weight enumerator functions of the $(7, 4)$ Hamming code and the dodecahedron code are shown in figures 13.1 and 13.2.

▶ 13.2 Obsession with distance

Since the minimum number of errors that a code can *guarantee* to correct, t, is related to its distance d by $t = \lfloor (d-1)/2 \rfloor$, many coding theorists focus on the distance of a code, searching for codes of a given size that have the biggest possible distance. Much of practical coding theory has focused on decoders that give the optimal decoding for all error patterns of weight up to the half-distance t of their codes.

Example:
The Hamming distance
between   00001111
and   11001101
is 3.

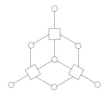

w	$A(w)$
0	1
3	7
4	7
7	1
Total	16

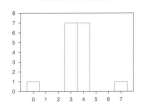

Figure 13.1. The graph of the $(7, 4)$ Hamming code, and its weight enumerator function.

$d = 2t + 1$ if d is odd, and $d = 2t + 2$ if d is even.

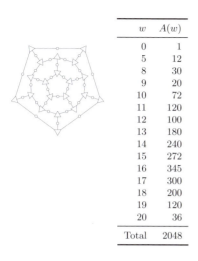

w	$A(w)$
0	1
5	12
8	30
9	20
10	72
11	120
12	100
13	180
14	240
15	272
16	345
17	300
18	200
19	120
20	36
Total	2048

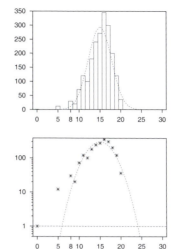

Figure 13.2. The graph defining the $(30, 11)$ dodecahedron code (the circles are the 30 transmitted bits and the triangles are the 20 parity checks, one of which is redundant) and the weight enumerator function (solid lines). The dotted lines show the average weight enumerator function of all random linear codes with the same size of generator matrix, which will be computed shortly. The lower figure shows the same functions on a log scale.

A bounded-distance decoder is a decoder that returns the closest codeword to a received binary vector $\mathbf{r}$ if the distance from $\mathbf{r}$ to that codeword is less than or equal to t; otherwise it returns a failure message.

The rationale for not trying to decode when more than t errors have occurred might be 'we can't *guarantee* that we can correct more than t errors, so we won't bother trying – who would be interested in a decoder that corrects some error patterns of weight greater than t, but not others?' This defeatist attitude is an example of *worst-case-ism*, a widespread mental ailment which this book is intended to cure.

The fact is that bounded-distance decoders cannot reach the Shannon limit of the binary symmetric channel; only a decoder that often corrects more than t errors can do this. The state of the art in error-correcting codes have decoders that work way beyond the minimum distance of the code.

Definitions of good and bad distance properties

Given a family of codes of increasing blocklength N, and with rates approaching a limit $R > 0$, we may be able to put that family in one of the following categories, which have some similarities to the categories of 'good' and 'bad' codes defined earlier (p.183):

A sequence of codes has 'good' distance if d/N tends to a constant greater than zero.

A sequence of codes has 'bad' distance if d/N tends to zero.

A sequence of codes has 'very bad' distance if d tends to a constant.

Figure 13.3. The graph of a rate-$1/2$ low-density generator matrix code. The rightmost M of the transmitted bits are each connected to a single distinct parity constraint.

Example 13.3. A *low-density generator-matrix code* is a linear code whose $K \times N$ generator matrix $\mathbf{G}$ has a small number d_0 of 1s per row, regardless of how big N is. The minimum distance of such a code is at most d_0, so low-density generator-matrix codes have 'very bad' distance.

While having large distance is no bad thing, we'll see, later on, why an emphasis on distance can be unhealthy.

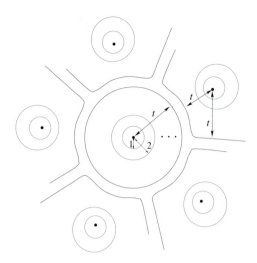

Figure 13.4. Schematic picture of part of Hamming space perfectly filled by t-spheres centred on the codewords of a perfect code.

▶ 13.3 Perfect codes

A t-sphere (or a sphere of radius t) in Hamming space, centred on a point $\mathbf{x}$, is the set of points whose Hamming distance from $\mathbf{x}$ is less than or equal to t.

The $(7, 4)$ Hamming code has the beautiful property that if we place 1-spheres about each of its 16 codewords, those spheres perfectly fill Hamming space without overlapping. As we saw in Chapter 1, every binary vector of length 7 is within a distance of $t = 1$ of exactly one codeword of the Hamming code.

A code is a perfect t-error-correcting code if the set of t-spheres centred on the codewords of the code fill the Hamming space without overlapping. (See figure 13.4.)

Let's recap our cast of characters. The number of codewords is $S = 2^K$. The number of points in the entire Hamming space is 2^N. The number of points in a Hamming sphere of radius t is

$$\sum_{w=0}^{t} \binom{N}{w}. \tag{13.1}$$

For a code to be perfect with these parameters, we require S times the number of points in the t-sphere to equal 2^N:

$$\text{for a perfect code, } \quad 2^K \sum_{w=0}^{t} \binom{N}{w} \; = \; 2^N \tag{13.2}$$

$$\text{or, equivalently, } \quad \sum_{w=0}^{t} \binom{N}{w} \; = \; 2^{N-K}. \tag{13.3}$$

For a perfect code, the number of noise vectors in one sphere must equal the number of possible syndromes. The $(7, 4)$ Hamming code satisfies this numerological condition because

$$1 + \binom{7}{1} = 2^3. \tag{13.4}$$

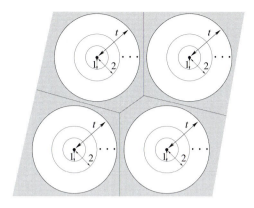

Figure 13.5. Schematic picture of Hamming space not perfectly filled by t-spheres centred on the codewords of a code. The grey regions show points that are at a Hamming distance of more than t from any codeword. This is a misleading picture, as, for any code with large t in high dimensions, the grey space between the spheres takes up almost all of Hamming space.

How happy we would be to use perfect codes

If there were large numbers of perfect codes to choose from, with a wide range of blocklengths and rates, then these would be the perfect solution to Shannon's problem. We could communicate over a binary symmetric channel with noise level f, for example, by picking a perfect t-error-correcting code with blocklength N and $t = f^* N$, where $f^* = f + \delta$ and N and δ are chosen such that the probability that the noise flips more than t bits is satisfactorily small.

However, *there are almost no perfect codes*. The only nontrivial perfect binary codes are

1. the Hamming codes, which are perfect codes with $t = 1$ and blocklength $N = 2^M - 1$, defined below; the rate of a Hamming code approaches 1 as its blocklength N increases;

2. the repetition codes of odd blocklength N, which are perfect codes with $t = (N - 1)/2$; the rate of repetition codes goes to zero as $1/N$; and

3. one remarkable 3-error-correcting code with 2^{12} codewords of blocklength $N = 23$ known as the binary Golay code. [A second 2-error-correcting Golay code of length $N = 11$ over a ternary alphabet was discovered by a Finnish football-pool enthusiast called Juhani Virtakallio in 1947.]

There are no other binary perfect codes. Why this shortage of perfect codes? Is it because precise numerological coincidences like those satisfied by the parameters of the Hamming code (13.4) and the Golay code,

$$1 + \binom{23}{1} + \binom{23}{2} + \binom{23}{3} = 2^{11}, \tag{13.5}$$

are rare? Are there plenty of 'almost-perfect' codes for which the t-spheres fill *almost* the whole space?

No. In fact, the picture of Hamming spheres centred on the codewords *almost* filling Hamming space (figure 13.5) is a misleading one: for most codes, whether they are good codes or bad codes, almost all the Hamming space is taken up by the space *between* t-spheres (which is shown in grey in figure 13.5).

Having established this gloomy picture, we spend a moment filling in the properties of the perfect codes mentioned above.

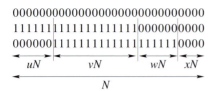

Figure 13.6. Three codewords.

The Hamming codes

The $(7, 4)$ Hamming code can be defined as the linear code whose 3×7 parity-check matrix contains, as its columns, all the 7 $(= 2^3 - 1)$ non-zero vectors of length 3. Since these 7 vectors are all different, any single bit-flip produces a distinct syndrome, so all single-bit errors can be detected and corrected.

We can generalize this code, with $M = 3$ parity constraints, as follows. The Hamming codes are single-error-correcting codes defined by picking a number of parity-check constraints, M; the blocklength N is $N = 2^M - 1$; the parity-check matrix contains, as its columns, all the N non-zero vectors of length M bits.

The first few Hamming codes have the following rates:

Checks, M	(N, K)	$R = K/N$	
2	$(3, 1)$	$1/3$	repetition code R_3
3	$(7, 4)$	$4/7$	$(7, 4)$ Hamming code
4	$(15, 11)$	$11/15$	
5	$(31, 26)$	$26/31$	
6	$(63, 57)$	$57/63$	

Exercise 13.4.[2, p.223] What is the probability of block error of the (N, K) Hamming code to leading order, when the code is used for a binary symmetric channel with noise density f?

▶ 13.4 Perfectness is unattainable – first proof

We will show in several ways that useful perfect codes do not exist (here, 'useful' means 'having large blocklength N, and rate close neither to 0 nor 1').

Shannon proved that, given a binary symmetric channel with any noise level f, there exist codes with large blocklength N and rate as close as you like to $C(f) = 1 - H_2(f)$ that enable communication with arbitrarily small error probability. For large N, the number of errors per block will typically by about fN, so these codes of Shannon are 'almost-certainly-fN-error-correcting' codes.

Let's pick the special case of a noisy channel with $f \in (1/3, 1/2)$. Can we find a large *perfect* code that is fN-error-correcting? Well, let's suppose that such a code has been found, and examine just three of its codewords. (Remember that the code ought to have rate $R \simeq 1 - H_2(f)$, so it should have an enormous number (2^{NR}) of codewords.) Without loss of generality, we choose one of the codewords to be the all-zero codeword and define the other two to have overlaps with it as shown in figure 13.6. The second codeword differs from the first in a fraction $u + v$ of its coordinates. The third codeword differs from the first in a fraction $v + w$, and from the second in a fraction $u + w$. A fraction x of the coordinates have value zero in all three codewords. Now, if the code is fN-error-correcting, its minimum distance must be greater

than $2fN$, so

$$u + v > 2f, \quad v + w > 2f, \quad \text{and} \quad u + w > 2f. \tag{13.6}$$

Summing these three inequalities and dividing by two, we have

$$u + v + w > 3f. \tag{13.7}$$

So if $f > 1/3$, we can deduce $u + v + w > 1$, so that $x < 0$, which is impossible. Such a code cannot exist. So the code cannot have *three* codewords, let alone 2^{NR}.

We conclude that, whereas Shannon proved there are plenty of codes for communicating over a binary symmetric channel with $f > 1/3$, *there are no perfect codes that can do this.*

We now study a more general argument that indicates that there are no large perfect linear codes for general rates (other than 0 and 1). We do this by finding the typical distance of a random linear code.

Figure 13.7. A random binary parity-check matrix.

13.5 Weight enumerator function of random linear codes

Imagine making a code by picking the binary entries in the $M \times N$ parity-check matrix $\mathbf{H}$ at random. What weight enumerator function should we expect?

The weight enumerator of one particular code with parity-check matrix $\mathbf{H}$, $A(w)_\mathbf{H}$, is the number of codewords of weight w, which can be written

$$A(w)_\mathbf{H} = \sum_{\mathbf{x}:|\mathbf{x}|=w} \mathbb{1}[\mathbf{H}\mathbf{x}=0], \tag{13.8}$$

where the sum is over all vectors $\mathbf{x}$ whose weight is w and the truth function $\mathbb{1}[\mathbf{H}\mathbf{x}=0]$ equals one if $\mathbf{H}\mathbf{x}=0$ and zero otherwise.

We can find the expected value of $A(w)$,

$$\langle A(w) \rangle = \sum_\mathbf{H} P(\mathbf{H}) A(w)_\mathbf{H} \tag{13.9}$$

$$= \sum_{\mathbf{x}:|\mathbf{x}|=w} \sum_\mathbf{H} P(\mathbf{H}) \mathbb{1}[\mathbf{H}\mathbf{x}=0], \tag{13.10}$$

by evaluating the probability that a particular word of weight $w > 0$ is a codeword of the code (averaging over all binary linear codes in our ensemble). By symmetry, this probability depends only on the weight w of the word, not on the details of the word. The probability that the entire syndrome $\mathbf{H}\mathbf{x}$ is zero can be found by multiplying together the probabilities that each of the M bits in the syndrome is zero. Each bit z_m of the syndrome is a sum (mod 2) of w random bits, so the probability that $z_m = 0$ is $1/2$. The probability that $\mathbf{H}\mathbf{x}=0$ is thus

$$\sum_\mathbf{H} P(\mathbf{H}) \mathbb{1}[\mathbf{H}\mathbf{x}=0] = (1/2)^M = 2^{-M}, \tag{13.11}$$

independent of w.

The expected number of words of weight w (13.10) is given by summing, over all words of weight w, the probability that each word is a codeword. The number of words of weight w is $\binom{N}{w}$, so

$$\langle A(w) \rangle = \binom{N}{w} 2^{-M} \quad \text{for any } w > 0. \tag{13.12}$$

For large N, we can use $\log \binom{N}{w} \simeq N H_2(w/N)$ and $R \simeq 1 - M/N$ to write

$$\log_2 \langle A(w) \rangle \simeq N H_2(w/N) - M \tag{13.13}$$
$$\simeq N[H_2(w/N) - (1-R)] \text{ for any } w > 0. \tag{13.14}$$

As a concrete example, figure 13.8 shows the expected weight enumerator function of a rate-1/3 random linear code with $N = 540$ and $M = 360$.

Gilbert–Varshamov distance

For weights w such that $H_2(w/N) < (1-R)$, the expectation of $A(w)$ is smaller than 1; for weights such that $H_2(w/N) > (1-R)$, the expectation is greater than 1. We thus expect, for large N, that the minimum distance of a random linear code will be close to the distance d_{GV} defined by

$$H_2(d_{\text{GV}}/N) = (1-R). \tag{13.15}$$

Definition. This distance, $d_{\text{GV}} \equiv N H_2^{-1}(1-R)$, is the *Gilbert–Varshamov distance* for rate R and blocklength N.

The *Gilbert–Varshamov conjecture*, widely believed, asserts that (for large N) it is not possible to create binary codes with minimum distance significantly greater than d_{GV}.

Definition. The *Gilbert–Varshamov rate* R_{GV} is the minimum rate at which you can reliably communicate with a bounded-distance decoder (as defined on p. 207), assuming that the Gilbert–Varshamov conjecture is true.

Why sphere-packing is a bad perspective, and an obsession with distance is inappropriate

If one uses a bounded-distance decoder, the maximum tolerable noise level will flip a fraction $f_{\text{bd}} = \frac{1}{2} d_{\text{min}}/N$ of the bits. So, assuming d_{min} is equal to the Gilbert distance d_{GV} (13.15), we have:

$$H_2(2 f_{\text{bd}}) = (1 - R_{\text{GV}}). \tag{13.16}$$

$$R_{\text{GV}} = 1 - H_2(2 f_{\text{bd}}). \tag{13.17}$$

Now, here's the crunch: what did Shannon say is achievable? He said the maximum possible rate of communication is the capacity,

$$C = 1 - H_2(f). \tag{13.18}$$

So for a given rate R, the maximum tolerable noise level, according to Shannon, is given by

$$H_2(f) = (1 - R). \tag{13.19}$$

Our conclusion: imagine a good code of rate R has been chosen; equations (13.16) and (13.19) respectively define the maximum noise levels tolerable by a bounded-distance decoder, f_{bd}, and by Shannon's decoder, f.

$$f_{\text{bd}} = f/2 \tag{13.20}$$

Those who use bounded-distance decoders can only ever cope with *half* the noise-level that Shannon proved is tolerable!

How does this relate to perfect codes? A code is perfect if there are t-spheres around its codewords that fill Hamming space without overlapping.

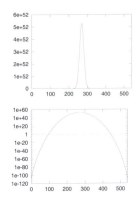

Figure 13.8. The expected weight enumerator function $\langle A(w) \rangle$ of a random linear code with $N = 540$ and $M = 360$. Lower figure shows $\langle A(w) \rangle$ on a logarithmic scale.

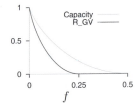

Figure 13.9. Contrast between Shannon's channel capacity C and the Gilbert rate R_{GV} – the minimum communication rate achievable using a bounded-distance decoder, as a function of noise level f. For any given rate, R, the minimum tolerable noise level for Shannon is twice as big as the minimum tolerable noise level for a 'worst-case-ist' who uses a bounded-distance decoder.

But when a typical random linear code is used to communicate over a binary symmetric channel near to the Shannon limit, the typical number of bits flipped is fN, and the minimum distance between codewords is also fN, or a little bigger, if we are a little below the Shannon limit. So the fN-spheres around the codewords overlap with each other sufficiently that each sphere almost contains the centre of its nearest neighbour! The reason why this overlap is not disastrous is because, in high dimensions, the volume associated with the overlap, shown shaded in figure 13.10, is a tiny fraction of either sphere, so the probability of landing in it is extremely small.

The moral of the story is that worst-case-ism can be bad for you, halving your ability to tolerate noise. You have to be able to decode *way* beyond the minimum distance of a code to get to the Shannon limit!

Nevertheless, the minimum distance of a code is of interest in practice, because, under some conditions, the minimum distance dominates the errors made by a code.

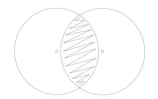

Figure 13.10. Two overlapping spheres whose radius is almost as big as the distance between their centres.

▶ ## 13.6 Berlekamp's bats

A blind bat lives in a cave. It flies about the centre of the cave, which corresponds to one codeword, with its typical distance from the centre controlled by a friskiness parameter f. (The displacement of the bat from the centre corresponds to the noise vector.) The boundaries of the cave are made up of stalactites that point in towards the centre of the cave. Each stalactite is analogous to the boundary between the home codeword and another codeword. The stalactite is like the shaded region in figure 13.10, but reshaped to convey the idea that it is a region of very small volume.

Decoding errors correspond to the bat's intended trajectory passing inside a stalactite. Collisions with stalactites at various distances from the centre are possible.

If the friskiness is very small, the bat is usually very close to the centre of the cave; collisions will be rare, and when they do occur, they will usually involve the stalactites whose tips are closest to the centre point. Similarly, under low-noise conditions, decoding errors will be rare, and they will typically involve low-weight codewords. Under low-noise conditions, the minimum distance of a code is relevant to the (very small) probability of error.

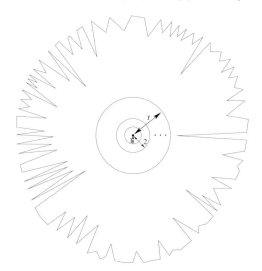

Figure 13.11. Berlekamp's schematic picture of Hamming space in the vicinity of a codeword. The jagged solid line encloses all points to which this codeword is the closest. The t-sphere around the codeword takes up a small fraction of this space.

If the friskiness is higher, the bat may often make excursions beyond the safe distance t where the longest stalactites start, but it will collide most frequently with more distant stalactites, owing to their greater number. There's only a tiny number of stalactites at the minimum distance, so they are relatively unlikely to cause the errors. Similarly, errors in a real error-correcting code depend on the properties of the weight enumerator function.

At very high friskiness, the bat is always a long way from the centre of the cave, and almost all its collisions involve contact with distant stalactites. Under these conditions, the bat's collision frequency has nothing to do with the distance from the centre to the closest stalactite.

▶ 13.7 Concatenation of Hamming codes

It is instructive to play some more with the concatenation of Hamming codes, a concept we first visited in figure 11.6, because we will get insights into the notion of good codes and the relevance or otherwise of the minimum distance of a code.

We can create a concatenated code for a binary symmetric channel with noise density f by encoding with several Hamming codes in succession.

The table recaps the key properties of the Hamming codes, indexed by number of constraints, M. All the Hamming codes have minimum distance $d = 3$ and can correct one error in N.

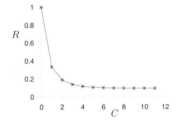

Figure 13.12. The rate R of the concatenated Hamming code as a function of the number of concatenations, C.

$N = 2^M - 1$	block length
$K = N - M$	number of source bits
$p_{\mathrm{B}} = \frac{3}{N}\binom{N}{2}f^2$	probability of block error to leading order

If we make a product code by concatenating a sequence of C Hamming codes with increasing M, we can choose those parameters $\{M_c\}_{c=1}^C$ in such a way that the rate of the product code

$$R_C = \prod_{c=1}^{C} \frac{N_c - M_c}{N_c} \qquad (13.21)$$

tends to a non-zero limit as C increases. For example, if we set $M_1 = 2$, $M_2 = 3$, $M_3 = 4$, etc., then the asymptotic rate is 0.093 (figure 13.12).

The block length N is a rapidly growing function of C, so these codes are somewhat impractical. A further weakness of these codes is that their minimum distance is not very good (figure 13.13). Every one of the constituent Hamming codes has minimum distance 3, so the minimum distance of the Cth product is 3^C. The blocklength N grows faster than 3^C, so the ratio d/N tends to zero as C increases. In contrast, for typical random codes, the ratio d/N tends to a constant such that $H_2(d/N) = 1 - R$. Concatenated Hamming codes thus have 'bad' distance.

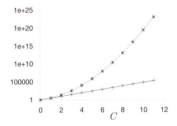

Figure 13.13. The blocklength N_C (upper curve) and minimum distance d_C (lower curve) of the concatenated Hamming code as a function of the number of concatenations C.

Nevertheless, it turns out that this simple sequence of codes yields good codes for some channels – but not very good codes (see section 11.4 to recall the definitions of the terms 'good' and 'very good'). Rather than prove this result, we will simply explore it numerically.

Figure 13.14 shows the bit error probability p_{b} of the concatenated codes assuming that the constituent codes are decoded in sequence, as described in section 11.4. [This one-code-at-a-time decoding is suboptimal, as we saw there.] The horizontal axis shows the rates of the codes. As the number of concatenations increases, the rate drops to 0.093 and the error probability drops towards zero. The channel assumed in the figure is the binary symmetric channel with $f = 0.0588$. This is the highest noise level that can be tolerated using this concatenated code.

The take-home message from this story is *distance isn't everything*. The minimum distance of a code, although widely worshipped by coding theorists, is not of fundamental importance to Shannon's mission of achieving reliable communication over noisy channels.

▷ Exercise 13.5.[3] Prove that there exist families of codes with 'bad' distance that are 'very good' codes.

13.8 Distance isn't everything

Let's get a quantitative feeling for the effect of the minimum distance of a code, for the special case of a binary symmetric channel.

The error probability associated with one low-weight codeword

Let a binary code have blocklength N and just two codewords, which differ in d places. For simplicity, let's assume d is even. What is the error probability if this code is used on a binary symmetric channel with noise level f?

Bit flips matter only in places where the two codewords differ. The error probability is dominated by the probability that $d/2$ of these bits are flipped. What happens to the other bits is irrelevant, since the optimal decoder ignores them.

$$P(\text{block error}) \simeq \binom{d}{d/2} f^{d/2} (1-f)^{d/2}. \tag{13.22}$$

This error probability associated with a single codeword of weight d is plotted in figure 13.15. Using the approximation for the binomial coefficient (1.16), we can further approximate

$$P(\text{block error}) \simeq \left[2f^{1/2}(1-f)^{1/2} \right]^d \tag{13.23}$$

$$\equiv [\beta(f)]^d, \tag{13.24}$$

where $\beta(f) = 2f^{1/2}(1-f)^{1/2}$ is called the Bhattacharyya parameter of the channel.

Now, consider a general linear code with distance d. Its block error probability must at least than $\binom{d}{d/2} f^{d/2}(1-f)^{d/2}$, independent of the blocklength N of the code. For this reason, a sequence of codes of increasing blocklength N and constant distance d (i.e., 'very bad' distance) cannot have a block error probability that tends to zero, on any binary symmetric channel. If we are interested in making superb error-correcting codes with tiny, tiny error probability, we might therefore shun codes with bad distance. However, being pragmatic, we should look more carefully at figure 13.15. In Chapter 1 we argued that codes for disk drives need an error probability smaller than about 10^{-18}. If the raw error probability in the disk drive is about 0.001, the error probability associated with one codeword at distance $d = 20$ is smaller than 10^{-24}. If the raw error probability in the disk drive is about 0.01, the error probability associated with one codeword at distance $d = 30$ is smaller than 10^{-20}. For practical purposes, therefore, it is not essential for a code to have good distance. For example, codes of blocklength $10\,000$, known to have many codewords of weight 32, can nevertheless correct errors of weight 320 with tiny error probability.

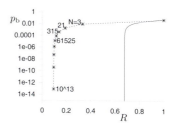

Figure 13.14. The bit error probabilities versus the rates R of the concatenated Hamming codes, for the binary symmetric channel with $f = 0.0588$. The solid line shows the Shannon limit for this channel.
The bit error probability drops to zero while the rate tends to 0.093, so the concatenated Hamming codes are a 'good' code family.

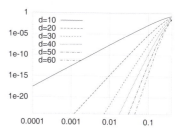

Figure 13.15. The error probability associated with a single codeword of weight d, $\binom{d}{d/2} f^{d/2}(1-f)^{d/2}$, as a function of f.

I wouldn't want you to think I am *recommending* the use of codes with bad distance; in Chapter 47 we will discuss low-density parity-check codes, my favourite codes, which have both excellent performance and *good* distance.

▶ 13.9 The union bound

The error probability of a code on the binary symmetric channel can be bounded in terms of its weight enumerator function by adding up appropriate multiples of the error probability associated with a single codeword (13.24):

$$P(\text{block error}) \leq \sum_{w>0} A(w)[\beta(f)]^{w}. \qquad (13.25)$$

This inequality, which is an example of a *union bound*, is accurate for low noise levels f, but inaccurate for high noise levels, because it overcounts the contribution of errors that cause confusion with more than one codeword at a time.

▷ Exercise 13.6.[3] Poor man's noisy-channel coding theorem.

Pretending that the union bound (13.25) *is* accurate, and using the average weight enumerator function of a random linear code (13.14) (section 13.5) as $A(w)$, estimate the maximum rate $R_{\text{UB}}(f)$ at which one can communicate over a binary symmetric channel.

Or, to look at it more positively, using the union bound (13.25) as an inequality, show that communication at rates up to $R_{\text{UB}}(f)$ is possible over the binary symmetric channel.

In the following chapter, by analysing the probability of error of *syndrome decoding* for a binary linear code, and using a union bound, we will prove Shannon's noisy-channel coding theorem (for symmetric binary channels), and thus show that *very good linear codes exist*.

▶ 13.10 Dual codes

A concept that has some importance in coding theory, though we will have no immediate use for it in this book, is the idea of the *dual* of a linear error-correcting code.

An (N, K) linear error-correcting code can be thought of as a set of 2^K codewords generated by adding together all combinations of K independent basis codewords. The generator matrix of the code consists of those K basis codewords, conventionally written as row vectors. For example, the $(7, 4)$ Hamming code's generator matrix (from p.10) is

$$\mathbf{G} = \begin{bmatrix} 1 & 0 & 0 & 0 & 1 & 0 & 1 \\ 0 & 1 & 0 & 0 & 1 & 1 & 0 \\ 0 & 0 & 1 & 0 & 1 & 1 & 1 \\ 0 & 0 & 0 & 1 & 0 & 1 & 1 \end{bmatrix} \qquad (13.26)$$

and its sixteen codewords were displayed in table 1.14 (p.9). The codewords of this code are linear combinations of the four vectors $[1\,0\,0\,0\,1\,0\,1]$, $[0\,1\,0\,0\,1\,1\,0]$, $[0\,0\,1\,0\,1\,1\,1]$, and $[0\,0\,0\,1\,0\,1\,1]$.

An (N, K) code may also be described in terms of an $M \times N$ parity-check matrix (where $M = N - K$) as the set of vectors $\{\mathbf{t}\}$ that satisfy

$$\mathbf{Ht} = \mathbf{0}. \qquad (13.27)$$

One way of thinking of this equation is that each row of $\mathbf{H}$ specifies a vector to which $\mathbf{t}$ must be orthogonal if it is a codeword.

> The generator matrix specifies K vectors *from which* all codewords can be built, and the parity-check matrix specifies a set of M vectors *to which* all codewords are orthogonal.
>
> The dual of a code is obtained by exchanging the generator matrix and the parity-check matrix.

Definition. The set of *all* vectors of length N that are orthogonal to all codewords in a code, $\mathcal{C}$, is called the dual of the code, $\mathcal{C}^\perp$.

If $\mathbf{t}$ is orthogonal to $\mathbf{h}_1$ and $\mathbf{h}_2$, then it is also orthogonal to $\mathbf{h}_3 \equiv \mathbf{h}_1 + \mathbf{h}_2$; so all codewords are orthogonal to any linear combination of the M rows of $\mathbf{H}$. So the set of all linear combinations of the rows of the parity-check matrix is the dual code.

For our Hamming $(7, 4)$ code, the parity-check matrix is (from p.12):

$$\mathbf{H} = [\ \mathbf{P}\ \ \mathbf{I}_3\ ] = \begin{bmatrix} 1 & 1 & 1 & 0 & 1 & 0 & 0 \\ 0 & 1 & 1 & 1 & 0 & 1 & 0 \\ 1 & 0 & 1 & 1 & 0 & 0 & 1 \end{bmatrix}. \tag{13.28}$$

The dual of the $(7, 4)$ Hamming code $\mathcal{H}_{(7,4)}$ is the code shown in table 13.16.

0000000	0101101	1001110	1100011
0010111	0111010	1011001	1110100

Table 13.16. The eight codewords of the dual of the $(7, 4)$ Hamming code. [Compare with table 1.14, p.9.]

A possibly unexpected property of this pair of codes is that the dual, $\mathcal{H}_{(7,4)}^\perp$, is contained within the code $\mathcal{H}_{(7,4)}$ itself: every word in the dual code is a codeword of the original $(7, 4)$ Hamming code. This relationship can be written using set notation:

$$\mathcal{H}_{(7,4)}^\perp \subset \mathcal{H}_{(7,4)}. \tag{13.29}$$

The possibility that the set of dual vectors can overlap the set of codeword vectors is counterintuitive if we think of the vectors as real vectors – how can a vector be orthogonal to itself? But when we work in modulo-two arithmetic, many non-zero vectors are indeed orthogonal to themselves!

▷ Exercise 13.7.[1, p.223] Give a simple rule that distinguishes whether a binary vector is orthogonal to itself, as is each of the three vectors $[1\,1\,1\,0\,1\,0\,0]$, $[0\,1\,1\,1\,0\,1\,0]$, and $[1\,0\,1\,1\,0\,0\,1]$.

Some more duals

In general, if a code has a systematic generator matrix,

$$\mathbf{G} = [\mathbf{I}_K | \mathbf{P}^\mathsf{T}], \tag{13.30}$$

where $\mathbf{P}$ is a $K \times M$ matrix, then its parity-check matrix is

$$\mathbf{H} = [\mathbf{P} | \mathbf{I}_M]. \tag{13.31}$$

Example 13.8. The repetition code R_3 has generator matrix

$$\mathbf{G} = \begin{bmatrix} 1 & 1 & 1 \end{bmatrix}; \qquad (13.32)$$

its parity-check matrix is

$$\mathbf{H} = \begin{bmatrix} 1 & 1 & 0 \\ 1 & 0 & 1 \end{bmatrix}. \qquad (13.33)$$

The two codewords are $[1\ 1\ 1]$ and $[0\ 0\ 0]$.

The dual code has generator matrix

$$\mathbf{G}^{\perp} = \mathbf{H} = \begin{bmatrix} 1 & 1 & 0 \\ 1 & 0 & 1 \end{bmatrix} \qquad (13.34)$$

or equivalently, modifying $\mathbf{G}^{\perp}$ into systematic form by row additions,

$$\mathbf{G}^{\perp} = \begin{bmatrix} 1 & 0 & 1 \\ 0 & 1 & 1 \end{bmatrix}. \qquad (13.35)$$

We call this dual code the *simple parity code* P_3; it is the code with one parity-check bit, which is equal to the sum of the two source bits. The dual code's four codewords are $[1\ 1\ 0]$, $[1\ 0\ 1]$, $[0\ 0\ 0]$, and $[0\ 1\ 1]$.

In this case, the only vector common to the code and the dual is the all-zero codeword.

Goodness of duals

If a sequence of codes is 'good', are their duals good too? Examples can be constructed of all cases: good codes with good duals (random linear codes); bad codes with bad duals; and good codes with bad duals. The last category is especially important: many state-of-the-art codes have the property that their duals are bad. The classic example is the low-density parity-check code, whose dual is a low-density generator-matrix code.

▷ Exercise 13.9.[3] Show that low-density generator-matrix codes are bad. A family of low-density generator-matrix codes is defined by two parameters j, k, which are the column weight and row weight of all rows and columns respectively of $\mathbf{G}$. These weights are fixed, independent of N; for example, $(j, k) = (3, 6)$. [Hint: show that the code has low-weight codewords, then use the argument from p.215.]

Exercise 13.10.[5] Show that low-density parity-check codes are good, and have good distance. (For solutions, see Gallager (1963) and MacKay (1999b).)

Self-dual codes

The $(7, 4)$ Hamming code had the property that the dual was contained in the code itself. A code is *self-orthogonal* if it is contained in its dual. For example, the dual of the $(7, 4)$ Hamming code is a self-orthogonal code. One way of seeing this is that overlap between any pair of rows of $\mathbf{H}$ is even. Codes that contain their duals are important in quantum error-correction (Calderbank and Shor, 1996).

It is intriguing, though not necessarily useful, to look at codes that are *self-dual*. A code $\mathcal{C}$ is self-dual if the dual of the code is identical to the code.

$$\mathcal{C}^{\perp} = \mathcal{C}. \qquad (13.36)$$

Some properties of self-dual codes can be deduced:

1. If a code is self-dual, then its generator matrix is also a parity-check matrix for the code.

2. Self-dual codes have rate $1/2$, i.e., $M = K = N/2$.

3. All codewords have even weight.

▷ Exercise 13.11.[2, p.223] What property must the matrix $\mathbf{P}$ satisfy, if the code with generator matrix $\mathbf{G} = [\mathbf{I}_K | \mathbf{P}^\mathsf{T}]$ is self-dual?

Examples of self-dual codes

1. The repetition code R_2 is a simple example of a self-dual code.

$$\mathbf{G} = \mathbf{H} = \begin{bmatrix} 1 & 1 \end{bmatrix}. \tag{13.37}$$

2. The smallest non-trivial self-dual code is the following $(8, 4)$ code.

$$\mathbf{G} = \begin{bmatrix} \mathbf{I}_4 \mid \mathbf{P}^\mathsf{T} \end{bmatrix} = \begin{bmatrix} 1 & 0 & 0 & 0 & 0 & 1 & 1 & 1 \\ 0 & 1 & 0 & 0 & 1 & 0 & 1 & 1 \\ 0 & 0 & 1 & 0 & 1 & 1 & 0 & 1 \\ 0 & 0 & 0 & 1 & 1 & 1 & 1 & 0 \end{bmatrix}. \tag{13.38}$$

▷ Exercise 13.12.[2, p.223] Find the relationship of the above $(8, 4)$ code to the $(7, 4)$ Hamming code.

Duals and graphs

Let a code be represented by a graph in which there are nodes of two types, parity-check constraints, and equality constraints, joined by edges which represent the bits of the code (not all of which need be transmitted).

The dual code's graph is obtained by replacing all parity-check nodes by equality nodes and *vice versa*. This type of graph is called a normal graph by Forney (2001).

Further reading

Duals are important in coding theory because functions involving a code (such as the posterior distribution over codewords) can be transformed by a Fourier transform into functions over the dual code. For an accessible introduction to Fourier analysis on finite groups, see Terras (1999). See also MacWilliams and Sloane (1977).

▶ 13.11 Generalizing perfectness to other channels

Having given up on the search for perfect codes for the binary symmetric channel, we could console ourselves by changing channel. We could call a code 'a perfect u-error-correcting code for the binary erasure channel' if it can restore any u erased bits, and never more than u. Rather than using the word perfect, however, the conventional term for such a code is a 'maximum distance separable code', or MDS code.

As we already noted in exercise 11.10 (p.190), the $(7, 4)$ Hamming code is *not* an MDS code. It can recover *some* sets of 3 erased bits, but not all. If any 3 bits corresponding to a codeword of weight 3 are erased, then one bit of information is unrecoverable. This is why the $(7, 4)$ code is a poor choice for a RAID system.

A tiny example of a maximum distance separable code is the simple parity-check code P_3 whose parity-check matrix is $\mathbf{H} = [1\,1\,1]$. This code has 4 codewords, all of which have even parity. All codewords are separated by a distance of 2. Any single erased bit can be restored by setting it to the parity of the other two bits. The repetition codes are also maximum distance separable codes.

▷ Exercise 13.13.[5, p.224] Can you make an (N, K) code, with $M = N - K$ parity symbols, for a q-ary erasure channel, such that the decoder can recover the codeword when *any* M symbols are erased in a block of N? [Example: for the channel with $q = 4$ symbols there is an $(N, K) = (5, 2)$ code which can correct any $M = 3$ erasures.]

For the q-ary erasure channel with $q > 2$, there are large numbers of MDS codes, of which the Reed–Solomon codes are the most famous and most widely used. As long as the field size q is bigger than the blocklength N, MDS block codes of any rate can be found. (For further reading, see Lin and Costello (1983).)

▶ **13.12 Summary**

Shannon's codes for the binary symmetric channel can almost always correct fN errors, but they are not fN-error-correcting codes.

Reasons why the distance of a code has little relevance

1. The Shannon limit shows you that you must be able to cope with a noise level twice as big as the maximum noise level for a bounded-distance decoder.

2. When the binary symmetric channel has $f > 1/4$, no code with a bounded-distance decoder can communicate at all; but Shannon says good codes exist for such channels.

3. Concatenation shows that we can get good performance even if the distance is bad.

The whole weight enumerator function is relevant to the question of whether a code is a good code.

The relationship between good codes and distance properties is discussed further in exercise 13.14 (p.220).

▶ **13.13 Further exercises**

Exercise 13.14.[3, p.224] A codeword $\mathbf{t}$ is selected from a linear (N, K) code $\mathcal{C}$, and it is transmitted over a noisy channel; the received signal is $\mathbf{y}$. We assume that the channel is a memoryless channel such as a Gaussian channel. Given an assumed channel model $P(\mathbf{y}\,|\,\mathbf{t})$, there are two decoding problems.

The codeword decoding problem is the task of inferring which codeword $\mathbf{t}$ was transmitted given the received signal.

The bitwise decoding problem is the task of inferring for each transmitted bit t_n how likely it is that that bit was a one rather than a zero.

Consider optimal decoders for these two decoding problems. Prove that the probability of error of the optimal bitwise-decoder is closely related to the probability of error of the optimal codeword-decoder, by proving the following theorem.

Theorem 13.1 *If a binary linear code has minimum distance $d_{\min}$, then, for any given channel, the codeword bit error probability of the optimal bitwise decoder, p_b, and the block error probability of the maximum likelihood decoder, p_B, are related by:*

$$p_B \geq p_b \geq \frac{1}{2} \frac{d_{\min}}{N} p_B. \qquad (13.39)$$

▷ **Exercise 13.15.**[1] What are the minimum distances of the $(15, 11)$ Hamming code and the $(31, 26)$ Hamming code?

▷ **Exercise 13.16.**[2] Let $A(w)$ be the average weight enumerator function of a rate-1/3 random linear code with $N = 540$ and $M = 360$. Estimate, from first principles, the value of $A(w)$ at $w = 1$.

Exercise 13.17.[3C] A code with minimum distance greater than d_{GV}. A rather nice $(15, 5)$ code is generated by this generator matrix, which is based on measuring the parities of all the $\binom{5}{3} = 10$ triplets of source bits:

$$\mathbf{G} = \begin{bmatrix} 1 & \cdot & \cdot & \cdot & \cdot & 1 & 1 & 1 & \cdot & \cdot & 1 & 1 & \cdot & 1 \\ \cdot & 1 & \cdot & \cdot & \cdot & \cdot & 1 & 1 & 1 & 1 & \cdot & 1 & 1 & \cdot \\ \cdot & \cdot & 1 & \cdot & \cdot & 1 & \cdot & 1 & 1 & \cdot & 1 & \cdot & 1 & 1 \\ \cdot & \cdot & \cdot & 1 & \cdot & 1 & 1 & \cdot & \cdot & 1 & 1 & \cdot & 1 & \cdot & 1 \\ \cdot & \cdot & \cdot & \cdot & 1 & 1 & 1 & 1 & \cdot & \cdot & 1 & 1 & \cdot & 1 & \cdot \end{bmatrix}. \qquad (13.40)$$

Find the minimum distance and weight enumerator function of this code.

Exercise 13.18.[3C] Find the minimum distance of the 'pentagonful' low-density parity-check code whose parity-check matrix is

$$\mathbf{H} = \left[\begin{array}{ccccc|ccccc|ccccc} 1 & \cdot & \cdot & \cdot & 1 & 1 & \cdot & \cdot & \cdot & \cdot & \cdot & \cdot & \cdot & \cdot & \cdot \\ 1 & 1 & \cdot & \cdot & \cdot & \cdot & 1 & \cdot & \cdot & \cdot & \cdot & \cdot & \cdot & \cdot & \cdot \\ \cdot & 1 & 1 & \cdot & \cdot & \cdot & \cdot & 1 & \cdot & \cdot & \cdot & \cdot & \cdot & \cdot & \cdot \\ \cdot & \cdot & 1 & 1 & \cdot & \cdot & \cdot & \cdot & 1 & \cdot & \cdot & \cdot & \cdot & \cdot & \cdot \\ \cdot & \cdot & \cdot & 1 & 1 & \cdot & \cdot & \cdot & \cdot & 1 & \cdot & \cdot & \cdot & \cdot & \cdot \\ \hline \cdot & \cdot & \cdot & \cdot & \cdot & 1 & \cdot & \cdot & \cdot & \cdot & 1 & \cdot & \cdot & \cdot & 1 \\ \cdot & \cdot & \cdot & \cdot & \cdot & \cdot & 1 & \cdot & 1 & 1 & \cdot & \cdot & \cdot \\ \cdot & \cdot & \cdot & \cdot & \cdot & \cdot & 1 & \cdot & \cdot & \cdot & \cdot & 1 & 1 & \cdot & \cdot \\ \cdot & \cdot & \cdot & \cdot & \cdot & \cdot & \cdot & \cdot & 1 & \cdot & \cdot & \cdot & 1 & 1 & \cdot \\ \cdot & \cdot & \cdot & \cdot & \cdot & \cdot & \cdot & 1 & \cdot & \cdot & \cdot & \cdot & \cdot & 1 & 1 \end{array} \right]. \qquad (13.41)$$

Show that nine of the ten rows are independent, so the code has parameters $N = 15$, $K = 6$. Using a computer, find its weight enumerator function.

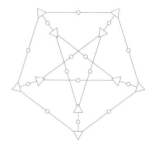

Figure 13.17. The graph of the pentagonful low-density parity-check code with 15 bit nodes (circles) and 10 parity-check nodes (triangles).

▷ **Exercise 13.19.**[3] Replicate the calculations used to produce figure 13.12. Check the assertion that the highest noise level that's correctable is 0.0588. Explore alternative concatenated sequences of codes. Can you find a better sequence of concatenated codes – better in the sense that it has either higher asymptotic rate R or can tolerate a higher noise level f?

Exercise 13.20.[3, p.226] Investigate the possibility of achieving the Shannon limit with linear block codes, using the following counting argument. Assume a linear code of large blocklength N and rate $R = K/N$. The code's parity-check matrix $\mathbf{H}$ has $M = N - K$ rows. Assume that the code's optimal decoder, which solves the syndrome decoding problem $\mathbf{Hn} = \mathbf{z}$, allows reliable communication over a binary symmetric channel with flip probability f.

How many 'typical' noise vectors $\mathbf{n}$ are there?

Roughly how many distinct syndromes $\mathbf{z}$ are there?

Since $\mathbf{n}$ is reliably deduced from $\mathbf{z}$ by the optimal decoder, the number of syndromes must be greater than or equal to the number of typical noise vectors. What does this tell you about the largest possible value of rate R for a given f?

▷ **Exercise 13.21.**[2] Linear binary codes use the input symbols 0 and 1 with equal probability, implicitly treating the channel as a symmetric channel. Investigate how much loss in communication rate is caused by this assumption, if in fact the channel is a highly asymmetric channel. Take as an example a Z-channel. How much smaller is the maximum possible rate of communication using symmetric inputs than the capacity of the channel? [Answer: about 6%.]

Exercise 13.22.[2] Show that codes with 'very bad' distance are 'bad' codes, as defined in section 11.4 (p.183).

Exercise 13.23.[3] One linear code can be obtained from another by *puncturing*. Puncturing means taking each codeword and deleting a defined set of bits. Puncturing turns an (N, K) code into an (N', K) code, where $N' < N$.

Another way to make new linear codes from old is *shortening*. Shortening means constraining a defined set of bits to be zero, and then deleting them from the codewords. Typically if we shorten by one bit, half of the code's codewords are lost. Shortening typically turns an (N, K) code into an (N', K') code, where $N - N' = K - K'$.

Another way to make a new linear code from two old ones is to make the *intersection* of the two codes: a codeword is only retained in the new code if it is present in both of the two old codes.

Discuss the effect on a code's distance properties of puncturing, shortening, and intersection. Is it possible to turn a code family with bad distance into a code family with good distance, or *vice versa*, by each of these three manipulations?

Exercise 13.24.[3, p.226] Todd Ebert's 'hat puzzle'.

Three players enter a room and a red or blue hat is placed on each person's head. The colour of each hat is determined by a coin toss, with the outcome of one coin toss having no effect on the others. Each person can see the other players' hats but not his own.

No communication of any sort is allowed, except for an initial strategy session before the group enters the room. Once they have had a chance to look at the other hats, the players must simultaneously guess their own hat's colour or pass. The group shares a $3 million prize if *at least one player guesses correctly and no players guess incorrectly.*

The same game can be played with any number of players. The general problem is to find a strategy for the group that maximizes its chances of winning the prize. Find the best strategies for groups of size **three** and **seven**.

[Hint: when you've done **three** and **seven**, you might be able to solve **fifteen**.]

> *If you already know the hat puzzle, you could try the 'Scottish version' of the rules in which the prize is only awarded to the group if they all guess correctly.*
>
> *In the 'Reformed Scottish version', all the players must guess correctly, and there are two rounds of guessing. Those players who guess during round one leave the room. The remaining players must guess in round two. What strategy should the team adopt to maximize their chance of winning?*

Exercise 13.25.[5] Estimate how many binary low-density parity-check codes have self-orthogonal duals. [Note that we don't expect a huge number, since almost all low-density parity-check codes are 'good', but a low-density parity-check code that contains its dual must be 'bad'.]

Exercise 13.26.[2] In figure 13.15 we plotted the error probability associated with a single codeword of weight d as a function of the noise level f of a binary symmetric channel. Make an equivalent plot for the case of the Gaussian channel, showing the error probability associated with a single codeword of weight d as a function of the rate-compensated signal to noise ratio E_b/N_0. Because E_b/N_0 depends on the rate, you have to choose a code rate. Choose $R = 1/2$, $2/3$, $3/4$, or $5/6$.

▶ 13.14 Solutions

Solution to exercise 13.4 (p.210). The probability of block error to leading order is $p_B = \frac{3}{N}\binom{N}{2}f^2$.

Solution to exercise 13.7 (p.217). A binary vector is perpendicular to itself if it has even weight, i.e., an even number of 1s.

Solution to exercise 13.11 (p.219). The self-dual code has two equivalent parity-check matrices, $\mathbf{H}_1 = \mathbf{G} = [\mathbf{I}_K|\mathbf{P}^\mathsf{T}]$ and $\mathbf{H}_2 = [\mathbf{P}|\mathbf{I}_K]$; these must be equivalent to each other through row additions, that is, there is a matrix $\mathbf{U}$ such that $\mathbf{U}\mathbf{H}_2 = \mathbf{H}_1$, so

$$[\mathbf{U}\mathbf{P}|\mathbf{U}\mathbf{I}_K] = [\mathbf{I}_K|\mathbf{P}^\mathsf{T}]. \tag{13.42}$$

From the right-hand sides of this equation, we have $\mathbf{U} = \mathbf{P}^\mathsf{T}$, so the left-hand sides become:

$$\mathbf{P}^\mathsf{T}\mathbf{P} = \mathbf{I}_K. \tag{13.43}$$

Thus if a code with generator matrix $\mathbf{G} = [\mathbf{I}_K|\mathbf{P}^\mathsf{T}]$ is self-dual then $\mathbf{P}$ is an *orthogonal* matrix, modulo 2, and *vice versa*.

Solution to exercise 13.12 (p.219). The $(8,4)$ and $(7,4)$ codes are intimately related. The $(8,4)$ code, whose parity-check matrix is

$$\mathbf{H} = [\ \mathbf{P}\ |\ \mathbf{I}_4\ ] = \begin{bmatrix} 0 & 1 & 1 & 1 & 1 & 0 & 0 & 0 \\ 1 & 0 & 1 & 1 & 0 & 1 & 0 & 0 \\ 1 & 1 & 0 & 1 & 0 & 0 & 1 & 0 \\ 1 & 1 & 1 & 0 & 0 & 0 & 0 & 1 \end{bmatrix}, \tag{13.44}$$

is obtained by (a) appending an extra parity-check bit which is the parity of all seven bits of the $(7,4)$ Hamming code; and (b) reordering the first four bits.

Solution to exercise 13.13 (p.220). If an (N, K) code, with $M = N - K$ parity symbols, has the property that the decoder can recover the codeword when *any* M symbols are erased in a block of N, then the code is said to be maximum distance separable (MDS).

No MDS binary codes exist, apart from the repetition codes and simple parity codes. For $q > 2$, some MDS codes can be found.

As a simple example, here is a $(9, 2)$ code for the 8-ary erasure channel. The code is defined in terms of the multiplication and addition rules of $GF(8)$, which are given in Appendix C.1. The elements of the input alphabet are $\{0, 1, A, B, C, D, E, F\}$ and the generator matrix of the code is

$$\mathbf{G} = \begin{bmatrix} 1 & 0 & 1 & A & B & C & D & E & F \\ 0 & 1 & 1 & 1 & 1 & 1 & 1 & 1 & 1 \end{bmatrix}. \tag{13.45}$$

The resulting 64 codewords are:

```
000000000  011111111  0AAAAAAAA  0BBBBBBBB  0CCCCCCCC  0DDDDDDDD  0EEEEEEEE  0FFFFFFFF
101ABCDEF  110BADCFE  1AB01EFCD  1BA10FEDC  1CDEF01AB  1DCFE10BA  1EFCDAB01  1FEDCBA10
A0ACEB1FD  A1BDFA0EC  AA0EC1BDF  AB1FD0ACE  ACE0AFDB1  ADF1BECA0  AECA0DF1B  AFDB1CE0A
B0BEDFC1A  B1AFCED0B  BA1CFDEB0  BB0DECFA1  BCFA1B0DE  BDEB0A1CF  BED0B1AFC  BFC1A0BED
C0CBFEAD1  C1DAEFBC0  CAE1DC0FB  CBF0CD1EA  CC0FBAE1D  CD1EABF0C  CEAD10CBF  CFBC01DAE
D0D1CAFBE  D1C0DBEAF  DAFBE0D1C  DBEAF1C0D  DC1D0EBFA  DD0C1FAEB  DEBFAC1D0  DFAEBD0C1
E0EF1DBAC  E1FE0CABD  EACDBF10E  EBDCAE01F  ECABD1FE0  EDBAC0EF1  EE01FBDCA  EF10EACDB
F0FDA1ECB  F1ECB0FDA  FADF0BCE1  FBCE1ADF0  FCB1EDA0F  FDA0FCB1E  FE1BCF0AD  FF0ADE1BC
```

Solution to exercise 13.14 (p.220). Quick, rough proof of the theorem. Let $\mathbf{x}$ denote the difference between the reconstructed codeword and the transmitted codeword. For any given channel output $\mathbf{r}$, there is a posterior distribution over $\mathbf{x}$. This posterior distribution is positive only on vectors $\mathbf{x}$ belonging to the code; the sums that follow are over codewords $\mathbf{x}$. The block error probability is:

$$p_{\mathrm{B}} = \sum_{\mathbf{x} \neq 0} P(\mathbf{x} \mid \mathbf{r}). \tag{13.46}$$

The average bit error probability, averaging over all bits in the codeword, is:

$$p_{\mathrm{b}} = \sum_{\mathbf{x} \neq 0} P(\mathbf{x} \mid \mathbf{r}) \frac{w(\mathbf{x})}{N}, \tag{13.47}$$

where $w(\mathbf{x})$ is the weight of codeword $\mathbf{x}$. Now the weights of the non-zero codewords satisfy

$$1 \geq \frac{w(\mathbf{x})}{N} \geq \frac{d_{\min}}{N}. \tag{13.48}$$

Substituting the inequalities (13.48) into the definitions (13.46, 13.47), we obtain:

$$p_{\mathrm{B}} \geq p_{\mathrm{b}} \geq \frac{d_{\min}}{N} p_{\mathrm{B}}, \tag{13.49}$$

which is a factor of two stronger, on the right, than the stated result (13.39). In making the proof watertight, I have weakened the result a little.

Careful proof. The theorem relates the performance of the optimal block decoding algorithm and the optimal bitwise decoding algorithm.

We introduce another pair of decoding algorithms, called the block-guessing decoder and the bit-guessing decoder. The idea is that these two algorithms are similar to the optimal block decoder and the optimal bitwise decoder, but lend themselves more easily to analysis.

We now define these decoders. Let $\mathbf{x}$ denote the inferred codeword. For any given code:

The optimal block decoder returns the codeword $\mathbf{x}$ that maximizes the posterior probability $P(\mathbf{x}\,|\,\mathbf{r})$, which is proportional to the likelihood $P(\mathbf{r}\,|\,\mathbf{x})$.

The probability of error of this decoder is called p_{B}.

The optimal bit decoder returns for each of the N bits, x_n, the value of a that maximizes the posterior probability $P(x_n\!=\!a\,|\,\mathbf{r}) = \sum_{\mathbf{x}} P(\mathbf{x}\,|\,\mathbf{r})\,\mathbb{1}[x_n\!=\!a]$.

The probability of error of this decoder is called p_{b}.

The block-guessing decoder returns a random codeword $\mathbf{x}$ with probability distribution given by the posterior probability $P(\mathbf{x}\,|\,\mathbf{r})$.

The probability of error of this decoder is called $p_{\mathrm{B}}^{\mathrm{G}}$.

The bit-guessing decoder returns for each of the N bits, x_n, a random bit from the probability distribution $P(x_n\!=\!a\,|\,\mathbf{r})$.

The probability of error of this decoder is called $p_{\mathrm{b}}^{\mathrm{G}}$.

The theorem states that the optimal bit error probability p_{b} is bounded above by p_{B} and below by a given multiple of p_{B} (13.39).

The left-hand inequality in (13.39) is trivially true – if a block is correct, all its constituent bits are correct; so if the optimal block decoder outperformed the optimal bit decoder, we could make a better bit decoder from the block decoder.

We prove the right-hand inequality by establishing that:

(a) the bit-guessing decoder is nearly as good as the optimal bit decoder:

$$p_{\mathrm{b}}^{\mathrm{G}} \leq 2p_{\mathrm{b}}. \tag{13.50}$$

(b) the bit-guessing decoder's error probability is related to the block-guessing decoder's by

$$p_{\mathrm{b}}^{\mathrm{G}} \geq \frac{d_{\min}}{N} p_{\mathrm{B}}^{\mathrm{G}}. \tag{13.51}$$

Then since $p_{\mathrm{B}}^{\mathrm{G}} \geq p_{\mathrm{B}}$, we have

$$p_{\mathrm{b}} > \frac{1}{2}p_{\mathrm{b}}^{\mathrm{G}} \geq \frac{1}{2}\frac{d_{\min}}{N}p_{\mathrm{B}}^{\mathrm{G}} \geq \frac{1}{2}\frac{d_{\min}}{N}p_{\mathrm{B}}. \tag{13.52}$$

We now prove the two lemmas.

Near-optimality of guessing: Consider first the case of a single bit, with posterior probability $\{p_0, p_1\}$. The optimal bit decoder has probability of error

$$P^{\mathrm{optimal}} = \min(p_0, p_1). \tag{13.53}$$

The guessing decoder picks from 0 and 1. The truth is also distributed with the same probability. The probability that the guesser and the truth match is $p_0^2 + p_1^2$; the probability that they mismatch is the guessing error probability,

$$P^{\mathrm{guess}} = 2p_0 p_1 \leq 2\min(p_0, p_1) = 2P^{\mathrm{optimal}}. \tag{13.54}$$

Since $p_{\mathrm{b}}^{\mathrm{G}}$ is the average of many such error probabilities, P^{guess}, and p_{b} is the average of the corresponding optimal error probabilities, P^{optimal}, we obtain the desired relationship (13.50) between $p_{\mathrm{b}}^{\mathrm{G}}$ and p_{b}. $\qquad\square$

Relationship between bit error probability and block error probability: The bit-guessing and block-guessing decoders can be combined in a single system: we can draw a sample x_n from the marginal distribution $P(x_n \,|\, \mathbf{r})$ by drawing a sample $(x_n, \mathbf{x})$ from the joint distribution $P(x_n, \mathbf{x} \,|\, \mathbf{r})$, then discarding the value of $\mathbf{x}$.

We can distinguish between two cases: the discarded value of $\mathbf{x}$ is the correct codeword, or not. The probability of bit error for the bit-guessing decoder can then be written as a sum of two terms:

$$
\begin{aligned}
p_{\mathrm{b}}^{\mathrm{G}} &= P(\mathbf{x}\ \text{correct})P(\text{bit error} \,|\, \mathbf{x}\ \text{correct}) \\
&\quad + P(\mathbf{x}\ \text{incorrect})P(\text{bit error} \,|\, \mathbf{x}\ \text{incorrect}) \\
&= 0 + p_{\mathrm{B}}^{\mathrm{G}} P(\text{bit error} \,|\, \mathbf{x}\ \text{incorrect}).
\end{aligned}
$$

Now, whenever the guessed $\mathbf{x}$ is incorrect, the true $\mathbf{x}$ must differ from it in at least d bits, so the probability of bit error in these cases is at least d/N. So

$$
p_{\mathrm{b}}^{\mathrm{G}} \geq \frac{d}{N} p_{\mathrm{B}}^{\mathrm{G}}.
$$

QED.   □

Solution to exercise 13.20 (p.222).   The number of 'typical' noise vectors $\mathbf{n}$ is roughly $2^{NH_2(f)}$. The number of distinct syndromes $\mathbf{z}$ is 2^M. So reliable communication implies

$$
M \geq NH_2(f),   \tag{13.55}
$$

or, in terms of the rate $R = 1 - M/N$,

$$
R \leq 1 - H_2(f),   \tag{13.56}
$$

a bound which agrees precisely with the capacity of the channel.

This argument is turned into a proof in the following chapter.

Solution to exercise 13.24 (p.222).   In the three-player case, it is possible for the group to win three-quarters of the time.

Three-quarters of the time, two of the players will have hats of the same colour and the third player's hat will be the opposite colour. The group can win every time this happens by using the following strategy. Each player looks at the other two players' hats. If the two hats are *different* colours, he passes. If they are the *same* colour, the player guesses his own hat is the *opposite* colour.

This way, every time the hat colours are distributed two and one, one player will guess correctly and the others will pass, and the group will win the game. When all the hats are the same colour, however, *all three* players will guess incorrectly and the group will lose.

When any particular player guesses a colour, it is true that there is only a 50:50 chance that their guess is right. The reason that the group wins 75% of the time is that their strategy ensures that when players are guessing wrong, a great many are guessing wrong.

For larger numbers of players, the aim is to ensure that most of the time no one is wrong and occasionally everyone is wrong at once. In the game with 7 players, there is a strategy for which the group wins 7 out of every 8 times they play. In the game with 15 players, the group can win 15 out of 16 times. If you have not figured out these winning strategies for teams of 7 and 15, I recommend thinking about the solution to the three-player game in terms of the locations of the winning and losing states on the three-dimensional hypercube, and thinking laterally.

If the number of players, N, is $2^r - 1$, the optimal strategy can be defined using a Hamming code of length N, and the probability of winning the prize is $N/(N+1)$. Each player is identified with a number $n \in 1 \ldots N$. The two colours are mapped onto 0 and 1. Any state of their hats can be viewed as a received vector out of a binary channel. A random binary vector of length N is either a codeword of the Hamming code, with probability $1/(N+1)$, or it differs in exactly one bit from a codeword. Each player looks at all the other bits and considers whether his bit can be set to a colour such that the state is a codeword (which can be deduced using the decoder of the Hamming code). If it can, then the player guesses that his hat is the *other* colour. If the state is actually a codeword, all players will guess and will guess wrong. If the state is a non-codeword, only one player will guess, and his guess will be correct. It's quite easy to train seven players to follow the optimal strategy if the cyclic representation of the $(7, 4)$ Hamming code is used (p.19).

About Chapter 14

In this chapter we will draw together several ideas that we've encountered so far in one nice short proof. We will simultaneously prove both Shannon's noisy-channel coding theorem (for symmetric binary channels) and his source coding theorem (for binary sources). While this proof has connections to many preceding chapters in the book, it's not essential to have read them all.

On the noisy-channel coding side, our proof will be more constructive than the proof given in Chapter 10; there, we proved that almost any random code is 'very good'. Here we will show that almost any *linear* code is very good. We will make use of the idea of typical sets (Chapters 4 and 10), and we'll borrow from the previous chapter's calculation of the weight enumerator function of random linear codes (section 13.5).

On the source coding side, our proof will show that *random linear hash functions* can be used for compression of compressible binary sources, thus giving a link to Chapter 12.

14

Very Good Linear Codes Exist

In this chapter we'll use a single calculation to prove simultaneously the source coding theorem and the noisy-channel coding theorem for the binary symmetric channel.

Incidentally, this proof works for much more general channel models, not only the binary symmetric channel. For example, the proof can be reworked for channels with non-binary outputs, for time-varying channels and for channels with memory, as long as they have binary inputs satisfying a symmetry property, c.f. section 10.6.

▶ 14.1 A simultaneous proof of the source coding and noisy-channel coding theorems

We consider a linear error-correcting code with binary parity-check matrix $\mathbf{H}$. The matrix has M rows and N columns. Later in the proof we will increase N and M, keeping $M \propto N$. The rate of the code satisfies

$$R \geq 1 - \frac{M}{N}. \tag{14.1}$$

If all the rows of $\mathbf{H}$ are independent then this is an equality, $R = 1 - M/N$. In what follows, we'll assume the equality holds. Eager readers may work out the expected rank of a random binary matrix $\mathbf{H}$ (it's very close to M) and pursue the effect that the difference $(M - \text{rank})$ has on the rest of this proof (it's negligible).

A codeword $\mathbf{t}$ is selected, satisfying

$$\mathbf{Ht} = \mathbf{0} \bmod 2, \tag{14.2}$$

and a binary symmetric channel adds noise $\mathbf{x}$, giving the received signal

$$\mathbf{r} = \mathbf{t} + \mathbf{x} \bmod 2. \tag{14.3}$$

In this chapter $\mathbf{x}$ denotes the noise added by the channel, not the input to the channel.

The receiver aims to infer both $\mathbf{t}$ and $\mathbf{x}$ from $\mathbf{r}$ using a syndrome decoding approach. Syndrome decoding was first introduced in section 1.2 (p.10 and 11). The receiver computes the syndrome

$$\mathbf{z} = \mathbf{Hr} \bmod 2 = \mathbf{Ht} + \mathbf{Hx} \bmod 2 = \mathbf{Hx} \bmod 2. \tag{14.4}$$

The syndrome only depends on the noise $\mathbf{x}$, and the decoding problem is to find the most probable $\mathbf{x}$ that satisfies

$$\mathbf{Hx} = \mathbf{z} \bmod 2. \tag{14.5}$$

This best estimate for the noise vector, $\hat{\mathbf{x}}$, is then subtracted from $\mathbf{r}$ to give the best guess for $\mathbf{t}$. Our aim is to show that, as long as $R < 1 - H(X) = 1 - H_2(f)$, where f is the flip probability of the binary symmetric channel, the optimal decoder for this syndrome decoding problem has vanishing probability of error, as N increases, for random $\mathbf{H}$.

We prove this result by studying a sub-optimal strategy for solving the decoding problem. Neither the optimal decoder nor this *typical set decoder* would be easy to implement, but the typical set decoder is easier to analyze. The typical set decoder examines the typical set T of noise vectors, the set of noise vectors $\mathbf{x}'$ that satisfy $\log 1/P(\mathbf{x}') \simeq NH(X)$, checking to see if any of those typical vectors $\mathbf{x}'$ satisfies the observed syndrome,

$$\mathbf{H}\mathbf{x}' = \mathbf{z}. \tag{14.6}$$

If exactly one typical vector $\mathbf{x}'$ does so, the typical set decoder reports that vector as the hypothesized noise vector. If no typical vector matches the observed syndrome, or more than one does, then the typical set decoder reports an error.

The probability of error of the typical set decoder, for a given matrix $\mathbf{H}$, can be written as a sum of two terms,

$$P_{\mathrm{TS}|\mathbf{H}} = P^{(I)} + P^{(II)}_{\mathrm{TS}|\mathbf{H}}, \tag{14.7}$$

where $P^{(I)}$ is the probability that the true noise vector $\mathbf{x}$ is itself not typical, and $P^{(II)}_{\mathrm{TS}|\mathbf{H}}$ is the probability that the true $\mathbf{x}$ is typical and at least one other typical vector clashes with it. The first probability vanishes as N increases, as we proved when we first studied typical sets (Chapter 4). We concentrate on the second probability. To recap, we're imagining a true noise vector, $\mathbf{x}$; and if *any* of the typical noise vectors $\mathbf{x}'$, different from $\mathbf{x}$, satisfies $\mathbf{H}(\mathbf{x}' - \mathbf{x}) = 0$, then we have an error. We use the truth function

$$\mathbb{1}\left[\mathbf{H}(\mathbf{x}' - \mathbf{x}) = 0\right], \tag{14.8}$$

whose value is one if the statement $\mathbf{H}(\mathbf{x}' - \mathbf{x}) = 0$ is true and zero otherwise. We can bound the number of type II errors made when the noise is $\mathbf{x}$ thus:

$$[\text{Number of errors given } \mathbf{x} \text{ and } \mathbf{H}] \le \sum_{\mathbf{x}':\,\substack{\mathbf{x}' \in T \\ \mathbf{x}' \neq \mathbf{x}}} \mathbb{1}\left[\mathbf{H}(\mathbf{x}' - \mathbf{x}) = 0\right]. \tag{14.9}$$

The number of errors is either zero or one; the sum on the right-hand side may exceed one, in cases where several typical noise vectors have the same syndrome.

We can now write down the probability of a type-II error by averaging over $\mathbf{x}$:

$$P^{(II)}_{\mathrm{TS}|\mathbf{H}} \le \sum_{\mathbf{x} \in T} P(\mathbf{x}) \sum_{\mathbf{x}':\,\substack{\mathbf{x}' \in T \\ \mathbf{x}' \neq \mathbf{x}}} \mathbb{1}\left[\mathbf{H}(\mathbf{x}' - \mathbf{x}) = 0\right]. \tag{14.10}$$

Now, we will find the average of this probability of type-II error over all linear codes by averaging over $\mathbf{H}$. By showing that the *average* probability of type-II error vanishes, we will thus show that there exist linear codes with vanishing error probability, indeed, that almost all linear codes are very good.

We denote averaging over all binary matrices $\mathbf{H}$ by $\langle \ldots \rangle_{\mathbf{H}}$. The average probability of type-II error is

$$\bar{P}^{(II)}_{\mathrm{TS}} = \sum_{\mathbf{H}} P(\mathbf{H}) P^{(II)}_{\mathrm{TS}|\mathbf{H}} = \left\langle P^{(II)}_{\mathrm{TS}|\mathbf{H}} \right\rangle_{\mathbf{H}} \tag{14.11}$$

We'll leave out the ϵs and βs that make a typical set definition rigorous. Enthusiasts are encouraged to revisit section 4.4 and put these details into this proof.

$$= \left\langle \sum_{\mathbf{x} \in T} P(\mathbf{x}) \sum_{\substack{\mathbf{x}': \mathbf{x}' \in T \\ \mathbf{x}' \neq \mathbf{x}}} \mathbb{1}\left[\mathbf{H}(\mathbf{x}' - \mathbf{x}) = 0\right] \right\rangle_{\mathbf{H}} \quad (14.12)$$

$$= \sum_{\mathbf{x} \in T} P(\mathbf{x}) \sum_{\substack{\mathbf{x}': \mathbf{x}' \in T \\ \mathbf{x}' \neq \mathbf{x}}} \left\langle \mathbb{1}\left[\mathbf{H}(\mathbf{x}' - \mathbf{x}) = 0\right] \right\rangle_{\mathbf{H}}. \quad (14.13)$$

Now, the quantity $\left\langle \mathbb{1}[\mathbf{H}(\mathbf{x}' - \mathbf{x}) = 0] \right\rangle_{\mathbf{H}}$ already cropped up when we were calculating the expected weight enumerator function of random linear codes (section 13.5): for any non-zero binary vector $\mathbf{v}$, the probability that $\mathbf{Hv} = 0$, averaging over all matrices $\mathbf{H}$, is 2^{-M}. So

$$\bar{P}_{\text{TS}}^{(II)} = \left(\sum_{\mathbf{x} \in T} P(\mathbf{x}) \right) (|T| - 1) \, 2^{-M} \quad (14.14)$$

$$\leq |T| \, 2^{-M}, \quad (14.15)$$

where $|T|$ denotes the size of the typical set. As you will recall from Chapter 4, there are roughly $2^{NH(X)}$ noise vectors in the typical set. So

$$\bar{P}_{\text{TS}}^{(II)} \leq 2^{NH(X)} 2^{-M}. \quad (14.16)$$

This bound on the probability of error either vanishes or grows exponentially as N increases (remembering that we are keeping M proportional to N as N increases). It vanishes if

$$H(X) < M/N. \quad (14.17)$$

Substituting $R = 1 - M/N$, we have thus established the noisy-channel coding theorem for the binary symmetric channel: very good linear codes exist for any rate R satisfying

$$R < 1 - H(X), \quad (14.18)$$

where $H(X)$ is the entropy of the channel noise, per bit. □

Exercise 14.1.[3] Redo the proof for a more general channel.

14.2 Data compression by linear hash codes

The decoding game we have just played can also be viewed as an *uncompression* game. The world produces a noise vector $\mathbf{x}$ from a source $P(\mathbf{x})$. The noise has redundancy (if the flip probability is not 0.5). We compress it with a linear compressor that maps the N-bit input $\mathbf{x}$ (the noise) to the M-bit output $\mathbf{z}$ (the syndrome). Our uncompression task is to recover the input $\mathbf{x}$ from the output $\mathbf{z}$. The rate of the compressor is

$$R_{\text{compressor}} \equiv M/N. \quad (14.19)$$

[We don't care about the possibility of linear redundancies in our definition of the rate, here.] The result that we just found, that the decoding problem can be solved, for almost any $\mathbf{H}$, with vanishing error probability, as long as $H(X) < M/N$, thus instantly proves a source coding theorem:

> Given a binary source X of entropy $H(X)$, and a required compressed rate $R > H(X)$, there exists a linear compressor $\mathbf{x} \to \mathbf{z} = \mathbf{Hx} \bmod 2$ having rate M/N equal to that required rate R, and an associated uncompressor, that is virtually lossless.

This theorem is true not only for a source of independent identically distributed symbols but also for any source for which a typical set can be defined: sources with memory, and time-varying sources, for example; all that's required is that the source be ergodic.

Notes

This method for proving that codes are good can be applied to other linear codes, such as low-density parity-check codes (MacKay, 1999b; Aji *et al.*, 2000). For each code we need an approximation of its expected weight enumerator function.

15

Further Exercises on Information Theory

The most exciting exercises, which will introduce you to further ideas in information theory, are towards the end of this chapter.

Refresher exercises on source coding and noisy channels

▷ Exercise 15.1.[2] Let X be an ensemble with $\mathcal{A}_X = \{0, 1\}$ and $\mathcal{P}_X = \{0.995, 0.005\}$. Consider source coding using the block coding of X^{100} where every $\mathbf{x} \in X^{100}$ containing 3 or fewer 1s is assigned a distinct codeword, while the other $\mathbf{x}$s are ignored.

    (a) If the assigned codewords are all of the same length, find the minimum length required to provide the above set with distinct codewords.

    (b) Calculate the probability of getting an $\mathbf{x}$ that will be ignored.

▷ Exercise 15.2.[2] Let X be an ensemble with $\mathcal{P}_X = \{0.1, 0.2, 0.3, 0.4\}$. The ensemble is encoded using the symbol code $\mathcal{C} = \{0001, 001, 01, 1\}$. Consider the codeword corresponding to $\mathbf{x} \in X^N$, where N is large.

    (a) Compute the entropy of the fourth bit of transmission.

    (b) Compute the conditional entropy of the fourth bit given the third bit.

    (c) Estimate the entropy of the hundredth bit.

    (d) Estimate the conditional entropy of the hundredth bit given the ninety-ninth bit.

Exercise 15.3.[2] Two fair dice are rolled by Alice and the sum is recorded. Bob's task is to ask a sequence of questions with yes/no answers to find out this number. Devise in detail a strategy that achieves the minimum possible average number of questions.

▷ Exercise 15.4.[2] How can you use a coin to draw straws among 3 people?

▷ Exercise 15.5.[2] In a magic trick, there are three participants: the magician, an assistant, and a volunteer. The assistant, who claims to have paranormal abilities, is in a soundproof room. The magician gives the volunteer six blank cards, five white and one blue. The volunteer writes a different integer from 1 to 100 on each card, as the magician is watching. The volunteer keeps the blue card. The magician arranges the five white cards in some order and passes them to the assistant. The assistant then announces the number on the blue card.

    How does the trick work?

▷ Exercise 15.6.[3] How does *this* trick work?

> 'Here's an ordinary pack of cards, shuffled into random order.
> Please choose five cards from the pack, any that you wish.
> Don't let me see their faces. No, don't give them to me: pass
> them to my assistant Esmerelda. She can look at them.
>
> 'Now, Esmerelda, show me four of the cards. Hmm... nine
> of spades, six of clubs, four of hearts, ten of diamonds. The
> hidden card, then, must be the queen of spades!'

The trick can be performed as described above for a pack of 52 cards.
Use information theory to give an upper bound on the number of cards
for which the trick can be performed.

▷ Exercise 15.7.[2] Find a probability sequence $\mathbf{p} = (p_1, p_2, \ldots)$ such that
$H(\mathbf{p}) = \infty$.

▷ Exercise 15.8.[2] Consider a discrete memoryless source with $\mathcal{A}_X = \{a, b, c, d\}$
and $\mathcal{P}_X = \{1/2, 1/4, 1/8, 1/8\}$. There are $4^8 = 65\,536$ eight-letter words
that can be formed from the four letters. Find the total number of such
words that are in the typical set $T_{N\beta}$ (equation 4.29) where $N = 8$ and
$\beta = 0.1$.

▷ Exercise 15.9.[2] Consider the source $\mathcal{A}_S = \{a, b, c, d, e\}$, $\mathcal{P}_S = \{1/3, 1/3, 1/9, 1/9, 1/9\}$ and the channel whose transition probability matrix
is

$$Q = \begin{bmatrix} 1 & 0 & 0 & 0 \\ 0 & 0 & 2/3 & 0 \\ 0 & 1 & 0 & 1 \\ 0 & 0 & 1/3 & 0 \end{bmatrix}. \tag{15.1}$$

Note that the source alphabet has five symbols, but the channel alphabet
$\mathcal{A}_X = \mathcal{A}_Y = \{0, 1, 2, 3\}$ has only four. Assume that the source produces
symbols at exactly $3/4$ the rate that the channel accepts channel sym-
bols. For a given (tiny) $\epsilon > 0$, explain how you would design a system
for communicating the source's output over the channel with an average error probability per source symbol less than ϵ. Be as explicit as
possible. In particular, *do not* invoke Shannon's noisy-channel coding
theorem.

▷ Exercise 15.10.[2] Consider a binary symmetric channel and a code $C = \{0000, 0011, 1100, 1111\}$; assume that the four codewords are used with
probabilities $\{1/2, 1/8, 1/8, 1/4\}$.

What is the decoding rule that minimizes the probability of decoding
error? [The optimal decoding rule depends on the noise level f of the
binary symmetric channel. Give the decoding rule for each range of
values of f, for f between 0 and $1/2$.]

▷ Exercise 15.11.[2] Find the capacity and optimal input distribution for the
three-input, three-output channel whose transition probabilities are:

$$Q = \begin{bmatrix} 1 & 0 & 0 \\ 0 & 2/3 & 1/3 \\ 0 & 1/3 & 2/3 \end{bmatrix}. \tag{15.2}$$

Exercise 15.12.[3, p.239] The input to a channel Q is a word of 8 bits. The output is also a word of 8 bits. Each time it is used, the channel flips *exactly one* of the transmitted bits, but the receiver does not know which one. The other seven bits are received without error. All 8 bits are equally likely to be the one that is flipped. Derive the capacity of this channel.

Show, by describing an *explicit* encoder *and* decoder that it is possible *reliably* (that is, with *zero* error probability) to communicate 5 bits per cycle over this channel.

▷ Exercise 15.13.[2] A channel with input $x \in \{a, b, c\}$ and output $y \in \{r, s, t, u\}$ has conditional probability matrix:

$$\mathbf{Q} = \begin{bmatrix} 1/2 & 0 & 0 \\ 1/2 & 1/2 & 0 \\ 0 & 1/2 & 1/2 \\ 0 & 0 & 1/2 \end{bmatrix}.$$

a →⟨ r, s
b →⟨ s, t
c →⟨ t, u

What is its capacity?

▷ Exercise 15.14.[3] The ten-digit number on the cover of a book known as the ISBN incorporates an error-detecting code. The number consists of nine source digits $x_1, x_2, \ldots, x_9$, satisfying $x_n \in \{0, 1, \ldots, 9\}$, and a tenth check digit whose value is given by

$$x_{10} = \left(\sum_{n=1}^{9} n x_n \right) \bmod 11.$$

0-521-64298-1
1-010-00000-4

Table 15.1. Some valid ISBNs. [The hyphens are included for legibility.]

Here $x_{10} \in \{0, 1, \ldots, 9, 10\}$. If $x_{10} = 10$ then the tenth digit is shown using the roman numeral X.

Show that a valid ISBN satisfies:

$$\left(\sum_{n=1}^{10} n x_n \right) \bmod 11 = 0.$$

Imagine that an ISBN is communicated over an unreliable human channel which sometimes *modifies* digits and sometimes *reorders* digits.

Show that this code can be used to detect (but not correct) all errors in which any one of the ten digits is modified (for example, 1-010-00000-4 → 1-010-00080-4).

Show that this code can be used to detect all errors in which any two adjacent digits are transposed (for example, 1-010-00000-4 → 1-100-00000-4).

What other transpositions of pairs of *non-adjacent* digits can be detected?

If the tenth digit were defined to be

$$x_{10} = \left(\sum_{n=1}^{9} n x_n \right) \bmod 10,$$

why would the code not work so well? (Discuss the detection of both modifications of single digits and transpositions of digits.)

Exercise 15.15.[3] A channel with input x and output y has transition probability matrix:

$$Q = \begin{bmatrix} 1-f & f & 0 & 0 \\ f & 1-f & 0 & 0 \\ 0 & 0 & 1-g & g \\ 0 & 0 & g & 1-g \end{bmatrix}.$$

Assuming an input distribution of the form

$$\mathcal{P}_X = \left\{ \frac{p}{2}, \frac{p}{2}, \frac{1-p}{2}, \frac{1-p}{2} \right\},$$

write down the entropy of the output, $H(Y)$, and the conditional entropy of the output given the input, $H(Y|X)$.

Show that the optimal input distribution is given by

$$p = \frac{1}{1 + 2^{-H_2(g)+H_2(f)}},$$

where $H_2(f) = f \log_2 \frac{1}{f} + (1-f) \log_2 \frac{1}{(1-f)}$.   Remember $\frac{d}{dp} H_2(p) = \log_2 \frac{1-p}{p}$.

Write down the optimal input distribution and the capacity of the channel in the case $f = 1/2$, $g = 0$, and comment on your answer.

▷ **Exercise 15.16.**[2] What are the differences in the redundancies needed in an error-detecting code (which can reliably detect that a block of data has been corrupted) and an error-correcting code (which can detect and correct errors)?

Further tales from information theory

The following exercises give you the chance to discover for yourself the answers to some more surprising results of information theory.

Exercise 15.17.[3] Communication of correlated information. Imagine that we want to communicate data from two data sources $X^{(A)}$ and $X^{(B)}$ to a central location C via noise-free one-way communication channels (figure 15.2a). The signals $x^{(A)}$ and $x^{(B)}$ are strongly correlated, so their joint information content is only a little greater than the marginal information content of either of them. For example, C is a weather collator who wishes to receive a string of reports saying whether it is raining in Allerton ($x^{(A)}$) and whether it is raining in Bognor ($x^{(B)}$). The joint probability of $x^{(A)}$ and $x^{(B)}$ might be

$$P(x^{(A)}, x^{(B)}):$$

		$x^{(A)}$	
		0	1
$x^{(B)}$	0	0.49	0.01
	1	0.01	0.49

$\qquad\qquad\qquad\qquad\qquad\qquad\qquad\qquad\qquad\qquad$ (15.3)

The weather collator would like to know N successive values of $x^{(A)}$ and $x^{(B)}$ exactly, but, since he has to pay for every bit of information he receives, he is interested in the possibility of avoiding buying N bits from source A and N bits from source B. Assuming that variables $x^{(A)}$ and $x^{(B)}$ are generated repeatedly from this distribution, can they be encoded at rates R_A and R_B in such a way that C can reconstruct all the variables, with the sum of information transmission rates on the two lines being less than two bits per cycle?

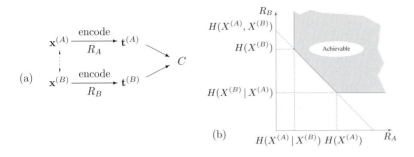

Figure 15.2. Communication of correlated information. (a) $x^{(A)}$ and $x^{(B)}$ are correlated sources (the correlation is represented by the dotted arrow). Strings of values of each variable are encoded using codes of rate R_A and R_B into transmissions $\mathbf{t}^{(A)}$ and $\mathbf{t}^{(B)}$, which are communicated over noise-free channels to a receiver C. (b) The achievable rate region. Both strings can be conveyed without error even though $R_A < H(X^{(A)})$ and $R_B < H(X^{(B)})$.

The answer, which you should demonstrate, is indicated in figure 15.2. In the general case of two correlated sources $X^{(A)}$ and $X^{(B)}$, there exist codes for the two transmitters that can achieve reliable communication of both $X^{(A)}$ and $X^{(B)}$ to C, as long as: the information rate from $X^{(A)}$, R_A, exceeds $H(X^{(A)} | X^{(B)})$; the information rate from $X^{(B)}$, R_B, exceeds $H(X^{(B)} | X^{(A)})$; and the total information rate $R_A + R_B$ exceeds the joint information $H(X^{(A)}, X^{(B)})$.

So in the case of $x^{(A)}$ and $x^{(B)}$ above, each transmitter must transmit at a rate greater than $H_2(0.02) = 0.14$ bits, and the total rate $R_A + R_B$ must be greater than 1.14 bits, for example $R_A = 0.6$, $R_B = 0.6$. There exist codes that can achieve these rates. Your task is to figure out why this is so.

Try to find an explicit solution in which one of the sources is sent as plain text, $\mathbf{t}^{(B)} = \mathbf{x}^{(B)}$, and the other is encoded.

Exercise 15.18.[3] Multiple access channels. Consider a channel with two sets of inputs and one output – for example, a shared telephone line (figure 15.3a). A simple model system has two binary inputs $x^{(A)}$ and $x^{(B)}$ and a ternary output y equal to the arithmetic sum of the two inputs, that's 0, 1 or 2. There is no noise. Users A and B cannot communicate with each other, and they cannot hear the output of the channel. If the output is a 0, the receiver can be certain that both inputs were set to 0; and if the output is a 2, the receiver can be certain that both inputs were set to 1. But if the output is 1, then it could be that the input state was $(0,1)$ or $(1,0)$. How should users A and B use this channel so that their messages can be deduced from the received signals? How fast can A and B communicate?

Clearly the total information rate from A and B to the receiver cannot be two bits. On the other hand it is easy to achieve a total information rate $R_A + R_B$ of one bit. Can reliable communication be achieved at rates (R_A, R_B) such that $R_A + R_B > 1$?

The answer is indicated in figure 15.3.

Some practical codes for multi-user channels are presented in Ratzer and MacKay (2003).

Exercise 15.19.[3] Broadcast channels. A broadcast channel consists of a single transmitter and two or more receivers. The properties of the channel are defined by a conditional distribution $Q(y^{(A)}, y^{(B)} | x)$. (We'll assume the channel is memoryless.) The task is to add an encoder and two decoders to enable reliable communication of a common message at rate R_0 to both receivers, an individual message at rate R_A to receiver A, and an individual message at rate R_B to receiver B. The *capacity* region of the broadcast channel is the convex hull of the set of achievable rate triplets (R_0, R_A, R_B).

A simple benchmark for such a channel is given by time-sharing (time-division signaling). If the capacities of the two channels, considered separately,

Figure 15.4. The broadcast channel. x is the channel input; $y^{(A)}$ and $y^{(B)}$ are the outputs.

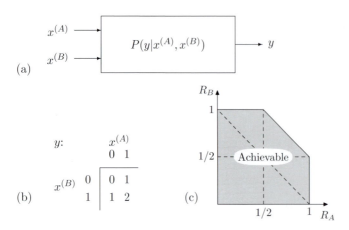

(a)

(b)

(c)

Figure 15.3. Multiple access channels. (a) A general multiple access channel with two transmitters and one receiver. (b) A binary multiple access channel with output equal to the sum of two inputs. (c) The achievable region.

are $C^{(A)}$ and $C^{(B)}$, then by devoting a fraction ϕ_A of the transmission time to channel A and $\phi_B = 1 - \phi_A$ to channel B, we can achieve $(R_0, R_A, R_B) = (0, \phi_A C^{(A)}, \phi_B C^{(B)})$.

We can do better than this, however. As an analogy, imagine speaking simultaneously to an American and a Belarusian; you are fluent in American and in Belarusian, but neither of your two receivers understands the other's language. If each receiver can distinguish whether a word is in their own language or not, then an extra binary file can be conveyed to both recipients by using its bits to decide whether the next transmitted word should be from the American source text or from the Belarusian source text. Each recipient can concatenate the words that they understand in order to receive their personal message, and can also recover the binary string.

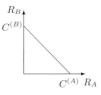

Figure 15.5. Rates achievable by simple timesharing.

An example of a broadcast channel consists of two binary symmetric channels with a common input. The two halves of the channel have flip probabilities f_A and f_B. We'll assume that A has the better half-channel, i.e., $f_A < f_B < 1/2$. [A closely related channel is a 'degraded' broadcast channel, in which the conditional probabilities are such that the random variables have the structure of a Markov chain,

$$x \to y^{(A)} \to y^{(B)}, \tag{15.4}$$

i.e., $y^{(B)}$ is a further degraded version of $y^{(A)}$.] In this special case, it turns out that whatever information is getting through to receiver B can also be recovered by receiver A. So there is no point distinguishing between R_0 and R_B: the task is to find the capacity region for the rate pair (R_0, R_A), where R_0 is the rate of information reaching both A and B, and R_A is the rate of the extra information reaching A.

The following exercise is equivalent to this one, and a solution to it is illustrated in figure 15.8.

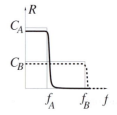

Figure 15.6. Rate of reliable communication R, as a function of noise level f, for Shannonesque codes designed to operate at noise levels f_A (solid line) and f_B (dashed line).

Exercise 15.20.[3] Variable-rate error-correcting codes for channels with unknown noise level. In real life, channels may sometimes not be well characterized before the encoder is installed. As a model of this situation, imagine that a channel is known to be a binary symmetric channel with noise level either f_A or f_B. Let $f_B > f_A$, and let the two capacities be C_A and C_B.

Those who like to live dangerously might install a system designed for noise level f_A with rate $R_A \simeq C_A$; in the event that the noise level turns out to be f_B, our experience of Shannon's theories would lead us to expect that there would be a catastrophic failure to communicate information reliably (solid line in figure 15.6).

A conservative approach would design the encoding system for the worst-case scenario, installing a code with rate $R_B \simeq C_B$ (dashed line in figure 15.6). In the event that the lower noise level, f_A, holds true, the managers would have a feeling of regret because of the wasted capacity difference $C_A - R_B$.

Is it possible to create a system that not only transmits reliably at some rate R_0 whatever the noise level, but also communicates some extra, 'lower-priority' bits if the noise level is low, as shown in figure 15.7? This code communicates the high-priority bits reliably at all noise levels between f_A and f_B, and communicates the low-priority bits also if the noise level is f_A or below.

This problem is mathematically equivalent to the previous problem, the degraded broadcast channel. The lower rate of communication was there called R_0, and the rate at which the low-priority bits are communicated if the noise level is low was called R_A.

An illustrative answer is shown in figure 15.8, for the case $f_A = 0.01$ and $f_B = 0.1$. (This figure also shows the achievable region for a broadcast channel whose two half-channels have noise levels $f_A = 0.01$ and $f_B = 0.1$.) I admit I find the gap between the simple time-sharing solution and the cunning solution disappointingly small.

In Chapter 50 we will discuss codes for a special class of broadcast channels, namely erasure channels, where every symbol is either received without error or erased. These codes have the nice property that they are *rateless* – the number of symbols transmitted is determined on the fly such that reliable comunication is achieved, whatever the erasure statistics of the channel.

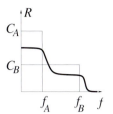

Figure 15.7. Rate of reliable communication R, as a function of noise level f, for a desired *variable-rate* code.

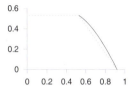

Figure 15.8. An achievable region for the channel with unknown noise level. Assuming the two possible noise levels are $f_A = 0.01$ and $f_B = 0.1$, the dashed lines show the rates R_A, R_B that are achievable using a simple time-sharing approach, and the solid line shows rates achievable using a more cunning approach.

Exercise 15.21.[3] Multiterminal information networks are both important practically and intriguing theoretically. Consider the following example of a two-way binary channel (figure 15.9a,b): two people both wish to talk over the channel, and they both want to hear what the other person is saying; but you can only hear the signal transmitted by the other person if you are transmitting a zero. What simultaneous information rates from A to B and from B to A can be achieved, and how? Everyday examples of such networks include the VHF channels used by ships, and computer ethernet networks (in which *all* the devices are unable to hear *anything* if two or more devices are broadcasting simultaneously).

Obviously, we can achieve rates of $^1/_2$ in both directions by simple time-sharing. But can the two information rates be made larger? Finding the capacity of a general two-way channel is still an open problem. However, we can obtain interesting results concerning achievable points for the simple binary channel discussed above, as indicated in figure 15.9c. There exist codes that can achieve rates up to the boundary shown. There may exist better codes too.

Solutions

Solution to exercise 15.12 (p.235). $C(Q) = 5$ bits.
Hint for the last part: a solution exists that involves a simple $(8, 5)$ code.

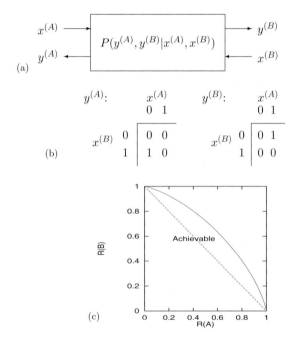

(a)

(b)

(c)

Figure 15.9. (a) A general
two-way channel. (b) The rules
for a binary two-way channel.
The two tables show the outputs
$y^{(A)}$ and $y^{(B)}$ that result for each
state of the inputs. (c) Achievable
region for the two-way binary
channel. Rates below the solid
line are achievable. The dotted
line shows the 'obviously
achievable' region which can be
attained by simple time-sharing.

16

Message Passing

One of the themes of this book is the idea of doing complicated calculations using simple distributed hardware. It turns out that quite a few interesting problems can be solved by *message-passing* algorithms, in which simple messages are passed locally among simple processors whose operations lead, after some time, to the solution of a global problem.

▶ 16.1 Counting

As an example, consider a line of soldiers walking in the mist. The commander wishes to perform the complex calculation of counting the number of soldiers in the line. This problem could be solved in two ways.

First there is a solution that uses expensive hardware: the loud booming voices of the commander and his men. The commander could shout 'all soldiers report back to me within one minute!', then he could listen carefully as the men respond 'Molesworth here sir!', 'Fotherington–Thomas here sir!', and so on. This solution relies on several expensive pieces of hardware: there must be a reliable communication channel to and from every soldier; the commander must be able to listen to all the incoming messages – even when there are hundreds of soldiers – and must be able to count; and all the soldiers must be well-fed if they are to be able to shout back across the possibly-large distance separating them from the commander.

The second way of finding this global function, the number of soldiers, does not require global communication hardware, high IQ, or good food; we simply require that each soldier can communicate single integers with the two adjacent soldiers in the line, and that the soldiers are capable of adding one to a number. Each soldier follows these rules:

---

1. If you are the front soldier in the line, say the number 'one' to the soldier behind you.

2. If you are the rearmost soldier in the line, say the number 'one' to the soldier in front of you.

3. If a soldier ahead of or behind you says a number to you, add one to it, and say the new number to the soldier on the other side.

Algorithm 16.1. Message-passing rule-set A.

If the clever commander can not only add one to a number, but also add two numbers together, then he can find the global number of soldiers by simply adding together:

> | | the number said to him by the soldier in front of him, | (which equals the total number of soldiers in front) |
> |---|---|---|
> | + | the number said to the commander by the soldier behind him, | (which is the number behind) |
> | + | one | (to count the commander himself). |

This solution requires only local communication hardware and simple computations (storage and addition of integers).

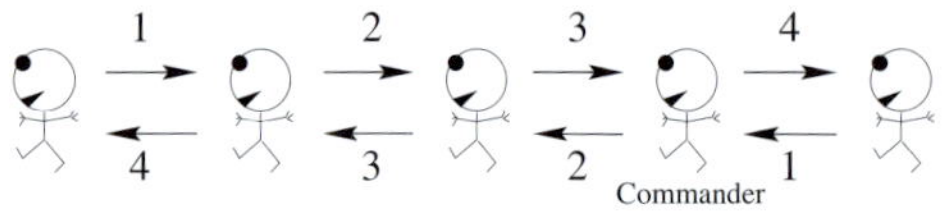

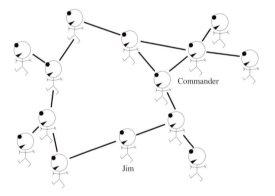

Figure 16.2. A line of soldiers counting themselves using message-passing rule-set A. The commander can add '3' from the soldier in front, '1' from the soldier behind, and '1' for himself, and deduce that there are 5 soldiers in total.

Separation

This clever trick makes use of a profound property of the total number of soldiers: that it can be written as the sum of the number of soldiers *in front* of a point and the number *behind* that point, two quantities which can be computed *separately*, because the two groups are separated by the commander.

If the soldiers were not arranged in a line but were travelling in a swarm, then it would not be easy to separate them into two groups in this way. The

Figure 16.3. A swarm of guerillas.

guerillas in figure 16.3 could not be counted using the above message-passing rule-set A, because, while the guerillas do have neighbours (shown by lines), it is not clear who is 'in front' and who is 'behind'; furthermore, since the *graph* of connections between the guerillas contains cycles, it is not possible for a guerilla in a cycle (such as 'Jim') to *separate* the group into two groups, 'those in front', and 'those behind'.

A swarm of guerillas *can* be counted by a modified message-passing algorithm *if they are arranged in a graph that contains no cycles*.

Rule-set B is a message-passing algorithm for counting a swarm of guerillas whose connections form a *cycle-free graph*, also known as a *tree*, as illustrated in figure 16.4. Any guerilla can deduce the total in the tree from the messages that they receive.

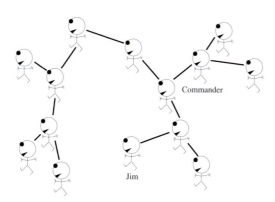

Figure 16.4. A swarm of guerillas whose connections form a tree.

1. Count your number of neighbours, N.

2. Keep count of the number of messages you have received from your neighbours, m, and of the values v_1, v_2, ..., v_N of each of those messages. Let V be the running total of the messages you have received.

3. If the number of messages you have received, m, is equal to $N - 1$, then identify the neighbour who has not sent you a message and tell them the number $V + 1$.

4. If the number of messages you have received is equal to N, then:

    (a) the number $V + 1$ is the required total.

    (b) for each neighbour n {
        say to neighbour n the number $V + 1 - v_n$.
    }

Algorithm 16.5. Message-passing rule-set B.

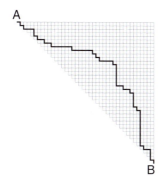

Figure 16.6. A triangular 41×41 grid. How many paths are there from A to B? One path is shown.

▶ 16.2 Path-counting

A more profound task than counting squaddies is the task of counting the number of paths through a grid, and finding how many paths pass through any given point in the grid.

Figure 16.6 shows a rectangular grid, and a path through the grid, connecting points A and B. A valid path is one that starts from A and proceeds to B by rightward and downward moves. Our questions are:

1. How many such paths are there from A to B?

2. If a random path from A to B is selected, what is the probability that it passes through a particular node in the grid? [When we say 'random', we mean that all *paths* have exactly the the same probability of being selected.]

3. How can a random path from A to B be selected?

Counting all the paths from A to B doesn't seem straightforward. The number of paths is expected to be pretty big – even if the permitted grid were a diagonal strip only three nodes wide, there would still be about $2^{N/2}$ possible paths.

The computational breakthrough is to realize that to find the *number* of paths, we do not have to enumerate all the paths explicitly. Pick a point P in the grid and consider the number of paths from A to P. Every path from A to P must come in to P through one of its upstream neighbours ('upstream' meaning above or to the left). So the number of paths from A to P can be found by adding up the number of paths from A to each of those neighbours.

This message-passing algorithm is illustrated in figure 16.8 for a simple grid with ten vertices connected by twelve directed edges. We start by sending the '1' message from A. When any node has received messages from all its upstream neighbours, it sends the *sum* of them on to its downstream neighbours. At B, the number 5 emerges: we have counted the number of paths from A to B without enumerating them all. As a sanity-check, figure 16.9 shows the five distinct paths from A to B.

Having counted all paths, we can now move on to more challenging problems: computing the probability that a random path goes through a given vertex, and creating a random path.

Probability of passing through a node

By making a backward pass as well as the forward pass, we can deduce how many of the paths go through each node; and if we divide that by the total number of paths, we obtain the probability that a randomly selected path passes through that node. Figure 16.10 shows the backward-passing messages in the lower-right corners of the tables, and the original forward-passing messages in the upper-left corners. By multiplying these two numbers at a given vertex, we find the total number of paths passing through that vertex. For example, four paths pass through the central vertex.

Figure 16.11 shows the result of this computation for the triangular 41 × 41 grid. The area of each blob is proportional to the probability of passing through each node.

Random path sampling

Exercise 16.1.[1, p.247] If one creates a 'random' path from A to B by flipping a fair coin at every junction where there is a choice of two directions, is

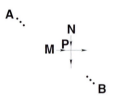

Figure 16.7. Every path from A to P enters P through an upstream neighbour of P, either M or N; so we can find the number of paths from A to P by adding the number of paths from A to M and from A to N.

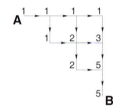

Figure 16.8. Messages sent in the forward pass.

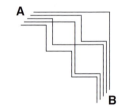

Figure 16.9. The five paths.

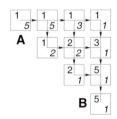

Figure 16.10. Messages sent in the forward and backward passes.

the resulting path a uniform random sample from the set of all paths? [Hint: imagine trying it for the grid of figure 16.8.]

There is a neat insight to be had here, and I'd like you to have the satisfaction of figuring it out.

Exercise 16.2.[2, p.247] Having run the forward and backward algorithms between points A and B on a grid, how can one draw one path from A to B *uniformly* at random? (Figure 16.11.)

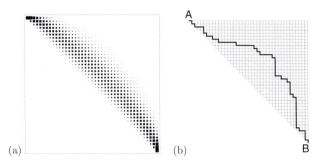

(a)   (b)

Figure 16.11. (a) The probability of passing through each node, and (b) a randomly chosen path.

The message-passing algorithm we used to count the paths to B is an example of the *sum–product algorithm*. The 'sum' takes place at each node when it adds together the messages coming from its predecessors; the 'product' was not mentioned, but you can think of the sum as a weighted sum in which all the summed terms happened to have weight 1.

▶ 16.3 Finding the lowest-cost path

Imagine you wish to travel as quickly as possible from Ambridge (A) to Bognor (B). The various possible routes are shown in figure 16.12, along with the cost in hours of traversing each edge in the graph. For example, the route A–I–L–N–B has a cost of 8 hours. We would like to find the lowest-cost path without explicitly evaluating the cost of all paths. We can do this efficiently by finding for each node what the cost of the lowest-cost path to that node from A is. These quantities can be computed by message-passing, starting from node A. The message-passing algorithm is called the *min–sum algorithm* or *Viterbi algorithm*.

For brevity, we'll call the cost of the lowest-cost path from node A to node x 'the cost of x'. Each node can broadcast its cost to its descendants once it knows the costs of all its possible predecessors. Let's step through the algorithm by hand. The cost of A is zero. We pass this news on to H and I. As the message passes along each edge in the graph, the cost of that edge is *added*. We find the costs of H and I are 4 and 1 respectively (figure 16.13a). Similarly then, the costs of J and L are found to be 6 and 2 respectively, but what about K? Out of the edge H–K comes the message that a path of cost 5 exists from A to K via H; and from edge I–K we learn of an alternative path of cost 3 (figure 16.13b). The min–sum algorithm sets the cost of K equal to the minimum of these (the 'min'), and records which was the smallest-cost route into K by retaining only the edge H–K and pruning away the other edges leading to K (figure 16.13c). Figure 16.13d and e show the remaining two iterations of the algorithm which reveal that there is a path from A to B with cost 6. [If the min–sum algorithm encounters a tie, where the minimum cost

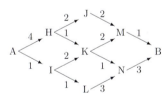

Figure 16.12. Route diagram from Ambridge to Bognor, showing the costs associated with the edges.

path to a node is achieved by more than one route to it, then the algorithm can pick any of those routes at random.]

We can recover this lowest-cost path by backtracking from B, following the trail of surviving edges back to A. We deduce that the lowest-cost path is A–I–K–M–B.

Other applications of the min–sum algorithm

Imagine that you manage the production of a product from raw materials via a large set of operations. You wish to identify the *critical path* in your process, that is, the subset of operations that are holding up production. If any operations on the critical path were carried out a little faster then the time to get from raw materials to product would be reduced.

The critical path of a set of operations can be found using the min–sum algorithm.

In Chapter 25 the min–sum algorithm will be used in the decoding of error-correcting codes.

▶ **16.4 Summary and related ideas**

Some global functions have a separability property. For example, the number of paths from A to P separates into the sum of the number of paths from A to M (the point to P's left) and the number of paths from A to N (the point above P). Such functions can be computed efficiently by message-passing. Other functions do not have such separability properties, for example

1. the number of pairs of soldiers in a troop who share the same birthday;

2. the size of the largest group of soldiers who share a common height (rounded to the nearest centimetre);

3. the length of the shortest tour that a travelling salesman could take that visits every soldier in a troop.

One of the challenges of machine learning is to find low-cost solutions to problems like these. The problem of finding a large subset variables that are approximately equal can be solved with a neural network approach (Hopfield and Brody, 2000; Hopfield and Brody, 2001). A neural approach to the travelling salesman problem will be discussed in section 42.9.

▶ **16.5 Further exercises**

▷ Exercise 16.3.[2] Describe the asymptotic properties of the probabilities depicted in figure 16.11a, for a grid in a triangle of width and height N.

▷ Exercise 16.4.[2] In image processing, the *integral image* $I(x, y)$ obtained from an image $f(x, y)$ (where x and y are pixel coordinates) is defined by

$$I(x, y) \equiv \sum_{u=0}^{x} \sum_{v=0}^{y} f(u, v). \qquad (16.1)$$

Show that the integral image $I(x, y)$ can be efficiently computed by message passing.

Show that, from the integral image, some simple functions of the image can be obtained. For example, give an expression for the sum of the image intensities $f(x, y)$ for all (x, y) in a rectangular region extending from (x_1, y_1) to (x_2, y_2).

(a)
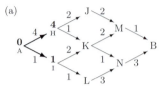

(b)
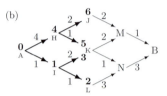

(c)
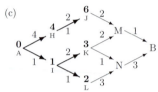

(d)
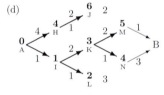

(e)
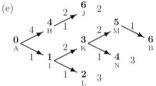

Figure 16.13. Min–sum message-passing algorithm to find the cost of getting to each node, and thence the lowest cost route from A to B.

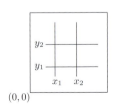

► **16.6 Solutions**

Solution to exercise 16.1 (p.244). Since there are five paths through the grid of figure 16.8, they must all have probability 1/5. But a strategy based on fair coin-flips will produce paths whose probabilities are powers of 1/2.

Solution to exercise 16.2 (p.245). To make a uniform random walk, each step of the walk should be chosen using a different biased coin at each junction, with the biases chosen in proportion to the *backward* messages emanating from the two options. For example, at the first choice after leaving A, there is a '3' message coming from the East, and a '2' coming from South, so one should go East with probability 3/5 and South with probability 2/5. This is how the path in figure 16.11 was generated.

17

Communication over Constrained
Noiseless Channels

In this chapter we study the task of communicating efficiently over a constrained noiseless channel – a constrained channel over which not all strings from the input alphabet may be transmitted.

We make use of the idea introduced in Chapter 16, that *global properties of graphs can be computed by a local message-passing algorithm.*

▶ ### 17.1 Three examples of constrained binary channels

A constrained channel can be defined by rules that define which strings are permitted.

Example 17.1. In Channel A every 1 must be followed by at least one 0.

A valid string for this channel is

$$00100101001010100010. \tag{17.1}$$

As a motivation for this model, consider a channel in which 1s are represented by pulses of electromagnetic energy, and the device that produces those pulses requires a recovery time of one clock cycle after generating a pulse before it can generate another.

Example 17.2. Channel B has the rule that all 1s must come in groups of two or more, and all 0s must come in groups of two or more.

A valid string for this channel is

$$00111001110011000011. \tag{17.2}$$

As a motivation for this model, consider a disk drive in which successive bits are written onto neighbouring points in a track along the disk surface; the values 0 and 1 are represented by two opposite magnetic orientations. The strings 101 and 010 are forbidden because a single isolated magnetic domain surrounded by domains having the opposite orientation is unstable, so that 101 might turn into 111, for example.

Example 17.3. Channel C has the rule that the largest permitted runlength is two, that is, each symbol can be repeated at most once.

A valid string for this channel is

$$10010011011001101001. \tag{17.3}$$

Channel A:
the substring 11 is forbidden.

Channel B:
101 and 010 are forbidden.

Channel C:
111 and 000 are forbidden.

A physical motivation for this model is a disk drive in which the rate of rotation of the disk is not known accurately, so it is difficult to distinguish between a string of two 1s and a string of three 1s, which are represented by oriented magnetizations of duration 2τ and 3τ respectively, where τ is the (poorly known) time taken for one bit to pass by; to avoid the possibility of confusion, and the resulting loss of synchronization of sender and receiver, we forbid the string of three 1s and the string of three 0s.

All three of these channels are examples of *runlength-limited channels*. The rules constrain the minimum and maximum numbers of successive 1s and 0s.

Channel	Runlength of 1s		Runlength of 0s	
	minimum	maximum	minimum	maximum
unconstrained	1	∞	1	∞
A	1	1	1	∞
B	2	∞	2	∞
C	1	2	1	2

In channel A, runs of 0s may be of any length but runs of 1s are restricted to length one. In channel B all runs must be of length two or more. In channel C, all runs must be of length one or two.

The capacity of the unconstrained binary channel is one bit per channel use. What are the capacities of the three constrained channels? [To be fair, we haven't defined the 'capacity' of such channels yet; please understand 'capacity' as meaning how many bits can be conveyed reliably per channel-use.]

Some codes for a constrained channel

Let us concentrate for a moment on channel A, in which runs of 0s may be of any length but runs of 1s are restricted to length one. We would like to communicate a random binary file over this channel as efficiently as possible.

A simple starting point is a $(2,1)$ code that maps each source bit into two transmitted bits, C_1. This is a rate-$^1/_2$ code, and it respects the constraints of channel A, so the capacity of channel A is at least 0.5. Can we do better?

C_1 is redundant because if the first of two received bits is a zero, we know that the second bit will also be a zero. We can achieve a smaller average transmitted length using a code that omits the redundant zeroes in C_1.

C_2 is such a *variable-length* code. If the source symbols are used with equal frequency then the average transmitted length per source bit is

$$L = \frac{1}{2}1 + \frac{1}{2}2 = \frac{3}{2}, \tag{17.4}$$

so the average communication rate is

$$R = {}^2/_3, \tag{17.5}$$

and the capacity of channel A must be at least $^2/_3$.

Can we do better than C_2? There are two ways to argue that the information rate could be increased above $R = {}^2/_3$.

The first argument assumes we are comfortable with the entropy as a measure of information content. The idea is that, starting from code C_2, we can reduce the average message length, without greatly reducing the entropy

Code C_1

s	t
0	00
1	10

Code C_2

s	t
0	0
1	10

of the message we send, by decreasing the fraction of 1s that we transmit. Imagine feeding into C_2 a stream of bits in which the frequency of 1s is f. [Such a stream could be obtained from an arbitrary binary file by passing the source file into the decoder of an arithmetic code that is optimal for compressing binary strings of density f.] The information rate R achieved is the entropy of the source, $H_2(f)$, divided by the mean transmitted length,

$$L(f) = (1 - f) + 2f = 1 + f. \tag{17.6}$$

Thus

$$R(f) = \frac{H_2(f)}{L(f)} = \frac{H_2(f)}{1 + f}. \tag{17.7}$$

The original code C_2, without preprocessor, corresponds to $f = 1/2$. What happens if we perturb f a little towards smaller f, setting

$$f = \frac{1}{2} + \delta, \tag{17.8}$$

for small negative δ? In the vicinity of $f = 1/2$, the denominator $L(f)$ varies linearly with δ. In contrast, the numerator $H_2(f)$ only has a second-order dependence on δ.

▷ **Exercise 17.4.**[1] Find, to order δ^2, the Taylor expansion of $H_2(f)$ as a function of δ.

To first order, $R(f)$ increases linearly with decreasing δ. It must be possible to increase R by decreasing f. Figure 17.1 shows these functions; $R(f)$ does indeed increase as f decreases and has a maximum of about 0.69 bits per channel use at $f \simeq 0.38$.

By this argument we have shown that the capacity of channel A is at least $\max_f R(f) = 0.69$.

▷ **Exercise 17.5.**[2, p.257] If a file containing a fraction $f = 0.5$ 1s is transmitted by C_2, what fraction of the transmitted stream is 1s?

What fraction of the transmitted bits is 1s if we drive code C_2 with a sparse source of density $f = 0.38$?

A second, more fundamental approach *counts* how many valid sequences of length N there are, S_N. We can communicate $\log S_N$ bits in N channel cycles by giving one name to each of these valid sequences.

▶ **17.2 The capacity of a constrained noiseless channel**

We defined the capacity of a noisy channel in terms of the mutual information between its input and its output, then we proved that this number, the capacity, was related to the number of distinguishable messages $S(N)$ that could be reliably conveyed over the channel in N uses of the channel by

$$C = \lim_{N \to \infty} \frac{1}{N} \log S(N). \tag{17.9}$$

In the case of the constrained noiseless channel, we can adopt this identity as our definition of the channel's capacity. However, the name s, which, when we were making codes for noisy channels (section 9.6), ran over messages $s = 1 \ldots S$, is about to take on a new role: labelling the states of our channel;

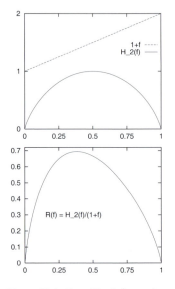

Figure 17.1. Top: The information content per source symbol and mean transmitted length per source symbol as a function of the source density. Bottom: The information content per transmitted symbol, in bits, as a function of f.

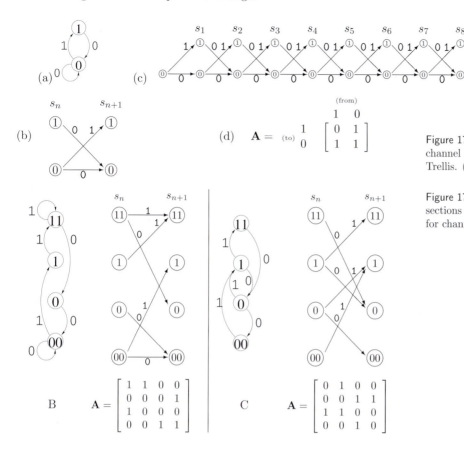

Figure 17.2. (a) State diagram for channel A. (b) Trellis section. (c) Trellis. (d) Connection matrix.

Figure 17.3. State diagrams, trellis sections and connection matrices for channels B and C.

so in this chapter we will denote the number of distinguishable messages of length N by M_N, and define the capacity to be:

$$C = \lim_{N \to \infty} \frac{1}{N} \log M_N. \tag{17.10}$$

Once we have figured out the capacity of a channel we will return to the task of making a practical code for that channel.

▶ 17.3 Counting the number of possible messages

First let us introduce some representations of constrained channels. In a *state diagram*, states of the transmitter are represented by circles labelled with the name of the state. Directed edges from one state to another indicate that the transmitter is permitted to move from the first state to the second, and a label on that edge indicates the symbol emitted when that transition is made. Figure 17.2a shows the state diagram for channel A. It has two states, 0 and 1. When transitions to state 0 are made, a 0 is transmitted; when transitions to state 1 are made, a 1 is transmitted; transitions from state 1 to state 1 are not possible.

We can also represent the state diagram by a *trellis section*, which shows two successive states in time at two successive horizontal locations (figure 17.2b). The state of the transmitter at time n is called s_n. The set of possible state sequences can be represented by a *trellis* as shown in figure 17.2c. A valid sequence corresponds to a path through the trellis, and the number of

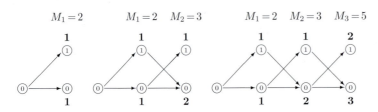

Figure 17.4. Counting the number of paths in the trellis of channel A. The counts next to the nodes are accumulated by passing from left to right across the trellises.

(a) Channel A

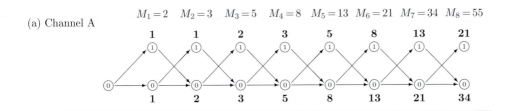

(b) Channel B

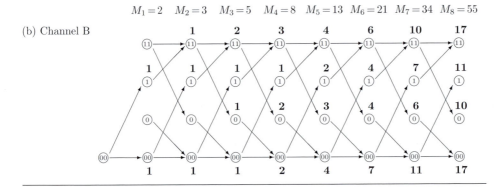

(c) Channel C

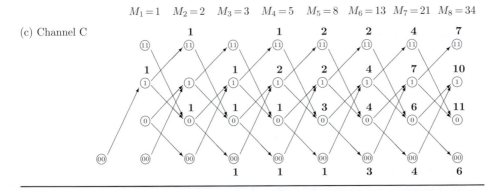

Figure 17.5. Counting the number of paths in the trellises of channels A, B, and C. We assume that at the start the first bit is preceded by 00, so that for channels A and B, any initial character is permitted, but for channel C, the first character must be a 1.

n	M_n	M_n/M_{n-1}	$\log_2 M_n$	$\frac{1}{n}\log_2 M_n$
1	2		1.0	1.00
2	3	1.500	1.6	0.79
3	5	1.667	2.3	0.77
4	8	1.600	3.0	0.75
5	13	1.625	3.7	0.74
6	21	1.615	4.4	0.73
7	34	1.619	5.1	0.73
8	55	1.618	5.8	0.72
9	89	1.618	6.5	0.72
10	144	1.618	7.2	0.72
11	233	1.618	7.9	0.71
12	377	1.618	8.6	0.71
100	9×10^{20}	1.618	69.7	0.70
200	7×10^{41}	1.618	139.1	0.70
300	6×10^{62}	1.618	208.5	0.70
400	5×10^{83}	1.618	277.9	0.69

Figure 17.6. Counting the number of paths in the trellis of channel A.

valid sequences is the number of paths. For the purpose of counting how many paths there are through the trellis, we can ignore the labels on the edges and summarize the trellis section by the *connection matrix* $\mathbf{A}$, in which $A_{ss'} = 1$ if there is an edge from state s to s', and $A_{ss'} = 0$ otherwise (figure 17.2d). Figure 17.3 shows the state diagrams, trellis sections and connection matrices for channels B and C.

Let's count the number of paths for channel A by message-passing in its trellis. Figure 17.4 shows the first few steps of this counting process, and figure 17.5a shows the number of paths ending in each state after n steps for $n = 1 \ldots 8$. The total number of paths of length n, M_n, is shown along the top. We recognize M_n as the Fibonacci series.

▷ Exercise 17.6.[1] Show that the ratio of successive terms in the Fibonacci series tends to the golden ratio,

$$\gamma \equiv \frac{1 + \sqrt{5}}{2} = 1.618. \qquad (17.11)$$

Thus, to within a constant factor, M_N scales as $M_N \sim \gamma^N$ as $N \to \infty$, so the capacity of channel A is

$$C = \lim \frac{1}{N} \log_2 \left[\text{constant} \cdot \gamma^N \right] = \log_2 \gamma = \log_2 1.618 = 0.694. \qquad (17.12)$$

How can we describe what we just did? The count of the number of paths is a vector $\mathbf{c}^{(n)}$; we can obtain $\mathbf{c}^{(n+1)}$ from $\mathbf{c}^{(n)}$ using:

$$\mathbf{c}^{(n+1)} = \mathbf{A}\mathbf{c}^{(n)}. \qquad (17.13)$$

So

$$\mathbf{c}^{(N)} = \mathbf{A}^N \mathbf{c}^{(0)}, \qquad (17.14)$$

where $\mathbf{c}^{(0)}$ is the state count before any symbols are transmitted. In figure 17.5 we assumed $\mathbf{c}^{(0)} = [0, 1]^\mathsf{T}$, i.e., that either of the two symbols is permitted at the outset. The total number of paths is $M_n = \sum_s c_s^{(n)} = \mathbf{c}^{(n)} \cdot \mathbf{n}$. In the limit, $\mathbf{c}^{(N)}$ becomes dominated by the principal right-eigenvector of $\mathbf{A}$.

$$\mathbf{c}^{(N)} \to \text{constant} \cdot \lambda_1^N \mathbf{e}_\mathsf{R}^{(0)}. \qquad (17.15)$$

Here, λ_1 is the principal eigenvalue of $\mathbf{A}$.

So to find the capacity of any constrained channel, all we need to do is find the principal eigenvalue, λ_1 of its connection matrix. Then

$$C = \log_2 \lambda_1. \tag{17.16}$$

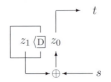

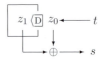

Figure 17.7. An accumulator and a differentiator.

▶ 17.4 Back to our model channels

Comparing figure 17.5a and figure 17.5b and c it looks as if channels B and C have the same capacity as channel A. The principal eigenvalues of the three trellises are the same (the eigenvectors for channels A and B are given at the bottom of table C.4, p.608). And indeed the channels are intimately related.

Equivalence of channels A and B

If we take any valid string $\mathbf{s}$ for channel A and pass it through an *accumulator*, obtaining $\mathbf{t}$ defined by:

$$\begin{aligned} t_1 &= s_1 \\ t_n &= t_{n-1} + s_n \bmod 2 \quad \text{for } n \geq 2, \end{aligned} \tag{17.17}$$

then the resulting string is a valid string for channel B, because there are no 11s in $\mathbf{s}$, so there are no isolated digits in $\mathbf{t}$. The accumulator is an invertible operator, so, similarly, any valid string $\mathbf{t}$ for channel B can be mapped onto a valid string $\mathbf{s}$ for channel A through the *binary differentiator*,

$$\begin{aligned} s_1 &= t_1 \\ s_n &= t_n - t_{n-1} \bmod 2 \quad \text{for } n \geq 2. \end{aligned} \tag{17.18}$$

Because $+$ and $-$ are equivalent in modulo 2 arithmetic, the differentiator is also a blurrer, convolving the source stream with the filter $(1, 1)$.

Channel C is also intimately related to channels A and B.

▷ Exercise 17.7.[1, p.257] What is the relationship of channel C to channels A and B?

▶ 17.5 Practical communication over constrained channels

OK, how to do it in practice? Since all three channels are equivalent, we can concentrate on channel A.

Fixed-length solutions

We start with explicitly-enumerated codes. The code in the table 17.8 achieves a rate of $3/5 = 0.6$.

s	$c(s)$
1	00000
2	10000
3	01000
4	00100
5	00010
6	10100
7	01010
8	10010

Table 17.8. A runlength-limited code for channel A.

▷ Exercise 17.8.[1, p.257] Similarly, enumerate all strings of length 8 that end in the zero state. (There are 34 of them.) Hence show that we can map 5 bits (32 source strings) to 8 transmitted bits and achieve rate $5/8 = 0.625$.

What rate can be achieved by mapping an integer number of source bits to $N = 16$ transmitted bits?

Optimal variable-length solution

The optimal way to convey information over the constrained channel is to find the optimal transition probabilities for all points in the trellis, $Q_{s'|s}$, and make transitions with these probabilities.

When discussing channel A, we showed that a sparse source with density $f = 0.38$, driving code C_2, would achieve capacity. And we know how to make sparsifiers (Chapter 6): we design an arithmetic code that is optimal for compressing a sparse source; then its associated decoder gives an optimal mapping from dense (i.e., random binary) strings to sparse strings.

The task of finding the optimal probabilities is given as an exercise.

Exercise 17.9.[3] Show that the optimal transition probabilities $\mathbf{Q}$ can be found as follows.

Find the principal right- and left-eigenvectors of $\mathbf{A}$, that is the solutions of $\mathbf{A}\mathbf{e}^{(R)} = \lambda\mathbf{e}^{(R)}$ and $\mathbf{e}^{(L)^{\mathsf{T}}}\mathbf{A} = \lambda\mathbf{e}^{(L)^{\mathsf{T}}}$ with largest eigenvalue λ. Then construct a matrix $\mathbf{Q}$ whose invariant distribution is proportional to $e_i^{(R)}e_i^{(L)}$, namely

$$Q_{s'|s} = \frac{e_{s'}^{(L)}A_{s's}}{\lambda e_s^{(L)}}. \tag{17.19}$$

[Hint: exercise 16.2 (p.245) might give helpful cross-fertilization here.]

▷ Exercise 17.10.[3, p.258] Show that when sequences are generated using the optimal transition probability matrix (17.19), the entropy of the resulting sequence is asymptotically $\log_2 \lambda$ per symbol. [Hint: consider the conditional entropy of just one symbol given the previous one, assuming the previous one's distribution is the invariant distribution.]

In practice, we would probably use finite-precision approximations to the optimal variable-length solution. One might dislike variable-length solutions because of the resulting unpredictability of the actual encoded length in any particular case. Perhaps in some applications we would like a guarantee that the encoded length of a source file of size N bits will be less than a given length such as $N/(C + \epsilon)$. For example, a disk drive is easier to control if all blocks of 512 bytes are known to take exactly the same amount of disk real-estate. For some constrained channels we can make a simple modification to our variable-length encoding and offer such a guarantee, as follows. We find two codes, two mappings of binary strings to variable-length encodings, having the property that for any source string $\mathbf{x}$, if the encoding of $\mathbf{x}$ under the first code is shorter than average, then the encoding of $\mathbf{x}$ under the second code is longer than average, and *vice versa*. Then to transmit a string $\mathbf{x}$ we encode the whole string with both codes and send whichever encoding has the shortest length, prepended by a suitably encoded single bit to convey which of the two codes is being used.

▷ Exercise 17.11.[3C, p.258] How many valid sequences of length 8 starting with a 0 are there for the run-length-limited channels shown in figure 17.9?

What are the capacities of these channels?

Using a computer, find the matrices $\mathbf{Q}$ for generating a random path through the trellises of the channel A, and the two run-length-limited channels shown in figure 17.9.

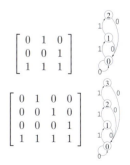

Figure 17.9. State diagrams and connection matrices for channels with maximum runlengths for 1s equal to 2 and 3.

▷ Exercise 17.12.[3, p.258] Consider the run-length-limited channel in which any length of run of 0s is permitted, and the maximum run length of 1s is a large number L such as nine or ninety.

Estimate the capacity of this channel. (Give the first two terms in a series expansion involving L.)

What, roughly, is the form of the optimal matrix $\mathbf{Q}$ for generating a random path through the trellis of this channel? Focus on the values of the elements $Q_{1|0}$, the probability of generating a 1 given a preceding 0, and $Q_{L|L-1}$, the probability of generating a 1 given a preceding run of $L-1$ 1s. Check your answer by explicit computation for the channel in which the maximum runlength of 1s is nine.

▶ 17.6 Variable symbol durations

We can add a further frill to the task of communicating over constrained channels by assuming that the symbols we send have different *durations*, and that our aim is to communicate at the maximum possible rate per unit time. Such channels can come in two flavours: unconstrained, and constrained.

Unconstrained channels with variable symbol durations

We encountered an unconstrained noiseless channel with variable symbol durations in exercise 6.18 (p.125). Solve that problem, and you've done this topic. The task is to determine the optimal frequencies with which the symbols should be used, given their durations.

    There is a nice analogy between this task and the task of designing an optimal symbol code (Chapter 4). When we make an binary symbol code for a source with unequal probabilities p_i, the optimal message lengths are $l_i^* = \log_2 1/p_i$, so

$$p_i = 2^{-l_i^*}. \tag{17.20}$$

Similarly, when we have a channel whose symbols have durations l_i (in some units of time), the optimal probability with which those symbols should be used is

$$p_i^* = 2^{-\beta l_i}, \tag{17.21}$$

where β is the capacity of the channel in bits per unit time.

Constrained channels with variable symbol durations

Once you have grasped the preceding topics in this chapter, you should be able to figure out how to define and find the capacity of these, the trickiest constrained channels.

Exercise 17.13.[3] A classic example of a constrained channel with variable symbol durations is the 'Morse' channel, whose symbols are

the dot	d,
the dash	D,
the short space (used between letters in morse code)	s, and
the long space (used between words)	S;

the constraints are that spaces may only be followed by dots and dashes.

Find the capacity of this channel in bits per unit time assuming (a) that all four symbols have equal durations; or (b) that the symbol durations are 2, 4, 3 and 6 time units respectively.

Exercise 17.14.[4] How well-designed is Morse code for English (with, say, the probability distribution of figure 2.1)?

Exercise 17.15.[3C] How difficult is it to get DNA into a narrow tube?

To an information theorist, the entropy associated with a constrained channel reveals how much information can be conveyed over it. In statistical physics, the same calculations are done for a different reason: to predict the thermodynamics of polymers, for example.

As a toy example, consider a polymer of length N that can either sit in a constraining tube, of width L, or in the open where there are no constraints. In the open, the polymer adopts a state drawn at random from the set of one dimensional random walks, with, say, 3 possible directions per step. The entropy of this walk is $\log 3$ per step, i.e., a total of $N \log 3$. [The free energy of the polymer is defined to be kT times this, where T is the temperature.] In the tube, the polymer's one-dimensional walk can go in 3 directions unless the wall is in the way, so the trellis section is, for example (if $L = 10$),

$$\begin{bmatrix} 1 & 1 & 0 & 0 & 0 & 0 & 0 & 0 & 0 & 0 \\ 1 & 1 & 1 & 0 & 0 & 0 & 0 & 0 & 0 & 0 \\ 0 & 1 & 1 & 1 & 0 & 0 & 0 & 0 & 0 & 0 \\ 0 & 0 & 1 & 1 & 1 & 0 & 0 & 0 & 0 & 0 \\ 0 & 0 & 0 & 1 & 1 & 1 & 0 & 0 & 0 & 0 \\ & & & \ddots & \ddots & \ddots & & & & \\ 0 & 0 & 0 & 0 & 0 & 0 & 0 & 1 & 1 & 1 \\ 0 & 0 & 0 & 0 & 0 & 0 & 0 & 0 & 1 & 1 \end{bmatrix}.$$

Now, what is the entropy of the polymer? What is the *change* in entropy associated with the polymer entering the tube? If possible, obtain an expression as a function of L. Use a computer to find the entropy of the walk for a particular value of L, e.g. 20, and plot the probability density of the polymer's transverse location in the tube.

Notice the difference in capacity between two channels, one constrained and one unconstrained, is directly proportional to the force required to pull the DNA into the tube.

Figure 17.10. Model of DNA squashed in a narrow tube. The DNA will have a tendency to pop out of the tube, because, outside the tube, its random walk has greater entropy.

▶ 17.7 Solutions

Solution to exercise 17.5 (p.250). A file transmitted by C_2 contains, on average, one-third 1s and two-thirds 0s.

If $f = 0.38$, the fraction of 1s is $f/(1+f) = (\gamma - 1.0)/(2\gamma - 1.0) = 0.2764$.

Solution to exercise 17.7 (p.254). A valid string for channel C can be obtained from a valid string for channel A by first inverting it $[1 \to 0;\ 0 \to 1]$, then passing it through an accumulator. These operations are invertible, so any valid string for C can also be mapped onto a valid string for A. The only proviso here comes from the edge effects. If we assume that the first character transmitted over channel C is preceded by a string of zeroes, so that the first character is forced to be a 1 (figure 17.5c) then the two channels are exactly equivalent only if we assume that channel A's first character must be a zero.

Solution to exercise 17.8 (p.254). With $N = 16$ transmitted bits, the largest integer number of source bits that can encoded is 10, so the maximum rate of a fixed length code with $N = 16$ is 0.625.

Solution to exercise 17.10 (p.255).   Let the invariant distribution be

$$P(s) = \alpha e_s^{(L)} e_s^{(R)}, \tag{17.22}$$

where α is a normalization constant. The entropy of S_t given S_{t-1}, assuming S_{t-1} comes from the invariant distribution, is

Here, as in Chapter 4, S_t denotes the ensemble whose random variable is the state s_t.

$$
\begin{aligned}
H(S_t|S_{t-1}) &= -\sum_{s,s'} P(s)P(s'|s) \log P(s'|s) \tag{17.23}\\
&= -\sum_{s,s'} \alpha e_s^{(L)} e_s^{(R)} \frac{e_{s'}^{(L)} A_{s's}}{\lambda e_s^{(L)}} \log \frac{e_{s'}^{(L)} A_{s's}}{\lambda e_s^{(L)}} \tag{17.24}\\
&= -\sum_{s,s'} \alpha \, e_s^{(R)} \frac{e_{s'}^{(L)} A_{s's}}{\lambda} \left[\log e_{s'}^{(L)} + \log A_{s's} - \log \lambda - \log e_s^{(L)} \right]. \tag{17.25}
\end{aligned}
$$

Now, $A_{s's}$ is either 0 or 1, so the contributions from the terms proportional to $A_{s's} \log A_{s's}$ are all zero. So

$$
\begin{aligned}
H(S_t|S_{t-1}) &= \log \lambda + -\frac{\alpha}{\lambda} \sum_{s'} \left(\sum_s A_{s's} e_s^{(R)} \right) e_{s'}^{(L)} \log e_{s'}^{(L)} + \\
&\quad \frac{\alpha}{\lambda} \sum_s \left(\sum_{s'} e_{s'}^{(L)} A_{s's} \right) e_s^{(R)} \log e_s^{(L)} \tag{17.26}\\
&= \log \lambda - \frac{\alpha}{\lambda} \sum_{s'} \lambda e_{s'}^{(R)} e_{s'}^{(L)} \log e_{s'}^{(L)} + \frac{\alpha}{\lambda} \sum_s \lambda e_s^{(L)} e_s^{(R)} \log e_s^{(L)} \tag{17.27}\\
&= \log \lambda. \tag{17.28}
\end{aligned}
$$

Solution to exercise 17.11 (p.255).   The principal eigenvalues of the connection matrices of the two channels are 1.839 and 1.928. The capacities ($\log \lambda$) are 0.879 and 0.947 bits.

Solution to exercise 17.12 (p.256).   The channel is similar to the unconstrained binary channel; runs of length greater than L are rare if L is large, so we only expect weak differences from this channel; these differences will show up in contexts where the run length is close to L. The capacity of the channel is very close to one bit.

A lower bound on the capacity is obtained by considering the simple variable-length code for this channel which replaces occurrences of the maximum runlength string 111...1 by 111...10, and otherwise leaves the source file unchanged. The average rate of this code is $1/(1+2^{-L})$ because the invariant distribution will hit the 'add an extra zero' state a fraction 2^{-L} of the time.

We can reuse the solution for the variable-length channel in exercise 6.18 (p.125). The capacity is the value of β such that the equation

$$Z(\beta) = \sum_{l=1}^{L+1} 2^{-\beta l} = 1 \tag{17.29}$$

is satisfied. The $L+1$ terms in the sum correspond to the $L+1$ possible strings that can be emitted, 0, 10, 110, ... , 11...10. The sum is exactly given by:

$$Z(\beta) = 2^{-\beta} \frac{\left(2^{-\beta}\right)^{L+1} - 1}{2^{-\beta} - 1}. \tag{17.30}$$

$$\left[\text{Here we used } \sum_{n=0}^{N} ar^n = \frac{a(r^{N+1} - 1)}{r - 1}.\right]$$

We anticipate that β should be a little less than 1 in order for $Z(\beta)$ to equal 1. Rearranging and solving approximately for β, using $\ln(1 + x) \simeq x$,

$$Z(\beta) = 1 \tag{17.31}$$
$$\Rightarrow \beta \simeq 1 - 2^{-(L+2)}/\ln 2. \tag{17.32}$$

We evaluated the true capacities for $L = 2$ and $L = 3$ in an earlier exercise. The table compares the approximate capacity β with the true capacity for a selection of values of L.

L	β	True capacity
2	0.910	0.879
3	0.955	0.947
4	0.977	0.975
5	0.9887	0.9881
6	0.9944	0.9942
9	0.9993	0.9993

The element $Q_{1|0}$ will be close to $1/2$ (just a tiny bit larger), since in the unconstrained binary channel $Q_{1|0} = 1/2$. When a run of length $L - 1$ has occurred, we effectively have a choice of printing 10 or 0. Let the probability of selecting 10 be f. Let us estimate the entropy of the *remaining* N characters in the stream as a function of f, assuming the rest of the matrix $\mathbf{Q}$ to have been set to its optimal value. The entropy of the next N characters in the stream is the entropy of the first bit, $H_2(f)$, plus the entropy of the remaining characters, which is roughly $(N-1)$ bits if we select 0 as the first bit and $(N-2)$ bits if 1 is selected. More precisely, if C is the capacity of the channel (which is roughly 1),

$$H(\text{the next } N \text{ chars}) \simeq H_2(f) + [(N - 1)(1 - f) + (N - 2)f]\, C$$
$$= H_2(f) + NC - fC \simeq H_2(f) + N - f. \tag{17.33}$$

Differentiating and setting to zero to find the optimal f, we obtain:

$$\log_2 \frac{1 - f}{f} \simeq 1 \;\Rightarrow\; \frac{1 - f}{f} \simeq 2 \;\Rightarrow f \simeq 1/3. \tag{17.34}$$

The probability of emitting a 1 thus decreases from about 0.5 to about $1/3$ as the number of emitted 1s increases.

Here is the optimal matrix:

$$\begin{bmatrix}
0 & .3334 & 0 & 0 & 0 & 0 & 0 & 0 & 0 \\
0 & 0 & .4287 & 0 & 0 & 0 & 0 & 0 & 0 \\
0 & 0 & 0 & .4669 & 0 & 0 & 0 & 0 & 0 \\
0 & 0 & 0 & 0 & .4841 & 0 & 0 & 0 & 0 \\
0 & 0 & 0 & 0 & 0 & .4923 & 0 & 0 & 0 \\
0 & 0 & 0 & 0 & 0 & 0 & .4963 & 0 & 0 \\
0 & 0 & 0 & 0 & 0 & 0 & 0 & .4983 & 0 \\
0 & 0 & 0 & 0 & 0 & 0 & 0 & 0 & .4993 & 0 \\
0 & 0 & 0 & 0 & 0 & 0 & 0 & 0 & 0 & .4998 \\
1 & .6666 & .5713 & .5331 & .5159 & .5077 & .5037 & .5017 & .5007 & .5002
\end{bmatrix}. \tag{17.35}$$

Our rough theory works.

18

Crosswords and Codebreaking

In this chapter we make a random walk through a few topics related to language modelling.

▶ 18.1 Crosswords

The rules of crossword-making may be thought of as defining a constrained channel. The fact that *many* valid crosswords can be made demonstrates that this constrained channel has a capacity greater than zero.

There are two archetypal crossword formats. In a 'type A' (or American) crossword, every row and column consists of a succession of words of length 2 or more separated by one or more spaces. In a 'type B' (or British) crossword, each row and column consists of a mixture of words and single characters, separated by one or more spaces, and every character lies in at least one word (horizontal or vertical). Whereas in a type A crossword every letter lies in a horizontal word *and* a vertical word, in a typical type B crossword only about half of the letters do so; the other half lie in one word only.

Type A crosswords are harder to *create* than type B because of the constraint that no single characters are permitted. Type B crosswords are generally harder to *solve* because there are fewer constraints per character.

Why are crosswords possible?

If a language has no redundancy, then any letters written on a grid form a valid crossword. In a language with high redundancy, on the other hand, it is hard to make crosswords (except perhaps a small number of trivial ones). The possibility of making crosswords in a language thus demonstrates a *bound on the redundancy* of that language. Crosswords are not normally written in genuine English. They are written in 'word-English', the language consisting of strings of words from a dictionary, separated by spaces.

▷ Exercise 18.1.[2] Estimate the capacity of word-English, in bits per character. [Hint: think of word-English as defining a constrained channel (Chapter 17) and see exercise 6.18 (p.125).]

The fact that many crosswords can be made leads to a lower bound on the entropy of word-English.

For simplicity, we now model word-English by Wenglish, the language introduced in section 4.1 which consists of W words all of length L. The entropy of such a language, per character, including inter-word spaces, is:

$$H_W \equiv \frac{\log_2 W}{L + 1}. \tag{18.1}$$

Figure 18.1. Crosswords of types A (American) and B (British).

260

We'll find that the conclusions we come to depend on the value of H_W and are not terribly sensitive to the value of L. Consider a large crossword of size S squares in area. Let the number of words be $f_w S$ and let the number of letter-occupied squares be $f_1 S$. For typical crosswords of types A and B made of words of length L, the two fractions f_w and f_1 have roughly the values in table 18.2.

We now estimate how many crosswords there are of size S using our simple model of Wenglish. We assume that Wenglish is created at random by generating W strings from a monogram (i.e., memoryless) source with entropy H_0. If, for example, the source used all $A = 26$ characters with equal probability then $H_0 = \log_2 A = 4.7$ bits. If instead we use Chapter 2's distribution then the entropy is 4.2. The redundancy of Wenglish stems from two sources: it tends to use some letters more than others; and there are only W words in the dictionary.

Let's now count how many crosswords there are by imagining filling in the squares of a crossword at random using the same distribution that produced the Wenglish dictionary and evaluating the probability that this random scribbling produces valid words in all rows and columns. The total number of *typical* fillings-in of the $f_1 S$ squares in the crossword that can be made is

$$|T| = 2^{f_1 S H_0}. \tag{18.2}$$

The probability that one word of length L is validly filled in is

$$\beta = \frac{W}{2^{L H_0}}, \tag{18.3}$$

and the probability that the whole crossword, made of $f_w S$ words, is validly filled in by a single typical in-filling is

$$\beta^{f_w S}. \tag{18.4}$$

So the log of the number of valid crosswords of size S is estimated to be

$$
\begin{aligned}
\log \beta^{f_w S} |T| &= S\left[(f_1 - f_w L)H_0 + f_w \log W\right] \log \beta^{f_w S} |T| \tag{18.5} \\
&= S\left[(f_1 - f_w L)H_0 + f_w (L+1) H_w\right] \tag{18.6}
\end{aligned}
$$

which is an increasing function of S only if

$$(f_1 - f_w L)H_0 + f_w (L+1) H_w > 0. \tag{18.7}$$

So arbitrarily many crosswords can be made only if there's enough words in the Wenglish dictionary that

$$H_W > \frac{(f_w L - f_1)}{f_w (L+1)} H_0. \tag{18.8}$$

Plugging in the values of f_1 and f_w from previous page, we find the following.

Crossword type	A	B
Condition for crosswords	$H_W > \frac{1}{2}\frac{L}{L+1}H_0$	$H_W > \frac{1}{4}\frac{L}{L+1}H_0$

If we set $H_0 = 4.2$ bits and assume there are $W = 4000$ words in a normal English-speaker's dictionary, all with length $L = 5$, then we find that the condition for crosswords of type B is satisfied, but the condition for crosswords of type A is *only just* satisfied. This fits with my experience that crosswords of type A usually contain more obscure words.

	A	B
f_w	$\dfrac{2}{L+1}$	$\dfrac{1}{L+1}$
f_1	$\dfrac{L}{L+1}$	$\dfrac{3}{4}\dfrac{L}{L+1}$

Table 18.2. Factors f_w and f_1 by which the number of words and number of letter-squares respectively are smaller than the total number of squares.

Further reading

These observations about crosswords were first made by Shannon (1948); I learned about them from Wolf and Siegel (1998). The topic is closely related to the capacity of two-dimensional constrained channels. An example of a two-dimensional constrained channel is a two-dimensional bar-code, as seen on parcels.

Exercise 18.2.[3] A two-dimensional channel is defined by the constraint that, of the eight neighbours of every interior pixel in an $N \times N$ rectangular grid, four must be black and four white. (The counts of black and white pixels around boundary pixels are not constrained.) A binary pattern satisfying this constraint is shown in figure 18.3. What is the capacity of this channel, in bits per pixel, for large N?

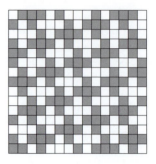

Figure 18.3. A binary pattern in which every pixel is adjacent to four black and four white pixels.

▶ ## 18.2 Simple language models

The Zipf–Mandelbrot distribution

The crudest model for a language is the monogram model, which asserts that each successive word is drawn independently from a distribution over words. What is the nature of this distribution over words?

  Zipf's law (Zipf, 1949) asserts that the probability of the rth most probable word in a language is approximately

$$P(r) = \frac{\kappa}{r^\alpha}, \qquad (18.9)$$

where the exponent α has a value close to 1, and κ is a constant. According to Zipf, a log–log plot of frequency versus word-rank should show a straight line with slope $-\alpha$.

  Mandelbrot's (1982) modification of Zipf's law introduces a third parameter v, asserting that the probabilities are given by

$$P(r) = \frac{\kappa}{(r+v)^\alpha}. \qquad (18.10)$$

For some documents, such as Jane Austen's *Emma*, the Zipf–Mandelbrot distribution fits well – figure 18.4.

  Other documents give distributions that are not so well fitted by a Zipf–Mandelbrot distribution. Figure 18.5 shows a plot of frequency versus rank for the LaTeX source of this book. Qualitatively, the graph is similar to a straight line, but a curve is noticeable. To be fair, this source file is not written in pure English – it is a mix of English, maths symbols such as 'x', and LaTeX commands.

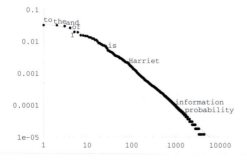

Figure 18.4. Fit of the Zipf–Mandelbrot distribution (18.10) (curve) to the empirical frequencies of words in Jane Austen's *Emma* (dots). The fitted parameters are $\kappa = 0.56$; $v = 8.0$; $\alpha = 1.26$.

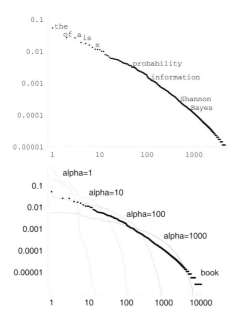

Figure 18.5. Log–log plot of frequency versus rank for the words in the LaTeX file of this book.

Figure 18.6. Zipf plots for four 'languages' randomly generated from Dirichlet processes with parameter α ranging from 1 to 1000. Also shown is the Zipf plot for this book.

The Dirichlet process

Assuming we are interested in monogram models for languages, what model should we use? One difficulty in modelling a language is the unboundedness of vocabulary. The greater the sample of language, the greater the number of words encountered. A generative model for a language should emulate this property. If asked 'what is the next word in a newly-discovered work of Shakespeare?' our probability distribution over words must surely include some non-zero probability for *words that Shakespeare never used before*. Our generative monogram model for language should also satisfy a consistency rule called *exchangeability*. If we imagine generating a new language from our generative model, producing an ever-growing corpus of text, all statistical properties of the text should be homogeneous: the probability of finding a particular word at a given location in the stream of text should be the same everywhere in the stream.

The Dirichlet process model is a model for a stream of symbols (which we think of as 'words') that satisfies the exchangeability rule and that allows the vocabulary of symbols to grow without limit. The model has one parameter α. As the stream of symbols is produced, we identify each new symbol by a unique integer w. When we have seen a stream of length F symbols, we define the probability of the next symbol in terms of the counts $\{F_w\}$ of the symbols seen so far thus: the probability that the next symbol is a new symbol, never seen before, is

$$\frac{\alpha}{F + \alpha}.$$ (18.11)

The probability that the next symbol is symbol w is

$$\frac{F_w}{F + \alpha}.$$ (18.12)

Figure 18.6 shows Zipf plots (i.e., plots of symbol frequency versus rank) for million-symbol 'documents' generated by Dirichlet process priors with values of α ranging from 1 to 1000.

It is evident that a Dirichlet process is not an adequate model for observed distributions that roughly obey Zipf's law.

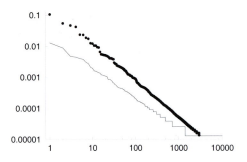

Figure 18.7. Zipf plots for the words of two 'languages' generated by creating successive characters from a Dirichlet process with $\alpha = 2$, and declaring one character to be the space character. The two curves result from two different choices of the space character.

With a small tweak, however, Dirichlet processes can produce rather nice Zipf plots. Imagine generating a language composed of elementary symbols using a Dirichlet process with a rather small value of the parameter α, so that the number of reasonably frequent symbols is about 27. If we then declare one of those symbols (now called 'characters' rather than words) to be a space character, then we can identify the strings between the space characters as 'words'. If we generate a language in this way then the frequencies of words often come out as very nice Zipf plots, as shown in figure 18.7. Which character is selected as the space character determines the slope of the Zipf plot – a less probable space character gives rise to a richer language with a shallower slope.

▶ 18.3 Units of information content

The information content of an outcome, x, whose probability is $P(x)$, is defined to be

$$h(x) = \log \frac{1}{P(x)}. \tag{18.13}$$

The entropy of an ensemble is an average information content,

$$H(X) = \sum_x P(x) \log \frac{1}{P(x)}. \tag{18.14}$$

When we compare hypotheses with each other in the light of data, it is often convenient to compare the log of the probability of the data under the alternative hypotheses,

$$\text{'log evidence for } \mathcal{H}_i\text{'} = \log P(D|\mathcal{H}_i), \tag{18.15}$$

or, in the case where just two hypotheses are being compared, we evaluate the 'log odds',

$$\log \frac{P(D|\mathcal{H}_1)}{P(D|\mathcal{H}_2)}, \tag{18.16}$$

which has also been called the 'weight of evidence in favour of $\mathcal{H}_1$'. The log evidence for a hypothesis, $\log P(D|\mathcal{H}_i)$ is the negative of the information content of the data D: if the data have large information content, given a hypothesis, then they are surprising to that hypothesis; if some other hypothesis is not so surprised by the data, then that hypothesis becomes more probable. 'Information content', 'surprise value', and log likelihood or log evidence are the same thing.

All these quantities are logarithms of probabilities, or weighted sums of logarithms of probabilities, so they can all be measured in the same units. The units depend on the choice of the base of the logarithm.

The names that have been given to these units are shown in table 18.8.

Unit	Expression that has those units
bit	$\log_2 p$
nat	$\log_e p$
ban	$\log_{10} p$
deciban (db)	$10 \log_{10} p$

Table 18.8. Units of measurement of information content.

The *bit* is the unit that we use most in this book. Because the word 'bit' has other meanings, a backup name for this unit is the *shannon*. A *byte* is 8 bits. A megabyte is $2^{20} \simeq 10^6$ bytes. If one works in natural logarithms, information contents and weights of evidence are measured in *nats*. The most interesting units are the *ban* and the *deciban*.

The history of the ban

Let me tell you why a factor of ten in probability is called a ban. When Alan Turing and the other codebreakers at Bletchley Park were breaking each new day's Enigma code, their task was a huge inference problem: to infer, given the day's cyphertext, which three wheels were in the Enigma machines that day; what their starting positions were; what further letter substitutions were in use on the steckerboard; and, not least, what the original German messages were. These inferences were conducted using Bayesian methods (of course!), and the chosen units were decibans or half-decibans, the deciban being judged the smallest weight of evidence discernible to a human. The evidence in favour of particular hypotheses was tallied using sheets of paper that were specially printed in Banbury, a town about 30 miles from Bletchley. The inference task was known as Banburismus, and the units in which Banburismus was played were called bans, after that town.

▶ 18.4 A taste of Banburismus

The details of the code-breaking methods of Bletchley Park were kept secret for a long time, but some aspects of Banburismus can be pieced together. I hope the following description of a small part of Banburismus is not too inaccurate.[1]

How much information was needed? The number of possible settings of the Enigma machine was about 8×10^{12}. To deduce the state of the machine, 'it was therefore necessary to find about 129 decibans from somewhere', as Good puts it. Banburismus was aimed not at deducing the entire state of the machine, but only at figuring out which wheels were in use; the logic-based bombes, fed with guesses of the plaintext (cribs), were then used to crack what the settings of the wheels were.

The Enigma machine, once its wheels and plugs were put in place, implemented a continually-changing permutation cypher that wandered deterministically through a state space of 26^3 permutations. Because an enormous number of messages were sent each day, there was a good chance that whatever state one machine was in when sending one character of a message, there would be another machine *in the same state* while sending a particular character in another message. Because the evolution of the machine's state was deterministic, the two machines would remain in same state as each other

---

[1] I've been most helped by descriptions given by Tony Sale (`http://www.codesandciphers.org.uk/lectures/`) and by Jack Good (1979), who worked with Turing at Bletchley.

for the rest of the transmission. The resulting correlations between the outputs of such pairs of machines provided a dribble of information-content from
which Turing and his co-workers extracted their daily 129 decibans.

How to detect that two messages came from machines with a common state sequence

The hypotheses are the null hypothesis, $\mathcal{H}_0$, which states that the machines
are in *different* states, and that the two plain messages are unrelated; and the
'match' hypothesis, $\mathcal{H}_1$, which says that the machines are in the *same* state,
and that the two plain messages are unrelated. No attempt is being made
here to infer what the state of either machine is. The data provided are the
two cyphertexts $\mathbf{x}$ and $\mathbf{y}$; let's assume they both have length T and that the
alphabet size is A (26 in Enigma). What is the probability of the data, given
the two hypotheses?

First, the null hypothesis. This hypothesis asserts that the two cyphertexts
are given by

$$\mathbf{x} = x_1 x_2 x_3 \ldots = c_1(u_1)c_2(u_2)c_3(u_3)\ldots \tag{18.17}$$

and

$$\mathbf{y} = y_1 y_2 y_3 \ldots = c_1'(v_1)c_2'(v_2)c_3'(v_3)\ldots, \tag{18.18}$$

where the codes c_t and c_t' are two unrelated time-varying permutations of the
alphabet, and $u_1 u_2 u_3 \ldots$ and $v_1 v_2 v_3 \ldots$ are the plaintext messages. An exact
computation of the probability of the data $(\mathbf{x}, \mathbf{y})$ would depend on a language
model of the plain text, and a model of the Enigma machine's guts, but if we
assume that each Enigma machine is an *ideal* random time-varying permutation, then the probability distribution of the two cyphertexts is uniform. All
cyphertexts are equally likely.

$$P(\mathbf{x}, \mathbf{y} | \mathcal{H}_0) = \left(\frac{1}{A}\right)^{2T} \quad \text{for all } \mathbf{x}, \mathbf{y} \text{ of length } T. \tag{18.19}$$

What about $\mathcal{H}_1$? This hypothesis asserts that a *single* time-varying permutation c_t underlies both

$$\mathbf{x} = x_1 x_2 x_3 \ldots = c_1(u_1)c_2(u_2)c_3(u_3)\ldots \tag{18.20}$$

and

$$\mathbf{y} = y_1 y_2 y_3 \ldots = c_1(v_1)c_2(v_2)c_3(v_3)\ldots. \tag{18.21}$$

What is the probability of the data $(\mathbf{x}, \mathbf{y})$? We have to make some assumptions
about the plaintext language. If it were the case that the plaintext language
was completely random, then the probability of $u_1 u_2 u_3 \ldots$ and $v_1 v_2 v_3 \ldots$ would
be uniform, and so would that of $\mathbf{x}$ and $\mathbf{y}$, so the probability $P(\mathbf{x}, \mathbf{y} | \mathcal{H}_1)$
would be equal to $P(\mathbf{x}, \mathbf{y} | \mathcal{H}_0)$, and the two hypotheses $\mathcal{H}_0$ and $\mathcal{H}_1$ would be
indistinguishable.

We make progress by assuming that the plaintext is not completely random. Both plaintexts are written in a language, and that language has redundancies. Assume for example that particular plaintext letters are used more
often than others. So, even though the two plaintext messages are unrelated,
they are slightly more likely to use the same letters as each other; if $\mathcal{H}_1$ is true,
two synchronized letters from the two cyphertexts are slightly more likely to
be identical. Similarly, if a language uses particular bigrams and trigrams
frequently, then the two plaintext messages will occasionally contain the same
bigrams and trigrams at the same time as each other, giving rise, if $\mathcal{H}_1$ is true,

u	LITTLE-JACK-HORNER-SAT-IN-THE-CORNER-EATING-A-CHRISTMAS-PIE--HE-PUT-IN-H
v	RIDE-A-COCK-HORSE-TO-BANBURY-CROSS-TO-SEE-A-FINE-LADY-UPON-A-WHITE-HORSE
matches:	.*....*..******.*.............*..........*................*..........

Table 18.9. Two aligned pieces of English plaintext, **u** and **v**, with matches marked by ∗. Notice that there are twelve matches, including a run of six, whereas the expected number of matches in two completely random strings of length $T = 74$ would be about 3. The two corresponding cyphertexts from two machines in identical states would also have twelve matches.

to a little burst of 2 or 3 identical letters. Table 18.9 shows such a coincidence in two plaintext messages that are unrelated, except that they are both written in English.

The codebreakers hunted among pairs of messages for pairs that were suspiciously similar to each other, counting up the numbers of matching monograms, bigrams, trigrams, etc. This method was first used by the Polish codebreaker Rejewski.

Let's look at the simple case of a monogram language model and estimate how long a message is needed to be able to decide whether two machines are in the same state. I'll assume the source language is monogram-English, the language in which successive letters are drawn i.i.d. from the probability distribution $\{p_i\}$ of figure 2.1. The probability of **x** and **y** is nonuniform: consider two single characters, $x_t = c_t(u_t)$ and $y_t = c_t(v_t)$; the probability that they are identical is

$$\sum_{u_t, v_t} P(u_t) P(v_t) \mathbb{1}[u_t = v_t] = \sum_i p_i^2 \equiv m. \tag{18.22}$$

We give this quantity the name m, for 'match probability'; for both English and German, m is about 2/26 rather than 1/26 (the value that would hold for a completely random language). Assuming that c_t is an ideal random permutation, the probability of x_t and y_t is, by symmetry,

$$P(x_t, y_t | \mathcal{H}_1) = \begin{cases} \frac{m}{A} & \text{if } x_t = y_t \\ \frac{(1-m)}{A(A-1)} & \text{for } x_t \neq y_t. \end{cases} \tag{18.23}$$

Given a pair of cyphertexts **x** and **y** of length T that match in M places and do not match in N places, the log evidence in favour of $\mathcal{H}_1$ is then

$$\log \frac{P(\mathbf{x}, \mathbf{y} | \mathcal{H}_1)}{P(\mathbf{x}, \mathbf{y} | \mathcal{H}_0)} = M \log \frac{m/A}{1/A^2} + N \log \frac{\frac{(1-m)}{A(A-1)}}{1/A^2} \tag{18.24}$$

$$= M \log mA + N \log \frac{(1-m)A}{A-1}. \tag{18.25}$$

Every match contributes $\log mA$ in favour of $\mathcal{H}_1$; every non-match contributes $\log \frac{A-1}{(1-m)A}$ in favour of $\mathcal{H}_0$.

Match probability for monogram-English	m	0.076
Coincidental match probability	$1/A$	0.037
log-evidence for $\mathcal{H}_1$ per match	$10 \log_{10} mA$	3.1 db
log-evidence for $\mathcal{H}_1$ per non-match	$10 \log_{10} \frac{(1-m)A}{(A-1)}$	−0.18 db

If there were $M = 4$ matches and $N = 47$ non-matches in a pair of length $T = 51$, for example, the weight of evidence in favour of $\mathcal{H}_1$ would be $+4$ decibans, or a likelihood ratio of 2.5 to 1 in favour.

The *expected* weight of evidence from a line of text of length $T = 20$ characters is the expectation of (18.25), which depends on whether $\mathcal{H}_1$ or $\mathcal{H}_0$ is true. If $\mathcal{H}_1$ is true then matches are expected to turn up at rate m, and the expected weight of evidence is 1.4 decibans per 20 characters. If $\mathcal{H}_0$ is true then spurious matches are expected to turn up at rate $1/A$, and the expected weight of evidence is -1.1 decibans per 20 characters. Typically, roughly 400 characters need to be inspected in order to have a weight of evidence greater than a hundred to one (20 decibans) in favour of one hypothesis or the other.

So, two English plaintexts have more matches than two random strings. Furthermore, because consecutive characters in English are not independent, the bigram and trigram statistics of English are nonuniform and the matches tend to occur in bursts of consecutive matches. [The same observations also apply to German.] Using better language models, the evidence contributed by runs of matches was more accurately computed. Such a scoring system was worked out by Turing and refined by Good. Positive results were passed on to automated and human-powered codebreakers. According to Good, the longest false-positive that arose in this work was a string of 8 consecutive matches between two machines that were actually in unrelated states.

Further reading

For further reading about Turing and Bletchley Park, see Hodges (1983) and Good (1979). For an in-depth read about cryptography, Schneier's (1996) book is highly recommended. It is readable, clear, and entertaining.

▶ **18.5 Exercises**

▷ Exercise 18.3.[2] Another weakness in the design of the Enigma machine, which was intended to emulate a perfectly random time-varying permutation, is that it never mapped a letter to itself. When you press Q, what comes out is always a different letter from Q. How much information per character is leaked by this design flaw? How long a crib would be needed to be confident that the crib is correctly aligned with the cyphertext? And how long a crib would be needed to be able confidently to identify the correct key?

[A *crib* is a guess for what the plaintext was. Imagine that the Brits know that a very important German is travelling from Berlin to Aachen, and they intercept Enigma-encoded messages sent to Aachen. It is a good bet that one or more of the original plaintext messages contains the string OBERSTURMBANNFUEHRERXGRAFXHEINRICHXVONXWEIZSAECKER, the name of the important chap. A crib could be used in a brute-force approach to find the correct Enigma key (feed the received messages through all possible Engima machines and see if any of the putative decoded texts match the above plaintext). This question centres on the idea that the crib can also be used in a much less expensive manner: slide the plaintext crib along all the encoded messages until a perfect *mismatch* of the crib and the encoded message is found; if correct, this alignment then tells you a lot about the key.]

19

Why have Sex? Information Acquisition and Evolution

Evolution has been happening on earth for about the last 10^9 years. Undeniably, *information has been acquired* during this process. Thanks to the tireless work of the Blind Watchmaker, some cells now carry within them all the information required to be outstanding spiders; other cells carry all the information required to make excellent octopuses. Where did this information come from?

The entire blueprint of all organisms on the planet has emerged in a teaching process in which the teacher is natural selection: fitter individuals have more progeny, the fitness being defined by the local environment (including the other organisms). The teaching signal is only a few bits per individual: an individual simply has a smaller or larger number of grandchildren, depending on the individual's fitness. 'Fitness' is a broad term that could cover

- the ability of an antelope to run faster than other antelopes and hence avoid being eaten by a lion;

- the ability of a lion to be well-enough camouflaged and run fast enough to catch one antelope per day;

- the ability of a peacock to attract a peahen to mate with it;

- the ability of a peahen to rear many young simultaneously.

The fitness of an organism is largely determined by its DNA – both the coding regions, or genes, and the non-coding regions (which play an important role in regulating the transcription of genes). We'll think of fitness as a function of the DNA sequence and the environment.

How does the DNA determine fitness, and how does information get from natural selection into the genome? Well, if the gene that codes for one of an antelope's proteins is defective, that antelope might get eaten by a lion early in life and have only two grandchildren rather than forty. The information content of natural selection is fully contained in a specification of which offspring survived to have children – an information content of *at most one bit per offspring*. The teaching signal does not communicate to the ecosystem any description of the imperfections in the organism that caused it to have fewer children. The bits of the teaching signal are highly redundant, because, throughout a species, unfit individuals who are similar to each other will be failing to have offspring for similar reasons.

So, how many bits per generation are acquired by the species as a whole by natural selection? How many bits has natural selection succeeded in conveying to the human branch of the tree of life, since the divergence between

269

Australopithecines and apes 4 000 000 years ago? Assuming a generation time of 10 years for reproduction, there have been about 400 000 generations of human precursors since the divergence from apes. Assuming a population of 10^9 individuals, each receiving a couple of bits of information from natural selection, the total number of bits of information responsible for modifying the genomes of 4 million B.C. into today's human genome is about 8×10^{14} bits. However, as we noted, natural selection is not smart at collating the information that it dishes out to the population, and there is a great deal of redundancy in that information. If the population size were twice as great, would it evolve twice as fast? No, because natural selection will simply be correcting the same defects twice as often.

John Maynard Smith has suggested that the rate of information acquisition by a species is independent of the population size, and is of order 1 bit per generation. This figure would only allow for 400 000 bits of difference between apes and humans, a number that is much smaller than the total size of the human genome – 6×10^9 bits. [One human genome contains about 3×10^9 nucleotides.] It is certainly the case that the genomic overlap between apes and humans is huge, but is the difference that small?

In this chapter, we'll develop a crude model of the process of information acquisition through evolution, based on the assumption that a gene with two defects is typically likely to be more defective than a gene with one defect, and an organism with two defective genes is likely to be less fit than an organism with one defective gene. Undeniably, this is a crude model, since real biological systems are baroque constructions with complex interactions. Nevertheless, we persist with a simple model because it readily yields striking results.

What we find from this simple model is that

1. John Maynard Smith's figure of 1 bit per generation is correct for an *asexually-reproducing* population;

2. in contrast, *if the species reproduces sexually*, the rate of information acquisition can be as large as $\sqrt{G}$ bits per generation, where G is the size of the genome.

We'll also find interesting results concerning the maximum mutation rate that a species can withstand.

▶ 19.1 The model

We study a simple model of a reproducing population of N individuals with a genome of size G bits: variation is produced by mutation or by recombination (i.e., sex) and truncation selection selects the N fittest children at each generation to be the parents of the next. We find striking differences between populations that have recombination and populations that do not.

The genotype of each individual is a vector $\mathbf{x}$ of G bits, each having a good state $x_g = 1$ and a bad state $x_g = 0$. The fitness $F(\mathbf{x})$ of an individual is simply the sum of her bits:

$$F(\mathbf{x}) = \sum_{g=1}^{G} x_g. \tag{19.1}$$

The bits in the genome could be considered to correspond either to genes that have good alleles ($x_g = 1$) and bad alleles ($x_g = 0$), or to the nucleotides of a genome. We will concentrate on the latter interpretation. The essential property of fitness that we are assuming is that it is locally a roughly linear function of the genome, that is, that there are many possible changes one could make to the genome, each of which has a small effect on fitness, and that these effects combine approximately linearly.

We define the normalized fitness $f(\mathbf{x}) \equiv F(\mathbf{x})/G$.

We consider evolution by natural selection under two models of variation.

Variation by mutation. The model assumes discrete generations. At each generation, t, every individual produces two children. The children's genotypes differ from the parent's by random mutations. Natural selection selects the fittest N progeny in the child population to reproduce, and a new generation starts.

[The selection of the fittest N individuals at each generation is known as truncation selection.]

The simplest model of mutations is that the child's bits $\{x_g\}$ are independent. Each bit has a small probability of being flipped, which, thinking of the bits as corresponding roughly to nucleotides, is taken to be a constant m, independent of x_g. [If alternatively we thought of the bits as corresponding to genes, then we would model the probability of the discovery of a good gene, $P(x_g = 0 \rightarrow x_g = 1)$, as being a smaller number than the probability of a deleterious mutation in a good gene, $P(x_g = 1 \rightarrow x_g = 0)$.]

Variation by recombination (or crossover, or sex). Our organisms are haploid, not diploid. They enjoy sex by recombination. The N individuals in the population are married into $M = N/2$ couples, at random, and each couple has C children – with $C = 4$ children being our standard assumption, so as to have the population double and halve every generation, as before. The C children's genotypes are independent given the parents'. Each child obtains its genotype $\mathbf{z}$ by random crossover of its parents' genotypes, $\mathbf{x}$ and $\mathbf{y}$. The simplest model of recombination has no linkage, so that:

$$z_g = \begin{cases} x_g & \text{with probability } 1/2 \\ y_g & \text{with probability } 1/2. \end{cases} \tag{19.2}$$

Once the MC progeny have been born, the parents pass away, the fittest N progeny are selected by natural selection, and a new generation starts.

We now study these two models of variation in detail.

▶ 19.2 Rate of increase of fitness

Theory of mutations

We assume that the genotype of an individual with normalized fitness $f = F/G$ is subjected to mutations that flip bits with probability m. We first show that if the average normalized fitness f of the population is greater than $1/2$, then the optimal mutation rate is small, and the rate of acquisition of information is at most of order one bit per generation.

Since it is easy to achieve a normalized fitness of $f = 1/2$ by simple mutation, we'll assume $f > 1/2$ and work in terms of the excess normalized fitness $\delta f \equiv f - 1/2$. If an individual with excess normalized fitness δf has a child and the mutation rate m is small, the probability distribution of the excess normalized fitness of the child has mean

$$\overline{\delta f}_{\text{child}} = (1 - 2m)\delta f \tag{19.3}$$

and variance

$$\frac{m(1-m)}{G} \simeq \frac{m}{G}. \tag{19.4}$$

If the population of parents has mean $\delta f(t)$ and variance $\sigma^2(t) \equiv \beta m/G$, then the child population, before selection, will have mean $(1-2m)\delta f(t)$ and variance $(1+\beta)m/G$. Natural selection chooses the upper half of this distribution, so the mean fitness and variance of fitness at the next generation are given by

$$\delta f(t+1) = (1-2m)\delta f(t) + \alpha\sqrt{(1+\beta)}\sqrt{\frac{m}{G}}, \tag{19.5}$$

$$\sigma^2(t+1) = \gamma(1+\beta)\frac{m}{G}, \tag{19.6}$$

where α is the mean deviation from the mean, measured in standard deviations, and γ is the factor by which the child distribution's variance is reduced by selection. The numbers α and γ are of order 1. For the case of a Gaussian distribution, $\alpha = \sqrt{2/\pi} \simeq 0.8$ and $\gamma = (1-2/\pi) \simeq 0.36$. If we assume that the variance is in dynamic equilibrium, i.e., $\sigma^2(t+1) \simeq \sigma^2(t)$, then

$$\gamma(1+\beta) = \beta, \text{ so } (1+\beta) = \frac{1}{1-\gamma}, \tag{19.7}$$

and the factor $\alpha\sqrt{(1+\beta)}$ in equation (19.5) is equal to 1, if we take the results for the Gaussian distribution, an approximation that becomes poorest when the discreteness of fitness becomes important, i.e., for small m. The rate of increase of normalized fitness is thus:

$$\frac{\mathrm{d}f}{\mathrm{d}t} \simeq -2m\,\delta f + \sqrt{\frac{m}{G}}, \tag{19.8}$$

which, assuming $G(\delta f)^2 \gg 1$, is maximized for

$$m_{\mathrm{opt}} = \frac{1}{16G(\delta f)^2}, \tag{19.9}$$

at which point,

$$\left(\frac{\mathrm{d}f}{\mathrm{d}t}\right)_{\mathrm{opt}} = \frac{1}{8G(\delta f)}. \tag{19.10}$$

So the rate of increase of fitness $F = fG$ is at most

$$\frac{\mathrm{d}F}{\mathrm{d}t} = \frac{1}{8(\delta f)} \text{ per generation.} \tag{19.11}$$

For a population with low fitness ($\delta f < 0.125$), the rate of increase of fitness may exceed 1 unit per generation. Indeed, if $\delta f \lesssim 1/\sqrt{G}$, the rate of increase, if $m = 1/2$, is of order $\sqrt{G}$; this initial spurt can only last of order $\sqrt{G}$ generations. For $\delta f > 0.125$, the rate of increase of fitness is smaller than one per generation. As the fitness approaches G, the optimal mutation rate tends to $m = 1/(4G)$, so that an average of $1/4$ bits are flipped per genotype, and the rate of increase of fitness is also equal to $1/4$; information is gained at a rate of about 0.5 bits per generation. It takes about $2G$ generations for the genotypes of all individuals in the population to attain perfection.

For fixed m, the fitness is given by

$$\delta f(t) = \frac{1}{2\sqrt{mG}}(1 - ce^{-2mt}), \tag{19.12}$$

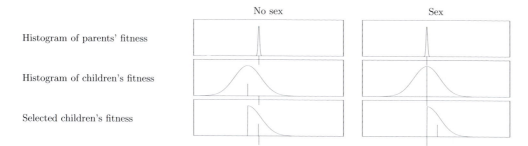

Figure 19.1. Why sex is better than sex-free reproduction. If mutations are used to create variation among children, then it is unavoidable that the average fitness of the children is lower than the parents' fitness; the greater the variation, the greater the average deficit. Selection bumps up the mean fitness again. In contrast, recombination produces variation without a decrease in average fitness. The typical amount of variation scales as $\sqrt{G}$, where G is the genome size, so after selection, the average fitness rises by $O(\sqrt{G})$.

subject to the constraint $\delta f(t) \leq 1/2$, where c is a constant of integration, equal to 1 if $f(0) = 1/2$. If the mean number of bits flipped per genotype, mG, exceeds 1, then the fitness F approaches an equilibrium value $F_{\text{eqm}} = (1/2 + 1/(2\sqrt{mG}))G$.

This theory is somewhat inaccurate in that the true probability distribution of fitness is non-Gaussian, asymmetrical, and quantized to integer values. All the same, the predictions of the theory are not grossly at variance with the results of simulations described below.

Theory of sex

The analysis of the sexual population becomes tractable with two approximations: first, we assume that the gene-pool mixes sufficiently rapidly that correlations between genes can be neglected; second, we assume *homogeneity*, i.e., that the fraction f_g of bits g that are in the good state is the same, $f(t)$, for all g.

Given these assumptions, if two parents of fitness $F = fG$ mate, the probability distribution of their children's fitness has mean equal to the parents' fitness, F; the variation produced by sex does not reduce the average fitness. The standard deviation of the fitness of the children scales as $\sqrt{Gf(1-f)}$. Since, after selection, the increase in fitness is proportional to this standard deviation, *the fitness increase per generation scales as the square root of the size of the genome*, $\sqrt{G}$. As shown in box 19.2, the mean fitness $\bar{F} = fG$ evolves in accordance with the differential equation:

$$\frac{\mathrm{d}\bar{F}}{\mathrm{d}t} \simeq \eta \sqrt{f(t)(1 - f(t))G}, \qquad (19.13)$$

where $\eta \equiv \sqrt{2/(\pi + 2)}$. The solution of this equation is

$$f(t) = \frac{1}{2}\left[1 + \sin\left(\frac{\eta}{\sqrt{G}}(t + c)\right)\right], \quad \text{for } t + c \in \left(-\frac{\pi}{2}\sqrt{G}/\eta, \frac{\pi}{2}\sqrt{G}/\eta\right), \ (19.14)$$

where c is a constant of integration, $c = \sin^{-1}(2f(0) - 1)$. So this idealized system reaches a state of eugenic perfection ($f = 1$) within a finite time: $(\pi/\eta)\sqrt{G}$ generations.

Simulations

Figure 19.3a shows the fitness of a sexual population of $N = 1000$ individuals with a genome size of $G = 1000$ starting from a random initial state with normalized fitness 0.5. It also shows the theoretical curve $f(t)G$ from equation (19.14), which fits remarkably well.

In contrast, figures 19.3(b) and (c) show the evolving fitness when variation is produced by mutation at rates $m = 0.25/G$ and $m = 6/G$ respectively. Note the difference in the horizontal scales from panel (a).

Box 19.2. Details of the theory of sex.

How does $f(t+1)$ depend on $f(t)$? Let's first assume the two parents of a child both have exactly $f(t)G$ good bits, and, by our homogeneity assumption, that those bits are independent random subsets of the G bits. The number of bits that are good in both parents is roughly $f(t)^2G$, and the number that are good in one parent only is roughly $2f(t)(1-f(t))G$, so the fitness of the child will be $f(t)^2G$ plus the sum of $2f(t)(1-f(t))G$ fair coin flips, which has a binomial distribution of mean $f(t)(1-f(t))G$ and variance $\frac{1}{2}f(t)(1-f(t))G$. The fitness of a child is thus roughly distributed as

$$F_{\text{child}} \sim \text{Normal}\left(\text{mean} = f(t)G, \text{variance} = \frac{1}{2}f(t)(1-f(t))G\right).$$

The important property of this distribution, contrasted with the distribution under mutation, is that the mean fitness is equal to the parents' fitness; the variation produced by sex does not reduce the average fitness.

If we include the parental population's variance, which we will write as $\sigma^2(t) = \beta(t)\frac{1}{2}f(t)(1-f(t))G$, the children's fitnesses are distributed as

$$F_{\text{child}} \sim \text{Normal}\left(\text{mean} = f(t)G, \text{variance} = \left(1 + \frac{\beta}{2}\right)\frac{1}{2}f(t)(1-f(t))G\right).$$

Natural selection selects the children on the upper side of this distribution. The mean increase in fitness will be

$$\bar{F}(t+1) - \bar{F}(t) = [\alpha(1 + \beta/2)^{1/2}/\sqrt{2}]\sqrt{f(t)(1-f(t))G},$$

and the variance of the surviving children will be

$$\sigma^2(t+1) = \gamma(1 + \beta/2)\frac{1}{2}f(t)(1-f(t))G,$$

where $\alpha = \sqrt{2/\pi}$ and $\gamma = (1-2/\pi)$. If there is dynamic equilibrium $[\sigma^2(t+1) = \sigma^2(t)]$ then the factor in (19.2) is

$$\alpha(1 + \beta/2)^{1/2}/\sqrt{2} = \sqrt{\frac{2}{(\pi + 2)}} \simeq 0.62.$$

Defining this constant to be $\eta \equiv \sqrt{2/(\pi + 2)}$, we conclude that, under sex and natural selection, the mean fitness of the population increases at a rate *proportional to the square root of the size of the genome,*

$$\frac{d\bar{F}}{dt} \simeq \eta\sqrt{f(t)(1-f(t))G} \text{ bits per generation.}$$

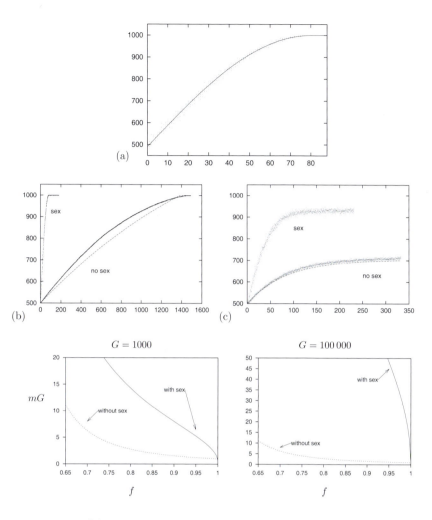

Figure 19.3. Fitness as a function of time. The genome size is $G = 1000$. The dots show the fitness of six randomly selected individuals from the birth population at each generation. The initial population of $N = 1000$ had randomly generated genomes with $f(0) = 0.5$ (exactly). (a) Variation produced by sex alone. Line shows theoretical curve (19.14) for infinite homogeneous population. (b,c) Variation produced by mutation, with and without sex, when the mutation rate is $mG = 0.25$ (b) or 6 (c) bits per genome. The dashed line shows the curve (19.12).

Figure 19.4. Maximal tolerable mutation rate, shown as number of errors per genome (mG), versus normalized fitness $f = F/G$. Left panel: genome size $G = 1000$; right: $G = 100\,000$. Independent of genome size, a parthenogenetic species (no sex) can only tolerate of order 1 error per genome per generation; a species that uses recombination (sex) can tolerate far greater mutation rates.

Exercise 19.1.[3] Dependence on population size. How do the results for a sexual population depend on the population size? We anticipate that there is a minimum population size above which the theory of sex is accurate.

In what way is that minimum population size related to G?

Exercise 19.2.[3] Dependence on crossover mechanism. In the simple model of sex, each bit is taken at random from one of the two parents, that is, we allow crossovers to occur with probability 50% between any two adjacent nucleotides. How is the model affected (a) if the crossover probability is smaller? (b) if crossovers exclusively occur at *hot-spots* located every d bits along the genome?

▶ **19.3 The maximal tolerable mutation rate**

What if we combine the two models of variation? What is the maximum mutation rate that can be tolerated by a species that has sex?

The rate of increase of fitness is given by

$$\frac{\mathrm{d}f}{\mathrm{d}t} \simeq -2m\,\delta f + \eta\sqrt{2}\sqrt{\frac{m + f(1-f)/2}{G}}, \qquad (19.15)$$

which is positive if the mutation rate satisfies

$$m < \eta \sqrt{\frac{f(1-f)}{G}}. \tag{19.16}$$

Let us compare this rate with the result in the absence of sex, which, from equation (19.8), is that the maximum tolerable mutation rate is

$$m < \frac{1}{G}\frac{1}{(2\,\delta f)^2}. \tag{19.17}$$

The tolerable mutation rate with sex is of order $\sqrt{G}$ times greater than that without sex!

A parthenogenetic (non-sexual) species could try to wriggle out of this bound on its mutation rate by increasing its litter sizes. But if mutation flips on average mG bits, the probability that no bits are flipped in one genome is roughly e^{-mG}, so a mother needs to have roughly e^{mG} offspring in order to have a good chance of having one child with the same fitness as her. The litter size of a non-sexual species thus has to be exponential in mG (if mG is bigger than 1), if the species is to persist.

So the maximum tolerable mutation rate is pinned close to $1/G$, for a non-sexual species, whereas it is a larger number of order $1/\sqrt{G}$, for a species with recombination.

Turning these results around, we can predict the largest possible genome size for a given fixed mutation rate, m. For a parthenogenetic species, the largest genome size is of order $1/m$, and for a sexual species, $1/m^2$. Taking the figure $m = 10^{-8}$ as the mutation rate per nucleotide per generation (Eyre-Walker and Keightley, 1999), and allowing for a maximum brood size of $20\,000$ (that is, $mG \simeq 10$), we predict that all species with more than $G = 10^9$ coding nucleotides make at least occasional use of recombination. If the brood size is 12, then this number falls to $G = 2.5 \times 10^8$.

▶ **19.4 Fitness increase and information acquisition**

For this simple model it is possible to relate increasing fitness to information acquisition.

If the bits are set at random, the fitness is roughly $F = G/2$. If evolution leads to a population in which all individuals have the maximum fitness $F = G$, then G bits of information have been acquired by the species, namely for each bit x_g, the species has figured out which of the two states is the better.

We define the information acquired at an intermediate fitness to be the amount of selection (measured in bits) required to select the perfect state from the gene pool. Let a fraction f_g of the population have $x_g = 1$. Because $\log_2(1/f)$ is the information required to find a black ball in an urn containing black and white balls in the ratio $f : 1-f$, we define the information acquired to be

$$I = \sum_g \log_2 \frac{f_g}{1/2} \text{bits}. \tag{19.18}$$

If all the fractions f_g are equal to F/G, then

$$I = G \log_2 \frac{2F}{G}, \tag{19.19}$$

which is well approximated by

$$\tilde{I} \equiv 2(F - G/2). \tag{19.20}$$

The rate of information acquisition is thus roughly two times the rate of increase of fitness in the population.

▶ **19.5 Discussion**

These results quantify the well known argument for why species reproduce
by sex with recombination, namely that recombination allows useful mutations to spread more rapidly through the species and allows deleterious mutations to be more rapidly cleared from the population (Maynard Smith, 1978;
Felsenstein, 1985; Maynard Smith, 1988; Maynard Smith and Száthmary,
1995). A population that reproduces by recombination can acquire information from natural selection at a rate of order $\sqrt{G}$ times faster than a parthenogenetic population, and it can tolerate a mutation rate that is of order $\sqrt{G}$
times greater. For genomes of size $G \simeq 10^8$ coding nucleotides, this factor of
$\sqrt{G}$ is substantial.

   This enormous advantage conferred by sex has been noted before by Kondrashov (1988), but this meme, which Kondrashov calls 'the deterministic
mutation hypothesis', does not seem to have diffused throughout the evolutionary research community, as there are still numerous papers in which the
prevalence of sex is viewed as a mystery to be explained by elaborate mechanisms.

'The cost of males' – stability of a gene for sex or parthenogenesis

Why do people declare sex to be a mystery? The main motivation for being
mystified is an idea called the 'cost of males'. Sexual reproduction is disad-
vantageous compared with asexual reproduction, it's argued, because of every
two offspring produced by sex, one (on average) is a useless male, incapable
of child-bearing, and only one is a productive female. In the same time, a
parthenogenetic mother could give birth to *two* female clones. To put it another way, the big advantage of parthenogenesis, from the point of view of
the individual, is that one is able to pass on 100% of one's genome to one's
children, instead of only 50%. Thus if there were two versions of a species, one
reproducing with and one without sex, the single mothers would be expected
to outstrip their sexual cousins. The simple model presented thus far did not
include either genders or the ability to convert from sexual reproduction to
asexual, but we can easily modify the model.

   We modify the model so that one of the G bits in the genome determines
whether an individual prefers to reproduce parthenogenetically ($x = 1$) or sexually ($x = 0$). The results depend on the number of children had by a single
parthenogenetic mother, K_p and the number of children born by a sexual
couple, K_s. Both ($K_p = 2$, $K_s = 4$) and ($K_p = 4$, $K_s = 4$) are reasonable models. The former ($K_p = 2$, $K_s = 4$) would seem most appropriate in the case
of unicellular organisms, where the cytoplasm of both parents goes into the
children. The latter ($K_p = 4$, $K_s = 4$) is appropriate if the children are solely
nurtured by one of the parents, so single mothers have just as many offspring
as a sexual pair. I concentrate on the latter model, since it gives the greatest
advantage to the parthenogens, who are supposedly expected to outbreed the
sexual community. Because parthenogens have four children per generation,
the maximum tolerable mutation rate for them is twice the expression (19.17)
derived before for $K_p = 2$. If the fitness is large, the maximum tolerable rate
is $mG \simeq 2$.

   Initially the genomes are set randomly with $F = G/2$, with half of the population having the gene for parthenogenesis. Figure 19.5 shows the outcome.
During the 'learning' phase of evolution, in which the fitness is increasing
rapidly, pockets of parthenogens appear briefly, but then disappear within
a couple of generations as their sexual cousins overtake them in fitness and

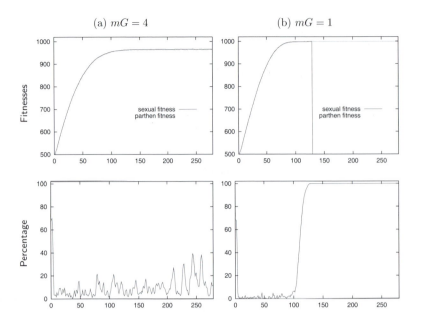

Figure 19.5. Results when there is a gene for parthenogenesis, and no interbreeding, *and single mothers produce as many children as sexual couples.* $G = 1000$, $N = 1000$. (a) $mG = 4$; (b) $mG = 1$. Vertical axis shows both fitness and percentage of the population that is parthenogenetic.

leave them behind. Once the population reaches its top fitness, however, the parthenogens can take over, if the mutation rate is sufficiently low ($mG = 1$).

In the presence of a higher mutation rate ($mG = 4$), however, the parthenogens never take over. The breadth of the sexual population's fitness is of order $\sqrt{G}$, so a mutant parthenogenetic colony arising with slightly above-average fitness will last for about $\sqrt{G}/(mG) = 1/(m\sqrt{G})$ generations before its fitness falls below that of its sexual cousins. As long as the population size is sufficiently large for some sexual individuals to survive for this time, sex will not die out.

In a sufficiently unstable environment, where the fitness function is continually changing, the parthenogens will always lag behind the sexual community. These results are consistent with the argument of Haldane and Hamilton that sex is helpful in an arms race with parasites. The parasites define an effective fitness function which changes with time, and a sexual population will always ascend the current fitness function more rapidly.

Additive fitness function

Of course, our results depend on the fitness function that we assume, and on our model of selection. Is it reasonable to model fitness, to first order, as a *sum* of independent terms? Maynard Smith (1968) argues that it is: the more good genes you have, the higher you come in the pecking order, for example. The directional selection model has been used extensively in theoretical population genetic studies (Bulmer, 1985). We might expect real fitness functions to involve interactions, in which case crossover might reduce the average fitness. However, since recombination gives the biggest advantage to species whose fitness functions are additive, we might predict that *evolution will have favoured species that used a representation of the genome that corresponds to a fitness function that has only weak interactions.* And even if there are interactions, it seems plausible that the fitness would still involve a sum of such interacting terms, with the number of terms being some fraction of the genome size G.

Exercise 19.3.[3C] Investigate how fast sexual and asexual species evolve if they have a fitness function with interactions. For example, let the fitness be a sum of exclusive-ors of pairs of bits; compare the evolving fitnesses with those of the sexual and asexual species with a simple additive fitness function.

Furthermore, if the fitness function were a highly nonlinear function of the genotype, it could be made more smooth and locally linear by the Baldwin effect. The Baldwin effect (Baldwin, 1896; Hinton and Nowlan, 1987) has been widely studied as a mechanism whereby *learning* guides evolution, and it could also act at the level of transcription and translation. Consider the evolution of a peptide sequence for a new purpose, assuming the effectiveness of the peptide is highly nonlinear function of the sequence, perhaps having a small island of good sequences surrounded by an ocean of equally bad sequences. In an organism whose transcription and translation machinery is flawless, the fitness will be an equally nonlinear function of the DNA sequence and evolution will wander around the ocean making progress towards the island only by a random walk. In contrast, an organism having the same DNA sequence, but whose DNA-to-RNA transcription or RNA-to-protein translation is 'faulty', will occasionally, by mistranslation or mistranscription, accidentally produce a working enzyme; and it will do so with greater probability if its DNA sequence is close to a good sequence. One cell might produce 1000 proteins from the one mRNA sequence, of which 999 have no enzymatic effect, and one does. The one working catalyst will be enough for that cell to have an increased fitness relative to rivals whose DNA sequence is further from the island of good sequences. For this reason I conjecture that, at least early in evolution, and perhaps still now, the genetic code was not implemented perfectly but was implemented noisily, with some codons coding for a distribution of possible amino acids. This noisy code could even be switched on and off from cell to cell in an organism by having multiple aminoacyl-tRNA synthetases, some more reliable than others.

Whilst our model assumed that the bits of the genome do not interact, ignored the fact that the information is represented redundantly, assumed that there is a direct relationship between phenotypic fitness and the genotype, and assumed that the crossover probability in recombination is high, I believe these qualitative results would still hold if more complex models of fitness and crossover were used: the relative benefit of sex will still scale as $\sqrt{G}$. Only in small, in-bred populations are the benefits of sex expected to be diminished.

In summary: Why have sex? Because sex is good for your bits!

Further reading

How did a high-information-content self-replicating system ever emerge in the first place? In the general area of the origins of life and other tricky questions about evolution, I highly recommend Maynard Smith and Száthmary (1995), Maynard Smith and Száthmary (1999), Kondrashov (1988), Maynard Smith (1988), Ridley (2000), Dyson (1985), Cairns-Smith (1985), and Hopfield (1978).

► **19.6 Further exercises**

Exercise 19.4.[3] How good must the error-correcting machinery in DNA replication be, given that mammals have not all died out long ago? Estimate the probability of nucleotide substitution, per cell division. [See Appendix C.4.]

Exercise 19.5.[4] Given that DNA replication is achieved by bumbling Brownian motion and ordinary thermodynamics in a biochemical porridge at a temperature of 35 C, it's astonishing that the error-rate of DNA replication is about 10^{-9} per replicated nucleotide. How can this reliability be achieved, given that the energetic difference between a correct base-pairing and an incorrect one is only one or two hydrogen bonds and the thermal energy kT is only about a factor of four smaller than the free energy associated with a hydrogen bond? If ordinary thermodynamics is what favours correct base-pairing, surely the frequency of incorrect base-pairing should be about

$$f = \exp(-\Delta E/kT), \qquad\qquad (19.21)$$

where ΔE is the free energy difference, i.e., an error frequency of $f \simeq 10^{-4}$? How has DNA replication cheated thermodynamics?

The situation is equally perplexing in the case of protein synthesis, which translates an mRNA sequence into a polypeptide in accordance with the genetic code. Two specific chemical reactions are protected against errors: the binding of tRNA molecules to amino acids, and the production of the polypeptide in the ribosome, which, like DNA replication, involves base-pairing. Again, the fidelity is high (an error rate of about 10^{-4}), and this fidelity can't be caused by the energy of the 'correct' final state being especially low – the correct polypeptide sequence is not expected to be significantly lower in energy than any other sequence. How do cells perform error correction? (See Hopfield (1974), Hopfield (1980)).

Exercise 19.6.[2] While the genome acquires information through natural selection at a rate of a few bits per generation, your brain acquires information at a greater rate.

Estimate at what rate new information can be stored in long term memory by your brain. Think of learning the words of a new language, for example.

▶ **19.7 Solutions**

Solution to exercise 19.1 (p.275). For small enough N, whilst the average fitness of the population increases, some unlucky bits become frozen into the bad state. (These bad genes are sometimes known as hitchhikers.) The homogeneity assumption breaks down. Eventually, all individuals have identical genotypes that are mainly 1-bits, but contain some 0-bits too. The smaller the population, the greater the number of frozen 0-bits is expected to be. How small can the population size N be if the theory of sex is accurate?

We find experimentally that the theory based on assuming homogeneity only fits poorly if the population size N is smaller than $\sim \sqrt{G}$. If N is significantly smaller than $\sqrt{G}$, information cannot possibly be acquired at a rate as big as $\sqrt{G}$, since the information content of the Blind Watchmaker's decisions cannot be any greater than $2N$ bits per generation, this being the number of bits required to specify which of the $2N$ children get to reproduce. Baum et al. (1995), analyzing a similar model, show that the population size N should be about $\sqrt{G}(\log G)^2$ to make hitchhikers unlikely to arise.

Part IV

Probabilities and Inference

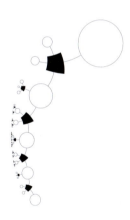

About Part IV

The number of inference problems that can (and perhaps should) be tackled by Bayesian inference methods is enormous. In this book, for example, we discuss the decoding problem for error-correcting codes, the task of inferring clusters from data, the task of interpolation through noisy data, and the task of classifying patterns given labelled examples. Most techniques for solving these problems can be categorized as follows.

Exact methods compute the required quantities directly. Only a few interesting problems have a direct solution, but exact methods are important as tools for solving subtasks within larger problems. Methods for the exact solution of inference problems are the subject of Chapters 21, 24, 25, and 26.

Approximate methods can be subdivided into

1. **deterministic approximations**, which include maximum likelihood (Chapter 22), Laplace's method (Chapters 27 and 28) and variational methods (Chapter 33); and

2. **Monte Carlo methods** – techniques in which random numbers play an integral part – which will be discussed in Chapters 29, 30, and 32.

This part of the book does not form a one-dimensional story. Rather, the ideas make up a web of interrelated threads which will recombine in subsequent chapters.

Chapter 3, which is an honorary member of this part, discussed a range of simple examples of inference problems and their Bayesian solutions.

To give further motivation for the toolbox of inference methods discussed in this part, Chapter 20 discusses the problem of clustering; subsequent chapters discuss the probabilistic interpretation of clustering as mixture modelling.

Chapter 21 discusses the option of dealing with probability distributions by completely enumerating all hypotheses. Chapter 22 introduces the idea of maximization methods as a way of avoiding the large cost associated with complete enumeration, and points out reasons why maximum likelihood is not good enough. Chapter 23 reviews the probability distributions that arise most often in Bayesian inference. Chapters 24, 25, and 26 discuss another way of avoiding the cost of complete enumeration: marginalization. Chapter 25 discusses message-passing methods appropriate for graphical models, using the decoding of error-correcting codes as an example. Chapter 26 combines these ideas with message-passing concepts from Chapters 16 and 17. These chapters are a prerequisite for the understanding of advanced error-correcting codes.

Chapter 27 discusses deterministic approximations including Laplace's method. This chapter is a prerequisite for understanding the topic of complexity control in learning algorithms, an idea that is discussed in general terms in Chapter 28.

Chapter 29 discusses Monte Carlo methods. Chapter 30 gives details of state-of-the-art Monte Carlo techniques.

Chapter 31 introduces the Ising model as a test-bed for probabilistic methods. An exact message-passing method and a Monte Carlo method are demonstrated. A motivation for studying the Ising model is that it is intimately related to several neural network models. Chapter 32 describes 'exact' Monte Carlo methods and demonstrates their application to the Ising model.

Chapter 33 discusses variational methods and their application to Ising models and to simple statistical inference problems including clustering. This chapter will help the reader understand the Hopfield network (Chapter 42) and the EM algorithm, which is an important method in latent-variable modelling. Chapter 34 discusses a particularly simple latent variable model called independent component analysis.

Chapter 35 discusses a ragbag of assorted inference topics. Chapter 36 discusses a simple example of decision theory. Chapter 37 discusses differences between sampling theory and Bayesian methods.

A theme: what inference is about

A widespread misconception is that the aim of inference is to find *the most probable explanation* for some data. While this most probable hypothesis may be of interest, and some inference methods do locate it, this hypothesis is just the peak of a probability distribution, and it is the whole distribution that is of interest. As we saw in Chapter 4, the *most probable* outcome from a source is often not a *typical* outcome from that source. Similarly, the most probable hypothesis given some data may be atypical of the whole set of reasonably-plausible hypotheses.

About Chapter 20

Before reading the next chapter, exercise 2.17 (p.36) and section 11.2 (inferring the input to a Gaussian channel) are recommended reading.

20

An Example Inference Task: Clustering

Human brains are good at finding regularities in data. One way of expressing
regularity is to put a set of objects into groups that are similar to each other.
For example, biologists have found that most objects in the natural world
fall into one of two categories: things that are brown and run away, and
things that are green and don't run away. The first group they call animals,
and the second, plants. We'll call this operation of grouping things together
clustering. If the biologist further sub-divides the cluster of plants into subclusters, we would call this 'hierarchical clustering'; but we won't be talking
about hierarchical clustering yet. In this chapter we'll just discuss ways to
take a set of N objects and group them into K clusters.

There are several motivations for clustering. First, a good clustering has
predictive power. When an early biologist encounters a new green thing he has
not seen before, his internal model of plants and animals fills in predictions for
attributes of the green thing: it's unlikely to jump on him and eat him; if he
touches it, he might get grazed or stung; if he eats it, he might feel sick. All of
these predictions, while uncertain, are useful, because they help the biologist
invest his resources (for example, the time spent watching for predators) well.
Thus, we perform clustering because we believe the underlying cluster labels
are meaningful, will lead to a more efficient description of our data, and will
help us choose better actions. This type of clustering is sometimes called
'mixture density modelling', and the objective function that measures how
well the predictive model is working is the information content of the data,
$\log 1/P(\{\mathbf{x}\})$.

Second, clusters can be a useful aid to communication because they allow
lossy compression. The biologist can give directions to a friend such as 'go to
the third *tree* on the right then take a right turn' (rather than 'go past the
large green thing with red berries, then past the large green thing with thorns,
then ...'). The brief category name 'tree' is helpful because it is sufficient to
identify an object. Similarly, in lossy image compression, the aim is to convey
in as few bits as possible a reasonable reproduction of a picture; one way to do
this is to divide the image into N small patches, and find a close match to each
patch in an alphabet of K image-templates; then we send a close fit to the
image by sending the list of labels $k_1, k_2, \ldots, k_N$ of the matching templates.
The task of creating a good library of image-templates is equivalent to finding
a set of cluster centres. This type of clustering is sometimes called 'vector
quantization'.

We can formalize a vector quantizer in terms of an *assignment rule* $\mathbf{x} \to$
$k(\mathbf{x})$ for assigning datapoints $\mathbf{x}$ to one of K codenames, and a *reconstruction
rule* $k \to \mathbf{m}^{(k)}$, the aim being to choose the functions $k(\mathbf{x})$ and $\mathbf{m}^{(k)}$ so as to

minimize the *expected distortion*, which might be defined to be

$$D = \sum_{\mathbf{x}} P(\mathbf{x}) \frac{1}{2} \left[\mathbf{m}^{(k(\mathbf{x}))} - \mathbf{x} \right]^2. \qquad (20.1)$$

[The ideal objective function would be to minimize the psychologically perceived distortion of the image. Since it is hard to quantify the distortion perceived by a human, vector quantization and lossy compression are not so crisply defined problems as data modelling and lossless compression.] In vector quantization, we don't necessarily believe that the templates $\{\mathbf{m}^{(k)}\}$ have any natural meaning; they are simply tools to do a job. We note in passing the similarity of the assignment rule (i.e., the encoder) of vector quantization to the *decoding* problem when decoding an error-correcting code.

A third reason for making a cluster model is that failures of the cluster model may highlight interesting objects that deserve special attention. If we have trained a vector quantizer to do a good job of compressing satellite pictures of ocean surfaces, then maybe patches of image that are not well compressed by the vector quantizer are the patches that contain ships! If the biologist encounters a green thing and sees it run (or slither) away, this misfit with his cluster model (which says green things don't run away) cues him to pay special attention. One can't spend all one's time being fascinated by things; the cluster model can help sift out from the multitude of objects in one's world the ones that really deserve attention.

A fourth reason for liking clustering algorithms is that they may serve as models of learning processes in neural systems. The clustering algorithm that we now discuss, the K-means algorithm, is an example of a *competitive learning* algorithm. The algorithm works by having the K clusters compete with each other for the right to own the data points.

Figure 20.1. $N = 40$ data points.

▶ 20.1 K-means clustering

The K-means algorithm is an algorithm for putting N data points in an I-dimensional space into K clusters. Each cluster is parameterized by a vector $\mathbf{m}^{(k)}$ called its mean.

The data points will be denoted by $\mathbf{x}^{(n)}$ where the superscript n runs from 1 to the number of data points N. Each vector $\mathbf{x}$ is a vector with I components x_i. We will assume that the space that $\mathbf{x}$ lives in is a real space and that we have a metric that defines distances between points, for example,

$$d(\mathbf{x}, \mathbf{y}) = \frac{1}{2} \sum_i (x_i - y_i)^2. \qquad (20.2)$$

About the name... As far as I know, the 'K' in K-means clustering simply refers to the chosen number of clusters. If Newton had followed the same naming policy, maybe we would learn at school about 'calculus for the variable x'. It's a silly name, but we are stuck with it.

To start the K-means algorithm (algorithm 20.2), the K means $\{\mathbf{m}^{(k)}\}$ are initialized in some way, for example to random values. K means is then an iterative two-step algorithm. In the *assignment step*, each data point n is assigned to the nearest mean. In the *update step*, the means are adjusted to match the sample means of the data points that they are responsible for.

The K-means algorithm is demonstrated for a toy two-dimensional data set in figure 20.3, where 2 means are used. The assignments of the points to the two clusters are indicated by two point styles, and the two means are shown by the circles. The algorithm converges after three iterations, at which point the assignments are unchanged so the means remain unmoved when updated. The K-means algorithm always converges to a fixed point.

Algorithm 20.2. The K-means
clustering algorithm.

Initialization. Set K means $\{\mathbf{m}^{(k)}\}$ to random values.

Assignment step. Each data point n is assigned to the nearest mean. We denote our guess for the cluster $k^{(n)}$ that the point $\mathbf{x}^{(n)}$ belongs to by $\hat{k}^{(n)}$.

$$\hat{k}^{(n)} = \operatorname*{argmin}_{k}\{d(\mathbf{m}^{(k)}, \mathbf{x}^{(n)})\}. \tag{20.3}$$

An alternative, equivalent representation of this assignment of points to clusters is given by 'responsibilities', which are indicator variables r_{nk}. In the assignment step, we set $r_k^{(n)}$ to one if mean k is the closest mean to datapoint $\mathbf{x}^{(n)}$; otherwise $r_k^{(n)}$ is zero.

$$r_k^{(n)} = \begin{cases} 1 & \text{if} \quad \hat{k}^{(n)} = k \\ 0 & \text{if} \quad \hat{k}^{(n)} \neq k. \end{cases} \tag{20.4}$$

What about ties? – We don't expect two means to be exactly the same distance from a data point, but if a tie does happen, $\hat{k}^{(n)}$ is set to the smallest of the winning $\{k\}$.

Update step. The model parameters, the means, are adjusted to match the sample means of the data points that they are responsible for.

$$\mathbf{m}^{(k)} = \frac{\sum_{n} r_k^{(n)} \mathbf{x}^{(n)}}{R^{(k)}} \tag{20.5}$$

where $R^{(k)}$ is the total responsibility of mean k,

$$R^{(k)} = \sum_{n} r_k^{(n)}. \tag{20.6}$$

What about means with no responsibilities? – If $R^{(k)} = 0$, then we leave the mean $\mathbf{m}^{(k)}$ where it is.

Repeat the assignment step and update step until the assignments do not change.

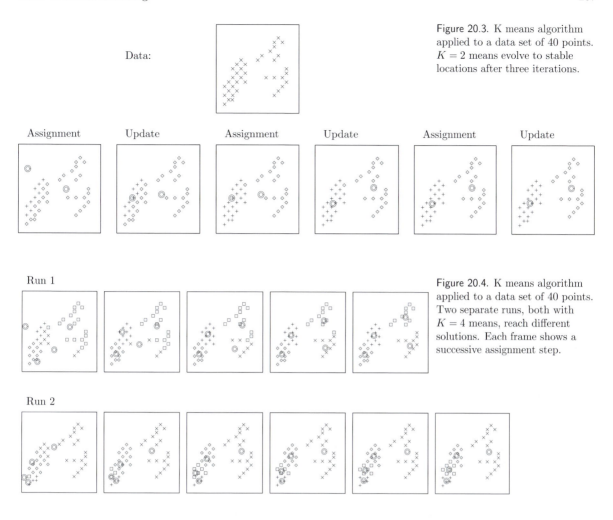

Data:

Figure 20.3. K means algorithm applied to a data set of 40 points. $K = 2$ means evolve to stable locations after three iterations.

Assignment   Update   Assignment   Update   Assignment   Update

Run 1

Figure 20.4. K means algorithm applied to a data set of 40 points. Two separate runs, both with $K = 4$ means, reach different solutions. Each frame shows a successive assignment step.

Run 2

Exercise 20.1.[4, p.291] See if you can prove that K-means always converges. [Hint: find a physical analogy and an associated Lyapunov function.]

[A Lyapunov function is a function of the state of the algorithm that decreases whenever the state changes and that is bounded below. If a system has a Lyapunov function then its dynamics converge.]

The K-means algorithm with a larger number of means, 4, is demonstrated in figure 20.4. The outcome of the algorithm depends on the initial condition. In the first case, after five iterations, a steady state is found in which the data points are fairly evenly split between the four clusters. In the second case, after six iterations, half the data points are in one cluster, and the others are shared among the other three clusters.

Questions about this algorithm

The K-means algorithm has several *ad hoc* features. Why does the update step set the 'mean' to the mean of the assigned points? Where did the distance d come from? What if we used a different measure of distance between $\mathbf{x}$ and $\mathbf{m}$? How can we choose the 'best' distance? [In vector quantization, the distance

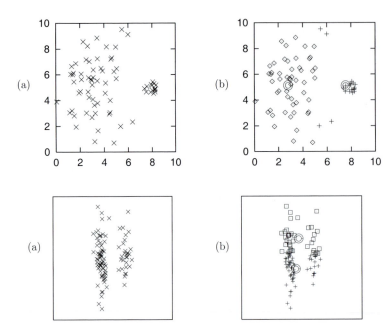

Figure 20.5. K means algorithm for a case with two dissimilar clusters. (a) The "little 'n' large" data. (b) A stable set of assignments and means. Note that four points belonging to the broad cluster have been incorrectly assigned to the narrower cluster.

Figure 20.6. Two elongated clusters, and the stable solution found by the K-means algorithm.

function is provided as part of the problem definition; but I'm assuming we are interested in data-modelling rather than vector quantization.] How do we choose K? Having found multiple alternative clusterings for a given K, how can we choose among them?

Cases where K-means might be viewed as failing.

Further questions arise when we look for cases where the algorithm behaves badly (compared with what the man in the street would call 'clustering'). Figure 20.5a shows a set of 75 data points generated from a mixture of two Gaussians. The right-hand Gaussian has less weight (only one fifth of the data points), and it is a less broad cluster. Figure 20.5b shows the outcome of using K-means clustering with $K = 2$ means. Four of the big cluster's data points have been assigned to the small cluster, and both means end up displaced to the left of the true centres of the clusters. The K-means algorithm takes account only of the distance between the means and the data points; it has no representation of the weight or breadth of each cluster. Consequently, data points which actually belong to the broad cluster are incorrectly assigned to the narrow cluster.

Figure 20.6 shows another case of K-means behaving badly. The data evidently falls into two elongated clusters. But the only stable state of the K-means algorithm is that shown in figure 20.6b: the two clusters have been sliced in half! These two examples show that there is something wrong with the distance d in the K-means algorithm. The K-means algorithm has no way of representing the size or shape of a cluster.

A final criticism of K-means is that it is a 'hard' rather than a 'soft' algorithm: points are assigned to exactly one cluster and all points assigned to a cluster are equals in that cluster. Points located near the border between two or more clusters should, arguably, play a *partial* role in determining the locations of all the clusters that they could plausibly be assigned to. But in the K-means algorithm, each borderline point is dumped in one cluster, and has an equal vote with all the other points in that cluster, and no vote in any other clusters.

▶ 20.2 Soft K-means clustering

These criticisms of K-means motivate the 'soft K-means algorithm', algorithm 20.7. The algorithm has one parameter, β, which we could term the *stiffness*.

Assignment step. Each data point $\mathbf{x}^{(n)}$ is given a soft 'degree of assignment' to each of the means. We call the degree to which $\mathbf{x}^{(n)}$ is assigned to cluster k the *responsibility* $r_k^{(n)}$ (the responsibility of cluster k for point n).

$$r_k^{(n)} = \frac{\exp\left(-\beta\, d(\mathbf{m}^{(k)}, \mathbf{x}^{(n)})\right)}{\sum_{k'} \exp\left(-\beta\, d(\mathbf{m}^{(k')}, \mathbf{x}^{(n)})\right)}. \tag{20.7}$$

The sum of the K responsibilities for the nth point is 1.

Update step. The model parameters, the means, are adjusted to match the sample means of the data points that they are responsible for.

$$\mathbf{m}^{(k)} = \frac{\sum_n r_k^{(n)} \mathbf{x}^{(n)}}{R^{(k)}} \tag{20.8}$$

where $R^{(k)}$ is the total responsibility of mean k,

$$R^{(k)} = \sum_n r_k^{(n)}. \tag{20.9}$$

Algorithm 20.7. Soft K-means algorithm, version 1.

Notice the similarity of this soft K-means algorithm to the hard K-means algorithm 20.2. The update step is identical; the only difference is that the responsibilities $r_k^{(n)}$ can take on values between 0 and 1. Whereas the assignment $\hat{k}^{(n)}$ in the K-means algorithm involved a 'min' over the distances, the rule for assigning the responsibilities is a 'soft-min' (20.7).

▷ Exercise 20.2.[2] Show that as the stiffness β goes to ∞, the soft K means algorithm becomes identical to the original hard K-means algorithm, except for the way in which means with no assigned points behave. Describe what those means do instead of sitting still.

Dimensionally, the stiffness β is an inverse-length-squared, so we can associate a lengthscale, $\sigma \equiv 1/\sqrt{\beta}$, with it. The soft K-means algorithm is demonstrated in figure 20.8. The lengthscale is shown by the radius of the circles surrounding the four means. Each panel shows the final fixed point reached for a different value of the lengthscale σ.

▶ 20.3 Conclusion

At this point, we may have fixed some of the problems with the original K-means algorithm by introducing an extra complexity-control parameter β. But how should we set β? And what about the problem of the elongated clusters,

Large σ ...

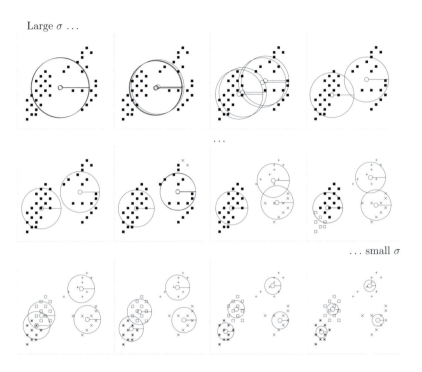

... small σ

Figure 20.8. Soft K-means
algorithm, version 1, applied to a
data set of 40 points. $K = 4$.
Implicit lengthscale parameter
$\sigma = 1/\beta^{1/2}$ varied from a large to
a small value. Each picture shows
the state of all four means, with
the implicit lengthscale shown by
the radius of the four circles, after
running the algorithm for several
tens of iterations. At the largest
lengthscale, all four means
converge exactly to the data
mean. Then the four means
separate into two groups of two.
At shorter lengthscales, each of
these pairs itself bifurcates into
subgroups.

and the clusters of unequal weight and width? Adding one stiffness parameter
β is not going to make all these problems go away.

We'll come back to these questions in a later chapter, as we develop the
mixture-density-modelling view of clustering.

Further reading

For a vector-quantization approach to clustering see (Luttrell, 1989; Luttrell,
1990).

▶ **20.4 Exercises**

▷ Exercise 20.3.[3, p.291] Explore the properties of the soft K-means algorithm,
version 1, assuming that the datapoints $\{\mathbf{x}\}$ come from a *single* separable
two-dimensional Gaussian distribution with mean zero and variances
$(\mathrm{var}(x_1), \mathrm{var}(x_2)) = (\sigma_1^2, \sigma_2^2)$, with $\sigma_1^2 > \sigma_2^2$. Set $K = 2$, assume N is
large, and investigate the fixed points of the algorithm as β is varied.
[Hint: assume that $\mathbf{m}^{(1)} = (m, 0)$ and $\mathbf{m}^{(2)} = (-m, 0)$.]

▷ Exercise 20.4.[3] Consider the soft K-means algorithm applied to a large
amount of one-dimensional data that comes from a mixture of two equal-
weight Gaussians with true means $\mu = \pm 1$ and standard deviation σ_P,
for example $\sigma_P = 1$. Show that the hard K-means algorithm with $K = 2$
leads to a solution in which the two means are further apart than the
two true means. Discuss what happens for other values of β, and find
the value of β such that the soft algorithm puts the two means in the
correct places.

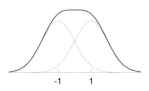

▶ 20.5 Solutions

Solution to exercise 20.1 (p.287).   We can associate an 'energy' with the state of the K-means algorithm by connecting a spring between each point $\mathbf{x}^{(n)}$ and the mean that is responsible for it. The energy of one spring is proportional to its squared-length, namely $\beta d(\mathbf{x}^{(n)}, \mathbf{m}^{(k)})$ where β is the stiffness of the spring. The total energy of all the springs is a *Lyapunov function* for the algorithm, because (a) the assignment step can only decrease the energy – a point only changes its allegiance if the length of its spring would be reduced; (b) the update step can only decrease the energy – moving $\mathbf{m}^{(k)}$ to the mean is the way to minimize the energy of its springs; and (c) the energy is bounded below – which is the second condition for a Lyapunov function. Since the algorithm has a Lyapunov function, it converges.

Solution to exercise 20.3 (p.290).   If the means are initialized to $\mathbf{m}^{(1)} = (m, 0)$ and $\mathbf{m}^{(1)} = (-m, 0)$, the assignment step for a point at location x_1, x_2 gives

$$r_1(\mathbf{x}) \;=\; \frac{\exp(-\beta(x_1 - m)^2/2)}{\exp(-\beta(x_1 - m)^2/2) + \exp(-\beta(x_1 + m)^2/2)} \tag{20.10}$$

$$=\; \frac{1}{1 + \exp(-2\beta m x_1)}, \tag{20.11}$$

and the updated m is

$$m' \;=\; \frac{\int \mathrm{d}x_1 \, P(x_1) \, x_1 \, r_1(\mathbf{x})}{\int \mathrm{d}x_1 \, P(x_1) \, r_1(\mathbf{x})} \tag{20.12}$$

$$=\; 2 \int \mathrm{d}x_1 \, P(x_1) \, x_1 \, \frac{1}{1 + \exp(-2\beta m x_1)}. \tag{20.13}$$

Now, $m = 0$ is a fixed point, but the question is, is it stable or unstable? For tiny m (that is, $\beta \sigma_1 m \ll 1$), we can Taylor expand

$$\frac{1}{1 + \exp(-2\beta m x_1)} \simeq \frac{1}{2}(1 + \beta m x_1) + \cdots \tag{20.14}$$

so

$$m' \;\simeq\; \int \mathrm{d}x_1 \, P(x_1) \, x_1 \, (1 + \beta m x_1) \tag{20.15}$$

$$=\; \sigma_1^2 \beta m. \tag{20.16}$$

For small m, m either grows or decays exponentially under this mapping, depending on whether $\sigma_1^2 \beta$ is greater than or less than 1. The fixed point $m = 0$ is *stable* if

$$\sigma_1^2 \leq 1/\beta \tag{20.17}$$

and *unstable* otherwise. [Incidentally, this derivation shows that this result is general, holding for any true probability distribution $P(x_1)$ having variance σ_1^2, not just the Gaussian.]

If $\sigma_1^2 > 1/\beta$ then there is a bifurcation and there are two stable fixed points surrounding the unstable fixed point at $m = 0$. To illustrate this bifurcation, figure 20.10 shows the outcome of running the soft K-means algorithm with $\beta = 1$ on one-dimensional data with standard deviation σ_1 for various values of σ_1. Figure 20.11 shows this pitchfork bifurcation from the other point of view, where the data's standard deviation σ_1 is fixed and the algorithm's lengthscale $\sigma = 1/\beta^{1/2}$ is varied on the horizontal axis.

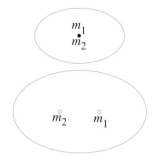

Figure 20.9. Schematic diagram of the bifurcation as the largest data variance σ_1 increases from below $1/\beta^{1/2}$ to above $1/\beta^{1/2}$. The data variance is indicated by the ellipse.

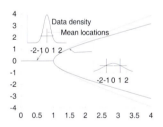

Figure 20.10. The stable mean locations as a function of σ_1, for constant β, found numerically (thick lines), and the approximation (20.22) (thin lines).

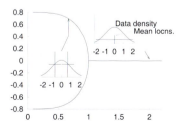

Figure 20.11. The stable mean locations as a function of $1/\beta^{1/2}$, for constant σ_1.

Here is a cheap theory to model how the fitted parameters $\pm m$ behave beyond the bifurcation, based on continuing the series expansion. This continuation of the series is rather suspect, since the series isn't necessarily expected to converge beyond the bifurcation point, but the theory fits well anyway.

We take our analytic approach one term further in the expansion

$$\frac{1}{1+\exp(-2\beta m x_1)} \simeq \frac{1}{2}(1+\beta m x_1 - \frac{1}{3}(\beta m x_1)^3) + \cdots \qquad (20.18)$$

then we can solve for the shape of the bifurcation to leading order, which depends on the fourth moment of the distribution:

$$m' \simeq \int dx_1\, P(x_1)x_1(1+\beta m x_1 - \frac{1}{3}(\beta m x_1)^3) \qquad (20.19)$$

$$= \sigma_1^2 \beta m - \frac{1}{3}(\beta m)^3 3\sigma_1^4. \qquad (20.20)$$

[At (20.20) we use the fact that $P(x_1)$ is Gaussian to find the fourth moment.] This map has a fixed point at m such that

$$\sigma_1^2 \beta(1 - (\beta m)^2 \sigma_1^2) = 1, \qquad (20.21)$$

i.e.,

$$m = \pm \beta^{-1/2} \frac{(\sigma_1^2 \beta - 1)^{1/2}}{\sigma_1^2 \beta}. \qquad (20.22)$$

The thin line in figure 20.10 shows this theoretical approximation. Figure 20.10 shows the bifurcation as a function of σ_1 for fixed β; figure 20.11 shows the bifurcation as a function of $1/\beta^{1/2}$ for fixed σ_1.

▷ Exercise 20.5.[2, p.292] Why does the pitchfork in figure 20.11 tend to the values $\sim \pm 0.8$ as $1/\beta^{1/2} \to 0$? Give an analytic expression for this asymptote.

Solution to exercise 20.5 (p.292). The asymptote is the mean of the rectified Gaussian,

$$\frac{\int_0^\infty \text{Normal}(x,1)x\,dx}{1/2} = \sqrt{2/\pi} \simeq 0.798. \qquad (20.23)$$

21

Exact Inference by Complete Enumeration

We open our toolbox of methods for handling probabilities by discussing a brute-force inference method: complete enumeration of all hypotheses, and evaluation of their probabilities. This approach is an exact method, and the difficulty of carrying it out will motivate the smarter exact and approximate methods introduced in the following chapters.

▶ ## 21.1 The burglar alarm

Bayesian probability theory is sometimes called 'common sense, amplified'. When thinking about the following questions, please ask your common sense what it thinks the answers are; we will then see how Bayesian methods confirm your everyday intuition.

Example 21.1. Fred lives in Los Angeles and commutes 60 miles to work. Whilst at work, he receives a phone-call from his neighbour saying that Fred's burglar alarm is ringing. What is the probability that there was a burglar in his house today? While driving home to investigate, Fred hears on the radio that there was a small earthquake that day near his home. 'Oh', he says, feeling relieved, 'it was probably the earthquake that set off the alarm'. What is the probability that there was a burglar in his house? (After Pearl, 1988).

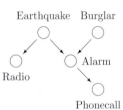

Figure 21.1. Belief network for the burglar alarm problem.

Let's introduce variables b (a burglar was present in Fred's house today), a (the alarm is ringing), p (Fred receives a phonecall from the neighbour reporting the alarm), e (a small earthquake took place today near Fred's house), and r (the radio report of earthquake is heard by Fred). The probability of all these variables might factorize as follows:

$$P(b, e, a, p, r) = P(b)P(e)P(a \,|\, b, e)P(p \,|\, a)P(r \,|\, e), \qquad (21.1)$$

and plausible values for the probabilities are:

1. Burglar probability:

$$P(b{=}1) = \beta, \quad P(b{=}0) = 1 - \beta, \qquad (21.2)$$

e.g., $\beta = 0.001$ gives a mean burglary rate of once every three years.

2. Earthquake probability:

$$P(e{=}1) = \epsilon, \quad P(e{=}0) = 1 - \epsilon, \qquad (21.3)$$

293

with, e.g., $\epsilon = 0.001$; our assertion that the earthquakes are independent of burglars, i.e., the prior probability of b and e is $P(b,e) = P(b)P(e)$, seems reasonable unless we take into account opportunistic burglars who strike immediately after earthquakes.

3. Alarm ringing probability: we assume the alarm will ring if *any* of the following three events happens: (a) a burglar enters the house, and triggers the alarm (let's assume the alarm has a reliability of $\alpha_b = 0.99$, i.e., 99% of burglars trigger the alarm); (b) an earthquake takes place, and triggers the alarm (perhaps $\alpha_e = 1\%$ of alarms are triggered by earthquakes?); or (c) some other event causes a false alarm; let's assume the false alarm rate f is 0.001, so Fred has false alarms from non-earthquake causes once every three years. [This type of dependence of a on b and e is known as a 'noisy-or'.] The probabilities of a given b and e are then:

$$
\begin{aligned}
P(a=0\,|\,b=0,e=0) &= (1-f), & P(a=1\,|\,b=0,e=0) &= f \\
P(a=0\,|\,b=1,e=0) &= (1-f)(1-\alpha_b), & P(a=1\,|\,b=1,e=0) &= 1-(1-f)(1-\alpha_b) \\
P(a=0\,|\,b=0,e=1) &= (1-f)(1-\alpha_e), & P(a=1\,|\,b=0,e=1) &= 1-(1-f)(1-\alpha_e) \\
P(a=0\,|\,b=1,e=1) &= (1-f)(1-\alpha_b)(1-\alpha_e), & P(a=1\,|\,b=1,e=1) &= 1-(1-f)(1-\alpha_b)(1-\alpha_e)
\end{aligned}
$$

or, in numbers,

$$
\begin{aligned}
P(a=0\,|\,b=0,e=0) &= 0.999, & P(a=1\,|\,b=0,e=0) &= 0.001 \\
P(a=0\,|\,b=1,e=0) &= 0.009\,99, & P(a=1\,|\,b=1,e=0) &= 0.990\,01 \\
P(a=0\,|\,b=0,e=1) &= 0.989\,01, & P(a=1\,|\,b=0,e=1) &= 0.010\,99 \\
P(a=0\,|\,b=1,e=1) &= 0.009\,890\,1, & P(a=1\,|\,b=1,e=1) &= 0.990\,109\,9.
\end{aligned}
$$

We assume the neighbour would never phone if the alarm is not ringing $[P(p=1\,|\,a=0) = 0]$; and that the radio is a trustworthy reporter too $[P(r=1\,|\,e=0) = 0]$; we won't need to specify the probabilities $P(p=1\,|\,a=1)$ or $P(r=1\,|\,e=1)$ in order to answer the questions above, since the outcomes $p=1$ and $r=1$ give us certainty respectively that $a=1$ and $e=1$.

We can answer the two questions about the burglar by computing the posterior probabilities of all hypotheses given the available information. Let's start by reminding ourselves that the probability that there is a burglar, before either p or r is observed, is $P(b=1) = \beta = 0.001$, and the probability that an earthquake took place is $P(e=1) = \epsilon = 0.001$, and these two propositions are *independent*.

First, when $p=1$, we know that the alarm is ringing: $a=1$. The posterior probability of b and e becomes:

$$
P(b,e\,|\,a=1) = \frac{P(a=1\,|\,b,e)P(b)P(e)}{P(a=1)}. \tag{21.4}
$$

The numerator's four possible values are

$$
\begin{aligned}
P(a=1\,|\,b=0,e=0) \times P(b=0) \times P(e=0) &= 0.001 & \times 0.999 \times 0.999 &= 0.000\,998 \\
P(a=1\,|\,b=1,e=0) \times P(b=1) \times P(e=0) &= 0.990\,01 & \times 0.001 \times 0.999 &= 0.000\,989 \\
P(a=1\,|\,b=0,e=1) \times P(b=0) \times P(e=1) &= 0.010\,99 & \times 0.999 \times 0.001 &= 0.000\,010\,979 \\
P(a=1\,|\,b=1,e=1) \times P(b=1) \times P(e=1) &= 0.990\,109\,9 \times 0.001 \times 0.001 &= 9.9 \times 10^{-7}.
\end{aligned}
$$

The normalizing constant is the sum of these four numbers, $P(a=1) = 0.002$, and the posterior probabilities are

$$
\begin{aligned}
P(b=0,e=0\,|\,a=1) &= 0.4993 \\
P(b=1,e=0\,|\,a=1) &= 0.4947 \\
P(b=0,e=1\,|\,a=1) &= 0.0055 \\
P(b=1,e=1\,|\,a=1) &= 0.0005.
\end{aligned} \tag{21.5}
$$

To answer the question, 'what's the probability a burglar was there?' we *marginalize* over the earthquake variable e:

$$
\begin{aligned}
P(b=0\,|\,a=1) &= P(b=0,e=0\,|\,a=1) + P(b=0,e=1\,|\,a=1) &= 0.505 \\
P(b=1\,|\,a=1) &= P(b=1,e=0\,|\,a=1) + P(b=1,e=1\,|\,a=1) &= 0.495.
\end{aligned}
\tag{21.6}
$$

So there is nearly a 50% chance that there was a burglar present. It is important to note that the variables b and e, which were independent *a priori*, are now *dependent*. The posterior distribution (21.5) is not a separable function of b and e. This fact is illustrated most simply by studying the effect of learning that $e = 1$.

When we learn $e=1$, the posterior probability of b is given by $P(b\,|\,e=1,a=1) = P(b,e=1\,|\,a=1)/P(e=1\,|\,a=1)$, i.e., by dividing the bottom two rows of (21.5), by their sum $P(e=1\,|\,a=1) = 0.0060$. The posterior probability of b is:

$$
\begin{aligned}
P(b=0\,|\,e=1,a=1) &= 0.92 \\
P(b=1\,|\,e=1,a=1) &= 0.08.
\end{aligned}
\tag{21.7}
$$

There is thus now an 8% chance that a burglar was in Fred's house. It is in accordance with everyday intuition that the probability that $b=1$ (a possible cause of the alarm) reduces when Fred learns that an earthquake, an alternative explanation of the alarm, has happened.

Explaining away

This phenomenon, that one of the possible causes ($b=1$) of some data (the data in this case being $a=1$) becomes *less* probable when another of the causes ($e=1$) becomes more probable, even though those two causes were independent variables *a priori*, is known as *explaining away*. Explaining away is an important feature of correct inferences, and one that any artificial intelligence should replicate.

If we believe that the neighbour and the radio service are unreliable or capricious, so that we are not certain that the alarm really is ringing or that an earthquake really has happened, the calculations become more complex, but the explaining-away effect persists; the arrival of the earthquake report r simultaneously makes it *more* probable that the alarm truly is ringing, and *less* probable that the burglar was present.

In summary, we solved the inference questions about the burglar by enumerating all four hypotheses about the variables (b,e), finding their posterior probabilities, and marginalizing to obtain the required inferences about b.

▷ Exercise 21.2.[2] After Fred receives the phone-call about the burglar alarm, but before he hears the radio report, what, from his point of view, is the probability that there was a small earthquake today?

▶ 21.2 Exact inference for continuous hypothesis spaces

Many of the hypothesis spaces we will consider are naturally thought of as continuous. For example, the unknown decay length λ of section 3.1 (p.48) lives in a continuous one-dimensional space; and the unknown mean and standard deviation of a Gaussian μ,σ live in a continuous two-dimensional space. In any practical computer implementation, such continuous spaces will necessarily be discretized, however, and so can, in principle, be enumerated – at a grid of parameter values, for example. In figure 3.2 we plotted the likelihood

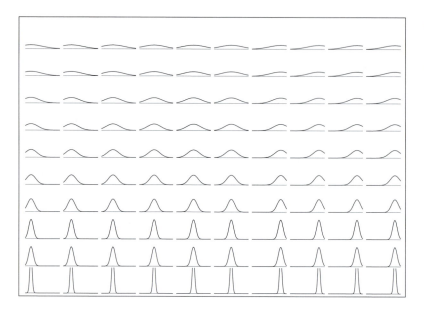

Figure 21.2. Enumeration of an entire (discretized) hypothesis space for one Gaussian with parameters μ (horizontal axis) and σ (vertical).

function for the decay length as a function of λ by evaluating the likelihood at a finely-spaced series of points.

A two-parameter model

Let's look at the Gaussian distribution as an example of a model with a two-dimensional hypothesis space. The one-dimensional Gaussian distribution is parameterized by a mean μ and a standard deviation σ:

$$P(x \mid \mu, \sigma) = \frac{1}{\sqrt{2\pi}\sigma} \exp\left(-\frac{(x-\mu)^2}{2\sigma^2}\right) \equiv \mathrm{Normal}(x; \mu, \sigma^2). \qquad (21.8)$$

Figure 21.2 shows an enumeration of one hundred hypotheses about the mean and standard deviation of a one-dimensional Gaussian distribution. These hypotheses are evenly spaced in a ten by ten square grid covering ten values of μ and ten values of σ. Each hypothesis is represented by a picture showing the probability density that it puts on x. We now examine the inference of μ and σ given data points x_n, $n = 1, \ldots, N$, assumed to be drawn independently from this density.

Figure 21.3. Five datapoints $\{x_n\}_{n=1}^5$. The horizontal coordinate is the value of the datum, x_n; the vertical coordinate has no meaning.

Imagine that we acquire data, for example the five points shown in figure 21.3. We can now evaluate the posterior probability of each of the one hundred subhypotheses by evaluating the likelihood of each, that is, the value of $P(\{x_n\}_{n=1}^5 \mid \mu, \sigma)$. The likelihood values are shown diagrammatically in figure 21.4 using the line thickness to encode the value of the likelihood. Subhypotheses with likelihood smaller than e^{-8} times the maximum likelihood have been deleted.

Using a finer grid, we can represent the same information by plotting the likelihood as a surface plot or contour plot as a function of μ and σ (figure 21.5).

A five-parameter mixture model

Eyeballing the data (figure 21.3), you might agree that it seems more plausible that they come not from a single Gaussian but from a mixture of two Gaussians, defined by two means, two standard deviations, and two mixing

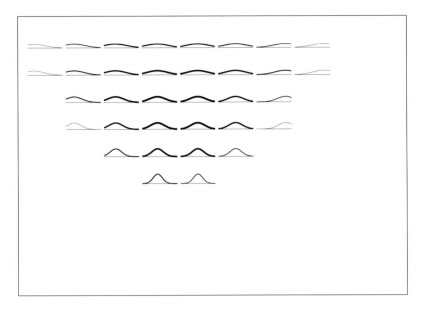

Figure 21.4. Likelihood function, given the data of figure 21.3, represented by line thickness. Subhypotheses having likelihood smaller than e^{-8} times the maximum likelihood are not shown.

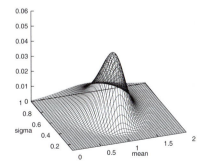 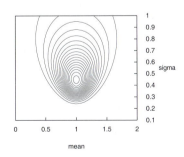

Figure 21.5. The likelihood function for the parameters of a Gaussian distribution. Surface plot and contour plot of the log likelihood as a function of μ and σ. The data set of $N = 5$ points had mean $\bar{x} = 1.0$ and $S^2 = \sum(x - \bar{x})^2 = 1.0$.

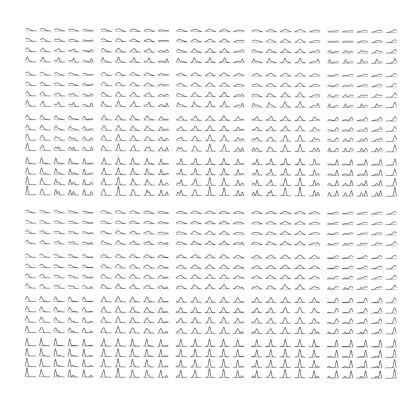

Figure 21.6. Enumeration of the entire (discretized) hypothesis space for a mixture of two Gaussians. Weight of the mixture components is $\pi_1, \pi_2 = 0.6, 0.4$ in the top half and $0.8, 0.2$ in the bottom half. Means μ_1 and μ_2 vary horizontally, and standard deviations σ_1 and σ_2 vary vertically.

coefficients π_1 and π_2, satisfying $\pi_1 + \pi_2 = 1$, $\pi_i \geq 0$.

$$P(x|\mu_1, \sigma_1, \pi_1, \mu_2, \sigma_2, \pi_2) = \frac{\pi_1}{\sqrt{2\pi}\sigma_1} \exp\left(-\frac{(x-\mu_1)^2}{2\sigma_1^2}\right) + \frac{\pi_2}{\sqrt{2\pi}\sigma_2} \exp\left(-\frac{(x-\mu_2)^2}{2\sigma_2^2}\right)$$

Let's enumerate the subhypotheses for this alternative model. The parameter space is five-dimensional, so it becomes challenging to represent it on a single page. Figure 21.6 enumerates 800 subhypotheses with different values of the five parameters $\mu_1, \mu_2, \sigma_1, \sigma_2, \pi_1$. The means are varied between five values each in the horizontal directions. The standard deviations take on four values each vertically. And π_1 takes on two values vertically. We can represent the inference about these five parameters in the light of the five datapoints as shown in figure 21.7.

If we wish to compare the one-Gaussian model with the mixture-of-two model, we can find the models' posterior probabilities by evaluating the marginal likelihood or evidence for each model $\mathcal{H}$, $P(\{x\} | \mathcal{H})$. The evidence is given by integrating over the parameters, $\boldsymbol{\theta}$; the integration can be implemented numerically by summing over the alternative enumerated values of $\boldsymbol{\theta}$,

$$P(\{x\} | \mathcal{H}) = \sum_{\boldsymbol{\theta}} P(\boldsymbol{\theta}) P(\{x\} | \boldsymbol{\theta}, \mathcal{H}), \tag{21.9}$$

where $P(\boldsymbol{\theta})$ is the prior distribution over the grid of parameter values, which I take to be uniform.

For the mixture of two Gaussians this integral is a five-dimensional integral; if it is to be performed at all accurately, the grid of points will need to be much finer than the grids shown in the figures. If the uncertainty about each of K parameters has been reduced by, say, a factor of ten by observing the data, then brute force integration requires a grid of at least 10^K points. This

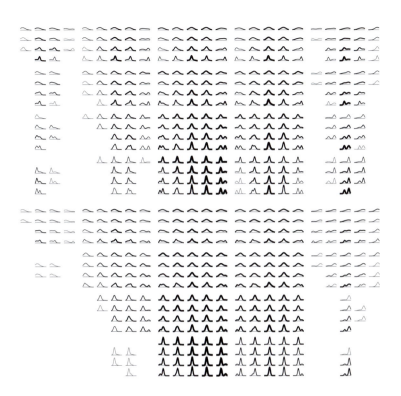

Figure 21.7. Inferring a mixture of two Gaussians. Likelihood function, given the data of figure 21.3, represented by line thickness. The hypothesis space is identical to that shown in figure 21.6. Subhypotheses having likelihood smaller than e^{-8} times the maximum likelihood are not shown, hence the blank regions, which correspond to hypotheses that the data have ruled out.

exponential growth of computation with model size is the reason why complete enumeration is rarely a feasible computational strategy.

Exercise 21.3.[1] Imagine fitting a mixture of ten Gaussians to data in a twenty-dimensional space. Estimate the computational cost of implementing inferences for this model by enumeration of a grid of parameter values.

22

***

Maximum Likelihood and Clustering

Rather than enumerate all hypotheses – which may be exponential in number – we can save a lot of time by homing in on one good hypothesis that fits the data well. This is the philosophy behind the maximum likelihood method, which identifies the setting of the parameter vector $\boldsymbol{\theta}$ that maximizes the likelihood, $P(\text{Data} \mid \boldsymbol{\theta}, \mathcal{H})$.

For some models the maximum likelihood parameters can be identified instantly from the data; for more complex models, finding the maximum likelihood parameters may require an iterative algorithm.

For any model, it is usually easiest to work with the *logarithm* of the likelihood rather than the likelihood, since likelihoods, being products of the probabilities of many data points, tend to be very small. Likelihoods multiply; log likelihoods add.

▶ 22.1 Maximum likelihood for one Gaussian

We return to the Gaussian for our first examples. Assume we have data $\{x_n\}_{n=1}^{N}$. The log likelihood is:

$$\ln P(\{x_n\}_{n=1}^{N} \mid \mu, \sigma) \;=\; -N\ln(\sqrt{2\pi}\sigma) - \sum_n (x_n - \mu)^2/(2\sigma^2). \quad (22.1)$$

The likelihood can be expressed in terms of two functions of the data, the sample mean

$$\bar{x} \equiv \sum_{n=1}^{N} x_n/N, \quad (22.2)$$

and the sum of square deviations

$$S \equiv \sum_n (x_n - \bar{x})^2 : \quad (22.3)$$

$$\ln P(\{x_n\}_{n=1}^{N} \mid \mu, \sigma) = -N\ln(\sqrt{2\pi}\sigma) - [N(\mu - \bar{x})^2 + S]/(2\sigma^2). \quad (22.4)$$

Because the likelihood depends on the data only through $\bar{x}$ and S, these two quantities are known as *sufficient statistics*.

Example 22.1. Differentiate the log likelihood with respect to μ and show that, if the standard deviation is known to be σ, the maximum likelihood mean μ of a Gaussian is equal to the sample mean $\bar{x}$, for any value of σ.

Solution.

$$\frac{\partial}{\partial \mu} \ln P \;=\; -\frac{N(\mu - \bar{x})}{\sigma^2} \quad (22.5)$$

$$=\; 0 \quad \text{when } \mu = \bar{x}. \qquad \square \quad (22.6)$$

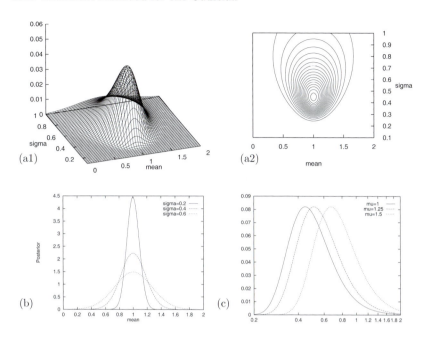

Figure 22.1. The likelihood function for the parameters of a Gaussian distribution.
(a1, a2) Surface plot and contour plot of the log likelihood as a function of μ and σ. The data set of $N = 5$ points had mean $\bar{x} = 1.0$ and $S^2 = \sum(x - \bar{x})^2 = 1.0$.
(b) The posterior probability of μ for various values of σ.
(c) The posterior probability of σ for various fixed values of μ.

If we Taylor-expand the log likelihood about the maximum, we can define approximate error bars on the maximum likelihood parameter: we use a quadratic approximation to estimate how far from the maximum-likelihood parameter setting we can go before the likelihood falls by some standard factor, for example $e^{1/2}$, or $e^{4/2}$, In the special case of a likelihood that is a Gaussian function of the parameters, the quadratic approximation is exact.

Example 22.2. Find the second derivative of the log likelihood with respect to μ, and find the error bars on μ, given the data and σ.

Solution.

$$\frac{\partial^2}{\partial \mu^2} \ln P = -\frac{N}{\sigma^2}. \qquad \Box \quad (22.7)$$

Comparing this curvature with the curvature of the log of a Gaussian distribution over μ of standard deviation σ_μ, $\exp(-\mu^2/(2\sigma_\mu^2))$, which is $1/\sigma_\mu^2$, we can deduce that the error bars on μ (derived from the likelihood function) are

$$\sigma_\mu = \frac{\sigma}{\sqrt{N}}. \qquad (22.8)$$

The error bars have this property: at the two points $\mu = \bar{x} \pm \sigma_\mu$, the likelihood is smaller than its maximum value by a factor of $e^{1/2}$.

Example 22.3. Find the maximum likelihood standard deviation σ of a Gaussian, whose mean is known to be μ, in the light of data $\{x_n\}_{n=1}^N$. Find the second derivative of the log likelihood with respect to $\ln \sigma$, and error bars on $\ln \sigma$.

Solution. The likelihood's dependence on σ is

$$\ln P(\{x_n\}_{n=1}^N \,|\, \mu, \sigma) = -N \ln(\sqrt{2\pi}\sigma) - \frac{S_{\text{tot}}}{(2\sigma^2)}, \qquad (22.9)$$

where $S_{\text{tot}} = \sum_n (x_n - \mu)^2$. To find the maximum of the likelihood, we can differentiate with respect to $\ln \sigma$. [It's often most hygienic to differentiate with respect to $\ln u$ rather than u, when u is a scale variable; we use $du^n/d(\ln u) = nu^n$.]

$$\frac{\partial \ln P(\{x_n\}_{n=1}^{N} \mid \mu, \sigma)}{\partial \ln \sigma} = -N + \frac{S_{\text{tot}}}{\sigma^2} \qquad (22.10)$$

This derivative is zero when

$$\sigma^2 = \frac{S_{\text{tot}}}{N}, \qquad (22.11)$$

i.e.,

$$\sigma = \sqrt{\frac{\sum_{n=1}^{N}(x_n - \mu)^2}{N}}. \qquad (22.12)$$

The second derivative is

$$\frac{\partial^2 \ln P(\{x_n\}_{n=1}^{N} \mid \mu, \sigma)}{\partial(\ln \sigma)^2} = -2\frac{S_{\text{tot}}}{\sigma^2}, \qquad (22.13)$$

and at the maximum-likelihood value of σ^2, this equals $-2N$. So error bars on $\ln \sigma$ are

$$\sigma_{\ln \sigma} = \frac{1}{\sqrt{2N}}. \qquad \Box \qquad (22.14)$$

▷ Exercise 22.4.[1] Show that the values of μ and $\ln \sigma$ that jointly maximize the likelihood are: $\{\mu, \sigma\}_{\text{ML}} = \left\{ \bar{x}, \sigma_N = \sqrt{S/N} \right\}$, where

$$\sigma_N \equiv \sqrt{\frac{\sum_{n=1}^{N}(x_n - \bar{x})^2}{N}}. \qquad (22.15)$$

▶ 22.2 Maximum likelihood for a mixture of Gaussians

We now derive an algorithm for fitting a mixture of Gaussians to one-dimensional data. In fact, this algorithm is so important to understand that, *you*, gentle reader, get to derive the algorithm. Please work through the following exercise.

Exercise 22.5.[2, p.310] A random variable x is assumed to have a probability distribution that is a *mixture of two Gaussians*,

$$P(x \mid \mu_1, \mu_2, \sigma) = \left[\sum_{k=1}^{2} p_k \frac{1}{\sqrt{2\pi\sigma^2}} \exp\left(-\frac{(x - \mu_k)^2}{2\sigma^2} \right) \right], \qquad (22.16)$$

where the two Gaussians are given the labels $k = 1$ and $k = 2$; the prior probability of the class label k is $\{p_1 = 1/2, p_2 = 1/2\}$; $\{\mu_k\}$ are the means of the two Gaussians; and both have standard deviation σ. For brevity, we denote these parameters by $\boldsymbol{\theta} \equiv \{\{\mu_k\}, \sigma\}$.

A data set consists of N points $\{x_n\}_{n=1}^{N}$ which are assumed to be independent samples from this distribution. Let k_n denote the unknown class label of the nth point.

Assuming that $\{\mu_k\}$ and σ are known, show that the posterior probability of the class label k_n of the nth point can be written as

$$
\begin{aligned}
P(k_n = 1 \mid x_n, \boldsymbol{\theta}) &= \frac{1}{1 + \exp[-(w_1 x_n + w_0)]} \\
P(k_n = 2 \mid x_n, \boldsymbol{\theta}) &= \frac{1}{1 + \exp[+(w_1 x_n + w_0)]},
\end{aligned}
\qquad (22.17)
$$

and give expressions for w_1 and w_0.

Assume now that the means $\{\mu_k\}$ are *not* known, and that we wish to infer them from the data $\{x_n\}_{n=1}^N$. (The standard deviation σ is known.) In the remainder of this question we will derive an iterative algorithm for finding values for $\{\mu_k\}$ that maximize the likelihood,

$$P(\{x_n\}_{n=1}^N|\{\mu_k\},\sigma) = \prod_n P(x_n|\{\mu_k\},\sigma). \qquad (22.18)$$

Let L denote the log of the likelihood. Show that the derivative of the log likelihood with respect to μ_k is given by

$$\frac{\partial}{\partial \mu_k}L = \sum_n p_{k|n}\frac{(x_n-\mu_k)}{\sigma^2}, \qquad (22.19)$$

where $p_{k|n} \equiv P(k_n=k|x_n,\boldsymbol{\theta})$ appeared above at equation (22.17).

Show, neglecting terms in $\frac{\partial}{\partial \mu_k}P(k_n=k|x_n,\boldsymbol{\theta})$, that the second derivative is approximately given by

$$\frac{\partial^2}{\partial \mu_k^2}L = -\sum_n p_{k|n}\frac{1}{\sigma^2}. \qquad (22.20)$$

Hence show that from an initial state μ_1,μ_2, an approximate Newton–Raphson step updates these parameters to μ'_1,μ'_2, where

$$\mu'_k = \frac{\sum_n p_{k|n}x_n}{\sum_n p_{k|n}}. \qquad (22.21)$$

[The Newton–Raphson method for maximizing $L(\mu)$ updates μ to $\mu' = \mu - \left[\frac{\partial L}{\partial \mu} \Big/ \frac{\partial^2 L}{\partial \mu^2}\right]$.]

Assuming that $\sigma = 1$, sketch a contour plot of the likelihood function L as a function of μ_1 and μ_2 for the data set shown above. The data set consists of 32 points. Describe the peaks in your sketch and indicate their widths.

Notice that the algorithm you have derived for maximizing the likelihood is identical to the soft K-means algorithm of section 20.4. Now that it is clear that clustering can be viewed as mixture-density-modelling, we are able to derive enhancements to the K-means algorithm, which rectify the problems we noted earlier.

▶ 22.3 Enhancements to soft K-means

Algorithm 22.2 shows a version of the soft-K-means algorithm corresponding to a modelling assumption that each cluster is a spherical Gaussian having its own width (each cluster has its own $\beta^{(k)} = 1/\sigma_k^2$). The algorithm updates the lengthscales σ_k for itself. The algorithm also includes cluster weight parameters $\pi_1, \pi_2, \ldots, \pi_K$ which also update themselves, allowing accurate modelling of data from clusters of unequal weights. This algorithm is demonstrated in figure 20.8 and figure 22.3 for two data sets that we've seen before. The second example shows that convergence can take a long time, but eventually the algorithm identifies the small cluster and the large cluster.

Assignment step. The responsibilities are

$$r_k^{(n)} = \frac{\pi_k \frac{1}{(\sqrt{2\pi}\sigma_k)^I} \exp\left(-\frac{1}{\sigma_k^2} d(\mathbf{m}^{(k)}, \mathbf{x}^{(n)})\right)}{\sum_{k'} \pi_k \frac{1}{(\sqrt{2\pi}\sigma_{k'})^I} \exp\left(-\frac{1}{\sigma_{k'}^2} d(\mathbf{m}^{(k')}, \mathbf{x}^{(n)})\right)} \quad (22.22)$$

where I is the dimensionality of $\mathbf{x}$.

Update step. Each cluster's parameters, $\mathbf{m}^{(k)}$, π_k, and σ_k^2, are adjusted to match the data points that it is responsible for.

$$\mathbf{m}^{(k)} = \frac{\sum_n r_k^{(n)} \mathbf{x}^{(n)}}{R^{(k)}} \quad (22.23)$$

$$\sigma_k^2 = \frac{\sum_n r_k^{(n)} (\mathbf{x}^{(n)} - \mathbf{m}^{(k)})^2}{I R^{(k)}} \quad (22.24)$$

$$\pi_k = \frac{R^{(k)}}{\sum_k R^{(k)}} \quad (22.25)$$

where $R^{(k)}$ is the total responsibility of mean k,

$$R^{(k)} = \sum_n r_k^{(n)}. \quad (22.26)$$

Algorithm 22.2. The soft K-means algorithm, version 2.

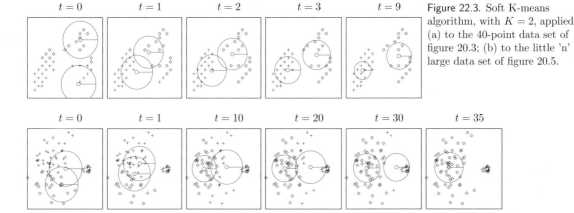

$t = 0$ $t = 1$ $t = 2$ $t = 3$ $t = 9$

$t = 0$ $t = 1$ $t = 10$ $t = 20$ $t = 30$ $t = 35$

Figure 22.3. Soft K-means algorithm, with $K = 2$, applied (a) to the 40-point data set of figure 20.3; (b) to the little 'n' large data set of figure 20.5.

$$r_k^{(n)} = \frac{\pi_k \frac{1}{\prod_{i=1}^I \sqrt{2\pi}\sigma_i^{(k)}} \exp\left(-\sum_{i=1}^I (m_i^{(k)} - x_i^{(n)})^2 \Big/ 2(\sigma_i^{(k)})^2\right)}{\sum_{k'} (\text{numerator, with } k' \text{ in place of } k)} \quad (22.27)$$

$$\sigma_i^{2(k)} = \frac{\sum_n r_k^{(n)} (x_i^{(n)} - m_i^{(k)})^2}{R^{(k)}} \quad (22.28)$$

Algorithm 22.4. The soft K-means algorithm, version 3, which corresponds to a model of axis-aligned Gaussians.

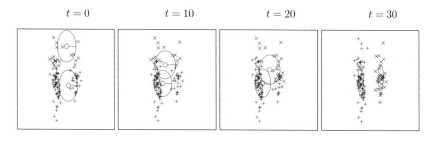

Figure 22.5. Soft K-means algorithm, version 3, applied to the data consisting of two cigar-shaped clusters. $K = 2$ (c.f. figure 20.6).

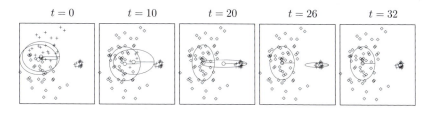

Figure 22.6. Soft K-means algorithm, version 3, applied to the little 'n' large data set. $K = 2$.

Soft K-means, version 2, is a maximum-likelihood algorithm for fitting a mixture of *spherical Gaussians* to data – 'spherical' meaning that the variance of the Gaussian is the same in all directions. This algorithm is still no good at modelling the cigar-shaped clusters of figure 20.6. If we wish to model the clusters by axis-aligned Gaussians with possibly-unequal variances, we replace the assignment rule (22.22) and the variance update rule (22.24) by the rules (22.27) and (22.28) displayed in algorithm 22.4.

A proof that the algorithm does indeed maximize the likelihood is deferred to section 33.7.

This third version of soft K-means is demonstrated in figure 22.5 on the 'two cigars' data set of figure 20.6. After 30 iterations, the algorithm has correctly located the two clusters. Figure 22.6 shows the same algorithm applied to the little 'n' large data set, where, again, the correct cluster locations are found.

▶ 22.4 A fatal flaw of maximum likelihood

Finally, figure 22.7 sounds a cautionary note: when we fit $K = 4$ means to our first toy data set, we sometimes find that very small clusters form, covering just one or two data points. This is a pathological property of soft K-means clustering, versions 2 and 3.

▷ Exercise 22.6.[2] Investigate what happens if one mean $\mathbf{m}^{(k)}$ sits exactly on top of one data point; show that if the variance σ_k^2 is sufficiently small, then no return is possible: σ_k^2 becomes ever smaller.

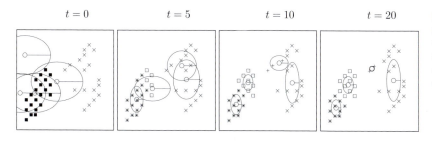

Figure 22.7. Soft K means algorithm applied to a data set of 40 points. $K = 4$. Notice that at convergence, one very small cluster has formed between two data points.

KABOOM!

Soft K-means can blow up. Put one cluster exactly on one data point and let its variance go to zero – you can obtain an arbitrarily large likelihood! Maximum likelihood methods can break down by finding highly tuned models that fit part of the data perfectly. This phenomenon is known as overfitting. The reason we are not interested in these solutions with enormous likelihood is this: sure, these parameter-settings may have enormous posterior probability *density*, but the density is large over only a very small *volume* of parameter space. So the probability *mass* associated with these likelihood spikes is usually tiny.

We conclude that maximum likelihood methods are not a satisfactory general solution to data modelling problems: the likelihood may be infinitely large at certain parameter settings. Even if the likelihood does not have infinitely-large spikes, the maximum of the likelihood is often unrepresentative, in high-dimensional problems.

Even in low-dimensional problems, maximum likelihood solutions can be unrepresentative. As you may know from basic statistics, the maximum likelihood estimator (22.15) for a Gaussian's standard deviation, σ_N, is a *biased* estimator, a topic that we'll take up in Chapter 24.

The maximum a posteriori (MAP) method

A popular replacement for maximizing the likelihood is maximizing the Bayesian posterior probability density of the parameters instead. However, multiplying the likelihood by a prior and maximizing the posterior does not make the above problems go away; the posterior density often also has infinitely-large spikes, and the maximum of the posterior probability density is often unrepresentative of the whole posterior distribution. Think back to the concept of typicality, which we encountered in Chapter 4: in high dimensions, most of the probability mass is in a typical set whose properties are quite different from the points that have the maximum probability density. Maxima are atypical.

A further reason for disliking the maximum *a posteriori* is that it is *basis-dependent*. If we make a nonlinear change of basis from the parameter θ to the parameter $u = f(\theta)$ then the probability density of θ is transformed to

$$P(u) = P(\theta) \left| \frac{\partial \theta}{\partial u} \right|. \qquad (22.29)$$

The maximum of the density $P(u)$ will usually not coincide with the maximum of the density $P(\theta)$. (For figures illustrating such nonlinear changes of basis, see the next chapter.) It seems undesirable to use a method whose answers change when we change representation.

Further reading

The soft K-means algorithm is at the heart of the automatic classification package, AutoClass (Hanson *et al.*, 1991b; Hanson *et al.*, 1991a).

▶ ## 22.5 Further exercises

Exercises where maximum likelihood may be useful

Exercise 22.7.[3] Make a version of the K-means algorithm that models the data as a mixture of K arbitrary Gaussians, i.e., Gaussians that are not constrained to be axis-aligned.

▷ Exercise 22.8.[2] (a) A photon counter is pointed at a remote star for one minute, in order to infer the brightness, i.e., the rate of photons arriving at the counter per minute, λ. Assuming the number of photons collected r has a Poisson distribution with mean λ,

$$P(r\,|\,\lambda) = \exp(-\lambda)\frac{\lambda^r}{r!}, \qquad (22.30)$$

what is the maximum likelihood estimate for λ, given $r=9$? Find error bars on $\ln\lambda$.

(b) Same situation, but now we assume that the counter detects not only photons from the star but also 'background' photons. The background rate of photons is known to be $b=13$ photons per minute. We assume the number of photons collected, r, has a Poisson distribution with mean $\lambda+b$. Now, given $r=9$ detected photons, what is the maximum likelihood estimate for λ? Comment on this answer, discussing also the Bayesian posterior distribution, and the 'unbiased estimator' of sampling theory, $\hat{\lambda} \equiv r - b$.

Exercise 22.9.[2] A bent coin is tossed N times, giving N_a heads and N_b tails. Assume a beta distribution prior for the probability of heads, p, for example the uniform distribution. Find the maximum likelihood and maximum *a posteriori* values of p, then find the maximum likelihood and maximum *a posteriori* values of the logit $a \equiv \ln[p/(1-p)]$. Compare with the predictive distribution, i.e., the probability that the next toss will come up heads.

▷ Exercise 22.10.[2] *Two men looked through prison bars; one saw stars, the other tried to infer where the window frame was.*

From the other side of a room, you look through a window and see stars at locations $\{(x_n, y_n)\}$. You can't see the window edges because it is totally dark apart from the stars. Assuming the window is rectangular and that the visible stars's locations are independently randomly distributed, what are the inferred values of $(x_{\min}, y_{\min}, x_{\max}, y_{\max})$, according to maximum likelihood? Sketch the likelihood as a function of $x_{\max}$, for fixed $x_{\min}$, $y_{\min}$, and $y_{\max}$.

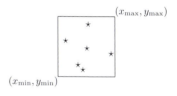

▷ Exercise 22.11.[3] A sailor infers his location (x, y) by measuring the bearings of three buoys whose locations (x_n, y_n) are given on his chart. Let the true bearings of the buoys be θ_n. Assuming that his measurement $\tilde{\theta}_n$ of each bearing is subject to Gaussian noise of small standard deviation σ, what is his inferred location, by maximum likelihood?

The sailor's rule of thumb says that the boat's position can be taken to be the centre of the cocked hat, the triangle produced by the intersection of the three measured bearings (figure 22.8). Can you persuade him that the maximum likelihood answer is better?

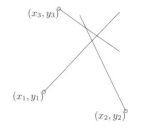

▷ Exercise 22.12.[3, p.310] Maximum likelihood fitting of an exponential-family model.

Assume that a variable $\mathbf{x}$ comes from a probability distribution of the form

$$P(\mathbf{x}\,|\,\mathbf{w}) = \frac{1}{Z(\mathbf{w})}\exp\left(\sum_k w_k f_k(\mathbf{x})\right), \qquad (22.31)$$

Figure 22.8. The standard way of drawing three slightly inconsistent bearings on a chart produces a triangle called a cocked hat. Where is the sailor?

where the functions $f_k(\mathbf{x})$ are given, and the parameters $\mathbf{w} = \{w_k\}$ are not known. A data set $\{\mathbf{x}^{(n)}\}$ of N points is supplied.

Show by differentiating the log likelihood that the maximum-likelihood parameters $\mathbf{w}_{\mathrm{ML}}$ satisfy

$$\sum_{\mathbf{x}} P(\mathbf{x} \,|\, \mathbf{w}_{\mathrm{ML}}) f_k(\mathbf{x}) = \frac{1}{N} \sum_n f_k(\mathbf{x}^{(n)}), \qquad (22.32)$$

where the left-hand sum is over *all* $\mathbf{x}$, and the right-hand sum is over the data points. A shorthand for this result is that each function-average under the fitted model must equal the function-average found in the data:

$$\langle f_k \rangle_{P(\mathbf{x} | \mathbf{w}_{\mathrm{ML}})} = \langle f_k \rangle_{\mathrm{Data}}. \qquad (22.33)$$

▷ Exercise 22.13.[3] 'Maximum entropy' fitting of models to constraints.

When confronted by a probability distribution $P(\mathbf{x})$ about which only a few facts are known, the *maximum entropy principle* (maxent) offers a rule for *choosing* a distribution that satisfies those constraints. According to maxent, you should select the $P(\mathbf{x})$ that maximizes the entropy

$$H = \sum_{\mathbf{x}} P(\mathbf{x}) \log 1/P(\mathbf{x}), \qquad (22.34)$$

subject to the constraints. Assuming the constraints assert that the *averages* of certain functions $f_k(\mathbf{x})$ are known, i.e.,

$$\langle f_k \rangle_{P(\mathbf{x})} = F_k, \qquad (22.35)$$

show, by introducing Lagrange multipliers (one for each constraint, including normalization), that the maximum-entropy distribution has the form

$$P(\mathbf{x})_{\mathrm{Maxent}} = \frac{1}{Z} \exp\left(\sum_k w_k f_k(\mathbf{x})\right), \qquad (22.36)$$

where the parameters Z and $\{w_k\}$ are set such that the constraints (22.35) are satisfied.

And hence the maximum entropy method gives identical results to maximum likelihood fitting of an exponential-family model (previous exercise).

The maximum entropy method has sometimes been recommended as a method for assigning prior distributions in Bayesian modelling. While the outcomes of the maximum entropy method are sometimes interesting and thought-provoking, I do not advocate maxent as *the* approach to assigning priors.

Maximum entropy is also sometimes proposed as a method for solving inference problems – for example, 'given that the mean score of this unfair six-sided die is 2.5, what is its probability distribution $(p_1, p_2, p_3, p_4, p_5, p_6)$?' I think it is a bad idea to use maximum entropy in this way; it can give very silly answers. The correct way to solve inference problems is to use Bayes' theorem.

Exercises where maximum likelihood and MAP have difficulties

▷ **Exercise 22.14.**[2] This exercise explores the idea that maximizing a probability density is a poor way to find a point that is representative of the density. Consider a Gaussian distribution in a k-dimensional space, $P(\mathbf{w}) = (1/\sqrt{2\pi}\,\sigma_W)^k \exp(-\sum_1^k w_i^2/2\sigma_W^2)$. Show that nearly all of the probability mass of a Gaussian is in a thin shell of radius $r = \sqrt{k}\sigma_W$ and of thickness proportional to $r/\sqrt{k}$. For example, in 1000 dimensions, 90% of the mass of a Gaussian with $\sigma_W = 1$ is in a shell of radius 31.6 and thickness 2.8. However, the probability *density* at the origin is $e^{k/2} \simeq 10^{217}$ times bigger than the density at this shell where most of the probability mass is.

Now consider two Gaussian densities in 1000 dimensions that differ in radius σ_W by just 1%, and that contain equal total probability mass. Show that the maximum probability density is greater at the centre of the Gaussian with smaller σ_W by a factor of $\sim\exp(0.01k) \simeq 20\,000$.

In ill-posed problems, a typical posterior distribution is often a weighted superposition of Gaussians with varying means and standard deviations, so the true posterior has a skew peak, with the maximum of the probability density located near the mean of the Gaussian distribution that has the smallest standard deviation, not the Gaussian with the greatest weight.

Scientist	x_n
A	−27.020
B	3.570
C	8.191
D	9.898
E	9.603
F	9.945
G	10.056

Figure 22.9. Seven measurements $\{x_n\}$ of a parameter μ by seven scientists each having his own noise-level σ_n.

▷ **Exercise 22.15.**[3] **The seven scientists.** N datapoints $\{x_n\}$ are drawn from N distributions, all of which are Gaussian with a common mean μ but with different unknown standard deviations σ_n. What are the maximum likelihood parameters $\mu, \{\sigma_n\}$ given the data?   For example, seven scientists (A, B, C, D, E, F, G) with wildly-differing experimental skills measure μ. You expect some of them to do accurate work (i.e., to have small σ_n), and some of them to turn in wildly inaccurate answers (i.e., to have enormous σ_n). Figure 22.9 shows their seven results. What is μ, and how reliable is each scientist?

I hope you agree that, intuitively, it looks pretty certain that A and B are both inept measurers, that D–G are better, and that the true value of μ is somewhere close to 10. But what does maximizing the likelihood tell you?

Exercise 22.16.[3] **Problems with MAP method.** A collection of widgets $i = 1\ldots k$ have a property called 'wodge', w_i, which we measure, widget by widget, in noisy experiments with a known noise level $\sigma_\nu = 1.0$. Our model for these quantities is that they come from a Gaussian prior $P(w_i \mid \alpha) = \text{Normal}(0, 1/\alpha)$, where $\alpha = 1/\sigma_W^2$ is not known. Our prior for this variance is flat over $\log \sigma_W$ from $\sigma_W = 0.1$ to $\sigma_W = 10$.

Scenario 1. Suppose four widgets have been measured and give the following data: $\{d_1, d_2, d_3, d_4\} = \{2.2, -2.2, 2.8, -2.8\}$. We are interested in inferring the wodges of these four widgets.

(a) Find the values of $\mathbf{w}$ and α that maximize the posterior probability $P(\mathbf{w}, \log \alpha \mid \mathbf{d})$.

(b) Marginalize over α and find the posterior probability density of $\mathbf{w}$ given the data. [Integration skills required. See MacKay (1999a) for solution.] Find maxima of $P(\mathbf{w} \mid \mathbf{d})$. [Answer: two maxima – one at $\mathbf{w}_{\text{MP}} = \{1.8, -1.8, 2.2, -2.2\}$, with error bars on all four parameters (obtained from Gaussian approximation to the posterior) ± 0.9; and one at $\mathbf{w}'_{\mathrm{MP}} = \{0.03, -0.03, 0.04, -0.04\}$ with error bars ± 0.1.]

Scenario 2. Suppose in addition to the four measurements above we are now informed that there are four more widgets that have been measured with a much less accurate instrument, having $\sigma'_\nu = 100.0$. Thus we now have both well-determined and ill-determined parameters, as in a typical ill-posed problem. The data from these measurements were a string of uninformative values, $\{d_5, d_6, d_7, d_8\} = \{100, -100, 100, -100\}$.

We are again asked to infer the wodges of the widgets. Intuitively, our inferences about the well-measured widgets should be negligibly affected by this vacuous information about the poorly-measured widgets. But what happens to the MAP method?

(a) Find the values of $\mathbf{w}$ and α that maximize the posterior probability $P(\mathbf{w}, \log \alpha \mid \mathbf{d})$.

(b) Find maxima of $P(\mathbf{w} \mid \mathbf{d})$. [Answer: only one maximum, $\mathbf{w}_{\mathrm{MP}} = \{0.03, -0.03, 0.03, -0.03, 0.0001, -0.0001, 0.0001, -0.0001\}$, with error bars on all eight parameters ± 0.11.]

▶ **22.6 Solutions**

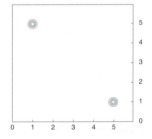

Figure 22.10. The likelihood as a function of μ_1 and μ_2.

Solution to exercise 22.5 (p.302). Figure 22.10 shows a contour plot of the likelihood function for the 32 data points. The peaks are pretty-near centred on the points $(1, 5)$ and $(5, 1)$, and are pretty-near circular in their contours. The width of each of the peaks is a standard deviation of $\sigma/\sqrt{16} = 1/4$. The peaks are roughly Gaussian in shape.

Solution to exercise 22.12 (p.307). The log likelihood is:

$$\ln P(\{\mathbf{x}^{(n)}\} \mid \mathbf{w}) = -N \ln Z(\mathbf{w}) + \sum_n \sum_k w_k f_k(\mathbf{x}^{(n)}). \tag{22.37}$$

$$\frac{\partial}{\partial w_k} \ln P(\{\mathbf{x}^{(n)}\} \mid \mathbf{w}) = -N \frac{\partial}{\partial w_k} \ln Z(\mathbf{w}) + \sum_n f_k(\mathbf{x}). \tag{22.38}$$

Now, the fun part is what happens when we differentiate the log of the normalizing constant:

$$\frac{\partial}{\partial w_k} \ln Z(\mathbf{w}) = \frac{1}{Z(\mathbf{w})} \sum_{\mathbf{x}} \frac{\partial}{\partial w_k} \exp\left(\sum_{k'} w_{k'} f_{k'}(\mathbf{x})\right)$$

$$= \frac{1}{Z(\mathbf{w})} \sum_{\mathbf{x}} \exp\left(\sum_{k'} w_{k'} f_{k'}(\mathbf{x})\right) f_k(\mathbf{x}) = \sum_{\mathbf{x}} P(\mathbf{x} \mid \mathbf{w}) f_k(\mathbf{x}), \tag{22.39}$$

so

$$\frac{\partial}{\partial w_k} \ln P(\{\mathbf{x}^{(n)}\} \mid \mathbf{w}) = -N \sum_{\mathbf{x}} P(\mathbf{x} \mid \mathbf{w}) f_k(\mathbf{x}) + \sum_n f_k(\mathbf{x}), \tag{22.40}$$

and at the maximum of the likelihood,

$$\sum_{\mathbf{x}} P(\mathbf{x} \mid \mathbf{w}_{\mathrm{ML}}) f_k(\mathbf{x}) = \frac{1}{N} \sum_n f_k(\mathbf{x}^{(n)}). \tag{22.41}$$

23

Useful Probability Distributions

In Bayesian data modelling, there's a small collection of probability distributions that come up again and again. The purpose of this chapter is to introduce these distributions so that they won't be intimidating when encountered in combat situations.

There is no need to memorize any of them, except perhaps the Gaussian; if a distribution is important enough, it will memorize itself, and otherwise, it can easily be looked up.

▶ 23.1 Distributions over integers

Binomial, Poisson, exponential

We already encountered the binomial distribution and the Poisson distribution on page 2.

The *binomial distribution* for an integer r with parameters f (the bias, $f \in [0, 1]$) and N (the number of trials) is:

$$P(r \mid f, N) = \binom{N}{r} f^r (1-f)^{N-r} \quad r \in \{0, 1, 2, \ldots, N\}. \quad (23.1)$$

The binomial distribution arises, for example, when we flip a bent coin, with bias f, N times, and observe the number of heads, r.

The *Poisson distribution* with parameter $\lambda > 0$ is:

$$P(r \mid \lambda) = e^{-\lambda} \frac{\lambda^r}{r!} \quad r \in \{0, 1, 2, \ldots\}. \quad (23.2)$$

The Poisson distribution arises, for example, when we count the number of photons r that arrive in a pixel during a fixed interval, given that the mean intensity on the pixel corresponds to an average number of photons λ.

The *exponential distribution on integers*,,

$$P(r \mid f) = f^r (1-f) \quad r \in (0, 1, 2, \ldots, \infty), \quad (23.3)$$

arises in waiting problems. How long will you have to wait until a six is rolled, if a fair six-sided dice is rolled? Answer: the probability distribution of the number of rolls, r, is exponential over integers with parameter $f = 5/6$. The distribution may also be written

$$P(r \mid f) = (1-f)\, e^{-\lambda r} \quad r \in (0, 1, 2, \ldots, \infty), \quad (23.4)$$

where $\lambda = \log(1/f)$.

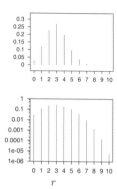

Figure 23.1. The binomial distribution $P(r \mid f = 0.3, N = 10)$, on a linear scale (top) and a logarithmic scale (bottom).

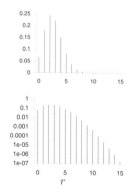

Figure 23.2. The Poisson distribution $P(r \mid \lambda = 2.7)$, on a linear scale (top) and a logarithmic scale (bottom).

▶ **23.2 Distributions over unbounded real numbers**

Gaussian, Student, Cauchy, biexponential, inverse-cosh.

The *Gaussian distribution* or normal distribution with mean μ and standard deviation σ is

$$P(x \mid \mu, \sigma) = \frac{1}{Z} \exp\left(-\frac{(x-\mu)^2}{2\sigma^2}\right) \quad x \in (-\infty, \infty), \qquad (23.5)$$

where

$$Z = \sqrt{2\pi\sigma^2}. \qquad (23.6)$$

It is sometimes useful to work with the quantity $\tau \equiv 1/\sigma^2$, which is called the *precision* parameter of the Gaussian.

A sample z from a standard univariate Gaussian can be generated by computing

$$z = \cos(2\pi u_1)\sqrt{2\ln(1/u_2)}, \qquad (23.7)$$

where u_1 and u_2 are uniformly distributed in $(0, 1)$. A second sample $z_2 = \sin(2\pi u_1)\sqrt{2\ln(1/u_2)}$, independent of the first, can then be obtained for free.

The Gaussian distribution is widely used and often asserted to be a very common distribution in the real world, but I am sceptical about this assertion. Yes, *unimodal* distributions may be common; but a Gaussian is a special, rather extreme, unimodal distribution. It has very light tails: the log-probability-density decreases quadratically. The typical deviation of x from μ is σ, but the respective probabilities that x deviates from μ by more than 2σ, 3σ, 4σ, and 5σ, are 0.046, 0.003, 6×10^{-5}, and 6×10^{-7}. In my experience, deviations from a mean four or five times greater than the typical deviation may be rare, but not as rare as 6×10^{-5}! I therefore urge caution in the use of Gaussian distributions: if a variable that is modelled with a Gaussian actually has a heavier-tailed distribution, the rest of the model will contort itself to reduce the deviations of the outliers, like a sheet of paper being crushed by a rubber band.

▷ Exercise 23.1.[1] Pick a variable that is supposedly bell-shaped in probability distribution, gather data, and make a plot of the variable's empirical distribution. Show the distribution as a histogram on a log scale and investigate whether the tails are well-modelled by a Gaussian distribution. [One example of a variable to study is the amplitude of an audio signal.]

One distribution with heavier tails than a Gaussian is a *mixture of Gaussians*. A mixture of two Gaussians, for example, is defined by two means, two standard deviations, and two *mixing coefficients* π_1 and π_2, satisfying $\pi_1 + \pi_2 = 1$, $\pi_i \geq 0$.

$$P(x \mid \mu_1, \sigma_1, \pi_1, \mu_2, \sigma_2, \pi_2) = \frac{\pi_1}{\sqrt{2\pi}\sigma_1} \exp\left(-\frac{(x-\mu_1)^2}{2\sigma_1^2}\right) + \frac{\pi_2}{\sqrt{2\pi}\sigma_2} \exp\left(-\frac{(x-\mu_2)^2}{2\sigma_2^2}\right).$$

If we take an appropriately weighted mixture of an infinite number of Gaussians, all having mean μ, we obtain a *Student-t distribution*,

$$P(x \mid \mu, s, n) = \frac{1}{Z} \frac{1}{(1 + (x-\mu)^2/(ns^2))^{(n+1)/2}}, \qquad (23.8)$$

where

$$Z = \sqrt{\pi n s^2} \frac{\Gamma(n/2)}{\Gamma((n+1)/2)} \qquad (23.9)$$

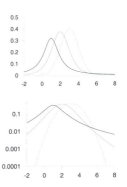

Figure 23.3. Three unimodal distributions. Two Student distributions, with parameters $(m, s) = (1, 1)$ (heavy line) (a Cauchy distribution) and $(2, 4)$ (light line), and a Gaussian distribution with mean $\mu = 3$ and standard deviation $\sigma = 3$ (dashed line), shown on linear vertical scales (top) and logarithmic vertical scales (bottom). Notice that the heavy tails of the Cauchy distribution are scarcely evident in the upper 'bell-shaped curve'.

and n is called the number of degrees of freedom and Γ is the gamma function. If $n > 1$ then the Student distribution (23.8) has a mean and that mean is μ. If $n > 2$ the distribution also has a finite variance, $\sigma^2 = ns^2/(n-2)$. As $n \to \infty$, the Student distribution approaches the normal distribution with mean μ and standard deviation s. The Student distribution arises both in classical statistics (as the sampling-theoretic distribution of certain statistics) and in Bayesian inference (as the probability distribution of a variable coming from a Gaussian distribution whose standard deviation we aren't sure of).

In the special case $n = 1$, the Student distribution is called the *Cauchy distribution*.

A distribution whose tails are intermediate in heaviness between Student and Gaussian is the *biexponential distribution*,

$$P(x \mid \mu, s) = \frac{1}{Z} \exp\left(-\frac{|x - \mu|}{s}\right) \quad x \in (-\infty, \infty) \tag{23.10}$$

where

$$Z = 2s. \tag{23.11}$$

The *inverse-cosh distribution*

$$P(x \mid \beta) \propto \frac{1}{[\cosh(\beta x)]^{1/\beta}} \tag{23.12}$$

is a popular model in independent component analysis. In the limit of large β, the probability distribution $P(x \mid \beta)$ becomes a biexponential distribution. In the limit $\beta \to 0$ $P(x \mid \beta)$ approaches a Gaussian with mean zero and variance $1/\beta$.

▶ 23.3 Distributions over positive real numbers

Exponential, gamma, inverse-gamma, and log-normal.

The *exponential distribution*,

$$P(x \mid s) = \frac{1}{Z} \exp\left(-\frac{x}{s}\right) \quad x \in (0, \infty), \tag{23.13}$$

where

$$Z = s, \tag{23.14}$$

arises in waiting problems. How long will you have to wait for a bus in Poissonville, given that buses arrive independently at random with one every s minutes on average? Answer: the probability distribution of your wait, x, is exponential with mean s.

The *gamma distribution* is like a Gaussian distribution, except whereas the Gaussian goes from $-\infty$ to ∞, gamma distributions go from 0 to ∞. Just as the Gaussian distribution has two parameters μ and σ which control the mean and width of the distribution, the gamma distribution has two parameters. It is the product of the one-parameter exponential distribution (23.13) with a polynomial, x^{c-1}. The exponent c in the polynomial is the second parameter.

$$P(x \mid s, c) = \Gamma(x; s, c) = \frac{1}{Z} \left(\frac{x}{s}\right)^{c-1} \exp\left(-\frac{x}{s}\right), \quad 0 \le x < \infty \tag{23.15}$$

where

$$Z = \Gamma(c)s. \tag{23.16}$$

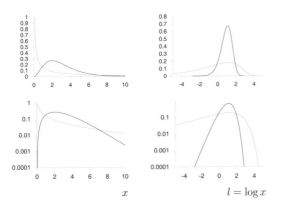

Figure 23.4. Two gamma distributions, with parameters $(s, c) = (1, 3)$ (heavy lines) and $10, 0.3$ (light lines), shown on linear vertical scales (top) and logarithmic vertical scales (bottom); and shown as a function of x on the left (23.15) and $l = \log x$ on the right (23.18).

This is a simple peaked distribution with mean sc and variance $s^2 c$.

It is often natural to represent a positive real variable x in terms of its logarithm $l = \log x$. The probability density of l is

$$P(l) \;=\; P(x(l)) \left| \frac{\partial x}{\partial l} \right| \;=\; P(x(l)) x(l) \tag{23.17}$$

$$=\; \frac{1}{Z_l} \left(\frac{x(l)}{s} \right)^c \exp\left(-\frac{x(l)}{s} \right), \tag{23.18}$$

where

$$Z_l \;=\; \Gamma(c). \tag{23.19}$$

[The gamma distribution is named after its normalizing constant – an odd convention, it seems to me!]

Figure 23.4 shows a couple of gamma distributions as a function of x and of l. Notice that where the original gamma distribution (23.15) may have a 'spike' at $x = 0$, the distribution over l never has such a spike. The spike is an artefact of a bad choice of basis.

In the limit $sc = 1, c \to 0$, we obtain the noninformative prior for a scale parameter, the $1/x$ prior. This improper prior is called noninformative because it has no associated length scale, no characteristic value of x, so it prefers all values of x equally. It is invariant under the reparameterization $x = mx$. If we transform the $1/x$ probability density into a density over $l = \log x$ we find the latter density is uniform.

▷ Exercise 23.2.[1] Imagine that we reparameterize a positive variable x in terms of its cube root, $u = x^{1/3}$. If the probability density of x is the improper distribution $1/x$, what is the probability density of u?

The gamma distribution is always a unimodal density over $l = \log x$, and, as can be seen in the figures, it is asymmetric. If x has a gamma distribution, and we decide to work in terms of the inverse of x, $v = 1/x$, we obtain a new distribution, in which the density over l is flipped left-for-right: the probability density of v is called an *inverse-gamma distribution*,

$$P(v \,|\, s, c) = \frac{1}{Z_v} \left(\frac{1}{sv} \right)^{c+1} \exp\left(-\frac{1}{sv} \right), \qquad 0 \le v < \infty \tag{23.20}$$

where

$$Z_v = \Gamma(c)/s. \tag{23.21}$$

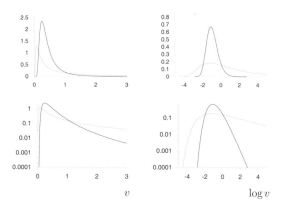

Figure 23.5. Two inverse gamma distributions, with parameters $(s, c) = (1, 3)$ (heavy lines) and $10, 0.3$ (light lines), shown on linear vertical scales (top) and logarithmic vertical scales (bottom); and shown as a function of x on the left and $l = \log x$ on the right.

Gamma and inverse gamma distributions crop up in many inference problems in which a positive quantity is inferred from data. Examples include inferring the variance of Gaussian noise from some noise samples, and inferring the rate parameter of a Poisson distribution from the count.

Gamma distributions also arise naturally in the distributions of waiting times between Poisson-distributed events. Given a Poisson process with rate λ, the probability density of the arrival time x of the mth event is

$$\frac{\lambda(\lambda x)^{m-1}}{(m-1)!} \, e^{-\lambda x}. \tag{23.22}$$

Log-normal distribution

Another distribution over a positive real number x is the *log-normal* distribution, which is the distribution that results when $l = \ln x$ has a normal distribution. We define m to be the median value of x, and s to be the standard deviation of $\ln x$.

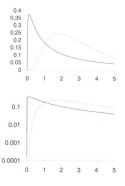

$$P(l \mid m, s) = \frac{1}{Z} \exp\left(-\frac{(l - \ln m)^2}{2s^2}\right) \quad l \in (-\infty, \infty), \tag{23.23}$$

where

$$Z = \sqrt{2\pi s^2}, \tag{23.24}$$

implies

$$P(x \mid m, s) = \frac{1}{x} \exp\left(-\frac{(\ln x - \ln m)^2}{2s^2}\right) \quad x \in (0, \infty). \tag{23.25}$$

Figure 23.6. Two log-normal distributions, with parameters $(m, s) = (3, 1.8)$ (heavy line) and $(3, 0.7)$ (light line), shown on linear vertical scales (top) and logarithmic vertical scales (bottom). [Yes, they really do have the same value of the median, $m = 3$.]

▶ 23.4 Distributions over periodic variables

A periodic variable θ is a real number $\in [0, 2\pi]$ having the property that $\theta = 0$ and $\theta = 2\pi$ are equivalent.

A distribution that plays for periodic variables the role played by the Gaussian distribution for real variables is the *Von Mises distribution*:

$$P(\theta \mid \mu, \beta) = \frac{1}{Z} \exp\left(\beta \cos(\theta - \mu)\right) \quad \theta \in (0, 2\pi). \tag{23.26}$$

The normalizing constant is $Z = 2\pi I_0(\beta)$, where $I_0(x)$ is a modified Bessel function.

A distribution that arises from Brownian diffusion around the circle is the wrapped Gaussian distribution,

$$P(\theta \,|\, \mu, \sigma) = \sum_{n=-\infty}^{\infty} \text{Normal}(\theta; (\mu + 2\pi n), \sigma) \quad \theta \in (0, 2\pi). \tag{23.27}$$

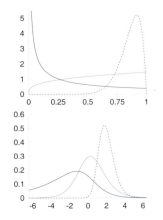

▶ 23.5 Distributions over probabilities

Beta distribution, Dirichlet distribution, entropic distribution

The *beta distribution* is a probability density over a variable p that is a probability, $p \in (0, 1)$:

$$P(p \,|\, u_1, u_2) = \frac{1}{Z(u_1, u_2)} p^{u_1 - 1}(1 - p)^{u_2 - 1}. \tag{23.28}$$

The parameters u_1, u_2 may take any positive value. The normalizing constant is the beta function.

$$Z(u_1, u_2) = \frac{\Gamma(u_1)\Gamma(u_2)}{\Gamma(u_1 + u_2)} \tag{23.29}$$

Special cases include the uniform distribution – $u_1 = 1, u_2 = 1$; the Jeffreys prior – $u_1 = 0.5, u_2 = 0.5$; and the improper Laplace prior – $u_1 = 0, u_2 = 0$. If we transform the beta distribution to the corresponding density over the logit $l \equiv \ln p / (1 - p)$, we find it is always a pleasant bell-shaped density over l, while the density over p may have singularities at $p = 0$ and $p = 1$ (figure 23.7).

More dimensions

The *Dirichlet distribution* is a density over an I-dimensional vector $\mathbf{p}$ whose I components are positive and sum to 1. The beta distribution is a special case of a Dirichlet distribution with $I = 2$. The Dirichlet distribution is parameterized by a measure $\mathbf{u}$ (a vector with all coefficients $u_i > 0$) which I will write here as $\mathbf{u} = \alpha \mathbf{m}$, where $\mathbf{m}$ is a normalized measure over the I components ($\sum m_i = 1$), and α is positive:

$$P(\mathbf{p} \,|\, \alpha \mathbf{m}) = \frac{1}{Z(\alpha \mathbf{m})} \prod_{i=1}^{I} p_i^{\alpha m_i - 1} \delta \left(\sum_i p_i - 1 \right) \equiv \text{Dirichlet}^{(I)}(\mathbf{p} | \alpha \mathbf{m}) \tag{23.30}$$

The function $\delta(x)$ is the Dirac delta function which restricts the distribution to the simplex such that $\mathbf{p}$ is normalized, i.e., $\sum_i p_i = 1$. The normalizing constant of the Dirichlet distribution is:

$$Z(\alpha \mathbf{m}) = \prod_i \Gamma(\alpha m_i) / \Gamma(\alpha). \tag{23.31}$$

The vector $\mathbf{m}$ is the mean of the probability distribution:

$$\int \text{Dirichlet}^{(I)}(\mathbf{p} | \alpha \mathbf{m}) \, \mathbf{p} \, d^I \mathbf{p} = \mathbf{m}. \tag{23.32}$$

When working with a probability vector $\mathbf{p}$, it is often helpful to work in the 'softmax basis', in which, for example, a three-dimensional probability $\mathbf{p} = (p_1, p_2, p_3)$ is represented by three numbers a_1, a_2, a_3 satisfying $a_1 + a_2 + a_3 = 0$ and

$$p_i = \frac{1}{Z} e^{a_i}, \text{ where } Z = \sum_i e^{a_i}. \tag{23.33}$$

This nonlinear transformation is analogous to the $\sigma \to \ln \sigma$ transformation for a scale variable and the logit transformation for a single probability, $p \to$

Figure 23.7. Three beta distributions, with $(u_1, u_2) = (0.3, 1)$, $(1.3, 1)$, and $(12, 2)$. The upper figure shows $P(p | u_1, u_2)$ as a function of p; the lower shows the corresponding density over the *logit*,

$$\ln \frac{p}{1 - p}.$$

Notice how well-behaved the densities are as a function of the logit.

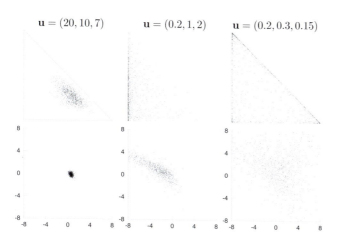

$\mathbf{u} = (20, 10, 7)$ $\mathbf{u} = (0.2, 1, 2)$ $\mathbf{u} = (0.2, 0.3, 0.15)$

Figure 23.8. Three Dirichlet distributions over a three-dimensional probability vector (p_1, p_2, p_3). The upper figures show 1000 random draws from each distribution, showing the values of p_1 and p_2 on the two axes. $p_3 = p_2 + p_1$. The triangle in the first figure is the simplex of legal probability distributions. The lower figures show the same points in the 'softmax' basis (equation (23.33)). The two axes show a_1 and a_2. $a_3 = -a_1 - a_2$.

$\ln \frac{p}{1-p}$. In the softmax basis, the ugly minus-ones in the exponents in the Dirichlet distribution (23.30) disappear, and the density is given by:

$$P(\mathbf{a} \,|\, \alpha \mathbf{m}) \propto \frac{1}{Z(\alpha \mathbf{m})} \prod_{i=1}^{I} p_i^{\alpha m_i} \delta \left(\sum_i a_i \right). \tag{23.34}$$

The role of α can be characterized in two ways. First, the parameter α measures the sharpness of the distribution (figure 23.8); it measures how different we expect typical samples $\mathbf{p}$ from the distribution to be from the mean $\mathbf{m}$, just as the precision $\tau = 1/\sigma^2$ of a Gaussian measures how far samples stray from its mean. A large value of α produces a distribution over $\mathbf{p}$ that is sharply peaked around $\mathbf{m}$. The effect of α in higher-dimensional situations can be visualized by drawing a typical sample from the distribution $\mathrm{Dirichlet}^{(I)}(\mathbf{p}|\alpha\mathbf{m})$, with $\mathbf{m}$ set to the uniform vector $m_i = 1/I$, and making a Zipf plot, that is, a ranked plot of the values of the components p_i. It is traditional to plot both p_i (vertical axis) and the rank (horizontal axis) on logarithmic scales so that power law relationships appear as straight lines. Figure 23.9 shows these plots for a single sample from ensembles with $I = 100$ and $I = 1000$ and with α from 0.1 to 1000. For large α, the plot is shallow with many components having similar values. For small α, typically one component p_i receives an overwhelming share of the probability, and of the small probability that remains to be shared among the other components, another component $p_{i'}$ receives a similarly large share. In the limit as α goes to zero, the plot tends to an increasingly steep power law.

Second, we can characterize the role of α in terms of the predictive distribution that results when we observe samples from $\mathbf{p}$ and obtain counts $\mathbf{F} = (F_1, F_2, \ldots, F_I)$ of the possible outcomes. The value of α defines the number of samples from $\mathbf{p}$ that are required in order that the data dominate over the prior in predictions.

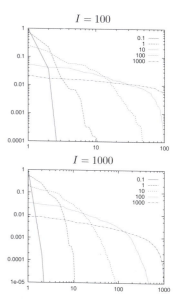

Figure 23.9. Zipf plots for random samples from Dirichlet distributions with various values of $\alpha = 0.1 \ldots 1000$. For each value of $I = 100$ or 1000 and each α, one sample $\mathbf{p}$ from the Dirichlet distribution was generated. The Zipf plot shows the probabilities p_i, ranked by magnitude, versus their rank.

Exercise 23.3.[3] The Dirichlet distribution satisfies a nice additivity property. Imagine that a biased six-sided die has two red faces and four blue faces. The die is rolled N times and two Bayesians examine the outcomes in order to infer the bias of the die and make predictions. One Bayesian has access to the red/blue colour outcomes only, and he infers a two-component probability vector (p_R, p_B). The other Bayesian has access to each full outcome: he can see which of the six faces came up, and he infers a six-component probability vector $(p_1, p_2, p_3, p_4, p_5, p_6)$, where

$p_R = p_1 + p_2$ and $p_B = p_3 + p_4 + p_5 + p_6$. Assuming that the second Bayesian assigns a Dirichlet distribution to $(p_1, p_2, p_3, p_4, p_5, p_6)$ with hyperparameters $(u_1, u_2, u_3, u_4, u_5, u_6)$, show that, in order for the first Bayesian's inferences to be consistent with those of the second Bayesian, the first Bayesian's prior should be a Dirichlet distribution with hyperparameters $((u_1 + u_2), (u_3 + u_4 + u_5 + u_6))$.

Hint: a brute-force approach is to compute the integral $P(p_R, p_B) = \int d^6\mathbf{p}\, P(\mathbf{p}\,|\,\mathbf{u})\, \delta(p_R - (p_1 + p_2))\, \delta(p_B - (p_3 + p_4 + p_5 + p_6))$. A cheaper approach is to compute the predictive distributions, given arbitrary data $(F_1, F_2, F_3, F_4, F_5, F_6)$, and find the condition for the two predictive distributions to match for all data.

The *entropic distribution* for a probability vector $\mathbf{p}$ is sometimes used in the 'maximum entropy' image reconstruction community.

$$P(\mathbf{p}\,|\,\alpha\mathbf{m}) = \frac{1}{Z(\alpha)} \exp[\alpha H(\mathbf{p})]\, \delta(\textstyle\sum_i p_i - 1), \qquad (23.35)$$

where $H(\mathbf{p}) = \sum_i p_i \log 1/p_i$.

Further reading

See (MacKay and Peto, 1995) for fun with Dirichlets.

▶ **23.6 Further exercises**

Exercise 23.4.[2] N datapoints $\{x_n\}$ are drawn from a gamma distribution $P(x\,|\,s, c) = \Gamma(x; s, c)$ with unknown parameters s and c. What are the maximum likelihood parameters s and c?

24

Exact Marginalization

How can we avoid the exponentially large cost of complete enumeration of all hypotheses? Before we stoop to approximate methods, we explore two approaches to exact marginalization: first, marginalization over continuous variables (sometimes known as nuisance parameters) by doing *integrals*; and second, summation over discrete variables by message-passing.

Exact marginalization over continuous parameters is a macho activity enjoyed by those who are fluent in definite integration. This chapter uses gamma distributions; as was explained in the previous chapter, gamma distributions are a lot like Gaussian distributions, except that whereas the Gaussian goes from $-\infty$ to ∞, gamma distributions go from 0 to ∞.

▶ ## 24.1 Inferring the mean and variance of a Gaussian distribution

We discuss again the one-dimensional Gaussian distribution, parameterized by a mean μ and a standard deviation σ:

$$P(x \mid \mu, \sigma) = \frac{1}{\sqrt{2\pi}\sigma} \exp\left(-\frac{(x-\mu)^2}{2\sigma^2}\right) \equiv \text{Normal}(x; \mu, \sigma^2). \qquad (24.1)$$

When inferring these parameters, we must specify their prior distribution. The prior gives us the opportunity to include specific knowledge that we have about μ and σ (from independent experiments, or on theoretical grounds, for example). If we have no such knowledge, then we can construct an appropriate prior that embodies our supposed ignorance. In section 21.2, we assumed a uniform prior over the range of parameters plotted. If we wish to be able to perform exact marginalizations, it may be useful to consider *conjugate priors*; these are priors whose functional form combines naturally with the likelihood such that the inferences have a convenient form.

Conjugate priors for μ and σ

The conjugate prior for a mean μ is a Gaussian: we introduce two 'hyperparameters', μ_0 and σ_μ, which parameterize the prior on μ, and write $P(\mu \mid \mu_0, \sigma_\mu) = \text{Normal}(\mu; \mu_0, \sigma_\mu)$. In the limit $\mu_0 = 0$, $\sigma_\mu \to \infty$, we obtain the *noninformative prior* for a location parameter, the flat prior. This is *noninformative* because it is *invariant* under the natural reparameterization $\mu' = \mu + c$. The prior $P(\mu) = \text{const.}$ is also an *improper* prior, that is, it is not normalizable.

The conjugate prior for a standard deviation σ is a gamma distribution, which has two parameters b_β and c_β. It is most convenient to define the prior density of the inverse variance (the *precision* parameter) $\beta = 1/\sigma^2$:

$$P(\beta) = \Gamma(\beta; b_\beta, c_\beta) = \frac{1}{\Gamma(c_\beta)} \frac{\beta^{c_\beta - 1}}{b_\beta^{c_\beta}} \exp\left(-\frac{\beta}{b_\beta}\right), \quad 0 \le \beta < \infty. \quad (24.2)$$

This is a simple peaked distribution with mean $b_\beta c_\beta$ and variance $b_\beta^2 c_\beta$. In the limit $b_\beta c_\beta = 1, c_\beta \to 0$, we obtain the noninformative prior for a scale parameter, the $1/\sigma$ prior. This is 'noninformative' because it is invariant under the reparameterization $\sigma' = c\sigma$. The $1/\sigma$ prior is less strange-looking if we examine the resulting density over $\log \sigma$, or $\log \beta$, which is flat. This is the prior that expresses ignorance about σ by saying 'well, it could be 10, or it could be 1, or it could be 0.1, ...' Scale variables such as σ are usually best represented in terms of their logarithm. Again, this noninformative $1/\sigma$ prior is improper.

In the following examples, I will use the improper noninformative priors for μ and σ. Using improper priors is viewed as distasteful in some circles, so let me excuse myself by saying it's for the sake of readability; if I included proper priors, the calculations could still be done but the key points would be obscured by the flood of extra parameters.

Maximum likelihood and marginalization: σ_N and σ_{N-1}

The task of inferring the mean and standard deviation of a Gaussian distribution from N samples is a familiar one, though maybe not everyone understands the difference between the σ_N and σ_{N-1} buttons on their calculator. Let us recap the formulae, then derive them.

Given data $D = \{x_n\}_{n=1}^N$, an 'estimator' of μ is

$$\bar{x} \equiv \sum_{n=1}^N x_n / N, \quad (24.3)$$

and two estimators of σ are:

$$\sigma_N \equiv \sqrt{\frac{\sum_{n=1}^N (x_n - \bar{x})^2}{N}} \quad \text{and} \quad \sigma_{N-1} \equiv \sqrt{\frac{\sum_{n=1}^N (x_n - \bar{x})^2}{N - 1}}. \quad (24.4)$$

There are two principal paradigms for statistics: sampling theory and Bayesian inference. In sampling theory (also known as 'frequentist' or orthodox statistics), one invents *estimators* of quantities of interest and then chooses between those estimators using some criterion measuring their sampling properties; there is no clear principle for deciding which criterion to use to measure the performance of an estimator; nor, for most criteria, is there any systematic procedure for the construction of optimal estimators. In Bayesian inference, in contrast, once we have made explicit all our assumptions about the model and the data, our inferences are mechanical. Whatever question we wish to pose, the rules of probability theory give a unique answer which consistently takes into account all the given information. Human-designed estimators and confidence intervals have no role in Bayesian inference; human input only enters into the important tasks of designing the hypothesis space (that is, the specification of the model and all its probability distributions), and figuring out how to do the computations that implement inference in that space. The answers to our questions are probability distributions over the quantities of interest. We often find that the estimators of sampling theory emerge automatically as modes or means of these posterior distributions when we choose a simple hypothesis space and turn the handle of Bayesian inference.

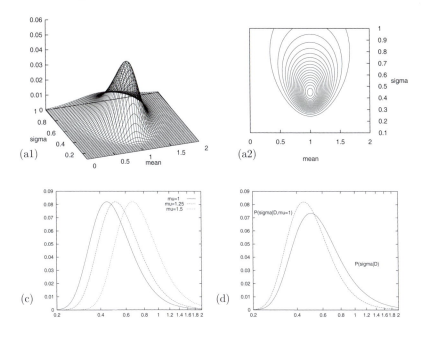

(a1)

(a2)

(c)

(d)

Figure 24.1. The likelihood function for the parameters of a Gaussian distribution, repeated from figure 21.5.

(a1, a2) Surface plot and contour plot of the log likelihood as a function of μ and σ. The data set of $N = 5$ points had mean $\bar{x} = 1.0$ and $S^2 = \sum(x - \bar{x})^2 = 1.0$. Notice that the maximum is skew in σ. The two estimators of standard deviation have values $\sigma_N = 0.45$ and $\sigma_{N-1} = 0.50$.
(c) The posterior probability of σ for various fixed values of μ.
(d) The posterior probability of σ, $P(\sigma \mid D)$, assuming a flat prior on μ, obtained by projecting the probability mass in (a) onto the σ axis. The maximum of $P(\sigma \mid D)$ is at σ_{N-1}. By contrast, the maximum of $P(\sigma \mid D, \mu = \bar{x}, \sigma)$ is at σ_N.

In sampling theory, the estimators above can be motivated as follows. $\bar{x}$ is an unbiased estimator of μ which, out of all the possible unbiased estimators of μ, has smallest variance (where this variance is computed by averaging over an ensemble of imaginary experiments in which the data samples are assumed to come from an unknown Gaussian distribution). The estimator $(\bar{x}, \sigma_N)$ is the maximum likelihood estimator for (μ, σ). The estimator σ_N is *biased*, however: the expectation of σ_N, given σ, averaging over many imagined experiments, is not σ.

 Exercise 24.1.[2, p.323] Give an intuitive explanation why the estimator σ_N is biased.

This bias motivates the invention, in sampling theory, of σ_{N-1}, which can be shown to be an unbiased estimator. Or to be precise, it is σ_{N-1}^2 that is an unbiased estimator of σ^2.

We now look at some Bayesian inferences for this problem, assuming non-informative priors for μ and σ. The emphasis is thus not on the priors, but rather on (a) the likelihood function, and (b) the concept of marginalization. The joint posterior probability of μ and σ is proportional to the likelihood function illustrated by a contour plot in figure 24.1a. The log likelihood is:

$$\ln P(\{x_n\}_{n=1}^N \mid \mu, \sigma) = -N \ln(\sqrt{2\pi}\sigma) - \sum_n (x_n - \mu)^2/(2\sigma^2), \qquad (24.5)$$

$$= -N \ln(\sqrt{2\pi}\sigma) - [N(\mu - \bar{x})^2 + S]/(2\sigma^2), \quad (24.6)$$

where $S \equiv \sum_n (x_n - \bar{x})^2$. Given the Gaussian model, the likelihood can be expressed in terms of the two functions of the data $\bar{x}$ and S, so these two quantities are known as 'sufficient statistics'. The posterior probability of μ and σ is, using the improper priors:

$$P(\mu, \sigma \mid \{x_n\}_{n=1}^N) = \frac{P(\{x_n\}_{n=1}^N \mid \mu, \sigma)P(\mu, \sigma)}{P(\{x_n\}_{n=1}^N)} \qquad (24.7)$$

$$= \frac{\frac{1}{(2\pi\sigma^2)^{N/2}} \exp\left(-\frac{N(\mu-\bar{x})^2 + S}{2\sigma^2}\right)\frac{1}{\sigma_\mu}\frac{1}{\sigma}}{P(\{x_n\}_{n=1}^N)}. \qquad (24.8)$$

This function describes the answer to the question, 'given the data, and the noninformative priors, what might μ and σ be?' It may be of interest to find the parameter values that maximize the posterior probability, though it should be emphasized that posterior probability maxima have no fundamental status in Bayesian inference, since their location depends on the choice of basis. Here we choose the basis $(\mu, \ln \sigma)$, in which our prior is flat, so that the posterior probability maximum coincides with the maximum of the likelihood. As we saw in exercise 22.4 (p.302), the maximum likelihood solution for μ and $\ln \sigma$ is $\{\mu, \sigma\}_{\mathrm{ML}} = \left\{ \bar{x}, \sigma_N = \sqrt{S/N} \right\}$.

There is more to the posterior distribution than just its mode. As can be seen in figure 24.1a, the likelihood has a skew peak. As we increase σ, the width of the conditional distribution of μ increases (figure 22.1b). And if we fix μ to a sequence of values moving away from the sample mean $\bar{x}$, we obtain a sequence of conditional distributions over σ whose maxima move to increasing values of σ (figure 24.1c).

The posterior probability of μ given σ is

$$P(\mu \mid \{x_n\}_{n=1}^N, \sigma) \quad = \quad \frac{P(\{x_n\}_{n=1}^N \mid \mu, \sigma) P(\mu)}{P(\{x_n\}_{n=1}^N \mid \sigma)} \tag{24.9}$$

$$\propto \quad \exp(-N(\mu - \bar{x})^2/(2\sigma^2)) \tag{24.10}$$

$$= \quad \mathrm{Normal}(\mu; \bar{x}, \sigma^2/N). \tag{24.11}$$

We note the familiar $\sigma/\sqrt{N}$ scaling of the error bars on μ.

Let us now ask the question 'given the data, and the noninformative priors, what might σ be?' This question differs from the first one we asked in that we are now not interested in μ. This parameter must therefore be *marginalized* over. The posterior probability of σ is:

$$P(\sigma \mid \{x_n\}_{n=1}^N) = \frac{P(\{x_n\}_{n=1}^N \mid \sigma) P(\sigma)}{P(\{x_n\}_{n=1}^N)}. \tag{24.12}$$

The data-dependent term $P(\{x_n\}_{n=1}^N \mid \sigma)$ appeared earlier as the normalizing constant in equation (24.9); one name for this quantity is the 'evidence', or marginal likelihood, for σ. We obtain the evidence for σ by integrating out μ; a noninformative prior $P(\mu) = $ constant is assumed; we call this constant $1/\sigma_\mu$, so that we can think of the prior as a top-hat prior of width σ_μ. The Gaussian integral, $P(\{x_n\}_{n=1}^N \mid \sigma) = \int P(\{x_n\}_{n=1}^N \mid \mu, \sigma) P(\mu) \, d\mu$, yields:

$$\ln P(\{x_n\}_{n=1}^N \mid \sigma) = -N \ln(\sqrt{2\pi}\sigma) - \frac{S}{2\sigma^2} + \ln \frac{\sqrt{2\pi}\sigma/\sqrt{N}}{\sigma_\mu}. \tag{24.13}$$

The first two terms are the best fit log likelihood (i.e., the log likelihood with $\mu = \bar{x}$). The last term is the log of the *Occam factor* which penalizes smaller values of σ. (We will discuss Occam factors more in Chapter 28.) When we differentiate the log evidence with respect to $\ln \sigma$, to find the most probable σ, the additional volume factor $(\sigma/\sqrt{N})$ shifts the maximum from σ_N to

$$\sigma_{N-1} = \sqrt{S/(N - 1)}. \tag{24.14}$$

Intuitively, the denominator $(N-1)$ counts the number of noise measurements contained in the quantity $S = \sum_n (x_n - \bar{x})^2$. The sum contains N residuals squared, but there are only $(N-1)$ effective noise measurements because the determination of one parameter μ from the data causes one dimension of noise to be gobbled up in unavoidable overfitting. In the terminology of classical statistics, the Bayesian's best guess for σ sets χ^2 (the measure of deviance defined by $\chi^2 \equiv \sum_n (x_n - \hat{\mu})^2/\hat{\sigma}^2$) equal to the number of degrees of freedom, $N - 1$.

Figure 24.1d shows the posterior probability of σ, which is proportional to the marginal likelihood. This may be contrasted with the posterior probability of σ with μ fixed to its most probable value, $\bar{x} = 1$, which is shown in figure 24.1c and d.

The final inference we might wish to make is 'given the data, what is μ?'

▷ **Exercise 24.2.**[3] Marginalize over σ and obtain the posterior marginal distribution of μ, which is a Student-t distribution:

$$P(\mu \,|\, D) \propto 1/\left(N(\mu - \bar{x})^2 + S\right)^{N/2}. \qquad (24.15)$$

Further reading

A bible of exact marginalization is Bretthorst's (1988) book on Bayesian spectrum analysis and parameter estimation.

▶ **24.2 Exercises**

▷ **Exercise 24.3.**[3] [This exercise requires macho integration capabilities.] Give a Bayesian solution to exercise 22.15 (p.309), where seven scientists of varying capabilities have measured μ with personal noise levels σ_n, and we are interested in inferring μ. Let the prior on each σ_n be a broad prior, for example a gamma distribution with parameters $(s, c) = (10, 0.1)$. Find the posterior distribution of μ. Plot it, and explore its properties for a variety of data sets such as the one given, and the data set $\{x_n\} = \{13.01, 7.39\}$.

[Hint: first find the posterior distribution of σ_n given μ and x_n, $P(\sigma_n \,|\, x_n, \mu)$. Note that the normalizing constant for this inference is $P(x_n \,|\, \mu)$. Marginalize over σ_n to find this normalizing constant, then use Bayes' theorem a second time to find $P(\mu \,|\, \{x_n\})$.]

▶ **24.3 Solutions**

Solution to exercise 24.1 (p.321). 1. The data points are distributed with mean squared deviation σ^2 about the true mean. 2. The sample mean is unlikely to exactly equal the true mean. 3. The sample mean is the value of μ that minimizes the sum squared deviation of the data points from μ. Any other value of μ (in particular, the true value of μ) will have a larger value of the sum-squared deviation that $\mu = \bar{x}$.

So the expected mean squared deviation from the sample mean is necessarily smaller than the mean squared deviation σ^2 about the true mean.

25

Exact Marginalization in Trellises

In this chapter we will discuss a few exact methods that are used in probabilistic modelling. As an example we will discuss the task of decoding a linear
error-correcting code. We will see that inferences can be conducted most efficiently by *message-passing algorithms*, which take advantage of the graphical
structure of the problem to avoid unnecessary duplication of computations
(see Chapter 16).

▶ ## 25.1 Decoding problems

A codeword $\mathbf{t}$ is selected from a linear (N, K) code $\mathcal{C}$, and it is transmitted
over a noisy channel; the received signal is $\mathbf{y}$. In this chapter we will assume
that the channel is a memoryless channel such as a Gaussian channel. Given
an assumed channel model $P(\mathbf{y} \mid \mathbf{t})$, there are two decoding problems.

The codeword decoding problem is the task of inferring which codeword
$\mathbf{t}$ was transmitted given the received signal.

The bitwise decoding problem is the task of inferring for each transmitted bit t_n how likely it is that that bit was a one rather than a zero.

As a concrete example, take the $(7, 4)$ Hamming code. In Chapter 1, we
discussed the codeword decoding problem for that code, assuming a binary
symmetric channel. We didn't discuss the bitwise decoding problem and we
didn't discuss how to handle more general channel models such as a Gaussian
channel.

Solving the codeword decoding problem

By Bayes' theorem, the posterior probability of the codeword $\mathbf{t}$ is

$$P(\mathbf{t} \mid \mathbf{y}) = \frac{P(\mathbf{y} \mid \mathbf{t})P(\mathbf{t})}{P(\mathbf{y})}. \tag{25.1}$$

Likelihood function. The first factor in the numerator, $P(\mathbf{y} \mid \mathbf{t})$, is the *likelihood* of the codeword, which, for any memoryless channel, is a separable
function,

$$P(\mathbf{y} \mid \mathbf{t}) = \prod_{n=1}^{N} P(y_n \mid t_n). \tag{25.2}$$

For example, if the channel is a Gaussian channel with transmissions $\pm x$
and additive noise of standard deviation σ, then the probability density

of the received signal y_n in the two cases $t_n = 0, 1$ is

$$P(y_n \mid t_n = 1) = \frac{1}{\sqrt{2\pi\sigma^2}} \exp\left(-\frac{(y_n - x)^2}{2\sigma^2}\right) \qquad (25.3)$$

$$P(y_n \mid t_n = 0) = \frac{1}{\sqrt{2\pi\sigma^2}} \exp\left(-\frac{(y_n + x)^2}{2\sigma^2}\right). \qquad (25.4)$$

From the point of view of decoding, all that matters is the *likelihood ratio*, which for the case of the Gaussian channel is

$$\frac{P(y_n \mid t_n = 1)}{P(y_n \mid t_n = 0)} = \exp\left(\frac{2xy_n}{\sigma^2}\right). \qquad (25.5)$$

Exercise 25.1.[2] Show that from the point of view of decoding, a Gaussian channel is equivalent to a time-varying binary symmetric channel with a known noise level f_n which depends on n.

Prior. The second factor in the numerator is the *prior* probability of the codeword, $P(\mathbf{t})$, which is usually assumed to be uniform over all valid codewords.

The denominator in (25.1) is the normalizing constant

$$P(\mathbf{y}) = \sum_{\mathbf{t}} P(\mathbf{y} \mid \mathbf{t}) P(\mathbf{t}). \qquad (25.6)$$

The complete solution to the codeword decoding problem is a list of all codewords and their probabilities as given by equation (25.1). Since the number of codewords in a linear code, 2^K, is often very large, and since we are not interested in knowing the detailed probabilities of all the codewords, we often restrict attention to a simplified version of the codeword decoding problem.

The MAP codeword decoding problem is the task of identifying *the most probable codeword* $\mathbf{t}$ given the received signal.

If the prior probability over codewords is uniform then this task is identical to the problem of *maximum likelihood decoding*, that is, identifying the codeword that maximizes $P(\mathbf{y} \mid \mathbf{t})$.

Example: In Chapter 1, for the $(7, 4)$ Hamming code and a binary symmetric channel we discussed a method for deducing the most probable codeword from the syndrome of the received signal, thus solving the MAP codeword decoding problem for that case. We would like a more general solution.

The MAP codeword decoding problem can be solved in exponential time (of order 2^K) by searching through all codewords for the one that maximizes $P(\mathbf{y} \mid \mathbf{t}) P(\mathbf{t})$. But we are interested in methods that are more efficient than this. In section 25.3, we will discuss an exact method known as the *min–sum algorithm* which may be able to solve the codeword decoding problem more efficiently; how much more efficiently depends on the properties of the code.

It is worth emphasizing that MAP codeword decoding for a *general* linear code is known to be NP-complete (which means in layman's terms that MAP codeword decoding has a complexity that scales exponentially with the block length, unless there is a revolution in computer science). So restricting attention to the MAP decoding problem hasn't necessarily made the task much less challenging; it simply makes the answer briefer to report.

Solving the bitwise decoding problem

Formally, the exact solution of the bitwise decoding problem is obtained from equation (25.1) by *marginalizing* over the other bits.

$$P(t_n \mid \mathbf{y}) = \sum_{\{t_{n'} : n' \neq n\}} P(\mathbf{t} \mid \mathbf{y}). \tag{25.7}$$

We can also write this marginal with the aid of a truth function $\mathbb{1}[S]$ that is one if the proposition S is true and zero otherwise.

$$P(t_n = 1 \mid \mathbf{y}) \;=\; \sum_{\mathbf{t}} P(\mathbf{t} \mid \mathbf{y}) \, \mathbb{1}[t_n = 1] \tag{25.8}$$

$$P(t_n = 1 \mid \mathbf{y}) \;=\; \sum_{\mathbf{t}} P(\mathbf{t} \mid \mathbf{y}) \, \mathbb{1}[t_n = 0]. \tag{25.9}$$

Computing these marginal probabilities by an explicit sum over all codewords $\mathbf{t}$ takes exponential time. But, for certain codes, the bitwise decoding problem can be solved much more efficiently using the *forward–backward algorithm*. We will describe this algorithm, which is an example of the *sum–product algorithm*, in a moment. Both the min–sum algorithm and the sum–product algorithm have widespread importance, and have been invented many times in many fields.

(a)

Repetition code R_3

▶ 25.2 Codes and trellises

In Chapters 1 and 11, we represented linear (N, K) codes in terms of their generator matrices and their parity-check matrices. In the case of a *systematic block code*, the first K transmitted bits in each block of size N are the source bits, and the remaining $M = N - K$ bits are the parity-check bits. This means that the generator matrix of the code can be written

(b)

Simple parity code P_3

$$\mathbf{G}^{\mathsf{T}} = \begin{bmatrix} \mathbf{I}_K \\ \mathbf{P} \end{bmatrix}, \tag{25.10}$$

and the parity-check matrix can be written

$$\mathbf{H} = \begin{bmatrix} \mathbf{P} & \mathbf{I}_M \end{bmatrix}, \tag{25.11}$$

(c)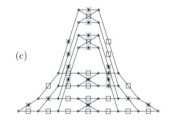

$(7, 4)$ Hamming code

where $\mathbf{P}$ is an $M \times K$ matrix.

In this section we will now study another representation of a linear code called a trellis. The codes that these trellises represent will not in general be systematic codes, but they can be mapped onto systematic codes if desired by a reordering of the bits in a block.

Figure 25.1. Examples of trellises. Each edge in a trellis is labelled by a zero (shown by a square) or a one (shown by a cross).

Definition of a trellis

Our definition will be quite narrow. For a more comprehensive view of trellises, the reader should consult Kschischang and Sorokine (1995).

A trellis is a *graph* consisting of *nodes* (also known as states or vertices) and *edges*. The nodes are grouped into vertical slices called *times*, and the times are ordered such that each edge connects a node in one time to a node in a neighbouring time. Every edge is labelled with a *symbol*. The leftmost and rightmost states contain only one node. Apart from these two extreme nodes, all nodes in the trellis have at least one edge connecting leftwards and at least one connecting rightwards.

A trellis with $N+1$ times defines a code of block length N as follows: a codeword is obtained by taking a path that crosses the trellis from left to right and reading out the symbols on the edges that are traversed. Each valid path through the trellis defines a codeword. We will number the leftmost time 'time 0' and the rightmost 'time N'. We will number the leftmost state 'state 0' and the rightmost 'state I', where I is the total number of states (vertices) in the trellis. The nth bit of the codeword is emitted as we move from time $n-1$ to time n.

The *width* of the trellis at a given time is the number of nodes in that time. The *maximal width* of a trellis is what it sounds like.

A trellis is called a *linear trellis* if the code it defines is a linear code. We will solely be concerned with linear trellises from now on, as nonlinear trellises are much more complex beasts. For brevity, we will only discuss binary trellises, that is, trellises whose edges are labelled with zeroes and ones. It is not hard to generalize the methods that follow to q-ary trellises.

Figures 25.1(a–c) show the trellises corresponding to the repetition code R_3 which has $(N, K) = (3, 1)$; the parity code P_3 with $(N, K) = (3, 2)$; and the $(7, 4)$ Hamming code.

▷ **Exercise 25.2.**[2] Confirm that the sixteen codewords listed in table 1.14 are generated by the trellis shown in figure 25.1c.

Observations about linear trellises

For any linear code the *minimal trellis* is the one that has the smallest number of nodes. In a minimal trellis, each node has at most two edges entering it and at most two edges leaving it. All nodes in a time have the same left degree as each other and they have the same right degree as each other. The width is always a power of two.

A minimal trellis for a linear (N, K) code cannot have a width greater than 2^K since every node has at least one valid codeword through it, and there are only 2^K codewords. Furthermore, if we define $M = N - K$, the minimal trellis's width is everywhere less than 2^M. This will be proved in section 25.4.

Notice that for the linear trellises in figure 25.1, all of which are minimal trellises, K is the number of times a binary branch point is encountered as the trellis is traversed from left to right or from right to left.

We will discuss the construction of trellises more in section 25.4. But we now know enough to discuss the decoding problem.

▶ 25.3 Solving the decoding problems on a trellis

We can view the trellis of a linear code as giving a causal description of the probabilistic process that gives rise to a codeword, with time flowing from left to right. Each time a divergence is encountered, a random source (the source of information bits for communication) determines which way we go.

At the receiving end, we receive a noisy version of the sequence of edge-labels, and wish to infer which path was taken, or to be precise, (a) we want to identify the most probable path in order to solve the codeword decoding problem; and (b) we want to find the probability that the transmitted symbol at time n was a zero or a one, to solve the bitwise decoding problem.

Example 25.3. Consider the case of a single transmission from the Hamming $(7, 4)$ trellis shown in figure 25.1c.

t	Likelihood	Posterior probability
0000000	0.0275562	0.25
0001011	0.0001458	0.0013
0010111	0.0013122	0.012
0011100	0.0030618	0.027
0100110	0.0002268	0.0020
0101101	0.0000972	0.0009
0110001	0.0708588	0.63
0111010	0.0020412	0.018
1000101	0.0001458	0.0013
1001110	0.0000042	0.0000
1010010	0.0030618	0.027
1011001	0.0013122	0.012
1100011	0.0000972	0.0009
1101000	0.0002268	0.0020
1110100	0.0020412	0.018
1111111	0.0000108	0.0001

Figure 25.2. Posterior probabilities over the sixteen codewords when the received vector **y** has normalized likelihoods $(0.1, 0.4, 0.9, 0.1, 0.1, 0.1, 0.3)$.

Let the normalized likelihoods be: $(0.1, 0.4, 0.9, 0.1, 0.1, 0.1, 0.3)$. That is, the ratios of the likelihoods are

$$\frac{P(y_1 \mid x_1 = 1)}{P(y_1 \mid x_1 = 0)} = \frac{0.1}{0.9}, \quad \frac{P(y_2 \mid x_2 = 1)}{P(y_2 \mid x_2 = 0)} = \frac{0.4}{0.6}, \quad \text{etc.} \qquad (25.12)$$

How should this received signal be decoded?

1. If we threshold the likelihoods at 0.5 to turn the signal into a binary received vector, we have $\mathbf{r} = (0, 0, 1, 0, 0, 0, 0)$, which decodes, using the decoder for the binary symmetric channel (Chapter 1), into $\hat{\mathbf{t}} = (0, 0, 0, 0, 0, 0, 0)$.

   This is not the optimal decoding procedure. Optimal inferences are always obtained by using Bayes' theorem.

2. We can find the posterior probability over codewords by explicit enumeration of all sixteen codewords. This posterior distribution is shown in figure 25.2. Of course, we aren't really interested in such brute-force solutions, and the aim of this chapter is to understand algorithms for getting the same information out in less than 2^K computer time.

   Examining the posterior probabilities, we notice that the most probable codeword is actually the string $\mathbf{t} = 0110001$. This is more than twice as probable as the answer found by thresholding, 0000000.

   Using the posterior probabilities shown in figure 25.2, we can also compute the posterior marginal distributions of each of the bits. The result is shown in figure 25.3. Notice that bits 1, 4, 5 and 6 are all quite confidently inferred to be zero. The strengths of the posterior probabilities for bits 2, 3, and 7 are not so great.   □

In the above example, the MAP codeword is in agreement with the bitwise decoding that is obtained by selecting the most probable state for each bit using the posterior marginal distributions. But this is not always the case, as the following exercise shows.

n	Likelihood		Posterior marginals	
	$P(y_n \mid t_n=1)$	$P(y_n \mid t_n=0)$	$P(t_n=1 \mid \mathbf{y})$	$P(t_n=0 \mid \mathbf{y})$
1	0.1	0.9	0.061	0.939
2	0.4	0.6	0.674	0.326
3	0.9	0.1	0.746	0.254
4	0.1	0.9	0.061	0.939
5	0.1	0.9	0.061	0.939
6	0.1	0.9	0.061	0.939
7	0.3	0.7	0.659	0.341

Figure 25.3. Marginal posterior probabilities for the 7 bits under the posterior distribution of figure 25.2.

 Exercise 25.4.[2, p.333] Find the most probable codeword in the case where the normalized likelihood is $(0.2, 0.2, 0.9, 0.2, 0.2, 0.2, 0.2)$. Also find or estimate the marginal posterior probability for each of the seven bits, and give the bit-by-bit decoding.

[Hint: concentrate on the few codewords that have the largest probability.]

We now discuss how to use message passing on a code's trellis to solve the decoding problems.

The min–sum algorithm

The MAP codeword decoding problem can be solved using the min–sum algorithm that was introduced in section 16.3. Each codeword of the code corresponds to a path across the trellis. Just as the cost of a journey is the sum of the costs of its constituent steps, the log likelihood of a codeword is the sum of the bitwise log likelihoods. By convention, we flip the sign of the log likelihood (which we would like to maximize) and talk in terms of a cost, which we would like to minimize.

We associate with each edge a cost $-\log P(y_n \mid t_n)$, where t_n is the transmitted bit associated with that edge, and y_n is the received symbol. The min–sum algorithm presented in section 16.3 can then identify the most probable codeword in a number of computer operations equal to the number of edges in the trellis. This algorithm is also known as the Viterbi algorithm (Viterbi, 1967).

The sum–product algorithm

To solve the bitwise decoding problem, we can make a small modification to the min–sum algorithm, so that the messages passed through the trellis define 'the probability of the data up to the current point' instead of 'the cost of the best route to this point'. We replace the costs on the edges, $-\log P(y_n \mid t_n)$, by the likelihoods themselves, $P(y_n \mid t_n)$. We replace the min and sum operations of the min–sum algorithm by a sum and product respectively.

Let i run over nodes/states, $i = 0$ be the label for the start state, $\mathcal{P}(i)$ denote the set of states that are parents of state i, and w_{ij} be the likelihood associated with the edge from node j to node i. We define the forward-pass messages α_i by

$$\alpha_0 = 1$$

$$\alpha_i = \sum_{j \in \mathcal{P}(i)} w_{ij} \alpha_j. \tag{25.13}$$

These messages can be computed sequentially from left to right.

▷ Exercise 25.5.[2] Show that for a node i whose time-coordinate is n, α_i is proportional to the joint probability that the codeword's path passed through node i and that the first n received symbols were $y_1, \ldots, y_n$.

The message α_i computed at the end node of the trellis is proportional to the marginal probability of the data.

▷ Exercise 25.6.[2] What is the constant of proportionality? [Answer: 2^K]

We define a second set of backward-pass messages β_i in a similar manner. Let node I be the end node.

$$\beta_I = 1$$
$$\beta_j = \sum_{i:j \in \mathcal{P}(i)} w_{ij} \beta_i. \tag{25.14}$$

These messages can be computed sequentially in a backward pass from right to left.

▷ Exercise 25.7.[2] Show that for a node i whose time-coordinate is n, β_i is proportional to the conditional probability, *given* that the codeword's path passed through node i, that the subsequent n received symbols were $y_{n+1} \cdots y_N$.

Finally, to find the probability that the nth bit was a 1 or 0, we do two summations of products of the forward and backward messages. Let i run over nodes at time n and j run over nodes at time $n-1$, and let t_{ij} be the value of t_n associated with the trellis edge from node j to node i. For each value of $t = 0/1$, we compute

$$r_n^{(t)} = \sum_{i,j: j \in \mathcal{P}(i), t_{ij} = t} \alpha_j w_{ij} \beta_i. \tag{25.15}$$

Then the posterior probability that t_n was $t = 0/1$ is

$$P(t_n = t \mid \mathbf{y}) = \frac{1}{Z} r_n^{(t)}, \tag{25.16}$$

where the normalizing constant $Z = r_n^{(0)} + r_n^{(1)}$ should be identical to the final forward message α_I that was computed earlier.

Exercise 25.8.[2] Confirm that the above sum–product algorithm does compute $P(t_n = t \mid \mathbf{y})$.

Other names for the sum–product algorithm presented here are 'the forward–backward algorithm', 'the BCJR algorithm', and 'belief propagation'.

▷ Exercise 25.9.[2, p.333] A codeword of the simple parity code P_3 is transmitted, and the received signal $\mathbf{y}$ has associated likelihoods shown in table 25.4. Use the min–sum algorithm and the sum–product algorithm in the trellis (figure 25.1) to solve the MAP codeword decoding problem and the bitwise decoding problem. Confirm your answers by enumeration of all codewords (000, 011, 110, 101). [Hint: use logs to base 2 and do the min–sum computations by hand. When working the sum–product algorithm by hand, you may find it helpful to use three colours of pen, one for the αs, one for the ws, and one for the βs.]

n	$P(y_n \mid t_n)$	
	$t_n = 0$	$t_n = 1$
1	$1/4$	$1/2$
2	$1/2$	$1/4$
3	$1/8$	$1/2$

Table 25.4. Bitwise likelihoods for a codeword of P_3.

► **25.4 More on trellises**

We now discuss various ways of making the trellis of a code. You may safely jump over this section.

The *span* of a codeword is the set of bits contained between the first bit in the codeword that is non-zero, and the last bit that is non-zero, inclusive. We can indicate the span of a codeword by a binary vector as shown in table 25.5.

Codeword	0000000	0001011	0100110	1100011	0101101
Span	0000000	0001111	0111110	1111111	0111111

Table 25.5. Some codewords and their spans.

A generator matrix is in *trellis-oriented form* if the spans of the rows of the generator matrix all start in different columns and the spans all end in different columns.

How to make a trellis from a generator matrix

First, put the generator matrix into trellis-oriented form by row-manipulations similar to Gaussian elimination. For example, our $(7,4)$ Hamming code can be generated by

$$\mathbf{G} = \begin{bmatrix} 1 & 0 & 0 & 0 & 1 & 0 & 1 \\ 0 & 1 & 0 & 0 & 1 & 1 & 0 \\ 0 & 0 & 1 & 0 & 1 & 1 & 1 \\ 0 & 0 & 0 & 1 & 0 & 1 & 1 \end{bmatrix} \tag{25.17}$$

but this matrix is not in trellis-oriented form – for example, rows 1, 3 and 4 all have spans that end in the same column. By subtracting lower rows from upper rows, we can obtain an equivalent generator matrix (that is, one that generates the same set of codewords) as follows:

$$\mathbf{G} = \begin{bmatrix} 1 & 1 & 0 & 1 & 0 & 0 & 0 \\ 0 & 1 & 0 & 0 & 1 & 1 & 0 \\ 0 & 0 & 1 & 1 & 1 & 0 & 0 \\ 0 & 0 & 0 & 1 & 0 & 1 & 1 \end{bmatrix}. \tag{25.18}$$

Now, each row of the generator matrix can be thought of as defining an $(N,1)$ subcode of the (N,K) code, that is, in this case, a code with two codewords of length $N = 7$. For the first row, the code consists of the two codewords 1101000 and 0000000. The subcode defined by the second row consists of 0100110 and 0000000. It is easy to construct the minimal trellises of these subcodes; they are shown in the left column of figure 25.6.

We build the trellis incrementally as shown in figure 25.6. We start with the trellis corresponding to the subcode given by the first row of the generator matrix. Then we add in one subcode at a time. The vertices within the span of the new subcode are all duplicated. The edge symbols in the original trellis are left unchanged and the edge symbols in the second part of the trellis are flipped wherever the new subcode has a 1 and otherwise left alone.

Another $(7,4)$ Hamming code can be generated by

$$\mathbf{G} = \begin{bmatrix} 1 & 1 & 1 & 0 & 0 & 0 & 0 \\ 0 & 1 & 1 & 1 & 1 & 0 & 0 \\ 0 & 0 & 1 & 0 & 1 & 1 & 0 \\ 0 & 0 & 0 & 1 & 1 & 1 & 1 \end{bmatrix}. \tag{25.19}$$

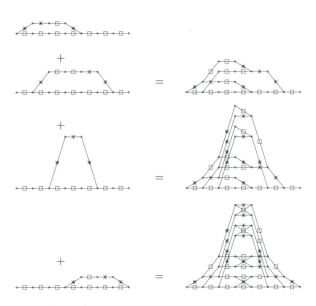

Figure 25.6. Trellises for four
subcodes of the $(7, 4)$ Hamming
code (left column), and the
sequence of trellises that are made
when constructing the trellis for
the $(7, 4)$ Hamming code (right
column).
Each edge in a trellis is labelled
by a zero (shown by a square) or
a one (shown by a cross).

The $(7, 4)$ Hamming code generated by this matrix differs by a permutation
of its bits from the code generated by the systematic matrix used in Chapter
1 and above. The parity-check matrix corresponding to this permutation is:

$$\mathbf{H} = \begin{bmatrix} 1 & 0 & 1 & 0 & 1 & 0 & 1 \\ 0 & 1 & 1 & 0 & 0 & 1 & 1 \\ 0 & 0 & 0 & 1 & 1 & 1 & 1 \end{bmatrix}. \tag{25.20}$$

The trellis obtained from the permuted matrix $\mathbf{G}$ given in equation (25.19) is
shown in figure 25.7a. Notice that the number of nodes in this trellis is smaller
than the number of nodes in the previous trellis for the Hamming $(7, 4)$ code
in figure 25.1c. We thus observe that *rearranging the order of the codeword
bits can sometimes lead to smaller, simpler trellises.*

Trellises from parity-check matrices

Another way of viewing the trellis is in terms of the syndrome. The syndrome
of a vector $\mathbf{r}$ is defined to be $\mathbf{Hr}$, where $\mathbf{H}$ is the parity-check matrix. A vector
is only a codeword if its syndrome is zero. As we generate a codeword we can
describe the current state by the *partial syndrome*, that is, the product of
$\mathbf{H}$ with the codeword bits thus far generated. Each state in the trellis is a
partial syndrome at one time coordinate. The starting and ending states are
both constrained to be the zero syndrome. Each node in a state represents a
different possible value for the partial syndrome. Since $\mathbf{H}$ is an $M \times N$ matrix,
where $M = N - K$, the syndrome is at most an M-bit vector. So we need at
most 2^M nodes in each state. We can construct the trellis of a code from its
parity-check matrix by walking from each end, generating two trees of possible
syndrome sequences. The intersection of these two trees defines the trellis of
the code.

In the pictures we obtain from this construction, we can let the vertical
coordinate represent the syndrome. Then any horizontal edge is necessarily
associated with a zero bit (since only a non-zero bit changes the syndrome)

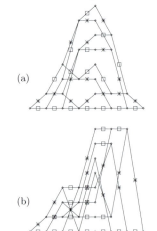

(a)

(b)

Figure 25.7. Trellises for the
permuted $(7, 4)$ Hamming code
generated from (a) the generator
matrix by the method of
figure 25.6; (b) the parity-check
matrix by the method on page
332.
Each edge in a trellis is labelled
by a zero (shown by a square) or
a one (shown by a cross).

and any non-horizontal edge is associated with a one bit. (Thus in this representation we no longer need to label the edges in the trellis.) Figure 25.7b shows the trellis corresponding to the parity-check matrix of equation (25.20).

▶ **25.5 Solutions**

t	Likelihood	Posterior probability
0000000	0.026	0.3006
0001011	0.00041	0.0047
0010111	0.0037	0.0423
0011100	0.015	0.1691
0100110	0.00041	0.0047
0101101	0.00010	0.0012
0110001	0.015	0.1691
0111010	0.0037	0.0423
1000101	0.00041	0.0047
1001110	0.00010	0.0012
1010010	0.015	0.1691
1011001	0.0037	0.0423
1100011	0.00010	0.0012
1101000	0.00041	0.0047
1110100	0.0037	0.0423
1111111	0.000058	0.0007

Table 25.8. The posterior probability over codewords for exercise 25.4.

Solution to exercise 25.4 (p.329). The posterior probability over codewords is shown in table 25.8. The most probable codeword is 0000000. The marginal posterior probabilities of all seven bits are:

n	Likelihood		Posterior marginals	
	$P(y_n \mid t_n = 1)$	$P(y_n \mid t_n = 0)$	$P(t_n = 1 \mid \mathbf{y})$	$P(t_n = 0 \mid \mathbf{y})$
1	0.2	0.8	0.266	0.734
2	0.2	0.8	0.266	0.734
3	0.9	0.1	0.677	0.323
4	0.2	0.8	0.266	0.734
5	0.2	0.8	0.266	0.734
6	0.2	0.8	0.266	0.734
7	0.2	0.8	0.266	0.734

So the bitwise decoding is 0010000, which is not actually a codeword.

Solution to exercise 25.9 (p.330). The MAP codeword is 101, and its likelihood is 1/8. The normalizing constant of the sum–product algorithm is $Z = \alpha_I = {}^3\!/_{16}$. The intermediate α_i are (from left to right) $1/2$, $1/4$, $5/16$, $4/16$; the intermediate β_i are (from right to left), $1/2$, $1/8$, $9/32$, $3/16$. The bitwise decoding is: $P(t_1 = 1 \mid \mathbf{y}) = 3/4$; $P(t_1 = 1 \mid \mathbf{y}) = 1/4$; $P(t_1 = 1 \mid \mathbf{y}) = 5/6$. The codewords's probabilities are $1/12$, $2/12$, $1/12$, $8/12$ for 000, 011, 110, 101.

26

Exact Marginalization in Graphs

We now take a more general view of the tasks of inference and marginalization. Before reading this chapter, you should read about message passing in Chapter 16.

▶ ## 26.1 The general problem

Assume that a function P^* of a set of N variables $\mathbf{x} \equiv \{x_n\}_{n=1}^N$ is defined as a product of M factors as follows:

$$P^*(\mathbf{x}) = \prod_{m=1}^M f_m(\mathbf{x}_m).$$

(26.1)

Each of the factors $f_m(\mathbf{x}_m)$ is a function of a subset $\mathbf{x}_m$ of the variables that make up $\mathbf{x}$. If P^* is a positive function then we may be interested in a second normalized function,

$$P(\mathbf{x}) \equiv \tfrac{1}{Z} P^*(\mathbf{x}) = \tfrac{1}{Z} \prod_{m=1}^M f_m(\mathbf{x}_m),$$

(26.2)

where the normalizing constant Z is defined by

$$Z = \sum_{\mathbf{x}} \prod_{m=1}^M f_m(\mathbf{x}_m).$$

(26.3)

As an example of the notation we've just introduced, here's a function on three binary variables x_1, x_2, x_3 defined by the five factors:

$$
\begin{aligned}
f_1(x_1) &= \begin{cases} 0.1 & x_1 = 0 \\ 0.9 & x_1 = 1 \end{cases} \\
f_2(x_2) &= \begin{cases} 0.1 & x_2 = 0 \\ 0.9 & x_2 = 1 \end{cases} \\
f_3(x_3) &= \begin{cases} 0.9 & x_3 = 0 \\ 0.1 & x_3 = 1 \end{cases} \\
f_4(x_1, x_2) &= \begin{cases} 1 & (x_1, x_2) = (0,0) \text{ or } (1,1) \\ 0 & (x_1, x_2) = (1,0) \text{ or } (0,1) \end{cases} \\
f_5(x_2, x_3) &= \begin{cases} 1 & (x_2, x_3) = (0,0) \text{ or } (1,1) \\ 0 & (x_2, x_3) = (1,0) \text{ or } (0,1) \end{cases} \\
P^*(\mathbf{x}) &= f_1(x_1) f_2(x_2) f_3(x_3) f_4(x_1, x_2) f_5(x_2, x_3) \\
P(\mathbf{x}) &= \tfrac{1}{Z} f_1(x_1) f_2(x_2) f_3(x_3) f_4(x_1, x_2) f_5(x_2, x_3).
\end{aligned}
$$

(26.4)

The five subsets of $\{x_1, x_2, x_3\}$ denoted by $\mathbf{x}_m$ in the general function (26.1) are here $\mathbf{x}_1 = \{x_1\}$, $\mathbf{x}_2 = \{x_2\}$, $\mathbf{x}_3 = \{x_3\}$, $\mathbf{x}_4 = \{x_1, x_2\}$, and $\mathbf{x}_5 = \{x_2, x_3\}$.

The function $P(\mathbf{x})$, by the way, may be recognized as the posterior probability distribution of the three transmitted bits in a repetition code (section 1.2) when the received signal is $\mathbf{r} = (1, 1, 0)$ and the channel is a binary symmetric channel with flip probability 0.1. The factors f_4 and f_5 respectively enforce the constraints that x_1 and x_2 must be identical and that x_2 and x_3 must be identical. The factors f_1, f_2, f_3 are the likelihood functions contributed by each component of $\mathbf{r}$.

A function of the factored form (26.1) can be depicted by a *factor graph*, in which the variables are depicted by circular nodes and the factors are depicted by square nodes. An edge is put between variable node n and factor node m if the function $f_m(\mathbf{x}_m)$ has any dependence on variable x_n. The factor graph for the example function (26.4) is shown in figure 26.1.

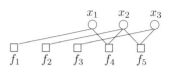

Figure 26.1. The factor graph associated with the function $g(\mathbf{x})$ (26.4).

The normalization problem

The first task to be solved is to compute the normalizing constant Z.

The marginalization problems

The second task to be solved is to compute the marginal function of any variable x_n, defined by

$$Z_n(x_n) = \sum_{\{x_{n'}\}, n' \neq n} P^*(\mathbf{x}). \tag{26.5}$$

For example, if f is a function of three variables then the marginal for $n = 1$ is defined by

$$Z_1(x_1) = \sum_{x_2, x_3} f(x_1, x_2, x_3). \tag{26.6}$$

This type of summation, over 'all the $x_{n'}$ except for x_n' is so important that it can be useful to have a special notation for it – the 'not-sum' or 'summary'.

The third task to be solved is to compute the normalized marginal of any variable x_n, defined by

$$P_n(x_n) \equiv \sum_{\{x_{n'}\}, n' \neq n} P(\mathbf{x}). \tag{26.7}$$

[We include the suffix 'n' in $P_n(x_n)$, departing from our normal practice in the rest of the book, where we would omit it.]

▷ Exercise 26.1.[1] Show that the normalized marginal is related to the marginal $Z_n(x_n)$ by

$$P_n(x_n) = \frac{Z_n(x_n)}{Z}. \tag{26.8}$$

We might also be interested in marginals over a subset of the variables, such as

$$Z_{12}(x_1, x_2) \equiv \sum_{x_3} P^*(x_1, x_2, x_3). \tag{26.9}$$

All these tasks are intractable in general. Even if every factor is a function of only three variables, the cost of computing exact solutions for Z and for the marginals is believed in general to grow exponentially with the number of variables N.

For certain functions P^*, however, the marginals can be computed efficiently by exploiting the factorization of P^*. The idea of how this efficiency arises is well illustrated by the message-passing examples of Chapter 16. The sum–product algorithm that we now review is a generalization of message-passing rule-set B (p.242). As was the case there, the sum–product algorithm is only valid if the graph is tree-like.

▶ 26.2 The sum–product algorithm

Notation

We identify the set of variables that the mth factor depends on, $\mathbf{x}_m$, by the set of their indices $\mathcal{N}(m)$. For our example function (26.4), the sets are $\mathcal{N}(1) = \{1\}$ (since f_1 is a function of x_1 alone), $\mathcal{N}(2) = \{2\}$, $\mathcal{N}(3) = \{3\}$, $\mathcal{N}(4) = \{1,2\}$, and $\mathcal{N}(5) = \{2,3\}$. Similarly we define the set of factors in which variable n participates, by $\mathcal{M}(n)$. We denote a set $\mathcal{N}(m)$ with variable n excluded by $\mathcal{N}(m)\backslash n$. We introduce the shorthand $\mathbf{x}_m\backslash n$ or $\mathbf{x}_{m\backslash n}$ to denote the set of variables in $\mathbf{x}_m$ with x_n excluded, i.e.,

$$\mathbf{x}_m\backslash n \equiv \{x_{n'} : n' \in \mathcal{N}(m)\backslash n\}. \tag{26.10}$$

The sum–product algorithm will involve messages of two types passing along the edges in the factor graph: messages $q_{n\to m}$ from variable nodes to factor nodes, and messages $r_{m\to n}$ from factor nodes to variable nodes. A message (of either type, q or r) that is sent along an edge connecting factor f_m to variable x_n is always a function of the variable x_n.

Here are the two rules for the updating of the two sets of messages.

From variable to factor:

$$q_{n\to m}(x_n) = \prod_{m'\in\mathcal{M}(n)\backslash m} r_{m'\to n}(x_n). \tag{26.11}$$

From factor to variable:

$$r_{m\to n}(x_n) = \sum_{\mathbf{x}_m\backslash n} \left(f_m(\mathbf{x}_m) \prod_{n'\in\mathcal{N}(m)\backslash n} q_{n'\to m}(x_{n'}) \right). \tag{26.12}$$

How these rules apply to leaves in the factor graph

A node that has only one edge connecting it to another node is called a leaf node.

Some factor nodes in the graph may be connected to only one variable node, in which case the set $\mathcal{N}(m)\backslash n$ of variables appearing in the factor message update (26.12) is an empty set, and the product of functions $\prod_{n'\in\mathcal{N}(m)\backslash n} q_{n'\to m}(x_{n'})$ is the empty product, whose value is 1. Such a factor node therefore always broadcasts to its one neighbour x_n the message $r_{m\to n}(x_n) = f_m(x_n)$.

Similarly, there may be variable nodes that are connected to only one factor node, so the set $\mathcal{M}(n)\backslash m$ in (26.11) is empty. These nodes perpetually broadcast the message $q_{n\to m}(x_n) = 1$.

Starting and finishing, method 1

The algorithm can be initialized in two ways. If the graph is tree-like then it must have nodes that are leaves. These leaf nodes can broadcast their

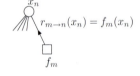

Figure 26.2. A factor node that is a leaf node perpetually sends the message $r_{m\to n}(x_n) = f_m(x_n)$ to its one neighbour x_n.

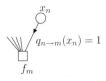

Figure 26.3. A variable node that is a leaf node perpetually sends the message $q_{n\to m}(x_n) = 1$.

messages to their respective neighbours from the start.

$$\text{For all leaf variable nodes } n: \quad q_{n \to m}(x_n) = 1 \qquad (26.13)$$
$$\text{For all leaf factor nodes } m: \quad r_{m \to n}(x_n) = f_m(x_n). \qquad (26.14)$$

We can then adopt the procedure used in Chapter 16's message-passing rule-set B (p.242): a message is created in accordance with the rules (26.11, 26.12) only if all the messages on which it depends are present. For example, in figure 26.4, the message from x_1 to f_1 will be sent only once the message from f_4 to x_1 has been received; and the message from x_2 to f_2, $q_{2 \to 2}$, can be sent only once the messages $r_{4 \to 2}$ and $r_{5 \to 2}$ have both been received.

Messages will thus flow through the tree, one in each direction along every edge, and after a number of steps equal to the diameter of the graph, every message will have been created.

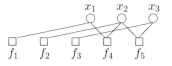

Figure 26.4. Our model factor graph for the function $g(\mathbf{x})$ (26.4).

The answers we require can then be read out. The marginal function of x_n is obtained by multiplying all the incoming messages at that node.

$$Z_n(x_n) = \prod_{m \in \mathcal{M}(n)} r_{m \to n}(x_n). \qquad (26.15)$$

The normalizing constant Z can be obtained by summing any marginal function, $Z = \sum_{x_n} Z_n(x_n)$, and the normalized marginals obtained from

$$P_n(x_n) = \frac{Z_n(x_n)}{Z}. \qquad (26.16)$$

▷ Exercise 26.2.[2] Apply the sum–product algorithm to the function defined in equation (26.4) and figure 26.1. Check that the normalized marginals are consistent with what you know about the repetition code R_3.

Exercise 26.3.[3] Prove that the sum–product algorithm correctly computes the marginal functions $Z_n(x_n)$ if the graph is tree-like.

Exercise 26.4.[3] Describe how to use the messages computed by the sum–product algorithm to obtain more complicated marginal functions in a tree-like graph, for example $Z_{1,2}(x_1, x_2)$, for two variables x_1 and x_2 that are connected to one common factor node.

Starting and finishing, method 2

Alternatively, the algorithm can be initialized by setting *all* the initial messages from variables to 1:

$$\text{for all } n, m: \quad q_{n \to m}(x_n) = 1, \qquad (26.17)$$

then proceeding with the factor message update rule (26.12), alternating with the variable message update rule (26.11). Compared with method 1, this lazy initialization method leads to a load of wasted computations, whose results are gradually flushed out by the correct answers computed by method 1.

After a number of iterations equal to the diameter of the factor graph, the algorithm will converge to a set of messages satisfying the sum–product relationships (26.11, 26.12).

Exercise 26.5.[2] Apply this second version of the sum–product algorithm to the function defined in equation (26.4) and figure 26.1.

The reason for introducing this lazy method is that (unlike method 1) it can be applied to graphs that are not tree-like. When the sum–product algorithm is run on a graph with cycles, the algorithm does not necessarily converge, and certainly does not in general compute the correct marginal functions; but it is nevertheless an algorithm of great practical importance, especially in the decoding of sparse graph codes.

Sum–product algorithm with on-the-fly normalization

If we are interested in only the *normalized* marginals, then another version of the sum–product algorithm may be useful. The factor-to-variable messages $r_{m \to n}$ are computed in just the same way (26.12), but the variable-to-factor messages are normalized thus:

$$q_{n \to m}(x_n) = \alpha_{nm} \prod_{m' \in \mathcal{M}(n) \backslash m} r_{m' \to n}(x_n) \qquad (26.18)$$

where α_{nm} is a scalar chosen such that

$$\sum_{x_n} q_{n \to m}(x_n) = 1. \qquad (26.19)$$

Exercise 26.6.[2] Apply this normalized version of the sum–product algorithm to the function defined in equation (26.4) and figure 26.1.

A factorization view of the sum–product algorithm

One way to view the sum–product algorithm is that it reexpresses the original factored function, the product of M factors $P^*(\mathbf{x}) = \prod_{m=1}^{M} f_m(\mathbf{x}_m)$, as another factored function which is the product of $M + N$ factors,

$$P^*(\mathbf{x}) = \prod_{m=1}^{M} \phi_m(\mathbf{x}_m) \prod_{n=1}^{N} \psi_n(x_n). \qquad (26.20)$$

Each factor ϕ_m is associated with a factor node m, and each factor $\psi_n(x_n)$ is associated with a variable node. Initially $\phi_m(\mathbf{x}_m) = f_m(\mathbf{x}_m)$ and $\psi_n(x_n) = 1$.

Each time a factor-to-variable message $r_{m \to n}(x_n)$ is sent, the factorization is updated thus:

$$\psi_n(x_n) = \prod_{m \in \mathcal{M}(n)} r_{m \to n}(x_n) \qquad (26.21)$$

$$\phi_m(\mathbf{x}_m) = \frac{f(\mathbf{x}_m)}{\prod_{n \in \mathcal{N}(m)} r_{m \to n}(x_n)}. \qquad (26.22)$$

And each message can be computed in terms of ϕ and ψ using

$$r_{m \to n}(x_n) = \sum_{\mathbf{x}_m \backslash n} \left(\phi_m(\mathbf{x}_m) \prod_{n' \in \mathcal{N}(m)} \psi_{n'}(x_{n'}) \right) \qquad (26.23)$$

which differs from the assignment (26.12) in that the product is over all $n' \in \mathcal{N}(m)$.

Exercise 26.7.[2] Confirm that the update rules (26.21–26.23) are equivalent to the sum–product rules (26.11–26.12). So $\psi_n(x_n)$ eventually becomes the marginal $Z_n(x_n)$.

This factorization viewpoint applies whether or not the graph is tree-like.

Computational tricks

On-the-fly normalization is a good idea from a computational point of view because if P^* is a product of many factors, its values are likely to be very large or very small.

Another useful computational trick involves passing the logarithms of the messages q and r instead of q and r themselves; the computations of the products in the algorithm (26.11, 26.12) are then replaced by simpler additions. The summations in (26.12) of course become more difficult: to carry them out and return the logarithm, we need to compute softmax functions like

$$l = \ln(e^{l_1} + e^{l_2} + e^{l_3}). \tag{26.24}$$

But this computation can be done efficiently using look-up tables along with the observation that the value of the answer l is typically just a little larger than $\max_i l_i$. If we store in look-up tables values of the function

$$\ln(1 + e^{\delta}) \tag{26.25}$$

(for negative δ) then l can be computed exactly in a number of look-ups and additions scaling as the number of terms in the sum. If look-ups and sorting operations are cheaper than `exp()` then this approach costs less than the direct evaluation (26.24). The number of operations can be further reduced by omitting negligible contributions from the smallest of the $\{l_i\}$.

A third computational trick applicable to certain error-correcting codes is to pass not the messages but the Fourier transform of the messages. This again makes the computations of the factor-to-variable messages quicker. A simple example of this Fourier transform trick is given in Chapter 47 at equation (47.9).

▶ ## 26.3 The min–sum algorithm

The sum–product algorithm solves the problem of finding the marginal function of a given product $P^*(\mathbf{x})$. This is analogous to solving the bitwise decoding problem of section 25.1. And just as there were other decoding problems (for example, the codeword decoding problem), we can define other tasks involving $P^*(\mathbf{x})$ that can be solved by modifications of the sum–product algorithm. For example, consider this task, analogous to the codeword decoding problem:

The maximization problem. Find the setting of $\mathbf{x}$ that maximizes the product $P^*(\mathbf{x})$.

This problem can be solved by replacing the two operations add and multiply everywhere they appear in the sum–product algorithm by another pair of operations that satisfy the distributive law, namely max and multiply. If we replace summation $(+, \sum)$ by maximization, we notice that the quantity formerly known as the normalizing constant,

$$Z = \sum_{\mathbf{x}} P^*(\mathbf{x}), \tag{26.26}$$

becomes $\max_{\mathbf{x}} P^*(\mathbf{x})$.

Thus the sum–product algorithm can be turned into a max–product algorithm that computes $\max_{\mathbf{x}} P^*(\mathbf{x})$, and from which the solution of the maximization problem can be deduced. Each 'marginal' $Z_n(x_n)$ then lists the maximum value that $P^*(\mathbf{x})$ can attain for each value of x_n.

In practice, the max–product algorithm is most often carried out in the negative log likelihood domain, where max and product and replaced by min and sum. The min–sum algorithm is also known as the Viterbi algorithm.

▶ 26.4 The junction tree algorithm

What should one do when the factor graph one is interested in is not a tree?

There are several options, and they divide into exact methods and approximate methods. The most widely used exact method for handling marginalization on graphs with cycles is called the junction tree algorithm. This algorithm works by agglomerating variables together until the agglomerated graph has no cycles. You can probably figure out the details for yourself; the complexity of the marginalization grows exponentially with the number of agglomerated variables. Read more about the junction tree algorithm in (Lauritzen, 1996; Jordan, 1998).

There are many approximate methods, and we'll visit some of them over the next few chapters – Monte Carlo methods and variational methods, to name a couple. However, the most amusing way of handling factor graphs to which the sum–product algorithm may not be applied is, as we already mentioned, to apply the sum–product algorithm! We simply compute the messages for each node in the graph, as if the graph were a tree, iterate, and cross our fingers. This so-called 'loopy' message passing has great importance in the decoding of error-correcting codes, and we'll come back to it in section 33.8 and Part VI.

Further reading

For further reading about factor graphs and the sum–product algorithm, see Kschischang *et al.* (2001), Yedidia *et al.* (2000c), Yedidia *et al.* (2000a), Yedidia *et al.* (2002), Wainwright *et al.* (2003), and Forney (2001).

See also Pearl (1988). A good reference for the fundamental theory of graphical models is Lauritzen (1996). A readable introduction to Bayesian networks is given by Jensen (1996).

Interesting message-passing algorithms that have different capabilities from the sum–product algorithm include *expectation propagation* (Minka, 2001) and *survey propagation* (Braunstein *et al.*, 2003). See also section 33.8.

▶ 26.5 Exercises

▷ Exercise 26.8.[2] Express the joint probability distribution from the burglar alarm and earthquake problem (example 21.1 (p.293)) as a factor graph, and find the marginal probabilities of all the variables as each piece of information comes to Fred's attention, using the sum–product algorithm with on-the-fly normalization.

27

Laplace's Method

The idea behind the Laplace approximation is simple. We assume that an unnormalized probability density $P^*(x)$, whose normalizing constant

$$Z_P \equiv \int P^*(x)\,dx \qquad (27.1)$$

is of interest, has a peak at a point x_0. We Taylor-expand the logarithm of $P^*(x)$ around this peak:

$$\ln P^*(x) \simeq \ln P^*(x_0) - \frac{c}{2}(x - x_0)^2 + \cdots, \qquad (27.2)$$

where

$$c = -\frac{\partial^2}{\partial x^2} \ln P^*(x)\bigg|_{x=x_0}. \qquad (27.3)$$

We then approximate $P^*(x)$ by an unnormalized Gaussian,

$$Q^*(x) \equiv P^*(x_0) \exp\left[-\frac{c}{2}(x - x_0)^2\right], \qquad (27.4)$$

and we approximate the normalizing constant Z_P by the normalizing constant of this Gaussian,

$$Z_Q = P^*(x_0)\sqrt{\frac{2\pi}{c}}. \qquad (27.5)$$

We can generalize this integral to approximate Z_P for a density $P^*(\mathbf{x})$ over a K-dimensional space $\mathbf{x}$. If the matrix of second derivatives of $-\ln P^*(\mathbf{x})$ at the maximum $\mathbf{x}_0$ is $\mathbf{A}$, defined by:

$$A_{ij} = -\frac{\partial^2}{\partial x_i \partial x_j} \ln P^*(\mathbf{x})\bigg|_{\mathbf{x}=\mathbf{x}_0}, \qquad (27.6)$$

so that the expansion (27.2) is generalized to

$$\ln P^*(\mathbf{x}) \simeq \ln P^*(\mathbf{x}_0) - \frac{1}{2}(\mathbf{x} - \mathbf{x}_0)^\mathsf{T}\mathbf{A}(\mathbf{x} - \mathbf{x}_0) + \cdots, \qquad (27.7)$$

then the normalizing constant can be approximated by:

$$Z_P \simeq Z_Q = P^*(\mathbf{x}_0)\frac{1}{\sqrt{\det \frac{1}{2\pi}\mathbf{A}}} = P^*(\mathbf{x}_0)\sqrt{\frac{(2\pi)^K}{\det \mathbf{A}}}. \qquad (27.8)$$

Predictions can be made using the approximation Q. Physicists also call this widely-used approximation the *saddle-point approximation*.

$P^*(x)$

$\ln P^*(x)$

$\ln P^*(x)$
& $\ln Q^*(x)$

$P^*(x)$
& $Q^*(x)$

The fact that the normalizing constant of a Gaussian is given by

$$\int d^K\mathbf{x}\ \exp\left[-\frac{1}{2}\mathbf{x}^\mathsf{T}\mathbf{A}\mathbf{x}\right] = \sqrt{\frac{(2\pi)^K}{\det \mathbf{A}}}\qquad(27.9)$$

can be proved by making an orthogonal transformation into the basis $\mathbf{u}$ in which $\mathbf{A}$ is transformed into a diagonal matrix. The integral then separates into a product of one-dimensional integrals, each of the form

$$\int du_i\ \exp\left[-\frac{1}{2}\lambda_i u_i^2\right] = \sqrt{\frac{2\pi}{\lambda_i}}.\qquad(27.10)$$

The product of the eigenvalues λ_i is the determinant of $\mathbf{A}$.

The Laplace approximation is basis-dependent: if x is transformed to a nonlinear function $u(x)$ and the density is transformed to $P(u) = P(x)\,|dx/du|$ then in general the approximate normalizing constants Z_Q will be different. This can be viewed as a defect – since the true value Z_P is basis-independent – or an opportunity – because we can hunt for a choice of basis in which the Laplace approximation is most accurate.

▶ 27.1 Exercises

Exercise 27.1.[2] (See also exercise 22.8 (p.307).) A photon counter is pointed at a remote star for one minute, in order to infer the rate of photons arriving at the counter per minute, λ. Assuming the number of photons collected r has a Poisson distribution with mean λ,

$$P(r\,|\,\lambda) = \exp(-\lambda)\frac{\lambda^r}{r!},\qquad(27.11)$$

and assuming the improper prior $P(\lambda) = 1/\lambda$, make Laplace approximations to the posterior distribution

(a) over λ
(b) over $\log\lambda$. [Note the improper prior transforms to $P(\log\lambda) =$ constant.]

▷ Exercise 27.2.[2] Use Laplace's method to approximate the integral

$$Z(u_1, u_2) = \int_{-\infty}^{\infty} da\ f(a)^{u_1}(1 - f(a))^{u_2},\qquad(27.12)$$

where $f(a) = 1/(1+e^{-a})$ and u_1, u_2 are positive. Check the accuracy of the approximation against the exact answer (23.29, p.316) for $(u_1, u_2) = (1/2, 1/2)$ and $(u_1, u_2) = (1, 1)$. Measure the accuracy $(\log Z_P - \log Z_Q)$ in bits.

▷ Exercise 27.3.[3] Linear regression. N datapoints $\{(x^{(n)}, t^{(n)})\}$ are generated by the experimenter choosing each $x^{(n)}$, then the world delivering a noisy version of the linear function

$$y(x) = w_0 + w_1 x,\qquad(27.13)$$

$$t^{(n)} \sim \text{Normal}(y(x^{(n)}), \sigma_\nu^2).\qquad(27.14)$$

Assuming Gaussian priors on w_0 and w_1, make the Laplace approximation to the posterior distribution of w_0 and w_1 (which is exact, in fact) and obtain the predictive distribution for the next datapoint $t^{(N+1)}$, given $x^{(N+1)}$.

(See MacKay (1992a) for further reading.)

28

Model Comparison and Occam's Razor

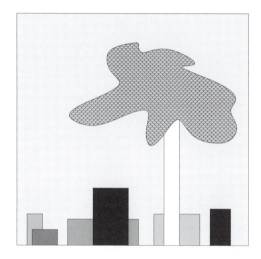

Figure 28.1. A picture to be interpreted. It contains a tree and some boxes.

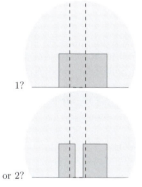

Figure 28.2. How many boxes are behind the tree?

▶ **28.1 Occam's razor**

How many boxes are in the picture (figure 28.1)? In particular, how many boxes are in the vicinity of the tree? If we looked with x-ray spectacles, would we see one or two boxes behind the trunk (figure 28.2)? (Or even more?) Occam's razor is the principle that states a preference for simple theories. 'Accept the simplest explanation that fits the data'. Thus according to Occam's razor, we should deduce that there is only one box behind the tree. Is this an ad hoc rule of thumb? Or is there a convincing reason for believing there is most likely one box? Perhaps your intuition likes the argument 'well, it would be a remarkable *coincidence* for the two boxes to be just the same height and colour as each other'. If we wish to make artificial intelligences that interpret data correctly, we must translate this intuitive feeling into a concrete theory.

Motivations for Occam's razor

If several explanations are compatible with a set of observations, Occam's razor advises us to buy the simplest. This principle is often advocated for one of two reasons: the first is aesthetic ('A theory with mathematical beauty is more likely to be correct than an ugly one that fits some experimental data'

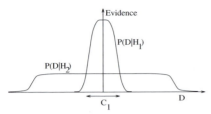

Figure 28.3. Why Bayesian
inference embodies Occam's razor.
This figure gives the basic
intuition for why complex models
can turn out to be less probable.
The horizontal axis represents the
space of possible data sets D.
Bayes' theorem rewards models in
proportion to how much they
predicted the data that occurred.
These predictions are quantified
by a normalized probability
distribution on D. This
probability of the data given
model $\mathcal{H}_i$, $P(D|\mathcal{H}_i)$, is called the
evidence for $\mathcal{H}_i$.
A simple model $\mathcal{H}_1$ makes only a
limited range of predictions,
shown by $P(D|\mathcal{H}_1)$; a more
powerful model $\mathcal{H}_2$, that has, for
example, more free parameters
than $\mathcal{H}_1$, is able to predict a
greater variety of data sets. This
means, however, that $\mathcal{H}_2$ does not
predict the data sets in region $\mathcal{C}_1$
as strongly as $\mathcal{H}_1$. Suppose that
equal prior probabilities have been
assigned to the two models. Then,
if the data set falls in region $\mathcal{C}_1$,
the *less powerful* model $\mathcal{H}_1$ will be
the *more probable* model.

(Paul Dirac)); the second reason is the past empirical success of Occam's razor. However there is a different justification for Occam's razor, namely:

> Coherent inference (as embodied by Bayesian probability) automatically embodies Occam's razor, quantitatively.

It is indeed *more probable* that there's one box behind the tree, and we can compute how much more probable one is than two.

Model comparison and Occam's razor

We evaluate the plausibility of two alternative theories $\mathcal{H}_1$ and $\mathcal{H}_2$ in the light of data D as follows: using Bayes' theorem, we relate the plausibility of model $\mathcal{H}_1$ given the data, $P(\mathcal{H}_1|D)$, to the predictions made by the model about the data, $P(D|\mathcal{H}_1)$, and the prior plausibility of $\mathcal{H}_1$, $P(\mathcal{H}_1)$. This gives the following probability ratio between theory $\mathcal{H}_1$ and theory $\mathcal{H}_2$:

$$\frac{P(\mathcal{H}_1|D)}{P(\mathcal{H}_2|D)} = \frac{P(\mathcal{H}_1)}{P(\mathcal{H}_2)}\frac{P(D|\mathcal{H}_1)}{P(D|\mathcal{H}_2)}. \tag{28.1}$$

The first ratio $(P(\mathcal{H}_1)/P(\mathcal{H}_2))$ on the right-hand side measures how much our initial beliefs favoured $\mathcal{H}_1$ over $\mathcal{H}_2$. The second ratio expresses how well the observed data were predicted by $\mathcal{H}_1$, compared to $\mathcal{H}_2$.

How does this relate to Occam's razor, when $\mathcal{H}_1$ is a simpler model than $\mathcal{H}_2$? The first ratio $(P(\mathcal{H}_1)/P(\mathcal{H}_2))$ gives us the opportunity, if we wish, to insert a prior bias in favour of $\mathcal{H}_1$ on aesthetic grounds, or on the basis of experience. This would correspond to the aesthetic and empirical motivations for Occam's razor mentioned earlier. But such a prior bias is not necessary: the second ratio, the data-dependent factor, embodies Occam's razor *automatically*. Simple models tend to make precise predictions. Complex models, by their nature, are capable of making a greater variety of predictions (figure 28.3). So if $\mathcal{H}_2$ is a more complex model, it must spread its predictive probability $P(D|\mathcal{H}_2)$ more thinly over the data space than $\mathcal{H}_1$. Thus, in the case where the data are compatible with both theories, the simpler $\mathcal{H}_1$ will turn out more probable than $\mathcal{H}_2$, without our having to express any subjective dislike for complex models. Our subjective prior just needs to assign equal prior probabilities to the possibilities of simplicity and complexity. Probability theory then allows the observed data to express their opinion.

Let us turn to a simple example. Here is a sequence of numbers:

$$-1, 3, 7, 11.$$

The task is to predict the next two numbers, and infer the underlying process that gave rise to this sequence. A popular answer to this question is the prediction '15, 19', with the explanation 'add 4 to the previous number'.

What about the alternative answer '$-19.9, 1043.8$' with the underlying rule being: 'get the next number from the previous number, x, by evaluating

$-x^3/11 + 9/11x^2 + 23/11$'? I assume that this prediction seems rather less
plausible. But the second rule fits the data $(-1, 3, 7, 11)$ just as well as the
rule 'add 4'. So why should we find it less plausible? Let us give labels to the
two general theories:

$\mathcal{H}_a$ – the sequence is an *arithmetic* progression, 'add n', where n is an integer.

$\mathcal{H}_c$ – the sequence is generated by a *cubic* function of the form $x \rightarrow cx^3 + dx^2 + e$, where c, d and e are fractions.

One reason for finding the second explanation, $\mathcal{H}_c$, less plausible, might be
that arithmetic progressions are more frequently encountered than cubic functions. This would put a bias in the prior probability ratio $P(\mathcal{H}_a)/P(\mathcal{H}_c)$ in
equation (28.1). But let us give the two theories equal prior probabilities, and
concentrate on what the data have to say. How well did each theory predict
the data?

To obtain $P(D|\mathcal{H}_a)$ we must specify the probability distribution that each
model assigns to its parameters. First, $\mathcal{H}_a$ depends on the added integer n,
and the first number in the sequence. Let us say that these numbers could
each have been anywhere between -50 and 50. Then since only the pair of
values $\{n=4,$ first number $= -1\}$ give rise to the observed data $D = (-1, 3,$
$7, 11)$, the probability of the data, given $\mathcal{H}_a$, is:

$$P(D|\mathcal{H}_a) = \frac{1}{101}\frac{1}{101} = 0.00010. \tag{28.2}$$

To evaluate $P(D|\mathcal{H}_c)$, we must similarly say what values the fractions c, d
and e might take on. [I choose to represent these numbers as fractions rather
than real numbers because if we used real numbers, the model would assign,
relative to $\mathcal{H}_a$, an infinitesimal probability to D. Real parameters are the
norm however, and are assumed in the rest of this chapter.] A reasonable
prior might state that for each fraction the numerator could be any number
between -50 and 50, and the denominator is any number between 1 and 50.
As for the initial value in the sequence, let us leave its probability distribution
the same as in $\mathcal{H}_a$. There are four ways of expressing the fraction $c = -1/11 =$
$-2/22 = -3/33 = -4/44$ under this prior, and similarly there are four and two
possible solutions for d and e, respectively. So the probability of the observed
data, given $\mathcal{H}_c$, is found to be:

$$P(D|\mathcal{H}_c) = \left(\frac{1}{101}\right)\left(\frac{4}{101}\frac{1}{50}\right)\left(\frac{4}{101}\frac{1}{50}\right)\left(\frac{2}{101}\frac{1}{50}\right)$$
$$= 0.0000000000025 = 2.5 \times 10^{-12}. \tag{28.3}$$

Thus comparing $P(D|\mathcal{H}_c)$ with $P(D|\mathcal{H}_a) = 0.00010$, even if our prior proba-
bilities for $\mathcal{H}_a$ and $\mathcal{H}_c$ are equal, the odds, $P(D|\mathcal{H}_a) : P(D|\mathcal{H}_c)$, in favour of
$\mathcal{H}_a$ over $\mathcal{H}_c$, given the sequence $D = (-1, 3, 7, 11)$, are about forty million to
one.   □

   This answer depends on several subjective assumptions; in particular, the
probability assigned to the free parameters n, c, d, e of the theories. Bayesians
make no apologies for this: there is no such thing as inference or prediction
without assumptions. However, the quantitative details of the prior probabilities have no effect on the qualitative Occam's razor effect; the complex
theory $\mathcal{H}_c$ always suffers an 'Occam factor' because it has more parameters,
and so can predict a greater variety of data sets (figure 28.3). This was only
a small example, and there were only four data points; as we move to larger

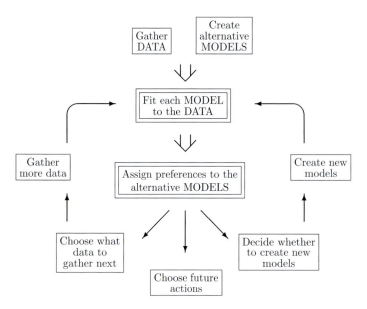

Figure 28.4. Where Bayesian inference fits into the data modelling process.
This figure illustrates an abstraction of the part of the scientific process in which data are collected and modelled. In particular, this figure applies to pattern classification, learning, interpolation, etc. The two double-framed boxes denote the two steps which involve *inference*. It is only in those two steps that Bayes' theorem can be used. Bayes does not tell you how to invent models, for example.
The first box, 'fitting each model to the data', is the task of inferring what the model parameters might be given the model and the data. Bayesian methods may be used to find the most probable parameter values, and error bars on those parameters. The result of applying Bayesian methods to this problem is often little different from the answers given by orthodox statistics.
The second inference task, model comparison in the light of the data, is where Bayesian methods are in a class of their own. This second inference problem requires a quantitative Occam's razor to penalize over-complex models. Bayesian methods can assign objective preferences to the alternative models in a way that automatically embodies Occam's razor.

and more sophisticated problems the magnitude of the Occam factors typically increases, and the degree to which our inferences are influenced by the quantitative details of our subjective assumptions becomes smaller.

Bayesian methods and data analysis

Let us now relate the discussion above to real problems in data analysis.

There are countless problems in science, statistics and technology which require that, given a limited data set, preferences be assigned to alternative models of differing complexities. For example, two alternative hypotheses accounting for planetary motion are Mr. Inquisition's geocentric model based on 'epicycles', and Mr. Copernicus's simpler model of the solar system with the sun at the centre. The epicyclic model fits data on planetary motion at least as well as the Copernican model, but does so using more parameters. Coincidentally for Mr. Inquisition, two of the extra epicyclic parameters for every planet are found to be identical to the period and radius of the sun's 'cycle around the earth'. Intuitively we find Mr. Copernicus's theory more probable.

The mechanism of the Bayesian razor: the evidence and the Occam factor

Two levels of inference can often be distinguished in the process of data modelling. At the first level of inference, we assume that a particular model is true, and we fit that model to the data, i.e., we infer what values its free parameters should plausibly take, given the data. The results of this inference are often summarized by the most probable parameter values, and error bars on those parameters. This analysis is repeated for each model. The second level of inference is the task of model comparison. Here we wish to compare the models in the light of the data, and assign some sort of preference or ranking to the alternatives.

Note that both levels of *inference* are distinct from *decision theory*. The goal of inference is, given a defined hypothesis space and a particular data set, to assign probabilities to hypotheses. Decision theory typically chooses between alternative *actions* on the basis of these probabilities so as to minimize the expectation of a 'loss function'. This chapter concerns inference alone and no loss functions are involved. When we discuss model comparison, this should not be construed as implying model *choice*. Ideal Bayesian predictions do not involve choice between models; rather, predictions are made by summing over all the alternative models, weighted by their probabilities.

Bayesian methods are able consistently and quantitatively to solve both the inference tasks. There is a popular myth that states that Bayesian methods only differ from orthodox statistical methods by the inclusion of subjective priors, which are difficult to assign, and which usually don't make much difference to the conclusions. It is true that, at the first level of inference, a Bayesian's results will often differ little from the outcome of an orthodox attack. What is not widely appreciated is how a Bayesian performs the second level of inference; this section will therefore focus on Bayesian model comparison.

Model comparison is a difficult task because it is not possible simply to choose the model that fits the data best: more complex models can always fit the data better, so the maximum likelihood model choice would lead us inevitably to implausible, over-parameterized models, which generalize poorly. Occam's razor is needed.

Let us write down Bayes' theorem for the two levels of inference described above, so as to see explicitly how Bayesian model comparison works. Each model $\mathcal{H}_i$ is assumed to have a vector of parameters $\mathbf{w}$. A model is defined by a collection of probability distributions: a 'prior' distribution $P(\mathbf{w}|\mathcal{H}_i)$, which states what values the model's parameters might be expected to take; and a set of conditional distributions, one for each value of $\mathbf{w}$, defining the predictions $P(D|\mathbf{w}, \mathcal{H}_i)$ that the model makes about the data D.

1. **Model fitting.** At the first level of inference, we assume that one model, the ith, say, is true, and we infer what the model's parameters $\mathbf{w}$ might be, given the data D. Using Bayes' theorem, the *posterior probability* of the parameters $\mathbf{w}$ is:

$$P(\mathbf{w}|D, \mathcal{H}_i) = \frac{P(D|\mathbf{w}, \mathcal{H}_i)P(\mathbf{w}|\mathcal{H}_i)}{P(D|\mathcal{H}_i)}, \qquad (28.4)$$

that is,

$$\text{Posterior} = \frac{\text{Likelihood} \times \text{Prior}}{\text{Evidence}}.$$

The normalizing constant $P(D|\mathcal{H}_i)$ is commonly ignored since it is irrelevant to the first level of inference, i.e., the inference of $\mathbf{w}$; but it becomes important in the second level of inference, and we name it the *evidence* for $\mathcal{H}_i$. It is common practice to use gradient-based methods to find the maximum of the posterior, which defines the most probable value for the parameters, $\mathbf{w}_{\mathrm{MP}}$; it is then usual to summarize the posterior distribution by the value of $\mathbf{w}_{\mathrm{MP}}$, and error bars or confidence intervals on these best fit parameters. Error bars can be obtained from the curvature of the posterior; evaluating the Hessian at $\mathbf{w}_{\mathrm{MP}}$, $\mathbf{A} = -\nabla\nabla \ln P(\mathbf{w}|D, \mathcal{H}_i)|_{\mathbf{w}_{\mathrm{MP}}}$, and Taylor-expanding the log posterior probability with $\Delta\mathbf{w} = \mathbf{w} - \mathbf{w}_{\mathrm{MP}}$:

$$P(\mathbf{w}|D, \mathcal{H}_i) \simeq P(\mathbf{w}_{\mathrm{MP}}|D, \mathcal{H}_i) \exp\left(-\frac{1}{2}\Delta\mathbf{w}^\mathsf{T}\mathbf{A}\Delta\mathbf{w}\right), \qquad (28.5)$$

we see that the posterior can be locally approximated as a Gaussian with covariance matrix (equivalent to error bars) $\mathbf{A}^{-1}$. [Whether this approximation is good or not will depend on the problem we are solving. Indeed, the maximum and mean of the posterior distribution have

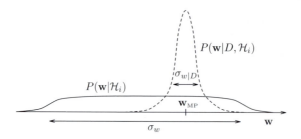

Figure 28.5. The Occam factor.
This figure shows the quantities
that determine the Occam factor
for a hypothesis $\mathcal{H}_i$ having a
single parameter $\mathbf{w}$. The prior
distribution (solid line) for the
parameter has width σ_w. The
posterior distribution (dashed
line) has a single peak at $\mathbf{w}_{\mathrm{MP}}$
with characteristic width $\sigma_{w|D}$.
The Occam factor is

no fundamental status in Bayesian inference – they both change under nonlinear reparameterizations. Maximization of a posterior probability is only useful if an approximation like equation (28.5) gives a good summary of the distribution.]

$$\sigma_{w|D} P(\mathbf{w}_{\mathrm{MP}}|\mathcal{H}_i) = \frac{\sigma_{w|D}}{\sigma_w}.$$

2. **Model comparison.** At the second level of inference, we wish to infer which model is most plausible given the data. The posterior probability of each model is:

$$P(\mathcal{H}_i|D) \propto P(D|\mathcal{H}_i)P(\mathcal{H}_i). \tag{28.6}$$

Notice that the data-dependent term $P(D|\mathcal{H}_i)$ is the evidence for $\mathcal{H}_i$, which appeared as the normalizing constant in (28.4). The second term, $P(\mathcal{H}_i)$, is the subjective prior over our hypothesis space, which expresses how plausible we thought the alternative models were before the data arrived. Assuming that we choose to assign equal priors $P(\mathcal{H}_i)$ to the alternative models, *models $\mathcal{H}_i$ are ranked by evaluating the evidence.* The normalizing constant $P(D) = \sum_i P(D|\mathcal{H}_i)P(\mathcal{H}_i)$ has been omitted from equation (28.6) because in the data modelling process we may develop new models after the data have arrived, when an inadequacy of the first models is detected, for example. Inference is open ended: we continually seek more probable models to account for the data we gather.

To repeat the key idea: to rank alternative models $\mathcal{H}_i$, a Bayesian evaluates the evidence $P(D|\mathcal{H}_i)$. This concept is very general: the evidence can be evaluated for parametric and 'non-parametric' models alike; whatever our data modelling task, a regression problem, a classification problem, or a density estimation problem, the evidence is a transportable quantity for comparing alternative models. In all these cases the evidence naturally embodies Occam's razor.

Evaluating the evidence

Let us now study the evidence more closely to gain insight into how the Bayesian Occam's razor works. The evidence is the normalizing constant for equation (28.4):

$$P(D|\mathcal{H}_i) = \int P(D|\mathbf{w},\mathcal{H}_i)P(\mathbf{w}|\mathcal{H}_i)\,\mathrm{d}\mathbf{w}. \tag{28.7}$$

For many problems the posterior $P(\mathbf{w}|D,\mathcal{H}_i) \propto P(D|\mathbf{w},\mathcal{H}_i)P(\mathbf{w}|\mathcal{H}_i)$ has a strong peak at the most probable parameters $\mathbf{w}_{\mathrm{MP}}$ (figure 28.5). Then, taking for simplicity the one-dimensional case, the evidence can be approximated, using Laplace's method, by the height of the peak of the integrand $P(D|\mathbf{w},\mathcal{H}_i)P(\mathbf{w}|\mathcal{H}_i)$ times its width, $\sigma_{w|D}$:

$$P(D|\mathcal{H}_i) \simeq \underbrace{P(D|\mathbf{w}_{\mathrm{MP}},\mathcal{H}_i)}_{} \times \underbrace{P(\mathbf{w}_{\mathrm{MP}}|\mathcal{H}_i)\,\sigma_{w|D}}_{}. \tag{28.8}$$

Evidence $\simeq$ Best fit likelihood $\times$ Occam factor

Thus the evidence is found by taking the best fit likelihood that the model can achieve and multiplying it by an 'Occam factor', which is a term with magnitude less than one that penalizes $\mathcal{H}_i$ for having the parameter $\mathbf{w}$.

Interpretation of the Occam factor

The quantity $\sigma_{w|D}$ is the posterior uncertainty in $\mathbf{w}$. Suppose for simplicity that the prior $P(\mathbf{w}|\mathcal{H}_i)$ is uniform on some large interval σ_w, representing the range of values of $\mathbf{w}$ that were possible *a priori*, according to $\mathcal{H}_i$ (figure 28.5). Then $P(\mathbf{w}_{\mathrm{MP}}|\mathcal{H}_i) = 1/\sigma_w$, and

$$\text{Occam factor} = \frac{\sigma_{w|D}}{\sigma_w}, \qquad (28.9)$$

i.e., *the Occam factor is equal to the ratio of the posterior accessible volume of $\mathcal{H}_i$'s parameter space to the prior accessible volume*, or the factor by which $\mathcal{H}_i$'s hypothesis space collapses when the data arrive. The model $\mathcal{H}_i$ can be viewed as consisting of a certain number of exclusive submodels, of which only one survives when the data arrive. The Occam factor is the inverse of that number. The logarithm of the Occam factor is a measure of the amount of information we gain about the model's parameters when the data arrive.

A complex model having many parameters, each of which is free to vary over a large range σ_w, will typically be penalized by a stronger Occam factor than a simpler model. The Occam factor also penalizes models that have to be finely tuned to fit the data, favouring models for which the required precision of the parameters $\sigma_{w|D}$ is coarse. The magnitude of the Occam factor is thus a measure of complexity of the model; it relates to the complexity of the predictions that the model makes in data space. This depends not only on the number of parameters in the model, but also on the prior probability that the model assigns to them. Which model achieves the greatest evidence is determined by a trade-off between minimizing this natural complexity measure and minimizing the data misfit. In contrast to alternative measures of model complexity, the Occam factor for a model is straightforward to evaluate: it simply depends on the error bars on the parameters, which we already evaluated when fitting the model to the data.

Figure 28.6 displays an entire hypothesis space so as to illustrate the various probabilities in the analysis. There are three models, $\mathcal{H}_1, \mathcal{H}_2, \mathcal{H}_3$, which have equal prior probabilities. Each model has one parameter $\mathbf{w}$ (each shown on a horizontal axis), but assigns a different prior range σ_W to that parameter. $\mathcal{H}_3$ is the most 'flexible' or 'complex' model, assigning the broadest prior range. A one-dimensional data space is shown by the vertical axis. Each model assigns a joint probability distribution $P(D, \mathbf{w}|\mathcal{H}_i)$ to the data and the parameters, illustrated by a cloud of dots. These dots represent random samples from the full probability distribution. The total number of dots in each of the three model subspaces is the same, because we assigned equal prior probabilities to the models.

When a particular data set D is received (horizontal line), we infer the posterior distribution of $\mathbf{w}$ for a model ($\mathcal{H}_3$, say) by reading out the density along that horizontal line, and normalizing. The posterior probability $P(\mathbf{w}|D, \mathcal{H}_3)$ is shown by the dotted curve at the bottom. Also shown is the prior distribution $P(\mathbf{w}|\mathcal{H}_3)$ (c.f. figure 28.5). [In the case of model $\mathcal{H}_1$ which is very poorly matched to the data, the shape of the posterior distribution will depend on the details of the tails of the prior $P(\mathbf{w}|\mathcal{H}_1)$ and the likelihood $P(D|\mathbf{w}, \mathcal{H}_1)$; the curve shown is for the case where the prior falls off more strongly.]

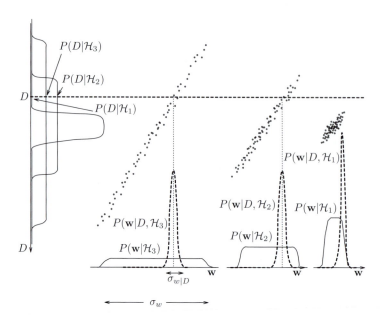

Figure 28.6. A hypothesis space consisting of three exclusive models, each having one parameter $\mathbf{w}$, and a one-dimensional data set D. The 'data set' is a single measured value which differs from the parameter $\mathbf{w}$ by a small amount of additive noise. Typical samples from the joint distribution $P(D, w, \mathcal{H})$ are shown by dots. (NB, these are not data points.) The observed 'data set' is a single particular value for D shown by the dashed horizontal line. The dashed curves below show the posterior probability of $\mathbf{w}$ for each model given this data set (c.f. figure 28.3). The evidence for the different models is obtained by marginalizing onto the D axis at the left-hand side (c.f. figure 28.5).

We obtain figure 28.3 by marginalizing the joint distributions $P(D, \mathbf{w}|\mathcal{H}_i)$ onto the D axis at the left-hand side. For the data set D shown by the dotted horizontal line, the evidence $P(D|\mathcal{H}_3)$ for the more flexible model $\mathcal{H}_3$ has a smaller value than the evidence for H_2. This is because $\mathcal{H}_3$ placed less predictive probability (fewer dots) on that line. In terms of the distributions over $\mathbf{w}$, model $\mathcal{H}_3$ has smaller evidence because the Occam factor $\sigma_{w|D}/\sigma_w$ is smaller for $\mathcal{H}_3$ than for $\mathcal{H}_2$. The simplest model $\mathcal{H}_1$ has the smallest evidence of all, because the best fit that it can achieve to the data D is very poor. Given this data set, the most probable model is $\mathcal{H}_2$.

Occam factor for several parameters

If the posterior is well approximated by a Gaussian, then the Occam factor is obtained from the determinant of the corresponding covariance matrix (c.f. equation (28.8) and Chapter 27):

$$P(D\,|\mathcal{H}_i) \simeq \underbrace{P(D\,|\mathbf{w}_{\mathrm{MP}}, H_i)}_{} \times \underbrace{P(\mathbf{w}_{\mathrm{MP}}|\mathcal{H}_i)\det^{-\frac{1}{2}}(\mathbf{A}/2\pi)}_{}, \qquad (28.10)$$

$$\text{Evidence} \simeq \text{Best fit likelihood} \times \qquad \text{Occam factor}$$

where $\mathbf{A} = -\nabla\nabla \ln P(\mathbf{w}|D, \mathcal{H}_i)$, the Hessian which we evaluated when we calculated the error bars on $\mathbf{w}_{\mathrm{MP}}$ (equation 28.5 and Chapter 27). As the amount of data collected increases, this Gaussian approximation is expected to become increasingly accurate.

In summary, Bayesian model comparison is a simple extension of maximum likelihood model selection: *the evidence is obtained by multiplying the best fit likelihood by the Occam factor.*

To evaluate the Occam factor we need only the Hessian $\mathbf{A}$, if the Gaussian approximation is good. Thus the Bayesian method of model comparison by evaluating the evidence is no more demanding computationally than the task of finding for each model the best fit parameters and their error bars.

► **28.2 Example**

Let's return to the example that opened this chapter. Are there one or two boxes behind the tree in figure 28.1? Why do coincidences make us suspicious?

Let's assume the image of the area round the trunk and box has a size of 50 pixels, that the trunk is 10 pixels wide, and that 16 different colours of boxes can be distinguished. The theory $\mathcal{H}_1$ that says there is one box near the trunk has four free parameters: three coordinates defining the top three edges of the box, and one parameter giving the box's colour. (If boxes could levitate, there would be five free parameters.)

The theory $\mathcal{H}_2$ that says there are two boxes near the trunk has eight free parameters (twice four), plus a ninth, a binary variable that indicates which of the two boxes is the closest to the viewer.

What is the evidence for each model? We'll do $\mathcal{H}_1$ first. We need a prior on the parameters to evaluate the evidence. For convenience, let's work in pixels. Let's assign a separable prior to the horizontal location of the box, its width, its height, and its colour. The height could have any of, say, 20 distinguishable values, so could the width, and so could the location. The colour could have any of 16 values. We'll put uniform priors over these variables. We'll ignore all the parameters associated with other objects in the image, since they don't come into the model comparison between $\mathcal{H}_1$ and $\mathcal{H}_2$. The evidence is

$$P(D|\mathcal{H}_1) = \frac{1}{20}\frac{1}{20}\frac{1}{20}\frac{1}{16} \tag{28.11}$$

since only one setting of the parameters fits the data, and it predicts the data perfectly.

As for model $\mathcal{H}_2$, six of its nine parameters are well-determined, and three of them are partly-constrained by the data. If the left-hand box is furthest away, for example, then its width is at least 8 pixels and at most 30; if it's the closer of the two boxes, then its width is between 8 and 18 pixels. (I'm assuming here that the visible portion of the left-hand box is about 8 pixels wide.) To get the evidence we need to sum up the prior probabilities of all viable hypotheses. To do an exact calculation, we need to be more specific about the data and the priors, but let's just get the ballpark answer, assuming that the two unconstrained real variables have half their values available, and that the binary variable is completely undetermined. (As an exercise, you can make an explicit model and work out the exact answer.)

$$P(D|\mathcal{H}_2) \simeq \frac{1}{20}\frac{1}{20}\frac{10}{20}\frac{1}{16}\frac{1}{20}\frac{1}{20}\frac{10}{20}\frac{1}{16}\frac{2}{2}. \tag{28.12}$$

Thus the posterior probability ratio is (assuming equal prior probability):

$$\frac{P(D|\mathcal{H}_1)P(\mathcal{H}_1)}{P(D|\mathcal{H}_2)P(\mathcal{H}_2)} = \frac{1}{\frac{1}{20}\frac{10}{20}\frac{10}{20}\frac{1}{16}} \tag{28.13}$$

$$= 20 \times 2 \times 2 \times 16 \simeq 1000/1. \tag{28.14}$$

So the data are roughly 1000 to 1 in favour of the simpler hypothesis. The four factors can be interpreted in terms of Occam factors. The more complex model has four extra parameters for sizes and colours – three for sizes, and one for colour. It has to pay two big Occam factors ($1/20$ and $1/16$) for the highly suspicious coincidences that the two box heights match exactly and the two colours match exactly; and it also pays two lesser Occam factors for the two lesser coincidences that both boxes happened to have one of their edges conveniently hidden behind a tree or behind each other.

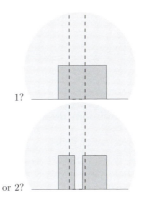

Figure 28.7. How many boxes are behind the tree?

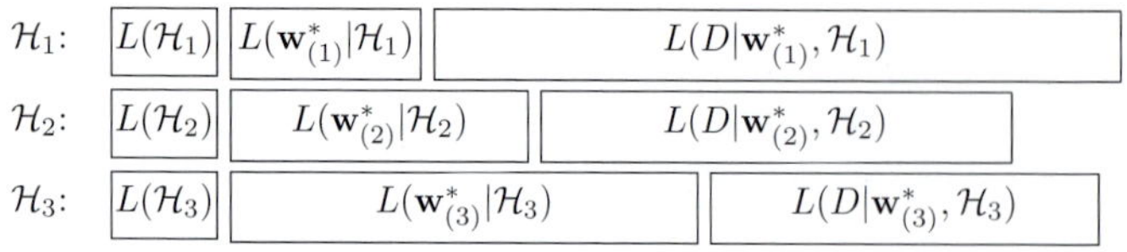

$\mathcal{H}_1$: | $L(\mathcal{H}_1)$ | $L(\mathbf{w}^*_{(1)}|\mathcal{H}_1)$ | $L(D|\mathbf{w}^*_{(1)}, \mathcal{H}_1)$

$\mathcal{H}_2$: | $L(\mathcal{H}_2)$ | $L(\mathbf{w}^*_{(2)}|\mathcal{H}_2)$ | $L(D|\mathbf{w}^*_{(2)}, \mathcal{H}_2)$

$\mathcal{H}_3$: | $L(\mathcal{H}_3)$ | $L(\mathbf{w}^*_{(3)}|\mathcal{H}_3)$ | $L(D|\mathbf{w}^*_{(3)}, \mathcal{H}_3)$

Figure 28.8. A popular view of model comparison by minimum description length. Each model $\mathcal{H}_i$ communicates the data D by sending the identity of the model, sending the best fit parameters of the model $\mathbf{w}^*$, then sending the data relative to those parameters. As we proceed to more complex models the length of the parameter message increases. On the other hand, the length of the data message decreases, because a complex model is able to fit the data better, making the residuals smaller. In this example the intermediate model $\mathcal{H}_2$ achieves the optimum trade-off between these two trends.

▶ ## 28.3 Minimum description length (MDL)

A complementary view of Bayesian model comparison is obtained by replacing probabilities of events by the lengths in bits of messages that communicate the events without loss to a receiver. Message lengths $L(\mathbf{x})$ correspond to a probabilistic model over events $\mathbf{x}$ via the relations:

$$P(\mathbf{x}) = 2^{-L(\mathbf{x})}, \quad L(\mathbf{x}) = -\log_2 P(\mathbf{x}). \tag{28.15}$$

The MDL principle (Wallace and Boulton, 1968) states that one should prefer models that can communicate the data in the smallest number of bits. Consider a two-part message that states which model, $\mathcal{H}$, is to be used, and then communicates the data D within that model, to some pre-arranged precision δD. This produces a message of length $L(D, \mathcal{H}) = L(\mathcal{H}) + L(D|\mathcal{H})$. The lengths $L(\mathcal{H})$ for different $\mathcal{H}$ define an implicit prior $P(\mathcal{H})$ over the alternative models. Similarly $L(D|\mathcal{H})$ corresponds to a density $P(D|\mathcal{H})$. Thus, a procedure for assigning message lengths can be mapped onto posterior probabilities:

$$L(D, \mathcal{H}) = -\log P(\mathcal{H}) - \log(P(D|\mathcal{H})\delta D) \tag{28.16}$$
$$= -\log P(\mathcal{H}|D) + \text{const.} \tag{28.17}$$

In principle, then, MDL can always be interpreted as Bayesian model comparison and *vice versa*. However, this simple discussion has not addressed how one would actually evaluate the key data-dependent term $L(D|\mathcal{H})$, which corresponds to the evidence for $\mathcal{H}$. Often, this message is imagined as being subdivided into a parameter block and a data block (figure 28.8). Models with a small number of parameters have only a short parameter block but do not fit the data well, and so the data message (a list of large residuals) is long. As the number of parameters increases, the parameter block lengthens, and the data message becomes shorter. There is an optimum model complexity ($\mathcal{H}_2$ in the figure) for which the sum is minimized.

This picture glosses over some subtle issues. We have not specified the precision to which the parameters $\mathbf{w}$ should be sent. This precision has an important effect (unlike the precision δD to which real-valued data D are sent, which, assuming δD is small relative to the noise level, just introduces an additive constant). As we decrease the precision to which $\mathbf{w}$ is sent, the parameter message shortens, but the data message typically lengthens because the truncated parameters do not match the data so well. There is a non-trivial optimal precision. In simple Gaussian cases it is possible to solve for this optimal precision (Wallace and Freeman, 1987), and it is closely related to the posterior error bars on the parameters, $\mathbf{A}^{-1}$, where $\mathbf{A} = -\nabla\nabla \ln P(\mathbf{w}|D, \mathcal{H})$. It turns out that the optimal parameter message length is virtually identical to the log of the Occam factor in equation (28.10). (The random element involved in parameter truncation means that the encoding is slightly sub-optimal.)

With care, therefore, one can replicate Bayesian results in MDL terms. Although some of the earliest work on complex model comparison involved the MDL framework (Patrick and Wallace, 1982), MDL has no apparent advantages over the direct probabilistic approach.

MDL does have its uses as a pedagogical tool. The description length concept is useful for motivating prior probability distributions. Also, different ways of breaking down the task of communicating data using a model can give helpful insights into the modelling process, as will now be illustrated.

On-line learning and cross-validation.

In cases where the data consist of a sequence of points $D = \mathbf{t}^{(1)}, \mathbf{t}^{(2)}, \ldots, \mathbf{t}^{(N)}$, the log evidence can be decomposed as a sum of 'on-line' predictive performances:

$$
\begin{aligned}
\log P(D|\mathcal{H}) \;=\;\; & \log P(\mathbf{t}^{(1)}|\mathcal{H}) + \log P(\mathbf{t}^{(2)}|\mathbf{t}^{(1)}, \mathcal{H}) \\
& + \log P(\mathbf{t}^{(3)}|\mathbf{t}^{(1)}, \mathbf{t}^{(2)}, \mathcal{H}) + \cdots + \log P(\mathbf{t}^{(N)}|\mathbf{t}^{(1)} \ldots \mathbf{t}^{(N-1)}, \mathcal{H}). \quad (28.18)
\end{aligned}
$$

This decomposition can be used to explain the difference between the evidence and 'leave-one-out cross-validation' as measures of predictive ability. Cross-validation examines the average value of just the last term, $\log P(\mathbf{t}^{(N)}|t^{(1)} \ldots \mathbf{t}^{(N-1)}, \mathcal{H})$, under random re-orderings of the data. The evidence, on the other hand, sums up how well the model predicted all the data, starting from scratch.

The 'bits back' encoding method.

Another MDL thought experiment (Hinton and van Camp, 1993) involves incorporating random bits into our message. The data are communicated using a parameter block and a data block. The parameter vector sent is a random sample from the posterior distribution $P(\mathbf{w}|D, \mathcal{H}) = P(D|\mathbf{w}, \mathcal{H})P(\mathbf{w}|\mathcal{H})/P(D|\mathcal{H})$. This sample $\mathbf{w}$ is sent to an arbitrary small granularity $\delta\mathbf{w}$ using a message length $L(\mathbf{w}|\mathcal{H}) = -\log[P(\mathbf{w}|\mathcal{H})\delta\mathbf{w}]$. The data are encoded relative to $\mathbf{w}$ with a message of length $L(D|\mathbf{w}, \mathcal{H}) = -\log[P(D|\mathbf{w}, \mathcal{H})\delta D]$. Once the data message has been received, the random bits used to generate the sample $\mathbf{w}$ from the posterior can be deduced by the receiver. The number of bits so recovered is $-\log[P(\mathbf{w}|D, \mathcal{H})\delta\mathbf{w}]$. These recovered bits need not count towards the message length, since we might use some other optimally encoded message as a random bit string, thereby communicating that message at the same time. The net description cost is therefore:

$$
\begin{aligned}
L(\mathbf{w}|\mathcal{H}) + L(D|\mathbf{w}, \mathcal{H}) - \text{`Bits back'} \;=\;\; & -\log \frac{P(\mathbf{w}|\mathcal{H})P(D|\mathbf{w}, \mathcal{H})\delta D}{P(\mathbf{w}|D, \mathcal{H})} \\
=\;\; & -\log P(D|\mathcal{H}) - \log \delta D. \quad (28.19)
\end{aligned}
$$

Thus this thought experiment has yielded the optimal description length. Bits back encoding has been turned into a practical compression method for data modelled with latent variable models by Frey (1998).

Further reading

Bayesian methods are introduced and contrasted with sampling-theory statistics in (Jaynes, 1983; Gull, 1988; Loredo, 1990). The Bayesian Occam's razor is demonstrated on model problems in (Gull, 1988; MacKay, 1992a). Useful textbooks are (Box and Tiao, 1973; Berger, 1985).

One debate worth understanding is the question of whether it's permissible to use improper priors in Bayesian inference (Dawid *et al.*, 1996). If we want to do model comparison (as discussed in this chapter), it is essential to use proper priors – otherwise the evidences and the Occam factors are meaningless. Only when one has no intention to do model comparison may it be safe to use improper priors, and even in such cases there are pitfalls, as Dawid *et al.* explain. I would agree with their advice to *always use proper priors*, tempered by an encouragement to be smart when making calculations, recognizing opportunities for approximation.

▶ **28.4 Exercises**

Exercise 28.1.[3] Random variables x come independently from a probability distribution $P(x)$. According to model $\mathcal{H}_0$, $P(x)$ is a uniform distribution

$$P(x|\mathcal{H}_0) = \frac{1}{2} \qquad x \in (-1,1). \tag{28.20}$$

According to model $\mathcal{H}_1$, $P(x)$ is a nonuniform distribution with an unknown parameter $m \in (-1,1)$:

$$P(x|m,\mathcal{H}_1) = \frac{1}{2}(1+mx) \qquad x \in (-1,1). \tag{28.21}$$

Given the data $D = \{0.3, 0.5, 0.7, 0.8, 0.9\}$, what is the evidence for $\mathcal{H}_0$ and $\mathcal{H}_1$?

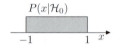

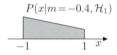

Exercise 28.2.[3] Datapoints (x,t) are believed to come from a straight line. The experimenter chooses x, and t is Gaussian-distributed about

$$y = w_0 + w_1 x \tag{28.22}$$

with variance σ_ν^2. According to model $\mathcal{H}_1$, the straight line is horizontal, so $w_1 = 0$. According to model $\mathcal{H}_2$, w_1 is a parameter with prior distribution Normal$(0,1)$. Both models assign a prior distribution Normal$(0,1)$ to w_0. Given the data set $D = \{(-8,8), (-2,10), (6,11)\}$, and assuming the noise level is $\sigma_\nu = 1$, what is the evidence for each model?

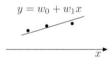

Exercise 28.3.[3] A six-sided die is rolled 30 times and the numbers of times each face came up were $\mathbf{F} = \{3, 3, 2, 2, 9, 11\}$. What is the probability that the die is a perfectly fair die ('$\mathcal{H}_0$'), assuming the alternative hypothesis $\mathcal{H}_1$ says that the die has a biased distribution $\mathbf{p}$, and the prior density for $\mathbf{p}$ is uniform over the simplex $p_i \geq 0$, $\sum_i p_i = 1$?

Solve this problem two ways: exactly, using the helpful Dirichlet formulae (23.30, 23.31), and approximately, using Laplace's method. Notice that your choice of basis for the Laplace approximation is important. See MacKay (1998a) for discussion of this exercise.

Exercise 28.4.[3] The influence of race on the imposition of the death penalty for murder in America has been much studied. The following three-way table classifies 326 cases in which the defendant was convicted of murder. The three variables are the defendant's race, the victim's race, and whether the defendant was sentenced to death. (Data from M. Radelet, 'Racial characteristics and imposition of the death penalty,' *American Sociological Review*, **46** (1981), pp.918-927.)

	White defendant		Black defendant		
	Death penalty			Death penalty	
	Yes	No		Yes	No
White victim	19	132	White victim	11	52
Black victim	0	9	Black victim	6	97

It seems that the death penalty was applied much more often when the victim was white then when the victim was black. When the victim was white 14% of defendants got the death penalty, but when the victim was black 6% of defendants got the death penalty. [Incidentally, these data provide an example of a phenomenon known as *Simpson's paradox*: a higher fraction of white defendants are sentenced to death overall, but in cases involving black victims a higher fraction of black defendants are sentenced to death and in cases involving white victims a higher fraction of black defendants are sentenced to death.]

Quantify the evidence for the four alternative hypotheses shown in figure 28.9. I should mention that I don't believe any of these models is adequate: several additional variables are important in murder cases, such as whether the victim and murderer knew each other, whether the murder was premeditated, and whether the defendant had a prior criminal record; none of these variables is included in the table. So this is an academic exercise in model comparison rather than a serious study of racial bias in the state of Florida.

The hypotheses are shown as graphical models, with arrows showing dependencies between the variables v (victim race), m (murderer race), and d (whether death penalty given). Model $\mathcal{H}_{00}$ has only one free parameter, the probability of receiving the death penalty; model $\mathcal{H}_{11}$ has four such parameters, one for each state of the variables v and m. Assign uniform priors to these variables. How sensitive are the conclusions to the choice of prior?

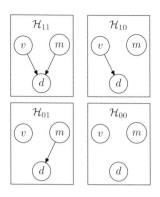

Figure 28.9. Four hypotheses concerning the dependence of the imposition of the death penalty d on the race of the victim v and the race of the convicted murderer m. $\mathcal{H}_{01}$, for example, asserts that the probability of receiving the death penalty does depend on the murderer's race, but not on the victim's.

About Chapter 29

The last couple of chapters have assumed that a Gaussian approximation to the probability distribution we are interested in is adequate. What if it is not? We have already seen an example – clustering – where the likelihood function is multimodal, and has nasty unboundedly high spikes in certain locations in the parameter space; so maximizing the posterior probability and fitting a Gaussian is not always going to work. This difficulty with Laplace's method is one motivation for being interested in Monte Carlo methods. In fact, Monte Carlo methods provide a general-purpose set of tools with applications in Bayesian data modelling and many other fields.

This chapter describes a sequence of methods: *importance sampling, rejection sampling, the Metropolis method, Gibbs sampling* and *slice sampling.* For each method, we discuss whether the method is expected to be useful for high-dimensional problems such as arise in inference with graphical models. [A graphical model is a probabilistic model in which dependencies and independencies of variables are represented by edges in a graph whose nodes are the variables.] Along the way, the terminology of Markov chain Monte Carlo methods is presented. The subsequent chapter gives a discussion of advanced methods for reducing random walk behaviour.

For details of Monte Carlo methods, theorems and proofs and a full list of references, the reader is directed to Neal (1993b), Gilks *et al.* (1996), and Tanner (1996).

In this chapter I will use the word 'sample' in the following sense: a sample from a distribution $P(\mathbf{x})$ is a single realization $\mathbf{x}$ whose probability distribution is $P(\mathbf{x})$. This contrasts with the alternative usage in statistics, where 'sample' refers to a collection of realizations $\{\mathbf{x}\}$.

When we discuss transition probability matrices, I will use a right-multiplication convention: I like my matrices to act to the right, preferring

$$\mathbf{u} = \mathbf{M}\mathbf{v} \tag{29.1}$$

to

$$\mathbf{u}^{\mathsf{T}} = \mathbf{v}^{\mathsf{T}}\mathbf{M}^{\mathsf{T}}. \tag{29.2}$$

A transition probability matrix T_{ij} or $T_{i|j}$ specifies the probability, given the current state is j, of making the transition from j to i. The columns of $\mathbf{T}$ are probability vectors. If we write down a transition probability density, we use the same convention for the order of its arguments: $T(x'; x)$ is a transition probability density from x to x'. This unfortunately means that you have to get used to reading from right to left – the sequence xyz has probability $T(z; y)T(y; x)\pi(x)$.

29

Monte Carlo Methods

▶ **29.1 The problems to be solved**

Monte Carlo methods are computational techniques that make use of random numbers. The aims of Monte Carlo methods are to solve one or both of the following problems.

Problem 1: to generate samples $\{\mathbf{x}^{(r)}\}_{r=1}^{R}$ from a given probability distribution $P(\mathbf{x})$.

Problem 2: to estimate expectations of functions under this distribution, for example

$$\Phi = \langle \phi(\mathbf{x}) \rangle \equiv \int \mathrm{d}^N\mathbf{x} \; P(\mathbf{x})\phi(\mathbf{x}). \tag{29.3}$$

The probability distribution $P(\mathbf{x})$, which we call the *target density*, might be a distribution from statistical physics or a conditional distribution arising in data modelling – for example, the posterior probability of a model's parameters given some observed data. We will generally assume that $\mathbf{x}$ is an N-dimensional vector with real components x_n, but we will sometimes consider discrete spaces also.

Simple examples of functions $\phi(\mathbf{x})$ whose expectations we might be interested in include the first and second moments of quantities that we wish to predict, from which we can compute means and variances; for example if some quantity t depends on $\mathbf{x}$, we can find the mean and variance of t under $P(\mathbf{x})$ by finding the expectations of the functions $\phi_1(\mathbf{x}) = t(\mathbf{x})$ and $\phi_2(\mathbf{x}) = (t(\mathbf{x}))^2$,

$$\Phi_1 \equiv \mathcal{E}[\phi_1(\mathbf{x})] \quad \text{and} \quad \Phi_2 \equiv \mathcal{E}[\phi_2(\mathbf{x})], \tag{29.4}$$

then using

$$\bar{t} = \Phi_1 \quad \text{and} \quad \mathrm{var}(t) = \Phi_2 - \Phi_1^2. \tag{29.5}$$

It is assumed that $P(\mathbf{x})$ is sufficiently complex that we cannot evaluate these expectations by exact methods; so we are interested in Monte Carlo methods.

We will concentrate on the first problem (sampling), because if we have solved it, then we can solve the second problem by using the random samples $\{\mathbf{x}^{(r)}\}_{r=1}^{R}$ to give the estimator

$$\hat{\Phi} \equiv \frac{1}{R}\sum_r \phi(\mathbf{x}^{(r)}). \tag{29.6}$$

If the vectors $\{\mathbf{x}^{(r)}\}_{r=1}^{R}$ are generated from $P(\mathbf{x})$ then the expectation of $\hat{\Phi}$ is Φ. Also, as the number of samples R increases, the variance of $\hat{\Phi}$ will decrease as σ^2/R, where σ^2 is the variance of ϕ,

$$\sigma^2 = \int \mathrm{d}^N\mathbf{x} \; P(\mathbf{x})(\phi(\mathbf{x}) - \Phi)^2. \tag{29.7}$$

357

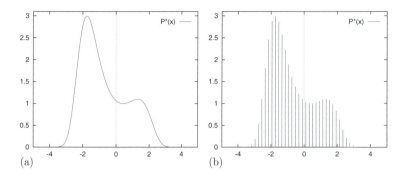

Figure 29.1. (a) The function
$P^*(x) =$
$\exp\left[0.4(x - 0.4)^2 - 0.08x^4\right]$. How
to draw samples from this
density? (b) The function $P^*(x)$
evaluated at a discrete set of
uniformly spaced points $\{x_i\}$.
How to draw samples from this
discrete distribution?

This is one of the important properties of Monte Carlo methods.

> The accuracy of the Monte Carlo estimate (29.6) depends only on
> the variance of ϕ, not on the dimensionality of the space sampled.
> To be precise, the variance of $\hat{\Phi}$ goes as σ^2/R. So regardless of the
> dimensionality of $\mathbf{x}$, it may be that as few as a dozen independent
> samples $\{\mathbf{x}^{(r)}\}$ suffice to estimate Φ satisfactorily.

We will find later, however, that high dimensionality can cause other difficulties for Monte Carlo methods. Obtaining independent samples from a given
distribution $P(\mathbf{x})$ is often not easy.

Why is sampling from $P(\mathbf{x})$ hard?

We will assume that the density from which we wish to draw samples, $P(\mathbf{x})$,
can be evaluated, at least to within a multiplicative constant; that is, we can
evaluate a function $P^*(\mathbf{x})$ such that

$$P(\mathbf{x}) = P^*(\mathbf{x})/Z. \qquad (29.8)$$

If we can evaluate $P^*(\mathbf{x})$, why can we not easily solve problem 1? Why is it in
general difficult to obtain samples from $P(\mathbf{x})$? There are two difficulties. The
first is that we typically do not know the normalizing constant

$$Z = \int d^N \mathbf{x} \ P^*(\mathbf{x}). \qquad (29.9)$$

The second is that, even if we did know Z, the problem of drawing samples
from $P(\mathbf{x})$ is still a challenging one, especially in high-dimensional spaces,
because there is no obvious way to sample from P without enumerating most
or all of the possible states. Correct samples from P will by definition tend
to come from places in $\mathbf{x}$-space where $P(\mathbf{x})$ is big; how can we identify those
places where $P(\mathbf{x})$ is big, without evaluating $P(\mathbf{x})$ *everywhere*? There are only
a few high-dimensional densities from which it is easy to draw samples, for
example the Gaussian distribution.

Let us start with a simple one-dimensional example. Imagine that we wish
to draw samples from the density $P(x) = P^*(x)/Z$ where

$$P^*(x) = \exp\left[0.4(x - 0.4)^2 - 0.08x^4\right], \quad x \in (-\infty, \infty). \qquad (29.10)$$

We can plot this function (figure 29.1a). But that does not mean we can draw
samples from it. To start with, we don't know the normalizing constant Z.

To give ourselves a simpler problem, we could discretize the variable x and ask for samples from the discrete probability distribution over a finite set of uniformly spaced points $\{x_i\}$ (figure 29.1b). How could we solve this problem? If we evaluate $p_i^* = P^*(x_i)$ at each point x_i, we can compute

$$Z = \sum_i p_i^* \qquad (29.11)$$

and

$$p_i = p_i^*/Z \qquad (29.12)$$

and we can then sample from the probability distribution $\{p_i\}$ using various methods based on a source of random bits (see section 6.3). But what is the cost of this procedure, and how does it scale with the dimensionality of the space, N? Let us concentrate on the initial cost of evaluating Z (29.11). To compute Z we have to visit every point in the space. In figure 29.1b there are 50 uniformly spaced points in one dimension. If our system had N dimensions, $N = 1000$ say, then the corresponding number of points would be 50^{1000}, an unimaginable number of evaluations of P^*. Even if each component x_n took only two discrete values, the number of evaluations of P^* would be 2^{1000}, a number that is still horribly huge. If every electron in the universe (there are about 2^{266} of them) were a 1000 gigahertz computer that could evaluate P^* for a trillion (2^{40}) states every second, and if we ran those 2^{266} computers for a time equal to the age of the universe (2^{58} seconds), they would still only visit 2^{364} states. We'd have to wait for more than $2^{636} \simeq 10^{190}$ universe ages to elapse before all 2^{1000} states had been visited.

Systems with 2^{1000} states are two a penny.* One example is a collection of 1000 spins such as a 30×30 fragment of an Ising model whose probability distribution is proportional to

$$P^*(\mathbf{x}) = \exp[-\beta E(\mathbf{x})] \qquad (29.13)$$

where $x_n \in \{\pm 1\}$ and

$$E(\mathbf{x}) = -\left[\frac{1}{2} \sum_{m,n} J_{mn} x_m x_n + \sum_n H_n x_n \right]. \qquad (29.14)$$

The energy function $E(\mathbf{x})$ is readily evaluated for any $\mathbf{x}$. But if we wish to evaluate this function at *all* states $\mathbf{x}$, the computer time required would be 2^{1000} function evaluations.

The Ising model is a simple model which has been around for a long time, but the task of generating samples from the distribution $P(\mathbf{x}) = P^*(\mathbf{x})/Z$ is still an active research area; the first 'exact' samples from this distribution were created in the pioneering work of Propp and Wilson (1996), as we'll describe in Chapter 32.

A useful analogy

Imagine the tasks of drawing random water samples from a lake and finding the average plankton concentration (figure 29.2). The depth of the lake at $\mathbf{x} = (x, y)$ is $P^*(\mathbf{x})$, and we assert (in order to make the analogy work) that the plankton concentration is a function of $\mathbf{x}$, $\phi(\mathbf{x})$. The required average concentration is an integral like (29.3), namely

$$\Phi = \langle \phi(\mathbf{x}) \rangle \equiv \frac{1}{Z} \int d^N \mathbf{x} \; P^*(\mathbf{x}) \phi(\mathbf{x}), \qquad (29.15)$$

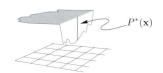

Figure 29.2. A lake whose depth at $\mathbf{x} = (x, y)$ is $P^*(\mathbf{x})$.

where $Z = \int dx\, dy\, P^*(\mathbf{x})$ is the volume of the lake. You are provided with a boat, a satellite navigation system, and a plumbline. Using the navigator, you can can take your boat to any desired location $\mathbf{x}$ on the map; using the plumbline you can measure $P^*(\mathbf{x})$ at that point. You can also measure the plankton concentration there.

Problem 1 is to draw $1\,\mathrm{cm}^3$ water samples at random from the lake, in such a way that each sample is equally likely to come from any point within the lake. Problem 2 is to find the average plankton concentration.

These are difficult problems to solve because at the outset we know nothing about the depth $P^*(\mathbf{x})$. Perhaps much of the volume of the lake is contained in narrow, deep underwater canyons (figure 29.3), in which case, to correctly sample from the lake and correctly estimate Φ our method must implicitly discover the canyons and find their volume relative to the rest of the lake. Difficult problems, yes; nevertheless, we'll see that clever Monte Carlo methods can solve them.

Figure 29.3. A slice through a lake that includes some canyons.

Uniform sampling

Having accepted that we cannot exhaustively visit every location $\mathbf{x}$ in the state space, we might consider trying to solve the second problem (estimating the expectation of a function $\phi(\mathbf{x})$) by drawing random samples $\{\mathbf{x}^{(r)}\}_{r=1}^{R}$ *uniformly* from the state space and evaluating $P^*(\mathbf{x})$ at those points. Then we could introduce a normalizing constant Z_R, defined by

$$Z_R = \sum_{r=1}^{R} P^*(\mathbf{x}^{(r)}), \qquad (29.16)$$

and estimate $\Phi = \int d^N\mathbf{x}\; \phi(\mathbf{x})P(\mathbf{x})$ by

$$\hat{\Phi} = \sum_{r=1}^{R} \phi(\mathbf{x}^{(r)})\frac{P^*(\mathbf{x}^{(r)})}{Z_R}. \qquad (29.17)$$

Is anything wrong with this strategy? Well, it depends on the functions $\phi(\mathbf{x})$ and $P^*(\mathbf{x})$. Let us assume that $\phi(\mathbf{x})$ is a benign, smoothly varying function and concentrate on the nature of $P^*(\mathbf{x})$. As we learnt in Chapter 4, a high-dimensional distribution is often concentrated in a small region of the state space known as its typical set T, whose volume is given by $|T| \simeq 2^{H(\mathbf{X})}$, where $H(\mathbf{X})$ is the entropy of the probability distribution $P(\mathbf{x})$. If almost all the probability mass is located in the typical set and $\phi(\mathbf{x})$ is a benign function, the value of $\Phi = \int d^N\mathbf{x}\; \phi(\mathbf{x})P(\mathbf{x})$ will be principally determined by the values that $\phi(\mathbf{x})$ takes on in the typical set. So uniform sampling will only stand a chance of giving a good estimate of Φ if we make the number of samples R sufficiently large that we are likely to hit the typical set at least once or twice. So, how many samples are required? Let us take the case of the Ising model again. (Strictly, the Ising model may not be a good example, since it doesn't necessarily have a typical set, as defined in Chapter 4; the definition of a typical set was that all states had log probability close to the entropy, which for an Ising model would mean that the *energy* is very close to the *mean energy*; but in the vicinity of phase transitions, the variance of energy, also known as the heat capacity, may diverge, which means that the energy of a random state is not necessarily expected to be very close to the mean energy.) The total size of the state space is 2^N states, and the typical set has size 2^H. So each sample has a chance of $2^H/2^N$ of falling in the typical set.

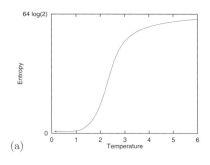
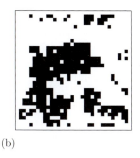

Figure 29.4. (a) Entropy of a 64-spin Ising model as a function of temperature. (b) One state of a 1024-spin Ising model.

The number of samples required to hit the typical set once is thus of order

$$R_{\min} \simeq 2^{N-H}. \tag{29.18}$$

So, what is H? At high temperatures, the probability distribution of an Ising model tends to a uniform distribution and the entropy tends to $H_{\max} = N$ bits, which means $R_{\min}$ is of order 1. Under these conditions, uniform sampling may well be a satisfactory technique for estimating Φ. But high temperatures are not of great interest. Considerably more interesting are intermediate temperatures such as the critical temperature at which the Ising model melts from an ordered phase to a disordered phase. The critical temperature of an infinite Ising model, at which it melts, is $\theta_c = 2.27$. At this temperature the entropy of an Ising model is roughly $N/2$ bits (figure 29.4). For this probability distribution the number of samples required simply to hit the typical set once is of order

$$R_{\min} \simeq 2^{N-N/2} = 2^{N/2}, \tag{29.19}$$

which for $N = 1000$ is about 10^{150}. This is roughly the square of the number of particles in the universe. Thus uniform sampling is utterly useless for the study of Ising models of modest size. And in most high-dimensional problems, if the distribution $P(\mathbf{x})$ is not actually uniform, uniform sampling is unlikely to be useful.

Overview

Having established that drawing samples from a high-dimensional distribution $P(\mathbf{x}) = P^*(\mathbf{x})/Z$ is difficult even if $P^*(\mathbf{x})$ is easy to evaluate, we will now study a sequence of more sophisticated Monte Carlo methods: *importance sampling*, *rejection sampling*, the *Metropolis method*, *Gibbs sampling*, and *slice sampling*.

▶ 29.2 Importance sampling

Importance sampling is not a method for generating samples from $P(\mathbf{x})$ (problem 1); it is just a method for estimating the expectation of a function $\phi(\mathbf{x})$ (problem 2). It can be viewed as a generalization of the uniform sampling method.

For illustrative purposes, let us imagine that the target distribution is a one-dimensional density $P(x)$. Let us assume that we are able to evaluate this density at any chosen point $\mathbf{x}$, at least to within a multiplicative constant; thus we can evaluate a function $P^*(x)$ such that

$$P(x) = P^*(x)/Z. \tag{29.20}$$

But $P(x)$ is too complicated a function for us to be able to sample from it directly. We now assume that we have a simpler density $Q(x)$ from which we *can* generate samples and which we can evaluate to within a multiplicative constant (that is, we can evaluate $Q^*(x)$, where $Q(x) = Q^*(x)/Z_Q$). An example of the functions P^*, Q^* and ϕ is shown in figure 29.5. We call Q the *sampler density*.

In importance sampling, we generate R samples $\{x^{(r)}\}_{r=1}^{R}$ from $Q(x)$. If these points were samples from $P(x)$ then we could estimate Φ by equation (29.6). But when we generate samples from Q, values of x where $Q(x)$ is greater than $P(x)$ will be *over-represented* in this estimator, and points where $Q(x)$ is less than $P(x)$ will be *under-represented*. To take into account the fact that we have sampled from the wrong distribution, we introduce *weights*

$$w_r \equiv \frac{P^*(x^{(r)})}{Q^*(x^{(r)})} \qquad (29.21)$$

which we use to adjust the 'importance' of each point in our estimator thus:

$$\hat{\Phi} \equiv \frac{\sum_r w_r \phi(x^{(r)})}{\sum_r w_r}. \qquad (29.22)$$

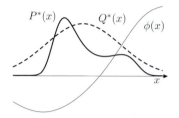

Figure 29.5. Functions involved in importance sampling. We wish to estimate the expectation of $\phi(x)$ under $P(x) \propto P^*(x)$. We can generate samples from the simpler distribution $Q(x) \propto Q^*(x)$. We can evaluate Q^* and P^* at any point.

▷ **Exercise 29.1.**[2, p.384] Prove that, if $Q(x)$ is non-zero for all x where $P(x)$ is non-zero, the estimator $\hat{\Phi}$ converges to Φ, the mean value of $\phi(x)$, as R increases. What is the variance of this estimator, asymptotically? Hint: consider the statistics of the numerator and the denominator separately. Is the estimator $\hat{\Phi}$ an unbiased estimator for small R?

A practical difficulty with importance sampling is that it is hard to estimate how reliable the estimator $\hat{\Phi}$ is. The variance of the estimator is unknown beforehand, because it depends on an integral over x of a function involving $P^*(x)$. And the variance of $\hat{\Phi}$ is hard to estimate, because the empirical variances of the quantities w_r and $w_r\phi(x^{(r)})$ are not necessarily a good guide to the true variances of the numerator and denominator in equation (29.22). If the proposal density $Q(x)$ is small in a region where $|\phi(x)P^*(x)|$ is large then it is quite possible, even after many points $x^{(r)}$ have been generated, that none of them will have fallen in that region. In this case the estimate of Φ would be drastically wrong, and there would be no indication in the *empirical* variance that the true variance of the estimator $\hat{\Phi}$ is large.

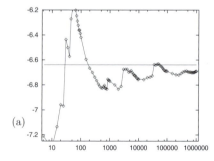

(a)

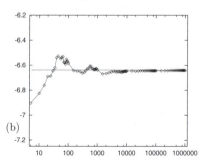

(b)

Figure 29.6. Importance sampling in action: (a) using a Gaussian sampler density; (b) using a Cauchy sampler density. Vertical axis shows the estimate $\hat{\Phi}$. The horizontal line indicates the true value of Φ. Horizontal axis shows number of samples on a log scale.

Cautionary illustration of importance sampling

In a toy problem related to the modelling of amino acid probability distributions with a one-dimensional variable x, I evaluated a quantity of interest using importance sampling. The results using a Gaussian sampler and a Cauchy sampler are shown in figure 29.6. The horizontal axis shows the number of samples on a log scale. In the case of the Gaussian sampler, after about 500 samples had been evaluated one might be tempted to call a halt; but evidently there are infrequent samples that make a huge contribution to $\hat{\Phi}$, and the value of the estimate at 500 samples is wrong. Even after a million samples have been taken, the estimate has still not settled down close to the true value. In contrast, the Cauchy sampler does not suffer from glitches; it converges (on the scale shown here) after about 5000 samples.

This example illustrates the fact that an importance sampler should have **heavy tails**.

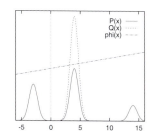

Figure 29.7. A multimodal distribution $P^*(x)$ and a unimodal sampler $Q(x)$.

> Exercise 29.2.[2, p.385] Consider the situation where $P^*(x)$ is multimodal, consisting of several widely separated peaks. (Probability distributions like this arise frequently in statistical data modelling.) Discuss whether it is a wise strategy to do importance sampling using a sampler $Q(x)$ that is a unimodal distribution fitted to one of these peaks. Assume that the function $\phi(x)$ whose mean Φ is to be estimated is a smoothly varying function of x such as $mx + c$. Describe the typical evolution of the estimator $\hat{\Phi}$ as a function of the number of samples R.

Importance sampling in many dimensions

We have already observed that care is needed in one-dimensional importance sampling problems. Is importance sampling a useful technique in spaces of higher dimensionality, say $N = 1000$?

Consider a simple case-study where the target density $P(\mathbf{x})$ is a uniform distribution inside a sphere,

$$P^*(\mathbf{x}) = \begin{cases} 1 & 0 \le \rho(\mathbf{x}) \le R_P \\ 0 & \rho(\mathbf{x}) > R_P, \end{cases} \qquad (29.23)$$

where $\rho(\mathbf{x}) \equiv (\sum_i x_i^2)^{1/2}$, and the proposal density is a Gaussian centred on the origin,

$$Q(\mathbf{x}) = \prod_i \text{Normal}(x_i; 0, \sigma^2). \qquad (29.24)$$

An importance sampling method will be in trouble if the estimator $\hat{\Phi}$ is dominated by a few large weights w_r. What will be the typical range of values of the weights w_r? We know from our discussions of typical sequences in Part I – see exercise 6.14 (p.124), for example – that if ρ is the distance from the origin of a sample from Q, the quantity ρ^2 has a roughly Gaussian distribution with mean and standard deviation:

$$\rho^2 \sim N\sigma^2 \pm \sqrt{2N}\sigma^2. \qquad (29.25)$$

Thus almost all samples from Q lie in a typical set with distance from the origin very close to $\sqrt{N}\sigma$. Let us assume that σ is chosen such that the typical set of Q lies inside the sphere of radius R_P. [If it does not, then the law of large numbers implies that almost all the samples generated from Q will fall outside R_P and will have weight zero.] Then we know that most samples from Q will have a value of Q that lies in the range

$$\frac{1}{(2\pi\sigma^2)^{N/2}} \exp\left(-\frac{N}{2} \pm \frac{\sqrt{2N}}{2}\right). \qquad (29.26)$$

Thus the weights $w_r = P^*/Q$ will typically have values in the range

$$(2\pi\sigma^2)^{N/2} \exp\left(\frac{N}{2} \pm \frac{\sqrt{2N}}{2}\right). \qquad (29.27)$$

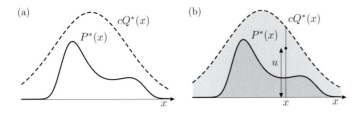

(a) $P^*(x)$ $cQ^*(x)$

(b) $P^*(x)$ $cQ^*(x)$ u

Figure 29.8. Rejection sampling.
(a) The functions involved in
rejection sampling. We desire
samples from $P(x) \propto P^*(x)$. We
are able to draw samples from
$Q(x) \propto Q^*(x)$, and we know a
value c such that $cQ^*(x) > P^*(x)$
for all x. (b) A point (x, u) is
generated at random in the lightly
shaded area under the curve
$cQ^*(x)$. If this point also lies
below $P^*(x)$ then it is accepted.

So if we draw a hundred samples, what will the typical range of weights be?
We can roughly estimate the ratio of the largest weight to the median weight
by doubling the standard deviation in equation (29.27). The largest weight
and the median weight will typically be in the ratio:

$$\frac{w_r^{\text{max}}}{w_r^{\text{med}}} = \exp\left(\sqrt{2N}\right). \qquad (29.28)$$

In $N = 1000$ dimensions therefore, the largest weight after one hundred samples is likely to be roughly 10^{19} times greater than the median weight. Thus an
importance sampling estimate for a high-dimensional problem will very likely
be utterly dominated by a few samples with huge weights.

In conclusion, importance sampling in high dimensions often suffers from
two difficulties. First, we need to obtain samples that lie in the typical set of P,
and this may take a long time unless Q is a good approximation to P. Second,
even if we obtain samples in the typical set, the weights associated with those
samples are likely to vary by large factors, because the probabilities of points
in a typical set, although similar to each other, still differ by factors of order
$\exp(\sqrt{N})$, so the weights will too, unless Q is a near-perfect approximation to
P.

▶ 29.3 Rejection sampling

We assume again a one-dimensional density $P(x) = P^*(x)/Z$ that is too complicated a function for us to be able to sample from it directly. We assume
that we have a simpler *proposal density* $Q(x)$ which we can evaluate (within a
multiplicative factor Z_Q, as before), and from which we can generate samples.
We further assume that we know the value of a constant c such that

$$c\,Q^*(x) > P^*(x), \quad \text{for all } x. \qquad (29.29)$$

A schematic picture of the two functions is shown in figure 29.8a.

We generate two random numbers. The first, x, is generated from the
proposal density $Q(x)$. We then evaluate $cQ^*(x)$ and generate a uniformly
distributed random variable u from the interval $[0, c\,Q^*(x)]$. These two random
numbers can be viewed as selecting a point in the two-dimensional plane as
shown in figure 29.8b.

We now evaluate $P^*(x)$ and accept or reject the sample x by comparing the
value of u with the value of $P^*(x)$. If $u > P^*(x)$ then x is rejected; otherwise
it is accepted, which means that we add x to our set of samples $\{x^{(r)}\}$. The
value of u is discarded.

Why does this procedure generate samples from $P(x)$? The proposed point
(x, u) comes with uniform probability from the lightly shaded area underneath
the curve $c\,Q^*(x)$ as shown in figure 29.8b. The rejection rule rejects all the
points that lie above the curve $P^*(x)$. So the points (x, u) that are accepted
are uniformly distributed in the heavily shaded area under $P^*(x)$. This implies

that the probability density of the x-coordinates of the accepted points must be proportional to $P^*(x)$, so the samples must be independent samples from $P(x)$.

Rejection sampling will work best if Q is a good approximation to P. If Q is very different from P then, for cQ to exceed P everywhere, c will necessarily have to be large and the frequency of rejection will be large.

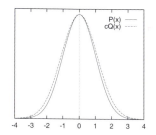

Rejection sampling in many dimensions

In a high-dimensional problem it is very likely that the requirement that cQ^* be an upper bound for P^* will force c to be so huge that acceptances will be very rare indeed. Finding such a value of c may be difficult too, since in many problems we know neither where the modes of P^* are located nor how high they are.

Figure 29.9. A Gaussian $P(x)$ and a slightly broader Gaussian $Q(x)$ scaled up by a factor c such that $cQ(x) \geq P(x)$.

As a case study, consider a pair of N-dimensional Gaussian distributions with mean zero (figure 29.9). Imagine generating samples from one with standard deviation σ_Q and using rejection sampling to obtain samples from the other whose standard deviation is σ_P. Let us assume that these two standard deviations are close in value – say, σ_Q is 1% larger than σ_P. [σ_Q must be larger than σ_P because if this is not the case, there is no c such that cQ exceeds P for all $\mathbf{x}$.] So, what value of c is required if the dimensionality is $N = 1000$? The density of $Q(\mathbf{x})$ at the origin is $1/(2\pi\sigma_Q^2)^{N/2}$, so for cQ to exceed P we need to set

$$c = \frac{(2\pi\sigma_Q^2)^{N/2}}{(2\pi\sigma_P^2)^{N/2}} = \exp\left(N \ln \frac{\sigma_Q}{\sigma_P}\right). \tag{29.30}$$

With $N = 1000$ and $\frac{\sigma_Q}{\sigma_P} = 1.01$, we find $c = \exp(10) \simeq 20{,}000$. What will the acceptance rate be for this value of c? The answer is immediate: since the acceptance rate is the ratio of the volume under the curve $P(\mathbf{x})$ to the volume under $cQ(\mathbf{x})$, the fact that P and Q are both normalized here implies that the acceptance rate will be $1/c$, for example, $1/20{,}000$. In general, c grows exponentially with the dimensionality N, so the acceptance rate is expected to be exponentially small in N.

Rejection sampling, therefore, whilst a useful method for one-dimensional problems, is not expected to be a practical technique for generating samples from high-dimensional distributions $P(\mathbf{x})$.

▶ **29.4 The Metropolis–Hastings method**

Importance sampling and rejection sampling work well only if the proposal density $Q(x)$ is similar to $P(x)$. In large and complex problems it is difficult to create a single density $Q(x)$ that has this property.

The Metropolis–Hastings algorithm instead makes use of a proposal density Q *which depends on the current state* $x^{(t)}$. The density $Q(x'; x^{(t)})$ might be a simple distribution such as a Gaussian centred on the current $x^{(t)}$. The proposal density $Q(x'; x)$ can be *any* fixed density from which we can draw samples. In contrast to importance sampling and rejection sampling, it is not necessary that $Q(x'; x^{(t)})$ look at all similar to $P(x)$ in order for the algorithm to be practically useful. An example of a proposal density is shown in figure 29.10; this figure shows the density $Q(x'; x^{(t)})$ for two different states $x^{(1)}$ and $x^{(2)}$.

As before, we assume that we can evaluate $P^*(x)$ for any x. A tentative new state x' is generated from the proposal density $Q(x'; x^{(t)})$. To decide

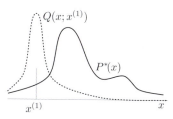

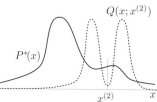

Figure 29.10. Metropolis–Hastings method in one dimension. The proposal distribution $Q(x'; x)$ is here shown as having a shape that changes as x changes, though this is not typical of the proposal densities used in practice.

whether to accept the new state, we compute the quantity

$$a = \frac{P^*(x')}{P^*(x^{(t)})} \frac{Q(x^{(t)}; x')}{Q(x'; x^{(t)})}. \tag{29.31}$$

If $a \geq 1$ then the new state is accepted.
Otherwise, the new state is accepted with probability a.

If the step is accepted, we set $x^{(t+1)} = x'$.
If the step is rejected, then we set $x^{(t+1)} = x^{(t)}$.

Note the difference from rejection sampling: in rejection sampling, rejected points are discarded and have no influence on the list of samples $\{x^{(r)}\}$ that we collected. Here, a rejection causes the current state to be written again onto the list.

Notation. I have used the superscript $r = 1, \ldots, R$ to label points that are *independent* samples from a distribution, and the superscript $t = 1, \ldots, T$ to label the sequence of states in a Markov chain. It is important to note that a Metropolis–Hastings simulation of T iterations does not produce T *independent* samples from the target distribution P. The samples are correlated.

To compute the acceptance probability (29.31) we need to be able to compute the probability ratios $P(x')/P(x^{(t)})$ and $Q(x^{(t)}; x')/Q(x'; x^{(t)})$. If the proposal density is a simple symmetrical density such as a Gaussian centred on the current point, then the latter factor is unity, and the Metropolis–Hastings method simply involves comparing the value of the target density at the two points. This special case is sometimes called the Metropolis method. However, with apologies to Hastings, I will call the general Metropolis–Hastings algorithm for asymmetric Q 'the Metropolis algorithm' since I believe important ideas deserve short names.

Convergence of the Metropolis method to the target density

It can be shown that for any positive Q (that is, any Q such that $Q(x'; x) > 0$ for all x, x'), as $t \to \infty$, the probability distribution of $x^{(t)}$ tends to $P(x) = P^*(x)/Z$. [This statement should not be seen as implying that Q *has* to assign positive probability to every point x' – we will discuss examples later where $Q(x'; x) = 0$ for some x, x'; notice also that we have said nothing about how rapidly the convergence to $P(x)$ takes place.]

The Metropolis method is an example of a *Markov chain Monte Carlo* method (abbreviated MCMC). In contrast to rejection sampling, where the accepted points $\{x^{(r)}\}$ are *independent* samples from the desired distribution, Markov chain Monte Carlo methods involve a Markov process in which a sequence of states $\{x^{(t)}\}$ is generated, each sample $x^{(t)}$ having a probability distribution that depends on the previous value, $x^{(t-1)}$. Since successive samples are correlated with each other, the Markov chain may have to be run for a considerable time in order to generate samples that are effectively independent samples from P.

Just as it was difficult to estimate the variance of an importance sampling estimator, so it is difficult to assess whether a Markov chain Monte Carlo method has 'converged', and to quantify how long one has to wait to obtain samples that are effectively independent samples from P.

Demonstration of the Metropolis method

The Metropolis method is widely used for high-dimensional problems. Many implementations of the Metropolis method employ a proposal distribution

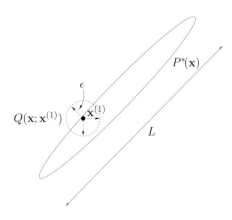

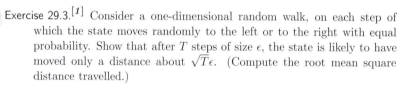

Figure 29.11. Metropolis method in two dimensions, showing a traditional proposal density that has a sufficiently small step size ϵ that the acceptance frequency will be about 0.5.

with a length scale ϵ that is short relative to the longest length scale L of the probable region (figure 29.11). A reason for choosing a small length scale is that for most high-dimensional problems, a large random step from a typical point (that is, a sample from $P(\mathbf{x})$) is very likely to end in a state that has very low probability; such steps are unlikely to be accepted. If ϵ is large, movement around the state space will only occur when such a transition to a low-probability state is actually accepted, or when a large random step chances to land in another probable state. So the rate of progress will be slow if large steps are used.

The disadvantage of small steps, on the other hand, is that the Metropolis method will explore the probability distribution by a *random walk*, and a random walk takes a long time to get anywhere, especially if the walk is made of small steps.

Exercise 29.3.[1] Consider a one-dimensional random walk, on each step of which the state moves randomly to the left or to the right with equal probability. Show that after T steps of size ϵ, the state is likely to have moved only a distance about $\sqrt{T}\epsilon$. (Compute the root mean square distance travelled.)

Recall that the first aim of Monte Carlo sampling is to generate a number of *independent* samples from the given distribution (a dozen, say). If the largest length scale of the state space is L, then we have to simulate a random-walk Metropolis method for a time $T \simeq (L/\epsilon)^2$ before we can expect to get a sample that is roughly independent of the initial condition – and that's assuming that every step is accepted: if only a fraction f of the steps are accepted on average, then this time is increased by a factor $1/f$.

> **Rule of thumb: lower bound on number of iterations of a Metropolis method.** If the largest length scale of the space of probable states is L, a Metropolis method whose proposal distribution generates a random walk with step size ϵ must be run for at least
>
> $$T \simeq (L/\epsilon)^2 \qquad (29.32)$$
>
> iterations to obtain an independent sample.

This rule of thumb gives only a lower bound; the situation may be much worse, if, for example, the probability distribution consists of several islands of high probability separated by regions of low probability.

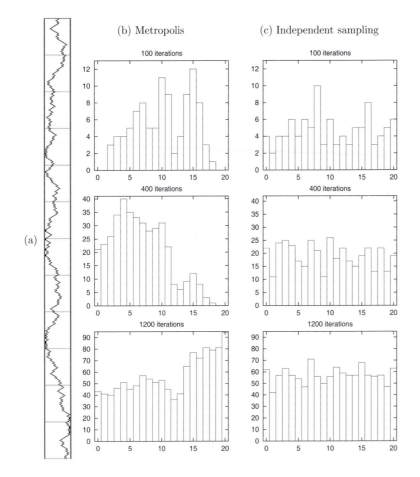

Figure 29.12. Metropolis method for a toy problem. (a) The state sequence for $t = 1, \ldots, 600$. Horizontal direction = states from 0 to 20; vertical direction = time from 1 to 600; the cross bars mark time intervals of duration 50. (b) Histogram of occupancy of the states after 100, 400 and 1200 iterations. (c) For comparison, histograms resulting when successive points are drawn *independently* from the target distribution.

To illustrate how slowly a random walk explores a state space, figure 29.12 shows a simulation of a Metropolis algorithm for generating samples from the distribution:

$$P(x) = \begin{cases} 1/21 & x \in \{0, 1, 2, \ldots, 20\} \\ 0 & \text{otherwise.} \end{cases} \tag{29.33}$$

The proposal distribution is

$$Q(x'; x) = \begin{cases} 1/2 & x' = x \pm 1 \\ 0 & \text{otherwise.} \end{cases} \tag{29.34}$$

Because the target distribution $P(x)$ is uniform, rejections occur only when the proposal takes the state to $x' = -1$ or $x' = 21$.

The simulation was started in the state $x_0 = 10$ and its evolution is shown in figure 29.12a. How long does it take to reach one of the end states $x = 0$ and $x = 20$? Since the distance is 10 steps, the rule of thumb (29.32) predicts that it will typically take a time $T \simeq 100$ iterations to reach an end state. This is confirmed in the present example: the first step into an end state occurs on the 178th iteration. How long does it take to visit *both* end states? The rule of thumb predicts about 400 iterations are required to traverse the whole state space; and indeed the first encounter with the other end state takes place on the 540th iteration. Thus effectively-independent samples are only generated by simulating for about four hundred iterations per independent sample.

This simple example shows that it is important to try to abolish random walk behaviour in Monte Carlo methods. A systematic exploration of the toy state space $\{0, 1, 2, \ldots, 20\}$ could get around it, using the same step sizes, in about twenty steps instead of four hundred. Methods for reducing random walk behaviour are discussed in the next chapter.

Metropolis method in high dimensions

The rule of thumb (29.32), which gives a lower bound on the number of iterations of a random walk Metropolis method, also applies to higher dimensional problems. Consider the simple case of a target distribution that is an N-dimensional Gaussian, and a proposal distribution that is a spherical Gaussian of standard deviation ϵ in each direction. Without loss of generality, we can assume that the target distribution is a separable distribution aligned with the axes $\{x_n\}$, and that it has standard deviation σ_n in direction n. Let $\sigma^{\max}$ and $\sigma^{\min}$ be the largest and smallest of these standard deviations. Let us assume that ϵ is adjusted such that the acceptance frequency is close to 1. Under this assumption, each variable x_n evolves independently of all the others, executing a random walk with step size about ϵ. The time taken to generate effectively independent samples from the target distribution will be controlled by the largest lengthscale $\sigma^{\max}$. Just as in the previous section, where we needed at least $T \simeq (L/\epsilon)^2$ iterations to obtain an independent sample, here we need $T \simeq (\sigma^{\max}/\epsilon)^2$.

Now, how big can ϵ be? The bigger it is, the smaller this number T becomes, but if ϵ is too big – bigger than $\sigma^{\min}$ – then the acceptance rate will fall sharply. It seems plausible that the optimal ϵ must be similar to $\sigma^{\min}$. Strictly, this may not be true; in special cases where the second smallest σ_n is significantly greater than $\sigma^{\min}$, the optimal ϵ may be closer to that second smallest σ_n. But our rough conclusion is this: where simple spherical proposal distributions are used, we will need at least $T \simeq (\sigma^{\max}/\sigma^{\min})^2$ iterations to obtain an independent sample, where $\sigma^{\max}$ and $\sigma^{\min}$ are the longest and shortest lengthscales of the target distribution.

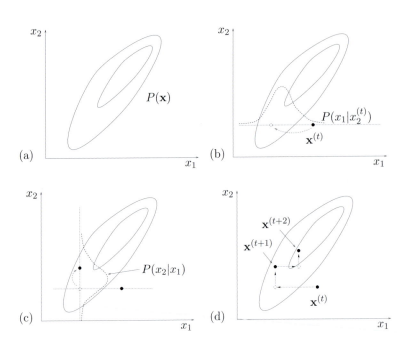

Figure 29.13. Gibbs sampling.
(a) The joint density $P(\mathbf{x})$ from
which samples are required. (b)
Starting from a state $\mathbf{x}^{(t)}$, x_1 is
sampled from the conditional
density $P(x_1|x_2^{(t)})$. (c) A sample
is then made from the conditional
density $P(x_2|x_1)$. (d) A couple of
iterations of Gibbs sampling.

This is good news and bad news. It is good news because, unlike the
cases of rejection sampling and importance sampling, there is no catastrophic
dependence on the dimensionality N. Our computer *will* give useful answers
in a time shorter than the age of the universe. But it is bad news all the same,
because this quadratic dependence on the lengthscale-ratio may still force us
to make very lengthy simulations.

Fortunately, there are methods for suppressing random walks in Monte
Carlo simulations, which we will discuss in the next chapter.

▶ 29.5 Gibbs sampling

We introduced importance sampling, rejection sampling and the Metropolis
method using one-dimensional examples. Gibbs sampling, also known as the
heat bath method or 'Glauber dynamics', is a method for sampling from distributions over at least two dimensions. Gibbs sampling can be viewed as a
Metropolis method in which a sequence of proposal distributions Q are defined
in terms of the *conditional* distributions of the joint distribution $P(\mathbf{x})$. It is
assumed that, whilst $P(\mathbf{x})$ is too complex to draw samples from directly, its
conditional distributions $P(x_i \,|\, \{x_j\}_{j \neq i})$ are tractable to work with. For many
graphical models (but not all) these one-dimensional conditional distributions
are straightforward to sample from. For example, if a Gaussian distribution
for some variables $\mathbf{d}$ has an unknown mean $\mathbf{m}$, and the prior distribution of $\mathbf{m}$
is Gaussian, then the conditional distribution of $\mathbf{m}$ given $\mathbf{d}$ is also Gaussian.
Conditional distributions that are not of standard form may still be sampled
from by *adaptive rejection sampling* if the conditional distribution satisfies
certain convexity properties (Gilks and Wild, 1992).

Gibbs sampling is illustrated for a case with two variables $(x_1, x_2) = \mathbf{x}$ in
figure 29.13. On each iteration, we start from the current state $\mathbf{x}^{(t)}$, and x_1 is
sampled from the conditional density $P(x_1|x_2)$, with x_2 fixed to $x_2^{(t)}$. A sample
x_2 is then made from the conditional density $P(x_2|x_1)$, using the new value of

x_1. This brings us to the new state $\mathbf{x}^{(t+1)}$, and completes the iteration.

In the general case of a system with K variables, a single iteration involves sampling one parameter at a time:

$$x_1^{(t+1)} \sim P(x_1 \,|\, x_2^{(t)}, x_3^{(t)}, \dots, x_K^{(t)}) \tag{29.35}$$

$$x_2^{(t+1)} \sim P(x_2 \,|\, x_1^{(t+1)}, x_3^{(t)}, \dots, x_K^{(t)}) \tag{29.36}$$

$$x_3^{(t+1)} \sim P(x_3 \,|\, x_1^{(t+1)}, x_2^{(t+1)}, \dots, x_K^{(t)}), \text{ etc.} \tag{29.37}$$

Convergence of Gibbs sampling to the target density

▷ Exercise 29.4.[2] Show that a single variable-update of Gibbs sampling can be viewed as a Metropolis method with target density $P(\mathbf{x})$, and that this Metropolis method has the property that every proposal is always accepted.

Because Gibbs sampling is a Metropolis method, the probability distribution of $\mathbf{x}^{(t)}$ tends to $P(\mathbf{x})$ as $t \to \infty$, as long as $P(\mathbf{x})$ does not have pathological properties.

▷ Exercise 29.5.[2, p.385] Discuss whether the syndrome decoding problem for a $(7, 4)$ Hamming code can be solved using Gibbs sampling. The syndrome decoding problem, if we are to solve it with a Monte Carlo approach, is to draw samples from the posterior distribution of the noise vector $\mathbf{n} = (n_1, \dots, n_n, \dots, n_N)$,

$$P(\mathbf{n} \,|\, \mathbf{f}, \mathbf{z}) = \frac{1}{Z} \prod_{n=1}^{N} f_n^{n_n} (1 - f_n)^{(1-n_n)} \mathbb{1}[\mathbf{Hn} = \mathbf{z}], \tag{29.38}$$

where f_n is the normalized likelihood for the nth transmitted bit and $\mathbf{z}$ is the observed syndrome. The factor $\mathbb{1}[\mathbf{Hn} = \mathbf{z}]$ is 1 if $\mathbf{n}$ has the correct syndrome $\mathbf{z}$ and 0 otherwise.

What about the syndrome decoding problem for any linear error-correcting code?

Gibbs sampling in high dimensions

Gibbs sampling suffers from the same defect as simple Metropolis algorithms – the state space is explored by a slow random walk, unless a fortuitous parameterization has been chosen that makes the probability distribution $P(\mathbf{x})$ separable. If, say, two variables x_1 and x_2 are strongly correlated, having marginal densities of width L and conditional densities of width ϵ, then it will take at least about $(L/\epsilon)^2$ iterations to generate an independent sample from the target density. Figure 30.3, p.390, illustrates the slow progress made by Gibbs sampling when $L \gg \epsilon$.

However Gibbs sampling involves no adjustable parameters, so it is an attractive strategy when one wants to get a model running quickly. An excellent software package, BUGS, makes it easy to set up almost arbitrary probabilistic models and simulate them by Gibbs sampling (Thomas *et al.*, 1992).[1]

---

[1] http://www.mrc-bsu.cam.ac.uk/bugs/

▶ 29.6 Terminology for Markov chain Monte Carlo methods

We now spend a few moments sketching the theory on which the Metropolis
method and Gibbs sampling are based. We denote by $p^{(t)}(\mathbf{x})$ the probability distribution of the state of a Markov chain simulator. (To visualize this
distribution, imagine running an infinite collection of identical simulators in
parallel.) Our aim is to find a Markov chain such that as $t \to \infty$, $p^{(t)}(\mathbf{x})$ tends
to the desired distribution $P(\mathbf{x})$.

A *Markov chain* can be specified by an *initial* probability distribution
$p^{(0)}(\mathbf{x})$ and a *transition probability* $T(\mathbf{x}';\mathbf{x})$.

The probability distribution of the state at the $(t{+}1)$th iteration of the
Markov chain, $p^{(t+1)}(\mathbf{x})$, is given by

$$p^{(t+1)}(\mathbf{x}') = \int \mathrm{d}^N\mathbf{x}\; T(\mathbf{x}';\mathbf{x})p^{(t)}(\mathbf{x}). \tag{29.39}$$

Example 29.6.   An example of a Markov chain is given by the Metropolis
demonstration of section 29.4 (figure 29.12), for which the transition probability is

$$\mathbf{T} = \begin{bmatrix} \ddots \end{bmatrix}$$

and the initial distribution was

$$p^{(0)}(x) = \begin{bmatrix} \cdots & \cdots & 1 & \cdots & \cdots \end{bmatrix}. \tag{29.40}$$

The probability distribution $p^{(t)}(x)$ of the state at the tth iteration is shown
for $t = 0, 1, 2, 3, 5, 10, 100, 200, 400$ in figure 29.14; an equivalent sequence of
distributions is shown in figure 29.15 for the chain that begins in initial state
$x_0 = 17$. Both chains converge to the target density, the uniform density, as
$t \to \infty$.

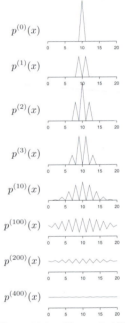

Figure 29.14. The probability
distribution of the state of the
Markov chain of example 29.6.

Required properties

When designing a Markov chain Monte Carlo method, we construct a chain
with the following properties:

1. The desired distribution $P(\mathbf{x})$ is an *invariant distribution* of the chain.

   A distribution $\pi(\mathbf{x})$ is an invariant distribution of the transition probability $T(\mathbf{x}';\mathbf{x})$ if

$$\pi(\mathbf{x}') = \int \mathrm{d}^N\mathbf{x}\; T(\mathbf{x}';\mathbf{x})\pi(\mathbf{x}). \tag{29.41}$$

   An invariant distribution is an eigenvector of the transition probability
   matrix that has eigenvalue 1.

2. The chain must also be *ergodic*, that is,

$$p^{(t)}(\mathbf{x}) \to \pi(\mathbf{x}) \text{ as } t \to \infty, \text{ for any } p^{(0)}(\mathbf{x}). \tag{29.42}$$

A couple of reasons why a chain might not be ergodic are:

(a) Its matrix might be *reducible*, which means that the state space contains two or more subsets of states that can never be reached from each other. Such a chain has many invariant distributions; which one $p^{(t)}(\mathbf{x})$ would tend to as $t \to \infty$ would depend on the initial condition $p^{(0)}(\mathbf{x})$.

The transition probability matrix of such a chain has more than one eigenvalue equal to 1.

(b) The chain might have a *periodic set*, which means that, for some initial conditions, $p^{(t)}(\mathbf{x})$ doesn't tend to an invariant distribution, but instead tends to a periodic limit-cycle.

A simple Markov chain with this property is the random walk on the N-dimensional hypercube. The chain T takes the state from one corner to a randomly chosen adjacent corner. The unique invariant distribution of this chain is the uniform distribution over all 2^N states, but the chain is not ergodic; it is periodic with period two: if we divide the states into states with odd parity and states with even parity, we notice that every odd state is surrounded by even states and *vice versa*. So if the initial condition at time $t = 0$ is a state with even parity, then at time $t = 1$ – and at all odd times – the state must have odd parity, and at all even times, the state will be of even parity.

The transition probability matrix of such a chain has more than one eigenvalue with magnitude equal to 1. The random walk on the hypercube, for example, has eigenvalues equal to $+1$ and -1.

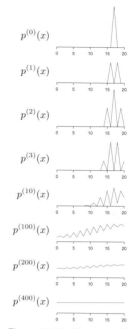

Figure 29.15. The probability distribution of the state of the Markov chain for initial condition $x_0 = 17$ (example 29.6 (p.372)).

Methods of construction of Markov chains

It is often convenient to construct T by *mixing* or *concatenating* simple *base transitions* B all of which satisfy

$$P(\mathbf{x}') = \int d^N\mathbf{x} \; B(\mathbf{x}'; \mathbf{x})P(\mathbf{x}), \tag{29.43}$$

for the desired density $P(\mathbf{x})$, i.e., they all have the desired density as an invariant distribution. These base transitions need not individually be ergodic.

T is a *mixture* of several base transitions $B_b(\mathbf{x}', \mathbf{x})$ if we make the transition by picking one of the base transitions at random, and allowing it to determine the transition, i.e.,

$$T(\mathbf{x}', \mathbf{x}) = \sum_b p_b B_b(\mathbf{x}', \mathbf{x}), \tag{29.44}$$

where $\{p_b\}$ is a probability distribution over the base transitions.

T is a *concatenation* of two base transitions $B_1(\mathbf{x}', \mathbf{x})$ and $B_2(\mathbf{x}', \mathbf{x})$ if we first make a transition to an intermediate state $\mathbf{x}''$ using B_1, and then make a transition from state $\mathbf{x}''$ to $\mathbf{x}'$ using B_2.

$$T(\mathbf{x}', \mathbf{x}) = \int d^N\mathbf{x}'' \; B_2(\mathbf{x}', \mathbf{x}'')B_1(\mathbf{x}'', \mathbf{x}). \tag{29.45}$$

Detailed balance

Many useful transition probabilities satisfy the *detailed balance* property:

$$T(\mathbf{x}_a; \mathbf{x}_b)P(\mathbf{x}_b) = T(\mathbf{x}_b; \mathbf{x}_a)P(\mathbf{x}_a), \text{ for all } \mathbf{x}_b \text{ and } \mathbf{x}_a. \qquad (29.46)$$

This equation says that if we pick (by magic) a state from the target density P and make a transition under T to another state, it is just as likely that we will pick $\mathbf{x}_b$ and go from $\mathbf{x}_b$ to $\mathbf{x}_a$ as it is that we will pick $\mathbf{x}_a$ and go from $\mathbf{x}_a$ to $\mathbf{x}_b$. Markov chains that satisfy detailed balance are also called *reversible* Markov chains. The reason why the detailed balance property is of interest is that detailed balance implies invariance of the distribution $P(\mathbf{x})$ under the Markov chain T, which is a necessary condition for the key property that we want from our MCMC simulation – that the probability distribution of the chain should converge to $P(\mathbf{x})$.

▷ Exercise 29.7.[2] Prove that detailed balance implies invariance of the distribution $P(\mathbf{x})$ under the Markov chain T.

Proving that detailed balance holds is often a key step when proving that a Markov chain Monte Carlo simulation will converge to the desired distribution. The Metropolis method satisfies detailed balance, for example. Detailed balance is not an essential condition, however, and we will see later that irreversible Markov chains can be useful in practice, because they may have different random walk properties.

▷ Exercise 29.8.[2] Show that, if we concatenate two base transitions B_1 and B_2 which satisfy detailed balance, it is not necessarily the case that the T thus defined (29.45) satisfies detailed balance.

Exercise 29.9.[2] Does Gibbs sampling, with several variables all updated in a deterministic sequence, satisfy detailed balance?

▶ 29.7 Slice sampling

Slice sampling (Neal, 1997a; Neal, 2003) is a Markov chain Monte Carlo method that has similarities to rejection sampling, Gibbs sampling and the Metropolis method. It can be applied wherever the Metropolis method can be applied, that is, to any system for which the target density $P^*(\mathbf{x})$ can be evaluated at any point $\mathbf{x}$; it has the advantage over simple Metropolis methods that it is more robust to the choice of parameters like step sizes. The simplest version of slice sampling is similar to Gibbs sampling in that it consists of one-dimensional transitions in the state space; however there is no requirement that the one-dimensional conditional distributions be easy to sample from, nor that they have any convexity properties such as are required for adaptive rejection sampling. And slice sampling is similar to rejection sampling in that it is a method that asymptotically draws samples from the volume under the curve described by $P^*(\mathbf{x})$; but there is no requirement for an upper-bounding function.

I will describe slice sampling by giving a sketch of a one-dimensional sampling algorithm, then giving a pictorial description that includes the details that make the method valid.

The skeleton of slice sampling

Let us assume that we want to draw samples from $P(x) \propto P^*(x)$ where x is a real number. A one-dimensional slice sampling algorithm is a method for making transitions from a two-dimensional point (x, u) lying under the curve $P^*(x)$ to another point (x', u') lying under the same curve, such that the probability distribution of (x, u) tends to a uniform distribution over the area under the curve $P^*(x)$, whatever initial point we start from – like the uniform distribution under the curve $P^*(x)$ produced by rejection sampling (section 29.3).

A single transition $(x, u) \rightarrow (x', u')$ of a one-dimensional slice sampling algorithm has the following steps, of which steps 3 and 8 will require further elaboration.

```
1: evaluate P*(x)
2: draw a vertical coordinate u' ~ Uniform(0, P*(x))
3: create a horizontal interval (xₗ, xᵣ) enclosing x
4: loop {
5:        draw x' ~ Uniform(xₗ, xᵣ)
6:        evaluate P*(x')
7:        if P*(x') > u' break out of loop 4-9
8:        else modify the interval (xₗ, xᵣ)
9: }
```

There are several methods for creating the interval (x_l, x_r) in step 3, and several methods for modifying it at step 8. The important point is that the overall method must satisfy detailed balance, so that the uniform distribution for (x, u) under the curve $P^*(x)$ is invariant.

The 'stepping out' method for step 3

In the 'stepping out' method for creating an interval (x_l, x_r) enclosing x, we step out in steps of length w until we find endpoints x_l and x_r at which P^* is smaller than u. The algorithm is shown in figure 29.16.

```
3a: draw r ~ Uniform(0, 1)
3b: xₗ := x − rw
3c: xᵣ := x + (1 − r)w
3d: while (P*(xₗ) > u) { xₗ := xₗ − w }
3e: while (P*(xᵣ) > u) { xᵣ := xᵣ + w }
```

The 'shrinking' method for step 8

Whenever a point x' is drawn such that (x', u') lies above the curve $P^*(x)$, we shrink the interval so that one of the end points is x', and such that the original point x is still enclosed in the interval.

```
8a: if (x' > x) { xᵣ := x' }
8b: else { xₗ := x' }
```

Properties of slice sampling

Like a standard Metropolis method, slice sampling gets around by a random walk, but whereas in the Metropolis method, the choice of the step size is

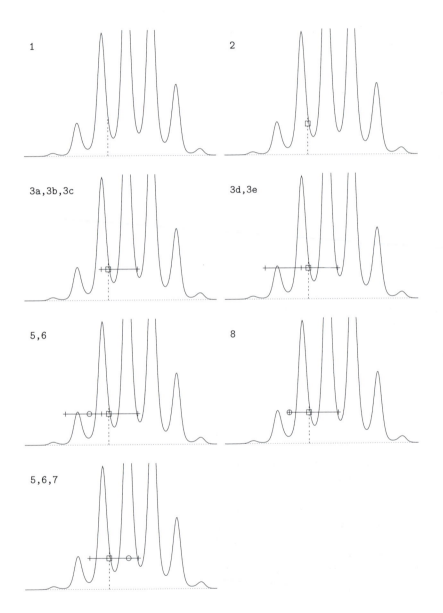

1

2

3a,3b,3c

3d,3e

5,6

8

5,6,7

Figure 29.16. Slice sampling. Each panel is labelled by the steps of the algorithm that are executed in it. At step 1, $P^*(x)$ is evaluated at the current point x. At step 2, a vertical coordinate is selected giving the point (x, u') shown by the box; At steps 3a–c, an interval of size w containing (x, u') is created at random. At step 3d, P^* is evaluated at the left end of the interval and is found to be larger than u', so a step to the left of size w is made. At step 3e, P^* is evaluated at the right end of the interval and is found to be smaller than u', so no stepping out to the right is needed. When step 3d is repeated, P^* is found to be smaller than u', so the stepping out halts. At step 5 a point is drawn from the interval, shown by a ∘. Step 6 establishes that this point is above P^* and step 8 shrinks the interval to the rejected point in such a way that the original point x is still in the interval. When step 5 is repeated, the new coordinate x' (which is to the right-hand side of the interval) gives a value of P^* greater than u', so this point x' is the outcome at step 7.

critical to the rate of progress, in slice sampling the step size is self-tuning. If the initial interval size w is too small by a factor f compared with the width of the probable region then the stepping-out procedure expands the interval size. The cost of this stepping-out is only linear in f, whereas in the Metropolis method the computer-time scales as the square of f if the step size is too small.

If the chosen value of w is too large by a factor F then the algorithm spends a time proportional to the logarithm of F shrinking the interval down to the right size, since the interval typically shrinks by a factor in the ballpark of 0.6 each time a point is rejected. In contrast, the Metropolis algorithm responds to a too-large step size by rejecting almost all proposals, so the rate of progress is exponentially bad in F. There are no rejections in slice sampling. The probability of staying in exactly the same place is very small.

Figure 29.17. $P^*(x)$.

▷ Exercise 29.10.[2] Investigate the properties of slice sampling applied to the density shown in figure 29.17. x is a real variable between 0.0 and 11.0. How long does it take typically for slice sampling to get from an x in the peak region $x \in (0, 1)$ to an x in the tail region $x \in (1, 11)$, and *vice versa*? Confirm that the probabilities of these transitions do yield an asymptotic probability density that is correct.

How slice sampling is used in real problems

An N-dimensional density $P(\mathbf{x}) \propto P^*(\mathbf{x})$ may be sampled with the help of one-dimensional slice sampling method presented above by picking a sequence of directions $\mathbf{y}^{(1)}, \mathbf{y}^{(2)}, \ldots$ and defining $\mathbf{x} = \mathbf{x}^{(t)} + x\mathbf{y}^{(t)}$. The function $P^*(x)$ above is replaced by $P^*(\mathbf{x}) = P^*(\mathbf{x}^{(t)} + x\mathbf{y}^{(t)})$. The directions may be chosen in various ways; for example, as in Gibbs sampling, the directions could be the coordinate axes; alternatively, the directions $\mathbf{y}^{(t)}$ may be selected at random in any manner such that the overall procedure satisfies detailed balance.

Computer-friendly slice sampling

The real variables of a probabilistic model will always be represented in a computer using a finite number of bits. In the following implementation of slice sampling due to Skilling, the stepping-out, randomization, and shrinking operations, described above in terms of floating-point operations, are replaced by binary and integer operations.

We assume that the variable x that is being slice-sampled is represented by a b-bit integer X taking on one of $B = 2^b$ values, $0, 1, 2, \ldots, B-1$, many or all of which correspond to valid values of x. Using an integer grid eliminates any errors in detailed balance that might ensue from variable-precision rounding of floating-point numbers. The mapping from X to x need not be linear; if it is nonlinear, we assume that the function $P^*(x)$ is replaced by an appropriately transformed function – for example, $P^{**}(X) \propto P^*(x)|\mathrm{d}x/\mathrm{d}X|$.

We assume the following operators on b-bit integers are available:

$X + N$	arithmetic sum, modulo B, of X and N.
$X - N$	difference, modulo B, of X and N.
$X \oplus N$	bitwise exclusive-or of X and N.
$N := \mathtt{randbits}(l)$	sets N to a random l-bit integer.

A slice-sampling procedure for integers is then as follows:

Given: a current point X and a height $Y = P^*(X) \times \mathsf{Uniform}(0, 1) \leq P^*(X)$

1:	$U := \mathtt{randbits}(b)$	Define a random translation U of the binary coordinate system.
2:	set l to a value $l \leq b$	Set initial l-bit sampling range.
3:	do {	
4:	$\quad N := \mathtt{randbits}(l)$	Define a random move within the current interval of width 2^l.
5:	$\quad X' := ((X - U) \oplus N) + U$	Randomize the lowest l bits of X (in the translated coordinate system).
6:	$\quad l := l - 1$	If X' is not acceptable, decrease l and try again
7:	} until $(X' = X)$ or $(P^*(X) \geq Y)$	with a smaller perturbation of X; termination at or before $l = 0$ is assured.

The translation U is introduced to avoid permanent sharp edges, where for example the adjacent binary integers 0111111111 and 1000000000 would otherwise be permanently in different sectors, making it difficult for X to move from one to the other.

The sequence of intervals from which the new candidate points are drawn is illustrated in figure 29.18. First, a point is drawn from the entire interval, shown by the top horizontal line. At each subsequent draw, the interval is halved in such a way as to contain the previous point X.

If preliminary stepping-out from the initial range is required, step 2 above can be replaced by the following similar procedure:

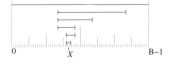

2a:	set l to a value $l < b$	l sets the initial width
2b:	do {	
2c:	$\quad N := \mathtt{randbits}(l)$	
2d:	$\quad X' := ((X - U) \oplus N) + U$	
2e:	$\quad l := l + 1$	
2f:	} until $(l = b)$ or $(P^*(X) < Y)$	

Figure 29.18. The sequence of intervals from which the new candidate points are drawn.

These shrinking and stepping out methods shrink and expand by a factor of two per evaluation. A variant is to shrink or expand by more than one bit each time, setting $l := l \pm \Delta l$ with $\Delta l > 1$. Taking Δl at each step from any pre-assigned distribution (which may include $\Delta l = 0$) allows extra flexibility.

Exercise 29.11.[4] In the shrinking phase, after an unacceptable X' has been produced, the choice of Δl is allowed to depend on the difference between the slice's height Y and the value of $P^*(X')$, without spoiling the algorithm's validity. (Prove this.) It might be a good idea to choose a larger value of Δl when $Y - P^*(X)$ is large. Investigate this idea theoretically or empirically.

A feature of using the integer representation is that, with a suitably extended number of bits, the single integer X can represent two or more real parameters – for example, by mapping X to (x_1, x_2, x_3) through a space-filling curve such as a Peano curve. Thus multi-dimensional slice sampling can be performed using the same software as for one dimension.

▶ **29.8 Practicalities**

Can we predict how long a Markov chain Monte Carlo simulation will take to equilibrate? By considering the random walks involved in a Markov chain Monte Carlo simulation we can obtain simple *lower bounds* on the time required for convergence. But predicting this time more precisely is a difficult problem, and most of the theoretical results giving upper bounds on the convergence time are of little practical use. The exact sampling methods of Chapter 32 offer a solution to this problem for certain Markov chains.

Can we diagnose or detect convergence in a running simulation? This is also a difficult problem. There are a few practical tools available, but none of them is perfect (Cowles and Carlin, 1996).

Can we speed up the convergence time and time between independent samples of a Markov chain Monte Carlo method? Here, there is good news, as described in the next chapter, which describes the Hamiltonian Monte Carlo method, overrelaxation, and simulated annealing.

▶ **29.9 Further practical issues**

Can the normalizing constant be evaluated?

If the target density $P(\mathbf{x})$ is given in the form of an unnormalized density $P^*(\mathbf{x})$ with $P(\mathbf{x}) = \frac{1}{Z}P^*(\mathbf{x})$, the value of Z may well be of interest. Monte Carlo methods do not readily yield an estimate of this quantity, and it is an area of active research to find ways of evaluating it. Techniques for evaluating Z include:

1. Importance sampling (reviewed by Neal (1993b)) and annealed importance sampling (Neal, 1998).

2. 'Thermodynamic integration' during simulated annealing, the 'acceptance ratio' method, and 'umbrella sampling' (reviewed by Neal (1993b)).

3. 'Reversible jump Markov chain Monte Carlo' (Green, 1995).

One way of dealing with Z, however, may be to find a solution to one's task that does not require that Z be evaluated. In Bayesian data modelling one might be able to avoid the need to evaluate Z – which would be important for model comparison – by not having more than one model. Instead of using several models (differing in complexity, for example) and evaluating their relative posterior probabilities, one can make a single *hierarchical* model having, for example, various continuous hyperparameters which play a role similar to that played by the distinct models (Neal, 1996). In noting the possibility of not computing Z, I am not endorsing this approach. The normalizing constant Z is often the single most important number in the problem, and I think every effort should be devoted to calculating it.

The Metropolis method for big models

Our original description of the Metropolis method involved a joint updating of all the variables using a proposal density $Q(\mathbf{x}'; \mathbf{x})$. For big problems it may be more efficient to use several proposal distributions $Q^{(b)}(\mathbf{x}'; \mathbf{x})$, each of which updates only some of the components of $\mathbf{x}$. Each proposal is individually accepted or rejected, and the proposal distributions are repeatedly run through in sequence.

▷ Exercise 29.12.[2, p.385] Explain why the rate of movement through the state space will be greater when B proposals $Q^{(1)}, \ldots, Q^{(B)}$ are considered *individually* in sequence, compared with the case of a single proposal Q^* defined by the concatenation of $Q^{(1)}, \ldots, Q^{(B)}$. Assume that each proposal distribution $Q^{(b)}(\mathbf{x}'; \mathbf{x})$ has an acceptance rate $f < 1/2$.

In the Metropolis method, the proposal density $Q(\mathbf{x}'; \mathbf{x})$ typically has a number of parameters that control, for example, its 'width'. These parameters are usually set by trial and error with the rule of thumb being to aim for a rejection frequency of about 0.5. It is *not* valid to have the width parameters be dynamically updated during the simulation in a way that depends on the history of the simulation. Such a modification of the proposal density would violate the detailed balance condition which guarantees that the Markov chain has the correct invariant distribution.

Gibbs sampling in big models

Our description of Gibbs sampling involved sampling one parameter at a time, as described in equations (29.35–29.37). For big problems it may be more efficient to sample *groups* of variables jointly, that is to use several proposal distributions:

$$x_1^{(t+1)}, \ldots, x_a^{(t+1)} \sim P(x_1, \ldots, x_a \mid x_{a+1}^{(t)}, \ldots, x_K^{(t)}) \qquad (29.47)$$
$$x_{a+1}^{(t+1)}, \ldots, x_b^{(t+1)} \sim P(x_{a+1}, \ldots, x_b \mid x_1^{(t+1)}, \ldots, x_a^{(t+1)}, x_{b+1}^{(t)}, \ldots, x_K^{(t)}), \quad \text{etc.}$$

How many samples are needed?

At the start of this chapter, we observed that the variance of an estimator $\hat{\Phi}$ depends only on the number of independent samples R and the value of

$$\sigma^2 = \int d^N \mathbf{x} \; P(\mathbf{x})(\phi(\mathbf{x}) - \Phi)^2. \qquad (29.48)$$

We have now discussed a variety of methods for generating samples from $P(\mathbf{x})$. How many independent samples R should we aim for?

In many problems, we really only need about twelve independent samples from $P(\mathbf{x})$. Imagine that $\mathbf{x}$ is an unknown vector such as the amount of corrosion present in each of 10 000 underground pipelines around Cambridge, and $\phi(\mathbf{x})$ is the total cost of repairing those pipelines. The distribution $P(\mathbf{x})$ describes the probability of a state $\mathbf{x}$ given the tests that have been carried out on some pipelines and the assumptions about the physics of corrosion. The quantity Φ is the expected cost of the repairs. The quantity σ^2 is the variance of the cost – σ measures by how much we should expect the actual cost to differ from the expectation Φ.

Now, how accurately would a manager like to know Φ? I would suggest there is little point in knowing Φ to a precision finer than about $\sigma/3$. After all, the true cost is likely to differ by $\pm\sigma$ from Φ. If we obtain $R = 12$ independent samples from $P(\mathbf{x})$, we can estimate Φ to a precision of $\sigma/\sqrt{12}$ – which is smaller than $\sigma/3$. So twelve samples suffice.

Allocation of resources

Assuming we have decided how many independent samples R are required, an important question is how one should make use of one's limited computer resources to obtain these samples.

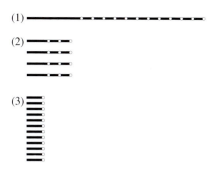

Figure 29.19. Three possible
Markov chain Monte Carlo
strategies for obtaining twelve
samples in a fixed amount of
computer time. Time is
represented by horizontal lines;
samples by white circles. (1) A
single run consisting of one long
'burn in' period followed by a
sampling period. (2) Four
medium-length runs with different
initial conditions and a
medium-length burn in period.
(3) Twelve short runs.

A typical Markov chain Monte Carlo experiment involves an initial period in which control parameters of the simulation such as step sizes may be
adjusted. This is followed by a 'burn in' period during which we hope the
simulation 'converges' to the desired distribution. Finally, as the simulation
continues, we record the state vector occasionally so as to create a list of states
$\{\mathbf{x}^{(r)}\}_{r=1}^{R}$ that we hope are roughly independent samples from $P(\mathbf{x})$.

There are several possible strategies (figure 29.19):

1. Make one long run, obtaining all R samples from it.

2. Make a few medium length runs with different initial conditions, obtaining some samples from each.

3. Make R short runs, each starting from a different random initial condition, with the only state that is recorded being the final state of each
   simulation.

The first strategy has the best chance of attaining 'convergence'. The last
strategy may have the advantage that the correlations between the recorded
samples are smaller. The middle path is popular with Markov chain Monte
Carlo experts (Gilks *et al.*, 1996) because it avoids the inefficiency of discarding
burn-in iterations in many runs, while still allowing one to detect problems
with lack of convergence that would not be apparent from a single run.

Finally, I should emphasize that there is no need to make the points nearly-
independent. Averaging over dependent points is fine – it won't lead to any
bias in the estimates. For example, when you use strategy 1 or 2, you may, if
you wish, include all the points between the first and last sample in each run.
Of course, estimating the accuracy of the estimate is harder when the points
are dependent.

▶ 29.10 Summary

- Monte Carlo methods are a powerful tool that allow one to sample from
  any probability distribution that can be expressed in the form $P(\mathbf{x}) =
  \frac{1}{Z}P^{*}(\mathbf{x})$.

- Monte Carlo methods can answer virtually any query related to $P(\mathbf{x})$ by
  putting the query in the form

$$\int \phi(\mathbf{x})P(\mathbf{x}) \simeq \frac{1}{R}\sum_{r}\phi(\mathbf{x}^{(r)}). \qquad (29.49)$$

- In high-dimensional problems the only satisfactory methods are those based on Markov chains, such as the Metropolis method, Gibbs sampling and slice sampling. Gibbs sampling is an attractive method because it has no adjustable parameters but its use is restricted to cases where samples can be generated from the conditional distributions. Slice sampling is attractive because, whilst it has step length parameters, its performance is not very sensitive to their values.

- Simple Metropolis algorithms and Gibbs sampling algorithms, although widely used, perform poorly because they explore the space by a slow random walk. The next chapter will discuss methods for speeding up Markov chain Monte Carlo simulations.

- Slice sampling does not avoid random walk behaviour, but it automatically chooses the largest appropriate step size, thus reducing the bad effects of the random walk compared with, say, a Metropolis method with a tiny step size.

▶ **29.11 Exercises**

Exercise 29.13.[2C, p.386] A study of importance sampling. We already established in section 29.2 that importance sampling is likely to be useless in high-dimensional problems. This exercise explores a further cautionary tale, showing that importance sampling can fail even in one dimension, even with friendly Gaussian distributions.

Imagine that we want to know the expectation of a function $\phi(x)$ under a distribution $P(x)$,

$$\Phi = \int dx\, P(x)\phi(x), \qquad (29.50)$$

and that this expectation is estimated by importance sampling with a distribution $Q(x)$. Alternatively, perhaps we wish to estimate the normalizing constant Z in $P(x) = P^*(x)/Z$ using

$$Z = \int dx\, P^*(x) = \int dx\, Q(x)\frac{P^*(x)}{Q(x)} = \left\langle \frac{P^*(x)}{Q(x)} \right\rangle_{x\sim Q}. \qquad (29.51)$$

Now, let $P(x)$ and $Q(x)$ be Gaussian distributions with mean zero and standard deviations σ_p and σ_q. Each point x drawn from Q will have an associated weight $P^*(x)/Q(x)$. What is the variance of the weights? [Assume that $P^* = P$, so P is actually normalized, and $Z = 1$, though we can pretend that we didn't know that.] What happens to the variance of the weights as $\sigma_q^2 \to \sigma_p^2/2$?

Check your theory by simulating this importance-sampling problem on a computer.

Exercise 29.14.[2] Consider the Metropolis algorithm for the one-dimensional toy problem of section 29.4, sampling from $\{0, 1, \dots, 20\}$. Whenever the current state is one of the end states, the proposal density given in equation (29.34) will propose with probability 50% a state that will be rejected.

To reduce this 'waste', Fred modifies the software responsible for generating samples from Q so that when $x = 0$, the proposal density is 100% on $x' = 1$, and similarly when $x = 20$, $x' = 19$ is always proposed.

Fred sets the software that implements the acceptance rule so that the software accepts all proposed moves. What probability $P'(x)$ will Fred's modified software generate samples from?

What is the correct acceptance rule for Fred's proposal density, in order to obtain samples from $P(x)$?

▷ Exercise 29.15.[3C] Implement Gibbs sampling for the inference of a single one-dimensional Gaussian, which we studied using maximum likelihood in section 22.1. Assign a broad Gaussian prior to μ and a broad gamma prior (24.2) to the precision parameter $\beta = 1/\sigma^2$. Each update of μ will involve a sample from a Gaussian distribution, and each update of σ requires a sample from a gamma distribution.

Exercise 29.16.[3C] **Gibbs sampling for clustering.** Implement Gibbs sampling for the inference of a mixture of K one-dimensional Gaussians, which we studied using maximum likelihood in section 22.2. Allow the clusters to have different standard deviations σ_k. Assign priors to the means and standard deviations in the same way as the previous exercise. Either fix the prior probabilities of the classes $\{\pi_k\}$ to be equal or put a uniform prior over the parameters π and include them in the Gibbs sampling.

Notice the similarity of Gibbs sampling to the soft K-means clustering algorithm (algorithm 22.2). We can alternately *assign* the class labels $\{k_n\}$ given the parameters $\{\mu_k, \sigma_k\}$, then *update* the parameters given the class labels. The assignment step involves sampling from the probability distributions defined by the responsibilities (22.22), and the update step updates the means and variances using probability distributions centred on the K-means algorithm's values (22.23, 22.24).

Do your experiments confirm that Monte Carlo methods bypass the overfitting difficulties of maximum likelihood discussed in section 22.4?

A solution to this exercise and the previous one, written in octave, is available.[2]

▷ Exercise 29.17.[3C] Implement Gibbs sampling for the **seven scientists** inference problem, which we encountered in exercise 22.15 (p.309), and which you may have solved by exact marginalization (exercise 24.3 (p.323)) [it's not essential to have done the latter].

▷ Exercise 29.18.[2] A Metropolis method is used to explore a distribution $P(\mathbf{x})$ that is actually a 1000-dimensional spherical Gaussian distribution of standard deviation 1 in all dimensions. The proposal density Q is a 1000-dimensional spherical Gaussian distribution of standard deviation ϵ. Roughly what is the step size ϵ if the acceptance rate is 0.5? Assuming this value of ϵ,

(a) roughly how long would the method take to traverse the distribution and generate a sample independent of the initial condition?

(b) By how much does $\ln P(\mathbf{x})$ change in a typical step? By how much should $\ln P(\mathbf{x})$ vary when $\mathbf{x}$ is drawn from $P(\mathbf{x})$?

(c) What happens if, rather than using a Metropolis method that tries to change all components at once, one instead uses a concatenation of Metropolis updates changing one component at a time?

---

[2] http://www.inference.phy.cam.ac.uk/mackay/itila/

▷ **Exercise 29.19.**[2] When discussing the time taken by the Metropolis algorithm to generate independent samples we considered a distribution with longest spatial length scale L being explored using a proposal distribution with step size ϵ. Another dimension that a MCMC method must explore is the range of possible values of the log probability $\ln P^*(\mathbf{x})$. Assuming that the state $\mathbf{x}$ contains a number of independent random variables proportional to N, when samples are drawn from $P(\mathbf{x})$, the 'asymptotic equipartition' principle tell us that the value of $-\ln P(\mathbf{x})$ is likely to be close to the entropy of $\mathbf{x}$, varying either side with a standard deviation that scales as $\sqrt{N}$. Consider a Metropolis method with a symmetrical proposal density, that is, one that satisfies $Q(\mathbf{x}; \mathbf{x}') = Q(\mathbf{x}'; \mathbf{x})$. Assuming that accepted jumps either increase $\ln P^*(\mathbf{x})$ by some amount or decrease it by a *small* amount, e.g. $\ln e = 1$ (is this a reasonable assumption?), discuss how long it must take to generate roughly independent samples from $P(\mathbf{x})$. Discuss whether Gibbs sampling has similar properties.

Exercise 29.20.[3] Markov chain Monte Carlo methods do not compute partition functions Z, yet they allow ratios of quantities like Z to be estimated. For example, consider a random-walk Metropolis algorithm in a state space where the energy is zero in a connected accessible region, and infinitely large everywhere else; and imagine that the accessible space can be chopped into two regions connected by one or more corridor states. The fraction of times spent in each region at equilibrium is proportional to the volume of the region. How does the Monte Carlo method manage to do this without measuring the volumes?

Exercise 29.21.[5] Philosophy.

One curious defect of these Monte Carlo methods – which are widely used by Bayesian statisticians – is that they are all non-Bayesian (O'Hagan, 1987). They involve computer experiments from which *estimators* of quantities of interest are derived. These estimators depend on the proposal distributions that were used to generate the samples and on the random numbers that happened to come out of our random number generator. In contrast, an alternative Bayesian approach to the problem would use the results of our computer experiments to infer the properties of the target function $P(\mathbf{x})$ and generate predictive distributions for quantities of interest such as Φ. This approach would give answers that would depend only on the computed values of $P^*(\mathbf{x}^{(r)})$ at the points $\{\mathbf{x}^{(r)}\}$; the answers would not depend on how those points were chosen.

Can you make a Bayesian Monte Carlo method? (See Rasmussen and Ghahramani (2003) for a practical attempt.)

▶ **29.12 Solutions**

Solution to exercise 29.1 (p.362). We wish to show that

$$\hat{\Phi} \equiv \frac{\sum_r w_r \phi(x^{(r)})}{\sum_r w_r} \tag{29.52}$$

converges to the expectation of Φ under P. We consider the numerator and the denominator separately. First, the denominator. Consider a single importance weight.

$$w_r \equiv \frac{P^*(x^{(r)})}{Q^*(x^{(r)})}. \tag{29.53}$$

What is its expectation, averaged under the distribution $Q = Q^*/Z_Q$ of the point $x^{(r)}$?

$$\langle w_r \rangle = \int dx\, Q(x) \frac{P^*(x)}{Q^*(x)} = \int dx\, \frac{1}{Z_Q} P^*(x) = \frac{Z_P}{Z_Q}. \qquad (29.54)$$

So the expectation of the denominator is

$$\left\langle \sum_r w_r \right\rangle = R \frac{Z_P}{Z_Q}. \qquad (29.55)$$

As long as the variance of w_r is finite, the denominator, divided by R, will converge to Z_P/Z_Q as R increases. [In fact, the estimate converges to the right answer even if this variance is infinite, as long as the expectation is well-defined.] Similarly, the expectation of one term in the numerator is

$$\langle w_r \phi(x) \rangle = \int dx\, Q(x) \frac{P^*(x)}{Q^*(x)} \phi(x) = \int dx\, \frac{1}{Z_Q} P^*(x)\phi(x) = \frac{Z_P}{Z_Q}\Phi, \qquad (29.56)$$

where Φ is the expectation of ϕ under P. So the numerator, divided by R, converges to $\frac{Z_P}{Z_Q}\Phi$ with increasing R. Thus $\hat{\Phi}$ converged to Φ.

The numerator and the denominator are unbiased estimators of RZ_P/Z_Q and $RZ_P/Z_Q\Phi$ respectively, but their ratio $\hat{\Phi}$ is not necessarily an unbiased estimator for finite R.

Solution to exercise 29.2 (p.363). When the true density P is multimodal, it is unwise to use importance sampling with a sampler density fitted to one mode, because on the rare occasions that a point is produced that lands in one of the other modes, the weight associated with that point will be enormous. The estimates will have enormous variance, but this enormous variance may not be evident to the user if no points in the other mode have been seen.

Solution to exercise 29.5 (p.371). The posterior distribution for the syndrome decoding problem is a pathological distribution from the point of view of Gibbs sampling. The factor $\mathbb{1}[\mathbf{Hn} = \mathbf{z}]$ is only 1 on a small fraction of the space of possible vectors $\mathbf{n}$, namely the 2^K points that correspond to the valid codewords. No two codewords are adjacent, so similarly, any single bit flip from a viable state $\mathbf{n}$ will take us to a state with zero probability and so the state will never move in Gibbs sampling.

A general code has exactly the same problem. The points corresponding to valid codewords are relatively few in number and they are not adjacent (at least for any useful code). So Gibbs sampling is no use for syndrome decoding for two reasons. First, finding *any* reasonably good hypothesis is difficult, and as long as the state is not near a valid codeword, Gibbs sampling cannot help since none of the conditional distributions is defined; and second, once we are in a valid hypothesis, Gibbs sampling will never take us out of it.

One could attempt to perform Gibbs sampling using the bits of the original message $\mathbf{s}$ as the variables. This approach would not get locked up in the way just described, but, for a good code, any single bit flip would substantially alter the reconstructed codeword, so if one had found a state with reasonably large likelihood, Gibbs sampling would take an impractically large time to escape from it.

Solution to exercise 29.12 (p.380). Each Metropolis proposal will take the energy of the state up or down by some amount. The total change in energy when B proposals are concatenated will be the end-point of a random walk with B steps in it. This walk might have mean zero, or it might have a tendency to drift upwards (if most moves increase the energy and only a few decrease it). In general the latter will hold, if the acceptance rate f is small: the mean change in energy from any one move will be some $\Delta E > 0$ and so the acceptance probability for the concatenation of B moves will be of order $1/(1 + \exp(-B\Delta E))$, which scales roughly as f^B. The mean-square-distance moved will be of order $f^B B \epsilon^2$, where ϵ is the typical step size. In contrast, the mean-square-distance moved when the moves are considered individually will be of order $f B \epsilon^2$.

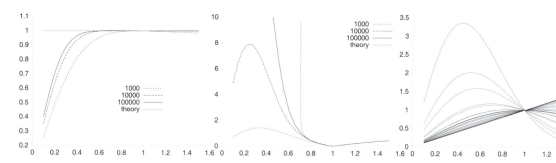

Figure 29.20. Importance sampling in one dimension. For $R = 1000$, 10^4, and 10^5, the normalizing constant of a Gaussian distribution (known in fact to be 1) was estimated using importance sampling with a sampler density of standard deviation σ_q (horizontal axis). The same random number seed was used for all runs. The three plots show (a) the estimated normalizing constant; (b) the *empirical* standard deviation of the R weights; (c) 30 of the weights.

Solution to exercise 29.13 (p.382). The weights are $w = P(x)/Q(x)$ and x is drawn from Q. The mean weight is

$$\int \mathrm{d}x\, Q(x)\,[P(x)/Q(x)] = \int \mathrm{d}x\, P(x) = 1, \qquad (29.57)$$

assuming the integral converges. The variance is

$$\mathrm{var}(w) \;=\; \int \mathrm{d}x\, Q(x) \left[\frac{P(x)}{Q(x)} - 1\right]^2 \qquad (29.58)$$

$$=\; \int \mathrm{d}x\, \frac{P(x)^2}{Q(x)} - 2P(x) + Q(x) \qquad (29.59)$$

$$=\; \left[\int \mathrm{d}x\, \frac{Z_Q}{Z_P^2} \exp\left(-\frac{x^2}{2}\left(\frac{2}{\sigma_p^2} - \frac{1}{\sigma_q^2}\right)\right)\right] - 1, \qquad (29.60)$$

where $Z_Q/Z_P^2 = \sigma_q/(\sqrt{2\pi}\sigma_p^2)$. The integral in (29.60) is finite only if the coefficient of x^2 in the exponent is positive, i.e., if

$$\sigma_q^2 > \frac{1}{2}\sigma_p^2. \qquad (29.61)$$

If this condition is satisfied, the variance is

$$\mathrm{var}(w) = \frac{\sigma_q}{\sqrt{2\pi}\sigma_p^2}\sqrt{2\pi}\left(\frac{2}{\sigma_p^2} - \frac{1}{\sigma_q^2}\right)^{-\frac{1}{2}} - 1 \;=\; \frac{\sigma_q^2}{\sigma_p\left(2\sigma_q^2 - \sigma_p^2\right)^{1/2}} - 1. \qquad (29.62)$$

As σ_q approaches the critical value – about $0.7\sigma_p$ – the variance becomes infinite. Figure 29.20 illustrates these phenomena for $\sigma_p = 1$ with σ_q varying from 0.1 to 1.5. *The same random number seed was used for all runs,* so the weights and estimates follow smooth curves. Notice that the *empirical* standard deviation of the R weights can look quite small and well-behaved (say, at $\sigma_q \simeq 0.3$) when the true standard deviation is nevertheless infinite.

30

Efficient Monte Carlo Methods

This chapter discusses several methods for reducing random walk behaviour in Metropolis methods. The aim is to reduce the time required to obtain effectively independent samples. For brevity, we will say 'independent samples' when we mean 'effectively independent samples'.

▶ 30.1 Hamiltonian Monte Carlo

The Hamiltonian Monte Carlo method is a Metropolis method, applicable to continuous state spaces, that makes use of gradient information to reduce random walk behaviour. [The Hamiltonian Monte Carlo method was originally called hybrid Monte Carlo, for historical reasons.]

For many systems whose probability $P(\mathbf{x})$ can be written in the form

$$P(\mathbf{x}) = \frac{e^{-E(\mathbf{x})}}{Z}, \tag{30.1}$$

not only $E(\mathbf{x})$ but also its gradient with respect to $\mathbf{x}$ can be readily evaluated. It seems wasteful to use a simple random-walk Metropolis method when this gradient is available – the gradient indicates which direction one should go in to find states with higher probability!

Overview of Hamiltonian Monte Carlo

In the Hamiltonian Monte Carlo method, the state space $\mathbf{x}$ is augmented by *momentum variables* $\mathbf{p}$, and there is an alternation of two types of proposal. The first proposal randomizes the momentum variable, leaving the state $\mathbf{x}$ unchanged. The second proposal changes both $\mathbf{x}$ and $\mathbf{p}$ using simulated Hamiltonian dynamics as defined by the Hamiltonian

$$H(\mathbf{x}, \mathbf{p}) = E(\mathbf{x}) + K(\mathbf{p}), \tag{30.2}$$

where $K(\mathbf{p})$ is a 'kinetic energy' such as $K(\mathbf{p}) = \mathbf{p}^{\mathsf{T}}\mathbf{p}/2$. These two proposals are used to create (asymptotically) samples from the joint density

$$P_H(\mathbf{x}, \mathbf{p}) = \frac{1}{Z_H} \exp[-H(\mathbf{x}, \mathbf{p})] = \frac{1}{Z_H} \exp[-E(\mathbf{x})] \exp[-K(\mathbf{p})]. \tag{30.3}$$

This density is separable, so the marginal distribution of $\mathbf{x}$ is the desired distribution $\exp[-E(\mathbf{x})]/Z$. So, simply discarding the momentum variables, we obtain a sequence of samples $\{\mathbf{x}^{(t)}\}$ that asymptotically come from $P(\mathbf{x})$.

```
g = gradE ( x ) ;              # set gradient using initial x
E = findE ( x ) ;              # set objective function too

for l = 1:L                    # loop L times
  p = randn ( size(x) ) ;      # initial momentum is Normal(0,1)
  H = p' * p / 2 + E ;         # evaluate H(x,p)

  xnew = x ;  gnew = g ;
  for tau = 1:Tau              # make Tau 'leapfrog' steps

    p = p - epsilon * gnew / 2 ; # make half-step in p
    xnew = xnew + epsilon * p ;  # make step in x
    gnew = gradE ( xnew ) ;      # find new gradient
    p = p - epsilon * gnew / 2 ; # make half-step in p

  endfor

  Enew = findE ( xnew ) ;      # find new value of H
  Hnew = p' * p / 2 + Enew ;
  dH = Hnew - H ;              # Decide whether to accept

  if ( dH < 0 )              accept = 1 ;
  elseif ( rand() < exp(-dH) ) accept = 1 ;
  else                       accept = 0 ;
  endif

  if ( accept )
    g = gnew ;   x = xnew ;   E = Enew ;
  endif
endfor
```

Algorithm 30.1. `Octave` source code for the Hamiltonian Monte Carlo method.

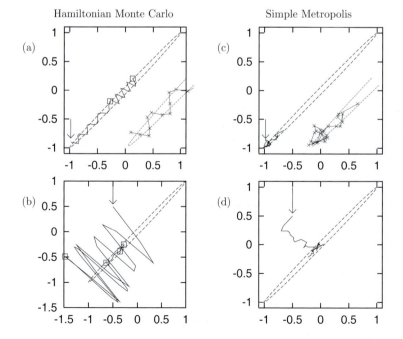

Hamiltonian Monte Carlo

Simple Metropolis

Figure 30.2. (a,b) Hamiltonian Monte Carlo used to generate samples from a bivariate Gaussian with correlation $\rho = 0.998$. (c,d) For comparison, a simple random-walk Metropolis method, given equal computer time.

Details of Hamiltonian Monte Carlo

The first proposal, which can be viewed as a Gibbs sampling update, draws a new momentum from the Gaussian density $\exp[-K(\mathbf{p})]/Z_K$. This proposal is always accepted. During the second, dynamical proposal, the momentum variable determines where the state $\mathbf{x}$ goes, and the *gradient* of $E(\mathbf{x})$ determines how the momentum $\mathbf{p}$ changes, in accordance with the equations

$$\dot{\mathbf{x}} = \mathbf{p} \tag{30.4}$$

$$\dot{\mathbf{p}} = -\frac{\partial E(\mathbf{x})}{\partial \mathbf{x}}. \tag{30.5}$$

Because of the persistent motion of $\mathbf{x}$ in the direction of the momentum $\mathbf{p}$ during each dynamical proposal, the state of the system tends to move a distance that goes *linearly* with the computer time, rather than as the square root.

The second proposal is accepted in accordance with the Metropolis rule. If the simulation of the Hamiltonian dynamics is numerically perfect then the proposals are accepted every time, because the total energy $H(\mathbf{x}, \mathbf{p})$ is a constant of the motion and so a in equation (29.31) is equal to one. If the simulation is imperfect, because of finite step sizes for example, then some of the dynamical proposals will be rejected. The rejection rule makes use of the change in $H(\mathbf{x}, \mathbf{p})$, which is zero if the simulation is perfect. The occasional rejections ensure that, asymptotically, we obtain samples $(\mathbf{x}^{(t)}, \mathbf{p}^{(t)})$ from the required joint density $P_H(\mathbf{x}, \mathbf{p})$.

The source code in figure 30.1 describes a Hamiltonian Monte Carlo method that uses the 'leapfrog' algorithm to simulate the dynamics on the function `findE(x)`, whose gradient is found by the function `gradE(x)`. Figure 30.2 shows this algorithm generating samples from a bivariate Gaussian whose energy function is $E(\mathbf{x}) = \frac{1}{2}\mathbf{x}^\mathsf{T}\mathbf{A}\mathbf{x}$ with

$$\mathbf{A} = \begin{bmatrix} 250.25 & -249.75 \\ -249.75 & 250.25 \end{bmatrix}, \tag{30.6}$$

corresponding to a variance–covariance matrix of

$$\begin{bmatrix} 1 & 0.998 \\ 0.998 & 1 \end{bmatrix}. \tag{30.7}$$

In figure 30.2a, starting from the state marked by the arrow, the solid line represents two successive trajectories generated by the Hamiltonian dynamics. The squares show the endpoints of these two trajectories. Each trajectory consists of `Tau = 19` 'leapfrog' steps with `epsilon = 0.055`. These steps are indicated by the crosses on the trajectory in the magnified inset. After each trajectory, the momentum is randomized. Here, both trajectories are accepted; the errors in the Hamiltonian were only $+0.016$ and -0.06 respectively.

Figure 30.2b shows how a sequence of four trajectories converges from an initial condition, indicated by the arrow, that is not close to the typical set of the target distribution. The trajectory parameters `Tau` and `epsilon` were randomized for each trajectory using uniform distributions with means 19 and 0.055 respectively. The first trajectory takes us to a new state, $(-1.5, -0.5)$, similar in energy to the first state. The second trajectory happens to end in a state nearer the bottom of the energy landscape. Here, since the potential energy E is smaller, the kinetic energy $K = \mathbf{p}^2/2$ is necessarily larger than it was at the start of the trajectory. When the momentum is randomized before the third trajectory, its kinetic energy becomes much smaller. After the fourth

(a)

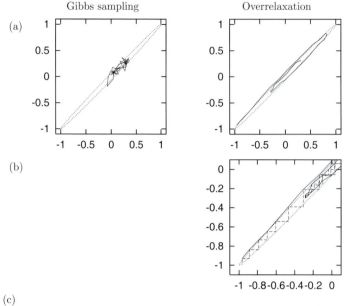

(b)

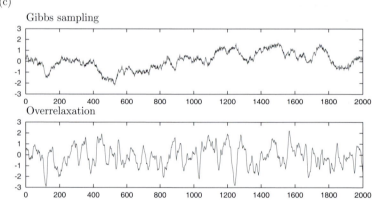

Figure 30.3. Overrelaxation contrasted with Gibbs sampling for a bivariate Gaussian with correlation $\rho = 0.998$. (a) The state sequence for 40 iterations, each iteration involving one update of both variables. The overrelaxation method had $\alpha = -0.98$. (This excessively large value is chosen to make it easy to see how the overrelaxation method reduces random walk behaviour.) The dotted line shows the contour $\mathbf{x}^{\mathsf{T}}\mathbf{\Sigma}^{-1}\mathbf{x} = 1$. (b) Detail of (a), showing the two steps making up each iteration. (c) Time-course of the variable x_1 during 2000 iterations of the two methods. The overrelaxation method had $\alpha = -0.89$. (After Neal (1995).)

(c)

trajectory has been simulated, the state appears to have become typical of the target density.

Figures 30.2(c) and (d) show a random-walk Metropolis method using a Gaussian proposal density to sample from the same Gaussian distribution, starting from the initial conditions of (a) and (b) respectively. In (c) the step size was adjusted such that the acceptance rate was 58%. The number of proposals was 38 so the total amount of computer time used was similar to that in (a). The distance moved is small because of random walk behaviour. In (d) the random-walk Metropolis method was used and started from the same initial condition as (b) and given a similar amount of computer time.

▶ 30.2 Overrelaxation

The method of *overrelaxation* is a method for reducing random walk behaviour in Gibbs sampling. Overrelaxation was originally introduced for systems in which all the conditional distributions are Gaussian.

An example of a joint distribution that is *not* Gaussian but whose conditional distributions *are* all Gaussian is $P(x, y) = \exp(-x^2 y^2 - x^2 - y^2)/Z$.

Overrelaxation for Gaussian conditional distributions

In ordinary Gibbs sampling, one draws the new value $x_i^{(t+1)}$ of the current variable x_i from its conditional distribution, ignoring the old value $x_i^{(t)}$. The state makes lengthy random walks in cases where the variables are strongly correlated, as illustrated in the left-hand panel of figure 30.3. This figure uses a correlated Gaussian distribution as the target density.

In Adler's (1981) overrelaxation method, one instead samples $x_i^{(t+1)}$ from a Gaussian that is biased to the *opposite* side of the conditional distribution. If the conditional distribution of x_i is Normal(μ, σ^2) and the current value of x_i is $x_i^{(t)}$, then Adler's method sets x_i to

$$x_i^{(t+1)} = \mu + \alpha(x_i^{(t)} - \mu) + (1 - \alpha^2)^{1/2}\sigma\nu, \tag{30.8}$$

where $\nu \sim$ Normal$(0, 1)$ and α is a parameter between -1 and 1, usually set to a negative value. (If α is positive, then the method is called under-relaxation.)

> Exercise 30.1.[2] Show that this individual transition leaves invariant the conditional distribution $x_i \sim$ Normal(μ, σ^2).

A single iteration of Adler's overrelaxation, like one of Gibbs sampling, updates each variable in turn as indicated in equation (30.8). The transition matrix $T(\mathbf{x}'; \mathbf{x})$ defined by a complete update of all variables in some fixed order does not satisfy detailed balance. Each individual transition for one coordinate just described *does* satisfy detailed balance – so the overall chain gives a valid sampling strategy which converges to the target density $P(\mathbf{x})$ – but when we form a chain by applying the individual transitions in a fixed sequence, the overall chain is not reversible. This temporal asymmetry is the key to why overrelaxation can be beneficial. If, say, two variables are positively correlated, then they will (on a short timescale) evolve in a directed manner instead of by random walk, as shown in figure 30.3. This may significantly reduce the time required to obtain independent samples.

> Exercise 30.2.[3] The transition matrix $T(\mathbf{x}'; \mathbf{x})$ defined by a complete update of all variables in some fixed order does not satisfy detailed balance. If the updates were in a *random order*, then T would be symmetric. Investigate, for the toy two-dimensional Gaussian distribution, the assertion that the advantages of overrelaxation are lost if the overrelaxed updates are made in a random order.

Ordered Overrelaxation

The overrelaxation method has been generalized by Neal (1995) whose *ordered overrelaxation* method is applicable to *any* system where Gibbs sampling is used. In ordered overrelaxation, instead of taking one sample from the conditional distribution $P(x_i|\{x_j\}_{j\neq i})$, we create K such samples $x_i^{(1)}, x_i^{(2)}, \ldots, x_i^{(K)}$, where K might be set to twenty or so. Often generating $K - 1$ extra samples adds a negligible computational cost to the initial computations required for making the first sample. The points $\{x_i^{(k)}\}$ are then sorted numerically, and the current value of x_i is inserted into the sorted list, giving a list of $K + 1$ points. We give them ranks $0, 1, 2, \ldots, K$. Let κ be the rank of the current value of x_i in the list. We set x_i' to the value that is an equal distance from the other end of the list, that is, the value with rank $K - \kappa$. The role played by Adler's α parameter is here played by the parameter K. When $K = 1$, we obtain ordinary Gibbs sampling. For practical purposes Neal estimates that ordered overrelaxation may speed up a simulation by a factor of ten or twenty.

▶ **30.3 Simulated annealing**

A third technique for speeding convergence is *simulated annealing*. In simulated annealing, a 'temperature' parameter is introduced which, when large, allows the system to make transitions that would be improbable at temperature 1. The temperature is set to a large value and gradually reduced to 1. This procedure is supposed to reduce the chance that the simulation gets stuck in an unrepresentative probability island.

We asssume that we wish to sample from a distribution of the form

$$P(\mathbf{x}) = \frac{e^{-E(\mathbf{x})}}{Z} \tag{30.9}$$

where $E(\mathbf{x})$ can be evaluated. In the simplest simulated annealing method, we instead sample from the distribution

$$P_T(\mathbf{x}) = \frac{1}{Z(T)} e^{-\frac{E(\mathbf{x})}{T}} \tag{30.10}$$

and decrease T gradually to 1.

Often the energy function can be separated into two terms,

$$E(\mathbf{x}) = E_0(\mathbf{x}) + E_1(\mathbf{x}), \tag{30.11}$$

of which the first term is 'nice' (for example, a separable function of $\mathbf{x}$) and the second is 'nasty'. In these cases, a better simulated annealing method might make use of the distribution

$$P_T'(\mathbf{x}) = \frac{1}{Z'(T)} e^{-E_0(\mathbf{x}) - E_1(\mathbf{x})/T} \tag{30.12}$$

with T gradually decreasing to 1. In this way, the distribution at high temperatures reverts to a well-behaved distribution defined by E_0.

Simulated annealing is often used as an optimization method, where the aim is to find an $\mathbf{x}$ that minimizes $E(\mathbf{x})$, in which case the temperature is decreased to zero rather than to 1.

As a Monte Carlo method, simulated annealing as described above doesn't sample exactly from the right distribution, because there is no guarantee that the probability of falling into one basin of the energy is equal to the total probability of all the states in that basin. The closely related 'simulated tempering' method (Marinari and Parisi, 1992) corrects the biases introduced by the annealing process by making the temperature itself a random variable that is updated in Metropolis fashion during the simulation. Neal's (1998) 'annealed importance sampling' method removes the biases introduced by annealing by computing importance weights for each generated point.

▶ **30.4 Skilling's multi-state leapfrog method**

A fourth method for speeding up Monte Carlo simulations, due to John Skilling, has a similar spirit to overrelaxation, but works in more dimensions. This method is applicable to sampling from a distribution over a continuous state space, and the sole requirement is that the energy $E(\mathbf{x})$ should be easy to evaluate. The gradient is not used. This leapfrog method is not intended to be used on its own but rather in sequence with other Monte Carlo operators.

Instead of moving just one state vector $\mathbf{x}$ around the state space, as was the case for all the Monte Carlo methods discussed thus far, Skilling's leapfrog method simultaneously maintains a *set* of S state vectors $\{\mathbf{x}^{(s)}\}$, where S

might be six or twelve. The aim is that all S of these vectors will represent independent samples from the same distribution $P(\mathbf{x})$.

Skilling's leapfrog makes a proposal for the new state $\mathbf{x}^{(s)'}$, which is accepted or rejected in accordance with the Metropolis method, by leapfrogging the current state $\mathbf{x}^{(s)}$ over another state vector $\mathbf{x}^{(t)}$:

$$\mathbf{x}^{(s)'} = \mathbf{x}^{(t)} + (\mathbf{x}^{(t)} - \mathbf{x}^{(s)}) = 2\mathbf{x}^{(t)} - \mathbf{x}^{(s)}. \qquad (30.13)$$

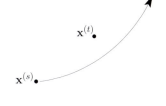

All the other state vectors are left where they are, so the acceptance probability depends only on the change in energy of $\mathbf{x}^{(s)}$.

Which vector, t, is the partner for the leapfrog event can be chosen in various ways. The simplest method is to select the partner at random from the other vectors. It might be better to choose t by selecting one of the nearest neighbours $\mathbf{x}^{(s)}$ – nearest by any chosen distance function – as long as one then uses an acceptance rule that ensures detailed balance by checking whether point t is still among the nearest neighbours of the new point, $\mathbf{x}^{(s)'}$.

Why the leapfrog is a good idea

Imagine that the target density $P(\mathbf{x})$ has strong correlations – for example, the density might be a needle-like Gaussian with width ϵ and length $L\epsilon$, where $L \gg 1$. As we have emphasized, motion around such a density by standard methods proceeds by a slow random walk.

Imagine now that our set of S points is lurking initially in a location that is probable under the density, but in an inappropriately small ball of size ϵ. Now, under Skilling's leapfrog method, a typical first move will take the point a little outside the current ball, perhaps doubling its distance from the centre of the ball. After all the points have had a chance to move, the ball will have increased in size; if all the moves are accepted, the ball will be bigger by a factor of two or so in all dimensions. The rejection of some moves will mean that the ball containing the points will probably have elongated in the needle's long direction by a factor of, say, two. After another cycle through the points, the ball will have grown in the long direction by another factor of two. So the typical distance travelled in the long dimension grows *exponentially* with the number of iterations.

Now, maybe a factor of two growth per iteration is on the optimistic side; but even if the ball only grows by a factor of, let's say, 1.1 per iteration, the growth is nevertheless exponential. It will only take a number of iterations proportional to $\log L / \log(1.1)$ for the long dimension to be explored.

▷ Exercise 30.3.[2, p.398] Discuss how the effectiveness of Skilling's method scales with dimensionality, using a correlated N-dimensional Gaussian distribution as an example. Find an expression for the rejection probability, assuming the Markov chain is at equilibrium. Also discuss how it scales with the strength of correlation among the Gaussian variables. [Hint: Skilling's method is invariant under affine transformations, so the rejection probability at equilibrium can be found by looking at the case of a *separable* Gaussian.]

This method has some similarity to the 'adaptive direction sampling' method of Gilks *et al.* (1994) but the leapfrog method is simpler and can be applied to a greater variety of distributions.

▶ **30.5 Monte Carlo algorithms as communication channels**

It may be a helpful perspective, when thinking about speeding up Monte Carlo methods, to think about the information that is being communicated. Two communications take place when a sample from $P(\mathbf{x})$ is being generated.

First, the selection of a particular $\mathbf{x}$ from $P(\mathbf{x})$ necessarily requires that at least $\log 1/P(\mathbf{x})$ random bits be consumed. [Recall the use of inverse arithmetic coding as a method for generating samples from given distributions (section 6.3).]

Second, the generation of a sample conveys information about $P(\mathbf{x})$ from the subroutine that is able to evaluate $P^*(\mathbf{x})$ (and from any other subroutines that have access to properties of $P^*(\mathbf{x})$).

Consider a dumb Metropolis method, for example. In a dumb Metropolis method, the proposals $Q(\mathbf{x}';\mathbf{x})$ have nothing to do with $P(\mathbf{x})$. Properties of $P(\mathbf{x})$ are only involved in the algorithm at the acceptance step, when the ratio $P^*(\mathbf{x}')/P^*(\mathbf{x})$ is computed. The channel from the true distribution $P(\mathbf{x})$ to the user who is interested in computing properties of $P(\mathbf{x})$ thus passes through a bottleneck: all the information about P is conveyed by the string of acceptances and rejections. If $P(\mathbf{x})$ were replaced by a different distribution $P_2(\mathbf{x})$, the only way in which this change would have an influence is that the string of acceptances and rejections would be changed. I am not aware of much use being made of this information-theoretic view of Monte Carlo algorithms, but I think it is an instructive viewpoint: if the aim is to obtain information about properties of $P(\mathbf{x})$ then presumably it is helpful to identify the channel through which this information flows, and maximize the rate of information transfer.

Example 30.4. The information-theoretic viewpoint offers a simple justification for the widely-adopted rule of thumb, which states that the parameters of a dumb Metropolis method should be adjusted such that the acceptance rate is about one half. Let's call the acceptance history, that is, the binary string of accept or reject decisions, $\mathbf{a}$. The information learned about $P(\mathbf{x})$ after the algorithm has run for T steps is less than or equal to the information content of $\mathbf{a}$, since all information about P is mediated by $\mathbf{a}$. And the information content of $\mathbf{a}$ is upper-bounded by $TH_2(f)$, where f is the acceptance rate. This bound on information acquired about P is maximized by setting $f = 1/2$.

Another helpful analogy for a dumb Metropolis method is an evolutionary one. Each proposal generates a progeny $\mathbf{x}'$ from the current state $\mathbf{x}$. These two individuals then compete with each other, and the Metropolis method uses a noisy survival-of-the-fittest rule. If the progeny $\mathbf{x}'$ is fitter than the parent (i.e., $P^*(\mathbf{x}') > P^*(\mathbf{x})$, assuming the Q/Q factor is unity) then the progeny replaces the parent. The survival rule also allows less-fit progeny to replace the parent, sometimes. Insights about the rate of evolution can thus be applied to Monte Carlo methods.

Exercise 30.5.[3] Let $\mathbf{x} \in \{0,1\}^G$ and let $P(\mathbf{x})$ be a separable distribution,

$$P(\mathbf{x}) = \prod_g p(x_g), \qquad (30.14)$$

with $p(0) = p_0$ and $p(1) = p_1$, for example $p_1 = 0.1$. Let the proposal density of a dumb Metropolis algorithm Q involve flipping a fraction m of the G bits in the state $\mathbf{x}$. Analyze how long it takes for the chain to converge to the target density as a function of m. Find the optimal m and deduce how long the Metropolis method must run for.

Compare the result with the results for an evolving population under natural selection found in Chapter 19.

The insight that the fastest progress that a standard Metropolis method can make, in information terms, is about one bit per iteration, gives a strong motivation for speeding up the algorithm. This chapter has already reviewed several methods for reducing random-walk behaviour. Do these methods also speed up the rate at which information is acquired?

Exercise 30.6.[4] Does Gibbs sampling, which is a smart Metropolis method whose proposal distributions do depend on $P(\mathbf{x})$, allow information about $P(\mathbf{x})$ to leak out at a rate faster than one bit per iteration? Find toy examples in which this question can be precisely investigated.

Exercise 30.7.[4] Hamiltonian Monte Carlo is another smart Metropolis method in which the proposal distributions depend on $P(\mathbf{x})$. Can Hamiltonian Monte Carlo extract information about $P(\mathbf{x})$ at a rate faster than one bit per iteration?

Exercise 30.8.[5] In importance sampling, the weight $w_r = P^*(\mathbf{x}^{(r)})/Q^*(\mathbf{x}^{(r)})$, a floating-point number, is computed and retained until the end of the computation. In contrast, in the dumb Metropolis method, the ratio $a = P^*(\mathbf{x}')/P^*(\mathbf{x})$ is reduced to a single bit ('is a bigger than or smaller than the random number u?'). Thus in principle importance sampling preserves more information about P^* than does dumb Metropolis. Can you find a toy example in which this extra information does indeed lead to faster convergence of importance sampling than Metropolis? Can you design a Markov chain Monte Carlo algorithm that moves around adaptively, like a Metropolis method, and that retains more useful information about the value of P^*, like importance sampling?

In Chapter 19 we noticed that an evolving population of N individuals can make faster evolutionary progress if the individuals engage in sexual reproduction. This observation motivates looking at Monte Carlo algorithms in which multiple parameter vectors $\mathbf{x}$ are evolved and interact.

▶ **30.6 Multi-state methods**

In a multi-state method, multiple parameter vectors $\mathbf{x}$ are maintained; they evolve individually under moves such as Metropolis and Gibbs; there are also interactions among the vectors. The intention is either that eventually all the vectors $\mathbf{x}$ should be samples from $P(\mathbf{x})$ (as illustrated by Skilling's leapfrog method), or that information associated with the final vectors $\mathbf{x}$ should allow us to approximate expectations under $P(\mathbf{x})$, as in importance sampling.

Genetic methods

Genetic algorithms are not often described by their proponents as Monte Carlo algorithms, but I think this is the correct categorization, and an ideal genetic algorithm would be one that can be proved to be a valid Monte Carlo algorithm that converges to a specified density.

I'll use R to denote the number of vectors in the population. We aim to have $P^*(\{\mathbf{x}^{(r)}\}_1^R) = \prod P^*(\mathbf{x}^{(r)})$. A genetic algorithm involves moves of two or three types.

First, individual moves in which one state vector is perturbed, $\mathbf{x}^{(r)} \to \mathbf{x}^{(r)'}$, which could be performed using any of the Monte Carlo methods we have mentioned so far.

Second, we allow crossover moves of the form $\mathbf{x}, \mathbf{y} \to \mathbf{x}', \mathbf{y}'$; in a typical crossover move, the progeny $\mathbf{x}'$ receives half his state vector from one parent, $\mathbf{x}$, and half from the other, $\mathbf{y}$; the secret of success in a genetic algorithm is that the parameter $\mathbf{x}$ must be encoded in such a way that the crossover of two independent states $\mathbf{x}$ and $\mathbf{y}$, both of which have good fitness P^*, should have a reasonably good chance of producing progeny who are equally fit. This constraint is a hard one to satisfy in many problems, which is why genetic algorithms are mainly talked about and hyped up, and rarely used by serious experts. Having introduced a crossover move $\mathbf{x}, \mathbf{y} \to \mathbf{x}', \mathbf{y}'$, we need to choose an acceptance rule. One easy way to obtain a valid algorithm is to accept or reject the crossover proposal using the Metropolis rule with $P^*(\{\mathbf{x}^{(r)}\}_1^R)$ as the target density – this involves comparing the fitnesses before and after the crossover using the ratio

$$\frac{P^*(\mathbf{x}')P^*(\mathbf{y}')}{P^*(\mathbf{x})P^*(\mathbf{y})}. \tag{30.15}$$

If the crossover operator is reversible then we have an easy proof that this procedure satisfies detailed balance and so is a valid component in a chain converging to $P^*(\{\mathbf{x}^{(r)}\}_1^R)$.

▷ Exercise 30.9.[3] Discuss whether the above two operators, individual variation and crossover with the Metropolis acceptance rule, will give a more efficient Monte Carlo method than a standard method with only one state vector and no crossover.

The reason why the sexual community could acquire information faster than the asexual community in Chapter 19 was because the crossover operation produced diversity with standard deviation $\sqrt{G}$, then the Blind Watchmaker was able to convey lots of information about the fitness function by *killing off* the less fit offspring. The above two operators do *not* offer a speed-up of $\sqrt{G}$ compared with standard Monte Carlo methods because there is no killing. What's required, in order to obtain a speed-up, is two things: multiplication and death; and at least one of these must operate *selectively*. Either we must kill off the less-fit state vectors, or we must allow the more-fit state vectors to give rise to more offspring. While it's easy to sketch these ideas, it is hard to define a valid method for doing it.

Exercise 30.10.[5] Design a birth rule and a death rule such that the chain converges to $P^*(\{\mathbf{x}^{(r)}\}_1^R)$.

I believe this is still an open research problem.

Particle filters

Particle filters, which are particularly popular in inference problems involving temporal tracking, are multistate methods that mix the ideas of importance sampling and Markov chain Monte Carlo. See Isard and Blake (1996), Isard and Blake (1998), Berzuini *et al.* (1997), Berzuini and Gilks (2001), Doucet *et al.* (2001).

▶ 30.7 Methods that do not necessarily help

It is common practice to use *many* initial conditions for a particular Markov chain (figure 29.19). If you are worried about sampling well from a complicated density $P(\mathbf{x})$, *can* you ensure the states produced by the simulations are well distributed about the typical set of $P(\mathbf{x})$ by ensuring that the initial points are 'well distributed about the whole state space'?

The answer is, unfortunately, no. In hierarchical Bayesian models, for example, a large number of parameters $\{x_n\}$ may be coupled together via another parameter β (known as a hyperparameter). For example, the quantities $\{x_n\}$ might be independent noise signals, and β might be the inverse-variance of the noise source. The joint distribution of β and $\{x_n\}$ might be

$$
\begin{aligned}
P(\beta, \{x_n\}) &= P(\beta) \prod_{n=1}^{N} P(x_n|\beta) \\
&= P(\beta) \prod_{n=1}^{N} \tfrac{1}{Z(\beta)} e^{-\beta x_n^2/2},
\end{aligned}
$$

where $Z(\beta) = \sqrt{2\pi/\beta}$ and $P(\beta)$ is a broad distribution describing our ignorance about the noise level. For simplicity, let's leave out all the other variables – data and such – that might be involved in a realistic problem. Let's imagine that we want to sample effectively from $P(\beta, \{x_n\})$ by Gibbs sampling – alternately sampling β from the conditional distribution $P(\beta|x_n)$ then sampling all the x_n from their conditional distributions $P(x_n|\beta)$. [The resulting marginal distribution of β should asymptotically be the broad distribution $P(\beta)$.]

If N is large then the conditional distribution of β given any particular setting of $\{x_n\}$ will be tightly concentrated on a particular most-probable value of β, with width proportional to $1/\sqrt{N}$. Progress up and down the β-axis will therefore take place by a slow random walk with steps of size $\propto 1/\sqrt{N}$.

So, to the initialization strategy. Can we finesse our slow convergence problem by using initial conditions located 'all over the state space'? Sadly, no. If we distribute the points $\{x_n\}$ widely, what we are actually doing is favouring an initial value of the noise level $1/\beta$ that is *large*. The random walk of the parameter β will thus tend, after the first drawing of β from $P(\beta|x_n)$, always to start off from one end of the β-axis.

Further reading

The Hamiltonian Monte Carlo method is reviewed in Neal (1993b). This excellent tome also reviews a huge range of other Monte Carlo methods, including the related topics of simulated annealing and free energy estimation.

▶ 30.8 Further exercises

Exercise 30.11.[4] An important detail of the Hamiltonian Monte Carlo method is that the simulation of the Hamiltonian dynamics, while it may be inaccurate, must be perfectly reversible, in the sense that if the initial condition $(\mathbf{x}, \mathbf{p}) \rightarrow (\mathbf{x}', \mathbf{p}')$, then the same simulator must take $(\mathbf{x}', -\mathbf{p}') \rightarrow (\mathbf{x}, -\mathbf{p})$, and the inaccurate dynamics must conserve state-space volume. [The leapfrog method in algorithm 30.1 satisfies these rules.]

Explain why these rules must be satisfied and create an example illustrating the problems that arise if they are not.

Exercise 30.12.[4] A multi-state idea for slice sampling. Investigate the following multi-state method for slice sampling. As in Skilling's multi-state
leapfrog method (section 30.4), maintain a set of S state vectors $\{\mathbf{x}^{(s)}\}$.
Update one state vector $\mathbf{x}^{(s)}$ by one-dimensional slice sampling in a direction $\mathbf{y}$ determined by picking two other state vectors $\mathbf{x}^{(v)}$ and $\mathbf{x}^{(w)}$
at random and setting $\mathbf{y} = \mathbf{x}^{(v)} - \mathbf{x}^{(w)}$. Investigate this method on toy
problems such as a highly-correlated multivariate Gaussian distribution.
Bear in mind that if $S - 1$ is smaller than the number of dimensions
N then this method will not be ergodic by itself, so it may need to be
mixed with other methods. Are there classes of problems that are better
solved by this slice sampling method than by the standard methods for
picking $\mathbf{y}$ such as cycling through the coordinate axes or picking $\mathbf{u}$ at
random from a Gaussian distribution?

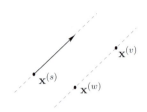

▶ 30.9 Solutions

Solution to exercise 30.3 (p.393). Consider the spherical Gaussian distribution
where all components have mean zero and variance 1. In one dimension, the
nth, if $x_n^{(1)}$ leapfrogs over $x_n^{(2)}$, we obtain the proposed coordinate

$$(x_n^{(1)})' = 2x_n^{(2)} - x_n^{(1)}. \tag{30.16}$$

Assuming that $x_n^{(1)}$ and $x_n^{(2)}$ are Gaussian random variables from $\text{Normal}(0,1)$,
$(x_n^{(1)})'$ is Gaussian from $\text{Normal}(0,\sigma^2)$, where $\sigma^2 = 2^2 + (-1)^2 = 5$. The change
in energy contributed by this one dimension will be

$$\frac{1}{2}\left[(2x_n^{(2)} - x_n^{(1)})^2 - (x_n^{(1)})^2\right] = 2(x_n^{(2)})^2 - 2x_n^{(2)}x_n^{(1)} \tag{30.17}$$

so the typical change in energy is $2\langle(x_n^{(2)})^2\rangle = 2$. This positive change is bad
news. In N dimensions, the typical change in energy when a leapfrog move is
made, at equilibrium, is thus $+2N$. The probability of acceptance of the move
scales as

$$e^{-2N}. \tag{30.18}$$

This implies that Skilling's method, as described, is not effective in very high-
dimensional problems – at least, not once convergence has occurred. Nevertheless it has the impressive advantage that its convergence properties are
independent of the strength of correlations between the variables – a property
that not even the Hamiltonian Monte Carlo and overrelaxation methods offer.

About Chapter 31

Some of the neural network models that we will encounter are related to Ising models, which are idealized magnetic systems. It is not essential to understand the statistical physics of Ising models to understand these neural networks, but I hope you'll find them helpful.

Ising models are also related to several other topics in this book. We will use exact tree-based computation methods like those introduced in Chapter 25 to evaluate properties of interest in Ising models. Ising models offer crude models for binary images. And Ising models relate to two-dimensional constrained channels (c.f. Chapter 17): a two-dimensional bar-code in which a black dot may not be completely surrounded by black dots and a white dot may not be completely surrounded by white dots is similar to an antiferromagnetic Ising model at low temperature. Evaluating the entropy of this Ising model is equivalent to evaluating the capacity of the constrained channel for conveying bits.

If you would like to jog your memory on statistical physics and thermodynamics, you might find Appendix B helpful. I also recommend the book by Reif (1965).

31

Ising Models

An Ising model is an array of spins (e.g., atoms that can take states ± 1) that are magnetically coupled to each other. If one spin is, say, in the $+1$ state then it is energetically favourable for its immediate neighbours to be in the same state, in the case of a ferromagnetic model, and in the opposite state, in the case of an antiferromagnet. In this chapter we discuss two computational techniques for studying Ising models.

Let the state $\mathbf{x}$ of an Ising model with N spins be a vector in which each component x_n takes values -1 or $+1$. If two spins m and n are neighbours we write $(m, n) \in \mathcal{N}$. The coupling between neighbouring spins is J. We define $J_{mn} = J$ if m and n are neighbours and $J_{mn} = 0$ otherwise. The energy of a state $\mathbf{x}$ is

$$E(\mathbf{x}; J, H) = -\left[\frac{1}{2}\sum_{m,n} J_{mn} x_m x_n + \sum_n H x_n\right], \tag{31.1}$$

where H is the applied field. If $J > 0$ then the model is ferromagnetic, and if $J < 0$ it is antiferromagnetic. We've included the factor of $^1\!/_2$ because each pair is counted twice in the first sum, once as (m, n) and once as (n, m). At equilibrium at temperature T, the probability that the state is $\mathbf{x}$ is

$$P(\mathbf{x}|\beta, J, H) = \frac{1}{Z(\beta, J, H)} \exp[-\beta E(\mathbf{x}; J, H)], \tag{31.2}$$

where $\beta = 1/k_{\mathrm{B}}T$, k_{B} is Boltzmann's constant, and

$$Z(\beta, J, H) \equiv \sum_{\mathbf{x}} \exp[-\beta E(\mathbf{x}; J, H)]. \tag{31.3}$$

Relevance of Ising models

Ising models are relevant for three reasons.

Ising models are important first as models of magnetic systems that have a phase transition. The theory of universality in statistical physics shows that all systems with the same dimension (here, two), and the same symmetries, have equivalent critical properties, i.e., the scaling laws shown by their phase transitions are identical. So by studying Ising models we can find out not only about magnetic phase transitions but also about phase transitions in many other systems.

Second, if we generalize the energy function to

$$E(\mathbf{x}; \mathbf{J}, \mathbf{h}) = -\left[\frac{1}{2}\sum_{m,n} J_{mn} x_m x_n + \sum_n h_n x_n\right], \tag{31.4}$$

where the couplings J_{mn} and applied fields h_n are not constant, we obtain a family of models known as 'spin glasses' to physicists, and as 'Hopfield networks' or 'Boltzmann machines' to the neural network community. In some of these models, all spins are declared to be neighbours of each other, in which case physicists call the system an 'infinite range' spin glass, and networkers call it a 'fully connected' network.

Third, the Ising model is also useful as a statistical model in its own right.

In this chapter we will study Ising models using two different computational techniques.

Some remarkable relationships in statistical physics

We would like to get as much information as possible out of our computations. Consider for example the heat capacity of a system, which is defined to be

$$C \equiv \frac{\partial}{\partial T}\bar{E}, \tag{31.5}$$

where

$$\bar{E} = \frac{1}{Z}\sum_{\mathbf{x}}\exp(-\beta E(\mathbf{x}))\,E(\mathbf{x}). \tag{31.6}$$

To work out the heat capacity of a system, we might naively guess that we have to increase the temperature and measure the energy change. Heat capacity, however, is intimately related to energy *fluctuations* at constant temperature. Let's start from the partition function,

$$Z = \sum_{\mathbf{x}}\exp(-\beta E(\mathbf{x})). \tag{31.7}$$

The mean energy is obtained by differentiation with respect to β:

$$\frac{\partial \ln Z}{\partial \beta} = \frac{1}{Z}\sum_{\mathbf{x}} -E(\mathbf{x})\exp(-\beta E(\mathbf{x})) = -\bar{E}. \tag{31.8}$$

A further differentiation spits out the variance of the energy:

$$\frac{\partial^2 \ln Z}{\partial \beta^2} = \frac{1}{Z}\sum_{\mathbf{x}} E(\mathbf{x})^2\exp(-\beta E(\mathbf{x})) - \bar{E}^2 = \langle E^2\rangle - \bar{E}^2 = \text{var}(E). \tag{31.9}$$

But the heat capacity is also the derivative of $\bar{E}$ with respect to temperature:

$$\frac{\partial \bar{E}}{\partial T} = -\frac{\partial}{\partial T}\frac{\partial \ln Z}{\partial \beta} = -\frac{\partial^2 \ln Z}{\partial \beta^2}\frac{\partial \beta}{\partial T} = -\text{var}(E)(-1/k_{\mathrm{B}}T^2). \tag{31.10}$$

So for any system at temperature T,

$$C = \frac{\text{var}(E)}{k_{\mathrm{B}}T^2} = k_{\mathrm{B}}\beta^2\,\text{var}(E). \tag{31.11}$$

Thus if we can observe the variance of the energy of a system at equilibrium, we can estimate its heat capacity.

I find this an almost paradoxical relationship. Consider a system with a finite set of states, and imagine heating it up. At high temperature, all states will be equiprobable, so the mean energy will be essentially constant and the heat capacity will be essentially zero. But on the other hand, with all states being equiprobable, there will certainly be fluctuations in energy. So how can the heat capacity be related to the fluctuations? The answer is in the words 'essentially zero' above. The heat capacity is not quite zero at high temperature, it just tends to zero. And it tends to zero as $\frac{\text{var}(E)}{k_{\mathrm{B}}T^2}$, with the quantity $\mathrm{var}(E)$ tending to a constant at high temperatures. This $1/T^2$ behaviour of the heat capacity of finite systems at high temperatures is thus very general.

The $1/T^2$ factor can be viewed as an accident of history. If only temperature scales had been defined using $\beta = \frac{1}{k_B T}$, then the definition of heat capacity would be

$$C^{(\beta)} \equiv \frac{\partial \bar{E}}{\partial \beta} = \mathrm{var}(E),\qquad\qquad (31.12)$$

and heat capacity and fluctuations would be identical quantities.

▷ Exercise 31.1.[2] [We will call the entropy of a physical system S rather than H, while we are in a statistical physics chapter; we set $k_B = 1$.]

The entropy of a system whose states are $\mathbf{x}$, at temperature $T = 1/\beta$, is

$$S = \sum p(\mathbf{x})[\ln 1/p(\mathbf{x})]\qquad\qquad (31.13)$$

where

$$p(\mathbf{x}) = \frac{1}{Z(\beta)} \exp[-\beta E(\mathbf{x})].\qquad\qquad (31.14)$$

(a) Show that
$$S = \ln Z(\beta) + \beta \bar{E}(\beta)\qquad\qquad (31.15)$$

where $\bar{E}(\beta)$ is the mean energy of the system.

(b) Show that
$$S = -\frac{\partial F}{\partial T},\qquad\qquad (31.16)$$

where the free energy $F = -kT \ln Z$ and $kT = 1/\beta$.

▶ 31.1 Ising models – Monte Carlo simulation

In this section we study two-dimensional planar Ising models using a simple Gibbs sampling method. Starting from some initial state, a spin n is selected at random, and the probability that it should be $+1$ given the state of the other spins and the temperature is computed,

$$P(+1|b_n) = \frac{1}{1 + \exp(-2\beta b_n)},\qquad\qquad (31.17)$$

where $\beta = 1/k_B T$ and b_n is the local field

$$b_n = \sum_{m:(m,n)\in\mathcal{N}} J x_m + H.\qquad\qquad (31.18)$$

[The factor of 2 appears in equation (31.17) because the two spin states are $\{+1, -1\}$ rather than $\{+1, 0\}$.] Spin n is set to $+1$ with that probability, and otherwise to -1; then the next spin to update is selected at random. After sufficiently many iterations, this procedure converges to the equilibrium distribution (31.2). An alternative to the Gibbs sampling formula (31.17) is the Metropolis algorithm, in which we consider the change in energy that results from flipping the chosen spin from its current state x_n,

$$\Delta E = 2x_n b_n,\qquad\qquad (31.19)$$

and adopt this change in configuration with probability

$$P(\text{accept}; \Delta E, \beta) = \begin{cases} 1 & \Delta E \leq 0 \\ \exp(-\beta \Delta E) & \Delta E > 0. \end{cases}\qquad\qquad (31.20)$$

This procedure has roughly double the probability of accepting energetically unfavourable moves, so may be a more efficient sampler – but at very low temperatures the relative merits of Gibbs sampling and the Metropolis algorithm may be subtle.

Rectangular geometry

I first simulated an Ising model with the rectangular geometry shown in figure 31.1, and with periodic boundary conditions. A line between two spins indicates that they are neighbours. I set the external field $H = 0$ and considered the two cases $J = \pm 1$ which are a ferromagnet and antiferromagnet respectively.

I started at a large temperature ($T = 33, \beta = 0.03$) and changed the temperature every I iterations, first decreasing it gradually to $T = 0.1, \beta = 10$, then increasing it gradually back to a large temperature again. This procedure gives a crude check on whether 'equilibrium has been reached' at each temperature; if not, we'd expect to see some hysteresis in the graphs we plot. It also gives an idea of the reproducibility of the results, if we assume that the two runs, with decreasing and increasing temperature, are effectively independent of each other.

At each temperature I recorded the mean energy per spin and the standard deviation of the energy, and the mean square value of the magnetization m,

$$m = \frac{1}{N} \sum_n x_n. \tag{31.21}$$

One tricky decision that has to be made is how soon to start taking these measurements after a new temperature has been established; it is difficult to detect 'equilibrium' – or even to give a clear definition of a system's being 'at equilibrium'! [But in Chapter 32 we will see a solution to this problem.] My crude strategy was to let the number of iterations at each temperature, I, be a few hundred times the number of spins N, and to discard the first $1/3$ of those iterations. With $N = 100$, I found I needed more than 100 000 iterations to reach equilibrium at any given temperature.

Results for small N with $J = 1$.

I simulated an $l \times l$ grid for $l = 4, 5, \ldots, 10, 40, 64$. Let's have a quick think about what results we expect. At low temperatures the system is expected to be in a ground state. The rectangular Ising model with $J = 1$ has two ground states, the all $+1$ state and the all -1 state. The energy per spin of either ground state is -2. At high temperatures, the spins are independent, all states are equally probable, and the energy is expected to fluctuate around a mean of 0 with a standard deviation proportional to $1/\sqrt{N}$.

Let's look at some results. In all figures temperature T is shown with $k_B = 1$. The basic picture emerges with as few as 16 spins (figure 31.3, top): the energy rises monotonically. As we increase the number of spins to 100 (figure 31.3, bottom) some new details emerge. First, as expected, the fluctuations at large temperature decrease as $1/\sqrt{N}$. Second, the fluctuations at intermediate temperature become relatively *bigger*. This is the signature of a 'collective phenomenon', in this case, a phase transition. Only systems with infinite N show true phase transitions, but with $N = 100$ we are getting a hint of the critical fluctuations. Figure 31.5 shows details of the graphs for $N = 100$ and $N = 4096$. Figure 31.2 shows a sequence of typical states from the simulation of $N = 4096$ spins at a sequence of decreasing temperatures.

Figure 31.1. Rectangular Ising model.

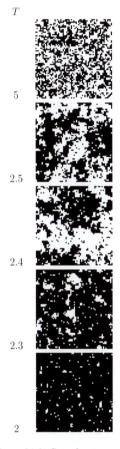

Figure 31.2. Sample states of rectangular Ising models with $J = 1$ at a sequence of temperatures T.

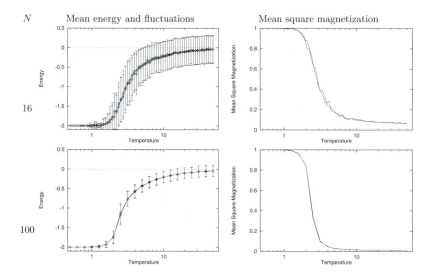

Figure 31.3. Monte Carlo simulations of rectangular Ising models with $J = 1$. Mean energy and fluctuations in energy as a function of temperature (left). Mean square magnetization as a function of temperature (right). In the top row, $N = 16$, and the bottom, $N = 100$. For even larger N, see later figures.

Contrast with Schottky anomaly

A peak in the heat capacity, as a function of temperature, occurs in any system that has a finite number of energy levels; a peak is not in itself evidence of a phase transition. Such peaks were viewed as anomalies in classical thermodynamics, since 'normal' systems with infinite numbers of energy levels (such as a particle in a box) have heat capacities that are either constant or increasing functions of temperature. In contrast, systems with a finite number of levels produced small blips in the heat capacity graph (figure 31.4).

Let us refresh our memory of the simplest such system, a two-level system with states $x = 0$ (energy 0) and $x = 1$ (energy ϵ). The mean energy is

$$E(\beta) = \epsilon \frac{\exp(-\beta\epsilon)}{1 + \exp(-\beta\epsilon)} = \epsilon \frac{1}{1 + \exp(\beta\epsilon)} \tag{31.22}$$

and the derivative with respect to β is

$$dE/d\beta = -\epsilon^2 \frac{\exp(\beta\epsilon)}{[1 + \exp(\beta\epsilon)]^2}. \tag{31.23}$$

So the heat capacity is

$$C = dE/dT = -\frac{dE}{d\beta}\frac{1}{k_{B}T^2} = \frac{\epsilon^2}{k_{B}T^2}\frac{\exp(\beta\epsilon)}{[1 + \exp(\beta\epsilon)]^2} \tag{31.24}$$

and the fluctuations in energy are given by $\mathrm{var}(E) = Ck_{B}T^2 = -dE/d\beta$, which was evaluated in (31.23). The heat capacity and fluctuations are plotted in figure 31.6. The take-home message at this point is that whilst Schottky anomalies do have a peak in the heat capacity, there is *no* peak in their *fluctuations*; the variance of the energy simply increases monotonically with temperature to a value proportional to the number of independent spins. Thus it is a peak in the *fluctuations* that is interesting, rather than a peak in the heat capacity. The Ising model has such a peak in its fluctuations, as can be seen in the second row of figure 31.5.

Rectangular Ising model with $J = -1$

What do we expect to happen in the case $J = -1$? The ground states of an infinite system are the two checkerboard patterns (figure 31.7), and they have

Figure 31.4. Schematic diagram to explain the meaning of a Schottky anomaly. The curve shows the heat capacity of two gases as a function of temperature. The lower curve shows a normal gas whose heat capacity is an increasing function of temperature. The upper curve has a small peak in the heat capacity, which is known as a Schottky anomaly (at least in Cambridge). The peak is produced by the gas having magnetic degrees of freedom with a finite number of accessible states.

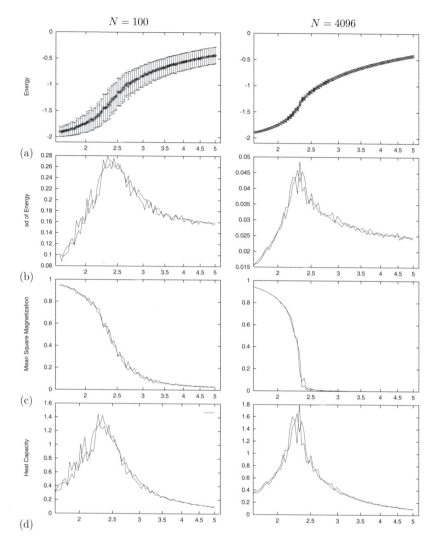

(a)

(b)

(c)

(d)

Figure 31.5. Detail of Monte Carlo simulations of rectangular Ising models with $J = 1$. (a) Mean energy and fluctuations in energy as a function of temperature. (b) Fluctuations in energy (standard deviation). (c) Mean square magnetization. (d) Heat capacity.

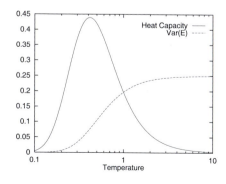

Figure 31.6. Schottky anomaly – Heat capacity and fluctuations in energy as a function of temperature for a two-level system with separation $\epsilon = 1$ and $k_{\mathrm{B}} = 1$.

energy per spin -2, like the ground states of the $J = 1$ model. Can this analogy be pressed further? A moment's reflection will confirm that the two systems are equivalent to each other under a checkerboard symmetry operation. If you take an infinite $J = 1$ system in some state and flip all the spins that lie on the black squares of an infinite checkerboard, and set $J = -1$ (figure 31.8), then the energy is unchanged. (The magnetization changes, of course.) So all thermodynamic properties of the two systems are expected to be identical in the case of zero applied field.

But there is a subtlety lurking here. Have you spotted it? We are simulating finite grids with periodic boundary conditions. If the size of the grid in any direction is *odd*, then the checkerboard operation is no longer a symmetry operation relating $J = +1$ to $J = -1$, because the checkerboard doesn't match up at the boundaries. This means that for systems of odd size, the ground state of a system with $J = -1$ will have degeneracy greater than 2, and the energy of those ground states will not be as low as -2 per spin. So we expect qualitative differences between the cases $J = \pm 1$ in odd sized systems. These differences are expected to be most prominent for small systems. The frustrations are introduced by the boundaries, and the length of the boundary grows as the square root of the system size, so the fractional influence of this boundary-related frustration on the energy and entropy of the system will decrease as $1/\sqrt{N}$. Figure 31.9 compares the energies of the ferromagnetic and antiferromagnetic models with $N = 25$. Here, the difference is striking.

Figure 31.7. The two ground states of a rectangular Ising model with $J = -1$.

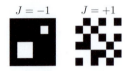

Figure 31.8. Two states of rectangular Ising models with $J = \pm 1$ that have identical energy.

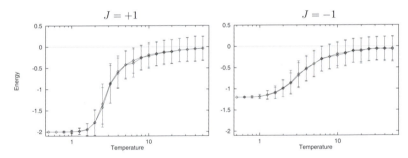

Figure 31.9. Monte Carlo simulations of rectangular Ising models with $J = \pm 1$ and $N = 25$. Mean energy and fluctuations in energy as a function of temperature. (a) $J = 1$. (b) $J = -1$.

Triangular Ising model

We can repeat these computations for a triangular Ising model. Do we expect the triangular Ising model with $J = \pm 1$ to show different physical properties from the rectangular Ising model? Presumably the $J = 1$ model will have broadly similar properties to its rectangular counterpart. But the case $J = -1$ is radically different from what's gone before. Think about it: *there is no unfrustrated ground state*; in any state, there *must* be frustrations – pairs of neighbours who have the same sign as each other. Unlike the case of the rectangular model with odd size, the frustrations are not introduced by the periodic boundary conditions. *Every set of three mutually neighbouring spins must be in a state of frustration,* as shown in figure 31.10. (Solid lines show 'happy' couplings which contribute $-|J|$ to the energy; dashed lines show 'unhappy' couplings which contribute $|J|$.) Thus we certainly expect different behaviour at low temperatures. In fact we might expect this system to have a non-zero entropy at absolute zero. ('Triangular model violates third law of thermodynamics!')

Let's look at some results. Sample states are shown in figure 31.12, and figure 31.11 shows the energy, fluctuations, and heat capacity for $N = 4096$.

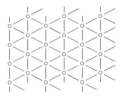

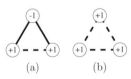

Figure 31.10. In an antiferromagnetic triangular Ising model, any three neighbouring spins are frustrated. Of the eight possible configurations of three spins, six have energy $-|J|$ (a), and two have energy $3|J|$ (b).

Note how different the results for $J = \pm 1$ are. There is no peak at all in the standard deviation of the energy in the case $J = -1$. This indicates that the antiferromagnetic system does not have a phase transition to a state with long-range order.

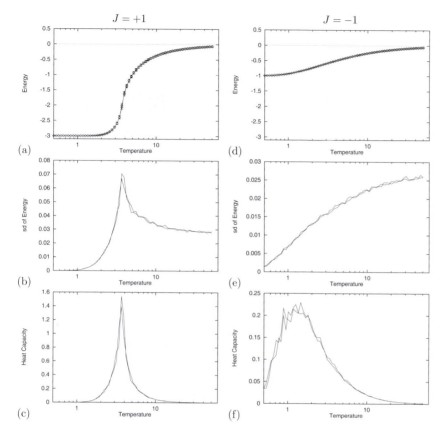

Figure 31.11. Monte Carlo simulations of triangular Ising models with $J = \pm 1$ and $N = 4096$. (a–c) $J = 1$. (d–f) $J = -1$. (a, d) Mean energy and fluctuations in energy as a function of temperature. (b, e) Fluctuations in energy (standard deviation). (c, f) Heat capacity.

▶ ## 31.2 Direct computation of partition function of Ising models

We now examine a completely different approach to Ising models. The *transfer matrix method* is an exact and abstract approach that obtains physical properties of the model from the partition function

$$Z(\beta, \mathbf{J}, \mathbf{b}) \equiv \sum_{\mathbf{x}} \exp[-\beta E(\mathbf{x}; \mathbf{J}, \mathbf{b})], \qquad (31.25)$$

where the summation is over all states $\mathbf{x}$, and the inverse temperature is $\beta = 1/T$. [As usual, Let $k_B = 1$.] The free energy is given by $F = -\frac{1}{\beta} \ln Z$. The number of states is 2^N, so direct computation of the partition function is not possible for large N. To avoid enumerating all global states explicitly, we can use a trick similar to the sum–product algorithm discussed in Chapter 25. We concentrate on models that have the form of a long thin strip of width W with periodic boundary conditions in both directions, and we iterate along the length of our model, working out a set of *partial partition functions* at one location l in terms of partial partition functions at the previous location $l-1$. Each iteration involves a summation over all the states at the boundary. This operation is exponential in the width of the strip, W. The final clever trick

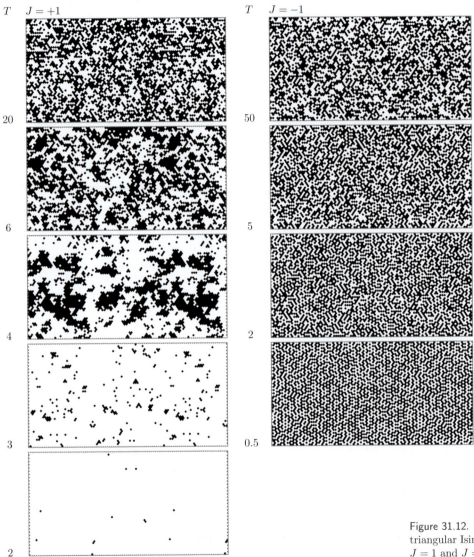

Figure 31.12. Sample states of
triangular Ising models with
$J = 1$ and $J = -1$.

is to note that if the system is translation-invariant along its length then we only need to do *one* iteration in order to find the properties of a system of *any* length.

The computational task becomes the evaluation of an $S \times S$ matrix, where S is the number of microstates that need to be considered at the boundary, and the computation of its eigenvalues. The eigenvalue of largest magnitude gives the partition function for an infinite-length thin strip.

Here is a more detailed explanation. Label the states of the C columns of the thin strip $s_1, s_2, \ldots, s_C$, with each s an integer from 0 to $2^W - 1$. The rth bit of s_c indicates whether the spin in row r, column c is up or down. The partition function is

$$Z = \sum_{\mathbf{x}} \exp(-\beta E(\mathbf{x})) \tag{31.26}$$

$$= \sum_{s_1} \sum_{s_2} \cdots \sum_{s_C} \exp\left(-\beta \sum_{c=1}^{C} \mathcal{E}(s_c, s_{c+1})\right) \tag{31.27}$$

where $\mathcal{E}(s_c, s_{c+1})$ is an appropriately defined energy, and, if we want periodic boundary conditions, s_{C+1} is defined to be s_1. One definition for $\mathcal{E}$ is:

$$\mathcal{E}(s_c, s_{c+1}) = \sum_{\substack{(m,n) \in \mathcal{N}: \\ m \in c, n \in c+1}} J x_m x_n + \frac{1}{4} \sum_{\substack{(m,n) \in \mathcal{N}: \\ m \in c, n \in c}} J x_m x_n + \frac{1}{4} \sum_{\substack{(m,n) \in \mathcal{N}: \\ m \in c+1, n \in c+1}} J x_m x_n. \tag{31.28}$$

This definition of the energy has the nice property that (for the rectangular Ising model) it defines a matrix that is symmetric in its two indices s_c, s_{c+1}. The factors of 1/4 are needed because vertical links are counted four times. Let us define

$$M_{ss'} = \exp\left(-\beta \mathcal{E}(s, s')\right). \tag{31.29}$$

Then continuing from equation (31.27),

$$Z = \sum_{s_1} \sum_{s_2} \cdots \sum_{s_C} \left[\prod_{c=1}^{C} M_{s_c, s_{c+1}}\right] \tag{31.30}$$

$$= \text{Trace}\left[\mathbf{M}^C\right] \tag{31.31}$$

$$= \sum_{a} \mu_a^C, \tag{31.32}$$

where $\{\mu_a\}_{a=1}^{2^W}$ are the eigenvalues of $\mathbf{M}$. As the length of the strip C increases, Z becomes dominated by the largest eigenvalue μ_{max}:

$$Z \to \mu_{\text{max}}^C. \tag{31.33}$$

So the free energy per spin in the limit of an infinite thin strip is given by:

$$f = -kT \ln Z / (WC) = -kTC \ln \mu_{\text{max}} / (WC) = -kT \ln \mu_{\text{max}} / W. \tag{31.34}$$

It's really neat that *all* the thermodynamic properties of a long thin strip can be obtained from just the largest eigenvalue of this matrix $\mathbf{M}$!

Computations

I computed the partition functions of *long thin strip* Ising models with the geometries shown in figure 31.14.

As in the last section, I set the applied field H to zero and considered the two cases $J = \pm 1$ which are a ferromagnet and antiferromagnet respectively. I computed the free energy per spin, $f(\beta, J, H) = F/N$ for widths from $W = 2$ to 8 as a function of β for $H = 0$.

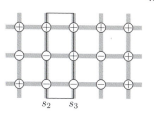

Figure 31.13. Illustration to help explain the definition (31.28). $\mathcal{E}(s_2, s_3)$ counts all the contributions to the energy in the rectangle. The total energy is given by stepping the rectangle along. Each horizontal bond inside the rectangle is counted once; each vertical bond is half-inside the rectangle (and will be half-inside an adjacent rectangle) so half its energy is included in $\mathcal{E}(s_2, s_3)$; the factor of 1/4 appears in the second term because m and n both run over all nodes in column c, so each bond is visited twice.

For the state shown here, $s_2 = (100)_2$, $s_3 = (110)_2$, the horizontal bonds contribute $+J$ to $\mathcal{E}(s_2, s_3)$, and the vertical bonds contribute $-J/2$ on the left and $-J/2$ on the right, assuming periodic boundary conditions between top and bottom. So $\mathcal{E}(s_2, s_3) = 0$.

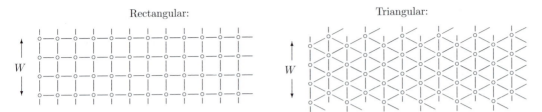

Rectangular: Triangular:

W W

Figure 31.14. Two long thin strip
Ising models. A line between two
spins indicates that they are
neighbours. The strips have width
W and infinite length.

Computational ideas:

Only the largest eigenvalue is needed. There are several ways of getting this
quantity, for example, iterative multiplication of the matrix by an initial vector. Because the matrix is all positive we know that the principal eigenvector
is all positive too (Frobenius–Perron theorem), so a reasonable initial vector is
$(1, 1, \ldots, 1)$. This iterative procedure may be faster than explicit computation
of all eigenvalues. I computed them all anyway, which has the advantage that
we can find the free energy of finite length strips – using equation (31.32) – as
well as infinite ones.

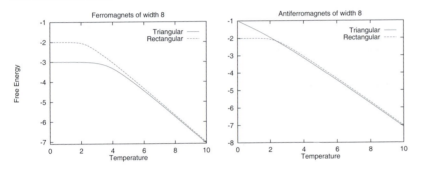

Figure 31.15. Free energy per spin
of long-thin-strip Ising models.
Note the non-zero gradient at
$T = 0$ in the case of the triangular
antiferromagnet.

Comments on graphs:

For large temperatures all Ising models should show the same behaviour: the
free energy is entropy-dominated, and the entropy per spin is $\ln(2)$. The mean
energy per spin goes to zero. The free energy per spin should tend to $-\ln(2)/\beta$.
The free energies are shown in figure 31.15.

One of the interesting properties we can obtain from the free energy is
the degeneracy of the ground state. As the temperature goes to zero, the
Boltzmann distribution becomes concentrated in the ground state. If the
ground state is degenerate (i.e., there are multiple ground states with identical

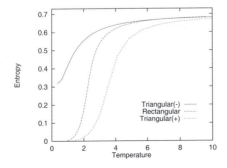

Figure 31.16. Entropies (in nats)
of width 8 Ising systems as a
function of temperature, obtained
by differentiating the free energy
curves in figure 31.15. The
rectangular ferromagnet and
antiferromagnet have identical
thermal properties. For the
triangular systems, the upper
curve $(-)$ denotes the
antiferromagnet and the lower
curve $(+)$ the ferromagnet.

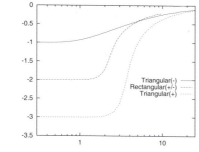

Figure 31.17. Mean energy versus temperature of long thin strip Ising models with width 8. Compare with figure 31.3.

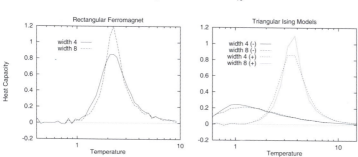

Figure 31.18. Heat capacities of (a) rectangular model; (b) triangular models with different widths, $(+)$ and $(-)$ denoting ferromagnet and antiferromagnet. Compare with figure 31.11.

energy) then the entropy as $T \to 0$ is non-zero. We can find the entropy from the free energy using $S = -\partial F/\partial T$.

The entropy of the triangular antiferromagnet at absolute zero appears to be about 0.3, that is, about half its high temperature value (figure 31.16). The mean energy as a function of temperature is plotted in figure 31.17. It is evaluated using the identity $\langle E \rangle = -\partial \ln Z/\partial \beta$.

Figure 31.18 shows the estimated heat capacity (taking raw derivatives of the mean energy) as a function of temperature for the triangular models with widths 4 and 8. Figure 31.19 shows the fluctuations in energy as a function of temperature. All of these figures should show smooth graphs; the roughness of the curves is due to inaccurate numerics. The nature of any phase transition is not obvious, but the graphs seem compatible with the assertion that the ferromagnet shows, and the antiferromagnet does not show a phase transition.

The pictures of the free energy in figure 31.15 give some insight into how we could predict the transition temperature. We can see how the two phases of the ferromagnetic systems each have simple free energies: a straight sloping line through $F = 0$, $T = 0$ for the high temperature phase, and a horizontal line for the low temperature phase. (The slope of each line shows what the entropy per spin of that phase is.) The phase transition occurs roughly at the intersection of these lines. So we predict the transition temperature to be linearly related to the ground state energy.

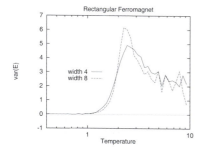

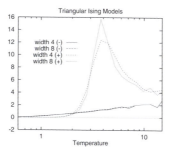

Figure 31.19. Energy variances, per spin, of (a) rectangular model; (b) triangular models with different widths, $(+)$ and $(-)$ denoting ferromagnet and antiferromagnet. Compare with figure 31.11.

Comparison with the Monte Carlo results

The agreement between the results of the two experiments seems very good. The two systems simulated (the long thin strip and the periodic square) are not quite identical. One could a more accurate comparison by finding all eigenvalues for the strip of width W and computing $\sum \lambda^W$ to get the partition function of a $W \times W$ patch.

▶ 31.3 Exercises

▷ Exercise 31.2.[4] What would be the best way to extract the entropy from the Monte Carlo simulations? What would be the best way to obtain the entropy and the heat capacity from the partition function computation?

Exercise 31.3.[3] An Ising model may be generalized to have a coupling J_{mn} between any spins m and n, and the value of J_{mn} could be different for each m and n. In the special case where all the couplings are positive we know that the system has two ground states, the all-up and all-down states. For a more general setting of J_{mn} it is conceivable that there could be *many* ground states.

Imagine that it is required to make a spin system whose local minima are a given list of states $\mathbf{x}_{(1)}, \mathbf{x}_{(2)}, \ldots, \mathbf{x}_{(S)}$. Can you think of a way of setting $\mathbf{J}$ such that the chosen states are low energy states? You are allowed to adjust all the $\{J_{mn}\}$ to whatever values you wish.

32

Exact Monte Carlo Sampling

▶ ## 32.1 The problem with Monte Carlo methods

For high-dimensional problems, the most widely used random sampling methods are Markov chain Monte Carlo methods like the Metropolis method, Gibbs sampling, and slice sampling.

The problem with all these methods is this: yes, a given algorithm can be guaranteed to produce samples from the target density $P(\mathbf{x})$ asymptotically, 'once the chain has converged to the equilibrium distribution'. But if one runs the chain for too short a time T, then the samples will come from some other distribution $P^{(T)}(\mathbf{x})$. For how long must the Markov chain be run before it has 'converged'? As was mentioned in Chapter 29, this question is usually very hard to answer. However, the pioneering work of Propp and Wilson (1996) allows one, for certain chains, to answer this very question; furthermore Propp and Wilson show how to obtain 'exact' samples from the target density.

▶ ## 32.2 Exact sampling concepts

Propp and Wilson's *exact sampling method* (also known as 'perfect simulation' or 'coupling from the past') depends on three ideas.

Coalescence of coupled Markov chains

First, if several Markov chains starting from different initial conditions share a single random-number generator, then their trajectories in state space may *coalesce*; and, having, coalesced, will not separate again. If *all* initial conditions lead to trajectories that coalesce into a single trajectory, then we can be sure that the Markov chain has 'forgotten' its initial condition. Figure 32.1a-i shows twenty-one Markov chains identical to the one described in section 29.4, which samples from $\{0, 1, \ldots, 20\}$ using the Metropolis algorithm (figure 29.12, p.368); each of the chains has a different initial condition but they are all driven by a single random number generator; the chains coalesce after about 80 steps. Figure 32.1(a-ii) shows the same Markov chains with a different random number seed; in this case, coalescence does not occur until 400 steps have elapsed (not shown). Figure 32.1b shows similar Markov chains, each of which has identical proposal density to those in section 29.4 and figure 32.1a; but in figure 32.1b, the proposed move at each step, 'left' or 'right', is obtained in the same way by all the chains at any timestep, independent of the current state. This coupling of the chains changes the statistics of coalescence. Because two neighbouring paths only merge when a rejection occurs, and rejections only occur at the walls (for this particular Markov chain), coa-

413

lescence will occur only when the chains are all in the leftmost state or all in
the rightmost state.

Coupling from the past

How can we use the coalescence property to find an exact sample from the
equilibrium distribution of the chain? The state of the system at the moment
when complete coalescence occurs is not a valid sample from the equilibrium
distribution; for example in figure 32.1b, final coalescence always occurs when
the state is against one of the two walls, because trajectories only merge at
the walls. So sampling forward in time until coalescence occurs is not a valid
method.

The second key idea of exact sampling is that we can obtain exact samples
by sampling *from a time T_0 in the past, up to the present.* If coalescence
has occurred, the present sample is an unbiased sample from the equilibrium
distribution; if not, we restart the simulation from a time T_0 further into
the past, *reusing the same random numbers.* The simulation is repeated at a
sequence of ever more distant times T_0, with a doubling of T_0 from one run to
the next being a convenient choice. When coalescence occurs at a time before
'the present', we can record $x(0)$ as an *exact sample* from the equilibrium
distribution of the Markov chain.

Figure 32.2 shows two exact samples produced in this way. In the leftmost
panel of figure 32.2a, we start twenty-one chains in all possible initial conditions at $T_0 = -50$ and run them forward in time. Coalescence does not occur.
We restart the simulation from all possible initial conditions at $T_0 = -100$, and
reset the random number generator in such a way that the random numbers
generated at each time t (in particular, from $t = -50$ to $t = 0$) will be identical
to what they were in the first run. Notice that the trajectories produced from
$t = -50$ to $t = 0$ by these runs that started from $T_0 = -100$ are identical to a
subset of the trajectories in the first simulation with $T_0 = -50$. Coalescence
still does not occur, so we double T_0 again to $T_0 = -200$. This time, all the
trajectories coalesce and we obtain an exact sample, shown by the arrow. If
we pick an earlier time such as $T_0 = -500$, all the trajectories must still end
in the same point at $t = 0$, since all trajectories must pass through some state
at $t = -200$, and all those states lead to the same final point. So if we ran
the Markov chain for an infinite time in the past, from any initial condition,
it would end in the same state. Figure 32.2b shows an exact sample produced
in the same way with the Markov chains of figure 32.1b.

This method, called *coupling from the past*, is important because it allows
us to obtain exact samples from the equilibrium distribution; but, as described
here, it is of little practical use, since we are obliged to simulate chains starting
in *all* initial states. In the examples shown, there are only twenty-one states,
but in any realistic sampling problem there will be an utterly enormous number
of states – think of the 2^{1000} states of a system of 1000 binary spins, for
example. The whole point of introducing Monte Carlo methods was to try to
avoid having to visit all the states of such a system!

Monotonicity

Having established that we can obtain valid samples by simulating forward
from times in the past, starting in *all* possible states at those times, the third
trick of Propp and Wilson, which makes the exact sampling method useful
in practice, is the idea that, for some Markov chains, it may be possible to
detect coalescence of all trajectories *without simulating all those trajectories.*

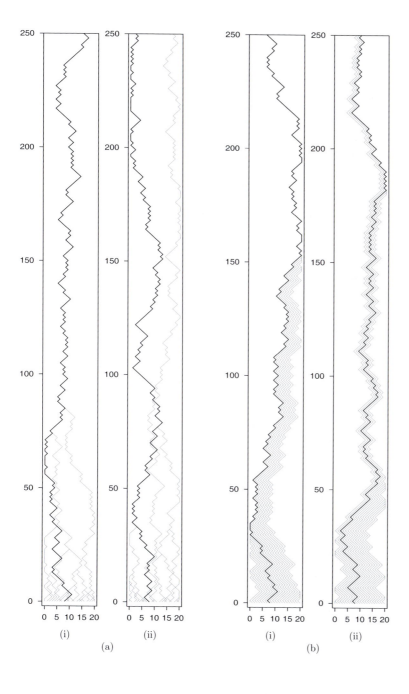

Figure 32.1. Coalescence, the first idea behind the exact sampling method. In the leftmost panel, coalescence occurred within 100 steps. Different coalescence properties are obtained depending on the way each state uses the random numbers it is supplied with. (a) Two runs of a Metropolis simulator in which the random bits that determine the proposed step depend on the current state; a different random number seed was used in each case. (b) In this simulator the random proposal ('left' or 'right') is the same for all states. In each panel, one of the paths, the one starting at location $x = 8$, has been highlighted.

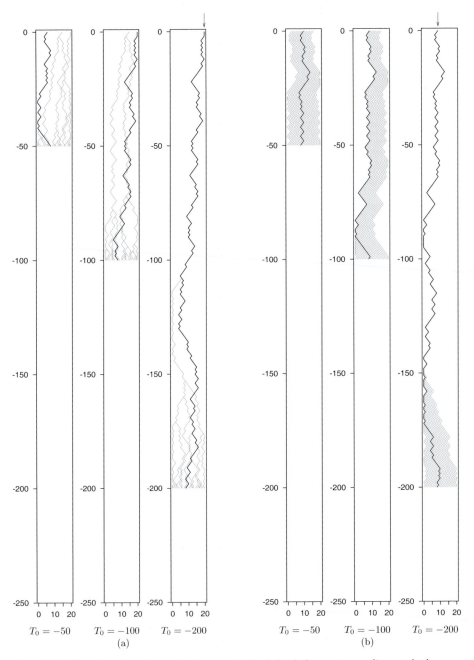

Figure 32.2. 'Coupling from the past', the second idea behind the exact sampling method.

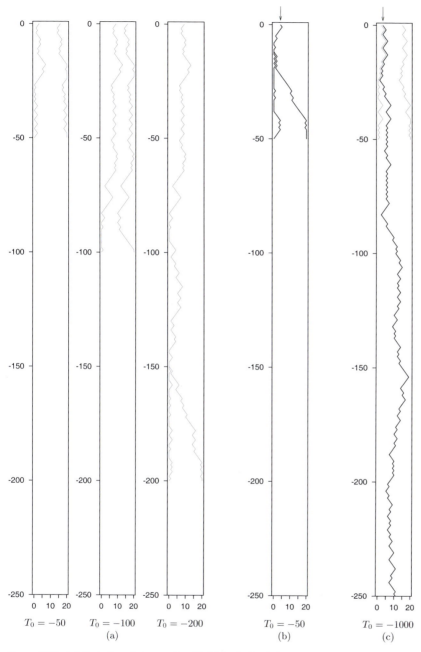

Figure 32.3. (a) Ordering of states, the third idea behind the exact sampling method. The trajectories shown here are the left-most and right-most trajectories of figure 32.2b. In order to establish what the state at time zero is, we only need to run simulations from $T_0 = -50$, $T_0 = -100$, and $T_0 = -200$, after which point coalescence occurs.

(b,c) Two more exact samples from the target density, generated by this method, and different random number seeds. The initial times required were $T_0 = -50$ and $T_0 = -1000$, respectively.

This property holds, for example, in the chain of figure 32.1b, which has the property that *two trajectories never cross*. So if we simply track the two trajectories starting from the leftmost and rightmost states, we will know that coalescence of *all* trajectories has occurred when *those two* trajectories coalesce. Figure 32.3a illustrates this idea by showing only the left-most and right-most trajectories of figure 32.2b. Figure 32.3(b,c) shows two more exact samples from the same equilibrium distribution generated by running the 'coupling from the past' method starting from the two end-states alone. In (b), two runs coalesced starting from $T_0 = -50$; in (c), it was necessary to try times up to $T_0 = -1000$ to achieve coalescence.

▶ **32.3 Exact sampling from interesting distributions**

In the toy problem we studied, the states could be put in a one-dimensional order such that no two trajectories crossed. The states of many interesting state spaces can also be put into a *partial order* and coupled Markov chains can be found that respect this partial order. [An example of a partial order on the four possible states of two spins is this: $(+,+) > (+,-) > (-,-)$; and $(+,+) > (-,+) > (-,-)$; and the states $(+,-)$ and $(-,+)$ are not ordered.] For such systems, we can show that coalescence has occurred merely by verifying that coalescence has occurred for all the histories whose initial states were 'maximal' and 'minimal' states of the state space.

As an example, consider the Gibbs sampling method applied to a ferromagnetic Ising spin system, with the partial ordering of states being defined thus: state **x** is 'greater than or equal to' state **y** if $x_i \geq y_i$ for all spins i. The maximal and minimal states are the the all-up and all-down states. The Markov chains are coupled together as shown in algorithm 32.4. Propp and Wilson (1996) show that exact samples can be generated for this system, although the time to find exact samples is large if the Ising model is below its critical temperature, since the Gibbs sampling method itself is slowly-mixing under these conditions. Propp and Wilson have improved on this method for the Ising model by using a Markov chain called the single-bond heat bath algorithm to sample from a related model called the random cluster model; they show that exact samples from the random cluster model can be obtained rapidly and can be converted into exact samples from the Ising model. Their ground-breaking paper includes an exact sample from a 16-million-spin Ising model at its critical temperature. A sample for a smaller Ising model is shown in figure 32.5.

A generalization of the exact sampling method for 'non-attractive' distributions

The method of Propp and Wilson for the Ising model, sketched above, can only be applied to probability distributions that are, as they call them, 'attractive'. Rather than define this term, let's say what it means, for practical purposes: the method can be applied to spin systems in which all the couplings are positive (e.g., the ferromagnet), and to a few special spin systems with negative couplings (e.g., as we already observed in Chapter 31, the rectangular ferromagnet and antiferromagnet are equivalent); but it cannot be applied to general spin systems in which some couplings are negative, because in such systems the trajectories followed by the all-up and all-down states are not guaranteed to be upper and lower bounds for the set of all trajectories. Fortunately, however, we do not need to be so strict. It is possible to re-express the Propp and Wilson algorithm in a way that generalizes to the case

---

> Compute $a_i := \sum_j J_{ij} x_j$
> Draw u from Uniform$(0, 1)$
> If $u < 1/(1 + e^{-a_i})$
> $x_i := +1$
> Else
> $x_i := -1$

Algorithm 32.4. Gibbs sampling coupling method. The Markov chains are coupled together by having all chains update the same spin i at each time step and having all chains sharing a common sequence of random numbers u.

Figure 32.5. An exact sample from the Ising model at its critical temperature, produced by D.B. Wilson. Such samples can be produced within seconds on an ordinary computer by exact sampling.

of spin systems with negative couplings. The idea the *summary state* version of the exact sampling method is still that we keep track of bounds on the set of all trajectories, and detect when these bounds are equal, so as to find exact samples. But the bounds will not themselves be actual trajectories, and they will not necessarily be *tight* bounds.

Instead of simulating two trajectories, each of which moves in a state space $\{-1, +1\}^N$, we simulate one *trajectory envelope* in an augmented state space $\{-1, +1, ?\}^N$, where the symbol *?* denotes 'either -1 or $+1$'. We call the state of this augmented system the 'summary state'. An example summary state of a six-spin system is ++-?+?. This summary state is shorthand for the set of states

$$++-+++, \; ++-++-, \; ++--++, \; ++--+- \; .$$

The update rule at each step of the Markov chain takes a single spin, enumerates all possible states of the neighbouring spins that are compatible with the current summary state, and, for each of these local scenarios, computes the new value (+ or -) of the spin using Gibbs sampling (coupled to a random number u as in algorithm 32.4). If all these new values agree, then the new value of the updated spin in the summary state is set to the unanimous value (+ or -). Otherwise, the new value of the spin in the summary state is '?'. The initial condition, at time T_0, is given by setting all the spins in the summary state to '?', which corresponds to considering all possible start configurations.

In the case of a spin system with positive couplings, this summary state simulation will be identical to the simulation of the uppermost state and lowermost states, in the style of Propp and Wilson, with coalescence occuring when all the '?' symbols have disappeared. The summary state method can be applied to general spin systems with any couplings. The only shortcoming of this method is that the envelope may describe an unnecessarily large set of states, so there is no guarantee that the summary state algorithm will converge; the time for coalescence to be *detected* may be considerably larger than the actual time taken for the underlying Markov chain to coalesce.

The summary state scheme has been applied to exact sampling in belief networks by Harvey and Neal (2000), and to the triangular antiferromagnetic Ising model by Childs *et al.* (2001).

Further reading

For further reading, impressive pictures of exact samples from other distributions, and generalizations of the exact sampling method, browse the perfectly-random sampling website.[1]

For beautiful exact-sampling demonstrations running live in your web-browser, see Jim Propp's website.[2]

Other uses for coupling

The idea of coupling together Markov chains by having them share a random number generator has other applications beyond exact sampling. Pinto and Neal (2001) have shown that the accuracy of estimates obtained from a Markov chain Monte Carlo simulation (the second problem discussed in section 29.1, p.357), using the estimator

$$\hat{\Phi}_P \equiv \frac{1}{T} \sum_t \phi(\mathbf{x}^{(t)}), \tag{32.1}$$

---

[1] http://www.dbwilson.com/exact/
[2] http://www.math.wisc.edu/∼propp/tiling/www/applets/

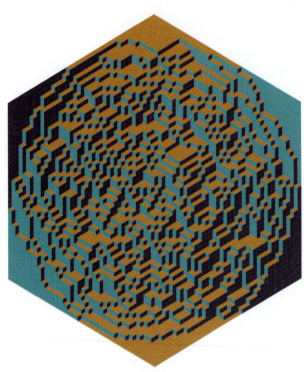

Figure 32.6. A perfectly random
tiling of a hexagon by lozenges,
provided by J.G. Propp and
D.B. Wilson.

can be improved by coupling the chain of interest, which converges to P, to a
second chain, which generates samples from a second, simpler distribution, Q.
The coupling must be set up in such a way that the states of the two chains
are strongly correlated. The idea is that we first estimate the expectations of
a function of interest, ϕ, under P and under Q in the normal way (32.1) and
compare the estimate under Q, $\hat{\Phi}_Q$, with the true value of the expectation
under Q, Φ_Q which we assume can be evaluated exactly. If $\hat{\Phi}_Q$ is an overestimate then it is likely that $\hat{\Phi}_P$ will be an overestimate too. The difference
$(\hat{\Phi}_Q - \Phi_Q)$ can thus be used to correct $\hat{\Phi}_P$.

▶ 32.4 Exercises

▷ Exercise 32.1.[2, p.421] Is there any relationship between the probability distribution of the time taken for all trajectories to coalesce, and the equilibration time of a Markov chain? Prove that there is a relationship, or
find a single chain that can be realized in two different ways that have
different coalescence times.

▷ Exercise 32.2.[2] Imagine that Fred ignores the requirement that the random
bits used at some time t, in every run from increasingly distant times
T_0, must be identical, and makes a coupled-Markov-chain simulator that
uses fresh random numbers every time T_0 is changed. Describe what
happens if Fred applies his method to the Markov chain that is intended
to sample from the uniform distribution over the states 0, 1, and 2, using
the Metropolis method, driven by a random bit source as in figure 32.1b.

Exercise 32.3.[5] Investigate the application of perfect sampling to linear regression in Holmes and Mallick (1998) and try to generalize it.

Exercise 32.4.[3] The concept of coalescence has many applications. Some surnames are more frequent than others, and some die out altogether. Make

a model of this process; how long will it take until everyone has the same surname?

Similarly, variability in any particular portion of the human genome (which forms the basis of forensic DNA fingerprinting) is inherited like a surname. A DNA fingerprint is like a string of surnames. Should the fact that these surnames are subject to coalescences, so that some surnames are by chance more prevalent than others, affect the way in which DNA fingerprint evidence is used in court?

▷ **Exercise 32.5.**[2] How can you use a coin to create a random ranking of 3 people? Construct a solution that uses exact sampling. For example, you could apply exact sampling to a Markov chain in which the coin is repeatedly used alternately to decide whether to switch first and second, then whether to switch second and third.

Exercise 32.6.[5] Finding the partition function Z of a probability distribution is a difficult problem. Many Markov chain Monte Carlo methods produce valid samples from a distribution without ever finding out what Z is.

Is there any probability distribution and Markov chain such that either the time taken to produce a perfect sample or the number of random bits used to create a perfect sample are related to the value of Z? Are there some situations in which the time to coalescence conveys information about Z?

▶ **32.5 Solutions**

Solution to exercise 32.1 (p.420). It is perhaps surprising that there is no direct relationship between the equilibration time and the time to coalescence. A simple example that proves this is the case of the uniform distribution over the integers $\mathcal{A} = \{0, 1, 2, \ldots, 20\}$. A Markov chain that converges to this distribution in exactly one iteration is the chain for which the probability of state s_{t+1} given s_t is the uniform distribution, for all s_t. Such a chain can be coupled to a random number generator in two ways: (a) we could draw a random integer $u \in \mathcal{A}$, and set s_{t+1} equal to u regardless of s_t; or (b) we could draw a random integer $u \in \mathcal{A}$, and set s_{t+1} equal to $(s_t + u) \bmod 21$. Method (b) would produce a cohort of trajectories locked together, similar to the trajectories in figure 32.1, except that no coalescence ever occurs. Thus, while the equilibration times of methods (a) and (b) are both one, the coalescence times are respectively one and infinity.

It seems plausible on the other hand that coalescence time provides some sort of upper bound on equilibration time.

33

Variational Methods

Variational methods are an important technique for the approximation of complicated probability distributions, having applications in statistical physics, data modelling and neural networks.

▶ ## 33.1 Variational free energy minimization

One method for approximating a complex distribution in a physical system is *mean field theory*. Mean field theory is a special case of a general *variational free energy* approach of Feynman and Bogoliubov which we will now study. The key piece of mathematics needed to understand this method is Gibbs' inequality, which we repeat here.

Gibbs' inequality first appeared in equation (1.24); see also exercise 2.26 (p. 37).

The relative entropy between two probability distributions $Q(x)$ and $P(x)$ that are defined over the same alphabet $\mathcal{A}_X$ is

$$D_{\mathrm{KL}}(Q||P) = \sum_x Q(x) \log \frac{Q(x)}{P(x)}. \qquad (33.1)$$

The relative entropy satisfies $D_{\mathrm{KL}}(Q||P) \geq 0$ (Gibbs' inequality) with equality only if $Q = P$. In general $D_{\mathrm{KL}}(Q||P) \neq D_{\mathrm{KL}}(P||Q)$.

In this chapter we will replace the log by ln, and measure the divergence in nats.

Probability distributions in statistical physics

In statistical physics one often encounters probability distributions of the form

$$P(\mathbf{x}|\beta, \mathbf{J}) = \frac{1}{Z(\beta, \mathbf{J})} \exp[-\beta E(\mathbf{x}; \mathbf{J})], \qquad (33.2)$$

where for example the state vector is $\mathbf{x} \in \{-1, +1\}^N$, and $E(\mathbf{x}; \mathbf{J})$ is some energy function such as

$$E(\mathbf{x}; \mathbf{J}) = -\frac{1}{2} \sum_{m,n} J_{mn} x_m x_n - \sum_n h_n x_n. \qquad (33.3)$$

The partition function (normalizing constant) is

$$Z(\beta, \mathbf{J}) \equiv \sum_{\mathbf{x}} \exp[-\beta E(\mathbf{x}; \mathbf{J})]. \qquad (33.4)$$

The probability distribution of equation (33.2) is complex. Not unbearably complex – we can, after all, evaluate $E(\mathbf{x}; \mathbf{J})$ for any particular $\mathbf{x}$ in a time

422

polynomial in the number of spins. But evaluating the normalizing constant $Z(\beta, \mathbf{J})$ is difficult, as we saw in Chapter 29, and describing the properties of the probability distribution is also hard. Knowing the value of $E(\mathbf{x}; \mathbf{J})$ at a few arbitrary points $\mathbf{x}$, for example, gives no useful information about what the average properties of the system are.

An evaluation of $Z(\beta, \mathbf{J})$ would be particularly desirable because from Z we can derive all the thermodynamic properties of the system.

Variational free energy minimization is a method for *approximating* the complex distribution $P(\mathbf{x})$ by a simpler ensemble $Q(\mathbf{x}; \boldsymbol{\theta})$ that is parameterized by adjustable parameters $\boldsymbol{\theta}$. We adjust these parameters so as to get Q to best approximate P, in some sense. A by-product of this approximation is a lower bound on $Z(\beta, \mathbf{J})$.

The variational free energy

The objective function chosen to measure the quality of the approximation is the *variational free energy*

$$\beta \tilde{F}(\boldsymbol{\theta}) = \sum_{\mathbf{x}} Q(\mathbf{x}; \boldsymbol{\theta}) \ln \frac{Q(\mathbf{x}; \boldsymbol{\theta})}{\exp[-\beta E(\mathbf{x}; \mathbf{J})]}. \tag{33.5}$$

This expression can be manipulated into a couple of interesting forms: first,

$$\beta \tilde{F}(\boldsymbol{\theta}) = \beta \sum_{\mathbf{x}} Q(\mathbf{x}; \boldsymbol{\theta}) E(\mathbf{x}; \mathbf{J}) - \sum_{\mathbf{x}} Q(\mathbf{x}; \boldsymbol{\theta}) \ln \frac{1}{Q(\mathbf{x}; \boldsymbol{\theta})} \tag{33.6}$$

$$\equiv \beta \langle E(\mathbf{x}; \mathbf{J}) \rangle_Q - S_Q, \tag{33.7}$$

where $\langle E(\mathbf{x}; \mathbf{J}) \rangle_Q$ is the average of the energy function under the distribution $Q(\mathbf{x}; \boldsymbol{\theta})$, and S_Q is the entropy of the distribution $Q(\mathbf{x}; \boldsymbol{\theta})$ (we set k_{B} to one in the definition of S so that it is identical to the definition of the entropy H in Part I).

Second, we can use the definition of $P(\mathbf{x}|\beta, \mathbf{J})$ to write:

$$\beta \tilde{F}(\boldsymbol{\theta}) = \sum_{\mathbf{x}} Q(\mathbf{x}; \boldsymbol{\theta}) \ln \frac{Q(\mathbf{x}; \boldsymbol{\theta})}{P(\mathbf{x}|\beta, \mathbf{J})} - \ln Z(\beta, \mathbf{J}) \tag{33.8}$$

$$= D_{\mathrm{KL}}(Q||P) + \beta F, \tag{33.9}$$

where F is the true free energy, defined by

$$\beta F \equiv -\ln Z(\beta, \mathbf{J}), \tag{33.10}$$

and $D_{\mathrm{KL}}(Q||P)$ is the relative entropy between the approximating distribution $Q(\mathbf{x}; \boldsymbol{\theta})$ and the true distribution $P(\mathbf{x}|\beta, \mathbf{J})$. Thus by Gibbs' inequality, the variational free energy $\tilde{F}(\boldsymbol{\theta})$ is bounded below by F and only attains this value for $Q(\mathbf{x}; \boldsymbol{\theta}) = P(\mathbf{x}|\beta, \mathbf{J})$.

Our strategy is thus to vary $\boldsymbol{\theta}$ in such a way that $\beta \tilde{F}(\boldsymbol{\theta})$ is minimized. The approximating distribution then gives a simplified approximation to the true distribution that may be useful, and the value of $\beta \tilde{F}(\boldsymbol{\theta})$ will be an upper bound for βF. Equivalently, $\tilde{Z} \equiv e^{-\beta \tilde{F}(\boldsymbol{\theta})}$ is a lower bound for Z.

Can $\beta \tilde{F}$ be evaluated?

We have already agreed that the evaluation of various interesting sums over $\mathbf{x}$ is intractable. For example, the partition function

$$Z = \sum_{\mathbf{x}} \exp(-\beta E(\mathbf{x}; \mathbf{J})), \tag{33.11}$$

the energy

$$\langle E \rangle_P = \frac{1}{Z} \sum_{\mathbf{x}} E(\mathbf{x}; \mathbf{J}) \exp(-\beta E(\mathbf{x}; \mathbf{J})), \qquad (33.12)$$

and the entropy

$$S \equiv \sum_{\mathbf{x}} P(\mathbf{x}|\beta, \mathbf{J}) \ln \frac{1}{P(\mathbf{x}|\beta, \mathbf{J})} \qquad (33.13)$$

are all presumed to be impossible to evaluate. So why should we suppose that this objective function $\beta \tilde{F}(\boldsymbol{\theta})$, which is also defined in terms of a sum over all $\mathbf{x}$ (33.5), should be a convenient quantity to deal with? Well, for a range of interesting energy functions, and for sufficiently simple approximating distributions, the variational free energy *can* be efficiently evaluated.

▶ 33.2 Variational free energy minimization for spin systems

An example of a tractable variational free energy is given by the spin system whose energy function was given in equation (33.3), which we can approximate with a *separable* approximating distribution,

$$Q(\mathbf{x}; \mathbf{a}) = \frac{1}{Z_Q} \exp \left(\sum_n a_n x_n \right). \qquad (33.14)$$

The variational parameters $\boldsymbol{\theta}$ of the variational free energy (33.5) are the components of the vector $\mathbf{a}$. To evaluate the variational free energy we need the entropy of this distribution,

$$S_Q = \sum_{\mathbf{x}} Q(\mathbf{x}; \mathbf{a}) \ln \frac{1}{Q(\mathbf{x}; \mathbf{a})} \qquad (33.15)$$

and the mean of the energy,

$$\langle E(\mathbf{x}; \mathbf{J}) \rangle_Q = \sum_{\mathbf{x}} Q(\mathbf{x}; \mathbf{a}) E(\mathbf{x}; \mathbf{J}). \qquad (33.16)$$

The entropy of the separable approximating distribution is simply the sum of the entropies of the individual spins (exercise 4.2, p.68),

$$S_Q = \sum_n H_2^{(e)}(q_n), \qquad (33.17)$$

where q_n is the probability that spin n is $+1$,

$$q_n = \frac{e^{a_n}}{e^{a_n} + e^{-a_n}} = \frac{1}{1 + \exp(-2a_n)}, \qquad (33.18)$$

and

$$H_2^{(e)}(q) = q \ln \frac{1}{q} + (1 - q) \ln \frac{1}{(1 - q)}. \qquad (33.19)$$

The mean energy under Q is easy to obtain because $\sum_{m,n} J_{mn} x_m x_n$ is a sum of terms each involving the product of two *independent* random variables. (There are no self-couplings, so $J_{mn} = 0$ when $m = n$.) If we define the mean value of x_n to be $\bar{x}_n$, which is given by

$$\bar{x}_n = \frac{e^{a_n} - e^{-a_n}}{e^{a_n} + e^{-a_n}} = \tanh(a_n) = 2q_n - 1, \qquad (33.20)$$

we obtain

$$\langle E(\mathbf{x}; \mathbf{J})\rangle_Q = \sum_{\mathbf{x}} Q(\mathbf{x}; \mathbf{a}) \left[-\frac{1}{2} \sum_{m,n} J_{mn} x_m x_n - \sum_n h_n x_n \right] \quad (33.21)$$

$$= -\frac{1}{2} \sum_{m,n} J_{mn} \bar{x}_m \bar{x}_n - \sum_n h_n \bar{x}_n. \quad (33.22)$$

So the variational free energy is given by

$$\beta \tilde{F}(\mathbf{a}) = \beta \langle E(\mathbf{x}; \mathbf{J})\rangle_Q - S_Q = \beta \left(-\frac{1}{2} \sum_{m,n} J_{mn} \bar{x}_m \bar{x}_n - \sum_n h_n \bar{x}_n \right) - \sum_n H_2^{(e)}(q_n). \quad (33.23)$$

We now consider minimizing this function with respect to the variational parameters $\mathbf{a}$. If $q = 1/(1 + e^{-2a})$, the derivative of the entropy is

$$\frac{\partial}{\partial q} H_2^e(q) = \ln \frac{1-q}{q} = -2a. \quad (33.24)$$

So we obtain

$$\frac{\partial}{\partial a_m} \beta \tilde{F}(\mathbf{a}) = \beta \left[-\sum_n J_{mn} \bar{x}_n - h_m \right] \left(2 \frac{\partial q_m}{\partial a_m} \right) - \ln \left(\frac{1-q_m}{q_m} \right) \left(\frac{\partial q_m}{\partial a_m} \right)$$

$$= 2 \left(\frac{\partial q_m}{\partial a_m} \right) \left[-\beta \left(\sum_n J_{mn} \bar{x}_n + h_m \right) + a_m \right]. \quad (33.25)$$

This derivative is equal to zero when

$$a_m = \beta \left(\sum_n J_{mn} \bar{x}_n + h_m \right). \quad (33.26)$$

So $\tilde{F}(\mathbf{a})$ is extremized at any point that satisfies equation (33.26) and

$$\bar{x}_n = \tanh(a_n). \quad (33.27)$$

The variational free energy $\tilde{F}(\mathbf{a})$ may be a multimodal function, in which case each stationary point (maximum, minimum or saddle) will satisfy equations (33.26) and (33.27). One way of using these equations, in the case of a system with an arbitrary coupling matrix $\mathbf{J}$, is to update each parameter a_m and the corresponding value of $\bar{x}_m$ using equation (33.26), one at a time. This *asynchronous updating of the parameters* is guaranteed to decrease $\beta \tilde{F}(\mathbf{a})$.

Equations (33.26) and (33.27) may be recognized as the mean field equations for a spin system. The variational parameter a_n may be thought of as the strength of a fictitious field applied to an isolated spin n. Equation (33.27) describes the mean response of spin n, and equation (33.26) describes how the field a_m is set in response to the mean state of all the other spins.

The variational free energy derivation is a helpful viewpoint for mean field theory for two reasons.

1. This approach associates an objective function $\beta \tilde{F}$ with the mean field equations; such an objective function is useful because it can help identify alternative dynamical systems that minimize the same function.

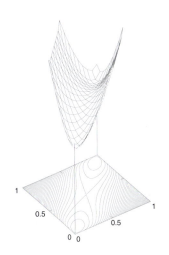

Figure 33.1. The variational free energy of the two-spin system whose energy is $E(\mathbf{x}) = -x_1 x_2$, as a function of the two variational parameters q_1 and q_2. The inverse-temperature is $\beta = 1.44$. The function plotted is

$$\beta \tilde{F} = -\beta \bar{x}_1 \bar{x}_2 - H_2^{(e)}(q_1) - H_2^{(e)}(q_2),$$

where $\bar{x}_n = 2q_n - 1$. Notice that for fixed q_2 the function is convex $\smile$ with respect to q_1, and for fixed q_1 it is convex $\smile$ with respect to q_2.

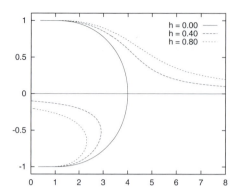

Figure 33.2. Solutions of the variational free energy extremization problem for the Ising model. Horizontal axis: temperature $T = 1/\beta$. Vertical axis: magnetization $\bar{x}$. The critical temperature found by mean field theory is $T_c^{\mathrm{mft}} = 4$.

2. The theory is readily generalized to other approximating distributions. We can imagine introducing a more complex approximation $Q(\mathbf{x}; \boldsymbol{\theta})$ that might for example capture correlations among the spins instead of modelling the spins as independent. One could then evaluate the variational free energy and optimize the parameters $\boldsymbol{\theta}$ of this more complex approximation. The more degrees of freedom the approximating distribution has, the tighter the bound on the free energy becomes. However, if the complexity of an approximation is increased, the evaluation of either the mean energy or the entropy typically becomes more challenging.

▶ 33.3 Example: mean field theory for the ferromagnetic Ising model

In the simple Ising model studied in Chapter 31, every coupling J_{mn} is equal to J if m and n are neighbours and zero otherwise. There is an applied field $h_n = h$ that is the same for all spins. A very simple approximating distribution is one with just a single variational parameter a, which defines a separable distribution

$$Q(\mathbf{x}; a) = \frac{1}{Z_Q} \exp\left(\sum_n a x_n\right) \tag{33.28}$$

in which all spins are independent and have the same probability

$$q_n = \frac{1}{1 + \exp(-2a)} \tag{33.29}$$

of being up. The mean magnetization is

$$\bar{x} = \tanh(a) \tag{33.30}$$

and the equation (33.26) which defines the minimum of the variational free energy becomes

$$a = \beta \left(C J \bar{x} + h\right), \tag{33.31}$$

where C is the number of couplings that a spin is involved in, $C = 4$ in the case of a rectangular two-dimensional Ising model. We can solve equations (33.30) and (33.31) for $\bar{x}$ numerically – in fact, it is easiest to vary $\bar{x}$ and solve for β – and obtain graphs of the free energy minima and maxima as a function of temperature as shown in figure 33.2. The solid line shows $\bar{x}$ versus $T = 1/\beta$ for the case $C = 4, J = 1$.

When $h = 0$, there is a pitchfork bifurcation at a critical temperature T_c^{mft}. [A pitchfork bifurcation is a transition like the one shown by the solid lines in figure 33.2, from a system with one minimum as a function of a (on the right) to a system (on the left) with two minima and one maximum; the maximum is the middle one of the three lines. The solid lines look like a pitchfork.] Above this temperature, there is only one minimum in the variational free energy, at $a = 0$ and $\bar{x} = 0$; this minimum corresponds to an approximating distribution that is uniform over all states. Below the critical temperature, there are two minima corresponding to approximating distributions that are symmetry-broken, with all spins more likely to be up, or all spins more likely to be down. The state $\bar{x} = 0$ persists as a stationary point of the variational free energy, but now it is a local *maximum* of the variational free energy.

When $h > 0$, there is a global variational free energy minimum at any temperature for a positive value of $\bar{x}$, shown by the upper dotted curves in figure 33.2. As long as $h < JC$, there is also a second local minimum in the free energy, if the temperature is sufficiently small. This second minimum corresponds to a self-preserving state of magnetization in the opposite direction to the applied field. The temperature at which the second minimum appears is smaller than T_c^{mft}, and when it appears, it is accompanied by a saddle point located between the two minima. A name given to this type of bifurcation is a saddle-node bifurcation.

The variational free energy per spin is given by

$$\beta \tilde{F} = \beta \left(-\frac{C}{2} J \bar{x}^2 - h \bar{x} \right) - H_2^{(e)} \left(\frac{\bar{x} + 1}{2} \right). \tag{33.32}$$

Exercise 33.1.[2] Sketch the variational free energy as a function of its one parameter $\bar{x}$ for a variety of values of the temperature T and the applied field h.

Figure 33.2 reproduces the key properties of the real Ising system – that, for $h = 0$, there is a critical temperature below which the system has long-range order, and that it can adopt one of two macroscopic states. However, by probing a little more we can reveal some inadequacies of the variational approximation. To start with, the critical temperature T_c^{mft} is 4, which is nearly a factor of 2 greater than the true critical temperature $T_c = 2.27$. Also, the variational model has equivalent properties in any number of dimensions, including $d = 1$, where the true system does not have a phase transition. So the bifurcation at T_c^{mft} should not be described as a phase transition.

For the case $h = 0$ we can follow the trajectory of the global minimum as a function of β and find the entropy, heat capacity and fluctuations of the approximating distribution and compare them with those of a real 8×8 fragment using the matrix method of Chapter 31. As shown in figure 33.3, one of the biggest differences is in the fluctuations in energy. The real system has large fluctuations near the critical temperature, whereas the approximating distribution has no correlations among its spins and thus has an energy-variance which scales simply linearly with the number of spins.

▶ **33.4 Variational methods in inference and data modelling**

In statistical data modelling we are interested in the posterior probability distribution of a parameter vector $\mathbf{w}$ given data D and model assumptions $\mathcal{H}$, $P(\mathbf{w} \mid D, \mathcal{H})$.

$$P(\mathbf{w} \mid D, \mathcal{H}) = \frac{P(D \mid \mathbf{w}, \mathcal{H}) P(\mathbf{w} \mid \mathcal{H})}{P(D \mid \mathcal{H})}. \tag{33.33}$$

In traditional approaches to model fitting, a single parameter vector $\mathbf{w}$ is optimized to find the mode of this distribution. What is really of interest is

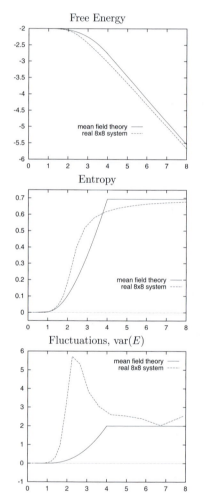

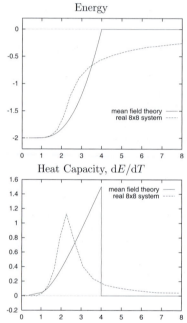

Figure 33.3. Comparison of
approximating distribution's
properties with those of a real
8×8 fragment. Notice that the
variational free energy of the
approximating distribution is
indeed an upper bound on the
free energy of the real system. All
quantities are shown 'per spin'.

the whole distribution. We may also be interested in its normalizing constant $P(D \mid \mathcal{H})$ if we wish to do model comparison. The probability distribution $P(\mathbf{w} \mid D, \mathcal{H})$ is often a complex distribution. In a variational approach to inference, we introduce an approximating probability distribution over the parameters, $Q(\mathbf{w}; \boldsymbol{\theta})$, and optimize this distribution (by varying its own parameters $\boldsymbol{\theta}$) so that it approximates the posterior distribution of the parameters $P(\mathbf{w} \mid D, \mathcal{H})$ well.

One objective function we may choose to measure the quality of the approximation is the variational free energy

$$\tilde{F}(\boldsymbol{\theta}) = \int d^k\mathbf{w}\, Q(\mathbf{w}; \boldsymbol{\theta}) \ln \frac{Q(\mathbf{w}; \boldsymbol{\theta})}{P(D \mid \mathbf{w}, \mathcal{H})P(\mathbf{w} \mid \mathcal{H})}. \tag{33.34}$$

The denominator $P(D \mid \mathbf{w}, \mathcal{H})P(\mathbf{w} \mid \mathcal{H})$ is, within a multiplicative constant, equal to the posterior probability $P(\mathbf{w} \mid D, \mathcal{H}) = P(D \mid \mathbf{w}, \mathcal{H})P(\mathbf{w} \mid \mathcal{H})/P(D \mid \mathcal{H})$. So the variational free energy $\tilde{F}(\boldsymbol{\theta})$ can be viewed as the sum of $-\ln P(D \mid \mathcal{H})$ and the relative entropy between $Q(\mathbf{w}; \boldsymbol{\theta})$ and $P(\mathbf{w} \mid D, \mathcal{H})$. $\tilde{F}(\boldsymbol{\theta})$ is bounded below by $-\ln P(D \mid \mathcal{H})$ and only attains this value for $Q(\mathbf{w}; \boldsymbol{\theta}) = P(\mathbf{w} \mid D, \mathcal{H})$. For certain models and certain approximating distributions, this free energy, and its derivatives with respect to the approximating distribution's parameters, can be evaluated.

The approximation of posterior probability distributions using variational free energy minimization provides a useful approach to approximating Bayesian inference in a number of fields ranging from neural networks to the decoding of error-correcting codes (Hinton and van Camp, 1993; Hinton and Zemel, 1994; Dayan *et al.*, 1995; Neal and Hinton, 1998; MacKay, 1995a). The method is sometimes called *ensemble learning* to contrast it with traditional learning processes in which a single parameter vector is optimized. Another name for it is *variational Bayes*. Let us examine how ensemble learning works in the simple case of a Gaussian distribution.

▶ 33.5 The case of an unknown Gaussian: approximating the posterior distribution of μ and σ

We will fit an approximating ensemble $Q(\mu, \sigma)$ to the posterior distribution that we studied in Chapter 24,

$$P(\mu, \sigma \mid \{x_n\}_{n=1}^N) = \frac{P(\{x_n\}_{n=1}^N \mid \mu, \sigma)P(\mu, \sigma)}{P(\{x_n\}_{n=1}^N)} \tag{33.35}$$

$$= \frac{\frac{1}{(2\pi\sigma^2)^{N/2}} \exp\left(-\frac{N(\mu - \bar{x})^2 + S}{2\sigma^2}\right) \frac{1}{\sigma_\mu} \frac{1}{\sigma}}{P(\{x_n\}_{n=1}^N)}. \tag{33.36}$$

We make the single assumption that the approximating ensemble is separable in the form $Q(\mu, \sigma) = Q_\mu(\mu)Q_\sigma(\sigma)$. No restrictions on the functional form of $Q_\mu(\mu)$ and $Q_\sigma(\sigma)$ are made.

We write down a variational free energy,

$$\tilde{F}(Q) = \int d\mu\, d\sigma\, Q_\mu(\mu)Q_\sigma(\sigma) \ln \frac{Q_\mu(\mu)Q_\sigma(\sigma)}{P(D \mid \mu, \sigma)P(\mu, \sigma)}. \tag{33.37}$$

We can find the optimal separable distribution Q by considering separately the optimization of $\tilde{F}$ over $Q_\mu(\mu)$ for fixed $Q_\sigma(\sigma)$, and then the optimization of $Q_\sigma(\sigma)$ for fixed $Q_\mu(\mu)$.

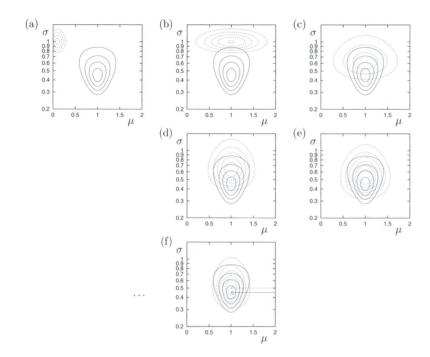

Figure 33.4. Optimization of an approximating distribution. The posterior distribution $P(\mu, \sigma \mid \{x_n\})$, which is the same as that in figure 24.1, is shown by solid contours. (a) Initial condition. The approximating distribution $Q(\mu, \sigma)$ (dotted contours) is an arbitrary separable distribution. (b) Q_μ has been updated, using equation (33.41). (c) Q_σ has been updated, using equation (33.44). (d) Q_μ updated again. (e) Q_σ updated again. (f) Converged approximation (after 15 iterations). The arrows point to the peaks of the two distributions, which are at $\sigma_N = 0.45$ (for P) and $\sigma_{N-1} = 0.5$ (for Q).

Optimization of $Q_\mu(\mu)$

As a functional of $Q_\mu(\mu)$, $\tilde{F}$ is:

$$\tilde{F} = -\int d\mu \, Q_\mu(\mu) \left[\int d\sigma \, Q_\sigma(\sigma) \ln P(D \mid \mu, \sigma) + \ln[P(\mu)/Q_\mu(\mu)] \right] + \kappa \quad (33.38)$$

$$= \int d\mu \, Q_\mu(\mu) \left[\int d\sigma \, Q_\sigma(\sigma) N \beta \frac{1}{2}(\mu - \bar{x})^2 + \ln Q_\mu(\mu) \right] + \kappa', \quad (33.39)$$

where $\beta \equiv 1/\sigma^2$ and κ denote constants that do not depend on $Q_\mu(\mu)$. The dependence on Q_σ thus collapses down to a simple dependence on the mean

$$\bar{\beta} \equiv \int d\sigma \, Q_\sigma(\sigma) 1/\sigma^2. \quad (33.40)$$

Now we can recognize the function $-N\bar{\beta}\frac{1}{2}(\mu - \bar{x})^2$ as the logarithm of a Gaussian identical to the posterior distribution for a particular value of $\beta = \bar{\beta}$. Since a relative entropy $\int Q \ln(Q/P)$ is minimized by setting $Q = P$, we can immediately write down the distribution $Q_\mu^{\mathrm{opt}}(\mu)$ that minimizes $\tilde{F}$ for fixed Q_σ:

$$Q_\mu^{\mathrm{opt}}(\mu) = P(\mu \mid D, \bar{\beta}, \mathcal{H}) = \mathrm{Normal}(\mu; \bar{x}, \sigma_{\mu|D}^2). \quad (33.41)$$

where $\sigma_{\mu|D}^2 = 1/(N\bar{\beta})$.

Optimization of $Q_\sigma(\sigma)$

We represent $Q_\sigma(\sigma)$ using the density over β, $Q_\sigma(\beta) \equiv Q_\sigma(\sigma) |d\sigma/d\beta| \propto 1/\beta$. As a functional of $Q_\sigma(\beta)$, $\tilde{F}$ is (neglecting additive constants):

$$\tilde{F} = -\int d\beta \, Q_\sigma(\beta) \left[\int d\mu \, Q_\mu(\mu) \ln P(D \mid \mu, \sigma) + \ln[P(\beta)/Q_\sigma(\beta)] \right] (33.42)$$

$$= \int d\beta \, Q_\sigma(\beta) \left[(N\sigma_{\mu|D}^2 + S)\beta/2 - \left(\tfrac{N}{2} - 1\right) \ln \beta + \ln Q_\sigma(\beta) \right] \quad (33.43)$$

where the integral over μ is performed assuming $Q_\mu(\mu) = Q_\mu^{\text{opt}}(\mu)$. Here, the β-dependent expression in square brackets can be recognized as the logarithm of a gamma distribution over β – see equation (23.15) – giving as the distribution that minimizes $\tilde{F}$ for fixed Q_μ:

$$Q_\sigma^{\text{opt}}(\beta) = \Gamma(\beta; b', c'), \qquad (33.44)$$

with

$$\frac{1}{b'} = \frac{1}{2}(N\sigma_{\mu|D}^2 + S) \quad \text{and} \quad c' = \frac{N}{2}. \qquad (33.45)$$

In figure 33.4, these two update rules (33.41, 33.44) are applied alternately, starting from an arbitrary initial condition. The algorithm converges to the optimal approximating ensemble in a few iterations.

Direct solution for the joint optimum $Q_\mu(\mu)Q_\sigma(\sigma)$

In this problem, we do not need to resort to iterative computation to find the optimal approximating ensemble. Equations (33.41) and (33.44) define the optimum implicitly. We must simultaneously have $\sigma_{\mu|D}^2 = 1/(N\bar{\beta})$, and $\bar{\beta} = b'c'$. The solution is:

$$1/\bar{\beta} = S/(N-1). \qquad (33.46)$$

This is similar to the true posterior distribution of σ, which is a gamma distribution with $c' = \frac{N-1}{2}$ and $1/b' = S/2$ (see equation 24.13). This true posterior also has a mean value of β satisfying $1/\bar{\beta} = S/(N-1)$; the only difference is that the approximating distribution's parameter c' is too large by $1/2$.

> The approximations given by variational free energy minimization always tend to be more compact than the true distribution.

In conclusion, ensemble learning gives an approximation to the posterior that agrees nicely with the conventional estimators. The approximate posterior distribution over β is a gamma distribution with mean $\bar{\beta}$ corresponding to a variance of $\sigma^2 = S/(N-1) = \sigma_{N-1}^2$. And the approximate posterior distribution over μ is a Gaussian with mean $\bar{x}$ and standard deviation $\sigma_{N-1}/\sqrt{N}$.

The variational free energy minimization approach has the nice property that it is parameterization-independent; it avoids the problem of basis-dependence from which MAP methods and Laplace's method suffer.

A convenient software package for automatic implementation of variational inference in graphical models is VIBES (Bishop and Winn, 2000; Bishop *et al.*, 2002; Bishop and Winn, 2003). It plays the same role for variational inference as BUGS plays for Monte Carlo inference.

▶ 33.6 Interlude

One of my students asked:

> How do you ever come up with a useful approximating distribution, given that the true distribution is so complex you can't compute it directly?

Let's answer this question in the context of Bayesian data modelling. Let the 'true' distribution of interest be the posterior probability distribution over a set of parameters $\mathbf{x}$, $P(\mathbf{x}\,|\,D)$. A standard data modelling practice is to find a single, 'best-fit' setting of the parameters, $\mathbf{x}^*$, for example, by finding the maximum of the likelihood function $P(D \mid \mathbf{x})$, or of the posterior distribution. One interpretation of this standard practice is that the full description of our knowledge about $\mathbf{x}$, $P(\mathbf{x} \mid D)$, is being approximated by a delta-function, a probability distribution concentrated on $\mathbf{x}^*$. From this perspective, *any* approximating distribution $Q(\mathbf{x}; \boldsymbol{\theta})$, no matter how crummy it is, *has* to be an improvement on the spike produced by the standard method! So even if we use only a simple Gaussian approximation, we are doing well.

We now study an application of the variational approach to a realistic example – data clustering.

▶ 33.7 K-means clustering and the expectation–maximization algorithm as a variational method

In Chapter 20, we introduced the soft K-means clustering algorithm, version 1. In Chapter 22, we introduced versions 2 and 3 of this algorithm, and motivated the algorithm as a maximum likelihood algorithm.

K-means clustering is an example of an 'expectation–maximization' (EM) algorithm, with the two steps, which we called 'assignment' and 'update', being known as the 'E-step' and the 'M-step' respectively.

We now give a more general view of K-means clustering, due to Neal and Hinton (1998), in which the algorithm is shown to optimize a variational objective function. Neal and Hinton's derivation applies to any EM algorithm.

The probability of everything

Let the parameters of the mixture model – the means, standard deviations, and weights – be denoted by $\boldsymbol{\theta}$. For each data point, there is a missing variable (also known as a latent variable), the class label k_n for that point. The probability of everything, given our assumed model $\mathcal{H}$, is

$$P(\{\mathbf{x}^{(n)}, k_n\}_{n=1}^{N}, \boldsymbol{\theta} \mid \mathcal{H}) = P(\boldsymbol{\theta} \mid \mathcal{H}) \prod_{n=1}^{N} \left[P(\mathbf{x}^{(n)} \mid k_n, \boldsymbol{\theta}) P(k_n \mid \boldsymbol{\theta}) \right]. \qquad (33.47)$$

The posterior probability of everything, given the data, is proportional to the probability of everything:

$$P(\{k_n\}_{n=1}^{N}, \boldsymbol{\theta} \mid \{\mathbf{x}^{(n)}\}_{n=1}^{N}, \mathcal{H}) = \frac{P(\{\mathbf{x}^{(n)}, k_n\}_{n=1}^{N}, \boldsymbol{\theta} \mid \mathcal{H})}{P(\{\mathbf{x}^{(n)}\}_{n=1}^{N} \mid \mathcal{H})}. \qquad (33.48)$$

We now approximate this posterior distribution by a separable distribution

$$Q_k(\{k_n\}_{n=1}^{N}) Q_{\boldsymbol{\theta}}(\boldsymbol{\theta}), \qquad (33.49)$$

and define a variational free energy in the usual way:

$$\tilde{F}(Q_k, Q_{\boldsymbol{\theta}}) = \sum_{\{k_n\}} \int \mathrm{d}^D \boldsymbol{\theta} \; Q_k(\{k_n\}_{n=1}^{N}) \, Q_{\boldsymbol{\theta}}(\boldsymbol{\theta}) \ln \frac{Q_k(\{k_n\}_{n=1}^{N}) Q_{\boldsymbol{\theta}}(\boldsymbol{\theta})}{P(\{\mathbf{x}^{(n)}, k_n\}_{n=1}^{N}, \boldsymbol{\theta} \mid \mathcal{H})}. \qquad (33.50)$$

$\tilde{F}$ is bounded below by minus the evidence, $\ln P(\{\mathbf{x}^{(n)}\}_{n=1}^{N} \mid \mathcal{H})$. We can now make an iterative algorithm with an 'assignment' step and an 'update' step. In the assignment step, $Q_k(\{k_n\}_{n=1}^{N})$ is adjusted to reduce $\tilde{F}$, for fixed $Q_{\boldsymbol{\theta}}$; in the update step, $Q_{\boldsymbol{\theta}}$ is adjusted to reduce $\tilde{F}$, for fixed Q_k.

If we wish to obtain exactly the soft K-means algorithm, we impose a further constraint on our approximating distribution: $Q_{\boldsymbol{\theta}}$ is constrained to be a delta function centred on a point estimate of $\boldsymbol{\theta}$, $\boldsymbol{\theta} = \boldsymbol{\theta}^*$:

$$Q_{\boldsymbol{\theta}}(\boldsymbol{\theta}) = \delta(\boldsymbol{\theta} - \boldsymbol{\theta}^*). \qquad (33.51)$$

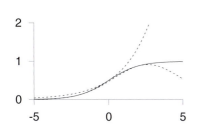

Upper bound

$$\frac{1}{1+e^{-a}} \leq \exp(\mu a - H_2^e(\mu)) \qquad \mu \in [0,1]$$

Lower bound

$$\frac{1}{1+e^{-a}} \geq g(\nu) \exp\left[(a-\nu)/2 - \lambda(\nu)(a^2 - \nu^2)\right]$$

where $\lambda(\nu) = \left[g(\nu) - 1/2\right]/2\nu$.

Figure 33.5. Illustration of the Jaakkola–Jordan variational method. Upper and lower bounds on the logistic function (solid line)

$$g(a) \equiv \frac{1}{1+e^{-a}}.$$

These upper and lower bounds are exponential or Gaussian functions of a, and so easier to integrate over. The graph shows the sigmoid function and upper and lower bounds with $\mu = 0.505$ and $\nu = -2.015$.

Unfortunately, this distribution contributes to the variational free energy an infinitely large integral $\int d^D \boldsymbol{\theta}\, Q_{\boldsymbol{\theta}}(\boldsymbol{\theta}) \ln Q_{\boldsymbol{\theta}}(\boldsymbol{\theta})$, so we'd better leave that term out of $\tilde{F}$, treating it as an additive constant. [Using a delta function $Q_{\boldsymbol{\theta}}$ is not a good idea if our aim is to minimize $\tilde{F}$!] Moving on, our aim is to derive the soft K-means algorithm.

▷ Exercise 33.2.[2] Show that, given $Q_{\boldsymbol{\theta}}(\boldsymbol{\theta}) = \delta(\boldsymbol{\theta} - \boldsymbol{\theta}^*)$, the optimal Q_k, in the sense of minimizing $\tilde{F}$, is a separable distribution in which the probability that $k_n = k$ is given by the responsibility $r_k^{(n)}$.

▷ Exercise 33.3.[4] Show that, given a separable Q_k as described above, the optimal $\boldsymbol{\theta}^*$, in the sense of minimizing $\tilde{F}$, is obtained by the update step of the soft K-means algorithm. (Assume a uniform prior on $\boldsymbol{\theta}$.)

Exercise 33.4.[4] We can instantly improve on the infinitely large value of $\tilde{F}$ achieved by soft K-means clustering by allowing $Q_{\boldsymbol{\theta}}$ to be a more general distribution than a delta-function. Derive an update step in which $Q_{\boldsymbol{\theta}}$ is allowed to be a separable distribution, a product of $Q_\mu(\{\mu\})$, $Q_\sigma(\{\sigma\})$, and $Q_\pi(\pi)$. Discuss whether this generalized algorithm still suffers from soft K-means's 'kaboom' problem, where the algorithm glues an ever-shrinking Gaussian to one data point.

Sadly, while it sounds like a promising generalization of the algorithm to allow $Q_{\boldsymbol{\theta}}$ to be a non-delta-function, and the 'kaboom' problem goes away, other artefacts can arise in this approximate inference method, involving local minima of $\tilde{F}$. For further reading, see (MacKay, 1997a; MacKay, 2001).

▶ **33.8 Variational methods other than free energy minimization**

There are other strategies for approximating a complicated distribution $P(\mathbf{x})$, in addition to those based on minimizing the relative entropy between an approximating distribution Q and P. One approach pioneered by Jaakkola and Jordan is to create adjustable upper and lower bounds Q^U and Q^L to P, as illustrated in figure 33.5. These bounds (which are unnormalized densities) are parameterized by variational parameters which are adjusted in order to obtain the tightest possible fit. The lower bound can be adjusted to *maximize*

$$\sum_{\mathbf{x}} Q^L(\mathbf{x}), \tag{33.52}$$

and the upper bound can be adjusted to *minimize*

$$\sum_{\mathbf{x}} Q^U(\mathbf{x}). \tag{33.53}$$

Using the normalized versions of the optimized bounds we then compute approximations to the predictive distributions. Further reading on such methods can be found in the references (Jaakkola and Jordan, 2000a; Jaakkola and Jordan, 2000b; Jaakkola and Jordan, 1996; Gibbs and MacKay, 2000).

Further reading

The Bethe and Kikuchi free energies

In Chapter 26 we discussed the sum–product algorithm for functions of the factor-graph form (26.1). If the factor graph is tree-like, the sum–product algorithm converges and correctly computes the marginal function of any variable x_n and can also yield the joint marginal function of subsets of variables that appear in a common factor, such as $\mathbf{x}_m$.

The sum–product algorithm may also be applied to factor graphs that are not tree-like. If the algorithm converges to a fixed point, it has been shown that that fixed point is a stationary point (usually a minimum) of a function of the messages called the Kikuchi free energy. In the special case where all factors in factor graph are functions of one or two variables, the Kikuchi free energy is called the Bethe free energy.

For articles on this idea, and new approximate inference algorithms motivated by it, see Yedidia (2000); Yedidia *et al.* (2000c); Welling and Teh (2001); Yuille (2001); Yedidia *et al.* (2000b); Yedidia *et al.* (2000a).

▶ 33.9 Further exercises

Exercise 33.5.[2, p.435] This exercise explores the assertion, made above, that the approximations given by variational free energy minimization always tend to be more compact than the true distribution. Consider a two dimensional Gaussian distribution $P(\mathbf{x})$ with axes aligned with the directions $\mathbf{e}^{(1)} = (1, 1)$ and $\mathbf{e}^{(2)} = (1, -1)$. Let the variances in these two directions be σ_1^2 and σ_2^2. What is the optimal variance if this distribution is approximated by a *spherical* Gaussian with variance σ_Q^2, optimized by variational free energy minimization? If we instead optimized the objective function

$$G = \int d\mathbf{x}\, P(\mathbf{x}) \ln \frac{P(\mathbf{x})}{Q(\mathbf{x}; \sigma^2)}, \tag{33.54}$$

what would be the optimal value of σ^2? Sketch a contour of the true distribution $P(\mathbf{x})$ and the two approximating distributions in the case $\sigma_1/\sigma_2 = 10$.

[Note that in general it is not possible to evaluate the objective function G, because integrals under the true distribution $P(\mathbf{x})$ are usually intractable.]

Exercise 33.6.[2, p.436] What do you think of the idea of using a variational method to optimize an approximating distribution Q which we then use as a proposal density for importance sampling?

Exercise 33.7.[2] Define the *relative entropy* or *Kullback–Leibler divergence* between two probability distributions P and Q, and state Gibbs' inequality.

Consider the problem of approximating a joint distribution $P(x, y)$ by a separable distribution $Q(x, y) = Q_X(x)Q_Y(y)$. Show that if the objective function for this approximation is

$$G(Q_X, Q_Y) = \sum_{x,y} P(x, y) \log_2 \frac{P(x, y)}{Q_X(x) Q_Y(y)}$$

that the minimal value of G is achieved when Q_X and Q_Y are equal to the marginal distributions over x and y.

Now consider the alternative objective function

$$F(Q_X, Q_Y) = \sum_{x,y} Q_X(x) Q_Y(y) \log_2 \frac{Q_X(x) Q_Y(y)}{P(x, y)};$$

the probability distribution $P(x, y)$ shown in the margin is to be approximated by a separable distribution $Q(x, y) = Q_X(x) Q_Y(y)$. State the value of $F(Q_X, Q_Y)$ if Q_X and Q_Y are set to the marginal distributions over x and y.

Show that $F(Q_X, Q_Y)$ has three distinct minima, identify those minima, and evaluate F at each of them.

$P(x, y)$		x		
	1	2	3	4
1	1/8	1/8	0	0
y 2	1/8	1/8	0	0
3	0	0	1/4	0
4	0	0	0	1/4

▶ **33.10 Solutions**

Solution to exercise 33.5 (p.434). We need to know the relative entropy between two one-dimensional Gaussian distributions:

$$\int dx \, \text{Normal}(x; 0, \sigma_Q) \ln \frac{\text{Normal}(x; 0, \sigma_Q)}{\text{Normal}(x; 0, \sigma_P)}$$

$$= \int dx \, \text{Normal}(x; 0, \sigma_Q) \left[\ln \frac{\sigma_P}{\sigma_Q} - \frac{1}{2} x^2 \left(\frac{1}{\sigma_Q^2} - \frac{1}{\sigma_P^2} \right) \right] \qquad (33.55)$$

$$= \frac{1}{2} \left(\ln \frac{\sigma_P^2}{\sigma_Q^2} - 1 + \frac{\sigma_Q^2}{\sigma_P^2} \right). \qquad (33.56)$$

So, if we approximate P, whose variances are σ_1^2 and σ_2^2, by Q, whose variances are both σ_Q^2, we find

$$F(\sigma_Q^2) = \frac{1}{2} \left(\ln \frac{\sigma_1^2}{\sigma_Q^2} - 1 + \frac{\sigma_Q^2}{\sigma_1^2} + \ln \frac{\sigma_2^2}{\sigma_Q^2} - 1 + \frac{\sigma_Q^2}{\sigma_2^2} \right); \qquad (33.57)$$

differentiating,

$$\frac{d}{d \ln(\sigma_Q^2)} F = \frac{1}{2} \left[-2 + \left(\frac{\sigma_Q^2}{\sigma_1^2} + \frac{\sigma_Q^2}{\sigma_2^2} \right) \right], \qquad (33.58)$$

which is zero when

$$\frac{1}{\sigma_Q^2} = \frac{1}{2} \left(\frac{1}{\sigma_1^2} + \frac{1}{\sigma_2^2} \right). \qquad (33.59)$$

Thus we set the approximating distribution's inverse variance to the mean inverse variance of the target distribution P.

In the case $\sigma_1 = 10$ and $\sigma_2 = 1$, we obtain $\sigma_Q \simeq \sqrt{2}$, which is just a factor of $\sqrt{2}$ larger than σ_2, pretty much *independent* of the value of the larger standard deviation σ_1. *Variational free energy minimization typically leads to approximating distributions whose length scales match the shortest length scale of the target distribution.* The approximating distribution might be viewed as *too compact*.

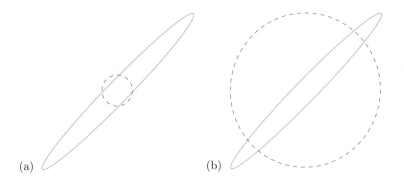

(a)   (b)

Figure 33.6. Two separable Gaussian approximations (dotted lines) to a bivariate Gaussian distribution (solid line). (a) The approximation that minimizes the variational free energy. (b) The approximation that minimizes the objective function G. In each figure, the lines show the contours at which $\mathbf{x}^\mathsf{T}\mathbf{A}\mathbf{x} = 1$, where $\mathbf{A}$ is the inverse covariance matrix of the Gaussian.

In contrast, if we use the objective function G then we find:

$$G(\sigma_Q^2) = \frac{1}{2}\left(\ln\sigma_Q^2 + \frac{\sigma_1^2}{\sigma_Q^2} + \ln\sigma_Q^2 + \frac{\sigma_2^2}{\sigma_Q^2}\right) + \text{constant},\qquad(33.60)$$

where the constant depends on σ_1 and σ_2 only. Differentiating,

$$\frac{\mathrm{d}}{\mathrm{d}\ln\sigma_Q^2}G = \frac{1}{2}\left[2 - \left(\frac{\sigma_1^2}{\sigma_Q^2} + \frac{\sigma_2^2}{\sigma_Q^2}\right)\right],\qquad(33.61)$$

which is zero when

$$\sigma_Q^2 = \frac{1}{2}\left(\sigma_1^2 + \sigma_2^2\right).\qquad(33.62)$$

Thus we set the approximating distribution's variance to the mean variance of the target distribution P.

In the case $\sigma_1 = 10$ and $\sigma_2 = 1$, we obtain $\sigma_Q \simeq 10/\sqrt{2}$, which is just a factor of $\sqrt{2}$ smaller than σ_1, independent of the value of σ_2.

The two approximations are shown to scale in figure 33.6.

Solution to exercise 33.6 (p.434). The best possible variational approximation is of course the target distribution P. Assuming that this is not possible, a good variational approximation is *more compact* than the true distribution. In contrast, a good sampler is *more heavy tailed* than the true distribution. An over-compact distribution would be a lousy sampler with a large variance.

34

Independent Component Analysis and Latent Variable Modelling

▶ 34.1 Latent variable models

Many statistical models are generative models (that is, models that specify a full probability density over all variables in the situation) that make use of *latent variables* to describe a probability distribution over observables.

Examples of latent variable models include Chapter 22's mixture models, which model the observables as coming from a superposed mixture of simple probability distributions (the latent variables are the unknown class labels of the examples); hidden Markov models (Rabiner and Juang, 1986; Durbin *et al.*, 1998); and factor analysis.

The decoding problem for error-correcting codes can also be viewed in terms of a latent variable model – figure 34.1. In that case, the encoding matrix $\mathbf{G}$ is normally known in advance. In latent variable modelling, the parameters equivalent to $\mathbf{G}$ are usually not known, and must be inferred from the data along with the latent variables $\mathbf{s}$.

Usually, the latent variables have a simple distribution, often a separable distribution. Thus when we fit a latent variable model, we are finding a description of the data in terms of 'independent components'. The 'independent component analysis' algorithm corresponds to perhaps the simplest possible latent variable model with continuous latent variables.

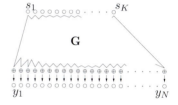

Figure 34.1. Error-correcting codes as latent variable models. The K latent variables are the independent source bits $s_1, \ldots, s_K$; these give rise to the observables via the generator matrix $\mathbf{G}$.

▶ 34.2 The generative model for independent component analysis

A set of N observations $D = \{\mathbf{x}^{(n)}\}_{n=1}^{N}$ are assumed to be generated as follows. Each J-dimensional vector $\mathbf{x}$ is a linear mixture of I underlying source signals, $\mathbf{s}$:

$$\mathbf{x} = \mathbf{G}\mathbf{s}, \tag{34.1}$$

where the matrix of mixing coefficients $\mathbf{G}$ is not known.

The simplest algorithm results if we assume that the number of sources is equal to the number of observations, i.e., $I = J$. Our aim is to recover the source variables $\mathbf{s}$ (within some multiplicative factors, and possibly permuted). To put it another way, we aim to create the inverse of $\mathbf{G}$ (within a post-multiplicative factor) given only a set of examples $\{\mathbf{x}\}$. We assume that the latent variables are independently distributed, with marginal distributions $P(s_i|\mathcal{H}) \equiv p_i(s_i)$. Here $\mathcal{H}$ denotes the assumed form of this model and the assumed probability distributions p_i of the latent variables.

The probability of the observables and the hidden variables, given $\mathbf{G}$ and

$\mathcal{H}$, is:

$$P(\{\mathbf{x}^{(n)}, \mathbf{s}^{(n)}\}_{n=1}^{N} \mid \mathbf{G}, \mathcal{H}) = \prod_{n=1}^{N} \left[P(\mathbf{x}^{(n)} \mid \mathbf{s}^{(n)}, \mathbf{G}, \mathcal{H}) P(\mathbf{s}^{(n)} \mid \mathcal{H}) \right] \qquad (34.2)$$

$$= \prod_{n=1}^{N} \left[\left(\prod_{j} \delta\left(x_j^{(n)} - \sum_i G_{ji} s_i^{(n)}\right) \right) \left(\prod_i p_i(s_i^{(n)}) \right) \right]. \qquad (34.3)$$

We assume that the vector $\mathbf{x}$ is generated *without noise*. This assumption is not usually made in latent variable modelling, since noise-free data are rare; but it makes the inference problem far simpler to solve.

The likelihood function

For learning about $\mathbf{G}$ from the data D, the relevant quantity is the likelihood function

$$P(D \mid \mathbf{G}, \mathcal{H}) = \prod_n P(\mathbf{x}^{(n)} \mid \mathbf{G}, \mathcal{H}) \qquad (34.4)$$

which is a product of factors each of which is obtained by marginalizing over the latent variables. When we marginalize over delta functions, remember that $\int ds\, \delta(x - vs) f(s) = \frac{1}{v} f(x/v)$. We adopt summation convention at this point, such that, for example, $G_{ji} s_i^{(n)} \equiv \sum_i G_{ji} s_i^{(n)}$. A single factor in the likelihood is given by

$$P(\mathbf{x}^{(n)} \mid \mathbf{G}, \mathcal{H}) = \int d^I \mathbf{s}^{(n)}\, P(\mathbf{x}^{(n)} \mid \mathbf{s}^{(n)}, \mathbf{G}, \mathcal{H}) P(\mathbf{s}^{(n)} \mid \mathcal{H}) \qquad (34.5)$$

$$= \int d^I \mathbf{s}^{(n)} \prod_j \delta\left(x_j^{(n)} - G_{ji} s_i^{(n)}\right) \prod_i p_i(s_i^{(n)}) \qquad (34.6)$$

$$= \frac{1}{|\det \mathbf{G}|} \prod_i p_i(G_{ij}^{-1} x_j) \qquad (34.7)$$

$$\Rightarrow \ln P(\mathbf{x}^{(n)} \mid \mathbf{G}, \mathcal{H}) = -\ln|\det \mathbf{G}| + \sum_i \ln p_i(G_{ij}^{-1} x_j). \qquad (34.8)$$

To obtain a maximum likelihood algorithm we find the gradient of the log likelihood. If we introduce $\mathbf{W} \equiv \mathbf{G}^{-1}$, the log likelihood contributed by a single example may be written:

$$\ln P(\mathbf{x}^{(n)} \mid \mathbf{G}, \mathcal{H}) = \ln|\det \mathbf{W}| + \sum_i \ln p_i(W_{ij} x_j). \qquad (34.9)$$

We'll assume from now on that $\det \mathbf{W}$ is positive, so that we can omit the absolute value sign. We will need the following identities:

$$\frac{\partial}{\partial G_{ji}} \ln \det \mathbf{G} = G_{ij}^{-1} = W_{ij} \qquad (34.10)$$

$$\frac{\partial}{\partial G_{ji}} G_{lm}^{-1} = -G_{lj}^{-1} G_{im}^{-1} = -W_{lj} W_{im} \qquad (34.11)$$

$$\frac{\partial}{\partial W_{ij}} f = -G_{jm} \left(\frac{\partial}{\partial G_{lm}} f\right) G_{li}. \qquad (34.12)$$

Let us define $a_i \equiv W_{ij} x_j$,

$$\phi_i(a_i) \equiv d \ln p_i(a_i)/da_i, \qquad (34.13)$$

Repeat for each datapoint **x**:

1. Put **x** through a linear mapping:

$$\mathbf{a} = \mathbf{W}\mathbf{x}.$$

2. Put **a** through a nonlinear map:

$$z_i = \phi_i(a_i),$$

where a popular choice for ϕ is $\phi = -\tanh(a_i)$.

3. Adjust the weights in accordance with

$$\Delta\mathbf{W} \propto [\mathbf{W}^{\mathsf{T}}]^{-1} + \mathbf{z}\mathbf{x}^{\mathsf{T}}.$$

Algorithm 34.2. Independent component analysis – online steepest ascents version. See also algorithm 34.4, which is to be preferred.

and $z_i = \phi_i(a_i)$, which indicates in which direction a_i needs to change to make the probability of the data greater. We may then obtain the gradient with respect to G_{ji} using equations (34.10) and (34.11):

$$\frac{\partial}{\partial G_{ji}} \ln P(\mathbf{x}^{(n)} \mid \mathbf{G}, \mathcal{H}) = -W_{ij} - a_i z_{i'} W_{i'j}. \qquad (34.14)$$

Or alternatively, the derivative with respect to W_{ij}:

$$\frac{\partial}{\partial W_{ij}} \ln P(\mathbf{x}^{(n)} \mid \mathbf{G}, \mathcal{H}) = G_{ji} + x_j z_i. \qquad (34.15)$$

If we choose to change **W** so as to ascend this gradient, we obtain the learning rule

$$\Delta\mathbf{W} \propto [\mathbf{W}^{\mathsf{T}}]^{-1} + \mathbf{z}\mathbf{x}^{\mathsf{T}}. \qquad (34.16)$$

The algorithm so far is summarized in algorithm 34.2.

Choices of ϕ

The choice of the function ϕ defines the assumed prior distribution of the latent variable s.

Let's first consider the *linear* choice $\phi_i(a_i) = -\kappa a_i$, which implicitly (via equation 34.13) assumes a Gaussian distribution on the latent variables. The Gaussian distribution on the latent variables is invariant under rotation of the latent variables, so there can be no evidence favouring any particular alignment of the latent variable space. The linear algorithm is thus uninteresting in that it will never recover the matrix **G** or the original sources. Our only hope is thus that the sources are non-Gaussian. Thankfully, most real sources have non-Gaussian distributions; often they have heavier tails than Gaussians.

We thus move on to the popular tanh nonlinearity. If

$$\phi_i(a_i) = -\tanh(a_i) \qquad (34.17)$$

then implicitly we are assuming

$$p_i(s_i) \propto 1/\cosh(s_i) \propto \frac{1}{e^{s_i} + e^{-s_i}}. \qquad (34.18)$$

This is a heavier-tailed distribution for the latent variables than the Gaussian distribution.

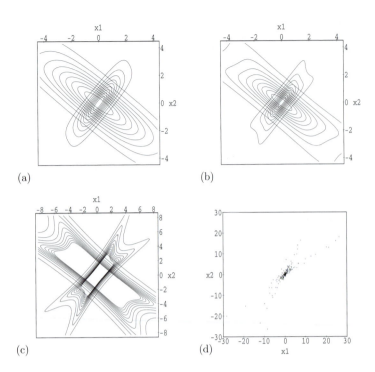

(a)

(b)

(c)

(d)

Figure 34.3. Illustration of the generative models implicit in the learning algorithm. (a) Distributions over two observables generated by $1/\cosh$ distributions on the latent variables, for

$$\mathbf{G} = \begin{bmatrix} 3/4 & 1/2 \\ 1/2 & 1 \end{bmatrix} \text{ (compact distribution) and}$$

$$\mathbf{G} = \begin{bmatrix} 2 & -1 \\ -1 & 3/2 \end{bmatrix} \text{ (broader distribution). (b) Contours of the}$$
generative distributions when the latent variables have Cauchy distributions. The learning algorithm fits this amoeboid object to the empirical data in such a way as to maximize the likelihood. The contour plot in (b) does not adequately represent this heavy-tailed distribution. (c) Part of the tails of the Cauchy distribution, giving the contours $0.01\ldots0.1$ times the density at the origin. (d) Some data from one of the generative distributions illustrated in (b) and (c). Can you tell which? 200 samples were created, of which 196 fell in the plotted region.

We could also use a tanh nonlinearity with gain β, that is, $\phi_i(a_i) = -\tanh(\beta a_i)$, whose implicit probabilistic model is $p_i(s_i) \propto 1/[\cosh(\beta s_i)]^{1/\beta}$. In the limit of large β, the nonlinearity becomes a step function and the probability distribution $p_i(s_i)$ becomes a biexponential distribution, $p_i(s_i) \propto \exp(-|s|)$. In the limit $\beta \to 0$, $p_i(s_i)$ approaches a Gaussian with mean zero and variance $1/\beta$. Heavier-tailed distributions than these may also be used. The Student and Cauchy distributions spring to mind.

Example distributions

Figures 34.3(a–c) illustrate typical distributions generated by the independent components model when the components have $1/\cosh$ and Cauchy distributions. Figure 34.3d shows some samples from the Cauchy model. The Cauchy distribution, being the more heavy-tailed, gives the clearest picture of how the predictive distribution depends on the assumed generative parameters $\mathbf{G}$.

▶ 34.3 A covariant, simpler, and faster learning algorithm

We have thus derived a learning algorithm that performs steepest descents on the likelihood function. The algorithm does not work very quickly, even on toy data; the algorithm is ill-conditioned and illustrates nicely the general advice that, *while finding the gradient of an objective function is a splendid idea, ascending the gradient directly may not be.* The fact that the algorithm is ill-conditioned can be seen in the fact that it involves a matrix inverse, which can be arbitrarily large or even undefined.

Covariant optimization in general

The principle of covariance says that a consistent algorithm should give the same results independent of the units in which quantities are measured (Knuth,

1968). A prime example of a *non*-covariant algorithm is the popular steepest descents rule. A dimensionless objective function $L(\mathbf{w})$ is defined, its derivative with respect to some parameters $\mathbf{w}$ is computed, and then $\mathbf{w}$ is changed by the rule

$$\Delta w_i = \eta \frac{\partial L}{\partial w_i}. \tag{34.19}$$

This popular equation is dimensionally inconsistent: the left-hand side of this equation has dimensions of $[w_i]$ and the right-hand side has dimensions $1/[w_i]$. The behaviour of the learning algorithm (34.19) is not covariant with respect to linear rescaling of the vector $\mathbf{w}$. Dimensional inconsistency is not the end of the world, as the success of numerous gradient descent algorithms has demonstrated, and indeed if η decreases with n (during on-line learning) as $1/n$ then the Munro–Robbins theorem (Bishop, 1992, p. 41) shows that the parameters will asymptotically converge to the maximum likelihood parameters. But the non-covariant algorithm may take a very large number of iterations to achieve this convergence; indeed many former users of steepest descents algorithms prefer to use algorithms such as conjugate gradients that adaptively figure out the curvature of the objective function. The defense of equation (34.19) that points out η could be a dimensional constant is untenable if not all the parameters w_i have the same dimensions.

The algorithm would be covariant if it had the form

$$\Delta w_i = \eta \sum_{i'} M_{ii'} \frac{\partial L}{\partial w_i}, \tag{34.20}$$

where $\mathbf{M}$ is a positive-definite matrix whose i, i' element has dimensions $[w_i w_{i'}]$. From where can we obtain such a matrix? Two sources of such matrices are *metrics* and *curvatures*.

Metrics and curvatures

If there is a natural metric that defines *distances* in our parameter space $\mathbf{w}$, then a matrix $\mathbf{M}$ can be obtained from the metric. There is often a natural choice. In the special case where there is a known quadratic metric defining the length of a vector $\mathbf{w}$, then the matrix can be obtained from the quadratic form. For example if the length is $\mathbf{w}^2$ then the natural matrix is $\mathbf{M} = \mathbf{I}$, and steepest descents is appropriate.

Another way of finding a metric is to look at the curvature of the objective function, defining $\mathbf{A} \equiv -\nabla\nabla L$ (where $\nabla \equiv \partial/\partial\mathbf{w}$). Then the matrix $\mathbf{M} = \mathbf{A}^{-1}$ will give a covariant algorithm; what is more, this algorithm is the Newton algorithm, so we recognize that it will alleviate one of the principal difficulties with steepest descents, namely its slow convergence to a minimum when the objective function is at all ill-conditioned. The Newton algorithm converges to the minimum in a single step if L is quadratic.

In some problems it may be that the curvature $\mathbf{A}$ consists of both data-dependent terms and data-independent terms; in this case, one might choose to define the metric using the data-independent terms only (Gull, 1989). The resulting algorithm will still be covariant but it will not implement an exact Newton step. Obviously there are many covariant algorithms; there is no unique choice. But covariant algorithms are a small subset of the set of *all* algorithms!

Back to independent component analysis

For the present maximum likelihood problem we have evaluated the gradient with respect to $\mathbf{G}$ and the gradient with respect to $\mathbf{W} = \mathbf{G}^{-1}$. Steepest ascents in $\mathbf{W}$ is not covariant. Let us construct an alternative, covariant algorithm with the help of the curvature of the log likelihood. Taking the second derivative of the log likelihood with respect to $\mathbf{W}$ we obtain two terms, the first of which is data-independent:

$$\frac{\partial G_{ji}}{\partial W_{kl}} = -G_{jk}G_{li}, \tag{34.21}$$

and the second of which is data-dependent:

$$\frac{\partial (z_i x_j)}{\partial W_{kl}} = x_j x_l \delta_{ik} z_i', \text{(no sum over } i) \tag{34.22}$$

where z' is the derivative of z. It is tempting to drop the data-dependent term and define the matrix $\mathbf{M}$ by $[M^{-1}]_{(ij)(kl)} = [G_{jk}G_{li}]$. However, this matrix is not positive definite (it has at least one non-positive eigenvalue), so it is a poor approximation to the curvature of the log likelihood, which must be positive definite in the neighbourhood of a maximum likelihood solution. We must therefore consult the data-dependent term for inspiration. The aim is to find a convenient approximation to the curvature and to obtain a covariant algorithm, not necessarily to implement an exact Newton step. What is the average value of $x_j x_l \delta_{ik} z_i'$? If the true value of $\mathbf{G}$ is $\mathbf{G}^*$, then

$$\left\langle x_j x_l \delta_{ik} z_i' \right\rangle = \left\langle G_{jm}^* s_m s_n G_{ln}^* \delta_{ik} z_i' \right\rangle. \tag{34.23}$$

We now make several severe approximations: we replace $\mathbf{G}^*$ by the present value of $\mathbf{G}$, and replace the correlated average $\langle s_m s_n z_i' \rangle$ by $\langle s_m s_n \rangle \langle z_i' \rangle \equiv \Sigma_{mn} D_i$. Here $\boldsymbol{\Sigma}$ is the variance–covariance matrix of the latent variables (which is assumed to exist), and D_i is the typical value of the curvature $\mathrm{d}^2 \ln p_i(a)/\mathrm{d}a^2$. Given that the sources are assumed to be independent, $\boldsymbol{\Sigma}$ and $\mathbf{D}$ are both diagonal matrices. These approximations motivate the matrix $\mathbf{M}$ given by:

$$[M^{-1}]_{(ij)(kl)} = G_{jm}\Sigma_{mn}G_{ln}\delta_{ik}D_i, \tag{34.24}$$

that is,

$$M_{(ij)(kl)} = W_{mj}\Sigma_{mn}^{-1}W_{nl}\delta_{ik}D_i^{-1}. \tag{34.25}$$

For simplicity, we further assume that the sources are similar to each other so that $\boldsymbol{\Sigma}$ and $\mathbf{D}$ are both homogeneous and that $\boldsymbol{\Sigma}\mathbf{D} = 1$. This will lead us to an algorithm that is covariant with respect to linear rescaling of the data $\mathbf{x}$, but not with respect to linear rescaling of the latent variables. We thus use:

$$M_{(ij)(kl)} = W_{mj}W_{ml}\delta_{ik}. \tag{34.26}$$

Multiplying this matrix by the gradient in equation (34.15) we obtain the following covariant learning algorithm:

$$\Delta W_{ij} = \eta \left(W_{ij} + W_{i'j}a_{i'}z_i \right). \tag{34.27}$$

Notice that this expression does not require any inversion of the matrix $\mathbf{W}$. The only additional computation once $\mathbf{z}$ has been computed is a single backward pass through the weights to compute the quantity

$$x_j' = W_{i'j}a_{i'} \tag{34.28}$$

Repeat for each datapoint $\mathbf{x}$:

1. Put $\mathbf{x}$ through a linear mapping:

    $$\mathbf{a} = \mathbf{W}\mathbf{x}.$$

2. Put $\mathbf{a}$ through a nonlinear map:

    $$z_i = \phi_i(a_i),$$

    where a popular choice for ϕ is $\phi = -\tanh(a_i)$.

3. Put $\mathbf{a}$ back through $\mathbf{W}$:

    $$\mathbf{x}' = \mathbf{W}^\mathsf{T}\mathbf{a}.$$

4. Adjust the weights in accordance with

    $$\Delta\mathbf{W} \propto \mathbf{W} + \mathbf{z}\mathbf{x}'^{\mathsf{T}}.$$

Algorithm 34.4. Independent component analysis – covariant version.

in terms of which the covariant algorithm reads:

$$\Delta W_{ij} = \eta \left(W_{ij} + x'_j z_i \right). \tag{34.29}$$

The quantity $\left(W_{ij} + x'_j z_i \right)$ on the right-hand side is sometimes called the *natural gradient*. The covariant independent component analysis algorithm is summarized in algorithm 34.4.

Further reading

ICA was originally derived using an information maximization approach (Bell and Sejnowski, 1995). Another view of ICA, in terms of energy functions, which motivates more general models, is given by Hinton *et al.* (2001). Another generalization of ICA can be found in Pearlmutter and Parra (1996, 1997).There is now an enormous literature on applications of ICA. A variational free energy minimization approach to ICA-like models is given in (Miskin, 2001; Miskin and MacKay, 2000; Miskin and MacKay, 2001). Further reading on blind separation, including non-ICA algorithms, can be found in (Jutten and Herault, 1991; Comon *et al.*, 1991; Hendin *et al.*, 1994; Amari *et al.*, 1996; Hojen-Sorensen *et al.*, 2002).

Infinite models

While latent variable models with a finite number of latent variables are widely used, it is often the case that our beliefs about the situation would be most accurately captured by a very large number of latent variables.

Consider clustering, for example. If we attack speech recognition by modelling words using a cluster model, how many clusters should we use? The number of possible words is unbounded (section 18.2), so we would really like to use a model in which it's always possible for new clusters to arise.

Furthermore, if we do a careful job of modelling the cluster corresponding to just one English word, we will probably find that the cluster for one word should itself be modelled as composed of clusters – indeed, a hierarchy of clusters within clusters. The first levels of the hierarchy would divide male speakers from female, and would separate speakers from different regions – India, Britain, Europe, and so forth. Within each of those clusters would be subclusters for the different accents within each region. The subclusters could have subsubclusters right down to the level of villages, streets, or families.

Thus we would often like to have infinite numbers of clusters; in some cases the clusters would have a hierarchical structure, and in other cases the hierarchy would be flat. So, how should such infinite models be implemented in finite computers? And how should we set up our Bayesian models so as to avoid getting silly answers?

Infinite mixture models for categorical data are presented in Neal (1991), along with a Monte Carlo method for simulating inferences and predictions. Infinite Gaussian mixture models with a flat hierarchical structure are presented in Rasmussen (2000). Neal (2001) shows how to use Dirichlet diffusion trees to define models of hierarchical clusters. Most of these ideas build on the Dirichlet process (section 18.2). This remains an active research area (Rasmussen and Ghahramani, 2002; Beal *et al.*, 2002).

▶ 34.4 Exercises

Exercise 34.1.[3] Repeat the derivation of the algorithm, but assume a small amount of noise in $\mathbf{x}$: $\mathbf{x} = \mathbf{Gs} + \mathbf{n}$; so the term $\delta\left(x_j^{(n)} - \sum_i G_{ji}s_i^{(n)}\right)$ in the joint probability (34.3) is replaced by a probability distribution over $x_j^{(n)}$ with mean $\sum_i G_{ji}s_i^{(n)}$. Show that, if this noise distribution has sufficiently small standard deviation, the identical algorithm results.

Exercise 34.2.[3] Implement the covariant ICA algorithm and apply it to toy data.

Exercise 34.3.[4-5] Create algorithms appropriate for the situations: (a) $\mathbf{x}$ includes substantial Gaussian noise; (b) more measurements than latent variables ($J > I$); (c) fewer measurements than latent variables ($J < I$).

Factor analysis assumes that the observations $\mathbf{x}$ can be described in terms of independent latent variables $\{s_k\}$ and independent additive noise. Thus the observable $\mathbf{x}$ is given by

$$\mathbf{x} = \mathbf{Gs} + \mathbf{n}, \tag{34.30}$$

where $\mathbf{n}$ is a noise vector whose components have a separable probability distribution. In factor analysis it is often assumed that the probability distributions of $\{s_k\}$ and $\{n_i\}$ are zero-mean Gaussians; the noise terms may have different variances σ_i^2.

Exercise 34.4.[4] Make a maximum likelihood algorithm for inferring $\mathbf{G}$ from data, assuming the generative model $\mathbf{x} = \mathbf{Gs} + \mathbf{n}$ is correct and that $\mathbf{s}$ and $\mathbf{n}$ have independent Gaussian distributions. Include parameters σ_j^2 to describe the variance of each n_j, and maximize the likelihood with respect to them too. Let the variance of each s_i be 1.

Exercise 34.5.[4C] Implement the infinite Gaussian mixture model of Rasmussen (2000).

35

Random Inference Topics

▶ **35.1 What do you know if you are ignorant?**

Example 35.1. A real variable x is measured in an accurate experiment. For example, x might be the half-life of the neutron, the wavelength of light emitted by a firefly, the depth of Lake Vostok, or the mass of Jupiter's moon Io.

What is the probability that the value of x starts with a '1', like the charge of the electron (in S.I. units),

$$e = 1.602\ldots \times 10^{-19}\,\mathrm{C},$$

and the Boltzmann constant,

$$k = 1.380\,66\ldots \times 10^{-23}\,\mathrm{J\,K^{-1}}?$$

And what is the probability that it starts with a '9', like the Faraday constant,

$$\mathcal{F} = 9.648\ldots \times 10^4\,\mathrm{C\,mol^{-1}}?$$

What about the second digit? What is the probability that the mantissa of x starts '1.1...', and what is the probability that x starts '9.9...'?

Solution. An expert on neutrons, fireflies, Antarctica, or Jove might be able to predict the value of x, and thus predict the first digit with some confidence, but what about someone with no knowledge of the topic? What is the probability distribution corresponding to 'knowing nothing'?

One way to attack this question is to notice that the units of x have not been specified. If the half-life of the neutron were measured in fortnights instead of seconds, the number x would be divided by 1 209 600; if it were measured in years, it would be divided by 3×10^7. Now, is our knowledge about x, and, in particular, our knowledge of its first digit, affected by the change in units? For the expert, the answer is yes; but let us take someone truly ignorant, for whom the answer is no; their predictions about the first digit of x are independent of the units. The arbitrariness of the units corresponds to *invariance* of the probability distribution when x is *multiplied* by any number.

If you don't know the units that a quantity is measured in, the probability of the first digit must be proportional to the length of the corresponding piece of logarithmic scale. The probability that the first digit of a number is 1 is thus

$$p_1 = \frac{\log 2 - \log 1}{\log 10 - \log 1} = \frac{\log 2}{\log 10}. \tag{35.1}$$

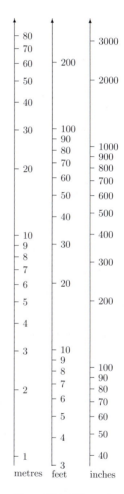

Figure 35.1. When viewed on a logarithmic scale, scales using different units are translated relative to each other.

Now, $2^{10} = 1024 \simeq 10^3 = 1000$, so without needing a calculator, we have $10 \log 2 \simeq 3 \log 10$ and

$$p_1 \simeq \frac{3}{10}. \tag{35.2}$$

More generally, the probability that the first digit is d is

$$(\log(d+1) - \log(d))/(\log 10 - \log 1) = \log_{10}(1 + 1/d). \tag{35.3}$$

This observation about initial digits is known as Benford's law. Ignorance does not correspond to a uniform probability distribution.   □

▷ Exercise 35.2.[2] A pin is thrown tumbling in the air. What is the probability distribution of the angle θ_1 between the pin and the vertical at a moment while it is in the air? The tumbling pin is photographed. What is the probability distribution of the angle θ_3 between the pin and the vertical as imaged in the photograph?

▷ Exercise 35.3.[2] Record breaking. Consider keeping track of the world record for some quantity x, say earthquake magnitude, or longjump distances jumped at world championships. If we assume that attempts to break the record take place at a steady rate, and if we assume that the underlying probability distribution of the outcome x, $P(x)$, is not changing – an assumption that I think is unlikely to be true in the case of sports endeavours, but an interesting assumption to consider nonetheless – and assuming no knowledge at all about $P(x)$, what can be predicted about successive intervals between the dates when records are broken?

▶ 35.2 The Luria–Delbrück distribution

Exercise 35.4.[3C, p.449] In their landmark paper demonstrating that bacteria could mutate from virus sensitivity to virus resistance, Luria and Delbrück (1943) wanted to estimate the mutation rate in an exponentially-growing population from the total number of mutants found at the end of the experiment. This problem is difficult because the quantity measured (the number of mutated bacteria) has a heavy-tailed probability distribution: a mutation occuring early in the experiment can give rise to a huge number of mutants. Unfortunately, Luria and Delbrück didn't know Bayes' theorem, and their way of coping with the heavy-tailed distribution involves arbitrary hacks leading to two different estimators of the mutation rate. One of these estimators (based on the mean number of mutated bacteria, averaging over several experiments) has appallingly large variance, yet sampling theorists continue to use it and base confidence intervals around it (Kepler and Oprea, 2001). In this exercise you'll do the inference right.

In each culture, a single bacterium that is *not resistant* gives rise, after g generations, to $N = 2^g$ descendants, all clones except for differences arising from mutations. The final culture is then exposed to a virus, and the number of resistant bacteria n is measured. According to the now accepted mutation hypothesis, these resistant bacteria got their resistance from random mutations that took place during the growth of the colony. The mutation rate (per cell per generation), a, is about one in a hundred million. The total number of opportunities to mutate is N, since $\sum_{i=0}^{g-1} 2^i \simeq 2^g = N$. If a bacterium mutates at the ith generation, its descendants all inherit the mutation, and the final number of resistant bacteria contributed by that one ancestor is 2^{g-i}.

Given M separate experiments, in each of which a colony of size N is created, and where the measured numbers of resistant bacteria are $\{n_m\}_{m=1}^M$, what can we infer about the mutation rate, a?

Make the inference given the following dataset from Luria and Delbrück, for $N = 2.4 \times 10^8$: $\{n_m\} = \{1, 0, 3, 0, 0, 5, 0, 5, 0, 6, 107, 0, 0, 0, 1, 0, 0, 64, 0, 35\}$. [A small amount of computation is required to solve this problem.]

▶ 35.3 Inferring causation

Exercise 35.5.[2, p.450] In the Bayesian graphical model community, the task of inferring which way the arrows point – that is, which nodes are parents, and which children – is one on which much has been written.

Inferring causation is tricky because of 'likelihood equivalence'. Two graphical models are likelihood-equivalent if for any setting of the parameters of either, there exists a setting of the parameters of the others such that the two joint probability distributions of all observables are identical. An example of a pair of likelihood-equivalent models are $A \rightarrow B$ and $B \rightarrow A$. The model $A \rightarrow B$ asserts that A is the parent of B, or, in very sloppy terminology, 'A causes B'. An example of a situation where '$B \rightarrow A$' is true is the case where B is the variable 'burglar in house' and A is the variable 'alarm is ringing'. Here it is literally true that B causes A. But this choice of words is confusing if applied to another example, $R \rightarrow D$, where R denotes 'it rained this morning' and D denotes 'the pavement is dry'. 'R causes D' is confusing. I'll therefore use the words 'B is a parent of A' to denote causation. Some statistical methods that use the likelihood alone are unable to use data to distinguish between likelihood-equivalent models. In a Bayesian approach, on the other hand, two likelihood-equivalent models may nevertheless be somewhat distinguished, in the light of data, since likelihood-equivalence does not force a Bayesian to use priors that assign equivalent densities over the two parameter spaces of the models.

However, many Bayesian graphical modelling folks, perhaps out of sympathy for their non-Bayesian colleagues, or from a latent urge not to appear different from them, deliberately discard this potential advantage of Bayesian methods – the ability to infer causation from data – by skewing their models so that the ability goes away; a widespread orthodoxy holds that one should identify the choices of prior for which 'prior equivalence' holds, i.e., the priors such that models that are likelihood-equivalent also have identical posterior probabilities, and then one should use one of those priors in inference and prediction. This argument motivates the use, as the prior over all probability vectors, of specially-constructed Dirichlet distributions.

In my view it is a philosophical error to use only those priors such that causation cannot be inferred. Priors should be set to describe one's assumptions; when this is done, it's likely that interesting inferences about causation *can* be made from data.

In this exercise, you'll make an example of such an inference.

Consider the toy problem where A and B are binary variables. The two models are $\mathcal{H}_{A \rightarrow B}$ and $\mathcal{H}_{B \rightarrow A}$. $\mathcal{H}_{A \rightarrow B}$ asserts that the marginal probability of A comes from a beta distribution with parameters $(1, 1)$, i.e., the uniform distribution; and that the two conditional distributions $P(b \,|\, a = 0)$ and $P(b \,|\, a = 1)$ also come independently from beta distributions with parameters $(1, 1)$. The other model assigns similar priors to the marginal probability of B and the conditional distributions of A given B. Data are gathered, and the counts, given $F = 1000$ outcomes, are

$$
\begin{array}{c|cc|c}
 & a=0 & a=1 & \\
\hline
b=0 & 760 & 5 & 765 \\
b=1 & 190 & 45 & 235 \\
\hline
 & 950 & 50 &
\end{array}
\qquad (35.4)
$$

What are the posterior probabilities of the two hypotheses?

> Hint: it's a good idea to work this exercise out symbolically in order to spot all the simplifications that emerge.

$$
\Psi(x) = \frac{d}{dx} \ln \Gamma(x) \simeq \ln(x) - \frac{1}{2x} + O(1/x^2). \qquad (35.5)
$$

The topic of inferring causation is a complex one. The fact that Bayesian inference can sensibly be used to infer the directions of arrows in graphs seems to be a neglected view, but it is certainly not the whole story. See Pearl (2000) for discussion of many other aspects of causality.

▶ 35.4 Further exercises

Exercise 35.6.[3] Photons arriving at a photon detector are believed to be emitted as a Poisson process with a time-varying rate,

$$
\lambda(t) = \exp(a + b \sin(\omega t + \phi)), \qquad (35.6)
$$

where the parameters a, b, ω, and ϕ are known. Data are collected during the time $t = 0 \ldots T$. Given that N photons arrived at times $\{t_n\}_{n=1}^N$, discuss the inference of a, b, ω, and ϕ. [Further reading: Gregory and Loredo (1992).]

▷ Exercise 35.7.[2] A data file consisting of two columns of numbers has been printed in such a way that the boundaries between the columns are unclear. Here are the resulting strings.

891.10.0	912.20.0	874.10.0	870.20.0	836.10.0	861.20.0
903.10.0	937.10.0	850.20.0	916.20.0	899.10.0	907.10.0
924.20.0	861.10.0	899.20.0	849.10.0	887.20.0	840.10.0
849.20.0	891.10.0	916.20.0	891.10.0	912.20.0	875.10.0
898.20.0	924.10.0	950.20.0	958.10.0	971.20.0	933.10.0
966.20.0	908.10.0	924.20.0	983.10.0	924.20.0	908.10.0
950.20.0	911.10.0	913.20.0	921.25.0	912.20.0	917.30.0
923.50.0					

Discuss how probable it is, given these data, that the correct parsing of each item is:

(a) 891.10.0 → 891. 10.0, etc.

(b) 891.10.0 → 891.1 0.0, etc.

[A parsing of a string is a grammatical interpretation of the string. For example, 'Punch bores' could be parsed as 'Punch (noun) bores (verb)', or 'Punch (imperative verb) bores (plural noun)'.]

▷ Exercise 35.8.[2] In an experiment, the measured quantities $\{x_n\}$ come independently from a biexponential distribution with mean μ,

$$
P(x \mid \mu) = \frac{1}{Z} \exp(-|x - \mu|),
$$

where Z is the normalizing constant, $Z = 2$. The mean μ is not known. An example of this distribution, with $\mu = 1$, is shown in figure 35.2.

Assuming the four datapoints are

$$\{x_n\} = \{0, 0.9, 2, 6\},$$

what do these data tell us about μ? Include detailed sketches in your answer. Give a range of plausible values of μ.

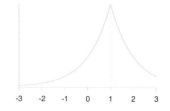

Figure 35.2. The biexponential distribution $P(x \mid \mu = 1)$.

35.5 Solutions

Solution to exercise 35.4 (p.446). A population of size N has N opportunities to mutate. The probability of the number of mutations that occurred, r, is roughly Poisson

$$P(r \mid a, N) = e^{-aN} \frac{(aN)^r}{r!}. \tag{35.7}$$

(This is slightly inaccurate because the descendants of a mutant cannot themselves undergo the same mutation.) Each mutation gives rise to a number of final mutant cells n_i that depends on the generation time of the mutation. If multiplication went like clockwork then the probability of n_i being 1 would be $1/2$, the probability of 2 would be $1/4$, the probability of 4 would be $1/8$, and $P(n_i) = 1/(2n)$ for all n_i that are powers of two. But we don't expect the mutant progeny to divide in exact synchrony, and we don't know the precise timing of the end of the experiment compared to the division times. A smoothed version of this distribution that permits all integers to occur is

$$P(n_i) = \frac{1}{Z} \frac{1}{n_i^2}, \tag{35.8}$$

where $Z = \pi^2/6 = 1.645$. [This distribution's moments are all wrong, since n_i can never exceed N, but who cares about moments? – only sampling theory statisticians who are barking up the wrong tree, constructing 'unbiased estimators' such as $\hat{a} = \bar{n}/\ln(N)$. The error that we introduce in the likelihood function by using the approximation to $P(n_i)$ is negligible.]

The observed number of mutants n is the sum

$$n = \sum_{i=1}^{r} n_i. \tag{35.9}$$

The probability distribution of n given r is the convolution of r identical distributions of the form (35.8). For example,

$$P(n \mid r = 2) = \sum_{n_1=1}^{n-1} \frac{1}{Z^2} \frac{1}{n_1^2} \frac{1}{(n-n_1)^2} \quad \text{for } n \geq 2. \tag{35.10}$$

The probability distribution of n given a, which is what we need for the Bayesian inference, is given by summing over r.

$$P(n \mid a) = \sum_{r=0}^{N} P(n \mid r) P(r \mid a, N). \tag{35.11}$$

This quantity can't be evaluated analytically, but for small a, it's easy to evaluate to any desired numerical precision by explicitly summing over r from

$r = 0$ to some $r_{\max}$, with $P(n\,|\,r)$ also being found for each r by $r_{\max}$ explicit convolutions for all required values of n; if $r_{\max} = n_{\max}$, the largest value of n encountered in the data, then $P(n\,|\,a)$ is computed exactly; but for this question's data, $r_{\max} = 9$ is plenty for an accurate result; I used $r_{\max} = 74$ to make the graphs in figure 35.3. Octave source code is available.[1] Incidentally, for data sets like the one in this exercise, which have a substantial number of zero counts, very little is lost by making Luria and Delbruck's second approximation, which is to retain only the count of how many n were equal to zero, and how many were non-zero. The likelihood function found using this weakened data set,

$$L(a) = (e^{-aN})^{11}(1 - e^{-aN})^9, \qquad (35.12)$$

is scarcely distinguishable from the likelihood computed using full information.

Solution to exercise 35.5 (p.447). From the six terms of the form

$$P(\mathbf{F}\,|\,\alpha\mathbf{m}) = \frac{\prod_i \Gamma(F_i + \alpha m_i)}{\Gamma(\sum_i F_i + \alpha)}\,\frac{\Gamma(\alpha)}{\prod_i \Gamma(\alpha m_i)}, \qquad (35.13)$$

most factors cancel and all that remains is

$$\frac{P(\mathcal{H}_{A\to B}\,|\,\text{Data})}{P(\mathcal{H}_{B\to A}\,|\,\text{Data})} = \frac{(765+1)(235+1)}{(950+1)(50+1)} = \frac{3.8}{1}. \qquad (35.14)$$

There is modest evidence in favour of $\mathcal{H}_{A\to B}$ because the three probabilities inferred for that hypothesis (roughly 0.95, 0.8, and 0.1) are more typical of the prior than are the three probabilities inferred for the other (0.24, 0.008, and 0.19). This statement sounds absurd if we think of the priors as 'uniform' over the three probabilities – surely, under a uniform prior, any settings of the probabilities are equally probable? But in the natural basis, the logit basis, the prior is proportional to $p(1-p)$, and the posterior probability ratio can be estimated by

$$\frac{0.95 \times 0.05 \times 0.8 \times 0.2 \times 0.1 \times 0.9}{0.24 \times 0.76 \times 0.008 \times 0.992 \times 0.19 \times 0.81} \simeq \frac{3}{1}, \qquad (35.15)$$

which is not exactly right, but it does illustrate where the preference for $A \to B$ is coming from.

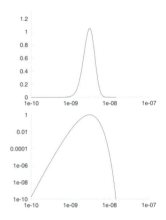

Figure 35.3. Likelihood of the mutation rate a on a linear scale and log scale, given Luria and Delbruck's data. Vertical axis: likelihood$/10^{-23}$; horizontal axis: a.

[1] www.inference.phy.cam.ac.uk/itprnn/code/octave/luria0.m

36

Decision Theory

Decision theory is trivial, apart from computational details (just like playing chess!).

You have a choice of various actions, a. The world may be in one of many states $\mathbf{x}$; which one occurs may be influenced by your action. The world's state has a probability distribution $P(\mathbf{x} \mid a)$. Finally, there is a utility function $U(\mathbf{x}, a)$ which specifies the payoff you receive when the world is in state $\mathbf{x}$ and you chose action a.

The task of decision theory is to select the action that maximizes the expected utility,

$$\mathcal{E}[U \mid a] = \int \mathrm{d}^K \mathbf{x}\, U(\mathbf{x}, a) P(\mathbf{x} \mid a). \tag{36.1}$$

That's all. The computational problem is to maximize $\mathcal{E}[U \mid a]$ over a. [Pessimists may prefer to define a loss function L instead of a utility function U and minimize the expected loss.]

Is there anything more to be said about decision theory?

Well, in a real problem, the choice of an appropriate utility function may be quite difficult. Furthermore, when a sequence of actions is to be taken, with each action providing information about $\mathbf{x}$, we have to take into account the effect that this anticipated information may have on our subsequent actions. The resulting mixture of forward probability and inverse probability computations in a decision problem is distinctive. In a realistic problem such as playing a board game, the tree of possible cogitations and actions that must be considered becomes enormous, and 'doing the right thing' is not simple because the expected utility of an action cannot be computed exactly (Russell and Wefald, 1991; Baum and Smith, 1993; Baum and Smith, 1997).

Let's explore an example.

▶ 36.1 Rational prospecting

Suppose you have the task of choosing the site for a Tanzanite mine. Your final action will be to select the site from a list of N sites. The nth site has a net value called the return x_n which is initially unknown, and will be found out exactly only after site n has been chosen. [x_n equals the revenue earned from selling the Tanzanite from that site, minus the costs of buying the site, paying the staff, and so forth.] At the outset, the return x_n has a probability distribution $P(x_n)$, based on the information already available.

Before you take your final action you have the opportunity to do some prospecting. Prospecting at the nth site has a cost c_n and yields data d_n which reduce the uncertainty about x_n. [We'll assume that the returns of the N sites are unrelated to each other, and that prospecting at one site only yields information about that site and doesn't affect the return from that site.]

Your decision problem is:

> given the initial probability distributions $P(x_1)$, $P(x_2)$, ..., $P(x_N)$, first, decide whether to prospect, and at which sites; then choose which site to mine.

For simplicity, let's make everything in the problem Gaussian and focus on the question of whether to prospect once or not. We'll assume our utility function is linear in x_n; we wish to maximize our expected return. The utility function is

$$U = x_{n_a}, \qquad (36.2)$$

The notation $P(y) = \text{Normal}(y; \mu, \sigma^2)$ indicates that y has Gaussian distribution with mean μ and variance σ^2.

if no prospecting is done, where n_a is the chosen 'action' site; and if prospecting is done the utility is

$$U = -c_{n_p} + x_{n_a}, \qquad (36.3)$$

where n_p is the site at which prospecting took place.

The prior distribution of the return of site n is

$$P(x_n) = \text{Normal}(x_n; \mu_n, \sigma_n^2). \qquad (36.4)$$

If you prospect at site n, the datum d_n is a noisy version of x_n:

$$P(d_n \mid x_n) = \text{Normal}(d_n; x_n, \sigma^2). \qquad (36.5)$$

▷ **Exercise 36.1.**[2] Given these assumptions, show that the prior probability distribution of d_n is

$$P(d_n) = \text{Normal}(d_n; \mu_n, \sigma^2 + \sigma_n^2) \qquad (36.6)$$

(mnemonic: when independent variables add, variances add), and that the posterior distribution of x_n given d_n is

$$P(x_n \mid d_n) = \text{Normal}\left(x_n; \mu_n', \sigma_n^{2'}\right) \qquad (36.7)$$

where

$$\mu_n' = \frac{d_n/\sigma^2 + \mu_n/\sigma_n^2}{1/\sigma^2 + 1/\sigma_n^2} \quad \text{and} \quad \frac{1}{\sigma_n^{2'}} = \frac{1}{\sigma^2} + \frac{1}{\sigma_n^2} \qquad (36.8)$$

(mnemonic: when Gaussians multiply, precisions add).

To start with let's evaluate the expected utility if we do no prospecting (i.e., choose the site immediately); then we'll evaluate the expected utility if we first prospect at one site and then make our choice. From these two results we will be able to decide whether to prospect once or zero times, and, if we prospect once, at which site.

So, first we consider the expected utility without any prospecting.

Exercise 36.2.[2] Show that the optimal action, assuming no prospecting, is to select the site with biggest mean

$$n_a = \underset{n}{\text{argmax}}\, \mu_n, \qquad (36.9)$$

and the expected utility of this action is

$$\mathcal{E}[U \mid \text{optimal } n] = \max_n \mu_n. \qquad (36.10)$$

[If your intuition says 'surely the optimal decision should take into account the different uncertainties σ_n too?', the answer to this question is 'reasonable – if so, then the utility function should be *nonlinear* in x'.]

Now the exciting bit. Should we prospect? Once we have prospected at site n_p, we will choose the site using the decision rule (36.9) with the value of mean μ_{n_p} replaced by the updated value μ'_n given by (36.8). What makes the problem exciting is that we don't yet know the value of d_n, so we don't know what our action n_a will be; indeed the whole value of doing the prospecting comes from the fact that the outcome d_n may alter the action from the one that we would have taken in the absence of the experimental information.

From the expression for the new mean in terms of d_n (36.8), and the known variance of d_n (36.6) we can compute the probability distribution of the key quantity, μ'_n, and can work out the expected utility by integrating over all possible outcomes and their associated actions.

Exercise 36.3.[2] Show that the probability distribution of the new mean μ'_n (36.8) is Gaussian with mean μ_n and variance

$$s^2 \equiv \sigma_n^2 \frac{\sigma_n^2}{\sigma^2 + \sigma_n^2}. \tag{36.11}$$

Consider prospecting at site n. Let the biggest mean of the other sites be μ_1. When we obtain the new value of the mean, μ'_n, we will choose site n and get an expected return of μ'_n if $\mu'_n > \mu_1$, and we will choose site 1 and get an expected return of μ_1 if $\mu'_n < \mu_1$.

So the expected utility of prospecting at site n, then picking the best site, is

$$\mathcal{E}[U \mid \text{prospect at } n] = -c_n + P(\mu'_n < \mu_1)\,\mu_1 + \int_{\mu_1}^{\infty} d\mu'_n\, \mu'_n\, \text{Normal}(\mu'_n; \mu_n, s^2). \tag{36.12}$$

The difference in utility between prospecting and not prospecting is the quantity of interest, and it depends on what we would have done without prospecting; and that depends on whether μ_1 is bigger than μ_n.

$$\mathcal{E}[U \mid \text{no prospecting}] = \begin{cases} -\mu_1 & \text{if } \mu_1 \geq \mu_n \\ -\mu_n & \text{if } \mu_1 \leq \mu_n. \end{cases} \tag{36.13}$$

So

$$\mathcal{E}[U \mid \text{prospect at } n] - \mathcal{E}[U \mid \text{no prospecting}]$$
$$= \begin{cases} -c_n + \int_{\mu_1}^{\infty} d\mu'_n\, (\mu'_n - \mu_1)\, \text{Normal}(\mu'_n; \mu_n, s^2) & \text{if } \mu_1 \geq \mu_n \\ -c_n + \int_{-\infty}^{\mu_1} d\mu'_n\, (\mu_1 - \mu'_n)\, \text{Normal}(\mu'_n; \mu_n, s^2) & \text{if } \mu_1 \leq \mu_n. \end{cases} \tag{36.14}$$

We can plot the change in expected utility due to prospecting (omitting c_n) as a function of the difference $(\mu_n - \mu_1)$ (horizontal axis) and the initial standard deviation σ_n (vertical axis). In the figure the noise variance is $\sigma^2 = 1$.

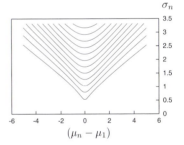

σ_n

$(\mu_n - \mu_1)$

Figure 36.1. Contour plot of the gain in expected utility due to prospecting. The contours are equally spaced from 0.1 to 1.2 in steps of 0.1. To decide whether it is worth prospecting at site n, find the contour equal to c_n (the cost of prospecting); all points $[(\mu_n - \mu_1), \sigma_n]$ above that contour are worthwhile.

▶ 36.2 Further reading

If the world in which we act is a little more complicated than the prospecting problem – for example, if multiple iterations of prospecting are possible, and the cost of prospecting is uncertain – then finding the optimal balance between exploration and exploitation becomes a much harder computational problem. *Reinforcement learning* addresses approximate methods for this problem (Sutton and Barto, 1998).

▶ 36.3 Further exercises

▷ Exercise 36.4.[2] The four doors problem.

A new game show uses rules similar to those of the three doors (exercise 3.8 (p.57)), but there are four doors, and the host explains: 'First you will point to one of the doors, and then I will open one of the other non-winners. Then you decide whether to stick with your original pick or switch to one of the remaining doors. Then I will open another (other than the current pick) non-winner. You will then make your final decision by sticking with the door picked on the previous decision or by switching to the only other remaining door.'

What is the optimal strategy? Should you switch on the first opportunity? Should you switch on the second opportunity?

▷ Exercise 36.5.[3, p.729] One of the challenges of decision theory is figuring out exactly what the utility function is. The utility of money, for example, is notoriously nonlinear for most people.

In fact, the behaviour of many people cannot be captured by a coherent utility function, as illustrated by the *Allias paradox*, which runs as follows.

Which of these choices do you find most attractive?
    A.   £1 million guaranteed.
    B.   89% chance of £1 million;
           10% chance of £2.5 million;
           1% chance of nothing.
Now consider these choices:
    C.   89% chance of nothing;
           11% chance of £1 million.
    D.   90% chance of nothing;
           10% chance of £2.5 million.

Many people prefer A to B and D to C. Prove that these preferences are inconsistent with any utility function $U(x)$ for money.

Exercise 36.6.[4] Optimal stopping.

A queue of N potential partners is waiting at your door, all asking to marry you. They have arrived in random order. As you meet each partner, you have to decide on the spot, based on the information so far, whether to marry them or say no. Each potential partner has a desirability d_n, which you find out if and when you meet them. You must marry one of them, but you are not allowed to go back to people you have said no to.

There are several ways to define the precise problem.

(a) Assuming your aim is to maximize the desirability d_n, i.e., your utility function is $d_{\hat{n}}$, where $\hat{n}$ is the partner selected, what strategy should you use?

(b) Assuming you wish very much to marry *the most desirable* person (i.e., your utility function is 1 if you achieve that, and zero otherwise); what strategy should you use?

(c) Assuming you wish very much to marry the most desirable person, and that your strategy will be 'strategy M':

> Strategy M – Meet the first M partners and say no to all of them. Memorize the maximum desirability d_{max} among them. Then meet the others in sequence, waiting until a partner with $d_n > d_{max}$ comes along, and marry them. If none more desirable comes along, marry the final Nth partner (and feel miserable).

– what is the optimal value of M?

Exercise 36.7.[3] **Regret as an objective function?**

The preceding exercise (parts b and c) involved a utility function based on regret. If one married the tenth most desirable candidate, the utility function asserts that one would feel regret for having not made chosen the most desirable.

Many people working in learning theory and decision theory use 'minimizing the maximal possible regret' as an objective function, but does this make sense?

Imagine that Fred has bought a lottery ticket, and offers to sell it to you before it's known whether the ticket is a winner. For simplicity say the probability that the ticket is a winner is $1/100$, and if it is a winner, it is worth £10. Fred offers to sell you the ticket for £1. Do you buy it?

The possible actions are 'buy' and 'don't buy'. The utilities of the four possible action–outcome pairs are shown in table 36.2. I have assumed that the utility of small amounts of money for you is linear. If you don't buy the ticket then the utility is zero regardless of whether the ticket proves to be a winner. If you do buy the ticket you either end up losing one pound (with probability $99/100$) or gaining nine (with probability $1/100$). In the minimax regret community, actions are chosen to minimize the maximum possible regret. The four possible regret outcomes are shown in table 36.3. If you buy the ticket and it doesn't win, you have a regret of £1, because if you had not bought it you would have been £1 better off. If you do not buy the ticket and it wins, you have a regret of £9, because if you had bought it you would have been £9 better off. The action that minimizes the maximum possible regret is thus to buy the ticket.

Discuss whether this use of regret to choose actions can be philosophically justified.

The above problem can be turned into an investment portfolio decision problem by imagining that you have been given one pound to invest in two possible funds for one day: Fred's lottery fund, and the cash fund. If you put £f_1 into Fred's lottery fund, Fred promises to return £$9f_1$ to you if the lottery ticket is a winner, and otherwise nothing. The remaining £f_0 (with $f_0 = 1 - f_1$) is kept as cash. What is the best investment? Show that the minimax regret community will invest $f_1 = 9/10$ of their money in the high risk, high return lottery fund, and only $f_0 = 1/10$ in cash. Can this investment method be justified?

Exercise 36.8.[3] **Gambling oddities** (from Cover and Thomas (1991)). A horse race involving I horses occurs repeatedly, and you are obliged to bet all your money each time. Your bet at time t can be represented by

	Action	
Outcome	Buy	Don't buy
No win	−1	0
Wins	+9	0

Table 36.2. Utility in the lottery ticket problem.

	Action	
Outcome	Buy	Don't buy
No win	1	0
Wins	0	9

Table 36.3. Regret in the lottery ticket problem.

a normalized probability vector $\mathbf{b}$ multiplied by your money $m(t)$. The odds offered by the bookies are such that if horse i wins then your return is $m(t+1) = b_i o_i m(t)$. Assuming the bookies' odds are 'fair', that is,

$$\sum_i \frac{1}{o_i} = 1, \tag{36.15}$$

and assuming that the probability that horse i wins is p_i, work out the optimal betting strategy if your aim is *Cover's aim*, namely, to maximize the *expected value of* $\log m(T)$. Show that the optimal strategy sets $\mathbf{b}$ equal to $\mathbf{p}$, independent of the bookies' odds $\mathbf{o}$. Show that when this strategy is used, the money is expected to grow exponentially as:

$$2^{nW(\mathbf{b},\mathbf{p})} \tag{36.16}$$

where $W = \sum_i p_i \log b_i o_i$.

If you only bet once, is the optimal strategy any different?

Do you think this optimal strategy makes sense? Do you think that it's 'optimal', in common language, to ignore the bookies' odds? What can you conclude about 'Cover's aim'?

Exercise 36.9.[3] Two ordinary dice are thrown repeatedly; the outcome of each throw is the sum of the two numbers. Joe Shark, who says that 6 and 8 are his lucky numbers, bets even money that a 6 will be thrown before the first 7 is thrown. If you were a gambler, would you take the bet? What is your probability of winning? Joe then bets even money that an 8 will be thrown before the first 7 is thrown. Would you take the bet?

Having gained your confidence, Joe suggests combining the two bets into a single bet: he bets a larger sum, still at even odds, that an 8 and a 6 will be thrown before two 7s have been thrown. Would you take the bet? What is your probability of winning?

37

Bayesian Inference and Sampling Theory

There are two schools of statistics. Sampling theorists concentrate on having methods guaranteed to work most of the time, given minimal assumptions. Bayesians try to make inferences that take into account all available information and answer the question of interest given the particular data set. As you have probably gathered, I strongly recommend the use of Bayesian methods.

Sampling theory is the widely used approach to statistics, and most papers in most journals report their experiments using quantities like confidence intervals, significance levels, and p-values. A p-value (e.g. $p = 0.05$) is the probability, given a null hypothesis for the probability distribution of the data, that the outcome would be as extreme as, or more extreme than, the observed outcome. Untrained readers – and perhaps, more worryingly, the authors of many papers – usually interpret such a p-value as if it is a Bayesian probability (for example, the posterior probability of the null hypothesis), an interpretation that both sampling theorists and Bayesians would agree is incorrect.

In this chapter we study a couple of simple inference problems in order to compare these two approaches to statistics.

While in some cases, the answers from a Bayesian approach and from sampling theory are very similar, we can also find cases where there are significant differences. We have already seen such an example in exercise 3.15 (p.59), where a sampling theorist got a p-value smaller than 7%, and viewed this as strong evidence *against* the null hypothesis, whereas the data actually *favoured* the null hypothesis over the simplest alternative. On p.64, another example was given where the p-value was smaller than the mystical value of 5%, yet the data again favoured the null hypothesis. Thus in some cases, sampling theory can be trigger-happy, declaring results to be 'sufficiently improbable that the null hypothesis should be rejected', when those results actually weakly support the null hypothesis. As we will now see, there are also inference problems where sampling theory fails to detect 'significant' evidence where a Bayesian approach and everyday intuition agree that the evidence is strong. Most telling of all are the inference problems where the 'significance' assigned by sampling theory changes depending on irrelevant factors concerned with the design of the experiment.

This chapter is only provided for those readers who are curious about the sampling theory / Bayesian methods debate. If you find any of this chapter tough to understand, please skip it. There is no point trying to understand the debate. Just use Bayesian methods – they are much easier to understand than the debate itself!

▶ 37.1 A medical example

We are trying to reduce the incidence of an unpleasant disease
called *microsoftus*. Two vaccinations, A and B, are tested on
a group of volunteers. Vaccination B is a control treatment, a
placebo treatment with no active ingredients. Of the 40 subjects,
30 are randomly assigned to have treatment A and the other 10
are given the control treatment B. We observe the subjects for one
year after their vaccinations. Of the 30 in group A, one contracts
microsoftus. Of the 10 in group B, three contract *microsoftus*.

Is treatment A better than treatment B?

Sampling theory has a go

The standard sampling theory approach to the question 'is A better than B?'
is to construct a *statistical test*. The test usually compares a hypothesis such
as

$\mathcal{H}_1$: 'A and B have different effectivenesses'

with a null hypothesis such as

$\mathcal{H}_0$: 'A and B have exactly the same effectivenesses as each other'.

A novice might object 'no, no, I want to compare the hypothesis "A is better
than B" with the alternative "B is better than A"!' but such objections are
not welcome in sampling theory.

Once the two hypotheses have been defined, the first hypothesis is scarcely
mentioned again – attention focuses solely on the null hypothesis. It makes me
laugh to write this, but it's true! The null hypothesis is accepted or rejected
purely on the basis of how unexpected the data were to $\mathcal{H}_0$, not on how much
better $\mathcal{H}_1$ predicted the data. One chooses a *statistic* which measures how
much a data set deviates from the null hypothesis. In the example here, the
standard statistic to use would be one called χ^2 (chi-squared). To compute
χ^2, we take the difference between each data measurement and its *expected*
value *assuming the null hypothesis to be true*, and divide the square of that
difference by the *variance* of the measurement, *assuming the null hypothesis to
be true*. In the present problem, the four data measurements are the integers
F_{A+}, F_{A-}, F_{B+}, and F_{B-}, that is, the number of subjects given treatment A
who contracted *microsoftus* (F_{A+}), the number of subjects given treatment A
who didn't (F_{A-}), and so forth. The definition of χ^2 is:

$$\chi^2 = \sum_i \frac{(F_i - \langle F_i \rangle)^2}{\langle F_i \rangle}. \tag{37.1}$$

Actually, in my elementary statistics book (Spiegel, 1988) I find Yates's correction is recommended:

$$\chi^2 = \sum_i \frac{(|F_i - \langle F_i \rangle| - 0.5)^2}{\langle F_i \rangle}. \tag{37.2}$$

In this case, given the null hypothesis that treatments A and B are equally
effective, and have rates f_+ and f_- for the two outcomes, the expected counts
are:

$$\begin{array}{ll}
\langle F_{A+} \rangle = f_+ N_A & \langle F_{A-} \rangle = f_- N_A \\
\langle F_{B+} \rangle = f_+ N_B & \langle F_{B-} \rangle = f_- N_B.
\end{array} \tag{37.3}$$

If you want to know about Yates's
correction, read a sampling theory
textbook. The point of this
chapter is not to teach sampling
theory; I merely mention Yates's
correction because it is what a
professional sampling theorist
might use.

The test accepts or rejects the null hypothesis on the basis of how big χ^2 is. To make this test precise, and give it a 'significance level', we have to work out what the *sampling distribution* of χ^2 is, taking into account the fact that the four data points are not independent (they satisfy the two constraints $F_{A+} + F_{A-} = N_A$ and $F_{B+} + F_{B-} = N_B$) and the fact that the parameters $f_{\pm}$ are not known. These three constraints reduce the *number of degrees of freedom* in the data from four to one. [If you want to learn more about computing the 'number of degrees of freedom', read a sampling theory book; in Bayesian methods we don't need to know all that, and quantities equivalent to the number of degrees of freedom pop straight out of a Bayesian analysis when they are appropriate.] These sampling distributions are tabulated by sampling theory gnomes and come accompanied by warnings about the conditions under which they are accurate. For example, standard tabulated distributions for χ^2 are only accurate if the expected numbers F_i are about 5 or more.

> The sampling distribution of a statistic is the probability distribution of its value under repetitions of the experiment, assuming that the null hypothesis is true.

Once the data arrive, sampling theorists estimate the unknown parameters $f_{\pm}$ of the null hypothesis from the data:

$$\hat{f}_+ = \frac{F_{A+} + F_{B+}}{N_A + N_B}, \quad \hat{f}_- = \frac{F_{A-} + F_{B-}}{N_A + N_B}, \tag{37.4}$$

and evaluate χ^2. At this point, the sampling theory school divides itself into two camps. One camp uses the following protocol: first, before looking at the data, pick the significance level of the test (e.g. 5%), and determine the critical value of χ^2 above which the null hypothesis will be rejected. (The significance level is the fraction of times that the statistic χ^2 would exceed the critical value, if the null hypothesis were true.) Then evaluate χ^2, compare with the critical value, and declare the outcome of the test, and its significance level (which was fixed beforehand).

The second camp looks at the data, finds χ^2, then looks in the table of χ^2-distributions for the significance level, p, for which the observed value of χ^2 would be the critical value. The result of the test is then reported by giving this value of p, which is the fraction of times that a result as extreme as the one observed, or more extreme, would be expected to arise if the null hypothesis were true.

Let's apply these two methods. First camp: let's pick 5% as our significance level. The critical value for χ^2 with one degree of freedom is $\chi^2_{0.05} = 3.84$. The estimated values of $f_{\pm}$ are

$$f_+ = 1/10, \quad f_- = 9/10. \tag{37.5}$$

The expected values of the four measurements are

$$\langle F_{A+} \rangle = 3 \tag{37.6}$$
$$\langle F_{A-} \rangle = 27 \tag{37.7}$$
$$\langle F_{B+} \rangle = 1 \tag{37.8}$$
$$\langle F_{B-} \rangle = 9 \tag{37.9}$$

and χ^2 (as defined in equation (37.1)) is

$$\chi^2 = 5.93. \tag{37.10}$$

Since this value exceeds 3.84, we reject the null hypothesis that the two treatments are equivalent at the 0.05 significance level. However, if we use Yates's correction, we find $\chi^2 = 3.33$, and therefore accept the null hypothesis.

Camp two runs a finger across the χ^2 table found at the back of any good sampling theory book and finds $\chi^2_{.10} = 2.71$. Interpolating between $\chi^2_{.10}$ and $\chi^2_{.05}$, camp two reports 'the p-value is $p = 0.07$'.

Notice that this answer does not say how much more effective A is than B, it simply says that A is 'significantly' different from B. And here, 'significant' means only 'statistically significant', not practically significant.

The man in the street, reading the statement that 'the treatment was significantly different from the control $(p = 0.07)$', might come to the conclusion that 'there is a 93% chance that the treatments differ in effectiveness'. But what '$p = 0.07$' actually means is 'if you did this experiment many times, and the two treatments *had* equal effectiveness, then 7% of the time you would find a value of χ^2 more extreme than the one that happened here'. This has almost nothing to do with what we want to know, which is how likely it is that treatment A is better than B.

Let me through, I'm a Bayesian

OK, now let's *infer* what we really want to know. We scrap the hypothesis that the two treatments have exactly equal effectivenesses, since we do not believe it. There are two unknown parameters, p_{A+} and p_{B+}, which are the probabilities that people given treatments A and B, respectively, contract the disease.

Given the data, we can infer these two probabilities, and we can answer questions of interest by examining the posterior distribution.

The posterior distribution is

$$P(p_{A+}, p_{B+} \mid \{F_i\}) = \frac{P(\{F_i\} \mid p_{A+}, p_{B+}) P(p_{A+}, p_{B+})}{P(\{F_i\})}. \qquad (37.11)$$

The likelihood function is

$$P(\{F_i\} \mid p_{A+}, p_{B+}) = \binom{N_A}{F_{A+}} p_{A+}^{F_{A+}} p_{A-}^{F_{A-}} \binom{N_B}{F_{B+}} p_{B+}^{F_{B+}} p_{B-}^{F_{B-}} \qquad (37.12)$$

$$= \binom{30}{1} p_{A+}^{1} p_{A-}^{29} \binom{10}{3} p_{B+}^{3} p_{B-}^{7}. \qquad (37.13)$$

What prior distribution should we use? The prior distribution gives us the opportunity to include knowledge from other experiments, or a prior belief that the two parameters p_{A+} and p_{B+}, while different from each other, are expected to have similar values.

Here we will use the simplest vanilla prior distribution, a uniform distribution over each parameter.

$$P(p_{A+}, p_{B+}) = 1. \qquad (37.14)$$

We can now plot the posterior distribution. Given the assumption of a separable prior on p_{A+} and p_{B+}, the posterior distribution is also separable:

$$P(p_{A+}, p_{B+} \mid \{F_i\}) = P(p_{A+} \mid F_{A+}, F_{A-}) P(p_{B+} \mid F_{B+}, F_{B-}). \qquad (37.15)$$

The two posterior distributions are shown in figure 37.1 (except the graphs are not normalized) and the joint posterior probability is shown in figure 37.2.

If we want to know the answer to the question 'how probable is it that p_{A+} is smaller than p_{B+}?', we can answer exactly that question by computing the posterior probability

$$P(p_{A+} < p_{B+} \mid \text{Data}), \qquad (37.16)$$

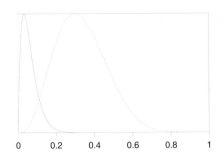

Figure 37.1. Posterior probabilities of the two effectivenesses. Treatment A – solid line; B – dotted line.

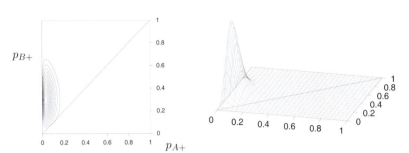

Figure 37.2. Joint posterior probability of the two effectivenesses – contour plot and surface plot.

which is the integral of the joint posterior probability $P(p_{A+}, p_{B+} \,|\, \text{Data})$ shown in figure 37.2 over the region in which $p_{A+} < p_{B+}$, i.e., the shaded triangle in figure 37.3. The value of this integral (obtained by a straightforward numerical integration of the likelihood function (37.13) over the relevant region) is $P(p_{A+} < p_{B+} \,|\, \text{Data}) = 0.990$.

Thus there is a 99% chance, given the data and our prior assumptions, that treatment A is superior to treatment B. In conclusion, according to our Bayesian model, the data (1 out of 30 contracted the disease after vaccination A, and 3 out of 10 contracted the disease after vaccination B) give very strong evidence – about 99 to one – that treatment A is superior to treatment B.

In the Bayesian approach, it is also easy to answer other relevant questions. For example, if we want to know 'how likely is it that treatment A is ten times more effective than treatment B?', we can integrate the joint posterior probability $P(p_{A+}, p_{B+} \,|\, \text{Data})$ over the region in which $p_{A+} < 10\, p_{B+}$ (figure 37.4).

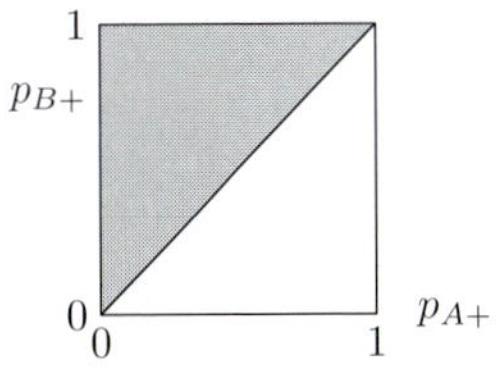

Figure 37.3. The proposition $p_{A+} < p_{B+}$ is true for all points in the shaded triangle. To find the probability of this proposition we integrate the joint posterior probability $P(p_{A+}, p_{B+} \,|\, \text{Data})$ (figure 37.2) over this region.

Model comparison

If there were a situation in which we really did want to compare the two hypotheses $\mathcal{H}_0$: $p_{A+} = p_{B+}$ and $\mathcal{H}_1$: $p_{A+} \neq p_{B+}$, we can of course do this directly with Bayesian methods also.

As an example, consider the data set:

D: One subject, given treatment A, subsequently contracted *microsoftus*.
One subject, given treatment B, did not.

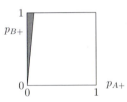

Figure 37.4. The proposition $p_{A+} < 10\, p_{B+}$ is true for all points in the shaded triangle.

Treatment	A	B
Got disease	1	0
Did not	0	1
Total treated	1	1

How strongly does this data set favour $\mathcal{H}_1$ over $\mathcal{H}_0$?

We answer this question by computing the evidence for each hypothesis. Let's assume uniform priors over the unknown parameters of the models. The first hypothesis $\mathcal{H}_0$: $p_{A+} = p_{B+}$ has just one unknown parameter, let's call it p.

$$P(p\,|\,\mathcal{H}_0) = 1 \quad p \in (0,1). \qquad (37.17)$$

We'll use the uniform prior over the two parameters of model $\mathcal{H}_1$ that we used before:

$$P(p_{A+}, p_{B+}\,|\,\mathcal{H}_1) = 1 \quad p_{A+} \in (0,1),\ p_{B+} \in (0,1). \qquad (37.18)$$

Now, the probability of the data D under model $\mathcal{H}_0$ is the normalizing constant from the inference of p given D:

$$P(D\,|\,\mathcal{H}_0) = \int \mathrm{d}p\, P(D\,|\,p)P(p\,|\,\mathcal{H}_0) \qquad (37.19)$$

$$= \int \mathrm{d}p\, p(1-p) \times 1 \qquad (37.20)$$

$$= 1/6. \qquad (37.21)$$

The probability of the data D under model $\mathcal{H}_1$ is given by a simple two-dimensional integral:

$$P(D\,|\,\mathcal{H}_1) = \int\!\!\int \mathrm{d}p_{A+}\,\mathrm{d}p_{B+}\, P(D\,|\,p_{A+}, p_{B+})P(p_{A+}, p_{B+}\,|\,\mathcal{H}_1) \quad (37.22)$$

$$= \int \mathrm{d}p_{A+}\, p_{A+} \int \mathrm{d}p_{B+}\, (1 - p_{B+}) \qquad (37.23)$$

$$= 1/2 \times 1/2 \qquad (37.24)$$

$$= 1/4. \qquad (37.25)$$

Thus the evidence ratio in favour of model $\mathcal{H}_1$, which asserts that the two effectivenesses are unequal, is

$$\frac{P(D\,|\,\mathcal{H}_1)}{P(D\,|\,\mathcal{H}_0)} = \frac{1/4}{1/6} = \frac{0.6}{0.4}. \qquad (37.26)$$

So if the prior probability over the two hypotheses was 50:50, the posterior probability is 60:40 in favour of $\mathcal{H}_1$.   □

Is it not easy to get sensible answers to well-posed questions using Bayesian methods?

[The sampling theory answer to this question would involve the identical significance test that was used in the preceding problem; that test would yield a 'not significant' result. I think it is greatly preferable to acknowledge what is obvious to the intuition, namely that the data D do give *weak* evidence in favour of $\mathcal{H}_1$. Bayesian methods quantify how weak the evidence is.]

▶ 37.2 Dependence of p-values on irrelevant information

In an expensive laboratory, Dr. Bloggs tosses a coin labelled a and b twelve times and the outcome is the string

$$aaabaaaabaab,$$

which contains three bs and nine as.

What evidence do these data give that the coin is biased in favour of a?

Dr. Bloggs consults his sampling theory friend who says 'let r be the number of bs and $n = 12$ be the total number of tosses; I view r as the random variable and find the probability of r taking on the value $r = 3$ or a more extreme value, assuming the null hypothesis $p_a = 0.5$ to be true'. He thus computes

$$P(r \leq 3 \,|\, n = 12, \mathcal{H}_0) = \sum_{r=0}^{3} \binom{n}{r} 1/2^n = \left(\binom{12}{0} + \binom{12}{1} + \binom{12}{2} + \binom{12}{3} \right) 1/2^{12}$$
$$= 0.07, \tag{37.27}$$

and reports 'at the significance level of 5%, there is not significant evidence of bias in favour of a'. Or, if the friend prefers to report p-values rather than simply compare p with 5%, he would report 'the p-value is 7%, which is not conventionally viewed as significantly small'. If a two-tailed test seemed more appropriate, he might compute the two-tailed area, which is twice the above probability, and report 'the p-value is 15%, which is not significantly small'. We won't focus on the issue of the choice between the one-tailed and two-tailed tests, as we have bigger fish to catch.

Dr. Bloggs pays careful attention to the calculation (37.27), and responds 'no, no, the random variable in the experiment was not r: I decided before running the experiment that I would keep tossing the coin until I saw three bs; the random variable is thus n'.

> Such experimental designs are not unusual. In my experiments on error-correcting codes I often simulate the decoding of a code until a chosen number r of block errors (bs) has occurred, since the error on the inferred value of $\log p_\mathrm{b}$ goes roughly as $\sqrt{r}$, independent of n.

Exercise 37.1.[2] Find the Bayesian inference about the bias p_a of the coin given the data, and determine whether a Bayesian's inferences depend on what stopping rule was in force.

According to sampling theory, a different calculation is required in order to assess the 'significance' of the result $n = 12$. The probability distribution of n given $\mathcal{H}_0$ is the probability that the first $n-1$ tosses contain exactly $r-1$ bs and then the nth toss is a b.

$$P(n \,|\, \mathcal{H}_0, r) = \binom{n-1}{r-1} 1/2^n. \tag{37.28}$$

The sampling theorist thus computes

$$P(n \geq 12 \,|\, r = 3, \mathcal{H}_0) = 0.03. \tag{37.29}$$

He reports back to Dr. Bloggs, 'the p-value is 3% – there *is* significant evidence of bias after all!'

What do you think Dr. Bloggs should do? Should he publish the result, with this marvellous p-value, in one of the journals that insists that all experimental results have their 'significance' assessed using sampling theory? Or should he boot the sampling theorist out of the door and seek a coherent method of assessing significance, one that does not depend on the stopping rule?

At this point the audience divides in two. Half the audience intuitively feel that the stopping rule is irrelevant, and don't need any convincing that the answer to exercise 37.1 (p.463) is 'the inferences about p_a do not depend on the stopping rule'. The other half, perhaps on account of a thorough training in sampling theory, intuitively feel that Dr. Bloggs's stopping rule, which stopped tossing the moment the third b appeared, may have biased the experiment somehow. If you are in the second group, I encourage you to reflect on the situation, and hope you'll eventually come round to the view that is consistent with the likelihood principle, which is that the stopping rule is not relevant to what we have learned about p_a.

As a thought experiment, consider some onlookers who (in order to save money) are spying on Dr. Bloggs's experiments: each time he tosses the coin, the spies update the values of r and n. The spies are eager to make inferences from the data as soon as each new result occurs. Should the spies' beliefs about the bias of the coin depend on Dr. Bloggs's intentions regarding the continuation of the experiment?

The fact that the p-values of sampling theory *do* depend on the stopping rule (indeed, whole volumes of the sampling theory literature are concerned with the task of assessing 'significance' when a complicated stopping rule is required – 'sequential probability ratio tests', for example) seems to me a compelling argument for having nothing to do with p-values at all. A Bayesian solution to this inference problem was given in sections 3.2 and 3.3 and exercise 3.15 (p.59).

Would it help clarify this issue if I added one more scene to the story? The janitor, who's been eavesdropping on Dr. Bloggs's conversation, comes in and says 'I happened to notice that just after you stopped doing the experiments on the coin, the Officer for Whimsical Departmental Rules ordered the immediate destruction of all such coins. Your coin was therefore destroyed by the departmental safety officer. There is no way you could have continued the experiment much beyond $n = 12$ tosses. Seems to me, you need to recompute your p-value?'

▶ 37.3 Confidence intervals

In an experiment in which data D are obtained from a system with an unknown parameter θ, a standard concept in sampling theory is the idea of a *confidence interval* for θ. Such an interval $(\theta_{\min}(D), \theta_{\max}(D))$ has associated with it a *confidence level* such as 95% which is informally interpreted as 'the probability that θ lies in the confidence interval'.

Let's make precise what the confidence level really means, then give an example. A confidence interval is a function $(\theta_{\min}(D), \theta_{\max}(D))$ of the data set D. The confidence level of the confidence interval is a property that we can compute before the data arrive. We imagine generating many data sets from a particular true value of θ, and calculating the interval $(\theta_{\min}(D), \theta_{\max}(D))$, and then checking whether the true value of θ lies in that interval. If, averaging over all these imagined repetitions of the experiment, the true value of θ lies in the confidence interval a fraction f of the time, and this property holds for all true values of θ, then the confidence level of the confidence interval is f.

For example, if θ is the mean of a Gaussian distribution which is known to have standard deviation 1, and D is a sample from that Gaussian, then $(\theta_{\min}(D), \theta_{\max}(D)) = (D-2, D+2)$ is a 95% confidence interval for θ.

Let us now look at a simple example where the meaning of the confidence level becomes clearer. Let the parameter θ be an integer, and let the data be a pair of points x_1, x_2, drawn independently from the following distribution:

$$P(x \mid \theta) = \begin{cases} \frac{1}{2} & x = \theta \\ \frac{1}{2} & x = \theta + 1 \\ 0 & \text{for other values of } x. \end{cases} \tag{37.30}$$

For example, if θ were 39, then we could expect the following data sets:

$$
\begin{aligned}
D = (x_1, x_2) &= (39, 39) \quad \text{with probability } 1/4; \\
(x_1, x_2) &= (39, 40) \quad \text{with probability } 1/4; \\
(x_1, x_2) &= (40, 39) \quad \text{with probability } 1/4; \\
(x_1, x_2) &= (40, 40) \quad \text{with probability } 1/4.
\end{aligned}
\tag{37.31}
$$

We now consider the following confidence interval:

$$
[\theta_{\min}(D), \theta_{\max}(D)] = [\min(x_1, x_2), \min(x_1, x_2)].
\tag{37.32}
$$

For example, if $(x_1, x_2) = (40, 39)$, then the confidence interval for θ would be $[\theta_{\min}(D), \theta_{\max}(D)] = [39, 39]$.

Let's think about this confidence interval. What is its confidence level? By considering the four possibilities shown in (37.31), we can see that there is a 75% chance that the confidence interval will contain the true value. The confidence interval therefore has a confidence level of 75%, by definition.

Now, what if the data we acquire are $(x_1, x_2) = (29, 29)$? Well, we can compute the confidence interval, and it is $[29, 29]$. So shall we report this interval, and its associated confidence level, 75%? This would be correct by the rules of sampling theory. But does this make sense? What do we actually know in this case? Intuitively, or by Bayes' theorem, it is clear that θ could either be 29 or 28, and both possibilities are equally likely (if the prior probabilities of 28 and 29 were equal). The posterior probability of θ is 50% on 29 and 50% on 28.

What if the data are $(x_1, x_2) = (29, 30)$? In this case, the confidence interval is still $[29, 29]$, and its associated confidence level is 75%. But in this case, by Bayes' theorem, or common sense, we are 100% sure that θ is 29.

In neither case is the probability that θ lies in the '75% confidence interval' equal to 75%!

Thus

1. the way in which many people interpret the confidence levels of sampling theory is *incorrect*;

2. given some data, what people usually want to know (whether they know it or not) is a Bayesian posterior probability distribution.

Are all these examples contrived? Am I making a fuss about nothing? If you are sceptical about the dogmatic views I have expressed, I encourage you to look at a case study: look in depth at exercise 35.4 (p.446) and the reference (Kepler and Oprea, 2001), in which sampling theory estimates and confidence intervals for a mutation rate are constructed. Try both methods on simulated data – the Bayesian approach based on simply computing the likelihood function, and the confidence interval from sampling theory; and let me know if you don't find that the Bayesian answer is always better than the sampling theory answer; and often much, much better. This suboptimality of sampling theory, achieved with great effort, is why I am passionate about Bayesian methods. Bayesian methods are straightforward, and they optimally use all the information in the data.

▶ **37.4 Some compromise positions**

Let's end on a conciliatory note. Many sampling theorists are pragmatic – they are happy to choose from a selection of statistical methods, choosing whichever has the 'best' long-run properties. In contrast, I have no problem with the idea that there is only *one* answer to a well-posed problem; but it's not essential to convert sampling theorists to this viewpoint: instead, we can offer them Bayesian estimators and Bayesian confidence intervals, and request that the sampling theoretical properties of these methods be evaluated. We don't need to mention that the methods are derived from a Bayesian perspective. If the sampling properties are good then the pragmatic sampling theorist will choose to use the Bayesian methods. It is indeed the case that many Bayesian methods have good sampling-theoretical properties. Perhaps it's not surprising that a method that gives the optimal answer for each individual case should also be good in the long run!

Another piece of common ground can be conceded: while I believe that most well-posed inference problems have a unique correct answer, which can be found by Bayesian methods, not all problems are well-posed. A common question arising in data modelling is 'am I using an appropriate model?' Model criticism, that is, hunting for defects in a current model, is a task that may be aided by sampling theory tests, in which the null hypothesis ('the current model is correct') is well defined, but the alternative model is not specified. One could use sampling theory measures such as p-values to guide one's search for the aspects of the model most in need of scrutiny.

Further reading

My favourite reading on this topic includes (Jaynes, 1983; Gull, 1988; Loredo, 1990; Berger, 1985; Jaynes, 2003). Treatises on Bayesian statistics from the statistics community include (Box and Tiao, 1973; O'Hagan, 1994).

▶ 37.5 Further exercises

▷ Exercise 37.2.[*3C*] A traffic survey records traffic on two successive days. On Friday morning, there are 12 vehicles in one hour. On Saturday morning, there are 9 vehicles in half an hour. Assuming that the vehicles are Poisson distributed with rates λ_F and λ_S (in vehicles per hour) respectively,

(a) is λ_S greater than λ_F?

(b) by what factor is λ_S bigger or smaller than λ_F?

▷ Exercise 37.3.[*3C*] Write a program to compare treatments A and B given data F_{A+}, F_{A-}, F_{B+}, F_{B-} as described in section 37.1. The outputs of the program should be (a) the probability that treatment A is more effective than treatment B; (b) the probability that $p_{A+} < 10\,p_{B+}$; (c) the probability that $p_{B+} < 10\,p_{A+}$.

Part V

Neural networks

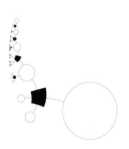

38

Introduction to Neural Networks

In the field of neural networks, we study the properties of networks of idealized 'neurons'.

Three motivations underlie work in this broad and interdisciplinary field.

Biology. The task of understanding how the brain works is one of the outstanding unsolved problems in science. Some neural network models are intended to shed light on the way in which computation and memory are performed by brains.

Engineering. Many researchers would like to create machines that can 'learn', perform 'pattern recognition' or 'discover patterns in data'.

Complex systems. A third motivation for being interested in neural networks is that they are complex adaptive systems whose properties are interesting in their own right.

I should emphasize several points at the outset.

- This book gives only a taste of this field. There are many interesting neural network models which we will not have time to touch on.

- The models that we discuss are not intended to be faithful models of biological systems. If they are at all relevant to biology, their relevance is on an abstract level.

- I will describe some neural network methods that are widely used in nonlinear data modelling, but I will not be able to give a full description of the state of the art. If you wish to solve real problems with neural networks, please read the relevant papers.

▶ 38.1 Memories

In the next few chapters we will meet several neural network models which come with simple learning algorithms which make them function as *memories*. Perhaps we should dwell for a moment on the conventional idea of memory in digital computation. A memory (a string of 5000 bits describing the name of a person and an image of their face, say) is stored in a digital computer at an *address*. To retrieve the memory you need to know the address. The address has nothing to do with the memory itself. Notice the properties that this scheme does *not* have:

1. Address-based memory is *not* associative. Imagine you know half of a memory, say someone's face, and you would like to recall the rest of the

memory – their name. If your memory is address-based then you can't get at a memory without knowing the address. [Computer scientists have devoted effort to wrapping traditional address-based memories inside cunning software to produce content-addressable memories, but content-addressability does not come naturally. It has to be added on.]

2. Address-based memory is *not* robust or fault-tolerant. If a one-bit mistake is made in specifying the *address* then a completely different memory will be retrieved. If one bit of a *memory* is flipped then whenever that memory is retrieved the error will be present. Of course, in all modern computers, error-correcting codes are used in the memory, so that small numbers of errors can be detected and corrected. But this error-tolerance is not an intrinsic property of the memory system. If minor damage occurs to certain hardware that implements memory retrieval, it is likely that all functionality will be catastrophically lost.

3. Address-based memory is not distributed. In a serial computer that is accessing a particular memory, only a tiny fraction of the devices participate in the memory recall: the CPU and the circuits that are storing the required byte. All the other millions of devices in the machine are sitting idle.

   Are there models of truly parallel computation, in which multiple devices participate in all computations? [Present-day parallel computers scarcely differ from serial computers from this point of view. Memory retrieval works in just the same way, and control of the computation process resides in CPUs. There are simply a few more CPUs. Most of the devices sit idle most of the time.]

Biological memory systems are completely different.

1. Biological memory is associative. Memory recall is *content-addressable*. Given a person's name, we can often recall their face; and *vice versa*. Memories are apparently recalled spontaneously, not just at the request of some CPU.

2. Biological memory recall is error-tolerant and robust.

   - Errors in the cues for memory recall can be corrected. An example asks you to recall 'An American politician who was very intelligent and whose politician father did not like broccoli'. Many people think of president Bush – even though one of the cues contains an error.

   - Hardware faults can also be tolerated. Our brains are noisy lumps of meat that are in a continual state of change, with cells being damaged by natural processes, alcohol, and boxing. While the cells in our brains and the proteins in our cells are continually changing, many of our memories persist unaffected.

3. Biological memory is parallel and distributed – not *completely* distributed throughout the whole brain: there does appear to be some functional specialization – but in the parts of the brain where memories are stored, it seems that many neurons participate in the storage of multiple memories.

These properties of biological memory systems motivate the study of 'artificial neural networks' – parallel distributed computational systems consisting of many interacting simple elements. The hope is that these model systems might give some hints as to how neural computation is achieved in real biological neural networks.

▶ ## 38.2 Terminology

Each time we describe a neural network algorithm we will typically specify three things. [If any of this terminology is hard to understand, it's probably best to dive straight into the next chapter.]

Architecture. The architecture specifies what variables are involved in the network and their topological relationships – for example, the variables involved in a neural net might be the *weights* of the connections between the neurons, along with the *activities* of the neurons.

Activity rule. Most neural network models have short time-scale dynamics: local rules define how the *activities* of the neurons change in response to each other. Typically the activity rule depends on the *weights* (the parameters) in the network.

Learning rule. The learning rule specifies the way in which the neural network's *weights* change with time. This learning is usually viewed as taking place on a longer time scale than the time scale of the dynamics under the activity rule. Usually the learning rule will depend on the *activities* of the neurons. It may also depend on the values of *target* values supplied by a *teacher* and on the current value of the weights.

Where do these rules come from? Often, activity rules and learning rules are invented by imaginative researchers. Alternatively, activity rules and learning rules may be *derived* from carefully chosen *objective functions*.

Neural network algorithms can be roughly divided into two classes.

Supervised neural networks are given data in the form of *inputs* and *targets*, the targets being a *teacher*'s specification of what the neural network's response to the input should be.

Unsupervised neural networks are given data in an undivided form – simply a set of examples $\{\mathbf{x}\}$. Some learning algorithms are intended simply to memorize these data in such a way that the examples can be recalled in the future. Other algorithms are intended to 'generalize', to discover 'patterns' in the data, or extract the underlying 'features' from them.

Some unsupervised algorithms are able to make predictions – for example, some algorithms can 'fill in' missing variables in an example $\mathbf{x}$ – and so can also be viewed as supervised networks.

39

The Single Neuron as a Classifier

▶ 39.1 The single neuron

We will study a single neuron for two reasons. First, many neural network models are built out of single neurons, so it is good to understand them in detail. And second, a single neuron is itself capable of 'learning' – indeed, various standard statistical methods can be viewed in terms of single neurons – so this model will serve as a first example of a *supervised neural network*.

Definition of a single neuron

We will start by defining the architecture and the activity rule of a single neuron, and we will then derive a learning rule.

Architecture. A single neuron has a number I of *inputs* x_i and one *output* which we will here call y. (See figure 39.1.) Associated with each input is a *weight* w_i $(i = 1, \ldots, I)$. There may be an additional parameter w_0 of the neuron called a *bias* which we may view as being the weight associated with an input x_0 which is permanently set to 1. The single neuron is a *feedforward* device – the connections are directed from the inputs to the output of the neuron.

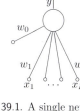

Figure 39.1. A single neuron

Activity rule. The activity rule has two steps.

1. First, in response to the imposed inputs **x**, we compute the *activation* of the neuron,
$$a = \sum_i w_i x_i, \tag{39.1}$$
where the sum is over $i = 0, \ldots, I$ if there is a bias and $i = 1, \ldots, I$ otherwise.

2. Second, the *output* y is set as a function $f(a)$ of the activation. The output is also called the *activity* of the neuron, not to be confused with the activation a. There are several possible *activation functions*; here are the most popular.

(a) Deterministic activation functions:

i. Linear.
$$y(a) = a. \tag{39.2}$$

ii. Sigmoid (logistic function).
$$y(a) = \frac{1}{1 + e^{-a}} \qquad (y \in (0,1)). \tag{39.3}$$

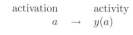

471

iii. Sigmoid (tanh).

$$y(a) = \tanh(a) \qquad (y \in (-1, 1)). \qquad (39.4)$$

iv. Threshold function.

$$y(a) = \Theta(a) \equiv \begin{cases} 1 & a > 0 \\ -1 & a \le 0. \end{cases} \qquad (39.5)$$

(b) Stochastic activation functions: y is stochastically selected from ± 1.

i. Heat bath.

$$y(a) = \begin{cases} 1 & \text{with probability } \dfrac{1}{1 + e^{-a}} \\ -1 & \text{otherwise.} \end{cases} \qquad (39.6)$$

ii. The Metropolis rule produces the output in a way that depends on the previous output state y:

> Compute $\Delta = ay$
> If $\Delta \le 0$, flip y to the other state
> Else flip y to the other state with probability $e^{-\Delta}$.

▶ 39.2 Basic neural network concepts

A neural network implements a function $y(\mathbf{x}; \mathbf{w})$; the 'output' of the network, y, is a nonlinear function of the 'inputs' $\mathbf{x}$; this function is parameterized by 'weights' $\mathbf{w}$.

We will study a single neuron which produces an output between 0 and 1 as the following function of $\mathbf{x}$:

$$y(\mathbf{x}; \mathbf{w}) = \frac{1}{1 + e^{-\mathbf{w} \cdot \mathbf{x}}}. \qquad (39.7)$$

 Exercise 39.1.[1] In what contexts have we encountered the function $y(\mathbf{x}; \mathbf{w}) = 1/(1 + e^{-\mathbf{w} \cdot \mathbf{x}})$ already?

Motivations for the linear logistic function

In section 11.2 we studied 'the best detection of pulses', assuming that one of two signals $\mathbf{x}_0$ and $\mathbf{x}_1$ had been transmitted over a Gaussian channel with variance–covariance matrix $\mathbf{A}^{-1}$. We found that the probability that the source signal was $s = 1$ rather than $s = 0$, given the received signal $\mathbf{y}$, was

$$P(s = 1 | \mathbf{y}) = \frac{1}{1 + \exp(-a(\mathbf{y}))}, \qquad (39.8)$$

where $a(\mathbf{y})$ was a linear function of the received vector,

$$a(\mathbf{y}) = \mathbf{w}^{\mathsf{T}} \mathbf{y} + \theta, \qquad (39.9)$$

with $\mathbf{w} \equiv \mathbf{A}(\mathbf{x}_1 - \mathbf{x}_0)$.

The linear logistic function can be motivated in several other ways – see the exercises.

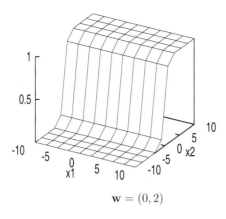

Figure 39.2. Output of a simple neural network as a function of its input.

$$\mathbf{w} = (0, 2)$$

Input space and weight space

For convenience let us study the case where the input vector $\mathbf{x}$ and the parameter vector $\mathbf{w}$ are both two-dimensional: $\mathbf{x} = (x_1, x_2)$, $\mathbf{w} = (w_1, w_2)$. Then we can spell out the function performed by the neuron thus:

$$y(\mathbf{x}; \mathbf{w}) = \frac{1}{1 + e^{-(w_1 x_1 + w_2 x_2)}}. \tag{39.10}$$

Figure 39.2 shows the output of the neuron as a function of the input vector, for $\mathbf{w} = (0, 2)$. The two horizontal axes of this figure are the inputs x_1 and x_2, with the output y on the vertical axis. Notice that on any line perpendicular to $\mathbf{w}$, the output is constant; and along a line in the direction of $\mathbf{w}$, the output is a sigmoid function.

We now introduce the idea of *weight space*, that is, the parameter space of the network. In this case, there are two parameters w_1 and w_2, so the weight space is two dimensional. This weight space is shown in figure 39.3. For a selection of values of the parameter vector $\mathbf{w}$, smaller inset figures show the function of $\mathbf{x}$ performed by the network when $\mathbf{w}$ is set to those values. Each of these smaller figures is equivalent to figure 39.2. Thus each *point* in $\mathbf{w}$ space corresponds to a *function* of $\mathbf{x}$. Notice that the gain of the sigmoid function (the gradient of the ramp) increases as the magnitude of $\mathbf{w}$ increases.

Now, the central idea of supervised neural networks is this. Given *examples* of a relationship between an input vector $\mathbf{x}$, and a target t, we hope to make the neural network 'learn' a model of the relationship between $\mathbf{x}$ and t. A successfully trained network will, for any given $\mathbf{x}$, give an output y that is close (in some sense) to the target value t. *Training* the network involves searching in the weight space of the network for a value of $\mathbf{w}$ that produces a function that fits the provided training data well.

Typically an *objective function* or *error function* is defined, as a function of $\mathbf{w}$, to measure how well the network with weights set to $\mathbf{w}$ solves the task. The objective function is a sum of terms, one for each input/target pair $\{\mathbf{x}, t\}$, measuring how close the output $y(\mathbf{x}; \mathbf{w})$ is to the target t. The training process is an exercise in *function minimization* – i.e., adjusting $\mathbf{w}$ in such a way as to find a $\mathbf{w}$ that minimizes the objective function. Many function-minimization algorithms make use not only of the objective function, but also its *gradient* with respect to the parameters $\mathbf{w}$. For general feedforward neural networks the *backpropagation* algorithm efficiently evaluates the gradient of the output y with respect to the parameters $\mathbf{w}$, and thence the gradient of the objective function with respect to $\mathbf{w}$.

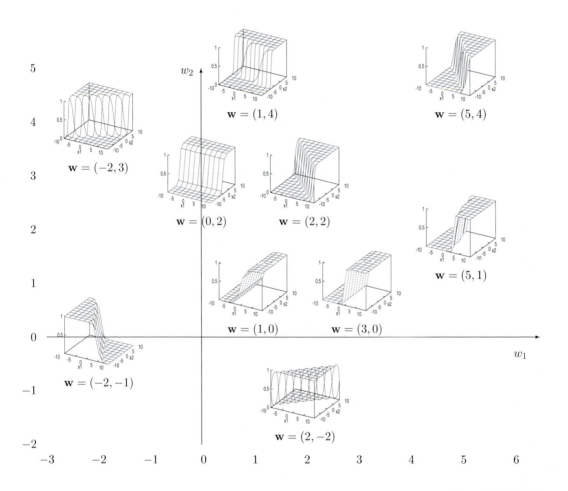

Figure 39.3. Weight space.

▶ **39.3 Training the single neuron as a binary classifier**

We assume we have a data set of inputs $\{\mathbf{x}^{(n)}\}_{n=1}^{N}$ with binary labels $\{t^{(n)}\}_{n=1}^{N}$, and a neuron whose output $y(\mathbf{x}; \mathbf{w})$ is bounded between 0 and 1. We can then write down the following *error function*:

$$G(\mathbf{w}) = -\sum_{n} \left[t^{(n)} \ln y(\mathbf{x}^{(n)}; \mathbf{w}) + (1 - t^{(n)}) \ln(1 - y(\mathbf{x}^{(n)}; \mathbf{w})) \right]. \quad (39.11)$$

Each term in this objective function may be recognized as the *information content* of one outcome. It may also be described as the relative entropy between the empirical probability distribution $(t^{(n)}, 1 - t^{(n)})$ and the probability distribution implied by the output of the neuron $(y, 1 - y)$. The objective function is bounded below by zero and only attains this value if $y(\mathbf{x}^{(n)}; \mathbf{w}) = t^{(n)}$ for all n.

We now differentiate this objective function with respect to $\mathbf{w}$.

Exercise 39.2.[2] The backpropagation algorithm. Show that the derivative $\mathbf{g} = \partial G/\partial \mathbf{w}$ is given by:

$$g_j = \frac{\partial G}{\partial w_j} = \sum_{n=1}^{N} -(t^{(n)} - y^{(n)}) x_j^{(n)}. \quad (39.12)$$

Notice that the quantity $e^{(n)} \equiv t^{(n)} - y^{(n)}$ is the *error* on example n – the difference between the target and the output. The simplest thing to do with a gradient of an error function is to *descend* it (even though this is often dimensionally incorrect, since a gradient has dimensions [1/parameter], whereas a change in a parameter has dimensions [parameter]). Since the derivative $\partial G/\partial \mathbf{w}$ is a sum of terms $\mathbf{g}^{(n)}$ defined by

$$g_j^{(n)} \equiv -(t^{(n)} - y^{(n)}) x_j^{(n)} \quad (39.13)$$

for $n = 1, \ldots, N$, we can obtain a simple on-line algorithm by putting each input through the network one at a time, and adjusting $\mathbf{w}$ a little in a direction opposite to $\mathbf{g}^{(n)}$.

We summarize the whole learning algorithm.

The on-line gradient-descent learning algorithm

Architecture. A single neuron has a number I of *inputs* x_i and one *output* y. Associated with each input is a weight w_i $(i = 1, \ldots, I)$.

Activity rule. 1. First, in response to the received inputs $\mathbf{x}$ (which may be arbitrary real numbers), we compute the *activation* of the neuron,

$$a = \sum_{i} w_i x_i, \quad (39.14)$$

where the sum is over $i = 0, \ldots, I$ if there is a bias and $i = 1, \ldots, I$ otherwise.

2. Second, the *output* y is set as a sigmoid function of the activation.

$$y(a) = \frac{1}{1 + e^{-a}}. \quad (39.15)$$

This output might be viewed as stating the probability, according to the neuron, that the given input is in class 1 rather than class 0.

Learning rule. The *teacher* supplies a *target* value $t \in \{0, 1\}$ which says what the correct answer is for the given input. We compute the *error signal*

$$e = t - y \tag{39.16}$$

then adjust the weights $\mathbf{w}$ in a direction that would reduce the magnitude of this error:

$$\Delta w_i = \eta e x_i, \tag{39.17}$$

where η is the 'learning rate'. Commonly η is set by trial and error to a constant value or to a decreasing function of simulation time τ such as η_0/τ.

The activity rule and learning rule are repeated for each input/target pair $(\mathbf{x}, t)$ that is presented. If there is a fixed data set of size N, we can cycle through the data multiple times.

Batch learning versus on-line learning

Here we have described the *on-line* learning algorithm, in which a change in the weights is made after every example is presented. An alternative paradigm is to go through a *batch* of examples, computing the outputs and errors and accumulating the changes specified in equation (39.17) which are then made at the end of the batch.

Batch learning for the single neuron classifier

For each input/target pair $(\mathbf{x}^{(n)}, t^{(n)})$ $(n = 1, \ldots, N)$, compute $y^{(n)} = y(\mathbf{x}^{(n)}; \mathbf{w})$, where

$$y(\mathbf{x}; \mathbf{w}) = \frac{1}{1 + \exp(-\sum_i w_i x_i)}, \tag{39.18}$$

define $e^{(n)} = t^{(n)} - y^{(n)}$, and compute for each weight w_i

$$g_i^{(n)} = -e^{(n)} x_i^{(n)}. \tag{39.19}$$

Then let

$$\Delta w_i = -\eta \sum_n g_i^{(n)}. \tag{39.20}$$

This batch learning algorithm is a *gradient descent algorithm*, whereas the on-line algorithm is a *stochastic gradient descent* algorithm. Source code implementing batch learning is given in algorithm 39.5. This algorithm is demonstrated in figure 39.4 for a neuron with two inputs with weights w_1 and w_2 and a bias w_0, performing the function

$$y(\mathbf{x}; \mathbf{w}) = \frac{1}{1 + e^{-(w_0 + w_1 x_1 + w_2 x_2)}}. \tag{39.21}$$

The bias w_0 is included, in contrast to figure 39.3, where it was omitted. The neuron is trained on a data set of ten labelled examples.

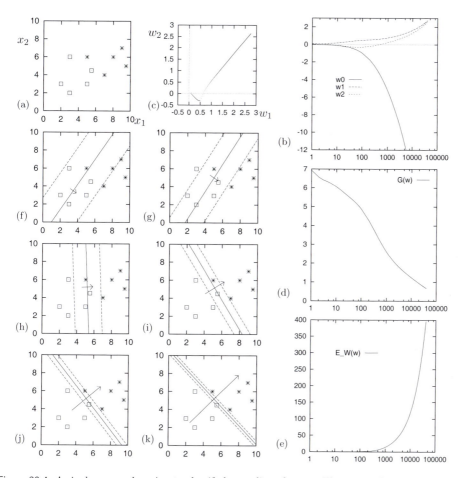

Figure 39.4. A single neuron learning to classify by gradient descent. The neuron has two weights w_1 and w_2 and a bias w_0. The learning rate was set to $\eta = 0.01$ and batch-mode gradient descent was performed using the code displayed in algorithm 39.5. (a) The training data. (b) Evolution of weights w_0, w_1 and w_2 as a function of number of iterations (on log scale). (c) Evolution of weights w_1 and w_2 in weight space. (d) The objective function $G(\mathbf{w})$ as a function of number of iterations. (e) The magnitude of the weights $E_W(\mathbf{w})$ as a function of time. (f–k) The function performed by the neuron (shown by three of its contours) after 30, 80, 500, 3000, 10 000 and 40 000 iterations. The contours shown are those corresponding to $a = 0, \pm 1$, namely $y = 0.5, 0.27$ and 0.73. Also shown is a vector proportional to (w_1, w_2). The larger the weights are, the bigger this vector becomes, and the closer together are the contours.

```
global x ;        # x is an N * I matrix containing all the input vectors
global t ;        # t is a vector of length N containing all the targets

for l = 1:L       # loop L times

  a = x * w  ;                    # compute all activations
  y = sigmoid(a) ;                # compute outputs
  e = t - y   ;                   # compute errors
  g = - x' * e ;                  # compute the gradient vector
  w = w - eta * ( g + alpha * w ) ;   # make step, using learning rate eta
                                  #    and weight decay alpha
endfor

function f = sigmoid ( v )
  f = 1.0 ./ ( 1.0 .+ exp ( - v ) ) ;
endfunction
```

Algorithm 39.5. Octave source code for a gradient descent optimizer of a single neuron, batch learning, with optional weight decay (rate `alpha`). Octave notation: the instruction `a = x * w` causes the $(N \times I)$ *matrix* x consisting of all the input vectors to be multiplied by the weight vector w, giving the *vector* a listing the activations for all N input vectors; x' means x-transpose; the single command `y = sigmoid(a)` computes the sigmoid function of all elements of the vector a.

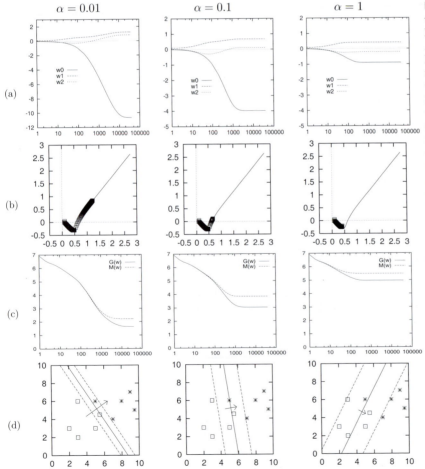

Figure 39.6. The influence of weight decay on a single neuron's learning. The objective function is $M(\mathbf{w}) = G(\mathbf{w}) + \alpha E_W(\mathbf{w})$. The learning method was as in figure 39.4. (a) Evolution of weights w_0, w_1 and w_2. (b) Evolution of weights w_1 and w_2 in weight space shown by points, contrasted with the trajectory followed in the case of zero weight decay, shown by a thin line (from figure 39.4). Notice that for this problem weight decay has an effect very similar to 'early stopping'. (c) The objective function $M(\mathbf{w})$ and the error function $G(\mathbf{w})$ as a function of number of iterations. (d) The function performed by the neuron after 40 000 iterations.

▶ **39.4 Beyond descent on the error function: regularization**

If the parameter η is set to an appropriate value, this algorithm works: the algorithm finds a setting of $\mathbf{w}$ which correctly classifies as many of the examples as possible.

If the examples are in fact *linearly separable* then the neuron finds this linear separation and its weights diverge to ever-larger values as the simulation continues. This can be seen happening in figure 39.4(f–k). This is an example of *overfitting*, where a model fits the data so well that its generalization performance is likely to be adversely affected.

This behaviour may be viewed as undesirable. How can it be rectified?

An ad hoc solution to overfitting is to use *early stopping*, that is, use an algorithm originally intended to minimize the error function $G(\mathbf{w})$, then prevent it from doing so by halting the algorithm at some point.

A more principled solution to overfitting makes use of *regularization*. Regularization involves modifying the objective function in such a way as to incorporate a bias against the sorts of solution $\mathbf{w}$ which we dislike. In the above example, what we dislike is the development of a very sharp decision boundary in figure 39.4k; this sharp boundary is associated with large weight values, so we use a regularizer that penalizes large weight values. We modify the objective function to:

$$M(\mathbf{w}) = G(\mathbf{w}) + \alpha E_W(\mathbf{w}) \tag{39.22}$$

where the simplest choice of regularizer is the *weight decay* regularizer

$$E_W(\mathbf{w}) = \frac{1}{2}\sum_i w_i^2. \tag{39.23}$$

The *regularization constant* α is called the weight decay rate. This additional term favours small values of $\mathbf{w}$ and decreases the tendency of a model to overfit fine details of the training data. The quantity α is known as a *hyperparameter*. Hyperparameters play a role in the learning algorithm but play no role in the activity rule of the network.

Exercise 39.3.[1] Compute the derivative of $M(\mathbf{w})$ with respect to w_i. Why is the above regularizer known as the 'weight decay' regularizer?

The gradient descent source code of algorithm 39.5 implements weight decay. This gradient descent algorithm is demonstrated in figure 39.6 using weight decay rates $\alpha = 0.01, 0.1$ and 1. As the weight decay rate is increased the solution becomes biased towards broader sigmoid functions with decision boundaries that are closer to the origin.

Note

Gradient descent with a step size η is in general *not* the most efficient way to minimize a function. A modification of gradient descent known as *momentum*, while improving convergence, is also not recommended. Most neural network experts use more advanced optimizers such as conjugate gradient algorithms. [Please do not confuse momentum, which is sometimes given the symbol α, with weight decay.]

▶ 39.5 Further exercises

More motivations for the linear neuron

▷ Exercise 39.4.[2] Consider the task of recognizing which of two Gaussian distributions a vector $\mathbf{z}$ comes from. Unlike the case studied in section 11.2, where the distributions had different means but a common variance–covariance matrix, we will assume that the two distributions have exactly the same mean but different variances. Let the probability of $\mathbf{z}$ given s ($s \in \{0, 1\}$) be

$$P(\mathbf{z}|s) = \prod_{i=1}^{I} \mathrm{Normal}(z_i; 0, \sigma_{si}^2), \tag{39.24}$$

where σ_{si}^2 is the variance of z_i when the source symbol is s. Show that $P(s = 1|\mathbf{z})$ can be written in the form

$$P(s = 1|\mathbf{z}) = \frac{1}{1 + \exp(-\mathbf{w}^\mathsf{T}\mathbf{x} + \theta)}, \tag{39.25}$$

where x_i is an appropriate function of z_i, $x_i = g(z_i)$.

Exercise 39.5.[2] **The noisy LED**.

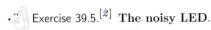

$$\mathbf{c}(2) = \quad \mathbf{c}(3) = \quad \mathbf{c}(8) =$$

Consider an LED display with 7 elements numbered as shown above. The state of the display is a vector $\mathbf{x}$. When the controller wants the display to show character number s, e.g. $s = 2$, each element x_j ($j = 1, \ldots, 7$) either adopts its intended state $c_j(s)$, with probability $1 - f$, or is flipped, with probability f. Let's call the two states of x '+1' and '−1'.

(a) Assuming that the intended character s is actually a 2 or a 3, what is the probability of s, given the state $\mathbf{x}$? Show that $P(s = 2|\mathbf{x})$ can be written in the form

$$P(s = 2|\mathbf{x}) = \frac{1}{1 + \exp(-\mathbf{w}^\mathsf{T}\mathbf{x} + \theta)}, \tag{39.26}$$

and compute the values of the weights $\mathbf{w}$ in the case $f = 0.1$.

(b) Assuming that s is one of $\{0, 1, 2, \ldots, 9\}$, with prior probabilities p_s, what is the probability of s, given the state $\mathbf{x}$? Put your answer in the form

$$P(s|\mathbf{x}) = \frac{e^{a_s}}{\sum_{s'} e^{a_{s'}}}, \tag{39.27}$$

where $\{a_s\}$ are functions of $\{c_j(s)\}$ and $\mathbf{x}$.

Could you make a better alphabet of 10 characters for a noisy LED, i.e., an alphabet less susceptible to confusion?

0	n̄
1	I₁
2	ᴗ
3	Π
4	ⲁ
5	⌐
6	⊐
7	⌐
8	8
9	c
10	ᴇ
11	⌐
12	⊔
13	⊐
14	⌐

Table 39.7. An alternative 15-character alphabet for the 7-element LED display.

▷ Exercise 39.6.[2] A $(3, 1)$ error-correcting code consists of the two codewords $\mathbf{x}^{(1)} = (1, 0, 0)$ and $\mathbf{x}^{(2)} = (0, 0, 1)$. A source bit $s \in \{1, 2\}$ having probability distribution $\{p_1, p_2\}$ is used to select one of the two codewords for transmission over a binary symmetric channel with noise level f. The received vector is $\mathbf{r}$. Show that the posterior probability of s given $\mathbf{r}$ can be written in the form

$$P(s = 1|\mathbf{r}) = \frac{1}{1 + \exp\left(-w_0 - \sum_{n=1}^{3} w_n r_n\right)},$$

and give expressions for the coefficients $\{w_n\}_{n=1}^{3}$ and the bias, w_0.

Describe, with a diagram, how this optimal decoder can be expressed in terms of a 'neuron'.

Problems to look at before Chapter 40

▷ Exercise 40.1.[2] What is $\sum_{K=0}^{N} \binom{N}{K}$?

[The symbol $\binom{N}{K}$ means the combination $\frac{N!}{K!(N-K)!}$.]

▷ Exercise 40.2.[2] If the top row of Pascal's triangle (which contains the single number '1') is denoted row zero, what is the sum of all the numbers in the triangle above row N?

▷ Exercise 40.3.[2] 3 points are selected at random on the surface of a sphere. What is the probability that all of them lie on a single hemisphere?

This chapter's material is originally due to Polya (1954) and Cover (1965) and the exposition that follows is Yaser Abu-Mostafa's.

40

Capacity of a Single Neuron

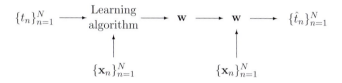

$$\{t_n\}_{n=1}^N \longrightarrow \boxed{\begin{array}{c}\text{Learning}\\\text{algorithm}\end{array}} \longrightarrow \mathbf{w} \longrightarrow \mathbf{w} \longrightarrow \{\hat{t}_n\}_{n=1}^N$$

Figure 40.1. Neural network learning viewed as communication.

▶ **40.1 Neural network learning as communication**

Many neural network models involve the adaptation of a set of weights $\mathbf{w}$ in response to a set of data points, for example a set of N target values $D_N = \{t_n\}_{n=1}^N$ at given locations $\{\mathbf{x}_n\}_{n=1}^N$. The adapted weights are then used to process subsequent input data. This process can be viewed as a communication process, in which the sender examines the data D_N and creates a message $\mathbf{w}$ that depends on those data. The receiver then uses $\mathbf{w}$; for example, the receiver might use the weights to try to reconstruct what the data D_N was. [In neural network parlance, this is using the neuron for 'memory' rather than for 'generalization'; 'generalizing' means extrapolating from the observed data to the value of t_{N+1} at some new location $\mathbf{x}_{N+1}$.] Just as a disk drive is a communication channel, the adapted network weights $\mathbf{w}$ therefore play the role of a communication channel, conveying information about the training data to a future user of that neural net. The question we now address is, 'what is the capacity of this channel?' – that is, 'how much information can be stored by training a neural network?'

If we had a learning algorithm that either produces a network whose response to all inputs is $+1$ or a network whose response to all inputs is 0, depending on the training data, then the weights allow us to distinguish between just two sorts of data set. The maximum information such a learning algorithm could convey about the data is therefore 1 bit, this information content being achieved if the two sorts of data set are equiprobable. How much more information can be conveyed if we make full use of a neural network's ability to represent other functions?

▶ **40.2 The capacity of a single neuron**

We will look at the simplest case, that of a single binary threshold neuron. We will find that the capacity of such a neuron is *two bits per weight*. A neuron with K inputs can store $2K$ bits of information.

To obtain this interesting result we lay down some rules to exclude less interesting answers, such as: 'the capacity of a neuron is infinite, because each of its weights is a real number and so can convey an infinite number of bits'. We exclude this answer by saying that the receiver is not able to examine the weights directly, nor is the receiver allowed to probe the weights by observing the output of the neuron for arbitrarily chosen inputs. We constrain the receiver to observe the output of the neuron at the same fixed set of N points $\{\mathbf{x}_n\}$ that were in the training set. What matters now is how many different distinguishable functions our neuron can produce, given that we can only observe the function at these N points. How many different binary labellings of N points can a linear threshold function produce? And how does this number compare with the maximum possible number of binary labellings, 2^N? If nearly all of the 2^N labellings can be realized by our neuron, then it is a communication channel that can convey all N bits (the target values $\{t_n\}$) with small probability of error. We will identify the capacity of the neuron as the maximum value that N can have such that the probability of error is very small. [We are departing a little from the definition of capacity in Chapter 9.]

We thus examine the following scenario. The sender is given a neuron with K inputs and a data set D_N which is a labelling of N points. The sender uses an adaptive algorithm to try to find a $\mathbf{w}$ that can reproduce this labelling exactly. We will assume the algorithm finds such a $\mathbf{w}$ if it exists. The receiver then evaluates the threshold function on the N input values. What is the probability that *all* N bits are correctly reproduced? How large can N become, for a given K, without this probability becoming substantially less than one?

General position

One technical detail needs to be pinned down: what set of inputs $\{\mathbf{x}_n\}$ are we considering? Our answer might depend on this choice. We will assume that the points are in *general position* (p.484), which means in $K = 3$ dimensions, for example, that no three points are colinear and no four points are coplanar.

Definition 40.1 *A set of points* $\{\mathbf{x}_n\}$ *in K-dimensional space are in* general position *if any subset of size $\leq K$ is linearly independent.*

In $K = 3$ dimensions, for example, a set of points are in general position if no three points are colinear and no four points are coplanar. The intuitive idea is that points in general position are like random points in the space, in terms of the linear dependences between points. You don't expect three random points in three dimensions to lie on a straight line.

The linear threshold function

The neuron we will consider performs the function

$$y = f\left(\sum_{k=1}^{K} w_k x_k\right) \tag{40.1}$$

where

$$f(a) = \begin{cases} 1 & a > 0 \\ 0 & a \leq 0. \end{cases} \tag{40.2}$$

We will not have a bias w_0; the capacity for a neuron with a bias can be obtained by replacing K by $K + 1$ in the final result below, i.e., considering one of the inputs to be fixed to 1. (These input points would not then be in general position; the derivation still works.)

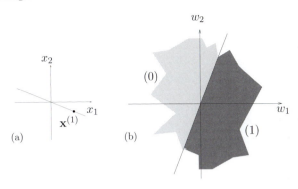

Figure 40.2. One data point in a two-dimensional input space, and the two regions of weight space that give the two alternative labellings of that point.

▶ **40.3 Counting threshold functions**

Let us denote by $T(N, K)$ the number of distinct threshold functions on N points in general position in K dimensions. We will derive a formula for $T(N, K)$.

To start with, let us work out a few cases by hand.

In $K = 1$ dimension, for any N

The N points lie on a line. By changing the sign of the one weight w_1 we can label all points on the right side of the origin 1 and the others 0, or *vice versa*. Thus there are two distinct threshold functions. $T(N, 1) = 2$.

With $N = 1$ point, for any K

If there is just one point $\mathbf{x}^{(1)}$ then we can realize both possible labellings by setting $\mathbf{w} = \pm\mathbf{x}^{(1)}$. Thus $T(1, K) = 2$.

In $K = 2$ dimensions

In two dimensions with N points, we are free to spin the separating line around the origin. Each time the line passes over a point we obtain a new function. Once we have spun the line through 360 degrees we reproduce the function we started from. Because the points are in general position, the separating plane (line) crosses only one point at a time. In one revolution, every point is passed over twice. There are therefore $2N$ distinct threshold functions. $T(N, 2) = 2N$.

Comparing with the total number of binary functions, 2^N, we may note that for $N \geq 3$, not all binary functions can be realized by a linear threshold function. One famous example of an unrealizable function with $N = 4$ and $K = 2$ is the exclusive-or function on the points $\mathbf{x} = (\pm 1, \pm 1)$. [These points are not in general position, but you may confirm that the function remains unrealizable even if the points are perturbed into general position.]

In $K = 2$ dimensions, from the point of view of weight space

There is another way of visualizing this problem. Instead of visualizing a plane separating points in the two-dimensional input space, we can consider the two-dimensional *weight space*, colouring regions in weight space different colours if they label the given datapoints differently. We can then count the number of threshold functions by counting how many distinguishable regions there are in weight space. Consider first the set of weight vectors in weight

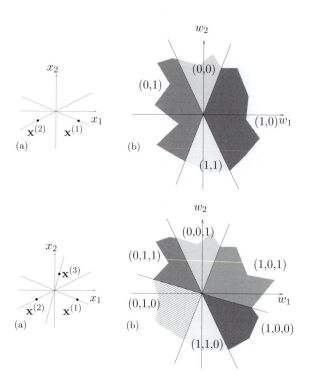

Figure 40.3. Two data points in a two-dimensional input space, and the four regions of weight space that give the four alternative labellings.

Figure 40.4. Three data points in a two-dimensional input space, and the six regions of weight space that give alternative labellings of those points. In this case, the labellings $(0,0,0)$ and $(1,1,1)$ cannot be realized. For any three points in general position there are always two labellings that cannot be realized.

space that classify a particular example $\mathbf{x}^{(n)}$ as a 1. For example, figure 40.2a shows a single point in our two-dimensional $\mathbf{x}$-space, and figure 40.2b shows the two corresponding sets of points in $\mathbf{w}$-space. One set of weight vectors occupy the half space

$$\mathbf{x}^{(n)}\cdot\mathbf{w} > 0, \tag{40.3}$$

and the others occupy $\mathbf{x}^{(n)}\cdot\mathbf{w} < 0$. In figure 40.3a we have added a second point in the input space. There are now 4 possible labellings: $(1,1)$, $(1,0)$, $(0,1)$, and $(0,0)$. Figure 40.3b shows the two hyperplanes $\mathbf{x}^{(1)}\cdot\mathbf{w} = 0$ and $\mathbf{x}^{(2)}\cdot\mathbf{w} = 0$ which separate the sets of weight vectors that produce each of these labellings. When $N = 3$ (figure 40.4), weight space is divided by three hyperplanes into six regions. Not all of the eight conceivable labellings can be realized. Thus $T(3,2) = 6$.

In $K = 3$ dimensions

We now use this weight space visualization to study the three dimensional case.

Let us imagine adding one point at a time and count the number of threshold functions as we do so. When $N = 2$, weight space is divided by two hyperplanes $\mathbf{x}^{(1)}\cdot\mathbf{w} = 0$ and $\mathbf{x}^{(2)}\cdot\mathbf{w} = 0$ into four regions; in any one region all vectors $\mathbf{w}$ produce the same function on the 2 input vectors. Thus $T(2,3) = 4$.

Adding a third point in general position produces a third plane in $\mathbf{w}$ space, so that there are 8 distinguishable regions. $T(3,3) = 8$. The three bisecting planes are shown in figure 40.5a.

At this point matters become slightly more tricky. As figure 40.5b illustrates, the fourth plane in the three-dimensional $\mathbf{w}$ space cannot transect all eight of the sets created by the first three planes. Six of the existing regions are cut in two and the remaining two are unaffected. So $T(4,3) = 14$. Two

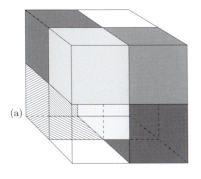

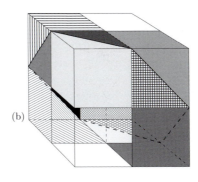

(a)

(b)

Figure 40.5. Weight space illustrations for $T(3,3)$ and $T(4,3)$. (a) $T(3,3) = 8$. Three hyperplanes (corresponding to three points in general position) divide 3-space into 8 regions, shown here by colouring the relevant part of the surface of a hollow, semi-transparent cube centred on the origin. (b) $T(4,3) = 14$. Four hyperplanes divide 3-space into 14 regions, of which this figure shows 13 (the 14th region is out of view on the right-hand face. Compare with figure 40.5a: all of the regions that are not coloured white have been cut into two.

				K				
N	1	2	3	4	5	6	7	8
1	2	2	2	2	2	2	2	2
2	2	4	4					
3	2	6	8					
4	2	8	14					
5	2	10						
6	2	12						

Table 40.6. Values of $T(N, K)$ deduced by hand.

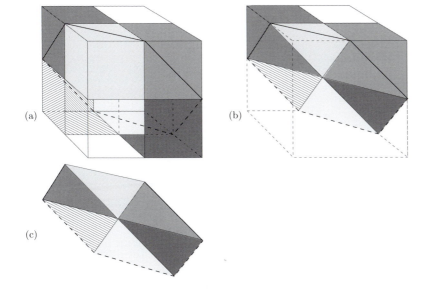

(a)

(b)

(c)

Figure 40.7. Illustration of the cutting process going from $T(3,3)$ to $T(4,3)$. (a) The eight regions of figure 40.5a with one added hyperplane. All of the regions that are not coloured white have been cut into two. (b) Here, the hollow cube has been made solid, so we can see which regions are cut by the fourth plane. The front half of the cube has been cut away. (c) This figure shows the new two dimensional hyperplane, which is divided into six regions by the three one-dimensional hyperplanes (lines) which cross it. Each of these regions corresponds to one of the three-dimensional regions in figure 40.7a which is cut into two by this new hyperplane. This shows that $T(4,3) - T(3,3) = 6$. Figure 40.7c should be compared with figure 40.4b.

of the binary functions on 4 points in 3 dimensions cannot be realized by a linear threshold function.

We have now filled in the values of $T(N, K)$ shown in table 40.6. Can we obtain any insights into our derivation of $T(4, 3)$ in order to fill in the rest of the table for $T(N, K)$? Why was $T(4, 3)$ greater than $T(3, 3)$ by six?

Six is the number of regions that the new hyperplane bisected in **w**-space (figure 40.7a b). Equivalently, if we look in the $K-1$ dimensional subspace that is the Nth hyperplane, that subspace is divided into six regions by the $N-1$ previous hyperplanes (figure 40.7c). Now this is a concept we have met before. Compare figure 40.7c with figure 40.4b. How many regions are created by $N-1$ hyperplanes in a $K-1$ dimensional space? Why, $T(N-1, K-1)$, of course! In the present case $N = 4$, $K = 3$, we can look up $T(3, 2) = 6$ in the previous section. So

$$T(4, 3) = T(3, 3) + T(3, 2). \tag{40.4}$$

Recurrence relation for any N, K

Generalizing this picture, we see that when we add an Nth hyperplane in K dimensions, it will bisect $T(N-1, K-1)$ of the $T(N-1, K)$ regions that were created by the previous $N-1$ hyperplanes. Therefore, the total number of regions obtained after adding the Nth hyperplane is $2T(N-1, K-1)$ (since $T(N-1, K-1)$ out of $T(N-1, K)$ regions are split in two) plus the remaining $T(N-1, K) - T(N-1, K-1)$ regions not split by the Nth hyperplane, which gives the following equation for $T(N, K)$:

$$T(N, K) = T(N-1, K) + T(N-1, K-1). \tag{40.5}$$

Now all that remains is to solve this recurrence relation given the boundary conditions $T(N, 1) = 2$ and $T(1, K) = 2$.

Does the recurrence relation (40.5) look familiar? Maybe you remember building Pascal's triangle by adding together two adjacent numbers in one row to get the number below. The N, K element of Pascal's triangle is equal to

$$C(N, K) \equiv \binom{N}{K} \equiv \frac{N!}{(N-K)!K!}. \tag{40.6}$$

Table 40.8. Pascal's triangle.

N	K							
	0	1	2	3	4	5	6	7
0	1							
1	1	1						
2	1	2	1					
3	1	3	3	1				
4	1	4	6	4	1			
5	1	5	10	10	5	1		

Combinations $\binom{N}{K}$ satisfy the equation

$$C(N, K) = C(N-1, K-1) + C(N-1, K), \quad \text{for all } N > 0. \tag{40.7}$$

[Here we are adopting the convention that $\binom{N}{K} \equiv 0$ if $K > N$ or $K < 0$.] So $\binom{N}{K}$ satisfies the required recurrence relation (40.5). This doesn't mean $T(N, K) = \binom{N}{K}$, since many functions can satisfy one recurrence relation.

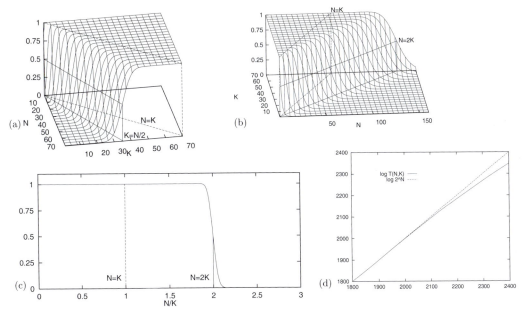

Figure 40.9. The fraction of functions on N points in K dimensions that are linear threshold functions, $T(N, K)/2^N$, shown from various viewpoints. In (a) we see the dependence on K, which is approximately an error function passing through 0.5 at $K = N/2$; the fraction reaches 1 at $K = N$. In (b) we see the dependence on N, which is 1 up to $N = K$ and drops sharply at $N = 2K$. Panel (c) shows the dependence on N/K for $K = 1000$. There is a sudden drop in the fraction of realizable labellings when $N = 2K$. Panel (d) shows the values of $\log_2 T(N, K)$ and $\log_2 2^N$ as a function of N for $K = 1000$. These figures were plotted using the approximation of $T/2^N$ by the error function.

But perhaps we can express $T(N, K)$ as a linear superposition of combination functions of the form $C_{\alpha,\beta}(N, K) \equiv \binom{N+\alpha}{K+\beta}$. By comparing tables 40.8 and 40.6 we can see how to satisfy the boundary conditions: we simply need to translate Pascal's triangle to the right by 1, 2, 3, ...; superpose; add; multiply by two, and drop the whole table by one line. Thus:

$$T(N, K) = 2 \sum_{k=0}^{K-1} \binom{N-1}{k}. \qquad (40.8)$$

Using the fact that the Nth row of Pascal's triangle sums to 2^N, that is, $\sum_{k=0}^{N-1} \binom{N-1}{k} = 2^{N-1}$, we can simplify the cases where $K-1 \geq N-1$.

$$T(N, K) = \begin{cases} 2^N & K \geq N \\ 2 \sum_{k=0}^{K-1} \binom{N-1}{k} & K < N. \end{cases} \qquad (40.9)$$

Interpretation

It is natural to compare $T(N, K)$ with the total number of binary functions on N points, 2^N. The ratio $T(N, K)/2^N$ tells us the probability that an arbitrary labelling $\{t_n\}_{n=1}^N$ can be memorized by our neuron. The two functions are equal for all $N \leq K$. The line $N = K$ is thus a special line, defining the maximum number of points on which *any* arbitrary labelling can be realized. This number of points is referred to as the *Vapnik–Chervonenkis dimension* (VC dimension) of the class of functions. The VC dimension of a binary threshold function on K dimensions is thus K.

What is interesting is (for large K) the number of points N such that *almost* any labelling can be realized. The ratio $T(N, K)/2^N$ is, for $N < 2K$, still greater than $1/2$, and for large K the ratio is very close to 1.

For our purposes the sum in equation (40.9) is well approximated by the error function,

$$\sum_0^K \binom{N}{k} \simeq 2^N \, \Phi\left(\frac{K - (N/2)}{\sqrt{N}/2}\right), \qquad (40.10)$$

where $\Phi(z) \equiv \int_{-\infty}^z \exp(-z^2/2)/\sqrt{2\pi}$. Figure 40.9 shows the realizable fraction $T(N, K)/2^N$ as a function of N and K. The take-home message is shown in figure 40.9c: although the fraction $T(N, K)/2^N$ is less than 1 for $N > K$, it is only negligibly less than 1 up to $N = 2K$; there, there is a catastrophic drop to zero, so that for $N > 2K$, only a tiny fraction of the binary labellings can be realized by the threshold function.

Conclusion

The capacity of a linear threshold neuron, for large K, is 2 bits per weight.

A single neuron can almost certainly memorize up to $N = 2K$ random binary labels perfectly, but will almost certainly fail to memorize more.

▶ 40.4 Further exercises

▷ Exercise 40.4.[2] Can a finite set of $2N$ distinct points in a two-dimensional space be split in half by a straight line

- if the points are in general position?
- if the points are not in general position?

Can $2N$ points in a K dimensional space be split in half by a $K - 1$ dimensional hyperplane?

Exercise 40.5.[2, p.491] Four points are selected at random on the surface of a sphere. What is the probability that all of them lie on a single hemisphere? How does this question relate to $T(N, K)$?

Exercise 40.6.[2] Consider the binary threshold neuron in $K = 3$ dimensions, and the set of points $\{\mathbf{x}\} = \{(1, 0, 0), (0, 1, 0), (0, 0, 1), (1, 1, 1)\}$. Find a parameter vector $\mathbf{w}$ such that the neuron memorizes the labels: (a) $\{t\} = \{1, 1, 1, 1\}$; (b) $\{t\} = \{1, 1, 0, 0\}$.

Find an unrealizable labelling $\{t\}$.

▷ Exercise 40.7.[3] In this chapter we constrained all our hyperplanes to go through the origin. In this exercise, we remove this constraint.

How many regions in a plane are created by N lines in general position?

Figure 40.10. Three lines in a plane create seven regions.

Exercise 40.8.[2] Estimate in bits the total sensory experience that you have had in your life – visual information, auditory information, etc. Estimate how much information you have memorized. Estimate the information content of the works of Shakespeare. Compare these with the capacity of your brain assuming you have 10^{11} neurons each making 1000 synaptic connections, and that the capacity result for one neuron (two bits per connection) applies. Is your brain full yet?

▷ Exercise 40.9.[*3*] What is the capacity of the axon of a spiking neuron, viewed as a communication channel, in bits per second? [See MacKay and McCulloch (1952) for an early publication on this topic.] Multiply by the number of axons in the optic nerve (about 10^6) or cochlear nerve (about 50 000 per ear) to estimate again the rate of acquisition sensory experience.

▶ 40.5 Solutions

Solution to exercise 40.5 (p.490). The probability that all four points lie on a single hemisphere is

$$T(4,3)/2^4 = 14/16 = 7/8. \qquad (40.11)$$

41

Learning as Inference

▶ ## 41.1 Neural network learning as inference

In Chapter 39 we trained a simple neural network as a classifier by minimizing an objective function

$$M(\mathbf{w}) = G(\mathbf{w}) + \alpha E_W(\mathbf{w}) \tag{41.1}$$

made up of an error function

$$G(\mathbf{w}) = -\sum_n \left[t^{(n)} \ln y(\mathbf{x}^{(n)}; \mathbf{w}) + (1 - t^{(n)}) \ln(1 - y(\mathbf{x}^{(n)}; \mathbf{w})) \right] \tag{41.2}$$

and a regularizer

$$E_W(\mathbf{w}) = \frac{1}{2} \sum_i w_i^2. \tag{41.3}$$

This neural network learning process can be given the following probabilistic interpretation.

We interpret the output $y(\mathbf{x}; \mathbf{w})$ of the neuron literally as defining (when its parameters $\mathbf{w}$ are specified) the probability that an input $\mathbf{x}$ belongs to class $t = 1$, rather than the alternative $t = 0$. Thus $y(\mathbf{x}; \mathbf{w}) \equiv P(t\!=\!1|\mathbf{x}, \mathbf{w})$. Then each value of $\mathbf{w}$ defines a different hypothesis about the probability of class 1 relative to class 0 as a function of $\mathbf{x}$.

We define the observed data D to be the *targets* $\{t\}$ – the inputs $\{\mathbf{x}\}$ are assumed to be given, and not to be modelled. To infer $\mathbf{w}$ given the data, we require a likelihood function and a prior probability over $\mathbf{w}$. The likelihood function measures how well the parameters $\mathbf{w}$ predict the observed data; it is the probability assigned to the observed t values by the model with parameters set to $\mathbf{w}$. Now the two equations

$$\begin{aligned} P(t = 1 \,|\, \mathbf{w}, \mathbf{x}) &= y \\ P(t = 0 \,|\, \mathbf{w}, \mathbf{x}) &= 1 - y \end{aligned} \tag{41.4}$$

can be rewritten as the single equation

$$P(t|\mathbf{w}, \mathbf{x}) = y^t (1 - y)^{1-t} = \exp[t \ln y + (1 - t) \ln(1 - y)] \,. \tag{41.5}$$

So the error function G can be interpreted as minus the log likelihood:

$$P(D|\mathbf{w}) = \exp[-G(\mathbf{w})]. \tag{41.6}$$

Similarly the regularizer can be interpreted in terms of a log prior probability distribution over the parameters:

$$P(\mathbf{w}|\alpha) = \frac{1}{Z_W(\alpha)} \exp(-\alpha E_W). \tag{41.7}$$

If E_W is quadratic as defined above, then the corresponding prior distribution is a Gaussian with variance $\sigma_W^2 = 1/\alpha$, and $1/Z_W(\alpha)$ is equal to $(\alpha/2\pi)^{K/2}$, where K is the number of parameters in the vector $\mathbf{w}$.

The objective function $M(\mathbf{w})$ then corresponds to the *inference* of the parameters $\mathbf{w}$, given the data:

$$P(\mathbf{w}|D, \alpha) = \frac{P(D|\mathbf{w})P(\mathbf{w}|\alpha)}{P(D|\alpha)} \tag{41.8}$$

$$= \frac{e^{-G(\mathbf{w})}\,e^{-\alpha E_W(\mathbf{w})}/Z_W(\alpha)}{P(D|\alpha)} \tag{41.9}$$

$$= \frac{1}{Z_M}\exp(-M(\mathbf{w})). \tag{41.10}$$

So the $\mathbf{w}$ found by (locally) minimizing $M(\mathbf{w})$ can be interpreted as the (locally) most probable parameter vector, $\mathbf{w}^*$. From now on we will refer to $\mathbf{w}^*$ as $\mathbf{w}_{\mathrm{MP}}$.

Why is it natural to interpret the error functions as *log* probabilities? Error functions are usually additive. For example, G is a *sum* of information contents, and E_W is a *sum* of squared weights. Probabilities, on the other hand, are multiplicative: for independent events X and Y, the joint probability is $P(x, y) = P(x)P(y)$. The logarithmic mapping maintains this correspondence.

The interpretation of $M(\mathbf{w})$ as a log probability has numerous benefits, some of which we will discuss in a moment.

▶ 41.2 Illustration for a neuron with two weights

In the case of a neuron with just two inputs and no bias,

$$y(\mathbf{x}; \mathbf{w}) = \frac{1}{1 + e^{-(w_1 x_1 + w_2 x_2)}}, \tag{41.11}$$

we can plot the posterior probability of $\mathbf{w}$, $P(\mathbf{w}|D, \alpha) \propto \exp(-M(\mathbf{w}))$. Imagine that we receive some data as shown in the left column of figure 41.1. Each data point consists of a two dimensional input vector $\mathbf{x}$ and a t value indicated by $\times$ ($t = 1$) or $\square$ ($t = 0$). The likelihood function $\exp(-G(\mathbf{w}))$ is shown as a function of $\mathbf{w}$ in the second column. It is a product of functions of the form (41.11).

The product of traditional learning is a point in $\mathbf{w}$-space, the estimator $\mathbf{w}^*$, which maximizes the posterior probability density. In contrast, in the Bayesian view, the product of learning is an *ensemble* of plausible parameter values (bottom right of figure 41.1). We do not choose one particular hypothesis $\mathbf{w}$; rather we evaluate their posterior probabilities. The posterior distribution is obtained by multiplying the likelihood by a prior distribution over $\mathbf{w}$ space (shown as a broad Gaussian at the upper right of figure 41.1). The posterior ensemble (within a multiplicative constant) is shown in the third column of figure 41.1, and as a contour plot in the fourth column. As the amount of data increases (from top to bottom), the posterior ensemble becomes increasingly concentrated around the most probable value $\mathbf{w}^*$.

▶ 41.3 Beyond optimization: making predictions

Let us consider the task of making predictions with the neuron which we trained as a classifier in section 39.3. This was a neuron with two inputs and a bias.

$$y(\mathbf{x}; \mathbf{w}) = \frac{1}{1 + e^{-(w_0 + w_1 x_1 + w_2 x_2)}}. \tag{41.12}$$

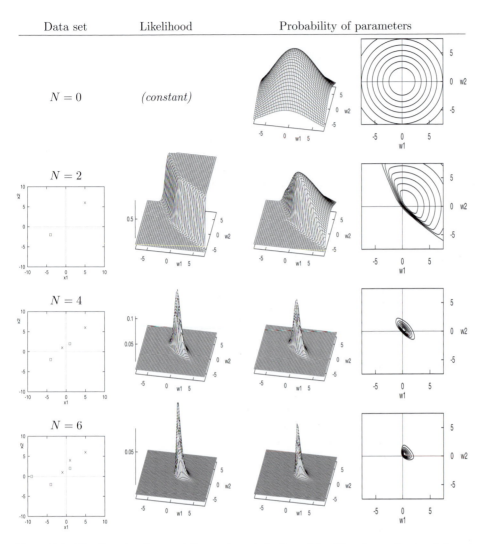

Figure 41.1. The Bayesian interpretation and generalization of traditional neural network learning.
Evolution of the probability distribution over parameters as data arrive.

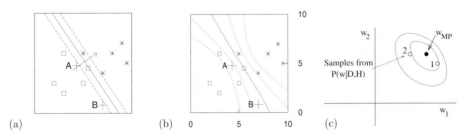

Figure 41.2. Making predictions. (a) The function performed by an optimized neuron $\mathbf{w}_{\mathrm{MP}}$ (shown by
three of its contours) trained with weight decay, $\alpha = 0.01$ (from figure 39.6). The contours
shown are those corresponding to $a = 0, \pm 1$, namely $y = 0.5, 0.27$ and 0.73. (b) Are these
predictions more reasonable? (Contours shown are for $y = 0.5, 0.27, 0.73, 0.12$ and 0.88.)
(c) The posterior probability of $\mathbf{w}$ (schematic); the Bayesian predictions shown in (b) were
obtained by averaging together the predictions made by each possible value of the weights
$\mathbf{w}$, with each value of $\mathbf{w}$ receiving a vote proportional to its probability under the posterior
ensemble. The method used to create (b) is described in section 41.4.

When we last played with it, we trained it by minimizing the objective function

$$M(\mathbf{w}) = G(\mathbf{w}) + \alpha E(\mathbf{w}). \tag{41.13}$$

The resulting optimized function for the case $\alpha = 0.01$ is reproduced in figure 41.2a.

We now consider the task of predicting the class $t^{(N+1)}$ corresponding to a new input $\mathbf{x}^{(N+1)}$. It is common practice, when making predictions, simply to use a neural network with its weights fixed to their optimized value $\mathbf{w}_{\mathrm{MP}}$, but this is not optimal, as can be seen intuitively by considering the predictions shown in figure 41.2a. Are these reasonable predictions? Consider new data arriving at points A and B. The best fit model assigns both of these examples probability 0.2 of being in class 1, because they have the same value of $\mathbf{w}_{\mathrm{MP}} \cdot \mathbf{x}$. If we really knew that $\mathbf{w}$ was equal to $\mathbf{w}_{\mathrm{MP}}$, then these predictions would be correct. But we do not know $\mathbf{w}$. The parameters are *uncertain*. Intuitively we might be inclined to assign a less confident probability (closer to 0.5) at B than at A, as shown in figure 41.2b, since point B is far from the training data. *The best fit parameters* $\mathbf{w}_{\mathrm{MP}}$ *often give over-confident predictions.* A non-Bayesian approach to this problem is to downweight all predictions uniformly, by an empirically determined factor (Copas, 1983). This is not ideal, since intuition suggests the strength of the predictions at B should be downweighted more than those at A. A Bayesian viewpoint helps us to understand the cause of the problem, and provides a straightforward solution. In a nutshell, we obtain Bayesian predictions by taking into account the whole posterior ensemble, shown schematically in figure 41.2c.

The Bayesian prediction of a new datum $\mathbf{t}^{(N+1)}$ involves *marginalizing* over the parameters (and over anything else about which we are uncertain). For simplicity, let us assume that the weights $\mathbf{w}$ are the only uncertain quantities – the weight decay rate α and the model $\mathcal{H}$ itself are assumed to be fixed. Then by the sum rule, the predictive probability of a new target $\mathbf{t}^{(N+1)}$ at a location $\mathbf{x}^{(N+1)}$ is:

$$P(\mathbf{t}^{(N+1)}|\mathbf{x}^{(N+1)}, D, \alpha) = \int d^K\mathbf{w}\, P(\mathbf{t}^{(N+1)}|\mathbf{x}^{(N+1)}, \mathbf{w}, \alpha) P(\mathbf{w}|D, \alpha), \tag{41.14}$$

where K is the dimensionality of $\mathbf{w}$, three in the toy problem. Thus the predictions are obtained by weighting the prediction for each possible $\mathbf{w}$,

$$\begin{aligned} P(\mathbf{t}^{(N+1)} = 1\,|\,\mathbf{x}^{(N+1)}, \mathbf{w}, \alpha) &= y(\mathbf{x}^{(N+1)}; \mathbf{w}) \\ P(\mathbf{t}^{(N+1)} = 0\,|\,\mathbf{x}^{(N+1)}, \mathbf{w}, \alpha) &= 1 - y(\mathbf{x}^{(N+1)}; \mathbf{w}), \end{aligned} \tag{41.15}$$

with a weight given by the posterior probability of $\mathbf{w}$, $P(\mathbf{w}|D, \alpha)$, which we most recently wrote down in equation (41.10). This posterior probability is

$$P(\mathbf{w}|D, \alpha) = \frac{1}{Z_M} \exp(-M(\mathbf{w})), \tag{41.16}$$

where

$$Z_M = \int d^K\mathbf{w} \exp(-M(\mathbf{w})). \tag{41.17}$$

In summary, we can get the Bayesian predictions if we can find a way of computing the integral

$$P(\mathbf{t}^{(N+1)} = 1|\mathbf{x}^{(N+1)}, D, \alpha) = \int d^K\mathbf{w}\; y(\mathbf{x}^{(N+1)}; \mathbf{w}) \frac{1}{Z_M} \exp(-M(\mathbf{w})), \tag{41.18}$$

which is the average of the output of the neuron at $\mathbf{x}^{(N+1)}$ under the posterior distribution of $\mathbf{w}$.

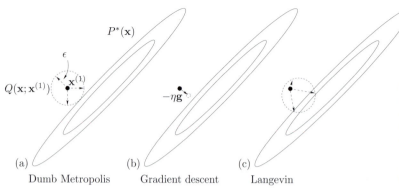

Figure 41.3. One step of the Langevin method in two dimensions (c), contrasted with a traditional 'dumb' Metropolis method (a) and with gradient descent (b). The proposal density of the Langevin method is given by 'gradient descent with noise'.

Implementation

How shall we compute the integral (41.18)? For our toy problem, the weight space is three dimensional; for a realistic neural network the dimensionality K might be in the thousands.

Bayesian inference for general data modelling problems may be implemented by exact methods (Chapter 25), by Monte Carlo sampling (Chapter 29), or by deterministic approximate methods, for example, methods that make Gaussian approximations to $P(\mathbf{w}|D, \alpha)$ using Laplace's method (Chapter 27) or variational methods (Chapter 33). For neural networks there are few exact methods. The two main approaches to implementing Bayesian inference for neural networks are the Monte Carlo methods developed by Neal (1996) and the Gaussian approximation methods developed by MacKay (1991).

▶ ## 41.4 Monte Carlo implementation of a single neuron

First we will use a Monte Carlo approach in which the task of evaluating the integral (41.18) is solved by treating $y(\mathbf{x}^{(N+1)}; \mathbf{w})$ as a function f of $\mathbf{w}$ whose mean we compute using

$$\langle f(\mathbf{w})\rangle \simeq \frac{1}{R}\sum_r f(\mathbf{w}^{(r)}) \qquad (41.19)$$

where $\{\mathbf{w}^{(r)}\}$ are samples from the posterior distribution $\frac{1}{Z_M}\exp(-M(\mathbf{w}))$ (c.f. equation (29.6)). We obtain the samples using a Metropolis method (section 29.4). As an aside, a possible disadvantage of this Monte Carlo approach is that it is a poor way of estimating the probability of an improbable event, i.e., a $P(t \mid D, \mathcal{H})$ that is very close to zero, if the improbable event is most likely to occur in conjunction with improbable parameter values.

How to generate the samples $\{\mathbf{w}^{(r)}\}$? Radford Neal introduced the *Hamiltonian Monte Carlo* method to neural networks. We met this sophisticated Metropolis method, which makes use of gradient information, in Chapter 30. The method we now demonstrate is a simple version of Hamiltonian Monte Carlo called the *Langevin Monte Carlo method*.

The Langevin Monte Carlo method

The Langevin method (algorithm 41.4) may be summarized as 'gradient descent with added noise', as shown pictorially in figure 41.3. A noise vector $\mathbf{p}$ is generated from a Gaussian with unit variance. The gradient $\mathbf{g}$ is computed,

```
g = gradM ( w ) ;              # set gradient using initial w
M = findM ( w ) ;              # set objective function too

for l = 1:L                    # loop L times
  p = randn ( size(w) ) ;      # initial momentum is Normal(0,1)
  H = p' * p / 2 + M ;         # evaluate H(w,p)

* p = p - epsilon * g / 2 ;    # make half-step in p
* wnew = w + epsilon * p ;     # make step in w
* gnew = gradM ( wnew ) ;      # find new gradient
* p = p - epsilon * gnew / 2 ; # make half-step in p

  Mnew = findM ( wnew ) ;      # find new objective function
  Hnew = p' * p / 2 + Mnew ;   # evaluate new value of H
  dH = Hnew - H ;              # decide whether to accept
  if ( dH < 0 )             accept = 1 ;
  elseif ( rand() < exp(-dH) ) accept = 1 ;  # compare with a uniform
  else                      accept = 0 ;  #              variate
  endif
  if ( accept )        g = gnew ;   w = wnew ;    M = Mnew ;    endif
endfor

function gM = gradM ( w )        # gradient of objective function
  a = x * w  ;                   # compute activations
  y = sigmoid(a) ;               # compute outputs
  e = t - y   ;                  # compute errors
  g = - x' * e ;                 # compute the gradient of G(w)
  gM = alpha * w + g ;
endfunction

function M = findM ( w )         # objective function
  G = - (t' * log(y) + (1-t') * log( 1-y )) ;
  EW = w' * w / 2 ;
  M = G + alpha * EW ;
endfunction
```

Algorithm 41.4. Octave source code for the Langevin Monte Carlo method. To obtain the Hamiltonian Monte Carlo method, we repeat the four lines marked * multiple times (algorithm 41.8).

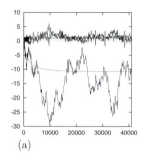 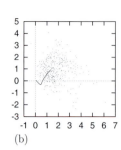 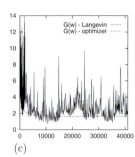 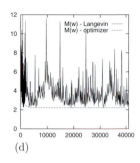

(a)   (b)   (c)   (d)

Figure 41.5.   A single neuron learning under the Langevin Monte Carlo method. (a) Evolution of
weights w_0, w_1 and w_2 as a function of number of iterations. (b) Evolution of weights w_1
and w_2 in weight space. Also shown by a line is the evolution of the weights using the
optimizer of figure 39.6. (c) The error function $G(\mathbf{w})$ as a function of number of iterations.
Also shown is the error function during the optimization of figure 39.6. (d) The objective
function $M(\mathbf{x})$ as a function of number of iterations. See also figures 41.6 and 41.7.

and a step in $\mathbf{w}$ is made, given by

$$\Delta\mathbf{w} = -\tfrac{1}{2}\epsilon^2\mathbf{g} + \epsilon\mathbf{p}. \qquad (41.20)$$

Notice that if the $\epsilon\mathbf{p}$ term were omitted this would simply be gradient descent
with learning rate $\eta = \tfrac{1}{2}\epsilon^2$. This step in $\mathbf{w}$ is accepted or rejected depending
on the change in the value of the objective function $M(\mathbf{w})$ and on the change
in gradient, with a probability of acceptance such that detailed balance holds.

The Langevin method has one free parameter, ϵ, which controls the typical
step size. If ϵ is set to too large a value, moves may be rejected. If it is set to
a very small value, progress around the state space will be slow.

Demonstration of Langevin method

The Langevin method is demonstrated in figures 41.5, 41.6 and 41.7. Here, the
objective function is $M(\mathbf{w}) = G(\mathbf{w}) + \alpha E_W(\mathbf{w})$, with $\alpha = 0.01$. These figures
include, for comparison, the results of the previous optimization method using
gradient descent on the same objective function (figure 39.6). It can be seen
that the mean evolution of $\mathbf{w}$ is similar to the evolution of the parameters
under gradient descent. The Monte Carlo method appears to have converged
to the posterior distribution after about 10 000 iterations.

The average acceptance rate during this simulation was 93%; only 7% of
the proposed moves were rejected. Probably, faster progress around the state
space would have been made if a larger step size ϵ had been used, but the
value was chosen so that the 'descent rate' $\eta = \tfrac{1}{2}\epsilon^2$ matched the step size of
the earlier simulations.

Making Bayesian predictions

From iteration 10,000 to 40,000, the weights were sampled every 1000 iterations and the corresponding functions of $\mathbf{x}$ are plotted in figure 41.6. There
is a considerable variety of plausible functions. We obtain a Monte Carlo approximation to the Bayesian predictions by averaging these thirty functions of
$\mathbf{x}$ together. The result is shown in figure 41.7 and contrasted with the predictions given by the optimized parameters. The Bayesian predictions become
satisfyingly moderate as we move away from the region of highest data density.

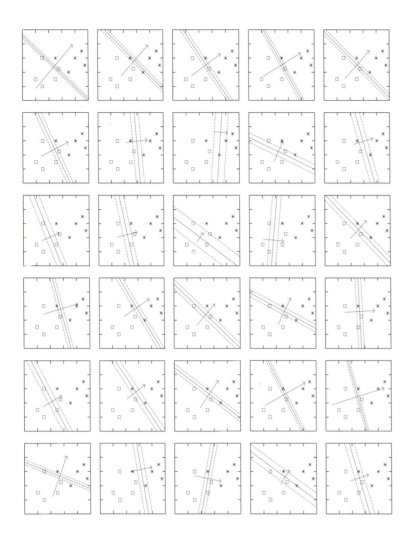

Figure 41.6. Samples obtained by the Langevin Monte Carlo method. The learning rate was set to $\eta = 0.01$ and the weight decay rate to $\alpha = 0.01$. The step size is given by $\epsilon = \sqrt{2\eta}$. The function performed by the neuron is shown by three of its contours every 1000 iterations from iteration 10 000 to 40 000. The contours shown are those corresponding to $a = 0, \pm 1$, namely $y = 0.5, 0.27$ and 0.73. Also shown is a vector proportional to (w_1, w_2).

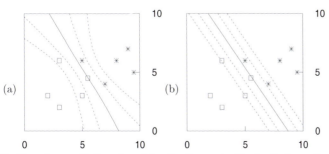

Figure 41.7. Bayesian predictions found by the Langevin Monte Carlo method compared with the predictions using the optimized parameters. (a) The predictive function obtained by averaging the predictions for 30 samples uniformly spaced between iterations 10 000 and 40 000, shown in figure 41.6. The contours shown are those corresponding to $a = 0, \pm 1, \pm 2$, namely $y = 0.5, 0.27, 0.73, 0.12$ and 0.88. (b) For contrast, the predictions given by the 'most probable' setting of the neuron's parameters, as given by optimization of $M(\mathbf{w})$.

```
    wnew = w ;
    gnew = g ;
    for tau = 1:Tau

        p = p - epsilon * gnew / 2 ;      # make half-step in p
        wnew = wnew + epsilon * p ;       # make step in w

        gnew = gradM ( wnew ) ;           # find new gradient
        p = p - epsilon * gnew / 2 ;      # make half-step in p

    endfor
```

Algorithm 41.8. Octave source code for the Hamiltonian Monte Carlo method. The algorithm is identical to the Langevin method in algorithm 41.4, except for the replacement of the four lines marked ∗ in that algorithm by the fragment shown here.

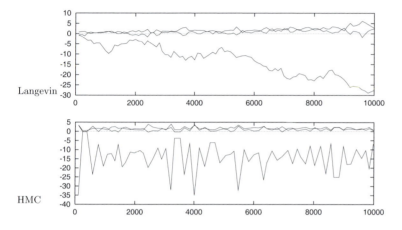

Langevin

HMC

Figure 41.9. Comparison of sampling properties of the Langevin Monte Carlo method and the Hamiltonian Monte Carlo (HMC) method. The horizontal axis is the number of gradient evaluations made. Each figure shows the weights during the first 10,000 iterations. The rejection rate during this Hamiltonian Monte Carlo simulation was 8%.

The Bayesian classifier is better able to identify the points where the classification is uncertain. This pleasing behaviour results simply from a mechanical application of the rules of probability.

Optimization and typicality

A final observation concerns the behaviour of the functions $G(\mathbf{w})$ and $M(\mathbf{w})$ during the Monte Carlo sampling process, compared with the values of G and M at the optimum $\mathbf{w}_{\mathrm{MP}}$ (figure 41.5). The function $G(\mathbf{w})$ fluctuates around the value of $G(\mathbf{w}_{\mathrm{MP}})$, though not in a symmetrical way. The function $M(\mathbf{w})$ also fluctuates, but it does not fluctuate *around* $M(\mathbf{w}_{\mathrm{MP}})$ – obviously it cannot, because M is minimized at $\mathbf{w}_{\mathrm{MP}}$, so M could not go any smaller – furthermore, M only rarely drops close to $M(\mathbf{w}_{\mathrm{MP}})$. In the language of information theory, *the typical set of $\mathbf{w}$ has different properties from the most probable state $\mathbf{w}_{\mathrm{MP}}$.*

A general message therefore emerges – applicable to all data models, not just neural networks: one should be cautious about making use of *optimized* parameters, as the properties of optimized parameters may be unrepresentative of the properties of typical, plausible parameters; and the predictions obtained using optimized parameters alone will often be unreasonably overconfident.

Reducing random walk behaviour using Hamiltonian Monte Carlo

As a final study of Monte Carlo methods, we now compare the Langevin Monte Carlo method with its big brother, the Hamiltonian Monte Carlo method. The change to Hamiltonian Monte Carlo is simple to implement, as shown in algorithm 41.8. Each single proposal makes use of multiple gradient evaluations along a dynamical trajectory in $\mathbf{w}, \mathbf{p}$ space, where $\mathbf{p}$ are the extra 'momentum' variables of the Langevin and Hamiltonian Monte Carlo methods. The number of steps 'Tau' was set at random to a number between 100 and 200 for each trajectory. The step size ϵ was kept fixed so as to retain comparability with the simulations that have gone before; it is recommended that one randomize the step size in practical applications, however.

Figure 41.9 compares the sampling properties of the Langevin and Hamiltonian Monte Carlo methods. The autocorrelation of the state of the Hamiltonian Monte Carlo simulation falls much more rapidly with simulation time than that of the Langevin method. For this toy problem, Hamiltonian Monte Carlo is at least ten times more efficient in its use of computer time.

▶ 41.5 Implementing inference with Gaussian approximations

Physicists love to take nonlinearities and locally linearize them, and they love to approximate probability distributions by Gaussians. Such approximations offer an alternative strategy for dealing with the integral

$$P(t^{(N+1)} = 1 \mid \mathbf{x}^{(N+1)}, D, \alpha) = \int d^K \mathbf{w} \, y(\mathbf{x}^{(N+1)}; \mathbf{w}) \frac{1}{Z_M} \exp(-M(\mathbf{w})), \quad (41.21)$$

which we just evaluated using Monte Carlo methods.

We start by making a Gaussian approximation to the posterior probability. We go to the minimum of $M(\mathbf{w})$ (using a gradient-based optimizer) and Taylor-expand M there:

$$M(\mathbf{w}) \simeq M(\mathbf{w}_{\mathrm{MP}}) + \frac{1}{2}(\mathbf{w} - \mathbf{w}_{\mathrm{MP}})^{\mathsf{T}}\mathbf{A}(\mathbf{w} - \mathbf{w}_{\mathrm{MP}}) + \cdots, \quad (41.22)$$

where $\mathbf{A}$ is the matrix of second derivatives, also known as the *Hessian*, defined by

$$A_{ij} \equiv \frac{\partial^2}{\partial w_i \partial w_j} M(\mathbf{w})\bigg|_{\mathbf{w} = \mathbf{w}_{\mathrm{MP}}}. \quad (41.23)$$

We thus define our Gaussian approximation:

$$Q(\mathbf{w}; \mathbf{w}_{\mathrm{MP}}, \mathbf{A}) = [\det(\mathbf{A}/2\pi)]^{1/2} \exp\left[-\frac{1}{2}(\mathbf{w} - \mathbf{w}_{\mathrm{MP}})^{\mathsf{T}}\mathbf{A}(\mathbf{w} - \mathbf{w}_{\mathrm{MP}})\right]. \quad (41.24)$$

We can think of the matrix $\mathbf{A}$ as defining *error bars* on $\mathbf{w}$. To be precise, Q is a normal distribution whose variance–covariance matrix is $\mathbf{A}^{-1}$.

Exercise 41.1.[2] Show that the second derivative of $M(\mathbf{w})$ with respect to $\mathbf{w}$ is given by

$$\frac{\partial^2}{\partial w_i \partial w_j} M(\mathbf{w}) = \sum_{n=1}^{N} f'(a^{(n)}) x_i^{(n)} x_j^{(n)} + \alpha \delta_{ij}, \quad (41.25)$$

where $f'(a)$ is the first derivative of $f(a) \equiv 1/(1 + e^{-a})$, which is

$$f'(a) = \frac{d}{da} f(a) = f(a)(1 - f(a)), \quad (41.26)$$

and

$$a^{(n)} = \sum_j w_j x_j^{(n)}. \quad (41.27)$$

Having computed the Hessian, our task is then to perform the integral (41.21) using our Gaussian approximation.

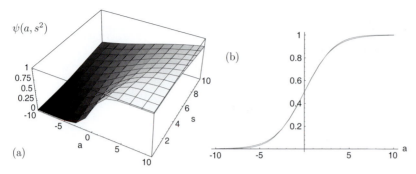

Figure 41.10. The marginalized probability, and an approximation to it. (a) The function $\psi(a, s^2)$, evaluated numerically. In (b) the functions $\psi(a, s^2)$ and $\phi(a, s^2)$ defined in the text are shown as a function of a for $s^2 = 4$. From MacKay (1992b).

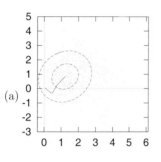
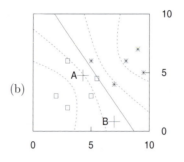

Figure 41.11. The Gaussian approximation in weight space and its approximate predictions in input space. (a) A projection of the Gaussian approximation onto the (w_1, w_2) plane of weight space. The one- and two-standard-deviation contours are shown. Also shown are the trajectory of the optimizer, and the Monte Carlo method's samples. (b) The predictive function obtained from the Gaussian approximation and equation (41.30). (c.f. figure 41.2.)

Calculating the marginalized probability

The output $y(\mathbf{x}; \mathbf{w})$ only depends on $\mathbf{w}$ through the scalar $a(\mathbf{x}; \mathbf{w})$, so we can reduce the dimensionality of the integral by finding the probability density of a. We are assuming a locally Gaussian posterior probability distribution over $\mathbf{w} = \mathbf{w}_{\mathrm{MP}} + \Delta\mathbf{w}$, $P(\mathbf{w} \mid D, \alpha) \simeq (1/Z_Q) \exp(-\frac{1}{2}\Delta\mathbf{w}^{\mathsf{T}}\mathbf{A}\Delta\mathbf{w})$. For our single neuron, the activation $a(\mathbf{x}; \mathbf{w})$ is a linear function of $\mathbf{w}$ with $\partial a/\partial\mathbf{w} = \mathbf{x}$, so for any $\mathbf{x}$, the activation a is Gaussian-distributed.

▷ Exercise 41.2.[2] Assuming $\mathbf{w}$ is Gaussian-distributed with mean $\mathbf{w}_{\mathrm{MP}}$ and variance–covariance matrix $\mathbf{A}^{-1}$, show that the probability distribution of $a(\mathbf{x})$ is

$$P(a \mid \mathbf{x}, D, \alpha) = \mathrm{Normal}(a_{\mathrm{MP}}, s^2) = \frac{1}{\sqrt{2\pi s^2}} \exp\left(-\frac{(a - a_{\mathrm{MP}})^2}{2s^2}\right), \tag{41.28}$$

where $a_{\mathrm{MP}} = a(\mathbf{x}; \mathbf{w}_{\mathrm{MP}})$ and $s^2 = \mathbf{x}^{\mathsf{T}}\mathbf{A}^{-1}\mathbf{x}$.

This means that the marginalized output is:

$$P(t=1 \mid \mathbf{x}, D, \alpha) = \psi(a_{\mathrm{MP}}, s^2) \equiv \int \mathrm{d}a\, f(a)\, \mathrm{Normal}(a_{\mathrm{MP}}, s^2). \tag{41.29}$$

This is to be contrasted with $y(\mathbf{x}; \mathbf{w}_{\mathrm{MP}}) = f(a_{\mathrm{MP}})$, the output of the most probable network. The integral of a sigmoid times a Gaussian can be approximated by:

$$\psi(a_{\mathrm{MP}}, s^2) \simeq \phi(a_{\mathrm{MP}}, s^2) \equiv f(\kappa(s)a_{\mathrm{MP}}) \tag{41.30}$$

with $\kappa = 1/\sqrt{1 + \pi s^2/8}$ (figure 41.10).

Demonstration

Figure 41.11 shows the result of fitting a Gaussian approximation at the optimum $\mathbf{w}_{\mathrm{MP}}$, and the results of using that Gaussian approximation and equation (41.30) to make predictions. Comparing these predictions with those of the Langevin Monte Carlo method (figure 41.7) we observe that, whilst qualitatively the same, the two are clearly numerically different. So at least one of the two methods is not completely accurate.

▷ Exercise 41.3.[2] Is the Gaussian approximation to $P(\mathbf{w} \mid D, \alpha)$ too heavy-tailed or too light-tailed, or both? It may help to consider $P(\mathbf{w} \mid D, \alpha)$ as a function of one parameter w_i and to think of the two distributions on a logarithmic scale. Discuss the conditions under which the Gaussian approximation is most accurate.

Why marginalize?

If the output is immediately used to make a $(0/1)$ decision and the costs associated with error are symmetrical, then the use of marginalized outputs under this Gaussian approximation will make no difference to the performance of the classifier, compared with using the outputs given by the most probable parameters, since both functions pass through 0.5 at $a_{\mathrm{MP}} = 0$. But these Bayesian outputs will make a difference if, for example, there is an option of saying 'I don't know', in addition to saying 'I guess 0' and 'I guess 1'. And even if there are just the two choices '0' and '1', if the costs associated with error are unequal, then the decision boundary will be some contour other than the 0.5 contour, and the boundary will be affected by marginalization.

Postscript on Supervised Neural Networks

One of my students, Robert, asked:

> Maybe I'm missing something fundamental, but supervised neural networks seem equivalent to fitting a pre-defined function to some given data, then extrapolating – what's the difference?

I agree with Robert. The supervised neural networks we have studied so far are simply parameterized nonlinear functions which can be fitted to data. Hopefully you will agree with another comment that Robert made:

> Unsupervised networks seem much more interesting than their supervised counterparts. I'm amazed that it works!

Hopfield Networks

We have now spent three chapters studying the single neuron. The time has come to connect multiple neurons together, making the output of one neuron be the input to another, so as to make neural networks.

Neural networks can be divided into two classes on the basis of their connectivity.

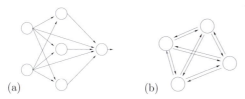

Figure 42.1. (a) A feedforward network. (b) A feedback network.

Feedforward networks. In a feedforward network, all the connections are directed such that the network forms a directed acyclic graph.

Feedback networks. Any network that is not a feedforward network will be called a feedback network.

In this chapter we will discuss a fully connected feedback network called the Hopfield network. The weights in the Hopfield network are constrained to be *symmetric*, i.e., the weight from neuron i to neuron j is equal to the weight from neuron j to neuron i.

Hopfield networks have two applications. First, they can act as *associative memories*. Second, they can be used to solve *optimization problems*. We will first discuss the idea of associative memory, also known as content-addressable memory.

▶ 42.1 Hebbian learning

In Chapter 38, we discussed the contrast between traditional digital memories and biological memories. Perhaps the most striking difference is the *associative* nature of biological memory.

A simple model due to Donald Hebb (1949) captures the idea of associative memory. Imagine that the weights between neurons whose activities are *positively correlated* are *increased*:

$$\frac{dw_{ij}}{dt} \sim \text{Correlation}(x_i, x_j). \tag{42.1}$$

Now imagine that when stimulus m is present (for example, the smell of a banana), the activity of neuron m increases; and that neuron n is associated with another stimulus, n (for example, the sight of a yellow object). If these two stimuli – a yellow sight and a banana smell – co-occur in the environment, then the Hebbian learning rule (42.1) will increase the weights w_{nm} and w_{mn}. This means that when, on a later occasion, stimulus n occurs in isolation, making the activity x_n large, the positive weight from n to m will cause neuron m also to be activated. Thus the response to the sight of a yellow object is an automatic association with the smell of a banana. We could call this 'pattern completion'. No teacher is required for this associative memory to work. No signal is needed to indicate that a correlation has been detected or that an association should be made. The unsupervised, local learning algorithm and the unsupervised, local activity rule spontaneously produce associative memory.

This idea seems so simple and so effective that it must be relevant to how memories work in the brain.

▶ 42.2 Definition of the binary Hopfield network

Convention for weights. Our convention in general will be that w_{ij} denotes the connection *from* neuron j *to* neuron i.

Architecture. A Hopfield network consists of I neurons. They are fully connected through *symmetric, bidirectional* connections with weights $w_{ij} = w_{ji}$. There are no self-connections, so $w_{ii} = 0$ for all i. Biases w_{i0} may be included (these may be viewed as weights from a neuron '0' whose activity is permanently $x_0 = 1$). We will denote the activity of neuron i (its output) by x_i.

Activity rule. Roughly, a Hopfield network's activity rule is for each neuron to update its state as if it were a single neuron with the threshold activation function

$$x(a) = \Theta(a) \equiv \begin{cases} 1 & a \geq 0 \\ -1 & a < 0. \end{cases} \tag{42.2}$$

Since there is *feedback* in a Hopfield network (every neuron's output is an input to all the other neurons) we will have to specify an order for the updates to occur. The updates may be synchronous or asynchronous.

Synchronous updates – all neurons compute their activations

$$a_i = \sum_j w_{ij} x_j \tag{42.3}$$

then update their states simultaneously to

$$x_i = \Theta(a_i). \tag{42.4}$$

Asynchronous updates – one neuron at a time computes its activation and updates its state. The sequence of selected neurons may be a fixed sequence or a random sequence.

The properties of a Hopfield network may be sensitive to the above choices.

Learning rule. The learning rule is intended to make a set of desired *memories* $\{\mathbf{x}^{(n)}\}$ be *stable states* of the Hopfield network's activity rule. Each memory is a binary pattern, with $x_i \in \{-1, 1\}$.

```
moscow------russia
lima----------peru
london-----england
tokyo--------japan
edinburgh-scotland
ottawa------canada
oslo--------norway
stockholm---sweden
paris-------france
```
(a)

(b)
```
moscow---::::::::::   ⟹   moscow------russia
:::::::::::--canada   ⟹   ottawa------canada
```

(c)
```
otowa-------canada   ⟹   ottawa------canada
egindurrh-sxotland   ⟹   edinburgh-scotland
```

Figure 42.2. Associative memory (schematic). (a) A list of desired memories. (b) The first purpose of an associative memory is pattern completion, given a partial pattern. (c) The second purpose of a memory is error correction.

The weights are set using the *sum of outer products* or *Hebb rule*,

$$w_{ij} = \eta \sum_n x_i^{(n)} x_j^{(n)}, \qquad (42.5)$$

where η is an unimportant constant. To prevent the largest possible weight from growing with N we might choose to set $\eta = 1/N$.

Exercise 42.1.[1] Explain why the value of η is not important for the Hopfield network defined above.

42.3 Definition of the continuous Hopfield network

Using the identical architecture and learning rule we can define a Hopfield network whose activities are real numbers between -1 and 1.

Activity rule. A Hopfield network's activity rule is for each neuron to update its state as if it were a single neuron with a sigmoid activation function. The updates may be synchronous or asynchronous, and involve the equations

$$a_i = \sum_j w_{ij} x_j \qquad (42.6)$$

and

$$x_i = \tanh(a_i). \qquad (42.7)$$

The learning rule is the same as in the binary Hopfield network, but the value of η becomes relevant. Alternatively, we may fix η and introduce a *gain* $\beta \in (0, \infty)$ into the activation function:

$$x_i = \tanh(\beta a_i). \qquad (42.8)$$

Exercise 42.2.[1] Where have we encountered equations 42.6, 42.7, and 42.8 before?

42.4 Convergence of the Hopfield network

The hope is that the Hopfield networks we have defined will perform associative memory recall, as shown schematically in figure 42.2. We hope that the activity rule of a Hopfield network will take a partial memory or a corrupted memory, and perform pattern completion or error correction to restore the original memory.

But why should we expect *any* pattern to be stable under the activity rule, let alone the desired memories?

We address the continuous Hopfield network, since the binary network is a special case of it. We have already encountered the activity rule (42.6, 42.8) when we discussed variational methods (section 33.2): when we approximated the spin system whose energy function was

$$E(\mathbf{x}; \mathbf{J}) = -\frac{1}{2} \sum_{m,n} J_{mn} x_m x_n - \sum_n h_n x_n \qquad (42.9)$$

with a separable distribution

$$Q(\mathbf{x}; \mathbf{a}) = \frac{1}{Z_Q} \exp\left(\sum_n a_n x_n\right) \qquad (42.10)$$

and optimized the latter so as to minimize the variational free energy

$$\beta \tilde{F}(\mathbf{a}) = \beta \sum_{\mathbf{x}} Q(\mathbf{x}; \mathbf{a}) E(\mathbf{x}; \mathbf{J}) - \sum_{\mathbf{x}} Q(\mathbf{x}; \mathbf{a}) \ln \frac{1}{Q(\mathbf{x}; \mathbf{a})}, \qquad (42.11)$$

we found that the pair of iterative equations

$$a_m = \beta \left(\sum_n J_{mn} \bar{x}_n + h_m\right) \qquad (42.12)$$

and

$$\bar{x}_n = \tanh(a_n) \qquad (42.13)$$

were guaranteed to decrease the variational free energy

$$\beta \tilde{F}(\mathbf{a}) = \beta \left(-\frac{1}{2} \sum_{m,n} J_{mn} \bar{x}_m \bar{x}_n - \sum_n h_n \bar{x}_n\right) - \sum_n H_2^{(e)}(q_n). \qquad (42.14)$$

If we simply replace J by w, $\bar{x}$ by x, and h_n by w_{i0}, we see that the equations of the Hopfield network are identical to a set of mean field equations that minimize

$$\beta \tilde{F}(\mathbf{x}) = -\beta \frac{1}{2} \mathbf{x}^\mathsf{T} \mathbf{W} \mathbf{x} - \sum_i H_2^{(e)}[(1 + x_i)/2]. \qquad (42.15)$$

There is a general name for a function that decreases under the dynamical evolution of a system and that is bounded below: such a function is a *Lyapunov function* for the system. It is useful to be able to prove the existence of Lyapunov functions: if a system has a Lyapunov function then its dynamics are bound to settle down to a *fixed point*, which is a local minimum of the Lyapunov function, or a *limit cycle*, along which the Lyapunov function is a constant. Chaotic behaviour is not possible for a system with a Lyapunov function. If a system has a Lyapunov function then its state space can be divided into *basins of attraction*, one basin associated with each attractor.

So, the continuous Hopfield network's activity rules (if implemented asynchronously) have a Lyapunov function. This Lyapunov function is a convex function of each parameter a_i so a Hopfield network's dynamics will always converge to a stable fixed point.

This convergence proof depends crucially on the fact that the Hopfield network's connections are *symmetric*. It also depends on the updates being made asynchronously.

Exercise 42.3.[2, p.520] Show by constructing an example that if a feedback network does not have symmetric connections then its dynamics may fail to converge to a fixed point.

Exercise 42.4.[2, p.521] Show by constructing an example that if a Hopfield network is updated synchronously that, from some initial conditions, it may fail to converge to a fixed point.

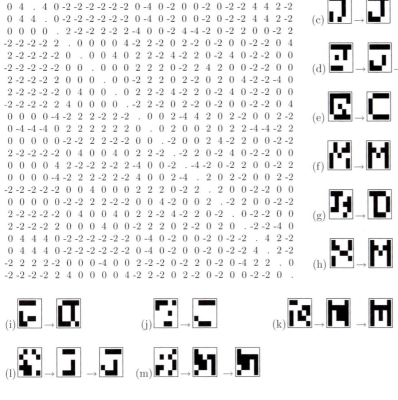

(a)

```
. 0 0 0 0-2 2-2 2 2-2 0 0 0 2 0 0-2 0 2 2 0 0-2-2
0 . 4 4 0-2-2-2-2-2-2 0-4 0-2 0 0-2 0-2-2 4 4 2-2
0 4 . 4 0-2-2-2-2-2-2 0-4 0-2 0 0-2 0-2-2 4 4 2-2
0 0 0 0 . 2-2-2 2 2-2-4 0 0-2 4-4-2 0-2 2 0 0-2 2
-2-2-2-2 2 . 0 0 0 0 4-2 2-2 0 2-2 0-2 0 0-2-2 0 4
2-2-2-2-2 0 . 0 0 4 0 2 2-2 4-2 2 0-2 4 0-2-2 0 0
-2-2-2-2-2 0 0 . 0 0 2 2 2 0-2 2 4 2 0 0-2-2 0 0
2-2-2-2 2 0 0 0 . 0 0-2 2 2 0 2-2 0 2 0 4-2-2-4 0
2-2-2-2 2 0 4 0 0 . 0 2 2-2 4-2 2 0-2 4 0-2-2 0 0
-2-2-2-2 2 4 0 0 0 0 .-2 2-2 0 2-2 0-2 0 0-2-2 0 4
0 0 0 0-4-2 2 2-2 2-2 . 0 0 2-4 4 2 0 2-2 0 0 2-2
0-4-4-4 0 2 2 2 2 2 2 0 . 0 2 0 0 2 0 2 2-4-4-2 2
0 0 0 0 0-2-2 2 2-2-2 0 0 .-2 0 0 2 4-2 2 0 0-2-2
2-2-2-2-2 0 4 0 0 4 0 2 2-2 .-2 2 0-2 4 0-2-4 0 0
0 0 0 0 4 2-2 2 2-2 2-4 0 0-2 .-4-2 0-2 2 0 0-2 2
0 0 0 0-4-2 2 2 2-2 2-4 0 0 2-4 . 2 0 2-2 0 0 2-2
-2-2-2-2-2 0 0 4 0 0 0 2 2 2 0-2 2 . 2 0 0-2-2 0 0
0 0 0 0 0-2-2 2 2-2-2 0 0 4-2 0 0 2 .-2 2 0 0-2-2
2-2-2-2-2 0 4 0 0 4 0 2 2-2 4-2 2 0-2 . 0-2-2 0 0
2-2-2-2 2 0 0 0 4 0 0-2 2 2 0 2-2 0 2 0 .-2-2-4 0
0 4 4 4 0-2-2-2-2-2-2 0-4 0-2 0 0-2 0-2-2 . 4 2-2
0 4 4 4 0-2-2-2-2-2-2 0-4 0-2 0 0-2 0-2-2 4 . 2-2
-2 2 2 2-2 0 0 0-4 0 0 2-2-2 0-2 2 0-2 2 0-2 0-4 2 2 . 0
-2-2-2-2 2 4 0 0 0 0 4-2 2-2 0 2-2 0-2 0 0-2-2 0 .
```

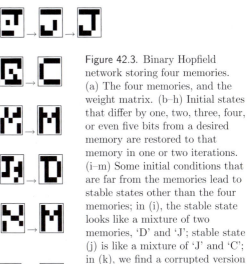

(b) D → D

(c) J → J

(d) J → J → J

Figure 42.3. Binary Hopfield network storing four memories. (a) The four memories, and the weight matrix. (b–h) Initial states that differ by one, two, three, four, or even five bits from a desired memory are restored to that memory in one or two iterations. (i–m) Some initial conditions that are far from the memories lead to stable states other than the four memories; in (i), the stable state looks like a mixture of two memories, 'D' and 'J'; stable state (j) is like a mixture of 'J' and 'C'; in (k), we find a corrupted version of the 'M' memory (two bits distant); in (l) a corrupted version of 'J' (four bits distant) and in (m), a state which looks spurious until we recognize that it is the inverse of the stable state (l).

(e) C → C

(f) M → M

(g) J → D

(h) M → M

(i) → (j) → (k) → →

(l) → → (m) → →

▶ 42.5 The associative memory in action

Figure 42.3 shows the dynamics of a 25-unit binary Hopfield network that
has learnt four patterns by Hebbian learning. The four patterns are displayed
as five by five binary images in figure 42.3a. For twelve initial conditions,
panels (b–m) show the state of the network, iteration by iteration, all 25
units being updated asynchronously in each iteration. For an initial condition
randomly perturbed from a memory, it often only takes one iteration for all
the errors to be corrected. The network has more stable states in addition
to the four desired memories: the inverse of any stable state is also a stable
state; and there are several stable states that can be interpreted as mixtures
of the memories.

Brain damage

The network can be severely damaged and still work fine as an associative
memory. If we take the 300 weights of the network shown in figure 42.3 and
randomly set 50 or 100 of them to zero, we still find that the desired memories
are attracting stable states. Imagine a digital computer that still works fine
even when 20% of its components are destroyed!

▷ Exercise 42.5.[2] Implement a Hopfield network and confirm this amazing robust error-correcting capability.

More memories

We can squash more memories into the network too. Figure 42.4a shows a
set of five memories. When we train the network with Hebbian learning, all
five memories are stable states, even when 26 of the weights are randomly
deleted (as shown by the 'x's in the figure). However, the basins of attraction
are smaller than before: figure 42.4(b–f) shows the dynamics resulting from
randomly chosen starting states close to each of the memories (3 bits flipped).
Only three of the memories are recovered correctly.

If we try to store too many patterns, the associative memory fails catastrophically. When we add a sixth pattern, as shown in figure 42.5, only one
of the patterns is stable; the others all flow into one of two spurious stable
states.

▶ 42.6 The continuous-time continuous Hopfield network

The fact that the Hopfield network's properties are not robust to the minor
change from asynchronous to synchronous updates might be a cause for concern; can this model be a useful model of biological networks? It turns out
that once we move to a continuous-time version of the Hopfield networks, this
issue melts away.

We assume that each neuron's activity x_i is a continuous function of time
$x_i(t)$ and that the activations $a_i(t)$ are computed instantaneously in accordance
with

$$a_i(t) = \sum_j w_{ij} x_j(t). \tag{42.16}$$

The neuron's response to its activation is assumed to be mediated by the
differential equation:

$$\frac{\mathrm{d}}{\mathrm{d}t} x_i(t) = -\frac{1}{\tau}(x_i(t) - f(a_i)), \tag{42.17}$$

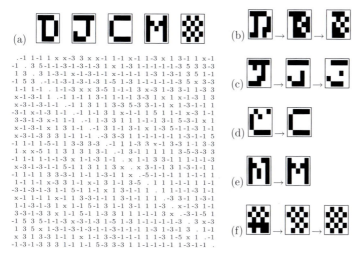

(a)

```
 .-1  1-1  1  x  x-3  3  x  x-1  1-1  x-1  1-3  x  1  3-1  1  x-1
-1  .  3  5-1-1-3-1-3-1-3  1  x  1-3  1-1-1-1-1-3  5  3  3-3
 1  3  .  3  1-3-1  x-1-3-1-1  x-1-1-1  1-3  1-3-1  3  5  1-1
-1  5  3  .-1-1-3-1-3-1-3  1-5  1-3  1-1-1-1-1-3  5  x  3-3
 1-1  1-1  .  1-1-3  x  x  3-5  1-1-1  3  x-3  1-3-3-1  1-3  3
 x-1-3-1  1  .-1  1-1  1  3-1  1-1-1  3-3  1  x  1  x-1-3  1  3
 x-3-1-3-1-1  .-1  1  3  1  1  3-3  5-3  3-1-1  x  1-3-1-1  1
-3-1  x-1-3  1-1  .-1  1-1  3  1  x-1-1  1  5  1  1-1  x-3  1-1
 3-3-1-3  x-1  1-1  .-1  1-3  3  1  1-1-1  3  1  5-3-1  x  1
 x-1-3-1  x  1  3  1-1  .-1  3  1  1-3-1  x  1-3  5-1-1-3  1-1
 x-3-1-3  3  3  1-1  1-1  .-3  3-3  1  1-1-1-1-1  1-3-1-1  5
-1  1-1  1-5-1  1  3-3  3-3  .-1  1  1-3  3  x-1  3-3  1-1  3-3
 1  x  x-5  1  1  3  1  3  1  3-1  .-1  3-1  1-1  3  1  3-5-3-3  3
-1  1-1  1-1-1-3  x  1-1-3  1-1  .  x  1-1  3  3-1  1  1-1-1-3
 x-3-1-3-1-1  5-1  1  3  1  1  3  x  .  x  3-1-1  3  1-3-1-1  1
-1  1-1  1  3  3-1  1-1  1-1-3-1  1  x  .-5-1-1-1  1  1-1-1  1
 1-1  1-1  x-3  3  1-1  x-1  3  1-1  3-5  .  1  1  1-1-1  1  1-1
-3-1-3-1-3  1-1  5-1  1-1  x  1  3-1-1  1  .  1  1-1-1-3  1-1
 x-1  1-1  1  x-1  1  3-3-1-1  1  3-1-1  1  1  .-3  3-1  1-3-1
 1-1-3-1-3  1  x  1-1  5-1  3  1-1  3-1  1  1-3  .  x-1-3  1-1
 3-3-1-3  3  x  1-1  5-1  1-3  3  1  1  1-1-1  3  x  .-3-1-5  1
-1  5  3  5-1-1-3  x-3-1-3  1-5  1-3  1-1-1-1-1-3  .  3  x-3
 1  3  5  x  1-3-1-3-1-3-1-1-3-1-1  1-3  1-3-1  3  .  1-1
 x  3  1  3-3  1-1  1  x  1-1  3-3-1-1-1  1  1-3  1-5  x  1  .-1
-1-3-1-3  3  3  1-1  1-1  5-3  3-3  1  1-1-1-1-1  1-3-1-1  .
```

(b)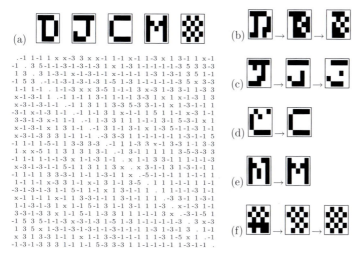

(c)

(d)

(e)

(f)

Figure 42.4. Hopfield network storing five memories, and suffering deletion of 26 of its 300 weights. (a) The five memories, and the weights of the network, with deleted weights shown by 'x'. (b–f) Initial states that differ by three random bits from a memory: some are restored, but some converge to other states.

Desired memories: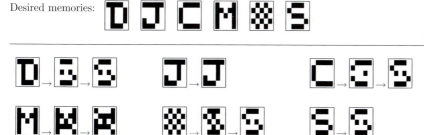

Figure 42.5. An overloaded Hopfield network trained on six memories, most of which are not stable.

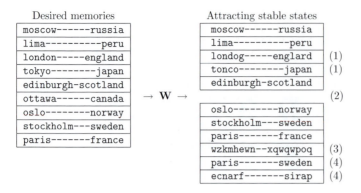

Desired memories
`moscow------russia`
`lima----------peru`
`london-----england`
`tokyo--------japan`
`edinburgh-scotland`
`ottawa------canada`
`oslo--------norway`
`stockholm---sweden`
`paris-------france`

$\rightarrow \mathbf{W} \rightarrow$

Attracting stable states	
`moscow------russia`	
`lima----------peru`	
`londog-----englard`	(1)
`tonco--------japan`	(1)
`edinburgh-scotland`	
	(2)
`oslo--------norway`	
`stockholm---sweden`	
`paris-------france`	
`wzkmhewn--xqwqwpoq`	(3)
`paris-------sweden`	(4)
`ecnarf-------sirap`	(4)

Figure 42.6. Failure modes of a Hopfield network (highly schematic). A list of desired memories, and the resulting list of attracting stable states. Notice (1) some memories that are retained with a small number of errors; (2) desired memories that are completely lost (there is no attracting stable state at the desired memory or near it); (3) spurious stable states unrelated to the original list; (4) spurious stable states that are confabulations of desired memories.

where $f(a)$ is the activation function, for example $f(a) = \tanh(a)$. For a steady activation a_i, the activity $x_i(t)$ relaxes exponentially to $f(a_i)$ with time-constant τ.

Now, here is the nice result: as long as the weight matrix is symmetric, this system has the variational free energy (42.15) as its Lyapunov function.

▷ **Exercise 42.6.**[1] By computing $\frac{d}{dt}\tilde{F}$, prove that the variational free energy $\tilde{F}(\mathbf{x})$ is a Lyapunov function for the continuous-time Hopfield network.

It is particularly easy to prove that a function L is a Lyapunov functions if the system's dynamics perform steepest descent on L, with $\frac{d}{dt}x_i(t) \propto \frac{\partial}{\partial x_i}L$. In the case of the continuous-time continuous Hopfield network, it is not quite so simple, but every component of $\frac{d}{dt}x_i(t)$ does have the same sign as $\frac{\partial}{\partial x_i}\tilde{F}$, which means that with an appropriately defined metric, the Hopfield network dynamics do perform steepest descents on $\tilde{F}(\mathbf{x})$.

▶ 42.7 The capacity of the Hopfield network

One way in which we viewed learning in the single neuron was as communication – communication of the labels of the training data set from one point in time to a later point in time. We found that the capacity of a linear threshold neuron was 2 bits per weight.

Similarly, we might view the Hopfield associative memory as a communication channel (figure 42.6). A list of desired memories is encoded into a set of weights $\mathbf{W}$ using the Hebb rule of equation (42.5), or perhaps some other learning rule. The receiver, receiving the weights $\mathbf{W}$ only, finds the stable states of the Hopfield network, which he interprets as the original memories. This communication system can fail in various ways, as illustrated in the figure.

1. Individual bits in some memories might be corrupted, that is, a stable state of the Hopfield network is displaced a little from the desired memory.

2. Entire memories might be absent from the list of attractors of the network; or a stable state might be present but have such a small basin of attraction that it is of no use for pattern completion and error correction.

3. Spurious additional memories unrelated to the desired memories might be present.

4. Spurious additional memories derived from the desired memories by operations such as mixing and inversion may also be present.

Of these failure modes, modes 1 and 2 are clearly undesirable, mode 2 especially so. Mode 3 might not matter so much as long as each of the desired memories has a large basin of attraction. The fourth failure mode might in some contexts actually be viewed as beneficial. For example, if a network is required to memorize examples of valid sentences such as 'John loves Mary' and 'John gets cake', we might be happy to find that 'John loves cake' was also a stable state of the network. We might call this behaviour 'generalization'.

The capacity of a Hopfield network with I neurons might be defined to be the number of random patterns N that can be stored without failure-mode 2 having substantial probability. If we also require failure-mode 1 to have tiny probability then the resulting capacity is much smaller. We now study these alternative definitions of the capacity.

The capacity of the Hopfield network – stringent definition

We will first explore the information storage capabilities of a binary Hopfield network that learns using the Hebb rule by considering the stability of just one bit of one of the desired patterns, assuming that the state of the network is set to that desired pattern $\mathbf{x}^{(n)}$. We will assume that the patterns to be stored are randomly selected binary patterns.

The activation of a particular neuron i is

$$a_i = \sum_j w_{ij} x_j^{(n)}, \tag{42.18}$$

where the weights are, for $i \neq j$,

$$w_{ij} = x_i^{(n)} x_j^{(n)} + \sum_{m \neq n} x_i^{(m)} x_j^{(m)}. \tag{42.19}$$

Here we have split $\mathbf{W}$ into two terms, the first of which will contribute 'signal', reinforcing the desired memory, and the second 'noise'. Substituting for w_{ij}, the activation is

$$a_i = \sum_{j \neq i} x_i^{(n)} x_j^{(n)} x_j^{(n)} + \sum_{j \neq i} \sum_{m \neq n} x_i^{(m)} x_j^{(m)} x_j^{(n)} \tag{42.20}$$

$$= (I - 1) x_i^{(n)} + \sum_{j \neq i} \sum_{m \neq n} x_i^{(m)} x_j^{(m)} x_j^{(n)}. \tag{42.21}$$

The first term is $(I - 1)$ times the desired state $x_i^{(n)}$. If this were the only term, it would keep the neuron firmly clamped in the desired state. The second term is a sum of $(I - 1)(N - 1)$ random quantities $x_i^{(m)} x_j^{(m)} x_j^{(n)}$. A moment's reflection confirms that these quantities are independent random binary variables with mean 0 and variance 1.

Thus, considering the statistics of a_i under the ensemble of random patterns, we conclude that a_i has mean $(I - 1) x_i^{(n)}$ and variance $(I - 1)(N - 1)$.

For brevity, we will now assume I and N are large enough that we can neglect the distinction between I and $I - 1$, and between N and $N - 1$. Then we can restate our conclusion: a_i is Gaussian-distributed with mean $I x_i^{(n)}$ and variance IN.

What then is the probability that the selected bit is stable, if we put the network into the state $\mathbf{x}^{(n)}$? The probability that bit i will flip on the first iteration of the Hopfield network's dynamics is

$$P(i \text{ unstable}) = \Phi\left(-\frac{I}{\sqrt{IN}}\right) = \Phi\left(-\frac{1}{\sqrt{N/I}}\right), \tag{42.22}$$

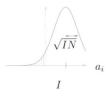

Figure 42.7. The probability density of the activation a_i in the case $x_i^{(n)} = 1$; the probability that bit i becomes flipped is the area of the tail.

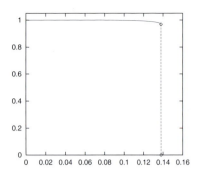 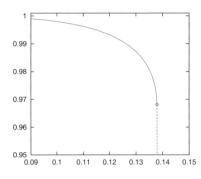

Figure 42.8. Overlap between a desired memory and the stable state nearest to it as a function of the loading fraction N/I. The overlap is defined to be the scaled inner product $\sum_i x_i x_i^{(n)}/I$, which is 1 when recall is perfect and zero when the stable state has 50% of the bits flipped. There is an abrupt transition at $N/I = 0.138$, where the overlap drops from 0.97 to zero.

where

$$\Phi(z) \equiv \int_{-\infty}^{z} dz\, \frac{1}{\sqrt{2\pi}}\, e^{-z^2/2}. \tag{42.23}$$

The important quantity N/I is the ratio of the number of patterns stored to the number of neurons. If, for example, we try to store $N \simeq 0.18I$ patterns in the Hopfield network then there is a chance of 1% that a specified bit in a specified pattern will be unstable on the first iteration.

   We are now in a position to derive our first capacity result, for the case where no corruption of the desired memories is permitted.

▷ Exercise 42.7.[2] Assume that we wish all the desired patterns to be completely stable – we don't want any of the bits to flip when the network is put into any desired pattern state – and the total probability of any error at all is required to be less than a small number ϵ. Using the approximation to the error function for large z,

$$\Phi(-z) \simeq \frac{1}{\sqrt{2\pi}}\frac{e^{-z^2/2}}{z}, \tag{42.24}$$

show that the maximum number of patterns that can be stored, $N_{\max}$, is

$$N_{\max} \simeq \frac{I}{4\ln I + 2\ln(1/\epsilon)}. \tag{42.25}$$

If, however, we allow a small amount of corruption of memories to occur, the number of patterns that can be stored increases.

The statistical physicists' capacity

The analysis that led to equation (42.22) tells us that if we try to store $N \simeq 0.18I$ patterns in the Hopfield network then, starting from a desired memory, about 1% of the bits will be unstable on the first iteration. Our analysis does not shed light on what is expected to happen on subsequent iterations. The flipping of these bits might make some of the other bits unstable too, causing an increasing number of bits to be flipped. This process might lead to an avalanche in which the network's state ends up a long way from the desired memory.

   In fact, when N/I is large, such avalanches do happen. When N/I is small, they tend not to – there is a stable state near to each desired memory. For the limit of large I, Amit *et al.* (1985) have used methods from statistical physics to find numerically the transition between these two behaviours. There is a sharp discontinuity at

$$N_{\text{crit}} = 0.138I. \tag{42.26}$$

Below this critical value, there is likely to be a stable state near every desired memory, in which a small fraction of the bits are flipped. When N/I exceeds 0.138, the system has only spurious stable states, known as *spin glass states*, none of which is correlated with any of the desired memories. Just below the critical value, the fraction of bits that are flipped when a desired memory has evolved to its associated stable state is 1.6%. Figure 42.8 shows the overlap between the desired memory and the nearest stable state as a function of N/I.

Some other transitions in properties of the model occur at some additional values of N/I, as summarized below.

For all N/I, stable spin glass states exist, uncorrelated with the desired memories.

For $N/I > 0.138$, these spin glass states are the only stable states.

For $N/I \in (0, 0.138)$, there are stable states close to the desired memories.

For $N/I \in (0, 0.05)$, the stable states associated with the desired memories have lower energy than the spurious spin glass states.

For $N/I \in (0.05, 0.138)$, the spin glass states dominate – there are spin glass states that have lower energy than the stable states associated with the desired memories.

For $N/I \in (0, 0.03)$, there are additional *mixture* states, which are combinations of several desired memories. These stable states do not have as low energy as the stable states associated with the desired memories.

In conclusion, the capacity of the Hopfield network with I neurons, if we define the capacity in terms of the abrupt discontinuity discussed above, is $0.138I$ random binary patterns, each of length I, each of which is received with 1.6% of its bits flipped. In bits, this capacity is

$$0.138I^2 \times (1 - H_2(0.016)) = 0.122\,I^2 \text{ bits.} \qquad (42.27)$$

Since there are $I^2/2$ weights in the network, we can also express the capacity as *0.24 bits per weight*.

▶ **42.8 Improving on the capacity of the Hebb rule**

The capacities discussed in the previous section are the capacities of the Hopfield network whose weights are set using the Hebbian learning rule. We can do better than the Hebb rule by defining an objective function that measures how well the network stores all the memories, and minimizing it.

For an associative memory to be useful, it must be able to correct at least one flipped bit. Let's make an objective function that measures whether flipped bits tend to be restored correctly. Our intention is that, for every neuron i in the network, the weights to that neuron should satisfy this rule:

> for every pattern $\mathbf{x}^{(n)}$, if the neurons other than i are set correctly to $x_j = x_j^{(n)}$, then the activation of neuron i should be such that its preferred output is $x_i = x_i^{(n)}$.

Is this rule a familiar idea? Yes, it is precisely what we wanted the single neuron of Chapter 39 to do. Each pattern $\mathbf{x}^{(n)}$ defines an input, target pair for the single neuron i. And it defines an input, target pair for all the other neurons too.

```
w = x' * x ;            # initialize the weights using Hebb rule

for l = 1:L             # loop L times

        for i=1:I             #
          w(i,i) = 0 ;        #  ensure the self-weights are zero.
        end                   #

        a  = x * w      ;     # compute all activations
        y  = sigmoid(a) ;     # compute all outputs
        e  = t - y      ;     # compute all errors
        gw = x' * e     ;     # compute the gradients
        gw = gw + gw'   ;     # symmetrize gradients

        w  = w + eta * ( gw - alpha * w ) ;   # make step

endfor
```

Algorithm 42.9. Octave source code for optimizing the weights of a Hopfield network, so that it works as an associative memory. c.f. algorithm 39.5. The data matrix x has I columns and N rows. The matrix t is identical to x except that -1s are replaced by 0s.

So, just as we defined an objective function (39.11) for the training of a single neuron as a classifier, we can define

$$G(\mathbf{W}) = -\sum_i \sum_n t_i^{(n)} \ln y_i^{(n)} + (1 - t_i^{(n)}) \ln(1 - y_i^{(n)})$$ (42.28)

where

$$t_i^{(n)} = \begin{cases} 1 & x_i^{(n)} = 1 \\ 0 & x_i^{(n)} = -1 \end{cases}$$ (42.29)

and

$$y_i^{(n)} = \frac{1}{1 + \exp(-a_i^{(n)})}, \quad \text{where } a_i^{(n)} = \sum_j w_{ij} x_j^{(n)}.$$ (42.30)

We can then steal the algorithm (algorithm 39.5, p.478) which we wrote for the single neuron, to write an algorithm for optimizing a Hopfield network, algorithm 42.9. The convenient syntax of Octave requires very few changes; the extra lines enforce the constraints that the self-weights w_{ii} should all be zero and that the weight matrix should be symmetrical ($w_{ij} = w_{ji}$).

As expected, this learning algorithm does a better job than the one-shot Hebbian learning rule. When the six patterns of figure 42.5, which cannot be memorized by the Hebb rule, are learned using algorithm 42.9, all six patterns become stable states.

Exercise 42.8.[4C] Implement this learning rule and investigate empirically its capacity for memorizing random patterns; also compare its avalanche properties with those of the Hebb rule.

▶ 42.9 Hopfield networks for optimization problems

Since a Hopfield network's dynamics minimize an energy function, it is natural to ask whether we can map interesting optimization problems onto Hopfield networks. Biological data processing problems often involve an element of *constraint satisfaction* – in scene interpretation, for example, one might wish to infer the spatial location, orientation, brightness and texture of each visible element, and which visible elements are connected together in objects. These inferences are constrained by the given data and by prior knowledge about continuity of objects.

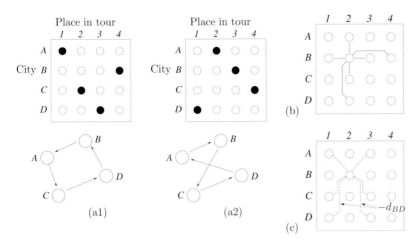

Figure 42.10. Hopfield network for solving a travelling salesman problem with $K = 4$ cities. (a1,2) Two solution states of the 16-neuron network, with activites represented by black = 1, white = 0; and the tours corresponding to these network states. (b) The negative weights between node $B2$ and other nodes; these weights enforce validity of a tour. (c) The negative weights that embody the distance objective function.

Hopfield and Tank (1985) suggested that one might take an interesting constraint satisfaction problem and design the weights of a binary or continuous Hopfield network such that the settling process of the network would minimize the objective function of the problem.

The travelling salesman problem

A classic constraint satisfaction problem to which Hopfield networks have been applied is the travelling salesman problem.

A set of K cities is given, and a matrix of the $K(K-1)/2$ distances between those cities. The task is to find a closed tour of the cities, visiting each city once, that has the smallest total distance. The travelling salesman problem is equivalent in difficulty to an NP-complete problem.

The method suggested by Hopfield and Tank is to represent a tentative solution to the problem by the state of a network with $I = K^2$ neurons arranged in a square, with each neuron representing the hypothesis that a particular city comes at a particular point in the tour. It will be convenient to consider the states of the neurons as being between 0 and 1 rather than -1 and 1. Two solution states for a four-city travelling salesman problem are shown in figure 42.10a.

The weights in the Hopfield network play two roles. First, they must define an energy function which is minimized only when the state of the network represents a *valid* tour. A valid state is one that looks like a permutation matrix, having exactly one '1' in every row and one '1' in every column. This rule can be enforced by putting large negative weights between any pair of neurons that are in the same row or the same column, and setting a positive bias for all neurons to ensure that K neurons do turn on. Figure 42.10b shows the negative weights that are connected to one neuron, '$B2$', which represents the statement 'city B comes second in the tour'.

Second, the weights must encode the objective function that we want to minimize – the total distance. This can be done by putting negative weights proportional to the appropriate distances between the nodes in adjacent columns. For example, between the B and D nodes in adjacent columns, the weight would be $-d_{BD}$. The negative weights that are connected to neuron $B2$ are shown in figure 42.10c. The result is that when the network is in a valid state, its total energy will be the total distance of the corresponding

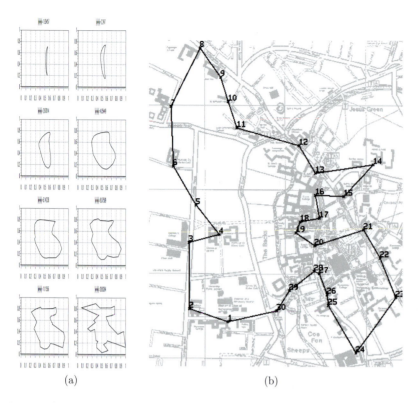

Figure 42.11. (a) Evolution of the state of a continuous Hopfield network solving a travelling salesman problem using Aiyer's (1991) graduated non-convexity method; the state of the network is projected into the two-dimensional space in which the cities are located by finding the centre of mass for each point in the tour, using the neuron activities as the mass function. (b) The travelling scholar problem. The shortest tour linking the 27 Cambridge Colleges, the Engineering Department, the University Library, and Sree Aiyer's house. From Aiyer (1991).

(a)   (b)

tour, plus a constant given by the energy associated with the biases.

Now, since a Hopfield network minimizes its energy, it is hoped that the binary or continuous Hopfield network's dynamics will take the state to a minimum that is a valid tour and which might be an optimal tour. This hope is not fulfilled for large travelling salesman problems, however, without some careful modifications. We have not specified the size of the weights that enforce the tour's validity, relative to the size of the distance weights, and setting this scale factor poses difficulties. If 'large' validity-enforcing weights are used, the network's dynamics will rattle into a valid state with little regard for the distances. If 'small' validity-enforcing weights are used, it is possible that the distance weights will cause the network to adopt an *invalid* state that has lower energy than any valid state. Our original formulation of the energy function puts the objective function and the solution's validity in potential conflict with each other. This difficulty has been resolved by the work of Sree Aiyer (1991), who showed how to modify the distance weights so that they would not interfere with the solution's validity, and how to define a continuous Hopfield network whose dynamics are at all times confined to a 'valid subspace'. Aiyer used a *graduated non-convexity* or *deterministic annealing* approach to find good solutions using these Hopfield networks. The deterministic annealing approach involves gradually increasing the gain β of the neurons in the network from 0 to ∞, at which point the state of the network corresponds to a valid tour. A sequence of trajectories generated by applying this method to a thirty-city travelling salesman problem is shown in figure 42.11a.

A solution to the 'travelling scholar problem' found by Aiyer using a continuous Hopfield network is shown in figure 42.11b.

▶ **42.10 Further exercises**

▷ Exercise 42.9.[3] Storing two memories.

Two binary memories $\mathbf{m}$ and $\mathbf{n}$ $(m_i, n_i \in \{-1, +1\})$ are stored by Hebbian learning in a Hopfield network using

$$w_{ij} = \begin{cases} m_i m_j + n_i n_j & \text{for } i \neq j \\ 0 & \text{for } i = j. \end{cases} \tag{42.31}$$

The biases b_i are set to zero.

The network is put in the state $\mathbf{x} = \mathbf{m}$. Evaluate the activation a_i of neuron i and show that in can be written in the form

$$a_i = \mu m_i + \nu n_i. \tag{42.32}$$

By comparing the signal strength, μ, with the magnitude of the noise strength, $|\nu|$, show that $\mathbf{x} = \mathbf{m}$ is a stable state of the dynamics of the network.

The network is put in a state $\mathbf{x}$ differing in D places from $\mathbf{m}$,

$$\mathbf{x} = \mathbf{m} + 2\mathbf{d}, \tag{42.33}$$

where the perturbation $\mathbf{d}$ satisfies $d_i \in \{-1, 0, +1\}$. D is the number of components of $\mathbf{d}$ that are non-zero, and for each d_i that is non-zero, $d_i = -m_i$. Defining the overlap between $\mathbf{m}$ and $\mathbf{n}$ to be

$$o_{\mathbf{mn}} = \sum_{i=1}^{I} m_i n_i, \tag{42.34}$$

evaluate the activation a_i of neuron i again and show that the dynamics of the network will restore $\mathbf{x}$ to $\mathbf{m}$ if the number of flipped bits satisfies

$$D < \frac{1}{4}(I - |o_{\mathbf{mn}}| - 2). \tag{42.35}$$

How does this number compare with the maximum number of flipped bits that can be corrected by the optimal decoder, assuming the vector $\mathbf{x}$ is either a noisy version of $\mathbf{m}$ or of $\mathbf{n}$?

Exercise 42.10.[3] Hopfield network as a collection of binary classifiers. This exercise explores the link between unsupervised networks and supervised networks. If a Hopfield network's desired memories are all attracting stable states, then every neuron in the network has weights going to it that solve a classification problem personal to that neuron. Take the set of memories and write them in the form $\mathbf{x}'^{(n)}, x_i^{(n)}$, where $\mathbf{x}'$ denotes all the components $x_{i'}$ for all $i' \neq i$, and let $\mathbf{w}'$ denote the vector of weights $w_{ii'}$, for $i' \neq i$.

Using what we know about the capacity of the single neuron, show that it is almost certainly impossible to store more than $2I$ random memories in a Hopfield network of I neurons.

Lyapunov functions

Exercise 42.11.[3] Erik's puzzle. In a stripped-down version of Conway's game
of life, cells are arranged on a square grid. Each cell is either alive or
dead. Live cells do not die. Dead cells become alive if two or more of
their immediate neighbours are alive. (Neighbours to north, south, east
and west.) What is the smallest number of live cells needed in order
that these rules lead to an entire $N \times N$ square being alive?

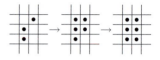

In a d-dimensional version of the same game, the rule is that if d neighbours are alive then you come to life. What is the smallest number of
live cells needed in order that an entire $N \times N \times \cdots \times N$ hypercube
becomes alive? (And how should those live cells be arranged?)

Figure 42.12. Erik's dynamics.

The southeast puzzle

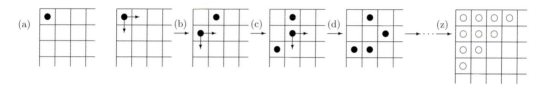

Figure 42.13. The southeast
puzzle.

The **southeast** puzzle is played on a semi-infinite chess board, starting at
its northwest (top left) corner. There are three rules:

1. In the starting position, one piece is placed in the northwest-most square
   (figure 42.13a).

2. It is not permitted for more than one piece to be on any given square.

3. At each step, you remove one piece from the board, and replace it with
   two pieces, one in the square immediately to the east, and one in the the
   square immediately to the south, as illustrated in figure 42.13b. Every
   such step increases the number of pieces on the board by one.

After move (b) has been made, either piece may be selected for the next move.
Figure 42.13c shows the outcome of moving the lower piece. At the next move,
either the lowest piece or the middle piece of the three may be selected; the
uppermost piece may not be selected, since that would violate rule 2. At move
(d) we have selected the middle piece. Now any of the pieces may be moved,
except for the leftmost piece.

   Now, here is the puzzle:

▷ Exercise 42.12.[4, p.521] Is it possible to obtain a position in which all the ten
   squares closest to the northwest corner, marked in figure 42.13z, are
   empty?

   [Hint: this puzzle has a connection to data compression.]

▶ 42.11 Solutions

Solution to exercise 42.3 (p.508). Take a binary feedback network with 2 neurons and let $w_{12} = 1$ and $w_{21} = -1$. Then whenever neuron 1 is updated,
it will match neuron 2, and whenever neuron 2 is updated, it will flip to the
opposite state from neuron 1. There is no stable state.

Solution to exercise 42.4 (p.508). Take a binary Hopfield network with 2 neurons and let $w_{12} = w_{21} = 1$, and let the initial condition be $x_1 = 1$, $x_2 = -1$. Then if the dynamics are synchronous, on every iteration both neurons will flip their state. The dynamics do not converge to a fixed point.

Solution to exercise 42.12 (p.520). The key to this problem is to notice its similarity to the construction of a binary symbol code. Starting from the empty string, we can build a binary tree by repeatedly splitting a codeword into two. Every codeword has an implicit probability 2^{-l}, where l is the depth of the codeword in the binary tree. Whenever we split a codeword in two and create two new codewords whose length is increased by one, the two new codewords each have implicit probability equal to half that of the old codeword. For a complete binary code, the Kraft equality affirms that the sum of these implicit probabilities is 1.

Similarly, in southeast, we can associate a 'weight' with each piece on the board. If we assign a weight of 1 to any piece sitting on the top left square; a weight of $1/2$ to any piece on a square whose distance from the top left is one; a weight of $1/4$ to any piece whose distance from the top left is two; and so forth, with 'distance' being the city-block distance; then every legal move in southeast leaves unchanged the total weight of all pieces on the board. Lyapunov functions come in two flavours: the function may be a function of state whose value is known to stay constant; or it may be a function of state that is bounded below, and whose value always decreases or stays constant. The total weight is a Lyapunov function of the second type.

The starting weight is 1, so now we have a powerful tool: a conserved function of the state. Is it possible to find a position in which the ten highest-weight squares are vacant, and the total weight is 1? What is the total weight if *all* the other squares on the board are occupied (figure 42.14)? The total weight would be $\sum_{l=4}^{\infty}(l+1)2^{-l}$. Which is equal to $3/4$. So it is impossible to empty all ten of those squares.

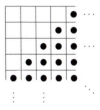

Figure 42.14. A possible position for the southeast puzzle?

43

Boltzmann Machines

▶ **43.1 From Hopfield networks to Boltzmann machines**

We have noticed that the binary Hopfield network minimizes an energy function

$$E(\mathbf{x}) = -\frac{1}{2}\mathbf{x}^\mathsf{T}\mathbf{W}\mathbf{x} \tag{43.1}$$

and that the continuous Hopfield network with activation function $x_n = \tanh(a_n)$ can be viewed as *approximating* the probability distribution associated with that energy function,

$$P(\mathbf{x}|\mathbf{W}) = \frac{1}{Z(\mathbf{W})}\exp[-E(\mathbf{x})] = \frac{1}{Z(\mathbf{W})}\exp\left[\frac{1}{2}\mathbf{x}^\mathsf{T}\mathbf{W}\mathbf{x}\right]. \tag{43.2}$$

These observations motivate the idea of working with a neural network model that actually *implements* the above probability distribution.

The *stochastic Hopfield network* or *Boltzmann machine* (Hinton and Sejnowski, 1986) has the following activity rule:

Activity rule of Boltzmann machine: after computing the activation a_n,

$$\text{set } x_n = +1 \text{ with probability } \frac{1}{1 + e^{-2a}}$$

$$\text{else set } x_n = -1. \tag{43.3}$$

This rule implements Gibbs sampling for the probability distribution (43.2).

Boltzmann machine learning

Given a set of examples $\{\mathbf{x}^{(n)}\}_1^N$ from the real world, we might be interested in adjusting the weights $\mathbf{W}$ such that the generative model

$$P(\mathbf{x}|\mathbf{W}) = \frac{1}{Z(\mathbf{W})}\exp\left[\frac{1}{2}\mathbf{x}^\mathsf{T}\mathbf{W}\mathbf{x}\right] \tag{43.4}$$

is well matched to those examples. We can derive a learning algorithm by writing down Bayes' theorem to obtain the posterior probability of the weights given the data:

$$P(\mathbf{W}|\{\mathbf{x}^{(n)}\}_1^N) = \frac{\left[\prod_{n=1}^N P(\mathbf{x}^{(n)}|\mathbf{W})\right]P(\mathbf{W})}{P(\{\mathbf{x}^{(n)}\}_1^N)}. \tag{43.5}$$

We concentrate on the first term in the numerator, the likelihood, and derive a maximum likelihood algorithm (though there might be advantages in pursuing a full Bayesian approach as we did in the case of the single neuron). We differentiate the logarithm of the likelihood,

$$\ln\left[\prod_{n=1}^{N} P(\mathbf{x}^{(n)}|\mathbf{W})\right] = \sum_{n=1}^{N}\left[\frac{1}{2}\mathbf{x}^{(n)\mathsf{T}}\mathbf{W}\mathbf{x}^{(n)} - \ln Z(\mathbf{W})\right], \tag{43.6}$$

with respect to w_{ij}, bearing in mind that $\mathbf{W}$ is defined to be symmetric with $w_{ji} = w_{ij}$.

Exercise 43.1.[2] Show that the derivative of $\ln Z(\mathbf{W})$ with respect to w_{ij} is

$$\frac{\partial}{\partial w_{ij}}\ln Z(\mathbf{W}) = \sum_{\mathbf{x}} x_i x_j P(\mathbf{x}|\mathbf{W}) = \langle x_i x_j\rangle_{P(\mathbf{x}|\mathbf{W})}. \tag{43.7}$$

[This exercise is similar to exercise 22.12 (p.307).]

The derivative of the log likelihood is therefore:

$$\frac{\partial}{\partial w_{ij}}\ln P(\{\mathbf{x}^{(n)}\}_1^N|\mathbf{W}) = \sum_{n=1}^{N}\left[x_i^{(n)}x_j^{(n)} - \langle x_i x_j\rangle_{P(\mathbf{x}|\mathbf{W})}\right] \tag{43.8}$$

$$= N\left[\langle x_i x_j\rangle_{\text{Data}} - \langle x_i x_j\rangle_{P(\mathbf{x}|\mathbf{W})}\right]. \tag{43.9}$$

This gradient is proportional to the difference of two terms. The first term is the *empirical* correlation between x_i and x_j,

$$\langle x_i x_j\rangle_{\text{Data}} \equiv \frac{1}{N}\sum_{n=1}^{N}\left[x_i^{(n)}x_j^{(n)}\right], \tag{43.10}$$

and the second term is the correlation between x_i and x_j under the current model,

$$\langle x_i x_j\rangle_{P(\mathbf{x}|\mathbf{W})} \equiv \sum_{\mathbf{x}} x_i x_j P(\mathbf{x}|\mathbf{W}). \tag{43.11}$$

The first correlation $\langle x_i x_j\rangle_{\text{Data}}$ is readily evaluated – it is just the empirical correlation between the activities in the real world. The second correlation, $\langle x_i x_j\rangle_{P(\mathbf{x}|\mathbf{W})}$, is not so easy to evaluate, but it can be estimated by Monte Carlo methods, that is, by observing the average value of $x_i x_j$ while the activity rule of the Boltzmann machine, equation (43.3), is iterated.

In the special case $\mathbf{W} = 0$, we can evaluate the gradient exactly because, by symmetry, the correlation $\langle x_i x_j\rangle_{P(\mathbf{x}|\mathbf{W})}$ must be zero. If the weights are adjusted by gradient descent with learning rate η, then, after one iteration, the weights will be

$$w_{ij} = \eta\sum_{n=1}^{N}\left[x_i^{(n)}x_j^{(n)}\right], \tag{43.12}$$

precisely the value of the weights given by the Hebb rule, equation (16.5), with which we trained the Hopfield network.

Interpretation of Boltzmann machine learning

One way of viewing the two terms in the gradient (43.9) is as 'waking' and 'sleeping' rules. While the network is 'awake', it measures the correlation between x_i and x_j in the real world, and weights are *increased* in proportion. While the network is 'asleep', it 'dreams' about the world using the generative model (43.4), and measures the correlations between x_i and x_j in the model world; these correlations determine a proportional *decrease* in the weights. If the second-order correlations in the dream world match the correlations in the real world, then the two terms balance and the weights do not change.

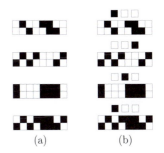

(a)   (b)

Figure 43.1. The 'shifter' ensembles. (a) Four samples from the plain shifter ensemble. (b) Four corresponding samples from the labelled shifter ensemble.

Criticism of Hopfield networks and simple Boltzmann machines

Up to this point we have discussed Hopfield networks and Boltzmann machines in which all of the neurons correspond to *visible* variables x_i. The result is a probabilistic model that, when optimized, can capture the second-order statistics of the environment. [The second-order statistics of an ensemble $P(\mathbf{x})$ are the expected values $\langle x_i x_j \rangle$ of all the pairwise products $x_i x_j$.] The real world, however, often has higher-order correlations that must be included if our description of it is to be effective. Often the second-order correlations in themselves may carry little or no useful information.

Consider, for example, the ensemble of binary images of chairs. We can imagine images of chairs with various designs – four-legged chairs, comfy chairs, chairs with five legs and wheels, wooden chairs, cushioned chairs, chairs with rockers instead of legs. A child can easily learn to distinguish these images from images of carrots and parrots. But I expect the second-order statistics of the raw data are useless for describing the ensemble. Second-order statistics only capture whether two pixels are likely to be in the same state as each other. Higher-order concepts are needed to make a good generative model of images of chairs.

A simpler ensemble of images in which high-order statistics are important is the 'shifter ensemble', which comes in two flavours. Figure 43.1a shows a few samples from the 'plain shifter ensemble'. In each image, the bottom eight pixels are a copy of the top eight pixels, either shifted one pixel to the left, or unshifted, or shifted one pixel to the right. (The top eight pixels are set at random.) This ensemble is a simple model of the visual signals from the two eyes arriving at early levels of the brain. The signals from the two eyes are similar to each other but may differ by small translations because of the varying depth of the visual world. This ensemble is simple to describe, but its second-order statistics convey no useful information. The correlation between one pixel and any of the three pixels above it is $1/3$. The correlation between any other two pixels is zero.

Figure 43.1b shows a few samples from the 'labelled shifter ensemble'. Here, the problem has been made easier by including an extra three neurons that label the visual image as being an instance of either the 'shift left', 'no shift', or 'shift right' sub-ensemble. But with this extra information, the ensemble is still not learnable using second-order statistics alone. The second-order correlation between any label neuron and any image neuron is zero. We need models that can capture higher-order statistics of an environment.

So, how can we develop such models? One idea might be to create models that directly capture higher-order correlations, such as:

$$P'(\mathbf{x}|\mathbf{W}, \mathbf{V}, \ldots) = \frac{1}{Z'} \exp\left(\frac{1}{2} \sum_{ij} w_{ij} x_i x_j + \frac{1}{6} \sum_{ij} v_{ijk} x_i x_j x_k + \cdots \right).$$

(43.13)

Such *higher-order Boltzmann machines* are equally easy to simulate using stochastic updates, and the learning rule for the higher-order parameters v_{ijk} is equivalent to the learning rule for w_{ij}.

▷ Exercise 43.2.[2] Derive the gradient of the log likelihood with respect to v_{ijk}.

It is possible that the spines found on biological neurons are responsible for detecting correlations between small numbers of incoming signals. However, to capture statistics of high enough order to describe the ensemble of images of chairs well would require an unimaginable number of terms. To capture merely the fourth-order statistics in a 128×128 pixel image, we need more than 10^7 parameters.

So measuring moments of images is *not* a good way to describe their underlying structure. Perhaps what we need instead or in addition are *hidden variables*, also known to statisticians as *latent variables*. This is the important innovation introduced by Hinton and Sejnowski (1986). The idea is that the high-order correlations among the visible variables are described by including extra hidden variables and sticking to a model that has only second-order interactions between its variables; the hidden variables induce higher-order correlations between the visible variables.

▶ 43.2 Boltzmann machine with hidden units

We now add *hidden neurons* to our stochastic model. These are neurons that do not correspond to observed variables; they are free to play any role in the probabilistic model defined by equation (43.4). They might actually take on interpretable roles, effectively performing 'feature extraction'.

Learning in Boltzmann machines with hidden units

The activity rule of a Boltzmann machine with hidden units is identical to that of the original Boltzmann machine. The learning rule can again be derived by maximum likelihood, but now we need to take into account the fact that the states of the hidden units are unknown. We will denote the states of the visible units by $\mathbf{x}$, the states of the hidden units by $\mathbf{h}$, and the generic state of a neuron (either visible or hidden) by y_i, with $\mathbf{y} \equiv (\mathbf{x}, \mathbf{h})$. The state of the network when the visible neurons are clamped in state $\mathbf{x}^{(n)}$ is $\mathbf{y}^{(n)} \equiv (\mathbf{x}^{(n)}, \mathbf{h})$. The likelihood of $\mathbf{W}$ given a single data example $\mathbf{x}^{(n)}$ is

$$P(\mathbf{x}^{(n)}|\mathbf{W}) = \sum_{\mathbf{h}} P(\mathbf{x}^{(n)}, \mathbf{h}|\mathbf{W}) = \sum_{\mathbf{h}} \frac{1}{Z(\mathbf{W})} \exp\left[\frac{1}{2}[\mathbf{y}^{(n)}]^{\mathsf{T}}\mathbf{W}\mathbf{y}^{(n)}\right], \quad (43.14)$$

where

$$Z(\mathbf{W}) = \sum_{\mathbf{x},\mathbf{h}} \exp\left[\frac{1}{2}\mathbf{y}^{\mathsf{T}}\mathbf{W}\mathbf{y}\right]. \quad (43.15)$$

Equation (43.14) may also be written

$$P(\mathbf{x}^{(n)}|\mathbf{W}) = \frac{Z_{\mathbf{x}^{(n)}}(\mathbf{W})}{Z(\mathbf{W})} \quad (43.16)$$

where

$$Z_{\mathbf{x}^{(n)}}(\mathbf{W}) = \sum_{\mathbf{h}} \exp\left[\frac{1}{2}[\mathbf{y}^{(n)}]^{\mathsf{T}}\mathbf{W}\mathbf{y}^{(n)}\right]. \quad (43.17)$$

Differentiating the likelihood as before, we find that the derivative with respect to any weight w_{ij} is again the difference between a 'waking' term and a 'sleeping' term,

$$\frac{\partial}{\partial w_{ij}} \ln P(\{\mathbf{x}^{(n)}\}_1^N|\mathbf{W}) = \sum_n \left\{ \langle y_i y_j \rangle_{P(\mathbf{h}|\mathbf{x}^{(n)},\mathbf{W})} - \langle y_i y_j \rangle_{P(\mathbf{x},\mathbf{h}|\mathbf{W})} \right\}. \quad (43.18)$$

The first term $\langle y_i y_j \rangle_{P(\mathbf{h}|\mathbf{x}^{(n)},\mathbf{W})}$ is the correlation between y_i and y_j if the Boltzmann machine is simulated with the visible variables clamped to $\mathbf{x}^{(n)}$ and the hidden variables freely sampling from their conditional distribution.

The second term $\langle y_i y_j \rangle_{P(\mathbf{x},\mathbf{h}|\mathbf{W})}$ is the correlation between y_i and y_j when the Boltzmann machine generates samples from its model distribution.

Hinton and Sejnowski demonstrated that non-trivial ensembles such as the labelled shifter ensemble can be learned using a Boltzmann machine with hidden units. The hidden units take on the role of feature detectors that spot patterns likely to be associated with one of the three shifts.

The Boltzmann machine is time-consuming to simulate because the computation of the gradient of the log likelihood depends on taking the difference of two gradients, both found by Monte Carlo methods. So Boltzmann machines are not in widespread use. It is an area of active research to create models that embody the same capabilities using more efficient computations (Hinton *et al.*, 1995; Dayan *et al.*, 1995; Hinton and Ghahramani, 1997; Hinton, 2001; Hinton and Teh, 2001).

▶ 43.3 Exercise

▷ Exercise 43.3.[3] Can the 'bars and stripes' ensemble (figure 43.2) be learned by a Boltzmann machine with no hidden units? [You may be surprised!]

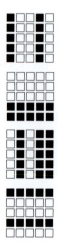

Figure 43.2. Four samples from the 'bars and stripes' ensemble. Each sample is generated by first picking an orientation, horizontal or vertical; then, for each row of spins in that orientation (each bar or stripe respectively), switching all spins on with probability $1/2$.

44

Supervised Learning in Multilayer Networks

▶ 44.1 Multilayer perceptrons

No course on neural networks could be complete without a discussion of supervised multilayer networks, also known as backpropagation networks.

The *multilayer perceptron* is a feedforward network. It has input neurons, hidden neurons and output neurons. The hidden neurons may be arranged in a sequence of layers. The most common multilayer perceptrons have a single hidden layer, and are known as 'two-layer' networks, the number 'two' counting the number of layers of neurons not including the inputs.

Such a feedforward network defines a nonlinear parameterized mapping from an input $\mathbf{x}$ to an output $\mathbf{y} = \mathbf{y}(\mathbf{x}; \mathbf{w}, \mathcal{A})$. The output is a continuous function of the input and of the parameters $\mathbf{w}$; the architecture of the net, i.e., the functional form of the mapping, is denoted by $\mathcal{A}$. Feedforward networks can be 'trained' to perform regression and classification tasks.

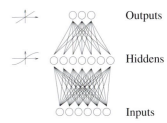

Figure 44.1. A typical two-layer network, with six inputs, seven hidden units, and three outputs. Each line represents one weight.

Regression networks

In the case of a regression problem, the mapping for a network with one hidden layer may have the form:

$$\text{Hidden layer:} \quad a_j^{(1)} = \sum_l w_{jl}^{(1)} x_l + \theta_j^{(1)}; \quad h_j = f^{(1)}(a_j^{(1)}) \tag{44.1}$$

$$\text{Output layer:} \quad a_i^{(2)} = \sum_j w_{ij}^{(2)} h_j + \theta_i^{(2)}; \quad y_i = f^{(2)}(a_i^{(2)}) \tag{44.2}$$

where, for example, $f^{(1)}(a) = \tanh(a)$, and $f^{(2)}(a) = a$. Here l runs over the inputs $x_1, \ldots, x_L$, j runs over the hidden units, and i runs over the outputs. The 'weights' w and 'biases' θ together make up the parameter vector $\mathbf{w}$. The nonlinear sigmoid function $f^{(1)}$ at the hidden layer gives the neural network greater computational flexibility than a standard linear regression model. Graphically, we can represent the neural network as a set of layers of connected neurons (figure 44.1).

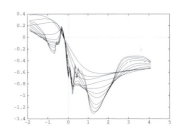

Figure 44.3. Samples from the prior over functions of a one-input network. For each of a sequence of values of $\sigma_{\text{bias}} = 8, 6, 4, 3, 2, 1.6, 1.2, 0.8, 0.4, 0.3, 0.2$, and $\sigma_{\text{in}} = 5\sigma_{\text{bias}}^w$, one random function is shown. The other hyperparameters of the network were $H = 400$, $\sigma_{\text{out}}^w = 0.05$.

What sorts of functions can these networks implement?

Just as we explored the weight space of the single neuron in Chapter 39, examining the functions it could produce, let us explore the weight space of a multilayer network. In figure 44.2 I take a network with one input and one output and a large number H of hidden units, set the biases and weights $\theta_j^{(1)}$,

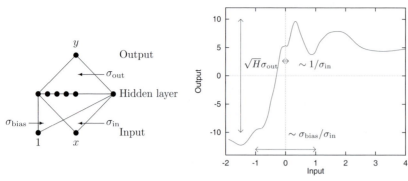

Figure 44.2. Properties of a function produced by a random network. The vertical scale of a typical function produced by the network with random weights is of order $\sqrt{H}\sigma_{\text{out}}$; the horizontal range in which the function varies significantly is of order $\sigma_{\text{bias}}/\sigma_{\text{in}}$; and the shortest horizontal length scale is of order $1/\sigma_{\text{in}}$. The function shown was produced by making a random network with $H = 400$ hidden units, and Gaussian weights with $\sigma_{\text{bias}} = 4$, $\sigma_{\text{in}} = 8$, and $\sigma_{\text{out}} = 0.5$.

$w_{jl}^{(1)}$, $\theta_i^{(2)}$ and $w_{ij}^{(2)}$ to random values, and plot the resulting function $y(x)$. I set the hidden unit biases $\theta_j^{(1)}$ to random values from a Gaussian with zero mean and standard deviation σ_{bias}; the input to hidden weights $w_{jl}^{(1)}$ to random values with standard deviation σ_{in}; and the bias and output weights $\theta_i^{(2)}$ and $w_{ij}^{(2)}$ to random values with standard deviation σ_{out}.

The sort of functions that we obtain depend on the values of σ_{bias}, σ_{in} and σ_{out}. As the weights and biases are made bigger we obtain more complex functions with more features and a greater sensitivity to the input variable. The vertical scale of a typical function produced by the network with random weights is of order $\sqrt{H}\sigma_{\text{out}}$; the horizontal range in which the function varies significantly is of order $\sigma_{\text{bias}}/\sigma_{\text{in}}$; and the shortest horizontal length scale is of order $1/\sigma_{\text{in}}$.

Radford Neal (1996) has also shown that in the limit as $H \to \infty$ the statistical properties of the functions generated by randomizing the weights are independent of the number of hidden units; so, interestingly, the complexity of the functions becomes independent of the number of parameters in the model. What determines the complexity of the typical functions is the characteristic magnitude of the weights. Thus we anticipate that when we fit these models to real data, an important way of controlling the complexity of the fitted function will be to control the characteristic magnitude of the weights.

Figure 44.3 shows one typical function produced by a network with two inputs and one output. This should be contrasted with the function produced by a traditional linear regression model, which is a flat plane. Neural networks can create functions with more complexity than a linear regression.

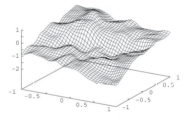

Figure 44.4. Samples from the prior of a two-input network. A typical function produced by a two-input network with $\{H, \sigma_{\text{in}}^w, \sigma_{\text{bias}}^w, \sigma_{\text{out}}^w\} = \{400, 8.0, 8.0, 0.05\}$.

▶ 44.2 How a regression network is traditionally trained

This network is trained using a data set $D = \{\mathbf{x}^{(n)}, \mathbf{t}^{(n)}\}$ by adjusting $\mathbf{w}$ so as to minimize an error function, e.g.,

$$E_D(\mathbf{w}) = \frac{1}{2}\sum_n \sum_i \left(t_i^{(n)} - y_i(\mathbf{x}^{(n)}; \mathbf{w})\right)^2. \tag{44.3}$$

This objective function is a sum of terms, one for each input/target pair $\{\mathbf{x}, \mathbf{t}\}$, measuring how close the output $\mathbf{y}(\mathbf{x}; \mathbf{w})$ is to the target $\mathbf{t}$.

This minimization is based on repeated evaluation of the gradient of E_D. This gradient can be efficiently computed using the *backpropagation* algorithm (Rumelhart *et al.*, 1986), which uses the chain rule to find the derivatives.

Often, regularization (also known as weight decay) is included, modifying the objective function to:

$$M(\mathbf{w}) = \beta E_D + \alpha E_W \tag{44.4}$$

where, for example, $E_W = \frac{1}{2}\sum_i w_i^2$. This additional term favours small values of $\mathbf{w}$ and decreases the tendency of a model to overfit noise in the training data.

Rumelhart *et al.* (1986) showed that multilayer perceptrons can be trained, by gradient descent on $M(\mathbf{w})$, to discover solutions to non-trivial problems such as deciding whether an image is symmetric or not. These networks have been successfully applied to real-world tasks as varied as pronouncing English textreading aloud (Sejnowski and Rosenberg, 1987) and focussing multiple-mirror telescopes (Angel *et al.*, 1990).

▶ 44.3 Neural network learning as inference

The neural network learning process above can be given the following probabilistic interpretation. [Here we repeat and generalize the discussion of Chapter 41.]

The error function is interpreted as defining a noise model. βE_D is the negative log likelihood:

$$P(D \mid \mathbf{w}, \beta, \mathcal{H}) = \frac{1}{Z_D(\beta)} \exp(-\beta E_D). \tag{44.5}$$

Thus, the use of the sum-squared error E_D (44.3) corresponds to an assumption of Gaussian noise on the target variables, and the parameter β defines a noise level $\sigma_\nu^2 = 1/\beta$.

Similarly the regularizer is interpreted in terms of a log prior probability distribution over the parameters:

$$P(\mathbf{w} \mid \alpha, \mathcal{H}) = \frac{1}{Z_W(\alpha)} \exp(-\alpha E_W). \tag{44.6}$$

If E_W is quadratic as defined above, then the corresponding prior distribution is a Gaussian with variance $\sigma_W^2 = 1/\alpha$. The probabilistic model $\mathcal{H}$ specifies the architecture $\mathcal{A}$ of the network, the likelihood (44.5), and the prior (44.6).

The objective function $M(\mathbf{w})$ then corresponds to the *inference* of the parameters $\mathbf{w}$, given the data:

$$P(\mathbf{w} \mid D, \alpha, \beta, \mathcal{H}) = \frac{P(D \mid \mathbf{w}, \beta, \mathcal{H}) P(\mathbf{w} \mid \alpha, \mathcal{H})}{P(D \mid \alpha, \beta, \mathcal{H})} \tag{44.7}$$

$$= \frac{1}{Z_M} \exp(-M(\mathbf{w})). \tag{44.8}$$

The $\mathbf{w}$ found by (locally) minimizing $M(\mathbf{w})$ is then interpreted as the (locally) most probable parameter vector, $\mathbf{w}_{\mathrm{MP}}$.

The interpretation of $M(\mathbf{w})$ as a log probability adds little new at this stage. But new tools will emerge when we proceed to other inferences. First, though, let us establish the probabilistic interpretation of classification networks, to which the same tools apply.

Binary classification networks

If the targets t in a data set are binary classification labels $(0, 1)$, it is natural to use a neural network whose output $y(\mathbf{x}; \mathbf{w}, \mathcal{A})$ is bounded between 0 and 1, and is interpreted as a probability $P(t=1 \mid \mathbf{x}, \mathbf{w}, \mathcal{A})$. For example, a network with one hidden layer could be described by the feedforward equations (44.1) and (44.2), with $f^{(2)}(a) = 1/(1 + e^{-a})$. The error function βE_D is replaced by the negative log likelihood:

$$G(\mathbf{w}) = - \left[\sum_n t^{(n)} \ln y(\mathbf{x}^{(n)}; \mathbf{w}) + (1 - t^{(n)}) \ln(1 - y(\mathbf{x}^{(n)}; \mathbf{w})) \right]. \quad (44.9)$$

The total objective function is then $M = G + \alpha E_W$. Note that this includes no parameter β (because there is no Gaussian noise).

Multi-class classification networks

For a multi-class classification problem, we can represent the targets by a vector, $\mathbf{t}$, in which a single element is set to 1, indicating the correct class, and all other elements are set to 0. In this case it is appropriate to use a 'softmax' network having coupled outputs which sum to one and are interpreted as class probabilities $y_i = P(t_i = 1 \mid \mathbf{x}, \mathbf{w}, \mathcal{A})$. The last part of equation (44.2) is replaced by:

$$y_i = \frac{e^{a_i}}{\sum_{i'} e^{a_{i'}}}. \quad (44.10)$$

The negative log likelihood in this case is

$$G(\mathbf{w}) = - \sum_n \sum_i t_i^{(n)} \ln y_i(\mathbf{x}^{(n)}; \mathbf{w}). \quad (44.11)$$

As in the case of the regression network, the minimization of the objective function $M(\mathbf{w}) = G + \alpha E_W$ corresponds to an inference of the form (44.8). A variety of useful results can be built on this interpretation.

▶ 44.4 Benefits of the Bayesian approach to supervised feedforward neural networks

From the statistical perspective, supervised neural networks are nothing more than nonlinear curve-fitting devices. Curve fitting is not a trivial task however. The effective complexity of an interpolating model is of crucial importance, as illustrated in figure 44.5. Consider a control parameter that influences the complexity of a model, for example a regularization constant α (weight decay parameter). As the control parameter is varied to increase the complexity of the model (descending from figure 44.5a–c and going from left to right across figure 44.5d), the best fit to the *training* data that the model can achieve becomes increasingly good. However, the empirical performance of the model, the *test error*, first decreases then *increases again*. *An over-complex model overfits the data and generalizes poorly.* This problem may also complicate the choice of architecture in a multilayer perceptron, the radius of the basis functions in a radial basis function network, and the choice of the input variables themselves in any multidimensional regression problem. Finding values for model control parameters that are appropriate for the data is therefore an important and non-trivial problem.

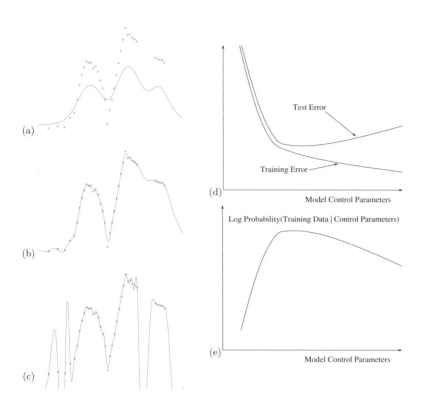

Figure 44.5. Optimization of model complexity. Panels (a–c) show a radial basis function model interpolating a simple data set with one input variable and one output variable. As the regularization constant is varied to increase the complexity of the model (from (a) to (c)), the interpolant is able to fit the training data increasingly well, but beyond a certain point the generalization ability (test error) of the model deteriorates. Probability theory allows us to optimize the control parameters without needing a test set.

The *overfitting problem* can be solved by using a Bayesian approach to control model complexity.

If we give a probabilistic interpretation to the model, then we can evaluate the evidence for alternative values of the control parameters. As was explained in Chapter 28, over-complex models turn out to be less probable, and the evidence $P(\text{Data} \mid \text{Control Parameters})$ can be used as an objective function for optimization of model control parameters (figure 44.5e). The setting of α that maximizes the evidence is displayed in figure 44.5b.

Bayesian optimization of model control parameters has four important advantages. (1) No 'test set' or 'validation set' is involved, so all available training data can be devoted to both model fitting and model comparison. (2) Regularization constants can be optimized on-line, i.e., simultaneously with the optimization of ordinary model parameters. (3) The Bayesian objective function is not noisy, in contrast to a cross-validation measure. (4) The gradient of the evidence with respect to the control parameters can be evaluated, making it possible to simultaneously optimize a large number of control parameters.

Probabilistic modelling also handles *uncertainty* in a natural manner. It offers a unique prescription, *marginalization*, for incorporating uncertainty about parameters into predictions; this procedure yields better predictions, as we saw in Chapter 41. Figure 44.6 shows error bars on the predictions of a trained neural network.

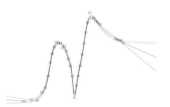

Figure 44.6. Error bars on the predictions of a trained regression network. The solid line gives the predictions of the best fit parameters of a multilayer perceptron trained on the data points. The error bars (dotted lines) are those produced by the uncertainty of the parameters $\mathbf{w}$. Notice that the error bars become larger where the data are sparse.

Implementation of Bayesian inference

As was mentioned in Chapter 41, Bayesian inference for multilayer networks may be implemented by Monte Carlo sampling, or by deterministic methods employing Gaussian approximations (Neal, 1996; MacKay, 1992c).

Within the Bayesian framework for data modelling, it is easy to improve our probabilistic models. For example, if we believe that some input variables in a problem may be irrelevant to the predicted quantity, but we don't know which, we can define a new model with multiple hyperparameters that captures the idea of uncertain input variable relevance (MacKay, 1994b; Neal, 1996; MacKay, 1995b); these models then infer automatically from the data which are the relevant input variables for a problem.

▶ 44.5 Exercises

Exercise 44.1.[4] How to measure a classifier's quality. You've just written a new classification algorithm and want to measure how well it performs on a test set, and compare it with other classifiers. What performance measure should you use? There are several standard answers. Let's assume the classifier gives an output $y(\mathbf{x})$, where $\mathbf{x}$ is the input, which we won't discuss further, and that the true target value is t. In the simplest discussions of classifiers, both y and t are binary variables, but you might care to consider cases where y and t are more general objects also.

The most widely used measure of performance on a test set is the *error rate* – the fraction of *misclassifications* made by the classifier. This measure forces the classifier to give a 0/1 output and ignores any additional information that the classifier might be able to offer – for example, an indication of the firmness of a prediction. Unfortunately, the error rate does not necessarily measure how *informative* a classifier's output is. Consider frequency tables showing the joint frequency of the 0/1 output of a classifier (horizontal axis), and the true 0/1 variable (vertical axis). The numbers that we'll show are percentages. The error rate e is the sum of the two off-diagonal numbers, which we could call the false positive rate e_+ and the false negative rate e_-.

Of the following three classifiers, A and B have the same error rate of 10% and C has a greater error rate of 12%.

Classifier A				Classifier B				Classifier C		
y	0	1		y	0	1		y	0	1
t				t				t		
0	90	0		0	80	10		0	78	12
1	10	0		1	0	10		1	0	10

But clearly classifier A, which simply guesses that the outcome is 0 for all cases, is conveying no information at all about t; whereas classifier B has an informative output: if $y = 0$ then we are sure that t really is zero; and if $y = 1$ then there is a 50% chance that $t = 1$, as compared to the prior probability $P(t = 1) = 0.1$. Classifier C is slightly less informative than B, but it is still much more useful than the information-free classifier A.

One way to improve on the error rate as a performance measure is to report the pair (e_+, e_-), the false positive error rate and the false negative error rate, which are $(0, 0.1)$ and $(0.1, 0)$ for classifiers A and B. It is especially important to distinguish between these two error probabilities in applications where the two sorts of error have different associated costs. However, there are a couple of problems with the 'error rate pair':

- First, if I simply told you that classifier A has error rates $(0, 0.1)$ and B has error rates $(0.1, 0)$, it would not be immediately evident that classifier A is actually utterly worthless. Surely we should have a performance measure that gives the worst possible score to A!

How common sense ranks the classifiers:

(best) $B > C > A$ (worst).

How error rate ranks the classifiers:

(best) $A = B > C$ (worst).

• Second, if we turn to a multiple-class classification problem such as digit recognition, then the number of types of error increases from two to $10 \times 9 = 90$ – one for each possible confusion of class t with t'. It would be nice to have some sensible way of collapsing these 90 numbers into a single rankable number that makes more sense than the error rate.

Another reason for not liking the error rate is that it doesn't give a classifier credit for accurately specifying its uncertainty. Consider classifiers that have three outputs available, '0', '1' and a *rejection* class, '?', which indicates that the classifier is not sure. Consider classifiers D and E with the following frequency tables, in percentages:

Classifier D

y	0	?	1
t			
0	74	10	6
1	0	1	9

Classifier E

y	0	?	1
t			
0	78	6	6
1	0	5	5

Both of these classifiers have $(e_+, e_-, r) = (6\%, 0\%, 11\%)$. But are they equally good classifiers? Compare classifier E with C. The two classifiers are equivalent. E is just C in disguise – we could make E by taking the output of C and tossing a coin when C says '1' in order to decide whether to give output '1' or '?'. So E is equal to C and thus inferior to B. Now compare D with B. Can you justify the suggestion that D is a more informative classifier than B, and thus is superior to E? Yet D and E have the same (e_+, e_-, r) scores.

People often plot *error-reject curves* (also known as ROC curves; ROC stands for 'receiver operating characteristic') which show the total $e = (e_+ + e_-)$ versus r as r is allowed to vary from 0 to 1, and use these curves to compare classifiers (figure 44.7). [In the special case of binary classification problems, e_+ may be plotted versus e_- instead.] But as we have seen, error rates can be undiscerning performance measures. Does plotting one error rate as a function of another make this weakness of error rates go away?

For this exercise, either construct an explicit example demonstrating that the error-reject curve, and the area under it, are not necessarily good ways to compare classifiers; or prove that they *are*.

As a suggested alternative method for comparing classifiers, consider the *mutual information* between the output and the target,

$$I(T; Y) \equiv H(T) - H(T|Y) = \sum_{y,t} P(y)P(t|y) \log \frac{P(t)}{P(t|y)}, \qquad (44.12)$$

which measures how many *bits* the classifier's output conveys about the target.

Evaluate the mutual information for classifiers A–E above.

Investigate this performance measure and discuss whether it is a useful one. Does it have practical drawbacks?

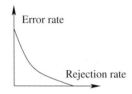

Figure 44.7. An error-reject curve. Some people use the area under this curve as a measure of classifier quality.

About Chapter 45

Feedforward neural networks such as multilayer perceptrons are popular tools for nonlinear regression and classification problems. From a Bayesian perspective, a choice of a neural network model can be viewed as defining a prior probability distribution over nonlinear functions, and the neural network's learning process can be interpreted in terms of the posterior probability distribution over the unknown function. (Some learning algorithms search for the function with maximum posterior probability and other Monte Carlo methods draw samples from this posterior probability.)

In the limit of large but otherwise standard networks, Neal (1996) has shown that the prior distribution over nonlinear functions implied by the Bayesian neural network falls in a class of probability distributions known as Gaussian processes. The hyperparameters of the neural network model determine the characteristic lengthscales of the Gaussian process. Neal's observation motivates the idea of discarding parameterized networks and working directly with Gaussian processes. Computations in which the parameters of the network are optimized are then replaced by simple matrix operations using the covariance matrix of the Gaussian process.

In this chapter I will review work on this idea by Williams and Rasmussen (1996), Neal (1997b), Barber and Williams (1997) and Gibbs and MacKay (2000), and will assess whether, for supervised regression and classification tasks, the feedforward network has been superceded.

▷ Exercise 45.1.[3] I regret that this chapter is rather dry. There's no simple explanatory examples in it, and few pictures. This exercise asks you to create interesting pictures to explain to yourself this chapter's ideas.

Source code for computer demonstrations written in the free language octave is available at:
http://www.inference.phy.cam.ac.uk/mackay/itprnn/software.html.
Radford Neal's software for Gaussian processes is available at:
http://www.cs.toronto.edu/~radford/.

Gaussian Processes

After the publication of Rumelhart, Hinton and Williams's (1986) paper on supervised learning in neural networks there was a surge of interest in the empirical modelling of relationships in high-dimensional data using nonlinear parametric models such as multilayer perceptrons and radial basis functions. In the Bayesian interpretation of these modelling methods, a nonlinear function $y(\mathbf{x})$ parameterized by parameters $\mathbf{w}$ is assumed to underlie the data $\{\mathbf{x}^{(n)}, t_n\}_{n=1}^N$, and the adaptation of the model to the data corresponds to an *inference* of the function given the data. We will denote the set of input vectors by $\mathbf{X}_N \equiv \{\mathbf{x}^{(n)}\}_{n=1}^N$ and the set of corresponding target values by the vector $\mathbf{t}_N \equiv \{t_n\}_{n=1}^N$. The inference of $y(\mathbf{x})$ is described by the posterior probability distribution

$$P(y(\mathbf{x}) \mid \mathbf{t}_N, \mathbf{X}_N) = \frac{P(\mathbf{t}_N \mid y(\mathbf{x}), \mathbf{X}_N) P(y(\mathbf{x}))}{P(\mathbf{t}_N \mid \mathbf{X}_N)}. \tag{45.1}$$

Of the two terms on the right-hand side, the first, $P(\mathbf{t}_N \mid y(\mathbf{x}), \mathbf{X}_N)$, is the probability of the target values given the function $y(\mathbf{x})$, which in the case of regression problems is often assumed to be a separable Gaussian distribution; and the second term, $P(y(\mathbf{x}))$, is the prior distribution on functions assumed by the model. This prior is implicit in the choice of parametric model and the choice of regularizers used during the model fitting. The prior typically specifies that the function $y(\mathbf{x})$ is expected to be continuous and smooth, and has less high frequency power than low frequency power, but the precise meaning of the prior is somewhat obscured by the use of the parametric model.

Now, for the prediction of future values of t, all that matters is the assumed prior $P(y(\mathbf{x}))$ and the assumed noise model $P(\mathbf{t}_N \mid y(\mathbf{x}), \mathbf{X}_N)$ – the parameterization of the function $y(\mathbf{x}; \mathbf{w})$ is irrelevant.

The idea of Gaussian process modelling is to place a prior $P(y(\mathbf{x}))$ directly on the space of functions, without parameterizing $y(\mathbf{x})$. The simplest type of prior over functions is called a Gaussian process. It can be thought of as the generalization of a Gaussian distribution over a finite vector space to a function space of infinite dimension. Just as a Gaussian distribution is fully specified by its mean and covariance matrix, a Gaussian process is specified by a mean and a *covariance function*. Here, the mean is a function of $\mathbf{x}$ (which we will often take to be the zero function), and the covariance is a function $C(\mathbf{x}, \mathbf{x}')$ that expresses the expected covariance between the values of the function y at the points $\mathbf{x}$ and $\mathbf{x}'$. The function $y(\mathbf{x})$ in any one data modelling problem is assumed to be a *single* sample from this Gaussian distribution. Gaussian processes are already well established models for various spatial and temporal problems – for example, Brownian motion, Langevin processes and Wiener processes are all examples of Gaussian processes; Kalman filters, widely used to model speech waveforms, also correspond to Gaussian process models; the method of 'kriging' in geostatistics is a Gaussian process regression method.

Reservations about Gaussian processes

It might be thought that it is not possible to reproduce the interesting properties of neural network interpolation methods with something so simple as a Gaussian distribution, but as we shall now see, many popular nonlinear interpolation methods are equivalent to particular Gaussian processes. (I use the term 'interpolation' to cover both the problem of 'regression' – fitting a curve through noisy data – and the task of fitting an interpolant that passes exactly through the given data points.)

It might also be thought that the computational complexity of inference when we work with priors over infinite-dimensional function spaces might be infinitely large. But by concentrating on the joint probability distribution of the observed data and the quantities we wish to predict, it is possible to make predictions with resources that scale as polynomial functions of N, the number of data points.

▶ 45.1 Standard methods for nonlinear regression

The problem

We are given N data points $\mathbf{X}_N, \mathbf{t}_N = \{\mathbf{x}^{(n)}, t_n\}_{n=1}^N$. The inputs $\mathbf{x}$ are vectors of some fixed input dimension I. The targets t are either real numbers, in which case the task will be a regression or interpolation task, or they are categorical variables, for example $t \in \{0, 1\}$, in which case the task is a classification task. We will concentrate on the case of regression for the time being.

Assuming that a function $y(\mathbf{x})$ underlies the observed data, the task is to infer the function from the given data, and predict the function's value – or the value of the observation t_{N+1} – at a new point $\mathbf{x}^{(N+1)}$.

Parametric approaches to the problem

In a parametric approach to regression we express the unknown function $y(\mathbf{x})$ in terms of a nonlinear function $y(\mathbf{x}; \mathbf{w})$ parameterized by parameters $\mathbf{w}$.

Example 45.2. Fixed basis functions. Using a set of basis functions $\{\phi_h(\mathbf{x})\}_{h=1}^H$, we can write

$$y(\mathbf{x}; \mathbf{w}) = \sum_{h=1}^H w_h \phi_h(\mathbf{x}). \qquad (45.2)$$

If the basis functions are nonlinear functions of $\mathbf{x}$ such as radial basis functions centred at fixed points $\{\mathbf{c}_h\}_{h=1}^H$,

$$\phi_h(\mathbf{x}) = \exp\left[-\frac{(\mathbf{x} - \mathbf{c}_h)^2}{2r^2}\right], \qquad (45.3)$$

then $y(\mathbf{x}; \mathbf{w})$ is a nonlinear function of $\mathbf{x}$; however, since the dependence of y on the parameters $\mathbf{w}$ is linear, we might sometimes refer to this as a 'linear' model. In neural network terms, this model is like a multilayer network whose connections from the input layer to the nonlinear hidden layer are fixed; only the output weights $\mathbf{w}$ are adaptive.

Other possible sets of fixed basis functions include polynomials such as $\phi_h(\mathbf{x}) = x_i^p x_j^q$ where p and q are integer powers that depend on h.

Example 45.3. Adaptive basis functions. Alternatively, we might make a function $y(\mathbf{x})$ from basis functions that depend on additional parameters included in the vector $\mathbf{w}$. In a two-layer feedforward neural network with nonlinear hidden units and a linear output, the function can be written

$$y(\mathbf{x}; \mathbf{w}) = \sum_{h=1}^{H} w_h^{(2)} \tanh \left(\sum_{i=1}^{I} w_{hi}^{(1)} x_i + w_{h0}^{(1)} \right) + w_0^{(2)} \qquad (45.4)$$

where I is the dimensionality of the input space and the weight vector $\mathbf{w}$ consists of the input weights $\{w_{hi}^{(1)}\}$, the hidden unit biases $\{w_{h0}^{(1)}\}$, the output weights $\{w_h^{(2)}\}$ and the output bias $w_0^{(2)}$. In this model, the dependence of y on $\mathbf{w}$ is nonlinear.

Having chosen the parameterization, we then infer the function $y(\mathbf{x}; \mathbf{w})$ by inferring the parameters $\mathbf{w}$. The posterior probability of the parameters is

$$P(\mathbf{w} \,|\, \mathbf{t}_N, \mathbf{X}_N) = \frac{P(\mathbf{t}_N \,|\, \mathbf{w}, \mathbf{X}_N) P(\mathbf{w})}{P(\mathbf{t}_N \,|\, \mathbf{X}_N)}. \qquad (45.5)$$

The factor $P(\mathbf{t}_N \,|\, \mathbf{w}, \mathbf{X}_N)$ states the probability of the observed data points when the parameters $\mathbf{w}$ (and hence, the function y) are known. This probability distribution is often taken to be a separable Gaussian, each data point t_n differing from the underlying value $y(\mathbf{x}^{(n)}; \mathbf{w})$ by additive noise. The factor $P(\mathbf{w})$ specifies the prior probability distribution of the parameters. This too is often taken to be a separable Gaussian distribution. If the dependence of y on $\mathbf{w}$ is nonlinear the posterior distribution $P(\mathbf{w} \,|\, \mathbf{t}_N, \mathbf{X}_N)$ is in general not a Gaussian distribution.

The inference can be implemented in various ways. In the Laplace method, we minimize an objective function

$$M(\mathbf{w}) = -\ln \left[P(\mathbf{t}_N \,|\, \mathbf{w}, \mathbf{X}_N) P(\mathbf{w}) \right] \qquad (45.6)$$

with respect to $\mathbf{w}$, locating the locally most probable parameters, then use the curvature of M, $\partial^2 M(\mathbf{w})/\partial w_i \partial w_j$, to define error bars on $\mathbf{w}$. Alternatively we can use more general Markov chain Monte Carlo techniques to create samples from the posterior distribution $P(\mathbf{w} \,|\, \mathbf{t}_N, \mathbf{X}_N)$.

Having obtained one of these representations of the inference of $\mathbf{w}$ given the data, predictions are then made by marginalizing over the parameters:

$$P(t_{N+1} \,|\, \mathbf{t}_N, \mathbf{X}_{N+1}) = \int d^H \mathbf{w} \, P(t_{N+1} \,|\, \mathbf{w}, \mathbf{x}^{(N+1)}) P(\mathbf{w} \,|\, \mathbf{t}_N, \mathbf{X}_N). \qquad (45.7)$$

If we have a Gaussian representation of the posterior distribution $P(\mathbf{w} \,|\, \mathbf{t}_N, \mathbf{X}_N)$, then this integral can typically be evaluated directly. In the alternative Monte Carlo approach, which generates R samples $\mathbf{w}^{(r)}$ that are intended to be samples from the posterior distribution $P(\mathbf{w} \,|\, \mathbf{t}_N, \mathbf{X}_N)$, we approximate the predictive distribution by

$$P(t_{N+1} \,|\, \mathbf{t}_N, \mathbf{X}_{N+1}) \simeq \frac{1}{R} \sum_{r=1}^{R} P(t_{N+1} \,|\, \mathbf{w}^{(r)}, \mathbf{x}^{(N+1)}). \qquad (45.8)$$

Nonparametric approaches.

In nonparametric methods, predictions are obtained without explicitly parameterizing the unknown function $y(\mathbf{x})$; $y(\mathbf{x})$ lives in the infinite-dimensional space of all continuous functions of $\mathbf{x}$. One well known nonparametric approach to the regression problem is the spline smoothing method (Kimeldorf and Wahba, 1970). A spline solution to a one-dimensional regression problem can be described as follows: we define the estimator of $y(\mathbf{x})$ to be the function $\hat{y}(\mathbf{x})$ that minimizes the functional

$$ M(y(x)) = \frac{1}{2}\beta\sum_{n=1}^{N}(y(x^{(n)}) - t_n)^2 + \frac{1}{2}\alpha\int \mathrm{d}x\,[y^{(p)}(x)]^2, \tag{45.9} $$

where $y^{(p)}$ is the pth derivative of y and p is a positive number. If p is set to 2 then the resulting function $\hat{y}(\mathbf{x})$ is a cubic spline, that is, a piecewise cubic function that has 'knots' – discontinuities in its second derivative – at the data points $\{x^{(n)}\}$.

This estimation method can be interpreted as a Bayesian method by identifying the prior for the function $y(x)$ as:

$$ \ln P(y(x)|\alpha) = -\frac{1}{2}\alpha\int \mathrm{d}x\,[y^{(p)}(x)]^2 + \mathrm{const}, \tag{45.10} $$

and the probability of the data measurements $\mathbf{t}_N = \{t_n\}_{n=1}^{N}$ assuming independent Gaussian noise as:

$$ \ln P(\mathbf{t}_N \mid y(x), \beta) = -\frac{1}{2}\beta\sum_{n=1}^{N}(y(x^{(n)}) - t_n)^2 + \mathrm{const}. \tag{45.11} $$

[The constants in equations (45.10) and (45.11) are functions of α and β respectively. Strictly the prior (45.10) is improper since addition of an arbitrary polynomial of degree $(p-1)$ to $y(x)$ is not constrained. This impropriety is easily rectified by the addition of $(p-1)$ appropriate terms to (45.10).] Given this interpretation of the functions in equation (45.9), $M(y(x))$ is equal to minus the log of the posterior probability $P(y(x)|\mathbf{t}_N, \alpha, \beta)$, within an additive constant, and the splines estimation procedure can be interpreted as yielding a Bayesian MAP estimate. The Bayesian perspective allows us additionally to put error bars on the splines estimate and to draw typical samples from the posterior distribution, and it gives an automatic method for inferring the hyperparameters α and β.

Comments

Splines priors are Gaussian processes

The prior distribution defined in equation (45.10) is our first example of a Gaussian process. Throwing mathematical precision to the winds, a Gaussian process can be defined as a probability distribution on a space of functions $y(x)$ that can be written in the form

$$ P(y(x)\,|\,\mu(x), A) = \frac{1}{Z}\exp\left[-\frac{1}{2}(y(x) - \mu(x))^{\mathsf{T}}A(y(x) - \mu(x))\right], \tag{45.12} $$

where $\mu(x)$ is the mean function and A is a linear operator, and where the inner product of two functions $y(x)^{\mathsf{T}}z(x)$ is defined by, for example, $\int \mathrm{d}x\, y(x)z(x)$.

Here, if we denote by D the linear operator that maps $y(x)$ to the derivative of $y(x)$, we can write equation (45.10) as

$$\ln P(y(x) \,|\, \alpha) = -\frac{1}{2}\alpha \int \mathrm{d}x \, [D^p y(x)]^2 + \text{const} = -\frac{1}{2}\, y(x)^\mathsf{T} A y(x) + \text{const},$$

$$(45.13)$$

which has the same form as equation (45.12) with $\mu(x) = 0$, and $A \equiv [D^p]^\mathsf{T} D^p$.

In order for the prior in equation (45.12) to be a proper prior, A must be a positive definite operator, i.e., one satisfying $y(x)^\mathsf{T} A y(x) > 0$ for all functions $y(x)$ other than $y(x) = 0$.

Splines can be written as parametric models

Splines may be written in terms of an infinite set of fixed basis functions, as in equation (45.2), as follows. First rescale the x axis so that the interval $(0, 2\pi)$ is much wider than the range of x values of interest. Let the basis functions be a Fourier set $\{\cos hx, \sin hx,\ h = 0, 1, 2, \ldots\}$, so the function is

$$y(x) = \sum_{h=0}^{\infty} w_{h(\cos)} \cos(hx) + \sum_{h=1}^{\infty} w_{h(\sin)} \sin(hx). \qquad (45.14)$$

Use the regularizer

$$E_W(\mathbf{w}) = \sum_{h=0}^{\infty} \frac{1}{2} h^{\frac{p}{2}} w^2_{h(\cos)} + \sum_{h=1}^{\infty} \frac{1}{2} h^{\frac{p}{2}} w^2_{h(\sin)} \qquad (45.15)$$

to define a Gaussian prior on $\mathbf{w}$,

$$P(\mathbf{w} \,|\, \alpha) = \frac{1}{Z_W(\alpha)} \exp(-\alpha E_W). \qquad (45.16)$$

If $p=2$ then we have the cubic splines regularizer $E_W(\mathbf{w}) = \int y^{(2)}(x)^2 \, \mathrm{d}x$, as in equation (45.9); if $p=1$ we have the regularizer $E_W(\mathbf{w}) = \int y^{(1)}(x)^2 \, \mathrm{d}x$, etc. (To make the prior proper we must add an extra regularizer on the term $w_{0(\cos)}$.) Thus in terms of the prior $P(y(x))$ there is no fundamental difference between the 'nonparametric' splines approach and other parametric approaches.

Representation is irrelevant for prediction

From the point of view of prediction at least, there are two objects of interest. The first is the conditional distribution $P(t_{N+1} \,|\, \mathbf{t}_N, \mathbf{X}_{N+1})$ defined in equation (45.7). The other object of interest, should we wish to compare one model with others, is the joint probability of all the observed data given the model, the evidence $P(\mathbf{t}_N \,|\, \mathbf{X}_N)$, which appeared as the normalizing constant in equation (45.5). Neither of these quantities makes any reference to the representation of the unknown function $y(x)$. So at the end of the day, our choice of representation is irrelevant.

The question we now address is, in the case of popular parametric models, what form do these two quantities take? We will see that for standard models with fixed basis functions and Gaussian distributions on the unknown parameters, the joint probability of all the observed data given the model, $P(\mathbf{t}_N \,|\, \mathbf{X}_N)$, is a multivariate Gaussian distribution with mean zero and with a covariance matrix determined by the basis functions; this implies that the conditional distribution $P(t_{N+1} \,|\, \mathbf{t}_N, \mathbf{X}_{N+1})$ is also a Gaussian distribution, whose mean depends linearly on the values of the targets $\mathbf{t}_N$. Standard parametric models are simple examples of Gaussian processes.

▶ 45.2 From parametric models to Gaussian processes

Linear models

Let us consider a regression problem using H fixed basis functions, for example one-dimensional radial basis functions as defined in equation (45.3).

Let us assume that a list of N input points $\{\mathbf{x}^{(n)}\}$ has been specified and define the $N \times H$ matrix $\mathbf{R}$ to be the matrix of values of the basis functions $\{\phi_h(\mathbf{x})\}_{h=1}^{H}$ at the points $\{\mathbf{x}_n\}$,

$$R_{nh} \equiv \phi_h(\mathbf{x}^{(n)}). \tag{45.17}$$

We define the vector $\mathbf{y}_N$ to be the vector of values of $y(\mathbf{x})$ at the N points,

$$y_n \equiv \sum_h R_{nh} w_h. \tag{45.18}$$

If the prior distribution of $\mathbf{w}$ is Gaussian with zero mean,

$$P(\mathbf{w}) = \text{Normal}(\mathbf{w}; \mathbf{0}, \sigma_w^2 \mathbf{I}), \tag{45.19}$$

then $\mathbf{y}$, being a linear function of $\mathbf{w}$, is also Gaussian distributed, with mean zero. The covariance matrix of $\mathbf{y}$ is

$$\begin{aligned}
\mathbf{Q} &= \langle \mathbf{y}\mathbf{y}^\mathsf{T} \rangle = \langle \mathbf{R}\mathbf{w}\mathbf{w}^\mathsf{T}\mathbf{R}^\mathsf{T} \rangle = \mathbf{R} \langle \mathbf{w}\mathbf{w}^\mathsf{T} \rangle \mathbf{R}^\mathsf{T} \tag{45.20} \\
&= \sigma_w^2 \mathbf{R}\mathbf{R}^\mathsf{T}. \tag{45.21}
\end{aligned}$$

So the prior distribution of $\mathbf{y}$ is:

$$P(\mathbf{y}) = \text{Normal}(\mathbf{y}; \mathbf{0}, \mathbf{Q}) = \text{Normal}(\mathbf{y}; \mathbf{0}, \sigma_w^2 \mathbf{R}\mathbf{R}^\mathsf{T}). \tag{45.22}$$

This result, that the vector of N function values $\mathbf{y}$ has a Gaussian distribution, is true for any selected points $\mathbf{X}_N$. This is the defining property of a Gaussian process. *The probability distribution of a function $y(\mathbf{x})$ is a Gaussian process if for any finite selection of points $\mathbf{x}^{(1)}, \mathbf{x}^{(2)}, \ldots, \mathbf{x}^{(N)}$, the density $P(y(\mathbf{x}^{(1)}), y(\mathbf{x}^{(2)}), \ldots, y(\mathbf{x}^{(N)}))$ is a Gaussian.*

Now, if the number of basis functions H is smaller than the number of data points N, then the matrix $\mathbf{Q}$ will not have full rank. In this case the probability distribution of $\mathbf{y}$ might be thought of as a flat elliptical pancake confined to an H-dimensional subspace in the N-dimensional space in which $\mathbf{y}$ lives.

What about the target values? If each target t_n is assumed to differ by additive Gaussian noise of variance σ_ν^2 from the corresponding function value y_n then $\mathbf{t}$ also has a Gaussian prior distribution,

$$P(\mathbf{t}) = \text{Normal}(\mathbf{t}; \mathbf{0}, \mathbf{Q} + \sigma_\nu^2 \mathbf{I}). \tag{45.23}$$

We will denote the covariance matrix of $\mathbf{t}$ by $\mathbf{C}$:

$$\mathbf{C} = \mathbf{Q} + \sigma_\nu^2 \mathbf{I} = \sigma_w^2 \mathbf{R}\mathbf{R}^\mathsf{T} + \sigma_\nu^2 \mathbf{I}. \tag{45.24}$$

Whether or not $\mathbf{Q}$ has full rank, the covariance matrix $\mathbf{C}$ has full rank since $\sigma_\nu^2 \mathbf{I}$ is full rank.

What does the covariance matrix $\mathbf{Q}$ look like? In general, the (n, n') entry of $\mathbf{Q}$ is

$$Q_{nn'} = [\sigma_w^2 \mathbf{R}\mathbf{R}^\mathsf{T}]_{nn'} = \sigma_w^2 \sum_h \phi_h(\mathbf{x}^{(n)}) \phi_h(\mathbf{x}^{(n')}) \tag{45.25}$$

and the (n, n') entry of $\mathbf{C}$ is

$$C_{nn'} = \sigma_w^2 \sum_h \phi_h(\mathbf{x}^{(n)})\phi_h(\mathbf{x}^{(n')}) + \delta_{nn'}\sigma_\nu^2, \qquad (45.26)$$

where $\delta_{nn'} = 1$ if $n = n'$ and 0 otherwise.

Example 45.4. Let's take as an example a one-dimensional case, with radial basis functions. The expression for $Q_{nn'}$ becomes simplest if we assume we have uniformly spaced basis functions with the basis function labelled h being centred on the point $x = h$ and take the limit $H \to \infty$, so that the sum over h becomes an integral; to avoid having a covariance that diverges with H, we had better make σ_w^2 scale as $S/(\Delta H)$, where ΔH is the number of basis functions per unit length of the x-axis, and S is a constant; then

$$Q_{nn'} = S \int_{h_{\min}}^{h_{\max}} dh\, \phi_h(x^{(n)})\phi_h(x^{(n')}) \qquad (45.27)$$

$$= S \int_{h_{\min}}^{h_{\max}} dh\, \exp\left[-\frac{(x^{(n)} - h)^2}{2r^2}\right] \exp\left[-\frac{(x^{(n')} - h)^2}{2r^2}\right]. \quad (45.28)$$

If we let the limits of integration be $\pm\infty$, we can solve this integral:

$$Q_{nn'} = \sqrt{\pi r^2}\, S \exp\left[-\frac{(x^{(n')} - x^{(n)})^2}{4r^2}\right]. \qquad (45.29)$$

We are arriving at a new perspective on the interpolation problem. Instead of specifying the prior distribution on functions in terms of basis functions and priors on parameters, the prior can be summarized simply by a covariance function,

$$C(x^{(n)}, x^{(n')}) \equiv \theta_1 \exp\left[-\frac{(x^{(n')} - x^{(n)})^2}{4r^2}\right], \qquad (45.30)$$

where we have given a new name, θ_1, to the constant out front.

Generalizing from this particular case, a vista of interpolation methods opens up. Given any valid covariance function $C(\mathbf{x}, \mathbf{x}')$ – we'll discuss in a moment what 'valid' means – we can define the covariance matrix for N function values at locations $\mathbf{X}_N$ to be the matrix $\mathbf{Q}$ given by

$$Q_{nn'} = C(\mathbf{x}^{(n)}, \mathbf{x}^{(n')}) \qquad (45.31)$$

and the covariance matrix for N corresponding target values, assuming Gaussian noise, to be the matrix $\mathbf{C}$ given by

$$C_{nn'} = C(\mathbf{x}^{(n)}, \mathbf{x}^{(n')}) + \sigma_\nu^2 \delta_{nn'}. \qquad (45.32)$$

In conclusion, the prior probability of the N target values $\mathbf{t}$ in the data set is:

$$P(\mathbf{t}) = \text{Normal}(\mathbf{t}; \mathbf{0}, \mathbf{C}) = \frac{1}{Z} e^{-\frac{1}{2}\mathbf{t}^{\mathsf{T}}\mathbf{C}^{-1}\mathbf{t}}. \qquad (45.33)$$

Samples from this Gaussian process and a few other simple Gaussian processes are displayed in figure 45.1.

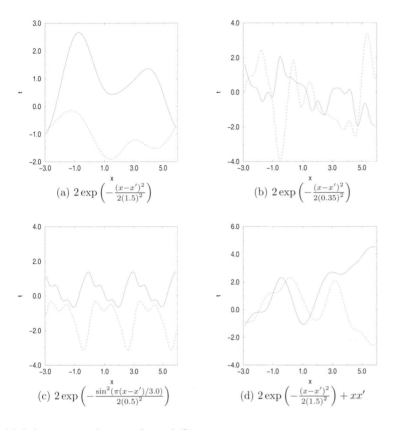

(a) $2\exp\left(-\frac{(x-x')^2}{2(1.5)^2}\right)$

(b) $2\exp\left(-\frac{(x-x')^2}{2(0.35)^2}\right)$

(c) $2\exp\left(-\frac{\sin^2(\pi(x-x')/3.0)}{2(0.5)^2}\right)$

(d) $2\exp\left(-\frac{(x-x')^2}{2(1.5)^2}\right)+xx'$

Figure 45.1. Samples drawn from Gaussian process priors. Each panel shows two functions drawn from a Gaussian process prior. The four corresponding covariance functions are given below each plot. The decrease in length scale from (a) to (b) produces more rapidly fluctuating functions. The periodic properties of the covariance function in (c) can be seen. The covariance function in (d) contains the non-stationary term xx' corresponding to the covariance of a straight line, so that typical functions include linear trends. From Gibbs (1997).

Multilayer neural networks and Gaussian processes

Figures 44.2 and 44.3 show some random samples from the prior distribution over functions defined by a selection of standard multilayer perceptrons with large numbers of hidden units. Those samples don't seem a million miles away from the Gaussian process samples of figure 45.1. And indeed Neal (1996) showed that the properties of a neural network with one hidden layer (as in equation (45.4)) converge to those of a Gaussian process as the number of hidden neurons tends to infinity, if standard 'weight decay' priors are assumed. The covariance function of this Gaussian process depends on the details of the priors assumed for the weights in the network and the activation functions of the hidden units.

▶ **45.3 Using a given Gaussian process model in regression**

We have spent some time talking about priors. We now return to our data and the problem of prediction. How do we make predictions with a Gaussian process?

Having formed the covariance matrix $\mathbf{C}$ defined in equation (45.32) our task is to infer t_{N+1} given the observed vector $\mathbf{t}_N$. The joint density $P(t_{N+1}, \mathbf{t}_N)$ is a Gaussian; so the conditional distribution

$$P(t_{N+1}\,|\,\mathbf{t}_N) = \frac{P(t_{N+1}, \mathbf{t}_N)}{P(\mathbf{t}_N)} \tag{45.34}$$

is also a Gaussian. We now distinguish between different sizes of covariance matrix $\mathbf{C}$ with a subscript, such that $\mathbf{C}_{N+1}$ is the $(N+1) \times (N+1)$ covariance matrix for the vector $\mathbf{t}_{N+1} \equiv (t_1, \ldots, t_{N+1})^{\mathsf{T}}$. We define submatrices of $\mathbf{C}_{N+1}$ as follows:

$$
\mathbf{C}_{N+1} \equiv
\begin{bmatrix}
\begin{bmatrix} \mathbf{C}_N \end{bmatrix} & \begin{bmatrix} \mathbf{k} \end{bmatrix} \\
\begin{bmatrix} \mathbf{k}^{\mathsf{T}} \end{bmatrix} & \begin{bmatrix} \kappa \end{bmatrix}
\end{bmatrix} .
\tag{45.35}
$$

The posterior distribution (45.34) is given by

$$
P(t_{N+1} \mid \mathbf{t}_N) \propto \exp\left[-\frac{1}{2} \begin{bmatrix} \mathbf{t}_N & t_{N+1} \end{bmatrix} \mathbf{C}_{N+1}^{-1} \begin{bmatrix} \mathbf{t}_N \\ t_{N+1} \end{bmatrix} \right] .
\tag{45.36}
$$

We can evaluate the mean and standard deviation of the posterior distribution of t_{N+1} by brute force inversion of $\mathbf{C}_{N+1}$. There is a more elegant expression for the predictive distribution, however, which is useful whenever predictions are to be made at a number of new points on the basis of the data set of size N. We can write $\mathbf{C}_{N+1}^{-1}$ in terms of $\mathbf{C}_N$ and $\mathbf{C}_N^{-1}$ using the partitioned inverse equations (Barnett, 1979)

$$
\mathbf{C}_{N+1}^{-1} = \begin{bmatrix} \mathbf{M} & \mathbf{m} \\ \mathbf{m}^{\mathsf{T}} & m \end{bmatrix}
\tag{45.37}
$$

where

$$
\begin{aligned}
m &= \left(\kappa - \mathbf{k}^T \mathbf{C}_N^{-1} \mathbf{k} \right)^{-1} & (45.38) \\
\mathbf{m} &= -m \, \mathbf{C}_N^{-1} \mathbf{k} & (45.39) \\
\mathbf{M} &= \mathbf{C}_N^{-1} + \frac{1}{m} \mathbf{m} \mathbf{m}^T . & (45.40)
\end{aligned}
$$

When we substitute this matrix into equation (45.36) we find

$$
P(t_{N+1} \mid \mathbf{t}_N) = \frac{1}{Z} \exp\left[-\frac{(t_{N+1} - \hat{t}_{N+1})^2}{2\sigma_{\hat{t}_{N+1}}^2} \right]
\tag{45.41}
$$

where

$$
\begin{aligned}
\hat{t}_{N+1} &= \mathbf{k}^T \mathbf{C}_N^{-1} \mathbf{t}_N & (45.42) \\
\sigma_{\hat{t}_{N+1}}^2 &= \kappa - \mathbf{k}^T \mathbf{C}_N^{-1} \mathbf{k} . & (45.43)
\end{aligned}
$$

The predictive mean at the new point is given by $\hat{t}_{N+1}$ and $\sigma_{\hat{t}_{N+1}}$ defines the error bars on this prediction. Notice that we do not need to invert $\mathbf{C}_{N+1}$ in order to make predictions at $\mathbf{x}^{(N+1)}$. Only $\mathbf{C}_N$ needs to be inverted. Thus Gaussian processes allow one to implement a model with a number of basis functions H much larger than the number of data points N, with the computational requirement being of order N^3, independent of H. [We'll discuss ways of reducing this cost later.]

The predictions produced by a Gaussian process depend entirely on the covariance matrix $\mathbf{C}$. We now discuss the sorts of covariance functions one might choose to define $\mathbf{C}$, and how we can automate the selection of the covariance function in response to data.

▶ 45.4 Examples of covariance functions

The only constraint on our choice of covariance function is that it must generate a non-negative-definite covariance matrix for any set of points $\{\mathbf{x}_n\}_{n=1}^N$.

We will denote the parameters of a covariance function by $\boldsymbol{\theta}$. The covariance matrix of $\mathbf{t}$ has entries given by

$$C_{mn} = C(\mathbf{x}^{(m)}, \mathbf{x}^{(n)}; \boldsymbol{\theta}) + \delta_{mn}\mathcal{N}(\mathbf{x}^{(n)}; \boldsymbol{\theta}) \qquad (45.44)$$

where C is the covariance function and $\mathcal{N}$ is a noise model which might be stationary or spatially varying, for example,

$$\mathcal{N}(\mathbf{x}; \boldsymbol{\theta}) = \begin{cases} \theta_3 & \text{for input-independent noise} \\ \exp\left(\sum_{j=1}^{J} \beta_j \phi_j(\mathbf{x})\right) & \text{for input-dependent noise.} \end{cases} \qquad (45.45)$$

The continuity properties of C determine the continuity properties of typical samples from the Gaussian process prior. An encyclopaedic paper on Gaussian processes giving many valid covariance functions has been written by Abrahamsen (1997).

Stationary covariance functions

A *stationary* covariance function is one that is translation invariant in that it satisfies

$$C(\mathbf{x}, \mathbf{x}'; \boldsymbol{\theta}) = D(\mathbf{x} - \mathbf{x}'; \boldsymbol{\theta}) \qquad (45.46)$$

for some function D, i.e., the covariance is a function of separation only, also known as the autocovariance function. If additionally C depends only on the *magnitude* of the distance between $\mathbf{x}$ and $\mathbf{x}'$ then the covariance function is said to be *homogenous*. Stationary covariance functions may also be described in terms of the Fourier transform of the function D, which is known as the power spectrum of the Gaussian process. This Fourier transform is necessarily a positive function of frequency. One way of constructing a valid stationary covariance function is to invent a positive function of frequency and define D to be its inverse Fourier transform.

Example 45.5. Let the power spectrum be a Gaussian function of frequency. Since the Fourier transform of a Gaussian is a Gaussian, the autocovariance function corresponding to this power spectrum is a Gaussian function of separation. This argument rederives the covariance function we derived at equation (45.30).

Generalizing slightly, a popular form for C with hyperparameters $\boldsymbol{\theta} = (\theta_1, \theta_2, \{r_i\})$ is

$$C(\mathbf{x}, \mathbf{x}'; \boldsymbol{\theta}) = \theta_1 \exp\left[-\frac{1}{2}\sum_{i=1}^{I}\frac{(x_i - x_i')^2}{r_i^2}\right] + \theta_2. \qquad (45.47)$$

$\mathbf{x}$ is an I-dimensional vector and r_i is a length scale associated with input x_i, the lengthscale in that direction on which y is expected to vary significantly. A very large length scale means that y is expected to be essentially a constant function of that input. Such an input could be said to be irrelevant, as in the automatic relevance determination method for neural networks (MacKay, 1994a; Neal, 1996). The θ_1 hyperparameter defines the vertical scale of variations of a typical function. The θ_2 hyperparameter allows the whole function to be offset away from zero by some unknown constant – to understand this term, examine equation (45.25) and consider the basis function $\phi(\mathbf{x}) = 1$.

Another stationary covariance function is

$$C(x, x') = \exp(-|x - x'|^\nu) \quad 0 < \nu \leq 2. \qquad (45.48)$$

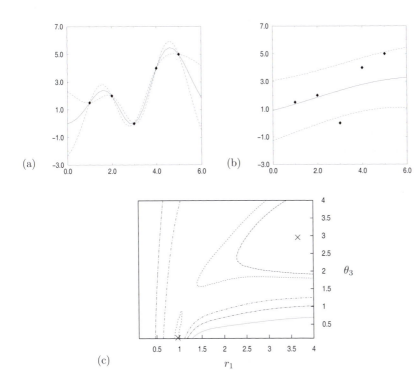

Figure 45.2. Multimodal likelihood functions for Gaussian processes. A data set of five points is modelled with the simple covariance function (45.47), with one hyperparameter θ_3 controlling the noise variance. Panels a and b show the most probable interpolant and its 1σ error bars when the hyperparameters $\boldsymbol{\theta}$ are set to two different values that (locally) maximize the likelihood $P(\mathbf{t}_N \mid \mathbf{X}_N, \boldsymbol{\theta})$: (a) $r_1 = 0.95$, $\theta_3 = 0.0$; (b) $r_1 = 3.5$, $\theta_3 = 3.0$. Panel c shows a contour plot of the likelihood as a function of r_1 and θ_3, with the two maxima shown by crosses. From Gibbs (1997).

For $\nu = 2$, this is a special case of the previous covariance function. For $\nu \in (1, 2)$, the typical functions from this prior are smooth but not analytic functions. For $\nu \leq 1$ typical functions are continuous but not smooth.

A covariance function that models a function that is periodic with known period λ_i in the ith input direction is

$$C(\mathbf{x}, \mathbf{x}'; \boldsymbol{\theta}) = \theta_1 \exp\left[-\frac{1}{2} \sum_i \left(\frac{\sin\left(\frac{\pi}{\lambda_i}(x_i - x_i') \right)}{r_i} \right)^2 \right]. \tag{45.49}$$

Figure 45.1 shows some random samples drawn from Gaussian processes with a variety of different covariance functions.

Nonstationary covariance functions

The simplest nonstationary covariance function is the one corresponding to a linear trend. Consider the plane $y(\mathbf{x}) = \sum_i w_i x_i + c$. If the $\{w_i\}$ and c have Gaussian distributions with zero mean and variances σ_w^2 and σ_c^2 respectively then the plane has a covariance function

$$C_{\text{lin}}(\mathbf{x}, \mathbf{x}'; \{\sigma_w, \sigma_c\}) = \sum_{i=1}^{I} \sigma_w^2 x_i x_i' + \sigma_c^2. \tag{45.50}$$

An example of random sample functions incorporating the linear term can be seen in figure 45.1d.

▶ ## 45.5 Adaptation of Gaussian process models

Let us assume that a form of covariance function has been chosen, but that it depends on undetermined hyperparameters $\boldsymbol{\theta}$. We would like to 'learn' these hyperparameters from the data. This learning process is equivalent to the inference of the hyperparameters of a neural network, for example, weight decay hyperparameters. It is a complexity control problem, one that is solved nicely by the Bayesian Occam's razor.

Ideally we would like to define a prior distribution on the hyperparameters and integrate over them in order to make our predictions, i.e., we would like to find

$$P(t_{N+1} \,|\, \mathbf{x}_{N+1}, \mathcal{D}) = \int P(t_{N+1} \,|\, \mathbf{x}_{N+1}, \boldsymbol{\theta}, \mathcal{D}) P(\boldsymbol{\theta} \,|\, \mathcal{D}) \, \mathrm{d}\boldsymbol{\theta}. \qquad (45.51)$$

But this integral is usually intractable. There are two approaches we can take.

1. We can approximate the integral by using the most probable values of hyperparameters.

$$P(t_{N+1} \,|\, \mathbf{x}_{N+1}, \mathcal{D}) \simeq P(t_{N+1} \,|\, \mathbf{x}_{N+1}, \mathcal{D}, \boldsymbol{\theta}_{\mathrm{MP}}) \qquad (45.52)$$

2. Or we can perform the integration over $\boldsymbol{\theta}$ numerically using Monte Carlo methods (Williams and Rasmussen, 1996; Neal, 1997b).

Either of these approaches is implemented most efficiently if the gradient of the posterior probability of $\boldsymbol{\theta}$ can be evaluated.

Gradient

The posterior probability of $\boldsymbol{\theta}$ is

$$P(\boldsymbol{\theta} \,|\, \mathcal{D}) \propto P(\mathbf{t}_N \,|\, \mathbf{X}_N, \boldsymbol{\theta}) P(\boldsymbol{\theta}). \qquad (45.53)$$

The log of the first term (the evidence for the hyperparameters) is

$$\ln P(\mathbf{t}_N \,|\, \mathbf{X}_N, \boldsymbol{\theta}) = -\frac{1}{2} \ln \det \mathbf{C}_N - \frac{1}{2} \mathbf{t}_N^T \mathbf{C}_N^{-1} \mathbf{t}_N - \frac{N}{2} \ln 2\pi, \qquad (45.54)$$

and its derivative with respect to a hyperparameter θ is

$$\frac{\partial}{\partial \theta} \ln P(\mathbf{t}_N \,|\, \mathbf{X}_N, \boldsymbol{\theta}) = -\frac{1}{2} \mathrm{Trace} \left(\mathbf{C}_N^{-1} \frac{\partial \mathbf{C}_N}{\partial \theta} \right) + \frac{1}{2} \mathbf{t}_N^T \mathbf{C}_N^{-1} \frac{\partial \mathbf{C}_N}{\partial \theta} \mathbf{C}_N^{-1} \mathbf{t}_N.$$
$$(45.55)$$

Comments

Assuming that finding the derivatives of the priors is straightforward, we can now search for $\boldsymbol{\theta}_{\mathrm{MP}}$. However there are two problems that we need to be aware of. Firstly, as illustrated in figure 45.2, the evidence may be multimodal. Suitable priors and sensible optimization strategies often eliminate poor optima. Secondly and perhaps most importantly the evaluation of the gradient of the log likelihood requires the evaluation of $\mathbf{C}_N^{-1}$. Any exact inversion method (such as Cholesky decomposition, LU decomposition or Gauss–Jordan elimination) has an associated computational cost that is of order N^3 and so calculating gradients becomes time consuming for large training data sets. Approximate methods for implementing the predictions (equations (45.42) and (45.43)) and gradient computation (equation (45.55)) are an active research area. One approach based on the ideas of Skilling (1993) makes approximations to $\mathbf{C}^{-1}\mathbf{t}$ and Trace $\mathbf{C}^{-1}$ using iterative methods with cost $\mathcal{O}(N^2)$ (Gibbs and MacKay, 1996; Gibbs, 1997). Further references on this topic are given at the end of the chapter.

▶ 45.6 Classification

Gaussian processes can be integrated into classification modelling once we
identify a variable that can sensibly be given a Gaussian process prior.

In a binary classification problem, we can define a quantity $a_n \equiv a(\mathbf{x}^{(n)})$
such that the probability that the class is 1 rather than 0 is

$$P(t_n = 1 \,|\, a_n) = \frac{1}{1 + e^{-a_n}}. \qquad (45.56)$$

Large positive values of a correspond to probabilities close to one; large negative values of a define probabilities that are close to zero. In a classification problem, we typically intend that the probability $P(t_n = 1)$ should be a
smoothly varying function of $\mathbf{x}$. We can embody this prior belief by defining
$a(\mathbf{x})$ to have a Gaussian process prior.

Implementation

It is not so easy to perform inferences and adapt the Gaussian process model
to data in a classification model as in regression problems because the likelihood function (45.56) is not a Gaussian function of a_n. So the posterior
distribution of $\mathbf{a}$ given some observations $\mathbf{t}$ is not Gaussian and the normal-
ization constant $P(\mathbf{t}_N \,|\, \mathbf{X}_N)$ cannot be written down analytically. Barber and
Williams (1997) have implemented classifiers based on Gaussian process priors
using Laplace approximations (Chapter 27). Neal (1997b) has implemented a
Monte Carlo approach to implementing a Gaussian process classifier. Gibbs
and MacKay (2000) have implemented another cheap and cheerful approach
based on the methods of Jaakkola and Jordan (section 33.8). In this *variational Gaussian process classifier*, we obtain tractable upper and lower bounds
for the unnormalized posterior density over $\mathbf{a}$, $P(\mathbf{t}_N \,|\, \mathbf{a})P(\mathbf{a})$. These bounds
are parameterized by variational parameters which are adjusted in order to
obtain the tightest possible fit. Using normalized versions of the optimized
bounds we then compute approximations to the predictive distributions.

Multi-class classification problems can also be solved with Monte Carlo
methods (Neal, 1997b) and variational methods (Gibbs, 1997).

▶ 45.7 Discussion

Gaussian processes are moderately simple to implement and use. Because very
few parameters of the model need to be determined by hand (generally only
the priors on the hyperparameters), Gaussian processes are useful tools for
automated tasks where fine tuning for each problem is not possible. We do
not appear to sacrifice any performance for this simplicity.

It is easy to construct Gaussian processes that have particular desired
properties; for example we can make a straightforward automatic relevance
determination model.

One obvious problem with Gaussian processes is the computational cost
associated with inverting an $N \times N$ matrix. The cost of direct methods of
inversion becomes prohibitive when the number of data points N is greater
than about 1000.

Have we thrown the baby out with the bath water?

According to the hype of 1987, neural networks were meant to be intelligent
models that discovered features and patterns in data. Gaussian processes in

contrast are simply smoothing devices. How can Gaussian processes possibly replace neural networks? Were neural networks over-hyped, or have we underestimated the power of smoothing methods?

I think both these propositions are true. The success of Gaussian processes shows that many real-world data modelling problems are perfectly well solved by sensible smoothing methods. The most interesting problems, the task of feature discovery for example, are not ones that Gaussian processes will solve. But maybe multilayer perceptrons can't solve them either. Perhaps a fresh start is needed, approaching the problem of machine learning from a paradigm different from the supervised feedforward mapping.

Further reading

The study of Gaussian processes for regression is far from new. Time series analysis was being performed by the astronomer T.N. Thiele using Gaussian processes in 1880 (Lauritzen, 1981). In the 1940s, Wiener–Kolmogorov prediction theory was introduced for prediction of trajectories of military targets (Wiener, 1948). Within the geostatistics field, Matheron (1963) proposed a framework for regression using optimal linear estimators which he called 'kriging' after D.G. Krige, a South African mining engineer. This framework is identical to the Gaussian process approach to regression. Kriging has been developed considerably in the last thirty years (see Cressie (1993) for a review) including several Bayesian treatments (Omre, 1987; Kitanidis, 1986). However the geostatistics approach to the Gaussian process model has concentrated mainly on low-dimensional problems and has largely ignored any probabilistic interpretation of the model. Kalman filters are widely used to implement inferences for stationary one-dimensional Gaussian processes, and are popular models for speech and music modelling (Bar-Shalom and Fortmann, 1988). Generalized radial basis functions (Poggio and Girosi, 1989), ARMA models (Wahba, 1990) and variable metric kernel methods (Lowe, 1995) are all closely related to Gaussian processes. See also O'Hagan (1978).

The idea of replacing supervised neural networks by Gaussian processes was first explored by Williams and Rasmussen (1996) and Neal (1997b). A thorough comparison of Gaussian processes with other methods such as neural networks and MARS was made by Rasmussen (1996). Methods for reducing the complexity of data modelling with Gaussian processes remain an active research area (Poggio and Girosi, 1990; Luo and Wahba, 1997; Tresp, 2000; Williams and Seeger, 2001; Smola and Bartlett, 2001; Rasmussen, 2002; Seeger et al., 2003; Opper and Winther, 2000).

A longer review of Gaussian processes is in (MacKay, 1998b). A review paper on regression with complexity control using hierarchical Bayesian models is (MacKay, 1992a).

Gaussian processes and *support vector learning machines* (Scholkopf et al., 1995; Vapnik, 1995) have a lot in common. Both are kernel-based predictors, the kernel being another name for the covariance function. A Bayesian version of support vectors, exploiting this connection, can be found in (Chu et al., 2001; Chu et al., 2002; Chu et al., 2003b; Chu et al., 2003a).

46

Deconvolution

▶ **46.1 Traditional image reconstruction methods**

Optimal linear filters

In many imaging problems, the data measurements $\{d_n\}$ are linearly related to the underlying image $\mathbf{f}$:

$$d_n = \sum_k R_{nk} f_k + n_n. \qquad (46.1)$$

The vector $\mathbf{n}$ denotes the inevitable noise that corrupts real data. In the case of a camera which produces a blurred picture, the vector $\mathbf{f}$ denotes the true image, $\mathbf{d}$ denotes the blurred and noisy picture, and the linear operator $\mathbf{R}$ is a convolution defined by the point spread function of the camera. In this special case, the true image and the data vector reside in the same space; but it is important to maintain a distinction between them. We will use the subscript $n = 1, \ldots, N$ to run over data measurements, and the subscripts $k, k' = 1, \ldots, K$ to run over image pixels.

   One might speculate that since the blur was created by a linear operation, then perhaps it might be deblurred by another linear operation. We can derive the *optimal linear filter* in two ways.

Bayesian derivation

We assume that the linear operator $\mathbf{R}$ is known, and that the noise $\mathbf{n}$ is Gaussian and independent, with a known standard deviation σ_ν.

$$P(\mathbf{d} \,|\, \mathbf{f}, \sigma_\nu, \mathcal{H}) = \frac{1}{(2\pi\sigma_\nu^2)^{N/2}} \exp\left(-\sum_n \left(d_n - \textstyle\sum_k R_{nk} f_k \right)^2 \Big/ (2\sigma_\nu^2) \right). \qquad (46.2)$$

We assume that the prior probability of the image is also Gaussian, with a scale parameter σ_f.

$$P(\mathbf{f} \,|\, \sigma_f, \mathcal{H}) = \frac{\det^{-\frac{1}{2}} \mathbf{C}}{(2\pi\sigma_f^2)^{K/2}} \exp\left(-\sum_{k,k'} f_k C_{kk'} f_{k'}' \Big/ (2\sigma_f^2) \right). \qquad (46.3)$$

If we assume no correlations among the pixels then the symmetric, full rank matrix $\mathbf{C}$ is equal to the identity matrix $\mathbf{I}$. The more sophisticated 'intrinsic correlation function' model uses $\mathbf{C} = [\mathbf{GG}^\mathsf{T}]^{-1}$, where $\mathbf{G}$ is a convolution that takes us from an imaginary 'hidden' image, which is uncorrelated, to the real correlated image. The intrinsic correlation function should not be confused with the point spread function $\mathbf{R}$ which defines the image-to-data mapping.

A zero-mean Gaussian prior is clearly a poor assumption if it is known that all elements of the image $\mathbf{f}$ are positive, but let us proceed. We can now write down the posterior probability of an image $\mathbf{f}$ given the data $\mathbf{d}$.

$$P(\mathbf{f} \,|\, \mathbf{d}, \sigma_\nu, \sigma_f, \mathcal{H}) = \frac{P(\mathbf{d} \,|\, \mathbf{f}, \sigma_\nu, \mathcal{H}) P(\mathbf{f} \,|\, \sigma_f, \mathcal{H}))}{P(\mathbf{d} \,|\, \sigma_\nu, \sigma_f, \mathcal{H})}. \tag{46.4}$$

In words,

$$\text{Posterior} = \frac{\text{Likelihood} \times \text{Prior}}{\text{Evidence}}. \tag{46.5}$$

The 'evidence' $P(\mathbf{d} \,|\, \sigma_\nu, \sigma_f, \mathcal{H})$ is the normalizing constant for this posterior distribution. Here it is unimportant, but it is used in a more sophisticated analysis to compare, for example, different values of σ_ν and σ_f, or different point spread functions $\mathbf{R}$.

Since the posterior distribution is the product of two Gaussian functions of $\mathbf{f}$, it is also a Gaussian, and can therefore be summarized by its mean, which is also the *most probable image*, $\mathbf{f}_{\text{MP}}$, and its covariance matrix:

$$\boldsymbol{\Sigma}_{\mathbf{f}|\mathbf{d}} \equiv [-\nabla\nabla \log P(\mathbf{f} \,|\, \mathbf{d}, \sigma_\nu, \sigma_f, \mathcal{H})]^{-1}, \tag{46.6}$$

which defines the joint error bars on $\mathbf{f}$. In this equation, the symbol ∇ denotes differentiation with respect to the image parameters $\mathbf{f}$. We can find $\mathbf{f}_{\text{MP}}$ by differentiating the log of the posterior, and solving for the derivative being zero. We obtain:

$$\mathbf{f}_{\text{MP}} = \left[\mathbf{R}^\mathsf{T}\mathbf{R} + \frac{\sigma_\nu^2}{\sigma_f^2} \mathbf{C} \right]^{-1} \mathbf{R}^\mathsf{T}\mathbf{d}. \tag{46.7}$$

The operator $\left[\mathbf{R}^\mathsf{T}\mathbf{R} + \frac{\sigma_\nu^2}{\sigma_f^2} \mathbf{C} \right]^{-1} \mathbf{R}^\mathsf{T}$ is called the optimal linear filter. When the term $\frac{\sigma_\nu^2}{\sigma_f^2} \mathbf{C}$ can be neglected, the optimal linear filter is the pseudoinverse $[\mathbf{R}^\mathsf{T}\mathbf{R}]^{-1} \mathbf{R}^\mathsf{T}$. The term $\frac{\sigma_\nu^2}{\sigma_f^2} \mathbf{C}$ regularizes this ill-conditioned inverse.

The optimal linear filter can also be manipulated into the form:

$$\text{Optimal linear filter} = \mathbf{C}^{-1}\mathbf{R}^\mathsf{T} \left[\mathbf{R}\mathbf{C}^{-1}\mathbf{R}^\mathsf{T} + \frac{\sigma_\nu^2}{\sigma_f^2} \mathbf{I} \right]^{-1}. \tag{46.8}$$

Minimum square error derivation

The non-Bayesian derivation of the optimal linear filter starts by assuming that we will 'estimate' the true image $\mathbf{f}$ by a linear function of the data:

$$\hat{\mathbf{f}} = \mathbf{W}\mathbf{d}. \tag{46.9}$$

The linear operator $\mathbf{W}$ is then 'optimized' by minimizing the expected sum-squared error between $\hat{\mathbf{f}}$ and the unknown true image . In the following equations, summations over repeated indices k, k', n are implicit. The expectation $\langle \cdot \rangle$ is over both the statistics of the random variables $\{n_n\}$, and the ensemble of images $\mathbf{f}$ which we expect to bump into. We assume that the noise is zero mean and uncorrelated to second order with itself and everything else, with $\langle n_n n_{n'} \rangle = \sigma_\nu^2 \delta_{nn'}$.

$$\langle E \rangle = \frac{1}{2} \left\langle (W_{kn} d_n - f_k)^2 \right\rangle \tag{46.10}$$

$$= \frac{1}{2} \left\langle (W_{kn} R_{nj} f_j - f_k)^2 \right\rangle + \frac{1}{2} W_{kn} W_{kn} \sigma_\nu^2. \tag{46.11}$$

Differentiating with respect to $\mathbf{W}$, and introducing $\mathbf{F} \equiv \langle f_{j'} f_j \rangle$ (c.f. $\sigma_f^2 \mathbf{C}^{-1}$ in the Bayesian derivation above), we find that the optimal linear filter is:

$$\mathbf{W}_{\mathrm{opt}} = \mathbf{F}\mathbf{R}^{\mathsf{T}} \left[\mathbf{R}\mathbf{F}\mathbf{R}^{\mathsf{T}} + \sigma_\nu^2 \mathbf{I} \right]^{-1}. \qquad (46.12)$$

If we identify $\mathbf{F} = \sigma_f^2 \mathbf{C}^{-1}$, we obtain the optimal linear filter (46.8) of the Bayesian derivation. The ad hoc assumptions made in this derivation were the choice of a quadratic error measure, and the decision to use a linear estimator. It is interesting that without explicit assumptions of Gaussian distributions, this derivation has reproduced the same estimator as the Bayesian posterior mode, $\mathbf{f}_{\mathrm{MP}}$.

The advantage of a Bayesian approach is that we can criticize these assumptions and modify them in order to make better reconstructions.

Other image models

The better matched our model of images $P(\mathbf{f} \mid \mathcal{H})$ is to the real world, the better our image reconstructions will be, and the less data we will need to answer any given question. The Gaussian models which lead to the optimal linear filter are spectacularly poorly matched to the real world. For example, the Gaussian prior (46.3) fails to specify that all pixel intensities in an image are positive. This omission leads to the most pronounced artefacts where the image under observation has high contrast or large black patches. Optimal linear filters applied to astronomical data give reconstructions with negative areas in them, corresponding to patches of sky that suck energy out of telescopes! The *maximum entropy* model for image deconvolution (Gull and Daniell, 1978) was a great success principally because this model forced the reconstructed image to be positive. The spurious negative areas and complementary spurious positive areas are eliminated, and the quality of the reconstruction is greatly enhanced.

The 'classic maximum entropy' model assigns an entropic prior

$$P(\mathbf{f} \mid \alpha, \mathbf{m}, \mathcal{H}_{\mathrm{Classic}}) = \exp(\alpha S(\mathbf{f}, \mathbf{m}))/Z, \qquad (46.13)$$

where

$$S(\mathbf{f}, \mathbf{m}) = \sum_i (f_i \ln(m_i/f_i) + f_i - m_i) \qquad (46.14)$$

(Skilling, 1989). This model enforces positivity; the parameter α defines a characteristic dynamic range by which the pixel values are expected to differ from the default image $\mathbf{m}$.

The 'intrinsic-correlation-function maximum-entropy' model (Gull, 1989) introduces an expectation of spatial correlations into the prior on $\mathbf{f}$ by writing $\mathbf{f} = \mathbf{G}\mathbf{h}$, where $\mathbf{G}$ is a convolution with an intrinsic correlation function, and putting a classic maxent prior on the underlying hidden image $\mathbf{h}$.

Probabilistic movies

Having found not only the most probable image $\mathbf{f}_{\mathrm{MP}}$ but also error bars on it, $\mathbf{\Sigma}_{\mathbf{f}|\mathbf{d}}$, one task is to visualize those error bars. Whether or not we use Monte Carlo methods to infer $\mathbf{f}$, a correlated random walk around the posterior distribution can be used to visualize the uncertainties and correlations. For a Gaussian posterior distribution, we can create a correlated sequence of unit normal random vectors $\mathbf{n}$ using

$$\mathbf{n}^{(t+1)} = c\mathbf{n}^{(t)} + s\mathbf{z}, \qquad (46.15)$$

where $\mathbf{z}$ is a unit normal random vector and $c^2 + s^2 = 1$ (c controls how persistent the memory of the sequence is). We then render the image sequence defined by

$$\mathbf{f}^{(t)} = \mathbf{f}_{\mathrm{MP}} + \boldsymbol{\Sigma}_{\mathbf{f}|\mathbf{d}}^{1/2} \mathbf{n}^{(t)} \tag{46.16}$$

where $\boldsymbol{\Sigma}_{\mathbf{f}|\mathbf{d}}^{1/2}$ is the Cholesky decomposition of $\boldsymbol{\Sigma}_{\mathbf{f}|\mathbf{d}}$.

▶ 46.2 Supervised neural networks for image deconvolution

Neural network researchers often exploit the following strategy. Given a problem currently solved with a standard algorithm: interpret the computations performed by the algorithm as a parameterized mapping from an input to an output, and call this mapping a neural network; then adapt the parameters to data so as to produce another mapping that solves the task better. By construction, the neural network can reproduce the standard algorithm, so this data-driven adaptation can only make the performance better.

There are several reasons why standard algorithms can be bettered in this way.

1. Algorithms are often not designed to optimize the real objective function. For example, in speech recognition, a hidden Markov model is designed to model the speech signal, and is fitted so as to to maximize the generative probability given the known string of words in the training data; but the real objective is to *discriminate* between different words. If an inadequate model is being used, the neural-net-style training of the model will focus the limited resources of the model on the aspects relevant to the discrimination task. Discriminative training of hidden Markov models for speech recognition does improve their performance.

2. The neural network can be more flexible than the standard model; some of the adaptive parameters might have been viewed as fixed features by the original designers. A flexible network can find properties in the data that were not included in the original model.

▶ 46.3 Deconvolution in humans

A huge fraction of our brain is devoted to vision. One of the neglected features of our visual system is that the raw image falling on the retina is severely blurred: while most people can see with a resolution of about *1 arcminute* (one sixtieth of a degree) under any daylight conditions, bright or dim, *the image on our retina is blurred through a point spread function of width as large as 5 arcminutes* (Wald and Griffin, 1947; Howarth and Bradley, 1986). It is amazing that we are able to resolve pixels that are twenty-five times smaller in area than the blob produced on our retina by any point source.

Isaac Newton was aware of this conundrum. It's hard to make a lens that does not have chromatic aberration, and our cornea and lens, like a lens made of ordinary glass, refract blue light more strongly than red. Typically our eyes focus correctly for the middle of the visible spectrum (green), so if we look at a single white dot made of red, green, and blue light, the image on our retina consists of a sharply focussed green dot surrounded by a broader red blob superposed on an even broader blue blob. The width of the red and blue blobs is proportional to the diameter of the pupil, which is largest under dim lighting conditions. [The blobs are roughly concentric, though most people have a slight bias, such that in one eye the red blob is centred a tiny distance to the left and the blue is centred a tiny distance to the right, and in the other eye it's the other way round. This slight bias explains why when we look at blue and red writing on a dark background most people perceive the blue writing to be at a slightly greater depth than the red. In a minority of people, this small bias is the other way round and the red/blue depth perception is reversed. But this effect (which many people are aware of, having noticed it in cinemas, for example) is *tiny* compared with the chromatic aberration we are discussing.]

You can vividly demonstrate to yourself how enormous the chromatic aberration in your eye is with the help of a sheet of card and a colour computer screen.

For the most impressive results – I guarantee you will be amazed – use a dim room with no light apart from the computer screen; a pretty strong effect will still be seen even if the room has daylight coming into it, as long as it is not bright sunshine. Cut a slit about 1.5 mm wide in the card. On the screen, display a few small coloured objects on a black background. I especially recommend thin vertical objects coloured pure red, pure blue, magenta (i.e., red plus blue), and white (red plus blue plus green). Include a little black-and-white text on the screen too. Stand or sit sufficiently far away that you can only just read the text – perhaps a distance of four metres or so, if you have normal vision. Now, hold the slit vertically in front of one of your eyes, and close the other eye. Hold the slit near to your eye – brushing your eyelashes – and look through it. Waggle the slit slowly to the left and to the right, so that the slit is alternately in front of the left and right sides of your pupil. What do you see? I see the red objects waggling to and fro, and the blue objects waggling to and fro, through *huge* distances and in opposite directions, while white objects appear to stay still and are negligibly distorted. Thin magenta objects can be seen splitting into their constituent red and blue parts. Measure how large the motion of the red and blue objects is – it's more than 5 minutes of arc for me, in a dim room. Then check how sharply you can see under these conditions – look at the text on the screen, for example: is it not the case that you can see (through your whole pupil) features far smaller than the distance through which the red and blue components were waggling? Yet when you are using the whole pupil, what is falling on your retina must be an image blurred with a blurring diameter equal to the waggling amplitude.

One of the main functions of early visual processing must be to deconvolve this chromatic aberration. Neuroscientists sometimes conjecture that the reason why retinal ganglion cells and cells in the lateral geniculate nucleus (the main brain area to which retinal ganglion cells project) have centre-surround receptive fields with colour opponency (long wavelength in the centre and medium wavelength in the surround, for example) is in order to perform 'feature extraction' or 'edge detection', but I think this view is mistaken. The reason we have centre-surround filters at the first stage of visual processing (in the fovea at least) is for the huge task of deconvolution of chromatic aberration.

I speculate that the *McCollough effect*, an extremely long-lasting association of colours with orientation (McCollough, 1965; MacKay and MacKay, 1974), is produced by the adaptation mechanism that tunes our chromatic-aberration-deconvolution circuits. Our deconvolution circuits must be rapidly tuneable, because the point spread function of our eye changes with our pupil diameter, which can change within seconds; and indeed the McCollough effect can be induced within 30 seconds. At the same time, the effect is long-lasting when an eye is covered, because it's in our interests that our deconvolution circuits should stay well-tuned while we sleep, so that we can see sharply the instant we wake up.

I also wonder whether the main reason that we evolved colour vision was not 'in order to see fruit better' but *'so as to be able to see black and white sharper'* – deconvolving chromatic aberration is easier, even in an entirely black and white world, if one has access to chromatic information in the image.

And a final speculation: why do our eyes make micro-saccades when we look at things? These miniature eye-movements are of an angular size bigger than the spacing between the cones in the fovea (which are spaced at roughly 1 minute of arc, the perceived resolution of the eye). The typical size of a microsaccade is 5–10 minutes of arc (Ratliff and Riggs, 1950). Is it a coincidence that this is the same as the size of chromatic aberration? Surely micro-saccades must play an essential role in the deconvolution mechanism that delivers our high-resolution vision.

▶ 46.4 Exercises

Exercise 46.1.[3] Blur an image with a circular (top hat) point spread function and add noise. Then deconvolve the blurry noisy image using the optimal linear filter. Find error bars and visualize them by making a probabilistic movie.

Part VI

Sparse Graph Codes

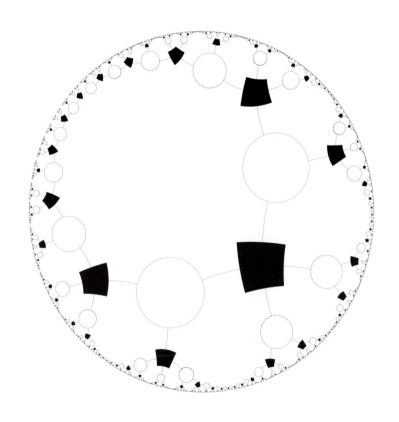

About Part VI

The central problem of communication theory is to construct an encoding and a decoding system that make it possible to communicate reliably over a noisy channel. During the 1990s, remarkable progress was made towards the Shannon limit, using codes that are defined in terms of sparse random graphs, and which are decoded by a simple probability-based message-passing algorithm.

In a *sparse graph code*, the nodes in the graph represent the transmitted bits and the constraints they satisfy. For a linear code with a codeword length N and rate $R = K/N$, the number of constraints is of order $M = N - K$. Any linear code can be described by a graph, but what makes a sparse graph code special is that each constraint only involves a small number of variables in the graph: so the number of edges in the graph scales roughly linearly with N, rather than quadratically.

In the following four chapters we will look at four families of sparse graph codes: three families that are excellent for error-correction: *low-density parity-check codes*, *turbo codes*, and *repeat–accumulate codes*; and the family of *digital fountain codes*, which are outstanding for erasure-correction.

All these codes can be decoded by a local message-passing algorithm on the graph, the sum–product algorithm, and, while this algorithm is not a perfect maximum likelihood decoder, the empirical results are record-breaking.

47

Low-Density Parity-Check Codes

A low-density parity-check code (or Gallager code) is a block code that has a parity-check matrix, $\mathbf{H}$, every row and column of which is 'sparse'.

A *regular* Gallager code is a low-density parity-check code in which every column of $\mathbf{H}$ has the same weight j and every row has the same weight k; regular Gallager codes are constructed at random subject to these constraints. A low-density parity-check code with $j = 3$ and $k = 4$ is illustrated in figure 47.1.

Figure 47.1. A low-density parity-check matrix and the corresponding graph of a rate-$^1/_4$ low-density parity-check code with blocklength $N = 16$, and $M = 12$ constraints. Each white circle represents a transmitted bit. Each bit participates in $j = 3$ constraints, represented by ⊞ squares. Each constraint forces the sum of the $k = 4$ bits to which it is connected to be even.

▶ ## 47.1 Theoretical properties

Low-density parity-check codes lend themselves to theoretical study. The following results are proved in Gallager (1963) and MacKay (1999b).

Low-density parity-check codes, in spite of their simple construction, are good codes, *given an optimal decoder* (good codes in the sense of section 11.4). Furthermore, they have good distance (in the sense of section 13.2). These two results hold for any column weight $j \geq 3$. Furthermore, there are sequences of low-density parity-check codes in which j increases gradually with N, in such a way that the ratio j/N still goes to zero, that are *very good* and that have very good distance.

However, we don't have an optimal decoder, and decoding low-density parity-check codes is an NP-complete problem. So what can we do in practice?

▶ ## 47.2 Practical decoding

Given a channel output $\mathbf{r}$, we wish to find the codeword $\mathbf{t}$ whose likelihood $P(\mathbf{r}\,|\,\mathbf{t})$ is biggest. All the effective decoding strategies for low-density parity-check codes are message-passing algorithms. The best algorithm known is the sum–product algorithm, also known as iterative probabilistic decoding or belief propagation.

We'll assume that the channel is a memoryless channel (though more complex channels can easily be handled by running the sum–product algorithm on a more complex graph that represents the expected correlations among the errors (Worthen and Stark, 1998)). For any memoryless channel, there are two approaches to the decoding problem both of which lead to the generic problem 'find the $\mathbf{x}$ that maximizes

$$P^*(\mathbf{x}) = P(\mathbf{x})\,\mathbb{1}[\mathbf{H}\mathbf{x} = \mathbf{z}]',\qquad(47.1)$$

where $P(\mathbf{x})$ is a separable distribution on a binary vector $\mathbf{x}$, and $\mathbf{z}$ is another binary vector. Each of these two approaches represents the decoding problem in terms of a factor graph (Chapter 26).

(a) The prior distribution over codewords

$$P(\mathbf{t}) \propto \mathbb{1}[\mathbf{Ht} = \mathbf{0}].$$

The variable nodes are the transmitted bits $\{t_n\}$.
Each $\boxplus$ node represents the factor $\mathbb{1}[\sum_{n \in \mathcal{N}(m)} t_n = 0 \bmod 2]$.

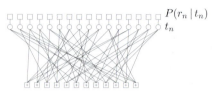

(b) The posterior distribution over codewords,

$$P(\mathbf{t} \,|\, \mathbf{r}) \propto P(\mathbf{t})P(\mathbf{r} \,|\, \mathbf{t}).$$

Each upper function node represents a likelihood factor $P(r_n \,|\, t_n)$.

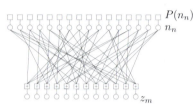

(c) The joint probability of the noise $\mathbf{n}$ and syndrome $\mathbf{z}$,

$$P(\mathbf{n}, \mathbf{z}) = P(\mathbf{n}) \, \mathbb{1}[\mathbf{z} = \mathbf{Hn}].$$

The top variable nodes are now the noise bits $\{n_n\}$.
The added variable nodes at the base are the syndrome values $\{z_m\}$.
Each definition $z_m = \sum_n H_{mn} n_n \bmod 2$ is enforced by a $\boxplus$ factor.

Figure 47.2. Factor graphs associated with a low-density parity-check code.

The codeword decoding viewpoint

First, we note that the prior distribution over codewords,

$$P(\mathbf{t}) \propto \mathbb{1}[\mathbf{Ht} = \mathbf{0} \bmod 2], \tag{47.2}$$

can be represented by a factor graph (figure 47.2a), with the factorization being

$$P(\mathbf{t}) \propto \prod_m \mathbb{1}[\sum_{n \in \mathcal{N}(m)} t_n = 0 \bmod 2]. \tag{47.3}$$

(We'll omit the 'mod 2's from now on.) The posterior distribution over codewords is given by multiplying this prior by the likelihood, which introduces another N factors, one for each received bit.

$$
\begin{aligned}
P(\mathbf{t} \,|\, \mathbf{r}) &\propto P(\mathbf{t})P(\mathbf{r} \,|\, \mathbf{t}) \\
&\propto \prod_m \mathbb{1}[\sum_{n \in \mathcal{N}(m)} t_n = 0] \prod_n P(r_n \,|\, t_n)
\end{aligned}
\tag{47.4}
$$

The factor graph corresponding to this function is shown in figure 47.2b. It is the same as the graph for the prior, except for the addition of likelihood 'dongles' to the transmitted bits.

In this viewpoint, the received signal r_n can live in any alphabet; all that matters are the values of $P(r_n \,|\, t_n)$.

The syndrome decoding viewpoint

Alternatively, we can view the channel output in terms of a binary received vector $\mathbf{r}$ and a noise vector $\mathbf{n}$, with a probability distribution $P(\mathbf{n})$ that can be derived from the channel properties and whatever additional information is available at the channel outputs.

For example, with a binary symmetric channel, we define the noise by $\mathbf{r} = \mathbf{t} + \mathbf{n}$, the syndrome $\mathbf{z} = \mathbf{Hr}$, and noise model $P(n_n) = f$. For other channels such as the Gaussian channel with output $\mathbf{y}$, we may define a received binary vector **r** however we wish and obtain an effective binary noise model $P(\mathbf{n})$ from **y** (exercises 9.18 (p.155) and 25.1 (p.325)).

The joint probability of the noise **n** and syndrome $\mathbf{z} = \mathbf{Hn}$ can be factored as

$$
\begin{aligned}
P(\mathbf{n}, \mathbf{z}) &= P(\mathbf{n})\,\mathbb{1}[\mathbf{z} = \mathbf{Hn}] \\
&= \prod_n P(n_n) \prod_m \mathbb{1}\Big[z_m = \sum_{n \in \mathcal{N}(m)} n_n\Big].
\end{aligned}
\tag{47.5}
$$

The factor graph of this function is shown in figure 47.2c. The variables **n** and **z** can also be drawn in a 'belief network' (also known as a 'Bayesian network', 'causal network', or 'influence diagram') similar to figure 47.2a, but with arrows on the edges from the upper circular nodes (which represent the variables **n**) to the lower square nodes (which now represent the variables **z**). We can say that every bit x_n is the parent of j checks z_m, and each check z_m is the child of k bits.

Both decoding viewpoints involve essentially the same graph. Either version of the decoding problem can be expressed as the generic decoding problem 'find the **x** that maximizes

$$
P^*(\mathbf{x}) = P(\mathbf{x})\,\mathbb{1}[\mathbf{Hx} = \mathbf{z}]';
\tag{47.6}
$$

in the codeword decoding viewpoint, **x** is the codeword **t**, and $\mathbf{z} = 0$; in the syndrome decoding viewpoint, **x** is the noise **n**, and **z** is the syndrome.

It doesn't matter which viewpoint we take when we apply the sum–product algorithm. The two decoding algorithms are isomorphic and will give equivalent outcomes (unless numerical errors intervene).

> I tend to use the syndrome decoding viewpoint because it has one advantage: one does not need to implement an *encoder* for a code in order to be able to simulate a decoding problem realistically.

We'll now talk in terms of the generic decoding problem.

▶ 47.3 Decoding with the sum–product algorithm

We aim, given the observed checks, to compute the marginal posterior probabilities $P(x_n = 1 \mid \mathbf{z}, \mathbf{H})$ for each n. It is hard to compute these exactly because the graph contains many cycles. However, it is interesting to implement the decoding algorithm that would be appropriate if there were no cycles, on the assumption that the errors introduced might be relatively small. This approach of ignoring cycles has been used in the artificial intelligence literature but is now frowned upon because it produces inaccurate probabilities. However, if we are decoding a good error-correcting code, we don't care about accurate marginal probabilities – we just want the correct codeword. Also, the posterior probability, in the case of a good code communicating at an achievable rate, is expected typically to be hugely concentrated on the most probable decoding; so we are dealing with a distinctive probability distribution to which experience gained in other fields may not apply.

The sum–product algorithm was presented in Chapter 26. We now write out explicitly how it works for solving the decoding problem

$$
\mathbf{Hx} = \mathbf{z} \pmod{2}.
$$

For brevity, we reabsorb the dongles hanging off the x and z nodes in figure 47.2c and modify the sum–product algorithm accordingly. The graph in which $\mathbf{x}$ and $\mathbf{z}$ live is then the original graph (figure 47.2a) whose edges are defined by the 1s in $\mathbf{H}$. The graph contains nodes of two types, which we'll call checks and bits. The graph connecting the checks and bits is a bipartite graph: bits connect only to checks, and *vice versa*. On each iteration, a probability ratio is propagated along each edge in the graph, and each bit node x_n updates its probability that it should be in state 1.

We denote the set of bits n that participate in check m by $\mathcal{N}(m) \equiv \{n : H_{mn} = 1\}$. Similarly we define the set of checks in which bit n participates, $\mathcal{M}(n) \equiv \{m : H_{mn} = 1\}$. We denote a set $\mathcal{N}(m)$ with bit n excluded by $\mathcal{N}(m)\backslash n$. The algorithm has two alternating parts, in which quantities q_{mn} and r_{mn} associated with each edge in the graph are iteratively updated. The quantity q_{mn}^x is meant to be the probability that bit n of $\mathbf{x}$ has the value x, given the information obtained via checks other than check m. The quantity r_{mn}^x is meant to be the probability of check m being satisfied if bit n of $\mathbf{x}$ is considered fixed at x and the other bits have a separable distribution given by the probabilities $\{q_{mn'} : n' \in \mathcal{N}(m)\backslash n\}$. The algorithm would produce the exact posterior probabilities of all the bits after a fixed number of iterations if the bipartite graph defined by the matrix $\mathbf{H}$ contained no cycles.

Initialization. Let $p_n^0 = P(x_n = 0)$ (the prior probability that bit x_n is 0), and let $p_n^1 = P(x_n = 1) = 1 - p_n^0$. If we are taking the syndrome decoding viewpoint and the channel is a binary symmetric channel then p_n^1 will equal f. If the noise level varies in a known way (for example if the channel is a binary input Gaussian channel with a real output) then p_n^1 is initialized to the appropriate normalized likelihood. For every (n, m) such that $H_{mn} = 1$ the variables q_{mn}^0 and q_{mn}^1 are initialized to the values p_n^0 and p_n^1 respectively.

Horizontal step. In the *horizontal* step of the algorithm (horizontal from the point of view of the matrix $\mathbf{H}$), we run through the checks m and compute for each $n \in \mathcal{N}(m)$ two probabilities: first, r_{mn}^0, the probability of the observed value of z_m arising when $x_n = 0$, given that the other bits $\{x_{n'} : n' \neq n\}$ have a separable distribution given by the probabilities $\{q_{mn'}^0, q_{mn'}^1\}$, defined by:

$$r_{mn}^0 = \sum_{\{x_{n'} : n' \in \mathcal{N}(m)\backslash n\}} P\left(z_m \,|\, x_n = 0, \{x_{n'} : n' \in \mathcal{N}(m)\backslash n\}\right) \prod_{n' \in \mathcal{N}(m)\backslash n} q_{mn'}^{x_{n'}}$$

(47.7)

and second, r_{mn}^1, the probability of the observed value of z_m arising when $x_n = 1$, defined by:

$$r_{mn}^1 = \sum_{\{x_{n'} : n' \in \mathcal{N}(m)\backslash n\}} P\left(z_m \,|\, x_n = 1, \{x_{n'} : n' \in \mathcal{N}(m)\backslash n\}\right) \prod_{n' \in \mathcal{N}(m)\backslash n} q_{mn'}^{x_{n'}}.$$

(47.8)

The conditional probabilities in these summations are either zero or one, depending on whether the observed z_m matches the hypothesized values for x_n and the $\{x_{n'}\}$.

These probabilities can be computed in various obvious ways based on equation (47.7) and (47.8). The computations may be done most efficiently (if $|\mathcal{N}(m)|$ is large) by regarding $z_m + x_n$ as the final state of a Markov chain with states 0 and 1, this chain being started in state 0, and undergoing transitions corresponding to additions of the various $x_{n'}$, with transition probabilities given by the corresponding $q_{mn'}^0$ and $q_{mn'}^1$. The probabilities for z_m having its observed value given either $x_n = 0$ or $x_n = 1$ can then be found efficiently by use of the forward–backward algorithm (section 25.3).

A particularly convenient implementation of this method uses forward and backward passes in which products of the differences $\delta q_{mn} \equiv q_{mn}^0 - q_{mn}^1$ are computed. We obtain $\delta r_{mn} \equiv r_{mn}^0 - r_{mn}^1$ from the identity:

$$\delta r_{mn} = (-1)^{z_m} \prod_{n' \in \mathcal{N}(m) \backslash n} \delta q_{mn'}. \tag{47.9}$$

This identity is derived by iterating the following observation: if $\zeta = x_\mu + x_\nu \bmod 2$, and x_μ and x_ν have probabilities q_μ^0, q_ν^0 and q_μ^1, q_ν^1 of being 0 and 1, then $P(\zeta\!=\!1) = q_\mu^1 q_\nu^0 + q_\mu^0 q_\nu^1$ and $P(\zeta\!=\!0) = q_\mu^0 q_\nu^0 + q_\mu^1 q_\nu^1$. Thus $P(\zeta\!=\!0) - P(\zeta\!=\!1) = (q_\mu^0 - q_\mu^1)(q_\nu^0 - q_\nu^1)$.

We recover r_{mn}^0 and r_{mn}^1 using

$$r_{mn}^0 = {}^{1}\!/{}_{2}(1 + \delta r_{mn}), \quad r_{mn}^1 = {}^{1}\!/{}_{2}(1 - \delta r_{mn}). \tag{47.10}$$

The transformations into differences δq and back from δr to $\{r\}$ may be viewed as a Fourier transform and an inverse Fourier transformation.

Vertical step. The *vertical* step takes the computed values of r_{mn}^0 and r_{mn}^1 and updates the values of the probabilities q_{mn}^0 and q_{mn}^1. For each n we compute:

$$q_{mn}^0 = \alpha_{mn} \, p_n^0 \prod_{m' \in \mathcal{M}(n) \backslash m} r_{m'n}^0 \tag{47.11}$$

$$q_{mn}^1 = \alpha_{mn} \, p_n^1 \prod_{m' \in \mathcal{M}(n) \backslash m} r_{m'n}^1 \tag{47.12}$$

where α_{mn} is chosen such that $q_{mn}^0 + q_{mn}^1 = 1$. These products can be efficiently computed in a downward pass and an upward pass.

We can also compute the 'pseudoposterior probabilities' q_n^0 and q_n^1 at this iteration, given by:

$$q_n^0 = \alpha_n \, p_n^0 \prod_{m \in \mathcal{M}(n)} r_{mn}^0, \tag{47.13}$$

$$q_n^1 = \alpha_n \, p_n^1 \prod_{m \in \mathcal{M}(n)} r_{mn}^1. \tag{47.14}$$

These quantities are used to create a tentative decoding $\hat{\mathbf{x}}$, the consistency of which is used to decide whether the decoding algorithm can halt. (Halt if $\mathbf{H}\hat{\mathbf{x}} = \mathbf{z}$.)

At this point, the algorithm repeats from the horizontal step.

The stop-when-it's-done decoding method. The recommended decoding procedure is to set $\hat{x}_n$ to 1 if $q_n^1 > 0.5$ and see if the checks $\mathbf{H}\hat{\mathbf{x}} = \mathbf{z} \bmod 2$ are all satisfied, halting when they are, and declaring a failure if some maximum number of iterations (e.g. 200 or 1000) occurs without successful decoding. In the event of a failure, we may still report $\hat{\mathbf{x}}$, but we flag the whole block as a failure.

We note in passing the difference between this decoding procedure and the widespread practice in the turbo code community, where the decoding algorithm is run for a *fixed* number of iterations (irrespective of whether the decoder finds a consistent state at some earlier time). This practice is wasteful of computer time, and it blurs the distinction between undetected and detected errors. In our procedure, 'undetected' errors occur if the decoder finds an $\hat{\mathbf{x}}$

Figure 47.3. Demonstration of encoding with a rate 1/2 Gallager code. The encoder is derived from a very sparse $10\,000 \times 20\,000$ parity-check matrix with three 1s per column. (a) The code creates transmitted vectors consisting of $10\,000$ source bits and $10\,000$ parity-check bits. (b) Here, the source sequence has been altered by changing the first bit. Notice that many of the parity-check bits are changed. Each parity bit depends on about half of the source bits. (c) The transmission for the case $\mathbf{s} = (1, 0, 0, \ldots, 0)$. This vector is the difference (modulo 2) between transmissions (a) and (b). [Dilbert image Copyright©1997 United Feature Syndicate, Inc., used with permission.]

satisfying $\mathbf{H}\hat{\mathbf{x}} = \mathbf{z}\bmod 2$ which is not equal to the true $\mathbf{x}$. 'Detected' errors occur if the algorithm runs for the maximum number of iterations without finding a valid decoding. Undetected errors are of scientific interest because they reveal distance properties of a code. And in engineering practice, it would seem preferable for the blocks that are known to contain detected errors to be so labelled if practically possible.

Cost. In a brute force approach, the time to create the generator matrix scales as N^3, where N is the block size. The encoding time scales as N^2, but encoding involves only binary arithmetic, so for the block lengths studied here it takes considerably less time than the simulation of the Gaussian channel. Decoding involves approximately $6Nj$ floating point multiplies per iteration, so the total number of operations per decoded bit (assuming 20 iterations) is about $120t/R$, independent of block length. For the codes presented in the next section, this is about 800 operations.

The encoding complexity can be reduced by clever encoding tricks invented by Richardson and Urbanke (2001b) or by specially constructing the parity-check matrix (MacKay *et al.*, 1999).

The decoding complexity can be reduced, with only a small loss in performance, by passing low-precision messages in place of real numbers (Richardson and Urbanke, 2001a).

▶ 47.4 Pictorial demonstration of Gallager codes

Figures 47.3–47.7 illustrate visually the conditions under which low-density parity-check codes can give reliable communication over binary symmetric channels and Gaussian channels. These demonstrations may be viewed as animations on the world wide web (MacKay, 1997b).

H =

Figure 47.4. A low-density parity-check matrix with $N = 20\,000$ columns of weight $j = 3$ and $M = 10\,000$ rows of weight $k = 6$.

Encoding

Figure 47.3 illustrates the encoding operation for the case of a Gallager code whose parity-check matrix is a $10\,000 \times 20\,000$ matrix with three 1s per column (figure 47.4). The high density of the *generator* matrix is illustrated in figure 47.3b and c by showing the change in the transmitted vector when one of the $10\,000$ source bits is altered. Of course, the source images shown here are highly redundant, and such images should really be compressed before encoding. Redundant images are chosen in these demonstrations to make it easier to see the correction process during the iterative decoding. The decoding algorithm does *not* take advantage of the redundancy of the source vector, and it would work in exactly the same way irrespective of the choice of source vector.

Iterative decoding

The transmission is sent over a channel with noise level $f = 7.5\%$ and the received vector is shown in the upper left of figure 47.5. The subsequent pictures in figure 47.5 show the iterative probabilistic decoding process. The sequence of figures shows the best guess, bit by bit, given by the iterative decoder, after 0, 1, 2, 3, 10, 11, 12, 13 iterations. The decoder halts after the 13th iteration when the best guess violates no parity checks. This final decoding is error free.

In the case of an unusually noisy transmission, the decoding algorithm fails to find a valid decoding. For this code and a channel with $f = 7.5\%$, such failures happen about once in every $100\,000$ transmissions. Figure 47.6 shows this error rate compared with the block error rates of classical error-correcting codes.

RECEIVED:

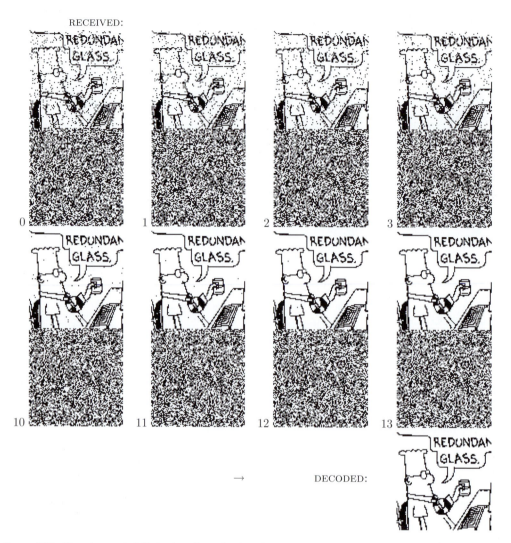

$\rightarrow$ DECODED:

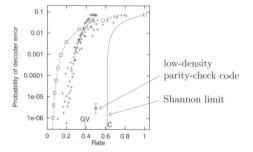

Figure 47.5. Iterative probabilistic decoding of a low–density parity–check code for a transmission received over a channel with noise level $f = 7.5\%$. The sequence of figures shows the best guess, bit by bit, given by the iterative decoder, after 0, 1, 2, 3, 10, 11, 12, 13 iterations. The decoder halts after the 13th iteration when the best guess violates no parity checks. This final decoding is error free.

Figure 47.6. Error probability of the low–density parity–check code (with error bars) for binary symmetric channel with $f = 7.5\%$, compared with algebraic codes. Squares: repetition codes and Hamming $(7, 4)$ code; other points: Reed–Muller and BCH codes.

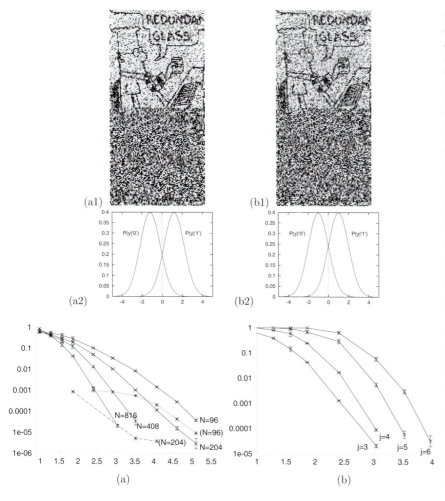

Figure 47.7. Demonstration of a Gallager code for a Gaussian channel. (a1) The received vector after transmission over a Gaussian channel with $x/\sigma = 1.185$ ($E_b/N_0 = 1.47$ dB). The greyscale represents the value of the normalized likelihood. This transmission can be perfectly decoded by the sum-product decoder. The empirical probability of decoding failure is about 10^{-5}. (a2) The probability distribution of the output y of the channel with $x/\sigma = 1.185$ for each of the two possible inputs. (b1) The received transmission over a Gaussian channel with $x/\sigma = 1.0$, which corresponds to the Shannon limit. (b2) The probability distribution of the output y of the channel with $x/\sigma = 1.0$ for each of the two possible inputs.

Figure 47.8. Performance of rate-$1/2$ Gallager codes on the Gaussian channel. Vertical axis: block error probability. Horizontal axis: signal to noise ratio E_b/N_0. (a) Dependence on blocklength N for $(j, k) = (3, 6)$ codes. From left to right: $N = 816$, $N = 408$, $N = 204$, $N = 96$. The dashed lines show the frequency of undetected errors, which is measurable only when the blocklength is as small as $N = 96$ or $N = 204$. (b) Dependence on column weight j for codes of blocklength $N = 816$.

Gaussian channel

In figure 47.7 the left picture shows the received vector after transmission over a Gaussian channel with $x/\sigma = 1.185$. The greyscale represents the value of the normalized likelihood, $\frac{P(y|t=1)}{P(y|t=1)+P(y|t=0)}$. This signal to noise ratio $x/\sigma = 1.185$ is a noise level at which this rate $1/2$ Gallager code communicates reliably (the probability of error is $\simeq 10^{-5}$). To show how close we are to the Shannon limit, the right panel shows the received vector when the signal to noise ratio is reduced to $x/\sigma = 1.0$, which corresponds to the Shannon limit for codes of rate $1/2$.

Variation of performance with code parameters

Figure 47.8 shows how the parameters N and j affect the performance of low–density parity–check codes. As Shannon would predict, increasing the blocklength leads to improved performance. The dependence on j follows a different pattern. Given an *optimal* decoder, the best performance would be obtained for the codes closest to random codes, that is, the codes with largest j. However, the sum–product decoder makes poor progress in dense graphs, so the best performance is obtained for a small value of j. Among the values

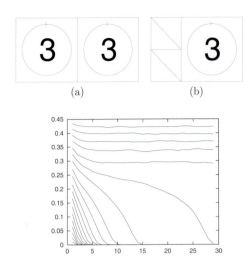

Figure 47.9. Schematic illustration of constructions (a) of a completely regular Gallager code with $j = 3$, $k = 6$ and $R = 1/2$; (b) of a nearly-regular Gallager code with rate $1/3$. Notation: an integer represents a number of permutation matrices superposed on the surrounding square. A diagonal line represents an identity matrix.

Figure 47.10. Monte Carlo simulation of density evolution, following the decoding process for $j = 4$, $k = 8$. Each curve shows the average entropy of a bit as a function of number of iterations, as estimated by a Monte Carlo algorithm using 10 000 samples per iteration. The noise level of the binary symmetric channel f increases by steps of 0.005 from bottom graph ($f = 0.010$) to top graph ($f = 0.100$). There is evidently a threshold at about $f = 0.075$, above which the algorithm cannot determine **x**. From MacKay (1999b).

of j shown in the figure, $j = 3$ is the best, for a blocklength of 816, down to a block error probability of 10^{-5}.

This observation motivates construction of Gallager codes with some columns of weight 2. A construction with $M/2$ columns of weight 2 is shown in figure 47.9b. Too many columns of weight 2 and the code becomes a much poorer code.

As we'll discuss later, we can do even better by making the code even more irregular.

▶ 47.5 Density evolution

One way to study the decoding algorithm is to imagine it running on an infinite tree-like graph with the same local topology as the Gallager code's graph. The larger the matrix **H**, the closer its decoding properties should approach those of the infinite graph.

Imagine an infinite belief network with no loops, in which every bit x_n connects to j checks and every check z_m connects to k bits (figure 47.11). We consider the iterative flow of information in this network, and examine the average entropy of one bit as a function of number of iterations. At each iteration, a bit has accumulated information from its local network out to a radius equal to the number of iterations. Successful decoding will occur only if the average entropy of a bit decreases to zero as the number of iterations increases.

The iterations of an infinite belief network can be simulated by Monte Carlo methods – a technique first used by Gallager (1963). Imagine a network of radius I (the total number of iterations) centred on one bit. Our aim is to compute the conditional entropy of the central bit x given the state **z** of all checks out to radius I. To evaluate the probability that the central bit is 1 given a *particular* syndrome **z** involves an I-step propagation from the outside of the network into the centre. At the ith iteration probabilities r at

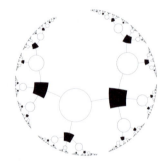

Figure 47.11. Local topology of the graph of a Gallager code with column weight $j = 3$ and row weight $k = 4$. White nodes represent bits, x_l; black nodes represent checks, z_m; each edge corresponds to a 1 in **H**.

radius $I - i + 1$ are transformed into qs and then into rs at radius $I - i$ in a way that depends on the states x of the unknown bits at radius $I - i$. In the Monte Carlo method, rather than simulating this network exactly, which would take a time that grows exponentially with I, we create for each iteration a representative sample (of size 100, say) of the values of $\{r, x\}$. In the case of a regular network with parameters j, k, each new pair $\{r, x\}$ in the list at the ith iteration is created by drawing the new x from its distribution and drawing at random with replacement $(j-1)(k-1)$ pairs $\{r, x\}$ from the list at the $(i-1)$th iteration; these are assembled into a tree fragment (figure 47.12) and the sum-product algorithm is run from top to bottom to find the new r value associated with the new node.

As an example, the results of runs with $j = 4$, $k = 8$ and noise densities f between 0.01 and 0.10, using 10 000 samples at each iteration, are shown in figure 47.10. Runs with low enough noise level show a collapse to zero entropy after a small number of iterations, and those with high noise level decrease to a non-zero entropy corresponding to a failure to decode.

The boundary between these two behaviours is called the *threshold* of the decoding algorithm for the binary symmetric channel. Figure 47.10 shows by Monte Carlo simulation that the threshold for regular $(j, k) = (4, 8)$ codes is about 0.075. Richardson and Urbanke (2001a) have derived thresholds for regular codes by a tour de force of direct analytic methods. Some of these thresholds are shown in table 47.13.

Approximate density evolution

For practical purposes, the computational cost of density evolution can be reduced by making Gaussian approximations to the probability distributions over the messages in density evolution, and updating only the parameters of these approximations. For further information about these techniques, which produce diagrams known as *EXIT charts*, see (ten Brink, 1999; Chung *et al.*, 2001; ten Brink *et al.*, 2002).

▶ ## 47.6 Improving Gallager codes

Since the rediscovery of Gallager codes, two methods have been found for enhancing their performance.

Clump bits and checks together

First, we can make Gallager codes in which the variable nodes are grouped together into metavariables consisting of say 3 binary variables, and the check nodes are similarly grouped together into metachecks. As before, a sparse graph can be constructed connecting metavariables to metachecks, with a lot of freedom about the details of how the variables and checks within are wired up. One way to set the wiring is to work in a finite field $GF(q)$ such as $GF(4)$ or $GF(8)$, define low-density parity-check matrices using elements of $GF(q)$, and translate our binary messages into $GF(q)$ using a mapping such as the one for $GF(4)$ given in table 47.14. Now, when messages are passed during decoding, those messages are probabilities and likelihoods over *conjunctions* of binary variables. For example if each clump contains three binary variables then the likelihoods will describe the likelihoods of the eight alternative states of those bits.

With carefully optimized constructions, the resulting codes over $GF(4)$,

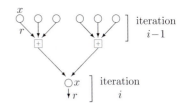

Figure 47.12. A tree-fragment constructed during Monte Carlo simulation of density evolution. This fragment is appropriate for a regular $j = 3$, $k = 4$ Gallager code.

(j, k)	$f_{\max}$
(3,6)	0.084
(4,8)	0.076
(5,10)	0.068

Table 47.13. Thresholds $f_{\max}$ for regular low–density parity–check codes, assuming sum–product decoding algorithm, from Richardson and Urbanke (2001a). The Shannon limit for rate-$^1/_2$ codes is $f_{\max} = 0.11$.

$GF(4)$	$\leftrightarrow$	binary
0	$\leftrightarrow$	00
1	$\leftrightarrow$	01
A	$\leftrightarrow$	10
B	$\leftrightarrow$	11

Table 47.14. Translation between binary and $GF(4)$ for message symbols.

$GF(4)$	$\rightarrow$	binary
0	$\rightarrow$	00 00
1	$\rightarrow$	10 01
A	$\rightarrow$	11 10
B	$\rightarrow$	01 11

Table 47.15. Translation between binary and $GF(4)$ for matrix entries. An $M \times N$ parity-check matrix over $GF(4)$ can be turned into a $2M \times 2N$ binary parity-check matrix in this way.

$$
\begin{aligned}
F^0 &= [f^0 + f^1] + [f^A + f^B] \\
F^1 &= [f^0 - f^1] + [f^A - f^B] \\
F^A &= [f^0 + f^1] - [f^A + f^B] \\
F^B &= [f^0 - f^1] - [f^A - f^B]
\end{aligned}
$$

Algorithm 47.16. The Fourier transform over $GF(4)$. The Fourier transform F of a function f over $GF(2)$ is given by $F^0 = f^0 + f^1$, $F^1 = f^0 - f^1$. Transforms over $GF(2^k)$ can be viewed as a sequence of binary transforms in each of k dimensions. The inverse transform is identical to the Fourier transform, except that we also divide by 2^k.

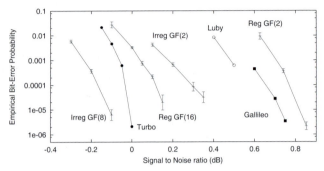

Figure 47.17. Comparison of regular binary Gallager codes with irregular codes, codes over $GF(q)$, and other outstanding codes of rate $1/4$. From left (best performance) to right: Irregular low–density parity–check code over $GF(8)$, blocklength 48 000 bits (Davey, 1999); JPL turbo code (JPL, 1996) blocklength 65 536; Regular low–density parity–check over $GF(16)$, blocklength 24 448 bits (Davey and MacKay, 1998); Irregular binary low–density parity–check code, blocklength 16 000 bits (Davey, 1999); Luby *et al.* (1998) irregular binary low–density parity–check code, blocklength 64 000 bits; JPL code for Galileo (in 1992, this was the best known code of rate 1/4); Regular binary low–density parity–check code: blocklength 40 000 bits (MacKay, 1999b). The Shannon limit is at about -0.79 dB. As of 2003, even better sparse-graph codes have been constructed.

$GF(8)$, and $GF(16)$ perform nearly one decibel better than comparable binary Gallager codes.

The computational cost for decoding in $GF(q)$ scales as $q \log q$, if the appropriate Fourier transform is used in the check nodes: the update rule for the check-to-variable message,

$$
r_{mn}^a = \sum_{\mathbf{x}:x_n=a} \mathbb{1}\left[\sum_{n' \in \mathcal{N}(m)} H_{mn'}x_{n'} = z_m\right] \prod_{j \in \mathcal{N}(m)\backslash n} q_{mj}^{x_j}, \tag{47.15}
$$

is a convolution of the quantities q_{mj}^a, so the summation can be replaced by a product of the Fourier transforms of q_{mj}^a for $j \in \mathcal{N}(m)\backslash n$, followed by an inverse Fourier transform. The Fourier transform for $GF(4)$ is shown in algorithm 47.16.

Make the graph irregular

The second way of improving Gallager codes, introduced by Luby *et al.* (2001b), is to make their graphs *irregular*. Instead of giving all variable nodes the same degree j, we can have some variable nodes with degree 2, some 3, some 4, and a few with degree 20. Check nodes can also be given unequal degrees – this helps improve performance on erasure channels, but it turns out that for the Gaussian channel, the best graphs have regular check connectivity.

Figure 47.17 illustrates the benefits offered by these two methods for improving Gallager codes, focussing on codes of rate $1/4$. Making the binary code irregular gives a win of about 0.4 dB; switching from $GF(2)$ to $GF(16)$ gives

DIFFERENCE SET CYCLIC CODES					
N	7	21	73	273	1057	4161
M	4	**10**	**28**	**82**	**244**	**730**
K	3	11	45	191	813	3431
d	4	**6**	**10**	**18**	34	66
k	3	**5**	**9**	17	33	65

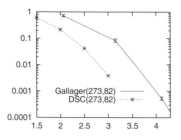

Figure 47.18. An algebraically constructed low-density parity-check code satisfying many redundant constraints outperforms an equivalent random Gallager code. The table shows the N, M, K, distance d, and row weight k of some difference-set cyclic codes, highlighting the codes that have large d/N, small k, and large N/M. In the comparison the Gallager code had $(j, k) = (4, 13)$, and rate identical to the $N = 273$ difference-set cyclic code.

about 0.6 dB; and Matthew Davey's code that combines both these features – it's irregular over $GF(8)$ – gives a win of about 0.9 dB over the regular binary Gallager code.

Methods for optimizing the *profile* of a Gallager code (that is, its number of rows and columns of each degree), have been developed by Richardson *et al.* (2001) and have led to low–density parity–check codes whose performance, when decoded by the sum–product algorithm, is within a hair's breadth of the Shannon limit.

Algebraic constructions of Gallager codes

The performance of regular Gallager codes can be enhanced in a third manner: by designing the code to have *redundant sparse constraints*. There is a difference-set cyclic code, for example, that has $N = 273$ and $K = 191$, but the code satisfies not $M = 82$ but N, i.e., *273* low-weight constraints (figure 47.18). It is impossible to make random Gallager codes that have anywhere near this much redundancy among their checks. The difference-set cyclic code performs about 0.7 dB better than an equivalent random Gallager code.

An open problem is to discover codes sharing the remarkable properties of the difference-set cyclic codes but with different blocklengths and rates. I call this task *the Tanner challenge*.

▶ 47.7 Fast encoding of low-density parity-check codes

We now discuss methods for fast encoding of low-density parity-check codes – faster than the standard method, in which a generator matrix **G** is found by Gaussian elimination (at a cost of order M^3) and then each block is encoded by multiplying it by **G** (at a cost of order M^2).

Staircase codes

Certain low-density parity-check matrices with M columns of weight 2 or less can be encoded easily in linear time. For example, if the matrix has a *staircase* structure as illustrated by the right-hand side of

$$\mathbf{H} = \begin{bmatrix} & & & & & & \\ & & & & & & \\ & & & & & & \\ & & & & & & \\ & & & & & & \\ & & & & & & \end{bmatrix}, \qquad (47.16)$$

and if the data $\mathbf{s}$ are loaded into the first K bits, then the M parity bits $\mathbf{p}$ can be computed from left to right in linear time.

$$
\begin{aligned}
p_1 &= & \sum_{n=1}^{K} H_{1n}s_n \\
p_2 &= p_1 + & \sum_{n=1}^{K} H_{2n}s_n \\
p_3 &= p_2 + & \sum_{n=1}^{K} H_{3n}s_n \\
&\vdots & \\
p_M &= p_{M-1}+ & \sum_{n=1}^{K} H_{Mn}s_n.
\end{aligned}
\tag{47.17}
$$

If we call two parts of the $\mathbf{H}$ matrix $[\mathbf{H}_s|\mathbf{H}_p]$, we can describe the encoding operation in two steps: first compute an intermediate parity vector $\mathbf{v} = \mathbf{H}_s\mathbf{s}$; then pass $\mathbf{v}$ through an accumulator to create $\mathbf{p}$.

The cost of this encoding method is linear if the sparsity of $\mathbf{H}$ is exploited when computing the sums in (47.17).

Fast encoding of general low-density parity-check codes

Richardson and Urbanke (2001b) demonstrated an elegant method by which the encoding cost of any low-density parity-check code can be reduced from the straightforward method's M^2 to a cost of $N + g^2$, where g, the *gap*, is hopefully a small constant, and in the worst cases scales as a small fraction of N.

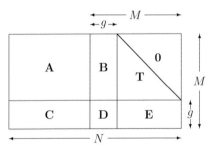

Figure 47.19. The parity-check matrix in approximate lower-triangular form.

In the first step, the parity-check matrix is rearranged, by row-interchange and column-interchange, into the *approximate lower-triangular form* shown in figure 47.19. The original matrix $\mathbf{H}$ was very sparse, so the six matrices $\mathbf{A}$, $\mathbf{B}$, $\mathbf{T}$, $\mathbf{C}$, $\mathbf{D}$, and $\mathbf{E}$ are also very sparse. The matrix $\mathbf{T}$ is lower triangular and has 1s everywhere on the diagonal.

$$
\mathbf{H} = \left[\begin{array}{ccc} \mathbf{A} & \mathbf{B} & \mathbf{T} \\ \mathbf{C} & \mathbf{D} & \mathbf{E} \end{array} \right].
\tag{47.18}
$$

The source vector $\mathbf{s}$ of length $K = N - M$ is encoded into a transmission $\mathbf{t} = [\mathbf{s}, \mathbf{p}_1, \mathbf{p}_2]$ as follows.

1. Compute the upper syndrome of the source vector,

$$
\mathbf{z}_A = \mathbf{A}\mathbf{s}.
\tag{47.19}
$$

   This can be done in linear time.

2. Find a setting of the second parity bits, $\mathbf{p}_2^A$, such that the upper syndrome is zero.

$$
\mathbf{p}_2^A = -\mathbf{T}^{-1}\mathbf{z}_A.
\tag{47.20}
$$

   This vector can be found in linear time by back-substitution, i.e., computing the first bit of $\mathbf{p}_2^A$, then the second, then the third, and so forth.

3. Compute the lower syndrome of the vector $[\mathbf{s}, \mathbf{0}, \mathbf{p}_2^A]$:

$$\mathbf{z}_B = \mathbf{C}\mathbf{s} - \mathbf{E}\mathbf{p}_2^A. \tag{47.21}$$

This can be done in linear time.

4. Now we get to the clever bit. Define the matrix

$$\mathbf{F} \equiv -\mathbf{E}\mathbf{T}^{-1}\mathbf{B} + \mathbf{D}, \tag{47.22}$$

and find its inverse, $\mathbf{F}^{-1}$. This computation needs to be done once only, and its cost is of order g^3. This inverse $\mathbf{F}^{-1}$ is a dense $g \times g$ matrix. [If $\mathbf{F}$ is not invertible then either $\mathbf{H}$ is not of full rank, or else further column permutations of $\mathbf{H}$ can produce an $\mathbf{F}$ that is invertible.]

Set the first parity bits, $\mathbf{p}_1$, to

$$\mathbf{p}_1 = -\mathbf{F}^{-1}\mathbf{z}_B. \tag{47.23}$$

This operation has a cost of order g^2.

Claim: At this point, we have found the correct setting of the first parity bits, $\mathbf{p}_1$.

5. Discard the tentative parity bits $\mathbf{p}_2^A$ and find the new upper syndrome,

$$\mathbf{z}_C = \mathbf{z}_A + \mathbf{B}\mathbf{p}_1. \tag{47.24}$$

This can be done in linear time.

6. Find a setting of the second parity bits, $\mathbf{p}_2$, such that the upper syndrome is zero,

$$\mathbf{p}_2 = -\mathbf{T}^{-1}\mathbf{z}_C \tag{47.25}$$

This vector can be found in linear time by back-substitution.

▶ 47.8 Further reading

Low-density parity-check codes codes were first studied in 1962 by Gallager, then were generally forgotten by the coding theory community. Tanner (1981) generalized Gallager's work by introducing more general constraint nodes; the codes that are now called turbo product codes should in fact be called Tanner product codes, since Tanner proposed them, and his colleagues (Karplus and Krit, 1991) implemented them in hardware. Publications on Gallager codes contributing to their 1990s rebirth include (Wiberg *et al.*, 1995; MacKay and Neal, 1995; MacKay and Neal, 1996; Wiberg, 1996; MacKay, 1999b; Spielman, 1996; Sipser and Spielman, 1996). Low-precision decoding algorithms and fast encoding algorithms for Gallager codes are discussed in (Richardson and Urbanke, 2001a; Richardson and Urbanke, 2001b). MacKay and Davey (2000) showed that low–density parity–check codes can outperform Reed–Solomon codes, even on the Reed–Solomon codes' home turf: high rate and short block lengths. Other important papers include (Luby *et al.*, 2001a; Luby *et al.*, 2001b; Luby *et al.*, 1997; Davey and MacKay, 1998; Richardson *et al.*, 2001; Chung *et al.*, 2001). Useful tools for the design of irregular low–density parity–check codes include (Chung *et al.*, 1999; Urbanke, 2001).

See (Wiberg, 1996; Frey, 1998; McEliece *et al.*, 1998) for further discussion of the sum-product algorithm.

For a view of low–density parity–check code decoding in terms of group theory and coding theory, see (Forney, 2001; Offer and Soljanin, 2000; Offer and Soljanin, 2001); and for background reading on this topic see (Hartmann and Rudolph, 1976; Terras, 1999). There is a growing literature on the practical design of low-density parity-check codes (Mao and Banihashemi, 2000; Mao and Banihashemi, 2001; ten Brink *et al.*, 2002); they are now being adopted for applications from hard drives to satellite communications.

For low–density parity–check codes applicable to quantum error-correction, see MacKay *et al.* (2003).

▶ 47.9 Exercises

Exercise 47.1.[2] The 'hyperbolic tangent' version of the decoding algorithm. In section 47.3, the sum–product decoding algorithm for low–density parity–check codes was presented first in terms of quantities $q_{mn}^{0/1}$ and $r_{mn}^{0/1}$, then in terms of quantities δq and δr. There is a third description, in which the $\{q\}$ are replaced by log probability-ratios,

$$l_{mn} \equiv \ln \frac{q_{mn}^0}{q_{mn}^1}. \qquad (47.26)$$

Show that

$$\delta q_{mn} \equiv q_{mn}^0 - q_{mn}^1 = \tanh(l_{mn}/2). \qquad (47.27)$$

Derive the update rules for $\{r\}$ and $\{l\}$.

Exercise 47.2.[2, p.572] I am sometimes asked 'why not decode *other* linear codes, for example algebraic codes, by transforming their parity-check matrices so that they are low-density, and applying the sum–product algorithm?' [Recall that any linear combination of rows of $\mathbf{H}$, $\mathbf{H}' = \mathbf{PH}$, is a valid parity-check matrix for a code, as long as the matrix $\mathbf{P}$ is invertible; so there are many parity check matrices for any one code.]

Explain why a random linear code does not have a low-density parity-check matrix. [Here, low-density means 'having row-weight at most k', where k is some small constant $\ll N$.]

Exercise 47.3.[3] Show that if a low-density parity-check code has more than M columns of weight 2 – say αM columns, where $\alpha > 1$ – then the code will have words with weight of order $\log M$.

Exercise 47.4.[5] In section 13.5 we found the expected value of the weight enumerator function $A(w)$, averaging over the ensemble of all random linear codes. This calculation can also be carried out for the ensemble of low-density parity-check codes (Gallager, 1963; MacKay, 1999b; Litsyn and Shevelev, 2002). It is plausible, however, that the mean value of $A(w)$ is not always a good indicator of the *typical* value of $A(w)$ in the ensemble. For example, if, at a particular value of w, 99% of codes have $A(w) = 0$, and 1% have $A(w) = 100\,000$, then while we might say the typical value of $A(w)$ is zero, the mean is found to be 1000. Find the *typical* weight enumerator function of low-density parity-check codes.

▶ 47.10 Solutions

Solution to exercise 47.2 (p.572). Consider codes of rate R and blocklength N, having $K = RN$ source bits and $M = (1-R)N$ parity-check bits. Let all the codes have their bits ordered so that the first K bits are independent, so that we could if we wish put the code in systematic form,

$$\mathbf{G} = [\mathbf{1}_K | \mathbf{P}^\mathsf{T}]; \;\; \mathbf{H} = [\mathbf{P} | \mathbf{1}_M]. \tag{47.28}$$

The number of *distinct* linear codes is the number of matrices $\mathbf{P}$, which is $\mathcal{N}_1 = 2^{MK} = 2^{N^2 R(1-R)}$. Can these all be expressed as distinct low–density parity–check codes? $\qquad \log \mathcal{N}_1 \simeq N^2 R(1-R)$

The number of low-density parity-check matrices with row-weight k is

$$\binom{N}{k}^M \tag{47.29}$$

and the number of distinct codes that they define is at most

$$\mathcal{N}_2 = \binom{N}{k}^M \bigg/ M!, \tag{47.30}$$

which is much smaller than $\mathcal{N}_1$, so, by the pigeon-hole principle, it is not possible for every random linear code to map on to a low-density $\mathbf{H}$. $\qquad \log \mathcal{N}_2 < Nk \log N$

48

Convolutional Codes and Turbo Codes

This chapter follows tightly on from Chapter 25. It makes use of the ideas of codes and trellises and the forward–backward algorithm.

▶ 48.1 Introduction to convolutional codes

When we studied linear block codes, we described them in three ways:

1. The generator matrix describes how to turn a string of K arbitrary source bits into a transmission of N bits.

2. The parity-check matrix specifies the $M = N - K$ parity-check constraints that a valid codeword satisfies.

3. The trellis of the code describes its valid codewords in terms of paths through a trellis with labelled edges.

A fourth way of describing some block codes, the algebraic approach, is not covered in this book (a) because it has been well covered by numerous other books in coding theory; (b) because, as this part of the book discusses, the state of the art in error-correcting codes makes little use of algebraic coding theory; and (c) because I am not competent to teach this subject.

We will now describe convolutional codes in two ways: first, in terms of mechanisms for generating transmissions $\mathbf{t}$ from source bits $\mathbf{s}$; and second, in terms of trellises that describe the constraints satisfied by valid transmissions.

▶ 48.2 Linear feedback shift registers

We generate a transmission with a convolutional code by putting a source stream through a linear filter. This filter makes use of a shift register, linear output functions, and, possibly, linear feedback.

I will draw the shift register in a right-to-left orientation: bits roll from right to left as time goes on.

Figure 48.1 shows three linear feedback shift registers which could be used to define convolutional codes. The rectangular box surrounding the bits $z_1 \ldots z_7$ indicate the *memory* of the filter, also known as its *state*. All three filters have one input and two outputs. On each clock cycle, the source supplies one bit, and the filter outputs two bits $t^{(a)}$ and $t^{(b)}$. By concatenating together these bits we can obtain from our source stream $s_1 s_2 s_3 \ldots$ a transmission stream $t_1^{(a)} t_1^{(b)} t_2^{(a)} t_2^{(b)} t_3^{(a)} t_3^{(b)} \ldots$. Because there are two transmitted bits for every source bit, the codes shown in figure 48.1 have rate $1/2$. Because these

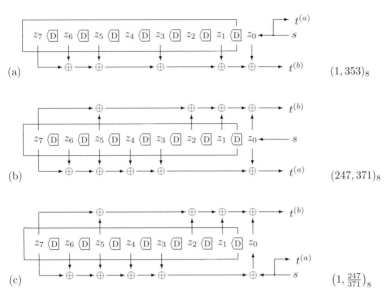

Figure 48.1. Linear feedback shift registers for generating convolutional codes with rate 1/2. The symbol $\boxed{\text{D}}$ indicates a copying with a delay of one clock cycle. The symbol $\oplus$ denotes linear addition modulo 2 with no delay.

filters require $k = 7$ bits of memory, the codes they define are known as a *constraint-length 7 codes.*

Convolutional codes come in three flavours, corresponding to the three types of filter in figure 48.1.

Systematic nonrecursive

The filter shown in figure 48.1a has no feedback. It also has the property that one of the output bits, $t^{(a)}$, is identical to the source bit s. This encoder is thus called *systematic*, because the source bits are reproduced transparently in the transmitted stream, and *nonrecursive*, because it has no feedback. The other transmitted bit $t^{(b)}$ is a linear function of the state of the filter. One way of describing that function is as a dot product (modulo 2) between two binary vectors of length $k + 1$: a binary vector $\mathbf{g}^{(b)} = (1, 1, 1, 0, 1, 0, 1, 1)$ and the state vector $\mathbf{z} = (z_k, z_{k-1}, \ldots, z_1, z_0)$. We include in the state vector the bit z_0 that will be put into the first bit of the memory on the next cycle. The vector $\mathbf{g}^{(b)}$ has $g_\kappa^{(b)} = 1$ for every κ where there is a tap (a downward pointing arrow) from state bit z_κ into the transmitted bit $t^{(b)}$.

A convenient way to describe these binary tap vectors is in octal. Thus, this filter makes use of the tap vector 353_8. I have drawn the delay lines from right to left to make it easy to relate the diagrams to these octal numbers.

$$11\ 101\ 011$$
$$\downarrow\quad\downarrow\quad\downarrow$$
$$3\quad 5\quad 3$$

Table 48.2. How taps in the delay line are converted to octal.

Nonsystematic nonrecursive

The filter shown in figure 48.1b also has no feedback, but it is not systematic. It makes use of two tap vectors $\mathbf{g}^{(a)}$ and $\mathbf{g}^{(b)}$ to create its two transmitted bits. This encoder is thus *nonsystematic* and *nonrecursive*. Because of their added complexity, nonsystematic codes can have error-correcting abilities superior to those of systematic nonrecursive codes with the same constraint length.

Systematic recursive

The filter shown in figure 48.1c is similar to the nonsystematic nonrecursive
filter shown in figure 48.1b, but it uses the taps that formerly made up $\mathbf{g}^{(a)}$
to make a linear signal that is fed back into the shift register along with the
source bit. The output $t^{(b)}$ is a linear function of the state vector as before.
The other output is $t^{(a)} = s$, so this filter is systematic.

A recursive code is conventionally identified by an octal ratio, e.g., figure 48.1c's code is denoted by $(247/371)_8$.

Equivalence of systematic recursive and nonsystematic nonrecursive codes

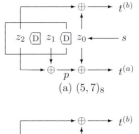

(a) $(5, 7)_8$

The two filters in figure 48.1b,c are *code-equivalent* in that the *sets* of codewords that they define are identical. For every codeword of the nonsystematic
nonrecursive code we can choose a source stream for the other encoder such
that its output is identical (and *vice versa*).

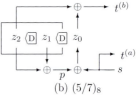

(b) $(5/7)_8$

To prove this, we denote by p the quantity $\sum_{\kappa=1}^{k} g_{\kappa}^{(a)} z_{\kappa}$, as shown in figure 48.3a and b, which shows a pair of smaller but otherwise equivalent filters.
If the two transmissions are to be equivalent – that is, the $t^{(a)}$s are equal in
both figures and so are the $t^{(b)}$s – then on every cycle the source bit in the
systematic code must be $s = t^{(a)}$. So now we must simply confirm that for
this choice of s, the systematic code's shift register will follow the same state
sequence as that of the nonsystematic code, assuming that the states match
initially. In figure 48.3a we have

Figure 48.3. Two rate $1/2$
convolutional codes with
constraint length $k = 2$:
(a) non-recursive; (b) recursive.
The two codes are equivalent.

$$t^{(a)} = p \oplus z_0^{\text{nonrecursive}} \tag{48.1}$$

whereas is figure 48.3b we have

$$z_0^{\text{recursive}} = t^{(a)} \oplus p. \tag{48.2}$$

Substituting for $t^{(a)}$, and using $p \oplus p = 0$ we immediately find

$$z_0^{\text{recursive}} = z_0^{\text{nonrecursive}}. \tag{48.3}$$

Thus, any codeword of a nonsystematic nonrecursive code is a codeword of
a systematic recursive code with the same taps – the same taps in the sense
that there are vertical arrows in all the same places in figure 48.3(a) and (b),
though one of the arrows points up instead of down in (b).

Now, while these two codes are equivalent, the two encoders behave differently. The nonrecursive encoder has a *finite impulse response*, that is, if
one puts in a string that is all zeroes except for a single one, the resulting
output stream contains a finite number of ones. Once the one bit has passed
through all the states of the memory, the delay line returns to the all-zero
state. Figure 48.4a shows the state sequence resulting from the source string
$\mathbf{s} = (0, 0, 1, 0, 0, 0, 0, 0)$.

Figure 48.4b shows the trellis of the recursive code of figure 48.3b and the
response of this filter to the same source string $\mathbf{s} = (0, 0, 1, 0, 0, 0, 0, 0)$. The
filter has an *infinite impulse response*. The response settles into a periodic
state with period equal to three clock cycles.

▷ Exercise 48.1.[1] What is the input to the recursive filter such that its state
sequence and the transmission are the same as those of the nonrecursive
filter? (Hint: see figure 48.5.)

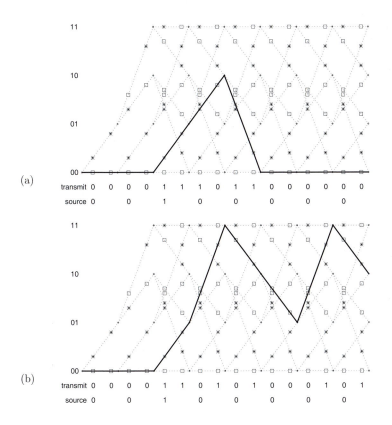

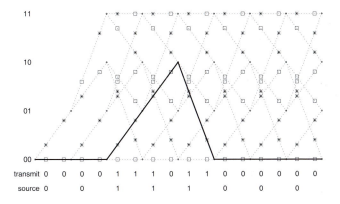

Figure 48.4. Trellises of the rate 1/2 convolutional codes of figure 48.3. It is assumed that the initial state of the filter is $(z_2, z_1) = (0, 0)$. Time is on the horizontal axis and the state of the filter at each time step is the vertical coordinate. On the line segments are shown the emitted symbols $t^{(a)}$ and $t^{(b)}$, with stars for '1' and boxes for '0'. The paths taken through the trellises when the source sequence is 00100000 are highlighted with a solid line. The light dotted lines show the state trajectories that are possible for other source sequences.

Figure 48.5. The source sequence for the systematic recursive code (00111000) produces the same path through the trellis as (00100000) does in the nonsystematic nonrecursive case.

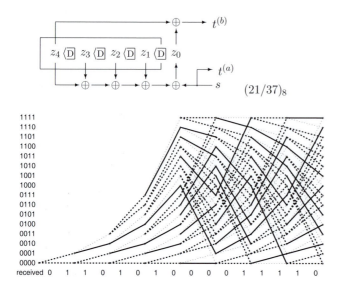

Figure 48.6. The trellis for a $k = 4$ code painted with the likelihood function when the received vector is equal to a codeword with just one bit flipped. There are three line styles, depending on the value of the likelihood: thick solid lines show the edges in the trellis that match the corresponding two bits of the received string exactly; thick dotted lines show edges that match one bit but mismatch the other; and thin dotted lines show the edges that mismatch both bits.

In general a linear feedback shift register with k bits of memory has an impulse response that is periodic with a period that is at most $2^k - 1$, corresponding to the filter visiting every non-zero state in its state space.

Incidentally, cheap pseudorandom number generators and cheap cryptographic products make use of exactly these periodic sequences, though with larger values of k than 7; the random number seed or cryptographic key selects the initial state of the memory. There is thus a close connection between certain cryptanalysis problems and the decoding of convolutional codes.

▶ 48.3 Decoding convolutional codes

The receiver receives a bit stream, and wishes to infer the state sequence and thence the source stream. The posterior probability of each bit can be found by the sum–product algorithm (also known as the forward–backward or BCJR algorithm), which was introduced in section 25.3. The most probable state sequence can be found using the min–sum algorithm of section 25.3 (also known as the Viterbi algorithm). The nature of this task is illustrated in figure 48.6, which shows the cost associated with each edge in the trellis for the case of a sixteen-state code; the channel is assumed to be a binary symmetric channel and the received vector is equal to a codeword except that one bit has been flipped. There are three line styles, depending on the value of the likelihood: thick solid lines show the edges in the trellis that match the corresponding two bits of the received string exactly; thick dotted lines show edges that match one bit but mismatch the other; and thin dotted lines show the edges that mismatch both bits. The min–sum algorithm seeks the path through the trellis that uses as many solid lines as possible; more precisely, it minimizes the cost of the path, where the cost is zero for a solid line, one for a thick dotted line, and two for a thin dotted line.

▷ Exercise 48.2.[1, p.581] Can you spot the most probable path and the flipped bit?

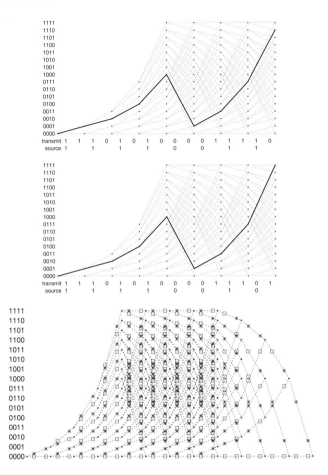

Figure 48.7. Two paths that differ in two transmitted bits only.

Figure 48.8. A terminated trellis.

Unequal protection

A defect of the convolutional codes presented thus far is that they offer unequal protection to the source bits. Figure 48.7 shows two paths through the trellis that differ in only two transmitted bits. The last source bit is less well protected than the other source bits. This unequal protection of bits motivates the *termination* of the trellis.

A terminated trellis is shown in figure 48.8. Termination slightly reduces the number of source bits used per codeword. Here, four source bits are turned into parity bits because the $k = 4$ memory bits must be returned to zero.

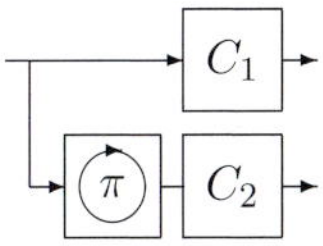

Figure 48.10. The encoder of a turbo code. Each box C_1, C_2, contains a convolutional code. The source bits are reordered using a permutation π before they are fed to C_2. The transmitted codeword is obtained by concatenating or interleaving the outputs of the two convolutional codes.

▶ 48.4 Turbo codes

An (N, K) turbo code is defined by a number of constituent convolutional encoders (often, two) and an equal number of *interleavers* which are $K \times K$ permutation matrices. Without loss of generality, we take the first interleaver to be the identity matrix. A string of K source bits is encoded by feeding them into each constituent encoder in the order defined by the associated interleaver, and transmitting the bits that come out of each constituent encoder. Often the first constituent encoder is chosen to be a systematic encoder, just like the recursive filter shown in figure 48.6, and the second is a non-systematic one of rate 1 that emits parity bits only. The transmitted codeword then consists of

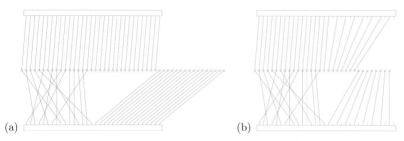

Figure 48.9. Rate-1/3 (a) and rate-1/2 (b) turbo codes represented as factor graphs. The circles
represent the codeword bits. The two rectangles represent trellises of rate 1/2 convolutional
codes, with the systematic bits occupying the left half of the rectangle and the parity bits
occupying the right half. The puncturing of these constituent codes in the rate 1/2 turbo
code is represented by the lack of connections to half of the parity bits in each trellis.

K source bits followed by M_1 parity bits generated by the first convolutional
code and M_2 parity bits from the second. The resulting turbo code has rate
$1/3$.

The turbo code can be represented by a factor graph in which the two
trellises are represented by two large rectangular nodes (figure 48.9a); the K
source bits and the first M_1 parity bits participate in the first trellis and the K
source bits and the last M_2 parity bits participate in the second trellis. Each
codeword bit participates in either one or two trellises, depending on whether
it is a parity bit or a source bit. Each trellis node contains a trellis exactly like
the terminated trellis shown in figure 48.8, except one thousand times as long.
[There are other factor graph representations for turbo codes that make use
of more elementary nodes, but the factor graph given here yields the standard
version of the sum–product algorithm used for turbo codes.]

If a turbo code of smaller rate such as $1/2$ is required, a standard modification to the rate-$1/3$ code is to *puncture* some of the parity bits (figure 48.9b).

Turbo codes are decoded using the sum–product algorithm described in
Chapter 26. On the first iteration, each trellis receives the channel likelihoods,
and runs the forward backward algorithm to compute, for each bit, the relative
likelihood of its being 1 or 0, given the information about the other bits.
These likelihoods are then passed across from each trellis to the other, and
multiplied by the channel likelihoods on the way. We are then ready for the
second iteration: the forward–backward algorithm is run again in each trellis
using the updated probabilities. After about ten or twenty such iterations, it's
hoped that the correct decoding will be found. It is common practice to stop
after some fixed number of iterations, but we can do better.

As a stopping criterion, the following procedure can be used at every iteration. For each time-step in each trellis, we identify the most probable edge,
according to the local messages. If these most probable edges join up into two
valid paths, one in each trellis, and if these two paths are consistent with each
other, it is reasonable to stop, as subsequent iterations are unlikely to take
the decoder away from this codeword. If a maximum number of iterations is
reached without this stopping criterion being satisfied, a decoding error can
be reported. This stopping procedure is recommended for several reasons: it
allows a big saving in decoding time with no loss in error probability; it allows
decoding failures that are detected by the decoder to be so identified – knowing
that a particular block is definitely corrupted is surely useful information for
the receiver! And when we distinguish between detected and undetected errors, the undetected errors give helpful insights into the low weight codewords

of the code, which may improve the process of code design.

Turbo codes as described here have excellent performance down to decoded error probabilities of about 10^{-5}, but randomly constructed turbo codes tend to have an *error floor* starting at that level. This error floor is caused by low-weight codewords. To reduce the height of the error floor, one can attempt to modify the random construction to increase the weight of these low-weight codewords. The tweaking of turbo codes is a black art, and it never succeeds in totalling eliminating low-weight codewords; more precisely, the low-weight codewords can only be eliminated by sacrificing the turbo code's excellent performance. In contrast, low-density parity-check codes rarely have error floors.

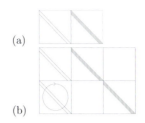

(a)

(b)

Figure 48.11. Schematic pictures of the parity-check matrices of (a) a convolutional code, rate 1/2, and (b) a turbo code, rate 1/3. Notation: A diagonal line represents an identity matrix. A band of diagonal lines represent a band of diagonal 1s. A circle inside a square represents the random permutation of all the columns in that square. A number inside a square represents the number of random permutation matrices superposed in that square. Horizontal and vertical lines indicate the boundaries of the blocks within the matrix.

48.5 Parity-check matrices of convolutional codes and turbo codes

We close by discussing the parity-check matrix of a rate-1/2 convolutional code viewed as a linear block code. We adopt the convention that the N bits of one block are made up of the $N/2$ bits $t^{(a)}$ followed by the $N/2$ bits $t^{(b)}$.

▷ Exercise 48.3.[2] Prove that a convolutional code has a low-density parity-check matrix as shown schematically in figure 48.11a.

> Hint: It's easiest to figure out the parity constraints satisfied by a convolutional code by thinking about the nonsystematic nonrecursive encoder (figure 48.1b). Consider putting through filter a a stream that's been through convolutional filter b, and *vice versa*; compare the two resulting streams. Ignore termination of the trellises.

The parity-check matrix of a turbo code can be written down by listing the constraints satisfied by the two constituent trellises (figure 48.11b). So turbo codes are also special cases of low-density parity-check codes. If a turbo code is punctured, it no longer necessarily has a low-density parity-check matrix, but it always has a *generalized parity-check matrix* that is sparse, as explained in the next chapter.

Further reading

For further reading about convolutional codes, Johannesson and Zigangirov (1999) is highly recommended. One topic I would have liked to include is *sequential decoding*. Sequential decoding explores only the most promising paths in the trellis, and backtracks when evidence accumulates that a wrong turning has been taken. Sequential decoding is used when the trellis is too big for us to be able to apply the maximum likelihood algorithm, the min–sum algorithm. You can read about sequential decoding in Johannesson and Zigangirov (1999).

For further information about the use of the sum–product algorithm in turbo codes, and the rarely-used but highly recommended stopping criteria for halting their decoding algorithm Frey (1998) is highly recommended. (And there's lots more good stuff in the same book!)

48.6 Solutions

Solution to exercise 48.2 (p.578). The first bit was flipped. The most probable path is the upper one in figure 48.7.

49

Repeat–Accumulate Codes

In Chapter 1 we discussed a very simple and not very effective method for communicating over a noisy channel: the repetition code. We now discuss a code that is almost as simple, and whose performance is outstandingly good.

Repeat–accumulate codes were studied by Divsalar *et al.* (1998) for theoretical purposes, as simple turbo-like codes that might be more amenable to analysis than messy turbo codes. Their practical performance turned out to be just as good as other sparse graph codes.

▶ 49.1 The encoder

1. Take K source bits.
$$s_1 s_2 s_3 \ldots s_K$$

2. Repeat each bit three times, giving $N = 3K$ bits.
$$s_1 s_1 s_1 s_2 s_2 s_2 s_3 s_3 s_3 \ldots s_K s_K s_K$$

3. Permute these N bits using a random permutation (a fixed random permutation – the same one for every codeword). Call the permuted string $\mathbf{u}$.
$$u_1 u_2 u_3 u_4 u_5 u_6 u_7 u_8 u_9 \ldots u_N$$

4. Transmit the *accumulated sum*.
$$
\begin{aligned}
t_1 &= u_1 \\
t_2 &= t_1 + u_2 \,(\mathrm{mod}\,2) \\
\ldots \quad t_n &= t_{n-1} + u_n \,(\mathrm{mod}\,2) \quad \ldots \qquad (49.1)\\
t_N &= t_{N-1} + u_N \,(\mathrm{mod}\,2).
\end{aligned}
$$

5. That's it!

▶ 49.2 Graph

Figure 49.1a shows the graph of a repeat–accumulate code, using four types of node: equality constraints ⊟, intermediate binary variables (black circles), parity constraints ⊞, and the transmitted bits (white circles).

The source sets the values of the black bits at the bottom, three at a time, and the accumulator computes the transmitted bits along the top.

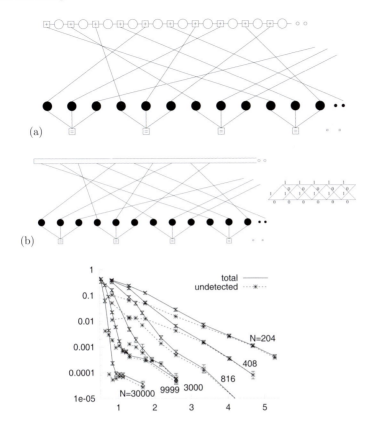

Figure 49.1. Factor graphs for a repeat–accumulate code with rate 1/3. (a) Using elementary nodes. Each white circle represents a transmitted bit. Each ⊞ constraint forces the sum of the 3 bits to which it is connected to be even. Each black circle represents an intermediate binary variable. Each ⊟ constraint forces the three variables to which it is connected to be equal.
(b) Factor graph normally used for decoding. The top rectangle represents the trellis of the accumulator, shown in the inset.

Figure 49.2. Performance of six rate-$1/3$ repeat–accumulate codes on the Gaussian channel. The blocklengths range from $N = 204$ to $N = 30\,000$. Vertical axis: block error probability; horizontal axis: E_b/N_0. The dotted lines show the frequency of undetected errors.

This graph is a factor graph for the prior probability over codewords, with the circles being binary variable nodes, and the squares representing two types of factor nodes. As usual, each ⊞ contributes a factor of the form $\mathbb{1}[\sum x = 0 \bmod 2]$; each ⊟ contributes a factor of the form $\mathbb{1}[x_1 = x_2 = x_3]$.

▶ 49.3 Decoding

The repeat–accumulate code is normally decoded using the sum–product algorithm on the factor graph depicted in figure 49.1b. The top box represents the trellis of the accumulator, including the channel likelihoods. In the first half of each iteration, the top trellis receives likelihoods for every transition in the trellis, and runs the forward–backward algorithm so as to produce likelihoods for each variable node. In the second half of the iteration, these likelihoods are multiplied together at the ⊟ nodes to produce new likelihood messages to send back to the trellis.

As with Gallager codes and turbo codes, the stop-when-it's-done decoding method can be applied, so it is possible to distinguish between undetected errors (which are caused by low-weight codewords in the code) and detected errors (where the decoder gets stuck and knows that it has failed to find a valid answer).

Figure 49.3 shows the performance of six randomly constructed repeat–accumulate codes on the Gaussian channel. If one does not mind the error floor which kicks in at about a block error probability of 10^{-4}, the performance is staggeringly good for such a simple code (c.f. figure 47.17).

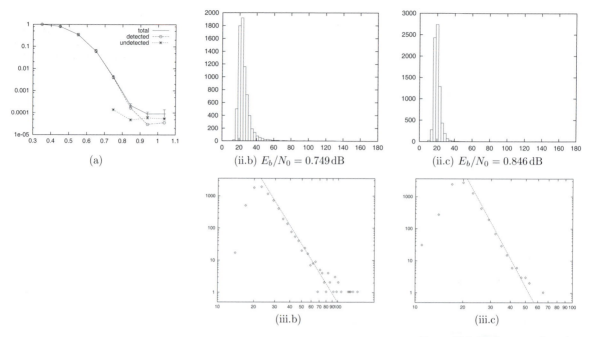

(a)   (ii.b) $E_b/N_0 = 0.749\,\text{dB}$ (ii.c) $E_b/N_0 = 0.846\,\text{dB}$

(iii.b)   (iii.c)

Figure 49.3. Histograms of number of iterations to find a valid decoding for a repeat–accumulate code with source block length $K = 10\,000$ and transmitted block length $N = 30\,000$. (a) Block error probability versus signal to noise ratio for the RA code. (ii.b) Histogram for $x/\sigma = 0.89$, $E_b/N_0 = 0.749\,\text{dB}$. (ii.c) $x/\sigma = 0.90$, $E_b/N_0 = 0.846\,\text{dB}$. (iii.b, iii.c) Fits of power laws to (ii.b) $(1/\tau^6)$ and (ii.c) $(1/\tau^9)$.

▶ **49.4 Empirical distribution of decoding times**

It is interesting to study the number of iterations τ of the sum–product algorithm required to decode a sparse graph code. Given one code and a set of channel conditions the decoding time varies randomly from trial to trial. We find that the histogram of decoding times follows a power law, $P(\tau) \propto \tau^{-p}$, for large τ. The power p depends on the signal to noise ratio and becomes smaller (so that the distribution is more heavy-tailed) as the signal to noise ratio decreases. We have observed power laws in repeat–accumulate codes and in irregular and regular Gallager codes. Figures 49.3(ii) and (iii) show the distribution of decoding times of a repeat–accumulate code at two different signal-to-noise ratios. The power laws extend over several orders of magnitude.

Exercise 49.1.[5] Investigate these power laws. Does density evolution predict them? Can the design of a code be used to manipulate the power law in a useful way?

▶ **49.5 Generalized parity-check matrices**

I find that it is helpful when relating sparse graph codes to each other to use a common representation for them all. Forney (2001) introduced the idea of a *normal graph* in which the only nodes are ⊞ and ⊟ and all variable nodes have degree one or two; variable nodes with degree two can be represented on edges that connect a ⊞ node to a ⊟ node. The *generalized parity-check matrix* is a graphical way of representing normal graphs. In a parity-check matrix, the columns are transmitted bits, and the rows are linear constraints. In a generalized parity-check matrix, additional columns may be included, which represent state variables that are not transmitted. One way of thinking of these state variables is that they are punctured from the code before transmission.

State variables are indicated by a horizontal line above the corresponding columns. The other pieces of diagrammatic notation for generalized parity-

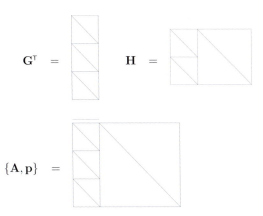

$$\mathbf{G}^{\mathsf{T}} \quad = \qquad \qquad \mathbf{H} \quad =$$

$$\{\mathbf{A}, \mathbf{p}\} \quad =$$

Figure 49.4. The generator matrix, parity-check matrix, and a generalized parity-check matrix of a repetition code with rate $^1/_3$.

check matrices are, as in (MacKay, 1999b; MacKay *et al.*, 1998):

- A diagonal line in a square indicates that that part of the matrix contains an identity matrix.

- Two or more parallel diagonal lines indicate a band-diagonal matrix with a corresponding number of 1s per row.

- A horizontal ellipse with an arrow on it indicates that the corresponding columns in a block are randomly permuted.

- A vertical ellipse with an arrow on it indicates that the corresponding rows in a block are randomly permuted.

- An integer surrounded by a circle represents that number of superposed random permutation matrices.

Definition. A generalized parity-check matrix is a pair $\{\mathbf{A}, \mathbf{p}\}$, where $\mathbf{A}$ is a binary matrix and $\mathbf{p}$ is a list of the punctured bits. The matrix defines a set of *valid vectors* $\mathbf{x}$, satisfying

$$\mathbf{A}\mathbf{x} = 0; \qquad (49.2)$$

for each valid vector there is a codeword $\mathbf{t}(\mathbf{x})$ that is obtained by puncturing from $\mathbf{x}$ the bits indicated by $\mathbf{p}$. For any one code there are many generalized parity-check matrices.

The *rate* of a code with generalized parity-check matrix $\{\mathbf{A}, \mathbf{p}\}$ can be estimated as follows. If $\mathbf{A}$ is $L \times M'$, and $\mathbf{p}$ punctures S bits and selects N bits for transmission ($L = N + S$), then the effective number of constraints on the codeword, M, is

$$M = M' - S, \qquad (49.3)$$

the number of source bits is

$$K = N - M = L - M', \qquad (49.4)$$

and the rate is greater than or equal to

$$R = 1 - \frac{M}{N} = 1 - \frac{M' - S}{L - S}. \qquad (49.5)$$

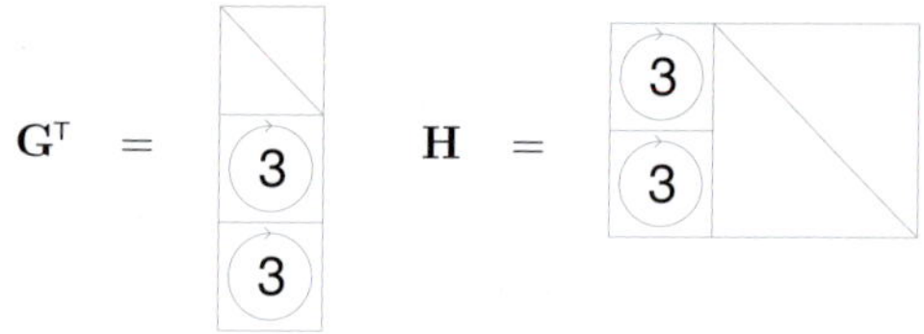

$$\mathbf{G}^{\mathsf{T}} = \boxed{\begin{array}{c} \\ \hline \boxed{3} \\ \hline \boxed{3} \end{array}} \qquad \mathbf{H} = \boxed{\begin{array}{cc} \boxed{3} & \\ \boxed{3} & \end{array}}$$

Figure 49.5. The generator matrix and parity-check matrix of a systematic low-density generator-matrix code. The code has rate $1/3$.

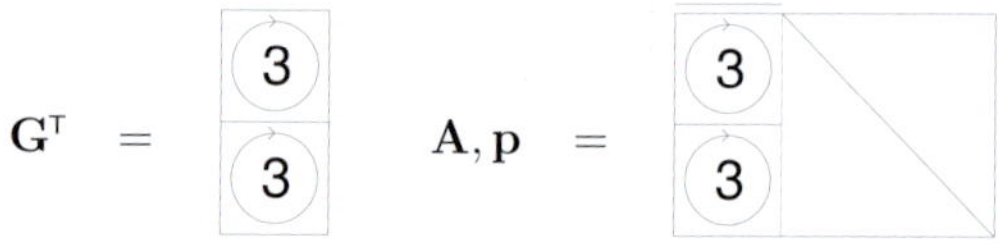

$$\mathbf{G}^{\mathsf{T}} = \boxed{\begin{array}{c} \boxed{3} \\ \hline \boxed{3} \end{array}} \qquad \mathbf{A}, \mathbf{p} = \boxed{\begin{array}{cc} \boxed{3} & \\ \boxed{3} & \end{array}}$$

Figure 49.6. The generator matrix and generalized parity-check matrix of a *non-systematic* low-density generator-matrix code. The code has rate $1/2$.

Examples

Repetition code. The generator matrix, parity-check matrix, and generalized parity-check matrix of a simple rate-$1/3$ repetition code are shown in figure 49.4.

Systematic low-density generator-matrix code. In an (N, K) systematic low-density generator-matrix code, there are no state variables. A transmitted codeword $\mathbf{t}$ of length N is given by

$$\mathbf{t} = \mathbf{G}^{\mathsf{T}}\mathbf{s}, \tag{49.6}$$

where

$$\mathbf{G}^{\mathsf{T}} = \left[\begin{array}{c} \mathbf{I}_K \\ \mathbf{P} \end{array} \right], \tag{49.7}$$

with $\mathbf{I}_K$ denoting the $K \times K$ identity matrix, and $\mathbf{P}$ being a very sparse $M \times K$ matrix, where $M = N - K$. The parity-check matrix of this code is

$$\mathbf{H} = [\mathbf{P}|\mathbf{I}_M]. \tag{49.8}$$

In the case of a rate $1/3$ code, this parity-check matrix might be represented as shown in figure 49.5.

Non-systematic low-density generator-matrix code. In an (N, K) non-systematic low-density generator-matrix code, a transmitted codeword $\mathbf{t}$ of length N is given by

$$\mathbf{t} = \mathbf{G}^{\mathsf{T}}\mathbf{s}, \tag{49.9}$$

where $\mathbf{G}^{\mathsf{T}}$ is a very sparse $N \times K$ matrix. The generalized parity-check matrix of this code is

$$\mathbf{A} = \left[\overline{\mathbf{G}^{\mathsf{T}}} | \mathbf{I}_N \right], \tag{49.10}$$

and the corresponding generalized parity-check equation is

$$\mathbf{A}\mathbf{x} = 0, \quad \text{where } \mathbf{x} = \left[\begin{array}{c} \mathbf{s} \\ \mathbf{t} \end{array} \right]. \tag{49.11}$$

Whereas the parity-check matrix of this simple code is typically a complex, dense matrix, the generalized parity-check matrix retains the underlying simplicity of the code.

In the case of a rate-$1/2$ code, this generalized parity-check matrix might be represented as shown in figure 49.6.

Low-density parity-check codes and linear MN codes. The parity-check matrix of a rate-1/3 low-density parity-check code is shown in figure 49.7a.

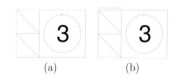

(a)　　　(b)

Figure 49.7. The generalized parity-check matrices of (a) a rate-$1/3$ Gallager code with $M/2$ columns of weight 2; (b) a rate-$1/2$ linear MN code.

A linear MN code is a non-systematic low-density parity-check code. The K state bits of an MN code are the source bits. Figure 49.7b shows the generalized parity-check matrix of a rate-1/2 linear MN code.

Convolutional codes. In a non-systematic, non-recursive convolutional code, the source bits, which play the role of state bits, are fed into a delay-line and two linear functions of the delay-line are transmitted. In figure 49.8a, these two parity streams are shown as two successive vectors of length K. [It is common to interleave these two parity streams, a bit-reordering that is not relevant here, and is not illustrated.]

Concatenation. 'Parallel concatenation' of two codes is represented in one of these diagrams by aligning the matrices of two codes in such a way that the 'source bits' line up, and by adding blocks of zero-entries to the matrix such that the state bits and parity bits of the two codes occupy separate columns. An example is given by the turbo code below. In 'serial concatenation', the columns corresponding to the *transmitted* bits of the first code are aligned with the columns corresponding to the *source* bits of the second code.

Turbo codes. A turbo code is the parallel concatenation of two convolutional codes. The generalized parity-check matrix of a rate-1/3 turbo code is shown in figure 49.8b.

Repeat–accumulate codes. The generalized parity-check matrices of a rate-1/3 repeat–accumulate code is shown in figure 49.9. Repeat-accumulate codes are equivalent to staircase codes (section 47.7, p.569).

Intersection. The generalized parity-check matrix of the intersection of two codes is made by stacking their generalized parity-check matrices on top of each other in such a way that all the transmitted bits' columns are correctly aligned, and any punctured bits associated with the two component codes occupy separate columns.

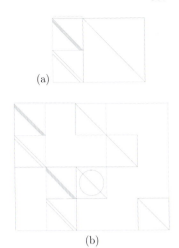

(a)

(b)

Figure 49.8. The generalized parity-check matrices of (a) a convolutional code with rate $^1/_2$. (b) a rate-$^1/_3$ turbo code built by parallel concatenation of two convolutional codes.

Figure 49.9. The generalized parity-check matrix of a repeat–accumulate code with rate $^1/_3$.

About Chapter 50

The following exercise provides a helpful background for digital fountain codes.

▷ Exercise 50.1.[3] An author proofreads his $K = 700$-page book by inspecting random pages. He makes N page-inspections, and does not take any precautions to avoid inspecting the same page twice.

(a) After $N = K$ page-inspections, what fraction of pages do you expect have never been inspected?

(b) After $N > K$ page-inspections, what is the probability that one or more pages have never been inspected?

(c) Show that in order for the probability that all K pages have been inspected to be $1 - \delta$, we require $N \simeq K \ln(K/\delta)$ page-inspections.

[This problem is commonly presented in terms of throwing N balls at random into K bins; what's the probability that every bin has at least one ball?]

Digital Fountain Codes

Digital fountain codes are record-breaking sparse-graph codes for channels with erasures.

Channels with erasures are of great importance. For example, files sent over the internet are chopped into packets, and each packet is either received without error or not received. A simple channel model describing this situation is a q-ary erasure channel, which has (for all inputs in the input alphabet $\{0, 1, 2, \ldots, q-1\}$) a probability $1 - f$ of transmitting the input without error, and probability f of delivering the output '?'. The alphabet size q is 2^l, where l is the number of bits in a packet.

Common methods for communicating over such channels employ a feedback channel from receiver to sender that is used to control the retransmission of erased packets. For example, the receiver might send back messages that identify the *missing* packets, which are then retransmitted. Alternatively, the receiver might send back messages that acknowledge each *received* packet; the sender keeps track of which packets have been acknowledged and retransmits the others until all packets have been acknowledged.

These simple retransmission protocols have the advantage that they will work regardless of the erasure probability f, but purists who have learned their Shannon theory will feel that these retransmission protocols are wasteful. If the erasure probability f is large, the number of feedback messages sent by the first protocol will be large. Under the second protocol, it's likely that the receiver will end up receiving multiple redundant copies of some packets, and heavy use is made of the feedback channel. According to Shannon, there is no need for the feedback channel: the capacity of the forward channel is $(1 - f)l$ bits, whether or not we have feedback.

The wastefulness of the simple retransmission protocols is especially evident in the case of a broadcast channel with erasures – channels where one sender broadcasts to many receivers, and each receiver receives a random fraction $(1 - f)$ of the packets. If every packet that is missed by one or more receivers has to be retransmitted, those retransmissions will be terribly redundant. Every receiver will have already received most of the retransmitted packets.

So, we would like to make erasure-correcting codes that require no feedback or almost no feedback. The classic block codes for erasure correction are called Reed–Solomon codes. An (N, K) Reed–Solomon code (over an alphabet of size $q = 2^l$) has the ideal property that if any K of the N transmitted symbols are received then the original K source symbols can be recovered. [See Berlekamp (1968) or Lin and Costello (1983) for further information; Reed–Solomon codes exist for $N < q$.] But Reed–Solomon codes have the disadvantage that they are practical only for small K, N, and q: standard implementations of encoding and decoding have a cost of order $K(N-K)\log_2 N$ packet operations. Furthermore, with a Reed–Solomon code, as with any block code, one must estimate the erasure probability f and choose the code rate $R = K/N$ *before* transmission. If we are unlucky and f is larger than expected and the receiver receives fewer than K symbols, what are we to do? We'd like a simple way to extend the code on the fly to create a lower-rate (N', K) code. For Reed–Solomon codes, no such on-the-fly method exists.

There is a better way, pioneered by Michael Luby (2002) at his company Digital Fountain, the first company whose business is based on sparse graph codes.

The digital fountain codes I describe here, *LT codes*, were invented by Luby in 1998. The idea of a digital fountain code is as follows. The encoder is a fountain that produces an endless supply of water drops (encoded packets); let's say the original source file has a size of Kl bits, and each drop contains l encoded bits. Now, anyone who wishes to receive the encoded file holds a bucket under the fountain and collects drops until the number of drops in the bucket is a little larger than K. They can then recover the original file.

LT stands for 'Luby transform'.

Digital fountain codes are *rateless* in the sense that the number of encoded packets that can be generated from the source message is potentially limitless; and the number of encoded packets generated can be determined on the fly. Regardless of the statistics of the erasure events on the channel, we can send as many encoded packets as are needed in order for the decoder to recover the source data. The source data can be decoded from any set of K' encoded packets, for K' slightly larger than K (in practice, about 5% larger).

Digital fountain codes also have fantastically small encoding and decoding complexities. With probability $1 - \delta$, K packets can be communicated with average encoding and decoding costs both of order $K \ln(K/\delta)$ packet operations.

Luby calls these codes *universal* because they are simultaneously near-optimal for every erasure channel, and they are very efficient as the file length K grows. The overhead $K' - K$ is of order $\sqrt{K}(\ln(K/\delta))^2$.

▶ 50.1 A digital fountain's encoder

> Each encoded packet t_n is produced from the source file $s_1 s_2 s_3 \dots s_K$ as follows:
>
> 1. Randomly choose the degree d_n of the packet from a degree distribution $\rho(d)$; the appropriate choice of ρ depends on the source file size K, as we'll discuss later.
>
> 2. Choose, uniformly at random, d_n distinct input packets, and set t_n equal to the bitwise sum, modulo 2 of those d_n packets. This sum can be done by successively exclusive-or-ing the packets together.

This encoding operation defines a graph connecting encoded packets to source packets. If the mean degree $\bar{d}$ is significantly smaller than K then the graph is sparse. We can think of the resulting code as an irregular low-density generator-matrix code.

The decoder needs to know the degree of each packet that is received, and which source packets it is connected to in the graph. This information can be communicated to the decoder in various ways. For example, if the sender and receiver have synchronized clocks, they could use identical pseudo-random number generators, seeded by the clock, to choose each random degree and each set of connections. Alternatively, the sender could pick a random key, κ_n, given which the degree and the connections are determined by a pseudo-random process, and send that key in the header of the packet. As long as the packet size l is much bigger than the key size (which need only be 32 bits or so), this key introduces only a small overhead cost.

50.2 The decoder

Decoding a sparse graph code is especially easy in the case of an erasure channel. The decoder's task is to recover $\mathbf{s}$ from $\mathbf{t} = \mathbf{Gs}$, where $\mathbf{G}$ is the matrix associated with the graph. The simple way to attempt to solve this problem is by message-passing. We can think of the decoding algorithm as the sum–product algorithm if we wish, but all messages are either *completely uncertain* messages or *completely certain* messages. Uncertain messages assert that a message packet s_k could have any value, with equal probability; certain messages assert that s_k has a particular value, with probablity one.

This simplicity of the messages allows a simple description of the decoding process. We'll call the encoded packets $\{t_n\}$ check nodes.

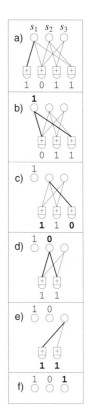

Figure 50.1. Example decoding for a digital fountain code with $K = 3$ source bits and $N = 4$ encoded bits.

---

1. Find a check node t_n that is connected to *only one* source packet s_k. (If there is no such check node, this decoding algorithm halts at this point, and fails to recover all the source packets.)

   (a) Set $s_k = t_n$.

   (b) Add s_k to all checks $t_{n'}$ that are connected to s_k:

   $$t_{n'} := t_{n'} + s_k \quad \text{for all } n' \text{ such that } G_{n'k} = 1. \quad (50.1)$$

   (c) Remove all the edges connected to the source packet s_k.

2. Repeat (1) until all $\{s_k\}$ are determined.

This decoding process is illustrated in figure 50.1 for a toy case where each packet is just one bit. There are three source packets (shown by the upper circles) and four received packets (shown by the lower check symbols), which have the values $t_1 t_2 t_3 t_4 = 1011$ at the start of the algorithm.

At the first iteration, the only check node that is connected to a sole source bit is the first check node (panel a). We set that source bit s_1 accordingly (panel b), discard the check node, then add the value of s_1 (1) to the checks to which it is connected (panel c), disconnecting s_1 from the graph. At the start of the second iteration (panel c), the fourth check node is connected to a sole source bit, s_2. We set s_2 to t_4 (0, in panel d), and add s_2 to the two checks it is connected to (panel e). Finally, we find that two check nodes are both connected to s_3, and they agree about the value of s_3 (as we would hope!), which is restored in panel f.

50.3 Designing the degree distribution

The probability distribution $\rho(d)$ of the degree is a critical part of the design: occasional encoded packets must have high degree (i.e., d similar to K) in order to ensure that there are not some source packets that are connected to no-one. Many packets must have low degree, so that the decoding process can get started, and keep going, and so that the total number of addition operations involved in the encoding and decoding is kept small. For a given degree distribution $\rho(d)$, the statistics of the decoding process can be predicted by an appropriate version of density evolution.

Ideally, to avoid redundancy, we'd like the received graph to have the property that just one check node has degree one at each iteration. At each iteration, when this check node is processed, the degrees in the graph are reduced in such a way that one new degree-one check node appears. *In expectation,* this ideal behaviour is achieved by the *ideal soliton distribution,*

$$
\begin{aligned}
\rho(1) &= 1/K \\
\rho(d) &= \frac{1}{d(d-1)} \quad \text{for } d = 2, 3, \ldots, K.
\end{aligned}
\tag{50.2}
$$

The expected degree under this distribution is roughly $\ln K$.

▷ Exercise 50.2.[2] Derive the ideal soliton distribution. At the first iteration ($t = 0$) let the number of packets of degree d be $h_0(d)$; show that (for $d > 1$) the expected number of packets of degree d that have their degree reduced to $d - 1$ is $h_0(d)d/K$; and at the tth iteration, when t of the K packets have been recovered and the number of packets of degree d is $h_t(d)$, the expected number of packets of degree d that have their degree reduced to $d - 1$ is $h_t(d)d/K - t$. Hence show that in order to have the expected number of packets of degree 1 satisfy $h_t(1) = 1$ for all $t \in \{0, \ldots K-1\}$, we must to start with have $h_0(1) = 1$ and $h_0(2) = K/2$; and more generally, $h_t(2) = (K - t)/2$; then by recursion solve for $h_0(d)$ for $d = 3$ upwards.

This degree distribution works poorly in practice, because fluctuations around the expected behaviour make it very likely that at some point in the decoding process there will be no degree-one check nodes; and, furthermore, a few source nodes will receive no connections at all. A small modification fixes these problems.

The *robust soliton distribution* has two extra parameters, c and δ; it is designed to ensure that the expected number of degree-one checks is about

$$
S \equiv c \ln(K/\delta)\sqrt{K},
\tag{50.3}
$$

rather than 1, throughout the decoding process. The parameter δ is a bound on the probability that the decoding fails to run to completion after a certain number K' of packets have been received. The parameter c is a constant of order 1, if our aim is to prove Luby's main theorem about LT codes; in practice however it can be viewed as a free parameter, with a value somewhat smaller than 1 giving good results. We define a positive function

$$
\tau(d) = \begin{cases}
\frac{S}{K}\frac{1}{d} & \text{for } d = 1, 2, \ldots (K/S)-1 \\
\frac{S}{K}\ln(S/\delta) & \text{for } d = K/S \\
0 & \text{for } d > K/S
\end{cases}
\tag{50.4}
$$

(see figure 50.2 and exercise 50.4 (p.594)) then add the ideal soliton distribution ρ to τ and normalize to obtain the robust soliton distribution, μ:

$$
\mu(d) = \frac{\rho(d) + \tau(d)}{Z},
\tag{50.5}
$$

where $Z = \sum_d \rho(d) + \tau(d)$. The number of encoded packets required at the receiving end to ensure that the decoding can run to completion, with probability at least $1 - \delta$, is $K' = KZ$.

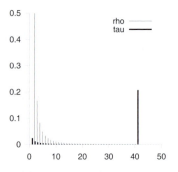

Figure 50.2. The distributions $\rho(d)$ and $\tau(d)$ for the case $K = 10\,000$, $c = 0.2$, $\delta = 0.05$, which gives $S = 244$, $K/S = 41$, and $Z \simeq 1.3$. The distribution τ is largest at $d = 1$ and $d = K/S$.

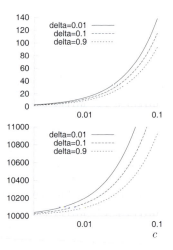

Figure 50.3. The number of degree-one checks S (upper figure) and the quantity K' (lower figure) as a function of the two parameters c and δ, for $K = 10\,000$. Luby's main theorem proves that there exists a value of c such that, given K' received packets, the decoding algorithm will recover the K source packets with probability $1 - \delta$.

Luby's (2002) analysis explains how the small-d end of τ has the role of ensuring that the decoding process gets started, and the spike in τ at $d = K/S$ is included to ensure that every source packet is likely to be connected to a check at least once. Luby's key result is that (for an appropriate value of the constant c) receiving $K' = K + 2\ln(S/\delta)S$ checks ensures that all packets can be recovered with probability at least $1 - \delta$. In the illustrative figures I have set the allowable decoder failure probability δ quite large, because the actual failure probability is much smaller than is suggested by Luby's conservative analysis.

In practice, LT can be tuned so that a file of original size $K \simeq 10\,000$ packets is recovered with an overhead of about 5%. Figure 50.4 shows histograms of the actual number of packets required for a couple of settings of the parameters, achieving mean overheads smaller than 5% and 10% respectively.

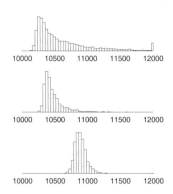

Figure 50.4. Histograms of the actual number of packets N required in order to recover a file of size $K = 10\,000$ packets. The parameters were as follows: top histogram: $c = 0.01$, $\delta = 0.5$ ($S = 10$, $K/S = 1010$, and $Z \simeq 1.01$); middle: $c = 0.03$, $\delta = 0.5$ ($S = 30$, $K/S = 337$, and $Z \simeq 1.03$); bottom: $c = 0.1$, $\delta = 0.5$ ($S = 99$, $K/S = 101$, and $Z \simeq 1.1$).

▶ 50.4 Applications

Digital fountain codes are an excellent solution in a wide variety of situations. Let's mention two.

Storage

You wish to make a backup of a large file, but you are aware that your magnetic tapes and hard drives are all unreliable in the sense that catastrophic failures, in which some stored packets are permanently lost within one device, occur at a rate of something like 10^{-3} per day. How should you store your file?

A digital fountain can be used to spray encoded packets all over the place, on every storage device available. Then to recover the backup file, whose size was K packets, one simply needs to find $K' \simeq K$ packets from anywhere. Corrupted packets do not matter; we simply skip over them and find more packets elsewhere.

This method of storage also has advantages in terms of *speed* of file recovery. In a hard drive, it is standard practice to store a file in successive sectors of a hard drive, to allow rapid reading of the file; but if, as occasionally happens, a packet is lost (owing to the reading head being off track for a moment, giving a burst of errors that cannot be corrected by the packet's error-correcting code), a whole revolution of the drive must be performed to bring back the packet to the head for a second read. The time taken for one revolution produces an undesirable delay in the file system.

If files were instead stored using the digital fountain principle, with the digital drops stored in one or more consecutive sectors on the drive, then one would never need to endure the delay of re-reading a packet; packet loss would become less important, and the hard drive could consequently be operated faster, with higher noise level, and with fewer resources devoted to noisy-channel coding.

▷ Exercise 50.3.[2] Compare the digital fountain method of robust storage on multiple hard drives with RAID (the redundant array of independent disks).

Broadcast

Imagine that ten thousand subscribers in an area wish to receive a digital movie from a broadcaster. The broadcaster can send the movie in packets over a broadcast network – for example, by a wide-bandwidth phone line, or by satellite.

Imagine that not all packets are received at all the houses. Let's say $f = 0.1\%$ of them are lost at each house. In a standard approach in which the file is transmitted as a plain sequence of packets with no encoding, each house would have to notify the broadcaster of the fK missing packets, and request that they be retransmitted. And with ten thousand subscribers all requesting such retransmissions, there would be a retransmission request for almost every packet. Thus the broadcaster would have to repeat the entire broadcast twice in order to ensure that most subscribers have received the whole movie, and most users would have to wait roughly twice as long as the ideal time before the download was complete.

If the broadcaster uses a digital fountain to encode the movie, each subscriber can recover the movie from *any* $K' \simeq K$ packets. So the broadcast needs to last for only, say, $1.1K$ packets, and every house is very likely to have successfully recovered the whole file.

Another application is broadcasting data to cars. Imagine that we want to send updates to in-car navigation databases by satellite. There are hundreds of thousands of vehicles, and they can only receive data when they are out on the open road; there are no feedback channels. A standard method for sending the data is to put it in a *carousel*, broadcasting the packets in a fixed periodic sequence. 'Yes, a car may go through a tunnel, and miss out on a few hundred packets, but it will be able to collect those missed packets an hour later when the carousel has gone through a full revolution (we hope); or maybe the following day...'

If instead the satellite uses a digital fountain, each car needs to receive only an amount of data equal to the original file size (plus 5%).

Further reading

The encoders and decoders sold by Digital Fountain have even higher efficiency than the LT codes described here, and they work well for all block lengths, not only large lengths such as $K \gtrsim 10\,000$. Shokrollahi (2003) presents *Raptor codes*, which are an extension of LT codes with linear time encoding and decoding.

▶ 50.5 Further exercises

▷ Exercise 50.4.[2] Understanding the robust soliton distribution.

Repeat the analysis of exercise 50.2 (p.592) but now aim to have the expected number of packets of degree 1 be $h_t(1) = 1+S$ for all t, instead of 1. Show that the initial required number of packets is

$$h_0(d) = \frac{K}{d(d-1)} + \frac{S}{d} \quad \text{for } d > 1. \tag{50.6}$$

The reason for truncating the second term beyond $d = K/S$ and replacing it by the spike at $d = K/S$ (see equation (50.4)) is to ensure that the decoding complexity does not grow larger than $O(K \ln K)$.

Estimate the expected number of packets $\sum_d h_0(d)$ and the expected number of edges in the sparse graph $\sum_d h_0(d)d$ (which determines the decoding complexity) if the histogram of packets is as given in (50.6). Compare with the expected numbers of packets and edges when the robust soliton distribution (50.4) is used.

Exercise 50.5.[4] Show that the spike at $d = K/S$ (equation (50.4)) is an adequate replacement for the tail of high-weight packets in (50.6).

Exercise 50.6.[3C] Investigate experimentally how necessary the spike at $d = K/S$ (equation (50.4)) is for successful decoding. Investigate also whether the tail of $\rho(d)$ beyond $d = K/S$ is necessary. What happens if all high-weight degrees are removed, both the spike at $d = K/S$ and the tail of $\rho(d)$ beyond $d = K/S$?

Exercise 50.7.[4] Fill in the details in the proof of Luby's main theorem, that receiving $K' = K + 2\ln(S/\delta)S$ checks ensures that all the source packets can be recovered with probability at least $1 - \delta$.

Exercise 50.8.[4C] Optimize the degree distribution of a digital fountain code for a file of $K = 10\,000$ packets. Pick a sensible objective function for your optimization, such as minimizing the mean of N, the number of packets required for complete decoding, or the 95th percentile of the histogram of N (figure 50.4).

▷ Exercise 50.9.[3] Make a model of the situation where a data stream is broadcast to cars, and quantify the advantage that the digital fountain has over the carousel method.

Exercise 50.10.[2] Construct a simple example to illustrate the fact that the digital fountain decoder of section 50.2 is suboptimal – it sometimes gives up even though the information available is sufficient to decode the whole file. How does the cost of the optimal decoder compare?

▷ Exercise 50.11.[2] If every transmitted packet were created by adding together source packets at random with probability $^1/_2$ of each source packet's being included, show that the probability that $K' = K$ received packets suffice for the optimal decoder to be able to recover the K source packets is just a little below $1/2$. [To put it another way, what is the probability that a random $K \times K$ matrix has full rank?]

Show that if $K' = K + \Delta$ packets are received, the probability that they will not suffice for the optimal decoder is roughly $2^{-\Delta}$.

▷ Exercise 50.12.[3C] Implement an optimal digital fountain decoder that uses the method of Richardson and Urbanke (2001b) derived for fast *encoding* of sparse graph codes (section 47.7) to handle the matrix inversion required for optimal decoding. Now that you have changed the decoder, you can reoptimize the degree distribution, using higher weight packets. By how much can you reduce the overhead? Confirm the assertion that this approach makes digital fountain codes viable as erasure-correcting codes for all blocklengths, not just the large blocklengths for which LT codes are excellent.

▷ Exercise 50.13.[5] Digital fountain codes are excellent rateless codes for erasure channels. Make a rateless code for a channel that has both erasures and *noise*.

▶ **50.6 Summary of sparse graph codes**

A simple method for designing error-correcting codes for noisy channels, first pioneered by Gallager (1962), has recently been rediscovered and generalized, and communication theory has been transformed. The practical performance of Gallager's low-density parity-check codes and their modern cousins is vastly better than the performance of the codes with which textbooks have been filled in the intervening years.

Which sparse graph code is 'best' for a noisy channel depends on the chosen rate and blocklength, the permitted encoding and decoding complexity, and the question of whether occasional undetected errors are acceptable. Low–density parity–check codes are the most versatile; it's easy to make a competitive low–density parity–check code with almost any rate and block-length, and low–density parity–check codes virtually never make undetected errors.

For the special case of the erasure channel, the sparse graph codes that are best are digital fountain codes.

▶ **50.7 Conclusion**

The best solution to the communication problem is:

> Combine a simple, pseudo-random code
> with a message-passing decoder.

Part VII

Appendices

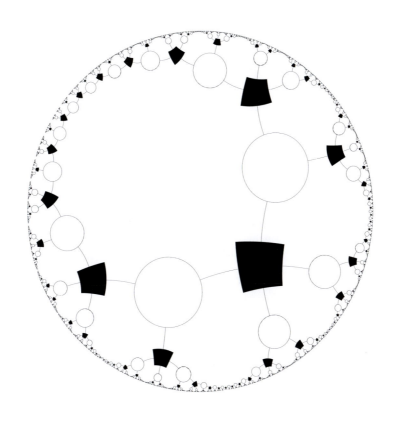

A

Notation

What does $P(A\,|\,B,C)$ **mean?** $P(A\,|\,B,C)$ is pronounced 'the probability that A is true *given that B is true and C is true*'. Or, more briefly, 'the probability of A given B and C'.

What do $\log$ **and** $\ln$ **mean?** In this book, $\log x$ means the base-two logarithm, $\log_2 x$; $\ln x$ means the natural logarithm, $\log_e x$.

What does $\hat{s}$ **mean?** Usually, a 'hat' over a variable denotes a guess or estimator. So $\hat{s}$ is a guess at the value of s.

Integrals. There is no difference between $\int f(u)\,\mathrm{d}u$ and $\int \mathrm{d}u\, f(u)$. The integrand is $f(u)$ in both cases.

What does $\displaystyle\prod_{n=1}^{N}$ **mean?** This is like the summation $\sum_{n=1}^{N}$ but it denotes a product. It's pronounced 'product over n from 1 to N'. So, for example,

$$\prod_{n=1}^{N} n = 1 \times 2 \times 3 \times \cdots \times N = N! = \exp\left[\sum_{n=1}^{N} \ln n\right]. \qquad (\text{A.1})$$

I like to choose the name of the free variable in a sum or a product – here, n – to be the lower case version of the range of the sum. So n usually runs from 1 to N, and m usually runs from 1 to M. This is a habit I learnt from Yaser Abu-Mostafa, and I think it makes formulae easier to understand.

What does $\dbinom{N}{n}$ **mean?** This is pronounced 'N choose n', and it is the number of ways of selecting an unordered set of n objects from a set of size N.

$$\binom{N}{n} = \frac{N!}{(N-n)!\,n!}. \qquad (\text{A.2})$$

This function is known as the combination function.

What is $\Gamma(x)$**?** The *gamma function* is defined by $\Gamma(x) \equiv \int_0^\infty \mathrm{d}u\, u^{x-1}e^{-u}$, for $x > 0$. The gamma function is an extension of the factorial function to real number arguments. In general, $\Gamma(x+1) = x\Gamma(x)$, and for integer arguments, $\Gamma(x+1) = x!$. The digamma function is defined by $\Psi(x) \equiv \frac{\mathrm{d}}{\mathrm{d}x}\log\Gamma(x)$.

For large x (for practical purposes, $0.1 \le x \le \infty$),

$$\log\Gamma(x) \simeq \left(x - \tfrac{1}{2}\right)\log(x) - x + \tfrac{1}{2}\log 2\pi + O(1/x); \qquad (\text{A.3})$$

and for small x (for practical purposes, $0 \leq x \leq 0.5$):

$$\log \Gamma(x) \simeq \log \frac{1}{x} - \gamma_e x + O(x^2) \tag{A.4}$$

where γ_e is Euler's constant.

What does $H_2^{-1}(1 - R/C)$ mean? Just as $\sin^{-1}(s)$ denotes the inverse function to $s = \sin(x)$, so $H_2^{-1}(h)$ is the inverse function to $h = H_2(x)$.

There is potential confusion when people use $\sin^2 x$ to denote $(\sin x)^2$, since then we might expect $\sin^{-1} s$ to denote $1/\sin(s)$; I therefore like to avoid using the notation $\sin^2 x$.

What does $f'(x)$ mean? The answer depends on the context. Often, a 'prime' is used to denote differentiation:

$$f'(x) \equiv \frac{\mathrm{d}}{\mathrm{d}x} f(x); \tag{A.5}$$

similarly, a dot denotes differentiation with respect to time, t:

$$\dot{x} \equiv \frac{\mathrm{d}}{\mathrm{d}t} x. \tag{A.6}$$

However, the prime is also a useful indicator for 'another variable', for example 'a new value for a variable'. So, for example, x' might denote 'the new value of x'. Also, if there are two integers that both range from 1 to N, I will often name those integers n and n'.

So my rule is: if a prime occurs in an expression that could be a function, such as $f'(x)$ or $h'(y)$, then it denotes differentiation; otherwise it indicates 'another variable'.

What is the error function? Definitions of this function vary. I define it to be the cumulative probability of a standard (variance $= 1$) normal distribution,

$$\Phi(z) \equiv \int_{-\infty}^{z} \exp(-z^2/2)/\sqrt{2\pi} \ \mathrm{d}z. \tag{A.7}$$

What does $\mathcal{E}(r)$ mean? $\mathcal{E}[r]$ is pronounced 'the expected value of r' or 'the expectation of r', and it is the mean value of r. Another symbol for 'expected value' is the pair of angle-brackets, $\langle r \rangle$.

What does $|x|$ mean? The vertical bars '$|\cdot|$' have two meanings. If $\mathcal{A}$ is a set, then $|\mathcal{A}|$ denotes the number of elements in the set; if x is a number, then $|x|$ is the absolute value of x.

What does $[\mathbf{A}|\mathbf{P}]$ mean? Here, $\mathbf{A}$ and $\mathbf{P}$ are matrices with the same number of rows. $[\mathbf{A}|\mathbf{P}]$ denotes the double-width matrix obtained by putting $\mathbf{A}$ alongside $\mathbf{P}$. The vertical bar is used to avoid confusion with the product $\mathbf{AP}$.

What does $\mathbf{x}^\mathsf{T}$ mean? The superscript T is pronounced 'transpose'. Transposing a row-vector turns it into a column vector:

$$(1, 2, 3)^\mathsf{T} = \begin{pmatrix} 1 \\ 2 \\ 3 \end{pmatrix}, \tag{A.8}$$

and *vice versa*. [Normally my vectors, indicated by bold face type ($\mathbf{x}$), are column vectors.]

Similarly, matrices can be transposed. If M_{ij} is the entry in row i and column j of matrix $\mathbf{M}$, and $\mathbf{N} = \mathbf{M}^\mathsf{T}$, then $N_{ji} = M_{ij}$.

What are $\text{Trace}\,\mathbf{M}$ **and** $\det\mathbf{M}$**?** The trace of a matrix is the sum of its diagonal elements,

$$\text{Trace}\,\mathbf{M} = \sum_i M_{ii}. \tag{A.9}$$

The determinant of $\mathbf{M}$ is denoted $\det\mathbf{M}$.

What does δ_{mn} **mean?** The δ matrix is the identity matrix.

$$\delta_{mn} = \begin{cases} 1 & \text{if } m = n \\ 0 & \text{if } m \neq n. \end{cases}$$

Another name for the identity matrix is $\mathbf{I}$ or $\mathbf{1}$. Sometimes I include a subscript on this symbol – $\mathbf{1}_K$ – which indicates the size of the matrix ($K \times K$).

What does $\delta(x)$ **mean?** The delta function has the property

$$\int dx\, f(x)\delta(x) = f(0). \tag{A.10}$$

Another possible meaning for $\delta(S)$ is the truth function, which is 1 if the proposition S is true but I have adopted another notation for that. After all, the symbol δ is quite busy already, with the two roles mentioned above in addition to its role as a small real number δ and an increment operator (as in δx)!

What does $\mathbb{1}[S]$ **mean?** $\mathbb{1}[S]$ is the truth function, which is 1 if the proposition S is true and 0 otherwise. For example, the number of positive numbers in the set $T = \{-2, 1, 3\}$ can be written

$$\sum_{x \in T} \mathbb{1}[x > 0]. \tag{A.11}$$

What is the difference between ':=' and '='? In an algorithm, $x := y$ means that the variable x is updated by assigning it the value of y.

In contrast, $x = y$ is a proposition, a statement that x is equal to y.

See Chapters 23 and 29 for further definitions and notation relating to probability distributions.

B

Some Physics

▶ B.1 About phase transitions

A system with states $\mathbf{x}$ in contact with a heat bath at temperature $T = 1/\beta$ has probability distribution

$$P(\mathbf{x}|\beta) = \frac{1}{Z(\beta)} \exp(-\beta E(\mathbf{x})). \tag{B.1}$$

The partition function is

$$Z(\beta) = \sum_{\mathbf{x}} \exp(-\beta E(\mathbf{x})). \tag{B.2}$$

The inverse temperature β can be interpreted as defining an exchange rate between entropy and energy. $(1/\beta)$ is the amount of energy that must be given to a heat bath to increase its entropy by one nat.

Often, the system will be affected by some other parameters such as the volume of the box it is in, V, in which case Z is a function of V too, $Z(\beta, V)$.

For any system with a finite number of states, the function $Z(\beta)$ is evidently a continuous function of β, since it is simply a sum of exponentials. Moreover, all the derivatives of $Z(\beta)$ with respect to β are continuous too.

What phase transitions are all about, however, is this: phase transitions correspond to values of β and V (called critical points) at which the derivatives of Z have discontinuities or divergences.

Immediately we can deduce:

> Only systems with an infinite number of states can show phase transitions.

Often, we include a parameter N describing the size of the system. Phase transitions may appear in the limit $N \to \infty$. Real systems may have a value of N like 10^{23}.

If we make the system large by simply grouping together N independent systems whose partition function is $Z_{(1)}(\beta)$, then nothing interesting happens. The partition function for N independent identical systems is simply

$$Z_{(N)}(\beta) = [Z_{(1)}(\beta)]^N. \tag{B.3}$$

Now, while this function $Z_{(N)}(\beta)$ may be a very rapidly varying function of β, that doesn't mean it is showing phase transitions. The natural way to look at the partition function is in the logarithm

$$\ln Z_{(N)}(\beta) = N \ln Z_{(1)}(\beta). \tag{B.4}$$

Duplicating the original system N times simply scales up all properties like the energy and heat capacity of the system by a factor of N. So if the original system showed no phase transitions then the scaled up system won't have any either.

> Only systems with long-range correlations show phase transitions.

Long-range correlations do not require long-range energetic couplings; for example, a magnet has only short-range couplings (between adjacent spins) but these are sufficient to create long-range order.

Why are points at which derivatives diverge interesting?

The derivatives of $\ln Z$ describe properties like the heat capacity of the system (that's the second derivative) or its fluctuations in energy. If the second derivative of $\ln Z$ diverges at a temperature $1/\beta$, then the heat capacity of the system diverges there, which means it can absorb or release energy without changing temperature (think of ice melting in ice water); when the system is at equilibrium at that temperature, its energy fluctuates a lot, in contrast to the normal law-of-large-numbers behaviour, where the energy only varies by one part in $\sqrt{N}$.

A toy system that shows a phase transition

Imagine a collection of N coupled spins that have the following energy as a function of their state $\mathbf{x} \in \{0, 1\}^N$.

$$E(\mathbf{x}) = \begin{cases} -N\epsilon & \mathbf{x} = (0, 0, 0, \dots, 0) \\ 0 & \text{otherwise.} \end{cases} \tag{B.5}$$

This energy function describes a ground state in which all the spins are aligned in the zero direction; the energy per spin in this state is $-\epsilon$. if any spin changes state then the energy is zero. This model is like an extreme version of a magnetic interaction, which encourages pairs of spins to be aligned.

We can contrast it with an ordinary system of N *independent* spins whose energy is:

$$E^0(\mathbf{x}) = \epsilon \sum_n (2x_n - 1). \tag{B.6}$$

Like the first system, the system of independent spins has a single ground state $(0, 0, 0, \dots, 0)$ with energy $-N\epsilon$, and it has roughly 2^N states with energy very close to 0, so the low-temperature and high-temperature properties of the independent-spin system and the coupled-spin system are virtually identical.

The partition function of the coupled-spin system is given by

$$Z(\beta) = e^{\beta N\epsilon} + 2^N - 1. \tag{B.7}$$

The function

$$\ln Z(\beta) = \ln\left(e^{\beta N\epsilon} + 2^N - 1\right) \tag{B.8}$$

is sketched in figure B.1a along with its low temperature behaviour,

$$\ln Z(\beta) \simeq N\beta\epsilon, \quad \beta \to \infty, \tag{B.9}$$

and its high temperature behaviour,

$$\ln Z(\beta) \simeq N \ln 2, \quad \beta \to 0. \tag{B.10}$$

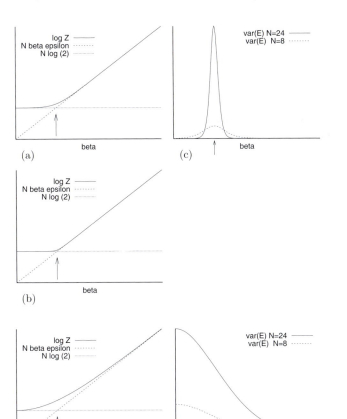

Figure B.1. (a) Partition function of toy system which shows a phase transition for large N. The arrow marks the point $\beta_c = \log 2/\epsilon$. (b) The same, for larger N. (c) The variance of the energy of the system as a function of β for two system sizes. As N increases the variance has an increasingly sharp peak at the critical point β_c. Contrast with figure B.2.

Figure B.2. The partition function (a) and energy-variance (b) of a system consisting of N independent spins. The partition function changes gradually from one asymptote to the other, regardless of how large N is; the variance of the energy does not have a peak. The fluctuations are largest at high temperature (small β) and scale linearly with system size N.

The arrow marks the point

$$\beta = \frac{\ln 2}{\epsilon} \tag{B.11}$$

at which these two asymptotes intersect. In the limit $N \to \infty$, the graph of $\ln Z(\beta)$ becomes more and more sharply bent at this point (figure B.1b).

The second derivative of $\ln Z$, which describes the variance of the energy of the system, has a peak value, at $\beta = \ln 2/\epsilon$, roughly equal to

$$\frac{N^2 \epsilon^2}{4}, \tag{B.12}$$

which corresponds to the system spending half of its time in the ground state and half its time in the other states.

At this critical point, the heat capacity of this system is thus proportional to N^2; the heat capacity per spin is proportional to N, which, for infinite N, is infinite, in contrast to the behaviour of systems away from phase transitions, whose capacity per atom is a finite number.

For comparison, figure B.2 shows the partition function and energy-variance of the ordinary independent-spin system.

More generally

Phase transitions can be categorized into 'first-order' and 'continuous' transitions. In a first-order phase transition, there is a discontinuous change of one or more order-parameters; in a continuous transition, all order-parameters change continuously. [What's an order-parameter? – a scalar function of the state of the system; or, to be precise, the expectation of such a function.]

In the vicinity of a critical point, the concept of 'typicality' defined in Chapter 4 does not hold. For example, our toy system, at its critical point, has a 50% chance of being in a state with energy $-N\epsilon$, and roughly a $1/2^{N+1}$ chance of being in each of the other states that have energy zero. It is thus not the case that $\ln 1/P(\mathbf{x})$ is very likely to be close to the entropy of the system at this point, unlike a system with N i.i.d. components.

Remember that information content $(\ln 1/P(\mathbf{x}))$ and energy are very closely related. If typicality holds, then the system's energy has negligible fluctuations, and *vice versa*.

C

Some Mathematics

► C.1 Finite field theory

Most linear codes are expressed in the language of Galois theory

Why are Galois fields an appropriate language for linear codes? First, a definition and some examples.

A field F is a set $F = \{0, F'\}$ such that

1. F forms an Abelian group under an addition operation '+', with 0 being the identity; [Abelian means all elements commute, i.e., satisfy $a + b = b + a$.]

2. F' forms an Abelian group under a multiplication operation '·'; multiplication of any element by 0 yields 0;

3. these operations satisfy the distributive rule $(a + b) \cdot c = a \cdot c + b \cdot c$.

For example, the real numbers form a field, with '+' and '·' denoting ordinary addition and multiplication.

A Galois field $GF(q)$ is a field with a finite number of elements q.

A unique Galois field exists for any $q = p^m$, where p is a prime number and m is a positive integer; there are no other finite fields.

$GF(2)$. The addition and multiplication tables for $GF(2)$ are shown in table C.1. These are the rules of addition and multiplication modulo 2.

$GF(p)$. For any prime number p, the addition and multiplication rules are those for ordinary addition and multiplication, modulo p.

$GF(4)$. The rules for $GF(p^m)$, with $m > 1$, are *not* those of ordinary addition and multiplication. For example the tables for $GF(4)$ (table C.2) are *not* the rules of addition and multiplication modulo 4. Notice that $1 + 1 = 0$, for example. So how can $GF(4)$ be described? It turns out that the elements can be related to *polynomials*. Consider polynomial functions of x of degree 1 and with coefficients that are elements of $GF(2)$. The polynomials shown in table C.3 obey the addition and multiplication rules of $GF(4)$ *if* addition and multiplication are modulo the polynomial $x^2 + x + 1$, and the coefficients of the polynomials are from $GF(2)$. For example, $B \cdot B = x^2 + (1 + 1)x + 1 = x = A$. Each element may also be represented as a bit pattern as shown in table C.3, with addition being bitwise modulo 2, and multiplication defined with an appropriate carry operation.

+	0	1
0	0	1
1	1	0

·	0	1
0	0	0
1	0	1

Table C.1. Addition and multiplication tables for $GF(2)$.

+	0	1	A	B
0	0	1	A	B
1	1	0	B	A
A	A	B	0	1
B	B	A	1	0

·	0	1	A	B
0	0	0	0	0
1	0	1	A	B
A	0	A	B	1
B	0	B	1	A

Table C.2. Addition and multiplication tables for $GF(4)$.

Element	Polynomial	Bit pattern
0	0	00
1	1	01
A	x	10
B	$x + 1$	11

Table C.3. Representations of the elements of $GF(4)$.

$GF(8)$. We can denote the elements of $GF(8)$ by $\{0, 1, A, B, C, D, E, F\}$. Each element can be mapped onto a polynomial over $GF(2)$. The multiplication and addition operations are given by multiplication and addition of the polynomials, modulo $x^3 + x + 1$. The multiplication table is given below.

element	polynomial	binary representation
0	0	000
1	1	001
A	x	010
B	$x + 1$	011
C	x^2	100
D	$x^2 + 1$	101
E	$x^2 + x$	110
F	$x^2 + x + 1$	111

$\cdot$	0	1	A	B	C	D	E	F
0	0	0	0	0	0	0	0	0
1	0	1	A	B	C	D	E	F
A	0	A	C	E	B	1	F	D
B	0	B	E	D	F	C	1	A
C	0	C	B	F	E	A	D	1
D	0	D	1	C	A	F	B	E
E	0	E	F	1	D	B	A	C
F	0	F	D	A	1	E	C	B

Why are Galois fields relevant to linear codes? Imagine generalizing a binary generator matrix $\mathbf{G}$ and binary vector $\mathbf{s}$ to a matrix and vector with elements from a larger set, and generalizing the addition and multiplication operations that define the product $\mathbf{Gs}$. In order to produce an appropriate input for a symmetric channel, it would be convenient if, for random $\mathbf{s}$, the product $\mathbf{Gs}$ produced all elements in the enlarged set with equal probability. This uniform distribution is easiest to guarantee if these elements form a group under both addition and multiplication, because then these operations do not break the symmetry among the elements. When two random elements of a multiplicative group are multiplied together, all elements are produced with equal probability. This is not true of other sets such as the integers, for which the multiplication operation is more likely to give rise to some elements (the composite numbers) than others. Galois fields, by their definition, avoid such symmetry-breaking effects.

▶ C.2 Eigenvectors and eigenvalues

A *right-eigenvector* of a square matrix $\mathbf{A}$ is a non-zero vector $\mathbf{e}_R$ that satisfies

$$\mathbf{A}\mathbf{e}_R = \lambda\mathbf{e}_R, \tag{C.1}$$

where λ is the eigenvalue associated with that eigenvector. The eigenvalue may be a real number or complex number and it may be zero. Eigenvectors may be real or complex.

A *left-eigenvector* of a matrix $\mathbf{A}$ is a vector $\mathbf{e}_L$ that satisfies

$$\mathbf{e}_L^{\mathsf{T}}\mathbf{A} = \lambda\mathbf{c}_L^{\mathsf{T}}. \tag{C.2}$$

The following statements for right-eigenvectors also apply to left-eigenvectors.

- If a matrix has two or more linearly independent right-eigenvectors with the same eigenvalue then that eigenvalue is called a degenerate eigenvalue of the matrix, or a repeated eigenvalue. Any linear combination of those eigenvectors is another right-eigenvector with the same eigenvalue.

- The principal right-eigenvector of a matrix is, by definition, the right-eigenvector with the largest associated eigenvalue.

- If a real matrix has a right-eigenvector with complex eigenvalue $\lambda = x + yi$ then it also has a right-eigenvector with the conjugate eigenvalue $\lambda^* = x - yi$.

Symmetric matrices

If $\mathbf{A}$ is a real symmetric $N \times N$ matrix then

1. all the eigenvalues and eigenvectors of $\mathbf{A}$ are real;

2. every left-eigenvector of $\mathbf{A}$ is also a right-eigenvector of $\mathbf{A}$ with the same eigenvalue, and *vice versa*;

3. a set of N eigenvectors and eigenvalues $\{\mathbf{e}^{(a)}, \lambda_a\}_{a=1}^N$ can be found that are orthonormal, that is,

$$\mathbf{e}^{(a)} \cdot \mathbf{e}^{(b)} = \delta_{ab}; \tag{C.3}$$

the matrix can be expressed as a weighted sum of outer products of the eigenvectors:

$$\mathbf{A} = \sum_{a=1}^N \lambda_a [\mathbf{e}^{(a)}][\mathbf{e}^{(a)}]^\mathsf{T}. \tag{C.4}$$

(Whereas I often use i and n as indices for sets of size I and N, I will use the indices a and b to run over eigenvectors, even if there are N of them. This is to avoid confusion with the components of the eigenvectors, which are indexed by n, e.g. $e_n^{(a)}$.)

General square matrices

An $N \times N$ matrix can have up to N distinct eigenvalues. Generically, there are N eigenvalues, all distinct, and each has one left-eigenvector and one right-eigenvector. In cases where two or more eigenvalues coincide, for each distinct eigenvalue that is non-zero there is at least one left-eigenvector and one right-eigenvector.

Left- and right-eigenvectors that have different eigenvalue are orthogonal, that is,

$$\text{if } \lambda_a \neq \lambda_b \text{ then } \mathbf{e}_\mathsf{L}^{(a)} \cdot \mathbf{e}_\mathsf{R}^{(b)} = 0. \tag{C.5}$$

Non-negative matrices

Definition. If all the elements of a non-zero matrix $\mathbf{C}$ satisfy $C_{mn} \geq 0$ then $\mathbf{C}$ is a non-negative matrix. Similarly, if all the elements of a non-zero vector $\mathbf{c}$ satisfy $c_i \geq 0$ then $\mathbf{c}$ is a non-negative vector.

Properties. A non-negative matrix has a principal eigenvector that is non-negative. It may also have other eigenvectors with the same eigenvalue that are not non-negative. But if the principal eigenvalue of a non-negative matrix is not degenerate, then the matrix has only one principal eigenvector $\mathbf{e}^{(1)}$, and it is non-negative.

Generically, all the other eigenvalues are smaller in absolute magnitude. [There can be several eigenvalues of identical magnitude in special cases.]

Transition probability matrices

An important example of a non-negative matrix is a transition probability matrix $\mathbf{Q}$.

Definition. A transition probability matrix $\mathbf{Q}$ has columns that are probability vectors, that is, it satisfies $\mathbf{Q} \geq 0$ and

$$\sum_i Q_{ij} = 1 \text{ for all } j. \tag{C.6}$$

Matrix	Eigenvalues and eigenvectors e_L, e_R
$\begin{bmatrix} 1 & 2 & 0 \\ 1 & 1 & 0 \\ 0 & 0 & 1 \end{bmatrix}$	**2.41** $\begin{bmatrix} .58 \\ .82 \\ 0 \end{bmatrix} \begin{bmatrix} .82 \\ .58 \\ 0 \end{bmatrix}$ **1** $\begin{bmatrix} 0 \\ 0 \\ 1 \end{bmatrix} \begin{bmatrix} 0 \\ 0 \\ 1 \end{bmatrix}$ **−0.41** $\begin{bmatrix} -.58 \\ .82 \\ 0 \end{bmatrix} \begin{bmatrix} -.82 \\ .58 \\ 0 \end{bmatrix}$
$\begin{bmatrix} 0 & 1 \\ 1 & 1 \end{bmatrix}$	**1.62** $\begin{bmatrix} .53 \\ .85 \end{bmatrix} \begin{bmatrix} .53 \\ .85 \end{bmatrix}$ **−0.62** $\begin{bmatrix} .85 \\ -.53 \end{bmatrix} \begin{bmatrix} .85 \\ -.53 \end{bmatrix}$
$\begin{bmatrix} 1 & 1 & 0 & 0 \\ 0 & 0 & 0 & 1 \\ 1 & 0 & 0 & 0 \\ 0 & 0 & 1 & 1 \end{bmatrix}$	**1.62** $\begin{bmatrix} .60 \\ .37 \\ .37 \\ .60 \end{bmatrix} \begin{bmatrix} .60 \\ .37 \\ .37 \\ .60 \end{bmatrix}$ **0.5+0.9i** $\begin{bmatrix} .1-.5i \\ -.3-.4i \\ .3+.4i \\ -.1+.5i \end{bmatrix} \begin{bmatrix} .1-.5i \\ .3+.4i \\ -.3-.4i \\ -.1+.5i \end{bmatrix}$ **0.5−0.9i** $\begin{bmatrix} .1+.5i \\ -.3+.4i \\ .3-.4i \\ -.1-.5i \end{bmatrix} \begin{bmatrix} .1+.5i \\ .3-.4i \\ -.3+.4i \\ -.1-.5i \end{bmatrix}$ **−0.62** $\begin{bmatrix} .37 \\ -.60 \\ -.60 \\ .37 \end{bmatrix} \begin{bmatrix} .37 \\ -.60 \\ -.60 \\ .37 \end{bmatrix}$

Table C.4. Some matrices and their eigenvectors.

Matrix	Eigenvalues and eigenvectors e_L, e_R
$\begin{bmatrix} 0 & .38 \\ 1 & .62 \end{bmatrix}$	**1** $\begin{bmatrix} .71 \\ .71 \end{bmatrix} \begin{bmatrix} .36 \\ .93 \end{bmatrix}$ **−0.38** $\begin{bmatrix} -.93 \\ .36 \end{bmatrix} \begin{bmatrix} -.71 \\ .71 \end{bmatrix}$
$\begin{bmatrix} 0 & .35 & 0 \\ 0 & 0 & .46 \\ 1 & .65 & .54 \end{bmatrix}$	**1** $\begin{bmatrix} .58 \\ .58 \\ .58 \end{bmatrix} \begin{bmatrix} .14 \\ .41 \\ .90 \end{bmatrix}$ **−0.2−0.3i** $\begin{bmatrix} -.8+.1i \\ -.2-.5i \\ .2+.2i \end{bmatrix} \begin{bmatrix} .2-.5i \\ -.6+.2i \\ .4+.3i \end{bmatrix}$ **−0.2+0.3i** $\begin{bmatrix} -.8-.1i \\ -.2+.5i \\ .2-.2i \end{bmatrix} \begin{bmatrix} .2+.5i \\ -.6-.2i \\ .4-.3i \end{bmatrix}$

Table C.5. Transition probability matrices for generating random paths through trellises.

This property can be rewritten in terms of the all-ones vector $\mathbf{n} = (1, 1, \ldots, 1)^{\mathsf{T}}$:

$$\mathbf{n}^{\mathsf{T}}\mathbf{Q} = \mathbf{n}^{\mathsf{T}}. \tag{C.7}$$

So $\mathbf{n}$ is the principal left-eigenvector of $\mathbf{Q}$ with eigenvalue $\lambda_1 = 1$.

$$\mathbf{e}_L^{(1)} = \mathbf{n}. \tag{C.8}$$

Because it is a non-negative matrix, $\mathbf{Q}$ has a principal right-eigenvector that is non-negative, $\mathbf{e}_R^{(1)}$. Generically, for Markov processes that are ergodic, this eigenvector is the only right-eigenvector with eigenvalue of magnitude 1 (see table C.6 for illustrative exceptions). This vector, if we normalize it such that $\mathbf{e}_R^{(1)} \cdot \mathbf{n} = 1$, is called the invariant distribution of the transition probability matrix. It is the probability density that is left unchanged under $\mathbf{Q}$. Unlike the principal left-eigenvector, which we explicitly identified above, we can't usually identify the principal right-eigenvector without computation.

The matrix may have up to $N - 1$ other right-eigenvectors all of which are orthogonal to the left-eigenvector $\mathbf{n}$, that is, they are zero-sum vectors.

▶ C.3 Perturbation theory

Perturbation theory is not used in this book, but it is useful in this book's fields. In this section we derive first order perturbation theory for the eigenvectors and eigenvalues of square, *not necessarily symmetric*, matrices. Most presentations of perturbation theory focus on symmetric matrices, but non-symmetric matrices (such as transition matrices) also deserve to be perturbed!

	Matrix	Eigenvalues and eigenvectors $\mathbf{e_L}, \mathbf{e_R}$			
(a)	$\begin{bmatrix} .90 & .20 & 0 & 0 \\ .10 & .80 & 0 & 0 \\ 0 & 0 & .90 & .20 \\ 0 & 0 & .10 & .80 \end{bmatrix}$	1 $\begin{bmatrix} 0 \\ 0 \\ .71 \\ .71 \end{bmatrix}\begin{bmatrix} 0 \\ 0 \\ .89 \\ .45 \end{bmatrix}$	1 $\begin{bmatrix} .71 \\ .71 \\ 0 \\ 0 \end{bmatrix}\begin{bmatrix} .89 \\ .45 \\ 0 \\ 0 \end{bmatrix}$	0.70 $\begin{bmatrix} .45 \\ -.89 \\ 0 \\ 0 \end{bmatrix}\begin{bmatrix} .71 \\ -.71 \\ 0 \\ 0 \end{bmatrix}$	0.70 $\begin{bmatrix} 0 \\ 0 \\ -.45 \\ .89 \end{bmatrix}\begin{bmatrix} 0 \\ 0 \\ -.71 \\ .71 \end{bmatrix}$
(a')	$\begin{bmatrix} .90 & .20 & 0 & 0 \\ .10 & .79 & .02 & 0 \\ 0 & .01 & .88 & .20 \\ 0 & 0 & .10 & .80 \end{bmatrix}$	1 $\begin{bmatrix} .50 \\ .50 \\ .50 \\ .50 \end{bmatrix}\begin{bmatrix} .87 \\ .43 \\ .22 \\ .11 \end{bmatrix}$	0.98 $\begin{bmatrix} -.18 \\ -.15 \\ .66 \\ .72 \end{bmatrix}\begin{bmatrix} -.66 \\ -.28 \\ .61 \\ .33 \end{bmatrix}$	0.70 $\begin{bmatrix} .20 \\ -.40 \\ -.40 \\ .80 \end{bmatrix}\begin{bmatrix} .63 \\ -.63 \\ -.32 \\ .32 \end{bmatrix}$	0.69 $\begin{bmatrix} -.19 \\ .41 \\ -.44 \\ .77 \end{bmatrix}\begin{bmatrix} -.61 \\ .65 \\ -.35 \\ .30 \end{bmatrix}$
(b)	$\begin{bmatrix} 0 & 0 & .90 & .20 \\ 0 & 0 & .10 & .80 \\ .90 & .20 & 0 & 0 \\ .10 & .80 & 0 & 0 \end{bmatrix}$	1 $\begin{bmatrix} .50 \\ .50 \\ .50 \\ .50 \end{bmatrix}\begin{bmatrix} .63 \\ .32 \\ .63 \\ .32 \end{bmatrix}$	0.70 $\begin{bmatrix} -.32 \\ .63 \\ -.32 \\ .63 \end{bmatrix}\begin{bmatrix} .50 \\ -.50 \\ .50 \\ -.50 \end{bmatrix}$	-0.70 $\begin{bmatrix} .32 \\ -.63 \\ -.32 \\ .63 \end{bmatrix}\begin{bmatrix} -.50 \\ .50 \\ .50 \\ -.50 \end{bmatrix}$	-1 $\begin{bmatrix} .50 \\ .50 \\ -.50 \\ -.50 \end{bmatrix}\begin{bmatrix} .63 \\ .32 \\ -.63 \\ -.32 \end{bmatrix}$

Table C.6. Illustrative transition probability matrices and their eigenvectors showing the two ways of being non-ergodic. (a) More than one principal eigenvector with eigenvalue 1 because the state space falls into two unconnected pieces. (a') A small perturbation breaks the degeneracy of the principal eigenvectors. (b) Under this chain, the density may oscillate between two parts of the state space. In addition to the invariant distribution, there is another right-eigenvector with eigenvalue -1. In general such circulating densities correspond to complex eigenvalues with magnitude 1.

We assume that we have an $N \times N$ matrix $\mathbf{H}$ that is a function $\mathbf{H}(\epsilon)$ of a real parameter ϵ, with $\epsilon = 0$ being our starting point. We assume that a Taylor expansion of $\mathbf{H}(\epsilon)$ is appropriate:

$$\mathbf{H}(\epsilon) = \mathbf{H}(0) + \epsilon \mathbf{V} + \cdots \qquad (C.9)$$

where

$$\mathbf{V} \equiv \frac{\partial \mathbf{H}}{\partial \epsilon}. \qquad (C.10)$$

We assume that for all ϵ of interest, $\mathbf{H}(\epsilon)$ has a complete set of N right-eigenvectors and left-eigenvectors, and that these eigenvectors and their eigenvalues are continuous functions of ϵ. This last assumption is not necessarily a good one: if $\mathbf{H}(0)$ has degenerate eigenvalues then it is possible for the eigenvectors to be discontinuous in ϵ; in such cases, degenerate perturbation theory is needed. That's a fun topic, but let's stick with the non-degenerate case here.

We write the eigenvectors and eigenvalues as follows:

$$\mathbf{H}(\epsilon)\mathbf{e}_R^{(a)}(\epsilon) = \lambda^{(a)}(\epsilon)\mathbf{e}_R^{(a)}(\epsilon), \qquad (C.11)$$

and we Taylor expand

$$\lambda^{(a)}(\epsilon) = \lambda^{(a)}(0) + \epsilon \mu^{(a)} + \cdots \qquad (C.12)$$

with

$$\mu^{(a)} \equiv \frac{\partial \lambda^{(a)}(\epsilon)}{\partial \epsilon} \qquad (C.13)$$

and

$$\mathbf{e}_R^{(a)}(\epsilon) = \mathbf{e}_R^{(a)}(0) + \epsilon \mathbf{f}_R^{(a)} + \cdots \qquad (C.14)$$

with

$$\mathbf{f}_R^{(a)} \equiv \frac{\partial \mathbf{e}_R^{(a)}}{\partial \epsilon}, \tag{C.15}$$

and similar definitions for $\mathbf{e}_L^{(a)}$ and $\mathbf{f}_L^{(a)}$. We define these left-vectors to be row vectors, so that the 'transpose' operation is not needed and can be banished.

We are free to constrain the magnitudes of the eigenvectors in whatever way we please. Each left-eigenvector and each right-eigenvector has an arbitrary magnitude. The natural constraints to use are as follows. First, we constrain the inner products with:

$$\mathbf{e}_L^{(a)}(\epsilon)\mathbf{e}_R^{(a)}(\epsilon) = 1, \quad \text{for all } a. \tag{C.16}$$

Expanding the eigenvectors in ϵ, equation (C.19) implies

$$(\mathbf{e}_L^{(a)}(0) + \epsilon\mathbf{f}_L^{(a)} + \cdots)(\mathbf{e}_R^{(a)}(0) + \epsilon\mathbf{f}_R^{(a)} + \cdots) = 1, \tag{C.17}$$

from which we can extract the terms in ϵ, which say:

$$\mathbf{e}_L^{(a)}(0)\mathbf{f}_R^{(a)} + \mathbf{f}_L^{(a)}\mathbf{e}_R^{(a)}(0) = 0 \tag{C.18}$$

We are now free to choose the two constraints:

$$\mathbf{e}_L^{(a)}(0)\mathbf{f}_R^{(a)} = 0, \quad \mathbf{f}_L^{(a)}\mathbf{e}_R^{(a)}(0) = 0, \tag{C.19}$$

which in the special case of a symmetric matrix correspond to constraining the eigenvectors to be of constant length, as defined by the Euclidean norm.

OK, now that we have defined our cast of characters, what do the defining equations (C.11) and (C.9) tell us about our Taylor expansions (C.13) and (C.15)? We expand equation (C.11) in ϵ.

$$(\mathbf{H}(0) + \epsilon\mathbf{V} + \cdots)(\mathbf{e}_R^{(a)}(0) + \epsilon\mathbf{f}_R^{(a)} + \cdots) = (\lambda^{(a)}(0) + \epsilon\mu^{(a)} + \cdots)(\mathbf{e}_R^{(a)}(0) + \epsilon\mathbf{f}_R^{(a)} + \cdots). \tag{C.20}$$

Identifying the terms of order ϵ, we have:

$$\mathbf{H}(0)\mathbf{f}_R^{(a)} + \mathbf{V}\mathbf{e}_R^{(a)}(0) = \lambda^{(a)}(0)\mathbf{f}_R^{(a)} + \mu^{(a)}\mathbf{e}_R^{(a)}(0). \tag{C.21}$$

We can extract interesting results from this equation by hitting it with $\mathbf{e}_L^{(b)}(0)$:

$$\mathbf{e}_L^{(b)}(0)\mathbf{H}(0)\mathbf{f}_R^{(a)} + \mathbf{e}_L^{(b)}(0)\mathbf{V}\mathbf{e}_R^{(a)}(0) = \mathbf{e}_L^{(b)}(0)\lambda^{(a)}(0)\mathbf{f}_R^{(a)} + \mu^{(a)}\mathbf{e}_L^{(b)}(0)\mathbf{e}_R^{(a)}(0).$$

$$\Rightarrow \lambda^{(b)}\mathbf{e}_L^{(b)}(0)\mathbf{f}_R^{(a)} + \mathbf{e}_L^{(b)}(0)\mathbf{V}\mathbf{e}_R^{(a)}(0) = \lambda^{(a)}(0)\mathbf{e}_L^{(b)}(0)\mathbf{f}_R^{(a)} + \mu^{(a)}\delta_{ab}. \tag{C.22}$$

Setting $b = a$ we obtain

$$\mathbf{e}_L^{(a)}(0)\mathbf{V}\mathbf{e}_R^{(a)}(0) = \mu^{(a)}. \tag{C.23}$$

Alternatively, choosing $b \neq a$, we obtain:

$$\mathbf{e}_L^{(b)}(0)\mathbf{V}\mathbf{e}_R^{(a)}(0) = \left[\lambda^{(a)}(0) - \lambda^{(b)}(0)\right]\mathbf{e}_L^{(b)}(0)\mathbf{f}_R^{(a)} \tag{C.24}$$

$$\Rightarrow \mathbf{e}_L^{(b)}(0)\mathbf{f}_R^{(a)} = \frac{1}{\lambda^{(a)}(0) - \lambda^{(b)}(0)}\mathbf{e}_L^{(b)}(0)\mathbf{V}\mathbf{e}_R^{(a)}(0). \tag{C.25}$$

Now, assuming that the right-eigenvectors $\{\mathbf{e}_R^{(b)}(0)\}_{b=1}^N$ form a complete basis, we must be able to write

$$\mathbf{f}_R^{(a)} = \sum_b w_b \mathbf{e}_R^{(b)}(0), \tag{C.26}$$

where
$$w_b = \mathbf{e}_L^{(b)}(0)\mathbf{f}_R^{(a)}, \tag{C.27}$$

so, comparing (C.25) and (C.27), we have:

$$\mathbf{f}_R^{(a)} = \sum_{b \neq a} \frac{\mathbf{e}_L^{(b)}(0)\mathbf{V}\mathbf{e}_R^{(a)}(0)}{\lambda^{(a)}(0) - \lambda^{(b)}(0)}\mathbf{e}_R^{(b)}(0). \tag{C.28}$$

Equations (C.23) and (C.28) are the solution to the first order perturbation theory problem, giving respectively the first derivative of the eigenvalue and the eigenvectors.

Second-order perturbation theory

If we expand the eigenvector equation (C.11) to second order in ϵ, and assume that the equation
$$\mathbf{H}(\epsilon) = \mathbf{H}(0) + \epsilon\mathbf{V} \tag{C.29}$$

is exact, that is, $\mathbf{H}$ is a purely linear function of ϵ, then we have:

$$(\mathbf{H}(0) + \epsilon\mathbf{V})(\mathbf{e}_R^{(a)}(0) + \epsilon\mathbf{f}_R^{(a)} + \frac{1}{2}\epsilon^2\mathbf{g}_R^{(a)} + \cdots)$$
$$= (\lambda^{(a)}(0) + \epsilon\mu^{(a)} + \frac{1}{2}\epsilon^2\nu^{(a)} + \cdots)(\mathbf{e}_R^{(a)}(0) + \epsilon\mathbf{f}_R^{(a)} + \frac{1}{2}\epsilon^2\mathbf{g}_R^{(a)} + \cdots) \tag{C.30}$$

where $\mathbf{g}_R^{(a)}$ and $\nu^{(a)}$ are the second derivatives of the eigenvector and eigenvalue. Equating the second order terms in ϵ in equation (C.30),

$$\mathbf{V}\mathbf{f}_R^{(a)} + \frac{1}{2}\mathbf{H}(0)\mathbf{g}_R^{(a)} = \frac{1}{2}\lambda^{(a)}(0)\mathbf{g}_R^{(a)} + \frac{1}{2}\nu^{(a)}\mathbf{e}_R^{(a)}(0) + \mu^{(a)}\mathbf{f}_R^{(a)} \tag{C.31}$$

Hitting this equation on the left with $\mathbf{e}_L^{(a)}(0)$, we obtain:

$$\mathbf{e}_L^{(a)}(0)\mathbf{V}\mathbf{f}_R^{(a)} + \frac{1}{2}\lambda^{(a)}\mathbf{e}_L^{(a)}(0)\mathbf{g}_R^{(a)}$$
$$= \frac{1}{2}\lambda^{(a)}(0)\mathbf{e}_L^{(a)}(0)\mathbf{g}_R^{(a)} + \frac{1}{2}\nu^{(a)}\mathbf{e}_L^{(a)}(0)\mathbf{e}_R^{(a)}(0) + \mu^{(a)}\mathbf{e}_L^{(a)}(0)\mathbf{f}_R^{(a)}. \tag{C.32}$$

The term $\mathbf{e}_L^{(a)}(0)\mathbf{f}_R^{(a)}$ is equal to zero because of our constraints (C.19), so

$$\mathbf{e}_L^{(a)}(0)\mathbf{V}\mathbf{f}_R^{(a)} = \frac{1}{2}\nu^{(a)}, \tag{C.33}$$

so the second derivative of the eigenvalue with respect to ϵ is given by

$$\frac{1}{2}\nu^{(a)} = \mathbf{e}_L^{(a)}(0)\mathbf{V}\sum_{b \neq a}\frac{\mathbf{e}_L^{(b)}(0)\mathbf{V}\mathbf{e}_R^{(a)}(0)}{\lambda^{(a)}(0) - \lambda^{(b)}(0)}\mathbf{e}_R^{(b)}(0) \tag{C.34}$$

$$= \sum_{b \neq a}\frac{[\mathbf{e}_L^{(b)}(0)\mathbf{V}\mathbf{e}_R^{(a)}(0)][\mathbf{e}_L^{(a)}(0)\mathbf{V}\mathbf{e}_R^{(b)}(0)]}{\lambda^{(a)}(0) - \lambda^{(b)}(0)}. \tag{C.35}$$

This is as far as we will take the perturbation expansion.

Summary

If we introduce the abbreviation V_{ba} for $\mathbf{e}_L^{(b)}(0)\mathbf{V}\mathbf{e}_R^{(a)}(0)$, we can write the eigenvectors of $\mathbf{H}(\epsilon) = \mathbf{H}(0) + \epsilon\mathbf{V}$ to first order as

$$\mathbf{e}_R^{(a)}(\epsilon) = \mathbf{e}_R^{(a)}(0) + \epsilon\sum_{b \neq a}\frac{V_{ba}}{\lambda^{(a)}(0) - \lambda^{(b)}(0)}\mathbf{e}_R^{(b)}(0) + \cdots \tag{C.36}$$

and the eigenvalues to second order as

$$\lambda^{(a)}(\epsilon) = \lambda^{(a)}(0) + \epsilon V_{aa} + \epsilon^2\sum_{b \neq a}\frac{V_{ba}V_{ab}}{\lambda^{(a)}(0) - \lambda^{(b)}(0)} + \cdots. \tag{C.37}$$

▶ C.4 Some numbers

	2^{8192}	10^{2466}	Number of distinct 1-kilobyte files
	2^{1024}	10^{308}	Number of states of a 2D Ising model with 32×32 spins
2^{1000}		10^{301}	Number of binary strings of length 1000
2^{500}		3×10^{150}	
	2^{469}	10^{141}	Number of binary strings of length 1000 having 100 1s and 900 0s
	2^{266}	10^{80}	Number of electrons in universe
2^{200}		1.6×10^{60}	
	2^{190}	10^{57}	Number of electrons in solar system
	2^{171}	3×10^{51}	Number of electrons in the earth
2^{100}		10^{30}	
	2^{98}	3×10^{29}	Age of universe/picoseconds
	2^{58}	3×10^{17}	Age of universe/seconds
2^{50}		10^{15}	
2^{40}		10^{12}	
		10^{11}	Number of neurons in human brain
		10^{11}	Number of bits stored on a DVD
		3×10^{10}	Number of bits in the wheat genome
		6×10^{9}	Number of bits in the human genome
	2^{32}	6×10^{9}	Population of earth
2^{30}		10^{9}	
		2.5×10^{8}	Number of fibres in the corpus callosum
		2×10^{8}	Number of bits in *C. Elegans* (a worm) genome
		2×10^{8}	Number of bits in *Arabidopsis thaliana* (a flowering plant related to broccoli) genome
	2^{25}	3×10^{7}	One year/seconds
		2×10^{7}	Number of bits in the compressed PostScript file that is this book
		2×10^{7}	Number of bits in unix kernel
		10^{7}	Number of bits in the *E. Coli* genome, or in a floppy disk
		4×10^{6}	Number of years since human/chimpanzee divergence
2^{20}		10^{6}	1 048 576
		2×10^{5}	Number of generations since human/chimpanzee divergence
		3×10^{4}	Number of genes in human genome
		3×10^{4}	Number of genes in *Arabidopsis thaliana* genome
		1.5×10^{3}	Number of base pairs in a gene
2^{10}	e^{7}	10^{3}	$2^{10} = 1024$; $e^{7} = 1096$
2^{0}		10^{0}	1
	2^{-2}	2.5×10^{-1}	Lifetime probability of dying from smoking one pack of cigarettes per day.
		10^{-2}	Lifetime probability of dying in a motor vehicle accident
2^{-10}		10^{-3}	
		10^{-5}	Lifetime probability of developing cancer because of drinking 2 litres per day of water containing 12 p.p.b. benzene
2^{-20}		10^{-6}	
		3×10^{-8}	Probability of error in transmission of coding DNA, per nucleotide, per generation
2^{-30}		10^{-9}	
2^{-60}		10^{-18}	Probability of undetected error in a hard disk drive, after error correction

Bibliography

ABRAHAMSEN, P. (1997) A review of Gaussian random fields and correlation functions. Technical Report 917, Norwegian Computing Center, Blindern, N-0314 Oslo, Norway. 2nd edition.

ABRAMSON, N. (1963) *Information Theory and Coding*. McGraw-Hill.

ADLER, S. L. (1981) Over-relaxation method for the Monte-Carlo evaluation of the partition function for multiquadratic actions. *Physical Review D – Particles and Fields* **23** (12): 2901–2904.

AIYER, S. V. B. (1991) *Solving Combinatorial Optimization Problems Using Neural Networks*. Cambridge Univ. Engineering Dept. PhD dissertation. CUED/F-INFENG/TR 89.

AJI, S., JIN, H., KHANDEKAR, A., McELIECE, R. J., and MACKAY, D. J. C. (2000) BSC thresholds for code ensembles based on 'typical pairs' decoding. In *Codes, Systems and Graphical Models*, ed. by B. Marcus and J. Rosenthal, volume 123 of *IMA Volumes in Mathematics and its Applications*, pp. 195–210. Springer.

AMARI, S., CICHOCKI, A., and YANG, H. H. (1996) A new learning algorithm for blind signal separation. In *Advances in Neural Information Processing Systems*, ed. by D. S. Touretzky, M. C. Mozer, and M. E. Hasselmo, volume 8, pp. 757–763. MIT Press.

AMIT, D. J., GUTFREUND, H., and SOMPOLINSKY, H. (1985) Storing infinite numbers of patterns in a spin glass model of neural networks. *Phys. Rev. Lett.* **55**: 1530–1533.

ANGEL, J. R. P., WIZINOWICH, P., LLOYD-HART, M., and SANDLER, D. (1990) Adaptive optics for array telescopes using neural-network techniques. *Nature* **348**: 221–224.

BAHL, L. R., COCKE, J., JELINEK, F., and RAVIV, J. (1974) Optimal decoding of linear codes for minimizing symbol error rate. *IEEE Trans. Info. Theory* **IT-20**: 284–287.

BALDWIN, J. (1896) A new factor in evolution. *American Naturalist* **30**: 441–451.

BAR-SHALOM, Y., and FORTMANN, T. (1988) *Tracking and Data Association*. Academic Press.

BARBER, D., and WILLIAMS, C. K. I. (1997) Gaussian processes for Bayesian classification via hybrid Monte Carlo. In *Neural Information Processing Systems 9*, ed. by M. C. Mozer, M. I. Jordan, and T. Petsche, pp. 340–346. MIT Press.

BARNETT, S. (1979) *Matrix Methods for Engineers and Scientists*. McGraw-Hill.

BATTAIL, G. (1993) We can think of good codes, and even decode them. In *Eurocode '92. Udine, Italy, 26-30 October*, ed. by P. Camion, P. Charpin, and S. Harari, number 339 in CISM Courses and Lectures, pp. 353–368. Springer.

BAUM, E., BONEH, D., and GARRETT, C. (1995) On genetic algorithms. In *Proc. Eighth Annual Conf. on Computational Learning Theory*, pp. 230–239. ACM.

BAUM, E. B., and SMITH, W. D. (1993) Best play for imperfect players and game tree search. Technical report, NEC, Princeton, NJ.

BAUM, E. B., and SMITH, W. D. (1997) A Bayesian approach to relevance in game playing. *Artificial Intelligence* **97** (1-2): 195–242.

BAUM, L. E., and PETRIE, T. (1966) Statistical inference for probabilistic functions of finite-state Markov chains. *Ann. Math. Stat.* **37**: 1559–1563.

BEAL, M. J., GHAHRAMANI, Z., and RASMUSSEN, C. E. (2002) The infinite hidden Markov model. In *Advances in Neural Information Processing Systems 14*. MIT Press.

BELL, A. J., and SEJNOWSKI, T. J. (1995) An information maximization approach to blind separation and blind deconvolution. *Neural Computation* **7** (6): 1129–1159.

BENTLEY, J. (2000) *Programming Pearls*. Addison-Wesley, second edition.

BERGER, J. (1985) *Statistical Decision theory and Bayesian Analysis*. Springer.

BERLEKAMP, E. R. (1968) *Algebraic Coding Theory*. McGraw-Hill.

BERLEKAMP, E. R. (1980) The technology of error-correcting codes. *IEEE Trans. Info. Theory* **68**: 564–593.

BERLEKAMP, E. R., McELIECE, R. J., and van TILBORG, H. C. A. (1978) On the intractability of certain coding problems. *IEEE Trans. Info. Theory* **24** (3): 384–386.

BERROU, C., and GLAVIEUX, A. (1996) Near optimum error correcting coding and decoding: Turbo-codes. *IEEE Trans. on Communications* **44**: 1261–1271.

BERROU, C., GLAVIEUX, A., and THITIMAJSHIMA, P. (1993) Near Shannon limit error-correcting coding and decoding: Turbo-codes. In *Proc. 1993 IEEE International Conf. on Communications, Geneva, Switzerland*, pp. 1064–1070.

BERZUINI, C., BEST, N. G., GILKS, W. R., and LARIZZA, C. (1997) Dynamic conditional independence models and Markov chain Monte Carlo methods. *J. American Statistical Assoc.* **92** (440): 1403–1412.

BERZUINI, C., and GILKS, W. R. (2001) Following a moving target – Monte Carlo inference for dynamic Bayesian models. *J. Royal Statistical Society Series B – Statistical Methodology* **63** (1): 127–146.

BHATTACHARYYA, A. (1943) On a measure of divergence between two statistical populations defined by their probability distributions. *Bull. Calcutta Math. Soc.* **35**: 99–110.

BISHOP, C. M. (1992) Exact calculation of the Hessian matrix for the multilayer perceptron. *Neural Computation* **4** (4): 494–501.

BISHOP, C. M. (1995) *Neural Networks for Pattern Recognition*. Oxford Univ. Press.

BISHOP, C. M., and WINN, J. M. (2000) Non-linear Bayesian image modelling. In *Proc. Sixth European Conf. on Computer Vision*, volume 1, pp. 3–17. Springer.

BISHOP, C. M., and WINN, J. M. (2003) Structured variational distributions in VIBES. In *Advances in Neural Information Processing Systems*.

BISHOP, C. M., WINN, J. M., and SPIEGELHALTER, D. (2002) VIBES: A variational inference engine for Bayesian networks. In *Advances in Neural Information Processing Systems XV*, ed. by S. Becker, S. Thrun, and K. Obermayer.

BLAHUT, R. E. (1987) *Principles and Practice of Information Theory*. Addison-Wesley.

BOTTOU, L., HOWARD, P. G., and BENGIO, Y. (1998) The Z-coder adaptive binary coder. In *Proc. Data Compression Conf., Snowbird, Utah, March 1998*, pp. 13–22.

BOX, G. E. P., and TIAO, G. C. (1973) *Bayesian Inference in Statistical Analysis*. Addison–Wesley.

BRAUNSTEIN, A., MÉZARD, M., and ZECCHINA, R., (2003) Survey propagation: an algorithm for satisfiability. cs.CC/0212002.

BRETTHORST, G. (1988) *Bayesian Spectrum Analysis and Parameter Estimation*. Springer. Also available at bayes.wustl.edu.

BRIDLE, J. S. (1989) Probabilistic interpretation of feedforward classification network outputs, with relationships to statistical pattern recognition. In *Neuro-computing: Algorithms, Architectures and Applications*, ed. by F. Fougelman-Soulie and J. Hérault. Springer–Verlag.

BULMER, M. (1985) *The Mathematical Theory of Quantitative Genetics*. Oxford Univ. Press.

BURROWS, M., and WHEELER, D. J. (1994) A block-sorting lossless data compression algorithm. Technical Report 124, Digital SRC.

BYERS, J., LUBY, M., MITZENMACHER, M., and REGE, A. (1998) A digital fountain approach to reliable distribution of bulk data. In *Proc. ACM SIGCOMM '98, September 2–4, 1998*.

CAIRNS-SMITH, A. G. (1985) *Seven Clues to the Origin of Life*. Cambridge Univ. Press.

CALDERBANK, A. R., and SHOR, P. W. (1996) Good quantum error-correcting codes exist. *Phys. Rev. A* **54**: 1098. quant-ph/9512032.

CARROLL, L. (1998) *Alice's Adventures in Wonderland; and, Through the Looking-glass: and what Alice Found There*. Macmillan Children's Books.

CHILDS, A. M., PATTERSON, R. B., and MACKAY, D. J. C. (2001) Exact sampling from non-attractive distributions using summary states. *Physical Review E* **63**: 036113.

CHU, W., KEERTHI, S. S., and ONG, C. J. (2001) A unified loss function in Bayesian framework for support vector regression. In *Proc. 18th International Conf. on Machine Learning*, pp. 51–58.

CHU, W., KEERTHI, S. S., and ONG, C. J. (2002) A new Bayesian design method for support vector classification. In *Special Section on Support Vector Machines of the 9th International Conf. on Neural Information Processing*.

CHU, W., KEERTHI, S. S., and ONG, C. J. (2003a) Bayesian support vector regression using a unified loss function. *IEEE Trans. on Neural Networks*. Submitted.

CHU, W., KEERTHI, S. S., and ONG, C. J. (2003b) Bayesian trigonometric support vector classifier. *Neural Computation*.

CHUNG, S.-Y., RICHARDSON, T. J., and URBANKE, R. L. (2001) Analysis of sum-product decoding of low-density parity-check codes using a Gaussian approximation. *IEEE Trans. Info. Theory* **47** (2): 657–670.

CHUNG, S.-Y., URBANKE, R. L., and RICHARDSON, T. J., (1999) LDPC code design applet. lids.mit.edu/~sychung/gaopt.html.

COMON, P., JUTTEN, C., and HERAULT, J. (1991) Blind separation of sources. 2. Problems statement. *Signal Processing* **24** (1): 11–20.

COPAS, J. B. (1983) Regression, prediction and shrinkage (with discussion). *J. R. Statist. Soc. B* **45** (3): 311–354.

COVER, T. M. (1965) Geometrical and statistical properties of systems of linear inequalities with applications in pattern recognition. *IEEE Trans. on Electronic Computers* **14**: 326–334.

COVER, T. M., and THOMAS, J. A. (1991) *Elements of Information Theory*. Wiley.

COWLES, M. K., and CARLIN, B. P. (1996) Markov-chain Monte-Carlo convergence diagnostics – a comparative review. *J. American Statistical Assoc.* **91** (434): 883–904.

COX, R. (1946) Probability, frequency, and reasonable expectation. *Am. J. Physics* **14**: 1–13.

CRESSIE, N. (1993) *Statistics for Spatial Data*. Wiley.

DAVEY, M. C. (1999) *Error-correction using Low-Density Parity-Check Codes*. Univ. of Cambridge PhD dissertation.

DAVEY, M. C., and MACKAY, D. J. C. (1998) Low density parity check codes over GF(q). *IEEE Communications Letters* **2** (6): 165–167.

DAVEY, M. C., and MACKAY, D. J. C. (2000) Watermark codes: Reliable communication over insertion/deletion channels. In *Proc. 2000 IEEE International Symposium on Info. Theory*, p. 477.

DAVEY, M. C., and MACKAY, D. J. C. (2001) Reliable communication over channels with insertions, deletions and substitutions. *IEEE Trans. Info. Theory* **47** (2): 687–698.

DAWID, A., STONE, M., and ZIDEK, J. (1996) Critique of E.T Jaynes's 'paradoxes of probability theory'. Technical Report 172, Dept. of Statistical Science, Univ. College London.

DAYAN, P., HINTON, G. E., NEAL, R. M., and ZEMEL, R. S. (1995) The Helmholtz machine. *Neural Computation* **7** (5): 889–904.

DIVSALAR, D., JIN, H., and MCELIECE, R. J. (1998) Coding theorems for 'turbo-like' codes. In *Proc. 36th Allerton Conf. on Communication, Control, and Computing, Sept. 1998*, pp. 201–210. Allerton House.

DOUCET, A., DE FREITAS, J., and GORDON, N. eds. (2001) *Sequential Monte Carlo Methods in Practice*. Springer.

DURBIN, R., EDDY, S. R., KROGH, A., and MITCHISON, G. (1998) *Biological Sequence Analysis. Probabilistic Models of Proteins and Nucleic Acids*. Cambridge Univ. Press.

DYSON, F. J. (1985) *Origins of Life*. Cambridge Univ. Press.

ELIAS, P. (1975) Universal codeword sets and representations of the integers. *IEEE Trans. Info. Theory* **21** (2): 194–203.

EYRE-WALKER, A., and KEIGHTLEY, P. (1999) High genomic deleterious mutation rates in hominids. *Nature* **397**: 344–347.

FELSENSTEIN, J. (1985) Recombination and sex: is Maynard Smith necessary? In *Evolution. Essays in Honour of John Maynard Smith*, ed. by P. J. Greenwood, P. H. Harvey, and M. Slatkin, pp. 209–220. Cambridge Univ. Press.

FERREIRA, H., CLARKE, W., HELBERG, A., ABDEL-GHAFFAR, K. S., and VINCK, A. H. (1997) Insertion/deletion correction with spectral nulls. *IEEE Trans. Info. Theory* **43** (2): 722–732.

FEYNMAN, R. P. (1972) *Statistical Mechanics*. Addison–Wesley.

FORNEY, JR., G. D. (1966) *Concatenated Codes*. MIT Press.

FORNEY, JR., G. D. (2001) Codes on graphs: Normal realizations. *IEEE Trans. Info. Theory* **47** (2): 520–548.

FREY, B. J. (1998) *Graphical Models for Machine Learning and Digital Communication*. MIT Press.

GALLAGER, R. G. (1962) Low density parity check codes. *IRE Trans. Info. Theory* **IT-8**: 21–28.

GALLAGER, R. G. (1963) *Low Density Parity Check Codes*. Number 21 in MIT Research monograph series. MIT Press. Available from www.inference.phy.cam.ac.uk/mackay/gallager/papers/.

GALLAGER, R. G. (1968) *Information Theory and Reliable Communication*. Wiley.

GALLAGER, R. G. (1978) Variations on a theme by Huffman. *IEEE Trans. Info. Theory* **IT-24** (6): 668–674.

GIBBS, M. N. (1997) *Bayesian Gaussian Processes for Regression and Classification*. Cambridge Univ. PhD dissertation. www.inference.phy.cam.ac.uk/mng10/.

GIBBS, M. N., and MACKAY, D. J. C., (1996) Efficient implementation of Gaussian processes for interpolation. www.inference.phy.cam.ac.uk/mackay/abstracts/gpros.html.

GIBBS, M. N., and MACKAY, D. J. C. (2000) Variational Gaussian process classifiers. *IEEE Trans. on Neural Networks* **11** (6): 1458–1464.

GILKS, W., ROBERTS, G., and GEORGE, E. (1994) Adaptive direction sampling. *Statistician* **43**: 179–189.

GILKS, W., and WILD, P. (1992) Adaptive rejection sampling for Gibbs sampling. *Applied Statistics* **41**: 337–348.

GILKS, W. R., RICHARDSON, S., and SPIEGELHALTER, D. J. (1996) *Markov Chain Monte Carlo in Practice*. Chapman and Hall.

GOLDIE, C. M., and PINCH, R. G. E. (1991) *Communication theory*. Cambridge Univ. Press.

GOLOMB, S. W., PEILE, R. E., and SCHOLTZ, R. A. (1994) *Basic Concepts in Information Theory and Coding: The Adventures of Secret Agent 00111*. Plenum Press.

GOOD, I. J. (1979) Studies in the history of probability and statistics. XXXVII. A.M. Turing's statistical work in World War II. *Biometrika* **66** (2): 393–396.

GRAHAM, R. L. (1966) On partitions of a finite set. *Journal of Combinatorial Theory* **1**: 215–223.

GRAHAM, R. L., and KNOWLTON, K. C., (1968) Method of identifying conductors in a cable by establishing conductor connection groupings at both ends of the cable. U.S. Patent 3,369,177.

GREEN, P. J. (1995) Reversible jump Markov chain Monte Carlo computation and Bayesian model determination. *Biometrika* **82**: 711–732.

GREGORY, P. C., and LOREDO, T. J. (1992) A new method for the detection of a periodic signal of unknown shape and period. In *Maximum Entropy and Bayesian Methods,*, ed. by G. Erickson and C. Smith. Kluwer. Also in *Astrophysical Journal*, **398**, pp. 146–168, Oct 10, 1992.

GULL, S. F. (1988) Bayesian inductive inference and maximum entropy. In *Maximum Entropy and Bayesian Methods in Science and Engineering, vol. 1: Foundations*, ed. by G. Erickson and C. Smith, pp. 53–74. Kluwer.

GULL, S. F. (1989) Developments in maximum entropy data analysis. In *Maximum Entropy and Bayesian Methods, Cambridge 1988*, ed. by J. Skilling, pp. 53–71. Kluwer.

GULL, S. F., and DANIELL, G. (1978) Image reconstruction from incomplete and noisy data. *Nature* **272**: 686–690.

HANSON, R., STUTZ, J., and CHEESEMAN, P. (1991a) Bayesian classification theory. Technical Report FIA–90-12-7-01, NASA Ames.

HANSON, R., STUTZ, J., and CHEESEMAN, P. (1991b) Bayesian classification with correlation and inheritance. In *Proc. 12th Intern. Joint Conf. on Artificial Intelligence, Sydney, Australia*, volume 2, pp. 692–698. Morgan Kaufmann.

HARTMANN, C. R. P., and RUDOLPH, L. D. (1976) An optimum symbol by symbol decoding rule for linear codes. *IEEE Trans. Info. Theory* **IT-22**: 514–517.

HARVEY, M., and NEAL, R. M. (2000) Inference for belief networks using coupling from the past. In *Uncertainty in Artificial Intelligence: Proc. Sixteenth Conf.*, pp. 256–263.

HEBB, D. O. (1949) *The Organization of Behavior*. Wiley.

HENDIN, O., HORN, D., and HOPFIELD, J. J. (1994) Decomposition of a mixture of signals in a model of the olfactory bulb. *Proc. Natl. Acad. Sci. USA* **91** (13): 5942–5946.

HERTZ, J., KROGH, A., and PALMER, R. G. (1991) *Introduction to the Theory of Neural Computation*. Addison-Wesley.

HINTON, G. (2001) Training products of experts by minimizing contrastive divergence. Technical Report 2000-004, Gatsby Computational Neuroscience Unit, Univ. College London.

HINTON, G., and NOWLAN, S. (1987) How learning can guide evolution. *Complex Systems* **1**: 495–502.

HINTON, G. E., DAYAN, P., FREY, B. J., and NEAL, R. M. (1995) The wake-sleep algorithm for unsupervised neural networks. *Science* **268** (5214): 1158–1161.

HINTON, G. E., and GHAHRAMANI, Z. (1997) Generative models for discovering sparse distributed representations. *Philosophical Trans. Royal Society B*.

HINTON, G. E., and SEJNOWSKI, T. J. (1986) Learning and relearning in Boltzmann machines. In *Parallel Distributed Processing*, ed. by D. E. Rumelhart and J. E. McClelland, pp. 282–317. MIT Press.

HINTON, G. E., and TEH, Y. W. (2001) Discovering multiple constraints that are frequently approximately satisfied. In *Uncertainty in Artificial Intelligence: Proc. Seventeenth Conf. (UAI-2001)*, pp. 227–234. Morgan Kaufmann.

HINTON, G. E., and VAN CAMP, D. (1993) Keeping neural networks simple by minimizing the description length of the weights. In *Proc. 6th Annual Workshop on Comput. Learning Theory*, pp. 5–13. ACM Press, New York, NY.

HINTON, G. E., WELLING, M., TEH, Y. W., and OSINDERO, S. (2001) A new view of ICA. In *Proc. International Conf. on Independent Component Analysis and Blind Signal Separation*, volume 3.

HINTON, G. E., and ZEMEL, R. S. (1994) Autoencoders, minimum description length and Helmholtz free energy. In *Advances in Neural Information Processing Systems 6*, ed. by J. D. Cowan, G. Tesauro, and J. Alspector. Morgan Kaufmann.

HODGES, A. (1983) *Alan Turing: The Enigma*. Simon and Schuster.

HOJEN-SORENSEN, P. A., WINTHER, O., and HANSEN, L. K. (2002) Mean field approaches to independent component analysis. *Neural Computation* **14**: 889–918.

HOLMES, C., and MALLICK, B. (1998) Perfect simulation for orthogonal model mixing. Technical report, Imperial College, London.

HOPFIELD, J. J. (1974) Kinetic proofreading: A new mechanism for reducing errors in biosynthetic processes requiring high specificity. *Proc. Natl. Acad. Sci. USA* **71** (10): 4135–4139.

HOPFIELD, J. J. (1978) Origin of the genetic code: A testable hypothesis based on tRNA structure, sequence, and kinetic proofreading. *Proc. Natl. Acad. Sci. USA* **75** (9): 4334–4338.

HOPFIELD, J. J. (1980) The energy relay: A proofreading scheme based on dynamic cooperativity and lacking all characteristic symptoms of kinetic proofreading in DNA replication and protein synthesis. *Proc. Natl. Acad. Sci. USA* **77** (9): 5248–5252.

HOPFIELD, J. J. (1982) Neural networks and physical systems with emergent collective computational abilities. *Proc. Natl. Acad. Sci. USA* **79**: 2554–8.

HOPFIELD, J. J. (1984) Neurons with graded response properties have collective computational properties like those of two-state neurons. *Proc. Natl. Acad. Sci. USA* **81**: 3088–92.

HOPFIELD, J. J. (1987) Learning algorithms and probability distributions in feed-forward and feed-back networks. *Proc. Natl. Acad. Sci. USA* **84**: 8429–33.

HOPFIELD, J. J., and BRODY, C. D. (2000) What is a moment? "Cortical" sensory integration over a brief interval. *Proc. Natl. Acad. Sci* **97**: 13919–13924.

HOPFIELD, J. J., and BRODY, C. D. (2001) What is a moment? Transient synchrony as a collective mechanism for spatiotemporal integration. *Proc. Natl. Acad. Sci* **98**: 1282–1287.

HOPFIELD, J. J., and TANK, D. W. (1985) Neural computation of decisions in optimization problems. *Biol. Cybernetics* **52**: 1–25.

HOWARTH, P., and BRADLEY, A. (1986) The longitudinal aberration of the human eye and its correction. *Vision Res.* **26**: 361–366.

ICHIKAWA, K., BHADESHIA, H. K. D. H., and MACKAY, D. J. C. (1996) Model for hot cracking in low-alloy steel weld metals. *Science and Technology of Welding and Joining* **1**: 43–50.

ISARD, M., and BLAKE, A. (1996) Visual tracking by stochastic propagation of conditional density. In *Proc. Fourth European Conf. Computer Vision*, pp. 343–356.

ISARD, M., and BLAKE, A. (1998) Condensation – conditional density propagation for visual tracking. *International Journal of Computer Vision* **29** (1): 5–28.

JAAKKOLA, T. S., and JORDAN, M. I. (1996) Computing upper and lower bounds on likelihoods in intractable networks. In *Proc. Twelfth Conf. on Uncertainty in AI*. Morgan Kaufman.

JAAKKOLA, T. S., and JORDAN, M. I. (2000a) Bayesian logistic regression: a variational approach. *Statistics and Computing* **10**: 25–37.

JAAKKOLA, T. S., and JORDAN, M. I. (2000b) Bayesian parameter estimation via variational methods. *Statistics and Computing* **10** (1): 25–37.

JAYNES, E. T. (1983) Bayesian intervals versus confidence intervals. In *E.T. Jaynes. Papers on Probability, Statistics and Statistical Physics*, ed. by R. D. Rosenkrantz, p. 151. Kluwer.

JAYNES, E. T. (2003) *Probability Theory: The Logic of Science*. Cambridge Univ. Press. Edited by G. Larry Bretthorst.

JENSEN, F. V. (1996) *An Introduction to Bayesian Networks*. UCL press.

JOHANNESSON, R., and ZIGANGIROV, K. S. (1999) *Fundamentals of Convolutional Coding*. IEEE Press.

JORDAN, M. I. ed. (1998) *Learning in Graphical Models*. NATO Science Series. Kluwer Academic Publishers.

JPL, (1996) Turbo codes performance. Available from www331.jpl.nasa.gov/public/TurboPerf.html.

JUTTEN, C., and HERAULT, J. (1991) Blind separation of sources. 1. An adaptive algorithm based on neuromimetic architecture. *Signal Processing* **24** (1): 1–10.

KARPLUS, K., and KRIT, H. (1991) A semi-systolic decoder for the PDSC–73 error-correcting code. *Discrete Applied Mathematics* **33**: 109–128.

KEPLER, T., and OPREA, M. (2001) Improved inference of mutation rates: I. An integral representation of the Luria-Delbrück distribution. *Theoretical Population Biology* **59**: 41–48.

KIMELDORF, G. S., and WAHBA, G. (1970) A correspondence between Bayesian estimation of stochastic processes and smoothing by splines. *Annals of Math. Statistics* **41** (2): 495–502.

KITANIDIS, P. K. (1986) Parameter uncertainty in estimation of spatial functions: Bayesian analysis. *Water Resources Research* **22**: 499–507.

KNUTH, D. E. (1968) *The Art of Computer Programming. Volume 1: Fundamental Algorithms*. Addison Wesley.

KONDRASHOV, A. S. (1988) Deleterious mutations and the evolution of sexual reproduction. *Nature* **336** (6198): 435–440.

KSCHISCHANG, F. R., FREY, B. J., and LOELIGER, H.-A. (2001) Factor graphs and the sum-product algorithm. *IEEE Trans. Info. Theory* **47** (2): 498–519.

KSCHISCHANG, F. R., and SOROKINE, V. (1995) On the trellis structure of block codes. *IEEE Trans. Info. Theory* **41** (6): 1924–1937.

LAURITZEN, S. L. (1981) Time series analysis in 1880, a discussion of contributions made by T. N. Thiele. *ISI Review* **49**: 319–333.

LAURITZEN, S. L. (1996) *Graphical Models*. Number 17 in Oxford Statistical Science Series. Clarendon Press.

LAURITZEN, S. L., and SPIEGELHALTER, D. J. (1988) Local computations with probabilities on graphical structures and their application to expert systems. *J. Royal Statistical Society B* **50**: 157–224.

LEVENSHTEIN, V. I. (1966) Binary codes capable of correcting deletions, insertions, and reversals. *Soviet Physics – Doklady* **10** (8): 707–710.

LIN, S., and COSTELLO, JR., D. J. (1983) *Error Control Coding: Fundamentals and Applications*. Prentice-Hall.

LITSYN, S., and SHEVELEV, V. (2002) On ensembles of low-density parity-check codes: asymptotic distance distributions. *IEEE Trans. Info. Theory* **48** (4): 887–908.

LOREDO, T. J. (1990) From Laplace to supernova SN 1987A: Bayesian inference in astrophysics. In *Maximum Entropy and Bayesian Methods, Dartmouth, U.S.A., 1989*, ed. by P. Fougere, pp. 81–142. Kluwer.

LOWE, D. G. (1995) Similarity metric learning for a variable kernel classifier. *Neural Computation* **7**: 72–85.

LUBY, M. (2002) LT codes. In *Proc. The 43rd Annual IEEE Symposium on Foundations of Computer Science, November 16–19 2002*, pp. 271–282.

LUBY, M. G., MITZENMACHER, M., SHOKROLLAHI, M. A., and SPIELMAN, D. A. (1998) Improved low-density parity-check codes using irregular graphs and belief propagation. In *Proc. IEEE International Symposium on Info. Theory*, p. 117.

LUBY, M. G., MITZENMACHER, M., SHOKROLLAHI, M. A., and SPIELMAN, D. A. (2001a) Efficient erasure correcting codes. *IEEE Trans. Info. Theory* **47** (2): 569–584.

LUBY, M. G., MITZENMACHER, M., SHOKROLLAHI, M. A., and SPIELMAN, D. A. (2001b) Improved low-density parity-check codes using irregular graphs and belief propagation. *IEEE Trans. Info. Theory* **47** (2): 585–584.

LUBY, M. G., MITZENMACHER, M., SHOKROLLAHI, M. A., SPIELMAN, D. A., and STEMANN, V. (1997) Practical loss-resilient codes. In *Proc. Twenty-Ninth Annual ACM Symposium on Theory of Computing (STOC)*.

LUO, Z., and WAHBA, G. (1997) Hybrid adaptive splines. *J. Amer. Statist. Assoc.* **92**: 107–116.

LURIA, S. E., and DELBRÜCK, M. (1943) Mutations of bacteria from virus sensitivity to virus resistance. *Genetics* **28**: 491–511. Reprinted in *Microbiology: A Centenary Perspective*, Wolfgang K. Joklik, ed., 1999, ASM Press, and available from www.esp.org/.

LUTTRELL, S. P. (1989) Hierarchical vector quantisation. *Proc. IEE Part I* **136**: 405–413.

LUTTRELL, S. P. (1990) Derivation of a class of training algorithms. *IEEE Trans. on Neural Networks* **1** (2): 229–232.

MACKAY, D. J. C. (1991) *Bayesian Methods for Adaptive Models*. California Institute of Technology PhD dissertation.

MACKAY, D. J. C. (1992a) Bayesian interpolation. *Neural Computation* **4** (3): 415–447.

MACKAY, D. J. C. (1992b) The evidence framework applied to classification networks. *Neural Computation* **4** (5): 698–714.

MACKAY, D. J. C. (1992c) A practical Bayesian framework for backpropagation networks. *Neural Computation* **4** (3): 448–472.

MACKAY, D. J. C. (1994a) Bayesian methods for backpropagation networks. In *Models of Neural Networks III*, ed. by E. Domany, J. L. van Hemmen, and K. Schulten, chapter 6, pp. 211–254. Springer.

MACKAY, D. J. C. (1994b) Bayesian non-linear modelling for the prediction competition. In *ASHRAE Trans., V.100, Pt.2*, pp. 1053–1062. American Society of Heating, Refrigeration, and Air-conditioning Engineers.

MACKAY, D. J. C. (1995a) Free energy minimization algorithm for decoding and cryptanalysis. *Electronics Letters* **31** (6): 446–447.

MACKAY, D. J. C. (1995b) Probable networks and plausible predictions – a review of practical Bayesian methods for supervised neural networks. *Network: Computation in Neural Systems* **6**: 469–505.

MACKAY, D. J. C., (1997a) Ensemble learning for hidden Markov models. www.inference.phy.cam.ac.uk/mackay/abstracts/ensemblePaper.html.

MACKAY, D. J. C., (1997b) Iterative probabilistic decoding of low density parity check codes. Animations available on world wide web. www.inference.phy.cam.ac.uk/mackay/codes/gifs/.

MacKay, D. J. C. (1998a) Choice of basis for Laplace approximation. *Machine Learning* **33** (1): 77–86.

MacKay, D. J. C. (1998b) Introduction to Gaussian processes. In *Neural Networks and Machine Learning*, ed. by C. M. Bishop, NATO ASI Series, pp. 133–166. Kluwer.

MacKay, D. J. C. (1999a) Comparison of approximate methods for handling hyperparameters. *Neural Computation* **11** (5): 1035–1068.

MacKay, D. J. C. (1999b) Good error correcting codes based on very sparse matrices. *IEEE Trans. Info. Theory* **45** (2): 399–431.

MacKay, D. J. C., (2000) An alternative to runlength-limiting codes: Turn timing errors into substitution errors. Available from www.inference.phy.cam.ac.uk/mackay/.

MacKay, D. J. C., (2001) A problem with variational free energy minimization. www.inference.phy.cam.ac.uk/mackay/abstracts/minima.html.

MacKay, D. J. C., and Davey, M. C. (2000) Evaluation of Gallager codes for short block length and high rate applications. In *Codes, Systems and Graphical Models*, ed. by B. Marcus and J. Rosenthal, volume 123 of *IMA Volumes in Mathematics and its Applications*, pp. 113–130. Springer.

MacKay, D. J. C., Mitchison, G., and McFadden, P. L., (2003) Sparse-graph codes for quantum error-correction. quant-ph/0304161. Submitted to *IEEE Trans. Info. Theory* May 8, 2003.

MacKay, D. J. C., and Neal, R. M. (1995) Good codes based on very sparse matrices. In *Cryptography and Coding. 5th IMA Conf., LNCS 1025*, ed. by C. Boyd, pp. 100–111. Springer.

MacKay, D. J. C., and Neal, R. M. (1996) Near Shannon limit performance of low density parity check codes. *Electronics Letters* **32** (18): 1645–1646. Reprinted *Electronics Letters*, **33**(6):457–458, March 1997.

MacKay, D. J. C., and Peto, L. (1995) A hierarchical Dirichlet language model. *Natural Language Engineering* **1** (3): 1–19.

MacKay, D. J. C., Wilson, S. T., and Davey, M. C. (1998) Comparison of constructions of irregular Gallager codes. In *Proc. 36th Allerton Conf. on Communication, Control, and Computing, Sept. 1998*, pp. 220–229. Allerton House.

MacKay, D. J. C., Wilson, S. T., and Davey, M. C. (1999) Comparison of constructions of irregular Gallager codes. *IEEE Trans. on Communications* **47** (10): 1449–1454.

MacKay, D. M., and MacKay, V. (1974) The time course of the McCollough effect and its physiological implications. *J. Physiol.* **237**: 38–39.

MacKay, D. M., and McCulloch, W. S. (1952) The limiting information capacity of a neuronal link. *Bull. Math. Biophys.* **14**: 127–135.

MacWilliams, F. J., and Sloane, N. J. A. (1977) *The Theory of Error-correcting Codes*. North-Holland.

Mandelbrot, B. (1982) *The Fractal Geometry of Nature*. W.H. Freeman.

Mao, Y., and Banihashemi, A. (2000) Design of good LDPC codes using girth distribution. In *IEEE International Symposium on Info. Theory, Italy, June, 2000*.

Mao, Y., and Banihashemi, A. (2001) A heuristic search for good LDPC codes at short block lengths. In *IEEE International Conf. on Communications*.

Marinari, E., and Parisi, G. (1992) Simulated tempering – a new Monte-Carlo scheme. *Europhysics Letters* **19** (6): 451–458.

Matheron, G. (1963) Principles of geostatistics. *Economic Geology* **58**: 1246–1266.

Maynard Smith, J. (1968) 'Haldane's dilemma' and the rate of evolution. *Nature* **219** (5159): 1114–1116.

Maynard Smith, J. (1978) *The Evolution of Sex*. Cambridge Univ. Press.

Maynard Smith, J. (1988) *Games, Sex and Evolution*. Harvester–Wheatsheaf.

Maynard Smith, J., and Száthmary, E. (1995) *The Major Transitions in Evolution*. Freeman.

Maynard Smith, J., and Száthmary, E. (1999) *The Origins of Life*. Oxford Univ. Press.

McCollough, C. (1965) Color adaptation of edge-detectors in the human visual system. *Science* **149**: 1115–1116.

McEliece, R. J. (2002) *The Theory of Information and Coding*. Cambridge Univ. Press, second edition.

McEliece, R. J., MacKay, D. J. C., and Cheng, J.-F. (1998) Turbo decoding as an instance of Pearl's 'belief propagation' algorithm. *IEEE Journal on Selected Areas in Communications* **16** (2): 140–152.

McMillan, B. (1956) Two inequalities implied by unique decipherability. *IRE Trans. Inform. Theory* **2**: 115–116.

Minka, T. (2001) *A family of algorithms for approximate Bayesian inference*. MIT PhD dissertation.

Miskin, J. W. (2001) *Ensemble Learning for Independent Component Analysis*. Dept. of Physics, Univ. of Cambridge PhD dissertation.

Miskin, J. W., and MacKay, D. J. C. (2000) Ensemble learning for blind image separation and deconvolution. In *Advances in Independent Component Analysis*, ed. by M. Girolami. Springer.

Miskin, J. W., and MacKay, D. J. C. (2001) Ensemble learning for blind source separation. In *ICA: Principles and Practice*, ed. by S. Roberts and R. Everson. Cambridge Univ. Press.

Mosteller, F., and Wallace, D. L. (1984) *Applied Bayesian and Classical Inference. The case of* The Federalist *papers*. Springer.

Neal, R. M. (1991) Bayesian mixture modelling by Monte Carlo simulation. Technical Report CRG–TR–91–2, Computer Science, Univ. of Toronto.

Neal, R. M. (1993a) Bayesian learning via stochastic dynamics. In *Advances in Neural Information Processing Systems 5*, ed. by C. L. Giles, S. J. Hanson, and J. D. Cowan, pp. 475–482. Morgan Kaufmann.

Neal, R. M. (1993b) Probabilistic inference using Markov chain Monte Carlo methods. Technical Report CRG–TR–93–1, Dept. of Computer Science, Univ. of Toronto.

Neal, R. M. (1995) Suppressing random walks in Markov chain Monte Carlo using ordered overrelaxation. Technical Report 9508, Dept. of Statistics, Univ. of Toronto.

Neal, R. M. (1996) *Bayesian Learning for Neural Networks*. Springer.

Neal, R. M. (1997a) Markov chain Monte Carlo methods based on 'slicing' the density function. Technical Report 9722, Dept. of Statistics, Univ. of Toronto.

Neal, R. M. (1997b) Monte Carlo implementation of Gaussian process models for Bayesian regression and classification. Technical Report CRG–TR–97–2, Dept. of Computer Science, Univ. of Toronto.

Neal, R. M. (1998) Annealed importance sampling. Technical Report 9805, Dept. of Statistics, Univ. of Toronto.

Neal, R. M. (2001) Defining priors for distributions using Dirichlet diffusion trees. Technical Report 0104, Dept. of Statistics, Univ. of Toronto.

Neal, R. M. (2003) Slice sampling. *Annals of Statistics* **31** (3): 705–767.

Neal, R. M., and Hinton, G. E. (1998) A new view of the EM algorithm that justifies incremental, sparse, and other variants. In *Learning in Graphical Models*, ed. by M. I. Jordan, NATO Science Series, pp. 355–368. Kluwer.

Nielsen, M., and Chuang, I. (2000) *Quantum Computation and Quantum Information*. Cambridge Univ. Press.

OFFER, E., and SOLJANIN, E. (2000) An algebraic description of iterative decoding schemes. In *Codes, Systems and Graphical Models*, ed. by B. Marcus and J. Rosenthal, volume 123 of *IMA Volumes in Mathematics and its Applications*, pp. 283–298. Springer.

OFFER, E., and SOLJANIN, E. (2001) LDPC codes: a group algebra formulation. In *Proc. Internat. Workshop on Coding and Cryptography WCC 2001, 8-12 Jan. 2001, Paris*.

O'HAGAN, A. (1978) On curve fitting and optimal design for regression. *J. Royal Statistical Society, B* **40**: 1–42.

O'HAGAN, A. (1987) Monte Carlo is fundamentally unsound. *The Statistician* **36**: 247–249.

O'HAGAN, A. (1994) *Bayesian Inference*, volume 2B of *Kendall's Advanced Theory of Statistics*. Edward Arnold.

OMRE, H. (1987) Bayesian kriging – merging observations and qualified guesses in kriging. *Mathematical Geology* **19**: 25–39.

OPPER, M., and WINTHER, O. (2000) Gaussian processes for classification: Mean-field algorithms. *Neural Computation* **12** (11): 2655–2684.

PATRICK, J. D., and WALLACE, C. S. (1982) Stone circle geometries: an information theory approach. In *Archaeoastronomy in the Old World*, ed. by D. C. Heggie, pp. 231–264. Cambridge Univ. Press.

PEARL, J. (1988) *Probabilistic Reasoning in Intelligent Systems: Networks of Plausible Inference*. Morgan Kaufmann.

PEARL, J. (2000) *Causality*. Cambridge Univ. Press.

PEARLMUTTER, B. A., and PARRA, L. C. (1996) A context-sensitive generalization of ICA. In *International Conf. on Neural Information Processing, Hong Kong*, pp. 151–157.

PEARLMUTTER, B. A., and PARRA, L. C. (1997) Maximum likelihood blind source separation: A context-sensitive generalization of ICA. In *Advances in Neural Information Processing Systems*, ed. by M. C. Mozer, M. I. Jordan, and T. Petsche, volume 9, p. 613. MIT Press.

PINTO, R. L., and NEAL, R. M. (2001) Improving Markov chain Monte Carlo estimators by coupling to an approximating chain. Technical Report 0101, Dept. of Statistics, Univ. of Toronto.

POGGIO, T., and GIROSI, F. (1989) A theory of networks for approximation and learning. Technical Report A.I. 1140, MIT.

POGGIO, T., and GIROSI, F. (1990) Networks for approximation and learning. *Proc. IEEE* **78**: 1481–1497.

POLYA, G. (1954) *Induction and Analogy in Mathematics*. Princeton Univ. Press.

PROPP, J. G., and WILSON, D. B. (1996) Exact sampling with coupled Markov chains and applications to statistical mechanics. *Random Structures and Algorithms* **9** (1-2): 223–252.

RABINER, L. R., and JUANG, B. H. (1986) An introduction to hidden Markov models. *IEEE ASSP Magazine* pp. 4–16.

RASMUSSEN, C. E. (1996) *Evaluation of Gaussian Processes and Other Methods for Non-Linear Regression*. Univ. of Toronto PhD dissertation.

RASMUSSEN, C. E. (2000) The infinite Gaussian mixture model. In *Advances in Neural Information Processing Systems 12*, ed. by S. Solla, T. Leen, and K.-R. Müller, pp. 554–560. MIT Press.

RASMUSSEN, C. E., (2002) Reduced rank Gaussian process learning. Unpublished manuscript.

RASMUSSEN, C. E., and GHAHRAMANI, Z. (2002) Infinite mixtures of Gaussian process experts. In *Advances in Neural Information Processing Systems 14*, ed. by T. G. Diettrich, S. Becker, and Z. Ghahramani. MIT Press.

RASMUSSEN, C. E., and GHAHRAMANI, Z. (2003) Bayesian Monte Carlo. In *Advances in Neural Information Processing Systems XV*, ed. by S. Becker, S. Thrun, and K. Obermayer.

RATLIFF, F., and RIGGS, L. A. (1950) Involuntary motions of the eye during monocular fixation. *J. Exptl. Psychol.* **40**: 687–701.

RATZER, E. A., and MACKAY, D. J. C. (2003) Sparse low-density parity-check codes for channels with cross-talk. In *Proc. 2003 IEEE Info. Theory Workshop, Paris*.

REIF, F. (1965) *Fundamentals of Statistical and Thermal Physics*. McGraw-Hill.

RICHARDSON, T., SHOKROLLAHI, M. A., and URBANKE, R. (2001) Design of capacity-approaching irregular low-density parity check codes. *IEEE Trans. Info. Theory* **47** (2): 619–637.

RICHARDSON, T., and URBANKE, R. (2001a) The capacity of low-density parity check codes under message-passing decoding. *IEEE Trans. Info. Theory* **47** (2): 599–618.

RICHARDSON, T., and URBANKE, R. (2001b) Efficient encoding of low-density parity-check codes. *IEEE Trans. Info. Theory* **47** (2): 638–656.

RIDLEY, M. (2000) *Mendel's Demon: gene justice and the complexity of life*. Phoenix.

RIPLEY, B. D. (1991) *Statistical Inference for Spatial Processes*. Cambridge Univ. Press.

RIPLEY, B. D. (1996) *Pattern Recognition and Neural Networks*. Cambridge Univ. Press.

RUMELHART, D. E., HINTON, G. E., and WILLIAMS, R. J. (1986) Learning representations by back-propagating errors. *Nature* **323**: 533–536.

RUSSELL, S., and WEFALD, E. (1991) *Do the Right Thing: Studies in Limited Rationality*. MIT Press.

SCHNEIER, B. (1996) *Applied Cryptography*. Wiley.

SCHOLKOPF, B., BURGES, C., and VAPNIK, V. (1995) Extracting support data for a given task. In *Proc. First International Conf. on Knowledge Discovery and Data Mining*, ed. by U. M. Fayyad and R. Uthurusamy. AAAI Press.

SCHOLTZ, R. A. (1982) The origins of spread-spectrum communications. *IEEE Trans. on Communications* **30** (5): 822–854.

SEEGER, M., WILLIAMS, C. K. I., and LAWRENCE, N. (2003) Fast forward selection to speed up sparse Gaussian process regression. In *Proc. Ninth International Workshop on Artificial Intelligence and Statistics*, ed. by C. Bishop and B. J. Frey. Society for Artificial Intelligence and Statistics.

SEJNOWSKI, T. J. (1986) Higher order Boltzmann machines. In *Neural networks for computing*, ed. by J. Denker, pp. 398–403. American Institute of Physics.

SEJNOWSKI, T. J., and ROSENBERG, C. R. (1987) Parallel networks that learn to pronounce English text. *Journal of Complex Systems* **1** (1): 145–168.

SHANNON, C. E. (1948) A mathematical theory of communication. *Bell Sys. Tech. J.* **27**: 379–423, 623–656.

SHANNON, C. E. (1993) The best detection of pulses. In *Collected Papers of Claude Shannon*, ed. by N. J. A. Sloane and A. D. Wyner, pp. 148–150. IEEE Press.

SHANNON, C. E., and WEAVER, W. (1949) *The Mathematical Theory of Communication*. Univ. of Illinois Press.

SHOKROLLAHI, A. (2003) Raptor codes. Technical report, Laboratoire d'algorithmique, École Polytechnique Fédérale de Lausanne, Lausanne, Switzerland. Available from `algo.epfl.ch/`.

SIPSER, M., and SPIELMAN, D. A. (1996) Expander codes. *IEEE Trans. Info. Theory* **42** (6.1): 1710–1722.

SKILLING, J. (1989) Classic maximum entropy. In *Maximum Entropy and Bayesian Methods, Cambridge 1988*, ed. by J. Skilling. Kluwer.

SKILLING, J. (1993) Bayesian numerical analysis. In *Physics and Probability*, ed. by W. T. Grandy, Jr. and P. Milonni. Cambridge Univ. Press.

SKILLING, J., and MACKAY, D. J. C. (2003) Slice sampling – a binary implementation. *Annals of Statistics* **31** (3): 753–755. Discussion of *Slice Sampling* by Radford M. Neal.

SMOLA, A. J., and BARTLETT, P. (2001) Sparse Greedy Gaussian Process Regression. In *Advances in Neural Information Processing Systems 13*, ed. by T. K. Leen, T. G. Diettrich, and V. Tresp, pp. 619–625. MIT Press.

SPIEGEL, M. R. (1988) *Statistics*. Schaum's outline series. McGraw-Hill, 2nd edition.

SPIELMAN, D. A. (1996) Linear-time encodable and decodable error-correcting codes. *IEEE Trans. Info. Theory* **42** (6.1): 1723–1731.

SUTTON, R. S., and BARTO, A. G. (1998) *Reinforcement Learning: An Introduction*. MIT Press.

SWANSON, L. (1988) A new code for Galileo. In *Proc. 1988 IEEE International Symposium Info. Theory*, pp. 94–95.

TANNER, M. A. (1996) *Tools for Statistical Inference: Methods for the Exploration of Posterior Distributions and Likelihood Functions*. Springer Series in Statistics. Springer, 3rd edition.

TANNER, R. M. (1981) A recursive approach to low complexity codes. *IEEE Trans. Info. Theory* **27** (5): 533–547.

TEAHAN, W. J. (1995) Probability estimation for PPM. In *Proc. NZCSRSC'95*. Available from `citeseer.nj.nec.com/teahan95probability.html`.

TEN BRINK, S. (1999) Convergence of iterative decoding. *Electronics Letters* **35** (10): 806–808.

TEN BRINK, S., KRAMER, G., and ASHIKHMIN, A., (2002) Design of low-density parity-check codes for multi-antenna modulation and detection. Submitted to *IEEE Trans. on Communications*.

TERRAS, A. (1999) *Fourier Analysis on Finite Groups and Applications*. Cambridge Univ. Press.

THOMAS, A., SPIEGELHALTER, D. J., and GILKS, W. R. (1992) BUGS: A program to perform Bayesian inference using Gibbs sampling. In *Bayesian Statistics 4*, ed. by J. M. Bernardo, J. O. Berger, A. P. Dawid, and A. F. M. Smith, pp. 837–842. Clarendon Press.

TRESP, V. (2000) A Bayesian committee machine. *Neural Computation* **12** (11): 2719–2741.

URBANKE, R., (2001) LdpcOpt – a fast and accurate degree distribution optimizer for LDPC code ensembles. `lthcwww.epfl.ch/research/ldpcopt/`.

VAPNIK, V. (1995) *The Nature of Statistical Learning Theory*. Springer.

VITERBI, A. J. (1967) Error bounds for convolutional codes and an asymptotically optimum decoding algorithm. *IEEE Trans. Info. Theory* **IT-13**: 260–269.

WAHBA, G. (1990) *Spline Models for Observational Data*. Society for Industrial and Applied Mathematics. CBMS-NSF Regional Conf. series in applied mathematics.

WAINWRIGHT, M. J., JAAKKOLA, T., and WILLSKY, A. S. (2003) Tree-based reparameterization framework for analysis of sum-product and related algorithms. *IEEE Trans. Info. Theory* **45** (9): 1120–1146.

WALD, G., and GRIFFIN, D. (1947) The change in refractive power of the eye in bright and dim light. *J. Opt. Soc. Am.* **37**: 321–336.

WALLACE, C., and BOULTON, D. (1968) An information measure for classification. *Comput. J.* **11** (2): 185–194.

WALLACE, C. S., and FREEMAN, P. R. (1987) Estimation and inference by compact coding. *J. R. Statist. Soc. B* **49** (3): 240–265.

WARD, D. J., BLACKWELL, A. F., and MACKAY, D. J. C. (2000) Dasher – A data entry interface using continuous gestures and language models. In *Proc. User Interface Software and Technology 2000*, pp. 129–137.

WARD, D. J., and MACKAY, D. J. C. (2002) Fast hands-free writing by gaze direction. *Nature* **418** (6900): 838.

WELLING, M., and TEH, Y. W. (2001) Belief optimization for binary networks: A stable alternative to loopy belief propagation. In *Uncertainty in Artificial Intelligence: Proc. Seventeenth Conf. (UAI-2001)*, pp. 554–561. Morgan Kaufmann.

WIBERG, N. (1996) *Codes and Decoding on General Graphs*. Dept. of Electrical Engineering, Linköping, Sweden PhD dissertation. Linköping Studies in Science and Technology No. 440.

WIBERG, N., LOELIGER, H.-A., and KÖTTER, R. (1995) Codes and iterative decoding on general graphs. *European Trans. on Telecommunications* **6**: 513–525.

WIENER, N. (1948) *Cybernetics*. Wiley.

WILLIAMS, C. K. I., and RASMUSSEN, C. E. (1996) Gaussian processes for regression. In *Advances in Neural Information Processing Systems 8*, ed. by D. S. Touretzky, M. C. Mozer, and M. E. Hasselmo. MIT Press.

WILLIAMS, C. K. I., and SEEGER, M. (2001) Using the Nyström Method to Speed Up Kernel Machines. In *Advances in Neural Information Processing Systems 13*, ed. by T. K. Leen, T. G. Diettrich, and V. Tresp, pp. 682–688. MIT Press.

WITTEN, I. H., NEAL, R. M., and CLEARY, J. G. (1987) Arithmetic coding for data compression. *Communications of the ACM* **30** (6): 520–540.

WOLF, J. K., and SIEGEL, P. (1998) On two-dimensional arrays and crossword puzzles. In *Proc. 36th Allerton Conf. on Communication, Control, and Computing, Sept. 1998*, pp. 366–371. Allerton House.

WORTHEN, A. P., and STARK, W. E. (1998) Low-density parity check codes for fading channels with memory. In *Proc. 36th Allerton Conf. on Communication, Control, and Computing, Sept. 1998*, pp. 117–125.

YEDIDIA, J. S. (2000) An idiosyncratic journey beyond mean field theory. Technical report, Mitsubishi Electric Research Laboratories. TR-2000-27.

YEDIDIA, J. S., FREEMAN, W. T., and WEISS, Y. (2000a) Bethe free energy, Kikuchi approximations and belief propagation algorithms. Technical report, Mitsubishi Electric Research Laboratories. TR-2001-16.

YEDIDIA, J. S., FREEMAN, W. T., and WEISS, Y. (2000b) Characterization of belief propagation and its generalizations. Technical report, Mitsubishi Electric Research Laboratories. TR-2001-15.

YEDIDIA, J. S., FREEMAN, W. T., and WEISS, Y. (2000c) Generalized belief propagation. Technical report, Mitsubishi Electric Research Laboratories. TR-2000-26.

YEDIDIA, J. S., FREEMAN, W. T., and WEISS, Y. (2002) Constructing free energy approximations and generalized belief propagation algorithms. Technical report, Mitsubishi Electric Research Laboratories. TR-2002-35.

YEUNG, R. W. (1991) A new outlook on Shannon-information measures. *IEEE Trans. Info. Theory* **37** (3.1): 466–474.

YUILLE, A. L. (2001) A double-loop algorithm to minimize the Bethe and Kikuchi free energies. In *Energy Minimization Methods in Computer Vision and Pattern Recognition. Proc. Third International Workshop, Sophia Antipolis France, September 3-5, 2001*, ed. by M. Figueiredo, J. Zerubia, and A. Jain, number 2134 in LNCS, pp. 3–18. Springer.

ZIPF, G. K. (1949) *Human Behavior and the Principle of Least Effort*. Addison-Wesley.

Index